QuickBooks® Complete 2010

For QuickBooks Pro and Premier Version 2010

Website: www.sleeter.com
Email: info@sleeter.com
888-484-5484

Product Name QuickBooks Complete - Version 2010

ISBN# 978-1-932487-72-5

Printed 6/15/2010 11:02:00 PM

Complete-10-1.docx

Developed and Written By Douglas Sleeter

Contributing Authors, Testers, and Reviewers Deborah Pembrook
Pat Carson

Table of Contents

Note:
Two additional chapters covering *Budgets, Forecasting and Business Planning* and *Adjustments and Year-End Procedures* as well as additional material on the *Inventory*, *Payroll Processing* and *Estimates* chapter are available online. Please see page xiii for more details.

Preface

On behalf of our whole team at The Sleeter Group, I would like to thank you for choosing this book. We work very hard each year to make it as understandable, complete, and relevant as possible, and we believe that after completing your study in this book, you will be prepared to apply your QuickBooks skills as a bookkeeper or as the owner of a small business.

Throughout the book, we've tried to include as many real-world transactions and situations as possible, so you can work through the issues before you face them in the real world. Also, we've included several optimized setup and data entry methods to help you streamline your bookkeeping and to ensure you keep accurate financial information. We hope to save you valuable time in your business by giving you the advantage of our many years of experience with QuickBooks.

Using This Book

Throughout this book, you will find tips from the experts on how to set up and use QuickBooks properly to provide managers with the data needed to make informed business decisions.

Each chapter covers how to manage a general part of your business. To allow you to learn the chapters in any order, each chapter uses a separate QuickBooks data file that you can open and use with QuickBooks to complete the practice lessons in the chapter. The data files are provided via download from the Internet.

Academy Photography, Inc. is the model company used throughout the chapters. By performing the in-chapter practices, students gain a hands-on experience with the topics discussed in the chapter, which are based on the day-to-day operations of this small corporation.

Each chapter is designed to aid understanding by providing a list of objectives, numerous hands-on tutorial practices, key terms, the "accounting behind the scenes," a chapter summary, and many extra notes throughout each chapter. The well-illustrated text includes step-by-step instructions in the hands-on computer exercises, which provide you with the practical experience needed to achieve operating skill.

The end-of-chapter applications include comprehension questions, multiple choice questions, completion sentences, discussion questions, and real-world problems that require the student to perform tasks with the software. Several chapters also include case studies that allow the student to apply their knowledge by reading about a real-world company and creating solutions to problems using QuickBooks.

The Horizon Business Simulation is a summary problem covering topics culled from all the chapters in this book.

The appendix contains keyboard shortcuts. The glossary provides a list of definitions for several accounting and QuickBooks-specific terms, and the Index provides comprehensive coverage of terms and topics covered throughout the book.

From using this book you will gain confidence in every aspect of QuickBooks by trying out each feature as you complete problems and simulations of a "real" business. You will want to keep this book for reference for years to come.

Installing QuickBooks Software

In order to practice what you will learn in this book, you'll need to first install QuickBooks 2010 on your computer and then open the practice file for the chapter you are studying. If you haven't installed the software yet, you should do so now so you will be prepared to work through the practice lessons in the book.

To install the software, insert the QuickBooks CD into your CD-ROM drive. The installation program will start automatically. If the installation program does not start automatically, select the **Windows Start Menu** and then select **Run.** Enter **[D]:\setup.exe** (where D is the drive letter of your CD-ROM drive), then click **OK.** Follow the onscreen instructions to complete the installation.

Working With the Practice Files

We have provided practice data files to work through the lessons in this book. You can access them by visiting The Sleeter Group website at www.sleeter.com/downloads and choosing this book title.

Follow the instructions on the Web page to download the installation file for this book to your local hard disk. After downloading the installation file, follow these steps to install the sample files:

Step 1. Double-click the file: **QuickBooks_2010_Classroom_Files.exe**. This launches the WinZip Self-Extractor.

Step 2. By default, the installation file will place your files in a directory called **C:\QuickBooks 2010 Classroom Files**. You can browse to another location by clicking the *Browse* button. If you are working on a classroom computer, ask your instructor where to put the classroom files.

Step 3. Click **Unzip**.

Important:
The Classroom Files are in QuickBooks Portable File Format. You cannot open these files by double-clicking them. For more on how to begin using these files, see page 10.

Computer Practices

Each chapter uses a separate practice file (e.g., Intro-10.QBW) for performing the in-chapter practices. In order to open this file, you must "restore" it as described in the first chapter (see page 10).

In the beginning of each chapter, the *Restore This File* instruction (see example below) instructs you to restore the practice file for that chapter to use with the computer practice lessons.

Example *Restore this file* instruction:

Restore this File

This chapter uses XXXXXXXXXXX-10.QBW. To open this file, restore the XXXXXXXXXXX -10.QBM file to your hard disk. See page 14 for instructions on restoring files.

The lessons are identified throughout the book with the words **COMPUTER PRACTICE**.

In some cases, concepts are presented in step form, but are not intended to be performed in your data file. In this case, you'll see a note at the top of the section that says:

> **DO NOT PERFORM THESE STEPS NOW. THEY ARE FOR REFERENCE ONLY.**

For these sections, you should look through and understand the material, but you should not enter any of the data in your practice file.

Supplemental Material

We've heard from many students that our previous editions were too large and bulky and that they wanted a book that was physically earlier to manage. As a result, we have moved several sections of this textbook, including the final two chapters, to supplemental material available online for download.

The supplemental materials are available at www.sleeter.com/downloads. Choose this title from the drop down list and choose the material you want to download.

Supplemental material includes:

- Unit of Measure and Inventory Assemblies (Supplemental material for the Inventory chapter)
- Paying Payroll Taxes (Supplemental material for the Payroll Processing chapter)
- Sales Orders (Supplemental material for the Estimates chapter)
- Budgeting, Forecasting and Business Planning Chapter
- Adjustments and Year-End Procedures Chapter
- Appendix, including a list of keyboard shortcuts, Answer Key to the End of Chapter Review questions, Glossary of terms and extensive coverage of QuickBooks Preferences.

Acknowledgements

I'd like to extend my heartfelt thanks to the co-authors, consultants, copy editors and contributors who have worked on all of our college textbooks over the years. Many people have put their head and their heart into each edition. All of you have improved and enhanced this textbook and I offer my gratitude.

This year's update was managed by The Sleeter Group's Manager of Educational Products, Deborah Pembrook. Updating this textbook is a labor of love for Deborah and I hope you see this reflected on the following pages.

My sincere thanks also goes to Pat Carson of Carson & Crew in San Jose, CA. Thank you, Pat, for being such a patient and deliberate eye at each stage of this book.

We hope you enjoy *QuickBooks Complete 2010.*

Chapter 1 Introducing QuickBooks

Objectives

In this chapter, you will learn about the following:

- An overview of the QuickBooks product line (page 1).
- Some of the basic principles of accounting (page 2).
- The accounting behind the scenes in QuickBooks (page 4).
- An overview of QuickBooks data files and types (page 6).
- Opening portable files (page 10).
- How to restore backup files (page 14).
- Entering transactions in QuickBooks (page 20).
- QuickBooks user interface features (page 25).
- About QuickBooks help and support (page 29).

QuickBooks is one of the most powerful tools you will use in managing your business. In addition to being a powerful bookkeeping program, QuickBooks is a *management tool.* When set up and used properly, QuickBooks allows you to track and manage income, expenses, bank accounts, receivables, inventory, fixed assets, payables, loans, payroll, billable time, and equity in your company. It also provides you with detailed reports that are essential to making good business decisions. Throughout this book, you will learn in detail about most of the features in QuickBooks.

QuickBooks helps small business owners run their businesses efficiently without worrying about the debits and credits of accounting entries. However, to use QuickBooks effectively, you still need to understand how QuickBooks is structured, how its files work, how to navigate in the system to do tasks, and how to retrieve information about your business. In this chapter you will explore the world of accounting and then you'll learn some of the basics of the QuickBooks program.

The QuickBooks Product Line

The QuickBooks family of products is designed to be easy to use, while providing a comprehensive set of accounting tools, including general ledger, inventory, accounts receivable, accounts payable, sales tax, and financial reporting. In addition, a variety of optional, fee-based payroll services, merchant account services, and other add-on products integrate with the QuickBooks software.

QuickBooks Editions

The QuickBooks product line includes five separate product editions: *QuickBooks Simple Start, QuickBooks Online Edition, QuickBooks Pro, QuickBooks Premier,* and *QuickBooks Enterprise Solutions*. The *Premier* and *Enterprise Solutions* editions are further broken down into six industry-specific editions for *Accounting Professionals, Contractors, Manufacturers/Wholesalers, Nonprofit Organizations, Professional Services,* and *Retailers*.

This book covers the features and usage of *QuickBooks Pro* and *Premier (non-industry specific)*, since most small businesses will use one of these editions. Also, once you learn how to use one of the editions, you'll be prepared to use *any* of the other editions, with the exception of the online edition. The online edition is a web-based software product, with different, yet similar features to the editions covered in this book. For a comparison of all editions and options, see www.quickbooks.com.

QuickBooks Releases

Occasionally, errors are found in the QuickBooks software after the product is released for sale. As errors are discovered, Intuit fixes the problem and provides program "patches" via the Internet. Each patch increases the **Release Level** of the QuickBooks application. To see what release level of the software you have, press **Ctrl+1** (or **F2**) while QuickBooks is running. At the top of the window, you will see the QuickBooks product information including the release level.

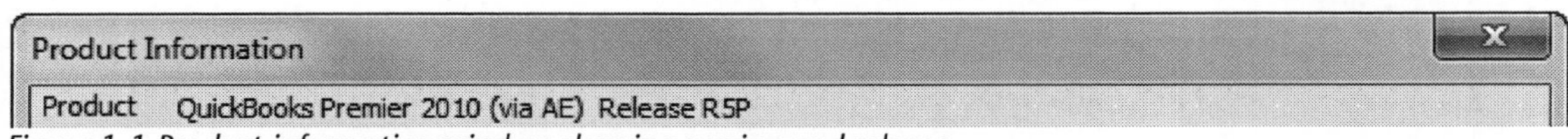

Figure 1-1 Product information window showing version and release

This book is based on QuickBooks Premier 2010 release R5P. If you have a newer (higher) release, you may see some slight differences compared to the screens in this book, but most likely you won't see any differences.

To patch your software with the latest maintenance release, download this release by selecting the *Help* menu and then selecting **Update QuickBooks**. Follow the instructions on these screens to download and install maintenance releases in QuickBooks via the Internet.

Accounting 101

Before we begin learning how to use QuickBooks, let's look at some of the background and key concepts of the accounting process.

Accounting's Focus

Accounting's primary concern is the accurate recording and categorizing of transactions so that you can produce reports that accurately portray the financial health of your organization. Put another way, accounting's focus is on whether your organization is succeeding and how well it is succeeding.

The examples in this book are about a *for-profit* company called Academy Photography, but similar needs for information and tracking rules apply to *not-for-profit organizations*.

The purpose of accounting is to serve management, investors, creditors, and government agencies. Accounting reports allow any of these groups to assess the financial position of the organization relative to its debts (liabilities), its capabilities to satisfy those debts and continue operations (assets), and the difference between them (net worth or equity).

The fundamental equation (called the *Accounting Equation*) that governs all accounting is:

Assets = Liabilities + Equity, or Equity = Assets - Liabilities.

Accounts, Accounts, Everywhere Accounts

Many factors go into making an organization work. Money and value are attached to everything that is associated with operating a company — cash, equipment, rent, utilities, wages, raw materials, merchandise, and so on. For an organization to understand its financial position, business transactions need to be recorded, summarized, balanced, and presented in reports according to the rules of accounting.

Business transactions (e.g., sales, purchases, operating expense payments) are recorded in several types of *ledgers*, called accounts. The summary of all transactions in all ledgers for a company is called the *General Ledger*. A listing of every account in the General Ledger is called the *Chart of Accounts*.

Each account summarizes transactions that increase or decrease the *equity* in your organization. The figure below shows a general picture of the effect your accounts have on the equity of your organization. Some accounts (those on the left) increase equity when they are increased, while others (those on the right) decrease equity when they are increased.

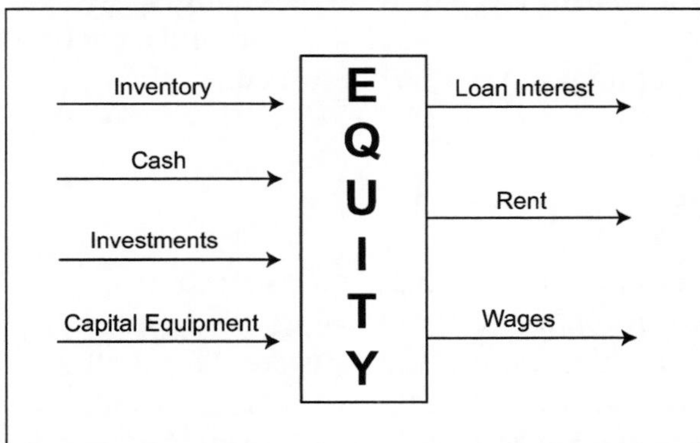

So let's return to the Accounting Equation. To understand the accounting equation, consider the following statement. **Everything a company owns was purchased by funds from creditors or by the owner's stake in the company.**

Account Types and Financial Reports

Each account in the general ledger has a type, which describes what kind of business transaction is stored in that account. There are primarily five types of account types: asset, liability, equity, income, or expense. Assets, liabilities, and equity accounts are associated with the **Balance Sheet** report which is used to analyze the net worth of a business. The income and expense accounts are associated with the **Profit and Loss** report (also called Income Statement) which is used to analyze the operating profit and loss for a business over a specific time range (month, quarter, year, etc.).

The Balance Sheet report preserves the fundamental accounting equation - **Total assets always equal the total liabilities plus equity**, between the accounts. This means that the total of the assets (which represent what the company "owns") is always equal to the sum of the liabilities (representing what the company owes) plus the equity (representing the owner's interest in the company). Although income and expense accounts are not directly shown in the accounting equation, they do affect this equation via the equity account as shown below.

The income and expenses are tracked throughout the year as business transactions occur and are totaled at the end of the year to calculate Net Income (or Loss). **Net income (total revenues minus total expenses) increases the owner's equity in the business and net loss (when expenses exceed revenues) does the opposite.** Thus the Income and Expense accounts indirectly affect the Equity component of the Accounting Equation Assets = Liabilities + Equity, where **Equity increases or decreases each year depending on whether the year's income exceeds expenses or not.**

At the end of the year, the balance of each income and expense account is reset to zero so these accounts can track the next year's transactions.

Double-Entry Accounting

Double-entry accounting is the technique that makes the Accounting Equation work. It divides each account into two sides. One side is a record of transactions that increase the account and the other side is a record of all transactions that decrease the account. One side (the left side) is for debits, and the other is for credits (the right side). Depending on the type of account, a debit might increase the account or decrease it. The same is true of credits. Therefore, debits are not always bad and credits are not always good. They are just part of the system of accounting. However, the rule of double-entry accounting is that **total debits must always equal total credits.** Every transaction creates a debit in one or more accounts and a credit in one or more accounts. If the debits and credits for any transaction are not equal, the transaction has an error or is incomplete.

Accounting Behind the Scenes

Recording and categorizing all of your business transactions into the proper accounts, summarizing and adjusting them, and then preparing financial statements can be an enormous, labor-intensive task without the help of a computer and software. This is where QuickBooks comes in. QuickBooks focuses on ease of use and hiding accounting details. To make all this possible, QuickBooks uses components like accounts, items, forms, registers and lists, which are discussed later in the chapter. Familiar-looking forms such as invoices, checks and bills are used for data entry. As you enter data in forms, QuickBooks handles the accounting entries for you. Thus business owners can use QuickBooks to efficiently run a business without getting bogged down with the debits and credits of accounting entries.

QuickBooks also handles double-entry for you. Every transaction you enter in the program automatically becomes a debit to one or more accounts and a credit to one or more other accounts, and QuickBooks won't let you record the transaction until the total of the debits equals the total of the credits. It means you can create reports that show the transactions in the full double-entry accounting format whenever you need them. This allows you to focus on the business transaction rather than the debits and credits in the General Ledger.

Cash or accrual method is handled in QuickBooks as a simple reporting option. You can create reports for either cash or accrual basis regardless of the method you use for taxes.

As the book introduces new transactions types (e.g., Invoices, Bills, or Checks), the text will include a section called "The accounting behind the scenes." For example, when you first learn about invoices you will see the following message:

The accounting behind the scenes:
When you create an **Invoice**, QuickBooks increases (with a debit) **Accounts Receivable** and increases (with a credit) the appropriate **income** account. If applicable, **Invoices** and **Sales Receipts** also increase (with a credit) the sales tax liability account.

Letting QuickBooks handle the accounting behind the scenes means you can focus on your organization and identify the important factors that will help you succeed. Once you identify these factors, you can use QuickBooks to monitor them and provide information that will guide you in managing your operations.

Accounting for the Future: Cash or Accrual?

Another critical aspect of accounting is managing for the future. Many times, your organization will have assets and liabilities that represent money owed to the company, or owed by the company, but are not yet due. For example, you may have sold something to a customer and sent an invoice, but the payment has not been received. In this case, you have an outstanding *receivable*. Similarly, you may have a bill for insurance that is not yet due. In this case, you have an outstanding *payable*.

An accounting system that uses the *accrual basis* method of accounting tracks these receivables and payables and uses them to evaluate a company's financial position. The *accrual basis* method specifies that revenues and expenses are *recognized* in the period in which the transactions occur, rather than in the period in which cash changes hands. So to help you manage the future and to more accurately reflect the true profitability of the business in each period, assets, liabilities, income, and expenses are entered when you know about them, and they are used to identify what you need on hand to meet both current, and known, future obligations.

In the *cash basis* method, revenues and expenses are not *recognized* until cash changes hands. So revenue is not recognized until the customer pays, and an expense is not recognized until you pay the bill for the expense. In most cash basis systems, you must use an outside system to track open invoices and unpaid bills, which means you cannot view both cash and accrual reports without going to several places to find information. However in QuickBooks, you can record transactions such as invoices and bills to facilitate *accrual basis* reporting, and with the same system, you can create *cash basis* reports that remove the receivables and payables.

Although certain types of organizations can use the cash basis method of accounting (many are not allowed to do so under IRS regulations), the accrual method provides the most accurate picture for managing your organization. You should check with your tax accountant to determine which accounting method (cash or accrual) is best for you.

Academy Photography Sample Company

Throughout this book, you will see references to a fictitious company called Academy Photography. Academy Photography is a photography studio that also sells camera equipment. This company uses QuickBooks for its accounting and business management. Academy Photography may not be exactly like your business; however, the examples in this text that focus on Academy Photography are generic enough to guide you on your own use of QuickBooks.

Academy Photography has two locations, one in San Jose and another in Walnut Creek. In order for management to separately track revenue and expenses for each store, Academy Photography uses **Classes** in QuickBooks. As you proceed through the book, you'll see how each transaction (bill, check, invoice, etc.) is tagged with what *Class* it belongs to, so that later you can create reports like Profit & Loss by Class. Classes can be used to separately track departments, profit-centers, store locations, or funds in any business.

Academy Photography also needs to separately track revenue and expenses for each job it performs. When a customer orders a photo shoot, Academy Photography needs to track all of the revenue and expenses specifically related to that job so it can look back and see how profitable the job was. This concept is called *job-costing*, and many different businesses need to track jobs in similar ways.

As you think through the examples with Academy Photography, ask yourself what parallels you see to your own organization. Certainly, areas such as salaries, supplies, equipment, and others will be appropriate for your setup, but the names and specifics of the accounts, items, lists, and forms will probably be different.

About QuickBooks Files

Before using QuickBooks, it is important for you to understand how QuickBooks files are structured and used. QuickBooks has three primary types of files described below. In the filename the letters after the dot (.) are referred to as the file extension and are used by Microsoft Windows to associate files with the appropriate application program. All filetypes can be opened using the *Open or Restore Company* option from the *File* menu.

1. *Working Data Files* – These files are used to enter transactions and create reports. The file extension for these files is ".QBW".
2. *Portable Company Files* –These files are a compact version of the company data files and are used to transport the file between computers or send as email attachment. The file extension for these files is ".QBM". These files should never be used to backup your QuickBooks data. These files must be "Restored" to a working data file to be used.
3. *Backup Files* –These files are compressed version of the company data files and are used as backup to safeguard the information. The file extension for these files is ".QBB". These files cannot be used directly within QuickBooks and must be "Restored" to working data file format.

This means, if you name your company file ABC, QuickBooks will store the working data file on disk as "ABC.QBW." When you back up your company file using the QuickBooks Backup function, QuickBooks will store your backup file with the name "ABC.QBB." If you create a portable data file using the QuickBooks Portable file creation function, the portable file "ABC.QBM" will be created and stored on the disk.

> **Important:**
> Each file type has a specific purpose and should be used accordingly. Working data files are used to enter data and run reports, backup files are used to safeguard the data, and portable files are compressed files used to transport data via the Internet where smaller files transfer faster.

Opening a QuickBooks Sample File

For learning purposes, QuickBooks provides sample data files that allow you to explore the program. To open a sample data file, follow these steps:

COMPUTER PRACTICE

Step 1. Launch the QuickBooks program by double-clicking the icon on your desktop or selecting it from the Windows Start menu.

Step 2. When QuickBooks opens, you will either see the ***No Company Open*** window (Figure 1-2) or the *last working data file* used.

No Company Open window is displayed if you are opening QuickBooks for the first time or if you closed the working data file *before* exiting in your last session. By default, the last working data file used will open, if you closed the QuickBooks *program* before closing the *file*.

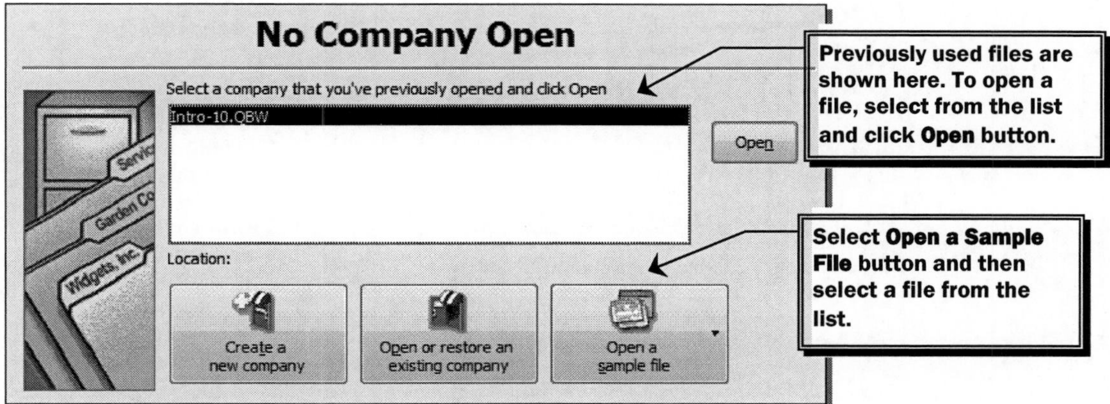

Figure 1-2 No Company Open window

Step 3. If you don't see the ***No Company Open*** window (Figure 1-2), select the **File** menu, and then select **Close Company**. Click **No** if you are prompted to back up your file.

Step 4. Click **Open a Sample file** button (Figure 1-2) and select one of the files from the list. The selected sample file will open with the *QuickBooks Information* screen (Figure 1-3).

Step 5. Click **OK** to continue.

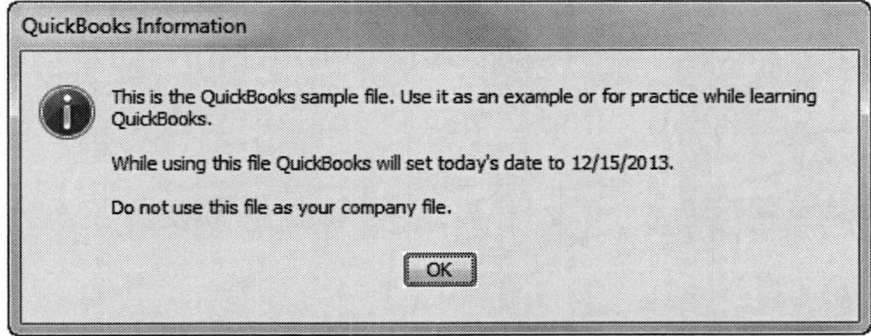

Figure 1-3 Sample File Information Screen

Step 6. The sample file you selected will open and then the Overview & Setup screen (Figure 1-4) may be displayed. This appears by default when you open a file, however, if you do not want to see it appear next time you open *this* file, you can uncheck the *Show this window at startup* box.

You can work with the tutorials available on this window to become familiar with the QuickBooks program. After you are done, close this window by clicking the *Begin Using QuickBooks* button at the bottom right corner of the window.

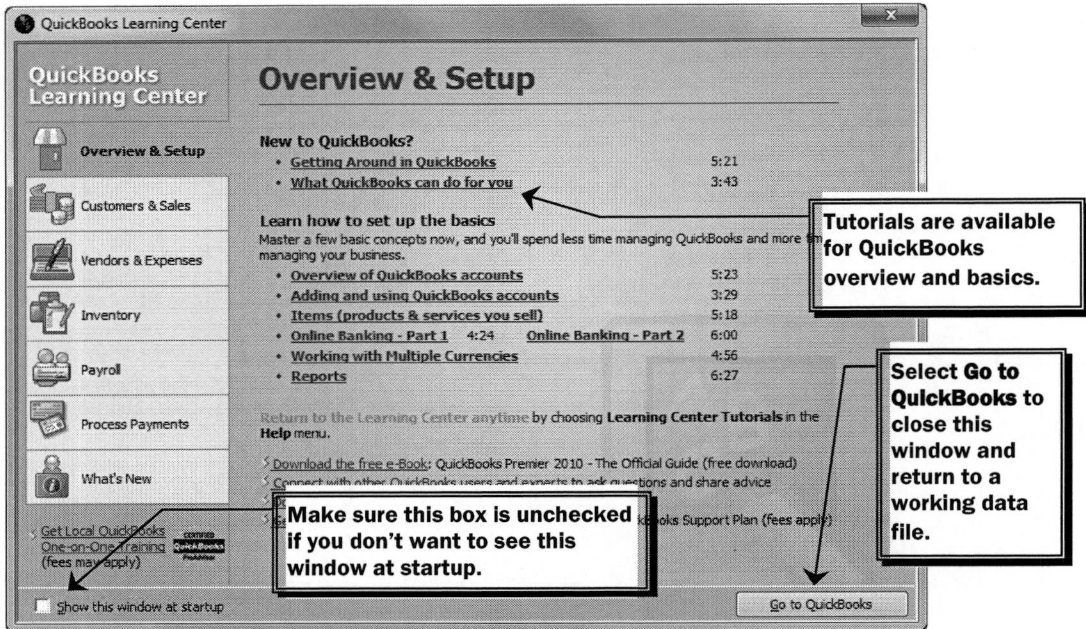

Figure 1-4 Welcome to QuickBooks Screen

Opening Other QuickBooks Data Files

If you want to open a QuickBooks company file other than the sample data files, you would follow the steps below. We will not complete these steps now, but will use a restored portable file in the next section.

DO NOT PERFORM THESE STEPS. THEY ARE FOR REFERENCE ONLY.

1. Launch the QuickBooks program by double-clicking the icon on your desktop or selecting it from the Windows Start menu. When QuickBooks opens, it launches the data file you previously had open when you last exited the program, unless you specifically closed the data file before exiting.
2. To open a different file, select the **File** menu and then select **Open or Restore Company** (see Figure 1-5).

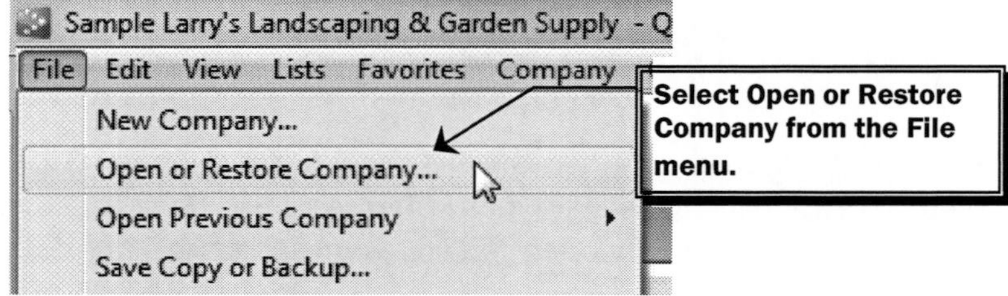

Figure 1-5 File menu

3. In the *Open or Restore Company* window, select **Open a company file** (.QBW) and click **Next.**

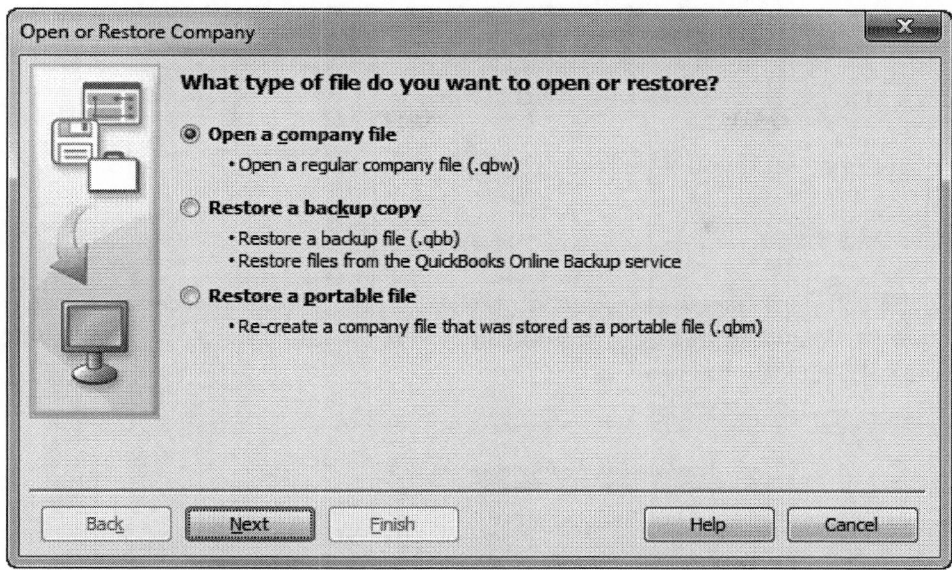

Figure 1-6 Open Company: Type window

4. Set the *Look in* field to the folder on your hard disk where you store your QuickBooks file (see Figure 1-7).

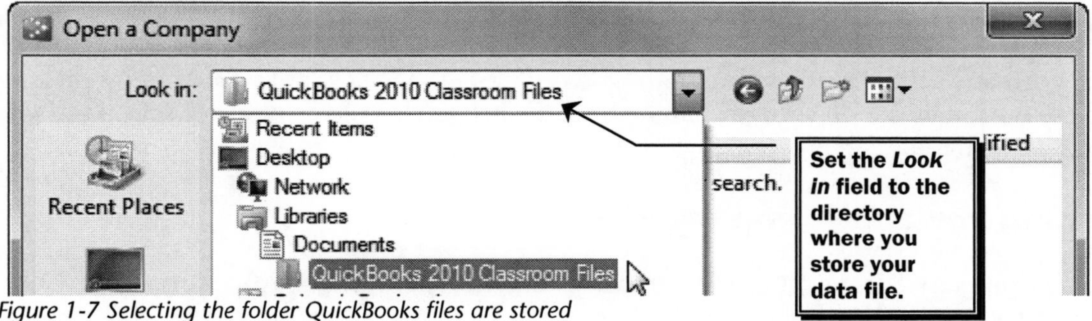

Figure 1-7 Selecting the folder QuickBooks files are stored

5. Select the file from the list of QuickBooks files (see Figure 1-8). Then click **Open**.

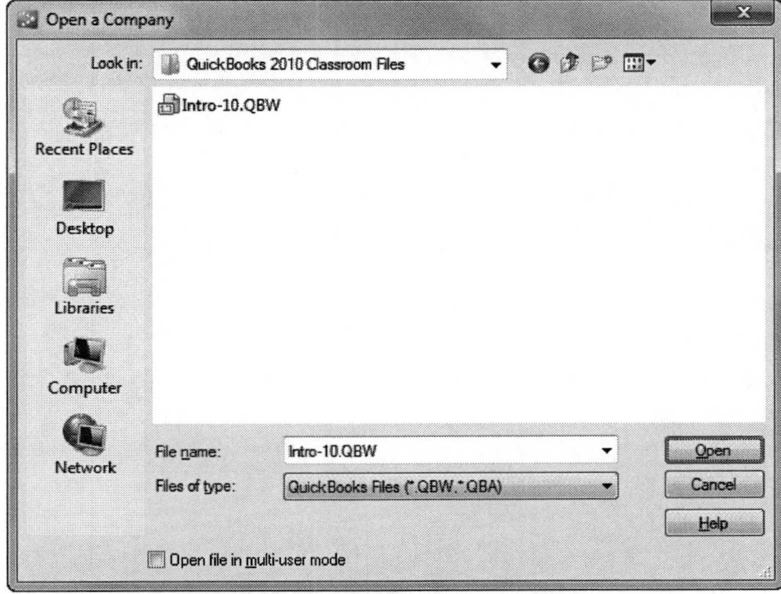

Figure 1-8 Open a Company window

Note: When you open a data file, depending on today's date, you may see one or more "Alerts" for learning to process credit cards, pay taxes, or similar activities. Click Mark as Done when you see these alerts.

Your company file will open, and you'll be ready to work with QuickBooks.

Closing QuickBooks Files

Step 1. Close the company data file by selecting **Close Company** from the *File* menu (see Figure 1-9). If you skip this step, this data file will open automatically next time when you start the QuickBooks program.

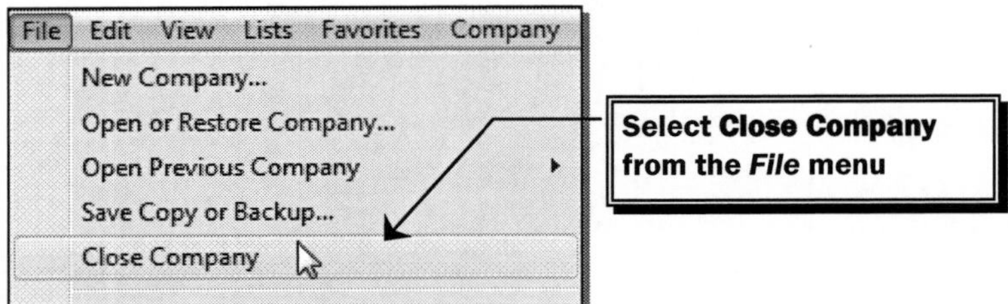

Figure 1-9 Close Company File option

Closing the QuickBooks Program

Just as with any other Windows program, you can close the QuickBooks program by clicking the close button at the upper right hand corner of the QuickBooks window or selecting **Exit** from the *File* menu.

Opening Portable Company Files

Portable Company Files are compact company data files that can be easily transported. The exercise files that accompany this book are portable files. You will need to open these exercise files at the start of each chapter and each problem.

When you move a data file from one computer (computer A) to another (computer B), any data you enter on computer B will cause the file on the computer A to become "obsolete." That is, the file on computer B has new data and there is no way to transfer that new data into the file on computer A, except by manually entering the data or by replacing the whole file on computer A with the new file. Therefore, when you copy data files from one computer to another, you cannot continue to work on the file in both places.

COMPUTER PRACTICE

To open portable files follow the steps below.

Step 1. Select the **Open or Restore Company** option from the *File* menu (see Figure 1-10).

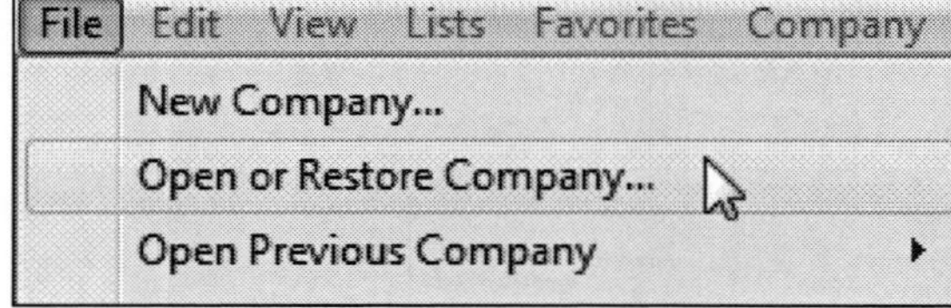

Figure 1-10 Open or Restore Company

Step 2. QuickBooks displays the *Open or Restore Company* window. Select **Restore a portable file (.QBM)** and click **Next.**

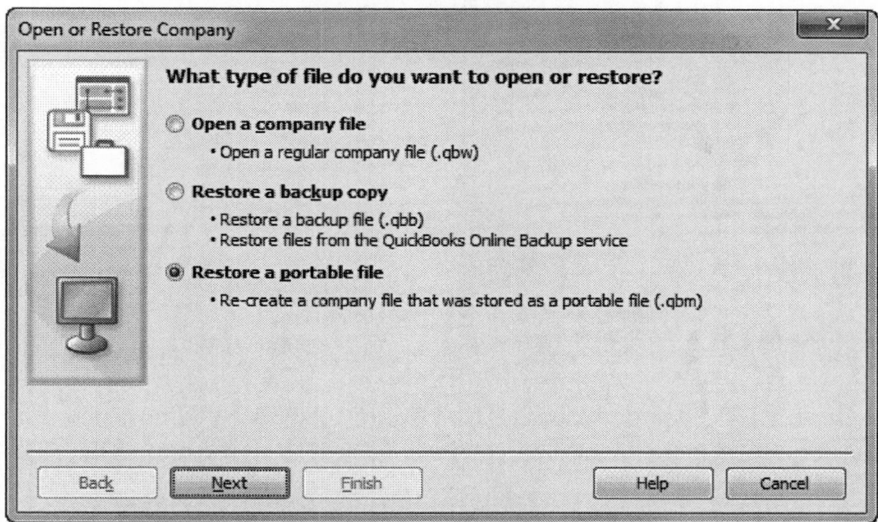

Figure 1-11 Open or Restore Company window

Step 3. QuickBooks displays the *Open Portable Company File* window (see Figure 1-12). Navigate to the location of your exercise files. You may need to ask your instructor if you do not know this location. Once you are viewing the contents of correct folder, select **Intro-10.QBM** and click **Open.**

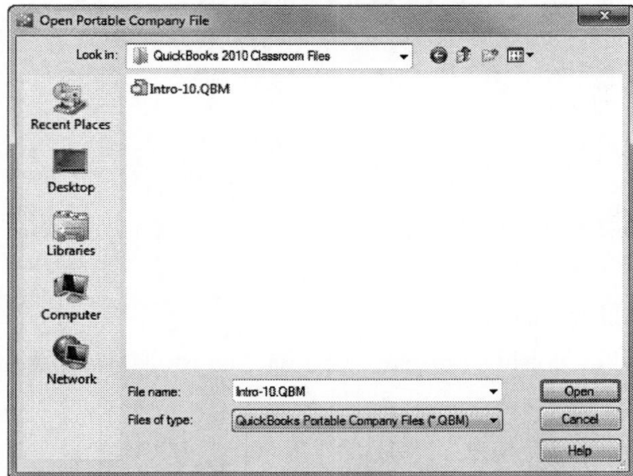

Figure 1-12 Open Portable Company File window

Step 4. Next you will need to tell QuickBooks where to save the working file that will be created from the portable file (see Figure 1-13). Click **Next** in the *Open or Restore Company* window to continue.

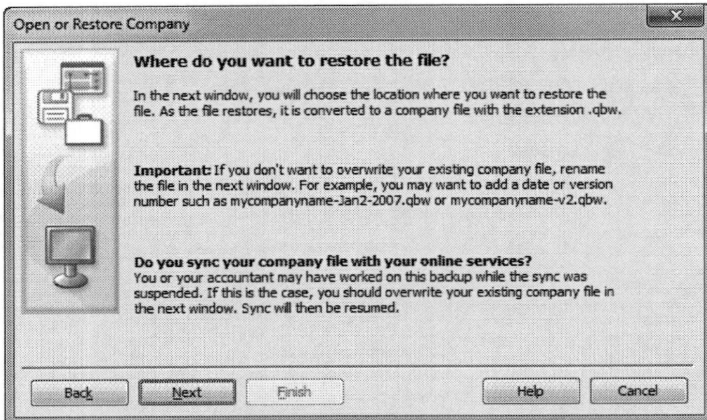

Figure 1-13 Open or Restore Company Location

Step 5. The *Save Company File as* window displays (see Figure 1-14). Ask your instructor or choose a location to save the file. When you have navigated to the appropriate folder, click **Save**.

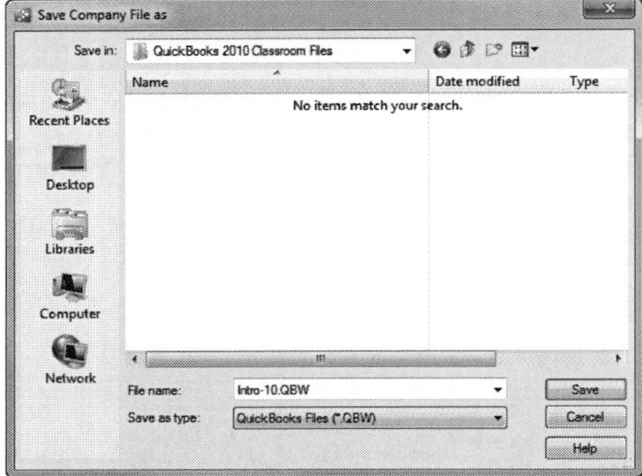

Figure 1-14 Save Company File as window

Step 6. If asked to update your company files, click **Yes**.

Step 7. Once the Intro-10.QBW company file finishes opening, you will see the Home page.

Creating Portable Company Files

Step 1. Select the **Save Copy or Backup** option from the *File* menu (see Figure 1-15).

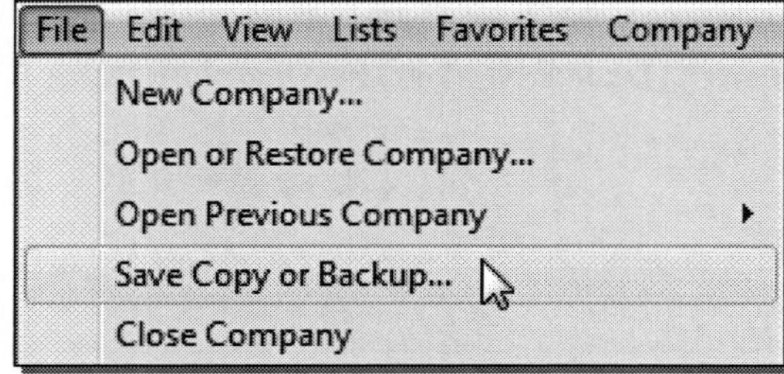

Figure 1-15 Save Copy or Backup option

Step 2. The *Save Copy or Backup* window displays. Select the **Portable company file** option and click **Next**.

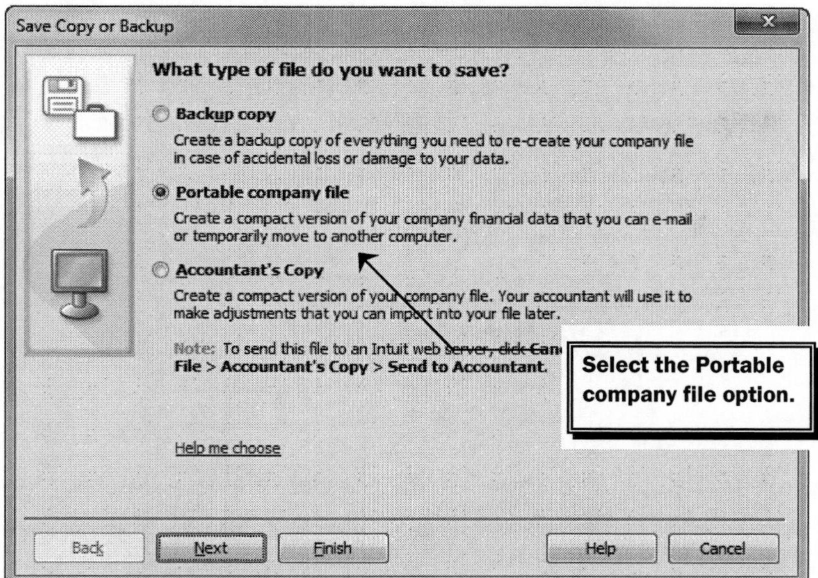

Figure 1-16 Save Copy or Backup window

Step 3. The *Save Portable Company File* window appears. The default file name in the *File name* field is the same as the working file name with "(Portable)" added to the end. For this exercise we will use the default file name.

Navigate to the student file location and click **Save**.

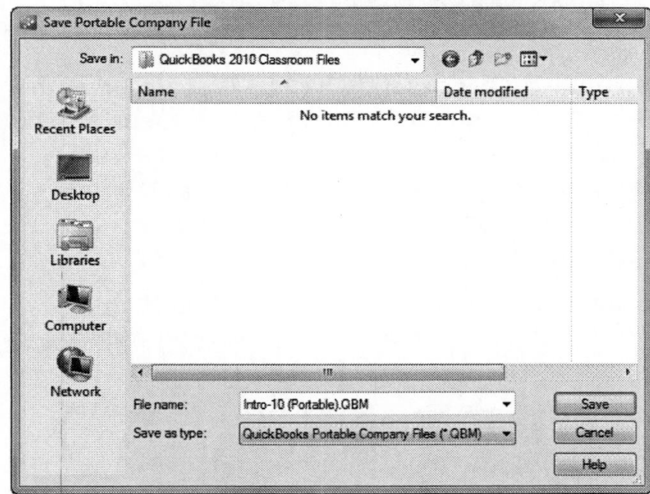

Figure 1-17 Save Portable Company File window

Step 4. The message shown in Figure 1-18 will appear before the portable file is created. Click **OK** to continue.

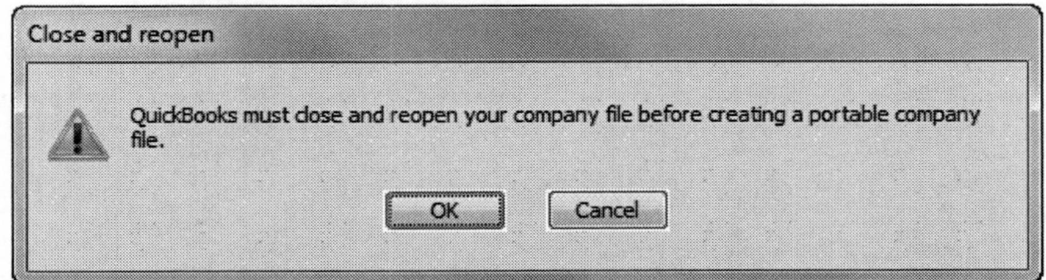

Figure 1-18 Message for creating portable company file

Step 5. QuickBooks displays the *QuickBooks Information* dialog box (see Figure 1-19). Click **OK** to return to the working data file.

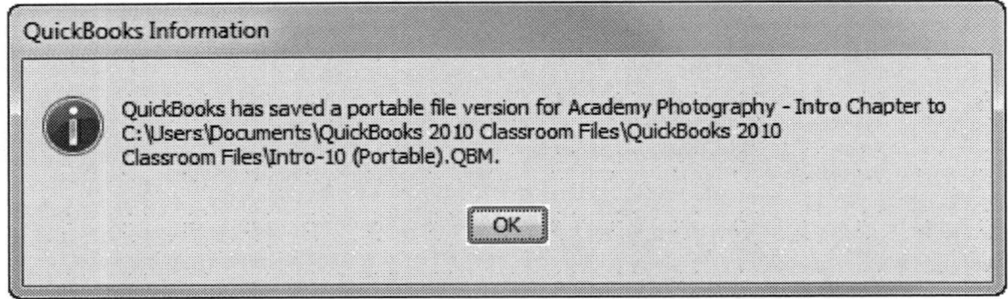

Figure 1-19 Message that the Portable File has been successfully created

Restoring Backup Files

When working with important financial information, creating backup files is a crucial safeguard against data loss. Every business should conduct regular backups of company information. QuickBooks has useful tools to automate this process.

In the event of an emergency, you may need to restore lost or damaged data. For example, if your computer's hard drive fails, you can restore your backup onto another computer and continue to work.

> **Important:**
> Restoring **does not add information** to your file, but **replaces your data** with a new file that has all of the data you had when you created the backup. Consequently, you should only restore a file when you are certain it is necessary.

Portable files should never be used as a substitute for backup files. Backup files are larger than portable files and hold more information about the company. When you create a backup file, QuickBooks resets a log file that tracks all the changes made to the file between backups. Intuit Customer Support can use this file to troubleshoot and help restore information in case you need to recreate your current company information from a restored backup.

In general, there are two main uses for QuickBooks backup files.

1. When you transfer files between computers and need more information than is contained within the portable file (for example, between accountant and client).
2. To recover damaged or lost data files.

> Note:
> In addition to the Backup and Restore process which moves the complete QuickBooks file between computers, QuickBooks also has a feature called the accountant's review. This feature enables an accountant to review and make corrections to a special copy of the client's company file while the client continues to work. Then the client can *merge* the accountant's changes back into the original file. See the QuickBooks Help Index for information on this feature.

Backing up Your Data File

Backing up your data is one of the most important safeguards you have to ensure the safety of your data.

DO NOT PERFORM THESE STEPS. THEY ARE FOR REFERENCE ONLY.

1. To backup your company file, select **Save Copy or Backup** from the *File* menu.
2. Choose **Backup** from the *Save File: Type* window. Click **Next.**
3. The *Save Copy or Backup* window displays (see Figure 1-20). You are given the option to save the backup to a local area, such as a removable disk, or an online backup using a fee-based service available from Intuit. Online backup is a good option for many companies. See the Appendix in the supplemental material (see page xiii) for more information about where to back up the file.

   Choose **Local backup** and click **Next.**

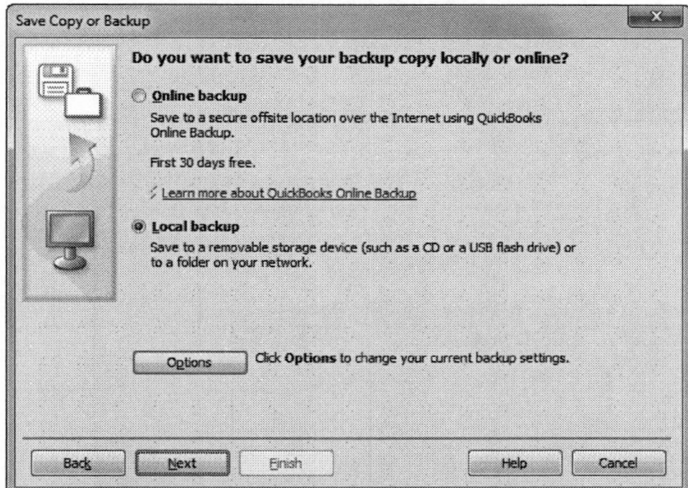

Figure 1-20 Save Copy or Backup window

4. The *Backup Options* window is displayed (see Figure 1-21). Under the *Local backup only* section, click the Browse button.

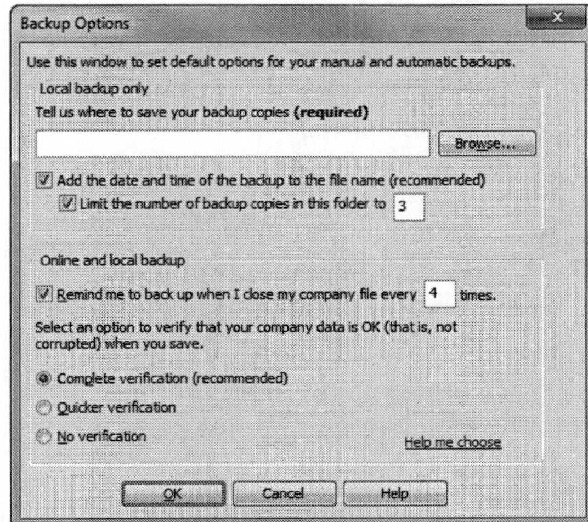

Figure 1-21 Backup Options window

5. Select the folder where you want to store your backup file (see Figure 1-22). You should store the backup files on a safe location, preferably on a different drive than your working data file. That way, if the drive with the working file is damaged, the backup will still be available.

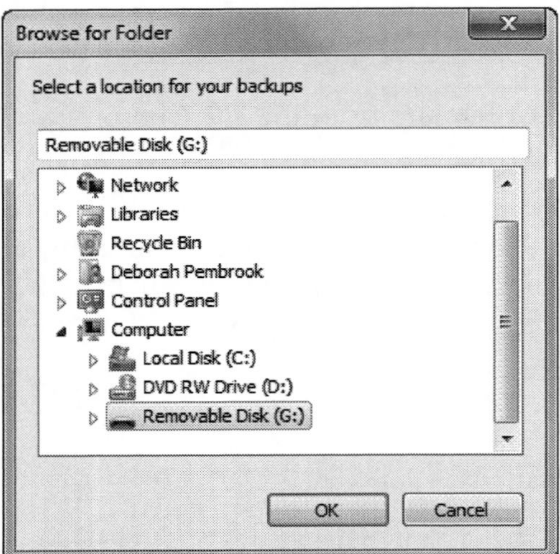

Figure 1-22 Backup options Browse for Folder window

6. When finished, click OK.
7. The *Save Copy or Backup* window is displayed (see Figure 1-23). You can save a backup now, schedule future backups, or both. Select **Only schedule future backups** and click **Next.**

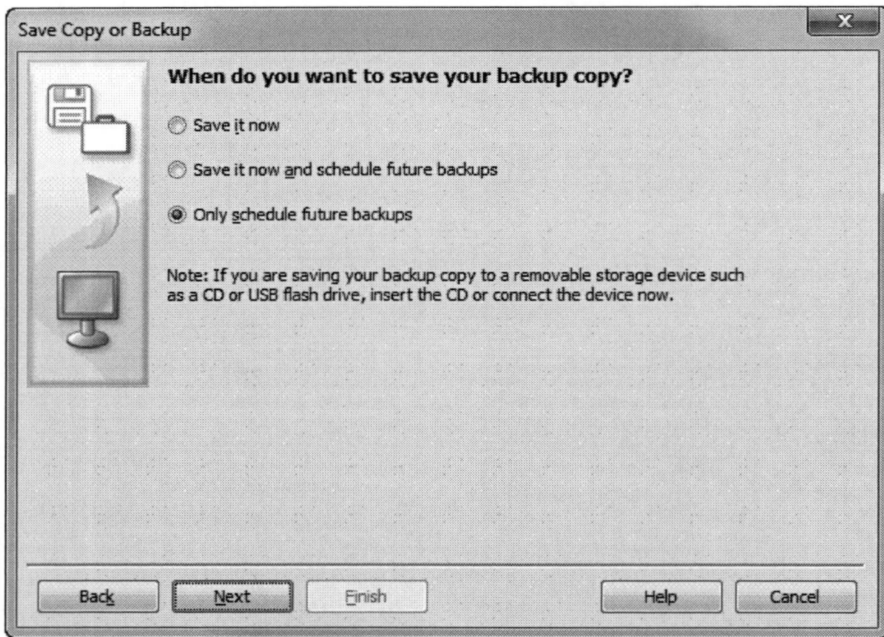

Figure 1-23 Save Copy or Backup window

8. In the *Save Copy or Backup* window, select **New** under the *Schedule Backup* area.

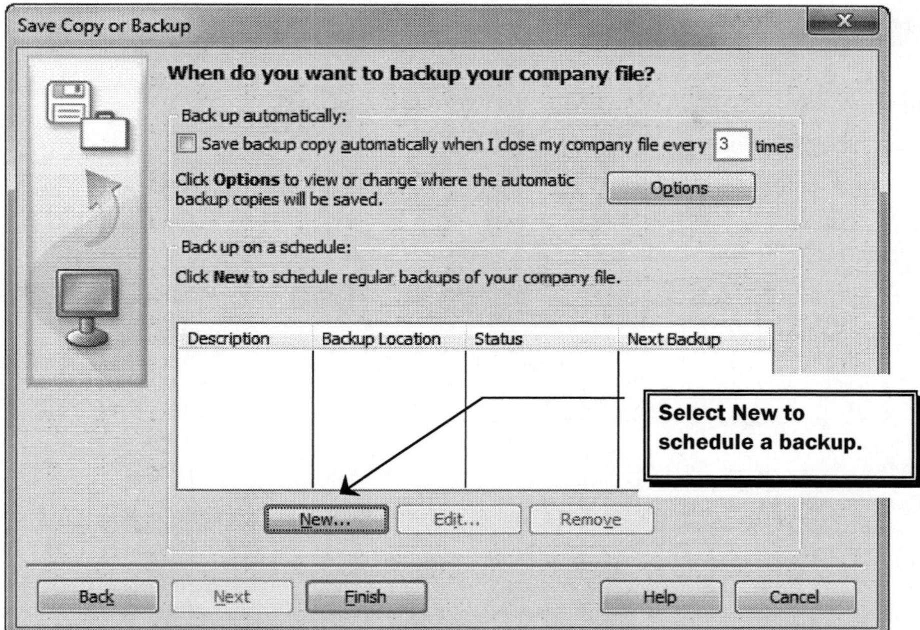

Figure 1-24 Save Copy or Backup window

9. The Schedule Backup window appears (see Figure 1-25). Enter a descriptive name for the backup, the location of the folder to contain the backups, and the time when the backup file will be created.

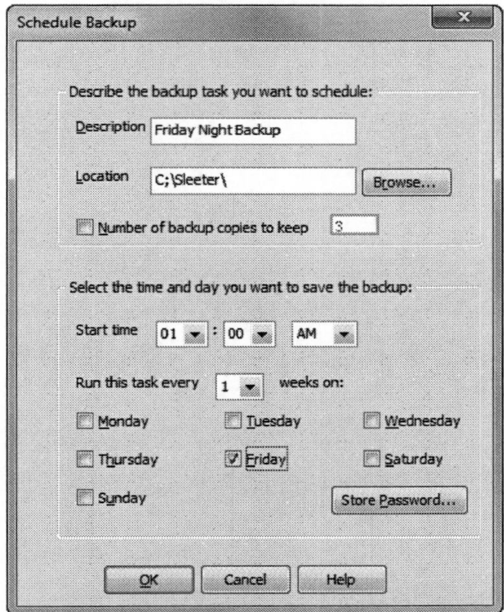

Figure 1-25 Schedule Backup window

10. When finished click **OK** to close the *Schedule Backup* window
11. Click **Finish** to close the *Schedule Backup* window.

Restoring a Backup File

To restore a QuickBooks backup file, follow these steps.

DO NOT PERFORM THESE STEPS. THEY ARE FOR REFERENCE ONLY.

1. Select the **File** menu and then select **Open or Restore Company**.
2. Choose **Restore a backup copy (.QBB)** from the *Open or Restore Company* window.
3. In the *Open or Restore Company* window (see Figure 1-26) you can specify whether the file is stored locally or if you use Intuit's fee-based *Online Backup* service. Choose **Local backup** and click **Next**.

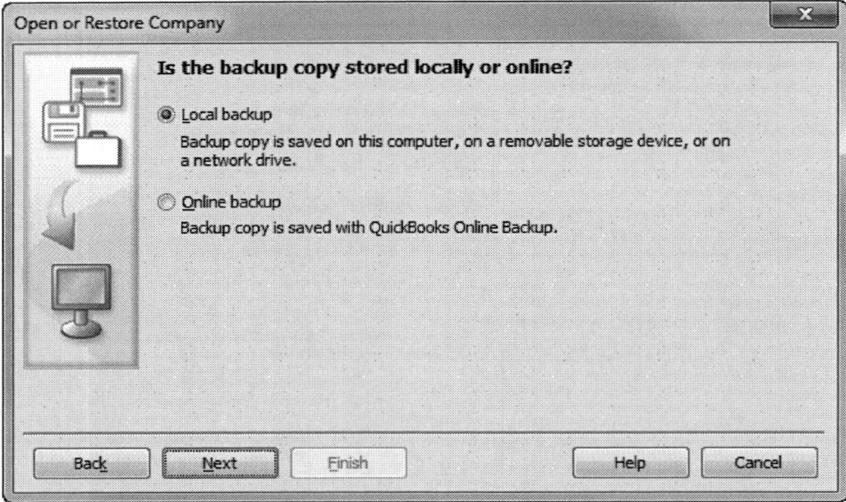

Figure 1-26 Open or Restore Company window

4. The *Open Backup Copy* window allows you to specify where the backup file is located (see Figure 1-27). Navigate to the folder that contains the file, select it and click **Open**.

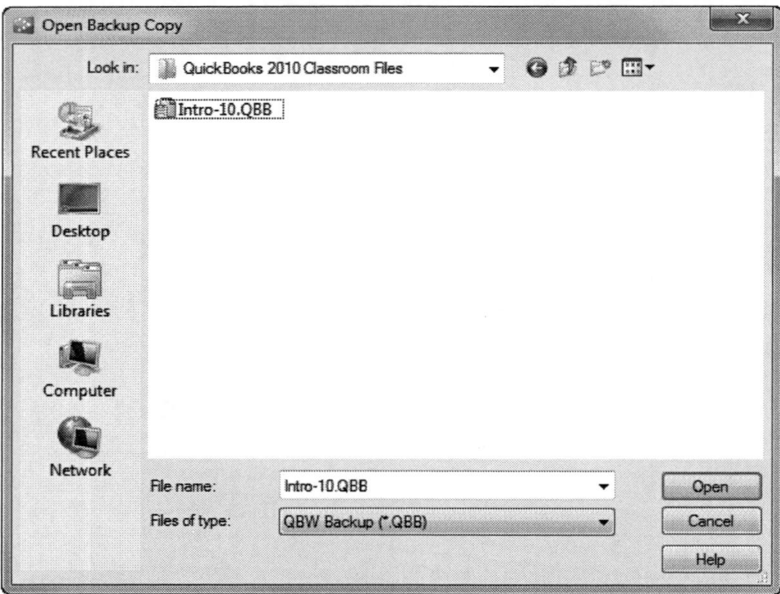

Figure 1-27 Open Backup Copy window

5. The *Open or Restore Company* window displays. Click **Next**.
6. The *Save Company File as* window allows you to specify where to restore the working files (see Figure 1-28). Navigate to the appropriate folder and click **Save**.

QuickBooks will then restore your backup file in the folder you specified. When QuickBooks restores the file, it creates a ".QBW" file.

Figure 1-28 Save Company File as window

7. If you receive the warning message shown in Figure 1-29, it means that QuickBooks is attempting to overwrite an existing file on your computer. If this is your intention, click **Yes**. If you do not intend to replace an existing file, click **No** and change the name of the restored file.

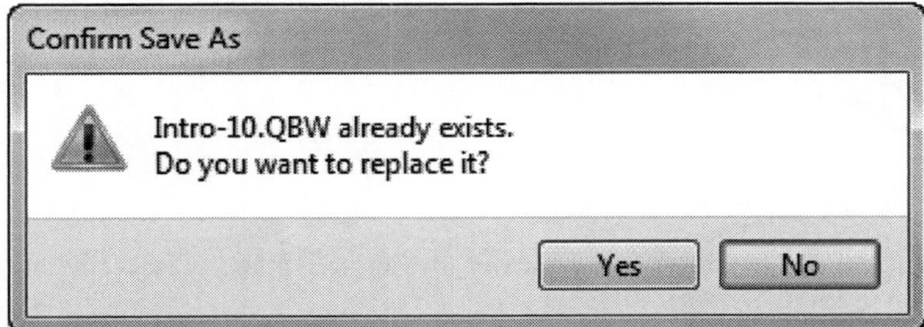

Figure 1-29 Restore To warning

> **Tip:** If you are not sure if you should replace a file, change the name of the restoring file slightly. For example *Intro-10 (version 2).QBW* would keep the file from being overwritten and indicate to users the most recent version.

8. After completion, a window displays that the new file has been successfully restored (see Figure 1-30).

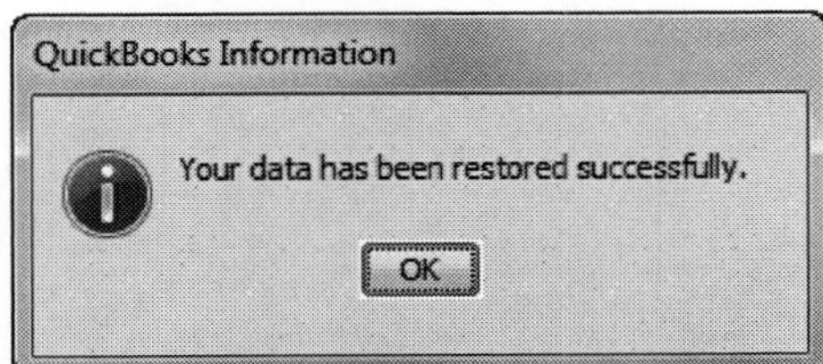

Figure 1-30 After restoring backup file

Note: When you restore a data file, depending on today's date, you may see one or more "Alerts" for learning to process credit cards, pay taxes, or similar activities. Click Mark as Done when you see these alerts.

Entering Transactions in QuickBooks

Whenever you buy or sell products or services, pay a bill, make a deposit at the bank, or transfer money, you enter a transaction into QuickBooks.

Forms

In QuickBooks, transactions are created by filling out familiar-looking forms such as invoices, bills, and checks. As you fill out forms, you choose names from *lists* such as the customer list, the item list, and the account list. When you finish filling out a form, QuickBooks automatically records the accounting entries behind the scenes. Most forms in QuickBooks have drop-down lists to allow you to pick items from lists instead of spelling the name of a customer, vendor, item, or account. The Pop-up calendar is another feature available on forms which allows you to pick a date on the calendar rather than entering the whole date.

COMPUTER PRACTICE

Step 1. Click the **Enter Bills** icon on the *Home* page (see Figure 1-31).

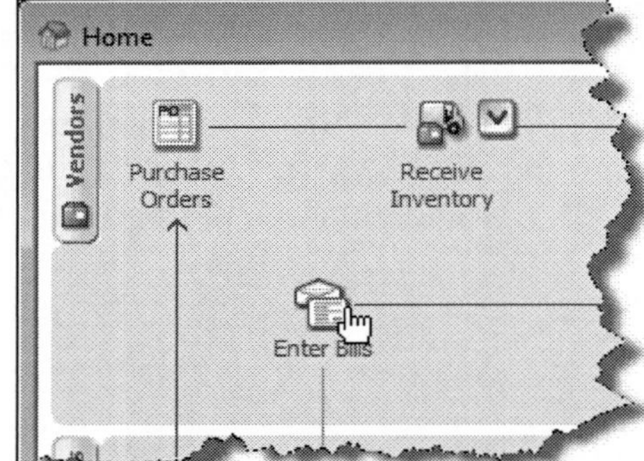

Figure 1-31 Enter Bills on the Home page

Step 2. Click the **Previous** button on the *Enter Bills* window until you see the previously entered bills in Figure 1-32.

Step 3. Click the down arrow next to the vendor field to see the dropdown list for vendors.

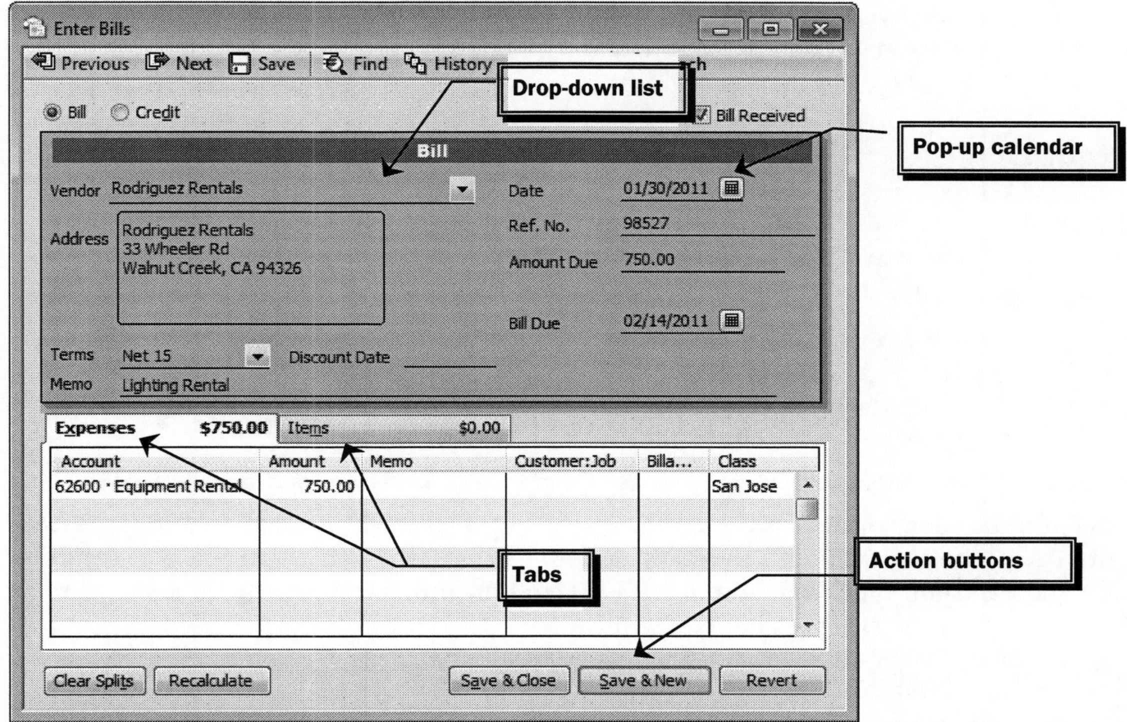

Figure 1-32 Bill form

Step 4. Click the calendar icon next to the date to see the calendar pop-up menu.

Step 5. When finished exploring, click the **Revert** button which will return the transaction to the last saved state.

Step 6. Close the Enter Bills window.

By using forms to enter transactions, you provide QuickBooks with *all of the details* of each transaction. For example, by using the Enter Bills form in Figure 1-32, QuickBooks will track the vendor balance, the due date of the bill, the discount terms, and the debits and credits in the General Ledger. This is a good example of how QuickBooks handles the accounting behind the scenes, and also provides management information beyond just the accounting entries.

Lists

Lists are one of the most important building blocks of QuickBooks that makes the program very powerful and efficient. Lists store information which is used again and again to fill out forms. For example, when you set up a customer's name, address, account number, etc. QuickBooks can use the information to automatically fill out an invoice. Similarly, when an Item is set up, QuickBooks can automatically fill in the Item's description, price, and associated account information. This helps speed up data entry and reduces errors.

> Note:
> There are two kinds of lists, **menu-based** and **center-based**. Menu-based lists are accessible through the *List* menu and include the *Item* list and *Terms* lists. Center-based lists include the *Customer Center* and *Vendor Center*, discussed on page 27.

Lists can be viewed by selecting an icon from the *Home* page (for example, the *Items & Services* button), choosing a menu option from the *Lists* menu, or viewing a list through one of the various QuickBooks Centers.

Accounts

QuickBooks provides the means to efficiently track all of your business transactions by categorizing them into *accounts*. The **Chart of Accounts** is the list of these accounts.

COMPUTER PRACTICE

Step 1. To display the Chart of Accounts, click the *Chart of Accounts* icon on the *Home* page.

Alternatively, you could select **Chart of Accounts** from the *List* menu, or press **Ctrl+A.**

Step 2. Scroll through the list. Leave the *Chart of Accounts* open for the next exercise.

By default, the Chart of Accounts is sorted *by account number* within each account type (see Figure 1-33). The *Name* column shows the account names that you assign; the *type* column shows their account type; and, and the *balance* column shows the balance for asset, liability, and equity accounts (except Retained Earnings).

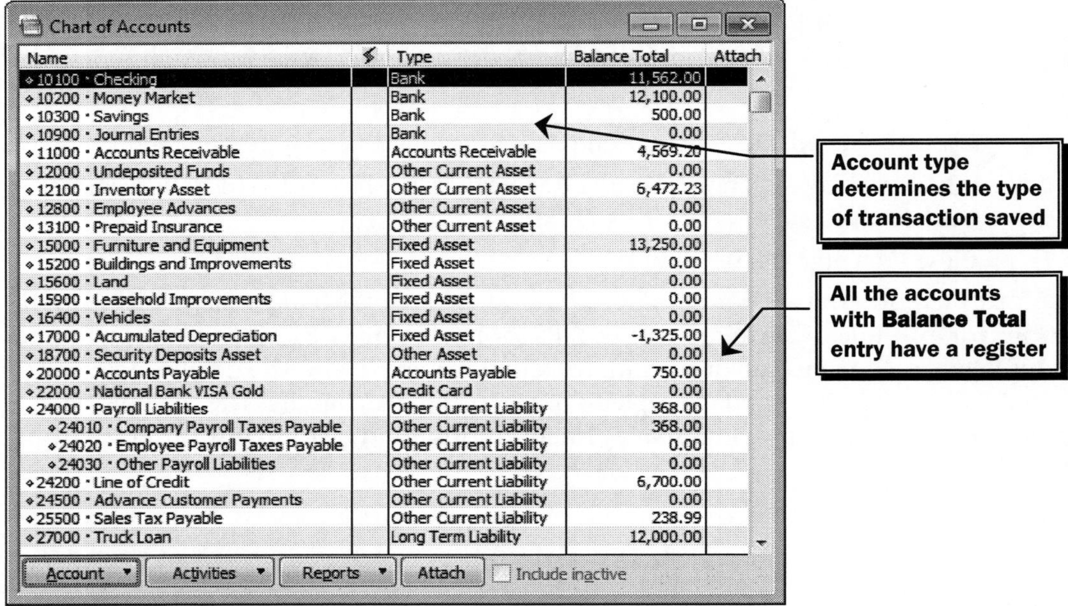

Chart of Accounts

Name	Type	Balance Total	Attach
10100 · Checking	Bank	11,562.00	
10200 · Money Market	Bank	12,100.00	
10300 · Savings	Bank	500.00	
10900 · Journal Entries	Bank	0.00	
11000 · Accounts Receivable	Accounts Receivable	4,569.20	
12000 · Undeposited Funds	Other Current Asset	0.00	
12100 · Inventory Asset	Other Current Asset	6,472.23	
12800 · Employee Advances	Other Current Asset	0.00	
13100 · Prepaid Insurance	Other Current Asset	0.00	
15000 · Furniture and Equipment	Fixed Asset	13,250.00	
15200 · Buildings and Improvements	Fixed Asset	0.00	
15600 · Land	Fixed Asset	0.00	
15900 · Leasehold Improvements	Fixed Asset	0.00	
16400 · Vehicles	Fixed Asset	0.00	
17000 · Accumulated Depreciation	Fixed Asset	-1,325.00	
18700 · Security Deposits Asset	Other Asset	0.00	
20000 · Accounts Payable	Accounts Payable	750.00	
22000 · National Bank VISA Gold	Credit Card	0.00	
24000 · Payroll Liabilities	Other Current Liability	368.00	
24010 · Company Payroll Taxes Payable	Other Current Liability	368.00	
24020 · Employee Payroll Taxes Payable	Other Current Liability	0.00	
24030 · Other Payroll Liabilities	Other Current Liability	0.00	
24200 · Line of Credit	Other Current Liability	6,700.00	
24500 · Advance Customer Payments	Other Current Liability	0.00	
25500 · Sales Tax Payable	Other Current Liability	238.99	
27000 · Truck Loan	Long Term Liability	12,000.00	

Figure 1-33 Chart of Accounts List

Registers

Each asset, liability and equity accounts (except Retained Earnings) has a *register*. Registers allow you to view and edit transactions in a single window. Income and expense accounts do not have registers; rather, their transactions must be viewed in a report.

COMPUTER PRACTICE

Step 1. To open the *Checking* account register, double-click on **10100 Checking** in the *Chart of Accounts* list.

Step 2. The **Checking** register opens (see Figure 1-34). Scroll through the register.

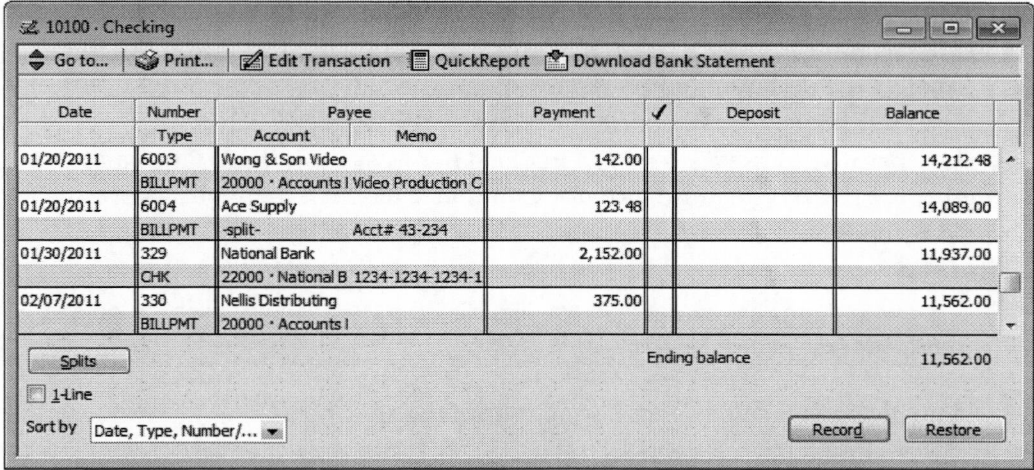

Figure 1-34 Checking account register

Step 3. Close the Checking account register by clicking the close button in the upper right corner.

Step 4. Double click the **40000 Services** account. This is an *Income* account.

Step 5. Instead of opening a register, QuickBooks opens a report (see Figure 1-35).

Step 6. If necessary, change the *Date* field to **All**.

Step 7. Close the report.

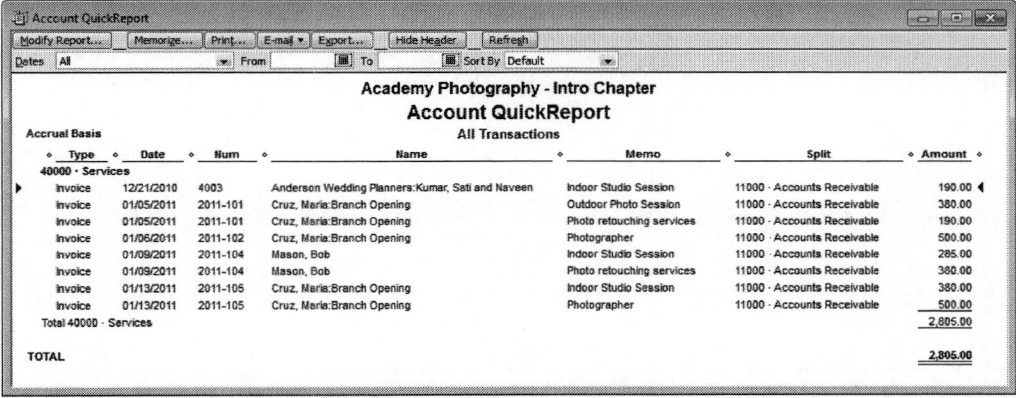

Figure 1-35 Services Account QuickReport – your screen may vary

Step 8. Close the *Chart of Accounts*.

Items

Items are used to track the detail behind QuickBooks transactions. Since every business has its own unique set of products and services, QuickBooks can be customized to your business by creating Items for each service or product your company buys or sells.

QuickBooks allows twelve item-types for Items associated with buying and selling: *Service, Inventory Part, Inventory Assembly* (Premier and Enterprise Solutions only), *Non-Inventory part, Fixed Asset, Other Charge, Subtotal, Group, Discount, Payment, Sales Tax Item,* and *Sales Tax Group*.

When you define Items, you associate Item names with Accounts in the Chart of Accounts. This association between Item names and Accounts is the "magic" that allows QuickBooks to automatically create the accounting entries behind each transaction.

For example, Figure 1-37 displays the *Item* list. The Item, **Camera SR32**, is associated, or linked, to the **Sales** account in the Chart of Accounts. Every time the **Camera SR32** Item is entered on an invoice, the dollar amount actually affects the **Sales** account in the Chart of Accounts.

Items are necessary because to use a sales form in QuickBooks (e.g., invoices, and sales receipts), you must use items. On an invoice, for example, every line item will have a QuickBooks Item which may represent products, services, discounts, or sales tax.

COMPUTER PRACTICE

Step 1. To see what Items are available in the file, click the **Item & Services** icon on the *Home page* (see Figure 1-36).

Alternatively, you could select **Item List** from the *Lists* menu.

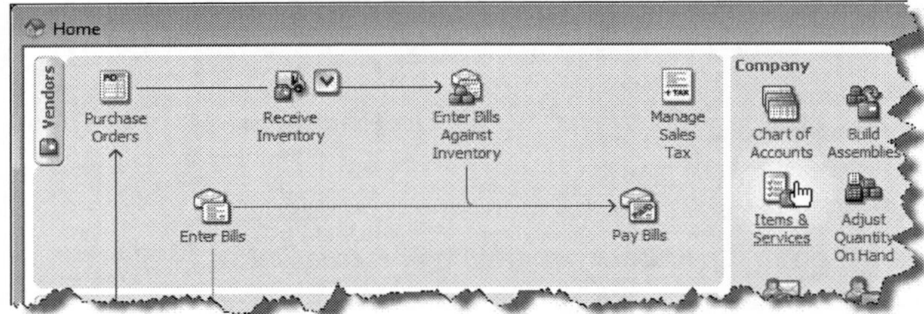

Figure 1-36 Items & Services button on Home page

Step 2. Figure 1-37 shows the *Item* list. Double click the **Camera SR32** item.

Item List

Look for [ ] in All fields | Search | Reset | Search within results

Name	Description	Type	Account	On Hand	On Sales Order	Price	Attach
◆Indoor Photo Session	Indoor Studio Session	Service	40000 · Services			95.00	
◆Outdoor Photo Session	Outdoor Photo Session	Service	40000 · Services			95.00	
◆Photographer	Photographer	Service	40000 · Services			125.00	
◆Retouching	Photo retouching services	Service	40000 · Services			95.00	
◆Camera SR32	Supra Digital Camera SR32	Inventory Part	45000 · Sales	9	0	695.99	
◆Case	Camera and Lens High Impact Case	Inventory Part	45000 · Sales	24	0	79.99	
◆Frame 5x7	Picture Frame - 5' x 7' Metal Frame	Inventory Part	45000 · Sales	22	0	5.99	
◆Lens	Supra Zoom Lens	Inventory Part	45000 · Sales	7	0	324.99	
◆Film 36C	200 ASA, 36 Color Film	Non-inventory Part	45000 · Sales			12.36	
◆Premium Photo Package	Premium Package of Photography from Session	Non-inventory Part	45000 · Sales			85.00	
◆Standard Photo Package	Standard Package of Photography from Session	Non-inventory Part	45000 · Sales			55.00	
◆Bad Debt	Bad Debt - Write off	Other Charge	60300 · Bad Debts			0.00	
◆Bounce Chg	Return Check Fee	Other Charge	45000 · Sales			0.00	
◆Contra Costa	Contra Costa County Sales Tax	Sales Tax Item	25500 · Sales Tax Payable			8.25%	
◆Out of State	Out-of-state sale, exempt from sales tax	Sales Tax Item	25500 · Sales Tax Payable			0.0%	
◆Santa Clara	Santa Clara County Sales Tax	Sales Tax Item	25500 · Sales Tax Payable			8.25%	

Item | Activities | Reports | Excel | Attach | Include inactive

Figure 1-37 Item List

Step 3. If the New Feature window opens, click **OK**.

Step 4. The *Edit Item* window opens (see Figure 1-38). Notice this item is linked to the Sales account. Every time this item is entered on an invoice, it changes the **Sales** account.

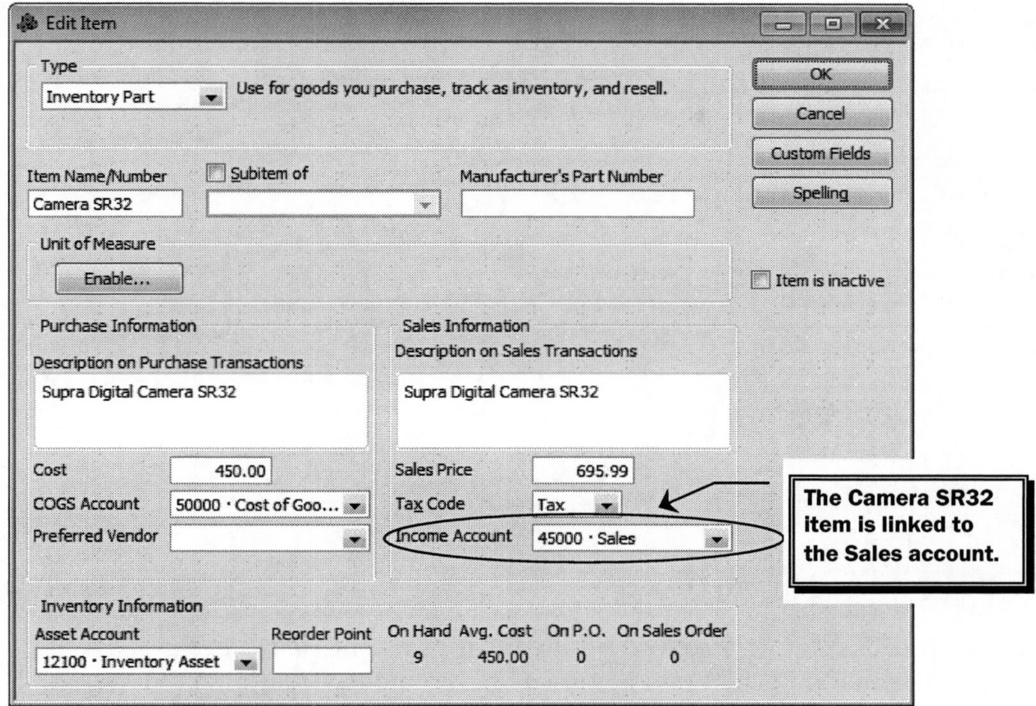

Figure 1-38 Camera SR32 Edit Item window – your screen may vary

Step 5. Close the *Edit Item* and *Item List* windows.

QuickBooks User Interface Features

QuickBooks provides a number of shortcuts and aids that assist the user in entering information and transactions. You should become familiar with these features so you can get to a task quickly.

There are various methods of accessing the data entry windows: the **Home** page, **Company Snapshot**, **Menus**, **QuickBooks Centers**, **Icon Bar**, and **Shortcut Keys**.

Home Page

As soon as you open a company file, QuickBooks displays the ***Home*** page (Figure 1-39). The ***Home*** page is broken into five sections – each dealing with a separate functional area of a business. These areas are: Vendors, Customers, Employees, Company, and Banking. Each area has icons to facilitate easy access to QuickBooks tasks. The *Home* page also displays a flow diagram showing the interdependency between tasks.

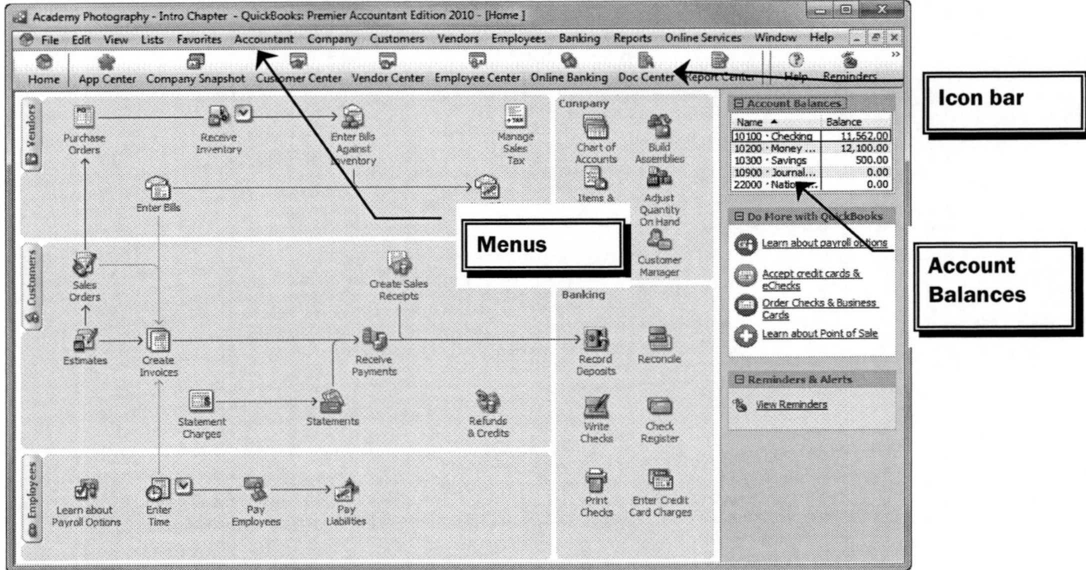

Figure 1-39 QuickBooks Premier 2010 Home page

To start a task, just click on its related icon on the *Home* page. The *Home* page displays the account balance information, which can be closed or even hidden based upon the user's access privileges (see Figure 1-40). If you close the *Home* page, it can be opened by clicking on the **Home** icon on the Icon bar.

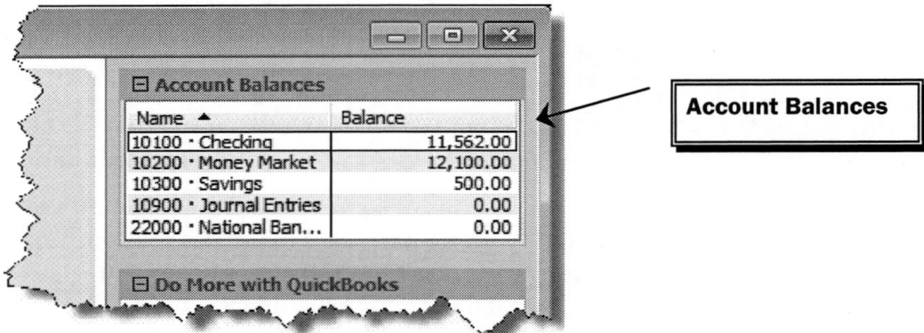

Figure 1-40 Account Balances on Home page

In addition to the tools shown above, you can use the Open Window List to access any open window on the screen. To view the open windows list, select the *View* menu, and then select **Open Windows List** (see Figure 1-41).

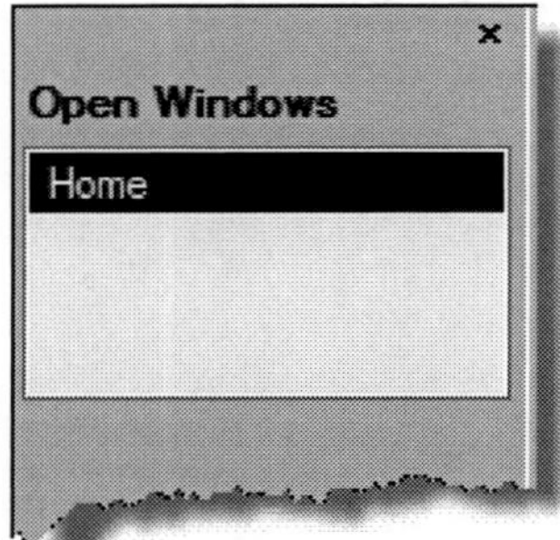

Figure 1-41 The Open Windows list

Menus

Menus run along the top of the screen. To open a menu, select the menu name and then choose the option desired (see Figure 1-42).

Figure 1-42 File menu in QuickBooks Premier 2010

Centers

There are several Centers in QuickBooks, such as the Customer Center and Vendor Center. Centers are organized to give pertinent information in one place.

Customer, Vendor and Employee Centers are very important since they provide the only way to access the Customer list, Vendor list, and Employee list. These three lists are referred to as the *Center-based Lists*. These Centers summarize general information and transactions in the same area. For example, the Customer Center shows the customer balance, their general information, and all transactions for that customer (see Figure 1-43).

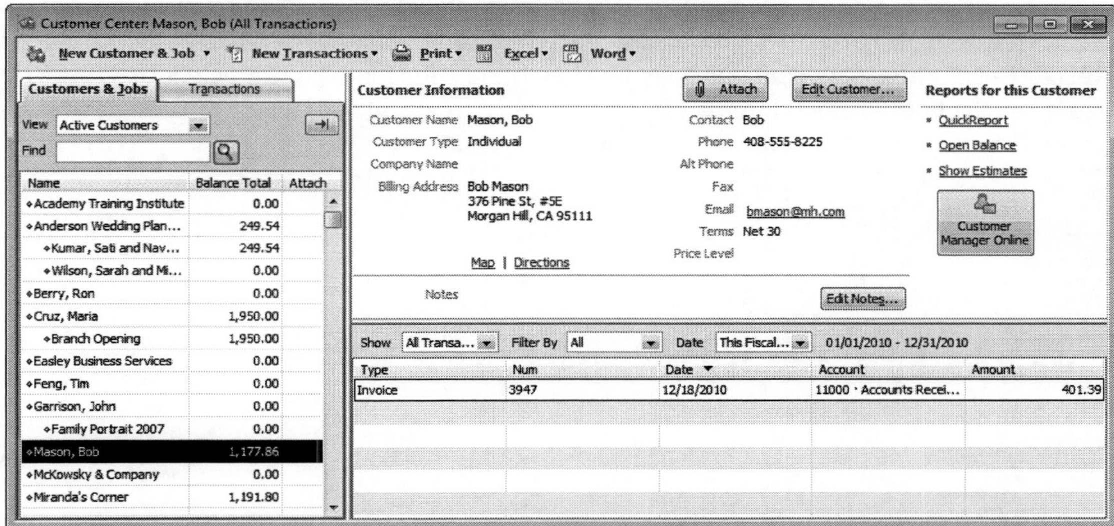

Figure 1-43 Customer Center

Other Centers include the *Application Center*, *Online Banking Center*, *Report Center* and the *Document Management Center*. These Centers will be addressed later in this book.

Company Snapshot

The *Company Snapshot* is a single screen summary of different aspects of a company. Charts such as *Income and Expense Trends*, *Previous Year Income Comparison* and *Expense Breakdown* are displayed along with important lists such as *Account Balances* and *Customers Who Owe Money*. The Company Snapshot can be easily customized to show the information that is of most interest to you and your company.

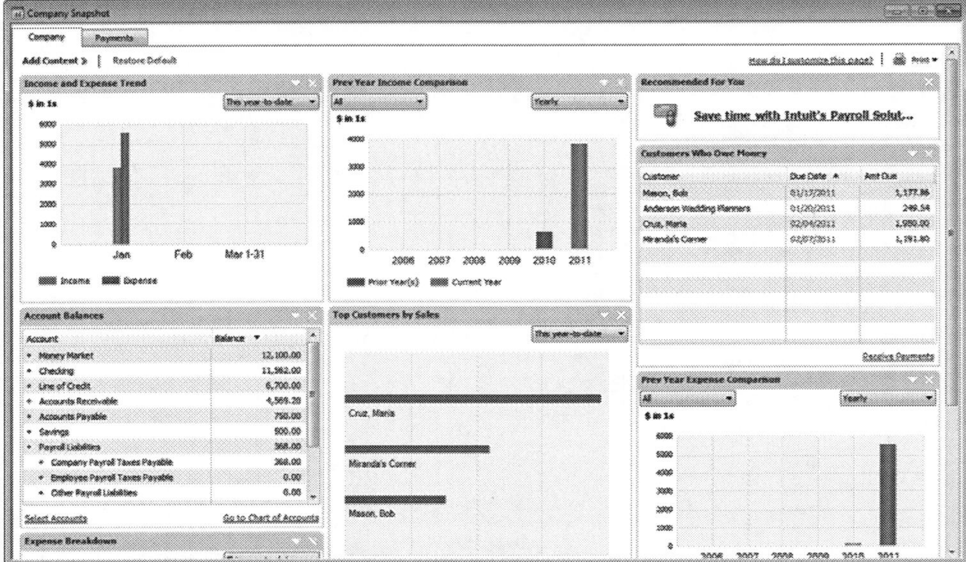

Figure 1-44 Company Snapshot - your screen may vary

Icon Bar

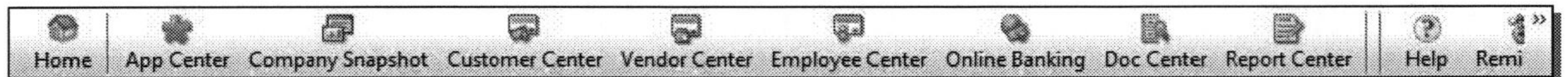

Figure 1-45 Icon Bar

The QuickBooks Icon Bar allows you to select activities and available services by clicking icons on the bar (see Figure 1-45). For example, you can open the Home page by clicking **Home** on the Icon Bar. To modify the contents or position of the icons on the Icon Bar, select the *View* menu, and then choose **Customize Icon Bar** (see Figure 1-46).

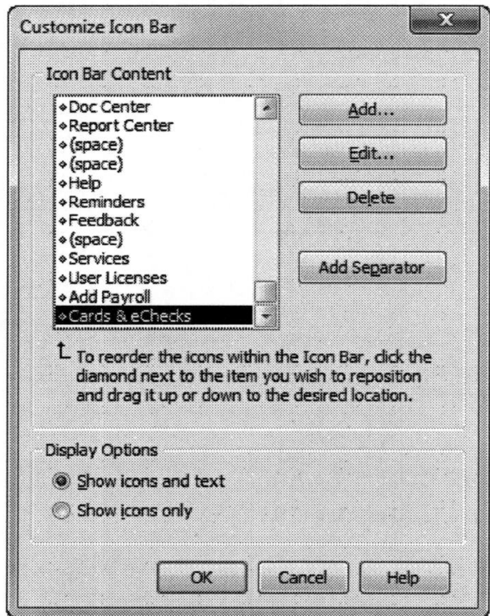

Figure 1-46 Customize Icon Bar

Shortcut Keys

You can use keyboard **Shortcut Keys** to select menu options. To use the keyboard, press the ALT key. This displays the menu with underlined letters under each menu item (see Figure

1-47). To display the options list under the appropriate menu, press the corresponding letter on the menu bar.

Figure 1-47 Menu bar with underlined menu items

Some menus items have control-key shortcuts that are indicated on the right side of the menu item. For example, to open a register, you can press **Ctrl+R** as indicated on the *Edit* menu (see Figure 1-48). A detailed list of Keyboard Shortcuts can be found in the Appendix.

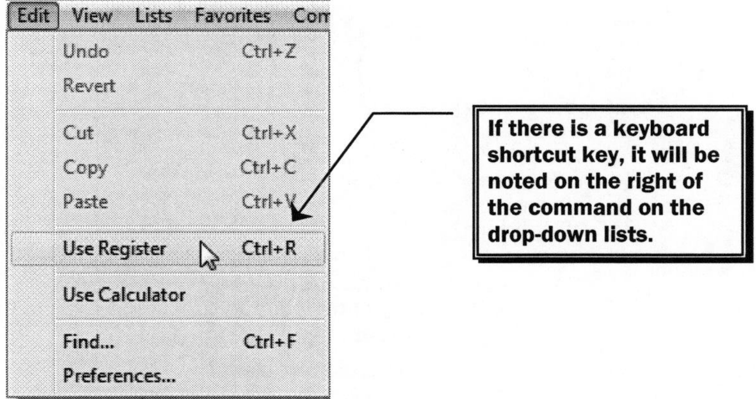

Figure 1-48 Menu showing shortcut keys

Open Previous Company

You can open a previous company file by selecting it from the **Open Previous Company** submenu of the *File* menu. QuickBooks lists the last few companies you have most recently accessed, allowing you to open any one of them without going to **Open Company** and navigating through your directory structure (see Figure 1-49). You can set the number of previous companies that show on the list from 1 to 20.

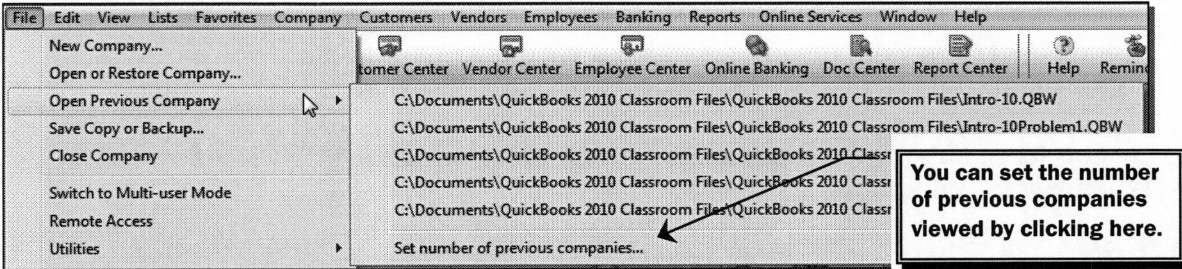

Figure 1-49 Open Previous Company list

> **Note:**
> When you access the Open Previous Companies list in your QuickBooks file, the previous companies you see may be different from those shown in Figure 1-49.

QuickBooks Help

Support Resources

QuickBooks provides a variety of support resources that assist in using the program. Some of these resources are on the Internet and others are stored in help files locally along with the QuickBooks software on your computer. To access the support resources, select the *Help* menu and then select **QuickBooks Help** (see Figure 1-50). Use the Index and Search tabs to find the topics you are looking for.

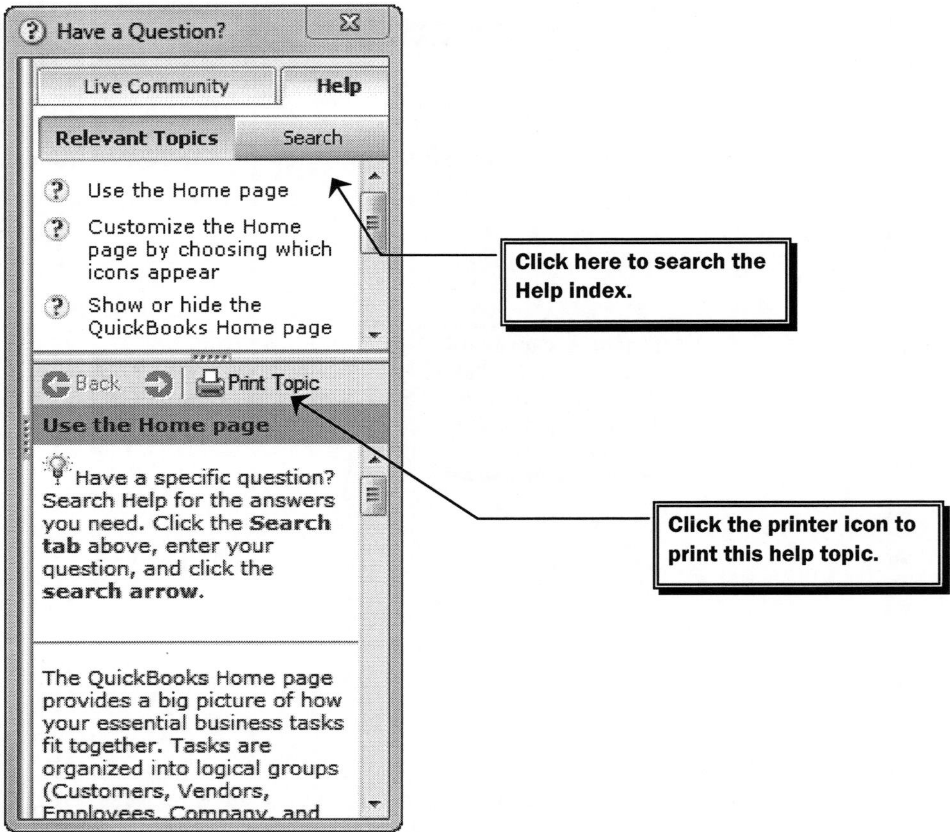

Figure 1-50 Help & Live Community window

QuickBooks Coach

QuickBooks transactions often occur in a specific order. For example, if you receive a check from a client, you will need to issue a *Sales Receipt* to record this transaction. After recording the *Sales Receipt*, you will need to deposit that check in a bank, which is recorded in the *Record Deposits* form. This process is called the *Payment with Sale Workflow*. There are several Workflows in QuickBooks.

QuickBooks Coach is an interactive help system that highlights these different Workflows. To use the QuickBooks Coach, complete the following steps.

COMPUTER PRACTICE

Step 1. Select the **Edit** menu, and then select **Preferences** (see Figure 1-51).

Step 2. Select the **Desktop View** preference from the choices on the left side of the window.

Step 3. Make sure the **My Preferences** tab is selected.

Step 4. Click the checkbox next to *Show Coach window and features.*

Step 5. Click **OK** to close the Preferences window.

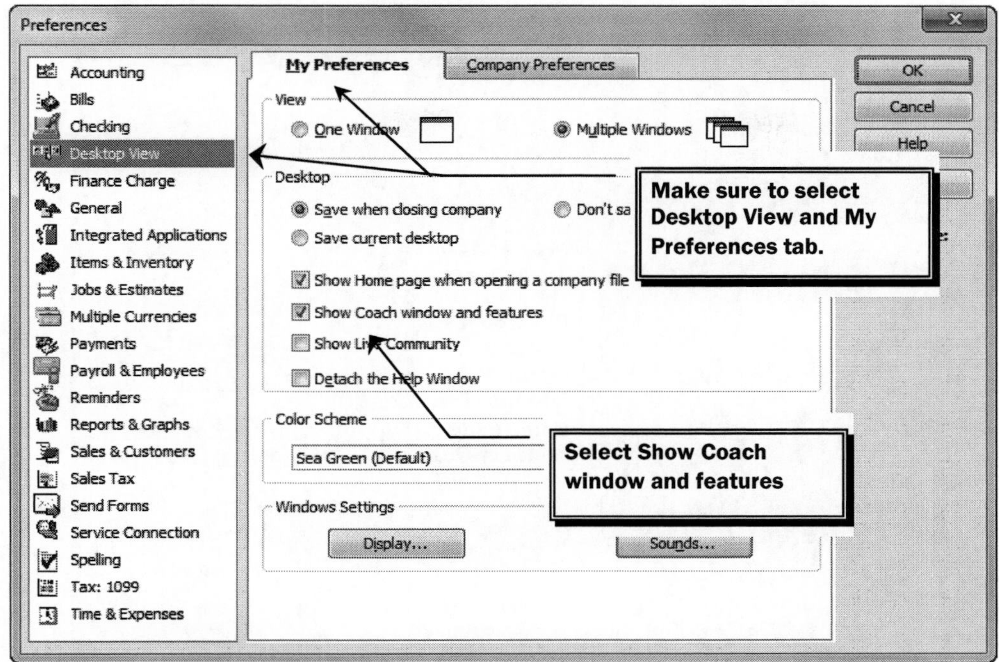

Figure 1-51 The Desktop View Preferences Window

> **Note:**
> You can customize many parts of your QuickBooks file through the Preferences. For more information about the various customizations available through the Preferences, see page 331.

Step 6. The *QuickBooks Coach* window opens (see Figure 1-52). Click the **Start Working** button.

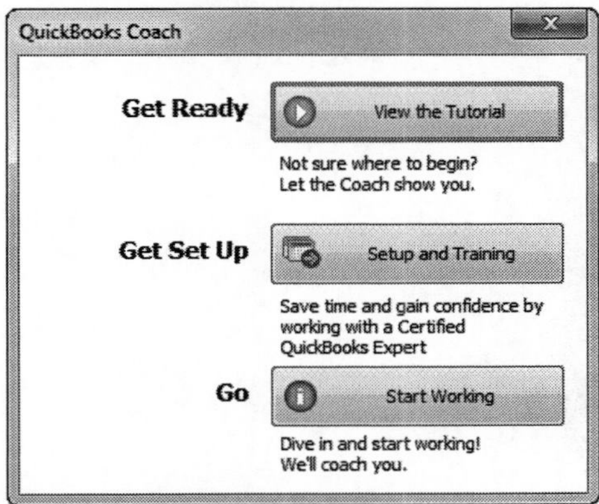

Figure 1-52 The QuickBooks Coach window

Step 7. The *QuickBooks Coach* integrates into the *Home Page* (see Figure 1-52). The Home Page changes to gray color scheme and some icons have a blue *Coach Icon.*

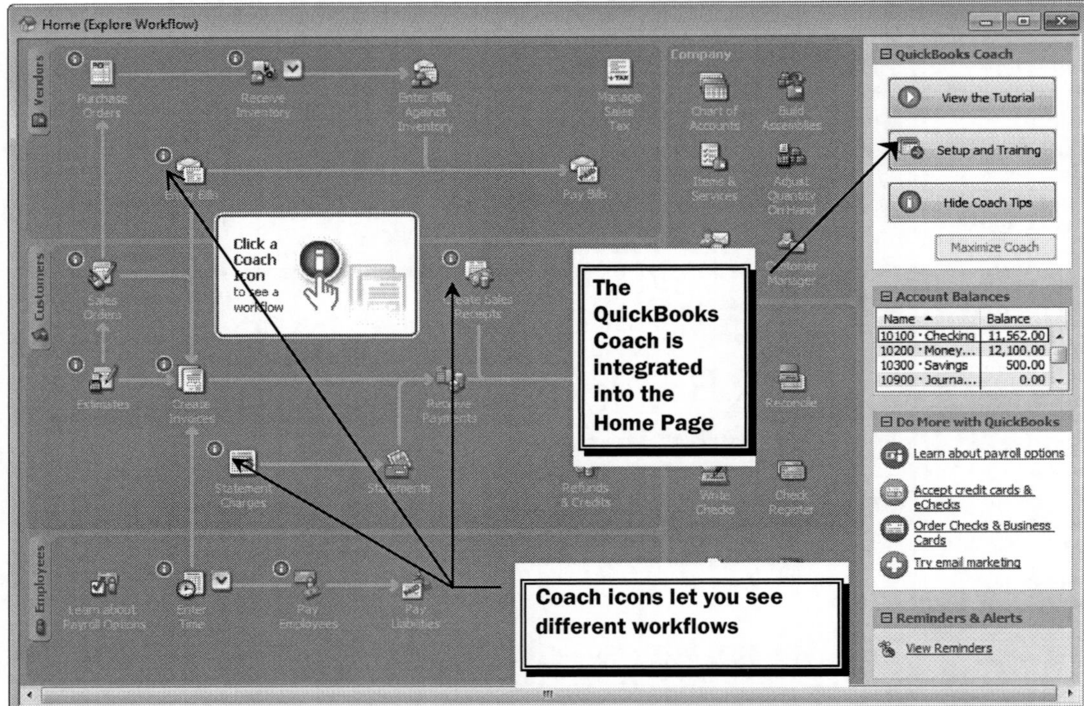

Figure 1-53 QuickBooks Coach and various Workflows

Step 8. Click on the **Coach** icon next to the *Enter Bills* icon on the *Home Page* (see Figure 1-53). The *Enter Bills* icon is on the left side of the *Home Page*, under the *Vendors* section.

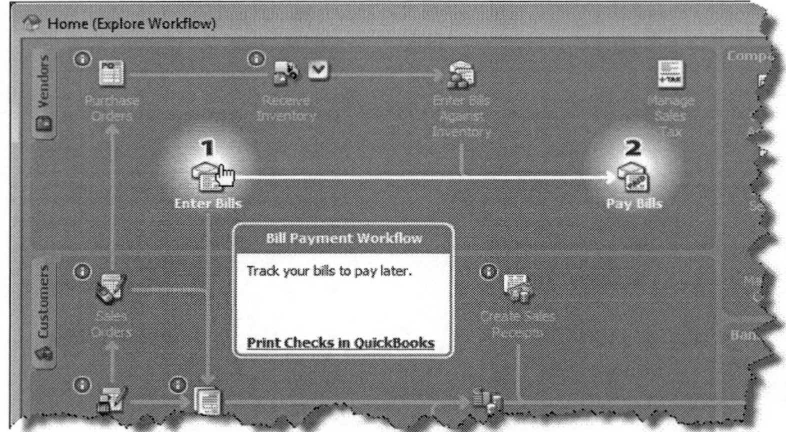

Figure 1-54 The Bill Payment Workflow Spotlight

Step 9. The *Bill Payment Workflow* is highlighted (see Figure 1-54). This workflow demonstrates that when you enter a bill, the next step is to pay the bill.

> **Note:**
> This book will address the workflows highlighted with the QuickBooks Coach in later chapters.

Step 10. When you are finished with the *QuickBooks Coach*, click the **Hide Coach Tips** button on the right side of the Home Page.

Step 11. If necessary, close the *QuickBooks Coach* window.

QuickBooks Learning Center

As you begin using QuickBooks, the first thing you see is the QuickBooks Learning Center (see Figure 1-4). This center provides interactive tutorials to help users learn how to use QuickBooks in common business scenarios. If you have deactivated the Learning Center so that it does not start once the program is launched, you can always access it by selecting **Learning Center Tutorials** from the *Help* menu.

QuickBooks Professional Advisors

QuickBooks Professional Advisors are independent consultants, accountants, bookkeepers, and educators who are proficient in QuickBooks and who can offer guidance to small businesses in various areas of business accounting. To find a ProAdvisor in your area use the following URL: http://www.quickbooks.com/findadvisor.

Another source of highly qualified advisors, certified by the author of this book can be found at The Sleeter Group's web site at www.sleeter.com.

Chapter Summary and Review

In this chapter, you learned about the key features in QuickBooks Pro and Premier 2010. This chapter also introduced much of the terminology used in the program. Review the following list of key concepts before proceeding to the next chapter.

- An overview of the QuickBooks product line (page 1).
- Some of the basic principles of accounting (page 2).
- The accounting behind the scenes in QuickBooks (page 4).
- An overview of QuickBooks data files and types (page 6).
- Opening portable files (page 10).
- How to restore backup files (page 14).
- Entering Transactions in QuickBooks (page 20).
- QuickBooks user interface features (page 25).
- About QuickBooks help and support (page 29).

Comprehension Questions

Answers to these review questions are available with the supplemental material. See page xiii for details.

1. Explain the difference between a QuickBooks working data file, a QuickBooks backup file and a QuickBooks portable file. How can you differentiate between the three types of files on your hard disk?
2. What is the main reason for creating portable files?
3. Explain the importance of the QuickBooks *Home* page.
4. Explain why it is important to enter transactions in QuickBooks using Forms rather than accounting entries.
5. Describe the primary purpose of accounting in business.

Multiple Choice

Select the best answer(s) for each of the following:

1. The fundamental accounting equation that governs all accounting is:
   a) Net income = Revenue - expenses.
   b) Assets + Liabilities = Equity.
   c) Assets = Liabilities + Equity.
   d) Assets = Liabilities - Equity.
2. Which of the following statement is true?
   a) Debits are bad because they reduce income.
   b) Equity is increased by a net loss.
   c) Debits - credits = 0.
   d) Assets are increased with a credit entry.

3. Under accrual accounting:
   a) A sale is not recorded until the customer pays the bill.
   b) Income and expenses are recognized when transactions occur.
   c) An expense is not recorded until you write the check.
   d) You must maintain two separate accounting systems.

4. QuickBooks is:
   a) A job-costing system.
   b) A payroll system.
   c) A double-entry accounting system.
   d) All of the above.

5. Which is not a method of accessing the data entry screens?
   a) Menus
   b) Home page
   c) Icon bar
   d) Data entry button

Completion Statements

1. As you enter data in familiar-looking ________, QuickBooks handles the __________ entries for you.

2. You should ________ your data file regularly because it is one of the most important safeguards you can do to ensure the safety of your data.

3. When you open your working data file, QuickBooks displays the _____ ______. This page is broken into five sections – each dealing with a separate functional area of a business.

4. ____________ are used in QuickBooks Sales forms and represent what the company buys and sells.

5. A list which shows all the accounts in your working data file is called the ______ ___ ______.

Introduction-Problem 1

APPLYING YOUR KNOWLEDGE

Restore **the Intro-10Problem1.QBM** file.

1. Select **Customer Center** from the QuickBooks *Icon* Bar. This will display *Customer & Jobs* list and related information.
   a) What is the first customer listed on the left of the Customer Center?

Note:
The answer to this first question **AAA Services**. If you don't see AAA Services in the *Customer Center*, make sure to restore *Intro-10Problem1.QBM* as directed in the box above. This book uses specific files for each Chapter and each Problem. If you don't restore the correct file, you will have trouble completing the exercises.

   b) In the Customers & Jobs list, click on **Miranda's Corner**. What is Miranda's Corner's balance?

c) Click the *Date* dropdown list above the transaction listing and scroll up to the top of the list to select **All**. How many transactions do you see and of what type?
d) Close the Customer Center.

2. Select **Vendor Center** from the QuickBooks *Icon* Bar. This displays the *Vendor* list and related information.
   a) Double-click *Sinclair Insurance*. This opens the *Edit Vendor* window. What is the Phone Number? Close the *Edit Vendor* window.
   b) What is the amount of bill of Bill number 8967 to *Sinclair Insurance*? (You may need to set the *Date* to **All** as in Step 1.)
   c) Close the Vendor Center.

3. From the *Home* page, click the **Chart of Accounts** icon to display the Chart of Accounts.
   a) What type of account is the **Checking** Account?
   b) How many accounts of type **Bank** are in the Chart of Accounts?
   c) How many account of type Other Current Asset are in the Chart of Accounts?

4. While still in the **Chart of Accounts**, Double-click the **Checking** account on the Chart of Accounts list. This will open the register for Checking account.
   a) Who was the payee for the check on 2/11/2011?
   b) What was the amount of the check?
   c) Close the checking account register and Chart of Accounts list.

5. Click the **Invoice** icon on the *Home page*, and then click **Previous** (top left).
   a) Who is the invoice billed to?
   b) What is the Balance Due for this invoice?
   c) Close the invoice.

6. Select the **Chart of Accounts** option from the *Lists* menu. Double-click on the **Checking** account.
   a) Which vendor was paid by the last bill payment in the register?
   b) What is the amount of the last bill payment in the register?
   c) Close the **Checking** register and close the **Chart of Accounts** list.

7. Click the **Write Checks** icon on the *Home* page and follow these steps:
   a) Click on the *Calendar* icon immediately to the right of the *Date* field. Select **tomorrow's date** in the *Date* field and press **Tab**.
   b) In the Pay to the Order of field, enter *Jones Office Supply*. Press **Tab**.
   c) Enter ***80.00*** in the *Amount* field and press **Tab**.
   d) Click in the **To be printed** check box.
   e) What is the city displayed in the Address field on the check for *Jones Office Supply*?
   f) Click **Clear** and then close the check window.

8. Select the **Chart of Accounts** option from the *Lists* menu and double-click on **Accounts Receivable**.
   a) What is the ending balance in the account?
   b) What is the date of the last transaction in the register?
   c) Close the register and the Chart of Accounts.
   d) Click the **Check Register** button on the Home page.
   e) Select **10100 – Checking** from the *Use Register* dialog box.
   f) What is the ending balance in the checking register?
   g) Close the **Checking Register**.

9. Close the working data file Intro-10Problem1.QBW.

Discussion Questions

These questions are designed to stimulate discussion about how you can apply QuickBooks to your own organization. They may help you think through some of the issues you'll encounter when using QuickBooks in your company.

1. Is your organization a for-profit or not-for-profit?
2. What is the equity in your company now? If you don't know how can you find out?
3. Approximately, what is the gross revenue your company earns each year? How many employees does your company employ? Do you think that QuickBooks is a good match for your company, given the size of your revenues and the number of employees?

Activity

Identify some of the transactions that occur in your organization. Create a list with ways in which you think QuickBooks can benefit your organization.

Chapter 2
The Sales Process

Objectives

After completing this chapter, you should be able to:

- Set up customer records in the Customer Center (page 43).
- Record Sales Receipts (page 52).
- Use the Undeposited Funds account to track your cash receipts (page 57).
- Record Invoices and Payments from customers (page 59).
- Record bank deposits of cash, check, and credit card receipts (page 74).

Restore this File

This chapter uses Sales-10.QBW. To open this file, restore the Sales-10.QBM file to your hard disk. See page 10 for instructions on restoring files.

Note: When you restore a data file, depending on today's date, you may see one or more "Alerts" for learning to process credit cards, pay taxes, or similar activities. Click Mark as Done when you see these alerts.

In this chapter, you will learn how QuickBooks can help you record and track revenues in your business.

Each time you sell products or services, you will record the transaction using one of QuickBooks' forms. When you fill out a QuickBooks **Invoice** or **Sales Receipt**, QuickBooks tracks the detail of each sale, allowing you to create reports about your sales.

Tracking Company Sales

Academy Photography tracks each sale individually on either an **Invoice** form (for sales to credit customers) or a **Sales Receipt** form (for customers who pay immediately using cash, checks, or credit cards).

The *Customers* section of the *Home* page window provides you with a graphical flow of the steps involved in the sales process.

When you open the sample file, the *Home* page is displayed. Academy Photography is a service and merchandising photo studio which sells products and provides services, so the home page displays activities likely to be used in this type of business (see Figure 2-1). The *Home* page is customized for each business type based on answers to questions in the setup interview. You'll learn about the company setup process later in this book.

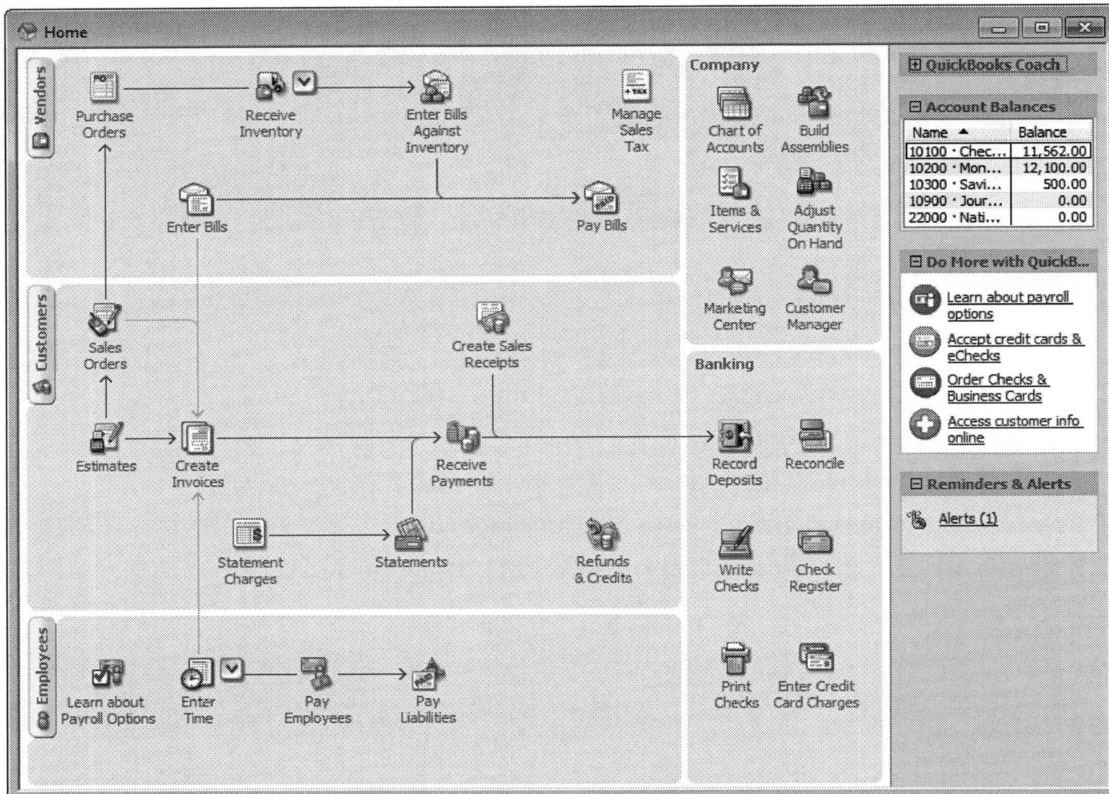

Figure 2-1 QuickBooks Home page

Sales are recorded two different ways, depending on whether the customer pays at the time of sale or service (called *Cash customers*), or if the customer pays after the sale or service (*Credit customers*). Transactions with Cash customers follow a specific process, called the *Payment with Sale Workflow*. At the time of sale, a Sale Receipt is issued, and then a deposit is recorded. The *Payment with Sale Workflow* is displayed in Figure 2-2 using the QuickBooks Coach (for more on the QuickBooks Coach, see 30).

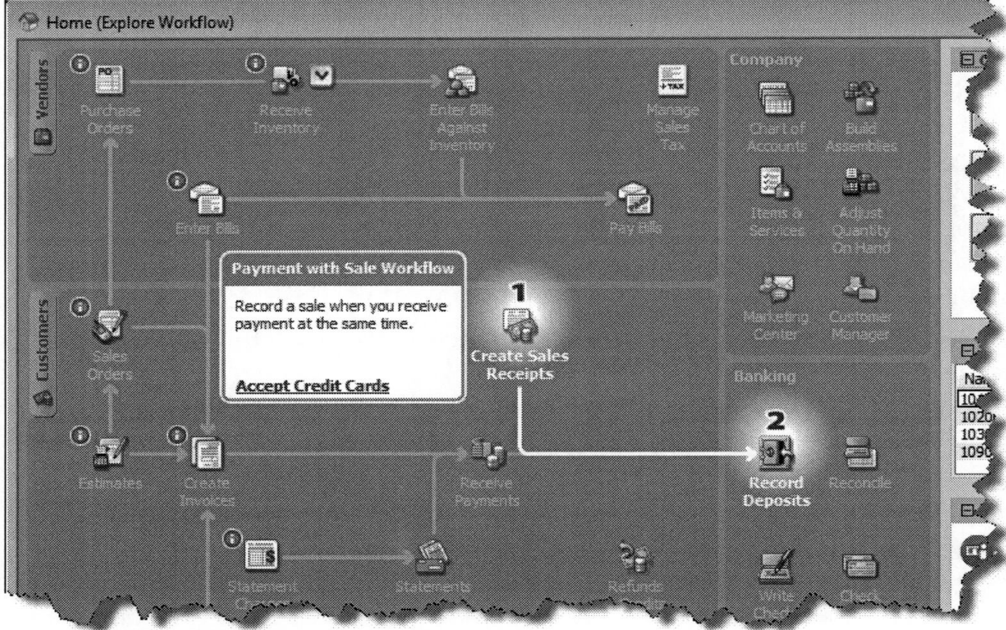

Figure 2-2 Payment with Sale Workflow

When working with a credit customer, who pays after the sale or service, the sales process is different. Often, the first step is to create an invoice. Once payment is received, the amount is applied to the invoice and the deposit is recorded. This is the *Invoicing Workflow*, displayed in Figure 2-3. This process can also begin with creating an Estimate.

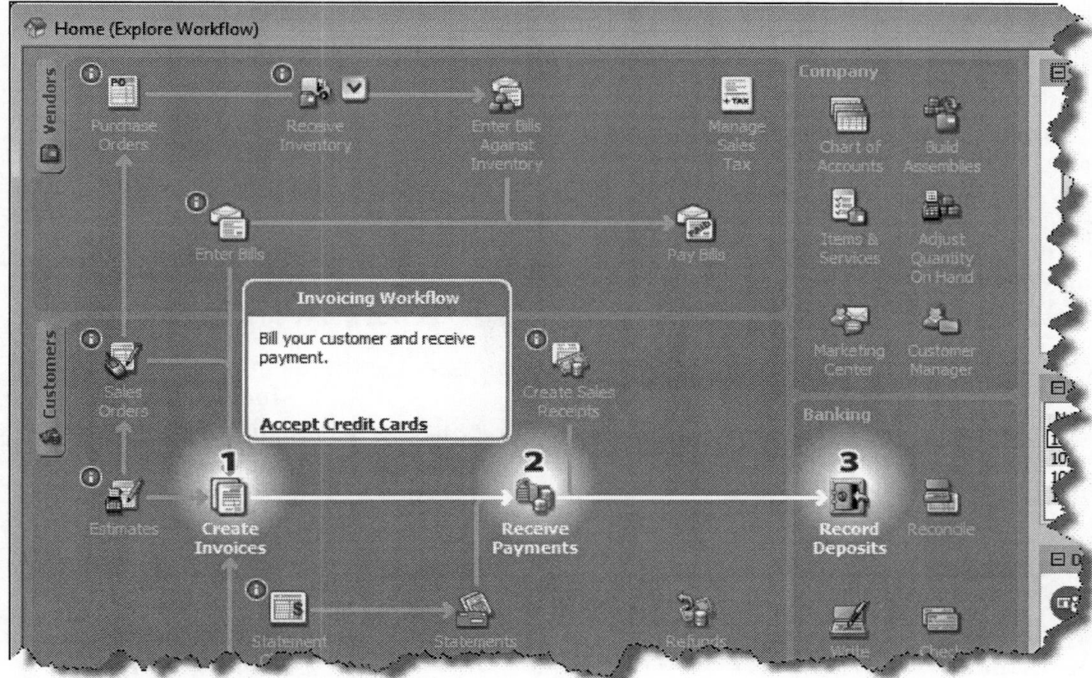

Figure 2-3 Invoicing Workflow

Table 2-1 provides more details about the Payment with Sales and Invoicing Workflow. In this table, you can see how to record business transactions for cash and credit customers. In addition, the table shows the *accounting behind the scenes* of each transaction. As discussed on page 4, the accounting behind the scenes is critical to your understanding of how QuickBooks converts the information on forms (invoices, sales receipts, etc.) into accounting entries.

Each row in the table represents a business transaction you might enter as you proceed through the sales process.

Business Transaction	Cash Customers (Pay by cash, check, or credit card at time of sale)		Credit Customers (Pay on a date after the sale date)	
	QuickBooks Transaction	Accounting Entry	QuickBooks Transaction	Accounting Entry
Customer Estimate (Optional)	Not Usually Used		Estimates	Non-posting entry used to record estimates (bids) for customers or jobs.
Customer Sales Order (Optional)	Not Usually Used		Sales Orders	Non-posting entry used to record customer orders.
Recording a Sale	Create Sales Receipts	Increase (debit) **Undeposited Funds**, increase (credit) *income* account.	Create Invoices	Increase (debit) **Accounts Receivable**, increase (credit) *income* account.
Receiving Money in Payment of an Invoice	No additional action is required on the sales form.		Receive Payments	Decrease (credit) **Accounts Receivable**, increase (debit) **Undeposited Funds.**
Depositing Money in the Bank	Record Deposits	Increase (debit) *bank* Account, decrease (credit) **Undeposited Funds.**	Record Deposits	Decrease (credit) **Undeposited Funds,** increase (debit) *bank* Account.

Table 2-1 Steps in the sales process

For cash customers, use the **Sales Receipt** form to record your sale. The *Sales Receipt* form records the details of what you've sold and to whom you sold it. By default, a special account called **Undeposited Funds** is used in these transactions. This account is an *Other Current Asset* account, and it can be thought of as a drawer where you keep your checks and other deposits before making a trip to the bank. See page 57 for more information on **Undeposited Funds.**

The accounting behind the scenes:
When you create a **Sales Receipt**, QuickBooks increases (with a debit) **a bank account or Undeposited Funds** (i.e., funds you have received from customers but have not yet deposited at your bank), and increases (with a credit) the appropriate *income* account. If the sale includes an Inventory Item, it also decreases (credits) the Inventory asset and increases (debits) the Cost of Goods Sold account.

For credit customers, create an **Invoice** for each sale. The **Invoice** form records the details of what you've sold and to whom you sold it.

> **The accounting behind the scenes:**
> When you create an **Invoice**, QuickBooks increases (with a debit) **Accounts Receivable** and increases (with a credit) the appropriate *income* account. If applicable, **Invoices** and **Sales Receipts** also increase (with a credit) the sales tax liability account. If the sale includes an Inventory Item, it also decreases (credits) the Inventory asset and increases (debits) the Cost of Goods Sold account.

As shown in Table 2-1, when you receive money from your credit customers, use the **Receive Payments** function to record the receipt.

> **The accounting behind the scenes:**
> When you record a **Payment**, QuickBooks increases (with a debit) **Undeposited Funds** or a bank account, and decreases (with a credit) **Accounts Receivable.**

If you post a **Sales Receipt** or a **Payment** to **Undeposited Funds**, which is the default option, the last step in the process is to make a **Deposit** to your bank account. This step is the same for both cash and credit customers. Use the **Make Deposits** function to record the deposit to your bank account.

If you prepare estimates (sometimes called bids) for customers or jobs, you can create an **Estimate** to track the details of what the sale will include. QuickBooks does not post **Estimates** to the **General Ledger**, but it helps you track the estimate until the job is complete. QuickBooks also provides reports that help you compare estimated vs. actual revenues and costs.

> **The accounting behind the scenes:**
> When you create an **Estimate**, QuickBooks records the estimate, but there is no accounting entry made. **Estimates** are "non-posting" entries.

If you use sales orders in your business, you can create a **Sales Order** form to track the details of what the sale will include. QuickBooks does not post **Sales Orders** to the **General Ledger**, but it helps you track your orders until they are shipped to the customer. **Sales Orders** are very similar to **Estimates** because they are both non-posting entries, and they both help you track future sales. **Sales Orders** are more appropriate for product businesses, and **Estimates** are more appropriate for service businesses. **Sales Orders** are only available in QuickBooks Premier and Enterprise Solutions.

> **The accounting behind the scenes:**
> When you create a **Sales Order**, QuickBooks records the sales order, but there is no accounting entry made. **Sales Orders** are "non-posting" entries.

In the following sections, you will learn about each step of the Payment with Sale and Invoicing workflows. For more information on Estimates and Sales Orders, see the Estimates and Sales Orders chapter beginning on page see 587.

Setting Up Customers

For each of your customers, create a record in the **Customers & Jobs** list of the *Customer Center*. Academy Photography has a new credit customer – Dr. Tim Feng. To add this new customer, follow these steps:

COMPUTER PRACTICE

Step 1. Select the **Customer Center** icon from the *Navigation bar*

Step 2. To add a new customer, select **New Customer** from the **New Customer & Job** drop-down menu (see Figure 2-4).

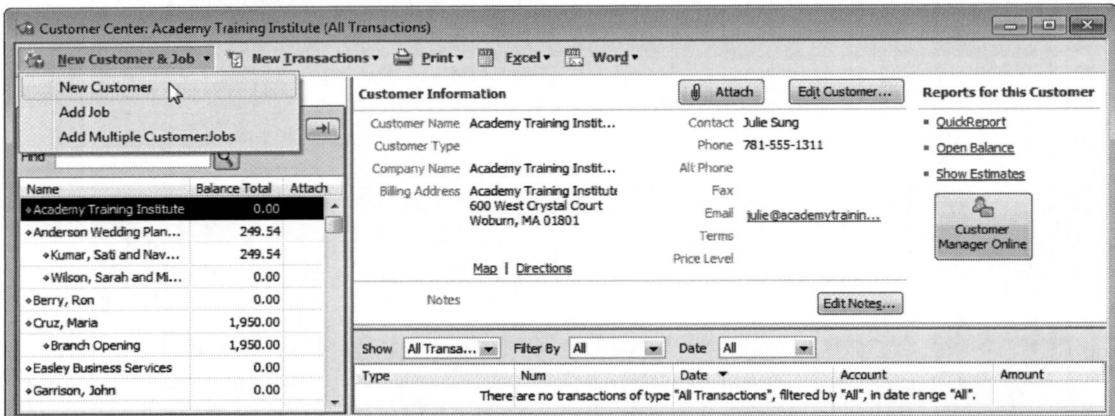

Figure 2-4 Adding a new customer record

Step 3. Enter ***Feng, Tim*** in the *Customer Name* field (see Figure 2-5) and then press **Tab**.

Step 4. Press **Tab** twice to skip the *Opening Balance* and *as of* fields.

The date in the *as of* field defaults to the current date. Since you will not enter an amount in the *Opening Balance* field, there is no need to change this date.

Do not enter anything in the *Opening Balance* field. It shows on the *New Customer* window so that you *could* enter the balance due from this customer, but it is much better to enter each open invoice for each customer. See the following important tip for a more thorough explanation.

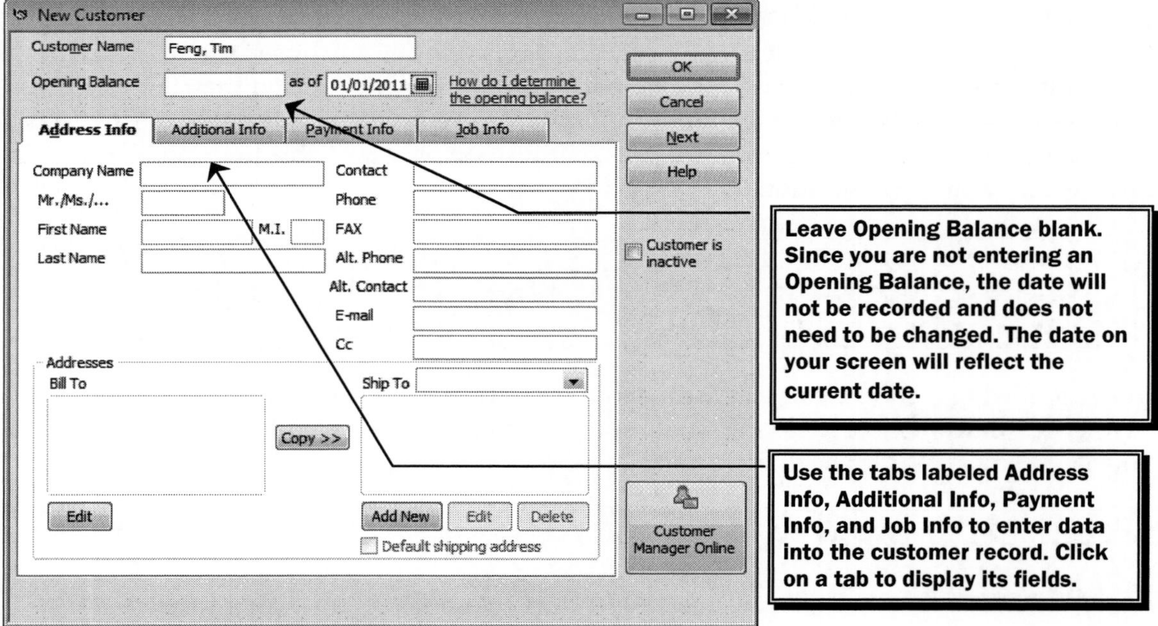

Figure 2-5 New Customer window

Important Tip:
It is best NOT to use the *Opening Balance* field in the customer record. When you enter an opening balance for a customer in the *Opening Balance* field, QuickBooks creates a new account in your Chart of Accounts called Uncategorized Income. Then, it creates an **Invoice** that increases (debits) **Accounts Receivable**, and increases (credits) **Uncategorized Income**.

It is preferable to enter the actual open Invoices for each customer when you set up your company file. That way, you will have all of the details of which invoice is open, and what items were sold on the open Invoices. When you use Invoices, the actual income accounts will be used instead of **Uncategorized Income**.

Step 5. Because this customer is an individual (i.e., not a company), press **Tab** to skip the *Company Name* field.

Step 6. Continue entering information in the rest of the fields using the data in Table 2-2. Press **Tab** after each entry.

Field	Data
Mr./Mrs.	Dr.
First Name	Tim
M.I.	S.
Last Name	Feng
Bill To Address **Hint**: Press **ENTER** to move to a new line in this field.	Tim S. Feng 300 Main St., Suite 3 San Jose, CA 95111
Contact	Tim S. Feng
Phone	408-555-8297
FAX	408-555-8298
Alt. Ph.	408-555-6711
Alt. Contact	Don Brewer
E-Mail	drf@df.com
Ship To	Click >>**Copy**>>. This displays *Add Ship To Address Information* field (see Figure 2-6). Type ***Office*** in the Address Name field and click **OK**. In QuickBooks, you can select multiple Ship To addresses for your customers.

Table 2-2 Data to complete the Address Info tab

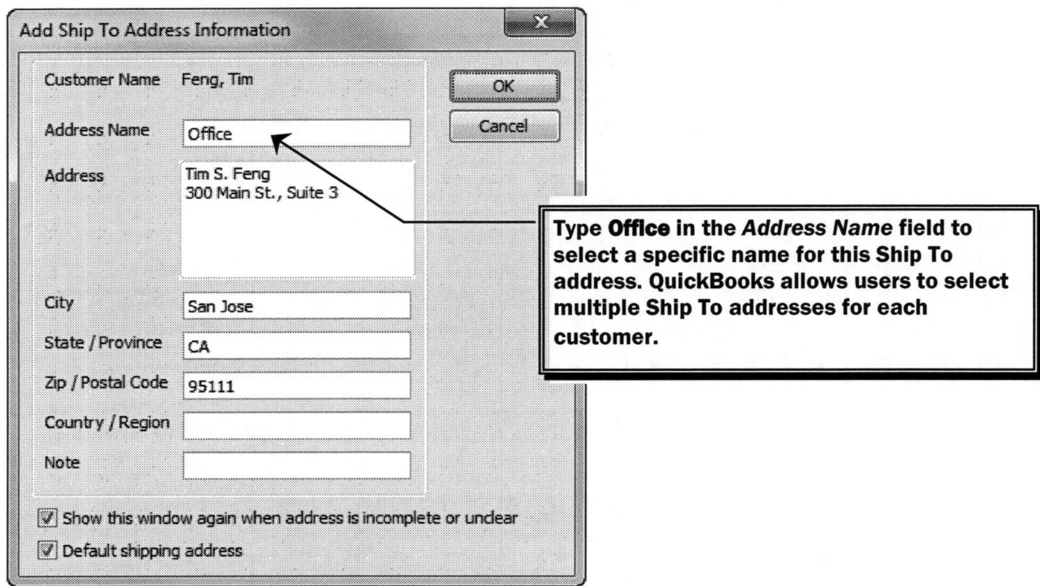

Figure 2-6 Add Ship To Address Information window

Figure 2-7 shows the finished Address Info section of the customer record. Verify that your screen matches Figure 2-7.

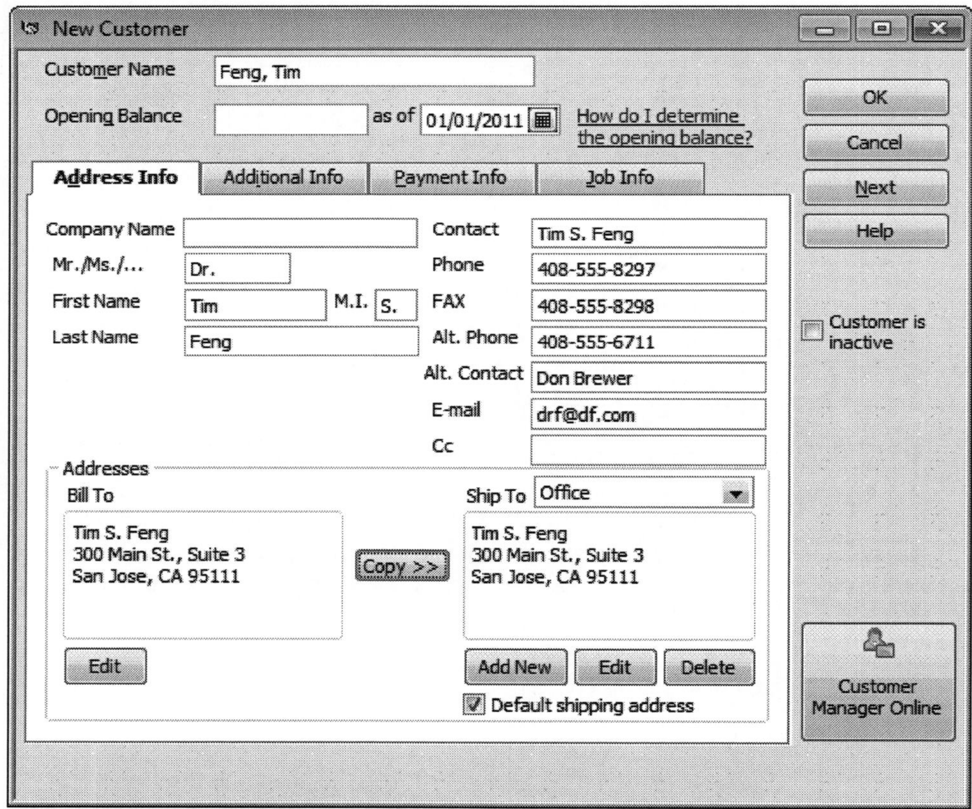

Figure 2-7 Completed Address Info tab

> **Tip:**
> There are four name lists in QuickBooks: **Vendor, Customer:Job, Employee,** and **Other Names**. After you enter a name in the *Customer Name* field of the *New Customer* window, you cannot use that name in any of the other three lists in QuickBooks.
>
> **When Customers are Vendors:**
> When you sell to and purchase from the same company, you'll need to create two records, one in the Vendor List, and one in the Customer:Job list. Make the two names slightly different. For example, you could enter Feng, Tim – C in the *New Customer* window and Feng, Tim – V in the *New Vendor* window. The vendor and customer records for Tim Feng can contain the same contact information.

Step 7. Click the **Additional Info** tab to continue entering information about this customer as shown in Figure 2-8.

Step 8. Select **Business** from the *Type* drop-down list and then press **Tab**.

QuickBooks allows you to group your customers into common types. By grouping your customers into types, you'll be able to create reports that focus on one or more types. For example, if you create two types of customers, Residential and Business, you are able to tag each customer with a type. Then you can create reports, statements, or mailing labels for all customers of a certain type.

Step 9. Select **Net 30** from the *Terms* drop-down list as the terms for this customer and then press **Tab**.

QuickBooks is *terms smart*. For example, if you enter terms of 2% 10 Net 30 and a customer pays within 10 days, QuickBooks will automatically calculate a 2% discount. For more information about setting up your Terms list, see page 349.

Step 10. Select **MM** in the *Rep* drop-down list and then press **Tab**.

The *Rep* field can contain the initials of one of your employees or vendors. Use this field to assign a sales rep to this customer. If you use the *Rep* field, you can create reports (e.g. Sales by Rep report) that provide the sales information you need to pay commissions. Each sales form (**Invoice** or **Sales Receipt**) can have a different name in the *Rep* field.

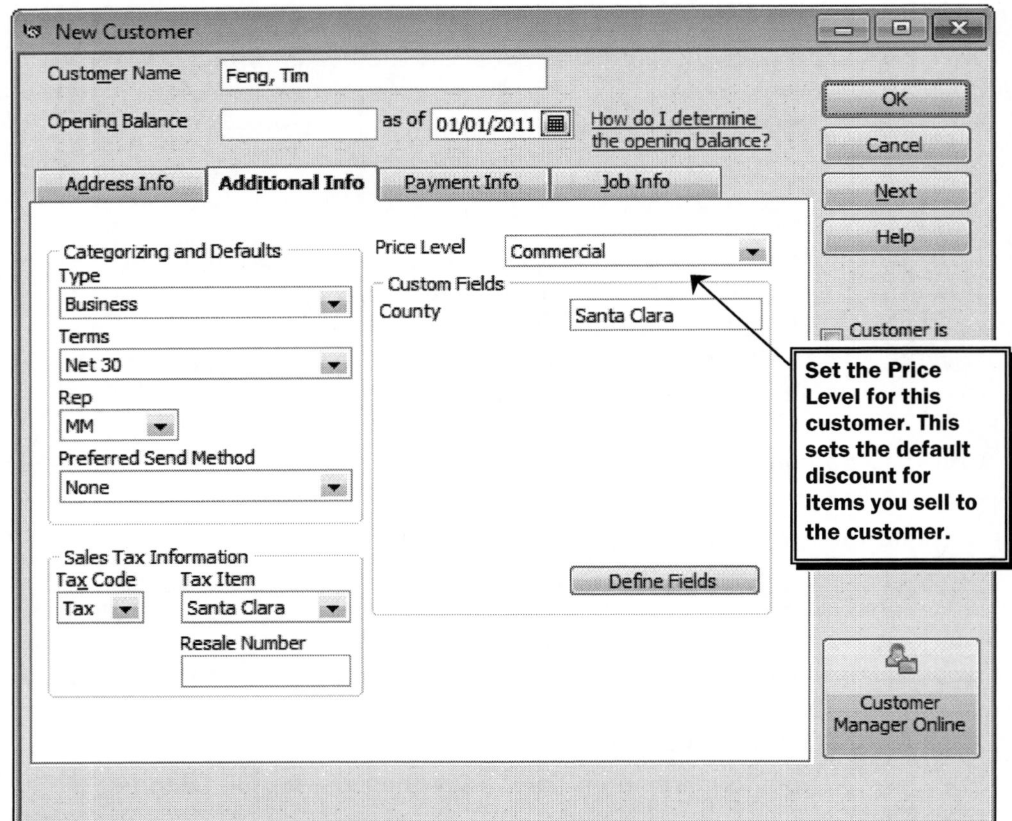

Figure 2-8 Completed Additional Info tab

Step 11. Press **Tab** to leave the default setting of **None** in the *Preferred Send Method* field.

You would use the *Preferred Send Method* field if you plan to email Invoices to a customer on a regular basis or if you plan to use QuickBooks' Invoice printing and mailing service.

> Note:
> For more information on the QuickBooks invoice payment and mailing service, select the **Help** menu and then select **Add QuickBooks Services**. You will then be directed online to the Intuit website. Scroll down and click on the **QuickBooks Billing Solutions** link under the *Financial Services* section. Additional transaction fees apply for this service.

Step 12. Press **Tab** to accept the **Tax** default **Sales Tax Code** in the *Tax Code* field.

Sales Tax Codes serve two purposes. First, they determine the default taxable status of a customer, item, or sale. Second, they are used to identify the type of tax exemption. For complete information on sales tax codes, see the Sales Tax Chapter beginning on page 407.

Step 13. Set the *Tax Item* field to **Santa Clara**. This indicates which sales tax rate to charge and which agency collects the tax. Press **Tab** when finished.

> **Tip:**
> In most states, you charge sales tax based on the delivery point of the shipment. Therefore, the **Sales Tax Item** should be chosen to match the tax charged in the county (or tax location) of the *Ship To* address on the *Address Info* tab.

Step 14. Press **Tab** to leave the *Resale Number* field blank.

If the customer is a reseller, you would enter his or her reseller number.

Step 15. Select **Commercial** from the *Price Level* drop-down list. See page 351 for information on setting up and using price levels. Press **Tab**.

Step 16. Enter ***Santa Clara*** in the *County* field.

The **Define Fields** button on the **Additional Information** tab allows you to define **Custom Fields** to track more information about your customers. For more information on setting up and using custom fields, see page 353.

Step 17. Verify that your screen matches Figure 2-8 and then click the **Payment Info** tab to continue entering information about this customer as shown in Figure 2-9.

Step 18. Enter ***3543*** in the *Account No.* field to assign a customer number by which you can sort or filter reports. Press **Tab**.

Step 19. Enter ***3,000.00*** in the *Credit Limit* field and press **Tab**.

QuickBooks will warn you if you record an Invoice to this customer when the balance due (plus the current sale) exceeds the credit limit. Even though QuickBooks warns you, you'll still be able to record the Invoice.

Step 20. Select ***VISA*** from the *Preferred Payment Method* drop-down list and then press **Tab**. When you set the fields on this window, you won't have to enter the credit card information each time you receive money from the customer.

> **Tip:**
> If more than one person accesses your QuickBooks file, set up a separate user name and password for each additional user. When you set up a user, you can restrict him or her from accessing *Sensitive Accounting Activities*. This will prevent the additional user from seeing the customer's credit card number. See page 315 for more information about setting up user names and passwords.

Step 21. Enter the remaining data as shown in Figure 2-9 in the *Preferred Payment Method* section.

> **Note:**
> If you track multiple jobs for each customer, it is best NOT to enter job information on the *Job Info* tab of the main customer record. If you want to track jobs for this customer, you can create separate job records in the **Customers & Jobs** list.

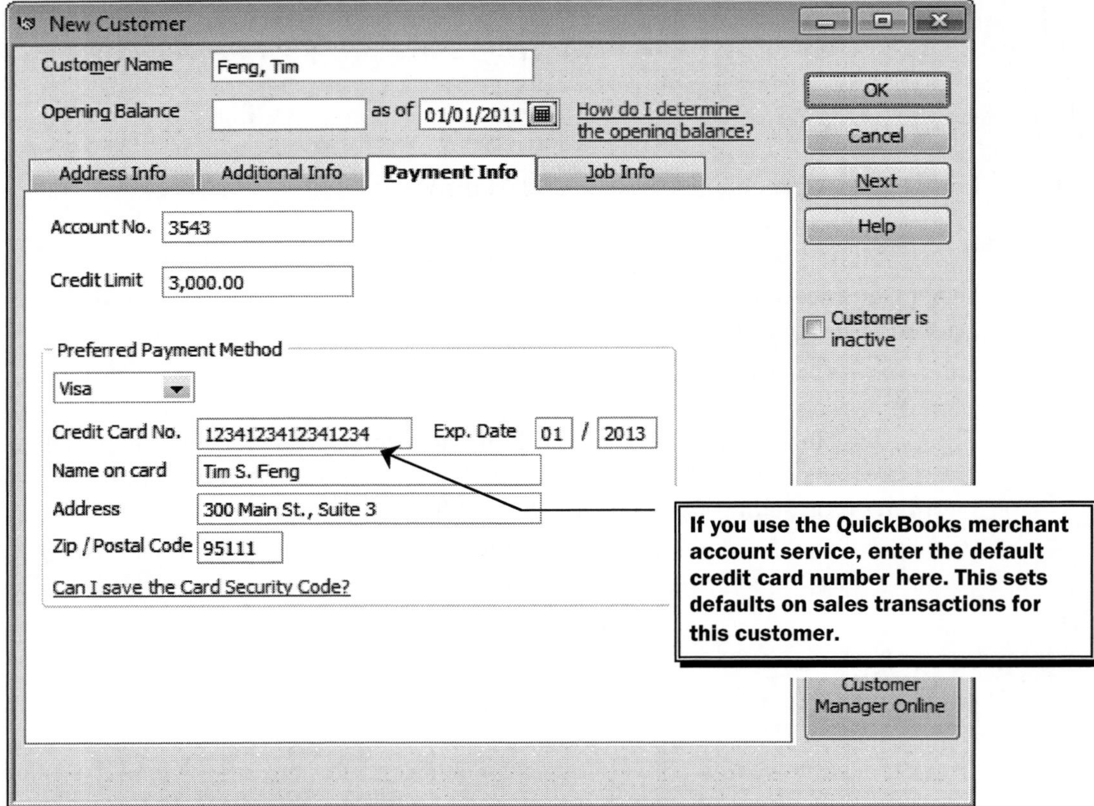

Figure 2-9 Completed Payment Info tab

Step 22. If you were adding several customers at a time, you would click **Next** to begin adding another customer. In this case, click **OK** to save and close the *New Customer* window.

> Note:
> If you see an error message when saving the Feng, Tim customer (see Figure 2-10), you may not be in the correct exercise file. Make sure you restore the correct file at the start of each chapter and problem, otherwise your exercises may not match the activities in this book. For this chapter, you should be using Sales-10.QBW. For instructions on restoring portable files, please see page 10.

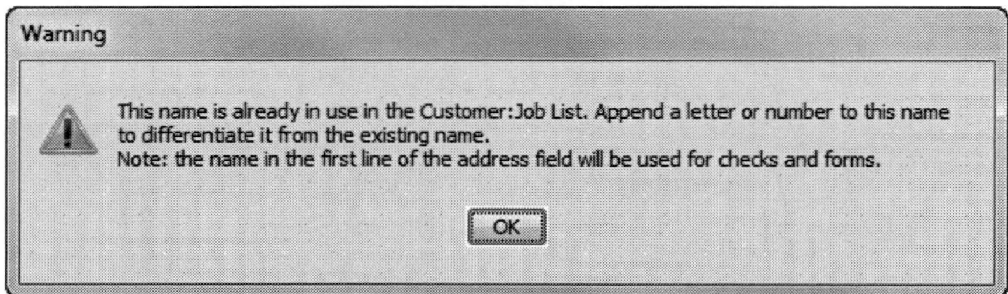

Figure 2-10 Error Message when saving a Name that already exists

Step 23. Close the Customer Center by clicking the close button (☒) on the *Customer Center* window or by pressing the **Esc** key.

Job Costing

QuickBooks tracks jobs in addition to customers. For each customer in the **Customers & Jobs** list, you can create one or more jobs. This helps you track income and expenses on each *Job*, so that you can create reports showing detailed or summarized information about each *Job*.

To create a job for an existing customer record, open the *Customer Center*, then select the customer, and then select **Add Job** from the **New Customer & Job** drop down menu. You don't need to do this now, because the sample data file already has jobs set up.

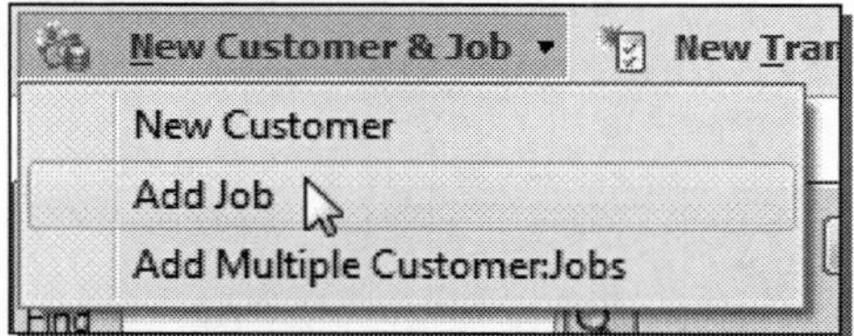

Figure 2-11 Adding a Job to an existing customer record

> **Key Term:**
> Tracking income and expenses separately for each job is known as *Job Costing*. If your company needs to track job costs, make sure you enter the job name on each income and expense transaction as you enter it.

In the **Name** column of the *Customers & Jobs* list, jobs are slightly indented under the Customer name.

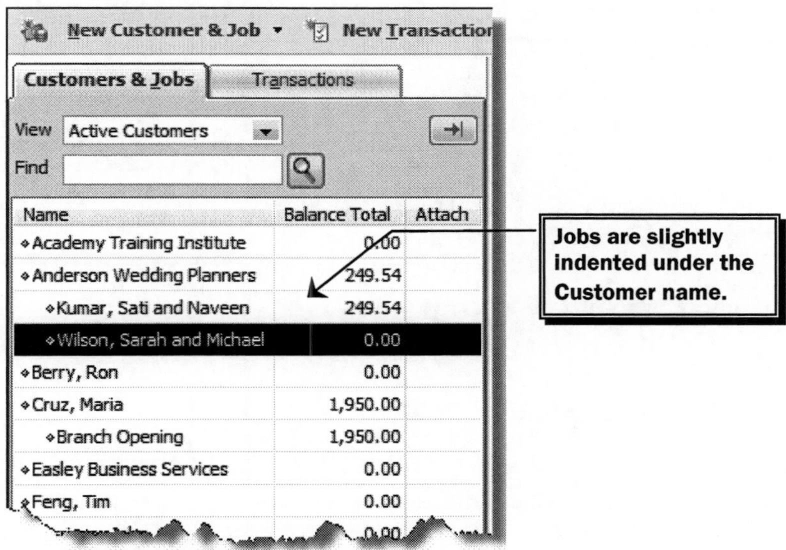

Figure 2-12 Customers & Jobs list

> **Did You Know?**
> To *Quick Add* a **Job** for a **Customer** on an invoice or sales receipt, enter the Customer's name followed by a colon (the Customer name must already exist in the Customer list first). After the colon, enter the name of the job. QuickBooks will then prompt you to either *Quick Add* or *Set Up* the job. If the *Customer* record includes job information on the Job tab, you won't be able to use *Quick Add* to create a job for the customer. In this case, you will need to create the job in the **Customers & Jobs** list before you begin entering sales.

Recording Sales

Now that you've set up your **Customers**, you're ready to begin entering sales. You don't have to have all your customers set up before you begin entering sales transactions. As you'll see, it's also possible to create a new customer record when you record the first sale to a customer. However, creating the customer records beforehand will significantly reduce the amount of time needed to record each sale.

There are two QuickBooks forms for recording sales transactions. The first is the **Sales Receipts** form. Use this form when you receive a cash, check, or credit card payment at the time of the sale. The other sales form is the **Invoice**. Use this form when you record credit sales to customers.

> **Note:** If you collect sales tax, turn on **Sales Tax** tracking in the **Preferences** window before recording your sales. For more information about Sales Tax, see the Sales Tax Chapter beginning on page 407.

Entering Sales Receipts

When customers pay at the time of the sale by cash, check, or credit card, create a **Sales Receipt** transaction.

COMPUTER PRACTICE

Step 1. Click the **Create Sales Receipts** icon in the *Customers* section on the *Home* page (see Figure 2-13). This opens the *Enter Sales Receipts* window (see Figure 2-14).

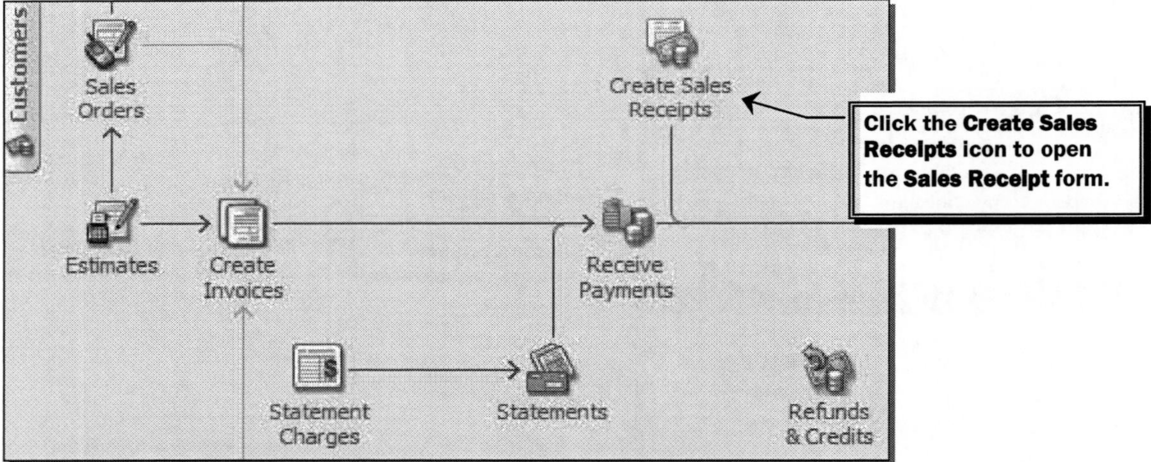

Figure 2-13 Selecting Sales Receipts icon on the Home page

Step 2. Enter ***Perez, Jerry*** in the *Customer:Job* field and press **Tab**.

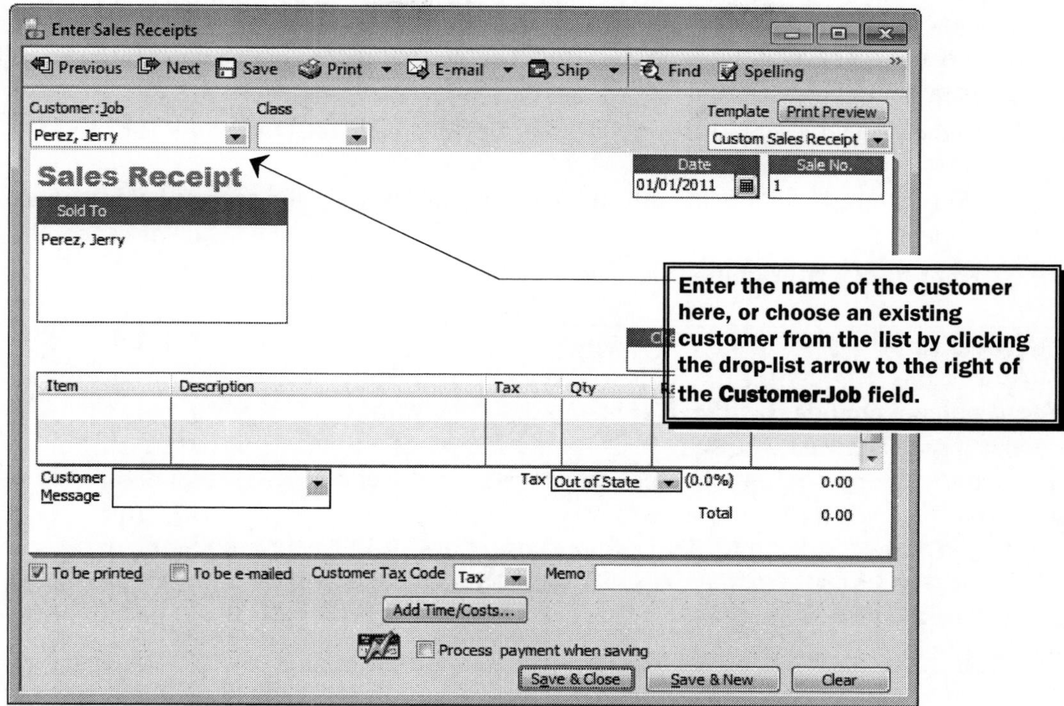

Figure 2-14 Sales Receipt form

Step 3. When the **Customer:Job Not Found** warning window appears (see Figure 2-15), click **Quick Add** to add this new customer to the *Customer:Job* list. If you choose this option, you can edit the customer record later to add more details.

> **Note:**
> **Quick Add** works on all your lists. Whenever you type a new name into any field on any form, QuickBooks prompts you to **Quick Add, Set up, or Cancel** the name.
>
> **Tip:**
> If your customer is an individual (i.e., not a business), it's a good idea to enter the customer's last name first. This way, your **Customer:Job** list sorts by last name so it will be easier to find names in the list.

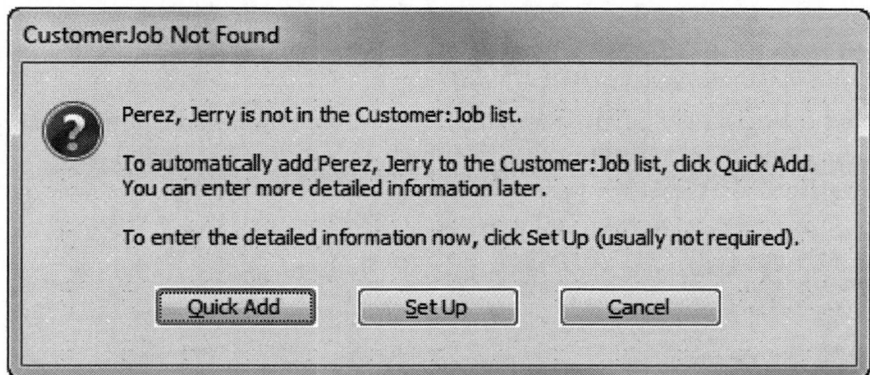

Figure 2-15 Use Quick Add to add new customers

Step 4. Enter ***San Jose*** in the *Class* field and then press **Tab** twice.

QuickBooks uses classes to separately track income and expenses for departments, functions, activities, locations, or profit centers. For more information on classes, see page 130.

Step 5. In the *Template* field, **Custom Sales Receipt** is already selected. Press **Tab**.

You can create your own custom forms, as you'll learn in the section beginning on page 355.

Step 6. Enter ***01/25/2011*** in the *Date* field and then press **Tab** (see Figure 2-16).

> **Did You Know?**
> Whenever you enter a date in QuickBooks, you can use any of several shortcut keys to quickly change the date. For example, if you want to change the date to the first day of the year, press **y**. "Y" is the first letter of the word "year," so it's easy to remember this shortcut. The same works for the end of the year. Press **r** since that's the last letter of the word "year." The same works for "month" (**m** and **h**) and "week" (**w** and **k**). You can also use the + and - keys to move the date one day forward or back. Finally, press **t** for "today." See the Appendix included with the supplemental material for this book (see page xiii) for a list of shortcut keys that help you quickly enter dates.

Step 7. ***Enter 2011-1*** in the *SALE NO.* field.
The first time you enter a **Sales Receipt**, enter any number you want in the *SALE NO.* field. QuickBooks will automatically number future Sales Receipts incrementally. You can change or reset the numbering at any time by overriding the *SALE NO.* on a Sales Receipt.

Step 8. Press **Tab** to skip the *SOLD TO* field.

QuickBooks automatically fills in this field, using the information in the *Bill To* field of the customer record. Since you used *Quick Add* to add this customer, there is no address information. You could enter an address in the *SOLD TO* field by entering it directly on the sales form. When you record the Sales Receipt, QuickBooks will give you the option of adding the address in the *Bill To* field of the customer record.

Step 9. Enter ***3612*** in the *CHECK NO.* field and then press **Tab**.

The number you enter here shows up on your printed deposit slips. If you were receiving a cash or credit card payment, you would leave this field blank.

Step 10. Select **Check** from the **PAYMENT METHOD** drop-down list and then press **Tab**.

If you wanted to add a new payment method, you would enter the new method in this field. QuickBooks would prompt you to either *Quick Add* or *Set Up* the new **Payment Method**.

Step 11. Select **Indoor Photo Session** from the **ITEM** drop-down list and then press **Tab**.

Step 12. Press **Tab** to accept the default description ***Indoor Studio Session*** in the **DESCRIPTION** column.

As soon as you enter an Item, QuickBooks enters the description, rate, and sales tax code using data from the Item that has already been set up.

Step 13. In the **Tax** column, the **Non** sales tax code is already selected. Press **Tab**.

Step 14. Enter ***1*** in the **QTY** (quantity) column and then press **Tab**.

Step 15. Leave the default rate at ***95.00*** in the **RATE** column and then press **Tab**.

Step 16. Press **Tab** to accept the calculated amount in the **AMOUNT** column.

After you enter the rate and press **Tab**, QuickBooks calculates the amount by multiplying the quantity by the rate. If you override the *AMOUNT* field, QuickBooks calculates a new rate by dividing the amount by the quantity.

Step 17. Select **Premium Photo Package** from the **ITEM** drop-down list and then press **Tab** three times.

Step 18. Enter ***2*** in the **QTY** (quantity) column and press **Tab**.

Step 19. Press **Tab** to accept the default rate of ***85.00***.

You can override this amount directly on the Sales Receipt if necessary. As with the line above, QuickBooks calculates the total in the **AMOUNT** column and QuickBooks uses the default sales tax code ***Non,*** which is set up for the ***Design*** Item.

Step 20. Select **Thank you for your business.** from the *Customer Message* drop-down list.

You can enter a message in the *Customer Message* field that shows on the printed **Sales Receipt**. This is typically a thank you message, but it can be whatever you want. If you type in a new message, **Quick Add** will prompt you to add your new message to the *Customer Message* list. If you want to edit an existing customer message, or if you want to remove a customer message from the list, select the **Lists** menu, then select **Customer & Vendor Profile Lists,** and then select **Customer Message List**.

Step 21. Press **Tab** and enter **Santa Clara** in the *Tax* field and to advance to the *Memo* field.

The Sales Tax item shown in the *Tax* field determines the rate of tax to be charged on all *Taxable* Items shown on the form. Each line in the body of the Invoice is marked with a Sales Tax Code that determines the taxability or non-taxability of the item on that line (see Figure 2-16).

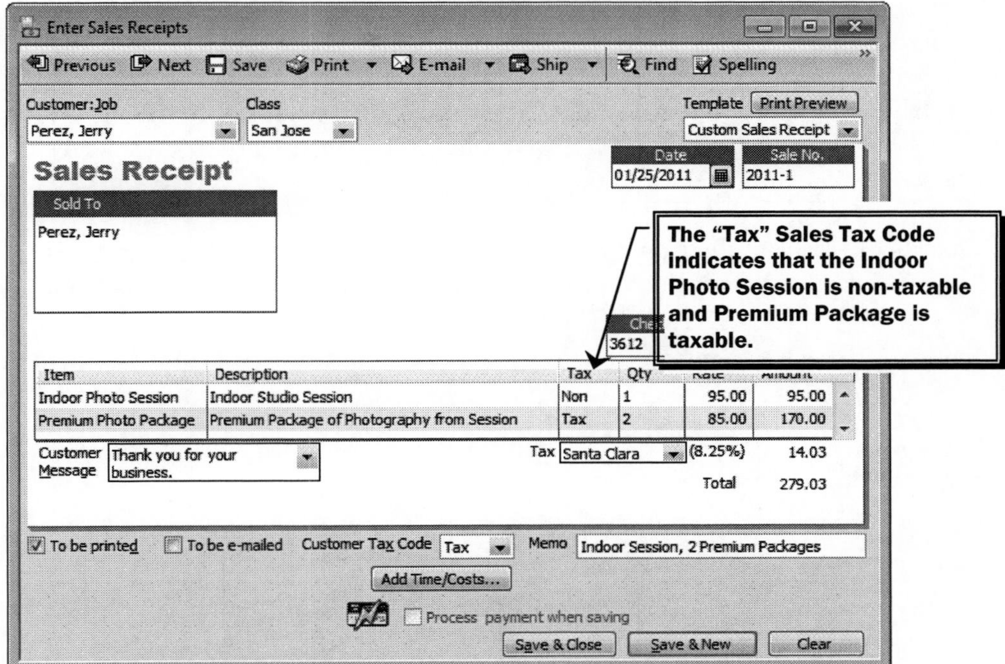

Figure 2-16 Completed Sales Receipt

Step 22. Press **Tab** so that the *To be printed* checkbox is selected. Enter the Spacebar on the keyboard to uncheck this box.

> Note:
> Entering the spacebar on the keyboard when a checkbox is selected will either check or uncheck that checkbox.

Step 23. Enter ***Indoor Session, 2 Premium Packages*** in the **Memo** field.

Step 24. To print the sale on blank paper or on a preprinted form, click the **Print** icon at the top of the **Sales Receipt** or select the **File** menu and then select **Print Sales Receipt**. If QuickBooks displays an information dialog box after you print the Sales Receipt, click **OK** to close the window and proceed to Step 25.

Alternatively, you could choose to print all your sales in one batch. To do this, save each Sales Receipt without printing and check the **To be printed** box on the sales receipts. Then print all of the forms together in one batch by selecting the *File* menu, then selecting **Print Forms**, and then selecting **Sales Receipts**.

> Note:
> If you are taking this course in a classroom environment (e.g., a computer lab) and your computer is not connected to a printer, skip Step 24. If you prefer, you can click the **Print** icon at the top of the **Sales Receipt** and then click **Preview** to view the Sales Receipt without printing.

Step 25. Click **Save & Close** to record the sale.

QuickBooks does not record any of the information on any form until you save the transaction by clicking **Save & Close**, **Save & New**, **Previous**, or **Next**.

> Note:
> If you prefer to use your keyboard over the mouse, you can use the *Alt* key on in combination with other keys to execute commands. QuickBooks will tell you which key can be used in connection with the *Alt* key by underlining the letter in the command. For example, in the Sale Receipt window, the *S* is underlined on the *Save & New* button. You can save the receipt and move to a new sales receipt window by pressing the **Alt** key followed by **S**.

Step 26. QuickBooks displays the *Name Information Changed* dialog box. This dialog box appears because you set the *Tax Item* field to *Santa Clara*. Click the **Yes** button.

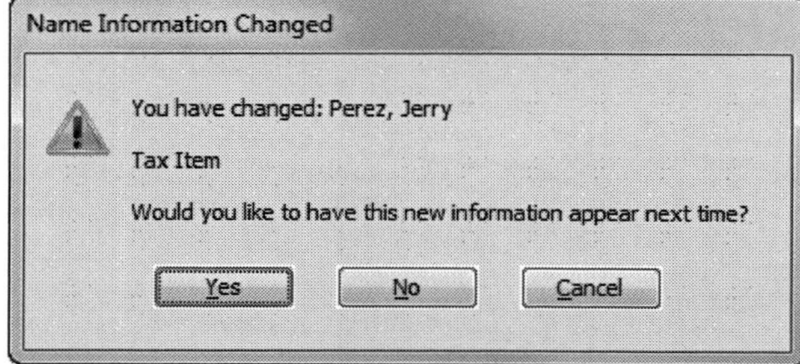

Figure 2-17 Name Information Changed dialog box

Undeposited Funds

The **Undeposited Funds** account is a special account that is automatically created by QuickBooks. The account works as a temporary holding account where QuickBooks tracks checks and other receipts before the money is deposited in a bank account.

As illustrated in Figure 2-18, as you record Payments and Sales Receipts, QuickBooks gives you a choice between (Option 1) grouping all receipts into the **Undeposited Funds** account or, (Option 2) immediately depositing the funds to one of your bank accounts.

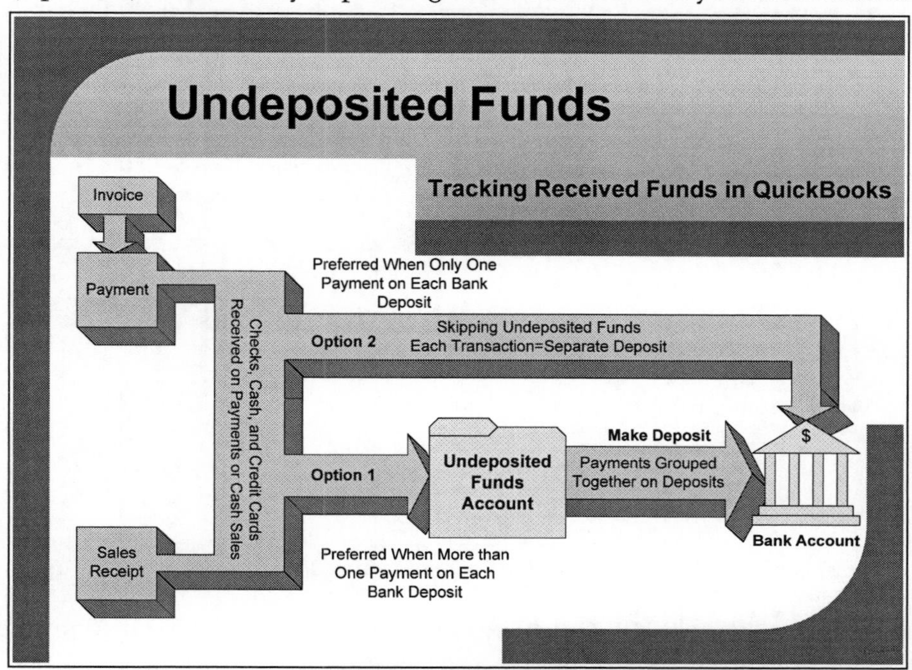

Figure 2-18 All funds from sales transactions go through **Undeposited Funds** *or directly to a bank account.*

There is a tradeoff here. When you use the **Undeposited Funds** account, you have to create a separate transaction (an additional step) to actually deposit money into a bank account. At first that might seem like extra work. However, when you skip the **Undeposited Funds** account, each sales transaction creates a separate deposit in your bank account.

Since it is most common to have multiple sales transactions per bank deposit, QuickBooks has a default preference setting that makes all Payments and Sales Receipts affect the balance in the **Undeposited Funds** account. Then when you actually make a deposit at the bank, you record a single deposit transaction in QuickBooks that empties the **Undeposited Funds** account into the bank account. This method makes it much easier to reconcile the bank account at the end of each month because the deposits on the bank statement will match the deposits in your QuickBooks bank account. Unless you only make one sale each day and your deposits include only the funds from that single sale, you will want to keep this default preference.

COMPUTER PRACTICE

You can modify the **Undeposited Funds** preference by following these steps:

Step 1. Select the *Edit* menu and then select **Preferences.**

Step 2. Select **Payments** in the *Preferences* window.

Step 3. In the **Company Preferences** tab, the box next to **Use Undeposited Funds as a default deposit to account** is checked (see Figure 2-19).

Step 4. If you prefer to deposit payments individually, uncheck the box next to **Use Undeposited Funds as a default deposit to account**. You will then have the option to select an account to deposit to in the *Sales Receipt* and *Receive Payment* windows.

Step 5. Click **Cancel** to leave default setting for the use of **Undeposited Funds.**

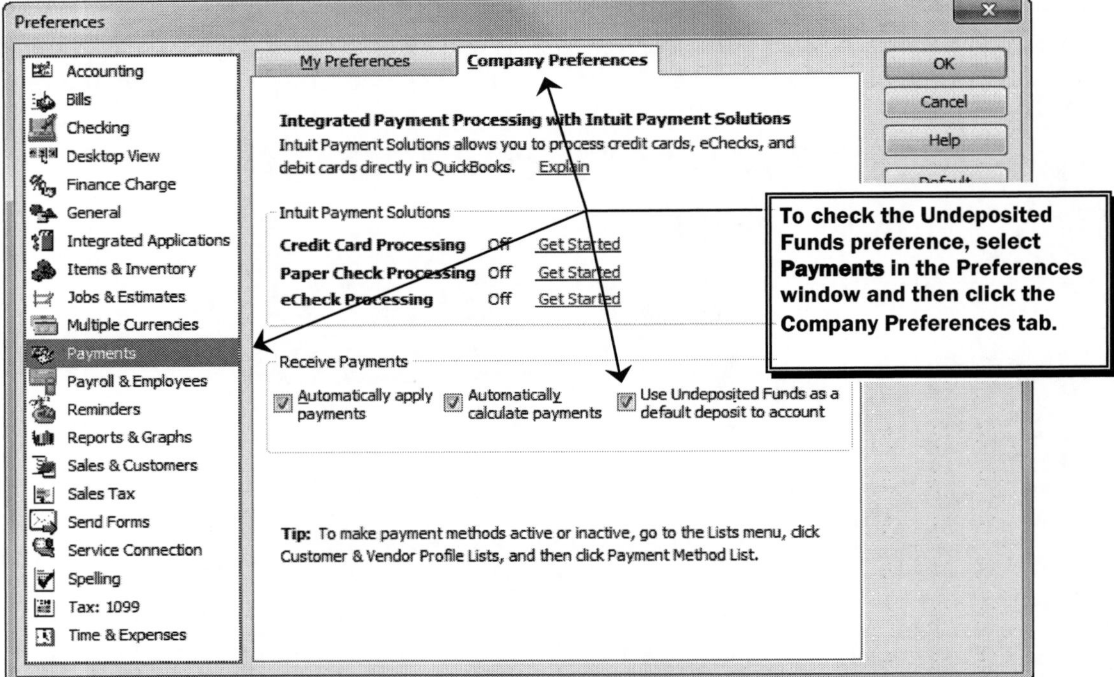

Figure 2-19 Preference for Payments to go to **Undeposited funds** *or another account*

When this preference is off (see Figure 2-20), QuickBooks displays the **Deposit To** field on the **Receive Payments** and **Enter Sales Receipt** windows (see Figure 2-21).

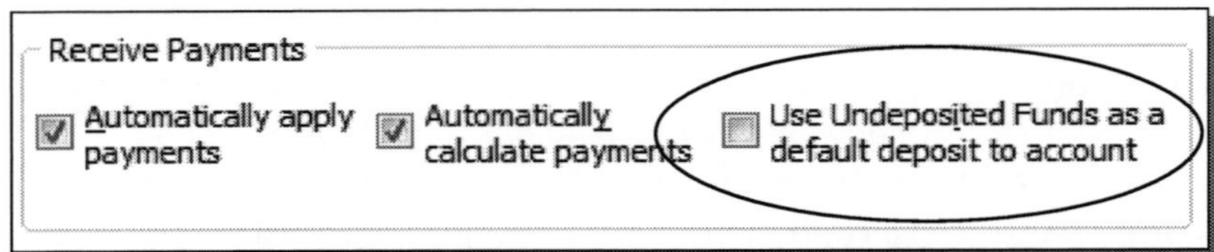

Figure 2-20 Setting for **Undeposited Funds** *on Company Preferences for Payments*

You must choose a destination account for the transaction from the *Deposit to* drop-down list.

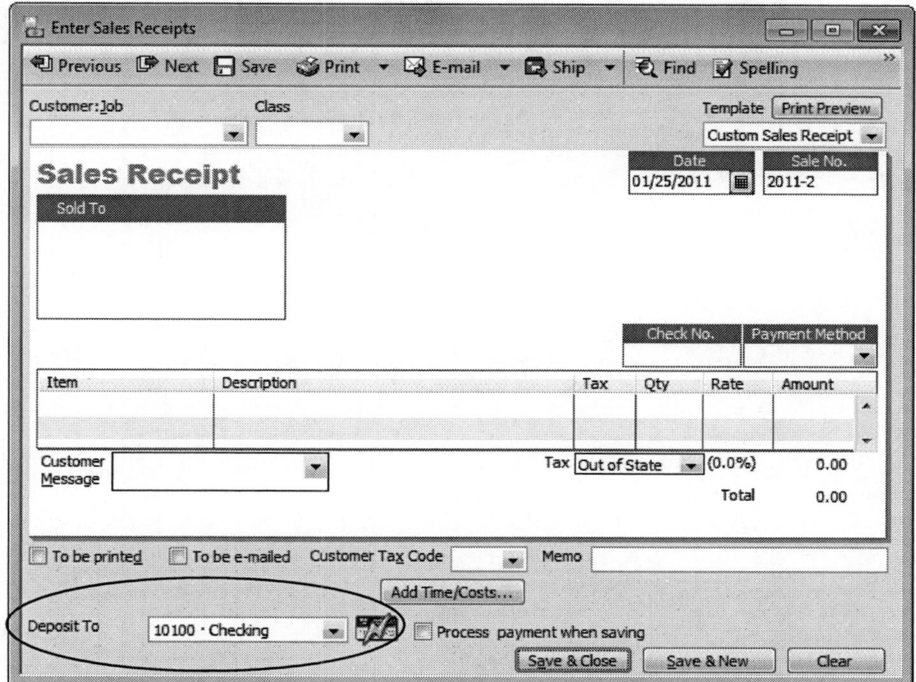

Figure 2-21 The ***Deposit To*** *field shows on Sales Receipts when this preference is off.*

Creating Invoices

Invoices are very similar to **Sales Receipts**. The only difference is that **Invoices** increase **Accounts Receivable** while **Sales Receipts** increase **Undeposited Funds** (or the specified bank account). You should use **Invoices** to record sales to your credit customers.

COMPUTER PRACTICE

To create an Invoice, follow these steps:

Step 1. From the *Customer Center* select **Mason, Bob** from the *Customers & Jobs* list. Then select **Invoices** from the *New Transactions* drop-down list.

Alternatively, click the **Create Invoices** icon on the *Home page* and select **Mason, Bob** from the *Customer:Job* drop-down list. Press **Tab** (see Figure 2-22).

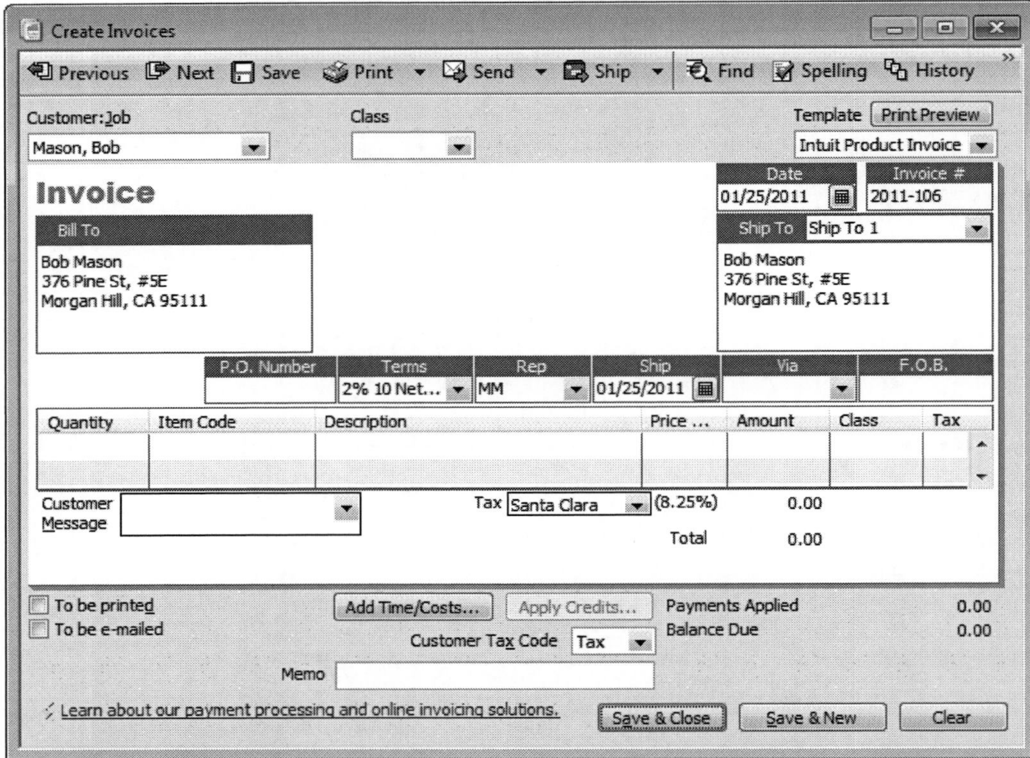

Figure 2-22 Invoice with Bob Mason selected

> **Did You Know?**
> When you type the first few characters of any field that has a list behind it, QuickBooks completes the field using a feature called **QuickFill**. QuickFill uses the first few characters you type to find the name in the list. If the name does not come up right away, keep typing until the correct name appears.

Step 2. Enter an *s* in the *Class* field. QuickBooks will QuickFill the field with the full word *San Jose*. Then press **Tab** twice.

Step 3. In the *Template* field, select **Academy Photo Service Invoice**. Press **Tab**.

Step 4. Enter ***01/26/2011*** in the *DATE* field and then press **Tab**.

Step 5. Leave ***2011-106*** in the *INVOICE #* field and then press **Tab**.

The first time you enter an Invoice, enter any number you want in the *INVOICE #* field. QuickBooks will automatically number future Invoices incrementally. You can change or reset the numbering at any time by overriding the number on a future Invoice.

Step 6. Press **Tab** to accept the default information in the *BILL TO* field.

QuickBooks automatically enters the address in this field, using the information in the *Bill To* field of the customer record. If necessary, change the *Bill To* address by typing over the existing data.

Step 7. Leave the *P.O. NO* field blank and then press **Tab**.

The P.O. (purchase order) number helps the customer identify your Invoice. When your customers use purchase orders, make sure you enter the P.O. numbers on their Invoices.

Warning:
Make sure you enter the P.O. number if your customer uses Purchase Orders. Some customers may reject Invoices that do not reference a P.O. number.

Step 8. In the *TERMS* field, **2%10 Net 30** is already selected. Press **Tab** to proceed to the next field.

The *TERMS* field on the **Invoice** indicates the due date for the Invoice and how long your customer can take to pay you. The entry in this field determines how this Invoice is reported on Customers and Receivables reports such as the **A/R Aging Summary** and the **Collections Report**. To learn more about the Terms list, and how to set up terms, see page 349.

Step 9. Enter the sale of 2 Hours for an Indoor Photo Session and 1 Standard Photo Package into the body of the Invoice as shown in Figure 2-23.

Step 10. Select ***Thank you for your business*** from the *Customer Message* drop-down list and then press **Tab**.

Step 11. **Santa Clara** in the *Tax* field is already selected. Press **Tab**.

As with Sales Receipts, QuickBooks selects the Sales Tax Item based on the defaults in Sales Tax Preferences or in the Customer's record. See the Sales Tax Chapter beginning on page 407.

Step 12. Enter ***2 Hr Indoor Session, 1 Standard Package*** in the *Memo* field at the bottom of the form.

Tip:
If you intend to send statements to your customers, the *Memo* field is extremely important. QuickBooks allows you to show line item detail from your customer's Invoices. However, if you want your statements to be more concise, you can choose not to show the line item detail and show the text from the *Memo* field instead. The text from the *Memo* field will show along with the information in the *INVOICE #,* and *DATE* fields. The customer's statement will also show a three-letter code "INV" representing the Invoice transaction. Therefore, it is best to include information about the products or services you sold to the customer in the *Memo* field.

Step 13. Compare your screen with the Invoice shown in Figure 2-23. If you see any errors, correct them. Otherwise, click **Save & Close** to record the Invoice.

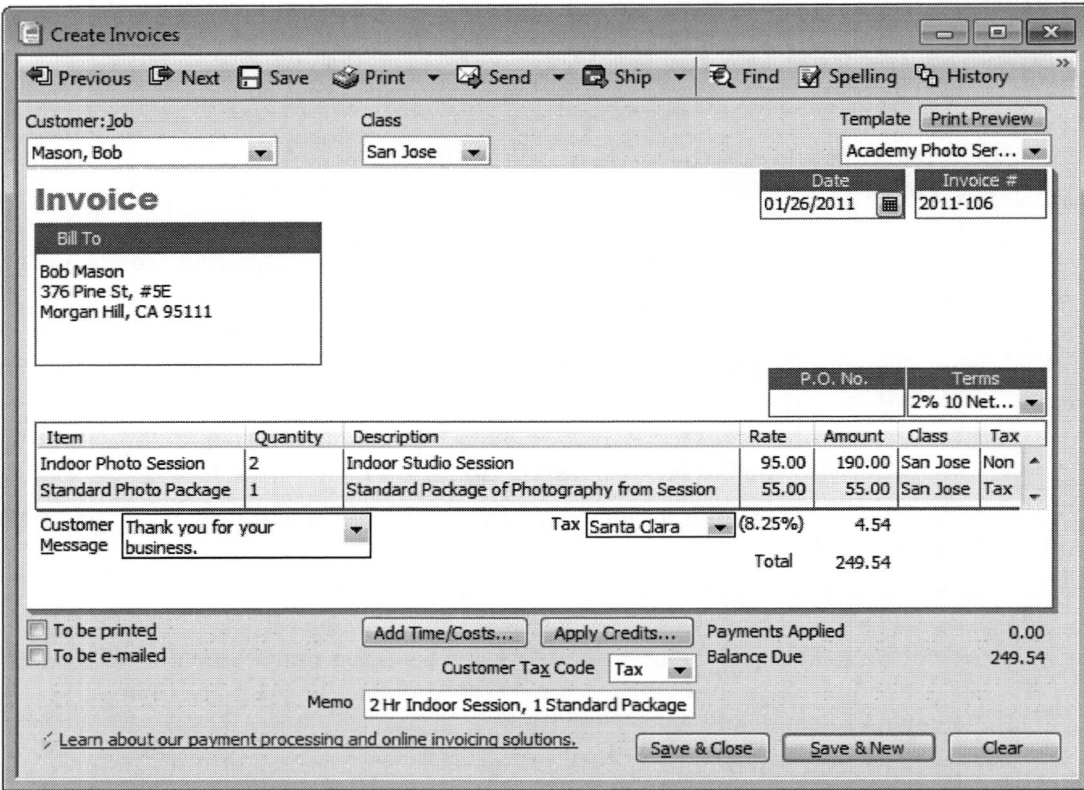

Figure 2-23 Completed Invoice

QuickBooks automatically tracks all of the accounting details behind this transaction so that all of your reports will immediately reflect the sale. For example, the Open Invoices report, the Profit & Loss Standard report, and the Balance Sheet Standard report will all change when you record this Invoice.

Adding Calculating Items to an Invoice

On the next Invoice, you'll learn how to add discounts and subtotals to an **Invoice**. Discounts and subtotals are called *Calculating Items.*

> **Key Term:**
> *Calculating Items* use the amount of the preceding line to calculate their amount. For example, if you enter 10% in the Discount item setup window and then enter the Discount item on an Invoice, QuickBooks will multiply the line just above the Discount item by 10% and enter that number, as a negative, in the **AMOUNT** column for the discount line.

COMPUTER PRACTICE

To create an Invoice with a calculating item, follow these steps:

Step 1. From the *Customer Center* select the **Branch Opening** job for Cruz, Maria from the *Customers & Jobs* list.

Step 2. Select **Invoices** from the *New Transactions* drop-down list; or, press Ctrl+ I.

Step 3. The Branch Opening job for Cruz, Maria is already selected. Press **Tab**.

Step 4. Enter ***Walnut Creek*** in the *Class* field and then press **Tab** twice.

Step 5. The Academy Photo Service Invoice template in the *Template* drop-down list is already selected. Press **Tab**.

Step 6. ***1/26/2011*** is already entered in the *DATE* field. Press **Tab**.

Step 7. Notice the *INVOICE #* is automatically entered for you with the next Invoice number (i.e. **2011-107**). Press **Tab** to skip to the next field.

Step 8. Press **Tab** to skip the ***BILL TO*** field.

Step 9. Press **Tab twice** to skip the ***P.O. NO and the Terms*** fields.

Step 10. Enter the two items shown in Table 2-3 in the body of the **Invoice**.

Item	Description	Qty	Rate	Amount
Camera SR32	Supra Digital Camera SR32	4	695.99	2,783.96
Lens	Supra Zoom Lens	1	324.99	324.99

Table 2-3 Data for use in the Invoice

Step 11. On the third line of the body of the Invoice, in the **ITEM** column, enter ***Subtotal*** to sum the previous two item lines, and press **Tab** twice.

Notice that QuickBooks automatically calculates the sum of the first two lines on the Invoice.

Step 12. Enter ***Disc 10%*** in the **ITEM** column and press **Tab**.

The ***Disc 10%*** Item is a special Calculating Item that calculates a percentage of the preceding line on sales forms. Since it is a **Discount Item**, QuickBooks performs the calculation and enters a negative amount for your discount. This subtracts the discount from the total of the Invoice and adjusts sales tax accordingly.

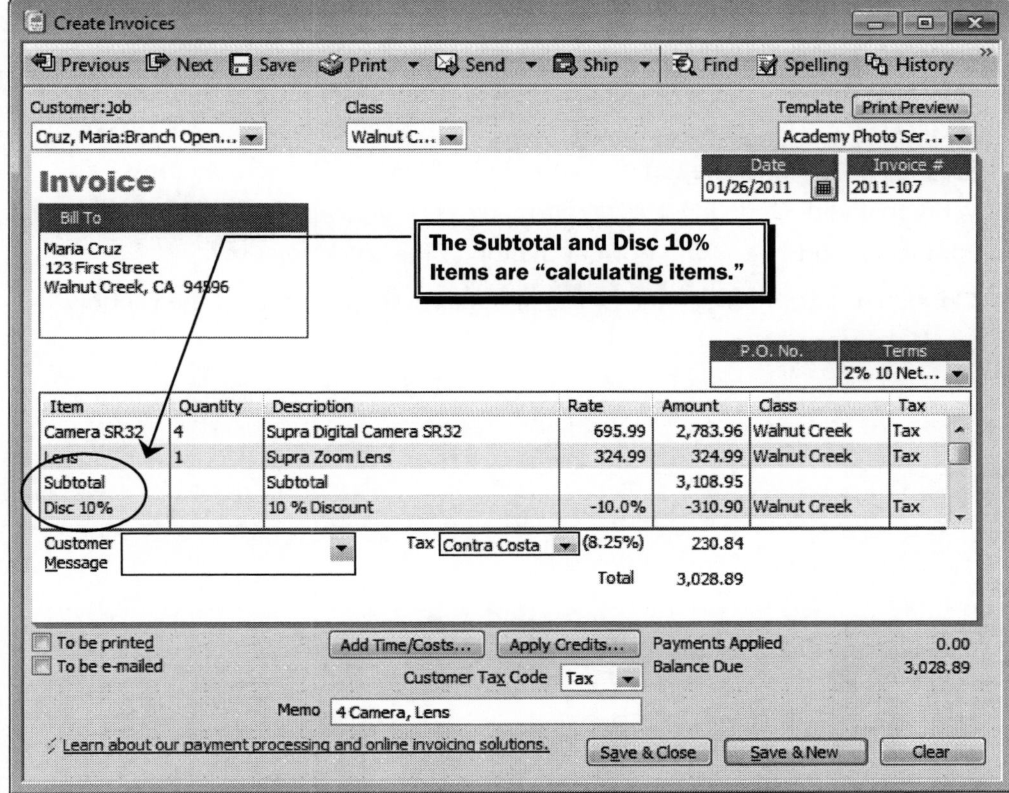

Figure 2-24 Completed Invoice with discount

Did You Know?
You can insert or delete lines on an Invoice (or any other form). To insert a line between two existing lines, click on the line that you want to move down and press Ctrl+INS (or select the **Edit** menu, and then select **Insert Line**). To delete a line, click on the line you want to delete and press Ctrl+DELETE (or select the **Edit** menu, and then select **Delete Line**).

Step 13. Leave the *Customer Message* field blank.

Step 14. Leave **Contra Costa** in the *Tax* field. Also leave **Tax** in the *Customer Tax Code* field.

Step 15. Enter ***4 Cameras, Lens*** in the *Memo* field.

Step 16. Verify that your screen matches Figure 2-24. To save the Invoice, click **Save & Close**.

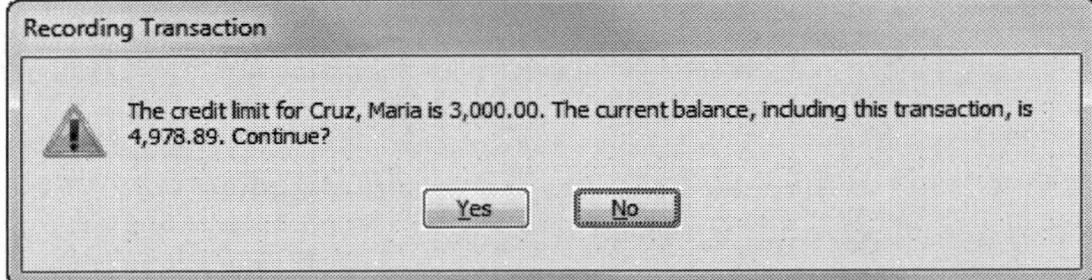

Figure 2-25 Recording Transaction window warns you about the customer's credit limit

Step 17. If you see the *Recording Transaction* warning about Maria Cruz exceeding her credit limit (Figure 2-25), click **Yes**.

Open Invoices Report

Now that you've entered Invoices for your customers, QuickBooks' reports reflect the Invoices that are "open" and the "age" of each Invoice. The Open Invoices report is shown in Figure 2-26.

COMPUTER PRACTICE

Step 1. Select the **Reports** menu, select **Customers & Receivables**, and then select **Open Invoices**.

Step 2. Set the *Dates* field at the top of the report to ***01/31/2011*** and then press **Tab**.

Step 3. Verify that your Open Invoices report matches Figure 2-26.

Step 4. Print this report by clicking **Print** at the top of the report window.

Step 5. Close the report by clicking the (☒) in the upper right corner of the window.

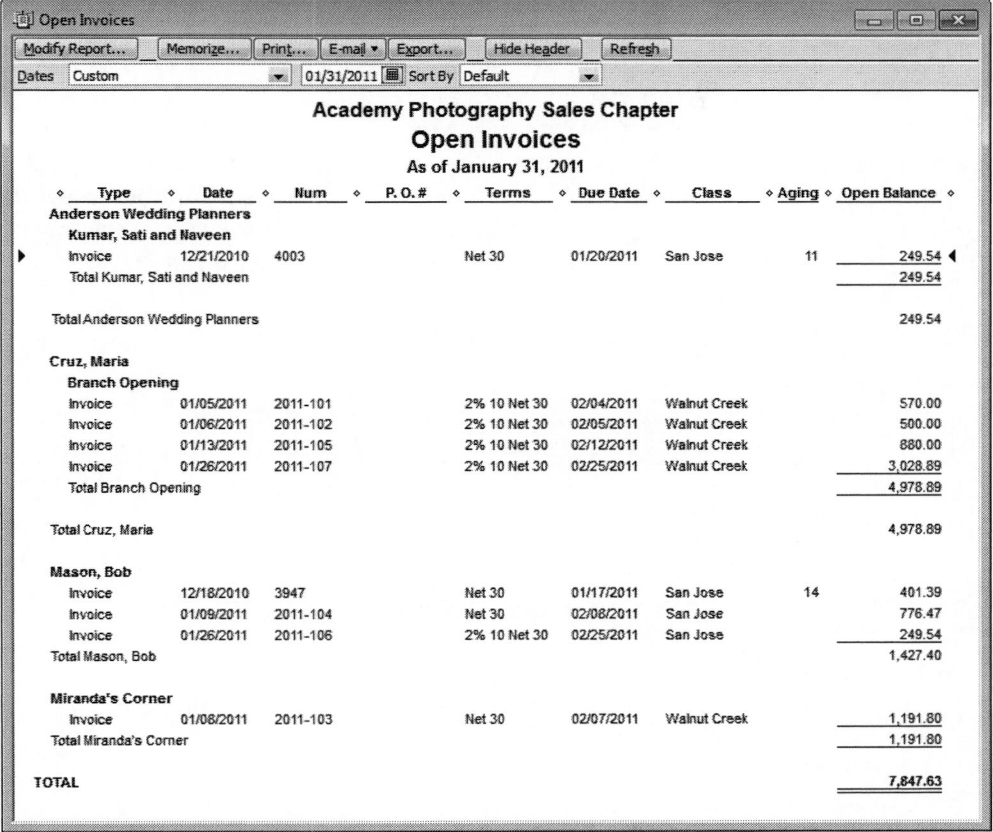

Academy Photography Sales Chapter

Open Invoices

As of January 31, 2011

Type	Date	Num	P. O. #	Terms	Due Date	Class	Aging	Open Balance
Anderson Wedding Planners								
Kumar, Sati and Naveen								
Invoice	12/21/2010	4003		Net 30	01/20/2011	San Jose	11	249.54
Total Kumar, Sati and Naveen								249.54
Total Anderson Wedding Planners								249.54
Cruz, Maria								
Branch Opening								
Invoice	01/05/2011	2011-101		2% 10 Net 30	02/04/2011	Walnut Creek		570.00
Invoice	01/06/2011	2011-102		2% 10 Net 30	02/05/2011	Walnut Creek		500.00
Invoice	01/13/2011	2011-105		2% 10 Net 30	02/12/2011	Walnut Creek		880.00
Invoice	01/26/2011	2011-107		2% 10 Net 30	02/25/2011	Walnut Creek		3,028.89
Total Branch Opening								4,978.89
Total Cruz, Maria								4,978.89
Mason, Bob								
Invoice	12/18/2010	3947		Net 30	01/17/2011	San Jose	14	401.39
Invoice	01/09/2011	2011-104		Net 30	02/08/2011	San Jose		776.47
Invoice	01/26/2011	2011-106		2% 10 Net 30	02/25/2011	San Jose		249.54
Total Mason, Bob								1,427.40
Miranda's Corner								
Invoice	01/08/2011	2011-103		Net 30	02/07/2011	Walnut Creek		1,191.80
Total Miranda's Corner								1,191.80
TOTAL								7,847.63

Figure 2-26 Open Invoices report

Step 6. If you see a *Memorize Report* dialog box, click the **No** button.

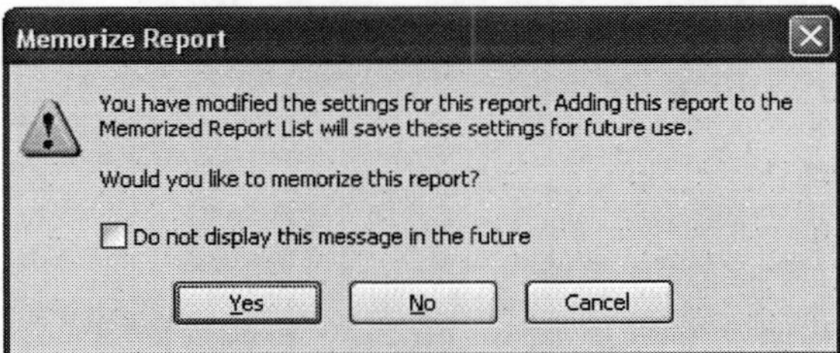

Figure 2-27 Memorized Reports window

> **Did You Know?**
> You can adjust the width of any column on the report by dragging the small diamond at the right of the column title to the left (narrowing the columns) or to the right (widening the columns).

Receiving Payments from Customers

Receiving Payments by Check

To record payments received from your customers and apply the payments to specific Invoices, follow these steps:

COMPUTER PRACTICE

Step 1. Click **Receive Payments** on the *Home* page. Alternatively, in the *Customer Center* select **Mason, Bob** from the *Customers & Jobs* list and select **Receive Payments** from the *New Transactions* drop-down list.

Step 2. Select **Mason, Bob** in the *Received From* field of the *Receive Payments* window (see Figure 2-28). Once a customer is selected, the *Customer Payment* window shows the open Invoices for that specific customer. This section shows the dates of the Invoices, along with the Invoice number, original amount, the last date for the prompt payment discount, and the amount due.

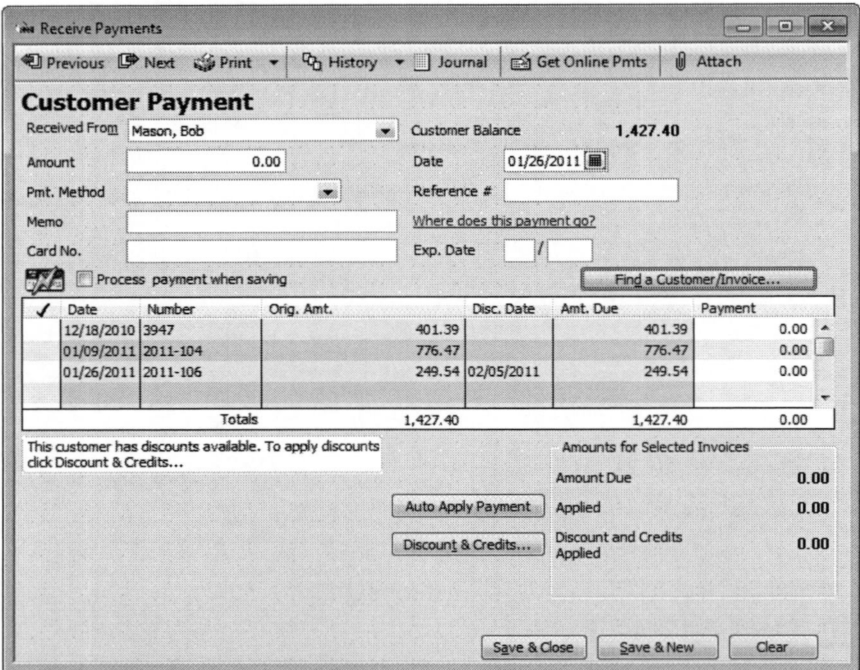

Figure 2-28 Receive Payments window

Step 3. Enter 401.39 in the *Amount* field and then press **Tab**.

Step 4. Enter ***1/27/2011*** in the *Date* field and then press **Tab** (see Figure 2-29).

Step 5. Select **Check** from the *Pmt. Method* drop-down list and then press **Tab**.

Step 6. Enter ***5256*** in the *Check No.* field and then press **Tab**.

Step 7. Enter ***Payment Received - Invoice #3947*** in the *Memo* field and then press **Tab**.

When entering a memo, type ***Payment Received*** followed by the Invoice number. Memos do not affect the application of payments to specific Invoices, but they are helpful in two very important ways. First, if you send your customers statements, only the information in the *Reference#, Date,* and *Memo* fields will show on statements, along with a three-letter code (PMT), representing the Payment transaction. Also, if you ever have to go back to the transaction and verify that you've applied the payment to the correct Invoice(s), you'll be able to look at the *Memo* field to see the Invoice(s) to which you *should* have applied the payments.

Step 8. Confirm that **Invoice #3947** is already checked.

> **Note:**
> **When One Payment Applies to More than One Invoice**
> You can apply one check from a customer to multiple Invoices. When you receive payments, you can override the amounts in the **Payment** column to apply the payment to Invoices in whatever combination is necessary.
>
> **When You Don't Want to Apply the Entire Amount of the Payment**
> If you don't want to apply the entire amount of the customer's check to the Invoice, reduce the amount in the **Payment** column. You can apply the remaining balance of the customer's check to additional Invoices. If you do not, QuickBooks will give you a choice to either hold the remaining balance as a credit for the customer or refund the amount to the customer.

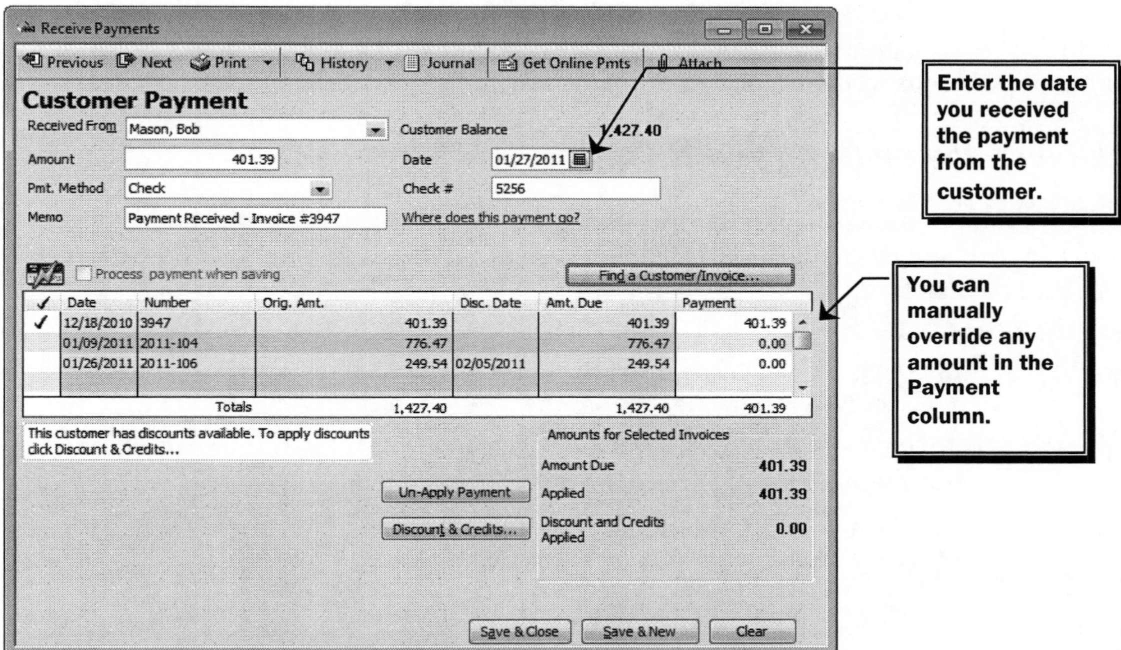

Figure 2-29 Completed Receive Payments window

Step 9. Verify that the **Amount Due** and **Payment** columns for the selected invoice both show ***$401.39***.

The checkmark to the left of the **Date** column indicates the Invoice to which QuickBooks will apply the payment. QuickBooks automatically selected this Invoice because the amount of the customer's check is the same as the unpaid amount of the Invoice. See *Preferences for Applying Payments* on page 69. You can deselect the Invoice by clicking on the checkmark. You can then select another Invoice from the list.

Step 10. Verify that your screen matches Figure 2-29. If you see errors, correct them.

Step 11. Click **Save & Close** to record the Payment transaction.

Handling Partial Payments

In the last example, Bob Mason paid Invoice #3947 in full.

However, if a customer pays only a portion of an Invoice, you should record the payment just as you did in the last example except that the amount would be less than the full amount due on any of the open invoices. Apply the payment to the appropriate Invoice. QuickBooks will give the option to either leave the invoice open or write off the unpaid amount. By clicking the *View Customer Contact Information* button, QuickBooks displays the *Edit Customer* window that allows you to see the customer's contact information. This is helpful if you need to contact the customer to ask a question about the partial payment (see Figure 2-30).

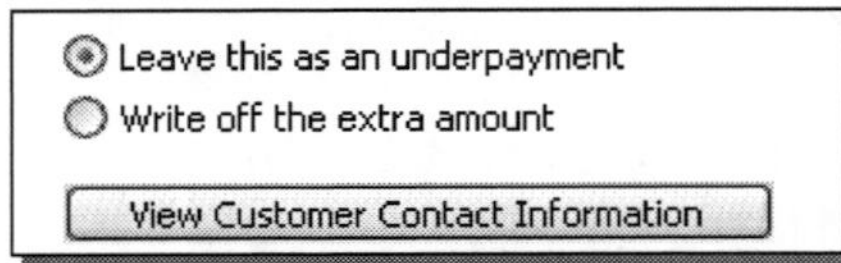

Figure 2-30 Partial Payment of Invoice

If you chose to leave the underpayment, the next time you use the **Receive Payments** function for that customer, the Invoice will show the remaining amount due. You can record additional payments to the Invoice in the same way as before.

Receiving Payments by Credit Card

The next example shows that Maria Cruz paid off the amount owing on the Branch Opening job. Maria Cruz used a credit card to pay her invoices, so this example shows how to receive credit card payments.

COMPUTER PRACTICE

Step 1. From the *Customer Center* select the **Branch Opening** job from the *Customers & Jobs* list. Select **Receive Payments** from the *New Transactions* drop-down list.

Step 2. Enter data into the *Received From, Amount,* and *Date* fields as shown in Figure 2-31.

Step 3. Enter ***American Express*** in the *Pmt. Method* field and then press **Tab**.

Step 4. Leave the *Reference#* field blank. Press **Tab**.

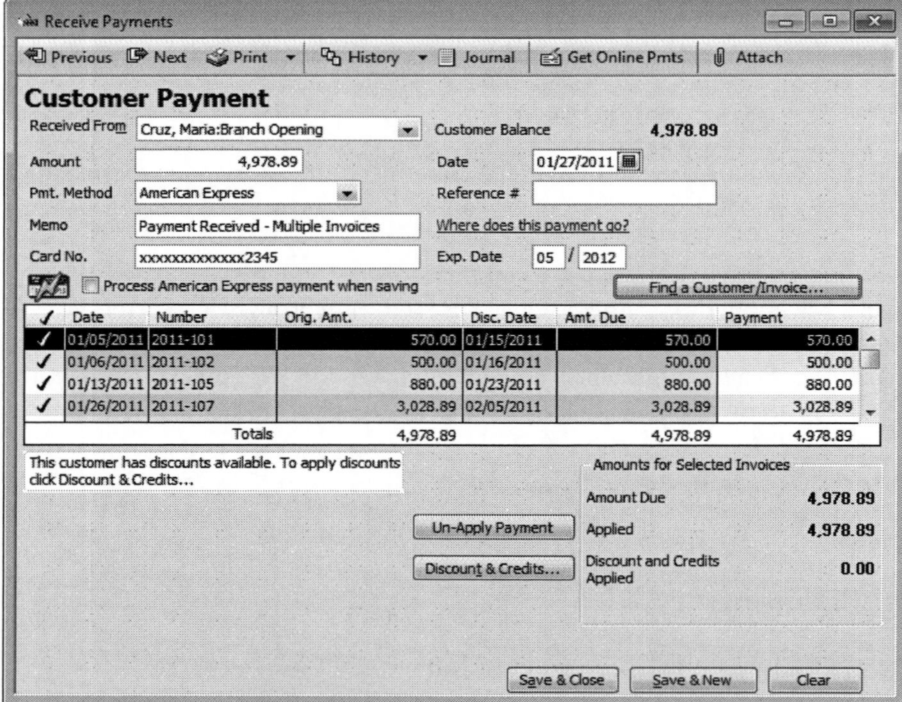

Figure 2-31 Customer Payment by Credit Card

Step 5. Enter ***Payment Received – multiple invoices*** in the *Memo* field. Press **Tab**.

Step 6. Enter ***1234-123456-12345*** in the *Card No.* field. Press **Tab**.

QuickBooks shows the credit card number with x's in the middle for security purposes.

Step 7. Enter ***05,*** then press **Tab** and enter ***2012*** in the *Exp. Date* fields.

Step 8. Verify that your screen matches Figure 2-31 and click **Save & Close**. If the Merchant Account Service Message appears, click the **Not Now** button.

> Note:
> If you want to keep a record of the customer's credit card information, including card number, expiration date, billing address and billing zip code, enter credit card information into the *Payment Info* tab of the Customer or Job record before you process the payment through the Receive Payments window. When you enter the customer or job name, QuickBooks will enter the credit card information automatically.

Where Do the Payments Go?

Recall the earlier discussion about **Undeposited Funds** beginning on page 57. Unless you turned off "Use **Undeposited Funds** as a default deposit to account" preference, QuickBooks does not increase your bank balance when you receive payments. Instead, when you record a payment transaction as shown above, QuickBooks reduces the balance in **Accounts Receivable** and increases the balance in **Undeposited Funds.** In order to have your payments show up in your bank account (and reduce **Undeposited Funds**), you must **Make Deposits.** See the section called *Making Bank Deposits* beginning on page 74.

> **The accounting behind the scenes:**
> Payments increase (debit) **Undeposited Funds** (or a bank/other current asset account) and decrease (credit) Accounts Receivable.

Preferences for Applying Payments

As soon as you enter the customer name at the top of the *Receive Payments* window and press **Tab**, QuickBooks displays all of the open Invoices for that customer in the lower section of the window. See Figure 2-32.

✓	Date	Number	Orig. Amt.	Disc. Date	Amt. Due	Payment
✓	01/05/2011	2011-101	570.00	01/15/2011	570.00	570.00
	01/06/2011	2011-102	500.00	01/16/2011	500.00	0.00
	01/13/2011	2011-105	880.00	01/23/2011	880.00	0.00
	01/26/2011	2011-107	3,028.89	02/05/2011	3,028.89	0.00
		Totals	4,978.89		4,978.89	570.00

Figure 2-32 Payment automatically applied to the oldest Invoice

Then, when you enter the payment amount, QuickBooks looks at all of the open Invoices for that customer. If it finds an amount due on an open Invoice that is the exact amount of the payment, it matches the payment with that Invoice. If there is no such match, it applies the payment to the *oldest* Invoice first and continues applying to the next oldest until the payment is completely applied. If this auto application of payments results in a partially paid

Invoice, QuickBooks holds the balance on that Invoice open for the unpaid amount. This is a feature called *Automatically Apply Payments.*

If you select an invoice in the Receive Payments form before entering an Amount Received, QuickBooks calculates the sum of the selected invoice(s) and enters that sum into the Amount Received field. This feature is called *Automatically Calculate Payments.*

COMPUTER PRACTICE

To modify the **Automatically Apply Payments** and **Automatically Calculate Payments** setting, change the **Company Preferences** for **Payments.**

Follow these steps:

Step 1. Select the *Edit* menu and then select **Preferences** (see Figure 2-33).

Step 2. Select the **Payments** icon from the preference category in the list on the left. Then click the **Company Preferences** tab.

Step 3. Check or uncheck the *Automatically apply payments* box to change it. For now, leave it checked.

With this feature disabled, you will have to click Auto Apply Payment in the Receive Payments window for each payment you process or you will have to manually apply payments to Invoices by clicking in the column to the left of the Invoice and modifying the amount in the Payment column as necessary.

Step 4. You can change the *Automatically calculate payments* box by checking or unchecking it. For now, leave it checked.

When this preference is on, QuickBooks will automatically calculate the payment received from the customer in the Amount field of the Receive Payments window as you select the invoices. When this preference is off, QuickBooks does not automatically calculate payments.

Step 5. Click OK.

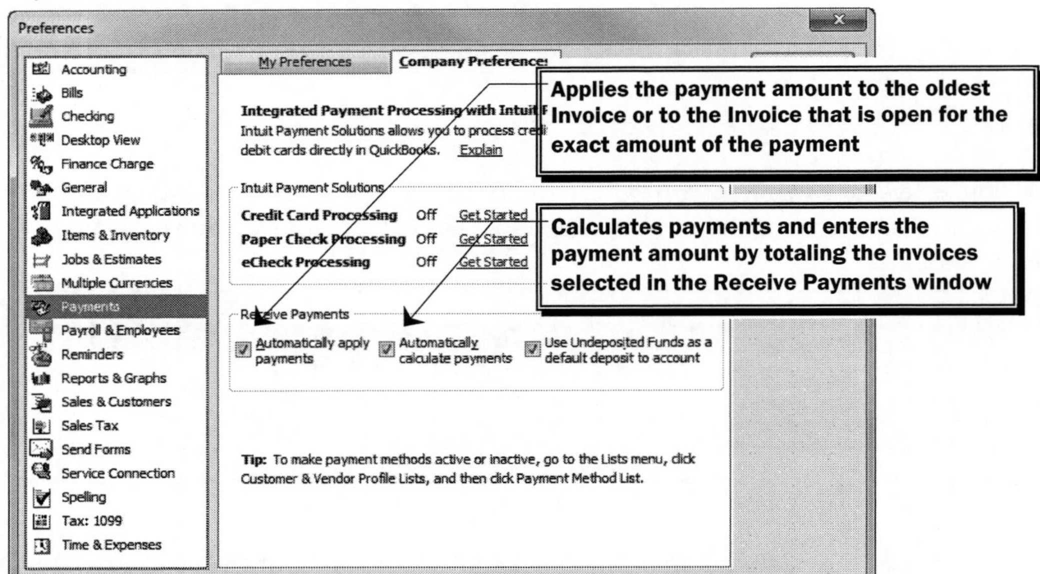

Figure 2-33 Preference for automatically applying payments

Recording Customer Discounts

What if your customer takes advantage of the discount you offer on your Invoice? In the next example, the payment you receive is less than the face amount of the Invoice because the customer took advantage of the 2% 10 Net 30 discount terms that Academy Photography offers.

COMPUTER PRACTICE

Follow these steps to record a payment on which the customer took a discount:

Step 1. From the *Customer Center* select **Mason, Bob** from the *Customers & Jobs* list. Then select **Receive Payments** from the *New Transactions* drop-down list.

Step 2. Enter all the customer payment information as shown in Figure 2-34. The customer is paying for Invoice #2011-106 after taking the discount allowed by the terms.

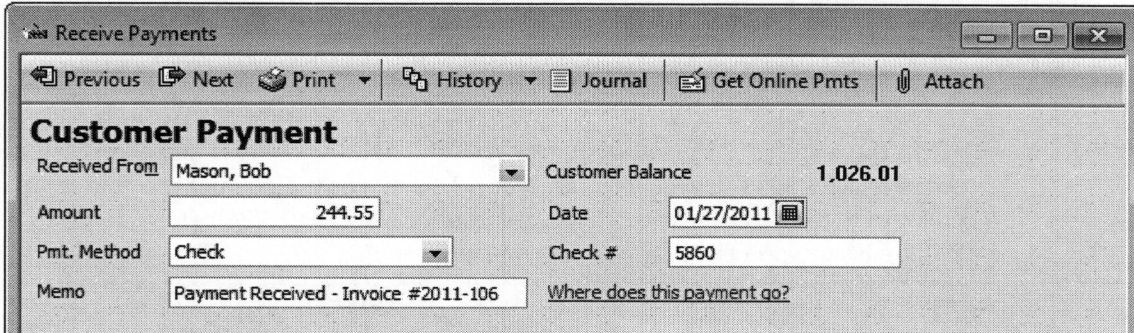

Figure 2-34 Top portion of the Receive Payments window

Step 3. The bottom portion of the *Receive Payments* window (see Figure 2-35) displays the open invoices for this customer. If the customer is eligible for discounts, a message will appear as shown just below the open invoices. The **Disc. Date** column shows the date through which the customer is eligible to take a discount.

If the amount paid is not an exact match with any Invoice balance, QuickBooks will automatically apply the payment to the oldest Invoices. Here, Invoice #2011-104 is automatically selected since the amount $244.55 does not match any open invoices. The underpayment is also displayed. We'll fix this in the next step.

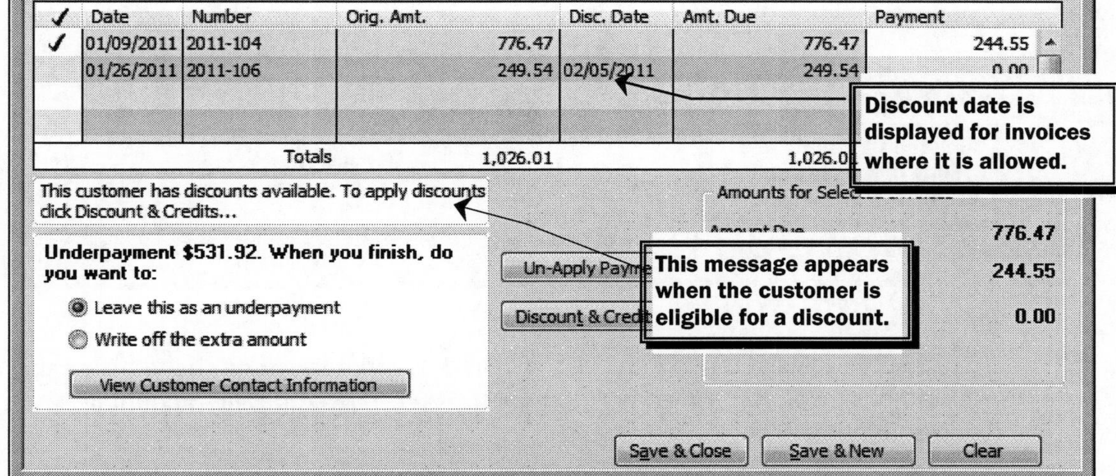

Figure 2-35 Show discount and credit information box, Invoice for payment and Underpayment

Note:
In the *Receive Payments* window the Underpayment amount is displayed with options to **Leave this as an underpayment** or **Write off the amount**. These options are displayed when the payment is less than the amount due on the selected Invoices. Similarly, Overpayment amounts are displayed with options to **Leave the credit to be used later** or **Refund the amount to customer** when the payment is more than the amount due on the selected Invoices.
Tip:
If the payment amount doesn't add up exactly to the discounted amount, you'll need to make a choice. If the payment is too high, you could reduce the amount of the discount by lowering the amount in the *Discounts and Credits* window. If the payment is too low, you could raise the amount in the *Discounts and Credits* window. If the payment amount is significantly different, you can apply the amount of the payment and then send a statement to the customer showing the balance due (if the payment is too low) or send a refund to the customer (if the payment is too high).

Step 4. Click in the column to the left of Invoice #**2011-104** to uncheck it and then click to check Invoice #**2011-106** (see Figure 2-36). This moves the payment so that it now applies to Invoice #2011-106. Make sure to uncheck #2011-104 before checking #2011-106, or you will see a Warning message.

✓	Date	Number	Orig. Amt.	Disc. Date	Amt. Due	Payment
	01/09/2011	2011-104	776.47		776.47	0.00
✓	01/26/2011	2011-106	249.54	02/05/2011	249.54	244.55
		Totals	1,026.01		1,026.01	244.55

Figure 2-36 Payment is now applied to the correct Invoice

Step 5. Since the customer took advantage of the 2% 10 Net 30 terms that Academy Photography offered him, you'll need to reduce the amount due by 2%. To apply the discount to this Invoice, click **Discount and Credits** on the bottom of the *Receive Payments* window (see Figure 2-37).

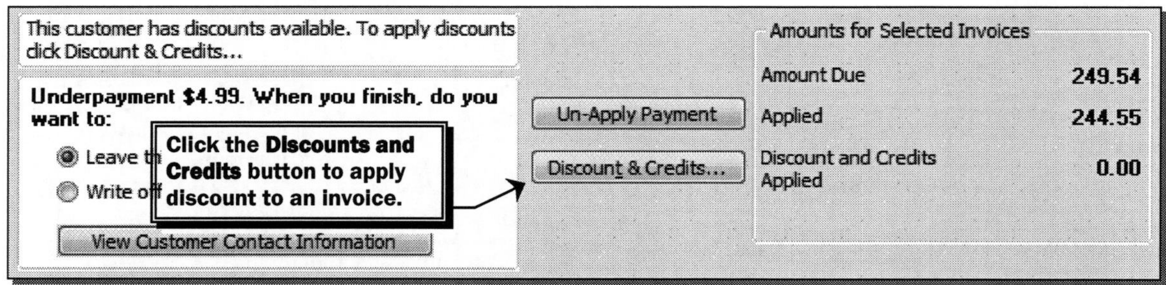

Figure 2-37 Discount and Credits Option

Step 6. QuickBooks calculates and enters a suggested discount based on the terms on the customer's Invoice as shown in Figure 2-38. You can override this amount if necessary. Press **Tab**.

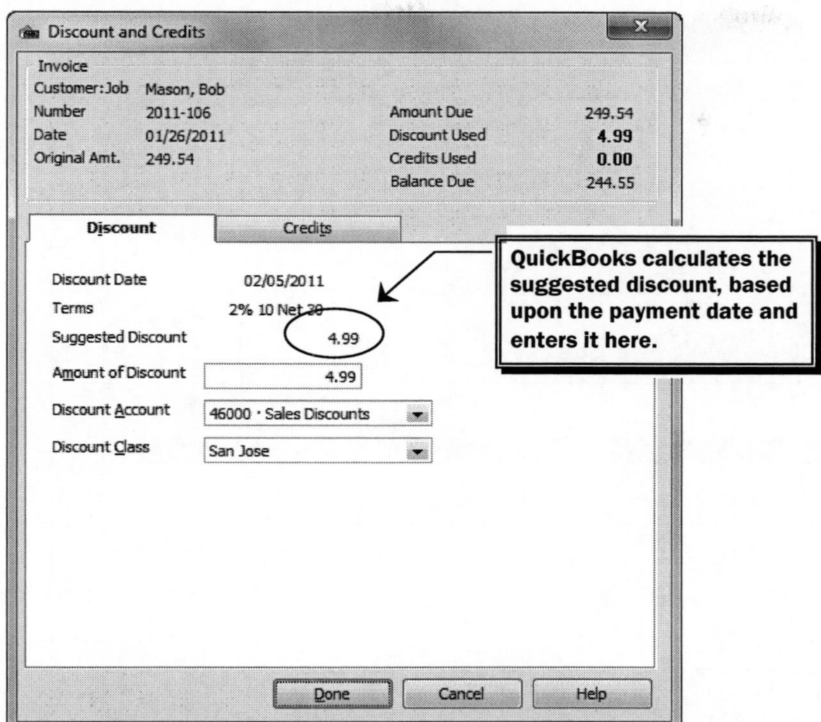

Figure 2-38 Discounts and Credits window

Step 7. Select **46000 Sales Discounts** in *the Discount Account* field. Press **Tab**.

The *Discount Account* field is where you assign an account that tracks the discounts you give to your customers.

Step 8. Enter ***San Jose*** in the *Class* field and then click **Done**.

Sales Discounts is a contra-income account. Since Academy Photography uses class tracking, you will need to enter the appropriate class in this field. If you do not classify this transaction, QuickBooks will display the amount in an *Unclassified* column on the **Profit & Loss by Class** report. Refer to the Invoice you are discounting to determine the class. Academy Photography uses the ***San Jose*** class when recording Invoice 2011-106.

After recording the discount, the *Receive Payments* window reflects Total Discount and Credits Applied at the bottom of the Receive Payments window.

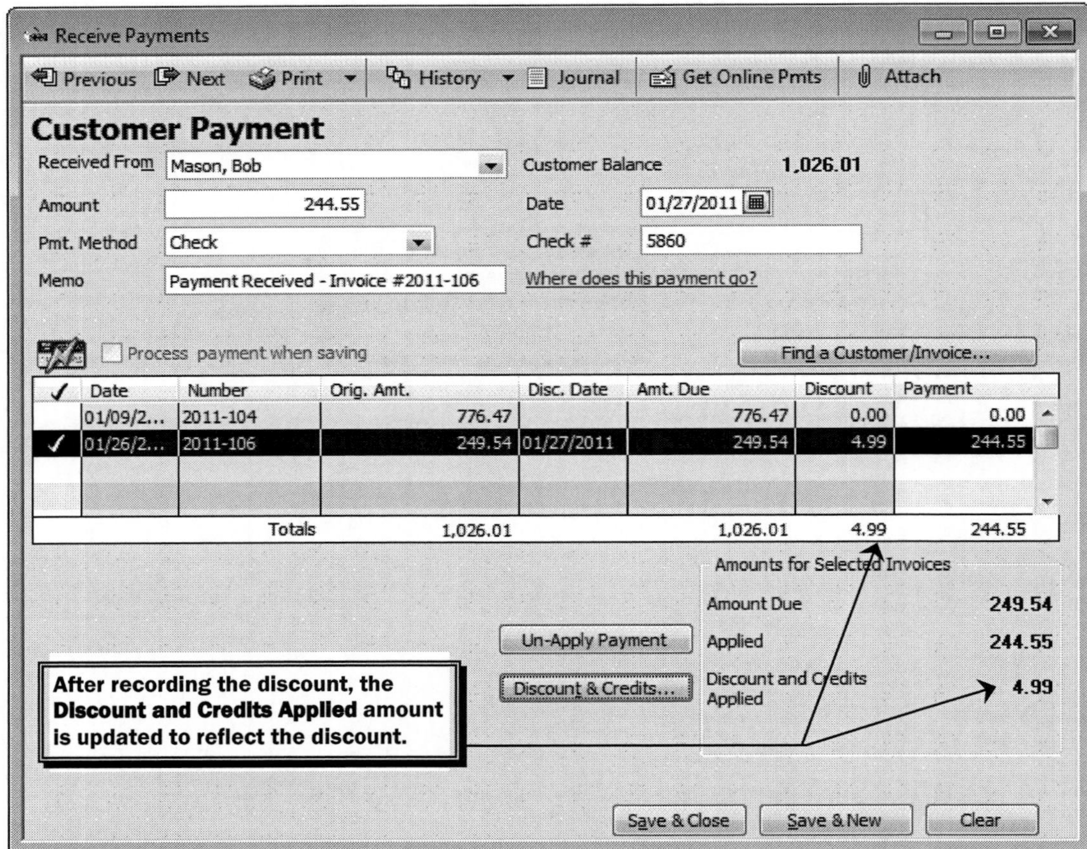

Figure 2-39 Receive Payments window after (recording the discount)

Step 9. Verify that your screen matches Figure 2-39.

Step 10. Click **Save & Close** to record the transaction.

Step 11. Close the Customer Center.

Making Bank Deposits

As you record payments from customers using the ***Enter Sales Receipts*** and ***Receive Payments*** windows, by default these payments are posted to a special QuickBooks account called **Undeposited Funds.** When you deposit these payments into your bank account, you will record a *Deposit* transaction. Deposit transactions move money from the **Undeposited Funds** account to the appropriate bank account. As you will see in this section, QuickBooks provides a special window (the *Payments to Deposit* window) to help you identify which payments are included on each deposit.

Since you will probably receive payments from your customers in several different ways (checks, cash, and credit cards), you'll want to record deposits of each payment type separately. This way, your deposits in QuickBooks will match what actually takes place at your bank, and your bank reconciliations will be much easier.

Therefore, when you make deposits, you'll deposit groups of each payment type together into deposits. Start with the checks and cash, followed by the MasterCard and VISA receipts, then the American Express receipts, and then the Discover receipts.

Depositing Checks and Cash

COMPUTER PRACTICE

To enter a deposit, follow these steps:

Step 1. From the *Home* page select **Record Deposits.**

Since you have payments stored in the **Undeposited Funds** account, QuickBooks displays the *Payments to Deposit* window (see Figure 2-40).

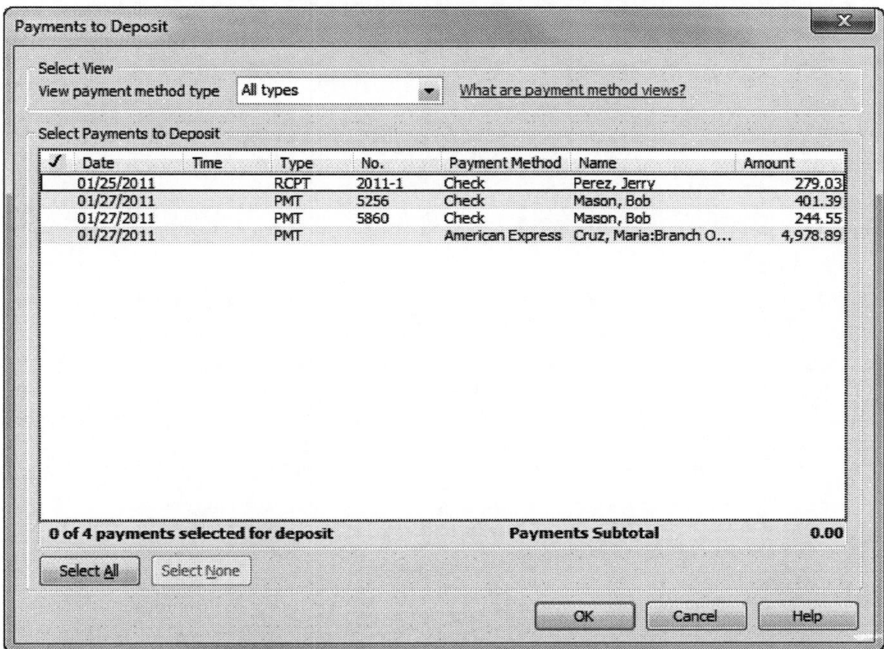

Figure 2-40 Select the payments to deposit

Step 2. Select **Cash and Check** from the *View Payment Method Type* drop-down list (see Figure 2-41).

Since the checks and cash you deposit in your bank account will post to your account separately from credit card receipts, it is best to filter the report by payment type and then create a separate deposit for each payment type. Depending on your merchant service, you will probably need to create a single deposit for your MasterCard and VISA receipts. Most merchant services combine MasterCard and VISA receipts when they credit your bank account.

Tip:
Since you can filter the *Payments to Deposit* window by only one payment method at a time, using a single **Payment Method** for *Checks* and *Cash* will allow you to filter for both payment methods on this window. Depending on your merchant service, you may want to create a single **Payment Method** for *MasterCard* and *VISA* as well. To edit **Payment Methods** select the *Lists* menu, then select **Customer & Vendor Profile Lists**, and then select **Payment Methods List**. Once the *Payment Method List* window opens, select the Payment Method and select **Edit Payment Method** from the *Payment Method* menu.

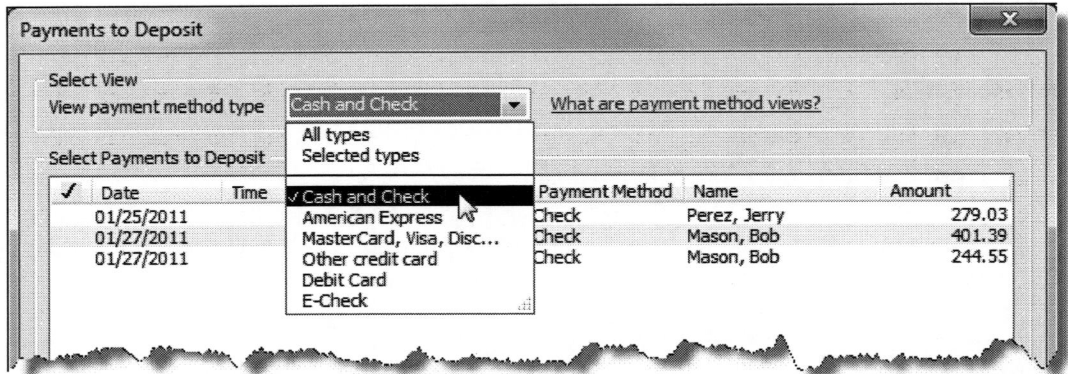

Figure 2-41 Cash and Check payments

Step 3. Click **Select All** to select all of the cash and check deposits. See Figure 2-42. Click **OK**.

A checkmark in the column on the left indicates that QuickBooks will include the payment on the deposit.

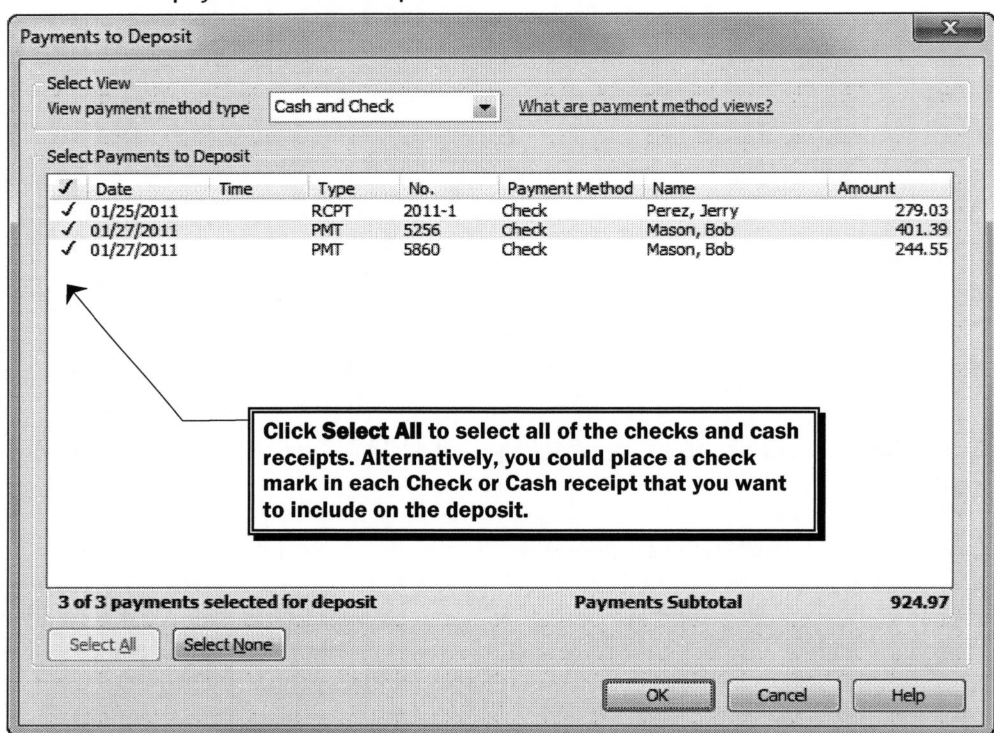

Figure 2-42 Select the payments to deposit

Step 4. In the *Make Deposits* window, the **Checking** account is already selected in the *Deposit To* field (see Figure 2-43). The payments will be deposited to this bank account. Press **Tab**.

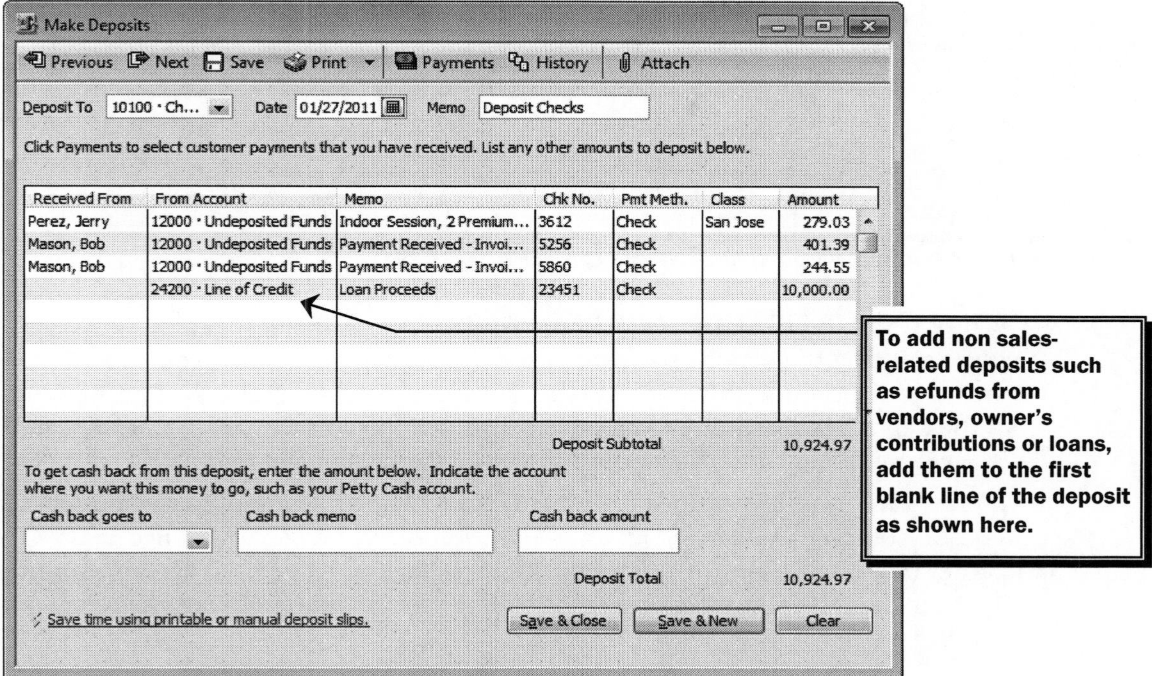

Figure 2-43 Make Deposits window

Step 5. Enter ***01/27/2011*** if it does not already display in the *Date* field and press **Tab**.

Step 6. Enter ***Deposit Checks*** in the *Memo* field and press **Tab**.

Step 7. On this deposit, we will add a non sales-related item, as follows:

a) On the first blank line, enter ***Line of Credit*** in the *From Account* column and press **Tab**.
The *From Account* column on the Make Deposits window shows the account that the deposit is coming "from."

b) Enter ***Loan Proceeds*** in the *Memo* column and press **Tab**.

c) Enter ***23451*** in the *Chk No.* column and press **Tab**.

d) Enter ***Check*** in the *Pmt Meth.* column and press **Tab**.

e) Press **Tab** to skip the *Class* column.

f) Enter ***10,000.00*** in the *Amount* column.

Step 8. Click **Save & Close** to record the deposit.

> **The accounting behind the scenes:**
> In the deposit transaction (Figure 2-43) the checking account will increase (with a debit) by the total deposit ($10,924.97). All of the customer checks are coming from the **Undeposited Funds** account, and the loan proceeds are coming from the Line of Credit account. The customer checks will decrease (credit) the balance in **Undeposited Funds** and the loan from the owner will increase (credit) the balance in the Line of Credit account.

Holding Cash Back from Deposits

If you hold cash back when you make your deposits to the bank, fill in the bottom part of the deposit slip indicating the account to which you want to post the cash (see Figure 2-44).

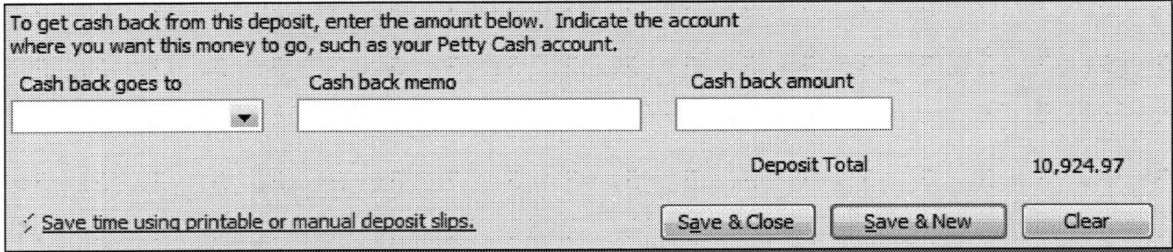

Figure 2-44 The bottom of the deposit slip deals with cash back

There are two ways you might use the cash back section of the deposit:

1. If you're splitting the deposit between two different bank accounts, you could enter the other bank account and amount here. For example, if you send part of the funds from the deposit to the Money Market account, you could enter ***Money Market*** in the *Cash back goes to* field and the amount in the *Cash back amount* field.
2. If you routinely hold back funds from your deposits and use them for several different purchases, you may want to set up a new QuickBooks bank account called **Petty Cash** and enter that account in the *Cash back goes to* field. The Petty Cash account is not really a bank account, but it's an account where you can track all your cash expenditures.

> Tip:
> It's not a good idea to hold cash back from deposits as "pocket money." If your business is a Sole Proprietorship, it's better to write a separate check (or ATM withdrawal) and then code it to **Owner's Draw**. This is a much cleaner way to track the money you take out for personal use. Discuss this with your QuickBooks ProAdvisor, or with your accountant.

Printing Deposit Slips

QuickBooks can print deposit slips on preprinted deposit slips.

To make this feature work for you, you'll need to order preprinted deposit slips that match the QuickBooks format.

COMPUTER PRACTICE

To print on preprinted deposit slips, follow these steps:

Step 1. Display the most recent deposit transaction by selecting the *Banking* menu and then selecting **Make Deposits.**

Click **Cancel** when you see the *Payments to Deposit* window. Then click the **Previous** button on the *Make Deposits* window. Alternatively, you could double-click the deposit transaction from the checking account register window.

Step 2. Click **Print** on the *Make Deposits* window (see Figure 2-45).

Step 3. Select **Deposit slip and deposit summary** on the window shown in Figure 2-46 and click **OK.**

Normally, you would load the preprinted deposit slips into the printer before printing. However, if you do not have a deposit slip print the deposit on blank paper.

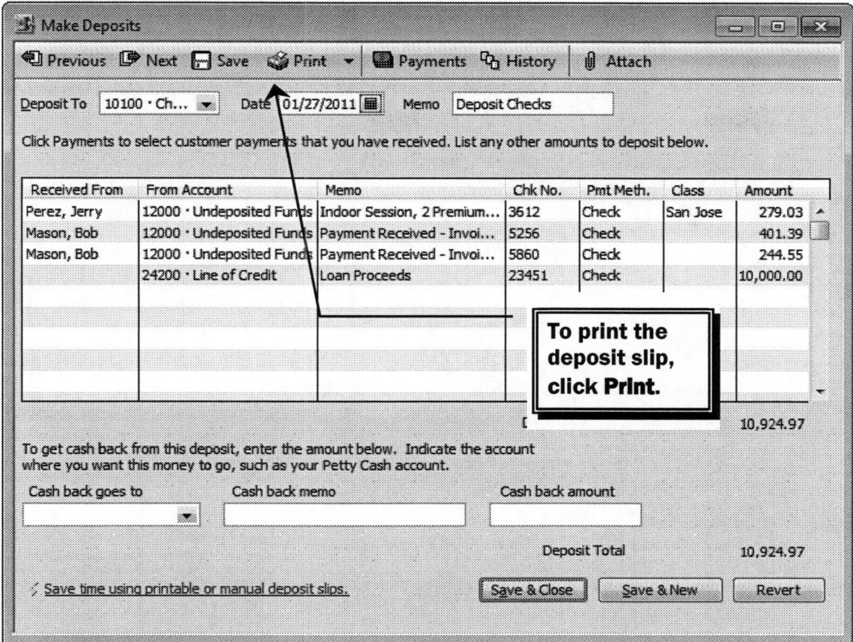

Figure 2-45 Printing a deposit

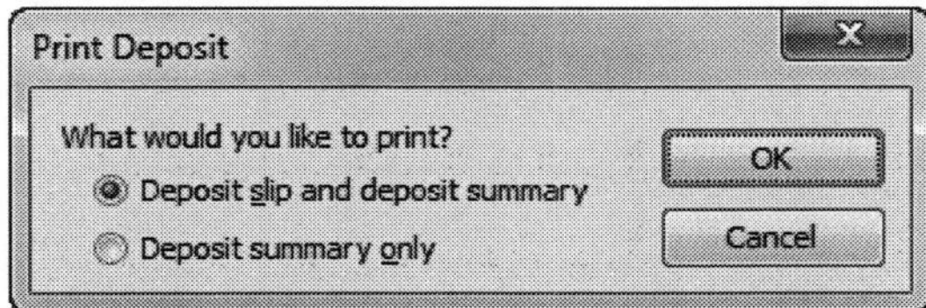

Figure 2-46 Print Deposit window for deposit slips

> **Tip:**
> Even if you don't have any preprinted deposit slips, it's still a good idea to keep a printed record of your deposits. To print a deposit record when you do not use preprinted deposit slips, select **Deposit summary only** on the *Print Deposit* window shown in Figure 2-46.

Step 4. Check the settings on the *Print Deposits Slips* window shown in Figure 2-47. Your *Printer name* will not be the same as the one shown here.

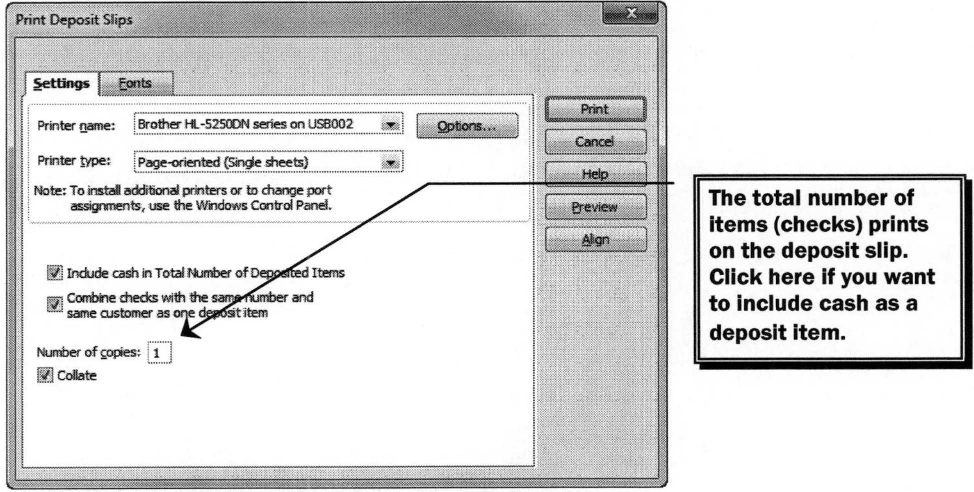

Figure 2-47 Settings on the Print Deposit Slips window

Step 5. Select your printer in the *Printer name* field. There is no need to change the *Printer type* field. The *Include cash in Total Number of Deposited Items* checkbox causes QuickBooks to include the cash you deposit (if any) as a separate Item on the deposit slip.

Step 6. Click **Print** to print the deposit slip (see Figure 2-48).

Step 7. Click **Save & Close** to save the Deposit.

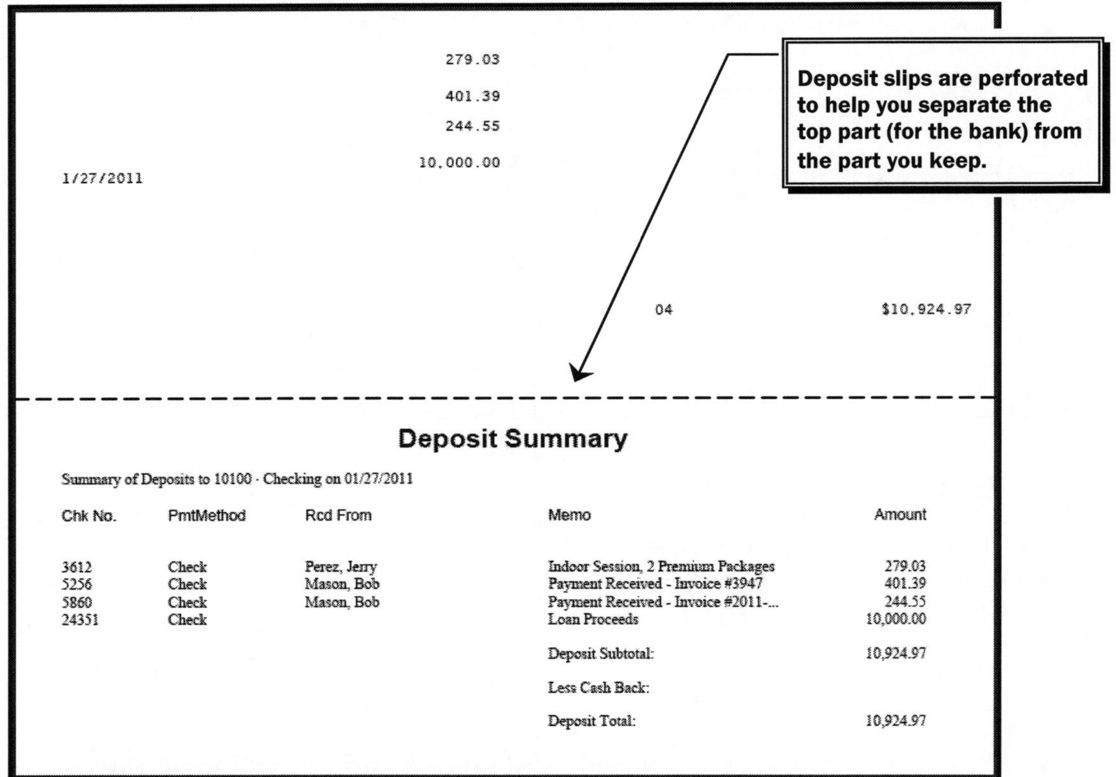

Deposit Summary

Summary of Deposits to 10100 · Checking on 01/27/2011

Chk No.	PmtMethod	Rcd From	Memo	Amount
3612	Check	Perez, Jerry	Indoor Session, 2 Premium Packages	279.03
5256	Check	Mason, Bob	Payment Received - Invoice #3947	401.39
5860	Check	Mason, Bob	Payment Received - Invoice #2011-...	244.55
24351	Check		Loan Proceeds	10,000.00
			Deposit Subtotal:	10,924.97
			Less Cash Back:	
			Deposit Total:	10,924.97

Figure 2-48 Deposit slip and deposit summary

Depositing Credit Card Payments

As mentioned previously, to ensure that your bank reconciliations go smoothly, you should always deposit your checks and cash separately from your credit card payments.

COMPUTER PRACTICE

Step 1. Select the **Banking** menu, and then select **Make Deposits**. The *Payments to Deposit* window opens.

Step 2. Click in the left column on the line to select the American Express receipt (see Figure 2-49). Then click **OK**. The *Make Deposits* window opens.

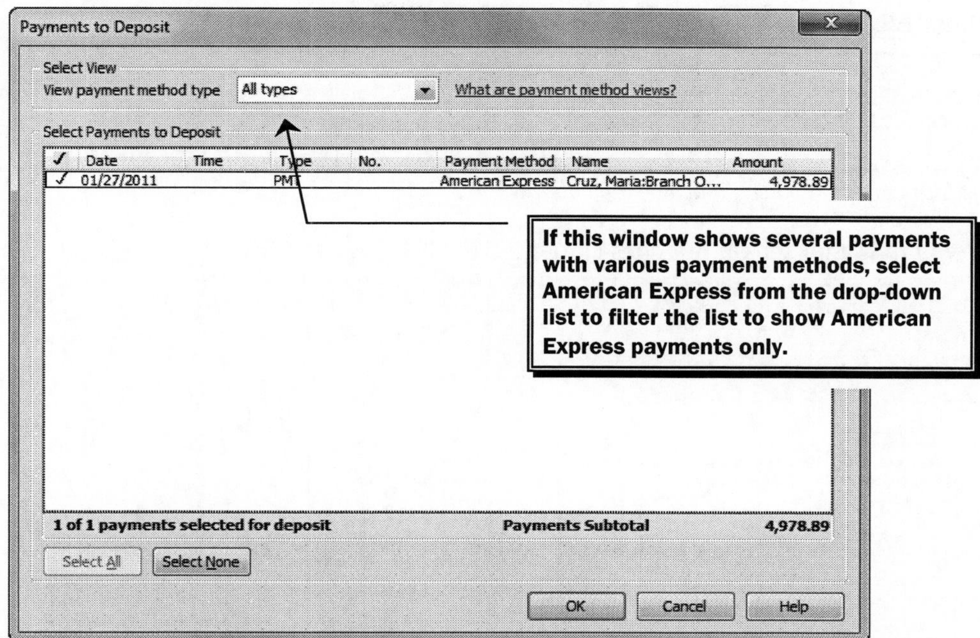

Figure 2-49 Payments to Deposit window

Step 3. The **Checking** account is already selected in the *Deposit to* field. Press **Tab**.

Step 4. Enter ***01/27/2011*** if it is not already entered in the *Date* field. Press **Tab**.

Step 5. Enter ***Deposit American Exp*** in the *Memo* field.

As stated earlier, make sure you group together receipts in a way that agrees with the actual deposits made to your bank. This is a critical step in making your bank reconciliation process go smoothly.

Step 6. On the first blank line of the deposit slip, enter ***Bankcard Fees*** in the **From Account** column and then press **Tab**.

You only need to create this line if your credit card processing company (or your bank) charges a discount fee on each credit card deposit rather than monthly.

Step 7. Enter ***Discount Fee*** in the **Memo** column and then press **Tab**.

Step 8. Press **Tab** to skip the **Chk No.** column.

Step 9. Enter ***American Express*** in the **Pmt Method** column and then press **Tab**.

Step 10. Enter ***Walnut Creek*** in the *Class* column and then press **Tab**.

Step 11. Enter ***4978.89 * -.02*** in the *Amount* column and press **ENTER.** You can use the QuickMath feature to enter the discount fee directly on the **Make Deposit** window.

QuickMath is a feature that helps you add, subtract, multiply, or divide in any QuickBooks Amount field. When you enter the first number (4978.89), it shows normally in the *Amount* column. Then when you enter the * (asterisk key or SHIFT+8), QuickMath shows a small adding machine tape on your screen (see Figure 2-50). Continue typing your formula for recording the discount fee. If the discount is 2%, enter ***-.02*** (minus point zero two) and press **ENTER**. The result of the calculation shows in the *Amount* column (-99.58). **The minus sign makes the result a negative number and reduces the amount of your deposit.** This also increases (debits) your **Bankcard Fees** expense account.

Step 12. Press **Tab** to have the total of the deposit updated automatically.

Received From	From Account	Memo	Chk No.	Pmt Meth.	Class	Amount
Cruz, Maria:Branch Opening	12000 · Undeposited Funds	Payment Received - Multiple Invoices		American Express		4,978.89
	60500 · Bankcard Fees	Discount Fee		American Ex...	Walnut..	* -.02

Figure 2-50 QuickMath makes an adding machine tape appear

Step 13. Verify that your screen matches Figure 2-51. Click **Save & Close**.

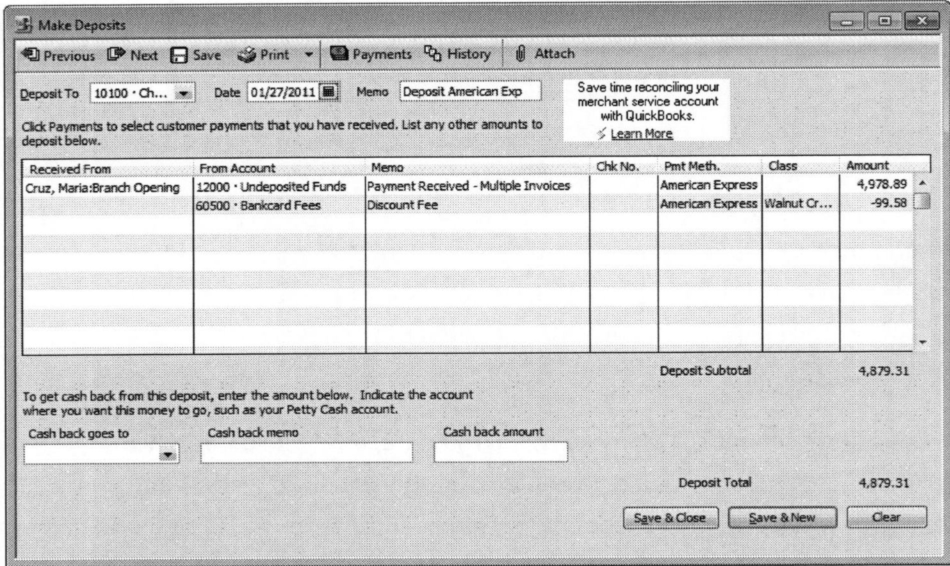

Figure 2-51 Make Deposits window after a credit card deposit

Now that you have entered your deposits, the checking account register shows each deposit and the updated balance in the account.

COMPUTER PRACTICE

To see the detail of a deposit, follow these steps:

Step 1. Click the **Chart of Accounts** Icon in the *Home* page.

Step 2. Double-click on the **Checking** account in the *Chart of Accounts* window.

Step 3. Scroll up until you see the two deposit transactions shown in Figure 2-52.

Step 4. Close the *Checking* register and Chart of Accounts.

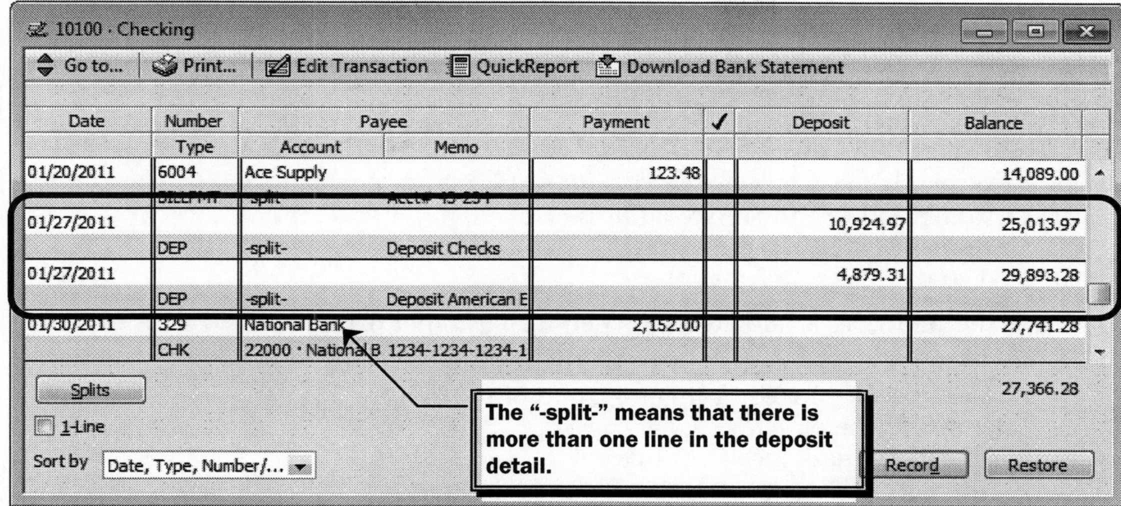

Figure 2-52 Checking register after entering deposits

Chapter Summary and Review

Summary of Key Points

In this chapter, you learned how to track sales in your company. You should now be familiar with how to use QuickBooks to do all of the following:

- Set up customer records in the Customer: Job list (page 43).
- Record Sales Receipts (page 52).
- Use the Undeposited Funds account as a default account to track your cash receipts (page 57).
- Record Invoices and Payments from customers (page 59).
- Record bank deposits of cash, check, and credit card receipts (page 74).

Comprehension Questions

> Answers to these review questions are available with the supplemental material. See page xiii for details.

1. When you make a sale to a customer who pays at the time of the sale, either by check or by credit card, which type of form should you use in QuickBooks to record the transaction?
2. Explain how the **Undeposited Funds** account works and why it is best to use the option, **Use Undeposited Funds as a default deposit to account**, as a *Payments* preference.
3. Why is it so important to use the memo field on transactions?
4. How does the *Automatically Apply Payments* feature work?
5. How does the *Automatically Calculate Payments* feature work?

Multiple Choice

Select the best answer(s) for each of the following:

1. In the *New Customer* window, you find everything except:
   a) Customer name.
   b) Customer Bill to and Ship to address.
   c) Customer active/inactive status.
   d) Year-to-date sales information.

2. You should record a Sales Receipt when the customer pays:
   a) By cash, check, or credit card at the time of sale.
   b) By cash, check, or credit card at the end of the month.
   c) Sales tax on the purchase.
   d) For the order upon receipt of Invoice.

3. Which statement is false?
   a) Invoices are very similar to the Sales Receipt form.
   b) Invoices decrease Accounts Receivable.
   c) Sales Receipts have no effect on Accounts Receivables.
   d) Invoices should be created when customers pay after the date of the initial sale.

4. You may specify payment terms on the *New Customer* window, however
   a) The payment terms will only show on Sales Receipt transactions.
   b) The terms can only be changed once a year.
   c) The sales representative must be informed.
   d) You are also permitted to override the terms on each sale.

5. Your company has just accepted a payment for an invoice. What should you do in QuickBooks to record this payment?
   a) Open the invoice by clicking the *Invoices* button on the *Home* page.
   b) Create a sales receipt by clicking the *Sales Receipt* button on the *Home* page.
   c) Make a deposit by clicking the *Record Deposits* button on the *Home* page.
   d) Receive the payment by clicking the *Receive Payment* button on the *Home* page.

6. Which statement is false?
   a) Many customers reject Invoices that do not reference a P.O. (purchase order) number.
   b) The P.O. number helps the customer identify your Invoice.
   c) The P.O. number is required on all Invoices.
   d) The P.O. number is generated by the customer's accounting system.

7. To record a deposit in QuickBooks:
   a) Make a separate deposit that includes both Checks and Cash receipts.
   b) Make a separate deposit that includes both VISA and MasterCard receipts.
   c) Make a separate deposit that includes American Express receipts.
   d) All of the above.

8. Your company has just received an order from a customer who will pay within 30 days. How should you record this transaction in QuickBooks?
   a) Open the invoice by clicking the *Invoices* button on the *Home* page.
   b) Create a sales receipt by clicking the *Sales Receipt* button on the *Home* page.
   c) Make a deposit by clicking the *Record Deposits* button on the *Home* page.
   d) Receive the payment by clicking the *Receive Payment* button on the *Home* page.

9. When you make a deposit, all of the following are true except:
   a) You must print a deposit slip in order to process a deposit.
   b) A "Make Deposit" transaction typically transfers money from **Undeposited Funds** into your bank account.
   c) You should separate your deposits by payment type.
   d) You should create deposits so that they match exactly with the deposits on your bank statement.

10. Which item is false regarding calculating items?
   a) Calculating items can be used on invoices, sales receipts, and credit memos.
   b) A calculating item calculates based upon the amount of the line directly above it.
   c) A discount item is a calculating item.
   d) An item of type *service charge* is a calculating item.

11. When creating a customer record, which statement is false:
   a) After you enter a name in the *Customer Name* field of the *New Customer* window, you cannot use that name in any of the other name lists in QuickBooks.
   b) The credit limit can be added in the new customer window.
   c) A sales rep must be selected when creating a new customer.
   d) When you sell to and purchase from the same company, you should create two records, one in the Vendor List, and one in the Customer: Job List.

12. When receiving payments from customers to whom you have sent invoices, you must:
   a) Receive the payment in full. Partial payments cannot be accepted in QuickBooks.
   b) Enter them directly into the checking account register.
   c) Enter the payment into the receive payments window and check off the appropriate invoice(s) to which the payment applies.
   d) Delete the invoice so it does not show on the customer's open records.

13. You need to calculate the amount of a bankcard fee by multiplying the amount of the received payments by -1%. What useful QuickBooks feature could you use?
   a) Calculating Items
   b) QuickMath
   c) QuickAdd
   d) The *Fees* button on the bottom of the *Make Deposit* window

14. The Undeposited Funds account tracks
   a) Bad debts.
   b) Funds that have been received but not deposited.
   c) Funds that have not been received or deposited.
   d) All company sales from the point an invoice is created until it is deposited in the bank.

15. After entering an existing customer in the *Customer:Job* field of an invoice, a *Customer:Job Not Found* dialog box opens to say the customer is not on the *Customer List*. What should you do?
   a) Click the *Quick Add* button to add the customer to the *Customer List*.
   b) Click the *Set Up* button to enter the customer's information in a *New Customer* window.
   c) Click *Cancel* to check the name you entered in the *Customer:Job* field for typos or other errors.
   d) None of the above.

Completion Statements

1. A new customer can be added to the customer list "on the fly" by clicking _____ ______ after entering a new customer name on a sales form.
2. When you create a Sales Receipt, QuickBooks increases (with a debit) a ________ account or the _________ _________ account.
3. Discounts and subtotals are called ________ Items.
4. Receiving payments reduces the balance in ________ __________ and increases the balance in the **Undeposited Funds** or a bank account.
5. ________ __________helps you add, subtract, multiply or divide numbers in an *Amount* field.

Sales-Problem 1

APPLYING YOUR KNOWLEDGE

Restore the Sales-10Problem1.QBM file and store it on your hard disk according to your instructor's directions.

1. Enter your own name and address information into the Customer Center List. Then print the Customer List by selecting the *Reports* menu, **List**, and then **Customer Contact List.**
2. Enter a Sales Receipt using the data in Table 2-4. The payment will be automatically grouped with other payments in **Undeposited Funds** account. You'll need to create the customer record using Quick Add, or by setting it up in the list before adding the sale. Print the sale on blank paper.

Field	Data
Customer Name	*Franklin, Steven*
Class	*Walnut Creek*
Date	*01/29/2011*
Sale #	*2011-1*
Sold To	*Steven Franklin* *1695 Blue Sky Pkwy* *Walnut Creek, CA 94599*
Check No	*477*
Payment Method	*Check*
Item	*Camera SR32, Qty 2, $695.99*
Item	*Case, Qty 2, $79.99*
Sales Tax	*Contra Costa (8.25%) – Auto Calculates*
Total Sale	*$1,680.00*
Customer Tax Code	*Tax*
Memo	*2 Cameras, 2 Cases*

Table 2-4 Use this data for a Sales Receipt in Step 2

3. Enter an Invoice using the data in the table below. Print the Invoice on blank paper.

Field	Data
Customer Name	*Pelligrini, George: 4266 Lake Drive*
Class	*San Jose*
Custom Template	*Academy Photo Service Invoice*
Date	*01/31/2011*
Invoice #	*2011-106*
Sold To	*Pelligrini Builders* *222 Santana Ave.* *Los Gatos, CA 94482*
PO Number	*8324*
Terms	*Net 30*
Item	*Indoor Photo Session, Qty 3, $95/hour*
Item	*Retouching, Qty 2 (hrs), $95/hour*
Sales Tax	*Santa Clara (8.25%) – Auto Calculates*
Total Sale	*$475*
Memo	*3 Hour Session, 2 Hours Retouching*

Table 2-5 Use this data for an Invoice in Step 3

4. Enter a second Invoice using the data in the table below. Print the Invoice on blank paper. You will need to add this customer either through *QuickAdd* or entering the customer information in the *Customer Center.*

Field	Data
Customer Name	*Feller, Nathan*
Class	*San Jose*
Custom Template	*Academy Photo Service Invoice*
Date	*01/31/2011*
Invoice #	*2011-107*
Sold To	*Nathan Feller* *99050 Market St.* *Santa Clara, CA 95111*
PO Number	*736555*
Terms	*2% 10 Net 30*
Item	*Indoor Photo Session, Qty 9, $95/hour*
Sales Tax	*Santa Clara (8.25%) – Auto Calculates*
Total Sale	*$855*
Memo	*9 Hour Session*

Table 2-6 Use this data for an Invoice in Step 4.

5. Record a payment dated ***2/15/2011*** for ***$855.00*** from Nathan Feller (check #5342) and apply it to Invoice **2011-107**.

6. On ***2/15/2011***, you received a partial payment from George Pelligrini for the 4266 Lake Drive Job for $300. American Express payment, card #4321-654321-54321, expires in 5/2014.

7. On ***2/15/2011***, deposit everything from the **Undeposited Funds** account using the following:

a) Deposit Cash and Check payments separately (Memo: Deposit Cash and Checks). Print **Deposit Slip and Deposit Summary** onto blank paper.

b) Deposit American Express payments separately (Memo- Deposit American Express). Record a 2% bankcard discount fee (use QuickMath to calculate) on the credit card deposit number (Account- Bankcard Fee, Payment Method - American Express, Memo-2% Discount Fee). This amount should be a negative number. Print **Deposit Summary Only** onto blank paper.

Workplace Applications

Discussion Questions

These questions are designed to stimulate discussion about how you can apply QuickBooks to your own organization. They may help you think through some of the issues you'll encounter when using QuickBooks in your company.

1. What products or services does your organization provide? Are sales of these services or products taxable?
2. How do customers in your organization pay for products and services? Do they pay at the time of the service or do you send Invoices later? What is the credit limit offered to each of your customers, if applicable?
3. Do any of your customers pay for more than one invoice at a time? What is your organization's policy regarding how to apply payments to open invoices? Oldest first? Specific matching? What is the policy regarding overpayments and underpayments? Are overpayments refunded?

Chapter 3 Tracking Revenue

Objectives

After completing this chapter, you should be able to:

- Process customer returns and credits (page 89).
- Write off customer invoices (record bad debts) (page 106).
- Create and print customer statements (page 109).
- Assess finance charges (page 111).
- Create Sales Reports (page 113).

Restore this File

This chapter uses Revenue-10.QBW. To open this file, restore the Revenue-10.QBM file to your hard disk. See page 10 for instructions on restoring files.

Note: When you restore a data file, depending on today's date, you may see one or more "Alerts" for learning to process credit cards, pay taxes, or similar activities. Click Mark as Done when you see these alerts.

In the last chapter, you learned about sales forms and the Accounts Receivable process. In this chapter, you will learn how QuickBooks can help you record customer returns and refunds, create customer statements and process sales reports. The sales reports show details of each sale, or you can see summaries of sales by customer, job, sales rep, class, or item.

Recording Customer Returns and Credits

To record customer returns or credits, use QuickBooks Credit Memos. Credit Memos can be used in the following situations:

- To record the cancellation of an order that has already been invoiced.
- To record a return of merchandise from a customer.
- To record a credit-on-account for a customer.
- To record the first step of making a refund to a customer.

Key Term:
Credit Memos are sales forms that reduce the amount owed to your company by a customer.

The accounting behind the scenes:
Credit Memos reduce (credit) Accounts Receivable and reduce (debit) income and, in some cases, Sales Tax Payable.

When you create a credit memo in QuickBooks, you must apply the credit to one or more invoices, or use it to give a refund to the Customer. Although this section will show several different methods of applying credits, it is usually best to apply credit memos at the time you create them.

In our first example, Maria Cruz canceled an order that Academy Photography recorded on Invoice 2011-107. Since this Invoice is unpaid, you *could* void or delete it, but accounting conventions dictate that instead of deleting the Invoice, you *should* add a new transaction (a Credit Memo) to your books to record the cancellation. Then you will need to apply the credit to the open Invoice.

COMPUTER PRACTICE

Step 1. From the *Home* page select **Refunds & Credits**. Alternatively, select **Create Credit Memos/Refunds** from the **Customer Menu**.

Credit Memos look similar to Invoices, but they perform the opposite function. That is, a Credit Memo reduces (debits) Sales, reduces (credits) Accounts Receivable, and in some cases reduces Sales Tax Payable. If Inventory is involved, a Credit Memos increases (debits) the Inventory asset and reduces (credits) the Cost of Goods Sold account.

Step 2. Select **Cruz, Maria: Branch Opening** from the *Customer: Job* drop-down list and then press **Tab** (see Figure 3-1).

Step 3. Enter ***Walnut Creek*** in the *Class* field and then press **Tab** twice.

Step 4. **Custom Credit Memo** is already selected in the *Template* field. Press **Tab**.

Step 5. Enter ***02/15/11*** if it is *not* already entered in the *DATE* field. Press **Tab**.

Step 6. Enter ***2011-107C*** in the *CREDIT NO.* field and then press **Tab**.

This credit transaction is included on statements and customer reports, so using the Invoice number followed by a "C" in the *CREDIT NO.* field helps identify which Invoice this Credit Memo should apply to.

> Note:
> By changing the *CREDIT NO.* field to use a "C" at the end, the next invoice number will not default to the next in sequence, but instead will default to the next number as you entered on your Credit Memo followed by a "C." You'll need to remember to reset your Invoice numbering sequence (to remove the "C") when you enter the next Invoice.

Step 7. Enter the data shown in Figure 3-1 into the body of the Credit Memo. If QuickBooks displays the Price Levels window, click **OK** to close the window and continue.

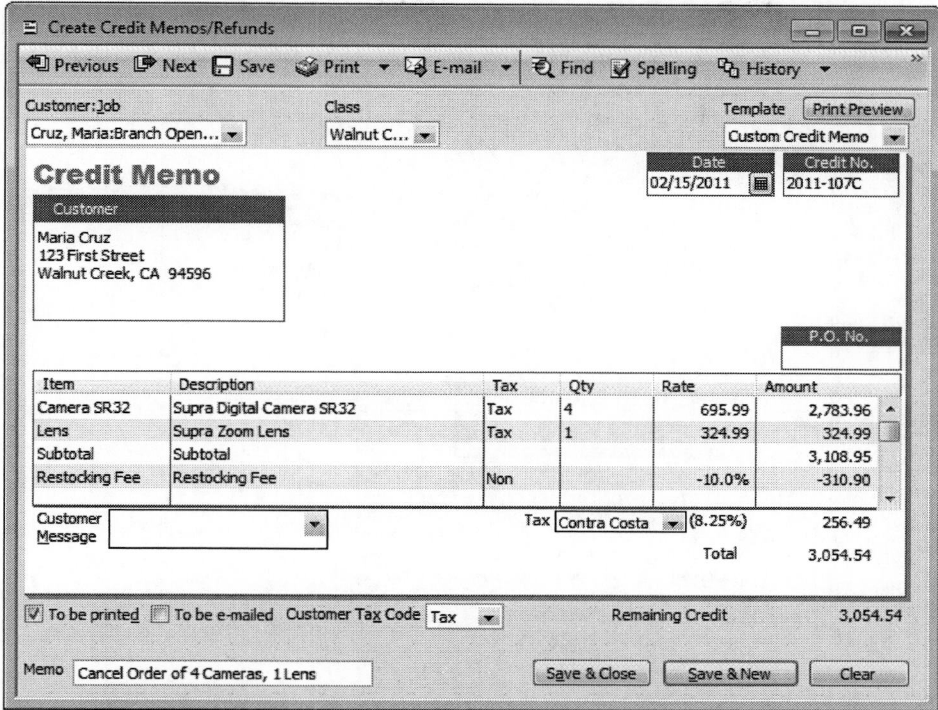

Figure 3-1 Credit Memos/Refunds window

Step 8. Enter ***Cancel Order of 4 Cameras, 1 Lens*** in the *Memo* field.

Step 9. Verify that all of the data on your screen matches Figure 3-1. Click **Save & Close** to record the Credit Memo.

Step 10. When the *Available Credit* window appears (see Figure 3-2), select the **Retain as an available credit** option and click **OK**. You will learn how to apply this Credit Memo to an Invoice in the section beginning on page 92.

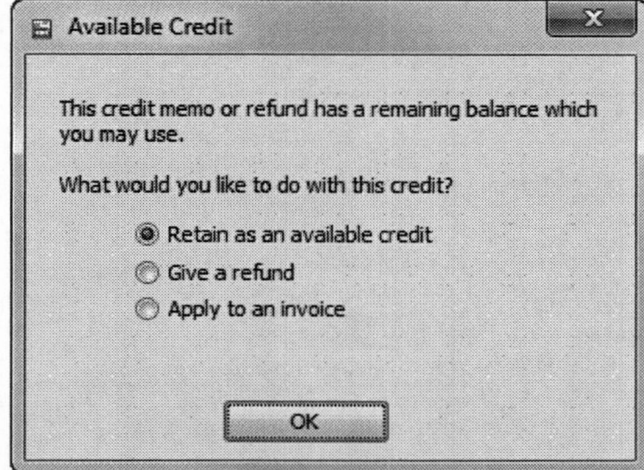

Figure 3-2 Available Credit Options

Customer Open Balance Report

Now, create a Customer Open Balance report to view the open Invoices and the Credit Memo for this customer.

Step 1. Display the **Customer Center** and then select **Cruz, Maria: Branch Opening** as shown in Figure 3-3.

Step 2. Under the *Reports for this Job* section, select the **Open Balance** link (see Figure 3-3). You may need to expand the window to see the Reports section. Note, you may need to stretch the window horizontally to display the *Reports for this Job* section of the customer center. If necessary, click and drag the right border of the *Customer Center* window to widen the window.

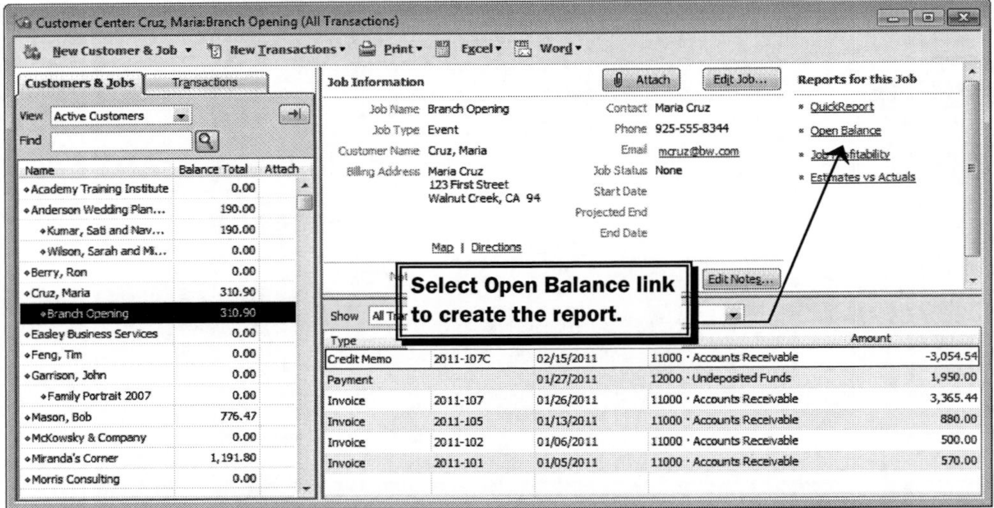

Figure 3-3 Select the job and click Reports in the **Customer Center**

Step 3. In the Open Balance report, notice that Invoice 2011-107 shows a balance of 3,365.44 and the Credit Memo 2011-107C shows an offsetting negative balance of -3,054.54 (see Figure 3-4).

The Credit Memo must be applied to the Invoice so all that remains is the $310.90 Restocking Fee for the cancelled order..

Step 4. Click the Close Window button (☒) at the top right of the window to close the report or press ESC to close the window.

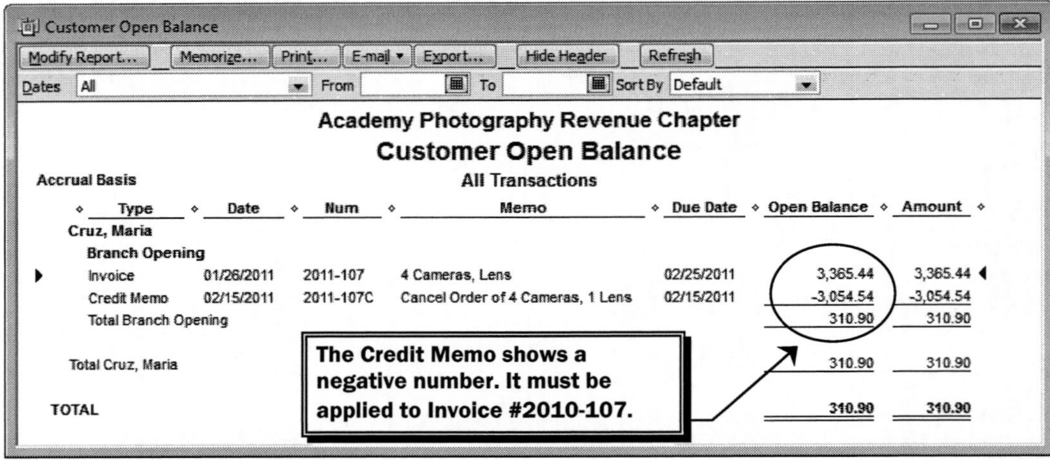

Type	Date	Num	Memo	Due Date	Open Balance	Amount
Cruz, Maria						
Branch Opening						
Invoice	01/26/2011	2011-107	4 Cameras, Lens	02/25/2011	3,365.44	3,365.44
Credit Memo	02/15/2011	2011-107C	Cancel Order of 4 Cameras, 1 Lens	02/15/2011	-3,054.54	-3,054.54
Total Branch Opening					310.90	310.90
Total Cruz, Maria					310.90	310.90
TOTAL					310.90	310.90

Figure 3-4 Customer Open Balance report

Applying an Existing Credit Memo to an Invoice

As mentioned earlier, when you create a credit memo, it does not automatically apply it to an invoice. There are several ways to apply an existing credit memo to one or more invoices.

1. Using the *Receive Payments* window
2. Using the *Credit Memo* window
3. Using the *Invoice* window

Applying a Credit Memo using Receive Payments Window

COMPUTER PRACTICE

To apply an existing Credit Memo to one or more Invoices using the *Receive Payments* window, follow these steps:

Step 1. From the *Customer Center* select **Cruz, Maria: Branch Opening** from the *Customers & Jobs* tab.

Step 2. Select **Receive Payments** from the *New Transactions* drop-down list.

Step 3. **Cruz, Maria: Branch Opening** already displays in the *Customer:Job* field. Press **Tab**.

Step 4. DO NOT enter an amount in the *Amount* field.

Step 5. Disregard the *Date* field. Dates only apply to transactions so there is no need to enter a date here. For this practice we are not creating a transaction; rather, we are only linking two existing transactions.

Step 6. Select Invoice# 2011-107 by clicking anywhere on the Invoice's row *except* the checkmark column (see Figure 3-5).

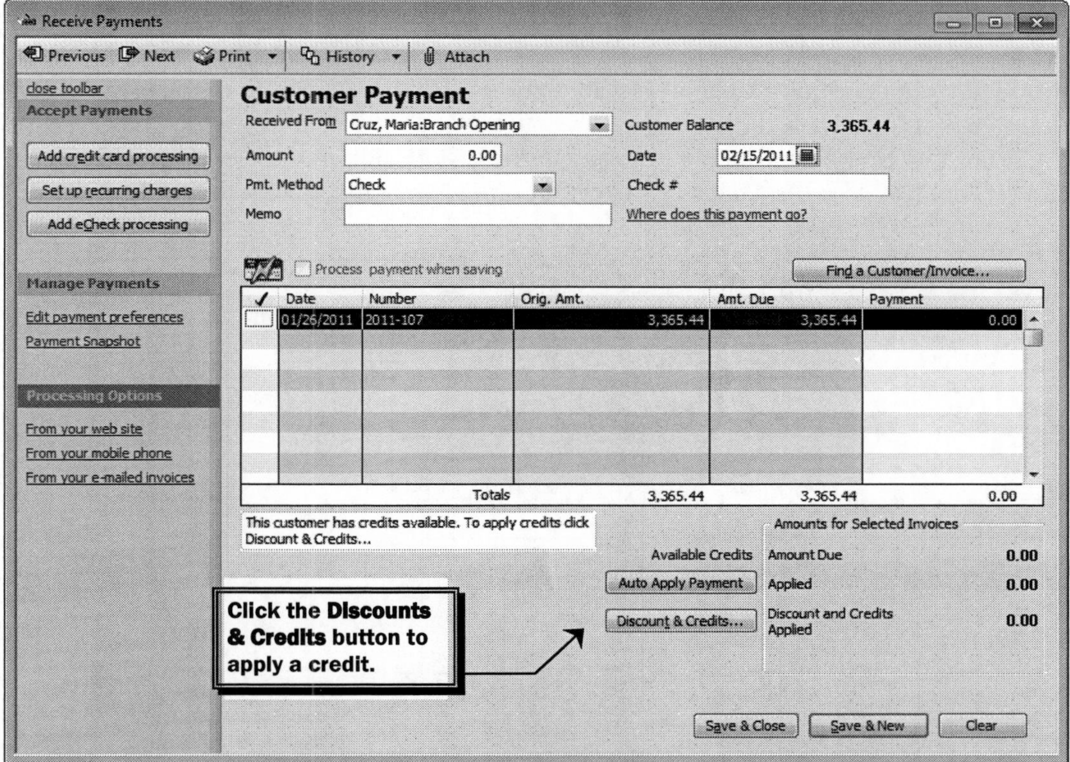

Figure 3-5 Receive Payment Window with Invoice Selected

> **Warning:**
> If QuickBooks displays the *Warning* window (see Figure 3-6), it means you clicked in the **Check (✓)** column to the left of the Invoice date on Figure 3-5. To select the invoice and complete this exercise, you need to click anywhere on the line, except the *Check* column.

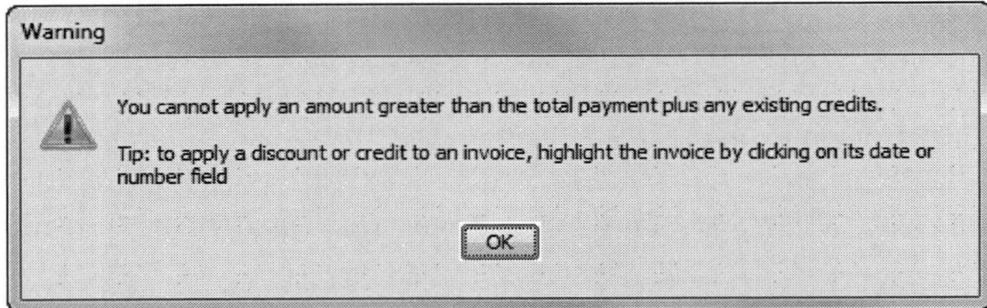

Figure 3-6 Message if selecting an invoice when no money is actually received

Step 7. Click **Discount & Credits** and verify that QuickBooks applied Credit Memo #2011-107C to Invoice #2011-107 (see Figure 3-7).

Since there is only one open (unapplied) Credit Memo for the Cruz, Maria: Branch Opening job, QuickBooks automatically applied the Credit Memo to Invoice #2011-107. If there were multiple Credit Memos for this job, QuickBooks would have auto-applied this Credit Memo to the Invoice using the same criteria as explained in **Preferences for Applying Payments** on page 69.

If the amount of the Credit Memo does not match the amount of the Invoice, or if the auto-apply feature is turned off, you may need to manually apply the Credit Memo to the appropriate Invoice. On the **Credits** Tab of the *Discounts and Credits* window, click the **Check (✓)** column on the line of the Invoice to which you wish to apply the credit.

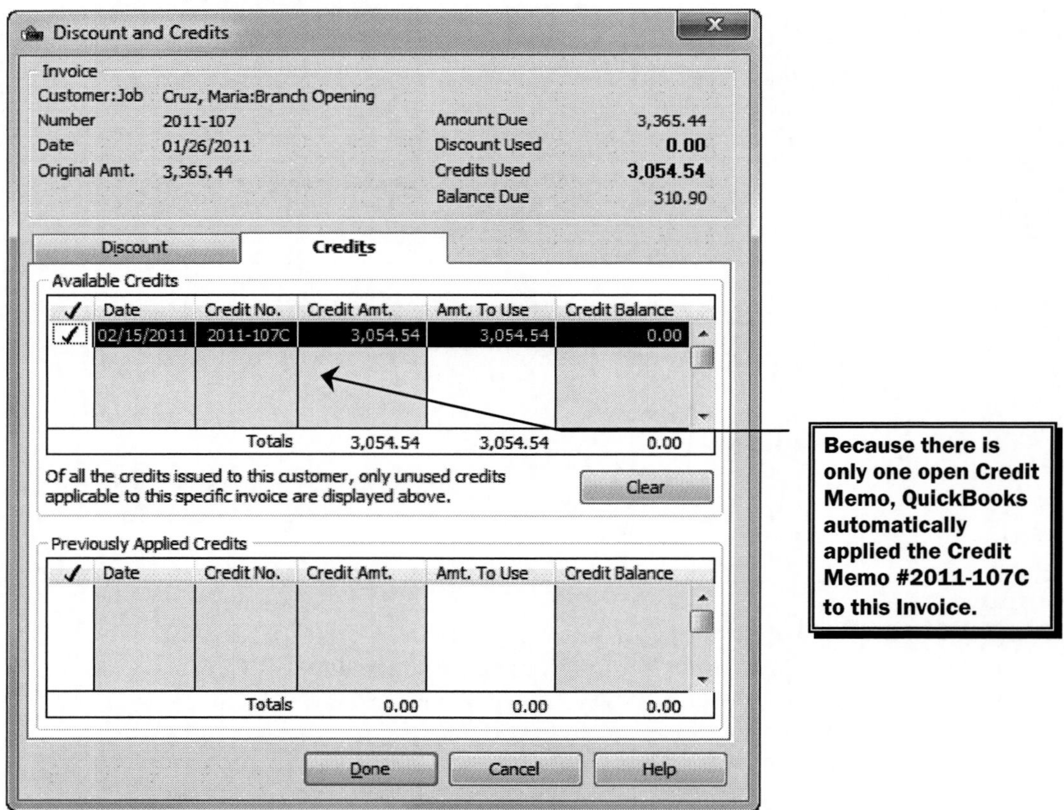

Figure 3-7 Credits tab of the Discounts and Credits window

Step 8. Click **Done** to return to the *Receive Payments* window.

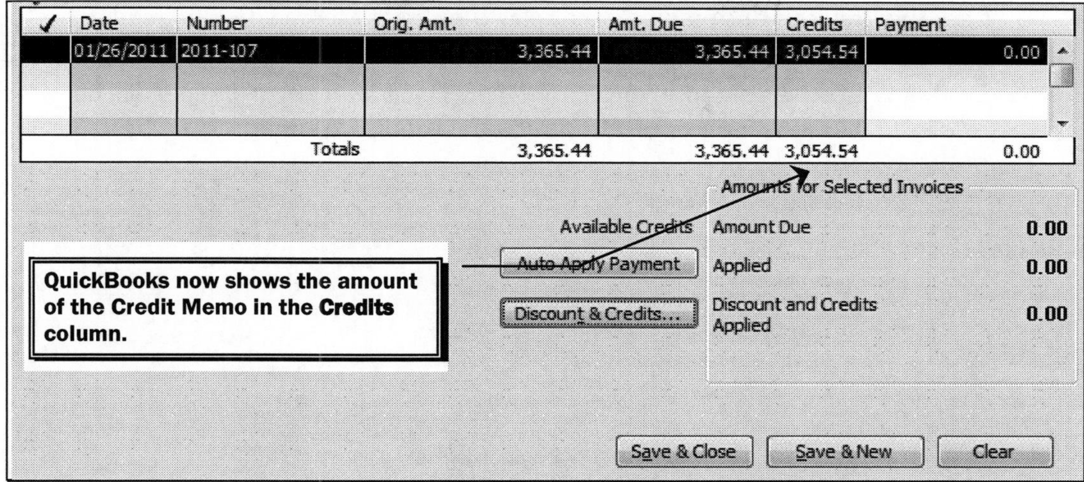

Figure 3-8 Applied To: section of Receive Payments window with Credit Memo applied

Step 9. Click **Save & Close** to apply the Credit Memo to the Invoice.

Applying a Credit Memo by Clicking the Use Credit to Button

COMPUTER PRACTICE

If you have an existing Credit Memo and you want to apply it to one or more invoices, you can display the credit memo and use the **Use Credit To** button to apply it to one or more invoices. Follow these steps:

First we have to create the Credit Memo to show the whole process.

Step 1. From the *Home* page select the **Refunds & Credits** icon.

Step 2. Create a credit memo for **Miranda's Corner job** as shown in Figure 3-9 by entering data in *Customer:Job, Class, Date, Credit No., Item, QTY,* and *Memo* fields.

Step 3. Click **Save & New** to save the Credit Memo and click **OK** on the *Available Credit* window when it is displayed.

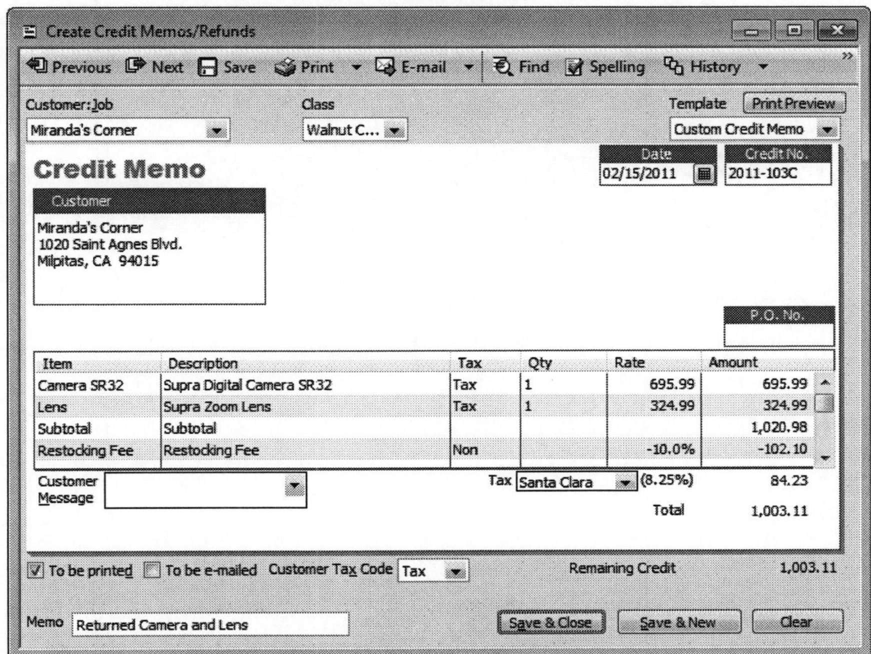

Figure 3-9 Credit Memo for Miranda's Corner

Step 4. Click the **Previous** button twice to display the Credit Memo you just created.

Step 5. Select the ***Use Credit to*** drop-down menu at the top of the Credit Memo (see Figure 3-10) and select **Apply to invoice**. The *Apply Credit to Invoices* window will be displayed. **Note**: You may need to stretch the window wider to see the *Use Credit to* button.

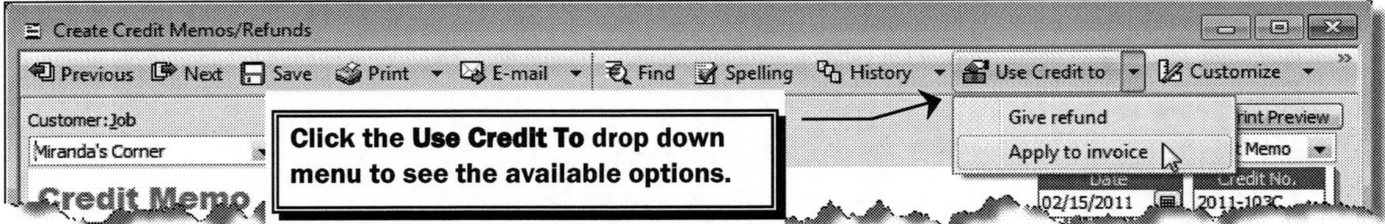

Figure 3-10 Use Credit to drop-down to Apply credit memo to invoice

Step 6. Make sure that Invoice # 2011-103 is selected (see Figure 3-11).

> **Note:**
> A credit memo can be applied to multiple invoices by selecting the invoices and entering the credit amount in the *Amt. Applied* column.

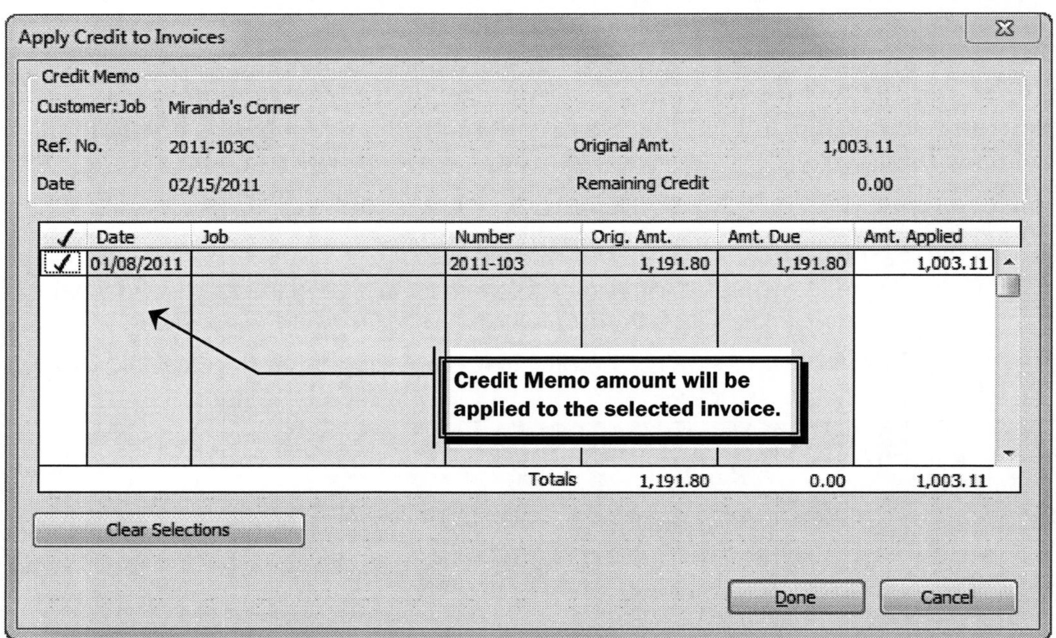

Figure 3-11 Applying the Credit Memo to the selected Invoice

Step 7. Click **Done** to return to Credit Memo window.

Step 8. When the Credit Memo has been fully applied, the remaining credit will be zero (see Figure 3-12).

Step 9. Click **Save & Close** to record the Credit Memo.

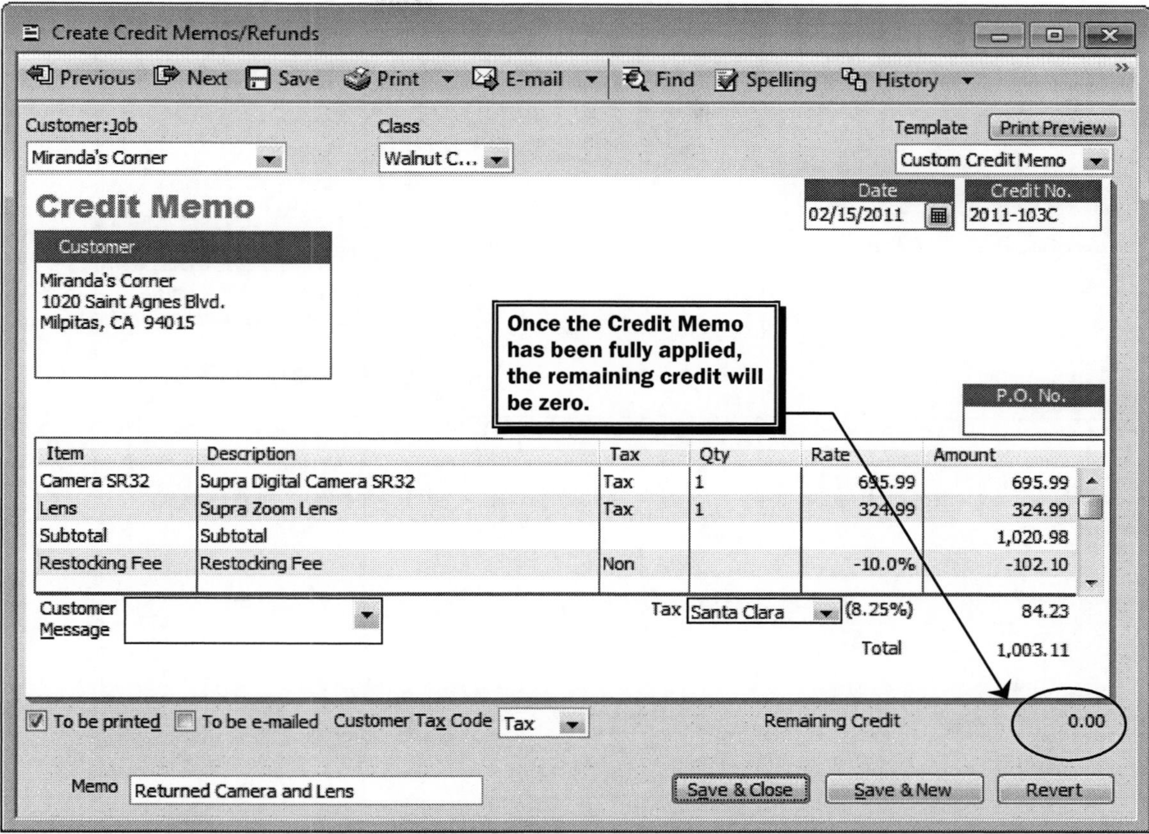

Figure 3-12 Credit Memo after it has been fully applied

Applying and Unapplying Credits Directly from an Invoice

COMPUTER PRACTICE

To apply or unapply credits to an Invoice, you can use the Apply Credits button at the bottom of the Invoice and then select which credits to apply or unapply. Follow these steps:

First let's find an Invoice for a customer known to have a credit already applied.

Step 1. From the *Home* page select **Invoices.**

Step 2. Click the **Find** icon shown in Figure 3-13.

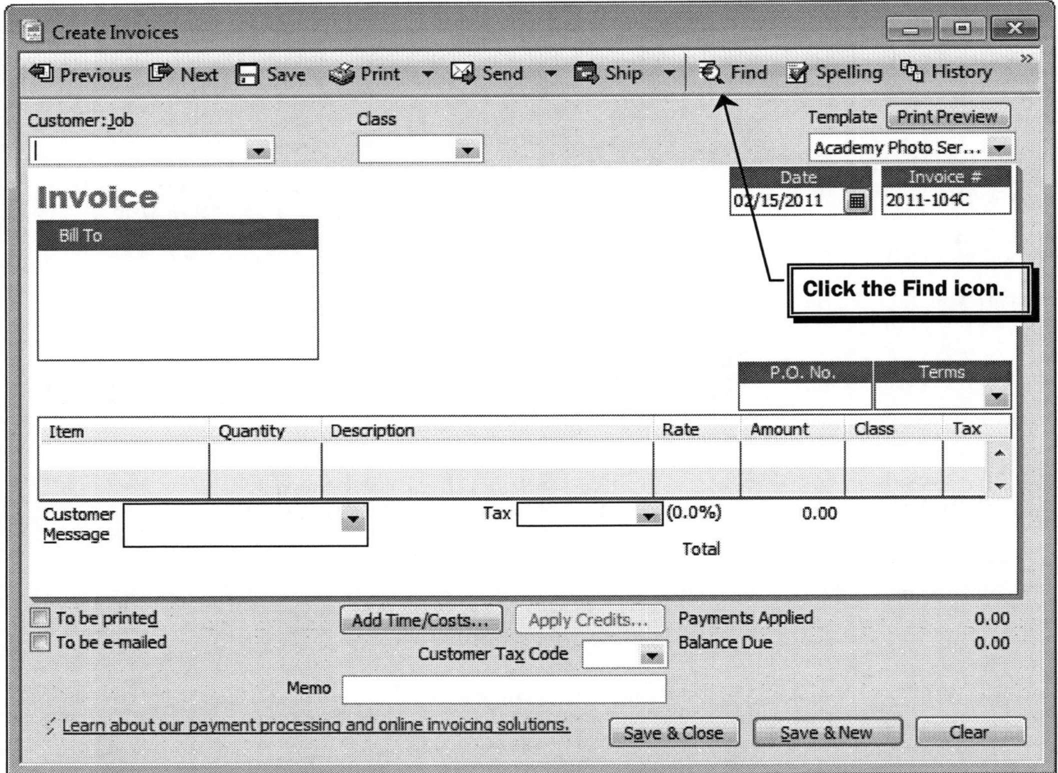

Figure 3-13 Finding an Invoice

Step 3. In the *Find Invoices* window (see Figure 3-14), enter **2011-103** in the *Invoice #* field. Click **Find**.

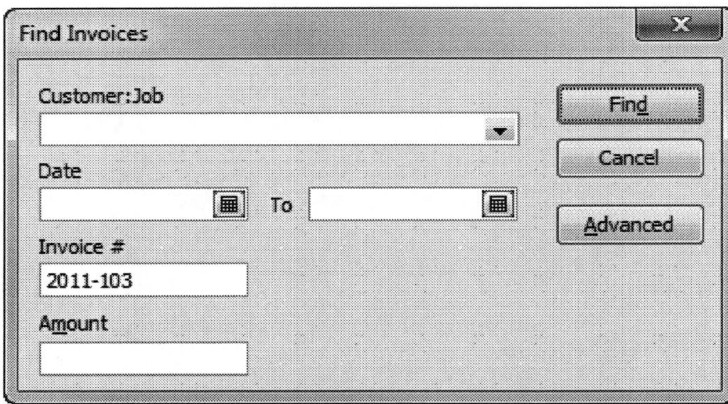

Figure 3-14 Find Invoices Window

Step 4. This displays Invoice #2011-103 (Figure 3-15) which shows that some payments (or credits) have already been applied. In addition, you can see that there is still a balance due on the invoice.

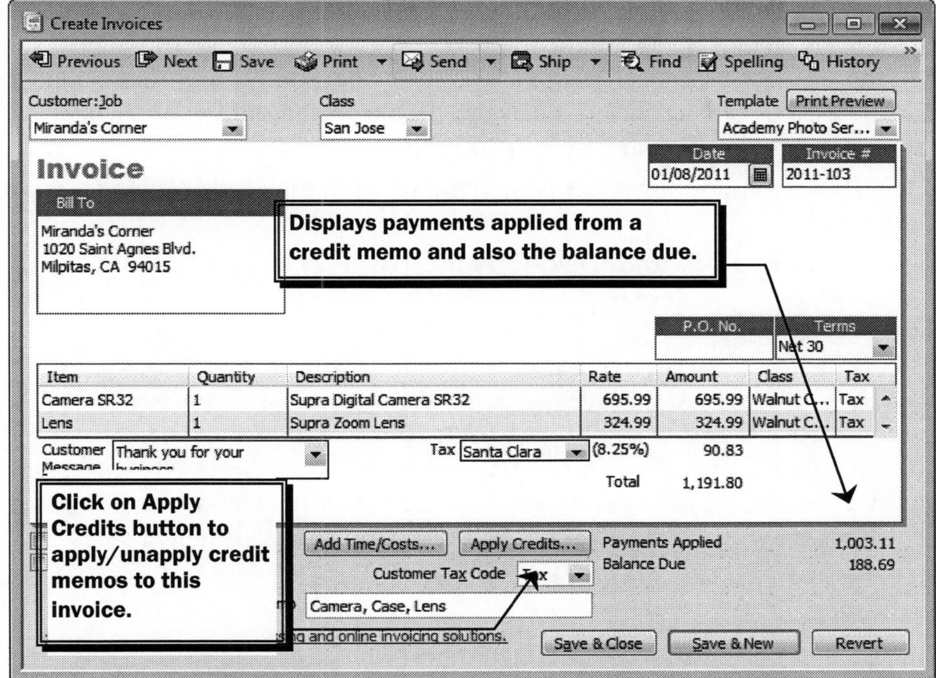

Figure 3-15 Invoice displayed using Find

Step 5. Click **Apply Credits** at the bottom of the invoice to apply or unapply credits.

Step 6. The *Apply Credits* window displays (see Figure 3-16).

Credit memo #2011-103C previously applied to this invoice displays in the **Previously Applied Credits** section. There are no other unapplied Credit Memos for this customer.

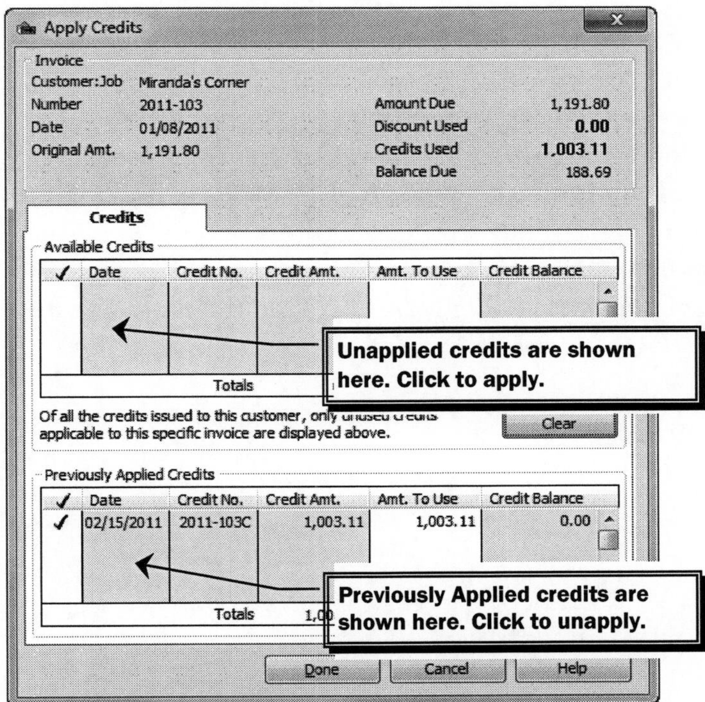

Figure 3-16 Apply Credit Window with available and used credits

Step 7. To apply a credit in this window, click the check mark in the first column of the *Available Credits* section (there are no available credits at this point). To unapply a credit in this window, place a checkmark next to the previously applied credit in the *Previously Applied Credits* section. You can also modify the amount to apply or unapply in the *Amt. to Use* column for each credit.

Step 8. Click **Cancel** to return to the Invoice without unapplying the Credit Memo (as shown in Figure 3-15).

Step 9. Click **Save & Close** to close the Invoice.

> **Did You Know?**
> A Credit Memo is not the only way to credit a customer's account. For example, if you receive a payment from a customer that exceeds their Accounts Receivable balance or if you record a payment and do not apply the full amount of the payment to the customer's Invoice(s), QuickBooks will create an unapplied credit for the customer. You then have two choices: (1) apply this credit to a future Invoice using the steps above; or, (2) issue the customer a refund check.

Refunding Customers

There are several situations when you may need to issue a refund to a customer:

1. When a customer pays for merchandise and then returns the merchandise.
2. When a customer requests a discount or refund on merchandise or services for which she has already paid.
3. When a customer overpays an Invoice and requests a refund.

If the customer paid with cash or check, you should issue a refund check. If the customer paid with a credit card, you should credit the customer's credit card.

Refunding by Check

COMPUTER PRACTICE

The first step in issuing a customer refund is to create a Credit Memo showing the detail of what is being refunded. Typically, the detail will include the products and/or services returned or discounted.

Step 1. Select **Refunds & Credits** from the *Home* page.

Step 2. Fill in the Credit Memo as displayed in Figure 3-17. Click **Save & New** to save the Credit Memo.

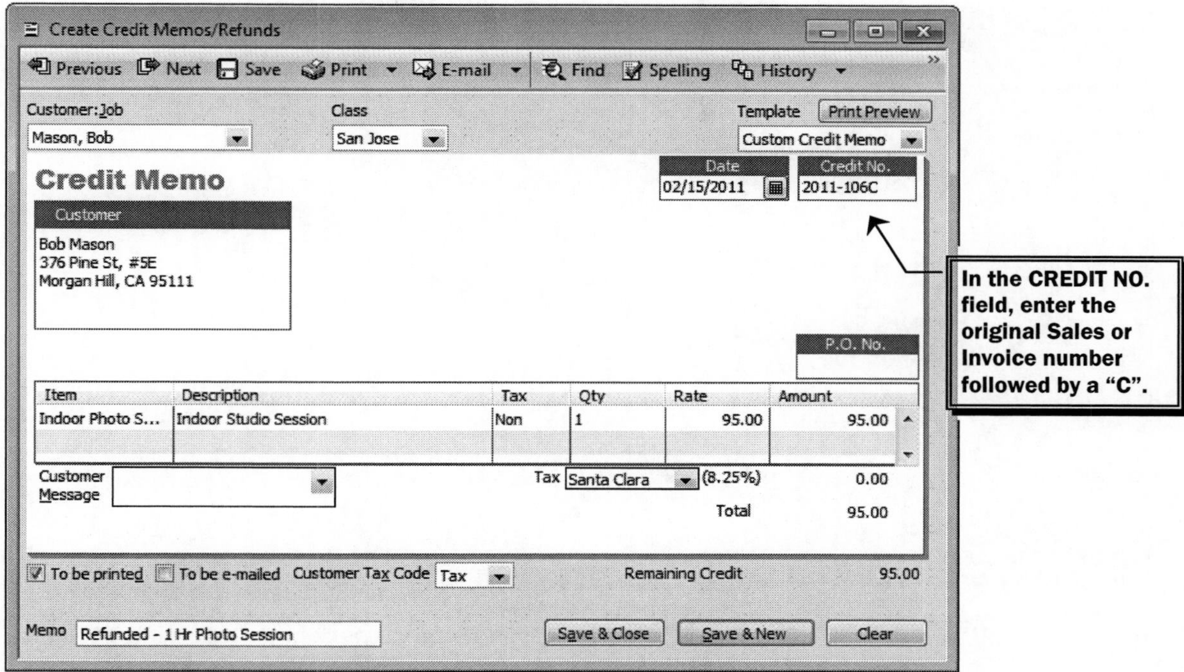

Figure 3-17 Use this data for the Credit Memo for Bob Mason

Step 3. After you save the Credit Memo, QuickBooks displays the *Available Credits* window (see Figure 3-18). Select *Give a Refund* and click **OK**.

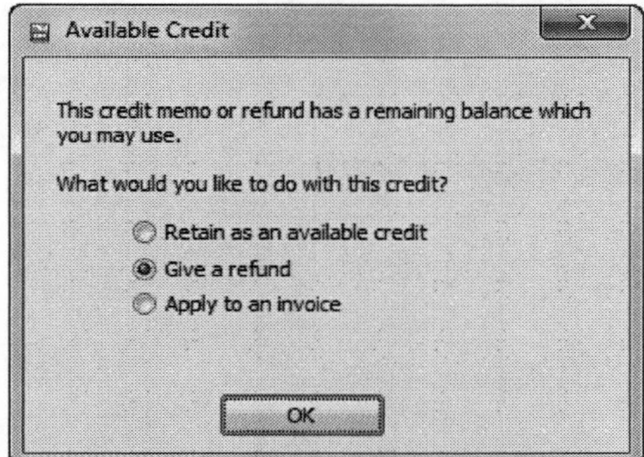

Figure 3-18 Give a refund option in Available Credit window

Step 4. QuickBooks opens the *Issue a Refund* window (see Figure 3-19). Most of the information is already filled in. Enter ***–Refunded – 1 Hr Photo Session*** in the Memo field. Click **OK** to record the refund check.

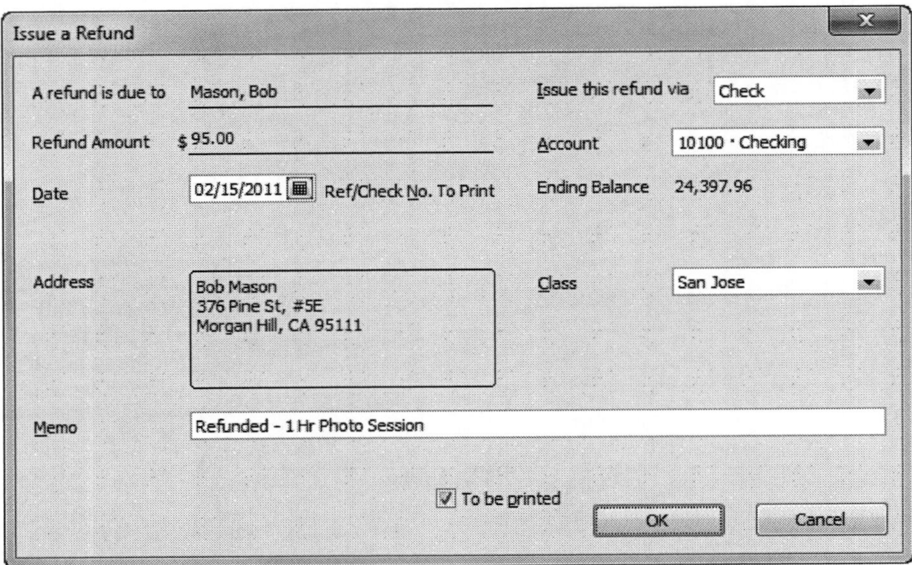

Figure 3-19 Issue a Refund for Photo Session

Step 5. When you click **OK**, QuickBooks creates the refund check in the checking account and records the Credit Memo.

Step 6. To redisplay the Credit Memo, click the **Previous** button twice in the *Credit Memo* window (see Figure 3-20).

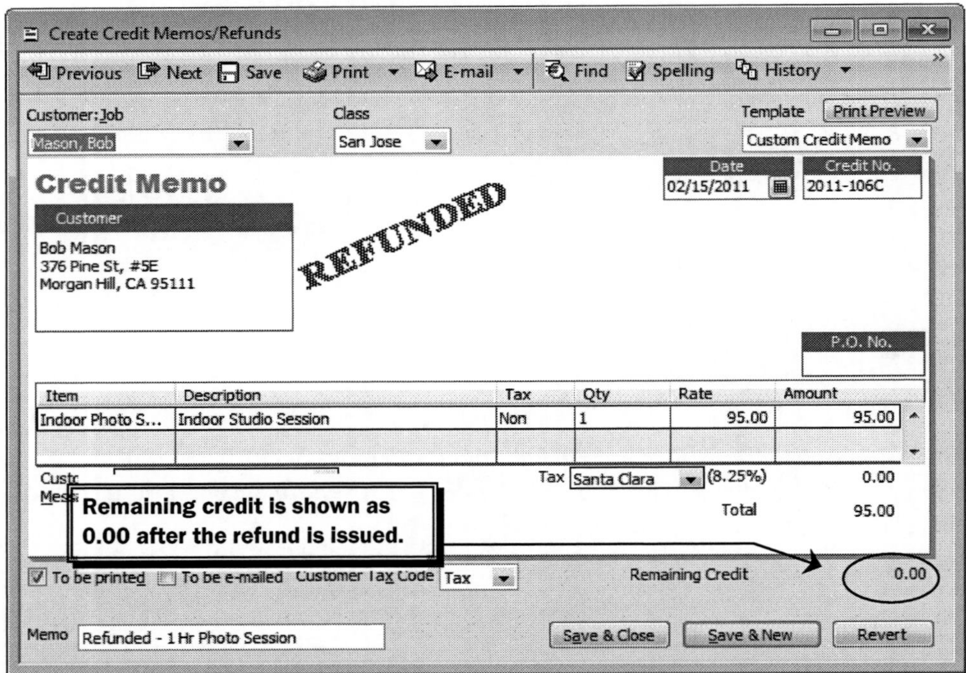

Figure 3-20 Credit Memo after the refund

Step 7. Close the *Credit Memo* window.

Step 8. Although you will not do it now, this is when you would print the refund check.

Refunding Credit Cards

> Note:
> This section does not apply if you use the QuickBooks Merchant Account Services for credit card processing. To process a credit refund using QuickBooks Merchant Account Services, click the **Process credit card refund when saving** field that will display at the bottom of the ***Issue a Refund*** window. See the onscreen help for more information.

The process for refunding a customer's credit card is similar to the last example on refunding by check, except while check refunds allow you to write a physical check to refund the customer, credit card refunds are held in the Undeposited Funds account and processed in a "batch" each day.

> DO NOT PERFORM THESE STEPS. THEY ARE FOR REFERENCE ONLY.

1. To give a customer a credit card refund, begin by creating a Credit Memo. In this example Maria Cruz: Branch Opening has been given a $190.00 refund for an Indoor Photo Session.
2. Select **Refunds & Credits** from the *Home* page.
3. Fill in the Credit Memo, such as the one displayed in Figure 3-21.

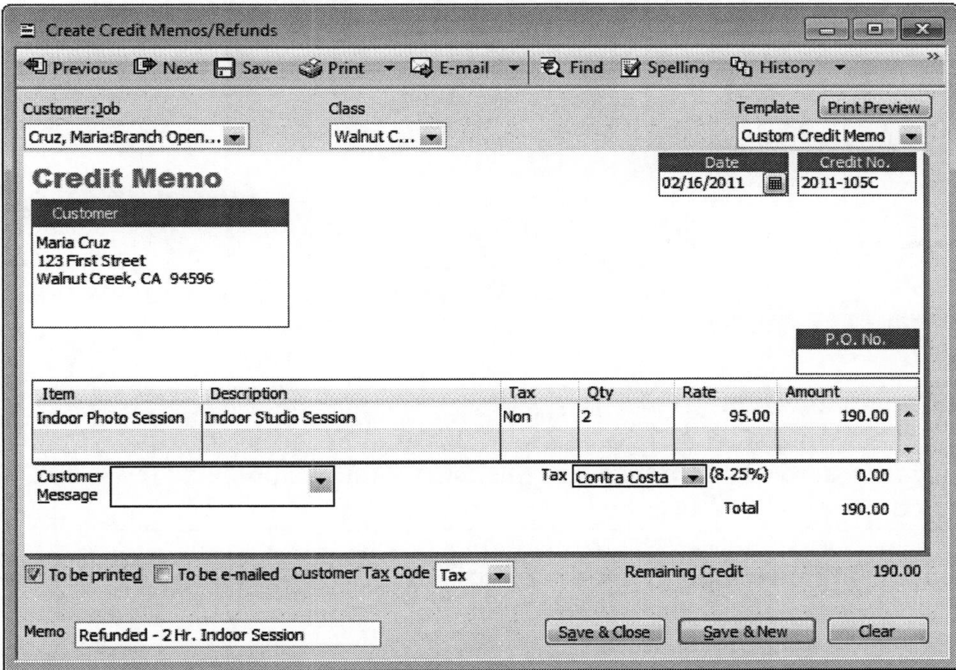

Figure 3-21 Maria Cruz Credit Memo for the credit card refund

4. Click **Save & New** to save the Credit Memo.
5. Select **Give a refund** in the *Available Credit* window and click **OK** (see Figure 3-22).

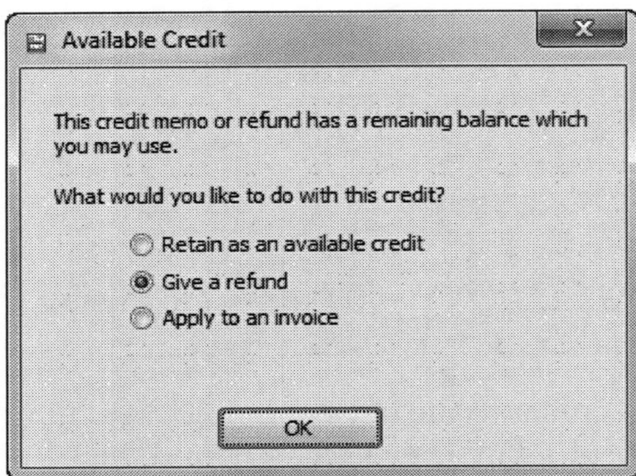

Figure 3-22 Available Credit window

6. In the *Issue a Refund* window fill in the needed information, such as Figure 3-23. Then click **OK**.

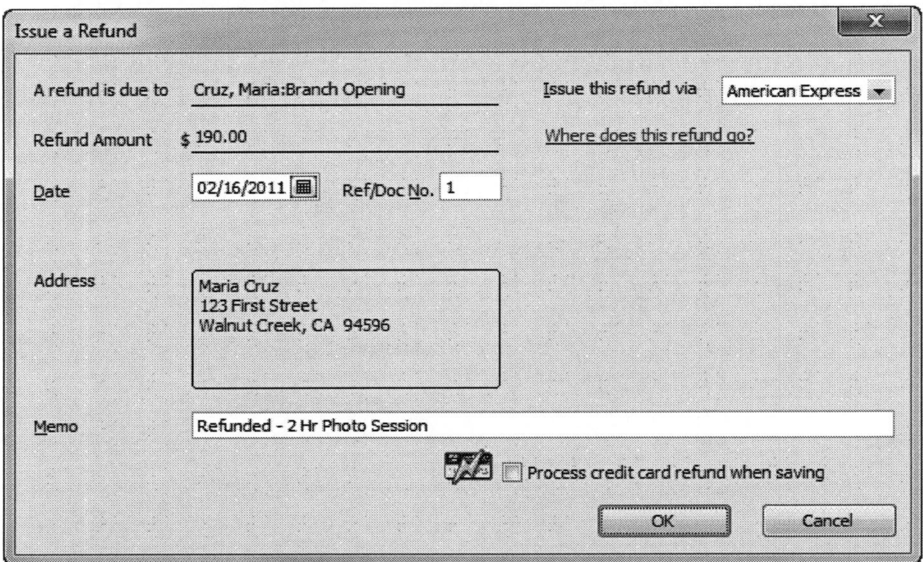

Figure 3-23 Issue a Refund window

> **The Accounting Behind the Scenes**
> Creating a Credit Memo and issuing a refund in this example decreases (or debits) the income account associated with the item on the Credit Memo (i.e. Services) and decreases (or credits) the Undeposited Funds account.

7. To record the credit card refund into the bank account, select **Make Deposits** from the *Banking* menu. Click on the credit card refund in the *Select Payments to Deposit* section and click **OK**.

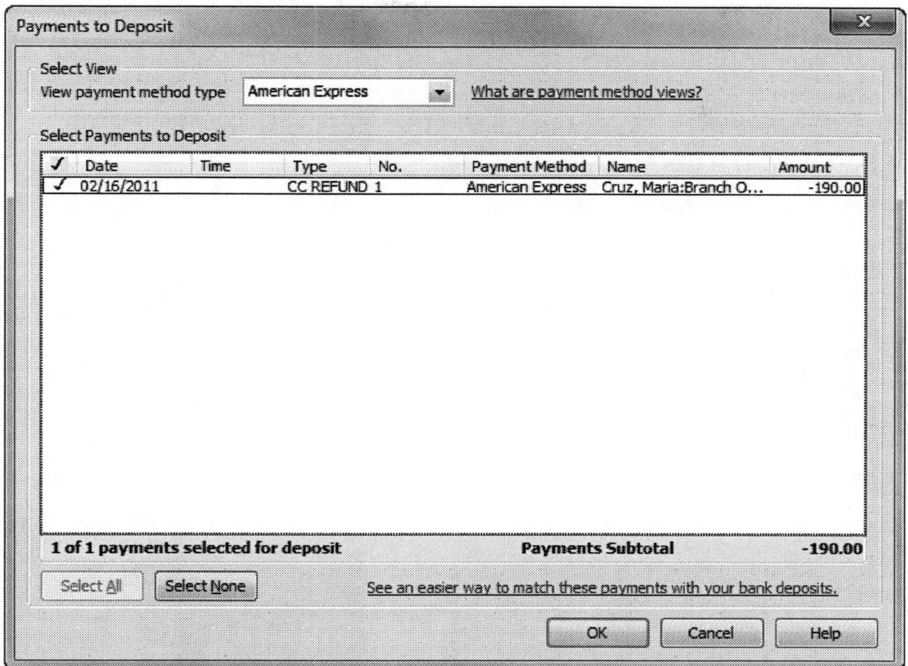
Figure 3-24 Payments to Deposit window with credit card refund

8. In the **Make Deposits** window, check to make sure your screen matches Figure 3-25.
9. Click **Save & Close**.

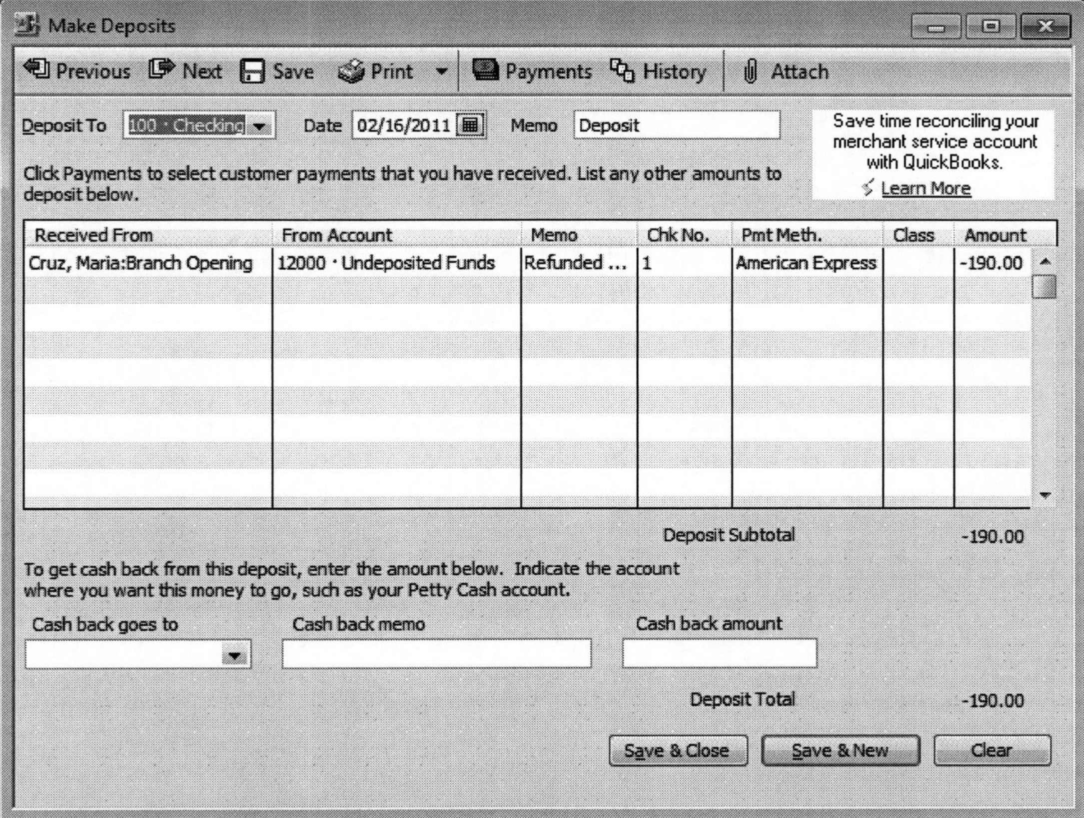
Figure 3-25 Make Deposits window

This example assumes that your merchant account service does not deduct a discount fee from each transaction. If your credit card company processes merchant discount fees with each transaction you will need to calculate the discount in the **Checking** account line and add a **Bankcard fees** account line recorded as a negative amount. Again, use this deposit method only if credit card returns exceed credit card payments.

10. Re-display the original Credit Memo. Notice that the **REFUNDED** stamp along the form confirms that the refund has been processed in QuickBooks.

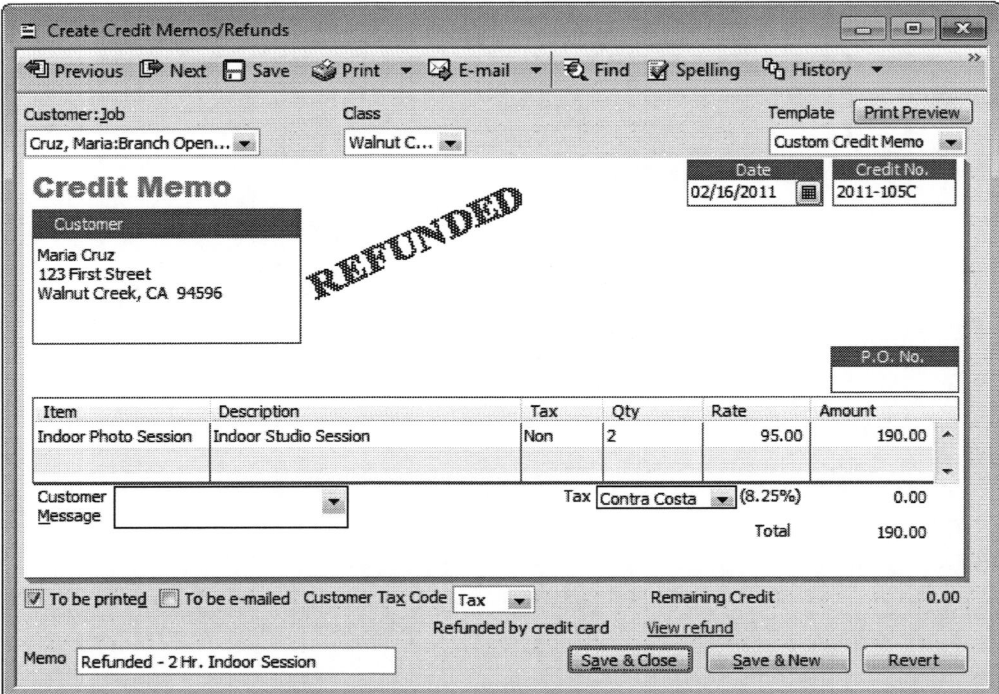

Figure 3-26 Credit Memo showing completed refund process

> **Did You Know?**
> Merchant services companies normally charge two types of fees for processing credit cards: a *transaction* fee and a *discount* fee. A **transaction** fee is a standard fee (like $.45) for each credit card transaction, regardless if it is a sale or refund. A **discount** fee (like 2.5%) is a percentage charge based upon the transaction amount. Some merchant services companies only charge a discount fee for credit card sales. Other companies, however, charge a discount fee for both credit card sales and refunds. Intuit's QuickBooks Merchant Account Services for credit card processing currently charges a discount fee for both sales and refunds.

Writing Off a Bad Debt

If an Invoice becomes uncollectible, you'll need to write off the debt. If you use the cash basis of accounting, the uncollectible invoice has not yet been recognized as income on your Profit & Loss report, and therefore, you *could* simply delete the invoice to remove it from your records. However, good accounting practice dictates that you enter a new entry to credit the customer balance and reverse the sale (and the sales tax if appropriate).

To properly write off the bad debt, use a **Credit Memo** and a *Bad Debt* Item as shown in the following practice. In the Customizing QuickBooks chapter, you'll learn more about Items, but for now, we'll set up a *Bad Debt* item the sample file.

COMPUTER PRACTICE

Step 1. From the *List* menu select **Item List.**

Step 2. Press **Ctrl+N** to display the New Item window.

Step 3. If the *New Feature* window displays, click **OK** to bypass this window.

Step 4. Create an *Other Charge* Item called **Bad Debt** as shown in Figure 3-27. Link the *Bad Debt* Item to the Bad Debts expense account. Click **OK.**

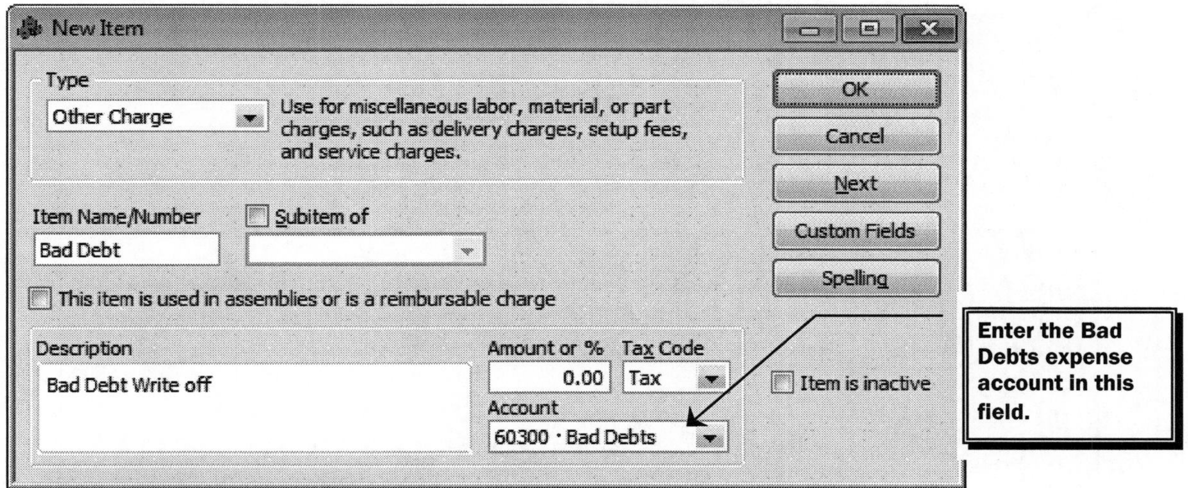

Figure 3-27 Bad Debt Other Charge Item

Step 5. Close the *Item List.*

Step 6. From the *Home* page select **Refunds & Credits.**

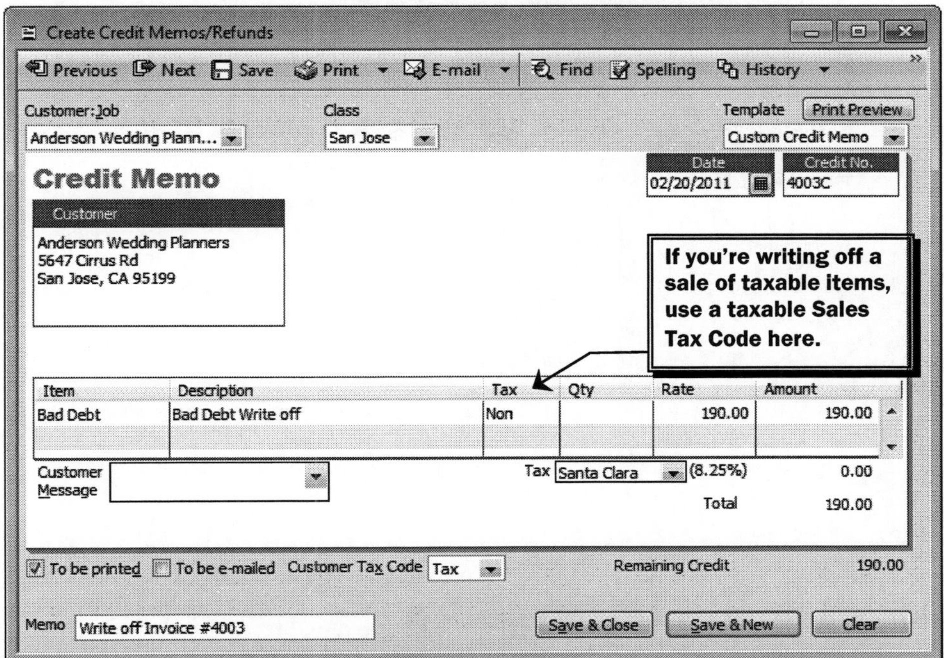

Figure 3-28 Write off a bad debt with a Credit Memo

Step 7. Fill out the **Credit Memo** as shown in Figure 3-28. Choose ***Anderson Wedding Planners: Kumar, Sati and Naveen*** in the *Customer:Job* field.

Step 8. QuickBooks displays a warning message because Invoices and Credit Memos normally increase or decrease Income accounts, rather than Expense accounts (see Figure 3-29). Click **OK**.

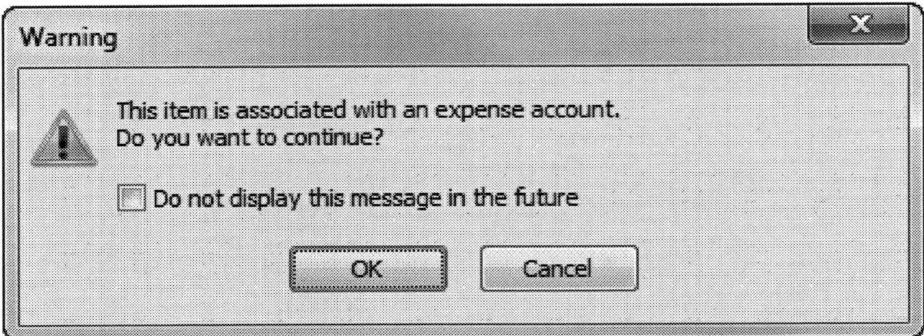

Figure 3-29 Warning about the Bad Debt Item pointing to an expense account

Note:
Under many circumstances, your Bad Debt write off should not affect sales tax. However, if the sale you are writing off does need to affect your sales tax liability, you'll need to use two lines on the credit memo.

On the first line of the Credit Memo, use the **Bad Debt** item and enter the total of all taxable items in the sale (not including the sales tax) in the amount column. Select **Tax** (or the appropriate Code) in the **Tax Code** column. QuickBooks will calculate the sales tax and reduce your liability by that amount.

On the second line, use the same **Bad Debt** Item and enter the total of the non-taxable items from the original invoice, including any shipping or miscellaneous charges (excluding sales tax). Select a non-taxable **Tax Code** for this line.

Step 9. Click **Save & Close** to record the Credit Memo. Available Credit window (see Figure 3-30) will be displayed. Select *Apply to an Invoice* option and click **OK**.

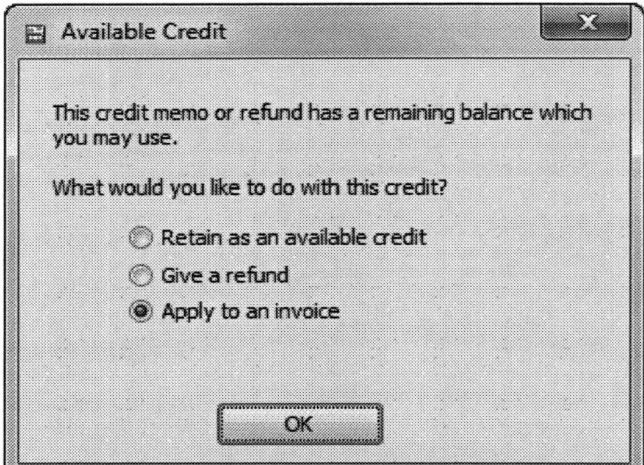

Figure 3-30 Apply to an Invoice option on Available Credit window

The accounting behind the scenes:
When you use the Bad Debt Item on a Credit Memo, the Credit Memo decreases (credit) Accounts Receivable and increase (debit) Bad Debts expense.

Applying the Bad Debt Credit Memo to an Open Invoice

COMPUTER PRACTICE

Step 1. *Apply Credit to Invoices* window is automatically displayed with Invoice #4003 **Check** (✓) column checked (see Figure 3-31).

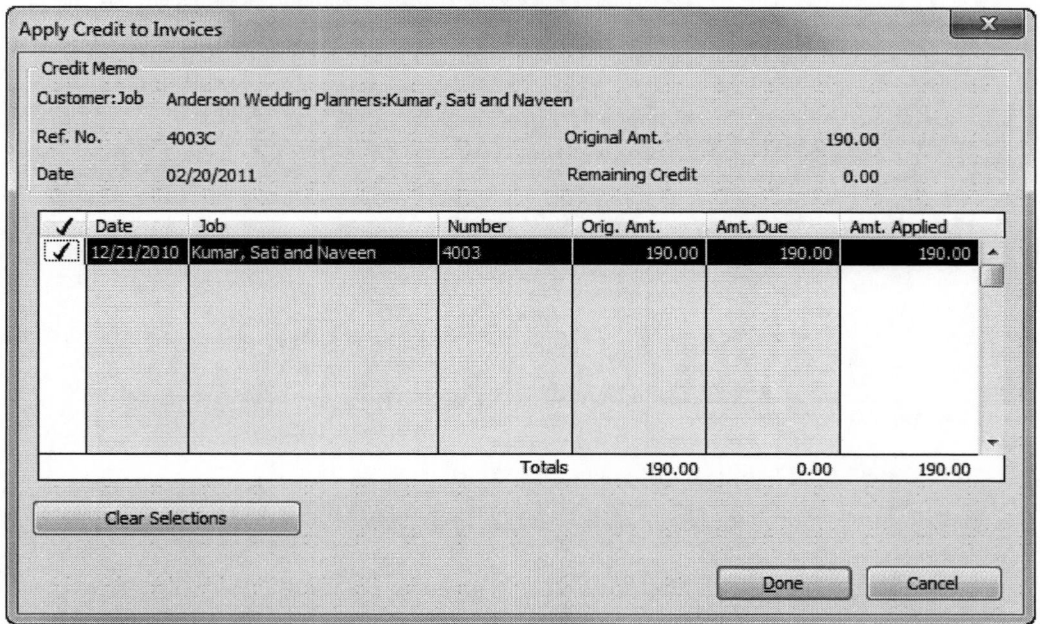

Figure 3-31 Apply Credit to Invoices window

Step 2. Click **Done** to apply the bad debt to the selected invoice.

Creating Customer Statements

QuickBooks customer statements provide a summary of the activity for an accounts receivable customer during the period you specify. When you create statements, you can show either all of the customer's accounts receivable activity or just the transactions that are currently open.

COMPUTER PRACTICE

Step 1. From the *Home* page click the **Statements** icon to open the *Create Statements* window (see Figure 3-32). Alternatively, click **Create Statements** from the *Customers* menu.

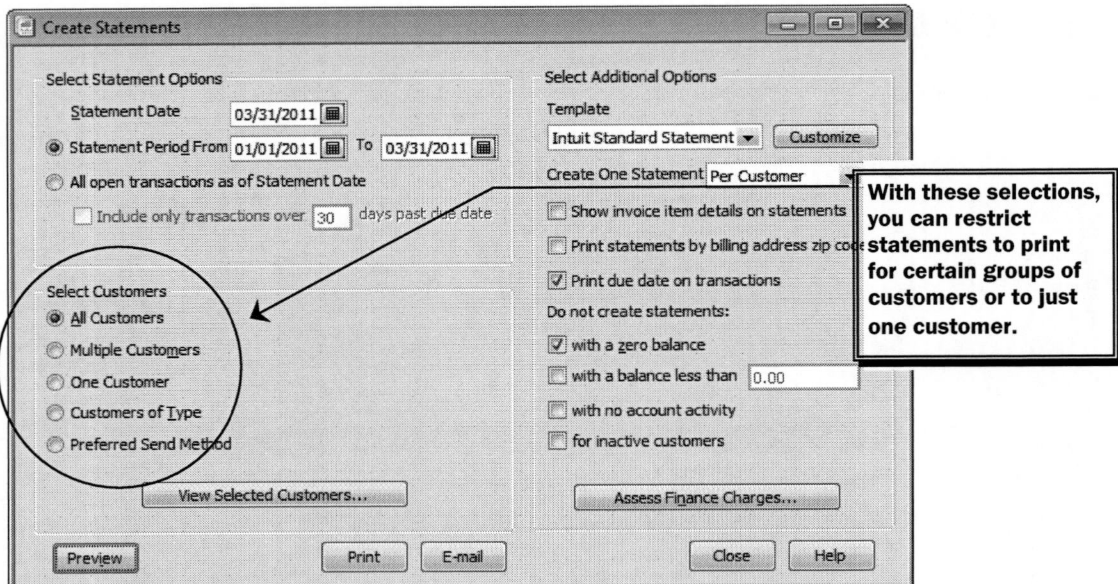

Figure 3-32 Create Statements window

Step 2. Enter **03/31/2011** in the *Statement Date* field.

Step 3. Set the *Statement Period From* and *To* fields to ***1/1/2011*** and ***3/31/2011*** respectively.

These dates include the period for which Accounts Receivable transactions will show on the customer statement.

Step 4. Leave **All Customers** selected in the *Select Customers* section.

> **Note:**
> If you want to print only the open Invoices for each customer select **All open transactions as of Statement Date** at the top left of the Create Statements window. If you want to show the detail from the invoice, make sure the *Show invoice item detail on statement* option is selected.

Step 5. Leave **Per Customer** selected in the *Create One Statement* drop-down list.

Step 6. Check the **with a zero balance** box in the *Do not create statements* section.

Step 7. Click **Preview**.

Step 8. After previewing the two pages of statements in the *Print Preview* window (see Figure 3-33), click the **Close** button. You will return to the *Create Statements* window. Leave this window open. You will use it in the next practice.

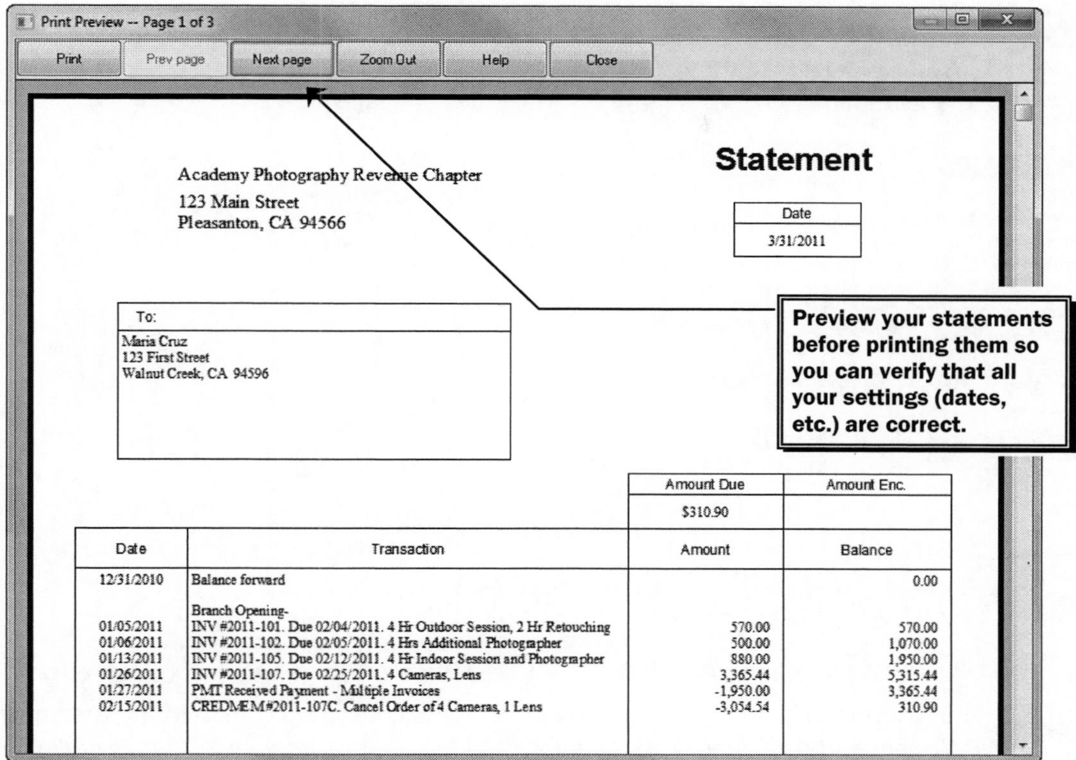

Figure 3-33 Preview your statements before printing

Assessing Finance Charges

When a customer is late in paying an invoice, you can assess finance charges. To set up your finance charge settings, follow these steps:

COMPUTER PRACTICE

Step 1. Click **Assess Finance Charges** button on the *Create Statements* window (see Figure 3-32).

Step 2. Click **Yes** in the *Set up Finance Charges* window (see Figure 3-34).

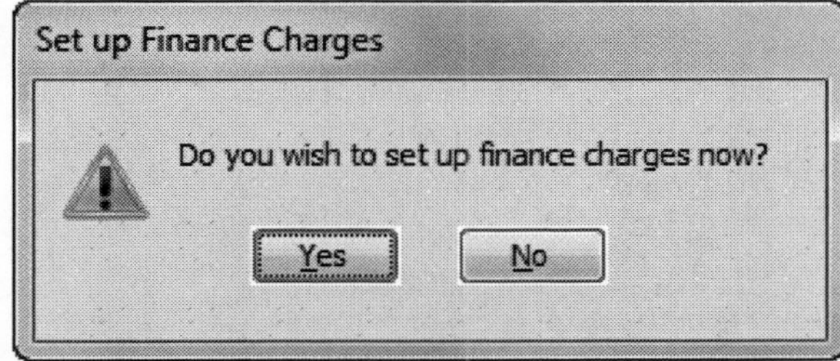

Figure 3-34 Set up Finance Charges window

> **Another Way:**
> You can also access the Finance Charge settings by selecting **Preferences** from the *Edit* menu. Select **Finance Charge** from the *Preferences* list and select the **Company Preferences** tab.

Step 3. The Finance Charges Company Preferences window is displayed. Enter the information in Figure 3-35.

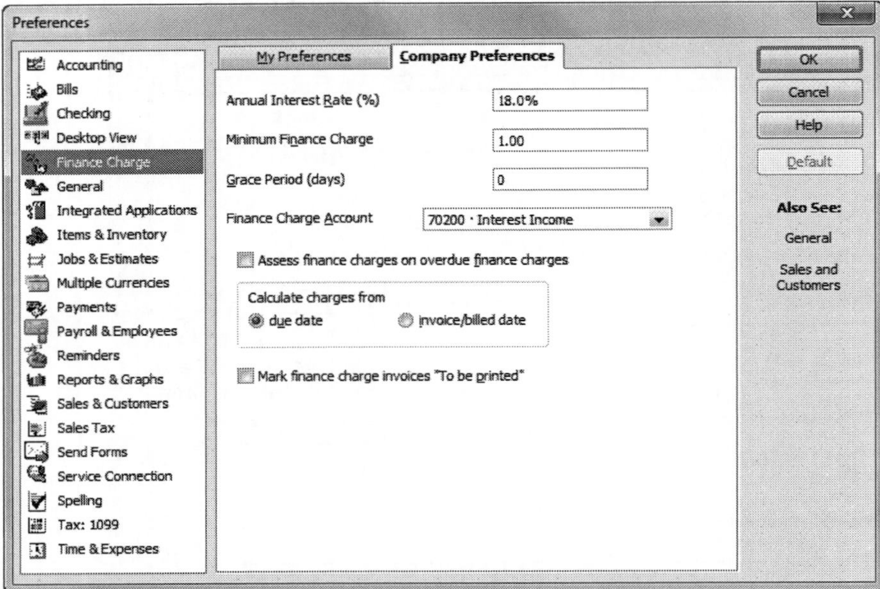

Figure 3-35 Finance Charge Company Preferences

Step 4. When finished entering, click **OK** to set the Finance Charge Company Preferences.

Step 5. The *Assess Finance Charges* window displays. The Enter ***03/31/2011*** in the *Assessment Date* field and then press **Tab**.

Step 6. All customers with overdue balances displays (see Figure 3-36). Review the finance charge amounts in the **Finance Charge** column. QuickBooks automatically calculated these amounts based on the amount in the *Annual Interest Rate (%)* field of the Finance Charge Company Preferences. You can override the amount of the finance charge for each customer by editing the amount in the **Finance Charge** column.

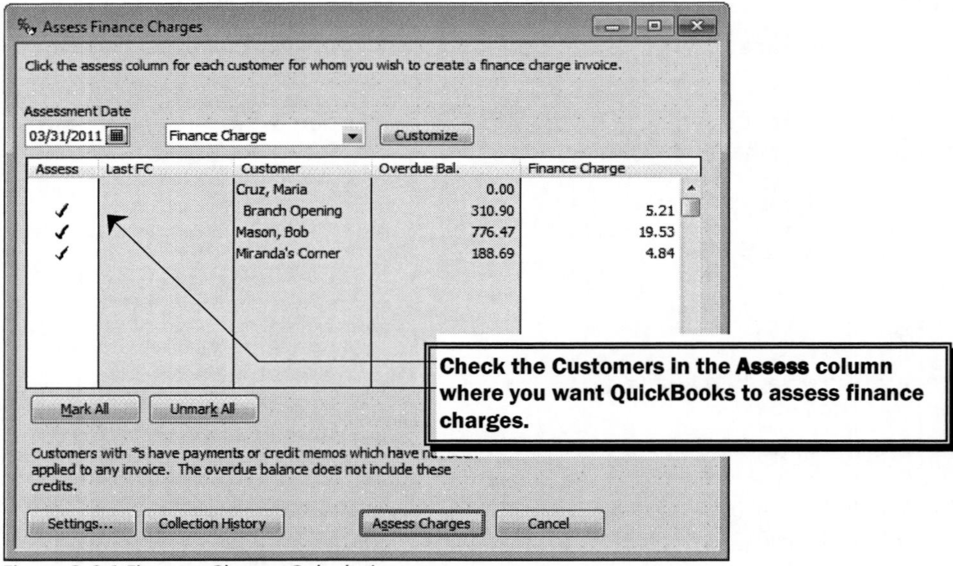

Figure 3-36 Finance Charge Calculation

Step 7. The **Assess** column for three customers is already selected. You can deselect each customer separately by clicking on the appropriate checkmarks in the **Assess** column or you can deselect all customers by clicking **Unmark All**. For now, leave these customers selected.

Step 8. Click the **Assess Charges** button to record the finance charges.

> **Note:**
> Finance Charges increase with time and are reset each time Finance Charges are applied. If you apply Finance Charges twice on the same *Assessment Date*, the second Finance Charges will be the minimum amount. In this exercise the minimum is $1. If your window looks different from Figure 3-34, it may be because you have already assessed Finance Charges. Finance Charges create invoices, so if you need to edit previously assess charges, you can edit their invoices.

Step 9. Click **Preview** again to view your statements on the *Print Preview* window as shown in Figure 3-37. Note that the statements now include assessed finance charges. You can print these at any time.

Step 10. Close all open windows.

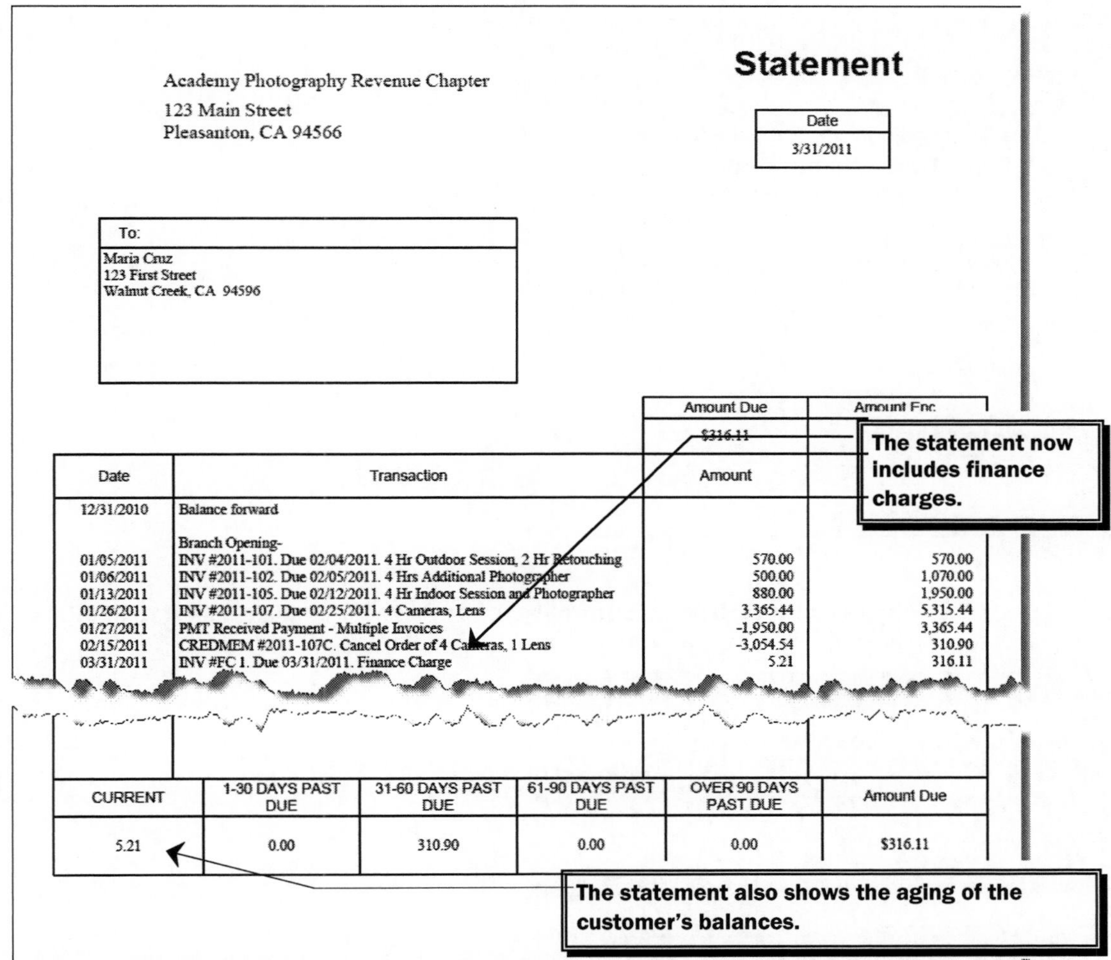

Statement

Academy Photography Revenue Chapter
123 Main Street
Pleasanton, CA 94566

Date
3/31/2011

To:
Maria Cruz
123 First Street
Walnut Creek, CA 94596

Amount Due	Amount Enc
$316.11	

Date	Transaction	Amount	
12/31/2010	Balance forward		
	Branch Opening-		
01/05/2011	INV #2011-101. Due 02/04/2011. 4 Hr Outdoor Session, 2 Hr Retouching	570.00	570.00
01/06/2011	INV #2011-102. Due 02/05/2011. 4 Hrs Additional Photographer	500.00	1,070.00
01/13/2011	INV #2011-105. Due 02/12/2011. 4 Hr Indoor Session and Photographer	880.00	1,950.00
01/26/2011	INV #2011-107. Due 02/25/2011. 4 Cameras, Lens	3,365.44	5,315.44
01/27/2011	PMT Received Payment - Multiple Invoices	-1,950.00	3,365.44
02/15/2011	CREDMEM #2011-107C. Cancel Order of 4 Cameras, 1 Lens	-3,054.54	310.90
03/31/2011	INV #FC 1. Due 03/31/2011. Finance Charge	5.21	316.11

CURRENT	1-30 DAYS PAST DUE	31-60 DAYS PAST DUE	61-90 DAYS PAST DUE	OVER 90 DAYS PAST DUE	Amount Due
5.21	0.00	310.90	0.00	0.00	$316.11

Figure 3-37 Customer after adding finance charges

Creating Sales Reports

In this section, you'll learn how to create reports that will help you analyze your company's sales.

Sales by Customer Summary Report

The **Sales by Customer Summary** report shows how much you have sold to each of your customers over a given date range.

COMPUTER PRACTICE

To create this report, follow these steps:

Step 1. From the *Report Center* select **Sales** from the category list and then double click the **Sales by Customer Summary** report in the *Sales by Customer* section.

Step 2. Enter ***01/1/2011*** in the *From* date field and then press **Tab**.

Step 3. Enter ***2/28/2011*** in the *To* date field and then press **Tab**.

Figure 3-38 shows the **Sales by Customer Summary** report for the first two months of 2011.

Step 4. To print the report, click **Print** at the top of the report.

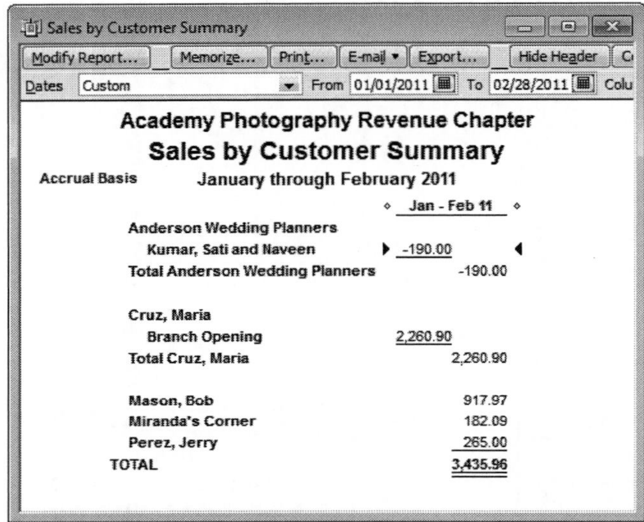

Figure 3-38 Your Sales by Customer Summary report should look like this

Step 5. Close the **Sales by Customer Summary** report. If the *Memorize Report* dialog box opens, click **No** (see Figure 3-39).

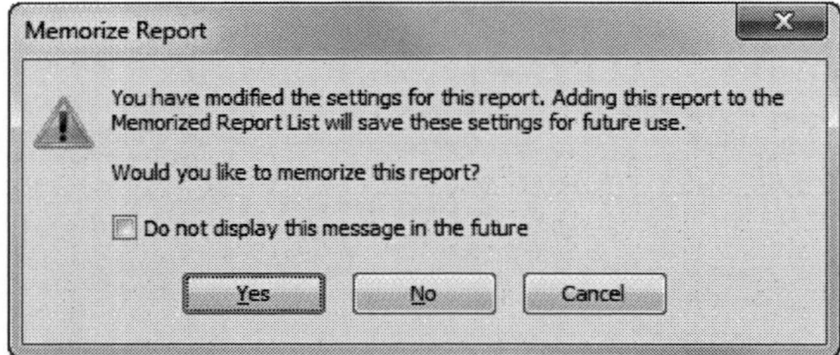

Figure 3-39 Memorize Report dialog box

Sales by Item Report

The **Sales by Item report** shows how much you have sold of each Item over a given date range. To create this report, follow these steps:

COMPUTER PRACTICE

Step 1. From the *Report Center* select **Sales** from the category list and then double click the **Sales by Item Summary** link in the *Sales by Item* section. You may need to scroll down.

Step 2. Enter ***1/1/2011*** in the *From* date field and then press **Tab.**

Step 3. Enter ***2/28/2011*** in the *To* date field and then press **Tab.**

Figure 3-40 shows the **Sales by Item Summary** report for the first two months of 2011.

Step 4. To print the report, click **Print** at the top of the report.

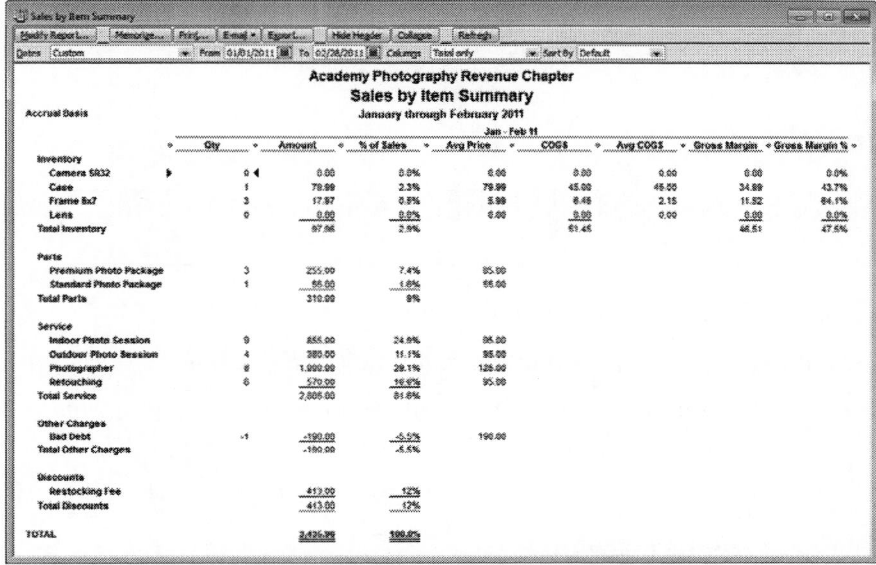

Academy Photography Revenue Chapter

Sales by Item Summary

January through February 2011

Accrual Basis

	Jan - Feb 11							
	Qty	Amount	% of Sales	Avg Price	COGS	Avg COGS	Gross Margin	Gross Margin %
Inventory								
Camera SR32	0	0.00	0.0%	0.00	0.00	0.00	0.00	0.0%
Case	1	79.99	2.3%	79.99	45.00	45.00	34.99	43.7%
Frame 5x7	3	17.97	0.5%	5.99	6.45	2.15	11.52	64.1%
Lens	0	0.00	0.0%	0.00	0.00	0.00	0.00	0.0%
Total Inventory		97.96	2.9%		51.45		46.51	47.5%
Parts								
Premium Photo Package	3	255.00	7.4%	85.00				
Standard Photo Package	1	55.00	1.6%	55.00				
Total Parts		310.00	9%					
Service								
Indoor Photo Session	9	855.00	24.9%	95.00				
Outdoor Photo Session	4	380.00	11.1%	95.00				
Photographer	8	1,000.00	29.1%	125.00				
Retouching	6	570.00	16.6%	95.00				
Total Service		2,805.00	81.6%					
Other Charges								
Bad Debt	-1	-190.00	-5.5%	190.00				
Total Other Charges		-190.00	-5.5%					
Discounts								
Restocking Fee		413.00	12%					
Total Discounts		413.00	12%					
TOTAL		3,435.96	100.0%					

Figure 3-40 Your Sales by Item Summary report should look like this

Step 5. Close the **Sales by Item Summary** report. If the *Memorize Report* dialog box opens, click **No.**

Chapter Summary and Review

Summary of Key Points

In this chapter, you learned how to track sales in your company. You should now be familiar with how to use QuickBooks to do all of the following:

- Process customer returns and credits (page 89).
- Write off customer invoices (record bad debts) (page 106).
- Create and print customer statements (page 109).
- Assess finance charges (page 111).
- Create Sales Reports (page 113).

Comprehension Questions

Answers to these review questions are available with the supplemental material. See page xiii for details.

1. How many ways can credit memos be applied to an invoice?
2. When would you choose to give a refund after creating a *Credit Memo*?
3. When would you choose to retain an available credit after creating a *Credit Memo*?

Multiple Choice

Select the best answer(s) for each of the following:

1. Customer Statements:
   a) Provide a summary of all Accounts Receivable activity for a customer during the period you specify.
   b) Are not available in QuickBooks.
   c) Automatically assess and calculate finance charges for overdue accounts without any user action.
   d) Should only be created and mailed if the customer's balance is over $500.
2. Which of the following options is not available on the *Available Credit* window?
   a) Give a refund.
   b) Retain as an available credit.
   c) Apply to an invoice.
   d) Use with Receive Payments.
3. What is the best way to write off a bad debt?
   a) Delete the original invoice.
   b) Create a *Credit Memo* using a *Bad Debt* item and applying the credit to the past due invoice.
   c) Create a *Credit Memo* for the amount of the past due invoice and retain the available credit.
   d) Any of the above.

4. In which of the following situations would you create a Credit Memo?
   a) You need to record a cancelled order that has already been invoiced but not paid.
   b) A customer returns merchandise and wants the return credited to a future invoice.
   c) A customer requests a refund.
   d) Any of the above.

5. The *Credit Memo Number* should be
   a) The next number after the *Credit Memo Number* on the last *Credit Memo*.
   b) The next number after the *Invoice Number* on the last *Invoice*, followed by a "C".
   c) Any unique number.
   d) The same number as the *Invoice* the *Credit Memo* is linked to, followed by a "C".

6. You need to issue a refund to a customer. The customer originally paid with a Visa card. How do you issue the credit?
   a) Pay the refund with your company's credit card.
   b) Pay the refund using any method of payment.
   c) Pay the refund by issuing a refund check.
   d) Pay the refund through the customer's credit card.

7. Your company policy is that each Finance Charge should be at least $5. Where is the best place to set this value in QuickBooks?
   a) Enter a value of at least $5 in the *Finance Charge* field in the *Assess Finance Charges* window.
   b) Enter ***$5*** in the *Minimum Finance Charge* field in the *Finance Charge Company Preferences* window.
   c) Enter ***$5*** on the last line of each statement.
   d) Enter ***$5*** in the *Minimum Finance Charge* field in the *Create Statements* window.

8. Which report would you run to see a summary of income by products and services?
   a) The Sales by Item Summary Report
   b) The Sale by Customer Summary Report
   c) The Customer Open Balance Report
   d) The Revenue by Item Summary Report

9. Which of the following is a way to issue a credit without creating a *Credit Memo*?
   a) Delete an open invoice.
   b) Deposit a check from a customer without receiving a payment.
   c) Receiving a payment from a customer for an amount greater than their Accounts Receivable balance.
   d) You can only issue a credit by creating a *Credit Memo*.

10. What is a Customer Statement?
    a) A summary of activity for an accounts receivable customer during a specific period.
    b) A list of a customer's open invoices.
    c) A list of all customer transaction during the last 3 years.
    d) An invoice that includes a customer's finance charges.

11. A past due invoice contains items that were taxed and items that were not taxed. How would you write off this invoice as a bad debt?
    a) Delete the original invoice.
    b) Delete the taxed items from the original invoice and then delete the entire invoice.

c) Create a *Credit Memo* with two *Bad Debt* items, the first set to non-taxable with the total of non-taxable items, the second set to taxable with the total of taxable items. Apply this *Credit Memo* to the original invoice.
d) Create a *Credit Memo* for the taxable amount from the original invoice. Apply the *Credit Memo* to the invoice, and then delete the invoice.

12. Which statement is true?
    a) If you assess Finance Charges for one past due customer, you have to assess them to all past due customers.
    b) You must preview statements before printing them.
    c) Finance Charges are assessed automatically when you create a statement.
    d) You can create a statement for a single customer.

13. After issuing a refund check
    a) The *Credit Memo* is marked **Refunded** and the *Remaining Credit* field is 0.00
    b) The *Credit Memo* is removed.
    c) The original *Invoice* is marked **Refunded** and the *Remaining Credit* field is 0.00.
    d) The *Total* field on the original invoice is 0.00.

14. Which of the following is true?
    a) You can only apply a *Credit Memo* to an *Invoice* if the *Remaining Credit* amount is equal to the *Amount Due.*
    b) *Credit Memos* are automatically applied to open invoices.
    c) *Credit Memos* look similar to invoices but perform the opposite function, reducing (debiting) Sales accounts and reducing (crediting) Accounts Receivable.
    d) You should not use a *Credit Memo* to write off a bad debt.

15. In which of the following situations would you assess a Finance Charge?
    a) A customer returns merchandise and you want to charge him or her a restocking fee.
    b) You want to write off a bad debt.
    c) A customer's invoice is 60 days past due.
    d) Any of the above.

Completion Statements

1. Regarding Refunds: If the customer paid by _______ or _______, you will need to issue a refund check. If the customer paid with a _______ _______, you will need to credit the customer's credit card account
2. _______ _________ are used to issue refunds or apply credits to existing invoices.
3. You can ___________ ___________ an uncollectible invoice as a bad debt.
4. When a customer is late paying an invoice, you can assess ___________ ___________.
5. A customer __________________ is a summary of all activity on an account in a specified period.

Revenue-Problem 1

EXTENDING YOUR KNOWLEDGE

Restore the Revenue-10Problem1.QBM file and store it on your hard disk according to your instructor's directions.

1. On **Feb 7, 2011**, create **Invoice #2011-108** to Morris Consulting. Use the Walnut Creek class, terms 2%10, Net 30. (**Note**: Special terms apply to this Invoice only.) The customer purchased a 4 hour Indoor Photo Session ($95 per hour) and 2 hours with a Photographer ($125 per hour). Use the Out of State Sales Tax Item. The invoice total is $630.00. Print the invoice.

2. On **Feb 9, 2011**, create **Invoice #2011-109** to Easley Business Services. Use the class San Jose. Terms are Net 30. The customer purchased 4 Camera ($695.99), 3 Lens ($324.99) and 3 Case ($79.99). Use the Out of State Sales Tax Item. The invoice total is $3,998.90. Print the invoice.

3. On **Feb 10, 2011**, receive check **#58621** in the amount of $617.40 from Morris Consulting in full payment of Invoice #2011-108. He took a 2% discount of $12.60. Use the Sales Discount account and the Walnut Creek class.

4. On **Feb 15, 2011**, Donald Easley of Easley Business Services called and gave his **VISA** credit card number to pay off the balance on his open invoices. The payment amount was $3,998.90; VISA #4444-3333-2222-1111; Exp. 05/2015.

5. On **Feb 23, 2011**, Morris Consulting requested a refund for two hours of Photographer services. Create Credit Memo #2011-108C and use the Walnut Creek class. Issue Morris Consulting a refund check.

6. On **Feb 26, 2011**, create a **Credit Memo** to write off Invoice 3696 to Ortega Services. You will need to create a Bad Debt item. Since Invoice 3696 included a taxable item, you will need to mark the Bad Debt item on the Credit Memo for the amount $695.99 and mark it as taxable. Use the Walnut Creek class. The entire amount of the write off is $753.41.

7. On **Feb 27, 2011**, receive payment for **$1,191.80** from Miranda's Corner in payment of Invoice #2011-103. She uses her Visa card number 7777-8888-9999-0000 expiration date 12/2011, to pay this invoice.

8. On **Feb 28, 2011**, issue **Credit Memo #2011-103C** to Miranda's Corner for Invoice #2011-103. The customer returned 1 Cameras ($695.99 each). A 10% restocking fee applies. Use the San Jose class and the Santa Clara County Sales tax. Issue a **refund** to **Miranda's Corner VISA** card on Credit Memo #2011-103C using the *Refunding Credit Cards* method discussed in the chapter. Total refund: **$683.81**. Print the credit memo after the refund.

9. Deposit the check in the **undeposited funds** account on **2/28/2011**. Total deposit amount is **$617.40**. Print the **Deposit Slip and Deposit Summary**.

10. Deposit all VISA receipts on **2/28/11**. Record a 2% bankcard **discount** fee (use QuickMath to calculate) on the credit card deposit. Total deposit amount is **$4,416.75**. Print the **Deposit Summary Only**.

11. Print **Sales by Customer Summary** for January through February 2011.

12. Print **Sales by Item Summary** for January through February 2011.

13. Create and print customer statements for the period of **February 1, 2011** through **February 28, 2011**. Assess finance charges of **18%**, with a **minimum $5** charge. The assessment date should be **February 28, 2011**. Then print statements for all customers who have a balance due: one for Anderson Weddings for **$195.00** and one for Bob Mason for **$784.13**.

Workplace Applications

Discussion Questions

These questions are designed to stimulate discussion about how you can apply QuickBooks to your own organization. They may help you think through some of the issues you'll encounter when using QuickBooks in your company.

1. What is your organization's return policy? Do you have many customer returns? If you don't have returnable products or services, how does your organization handle dissatisfied customers?
2. Does your organization use its own invoice or sales receipt layout? How does your company's form differ from the Sales Receipt and Invoice forms in QuickBooks? Will your organization continue to use their current forms? If not, how will they change? Will you purchase preprinted forms, or will you use blank paper to print your sales from QuickBooks?

Chapter 4 Managing Expenses

Objectives

After completing this chapter, you should be able to:

- Set up vendors in the Vendor list (page 124).
- Understand how to use classes in QuickBooks (page 130).
- Use QuickBooks for job costing (page 134).
- Enter expense transactions in several different ways (page 134).
- Manage Accounts Payable transactions (page 139).
- Print checks (page 148).
- Void checks (page 152).
- Create and apply vendor credits (page 156).
- Handle deposits and refunds from vendors (page 160).
- Track petty cash (page 165).
- Track credit card charges and payments (page 166).
- Create reports about vendor transactions (page 169).
- Track Loans using the QuickBooks Loan Manager (page 171).

Restore this File

This chapter uses Expenses-10.QBW. To open this file, restore the Expenses-10.QBM file to your hard disk. See page 10 for instructions on restoring files.

In this chapter, we will discuss several ways to track your company's expenditures and vendors. We will start by adding vendors to your file, and then discuss several methods of paying them. In addition, this chapter shows you how to track expenses by job.

Entering Expenses in QuickBooks

QuickBooks provides several tools to help you track and manage the expenses in your business. These tools allow you to track your expenses in detail so that you can create extensive reports that help you manage your vendor relationships and control the costs in your business.

The Process of Entering Expenses in QuickBooks

The *Vendors* section of the *Home* page window provides you with a graphical flow of the steps involved in managing vendors, purchases, and payments (see Figure 4-1). The QuickBooks Coach tips clearly display this workflow. See page 30 for more about the QuickBooks Coach.

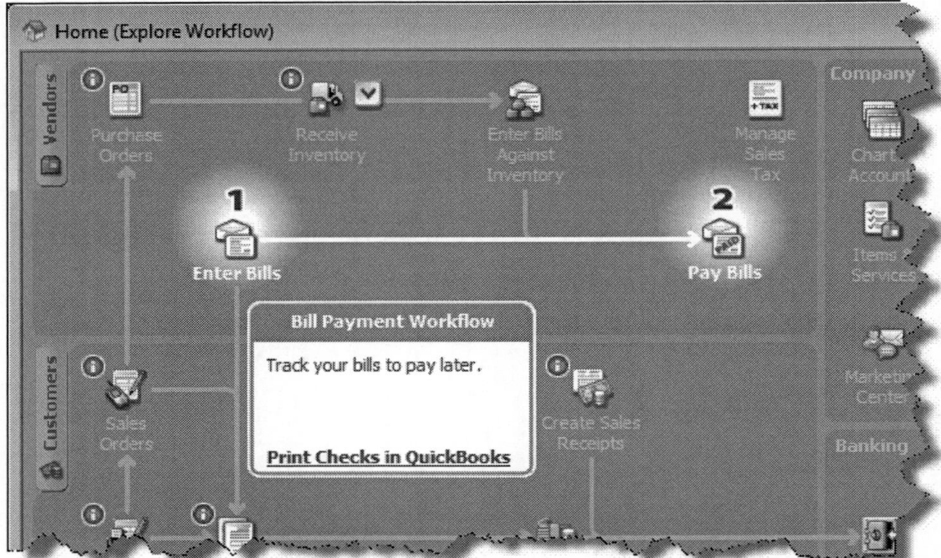

Figure 4-1 QuickBooks Home page

Clicking the *Vendors* icon on the *Home* page displays the **Vendor Center** (see Figure 4-2). The Vendor Center displays information about all of your vendors and their transactions in a single place. You can add a new vendor, add a transaction to an existing vendor, or print the vendor list or transaction list.

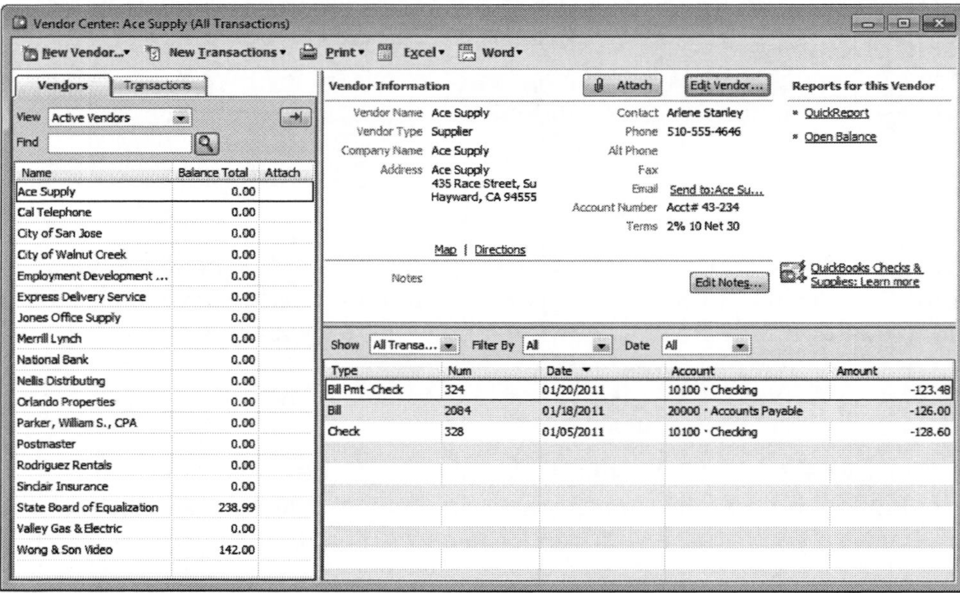

Figure 4-2 Vendor Center

In addition to the Vendor Center, the *Banking* section of the *Home* page contains options to help you navigate making deposits, writing checks, opening a check register, and reconciling with the bank statement. Figure 4-3 displays the *Banking* section of the *Home* page.

Figure 4-3 Banking section of the Home page

Table 4-1 shows many of the business transactions that might occur in dealing with vendors to process expenses in QuickBooks.

For illustrative purposes, we have defined two major groups of Vendors – **Cash Vendors,** and **Credit Vendors.** Table 4-1 shows how to enter transactions for each of these two groups of Vendors. The table also shows what QuickBooks does "behind the scenes" to record these transactions.

For some of vendors, you will decide to track bills and bill payments. This means the Accounts Payable account will be used to track how much you owe these Vendors. We will refer to these as your **Credit Vendors.**

With other Vendors, you will skip the Accounts Payable account and just write checks, coding the checks to the appropriate expense accounts. We will refer to these as your **Cash Vendors.** Although you probably will not pay these vendors with cash, we will use the term **Cash Vendor** to distinguish them from Credit Vendors described previously.

Business Transaction	**Cash Vendors**		**Credit Vendors**	
	QuickBooks Transaction	**Accountin g Entry**	**QuickBooks Transaction**	**Accounting Entry**
Recording a Purchase Order	Not Usually Used		Purchase Orders	Non-posting entry used to track Purchase Orders.
Recording a Bill from a Vendor	Not Usually Used		Enter Bills	Increase (debit) **Expenses,** Increase (credit) **Accounts Payable.**
Paying Bills	Write Checks	Increase (debit) **Expense,** Decrease (credit) **Checking.**	Pay Bills	Decrease (debit) **Accounts Payable,** Decrease (credit) the **Checking Account.**

Table 4-1 Steps for entering expenses

Recording Transactions

The first row in Table 4-1 references **Recording a Purchase Order**. Some vendors require **Purchase Orders** so they can properly process orders. When a Purchase Orders is recorded, no accounting transaction is entered into QuickBooks; rather, a "memo" entry is made to track the Purchase Order. For details on using Purchase Orders, refer to the **Inventory** chapter beginning on page 369.

The second row references **Recording a Bill from a Vendor**. When you receive a bill from a vendor, you will record it using the *Enter Bills* window. Then, when it is time to pay your bills, you will use the *Pay Bills* window in QuickBooks to select the bills you want to pay. As shown below in Figure 4-4, both of these commands are available from the **New Transactions** drop-down menu in the Vendor Center.

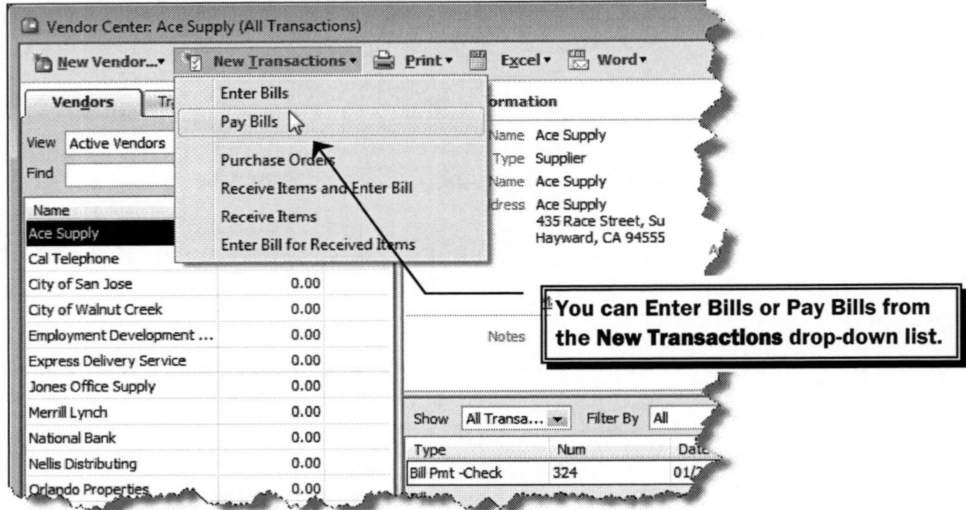

Figure 4-4 New Transactions Menu drop-down list in the Vendor Center

The third row references **Paying Bills**. Sometimes you will need to write a check that is not for the payment of a bill. In that case, you will use the *Write Checks* window. *Write Checks* is accessible by clicking the **Check** icon in the icon bar, the **Write Checks** icon from the *Home* page, the **Write Checks** option from the *Banking* menu, or by pressing **Ctrl+W**.

Setting Up Vendors

Vendors include everyone from whom you purchase products or services, including trade vendors, service vendors, and 1099 contract workers. Before you record any transactions to a Vendor in QuickBooks, you must set them up in the *Vendor Center.*

> **Tip:**
> When a vendor is also a customer, you will need to set up two separate records: a vendor record in the Vendor Center and a customer record in the Customer Center. The customer name must be slightly different from the vendor name. For example, you could enter Boswell Consulting as "Boswell Insulation-V" for the vendor name in the *New Vendor* window, and "Boswell Insulation-C" for the customer name in the *New Customer* window. The contact information for both customer and vendor record can be identical.

To set up a vendor, follow these steps:

COMPUTER PRACTICE

Step 1. To display the *Vendor Center*, select the **Vendors** icon in the Vendors section of the *Home* page (see Figure 4-5). Alternately, click on the **Vendor Center** icon on the Navigation Bar.

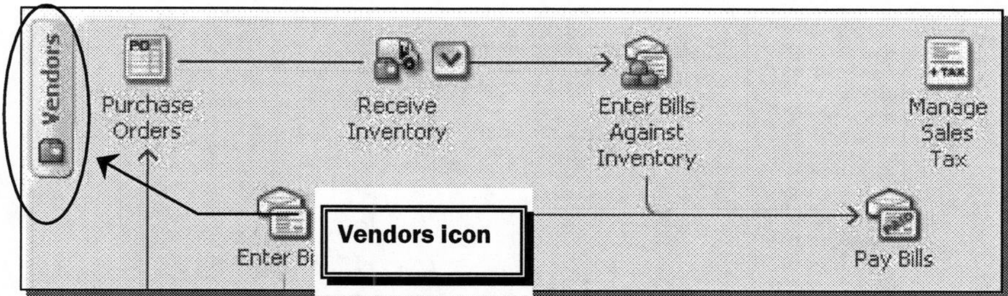

Figure 4-5 Vendors section of the Home page

Step 2. Click **New Vendor** in the *Vendor Center* (see Figure 4-6).

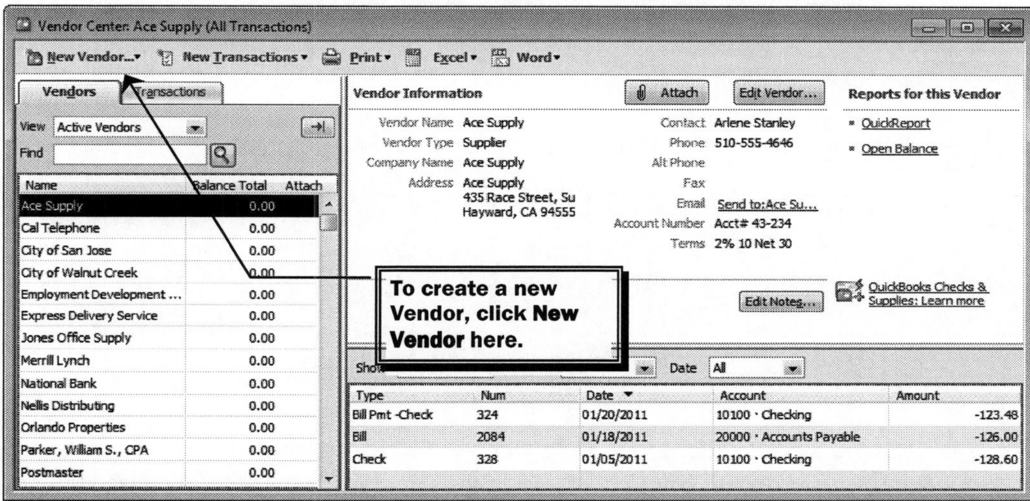

Figure 4-6 Add New Vendor to the Vendor list

Step 3. The *New Vendor* window displays (see Figure 4-7). Notice there are three tabs labeled *Address Info, Additional Info* and *Account Prefill.*

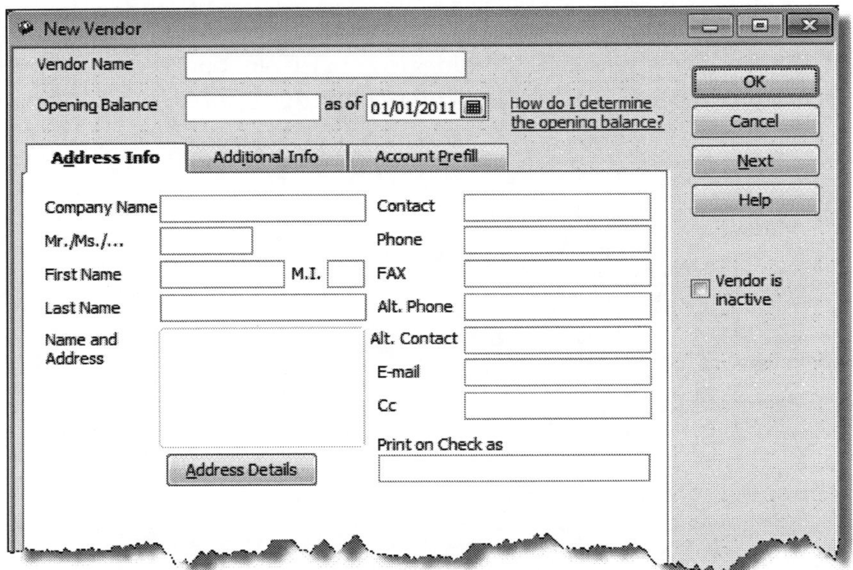

Figure 4-7 The New Vendor window

Step 4. Enter ***Boswell Consulting*** in the *Vendor Name* field and press **Tab**.

> **Tip:**
> The **Vendor** list sorts alphabetically, just like the **Customer** list. Therefore, if your vendor is an individual person, enter the last name first, followed by the first name.

Step 5. Press **Tab** twice to skip the *Opening Balance* and *as of* fields (see Figure 4-8).

The *Opening Balance* field shows only when you create a new *Vendor* record. You will not see this field on the *Edit Vendor* windows. The date in the *as of* field defaults to the current date. Since you will not enter an amount in the *Opening Balance* field there is no need to change this date.

> **Important:**
> It is best *not* to use the *Opening Balance* field in the *New Vendor* window. If you *do* enter an opening balance for a vendor in the *Opening Balance* field, QuickBooks creates a Bill that increases (credits) Accounts Payable, and increases (debits) Uncategorized Expense. Instead, enter each unpaid bill separately after you create the vendor record.

Step 6. Enter ***Boswell Consulting*** in the *Company Name* field and press **Tab**.

Step 7. Continue entering data in the rest of the fields on the Vendor record, as shown in Figure 4-8. Press **Tab** after each entry.

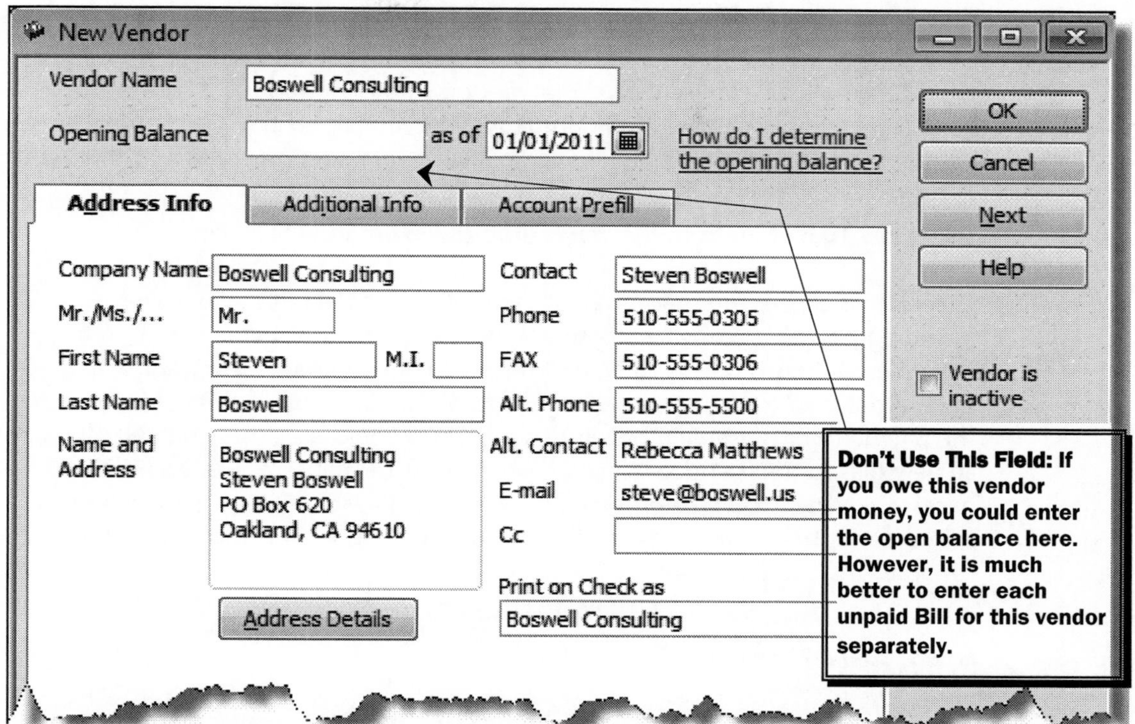

Figure 4-8 New Vendor window after it has been completed

Step 8. Click the **Additional Info** tab to continue entering information about this vendor (see Figure 4-9).

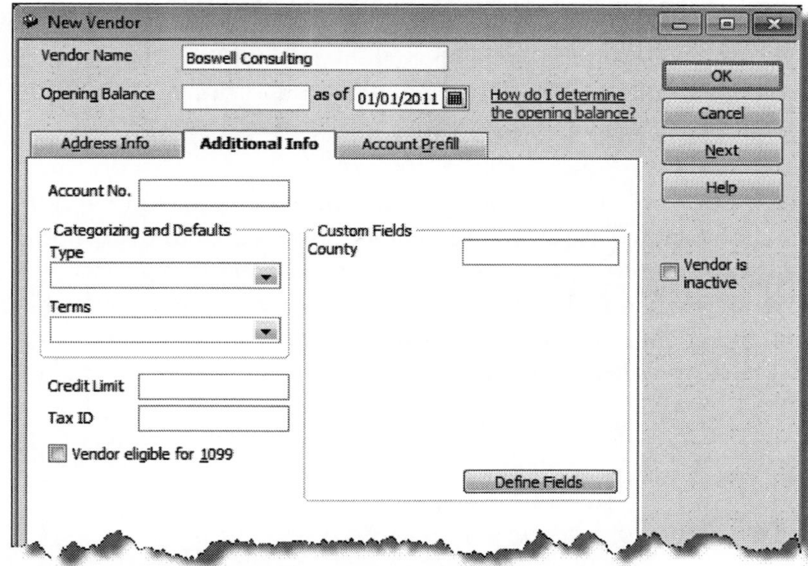

Figure 4-9 The Additional Info tab of the New Vendor window

Step 9. Enter ***66-112*** in the *Account No.* field and press **Tab**.

In this field, enter the number that your vendor uses to track you as a customer. If your vendor requires you to enter your account number on the checks you send, enter it here. QuickBooks prints the contents of this field on the memo of the check when you pay this vendor's bill.

Step 10. Select **Consultant** from the *Type* drop-down list and press **Tab**.

QuickBooks allows you to group your vendors into common types. For example, if you create a Vendor type called *Consultant* and you tag each of your consultants' Vendor records with this type, you could later create a report specific to this Vendor Type.

Step 11. Select **2% 10 Net 30** from the *Terms* drop-down list and press **Tab**.

QuickBooks allows you to establish different types of default payment terms, including payment terms to accommodate discounts for early payment. In this example, the terms of 2% 10 Net 30 means that if you pay this vendor within 10 days of the invoice date, you are eligible for a 2% discount. In this field, you can set the payment terms default for this vendor. QuickBooks uses these default terms on all new bills for this vendor. You can override the default terms on each bill as necessary. When you create reports for Accounts Payable (A/P), QuickBooks takes into account the terms on each bill. To learn more about the Terms list, and how to set up terms, see page 349.

Step 12. Press **Tab** to leave the *Credit Limit* field blank.

Step 13. Enter ***123-12-1234*** in the *TaxID* field.

The *Tax ID* field is where you enter the social security or taxpayer identification number of your Form 1099-MISC recipients. QuickBooks prints this number on the Form 1099-MISC at the end of the year.

Step 14. Check the box next to *Vendor eligible for 1099*.

Select this box for all vendors for whom you expect to file Forms 1099-MISC. See the Customizing chapter (included in the supplemental material for this book explained on page xiii) for more information about tracking and printing Forms 1099-MISC.

Step 15. Enter ***Alameda*** in the *County* field and press **Tab**.

The *County* field is a Custom Field. The **Define Fields** button on the New Vendor Additional Information window allows you to define Custom Fields to track more information about your vendors. In the *County* field, you will tag each vendor with the county in which it is located. This allows you to create reports later that include geographic information about purchases from vendors. For more information on setting up and using custom fields, see page 353.

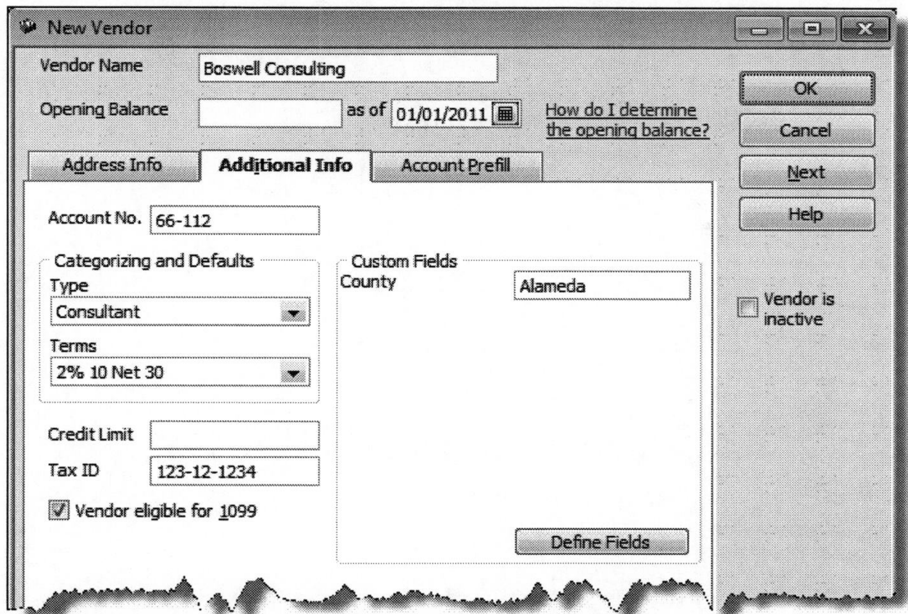

Figure 4-10 The Completed Boswell Consulting Additional Info tab

Step 16. Verify that your screen matches Figure 4-10, and then click the **Account Prefill** tab (see Figure 4-11).

The Account Prefill tab allows you to set a default expense account for future transactions with this vendor.

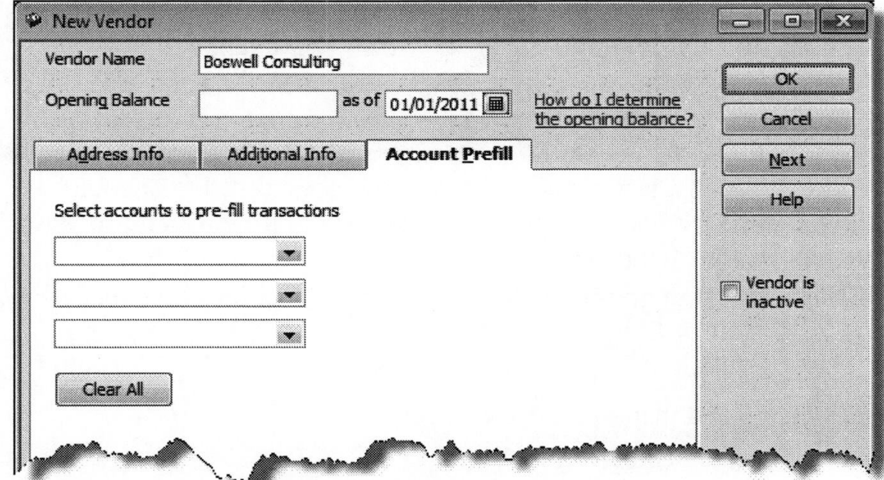

Figure 4-11 The Account Prefill tab of the New Vendor window

Step 17. Select **Professional Fees** from the first *Select accounts to pre-fill transactions* field.

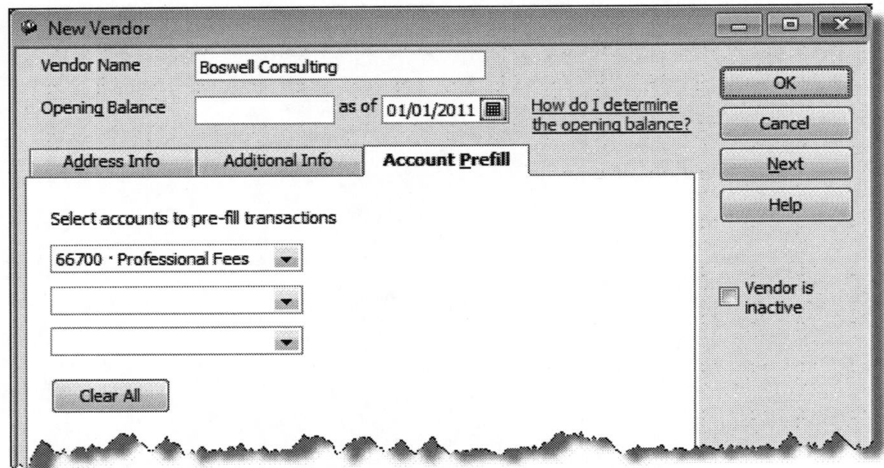

Figure 4-12 The Completed Boswell Consulting Account Prefill tab

Step 18. When finished, click **OK**.

If you were adding several vendors at this time, you would click **Next** instead, and begin adding another vendor. Close the *New Vendor* window.

Activating Class Tracking

In QuickBooks, classes give you a way to segregate your transactions other than by account name. You can use QuickBooks **Classes** to separate your income and expenses by line of business, department, location, profit center, or any other meaningful breakdown of your business. Alternatively, if your business is a not-for-profit organization, you could use Classes to separately track transactions for each *Program* or *Activity* within the organization.

For example, a dentist might classify all income and expenses as relating to either the dentistry or hygiene department. A law firm formed as a partnership might classify all income and expenses according to which partner generated the business. If you use Classes, you'll be able to create separate reports for each Class of the business. Therefore, the dentist could create separate Profit & Loss reports for the dentistry and hygiene departments, and the law firm could create separate reports for each partner.

In our sample company, Academy Photography uses Classes to track income and expenses for each of its stores - San Jose and Walnut Creek.

COMPUTER PRACTICE

Step 1. Select the **Edit** menu, and then select **Preferences.**

Step 2. Select the **Accounting** preference.

Step 3. Select the *Company Preferences* tab, and check the box next to *Use class tracking* (see Figure 4-13). When you use classes on each transaction (Checks, Bills, Invoices, etc.), the **Profit & Loss by Class** report shows the income and expenses for each class.

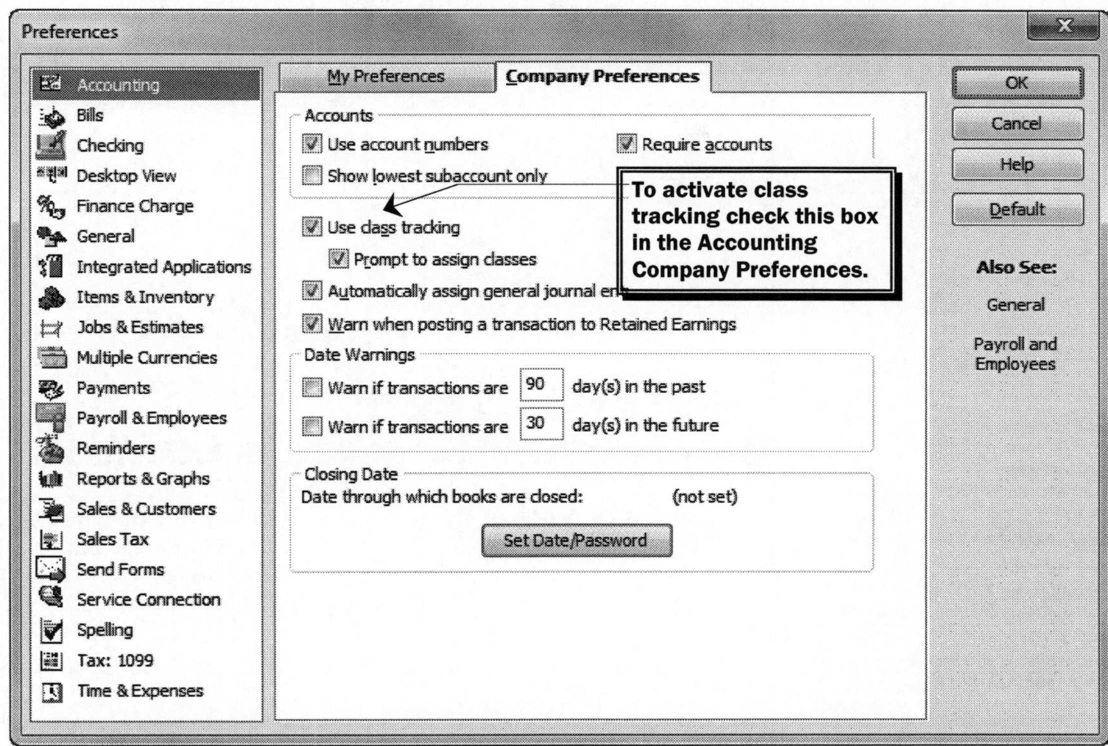

Figure 4-13 Activating class tracking in Accounting preferences

Step 4. The *Prompt to assign classes* field is already checked. Leave the checkmark in this box.

With this setting, QuickBooks prompts you if you fail to assign a Class on any line of the transaction.

Step 5. Click **OK**.

To illustrate class tracking, select **Wong & Son Video** from the *Vendor* list. Select **All** from the Date field drop-down list (scroll the list to the top) and see bill #2342 (see Figure 4-14). Double-click on bill #2342 to display the bill.

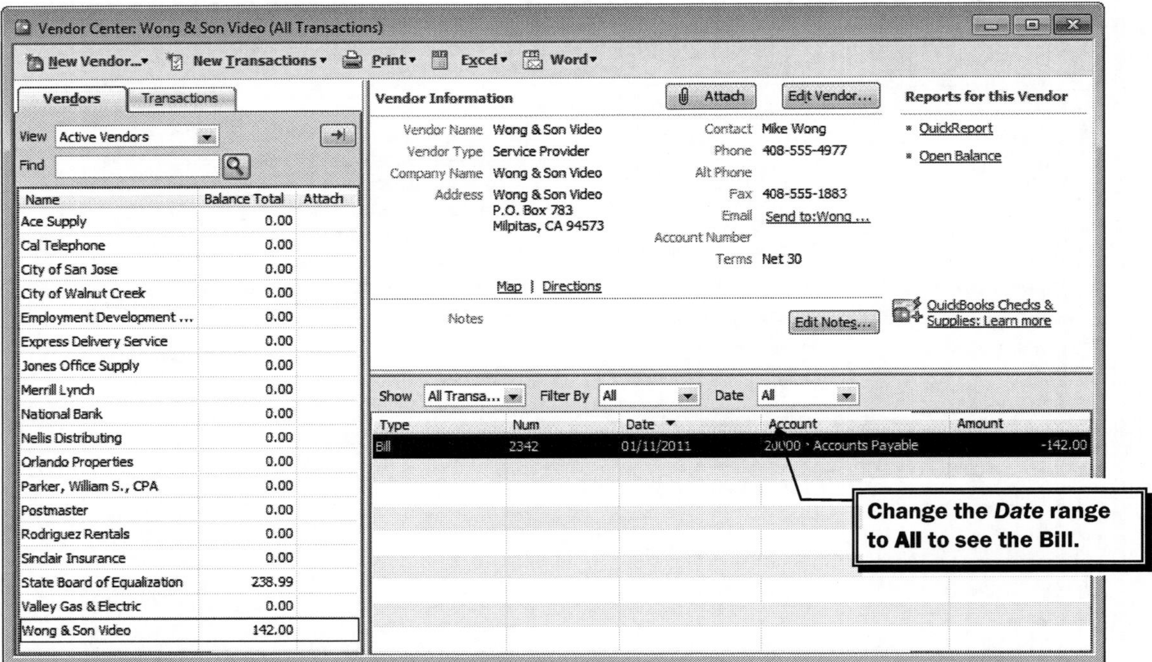

Figure 4-14 Vendor Center with Wong & Son Video displayed

In Figure 4-15, **San Jose** is selected in the *Class*. This tracks the expense to the *San Jose* Class (i.e. the San Jose store) so that the ***Profit & Loss by Class*** report shows the expense under the column for the *San Jose* class. Close the Enter Bills and Vendor Center windows.

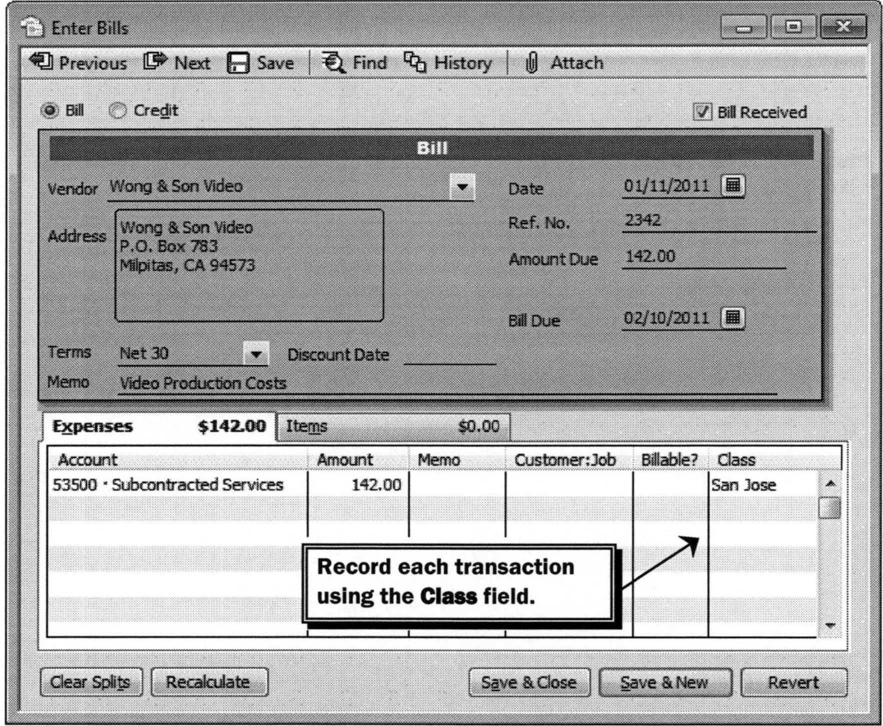

Figure 4-15 The Class field shows on many windows in QuickBooks, including Enter Bills

To view the Profit & Loss by Class report, select the *Reports* menu, then select **Company & Financial**, and then select **Profit & Loss by Class** (see Figure 4-16).

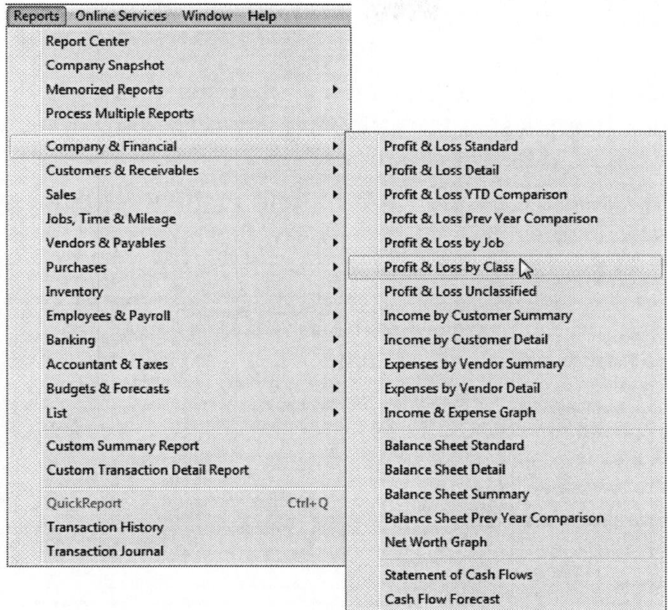

Figure 4-16 Profit & Loss by Class report

Set the *From* and *To* dates to ***01/01/2011*** and ***01/31/2011*** respectively (see Figure 4-17). Close the window after reviewing the report.

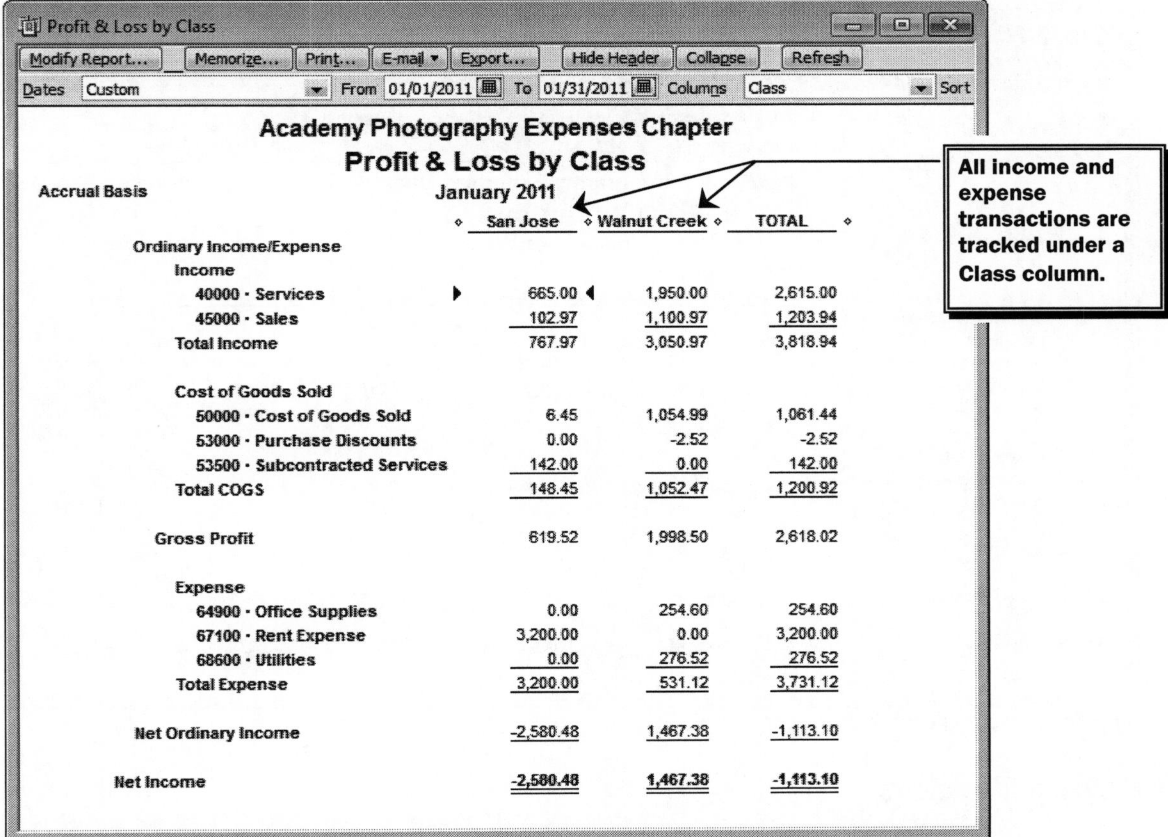

Academy Photography Expenses Chapter
Profit & Loss by Class
Accrual Basis — January 2011

	San Jose	Walnut Creek	TOTAL
Ordinary Income/Expense			
Income			
40000 · Services	665.00	1,950.00	2,615.00
45000 · Sales	102.97	1,100.97	1,203.94
Total Income	767.97	3,050.97	3,818.94
Cost of Goods Sold			
50000 · Cost of Goods Sold	6.45	1,054.99	1,061.44
53000 · Purchase Discounts	0.00	-2.52	-2.52
53500 · Subcontracted Services	142.00	0.00	142.00
Total COGS	148.45	1,052.47	1,200.92
Gross Profit	619.52	1,998.50	2,618.02
Expense			
64900 · Office Supplies	0.00	254.60	254.60
67100 · Rent Expense	3,200.00	0.00	3,200.00
68600 · Utilities	0.00	276.52	276.52
Total Expense	3,200.00	531.12	3,731.12
Net Ordinary Income	-2,580.48	1,467.38	-1,113.10
Net Income	-2,580.48	1,467.38	-1,113.10

Figure 4-17 Profit & Loss by Class report

Tracking Job Costs

If you want to track the expenses for each customer or job (i.e., track job costs), link each expense with the customer or job to which it applies. In the following sections, you will learn about recording expense transactions in several different situations.

When you record an expense transaction, use the **Customer:Job** column to link each expense account or Item with a customer or job (see Figure 4-18).

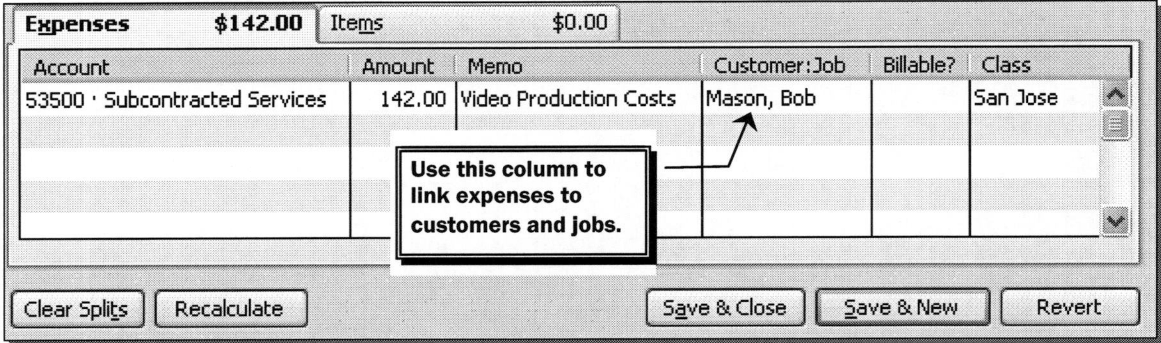

Figure 4-18 Linking expenses to customers and job (i.e. job costing)

When you track job costs, you can create reports such as the **Profit & Loss by Job** report that shows income and expenses separately for each job (see Figure 4-19). From the *Report* menu, select **Company & Financial** and then select **Profit & Loss by Job**. Set the *From* and *To* dates to ***01/01/2011*** and ***01/31/2011*** respectively. Close the window after reviewing the report.

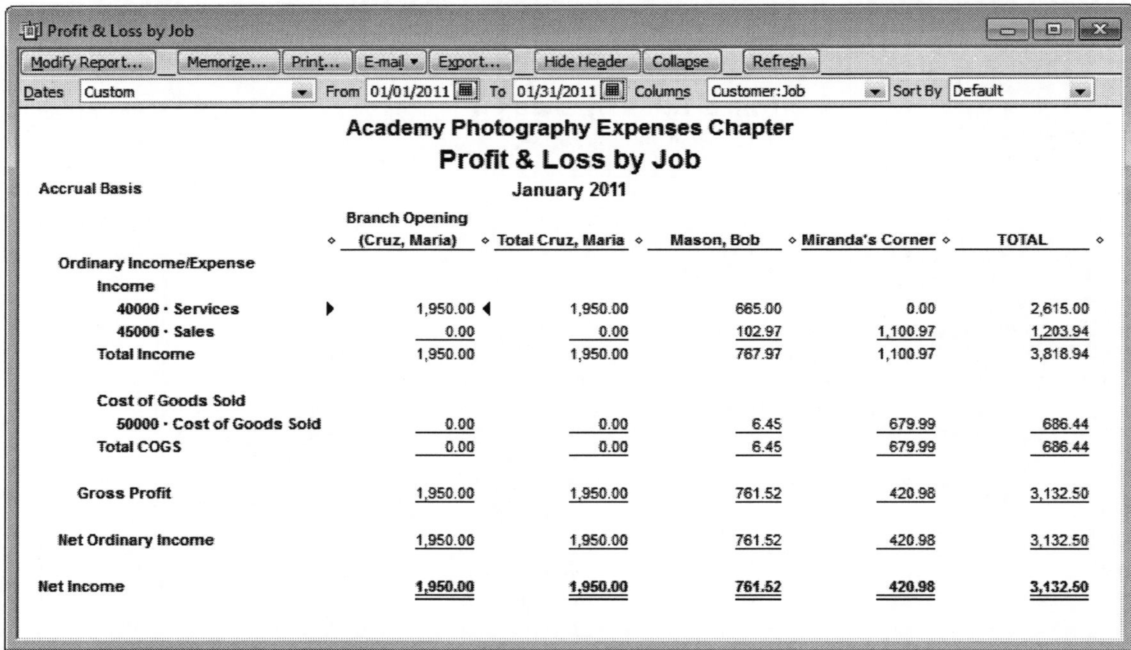

Profit & Loss by Job

Modify Report... Memorize... Print... E-mail Export... Hide Header Collapse Refresh

Dates Custom From 01/01/2011 To 01/31/2011 Columns Customer:Job Sort By Default

Academy Photography Expenses Chapter

Profit & Loss by Job

Accrual Basis

January 2011

	Branch Opening (Cruz, Maria)	Total Cruz, Maria	Mason, Bob	Miranda's Corner	TOTAL
Ordinary Income/Expense					
Income					
40000 · Services	1,950.00	1,950.00	665.00	0.00	2,615.00
45000 · Sales	0.00	0.00	102.97	1,100.97	1,203.94
Total Income	1,950.00	1,950.00	767.97	1,100.97	3,818.94
Cost of Goods Sold					
50000 · Cost of Goods Sold	0.00	0.00	6.45	679.99	686.44
Total COGS	0.00	0.00	6.45	679.99	686.44
Gross Profit	1,950.00	1,950.00	761.52	420.98	3,132.50
Net Ordinary Income	1,950.00	1,950.00	761.52	420.98	3,132.50
Net Income	1,950.00	1,950.00	761.52	420.98	3,132.50

Figure 4-19 Profit & Loss by Job report

Paying Vendors

With QuickBooks, you can pay your vendors in several ways. You can pay by check, credit card, electronic funds transfer, or, though not recommended, cash.

Most of the time, you'll pay your vendors from a checking account, so this section covers three different situations for recording payments out of your checking account. The three situations are:

- Manually writing a check or initiating an electronic funds transfer and recording the transaction in a QuickBooks account register.
- Using the *Write Checks* function to record and print checks.
- Recording Accounts Payable bills through the *Enter Bills* window and using the *Pay Bills* function to pay these bills.

Using Registers

In this example, you will manually write a check and then record the transaction in the QuickBooks *Checking* account register.

COMPUTER PRACTICE

After you have written a manual check, or made a payment made by electronic funds transfer, you will record the transaction in QuickBooks.

Step 1. Select the **Check Register** icon from the *Home* page. Alternatively, key **Ctrl+R** on your keyboard.

Step 2. In the *Use Register* dialog box, make sure **Checking** displays in the *Select Account* field and click **OK** (see Figure 4-20).

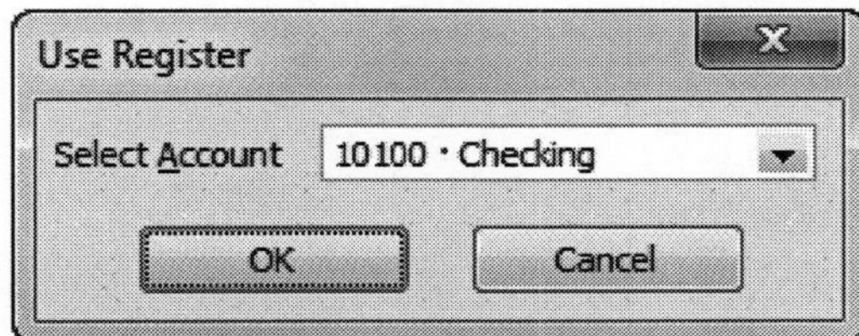

Figure 4-20 Use Register dialog box

Step 3. Enter ***02/05/2011*** in the first empty line of *Date* column and press **Tab** (see Figure 4-21).

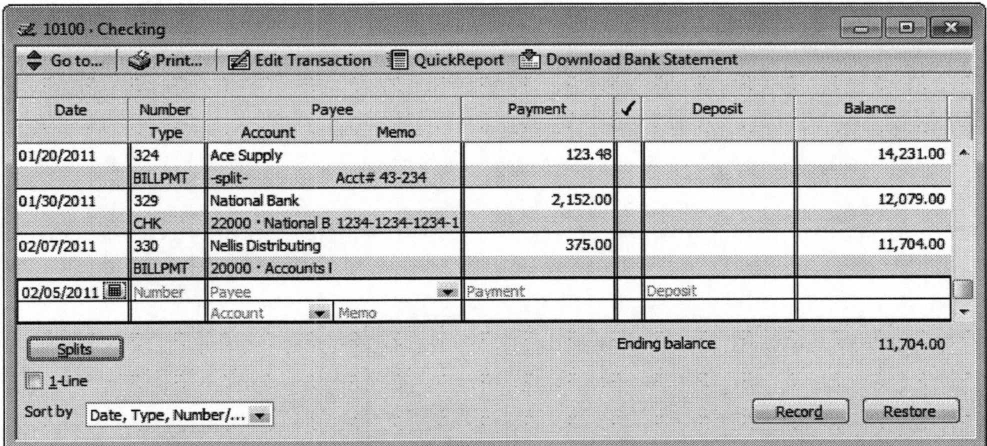

Figure 4-21 Entering in manual check information

Step 4. Enter ***331*** in the *Number* column and press **Tab**.

If you are entering a previously handwritten check, make sure this number matches the number on the physical check. If you are entering an electronic funds transfer or an ATM withdrawal, enter ***EFT*** in the check number field.

Step 5. Enter ***Bay Office Supply*** in the *Payee* column and press **Tab**.

Since ***Bay Office Supply*** is not in the *Vendor List*, QuickBooks prompts you to *Quick Add* or *Set Up* the Vendor (see Figure 4-22). Click **Quick Add** on the *Name Not Found* dialog box.

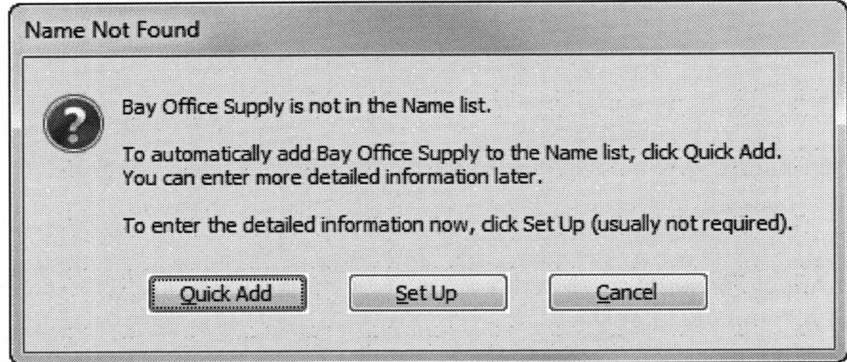

Figure 4-22 Name Not Found dialog box

Step 6. Clicking **Quick Add** will add this Vendor without entering the address and other information to completely set up the vendor. You can always go back later and add the other information by editing the Vendor record. Click **OK** on the *Select Name Type* dialog box to add Bay Office Supply to the *Vendor Center* (see Figure 4-23).

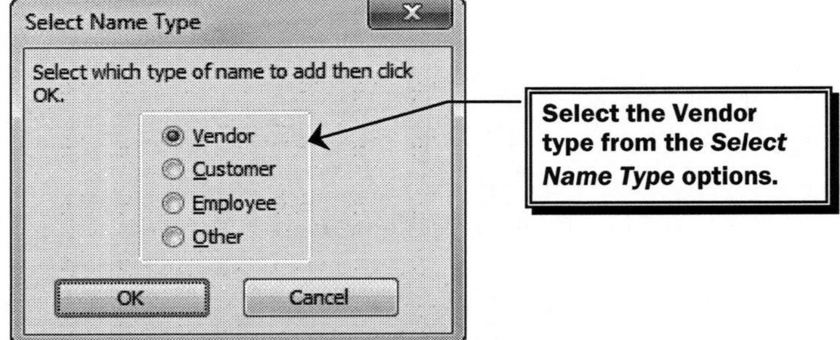

Figure 4-23 Select Name Type options - choose Vendor

Step 7. Enter ***128.60*** in the *Payment* column and press **Tab**.

Step 8. Enter ***Office Supplies*** in the *Account* column and press **Tab**.

After you enter the first few characters of the word "**Office**" in the *Account* field, notice that QuickBooks automatically fills in the rest of the field with "Office Supplies." This QuickFill feature helps you to enter data faster.

Step 9. Enter ***Printer Paper*** in the **Memo** column.

Step 10. Verify that you've entered all of the fields in the transaction correctly, and click **Record** to save the transaction (see Figure 4-24). If the Set Check Reminder dialog box opens, click **Cancel**.

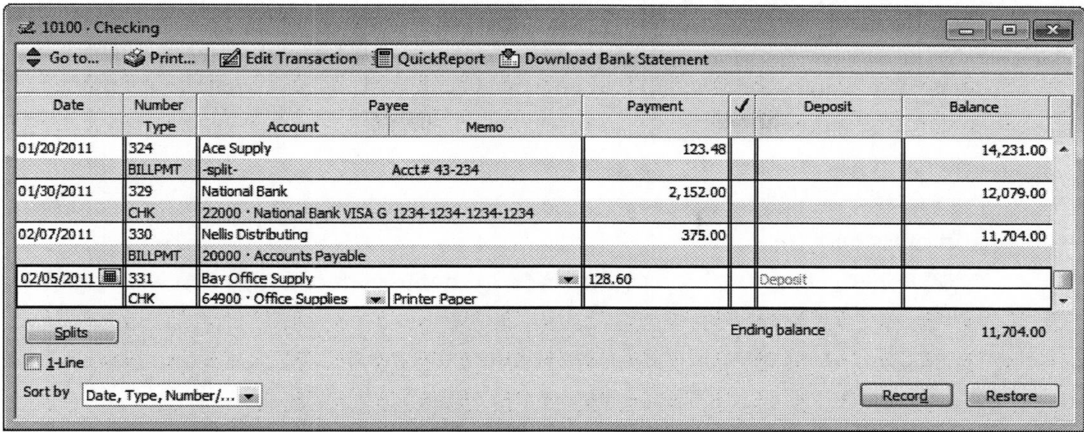

Figure 4-24 Bay Office Supply enter in the Checkbook register

Notice that QuickBooks automatically updates your account balance after you record the transaction.

Splitting Transactions

Sometimes you will need to split your purchase to more than one account. Let's say that the check you just wrote to Bay Office Supply was actually for the following expenses:

- $100.00 for printer paper, to be used in the San Jose store (Class).
- $28.60 for computer cables for the Walnut Creek store (Class).

In order to track your printing costs separately from your office supplies, you must *split* the expenses and assign each expense to a separate account.

COMPUTER PRACTICE

Step 1. With the *Checking* register open, click on check #**331** to select it.

Step 2. Click the **Splits** button as highlighted in Figure 4-25.

QuickBooks displays an area below the check where you can add several lines, memos, and amounts for *splitting* the expenses among multiple accounts.

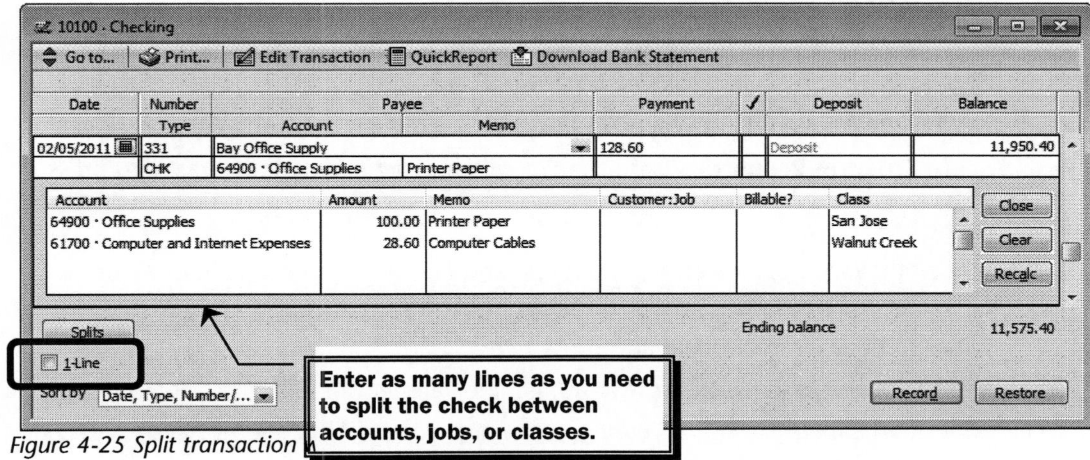

Figure 4-25 Split transaction

Step 3. Change the amount on the first line from ***128.60*** to ***100.00***. Then press **Tab**.

Step 4. Enter ***Printer Paper*** in the *Memo* column and press **Tab**.

Step 5. Skip the *Customer:Job* column by pressing **Tab**.

This is the column where you can enter the customer or job name where this expense should apply.

Step 6. Enter ***San Jose*** in the *Class* column and press **Tab**.

Step 7. On the second line, enter ***Computer and Internet Expenses*** in the *Account* column and press **Tab**.

Step 8. QuickBooks calculates the amount **28.60** in the *Amount* column. This is correct so press **Tab** to leave it and move to the next field.

Step 9. Enter ***Computer Cables*** in the *Memo* column and press **Tab**.

Step 10. Press **Tab** to skip to the **Class** column and enter ***Walnut Creek***.

Step 11. Verify that your screen matches Figure 4-25, and then press **Record**.

Step 12. QuickBooks displays a dialog box asking if you want to record the changes to the previously recorded transaction. Click **Yes**.

Step 13. Close the *Checking* register.

Using Write Checks Without Using Accounts Payable

If you are tracking job costs or classes and are not using the Accounts Payable feature, it may be best to use the *Write Checks* window to record your expenses. If you use Items to track purchases and you are not using the Accounts Payable feature, you *must* use either *Write Checks* or the *Enter Credit Card Charges* window. See page 166 for more information about tracking credit cards.

COMPUTER PRACTICE

Step 1. To display the *Write Checks* window, click on the **Write Checks** icon on the *Home* page. Alternatively, press **Ctrl+W**.

Step 2. **Checking** in the *Bank Account* field is already selected. Press **Tab**.

Step 3. Enter ***To Print*** in the *No.* field and press **Tab**. Alternately, click the **To be printed** box to the right of the *Items* tab.

This indicates that you want QuickBooks to print this check on your printer. When you print the check, QuickBooks will assign the next check number in the sequence of your checks.

Step 4. ***02/05/2011*** is already displayed in the *Date* field. Press **Tab**.

Step 5. Select **Orlando Properties** from the *Pay to the Order of* drop-down list and press **Tab**.

Notice that QuickBooks enters the name and address from the Vendor record as soon as you choose the Vendor name from the list.

Step 6. Enter ***3,200.00*** in the *$* field and press **Tab**.

Step 7. Press **Tab** to skip the Address, Memo, Online Payment, and To be printed fields.

Step 8. Enter ***Rent Expense*** in the *Account* column of the Expenses tab if not already selected and press **Tab**.

If necessary, when you enter your own expenses, use the bottom part of the check to split the payment between several different accounts, jobs, and classes.

Step 9. Leave the *Amount* column set to ***3,200.00*** and press **Tab**.

Step 10. Enter ***San Jose Rent*** in the *Memo* column, and press **Tab** twice.

Step 11. Enter ***San Jose*** in the *Class* column.

Step 12. Verify that your screen matches Figure 4-26. Do not print the check now; we will print it later.

Step 13. Click **Save & Close** to record the transaction.

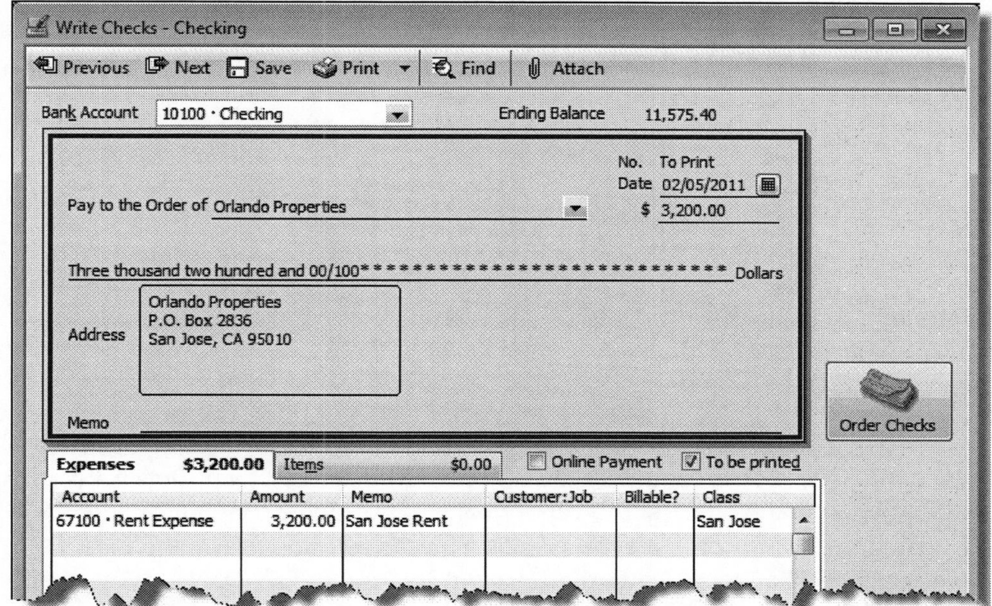

Figure 4-26 Write Checks window for Orlando Properties rent payment

> **Note:**
> In the example above, you recorded the check with a **To be printed** status, so that you can print it later, perhaps in a batch with other checks. If you wanted to print the check immediately after you entered it, you would have clicked **Print** at the top of the *Write Checks* window. QuickBooks would ask you to enter the check number.

Managing Accounts Payable

You can also use QuickBooks to track Accounts Payable.

When you receive a bill from a vendor, enter it into QuickBooks using the *Enter Bills* window. Recording a bill allows QuickBooks to track the amount you owe to the vendor along with the detail of what you purchased. For a bill to be considered paid by QuickBooks, you must pay it using the *Pay Bills* window, as discussed here.

Entering Bills

When a bill arrives from your vendor, enter it into QuickBooks using the *Enter Bills* window.

COMPUTER PRACTICE

Step 1. Select the **Vendors** icon from the *Home* page to display the Vendor Center. Select the vendor, **Ace Supply**, and then select **Enter Bills** from the *New Transactions* drop-down list (see Figure 4-27). Alternatively, you can click the **Enter Bills** icon on the *Home* page and select **Ace Supply** from the Vendor drop-down field.

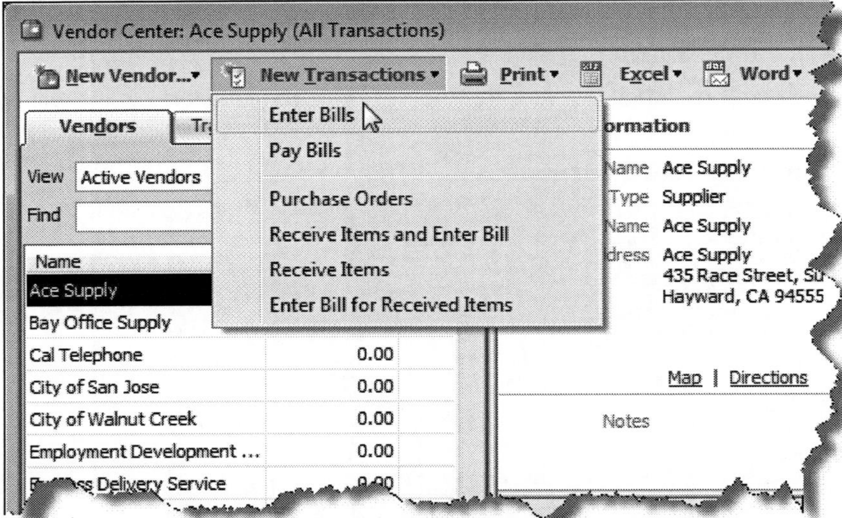

Figure 4-27 Selecting Enter Bills from the New Transaction drop-down list

Step 2. Verify that Ace Supply is displayed in the *Vendor* field and press **Tab**.

Notice that QuickBooks completes the *Bill Due, Terms,* and *Discount Date* fields automatically when you enter the Vendor name. QuickBooks uses information from the Vendor record to complete these fields. You can override this information if necessary. QuickBooks calculates the *Discount Date* and the *Bill Due* fields by adding the terms information to the date entered in the *Date* field. If the terms do not include a discount, the *Discount Date* will not appear.

Step 3. Enter ***02/05/2011*** in the *Date* field and press **Tab**.

Step 4. Enter ***2085*** in the *Ref. No.* field and press **Tab**.

> **Tip:**
> When an A/P transaction increases what we owe, we call it a "bill." However, our vendors call them "invoices." Therefore, the *Ref. No.* field should match the number on the invoice you received from the vendor. The *Ref. No.* field is important for two reasons. First, it is the number used to identify this bill in the *Pay Bills* window, and second, it is the number that shows on the voucher of the *Bill Payment* check.

Step 5. Enter ***360.00*** in the *Amount Due* field and press **Tab**.

Step 6. Press **Tab** to skip the *Bill Due* field and to accept the due date that QuickBooks has calculated.

Step 7. Press **Tab** to accept the **2% 10 Net 30** terms already selected.

Step 8. Enter Photo Materials for Jerry Perez job in the Memo field and press Tab.

> **Important:**
> If your vendor requires you to enter your account number on the checks you send, enter it in the **Acct#** field in the Vendor record. QuickBooks will print the contents of that field on bill payments to the vendor. If you enter a memo in this field on the Bill, it will override the Account # field in the Vendor record.

Step 9. Enter ***Cost of Goods Sold*** in the *Account* column of the *Expenses* tab and press **Tab**.

Step 10. Press **Tab** to accept ***360.00*** already entered in the *Amount* column.

Step 11. Enter ***Photo Materials*** in the *Memo* column and press **Tab.**

Step 12. To job cost this purchase, enter ***Perez, Jerry*** in the *Customer:Job* column and press **Tab.**

Step 13. Enter ***Walnut Creek*** in the *Class* column.

Step 14. Verify that your screen matches that shown in Figure 4-28. Click **Save & Close** to record the **Bill**. Close the **Vendor Center** window.

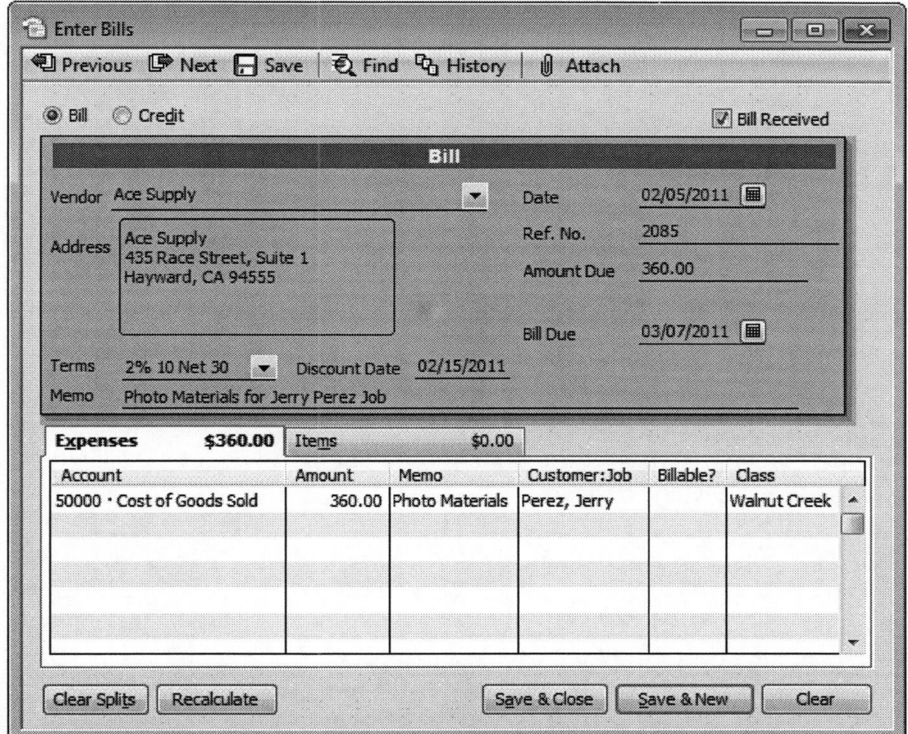

Figure 4-28 Recording Ace Supply bill

The Unpaid Bills Detail Report

To view a list of your unpaid bills, use the *Unpaid Bills Detail* report.

COMPUTER PRACTICE

Step 1. From the *Reports* menu, select **Vendors & Payables** and then select **Unpaid Bills Detail** (see Figure 4-29).

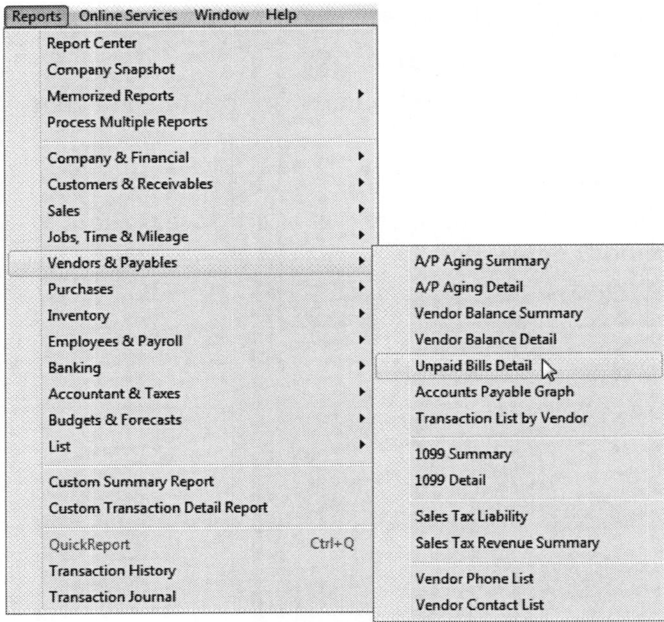

Figure 4-29 Selecting the Unpaid Bill Detail report

Step 2. Enter ***02/10/2011*** in the *Date* field and press **Tab**.

Step 3. Verify that your screen matches Figure 4-30. Close the report window. Click **No**, if the *Memorize Report* message appears.

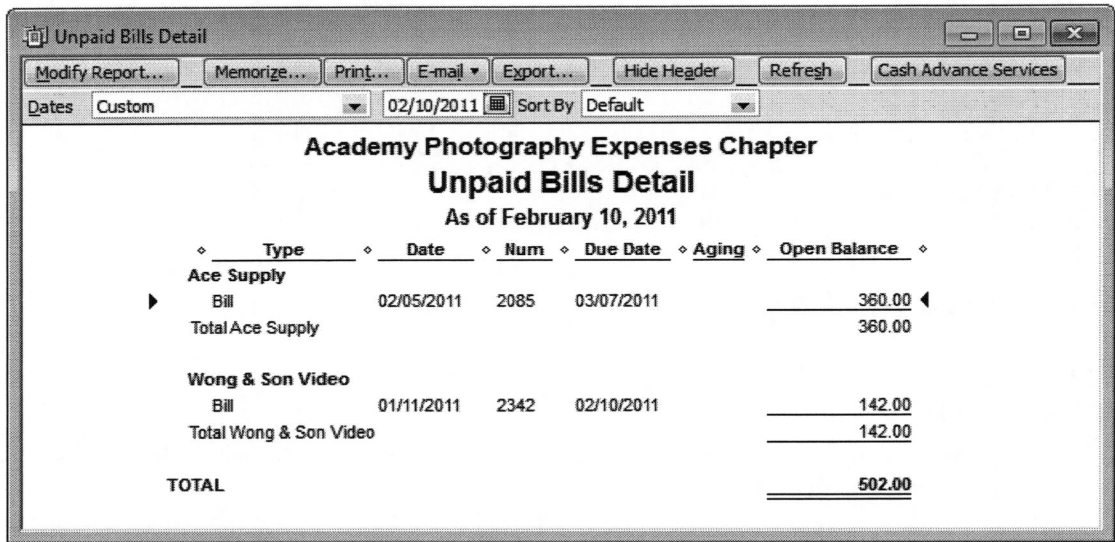

Type	Date	Num	Due Date	Aging	Open Balance
Ace Supply					
Bill	02/05/2011	2085	03/07/2011		360.00
Total Ace Supply					360.00
Wong & Son Video					
Bill	01/11/2011	2342	02/10/2011		142.00
Total Wong & Son Video					142.00
TOTAL					502.00

Figure 4-30 Unpaid Bills Detail report

Paying Bills

QuickBooks keeps track of all your bills in the Accounts Payable account. When you pay your bills, you will reduce the balance in Accounts Payable by creating Bill Payment checks.

COMPUTER PRACTICE

Step 1. Select the **Vendors** icon from the *Home* page to display the **Vendor Center**. Select **Pay Bills** from the *New Transactions* drop-down list (see Figure 4-31). You *do not* need to select a vendor first. Alternatively, you can click the **Pay Bills** icon on the *Home* page.

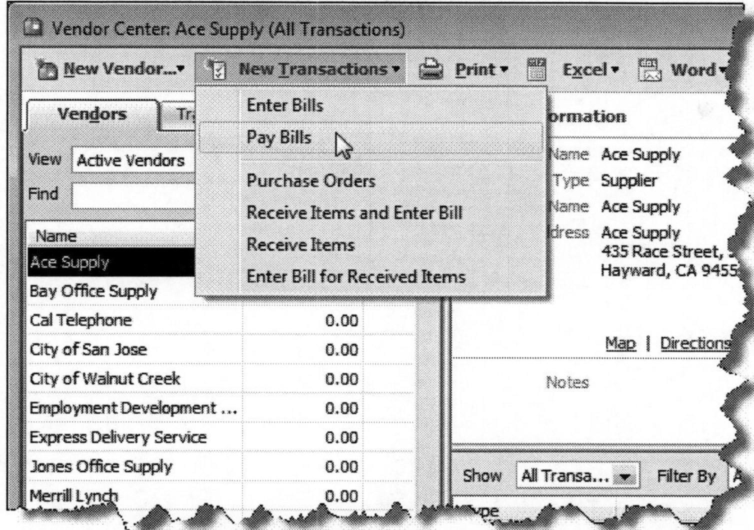

Figure 4-31 Selecting Pay Bills from the New Transaction drop-down list

Step 2. QuickBooks displays the *Pay Bills* window.

Step 3. Click on the radio button *Due on or before* and enter ***03/10/2011*** in the *Due on or before* date field (see Figure 4-32). QuickBooks allows you to filter the *Pay Bills* window so only the bills due on or before a given date are shown.

> **Note:**
> The *Due on or before* field applies only to the bill due date. There is no way to show only the bills whose *discounts* expire on or before a certain date. However, you can sort the list of bills by the discount dates in the *Pay Bills* window by selecting **Discount Date** from the *Sort Bills by* drop-down list.

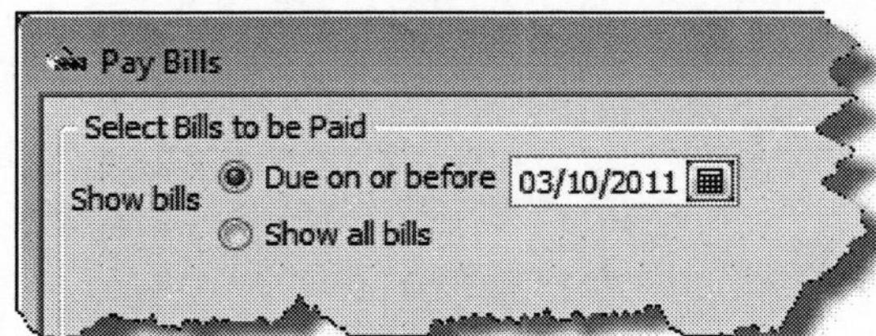

Figure 4-32 Entering the date in the Due on or before field

Step 4. As shown Figure 4-33, *Filter By* is set to **All Vendors**. You can filter the *Pay Bills* window to only show specific vendors. Also, **Due Date** is already selected from the *Sort Bills By* drop-down list. If you have several bills from the same vendor, it is sometimes easier to see all of the bills sorted by **Vendor**. You can also sort the bills by **Discount Date** or **Amount Due**.

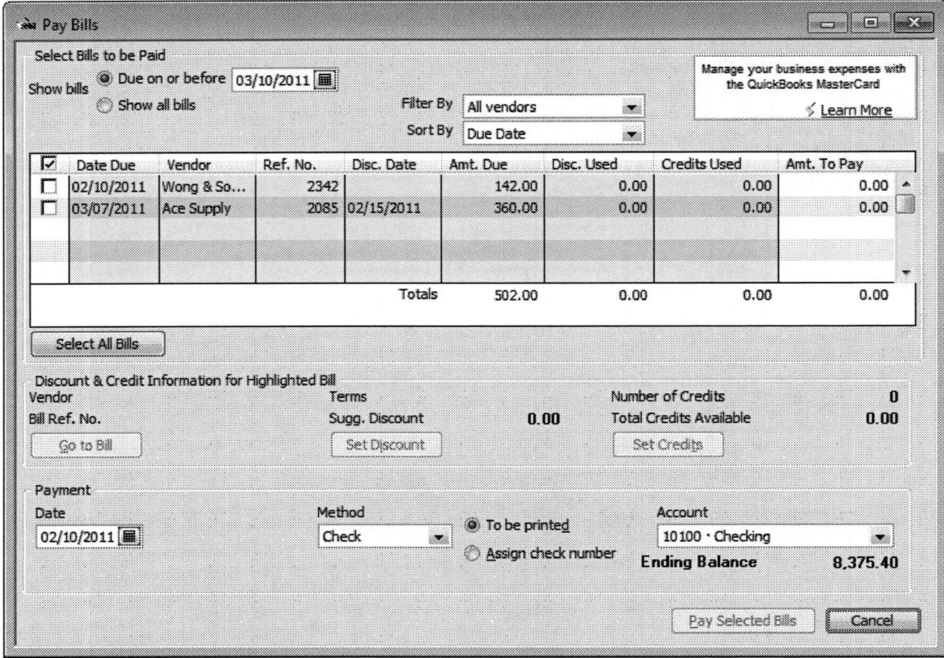

Figure 4-33 Pay Bills window

Step 5. Leave ***Check*** in the *Payment Method* field selected. Ensure that the *To be printed* radio button is selected.

Step 6. Leave **Checking** in the *Payment Account* field.

> **Note:**
> The *Payment Method* field allows you to choose to pay the bills by check or credit card. If you pay by check, QuickBooks automatically creates a check in your Checking account for each bill selected for payment. To pay by credit card, select **Credit Card** and select the name of the credit card you want to use for the bill payments. QuickBooks will then create a separate credit card charge for each bill payment.

Step 7. Enter **02/10/2011** in the Payment Date field.

Step 8. Click the **Select All Bills** button at the bottom to select all both bills displayed. Alternately, place a checkmark in front of the bills you want to pay.

> **Tip:**
> If you want to display the original bill, select the bill on the *Pay Bills* window and click **Go to Bill**. This displays the original bill so you can edit it if necessary.
>
> If you want to make a partial payment on a bill, enter only the amount you want to pay in the *Amt. To Pay* column. If you pay less than the full amount due, QuickBooks will track the remaining amount due for that bill in Accounts Payable. The next time you go to the *Pay Bills* window, the partially paid bills will show with the remaining amount due.

Step 9. To record a discount on the Ace Supply bill, click on the bill to select it. Notice the **Discount & Credit Information for Highlighted Bill** section (see Figure 4-34). Notice that QuickBooks displays the terms and a suggested discount for the bill.

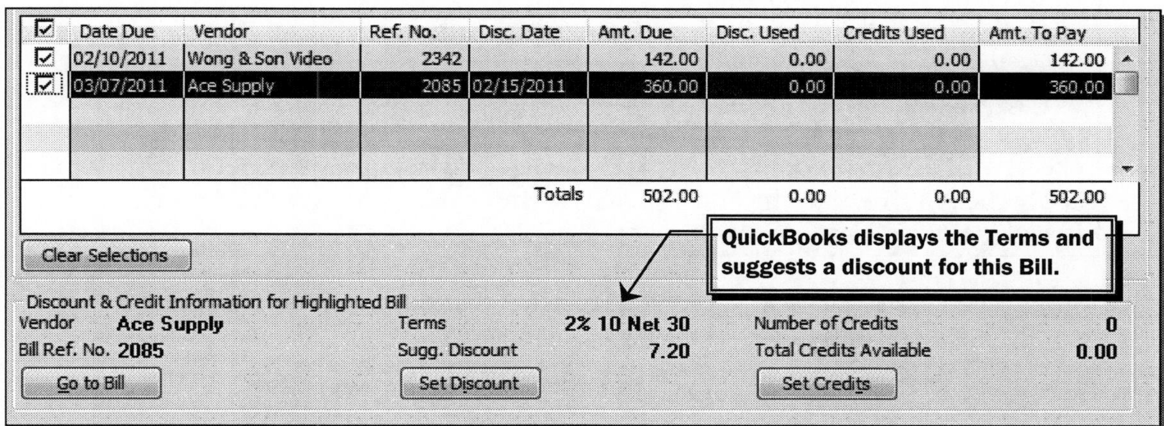

Figure 4-34 Discount section for Ace Supply bill

Step 10. Click **Set Discount**.

In the *Discounts and Credits* window, notice that QuickBooks calculates the discount according to the terms set on the Bill (see Figure 4-35). In this case, the terms are *2% 10 Net 30*.

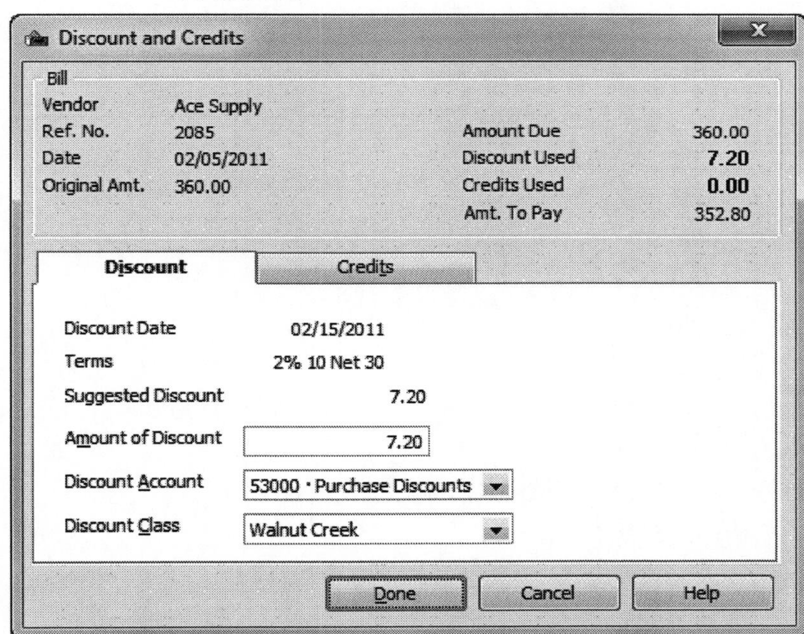

Figure 4-35 Discount and Credits window

Step 11. Select **Purchase Discounts** in the *Discount Account* field to assign this discount to the proper account.

Step 12. Enter ***Walnut Creek*** in the *Class* field to assign this discount to the proper class.

Refer to the Bill to determine the class. The bill being discounted was originally assigned to the *Walnut Creek* class so the discount should use that class as well.

Step 13. Click **Done**. This returns you to the *Pay Bills* window.

> **Note:**
> In some cases, it is better to use a Bill Credit instead of a discount. For example, when you want to associate the discount with a job, or if you want to track discount items, use Bill Credits instead of using discounts in the *Pay Bills* process. You can record items, accounts, classes, and job information on the Bill Credit, just as you do on Bills. Then, in the *Pay Bills* window, click **Set Credits** to apply the Bill Credit to the Bill. To see how this would work, see the section on *Applying Vendor Credits* beginning on page 156.

Step 14. Verify that your *Pay Bills* window matches that shown in Figure 4-36. Click **Pay Selected Bills** to record the Bill Payments.

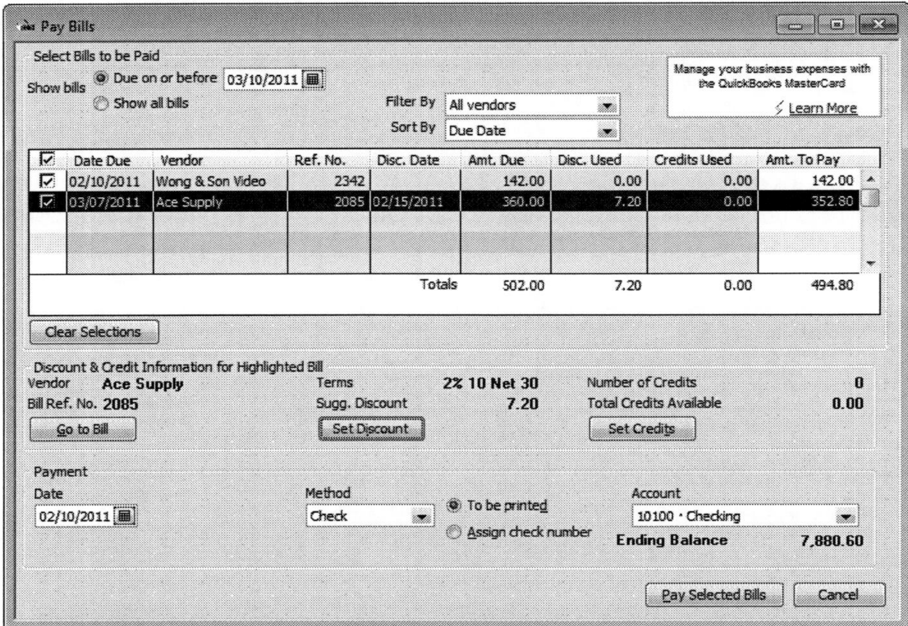

Figure 4-36 Pay Bills window after setting the discount

Step 15. QuickBooks displays a *Payment* Summary dialog box as shown in Figure 4-37. Review the payments and click **Done**.

Step 16. Close all windows except for the *Home* page.

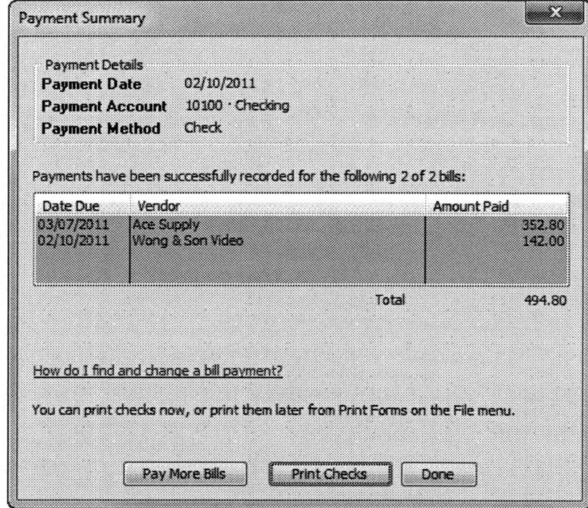

Figure 4-37 Payment Summary dialog box

> **Note:**
> If you select more than one Bill for the same vendor, QuickBooks combines all of the amounts onto a single Bill Payment.

When you use a check to pay bills, QuickBooks records each Bill Payment in the Checking account register and in the Accounts Payable account register (see Figure 4-38 and Figure 4-39). Bill Payments *reduce* the balance in both the Checking account and the Accounts Payable account.

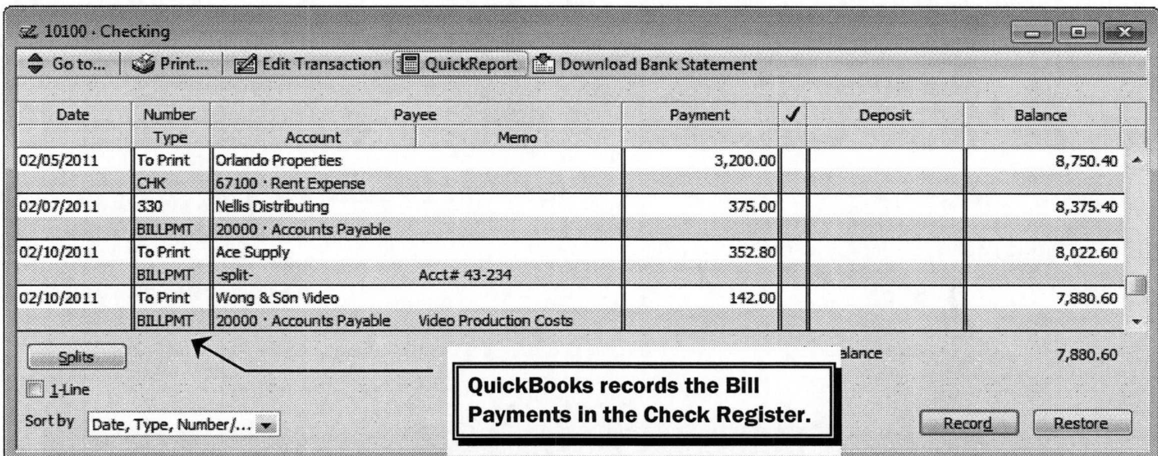

Figure 4-38 Checking account register after Bill Pay

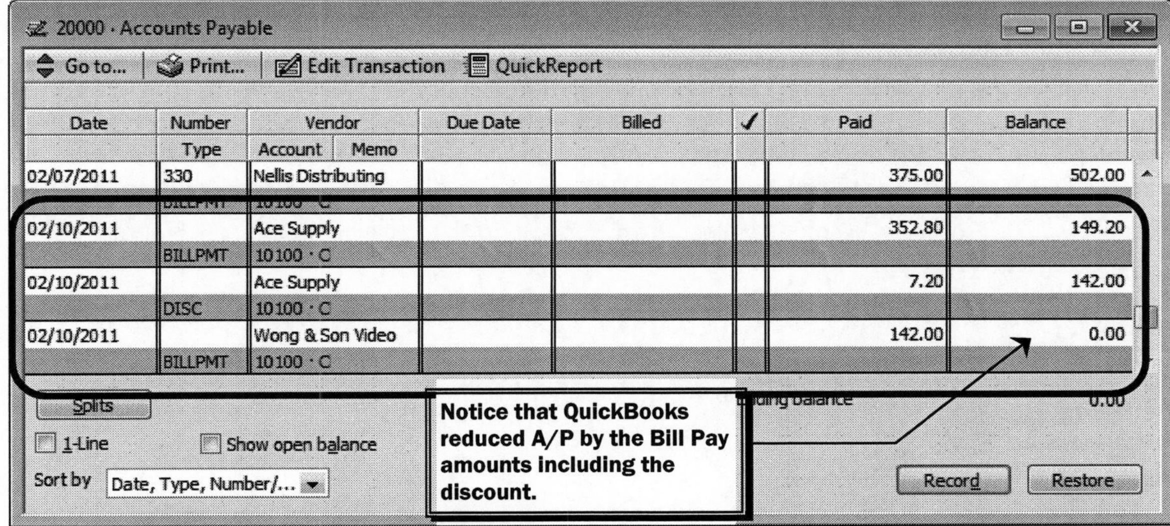

Figure 4-39 Accounts Payable register after Bill Pay

Printer Setup

Before printing checks for the first time, you'll need to configure your printer settings.

COMPUTER PRACTICE

Step 1. Select the **File** menu and then select **Printer Setup**. The *Printer Setup* window displays.

Step 2. Select **Check/PayCheck** from the *Form Name* drop-down list.

Step 3. In the *Printer Setup* window you will indicate the type of printer and checks you have. Most businesses should use voucher checks. You will need to order preprinted checks from Intuit or from another vendor that supplies QuickBooks-compatible checks. The appearance of the window in Figure 4-40 will vary depending on your printer. Select the settings you want for your checks and then click **OK**.

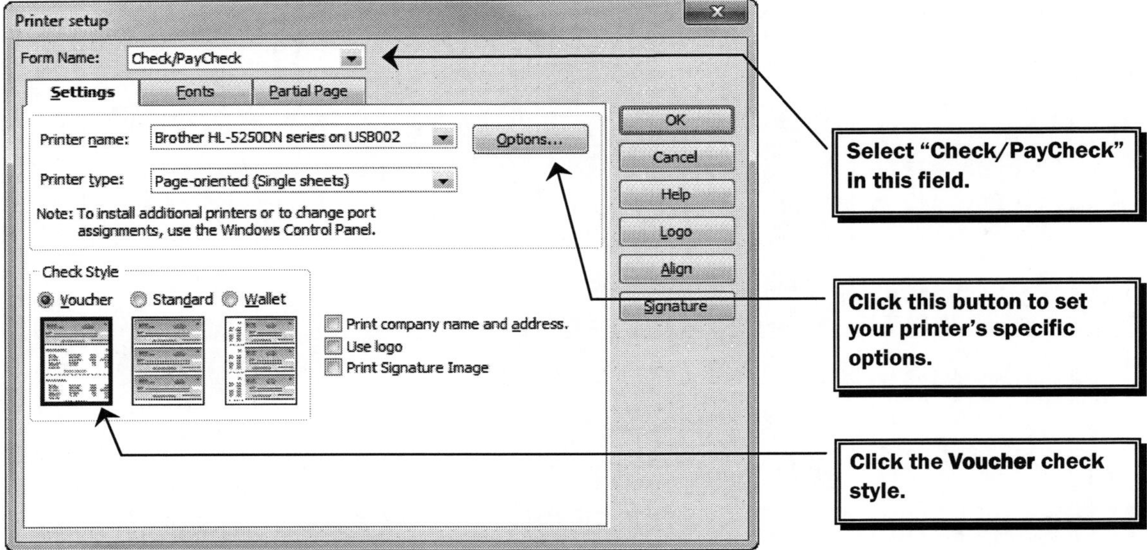

Figure 4-40 Printer setup window

Printing Checks

COMPUTER PRACTICE

You do not need to print each check or bill payment separately. As you write checks and pay bills, you have the option to record each check with a *To be Printed* status. Follow these steps to print checks and bill payments that you have previously recorded with a *To be Printed* status:

Step 1. From the *File* menu, select **Print Forms** and then select **Checks** (see Figure 4-41).

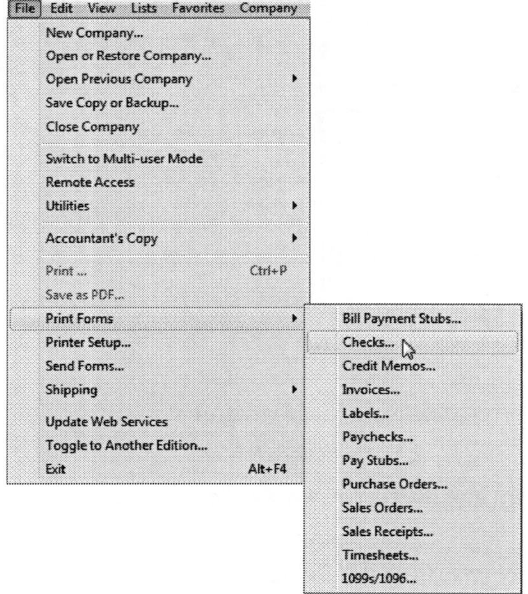

Figure 4-41 Menu selection to print checks

Step 2. **Checking** in the *Bank Account* field is already selected (see Figure 4-42). This is the bank account on which the checks are written. Press **Tab**.

Step 3. Enter ***6001*** in the *First Check Number* field, if necessary.

The *First Check Number* field is where you set the number of the first check you put in the printer.

> **Note:**
> QuickBooks assigns check numbers when it prints checks. You have the opportunity to set the check number just before you print the checks and after you assign a check number. QuickBooks keeps track of each check it prints and keeps the check number up to date.

Step 4. QuickBooks automatically selects all of the checks for printing. Click **OK**.

To prevent one or more checks from printing, you can click in the left column to remove the checkmark for each check you don't want to print.

Since we did not print the rent check, it shows in Figure 4-42 along with the two Bill Payments. We will include it here so we can "batch print" all checks together.

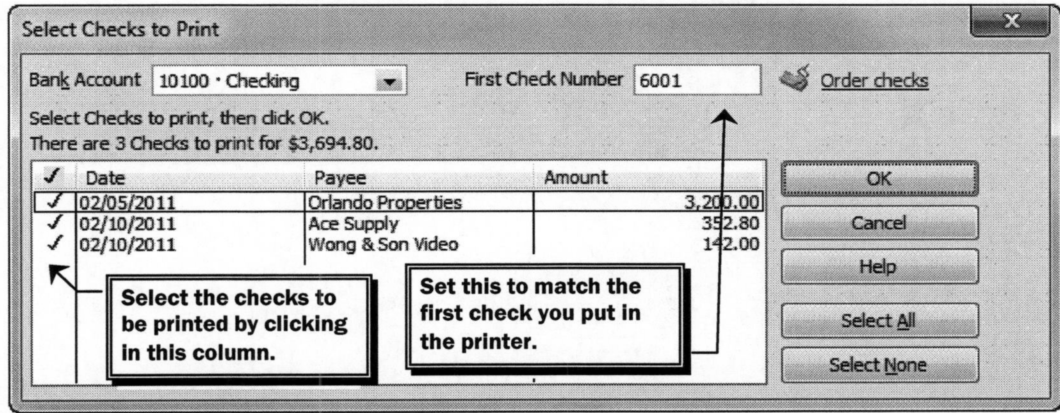

Figure 4-42 Select Checks to Print window

Step 5. When the *Print Checks* window displays, click **Signature** on the right side of the window (see Figure 4-43).

You can automatically print singed checks by uploading a graphic file of a signature during the printing process.

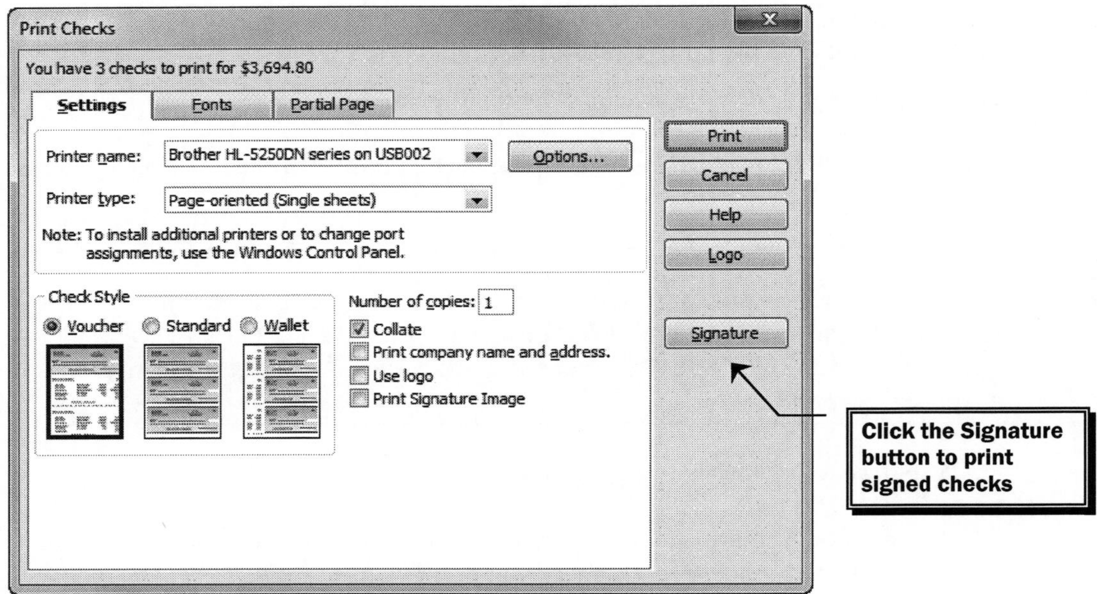

Figure 4-43 Signature Button in Print Checks window

Step 6. In the *Signature* window, click the **File** button to upload the graphic file (see Figure 4-44).

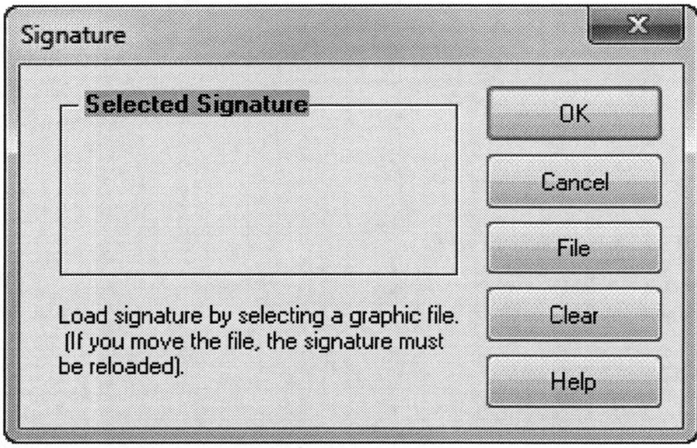

Figure 4-44 Signature window

Step 7. In the *Open File* window, navigate to where you store your exercise files and open **Sign.png**.

Step 8. If QuickBooks displays a warning window, click **OK**. QuickBooks will copy the image file to a new folder called *Expenses-10 – Images.*

Step 9. The *Signature* window now displays an image of the uploaded signature file (see Figure 4-45). Click **OK**.

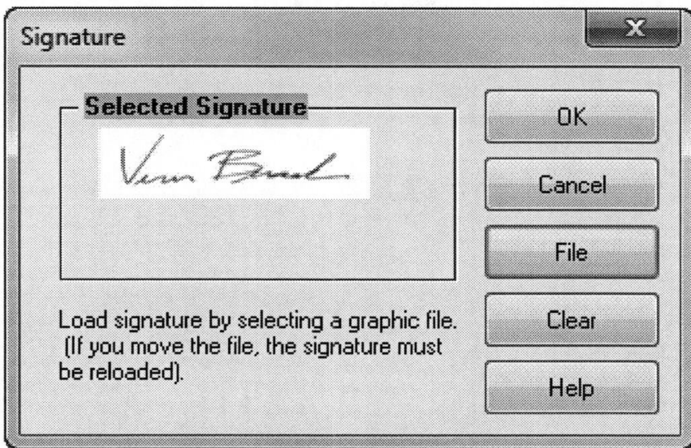

Figure 4-45 Signature window with file uploaded

Note:
Once you select the signature, QuickBooks will leave the box checked to always print the signature unless you uncheck the *Print Signature Image* shown in Figure 4-46.

Step 10. Confirm your printer settings on the *Print Checks* window (see Figure 4-46), and click **Print** when you are ready to print. Your **Printer name** will most likely be different than what is displayed in Figure 4-46.

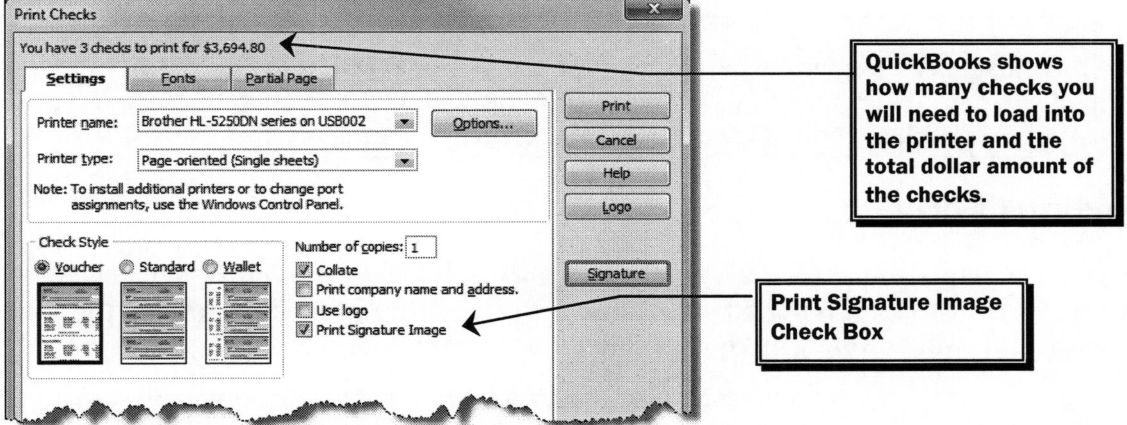

Figure 4-46 Print Checks window

Tip:
Make sure your checks are oriented correctly in the printer. With some printers, you feed the top of the page in first, and some you feed in bottom first. With some printers, you must insert the check face up, and with others, face down.

Step 11. When QuickBooks has finished printing the checks, you will see the *Print Checks – Confirmation* dialog box in Figure 4-47.

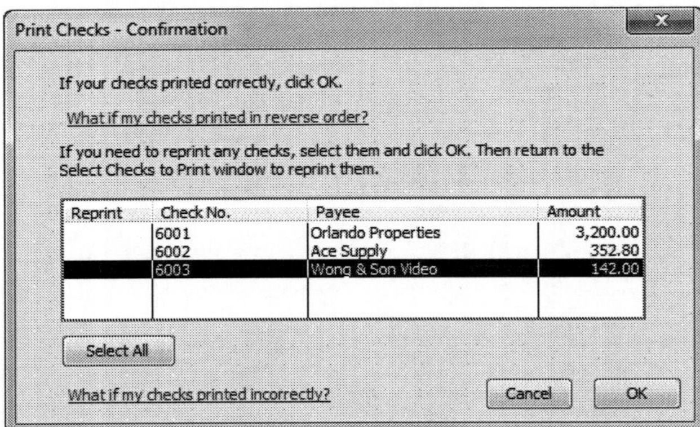

Figure 4-47 Print Checks - Confirmation dialog box

Step 12. If the Set Check Reminder dialog box opens, click **Cancel**.

Step 13. Click **OK**.

> **Note:**
> If your printer damages your checks and you selected checks for reprinting, you will need to re-enter and void each damaged check in the bank account register or on the *Write Checks* window.

> Tip:
> If you are paying multiple bills on a single check and you want the vendor to be able to identify these bills, you can print a *Bill Payment Stub* by choosing **Bill Payment Stub** from the *Print Forms* submenu on the *File* menu.

Voiding Checks

QuickBooks allows you to keep the information about voided checks so that you retain a record of these checks. It is important to enter each check into your register even if the check is voided. This will prevent gaps in your check number sequence.

> **Did You Know?**
> QuickBooks has a special report called Missing Checks that allows you to view all of your checks sorted by check number. The report highlights any gaps in the check number sequence. To view this report, select the *Reports* menu, then select **Banking**, and then select **Missing Checks**.

COMPUTER PRACTICE

Step 1. Open the Checking account register and then select check 6003 by clicking anywhere on that record. You will be able to tell that the record has been selected as it will be outlined in the register.

Step 2. From the *Edit* menu select **Void Bill Pmt-Check** (see Figure 4-48).

When you void a check, QuickBooks changes the amount to zero, marks the check cleared, and adds **VOID** to the *Memo* field.

Step 3. Click **Record** to save your changes.

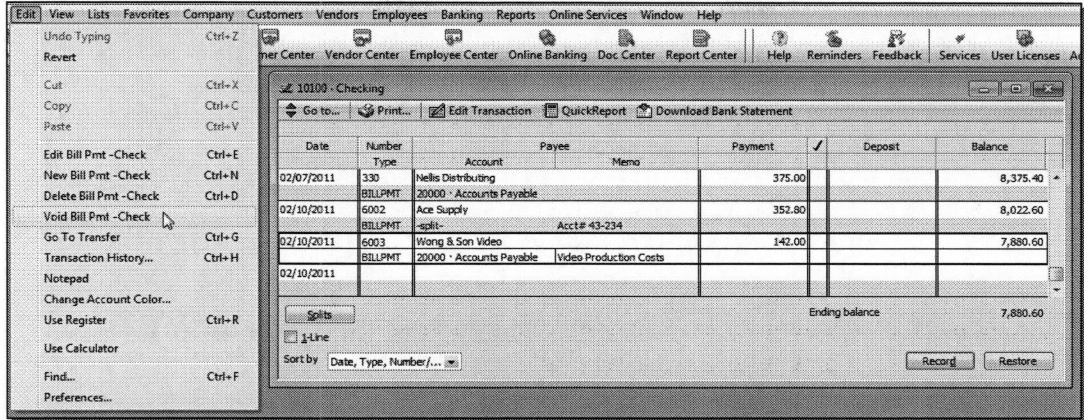

Figure 4-48 Voiding a check from the Edit menu

Since you are voiding a Bill Payment, QuickBooks warns you that this change will affect the application of this check to the Bills (see Figure 4-49). In other words, voiding a **Bill Payment** will make the **Bill** payable again.

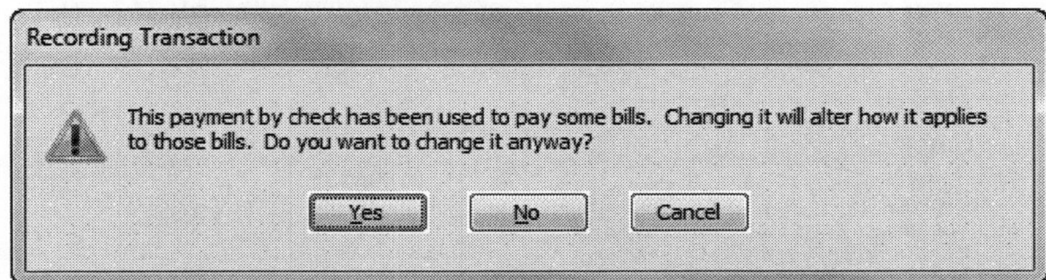

Figure 4-49 Recording Transaction dialog box about voiding BILLPMT check 6003

Step 4. Click **Yes.**

Notice that the transaction shows as cleared in the register, and that QuickBooks set the amount of the check to zero (see Figure 4-50).

Step 5. Close all open windows except the *Home* page.

10100 · Checking

Go to... | Print... | Edit Transaction | QuickReport | Download Bank Statement

Date	Number / Type	Payee / Account	Memo	Payment	✓	Deposit	Balance
02/05/2011	6001	Orlando Properties		3,200.00			8,750.40
	CHK	67100 · Rent Expense					
02/07/2011	330	Nellis Distributing		375.00			8,375.40
	BILLPMT	20000 · Accounts Payable					
02/10/2011	6002	Ace Supply		352.80			8,022.60
	BILLPMT	-split-	Acct# 43-234				
02/10/2011	6003	Wong & Son Video		0.00	✓		8,022.60
	BILLPMT	20000 · Accounts Payable	VOID: Video Production Costs				

Splits | Ending balance 8,022.60

1-Line

Sort by Date, Type, Number/... | Record | Restore

Figure 4-50 Check register after voided transaction

To repay the Bill, repeat the bill paying, discount, and printing process by following the steps below.

COMPUTER PRACTICE

Step 1. Select the **Pay Bills** icon on the *Home* page.

Step 2. Complete the *Pay Bills* window for the **Wong & Son Video** bill per the instructions given in the **Paying Bills** section beginning on page 142. Verify that your screen matches Figure 4-51. Set the Payment Date to ***02/16/2011***.

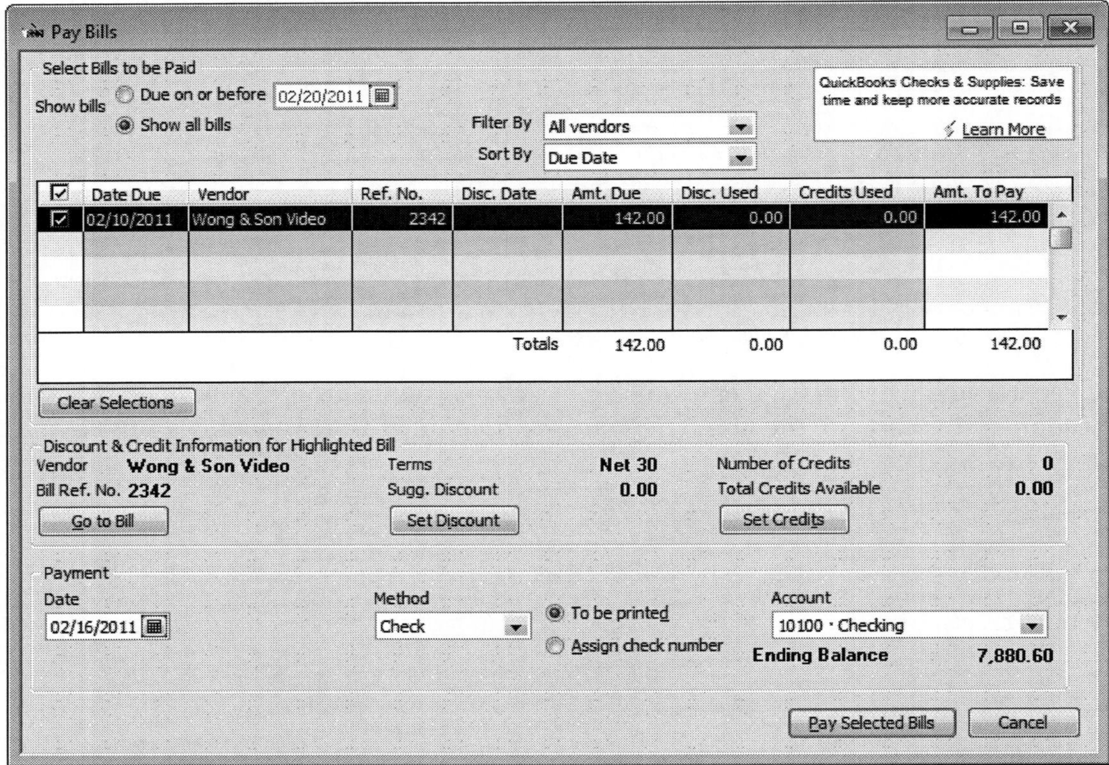

Figure 4-51 Completed Pay Bills window

Step 3. Click **Pay Selected Bills** on the *Pay Bills* window to record the bill payment.

Step 4. Click **Done** on the Payment Summary dialog box.

Step 5. To print the new Bill Payment check, select the *File* menu, select **Print Forms**, and then select **Checks**.

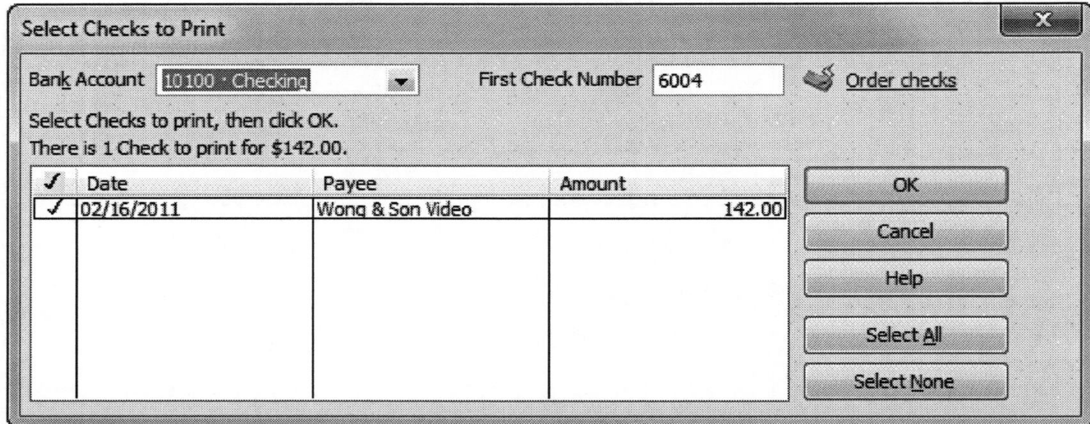

Figure 4-52 Select Checks to Print window for Ace Supply bill

Step 6. Click **OK** on the *Select Checks to Print* window (see Figure 4-52).

Step 7. Click **Print** to print the check.

Step 8. Click **OK** in the *Print Checks – Confirmation* dialog box.

Attaching Documents

The Sleeter Group has long advocated both doing transactions and keeping documents electronically. Going "paperless" greatly increases efficiency and eliminates costly storage of paper documentation.

QuickBooks 2010 allows you to attach electronic documents to QuickBooks transactions, such as bills, invoices and other QuickBooks forms. The attached documents are stored on a secure server managed by Intuit using QuickBooks Document Management. At the time of this writing, up to 100 MB of storage is available for free, and a tiered monthly fee is required for larger amounts of storage.

DO NOT COMPLETE THESE STEPS. THEY ARE FOR REFERENCE ONLY.

1. From the *Home* page, select **Enter Bills.**
2. Open the desired QuickBooks form (such as a bill).
3. Click the **Attach** button (see Figure 4-53).

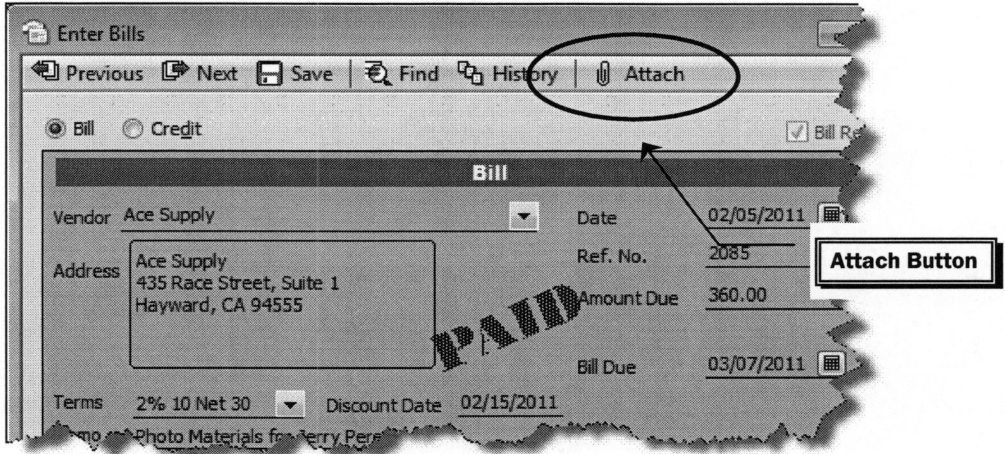

Figure 4-53 Attach button in Enter Bills window

4. The *QuickBooks Document Management* window opens. You will need to sign in or create a Document Management account.
5. After logging in, the *Attachments* window opens (see Figure 4-54). From this window, you can scan documents, open files on your local desktop or use the Intuit Online Document Inbox.

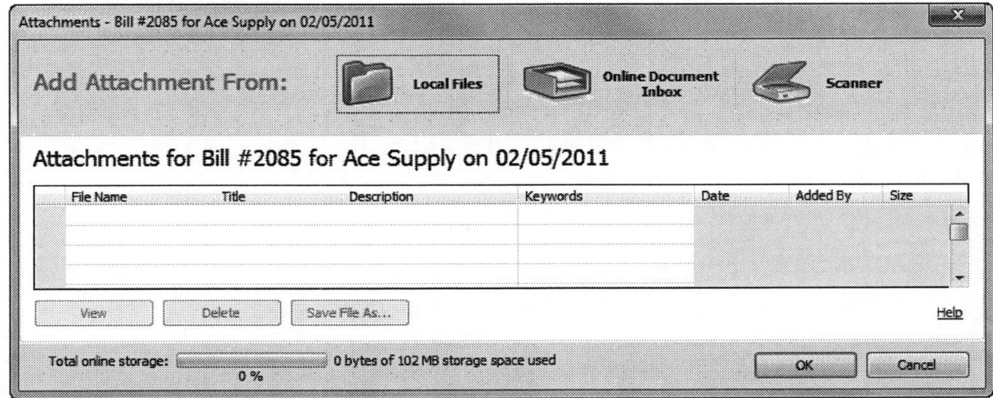

Figure 4-54 Attachments window

6. Click **Local Files** to attach a file located on your computer or local server.
7. Navigate to the desired file and click **OK**. The file uploads and is displayed in the *Attachments* window (see Figure 4-55).

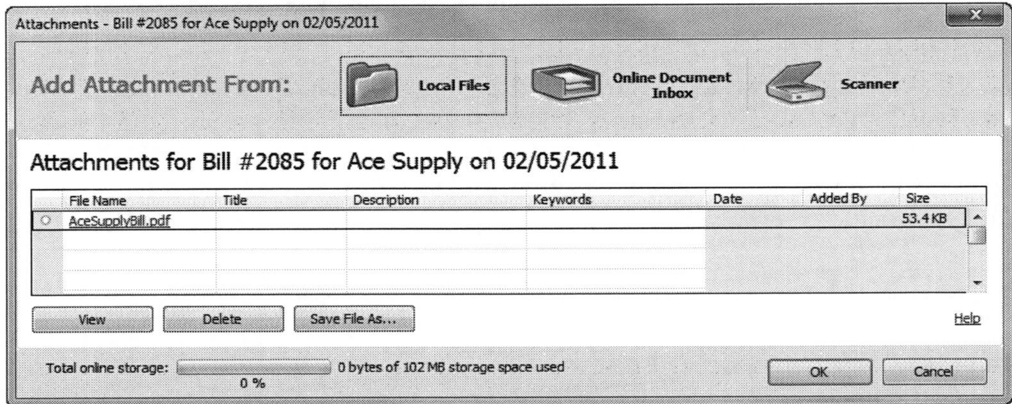

Figure 4-55 Attachment window with document uploaded

8. When finished, click **OK** to close the *Attachments* window.
9. Notice that the form now has a green paperclip image next to the Attach button. This shows that the bill has a document attached (see Figure 4-56).

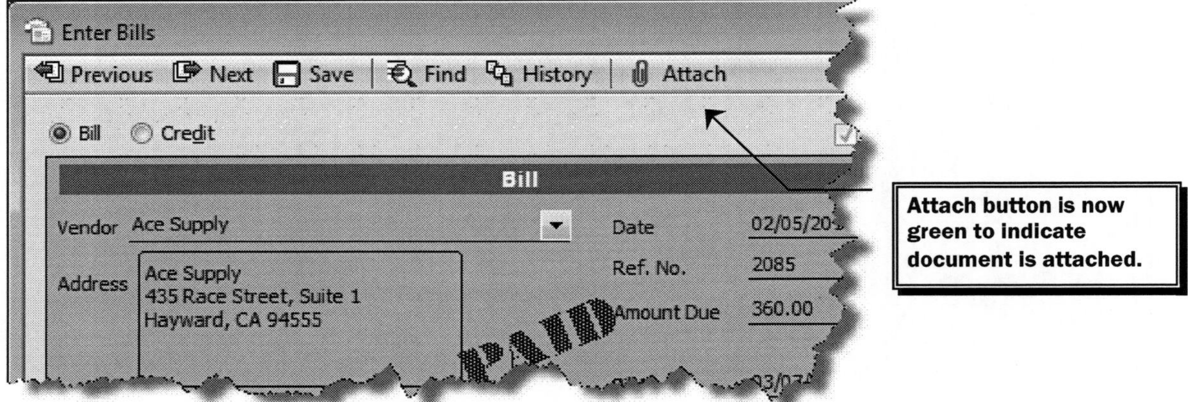

Figure 4-56 Attach button after document is uploaded

10. When finished, close the bill.

Applying Vendor Credits

When a vendor credits your account, you should record the transaction in the *Enter Bills* window as a *Credit* and apply it to one of your unpaid bills.

In some situations, it is best to use a Bill Credit instead of the *Discount* window to record certain vendor credits, because the *Discount* window does not allow you to record any of the following information:

- Reference numbers or memos – These may be important for reference later.
- Allocation of the credit to multiple accounts.
- Allocation to customers or jobs – This may be critical in many situations.
- The ability to use Items.

COMPUTER PRACTICE

First, create a Bill from Nellis Distributing for a Custom Window.

Step 1. Click on the **Enter Bills** icon on the *Home* page.

Step 2. Enter the Bill shown in Figure 4-57.

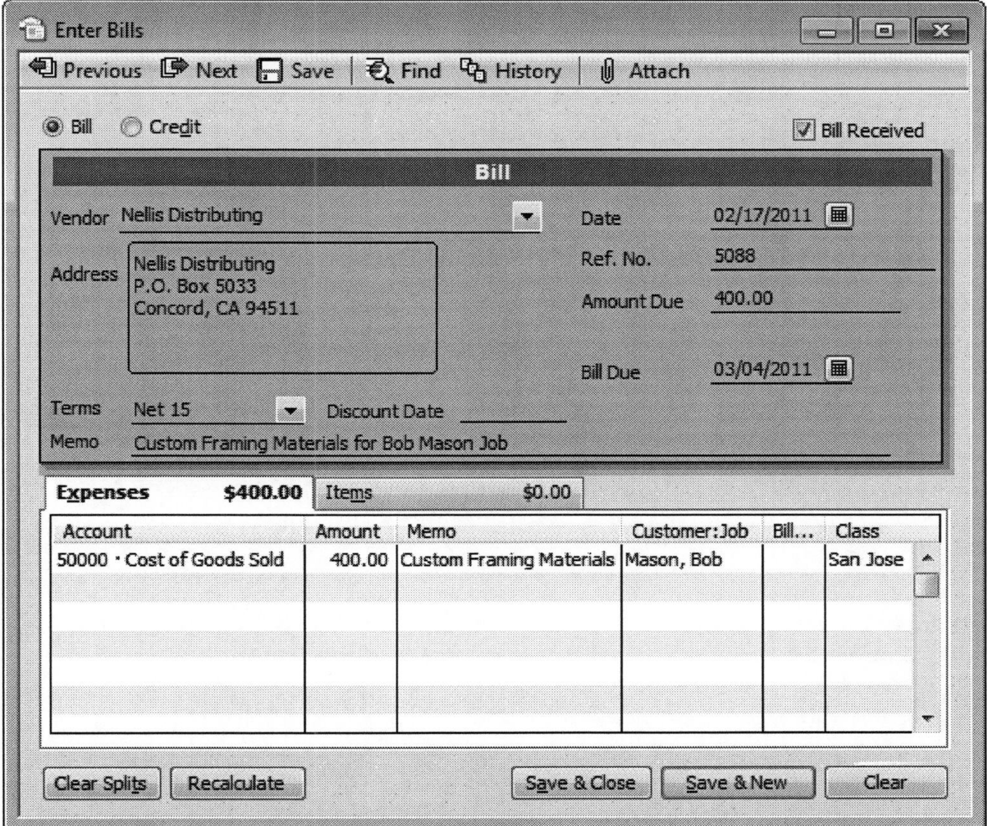

Figure 4-57 Bill from Nellis Distributing for Bob Mason job

Step 3. When you're finished entering the data in Figure 4-57, click **Save & New**.

Now, enter a Bill Credit.

Step 1. On the next (blank) **Bill** form, select the **Credit** radio button at the top right of the window.

Step 2. Fill in the Bill Credit information as shown in Figure 4-58. Click **Save & Close** to record the credit.

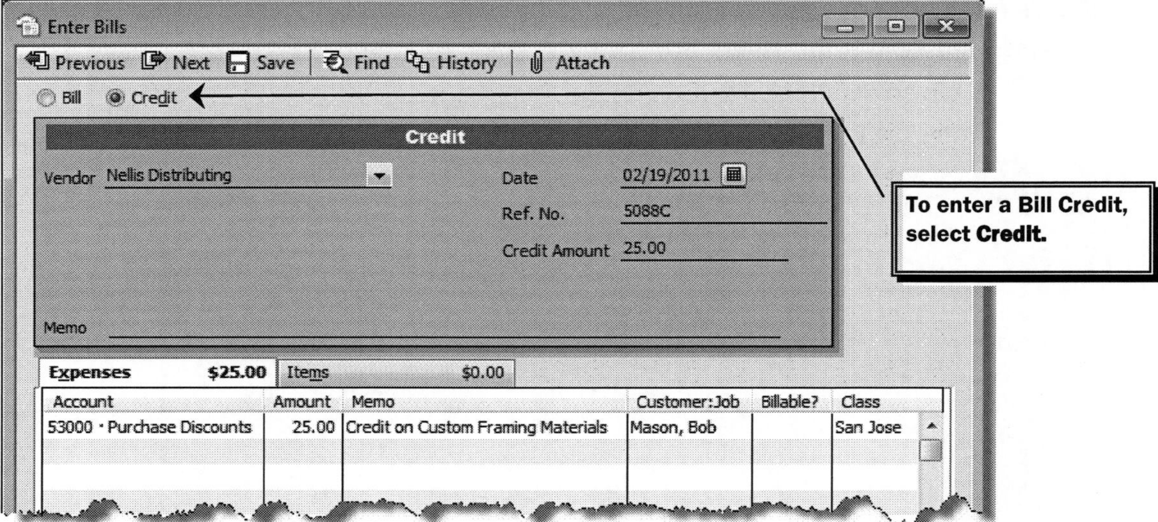

Figure 4-58 Creating a Bill Credit

> **The accounting behind the scenes:**
> When you record the **Bill Credit** shown in Figure 4-58, QuickBooks reduces (debits) Accounts Payable and reduces (credits) Purchase Discounts – a Cost of Goods Sold account.

Step 3. To apply the Bill Credit to a Bill for that vendor, select **Pay Bills** from the *Home* page (See Figure 4-59).

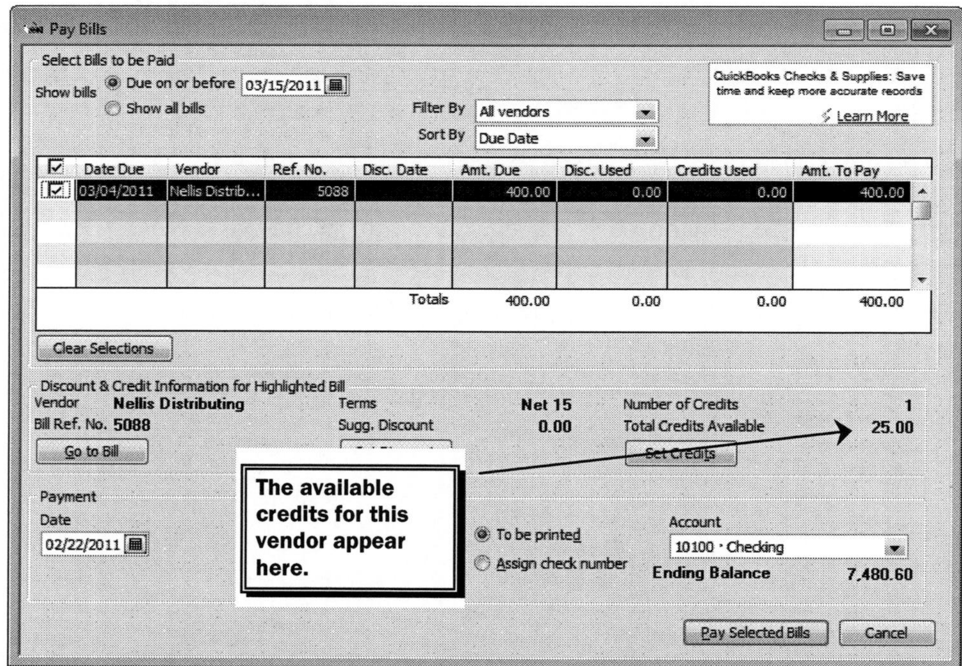

Figure 4-59 Pay Bills window for Nellis Distributing

Step 4. Enter ***03/15/2011*** in the *Due on or before* field and press **Tab**.

Step 5. Leave **Check** in the Payment Method field and **Checking** in the Payment Account field. Enter **02/22/2011** in the Payment Date field.

> **Important:**
> In order to apply a Bill Credit, the vendor name must be the same on both the Bill and the Bill Credit.

Step 6. Select the unpaid Bill for **Nellis Distributing** as shown in Figure 4-59.

When you select a Bill from a vendor for whom one or more unapplied credits exist, QuickBooks displays the total amount of all credits for the vendor in the *Total Credits Available* section. Notice the credit of $25.00 in Figure 4-59 for Nellis Distributing which we created above.

Step 7. Click Set Credits.

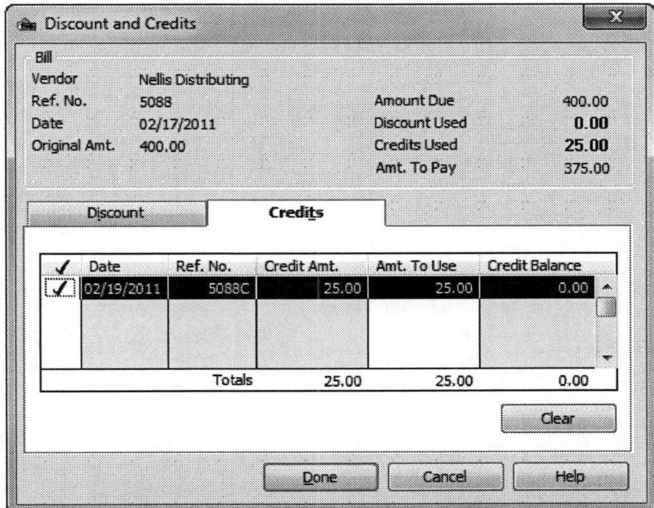

Figure 4-60 Discount and Credits window to set Bill Credit

On the *Discounts and Credits* window, QuickBooks automatically selected the credits to be applied to the bill. You can override what is shown by deselecting the credit (removing the checkmark), or by entering a different amount in the *Amt. To Use* column.

Step 8. Leave the credit selected as shown in Figure 4-60 and click **Done**.

QuickBooks has applied the $25.00 credit to Bill #5088 and reduced the amount in the *Amt. To Pay* column to $375.00 (see Figure 4-61).

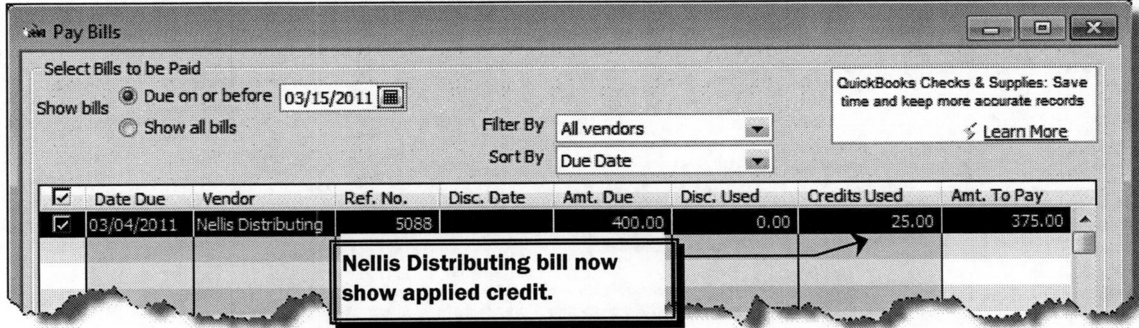

Figure 4-61 Pay Bills window after Bill Credit has been applied

Step 9. Click **Pay Selected Bills** to pay the bill.

Step 10. Click **Done** on the *Payment Summary* dialog box.

> **Note:**
> If you want to apply the credit without paying the bill, reduce the *Amt. To Pay* column to zero.

Handling Deposits and Refunds from Vendors

This section covers how to handle more complicated transactions between you and your vendors. These transactions include deposits paid to vendors in advance of receiving the bill, refunds received from vendors for overpayment of a bill, and refunds received from vendors when Accounts Payable is not involved.

Vendor Deposits — When You Use Accounts Payable

Sometimes vendors require you to give them a deposit before they will provide you with services or products. To do this, create a check for the vendor and code it to Accounts Payable. This creates a credit in QuickBooks for the vendor that you can apply to the bill when it arrives.

COMPUTER PRACTICE

Step 1. Click on the **Write Checks** icon on the *Home* page.

Step 2. Enter the data as shown in Figure 4-62. Notice that this check is coded to Accounts Payable. You only code checks to A/P when you are sending deposits to a vendor prior to receiving the bill.

Step 3. In this example, a manual check (#332) was written for the deposit. Uncheck the *To be printed* checkbox, if necessary, for QuickBooks to display the next manual check number in the *Checking* register.

Step 4. Click Save & Close.

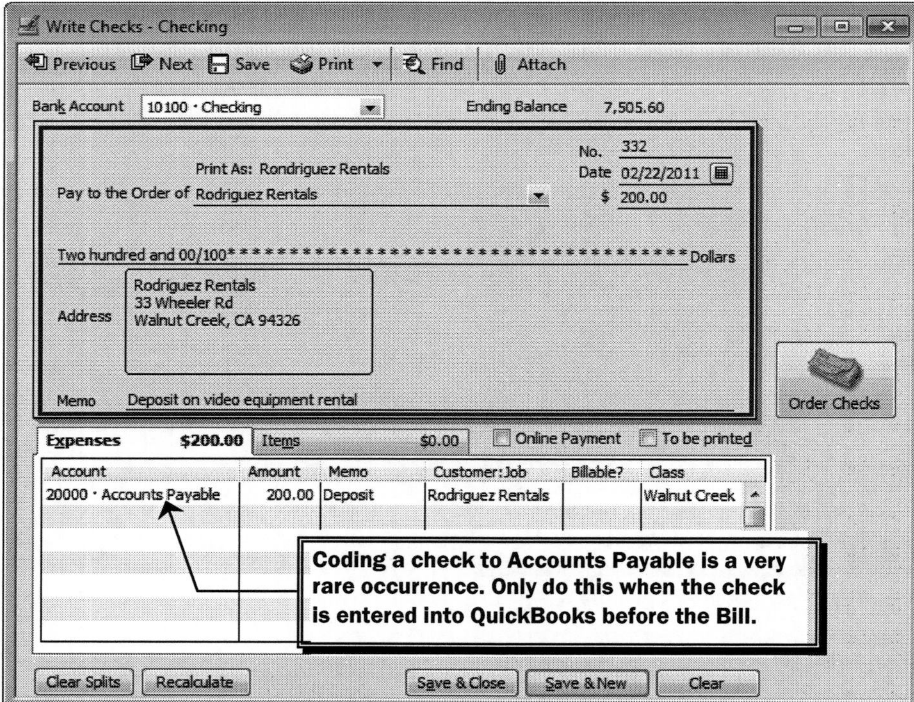

Figure 4-62 Coding check to Accounts Payable

Later, when the Bill is received from the vendor, enter it as you would any other Bill. Then apply the credit resulting from the check created above to the Bill by using the procedures outlined in the **Applying Vendor Credits** section of this chapter, beginning on page 156.

Vendor Refunds — When You Use Accounts Payable

When you receive a refund from a vendor, the kind of transaction you enter in QuickBooks will depend on how you originally paid the vendor.

If you prepaid the vendor using the method above and the amount of your prepayment was more than the bill, your Accounts Payable account will have a negative (debit) balance for that vendor. In this case, you will apply the refund check from the vendor to this credit balance in Accounts Payable.

On the other hand, if you simply wrote a check to the vendor and coded the check to an expense account, you will need to reduce the expense by the amount of the refund. The following tutorials address each of these situations.

To record a refund from a vendor that you prepaid using the deposit check in Figure 4-62, follow the steps below. In this example, you paid Rodriguez Rentals $200.00 in advance of receiving the bill. On a later date, Rodriguez Rentals sent a bill for $185.00. Since your deposit was more than the bill, the vendor also sent you a refund check for $15.00.

Start by entering the bill from the vendor just like any other bill. Then use the *Make Deposits* window to record your refund from the vendor.

COMPUTER PRACTICE

Step 1. Open the *Enter Bills* window and enter the bill from Rodriguez Rentals as shown in Figure 4-63. Click **Save & Close** to record the bill.

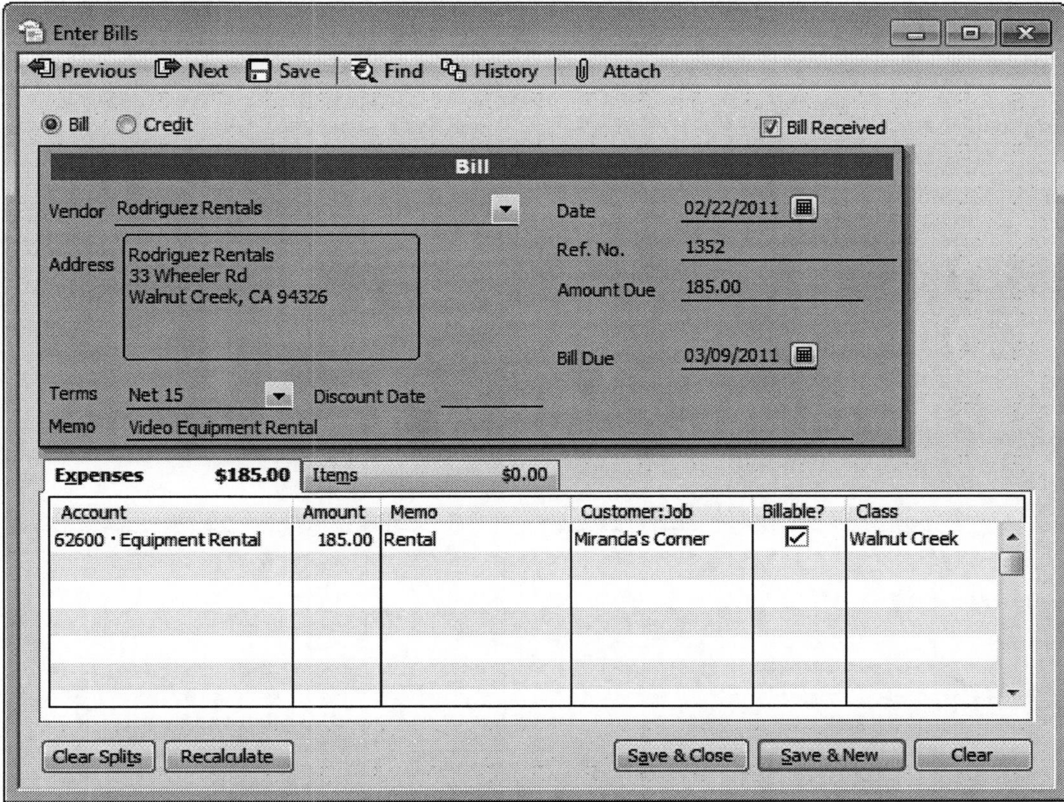

Figure 4-63 Enter Bill received from Rodriguez Rentals

Step 2. Select the **Record Deposit** icon in the *Banking* section of the *Home* page.

Step 3. Press **Tab** to leave *Checking* selected in the *Deposit To* field (see Figure 4-64).

Step 4. Press **Tab** to leave **02/22/2011** in the *Date* field.

Step 5. Enter ***Refund from Rodriguez*** in the *Memo* field and press **Tab**.

Step 6. Enter in the remaining data as shown in Figure 4-64.

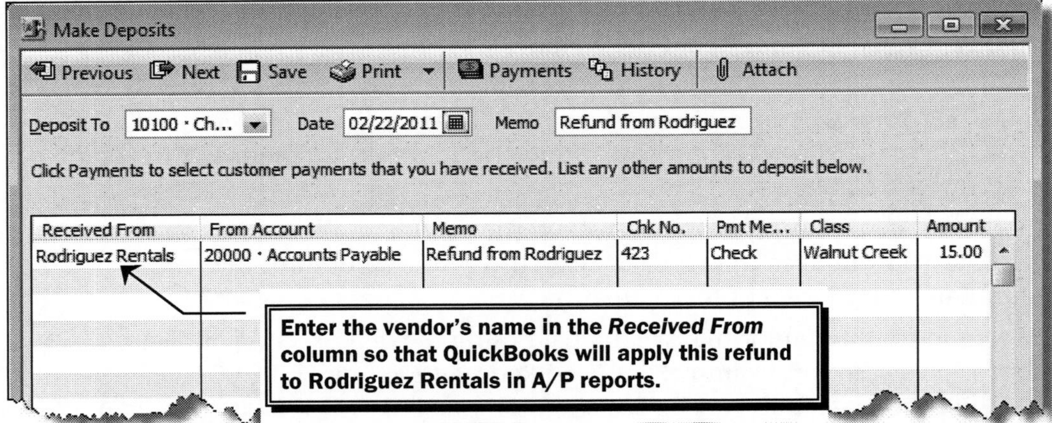

Figure 4-64 Make Deposits window to deposit refund check

Step 7. Click **Save & Close** at the bottom of the window.

After you have recorded the deposit in Figure 4-64, apply the $200.00 prepayment check to both the bill and the refund check you just received (i.e. use the $200.00 prepayment check to *pay* the bill and the refund). Your Accounts Payable reports will not be correct until you make this application.

COMPUTER PRACTICE

Step 1. Select the **Pay Bills** icon from the *Home* page.

Step 2. Enter ***03/15/2011*** in the *Due on or before date* field and press **Tab**.

Step 3. Leave **Check** in the *Payment Method* field and **Checking** in the *Payment Account* column.

Step 4. Enter ***02/24/2011*** in the *Payment Date* field.

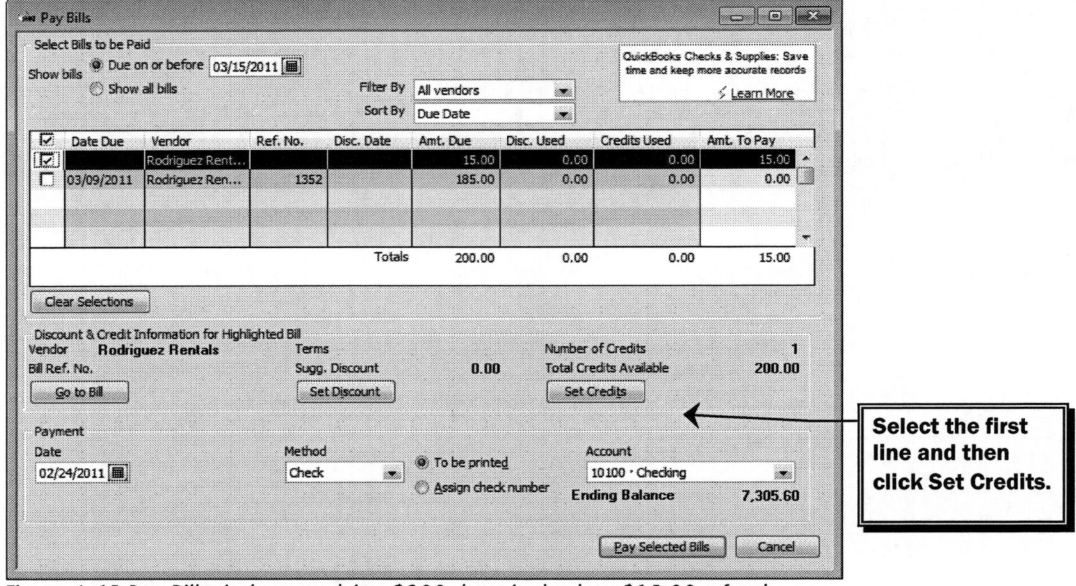

Figure 4-65 Pay Bill window; applying $200 deposit check to $15.00 refund

Step 5. Place a checkmark on the first line in the *Pay Bills* window ($15.00 deposit) and click **Set Credits** as shown in Figure 4-65.

Though this window seems to show two bills for Rodriguez Rentals, the first line is actually the refund check you recorded using the *Make Deposits* window as shown in Figure 4-64.

Step 6. In the *Discounts and Credits* window, QuickBooks automatically applies $15.00 of the $200.00 credit to the refund check (see Figure 4-66).

Step 7. Click **Done**.

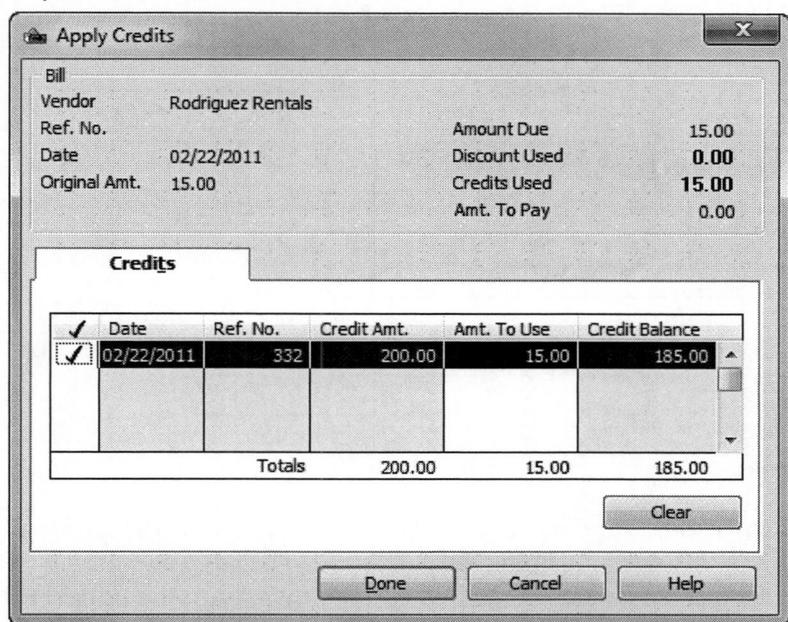

Figure 4-66 Apply Credits window

Step 8. The second line in the *Pay Bills* window is the actual Bill from Rodriguez Rentals. Select this Bill and click **Set Credits** (Figure 4-67).

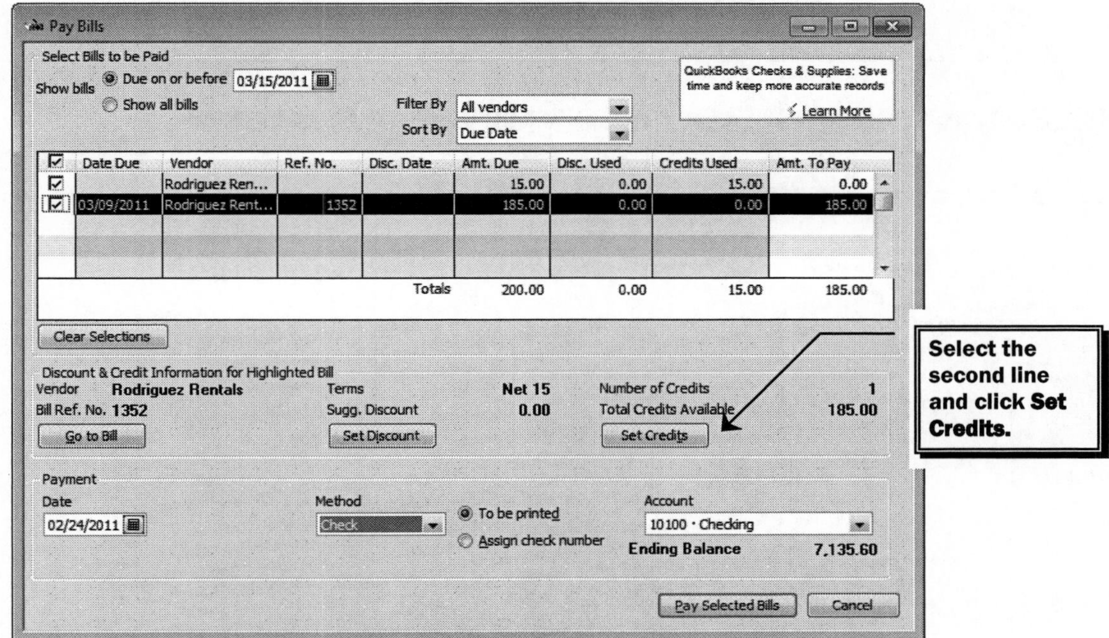

Figure 4-67 Pay Bill window; applying the $200.00 deposit to the $185.00 bill

Step 9. In the *Discounts and Credits* window, QuickBooks automatically applies $185.00 of the $200.00 credit to Bill #1352 (see Figure 4-68).

Step 10. Click **Done**.

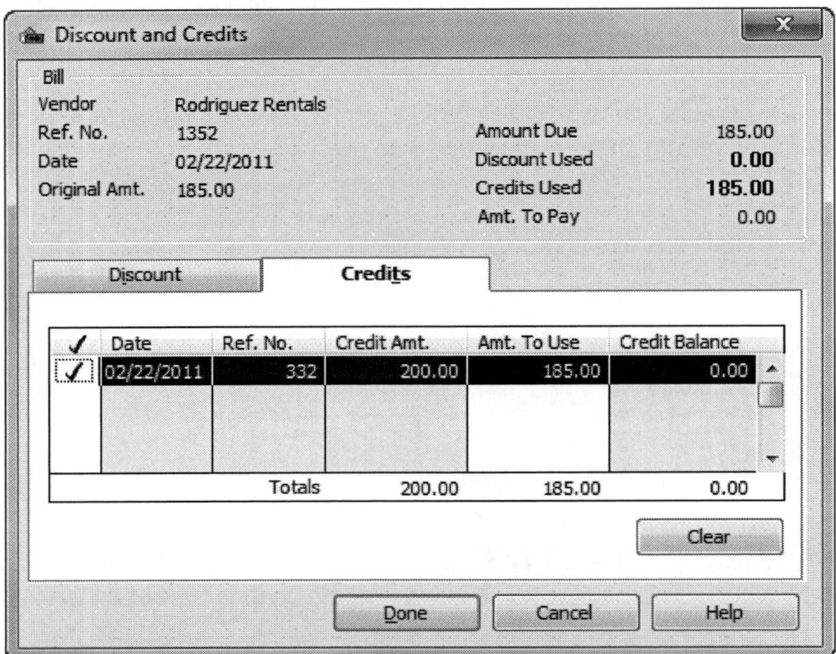

Figure 4-68 Discounts and Credits window

Step 11. Since the amount of the prepayment ($200.00) is the same as the bill ($185.00) plus the refund check ($15.00), the total in the *Amt. To Pay* field is zero (see Figure 4-69). QuickBooks will link these transactions together, clearing them from the Unpaid Bills and Accounts Payable Aging reports, but will not create a Bill Payment.

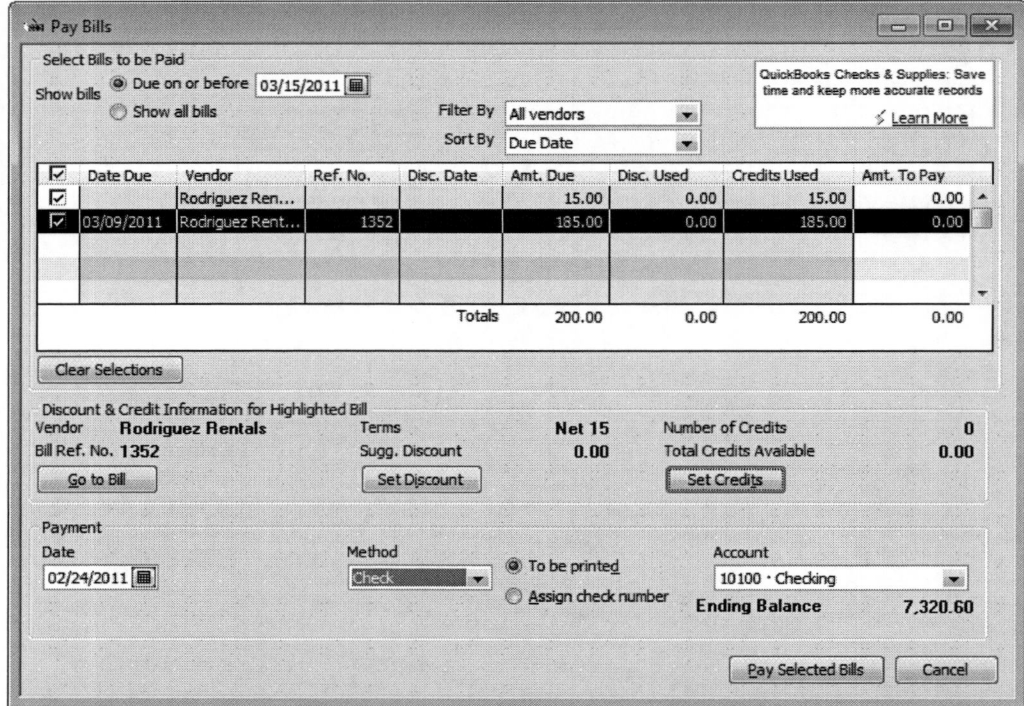

Figure 4-69 Pay and Close window applying the $200.00 deposit to the $185.00 bill

Step 12. Click Pay Selected Bills.

Step 13. Click **Done** on the Payment Summary dialog box.

Step 14. If QuickBooks displays the *Bills Paid By Credits* message shown in Figure 4-70, read it carefully and click **OK**.

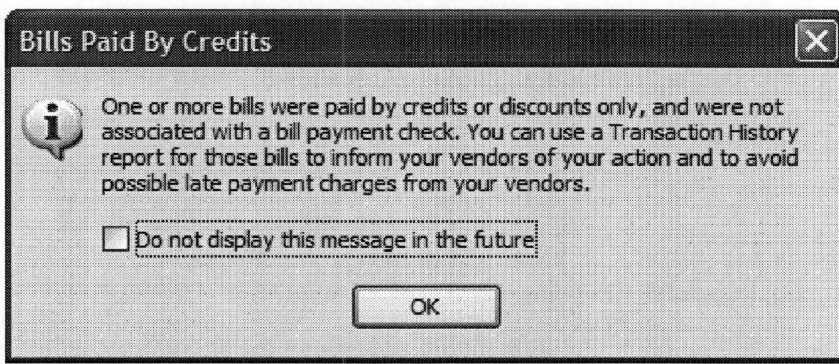

Figure 4-70 Bills Paid By Credits window

Vendor Refunds — When You Directly Expensed Payment

If you did not use the Accounts Payable features, but instead wrote a check to the vendor and coded the check to an expense account, record the refund using a deposit transaction. Use the same expense account you used on the original payment to the vendor (see Figure 4-71). For this exercise, **do not** save this transaction. Click the **Clear** button and close the *Make Deposits* window.

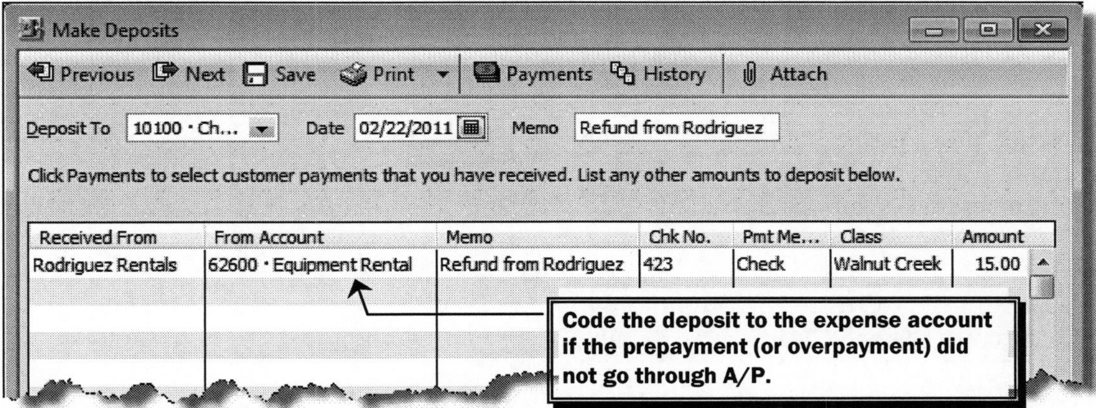

Figure 4-71 Make Deposit window coding the refund to an expense account

Tracking Petty Cash

It is sometimes necessary to use cash for minor expenditures, such as office supplies, postage, parking, or other small items. In order to track these expenditures, you can set up a separate bank account in QuickBooks called *Petty Cash.*

To track a deposit to your Petty Cash account (and the withdrawal of cash from your Checking account), simply write a check to a designated person, the *custodian,* who will cash the check at a local bank and place the money into Petty Cash. Code the check to the Petty Cash account.

When you use Petty Cash for a company expense, enter the expenditure in the *Payment* column of the Petty Cash account register. This reduces the balance in the Petty Cash account so that it always agrees with the actual amount of cash you have on hand. Code each cash expenditure to the appropriate *payee, account, class* and *job.* Click the **Splits** button to split the expenditure among multiple accounts or to assign customer names or classes to the transaction.

Tracking Company Credit Cards

To track charges and payments on your company credit card, set up a separate credit card account in QuickBooks for each card. Then enter each charge individually using the *Enter Credit Card Charges* window. To pay the credit card bill, use **Write Checks** and code the check to the credit card account.

Another Way:
You can also pay your credit card bill by using *Pay Bills* after recording a bill for the balance due, coded to the credit card liability account.

Did You Know?
Many Credit Cards allow you to download your credit card charges into QuickBooks through the Internet, eliminating the need to enter each charge manually. For more information about the QuickBooks Credit Card, select the *Banking* menu, select **Online Banking Services**, and then select **Set Up Account for Online Access.**

Entering Credit Card Charges

Each time you use a company credit card, use the *Enter Credit Card Charges* window to record the transaction.

The accounting behind the scenes:
When you record credit card charges, QuickBooks increases (credits) your Credit Card Payable liability account and increases (debits) the expense account shown at the bottom of the window.

Note:
You will need to create an account on your *Chart of Accounts* for each company credit card. Use the *Credit Card* type when creating the account.

COMPUTER PRACTICE

Step 1. From the *Banking* menu, select **Enter Credit Card Charges.**

Step 2. Press **Tab** to accept **National Bank VISA Gold** in the *Credit Card* field.

Step 3. **Purchase/Charge** is already selected. Press **Tab** twice.

If you used your card when receiving a refund or credit from a vendor, you would select **Credit** instead of **Charge** on this step. QuickBooks will then reduce the balance on your credit card when you record a Credit transaction.

Step 4. Enter ***Bay Office Supply*** in the *Purchased From* field and press **Tab.**

Step 5. Press **Tab** to accept ***02/24/2011*** in the *Date* field.

Step 6. Enter ***65432*** in the *Ref No.* field and press **Tab.**

The *Ref No.* field is optional. Its purpose is to tag each charge with the number on the charge slip.

Step 7. Enter ***86.48*** in the *Amount* field and press **Tab.**

Step 8. Enter ***Purchase Office Supplies*** in *Memo* field and press **Tab.**

Step 9. Enter the *Account, Amount, Memo,* and *Class* fields as displayed in Figure 4-72.

Step 10. Verify that your screen matches Figure 4-72. Click **Save & New** to record the credit card charge.

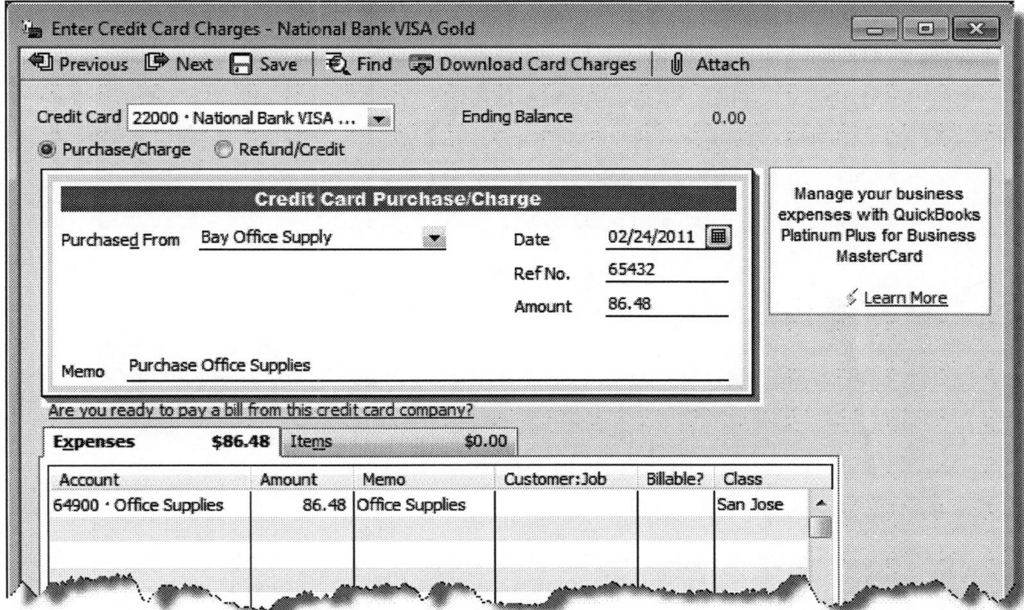

Figure 4-72 Enter Credit Card Charges window for Bay Office Supply purchase

Step 11. Enter another credit card charge that matches Figure 4-73. Click **Save & Close.**

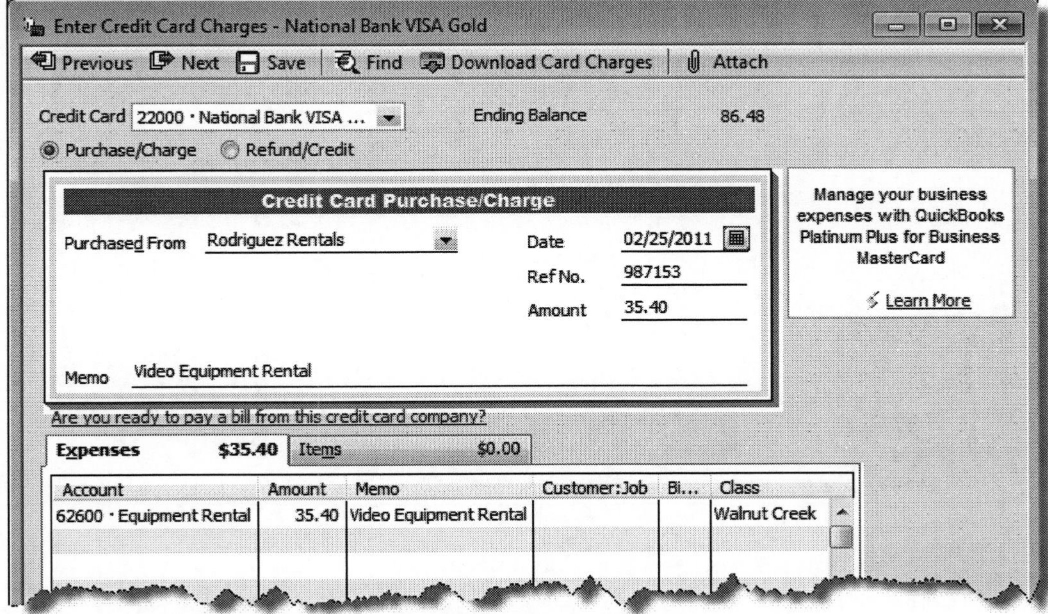

Figure 4-73 Enter Credit Card Charges window for equipment rental

Paying the Credit Card Bill

Follow the steps below to write a check to pay your credit card bill.

> **The accounting behind the scenes:**
> When you record a credit card payment, QuickBooks reduces (credits) the Checking account and reduces (debits) the Credit Card liability account.
> **Note:** There is another method of paying the credit card bill that is part of the reconciliation process. In the reconciliation chapter, you'll learn more about reconciling the credit card account, and then creating a Bill for the balance due.

COMPUTER PRACTICE

Step 1. Click the **Write Checks** icon on the *Home* page.

Step 2. Enter the check as shown in Figure 4-74. Notice that you will enter the credit card account name in the *Account* column of the *Expenses* Tab.

> **Note:**
> When you enter ***National Bank*** in the *Pay to the Order of* field, QuickBooks recalls the last transaction you recorded to National Bank. In your sample company file, the last transaction was the loan payment made through the *Loan Manager*. Clear each line in the expenses tab by clicking anywhere on the first line and pressing Ctrl+DEL twice to remove the split detail lines on the *Expenses* tab. Then, complete the *Expenses* tab as shown in Figure 4-74.

Step 3. Click **Save & Close** to record the transaction.

Step 4. Click **Save Anyway** to bypass *Items not assigned to classes* window.

You do not need to enter a class when posting to a credit card account or any other Balance Sheet account.

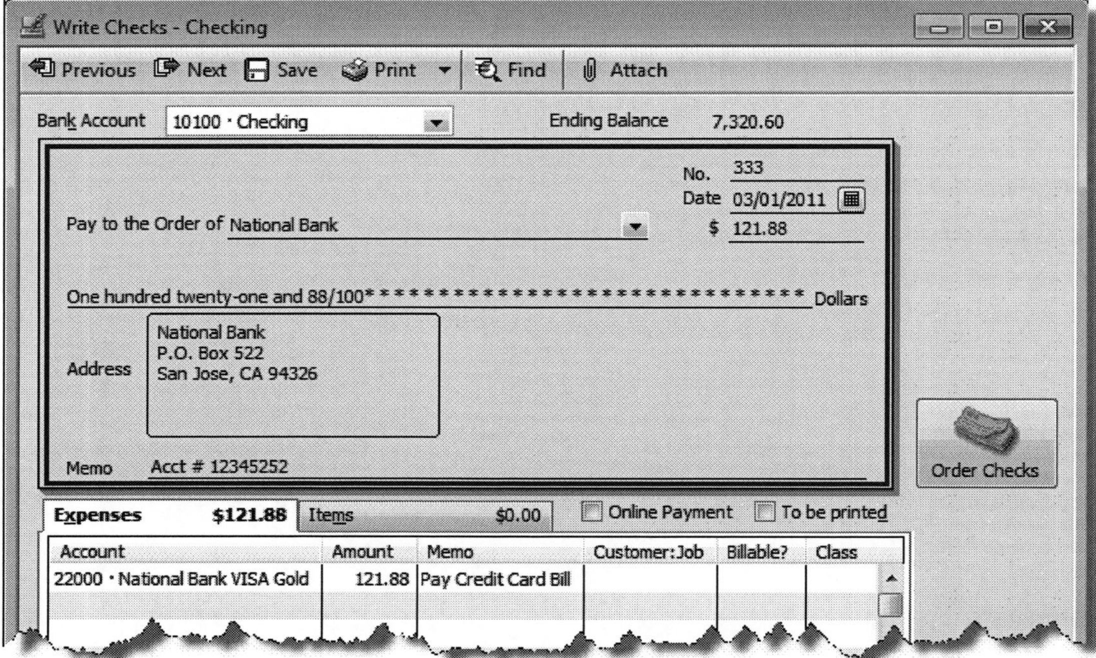

Figure 4-74 Write Checks window to pay credit card bill

To see the detail of your credit card charges and payments, look in the *National Bank VISA Gold* account register (see Figure 4-75). This register can be access by pressing **Ctrl+A** to open the Chart of Accounts, and then double-clicking on the *National Bank Visa Gold* credit card account.

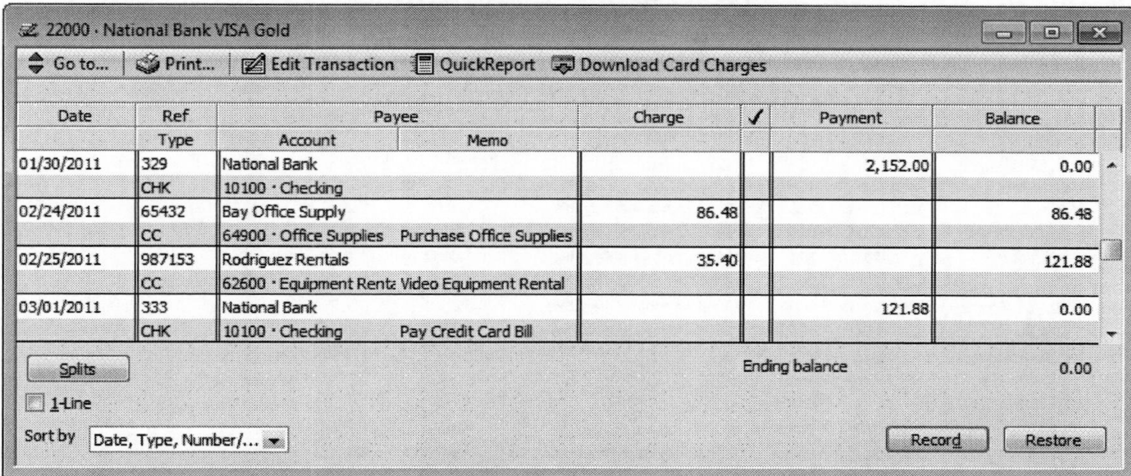

Figure 4-75 National Bank VISA Gold account register

Accounts Payable Reports

QuickBooks has several reports that you can use to analyze and track your purchases and vendors. Following are two sample reports for you to create. See the Reports chapter for more information on creating reports.

Vendor Balance Detail

The **Vendor Balance Detail** report shows the detail of each Bill and Bill Payment to each vendor. However, this report only includes transactions that "go through" Accounts Payable. That is, it only shows transactions such as ***Bills*** and *Bill Payments*. If you write checks to your vendors directly--without first entering a bill--those transactions will not show in this report.

COMPUTER PRACTICE

Step 1. From the *Reports* menu, select **Vendors & Payables** and then select **Vendor Balance Detail** (see Figure 4-76).

Step 2. To print the report, click **Print** at the top of the report. Close the report and click **No**, if the *Memorize Report* message appears.

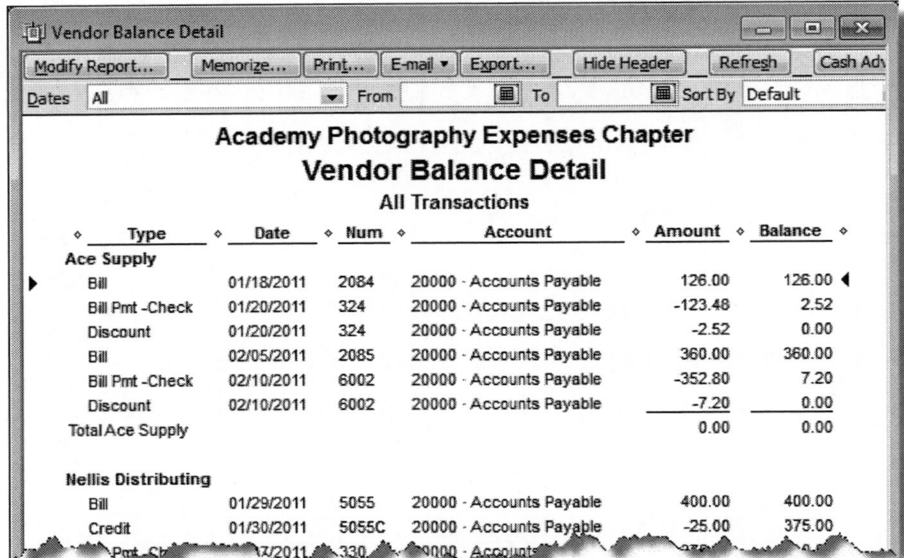

Academy Photography Expenses Chapter
Vendor Balance Detail
All Transactions

Type	Date	Num	Account	Amount	Balance
Ace Supply					
Bill	01/18/2011	2084	20000 · Accounts Payable	126.00	126.00
Bill Pmt -Check	01/20/2011	324	20000 · Accounts Payable	-123.48	2.52
Discount	01/20/2011	324	20000 · Accounts Payable	-2.52	0.00
Bill	02/05/2011	2085	20000 · Accounts Payable	360.00	360.00
Bill Pmt -Check	02/10/2011	6002	20000 · Accounts Payable	-352.80	7.20
Discount	02/10/2011	6002	20000 · Accounts Payable	-7.20	0.00
Total Ace Supply				0.00	0.00
Nellis Distributing					
Bill	01/29/2011	5055	20000 · Accounts Payable	400.00	400.00
Credit	01/30/2011	5055C	20000 · Accounts Payable	-25.00	375.00

Figure 4-76 Vendor Balance Detail Report

Transaction List by Vendor

The **Transaction List by Vendor** report shows all transactions associated with your vendors, even if the transactions did not "go through" Accounts Payable (e.g., checks and credit card charges).

COMPUTER PRACTICE

Step 1. From the *Reports* menu, select **Vendors & Payables** and then select **Transaction List by Vendor** (see Figure 4-77).

Step 2. Set the date fields on the report to *01/01/2011* through *03/31/2011*.

Step 3. Close all open windows and click **No** if the *Memorize Report* message appears.

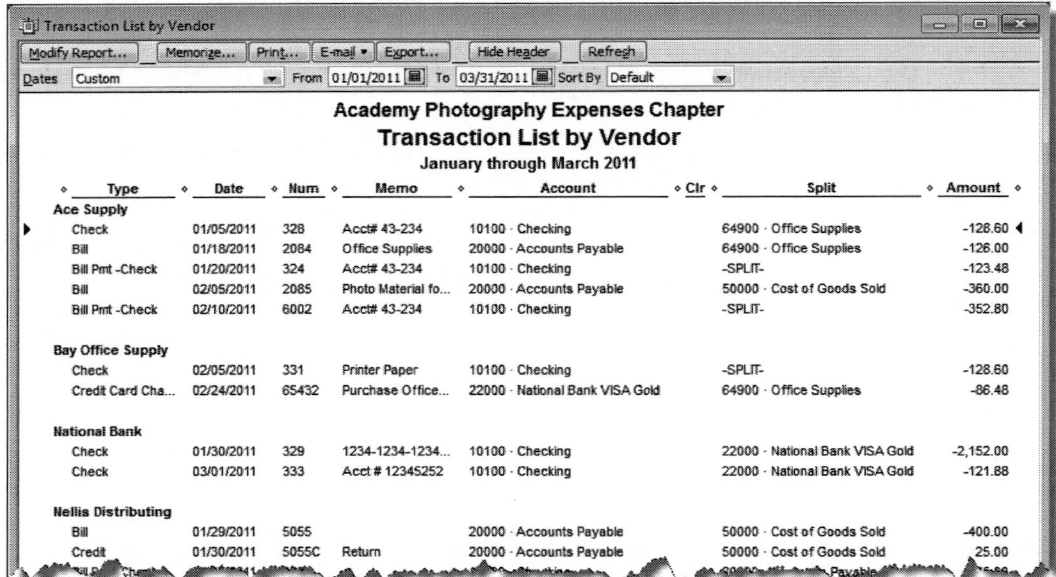

Academy Photography Expenses Chapter
Transaction List by Vendor
January through March 2011

Type	Date	Num	Memo	Account	Clr	Split	Amount
Ace Supply							
Check	01/05/2011	328	Acct# 43-234	10100 · Checking		64900 · Office Supplies	-128.60
Bill	01/18/2011	2084	Office Supplies	20000 · Accounts Payable		64900 · Office Supplies	-126.00
Bill Pmt -Check	01/20/2011	324	Acct# 43-234	10100 · Checking		-SPLIT-	-123.48
Bill	02/05/2011	2085	Photo Material fo...	20000 · Accounts Payable		50000 · Cost of Goods Sold	-360.00
Bill Pmt -Check	02/10/2011	6002	Acct# 43-234	10100 · Checking		-SPLIT-	-352.80
Bay Office Supply							
Check	02/05/2011	331	Printer Paper	10100 · Checking		-SPLIT-	-128.60
Credit Card Cha...	02/24/2011	65432	Purchase Office...	22000 · National Bank VISA Gold		64900 · Office Supplies	-86.48
National Bank							
Check	01/30/2011	329	1234-1234-1234...	10100 · Checking		22000 · National Bank VISA Gold	-2,152.00
Check	03/01/2011	333	Acct # 12345252	10100 · Checking		22000 · National Bank VISA Gold	-121.88
Nellis Distributing							
Bill	01/29/2011	5055		20000 · Accounts Payable		50000 · Cost of Goods Sold	-400.00
Credit	01/30/2011	5055C	Return	20000 · Accounts Payable		50000 · Cost of Goods Sold	25.00

Figure 4-77 Transaction List by Vendor report

Tracking Loans using the Loan Manager

If you have QuickBooks Pro or Premier, you can track detailed information about your loans. You can individually track and amortize each of your loans so that QuickBooks will automatically allocate the principal and interest on each payment.

Setting up a Loan in the Loan Manager

The details of each loan can be set up in the **QuickBooks Loan Manager** to automatically amortize and track each loan. If you plan to have QuickBooks track loan details using the Loan Manager, you'll need to gather the details on each loan so that you have all of the information shown in Table 4-2.

Truck Loan Detail	
Account Name	Truck Loan
Lender	National Bank
Origination Date	12/31/2010
Original Amount	$ 12,000.00
Term	36 Months
Due Date of Next Payment	01/31/2011
Payment Amount	$ 370.53
Next Payment Number	1
Payment Period	Monthly
Does loan have escrow payment?	No
Alert me 10 days before a payment is due	Leave checked
Interest Rate	7%
Compounding period	Monthly
Payment Account	Checking
Interest Expense Account	Interest Expense
Fees/Charges Expense Account	Bank Service Charges

Table 4-2 Truck Loan Balance Detail

COMPUTER PRACTICE

For this example, Academy Photography owns a Delivery Truck that they purchased on 12/31/2010. When they purchased the truck, they took out a loan with National Bank for $12,000.00 that carries an interest rate of 7% per year, for 3 years.

Step 1. From the *Banking Menu*, select **Loan Manager** (see Figure 4-78).

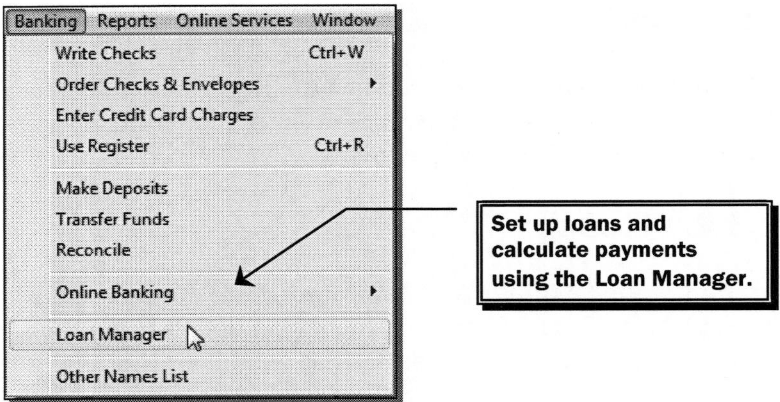

Figure 4-78 Selecting Loan Manager from Banking menu

Step 2. In the *Loan Manage* setup window, click **Add a Loan**.

> **Note:**
> The liability account and the balance for this loan were set up in the data file for this chapter. It is necessary to set up the account and the beginning balance first to ensure correct linking of the loan detail to the General Ledger. For more information click **What you need to do before you add a loan** on the *Loan Manager* setup window (see Figure 4-79).

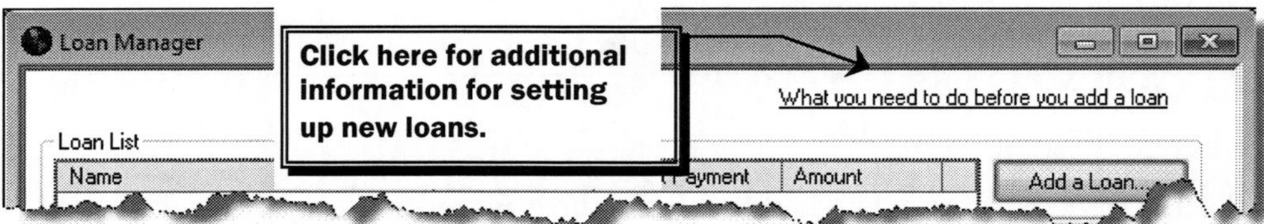

Figure 4-79 Loan Manager setup window

Step 3. Complete the loan information in the *Add Loan* window using the data from Table 4-2. Complete the *Enter account information for this* loan section. When completed your screen should look like Figure 4-80.

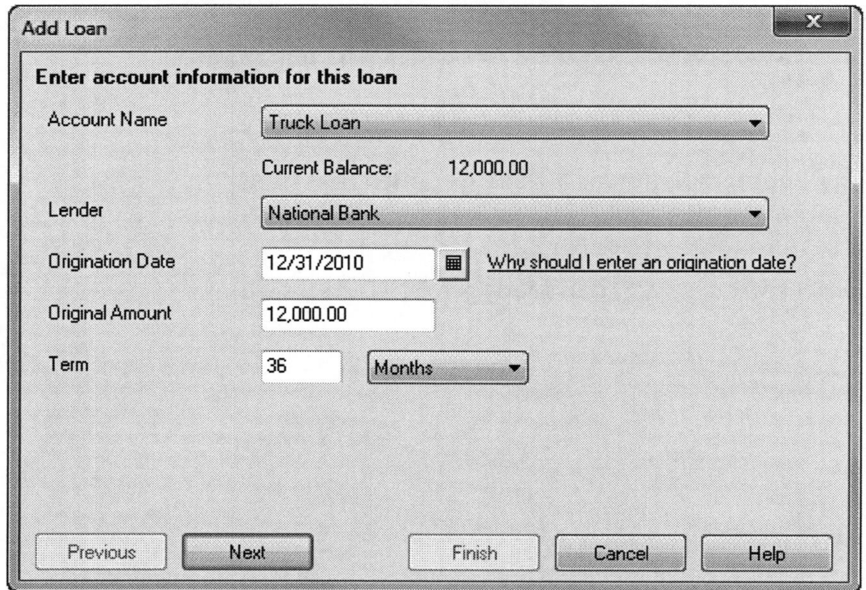

Figure 4-80 Truck loan information – your screen may vary

Step 4. Click **Next.**

Step 5. Complete the *Enter payment information for this* loan section using data from Table 4-2. When completed, your screen should look like Figure 4-81. For this exercise, uncheck *Alert me 10 days before payment is due.*

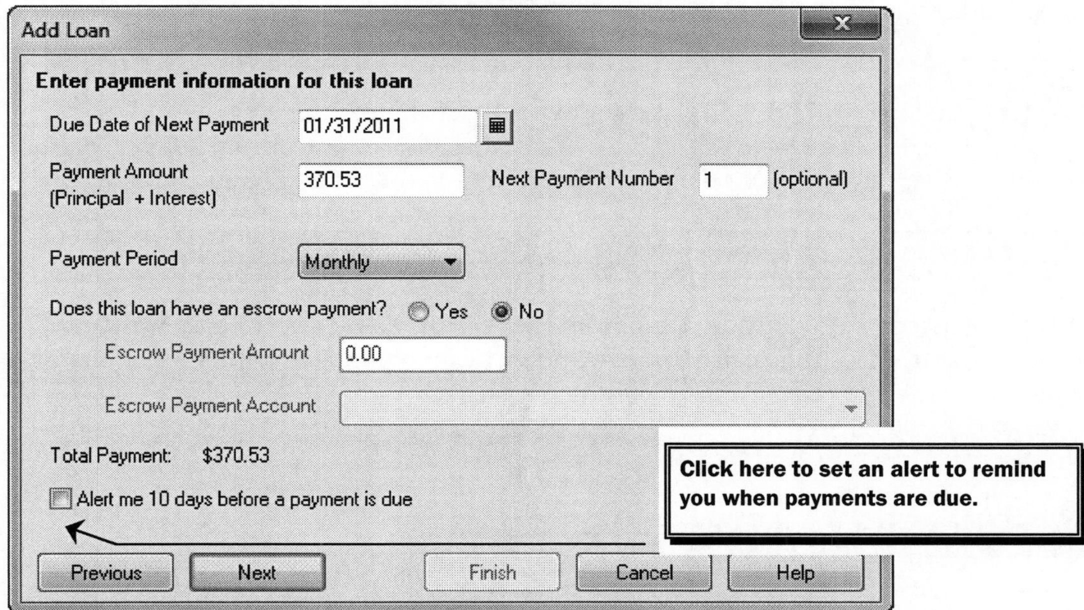

Figure 4-81 Payment information for Truck loan

> **Note:**
> QuickBooks allows you to track escrow amounts separately from principal and interest so you can automatically record these expenditures with each payment. For example, taxes added to your mortgage payment automatically could be posted each month, rather than by a separate manual entry.

Step 6. Click **Next.**

Step 7. Complete the *Enter interest information for this* loan section using data from Table 4-2. When completed, your screen should look like Figure 4-82.

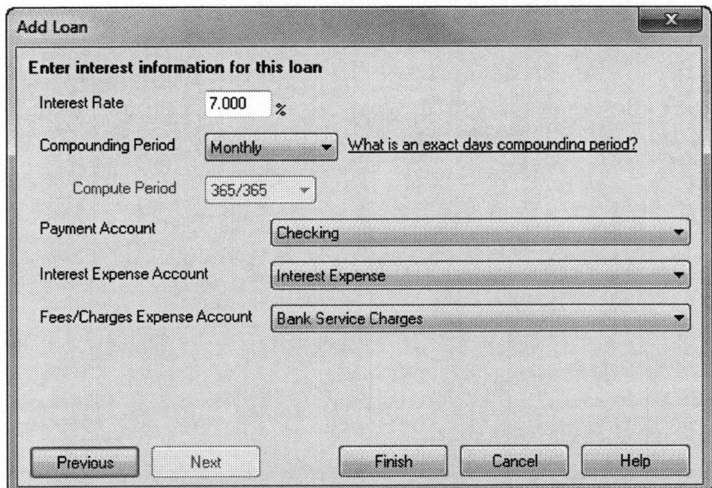

Figure 4-82 Interest information for Truck loan

Step 8. Click **Finish** to save the Truck Loan.

Making Loan Payments using the Loan Manager

In our example, Academy Photography purchased a truck and took out a loan with National Bank for $12,000.00. The loan has been set up in Loan Manager; therefore, all payments on the loan should originate in Loan Manager.

> **Note:**
> The loan manager will only display the Payment Schedule until after the origination date of the loan. If you are completing this exercise during 2010, you should read through the following section but not complete the steps.

DO NOT PERFORM THESE STEPS. THEY ARE FOR PRACTICE ONLY.

1. If Loan Manager is not already open, from the *Banking* menu select **Loan Manager**. QuickBooks displays the *Loan Manager* window as shown in Figure 4-83. Click the *Payment Schedule* tab to see a list of all the payments.

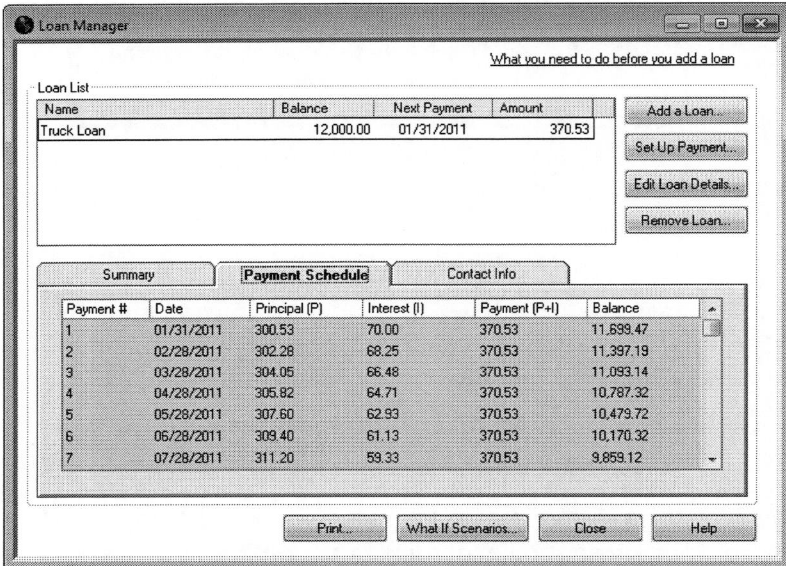

Figure 4-83 Loan Manager window – your screen may vary

2. **Truck Loan** in the *Loan List* is already selected. Click **Set Up Payment** to make a payment for the Truck Loan. QuickBooks displays the window shown in Figure 4-84.
3. Confirm that **A regular payment** is selected in the *This payment is* drop-down list as shown in Figure 4-84.

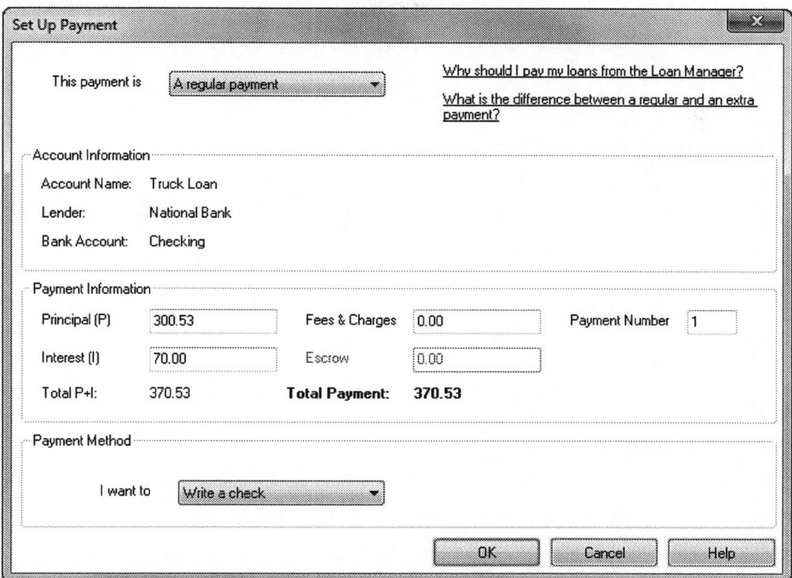

Figure 4-84 Set Up Payment window

> **Note:**
> Select **An extra payment** when you are making a payment in addition to your regular monthly amount.
>
> QuickBooks automatically calculates the amounts for the *Principal* and *Interest* fields based on the information you entered when you set up the loan. Confirm that these amounts agree to your loan statement and enter any fees or charges for the month in the *Fees & Charges* field.

4. In the *I want to* field, leave **Write a check** selected.
5. Click **OK** to create a check to make a payment for this loan. QuickBooks displays the *Write Checks* window and populates each field with the correct information as shown in Figure 4-85. If a manual check number displays in the **No.** field, check the *To be printed* box so that a voucher check can be used.

> **Note:**
> If you want to enter a Bill instead of a Check, select **Enter a bill** in the *I want to* drop-down list.

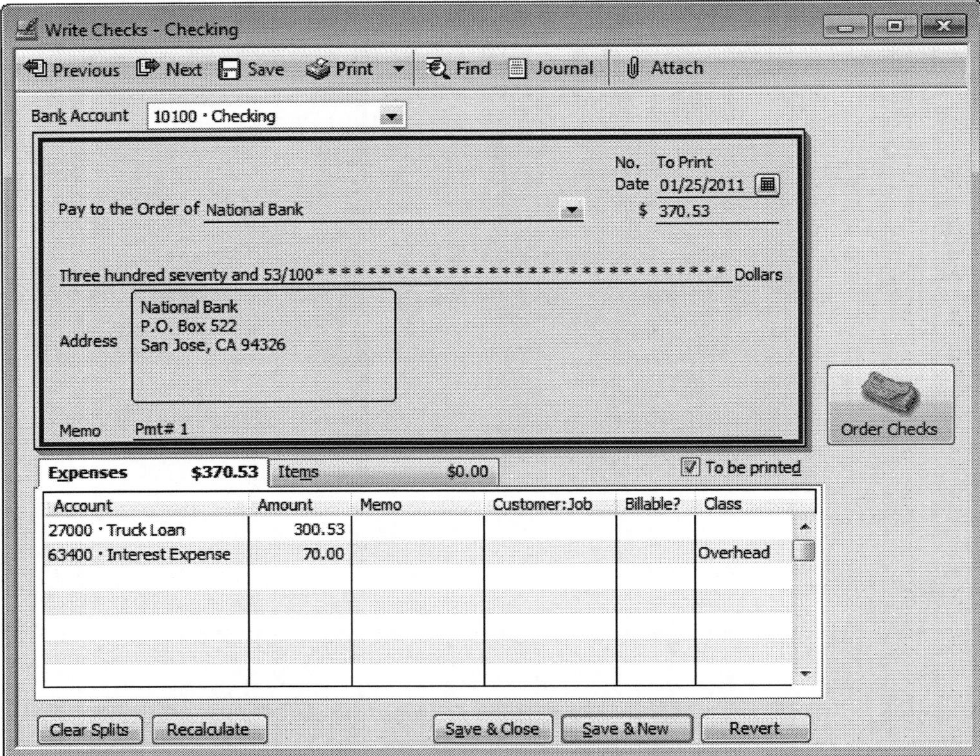

Figure 4-85 Write Checks window for Truck loan payment

6. Enter ***01/25/2011*** in the *Date* field.

   QuickBooks uses the current date when creating a **Check** or **Bill** through the *Loan Manager*. Edit the date field as necessary so the **Check** or **Bill** has the correct date.

7. On the Interest Expense line of the *Expenses* tab, select **Overhead** from the *Class* column drop-down list as shown in Figure 4-85.
8. Confirm that your screen matches Figure 4-85.
9. Click **Clear** and close the window. For this exercise you will not save your changes.

Chapter Summary and Review

Summary of Key Points

In this chapter, you learned how to track the expenses in your company. You should now be familiar with how to use QuickBooks to do all of the following:

- Set up vendors in the Vendor list (page 124).
- Understand how to use classes in QuickBooks (page 130).
- Use QuickBooks for job costing (page 134).
- Enter expense transactions in several different ways (page 134).
- Manage Accounts Payable transactions (page 139).
- Print checks (page 148).
- Void checks (page 152).
- Create and apply vendor credits (page 156).

- Handle deposits and refunds from vendors (page 160).
- Track petty cash (page 165).
- Track credit card charges and payments (page 166).
- Create reports about vendor transactions (page 169).
- Track Loans using the QuickBooks Loan Manager (page 171).

Comprehension Questions

> Answers to these review questions are available with the supplemental material. See page xiii for details.

1. Describe how classes are used in QuickBooks.
2. Describe how to track expenses by job in QuickBooks.
3. Describe the steps in tracking Accounts Payable transactions in QuickBooks.
4. Under what circumstances is it important to use Bill Credits to record discounts?
5. To track credit card charges and payments in a separate liability account, describe the steps you must use to record charges and payments on the credit card.

Multiple Choice

Select the best answer(s) for each of the following:

1. You may record payments to your vendors by:
   a) Recording a manual entry directly into the check register.
   b) Using *Write Checks* to write and print a check without using Accounts Payable.
   c) Using *Enter Bills* to record Accounts Payable and then using *Pay Bills* to pay open Bills.
   d) a, b, or c.
2. To display the *Vendor Center:*
   a) Click Vendors on the QuickBooks *Home* Page.
   b) Click the **Vendor Center** icon on the Navigation Bar.
   c) Select the *Vendor* menu and then select **Vendor Center**.
   d) a, b, or c.
3. You can add a vendor:
   a) Only at the beginning of the fiscal year.
   b) Only if you will purchase over $600 from that particular vendor and a Form 1099 will be issued.
   c) Only at the beginning of the month.
   d) At any time by selecting *New Vendor* in the **Vendor Center**.
4. Which statement is true?
   a) QuickBooks records each Bill Payment in a bank account register (or credit card account register) and the Accounts Payable register.
   b) Bill Payments increase the balance in both the Checking Account and the Accounts Payable account.
   c) You should assign jobs to all discounts taken.
   d) You cannot make partial payments on a Bill.

5. Which QuickBooks feature allows you to separate your income and expenses by line of business, department, location, profit centers, or any other meaningful breakdown of your business:
   a) Job Costing.
   b) Class tracking.
   c) Customer types.
   d) Vendor types.
6. If you void a Bill Payment check, all of the following occur, except:
   a) QuickBooks retains a trail of the check number, but the amount becomes zero.
   b) The Bill becomes unpaid.
   c) The Checking account balance increases.
   d) The Accounts Payable account decreases.
7. If you want to track the expenses for each customer or job:
   a) Enter each expense in the job-cost section.
   b) Use the pay liabilities function.
   c) Link each expense with the customer or job to which it applies.
   d) Create a separate expense account for each job.
8. To make a loan payment, you can:
   a) Select the loan liability account in the Chart of Accounts and choose Make Deposit from the Activities Menu.
   b) Choose Pay Loan from the Banking Menu.
   c) Use the **Loan Manager** to calculate the interest and principal amounts. Select the **Loan Manager**, then select the Loan to pay, and then select **Set Up Payment**.
   d) All of the Above.
9. When a vendor credits your account, you record it in:
   a) The *Write Checks* window.
   b) The *Enter Bills* window.
   c) The *Pay Bills* window.
   d) The *Accounts Payable* Register.
10. Which Account-type should you use to track Petty Cash:
    a) Credit Card.
    b) Equity.
    c) Bank.
    d) Checking.
11. The Vendor Balance Detail Report:
    a) Shows the detail of each Bill, Bill Credit, Discount, and Bill Payment to each vendor.
    b) Shows the detail of each payment created using the *Write Checks* window.
    c) Can be created by selecting *Vendor Balance Detail* report from the **Vendor Center**.
    d) None of the above.
12. What is the accounting behind the scenes for the *Pay Bills* window:
    a) Increase (debit) Accounts Payable, Decrease (credit) the Checking Account.
    b) Decrease (debit) Accounts Payable, Decrease (credit) the Checking Account.
    c) Decrease (debit) Accounts Payable, Increase (credit) the Checking Account.
    d) Decrease (debit) Accounts Payable, Decrease (debit) the Checking Account.
13. It's best not to use which field in the new vendor setup window:
    a) Opening Balance.

b) Vendor Name.
c) Address.
d) Terms.

14. In the *Pay Bills* window, you can sort the Bills by:
    a) Due Date.
    b) Vendor.
    c) Discount Date.
    d) All of the above.

15. Which statement is true regarding bill payments:
    a) Bill Payments *increase* the balance in the Accounts Payable account.
    b) When you use a check to pay bills, QuickBooks records each Bill Payment in the Checking account register and in the Accounts Payable account register.
    c) If you select more than one Bill for the same vendor, QuickBooks creates a separate Bill Payment for each Bill.
    d) Bill Credits that are created from a vendor are automatically applied to Bills that are due for that same vendor.

Completion Statements

1. The ______ _______ shows a graphical representation of the steps involved in recording your expenses.
2. Terms of 2% 10 Net 30 on a bill means that if you pay the bill within _________ days, you are eligible for a ________ discount.
3. To separately track income and expenses for multiple departments, locations, or profit centers, use _________ tracking.
4. To track job costs in QuickBooks, link each expense with the _________ or _______ to which it applies.
5. For a Bill to be considered paid by QuickBooks, you must pay the Bill using the _______ _________ window.

Expenses-Problem 1

APPLYING YOUR KNOWLEDGE

Restore the Expenses-10Problem1.QBM file according to your instructor's directions.

1. Activate Class tracking in the data file.
2. Add a new Vendor to the Vendor list using the data in the table below.

Field Name	Data
Vendor Name	*Jordan Photography Services*
Company Name	*Jordan Photography Services*
Mr./Ms./...	*Ms.*
First Name	*Kate*
M.I.	
Last Name	*Jordan*
Name and Address	*Jordan Photography Services* *Kate Jordan* *1425 14th Ave.* *Castro Valley, CA 94500*
Contact	*Kate Jordan*
Phone	*(510) 555-1414*
Fax	
Alt Ph.	
Alt. Contact	
Email	*kate@jordanphoto.biz*
Cc	
Print on Check as	*Jordan Photography Services*
Account #	*89766-46*
Vendor Type	*Consultant*
Terms	*Net 30*
Credit Limit	
Tax ID	*111-22-3333*
Check Box	*Vendor eligible for 1099*
County	*Alameda*
Account Prefill	*Professional Fees*

Table 4-3 Use this data to enter a new vendor

3. Print the Vendor List. (From the *Reports* menu, select **Vendors & Payables** and then select **Vendor Contact List.**)

4. Enter check #*331* directly in the *Checking* register on ***01/12/2011*** to ***Michael's Hardware*** for $*485.00*. Use **QuickAdd** to add the Vendor. Split the expense to $*100.00* for **Office Supplies** for the **San Jose** store and $*385.00* for **Repairs and Maintenance** for the **Walnut Creek** store.
5. Using **Write Checks**, enter a check (**to be printed**) to ***Orlando Properties***, dated ***01/12/2011*** for $*1,500.00*, for **Rent** at the **San Jose** store. Make the check printable, but don't print the check.
6. Enter **Bill #*1500*** from ***Nellis Distributing*** on ***01/18/2011*** for ***$732.00*** with terms of **Net 15**. The Bill is for the purchase of supplies for the Bob Mason job, so code the Bill to **Cost of Goods Sold**. Bob Mason is a customer in the San Jose store, so link the cost with the appropriate job and class.
7. Enter **Bill #*3453*** from ***Sinclair Insurance*** on ***01/19/2011*** for $*1,250.00* with terms of **Net 30**. Code the Bill to **Insurance Expense**. Allocate 100% of the cost to the **San Jose** store.
8. Create and print an **Unpaid Bills Detail** report dated 1/20/2011.
9. Pay all of the Bills due on or before **02/28/2011**. Pay the Bills from the *Checking* account on 01/19/2011. Make the Bill Payments "printable" checks.
10. Print all of the checks that you recorded with a "to be printed" status. Print them on blank paper and start the check numbers at ***6001***.
11. Enter a credit card charge on the **National Bank VISA** card from **Bay Office Supply** (Use Quick Add to add the vendor), reference #*1234*, dated ***1/25/2011***. The purchase was for $*87.55* for office supplies for the Walnut Creek store.
12. Enter Bill #*4635* from ***Ace Supply*** on ***01/25/2011*** for $*1,776.50* with terms of **Net 30.** Code the Bill to **Cost of Goods Sold** since it was for supplies for the **Ron Berry** job. Ron Berry is a customer at the **San Jose** store. Keep the default terms for Ace Supply.
13. Enter a *Bill Credit* from ***Ace Supply*** on ***01/30/2011*** for ***$650.00***. Use reference number ***4635C*** on the credit. Code the credit to **Cost of Goods Sold** and link the credit with the **Ron Berry** job and the **San Jose** class.
14. Apply the credit to Bill **#4635** and pay the remainder of the Bill on ***01/30/2011*** using a printable check.
15. Print check **#6005** on blank paper.
16. Print a **Vendor Balance Detail** report for **All** transactions.

Workplace Applications

Discussion Questions

These questions are designed to stimulate discussion about how you can apply QuickBooks to your own organization. They may help you think through some of the issues you'll encounter when using QuickBooks in your company.

1. How many locations does your organization have? Does your organization track purchases or costs by each location?

2. Does your organization keep track of specific job or project costs for a customer? If so, how does your organization use that information? Does it affect the estimates or prices for future jobs or projects? If yes, what is the process you follow?
3. Which of your vendors send you bills? Do they offer you discount terms? If so, list some of the different discount terms you receive.
4. What is your organization's cash management policy that determines when you will pay your bills?
5. Does your organization have vendor returns or disputes that result in vendor credits? How do you receive them? Are they separate pieces of paper, are they listed on each customer statement, or do you receive refunds?
6. Does your organization have company credit cards? How many? Are they issued in an individual's name or only in the organization's name? How are the credit cards controlled? In what ways will QuickBooks' credit card-tracking function improve your ability to manage credit card expenditures?

Case Study

Music Central

Music Central sells and services musical instruments and teaches music lessons. One of the store's piano students, Peter Cornish, who has been a long-time customer, has just mentioned that he sells guitar strings. He will sell Music Central 100 strings for only $500. However, if they pay the bill in 10 days, he will give a discount of $50.

1. If you chose Peter Cornish as a vendor, do you have to enter him as a vendor since he is already in QuickBooks as a customer? Do you enter his name the same or differently?
2. How would you enter the terms that Cornish specified for payment?
3. Since Cornish wants a check, do you need to enter this as Account Payable or just write a check from the *Checking* register?
4. If you have a *Petty Cash* account and one of your assistants paid Cornish from *Petty Cash,* what steps should you take to record the transaction?

Chapter 5 Bank Reconciliation

Objectives

After completing this chapter, you should be able to:

- Reconcile your checking account (page 184).
- Create bank reconciliation reports (page 190).
- Find errors during reconciliation (page 192).
- Correct errors found during reconciliation (page 196).
- Make corrections when QuickBooks automatically adjusts the balance in a bank account (page 200).
- Handle bounced checks (page 200).
- Reconcile credit card accounts and record a bill for later payment (page 206).
- Improve efficiency with Online Banking (page 210)

Restore this File

This chapter uses BankRec-10.QBW. To open this file, restore the BankRec-10.QBM file to your hard disk. See page 10 for instructions on restoring files.

As you write checks, withdraw money, make deposits, and incur bank charges, each of these transactions are recorded in QuickBooks. Then, at the end of each month, you must compare these transactions with your bank statement to ensure that each QuickBooks transaction matches the bank's records.

This process is called *reconciling.* It is a very important step in the overall accounting process and its primary goal is to ensure the accuracy of your accounting records.

In addition to reconciling bank accounts, you can also reconcile other accounts such as credit card accounts using the same process. For example, if you track each credit card transaction (charges, payments, interest charges, etc.) in a separate credit card liability account in QuickBooks, you should reconcile your QuickBooks credit card accounts with your monthly credit card statement.

In fact, you can reconcile almost any Other Current Asset, Fixed Asset, Credit Card, Other Current Liability, Long Term Liability, or Equity account using the same process presented in this chapter. However, even though QuickBooks *allows* you to reconcile many accounts, the primary accounts you'll reconcile are bank and credit card accounts since these types of accounts always have monthly statements.

In this chapter, you'll learn how to reconcile bank and credit card accounts as well as how to find and correct errors in the reconciliation process.

Reconciling Bank Accounts

Figure 5-1 shows Academy Photography's bank statement for the checking account as of January 31, 2011. Before reconciling the account in QuickBooks, make sure you've entered all of the transactions for that account. For example, if you have automatic payments from your checking account (EFTs) or automatic charges on your credit card, it is best to enter those transactions before you start the reconciliation.

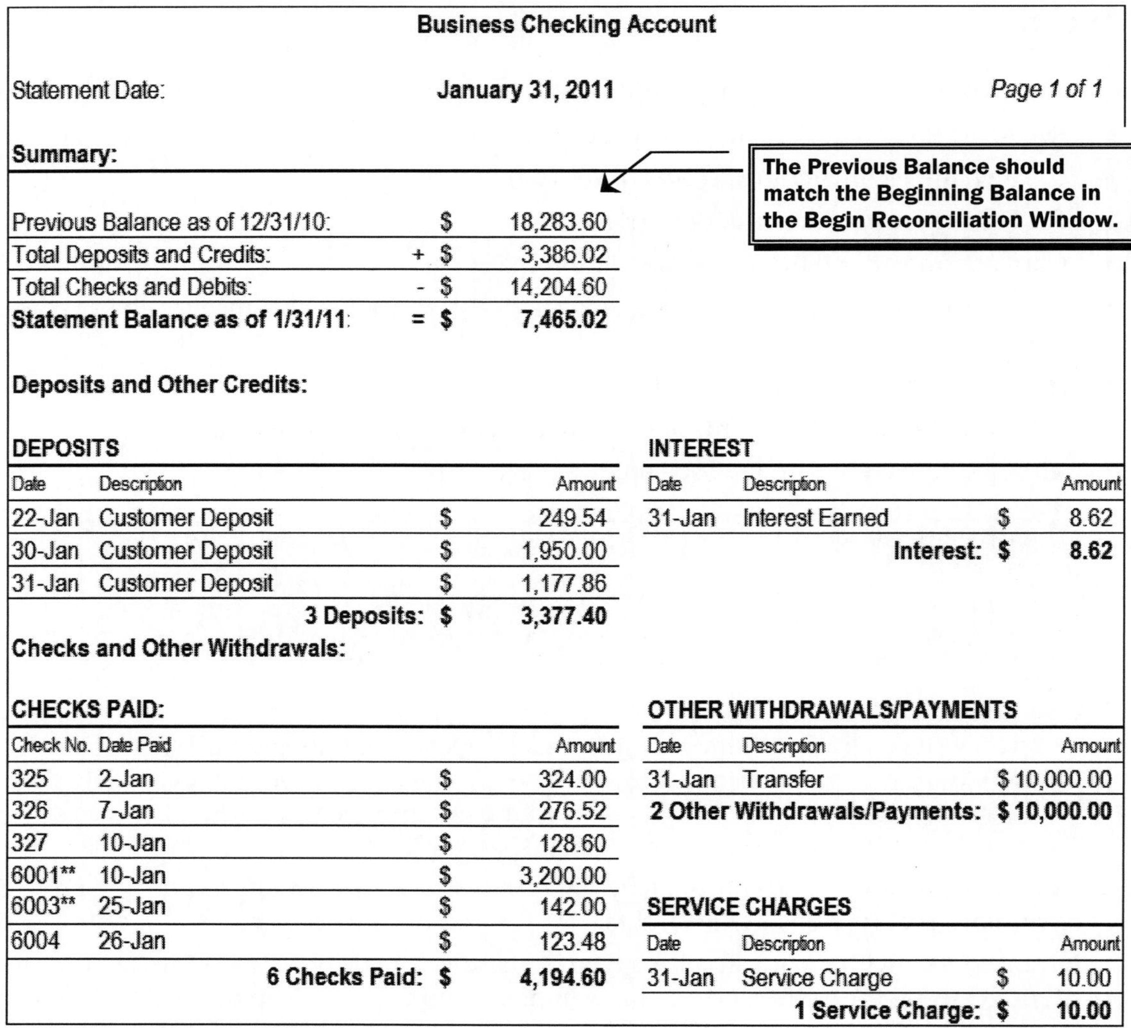

Business Checking Account

Statement Date: **January 31, 2011** *Page 1 of 1*

Summary:

Previous Balance as of 12/31/10:		$	18,283.60
Total Deposits and Credits:	+	$	3,386.02
Total Checks and Debits:	-	$	14,204.60
Statement Balance as of 1/31/11:	**=**	**$**	**7,465.02**

Deposits and Other Credits:

DEPOSITS

Date	Description		Amount
22-Jan	Customer Deposit	$	249.54
30-Jan	Customer Deposit	$	1,950.00
31-Jan	Customer Deposit	$	1,177.86
	3 Deposits:	**$**	**3,377.40**

INTEREST

Date	Description		Amount
31-Jan	Interest Earned	$	8.62
	Interest:	**$**	**8.62**

Checks and Other Withdrawals:

CHECKS PAID:

Check No.	Date Paid		Amount
325	2-Jan	$	324.00
326	7-Jan	$	276.52
327	10-Jan	$	128.60
6001**	10-Jan	$	3,200.00
6003**	25-Jan	$	142.00
6004	26-Jan	$	123.48
	6 Checks Paid:	**$**	**4,194.60**

OTHER WITHDRAWALS/PAYMENTS

Date	Description	Amount
31-Jan	Transfer	$ 10,000.00
	2 Other Withdrawals/Payments:	**$ 10,000.00**

SERVICE CHARGES

Date	Description		Amount
31-Jan	Service Charge	$	10.00
	1 Service Charge:	**$**	**10.00**

Figure 5-1 Sample bank statement

COMPUTER PRACTICE

Using the sample data file for this chapter, follow these steps to reconcile the QuickBooks Checking account with the bank statement shown in Figure 5-1.

Step 1. Before you begin the reconciliation process, first review the account register to verify that all of the transactions for the statement period have been entered (e.g., deposits, checks, other withdrawals, and payments). You don't need to record the "bank originated" transactions such as interest received and bank charges, because these transactions can be recorded during the reconciliation.

The Academy Photography sample data file for this section already has the deposits, checks, other withdrawals, and payments entered into the register.

Step 2. If the *Home* page is not already open, select the **Company** menu and then select **Home Page**.

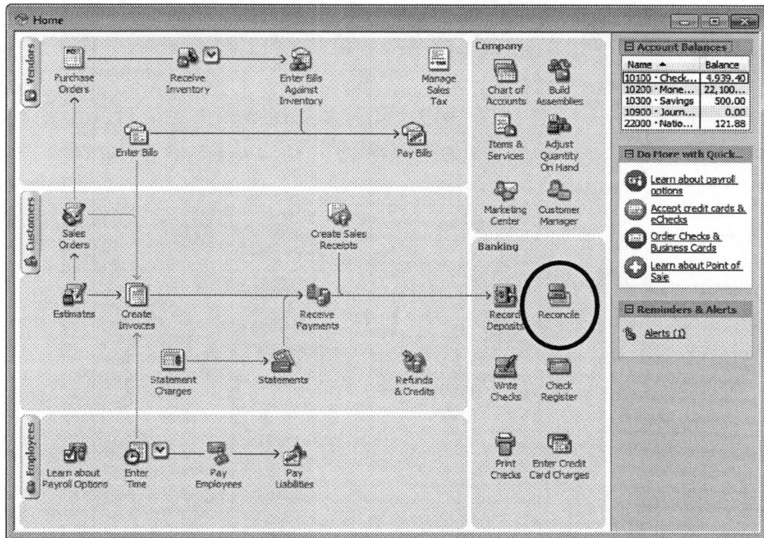

Figure 5-2 The Home Page

Step 3. Click the **Reconcile** Icon on the *Banking* section of the *Home* page (see Figure 5-2).

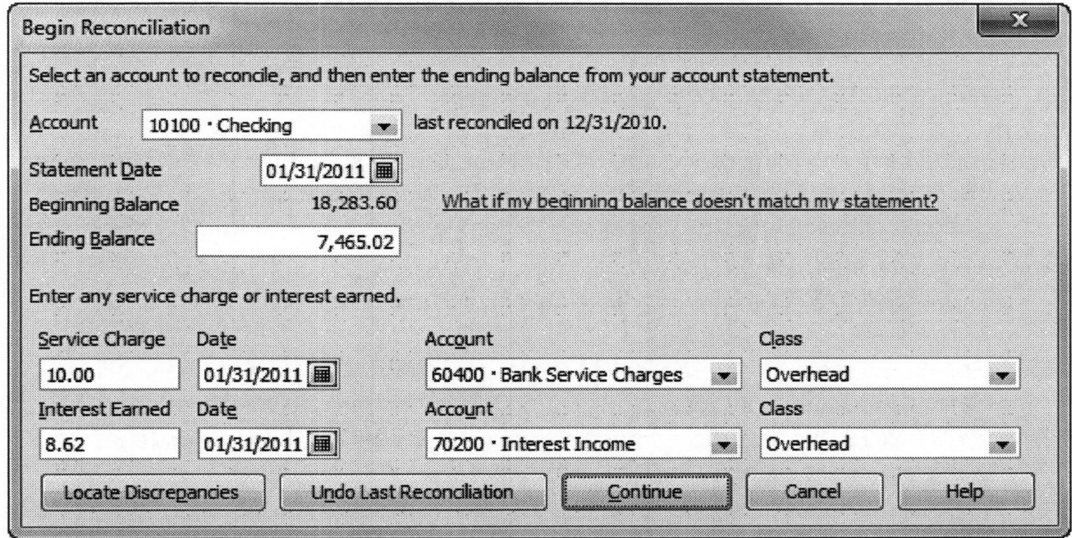

Figure 5-3 Begin Reconciliation window

Step 4. In the ***Begin Reconciliation*** window (see Figure 5-3), the *Account* field already shows **Checking**. The account drop-down list allows you to select other accounts to reconcile, however since **Checking** is the account you're reconciling, you don't need to change it now. Press **Tab**.

Step 5. Leave **01/31/2011** in the *Statement Date* field and press **Tab**.

The default statement date is one month after your last reconciliation date. Since this account was last reconciled on 12/31/2010, QuickBooks entered ***01/31/2011***. Before proceeding to the next field, confirm this date matches your bank statement date. Correct it if necessary.

> **Tip:**
> If your bank does not date statements at the end of the month, ask the bank to change your statement date to the end of the month. This makes it easier to match the bank statement with your month-end reports in QuickBooks.

Step 6. Look for the *Previous Balance as of 12/31/10* on the bank statement (see Figure 5-1). Compare this amount with the *Beginning Balance* amount in the *Begin Reconciliation* window (see Figure 5-3). Notice that they are the same.

> **Note:**
> QuickBooks calculates the *Beginning Balance* field in the *Begin Reconciliation* window by adding and subtracting all previously reconciled transactions. If the beginning balance does not match the bank statement, you probably made changes to previously cleared transactions. See *Finding Errors During Bank Reconciliation* on page 192 for more information.

Step 7. Enter ***7,465.02*** in the *Ending Balance* field. This amount is the *Statement Balance as of 1/31/11* shown on the bank statement in Figure 5-1. Press **Tab**.

> **Note:**
> If you already recorded bank charges in the check register, skip Step 8 through Step 11 to avoid duplicate entry of the charges.

Step 8. Enter ***10.00*** in the *Service Charge* field and press **Tab**.

If you have any bank service charges or interest earned in the bank account, enter those amounts in the appropriate fields in the *Begin Reconciliation* window. When you enter these amounts, QuickBooks adds the corresponding transactions to your bank account register.

Step 9. Leave **01/31/2011** in the *Date* field and press **Tab**.

The default date for the service charge is one month after your last reconciliation. Since this account was last reconciled on 12/31/2010, QuickBooks entered ***01/31/2011***. Before proceeding to the next field, confirm this date matches your bank statement date. Correct it if necessary.

Step 10. Select ***Bank Service Charges*** from the *Account* drop-down list and press **Tab**.

Each time you reconcile, this field will default to the account you used on the last bank reconciliation. Confirm that this is the correct expense account before proceeding to the next field.

Step 11. Select ***Overhead*** from the *Class* drop-down list and press **Tab**.

> **Note:**
> If you already recorded interest income in the check register, skip Step 12 through Step 15 to avoid duplicate entry of the interest income.

Step 12. Enter ***8.62*** in the *Interest Earned* field and press **Tab**.

Step 13. Leave **01/31/2011** in the *Date* field and press **Tab**.

Step 14. Select ***Interest Income*** from the *Account* drop-down list and press **Tab**.

Step 15. Select ***Overhead*** from the *Class* drop-down list and click **Continue**.

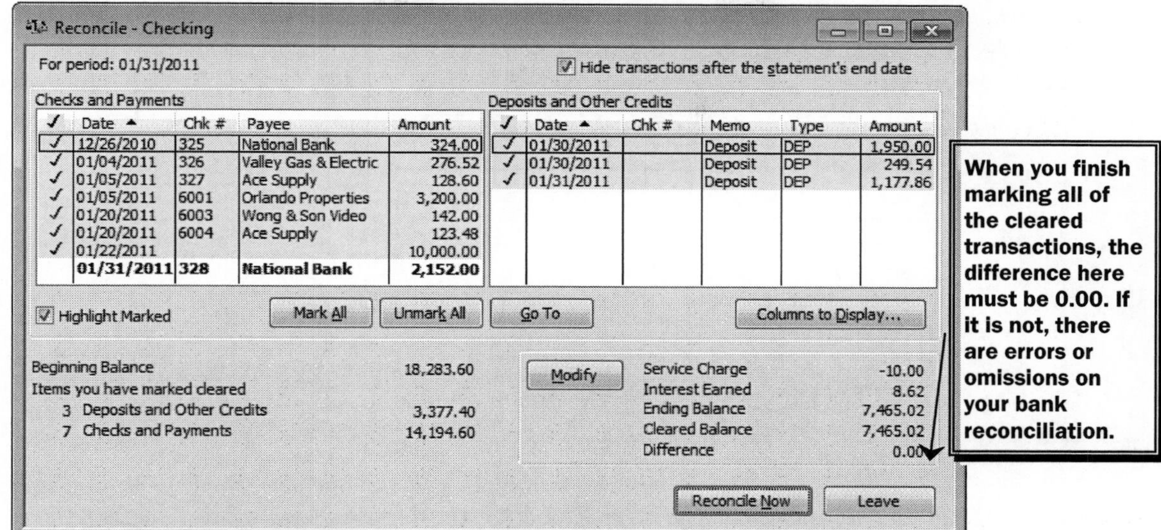

Figure 5-4 Reconcile – Checking window

Step 16. At the top of the *Reconcile – Checking* window (see Figure 5-4), check the box labeled "Hide transactions after the statement ending date".

Hide transactions after the statement's end date

This removes transactions dated after the statement date from being displayed on the screen. Since they could not possibly have cleared, this simplifies your life so you only have to look at transactions that *could* have cleared the bank as of the statement date.

Step 17. In the *Deposits, Interest, and Other Credits* section of the *Reconcile – Checking* window, match the deposits and other credits on the bank statement (see Figure 5-1 on page 184) with the associated QuickBooks transactions. Click anywhere on a line to mark it cleared. The checkmark (✓) indicates which transactions have cleared.

Step 18. In the *Checks, Payments, and Service Charges* section of the *Reconcile – Checking* window, match the checks and other withdrawals on the bank statement with the associated QuickBooks transactions.

Tip:
Notice that QuickBooks calculates the sum of your marked items at the bottom of the window in the *Items you have marked cleared* section. This section also shows the number of deposits and checks you have marked cleared. Compare the figures to your bank statement. If you find a discrepancy with these totals, you most likely have an error. Search for an item you forgot to mark or one that you marked in error.

Tip:
You can sort the columns in the *Reconcile - Checking* window by clicking the column heading. If you would like to change the columns displayed in the *Reconcile – Checking* window, click the **Columns to Display** button. This will allow you to select which columns you would like to see when you are reconciling (see Figure 5-5).

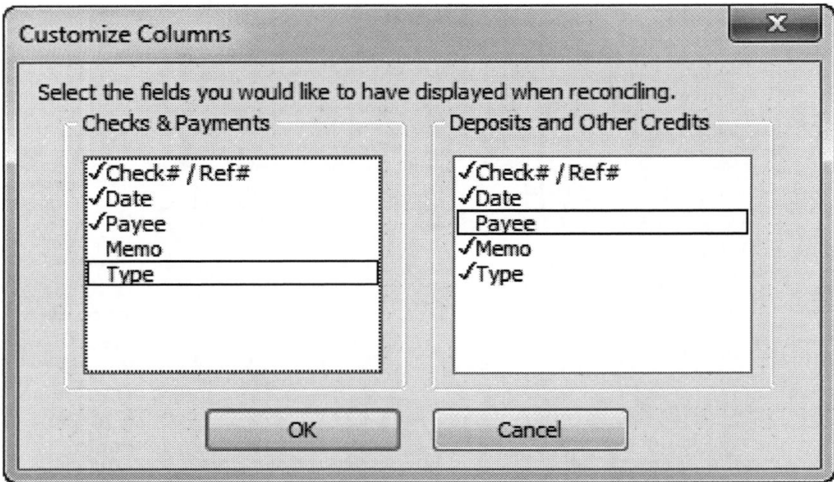

Figure 5-5 Customizing the Bank Reconciliation with Columns to Display

Step 19. After you've marked all the cleared checks and deposits, look at the *Difference* field. It should be **0.00**, indicating that your bank account is reconciled.

If the *Difference* field is not zero, check for errors. For help in troubleshooting your bank reconciliation, see *Finding Errors During Bank Reconciliation* on page 192.

> **Tip:**
> If you need to wait until another time to complete the bank reconciliation, you can click **Leave**. When you click **Leave**, QuickBooks will save all of your changes so you can complete the reconciliation later.

Step 20. If the *Difference* field is zero, you've successfully reconciled. Click ***Reconcile Now***. If you see a window offering online banking, click **OK** to close.

> **Note:**
> It is very important that you do not click **Reconcile Now** unless the *Difference* field shows **0.00**. Doing so will cause discrepancies in your accounting records. See page 200 for more information.

Step 21. The *Select Reconciliation Report* dialog box displays. The **Both** option is already selected, so click **Display** to view your reports on the screen (see Figure 5-6).

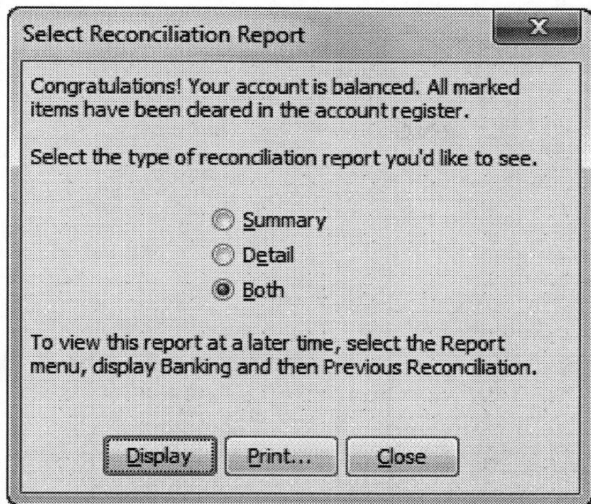

Figure 5-6 Select Reconciliation Report window

Step 22. Click **OK** on the *Reconciliation Report* dialog box (see Figure 5-7).

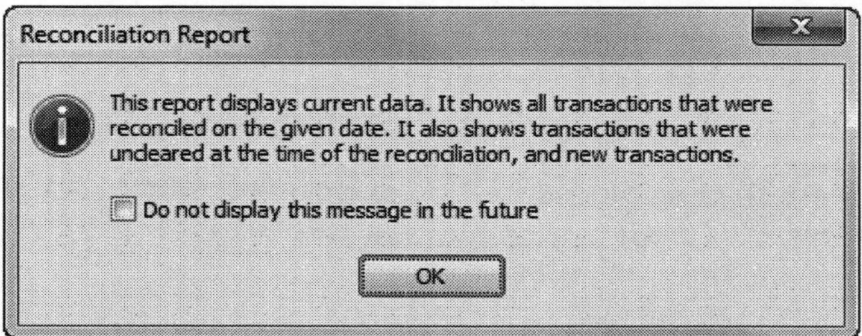

Figure 5-7 Reconciliation Report information window

Step 23. QuickBooks creates both a **Reconciliation Summary** report (Figure 5-8) and a **Reconciliation Detail** report (Figure 5-9). The length of the detail report will depend on how many transactions you cleared on this reconciliation and how many uncleared transactions remain in the account.

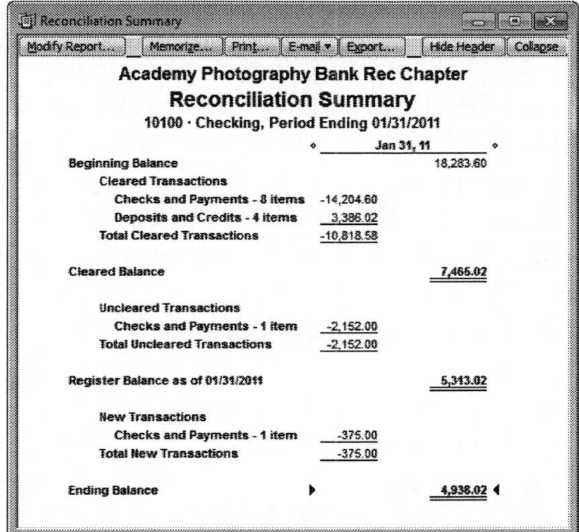

Academy Photography Bank Rec Chapter

Reconciliation Summary

10100 · Checking, Period Ending 01/31/2011

		Jan 31, 11
Beginning Balance		18,283.60
Cleared Transactions		
Checks and Payments - 8 items	-14,204.60	
Deposits and Credits - 4 items	3,386.02	
Total Cleared Transactions	-10,818.58	
Cleared Balance		7,465.02
Uncleared Transactions		
Checks and Payments - 1 item	-2,152.00	
Total Uncleared Transactions	-2,152.00	
Register Balance as of 01/31/2011		5,313.02
New Transactions		
Checks and Payments - 1 item	-375.00	
Total New Transactions	-375.00	
Ending Balance		4,938.02

Figure 5-8 Reconciliation Summary report

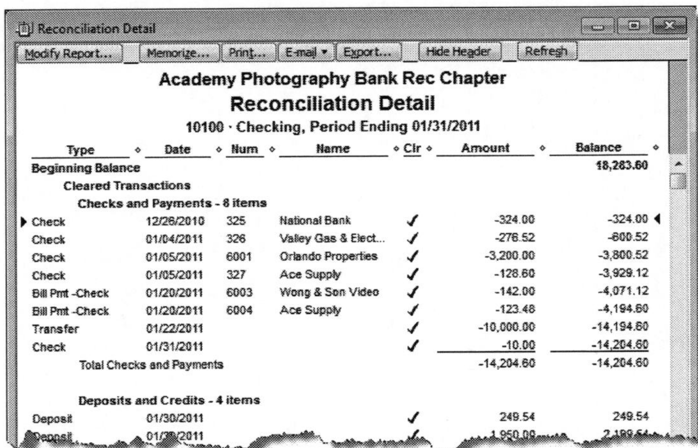
Reconciliation Detail

Modify Report... | Memorize... | Print... | E-mail ▾ | Export... | Hide Header | Refresh

Academy Photography Bank Rec Chapter
Reconciliation Detail
10100 · Checking, Period Ending 01/31/2011

Type	Date	Num	Name	Clr	Amount	Balance
Beginning Balance						18,283.60
Cleared Transactions						
Checks and Payments - 8 items						
Check	12/26/2010	325	National Bank	✓	-324.00	-324.00
Check	01/04/2011	326	Valley Gas & Elect...	✓	-276.52	-600.52
Check	01/05/2011	6001	Orlando Properties	✓	-3,200.00	-3,800.52
Check	01/05/2011	327	Ace Supply	✓	-128.60	-3,929.12
Bill Pmt -Check	01/20/2011	6003	Wong & Son Video	✓	-142.00	-4,071.12
Bill Pmt -Check	01/20/2011	6004	Ace Supply	✓	-123.48	-4,194.60
Transfer	01/22/2011			✓	-10,000.00	-14,194.60
Check	01/31/2011			✓	-10.00	-14,204.60
Total Checks and Payments					-14,204.60	-14,204.60
Deposits and Credits - 4 items						
Deposit	01/30/2011			✓	249.54	249.54
Deposit	01/30/2011			✓	1,950.00	2,199.54

Figure 5-9 Reconciliation Detail report

Step 24. To print the reports, click **Print** at the top of each report.

Step 25. Close all open report windows.

Bank Reconciliation Reports

Each time you complete a bank reconciliation, QuickBooks walks you through creating a bank reconciliation report for that reconciliation. You can recreate your bank reconciliation reports at any time by following the steps below.

> Note:
> If you are using QuickBooks Pro you can create Bank Reconciliation reports for the most recently reconciled month only. QuickBooks Premier allows you to view and print bank reconciliation reports for all bank reconciliations performed using QuickBooks versions 2002 or later. The examples and screenshots in this section apply to QuickBooks Premier.

COMPUTER PRACTICE

Step 1. From the *Reports* menu select **Banking** and then select **Previous Reconciliation**. The **Select Previous Reconciliation Report** window displays (see Figure 5-10).

Step 2. Confirm that **Checking** is selected in the *Account* field.

If you have more than one bank account, you can select another bank account using the *Account* drop-down list.

Step 3. Confirm that **01/31/2011** is selected in the *Statement Ending Date* field.

QuickBooks automatically selects the report for your most recent bank reconciliation. You can select another report by highlighting the statement date in this section.

Step 4. Confirm that **Detail** is selected in the *Type of Report* section.

Step 5. Confirm that **Transactions cleared at the time of reconciliation** in the *In this report, include* section is selected. When you select this option, QuickBooks displays an Adobe Acrobat PDF file with the contents of the reconciliation report. The Acrobat (PDF) report does not include any changes you may have made to reconciled transactions. See Figure 5-10.

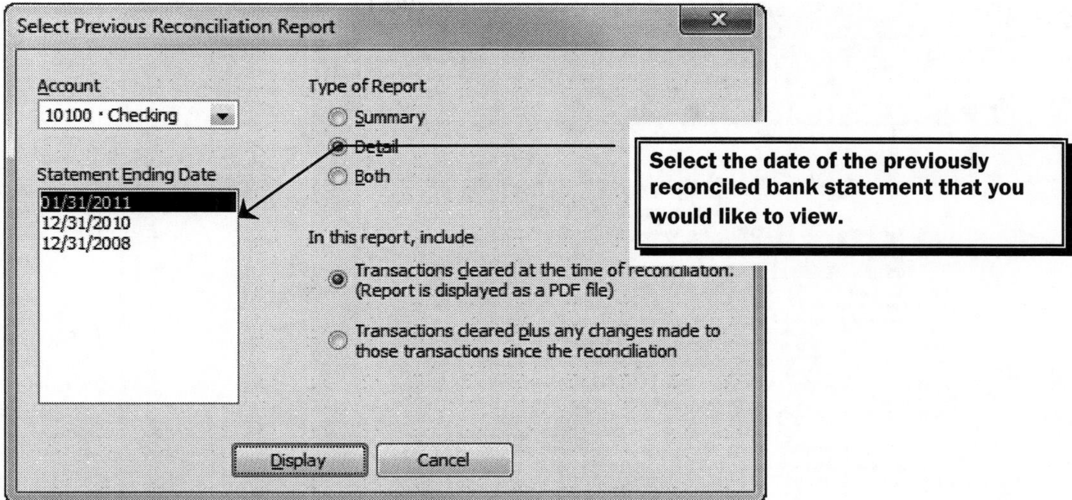

Figure 5-10 Printing a Previous Bank Reconciliation

Step 6. Click **Display** to view your bank reconciliation reports on screen.

Note:
If your screen does not show the Balance column in the window shown in Figure 5-11, you need to set your Printer Setup settings to fit the report to 1 page wide before you perform the bank reconciliation. This is because Acrobat creates the report when you finish the reconciliation and uses the settings in your Printer Setup to determine how to lay out the page.

If you have already created the report you can undo the reconciliation (see page 193) and then select **Printer Setup** from the *File* menu. When the *Printer setup* window displays select **Report** from the *Form Name* drop down list. At the bottom of the window you can check the **Fit report to** option and enter ***1*** for the number of pages wide you want reports to display, as illustrated below.

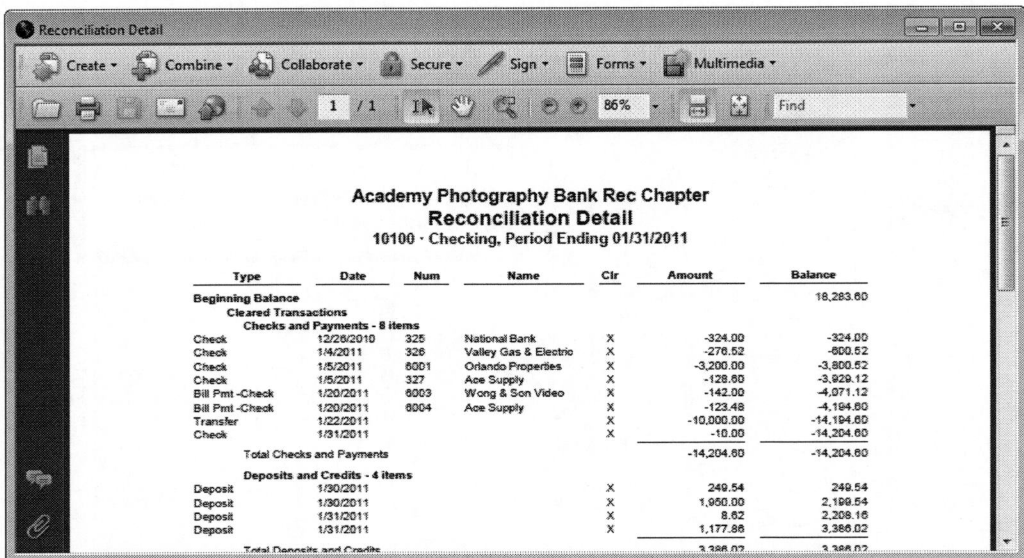

Academy Photography Bank Rec Chapter
Reconciliation Detail
10100 · Checking, Period Ending 01/31/2011

Type	Date	Num	Name	Clr	Amount	Balance
Beginning Balance						18,283.60
Cleared Transactions						
Checks and Payments - 8 items						
Check	12/28/2010	325	National Bank	X	-324.00	-324.00
Check	1/4/2011	326	Valley Gas & Electric	X	-276.52	-600.52
Check	1/5/2011	6001	Orlando Properties	X	-3,200.00	-3,800.52
Check	1/5/2011	327	Ace Supply	X	-128.60	-3,929.12
Bill Pmt -Check	1/20/2011	6003	Wong & Son Video	X	-142.00	-4,071.12
Bill Pmt -Check	1/20/2011	6004	Ace Supply	X	-123.48	-4,194.60
Transfer	1/22/2011			X	-10,000.00	-14,194.60
Check	1/31/2011			X	-10.00	-14,204.60
Total Checks and Payments					-14,204.60	-14,204.60
Deposits and Credits - 4 items						
Deposit	1/30/2011			X	249.54	249.54
Deposit	1/30/2011			X	1,950.00	2,199.54
Deposit	1/31/2011			X	8.62	2,208.16
Deposit	1/31/2011			X	1,177.86	3,386.02
Total Deposits and Credits					3,386.02	3,386.02

Figure 5-11 Adobe Acrobat (PDF) bank reconciliation report – your screen may vary

Step 7. With the report displayed, click the **Print** icon to print the report. Then, close the **Reconciliation Detail** report.

> Note:
> If you prefer to create a normal QuickBooks reconciliation report (as opposed to an Acrobat PDF report), select the option, **Transactions cleared plus any changes made to those transactions since the reconciliation** in Step 5 above.

Finding Errors During Bank Reconciliation

If you have finished checking off all of the deposits and checks but the *Difference* field at the bottom of the window does not equal zero, there is an error (or discrepancy) that must be found and corrected. To find errors in your bank reconciliation, try the following steps:

Step 1: Review the Beginning Balance Field

Verify that the amount in the *Beginning Balance* field matches the beginning balance on your bank statement. If it does not, you are not ready to reconcile. There are two possibilities for why the beginning balance will no longer match to the bank statement:

1. One or more reconciled transactions were voided, deleted, or changed since the last reconciliation; and/or,
2. The checkmark on one or more reconciled transactions in the account register was removed since the last reconciliation.

To correct the problem you have two options:

Option 1: Use the Reconciliation Discrepancy Report to Troubleshoot

> DO NOT PERFORM THESE STEPS NOW. THEY ARE FOR REFERENCE ONLY.

1. From the **Reports** menu select **Banking** and then select **Reconciliation Discrepancy**. QuickBooks displays the window shown in Figure 5-12.
2. Select the appropriate account from the *Specify Account* drop-down list and click **OK**.

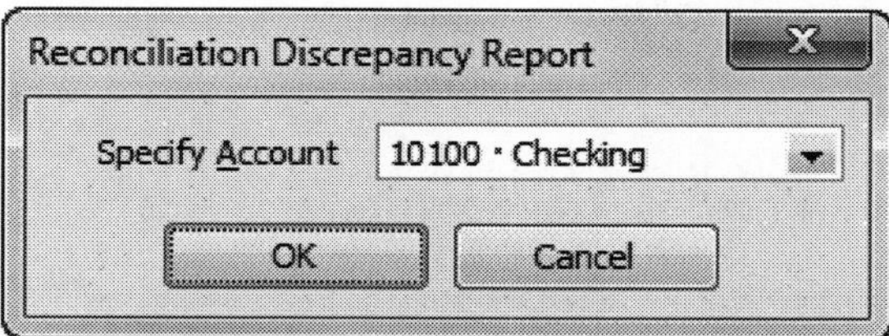

Figure 5-12 Reconciliation Discrepancy Report Account Selection window

3. QuickBooks displays the **Previous Reconciliation Discrepancy** report shown in Figure 5-13.

> **Note:**
> If you're using the sample data file for this chapter (BankRec-10.QBW), this report will be blank because the reconciled transactions have not been modified. However, these steps can be used on your own file to troubleshoot reconciliation problems.

Review the report for any changes or deletions to cleared transactions. The *Type of Change* column shows the nature of the change to the transaction. Notice on the first line that a user deleted a cleared check. On the second line of the report a user changed the amount of a check.

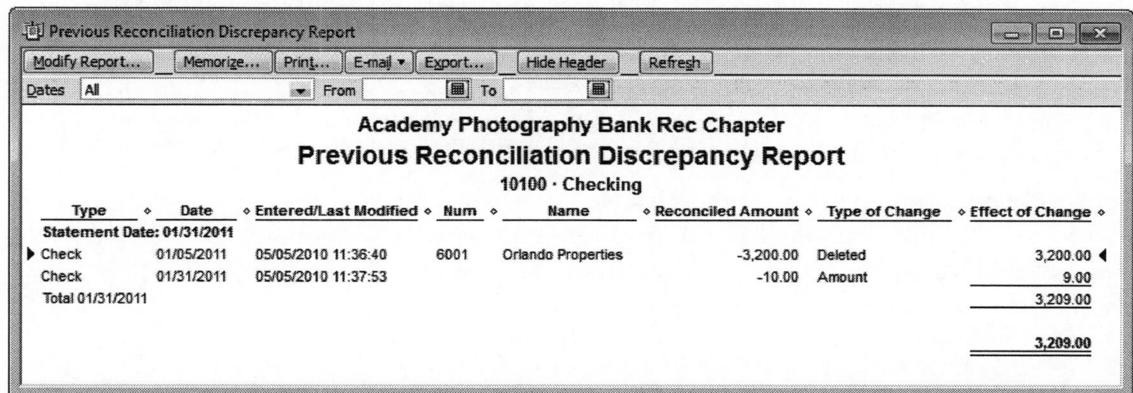

Academy Photography Bank Rec Chapter
Previous Reconciliation Discrepancy Report
10100 · Checking

Type	Date	Entered/Last Modified	Num	Name	Reconciled Amount	Type of Change	Effect of Change
Statement Date: 01/31/2011							
Check	01/05/2011	05/05/2010 11:36:40	6001	Orlando Properties	-3,200.00	Deleted	3,200.00
Check	01/31/2011	05/05/2010 11:37:53			-10.00	Amount	9.00
Total 01/31/2011							3,209.00
							3,209.00

Figure 5-13 Reconciliation Discrepancy report

4. For each line of the report with "Deleted" in the *Type of Change* column, re-enter the deleted transaction. Then, use the *Bank Reconciliation* window to re-reconcile the transaction that had been deleted.
5. For each line of the report with "Amount" in the *Type of Change* column, double-click the transaction in the **Reconciliation Discrepancy** report to open it (i.e., QuickZoom). Then, change the amount back to the reconciled amount.

After returning all transactions to their original state (as they were at the time of the last reconciliation), then you can proceed to investigate whether the changes were necessary, and if so, enter adjustment transactions. For instructions on how to adjust for errors, see the **Adjustments** chapter included with the supplemental material for this book (see page xiii).

Option 2: Undo the Bank Reconciliation

> DO NOT PERFORM THESE STEPS NOW. THEY ARE FOR REFERENCE ONLY.

The **Previous Reconciliation Discrepancy** report only shows changes to cleared transactions since your most recent bank reconciliation. If the beginning balance was incorrect when you performed previous bank reconciliations, the **Previous Reconciliation Discrepancy** report will not fully explain the problem.

If this is the case, the best way to find and correct the problem is to undo the previous reconciliation(s). Perform the following steps to restore the beginning balance:

> **Note:**
> If you're using the sample data file for this chapter (BankRec-10.QBW), you can perform steps 1-4 to see how the process works, but do not perform step 5 or after. Instead, just cancel out after step 4. These steps can be used on your own file to troubleshoot reconciliation problems.

1. Select the **Banking** menu, and then select **Reconcile**.
2. In the *Begin Reconciliation* window, confirm that **Checking** is selected in the *Account* field. See Figure 5-14.
3. Click the **Locate Discrepancies** button.

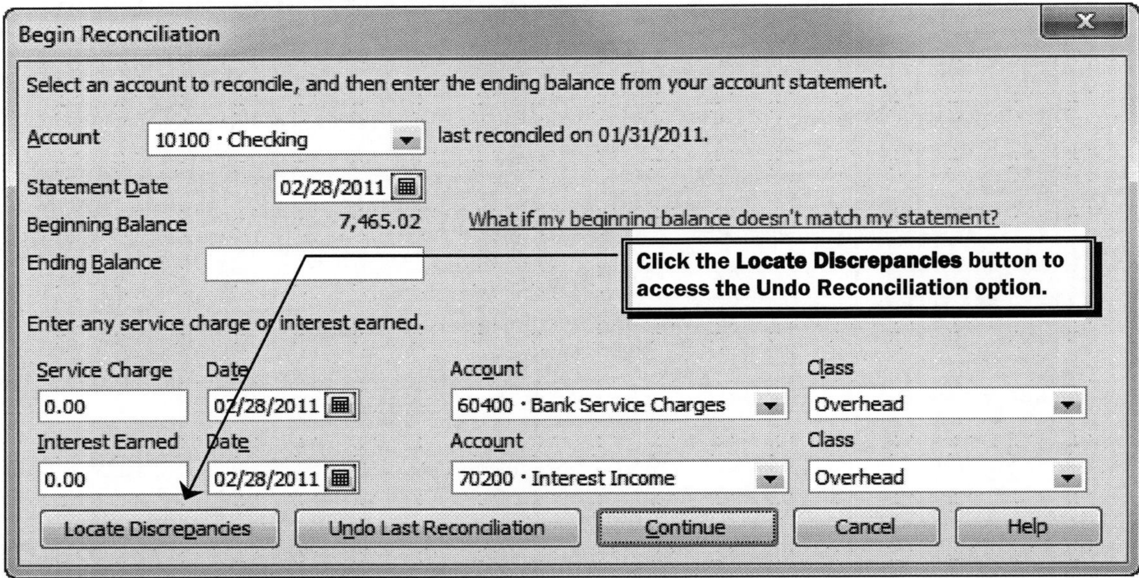

Figure 5-14 Begin Reconciliation window

4. Click the **Undo Last Reconciliation** button (see Figure 5-15).

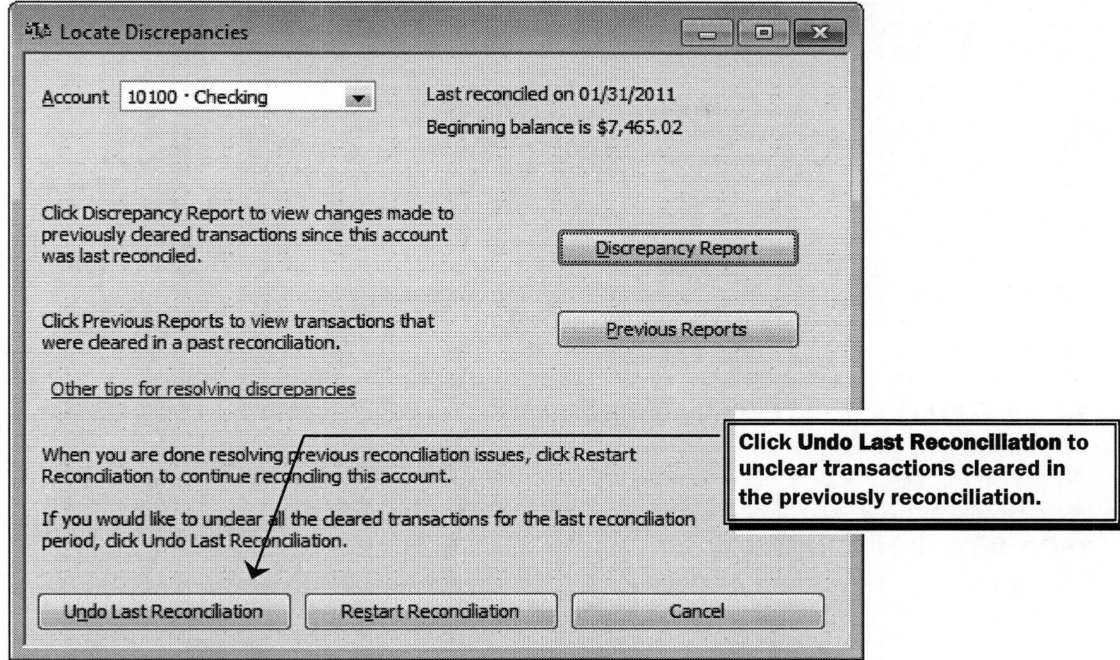

Figure 5-15 Locate Discrepancies window

5. Click **Continue** on the *Undo Previous Reconciliation* window (see Figure 5-16).

   Notice that QuickBooks shows both the *Current Beginning Balance* and the *Previous Beginning Balance*. If the *Previous Beginning Balance* is incorrect (i.e., does not match the previous bank statement balance), you may need to undo more than one bank reconciliation until the *Previous Beginning Balance* matches a previous bank statement.

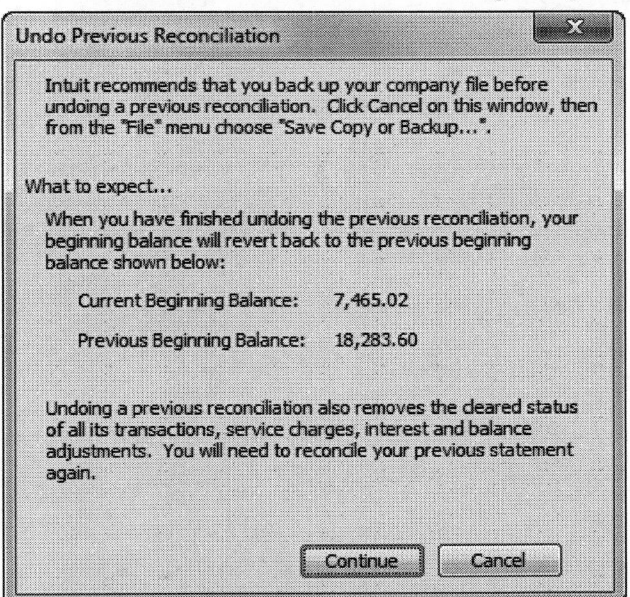

Figure 5-16 Undo Previous Reconciliation window

6. When the undo reconciliation is complete, QuickBooks displays the dialog box shown in Figure 5-17. Click **OK**.

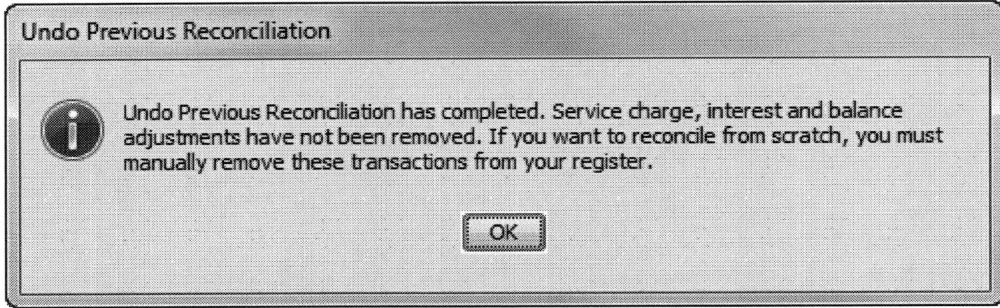

Figure 5-17 Undo Previous Reconcile Complete window

7. QuickBooks displays the *Locate Discrepancy* window (Figure 5-15). Click **Restart Reconciliation** to re-perform the bank reconciliation from the previous period.

> Note:
> When you undo a reconciliation, QuickBooks resets your beginning balance to the previous period. However, the bank service charges and interest income that you entered in the prior reconciliation will remain in the check register and will not be deleted.
>
> Therefore, do not enter bank services charges and interest income when repeating the bank reconciliation. Instead, clear those transactions along with the other checks and deposits when you re-reconcile the account.

> Also Note:
> If there is an entry in your bank account register coded to *Reconciliation Discrepancies* expense account with a memo that reads "Balance Adjustment," see *When QuickBooks Automatically Adjusts your Balance* on page 200 for more information.

Step 2: Locate and Edit Incorrectly Recorded Transactions

When you find a discrepancy between a transaction in QuickBooks and a transaction on the bank statement, you need to correct it. You will use different methods to correct the error depending on the date of the transaction.

Correcting or Voiding Transactions in the Current Accounting Period

If you find that you need to correct a transaction in QuickBooks and the transaction is dated in the **current accounting period** (i.e., a period for which financial statements and/or tax returns have not yet been issued), correct the error as described in the following paragraphs.

If You Made the Error

If you made an error in your records, you must make a correction in QuickBooks so that your records will agree with the bank. For example, if you wrote a check for $400.00, but you recorded it in QuickBooks as $40.00, you will need to change the check in QuickBooks. Double-click the transaction in the *Reconcile* window, or highlight the transaction and click **Go To.** Make the correction, and then click **Save & Close**. This will return you to the *Reconcile* window and you will see the updated amount.

If the Bank Made the Error

If the bank made an error, enter a transaction in the bank account register to adjust your balance for the error and continue reconciling the account. Then, call or write to the bank and ask them to post an adjustment to your account. When you receive the bank statement showing the correction, enter a subsequent entry in the bank account register to record the bank's adjustment. This register entry will show on your next bank reconciliation, and you can clear it like any other transaction.

For example, Figure 5-18 displays a check register with an adjusting entry of $90.00 on 1/31/2011 where the bank made a deposit error during the month. The $90.00 shortage is recorded on the *Payment* side of the check register so that the register will reconcile with the bank statement. Subsequently, another adjusting entry is made on the *Deposit* side of the check register to record the bank's correction of the previous month's deposit. The $90.00 deposit will show on February's bank statement and can be cleared during the reconciliation process. Notice that *both* adjusting entries in the register are recorded to the same account, *Reconciliation Discrepancies*.

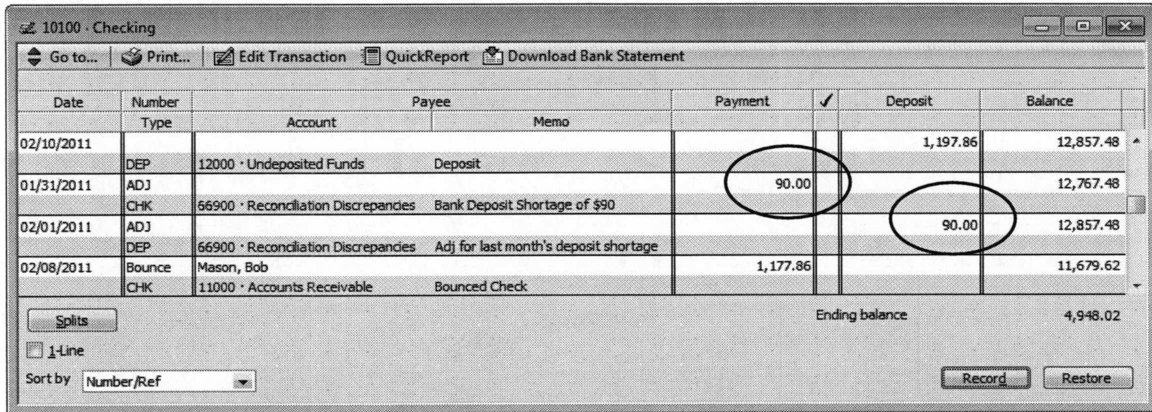

Figure 5-18 Adjusting entries for bank deposit error

Voiding Checks and Stop Payments

When you find a check dated in the **current accounting period** that you know will not clear the bank (e.g., if you stop payment on a check) you will need to void the check. Double-click the check from the *Reconcile* window. Select the **Edit** menu and then select **Void Check**. Click **Save & Close** to return to the *Reconcile* window.

Correcting or Voiding Transactions in Closed Accounting Periods

A *closed accounting period* is the period prior to and including the date on which a company officially "closes" its books (for example, 12/31/2010), creates its final financial reports, and presents its finalized reports to external stakeholders such as the IRS and investors. You do not want to change transactions dated in a closed accounting period because doing so will change financial reports during a period for which you have already issued financial statements or filed tax returns.

In QuickBooks, you can use the *closing date* to indicate the date on which you last closed the accounting period. For example, if you issued financial statements on 12/31/2010, you can set the closing date in QuickBooks to 12/31/2010. This will essentially "lock" your QuickBooks file so that only the administrator (or other authorized users) will be able to modify transactions before 12/31/2010. For more information on setting the closing date, see the

Adjustments Chapter, available with this books supplemental material (see page xiii for more information).

To correct or void a check that is dated in a **closed accounting period**, follow the procedure described below.

DO NOT PERFORM THESE STEPS NOW. THEY ARE FOR REFERENCE ONLY.

1. Display the check in the register as shown in Figure 5-19 and click on the transaction that needs to be voided to select it.

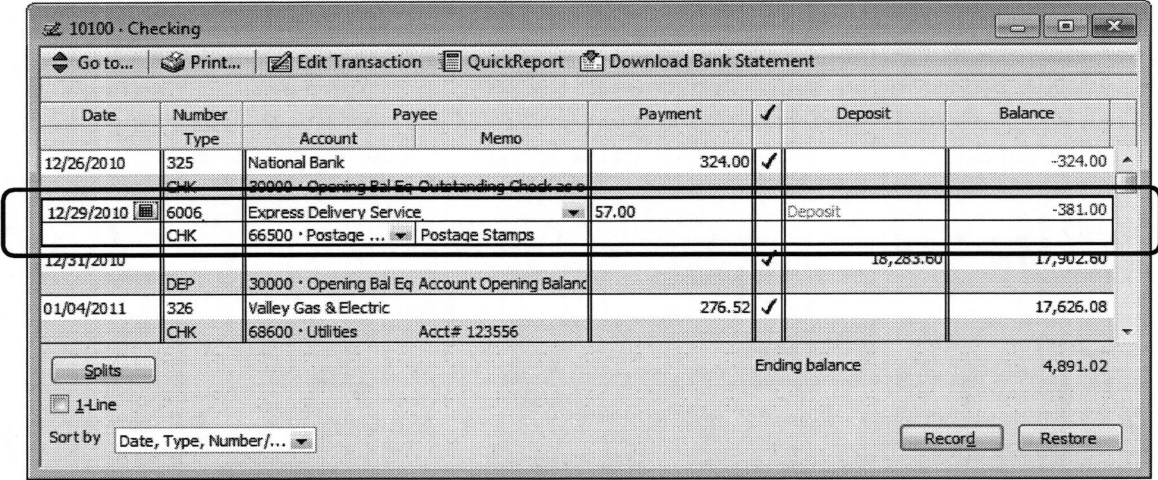

Figure 5-19 Uncleared Check #6006 from Previous Reporting Period

2. From the **Edit** menu, select **Void Check**. QuickBooks zeros all dollar amounts and adds a "VOID" note in the Memo field as shown in Figure 5-20. Click **Record**.

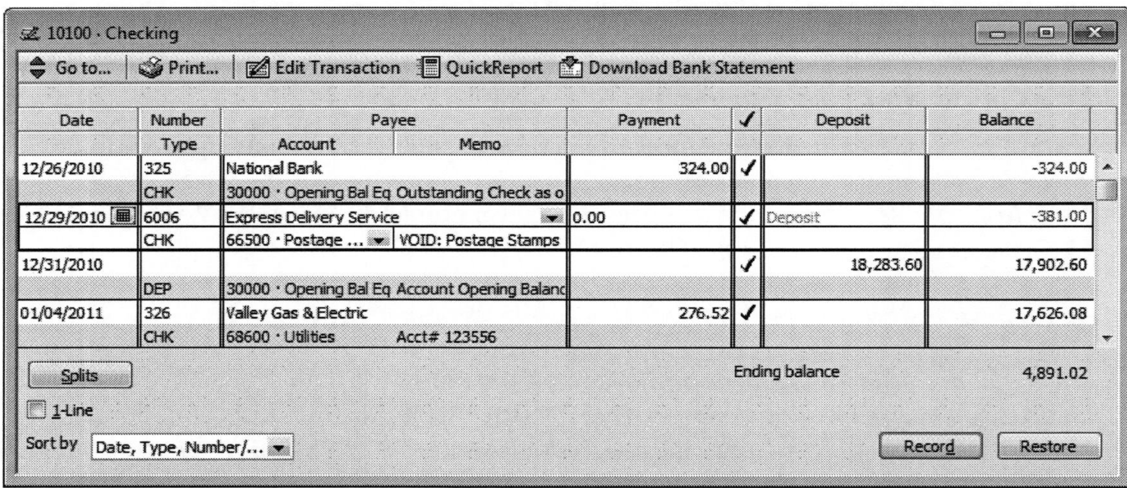

Figure 5-20 Voided Check - #6006

3. QuickBooks prompts you that the transaction you are voiding is cleared and that it is dated in a closed accounting period (Figure 5-21). Click **Yes**.

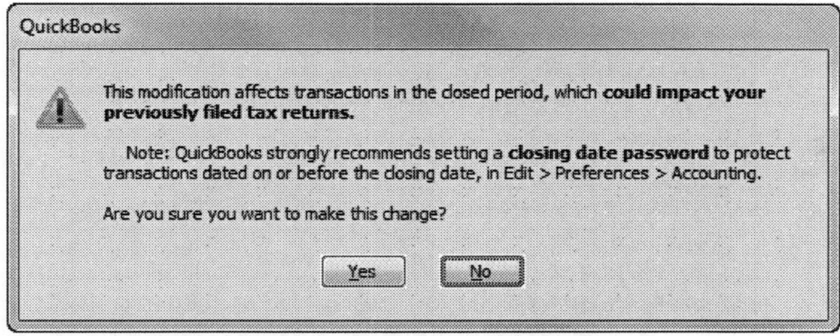

Figure 5-21 Voided Check in Closed Period Prompt

4. QuickBooks then displays the window shown in Figure 5-22. Click **Yes (Recommended).** This is the default response.

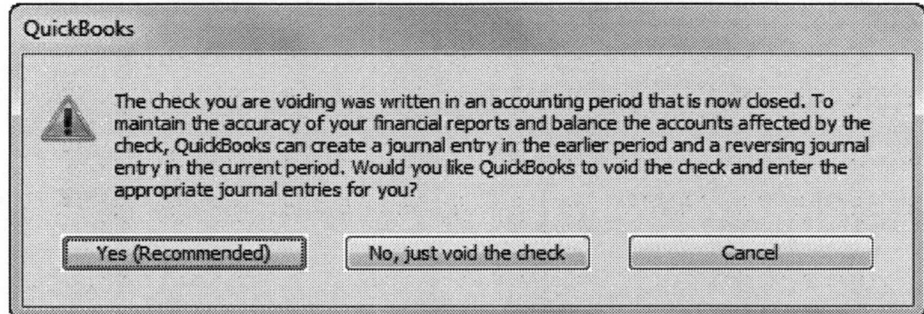

Figure 5-22 Voided Check Adjustment Prompt

5. QuickBooks performs three actions when you click **Yes (Recommended)** on the window shown in Figure 5-22 above.
   a) QuickBooks adds wording to the Memo field of the check showing that the program reversed the impact of the void on the General Ledger.

Figure 5-23 Voided Check - Additional Memo Text

   b) QuickBooks posts a General Journal Entry (GJE) dated the same date that reverses the impact on the General Ledger caused by the voided check.

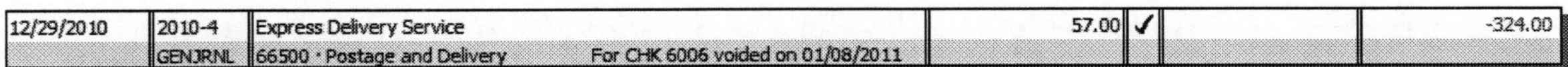

Figure 5-24 Journal Entry - Reverses GL Changes from Voiding the Check

   c) QuickBooks then enters a Reversing General Journal Entry (RGJE) in the current period. The default date for the reversing entry is "today."

Figure 5-25 Journal Entry that "moves" the GL Change to the Current Reporting Period

Note
QuickBooks clears all entries. However, the entries will appear in the Bank Reconciliation window until the client reconciles them using the Bank Reconciliation feature.

Important:
The Void Checks tool only works with *Check(CHK)* transactions that are coded to one or more *Expense* and/or *Other Expense* accounts. The following transactions are not protected with the Void Checks tool:
1. Checks coded to accounts other than Expense/Other Expense
2. Checks that include Items
3. Checks that are not "Check" transaction types (e.g., Bill Payment, Payroll Liability Payment, Sales Tax Payment, Paycheck)

6. Next, enter the correct amount in a new transaction. Use the date of the current bank statement for the new transaction.

When QuickBooks Automatically Adjusts your Balance

If the difference is not zero when you click **Reconcile Now** in the *Reconcile* window, QuickBooks creates a transaction in the bank account for the difference. The transaction is coded to the *Reconciliation Discrepancies* expense account. You should not leave this transaction in the register, but research why the discrepancy exists and properly account for it. A balance in this account usually indicates an over or understatement in net income.

Perform the following steps to correct the problem:

DO NOT PERFORM THESE STEPS NOW. THEY ARE FOR REFERENCE ONLY.

1. Delete the transaction that is coded to *Reconciliation Discrepancies*. (To locate this transaction, double-click the *Reconciliation Discrepancies* account from the Chart of Accounts.) The memo on the transaction will say "Balance Adjustment."
2. Undo the Last Reconciliation. See page 193 for more information.
3. Perform the bank reconciliation again correctly, ensuring that the *Difference* field shows **0.00** before clicking **Reconcile Now**.

Handling Bounced Checks

Banks and accountants often refer to bounced checks as NSF (non-sufficient funds) transactions. This means there are insufficient funds in the account to cover the check.

When Your Customer's Check Bounces

If your bank returns a check from one of your customers, enter an NSF transaction in the banking account register.

For example, Bob Mason bounced the check #2526 for $1,177.86 and the bank charged the Company $10.00. Complete the steps below to complete the NSF transaction.

COMPUTER PRACTICE

Step 1. Open the **Checking** check register.

Step 2. If necessary, choose **Date, Type, Number** from the *Sort by* drop down list.

Step 3. Enter two transactions, both dated 2/8/2011, as shown in Figure 5-26 – one for the amount of the check that bounced, and one for the fee charged by the bank.

Notice that the bounced check is coded to Accounts Receivable. This transaction creates a receivable from the customer that will show in your A/R reports and customer statements until the customer repays you.

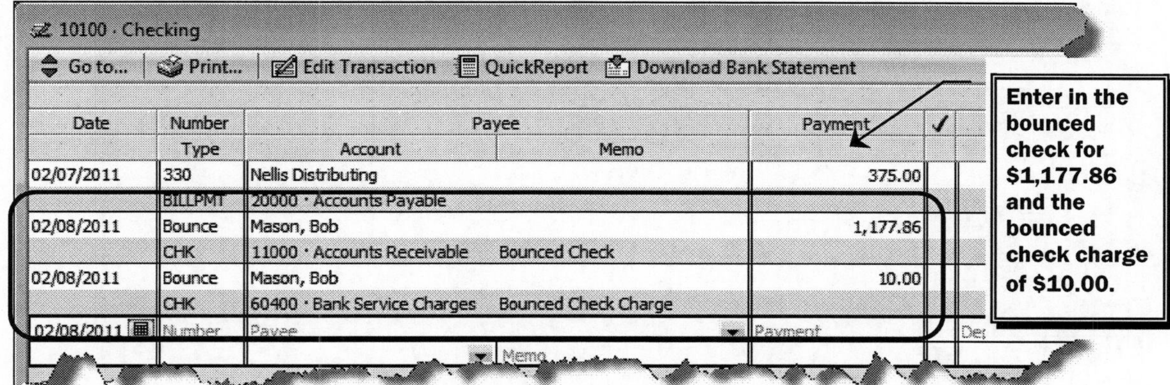

Figure 5-26 Add two transactions to your Checking register

> **Note:**
> If the bounced check was *not* a payment for one of your invoices (i.e. not recorded to Accounts Receivable), skip Step 4 through Step 9.

Step 4. After you enter the Bounced Check, select the **Reports** menu, select **Customers and Receivables,** and then select **Customer Balance Detail** (see Figure 5-27).

Step 5. Double-click the payment transaction (#2526 on 01/30/2011) in the **Customer Balance Detail** report to view the *Receive Payments* window you used to record the check from your customer (see Figure 5-27). You may need to scroll to the bottom of the report.

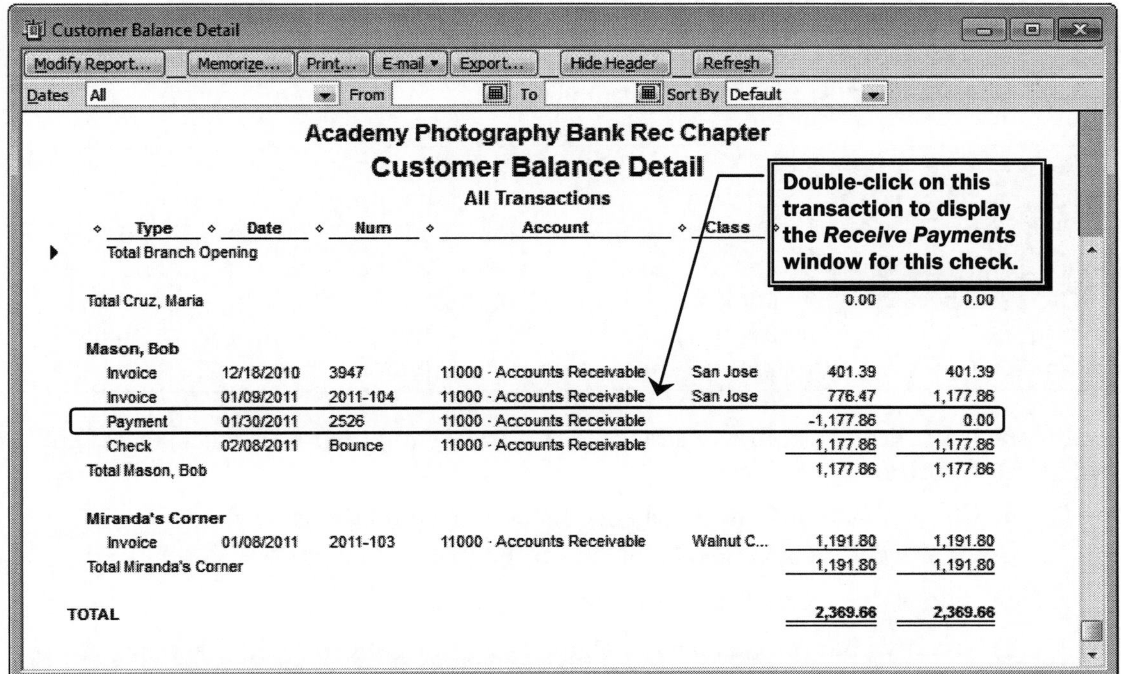

Figure 5-27 Customer Balance Detail report

Step 6. In the *Receive Payments* window click in the check column (✓) next to the original invoices, both 3947 on 12/18/2010 and 2011-104 on 1/9/2011 to un-apply the payments (see Figure 5-28).

Step 7. Next, click in the checkmark column (✓) next to the bounced check transaction you recorded in Step 3 above. You'll see this transaction in the *Receive Payments* window.

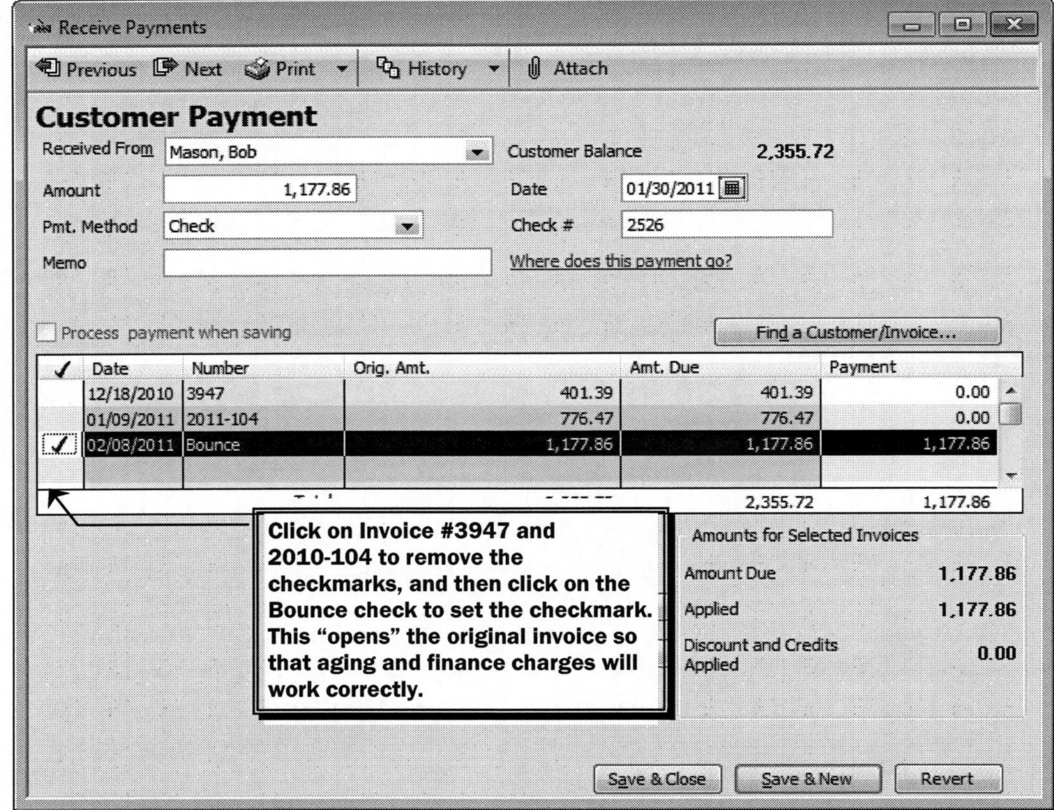

Figure 5-28 Select *the Bounced Check to apply to the original payment*

Step 8. Click **Save & Close** and then click **Yes** in the *Recording Transaction* dialog box.

Step 9. Close the **Customer Balance Detail** report.

> **Note:**
> The payment is reapplied to the bounced check so that the aging and finance charge calculations of the original invoice are restored. If you did not edit the *Receive Payment* window in this way, the Accounts Receivable aging would be incorrect because QuickBooks would still think the original check (the one that bounced) had paid the invoice. Since that check bounced, we want the original invoice to show as unpaid until the customer actually makes payment.

Next, if you charge your customers a service fee for processing their NSF check, create an Invoice for the customer as follows:

Step 10. Create an **Other Charge** Item called ***NSF Charge,*** as shown in Figure 5-29.

a) Click the **Item & Services** icon on the Home Page.

b) Press **Ctrl+N** to display the *New Item* window.

c) Verify your screen matches Figure 5-29. Click **OK** to create the new item.

d) Close the *Item List.*

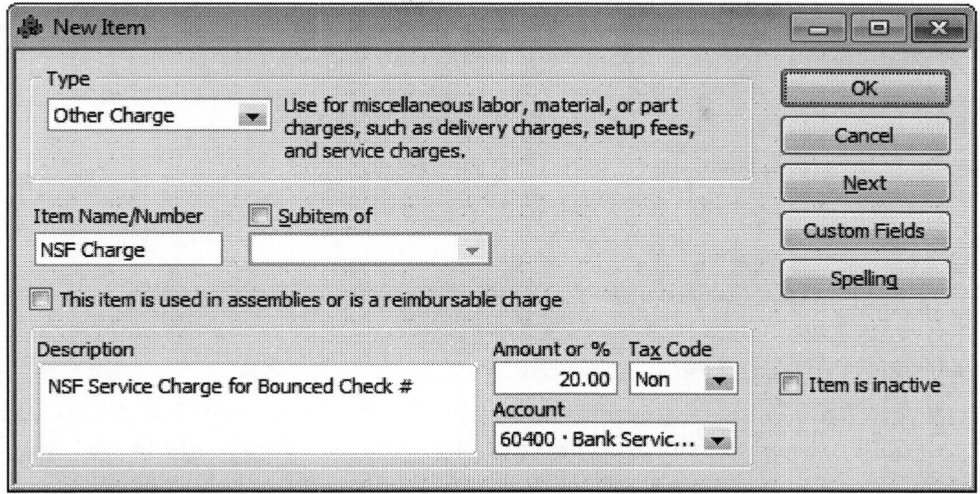

Figure 5-29 Use an Other Charge Item to charge your customers an NSF fee

Step 11. If you see a window offer *Professional Service Forms*, press **OK** to clear the window.

Step 12. Create an Invoice for the amount for the NSF charge as shown in Figure 5-30. Change the Invoice number to ***2526Bounce*** and the terms to **Due Upon Receipt**. If necessary, choose **Academy Photo Service Template** in the *Template* field.

Step 13. Fill out the rest of the fields on the Invoice to match Figure 5-30.

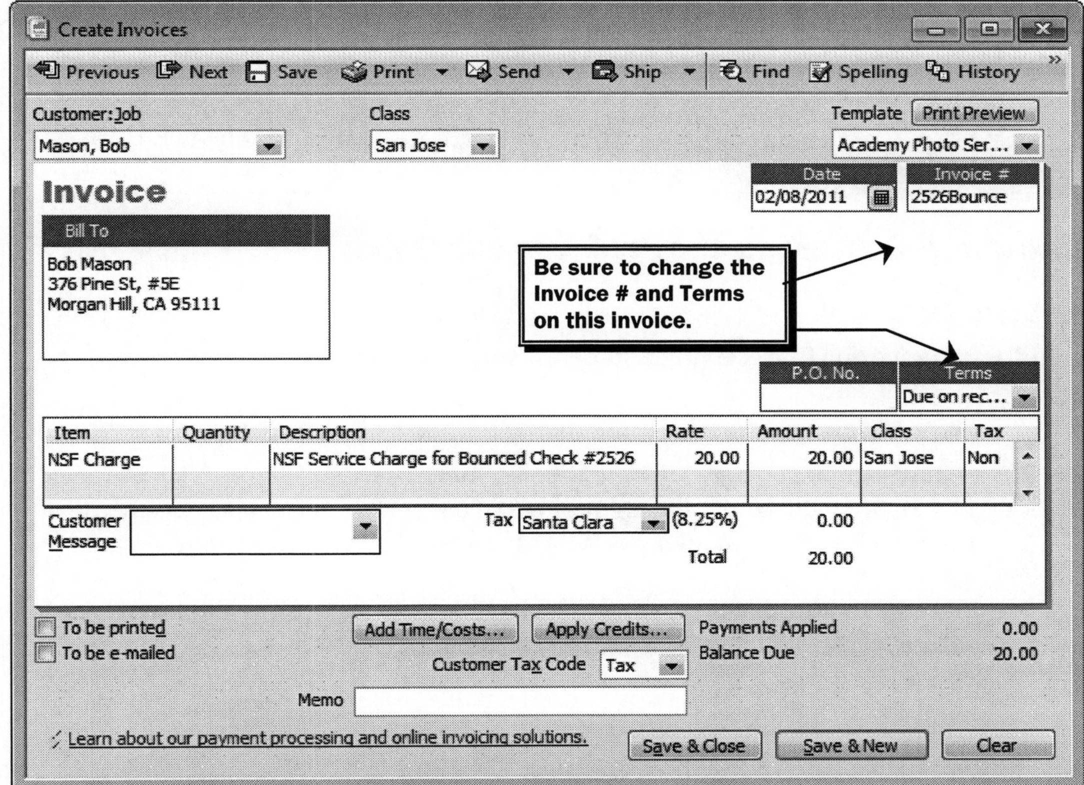

Figure 5-30 Invoice to charge the customer an NSF service charge

Step 14. When you add the **NSF Charge** Item to the Invoice, QuickBooks displays a warning that says the Item is associated with an expense account. Click **OK**.

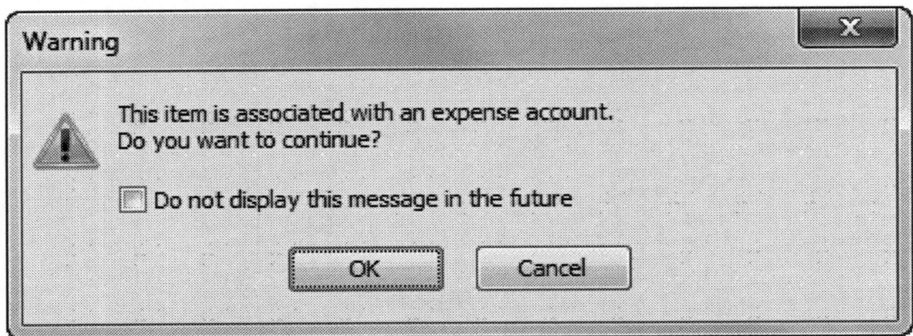

Figure 5-31 Warning dialog box

Step 15. Click **Save & Close** to record the Invoice.

Step 16. Since you changed the terms on this Invoice to **Due Upon Receipt** QuickBooks asks if you want to make the Due Upon Receipt terms the default for Bob Mason. Click **No** on this window since you will use the Net 30 terms on future Invoices for this customer.

> **Tip:**
> You will need to notify the customer of bounced check and the NFS fee. You can do this by sending the customer a statement. For more information on printing statements, see page 109
>
> **The accounting behind the scenes:**
> The bounced check you entered in the register increases (debits) Accounts Receivable and it reduces (credits) the Checking account for the amount of the original check that bounced. The Invoice increases (debits) Accounts Receivable and decreases (credits) Bank Service Charges for the amount of NSF fees you are charging the customer.

Receiving and Depositing the Replacement Check

COMPUTER PRACTICE

To record the transactions for receiving and depositing a replacement check, follow these steps:

Step 1. Select the **Customers** menu, and then select **Receive Payments.**

Step 2. In this example, Bob Mason sent a replacement check #2538 on 2/10/11 for $1,197.86 that includes the amount of the check plus the NSF service charge of $20.00. Fill in the customer payment information as shown in Figure 5-32.

Make sure you apply the payment against the original invoices and the service charge invoice you just created in Figure 5-30.

Step 3. Click **Save & Close.**

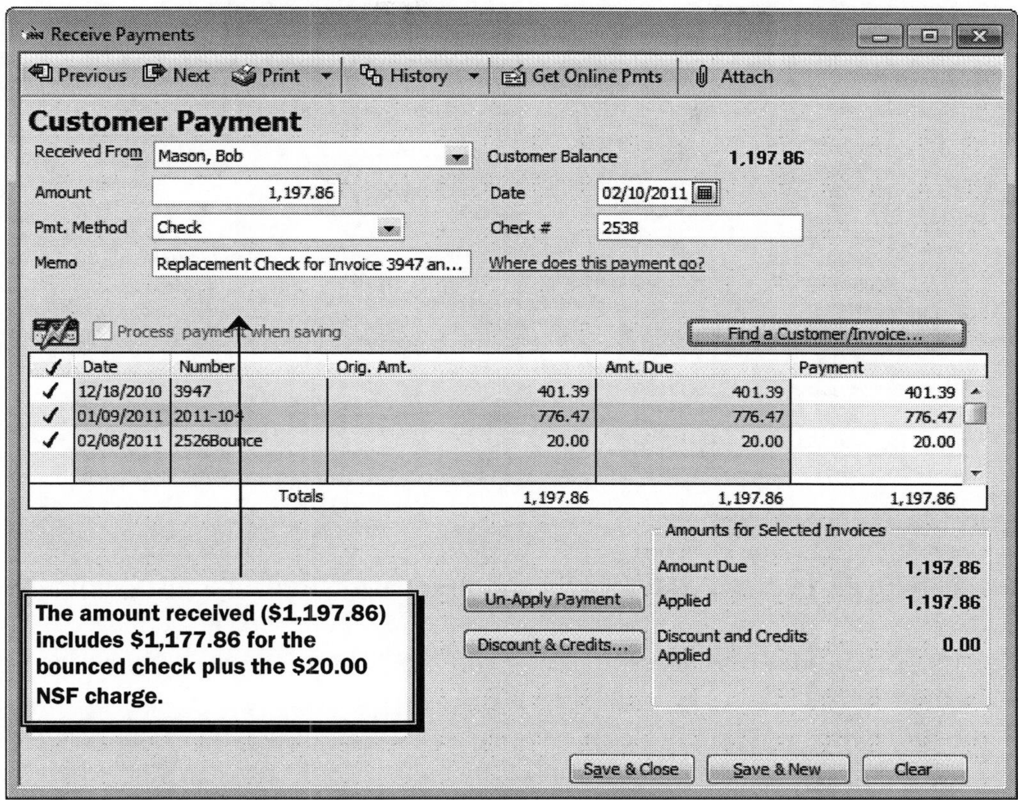

Figure 5-32 The Receive Payments window showing the replacement check

Next, add the replacement check to your next deposit just as you would any other check.

Step 4. Select the **Banking** menu and then select **Make Deposits** (see Figure 5-33).

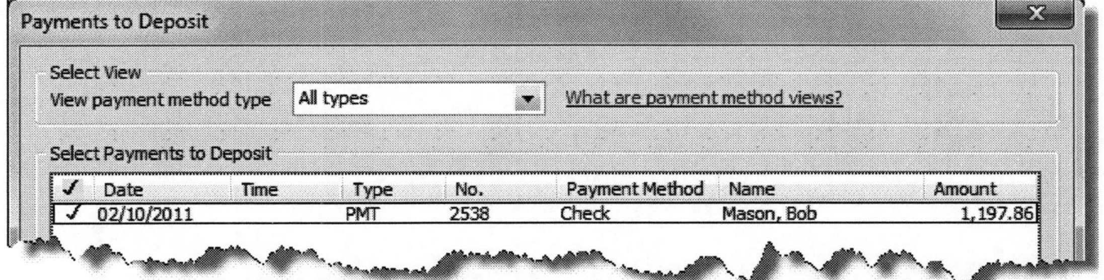

Figure 5-33 Add the replacement check to your deposit

Step 5. In the *Payments to Deposit* window, select check #2538 as shown in Figure 5-33 and then click **OK** at the bottom of the window.

Step 6. In the *Make Deposits* window, confirm that **Checking** in the *Deposit to* field is selected and that 02/10/2011 displays in the date field (see Figure 5-34). Then, click **Save & Close** at the bottom of the window.

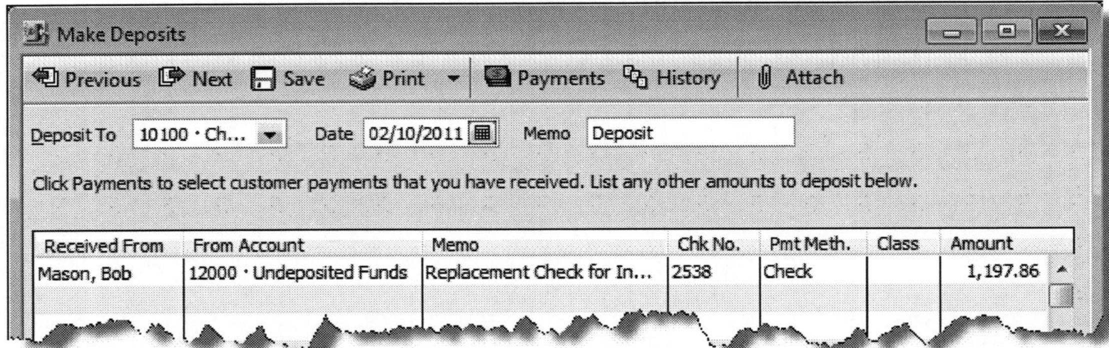

Figure 5-34 Make Deposits window

Step 7. Close the Checking register.

When Your Check Bounces

If you write a check that overdraws your account and your bank returns the check, follow these steps:

1. Decide with your vendor how you will handle the NSF Check. (e.g., send a new check, redeposit the same check, or pay by credit card).
2. When the bank sends you the notice that your check was returned, there will be a charge from your bank. Enter a transaction in the bank account register. Code the transaction to Bank Service Charges and use the actual date that the bank charged your account.
3. If your balance is sufficient for the check to clear, tell the vendor to redeposit the check.
4. If your balance is not sufficient, consider other ways of paying the vendor, such as paying with a credit card. Alternatively, negotiate delayed payment terms with your vendor.
5. If your vendor charges an extra fee for bouncing a check, enter a Bill (or use Write Checks) and code the charge to the Bank Service Charge account.
6. If you bounce a payroll check, use the same process as described. Offer to reimburse your employee for any bank fees incurred as a result of your mistake.

Reconciling Credit Card Accounts and Paying the Bill

If you use a credit card liability account to track all of your credit card charges and payments, you should reconcile the account every month just as you do with your bank account. The credit card reconciliation process is very similar to the bank account reconciliation, except that when you finish the reconciliation, QuickBooks asks you if you want to pay the credit card immediately or if you want to enter a bill for the balance of the credit card.

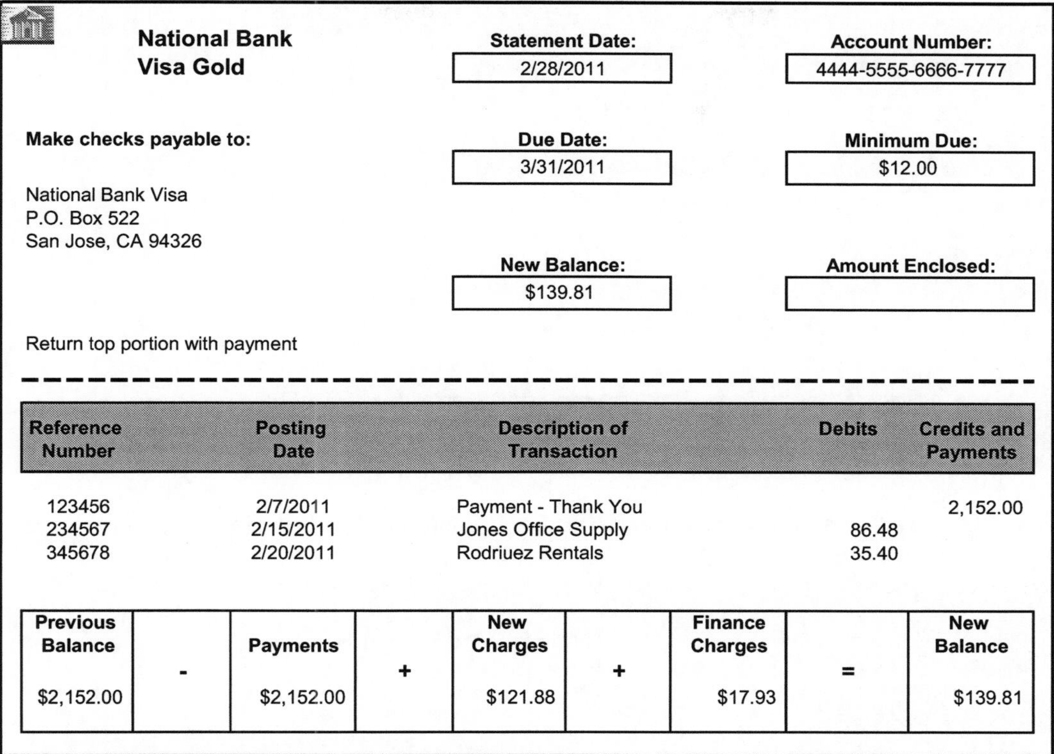

National Bank
Visa Gold

Statement Date: 2/28/2011

Account Number: 4444-5555-6666-7777

Make checks payable to:

National Bank Visa
P.O. Box 522
San Jose, CA 94326

Due Date: 3/31/2011

Minimum Due: $12.00

New Balance: $139.81

Amount Enclosed:

Return top portion with payment

Reference Number	Posting Date	Description of Transaction	Debits	Credits and Payments
123456	2/7/2011	Payment - Thank You		2,152.00
234567	2/15/2011	Jones Office Supply	86.48	
345678	2/20/2011	Rodriuez Rentals	35.40	

Previous Balance		Payments		New Charges		Finance Charges		New Balance
$2,152.00	-	$2,152.00	+	$121.88	+	$17.93	=	$139.81

Figure 5-35 National Bank Visa credit card statement

Use the National Bank Visa Gold credit card statement shown in Figure 5-35 to reconcile your account.

COMPUTER PRACTICE

Step 1. Select the **Banking** menu and then select **Reconcile**.

Step 2. On the Begin Reconciliation window, enter ***National Bank VISA Gold*** in the *Account* field and press **Tab**.

Step 3. Verify that **02/28/2011** displays in the *Statement Date* field and press **Tab**.

Step 4. Verify that the *Beginning Balance* field shows **2,152.00**.

Step 5. Enter ***139.81*** in the *Ending Balance* field and press **Tab**.

In this field, enter the ending balance for the credit card that shows on your credit card statement.

Step 6. Enter ***17.93*** in the *Finance Charge* field and press **Tab**.

Step 7. Verify that **02/28/2011** is entered in the *Date* field and press **Tab**.

Step 8. Enter ***Interest Expense*** in the *Account* field and press **Tab**.

Step 9. Enter ***Overhead*** in the *Class* field and press **Tab**.

Step 10. Verify that your screen matches Figure 5-36 and click **Continue**.

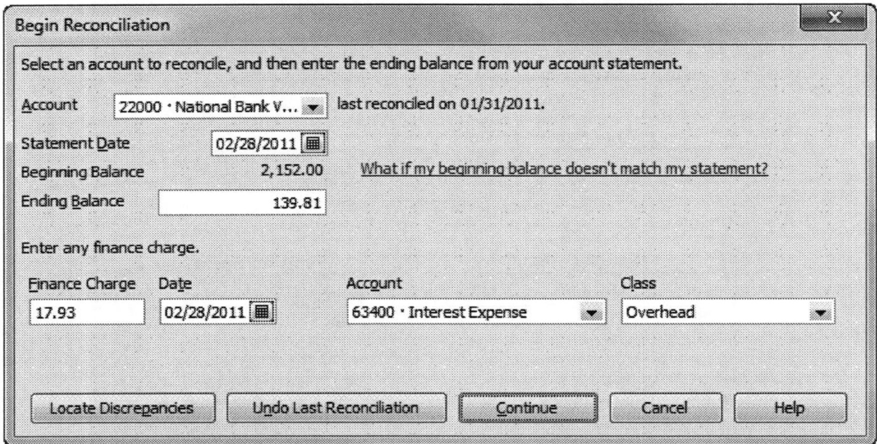

Figure 5-36 Enter your credit card statement information on the Begin Reconciliation window

Step 11. Click each cleared transaction in the *Reconcile Credit Card* window as you match it with the credit card statement.

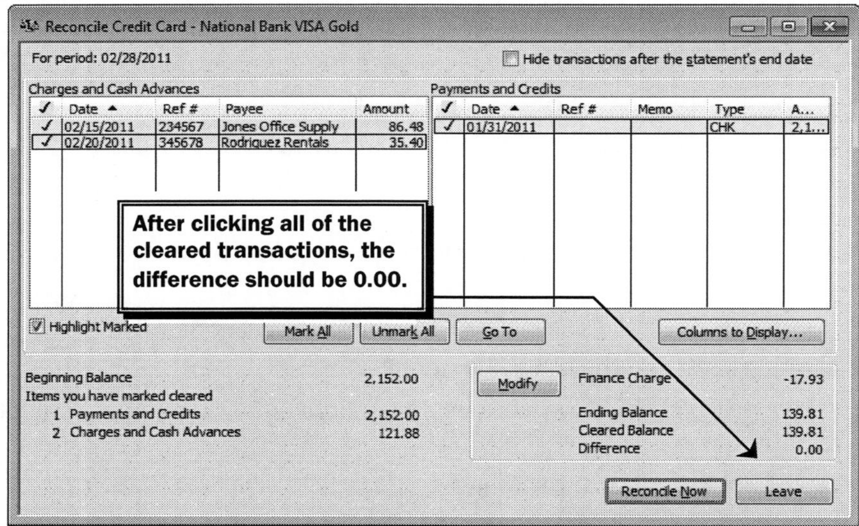

Figure 5-37 The Difference field should show a difference of 0.00 after reconciling

Step 12. Verify that the *Difference* field shows **0.00** (see Figure 5-37). If it doesn't, look for discrepancies between your records and the credit card statement.

Step 13. Verify that your screen looks like Figure 5-37 and click **Reconcile Now**.

Step 14. On the *Make Payment* dialog box, click to select **Enter a bill for payment later** and click **OK** (see Figure 5-38).

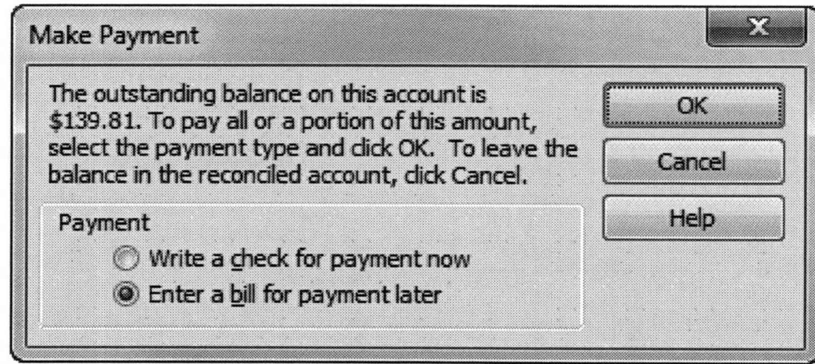

Figure 5-38 Make Payment window

Step 15. On the *Select Reconciliation Report* window, click **Close.**

Normally you would select **Both** and then click **Print**. However, for this exercise, skip this step. See page 190 for more information about Bank Reconciliation reports.

Step 16. Enter the additional information to complete the **Bill** for the VISA payment as shown in Figure 5-39.

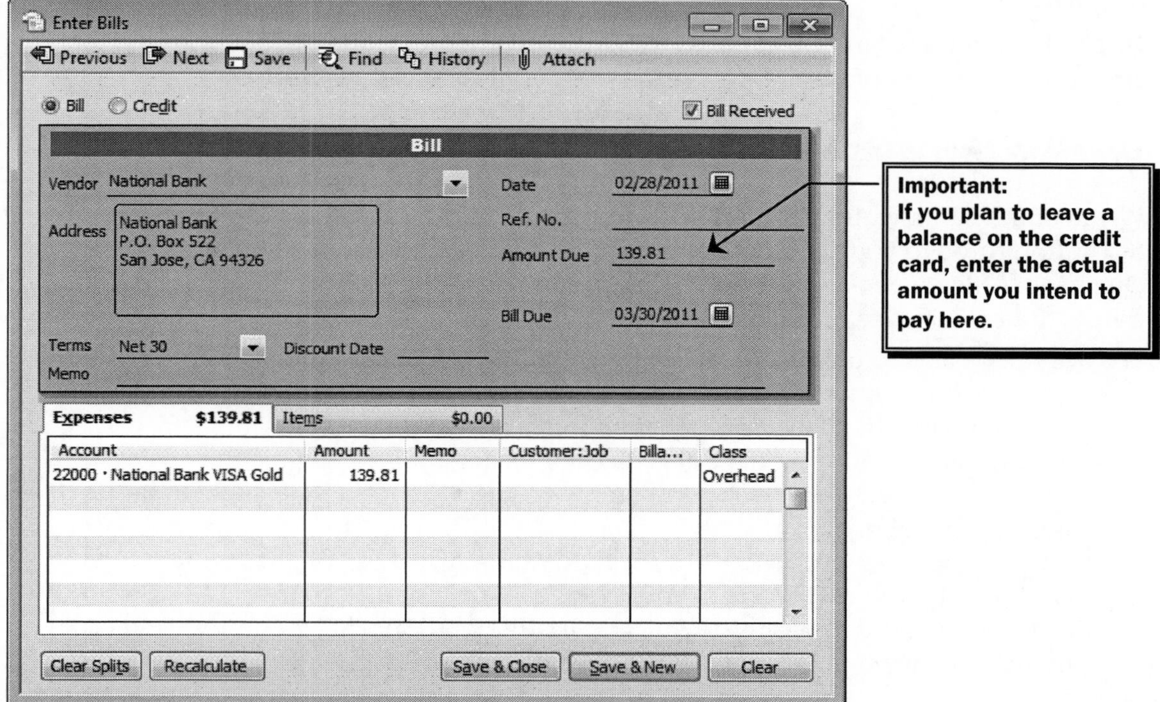

Figure 5-39 Use this data to pay the VISA Bill

> **The accounting behind the scenes:**
> QuickBooks selects the **National Bank VISA Gold** account on the Expenses tab. This reduces the Credit Card liability account (debit) and increases Accounts Payable (credit).
> **Note:**
> Although the bill in Figure 5-39 includes the Overhead class, the transaction will not affect the **Profit & Loss by Class** report because the bill does not post to any income or expense accounts.

Step 17. Click **Save & Close** to record the Bill.

This bill for $139.81 will display in the *Pay Bills* window the next time you select **Pay Bills** from the *Vendor* menu.

> **Important tip for partial payments of credit card bills:**
> If you don't want to pay the whole amount due on a credit card, don't just change the amount in the Pay Bills window. Instead, edit the original Bill to match the amount you actually intend to pay. By changing the Bill, you reduce the amount that is transferred out of the Credit Card account (and into A/P) to the exact amount that is paid. This way, the amount you don't pay remains in the balance of the Credit Card liability account and will match the account balance on your next credit card statement.

Online Banking

The QuickBooks Online Banking feature allows you to process online transactions, such as payments and transfers, and download bank transactions into your QuickBooks file. Downloaded transactions save you time by decreasing manual entry and increasing accuracy. It is important to review each downloaded transaction to avoid bringing errors into your company file.

Online Banking is secure. QuickBooks uses a secure internet connection and a high level of encryption when transferring information from your financial institution.

Opening the Sample File

With Online Banking, transactions are processed and downloaded directly from your financial institution through your internet connection. For this section, we will open a sample QuickBooks file for *Sample Rock Castle Construction Company*. This file has downloaded transactions pre-loaded in the file.

We will not be able to use this file to set up an online banking connection or to send or receive transactions, since this would require a live account at a financial institution and cannot be simulated in an educational environment. We will use this sample file to process downloaded transactions that have already been loaded into the sample file.

> **Restore this File**
> This chapter uses **OnlineBanking-10.QBW**. To open this file, restore the OnlineBanking-10.QBM file to your hard disk. See page 10 for instructions on restoring files. Click *OK* in the QuickBooks Information window notifying you that the file will use 12/15/2012 as the date. For more on sample files see page 6.

Online Banking Setup

To begin to use Online Banking, you will need to set up the appropriate accounts to communicate with the bank. Steps vary by institution. To complete this process, refer to the QuickBooks help files or the video tutorial.

Processing Online Transactions

You may have the option to enter online transactions, such as online payments, bill payments or transfers (depending on your financial institution). Figure 5-40 displays an example of an online payment. You can create an online payment by opening the *Write Checks* window and checking **Online Payment**. Notice that there are several differences between a standard check form and an online payment form. For example, the check number field displays the word *SEND*.

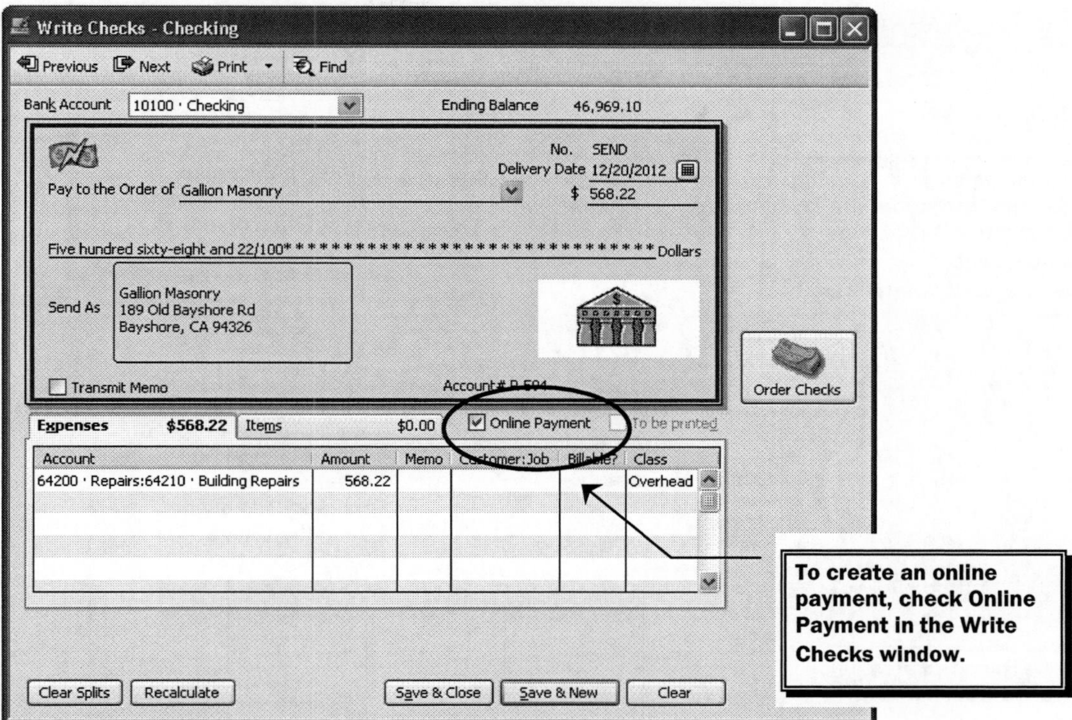

Figure 5-40 Check to be sent as an Online Payment

After saving an online payment, the transaction is queued up in the *Online Banking Center*. By clicking the *Send/Receive Transactions* button in the *Online Banking Center*, you can send the online payments and other online transactions, as well as download transactions from your financial institution.

Your financial institution may require additional steps. Follow any guidelines given after clicking the *Send/Receive Transactions* button. Do not click the *Send/Receive Transactions* button now.

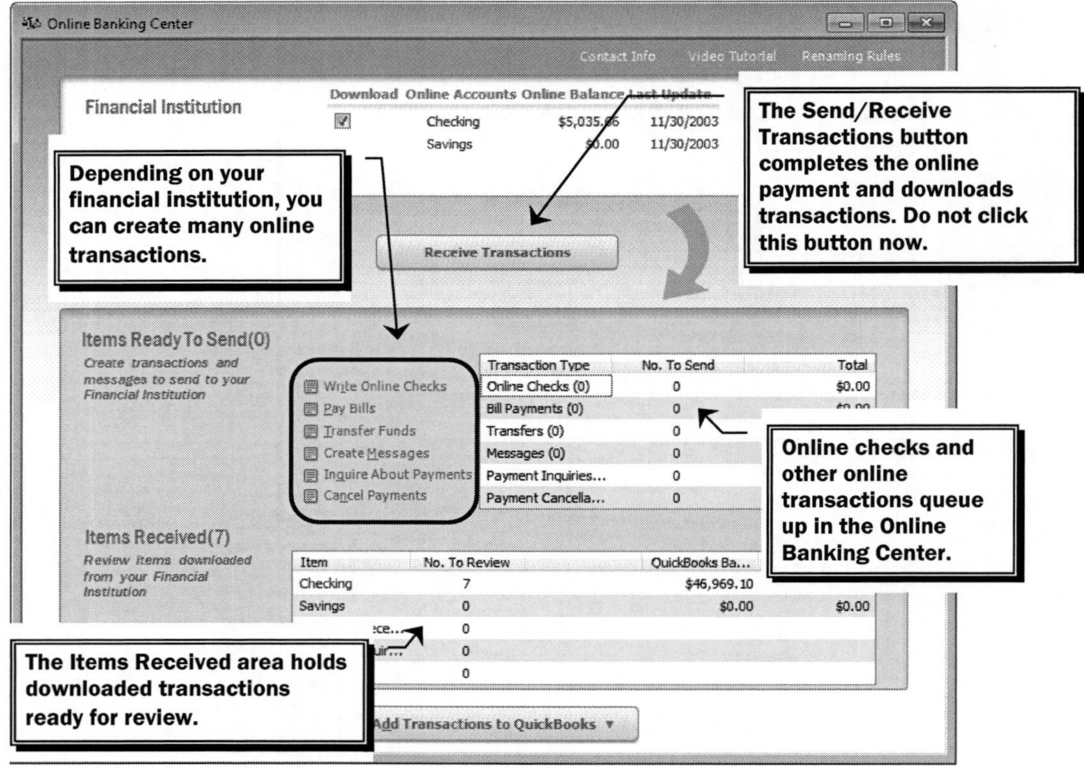

Figure 5-41 Online Banking Center – your screen may vary

Downloaded Transactions

When you click the *Send/Receive Transactions* button in the *Online Banking Center*, you download all the new transactions from your financial institution. After downloading, the transactions are ready for review. (Do not click the *Send/Receive Transactions* button now.)

As the transactions are downloaded, QuickBooks searches for similar transactions that have previously been entered. If an existing transaction is similar to the downloaded transaction, such as by having the same date and amount, QuickBooks ***matches*** the downloaded transaction with this entry. Any downloaded transaction that is unpaired with an existing entry is ***unmatched***.

> Note:
> Some transactions will be downloaded with payee names that do not match the names in the *Vendor Center*. Downloaded transactions often include names appended with a numerical code. It is important to avoid creating duplicate vendors. QuickBooks 2010 allows you to create ***renaming rules*** so that these downloaded transactions are linked to the appropriate existing vendor. You can access the renaming rules by clicking the link in the upper right of the *Online Banking Center*; however, the renaming rules window is not accessible in the sample file.

COMPUTER PRACTICE

Step 1. Select **Online Banking Center** from the *Online Banking* option under the *Banking* menu.

Step 2. The *Choose Your Online Banking Mode* opens. Choose *Side-by-Side Mode* and click **Continue** (see Figure 5-42).

Intuit redesigned the Online Banking Center for the QuickBooks 2009 version. After hearing from many QuickBooks users who preferred the earlier layout, Intuit enabled QuickBooks 2010 to offer a choice between both layouts. For this exercise, we will use the Side-by-Side Mode. You can try both modes to see which one you prefer.

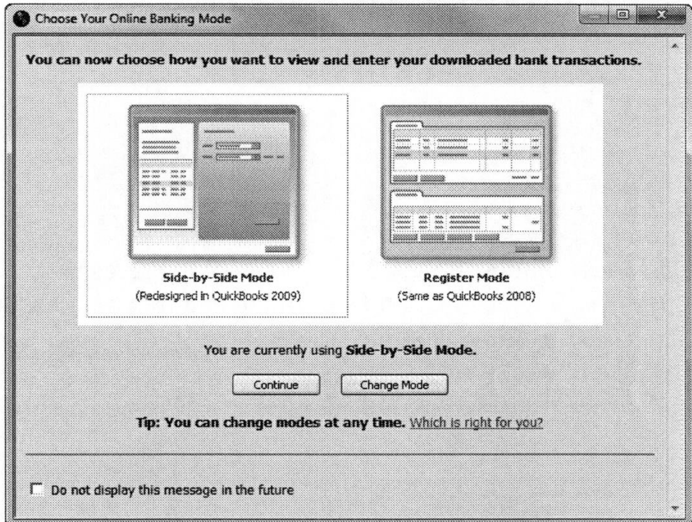

Figure 5-42 Choose Your Online Banking Mode window

Step 3. The *Online Banking Center* opens (see Figure 5-43).

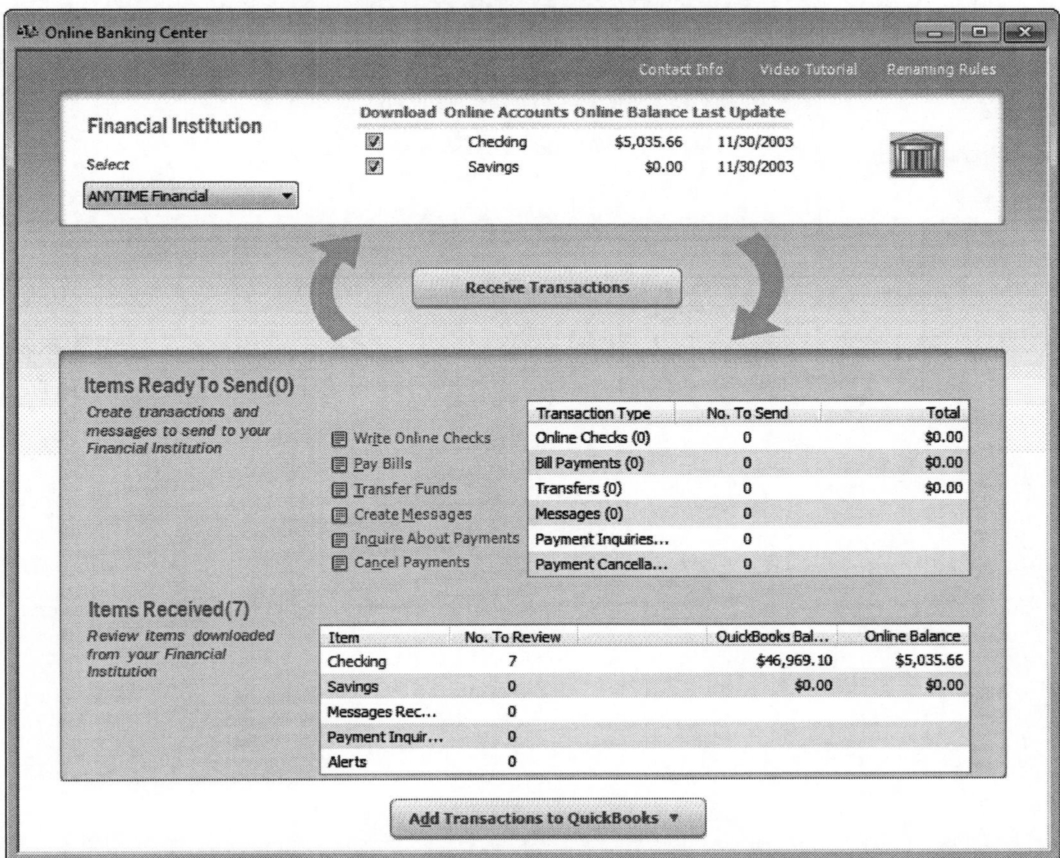

Figure 5-43 Online Banking Center

Step 4. The number of downloaded transactions to be reviewed is listed under the *Items Received* area at the bottom of the Online Banking Center. Click **Checking** (see Figure 5-44).

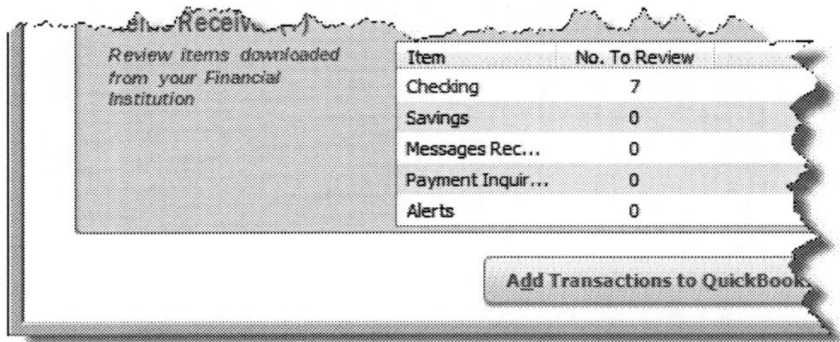

Figure 5-44 Items Received section of the Online Banking Center

Step 5. The *Add Transactions to QuickBooks* window opens. The left side of the screen lists downloaded transactions. There is one matched and six unmatched transactions. To see the matched transaction, click the **Show** link (see Figure 5-45).

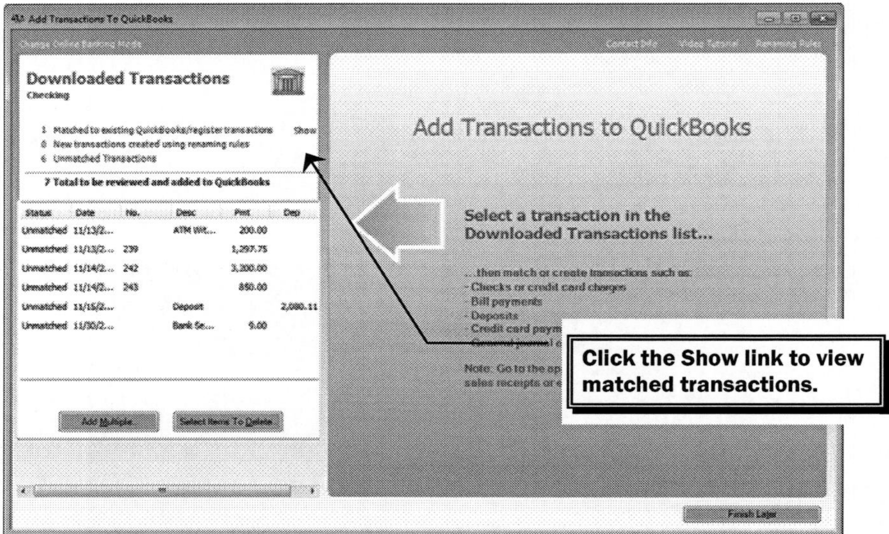

Figure 5-45 The Add Transactions To QuickBooks window

Step 6. If necessary, select the matched $5,000.00 transfer dated 11/5/2003 on the left side of the screen. The right side of the screen displays the existing transaction (see Figure 5-46).

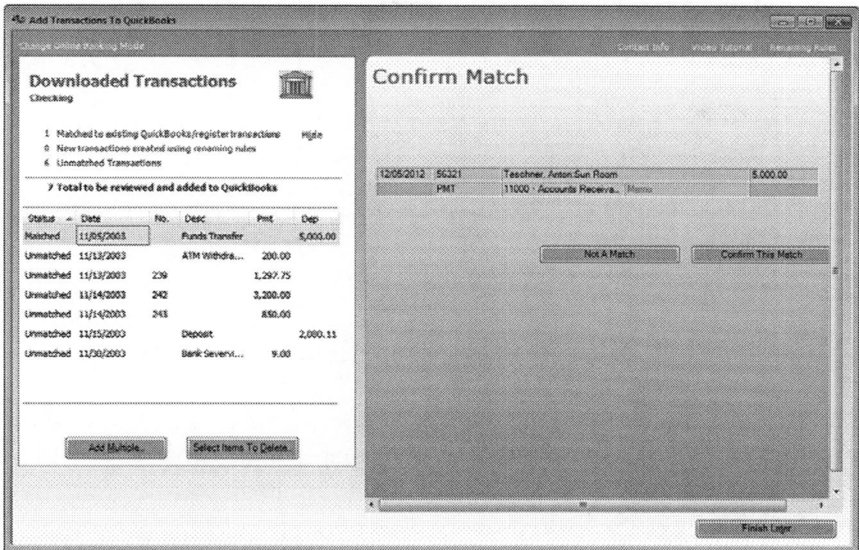

Figure 5-46 Matched transaction in Add Transactions To QuickBooks window

> **Note:**
> Observant readers may notice that the downloaded transactions are dated 2003, while most of the transactions in the sample file are dated 2012. Please disregard this discrepancy in the sample file.

Step 7. Confirm that the existing transaction matches the downloaded transaction and click **Confirm This Match**.

Step 8. QuickBooks automatically selects the next downloaded transaction, an ATM withdrawal of $200.00 on 11/13/2003. Under *Record an Expense* on the right side of the *Add Transactions To QuickBooks* window, you can designate the proper Account for the ATM withdrawal. Select **Petty Cash** from the *Account* drop-down list.

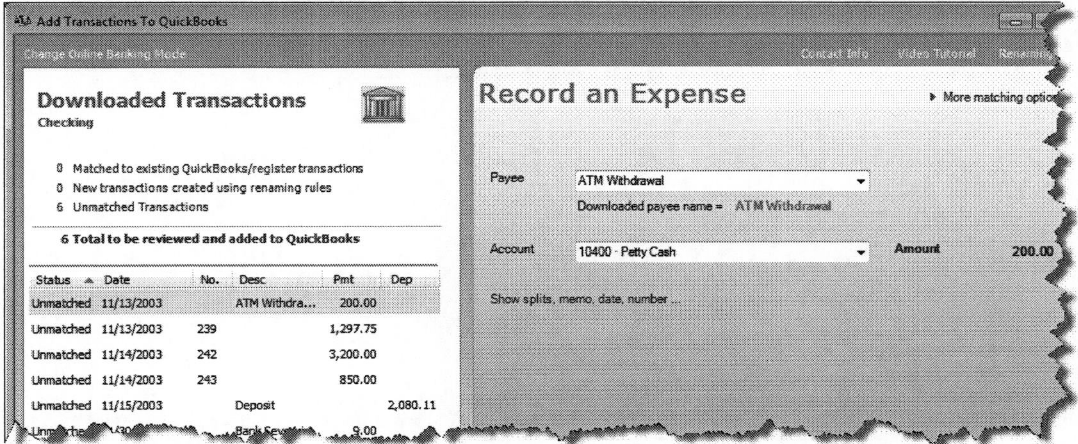

Figure 5-47 An unmatched transaction in the Add Transaction To QuickBooks window

Step 9. Click **Add to QuickBooks** in the bottom right of the *Add Transactions To QuickBooks* window.

The transaction is now saved to the QuickBooks file.

Step 10. QuickBooks selects an unmatched check for $1,297.75 processed on 11/13/2003. You will need to enter more information for this check.

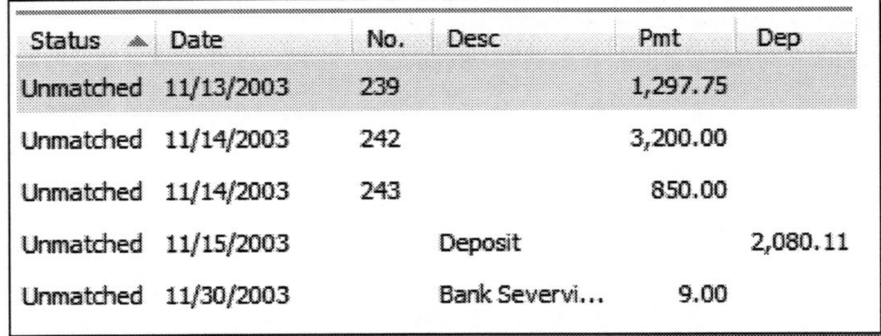

Status	Date	No.	Desc	Pmt	Dep
Unmatched	11/13/2003	239		1,297.75	
Unmatched	11/14/2003	242		3,200.00	
Unmatched	11/14/2003	243		850.00	
Unmatched	11/15/2003		Deposit		2,080.11
Unmatched	11/30/2003		Bank Severvi...	9.00	

Figure 5-48 Unmatched Downloaded Transaction

Step 11. Select **Holly Heating and Electric** in the *Payee* drop down list.

You can do this by entering the beginning of the vendor name or selecting it from the drop-down list. Note that you will need to scroll below the customers and to the vendors to find *Holly Heating and Electric* in the *Payee* drop down list.

Step 12. Select **Building Repairs** (a subaccount under *Repairs*) from the *Accounts* drop down list (see Figure 5-49).

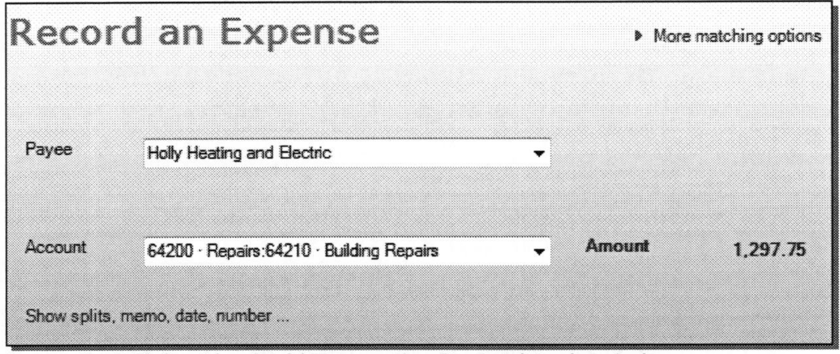

Figure 5-49 Right side of Add Transaction To QuickBooks window

Step 13. Click the *Show splits, memo, date, number...* link.

Step 14. Enter **Final Payment** in the *Memo*.

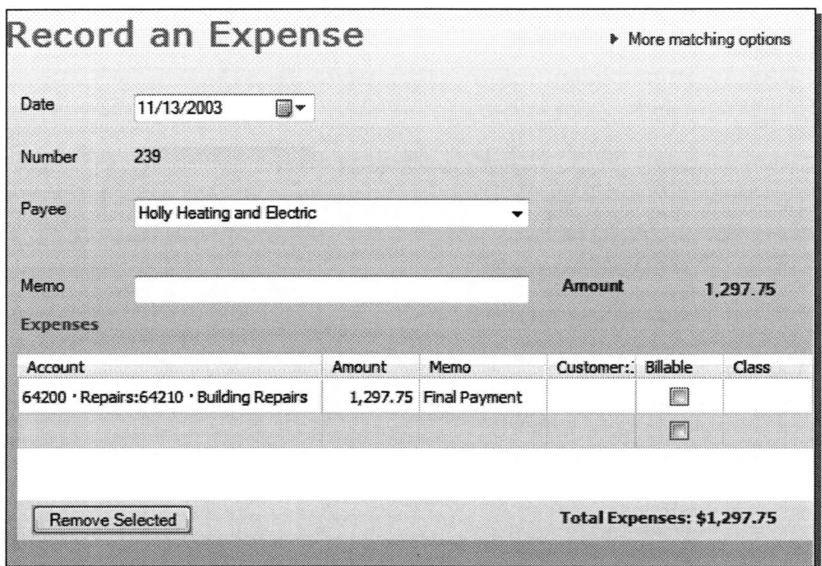

Figure 5-50 Right side of Add Transaction To QuickBooks window with detail

Step 15. Click **Add to QuickBooks**.

Step 16. You can leave the *Add Transactions To QuickBooks* window with unaccepted downloaded transactions and return to them later to complete.

Click **Finish Later.**

Step 17. Close the Online Banking Center.

Chapter Summary and Review

Summary of Key Points

In this chapter, you learned how to reconcile your bank accounts. Reconciling is one of the *most important* parts of keeping your QuickBooks file working well.

You should now be familiar with using QuickBooks to do all of the following:

- Reconcile your checking account (page 184).
- Create bank reconciliation reports (page 190).
- Find errors during reconciliation (page 192).
- Correct errors found during reconciliation (page 196).
- Make corrections when QuickBooks automatically adjusts the balance in a bank account (page 200).
- Handle bounced checks (page 200).
- Reconcile credit card accounts and record a bill for later payment (page 206).
- Improve efficiency with Online Banking (page 210)

Comprehension Questions

Answers to these review questions are available with the supplemental material. See page xiii for details.

1. Explain how QuickBooks calculates the *Beginning Balance* field in the *Begin Reconciliation* window. Why might the beginning balance calculated by QuickBooks differ from the beginning balance on your bank statement?
2. Explain why it's important not to change transactions in closed accounting periods.
3. How is the credit card reconciliation process different from the bank account reconciliation?

Multiple Choice

Select the best answer(s) for each of the following:

1. When the *Beginning Balance* field on the *Begin Reconciliation* window doesn't match the beginning balance on the bank statement, you should:
   a) Call the bank.
   b) Change the number in QuickBooks to match the bank's number.
   c) Click **Locate Discrepancies** in the *Begin Reconciliation* window. Click **Discrepancy Report** and/or **Previous Reports** to research what has been changed since the last reconciliation. Then fix the problem before reconciling.
   d) Select the **Banking** menu and then select **Enter Statement Charges**.

2. Which statement is false?
   a) You can enter bank service charges using ***Enter Statement Charges***.
   b) You can enter bank service charges on the *Begin Reconciliation* window.
   c) You can enter bank service charges using the **Splits** button on a register transaction.
   d) You can enter bank service charges using **Write Checks** before you start your reconciliation.

3. When you find an erroneous amount on a transaction while reconciling, correct the amount by:
   a) Selecting the **Banking** menu and then selecting **Correct Error**.
   b) Double-clicking on the entry and changing the amount on the transaction.
   c) Selecting the entry in the *Reconcile* window, then clicking **Go To** and changing the amount on the transaction.
   d) Performing either b or c.

4. To properly record a voided check from a closed accounting period:
   a) Delete the check in the register.
   b) Make a deposit in the current period and code it to the same account as the original check you want to void. Then delete both transactions in the *Reconciliation* window.
   c) Find the check in the register, select the **Edit** Menu, and then select **Void Check.**
   d) Change the amount of the check to zero.

5. Which of the following columns cannot be displayed in the *Checks and Payments* section of the *Reconcile* window:
   a) Check #.
   b) Class.
   c) Date.
   d) Payee.

6. You know you have reconciled your bank account correctly when:
   a) You make a *Balance Adjustment* entry.
   b) The *Difference* field shows **0.00.**
   c) There are no more register entries to select in the *Reconcile* window.
   d) All of the above.

7. The **Reconciliation Summary** report shows:
   a) The Beginning Balance shown on the Bank Statement.
   b) Detail of all the entries for the month in the register.
   c) The Ending Balance shown in the register in QuickBooks.
   d) Both a) and c).

8. What accounts should be reconciled?
   a) Any account that receives regular statements.
   b) Any bank, income or expense account.
   c) Only bank accounts can be reconciled.
   d) Reconciling is optional for all account types.

9. When you "undo" a bank reconciliation, which statement is true?
   a) Undoing a bank reconciliation does not affect the Beginning Balance.
   b) Balance Adjustments are deleted from the check register.
   c) Interest Income amounts that are entered during the prior bank reconciliation are deleted.
   d) Undoing a bank reconciliation does not delete the Bank Service Charges recorded on the "undone" bank reconciliation.

10. When a customer bounces a check, you should:
    a) Add a transaction to your check register for the amount of the bounced check.
    b) Add a transaction to your check register for any fees the bank charges you for bounced checks.
    c) Create an invoice to the customer for NSF charges.
    d) All of the above.

11. When you finish reconciling a credit card account, you:
    a) Can only create a check for the total amount due.
    b) Can create a check for an amount equal to or less than the total amount due.
    c) Cannot choose to bypass making a payment.
    d) Cannot choose to enter a bill for later payment.

12. What is the accounting behind the scenes for a Bill coded to a Credit Card liability account:
    a) Decrease (debit) Accounts Payable, Increase (credit) Credit Card liability.
    b) Decrease (debit) Accounts Payable, Decrease (credit) Credit Card liability.
    c) Increase (credit) Accounts Payable, Decrease (debit) Credit Card liability.
    d) Increase (credit) Accounts Payable, Increase (credit) Credit Card liability.

13. What account is a transaction created in if you complete a reconciliation and your difference is not 0.00:
    a) Opening Balance Equity.
    b) Uncategorized Income.
    c) Reconciliation Discrepancies.
    d) Other Expense.

14. When you void a check written in a closed accounting period, QuickBooks automatically creates
    a) An adjustment in the *Reconciliation Discrepancies* account.
    b) A new check to be dated to the current date.
    c) Two journal entries in the closed accounting period.
    d) A journal entry in the closed accounting period and a journal entry during the open accounting period.

15. After notifying a customer that his check bounced, he asks you to deposit it again. What should you record in QuickBooks?
    a) Enter the same transactions as you would for any bounced check and receive the check as a new payment or create a new deposit using the current date.
    b) Delete the original deposit.
    c) Change the date on the original deposit to the current date.
    d) You do not need to record the deposit in QuickBooks because the check was previously deposited.

Completion Statements

1. QuickBooks calculates the *Beginning Balance* field in the *Begin Reconciliation* window by adding and subtracting all previously __________ transactions.

2. Voiding, deleting, or changing the amount of a transaction you previously cleared in a bank reconciliation causes the __________ __________ field on the *Begin Reconciliation* window to disagree with your bank statement.

3. The **Previous Reconciliation Discrepancy** report shows changes to cleared transactions since your most recent bank ____________.

4. You don't want to change transactions dated in a _______ accounting period because doing so would change net income in a period for which you have already issued _________ statements and/or filed the tax returns.

5. Banks and accountants often refer to bounced checks as ______ transactions.

Bank Rec-Problem 1

APPLYING YOUR KNOWLEDGE

> Restore the BankRec-10Problem1.QBM file and store it on your hard disk according to your instructor's directions.

1. Using the sample bank statement shown on below, reconcile the checking account for 01/31/2011.

Business Checking Account

Statement Date: **January 31, 2011** *Page 1 of 1*

Summary:

Previous Balance as of 12/31/10:	$	18,283.60
Total Deposits and Credits	+ $	4,561.08
Total Checks and Debits	- $	8,076.12
Statement Balance as of 1/31/10:	**= $**	**14,768.56**

Deposits and Other Credits:

DEPOSITS

Date	Description		Amount
12-Jan	Customer Deposit	$	1,709.53
30-Jan	Customer Deposit	$	2,848.27
	2 Deposits:	**$**	**4,557.80**

INTEREST

Date	Description		Amount
31-Jan	Interest Earned	$	3.28
	Interest:	**$**	**3.28**

Checks and Other Withdrawals:

CHECKS PAID:

Check No.	Date Paid		Amount
325	2-Jan	$	324.00
326	7-Jan	$	276.52
327	17-Jan	$	128.60
6001**	25-Jan	$	3,200.00
6003**	25-Jan	$	142.00
	5 Checks Paid:	**$**	**4,071.12**

OTHER WITHDRAWALS/PAYMENTS

Date	Description		Amount
31-Jan	Transfer	$	4,000.00
	1 Other Withdrawals/Payments:	**$**	**4,000.00**

SERVICE CHARGES

Date	Description		Amount
31-Jan	Service Charge	$	5.00
	1 Service Charge:	**$**	**5.00**

Figure 5-51 Bank statement for January 31, 2011

2. Print a **Reconciliation Detail Report** dated 1/31/2011.

3. On **02/12/2011**, Miranda's Corner's payment bounced (check #4523, received on 1/25/11 for Invoice #2011-103). The amount of the check was **$1,191.80**. The bank charged you an NSF Fee of **$10.00**. Using this information, record the following:

   a) Enter the bounced check and NSF fee your bank charged you in your check register by using **Miranda's Corner** as the *Payee.*

   b) Unapply the original payment for *Invoice #2011-103* and then apply this same payment to the bounced check transaction you just created.

c) Create an *Other Charge* item called NSF Charge with an amount of $20.00. The description should read ***"NSF Service Charge for Bounced Check #."*** Use the **Non** sales tax code, and associate the item with the **Bank Service Charge** expense account.

d) Create Invoice ***#2011-103B*** dated ***2/12/2011 and code it to*** the **Walnut Creek** class for the **Miranda's Corner**. Select the ***NSF Charge*** item and charge Miranda's Corner **$20.00** for the bounced check. Change the Terms to **Due Upon Receipt** for this invoice only.

4. Enter the transactions necessary to record the receipt and redeposit of Miranda's Corner's replacement check (Check ***#4543***) that did not include the bounce charge. Date the payment ***02/14/2011*** and apply it to invoice **#2011-103.** Date the deposit on ***02/14/2011.***

5. Using the sample bank statement shown below, reconcile the checking account for 02/28/2011.

Business Checking Account

Statement Date:	**February 28, 2011**	*Page 1 of 1*

Summary:

Previous Balance as of 1/31/11:	$	14,768.56
Total Deposits and Credits: 6	+ $	6,032.00
Total Checks and Debits: 7	- $	4,879.56
Statement Balance as of 2/28/11:	**= $**	**15,921.00**

Deposits and Other Credits:

DEPOSITS

Date	Description		Amount
3-Feb	Customer Deposit	$	119.08
4-Feb	Customer Deposit	$	2,460.13
10-Feb	Customer Deposit	$	809.03
11-Feb	Customer Deposit	$	753.41
13-Feb	Customer Deposit	$	695.99
14-Feb	Customer Deposit	$	1,191.80
	6 Deposits:	**$**	**6,029.44**

INTEREST

Date	Description		Amount
28-Feb	Interest Earned	$	2.56
	Interest:	**$**	**2.56**

Checks and Other Withdrawals:

CHECKS PAID:

Check No.	Date Paid		Amount
329	14-Feb	$	2,152.00
330	15-Feb	$	377.28
331	24-Feb	$	375.00
332 **	28-Feb	$	645.00
6004	2-Feb	$	123.48
	5 Checks Paid:	**$**	**3,672.76**

OTHER WITHDRAWALS/PAYMENTS

Date	Description		Amount
12-Feb	Returned Item	$	1,191.80
12-Feb	NSF Charge	$	10.00
	2 Other Withdrawals/Payments:	**$**	**1,201.80**

SERVICE CHARGES

Date	Description		Amount
28-Feb	Service Charge	$	5.00
	1 Service Charge:	**$**	**5.00**

Figure 5-52 Bank statement for February 28, 2011

6. Print a *Reconciliation Detail* Report dated 02/28/2011.

7. Print a customer statement for Miranda's Corner for the period 01/1/2011 through 02/28/2011.

Discussion Questions

These questions are designed to stimulate discussion about how you can apply QuickBooks to your own organization. They may help you think through some of the issues you'll encounter when using QuickBooks in your company.

1. How many bank accounts does your organization have? With how many banks? List all the banks your organization uses and what types of accounts are held at each.
2. How many bank statements does your organization receive? What is your organization's policy for how quickly statements should be reconciled?
3. What service charges do the banks charge your company for maintaining the accounts? Are there charges per transaction (check, deposit, etc.)?

ACTIVITY

Research your company's policy with regard to outstanding transactions. Identify any checks that have been outstanding for more than three months.

Research your company's policy with regard to non-sufficient funds. Identify any NSF checks.

Case Study

Software Support, Incorporated

Software Support, Inc. is a company that provides computer consulting services for clients throughout the Chicago metropolitan area. The company provides computer setup, training, and troubleshooting services for small business clients.

On February 23, 2011, a customer named Andre Wise paid invoice #2011-202 for 800.00 with check #2433. This check was deposited that day to the company's checking account. On the next day, the bank returned the check with a note explaining that the account on which the check was drawn did not have sufficient funds to pay the check. The bank charged the account a $10.00 returned check fee.

On 02/27/2011, you received a replacement check (#2438) from Mr. Wise for $820.00 to cover the check plus the service charge.

1. What transactions would you enter in Software Support's QuickBooks file to record the bounced check, and to pass on a $20.00 fee to Andre Wise?
2. How would you record the receipt of the replacement check?

Chapter 6 Reports and Graphs

Objectives

After completing this chapter, you should be able to:

- Describe several types of QuickBooks reports (page 223).
- Set QuickBooks preferences for cash or accrual basis reports (page 224).
- Create several different accounting reports (page 227).
- Create several different business management reports (page 238).
- Create graphs (page 244).
- Customize the look of reports and filter the data on reports (page 246).
- Memorize and group reports (page 253).
- Process and print multiple reports in batches (page 255).
- Print reports (page 257).
- Use the Find command to find transactions (page 259).
- Use QuickZoom to see the "numbers behind the numbers" on reports (page 266).
- Export reports to spreadsheets for further analysis (page 267).

Restore this File

This chapter uses Reports-10.QBW. To open this file, restore the Reports-10.QBM file to your hard disk. See page 10 for instructions on restoring files.

QuickBooks reports allow you to get the information you need to make critical business decisions. In this chapter, you'll learn how to create a variety of reports to help you manage your business. Every report in QuickBooks gives you immediate, up-to-date information about your company's performance.

There are literally hundreds of reports available in QuickBooks. These allow you to manipulate the numbers so that you can look at your data in any way you wish. In addition to the built-in reports, you can *modify* reports to include or exclude whatever data you want. To control the look of your reports, you can customize the formatting of headers, footers, fonts, or columns.

When you get a report looking just the way you want, you can *memorize* it so that you can quickly create it again later.

Types of Reports

There are two major types of reports in QuickBooks – Accounting Reports and Business Management Reports. In addition, most reports have a "detail" or "summary" style. **Detail** reports show individual transactions, and **summary** reports show totals for a group of transactions.

Accounting reports contain information about transactions and accounts. For example, the Profit & Loss report is a summary report of all transactions coded to income and expense accounts for a specified period of time. Your accountant or tax preparer will need several accounting reports from QuickBooks in order to provide accounting and tax services for your company.

Business Management reports are used to monitor different activities of a business to help plan workflow and review transactions that have already occurred. These reports provide critical information that you need to operate your business. For example, the Customer Contact List report shows addresses, phone numbers, fax numbers, and other information about Customers. The Collections Report provides information you need to follow up on invoices that are past due. The Sales by Item report shows business managers how well each product and service is selling.

Report Type	Example Reports
Accounting	Profit & Loss, Balance Sheet, Trial Balance, Cash Flow Forecast, General Ledger, Trial Balance
Business Management	Open Invoices, Unpaid Bills Detail, Check Detail, Sales by Item Detail, Item Profitability, Customer Contact List, Item Price List, Time by Name, Stock Status by Item

Table 6-1 Types of QuickBooks reports

Cash versus Accrual Reports

QuickBooks can automatically convert reports from the accrual basis to the cash basis, depending on how you set your preferences or how you customize reports.

If you use **Cash Basis** accounting, you regard income or expenses as occurring at the time you actually receive a payment from a customer or pay a bill from a vendor. The cash basis records (or recognizes) income or expense only when cash is received or paid, no matter when the original transaction occurred. If you use **Accrual Basis** accounting, you regard income or expenses as occurring at the time you ship a product, render a service, or receive a bill from your vendors. Under this method, the date that you enter a transaction and the date that you actually pay or receive cash may be two separate dates, but income (or expense) is recognized on the day of the original transaction.

You can set the default for all QuickBooks summary reports to the cash or accrual basis by selecting **Cash** or **Accrual** in the **Summary Reports Basis** section of the *Reports & Graphs Preferences* window. Follow these steps:

COMPUTER PRACTICE

Step 1. Select the **Edit** menu and then select **Preferences.**

Step 2. Click on the **Reports and Graphs** preference.

Step 3. Click the Company Preferences tab.

> **Note:**
> If you are in multi-user mode you will need to first switch to single-user mode to change company preferences.

Step 4. To set the basis to match your company's finances, click **Cash** or **Accrual** in the *Summary Reports Basis* section (see Figure 6-1). For this chapter, leave the basis set to **Accrual**.

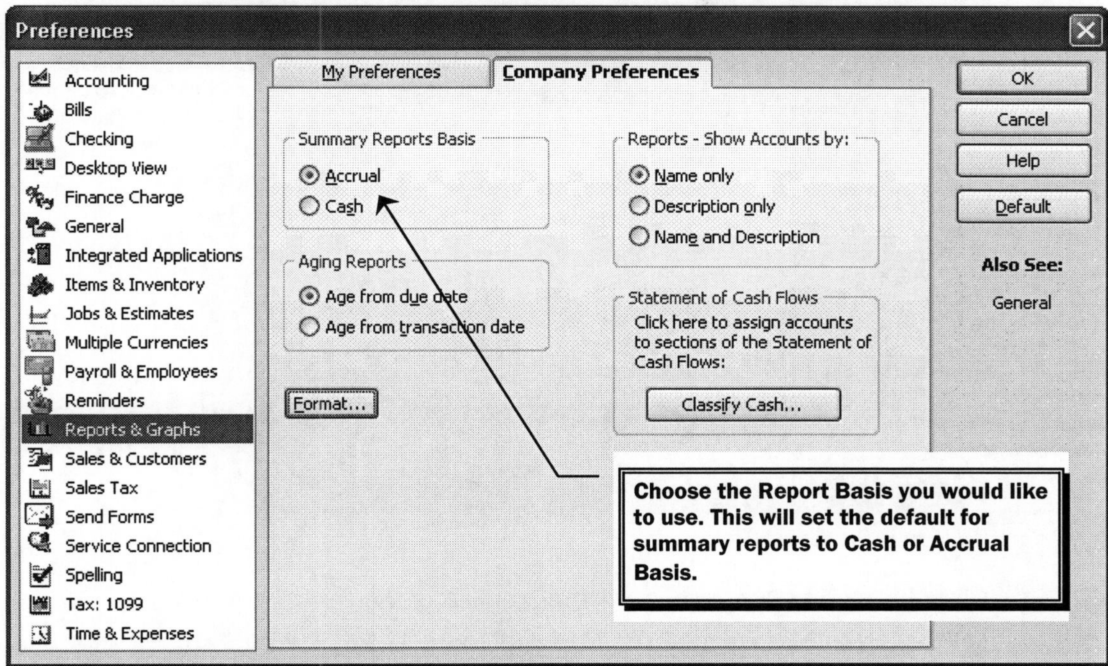

Figure 6-1 Preferences for Reports and Graphs

Step 5. Click **OK** to save your changes (if any) and close the Preferences window.

> **Did You Know?**
> In QuickBooks, you can leave the reporting preferences set to the accrual basis for internal management reporting purposes and then create cash-basis reports for tax purposes.

Irrespective of the default setting in your preferences, you can always switch between cash and accrual reports by modifying reports. To convert a report basis from accrual to cash on any report, follow these steps:

COMPUTER PRACTICE

Step 1. Click the *Report Center* icon on the Navigation Bar.

The *Report Center* has been redesigned in QuickBooks 2010. There are now three different views for previewing the reports, *Carousel*, *List* and *Grid*.

Step 2. Click on **Carousel View** in the upper right corner of the *Report Center*.

Step 3. Select **Company & Financial** from the list on the left of the window. Profit & Loss Standard is the first report (see Figure 6-2).

You can choose other reports by moving the slider at the bottom the window. You can also choose a date range from the *Dates* fields at the bottom of the window.

Step 4. Double click the **Profit & Loss Standard** report image in the *Report Center*.

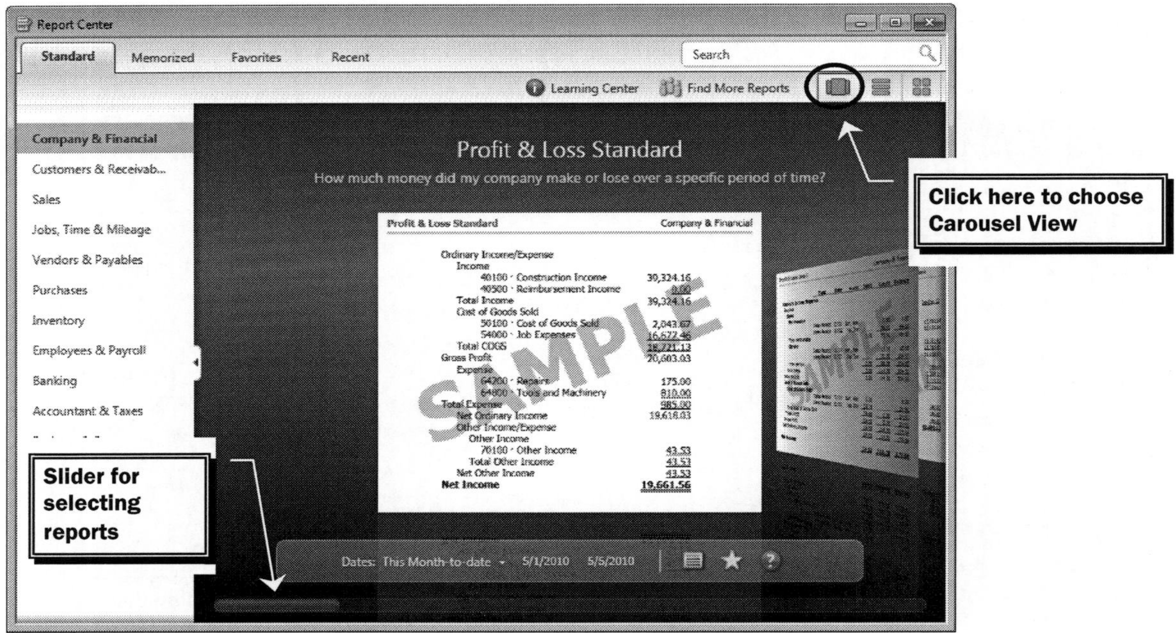

Figure 6-2 Carousel View in the Report Center

Step 5. Click the **Modify Report** button at the top left of the *Profit & Loss* window.

Step 6. Set the *Dates* fields *From* ***01/01/2011*** and *To* ***01/31/2011***. Press **Tab**.

Step 7. Click **Cash** in the *Report Basis* section (see Figure 6-3).

Step 8. Click **OK** to save your changes and display a Cash Basis Profit & Loss report for January 2011.

Step 9. Close the *Profit & Loss* report window.

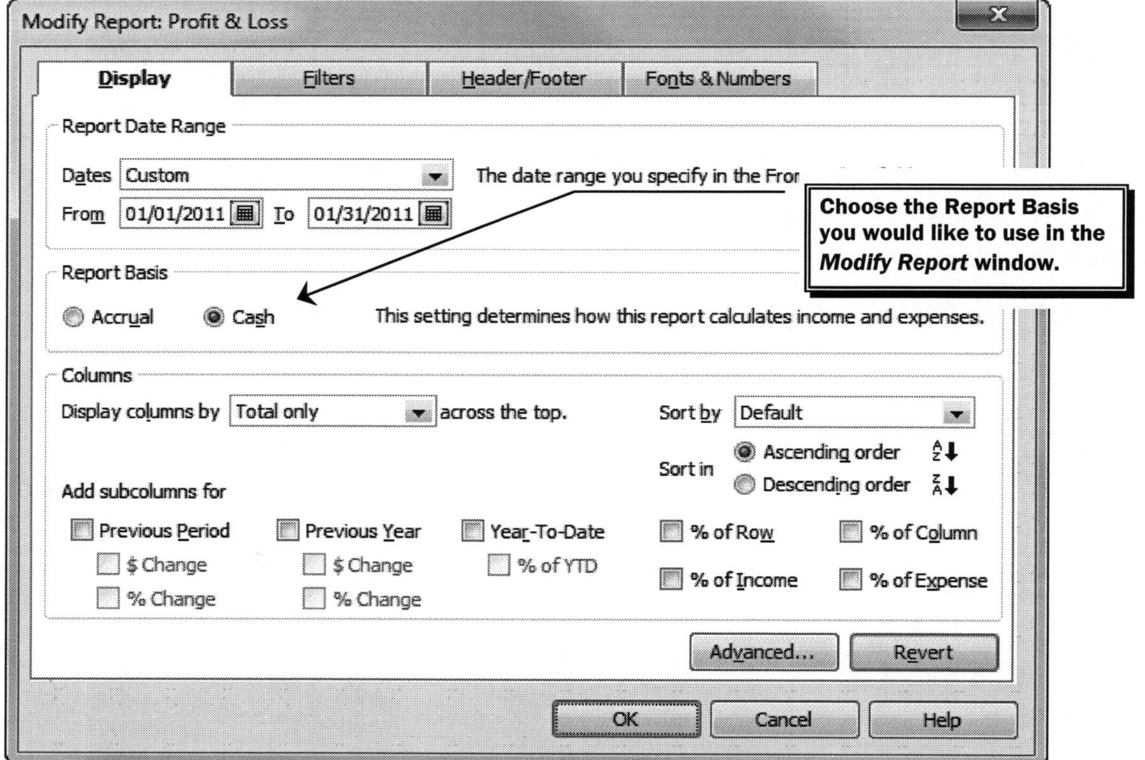

Figure 6-3 Select the Cash report basis in the Modify Report window

Accounting Reports

There are several built-in reports that summarize a group of transactions. These reports help you analyze the performance of your business.

Profit & Loss

The **Profit & Loss** report (also referred to as the *Income Statement*) shows all your income and expenses for a given period.

As discussed earlier, the goal of accounting is to provide the financial information you need to measure the success (or failure) of your organization. The Profit & Loss report is one of the most valuable sources of this financial information.

COMPUTER PRACTICE

Step 1. From the *Report Center,* click Grid View to choose a report from a different view (see Figure 6-4).

Step 2. Select **Company & Financial** from the list on the left of the window and then double click the **Profit & Loss Standard** report in the upper left of the Grid View.

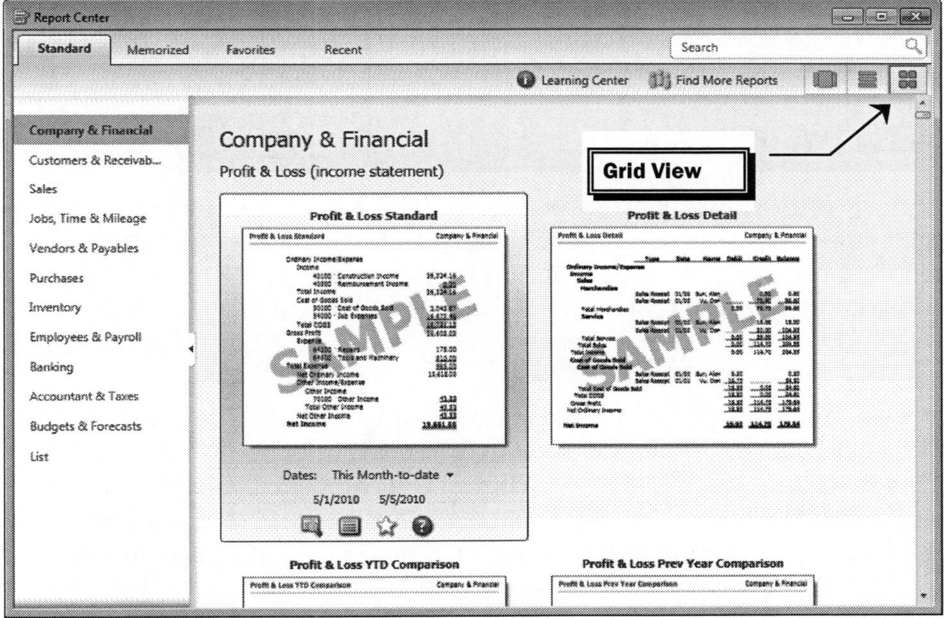

Figure 6-4 Grid View of the Report Center

Step 3. Set the *Dates* fields *From* ***01/01/2011*** and *To* ***01/31/2011***. Press **Tab**.

Step 4. The Profit & Loss report (see Figure 6-5) summarizes the totals of all your Income accounts, followed by Cost of Goods Sold accounts, then Expenses, then Other Income, and finally, Other Expenses. The total at the bottom of the report is your Net Income (or loss) for the period you specified in the *Dates* fields. The Profit & Loss report is a company's operating results, normally for a period of 12 months or less.

Note that the window shown in Figure 6-5 is not the complete report. You will have to scroll down to see the remainder of the report. Do not close this report.

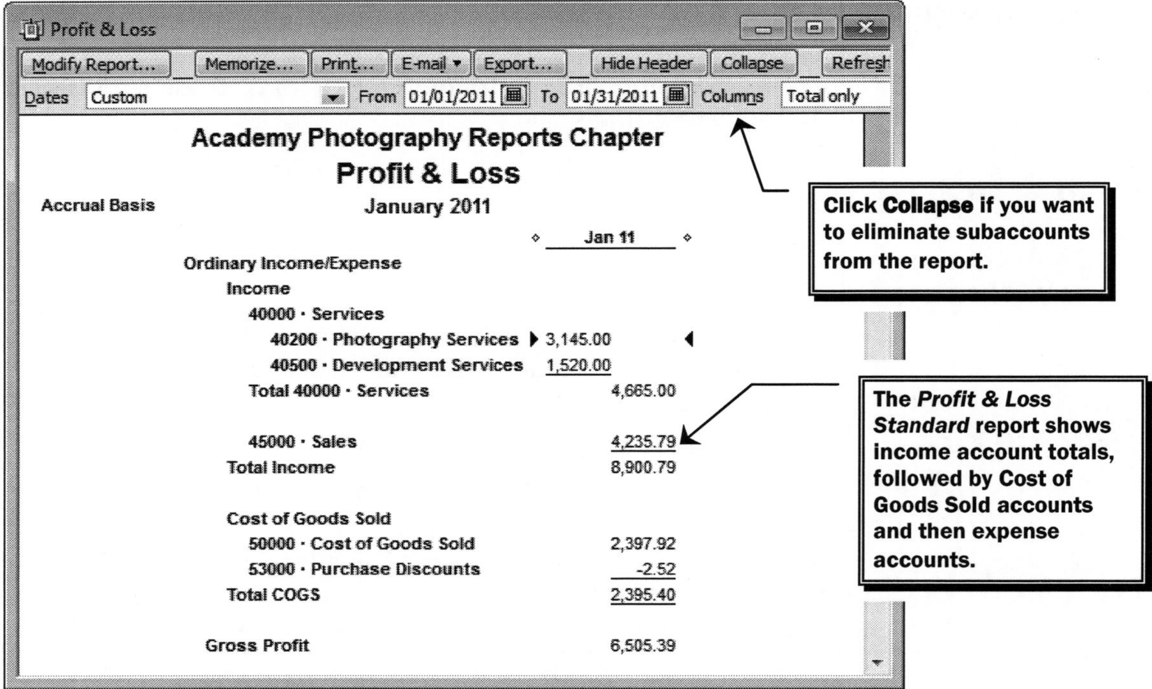

Academy Photography Reports Chapter
Profit & Loss
Accrual Basis — January 2011

		Jan 11
Ordinary Income/Expense		
Income		
40000 · Services		
40200 · Photography Services	3,145.00	
40500 · Development Services	1,520.00	
Total 40000 · Services		4,665.00
45000 · Sales		4,235.79
Total Income		8,900.79
Cost of Goods Sold		
50000 · Cost of Goods Sold		2,397.92
53000 · Purchase Discounts		-2.52
Total COGS		2,395.40
Gross Profit		6,505.39

Figure 6-5 Upper portion of the Profit & Loss report (scroll down to see the remainder)

Analyzing the Profit & Loss Report

The first section of the **Profit & Loss** report shows the total of each of your income accounts for the period specified on the report. If you have subaccounts, QuickBooks indents those accounts on the report and subtotals them. Notice on Figure 6-5 that the Services income category has two subaccounts: Photography Services and Development Services. To hide subaccounts on this report (or any summary report), click the **Collapse** button at the top of the report.

The next section of the report shows your **Cost of Goods Sold** accounts. You use these accounts to record the costs of the products and services you sell in your business (e.g., inventory, cost of labor, etc.). If you use Inventory Items, QuickBooks calculates Cost of Goods Sold as each Inventory Item is sold, using the *average cost method.* (See the **Inventory** chapter beginning on page 369 for more information on how QuickBooks calculates average cost.)

The next section of the report shows your **Expenses** of the business. Use these accounts to record costs associated with operating your business (e.g. rent, salaries, supplies, etc.). Expenses are generally recorded in QuickBooks as you write checks or enter bills, but can also be recorded directly into a register or as a journal entry.

The next section of the report shows your **Other Income/Expenses** accounts. Use these accounts to record income and expenses that are generated outside the normal operation of your business. For example, if you provide accounting services but sold an old business computer to a relative, the income generated from the sale would be classified as *Other Income* because it was generated outside the normal operation of your business.

At the bottom of the report, QuickBooks calculates your *Net Income* – the amount of your revenue less your Cost of Goods Sold and your operating expenses. You may want to view your expenses (such as rent, office supplies, employee salaries, etc.) as a percentage of total income to help you locate excessive expenses in your business.

COMPUTER PRACTICE

Step 1. Click the **Modify Report** button at the top left of the *Profit & Loss* report.

Step 2. Click the **% of Income** box (see Figure 6-6).

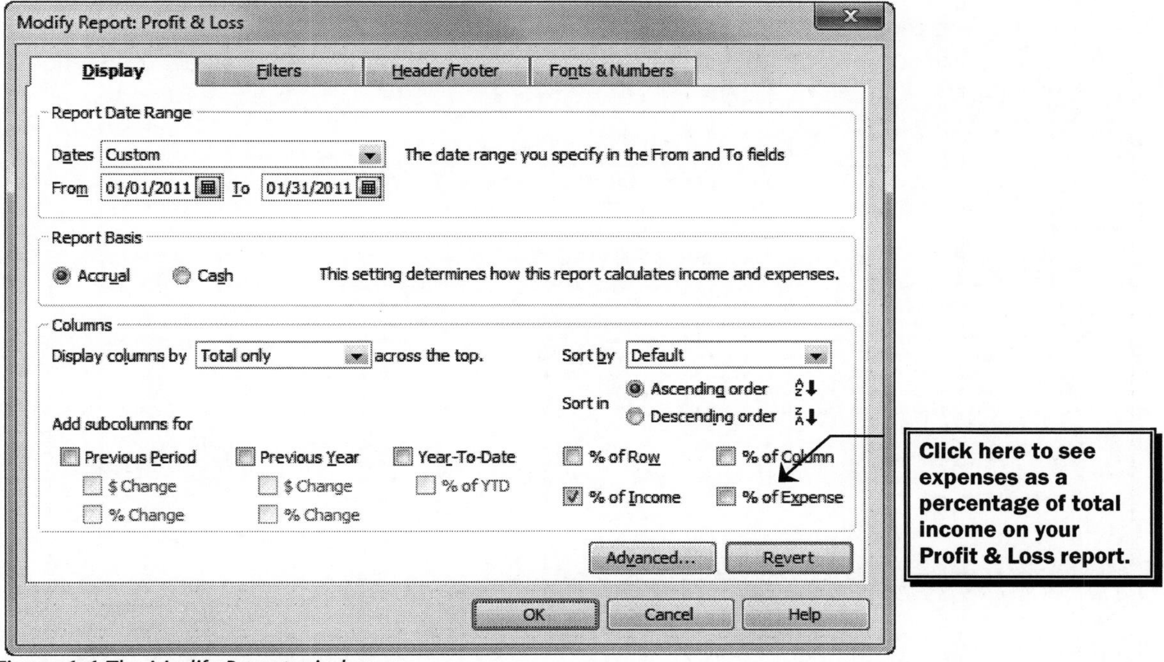

Figure 6-6 The Modify Report window

Step 3. Click OK.

The **Profit & Loss** report now has a **% of Income** column (see Figure 6-7) allowing you to quickly identify numbers that deviate from the norm. Familiarize yourself with the percentages of expenses in your business and review this report periodically to make sure you stay in control of your expenses.

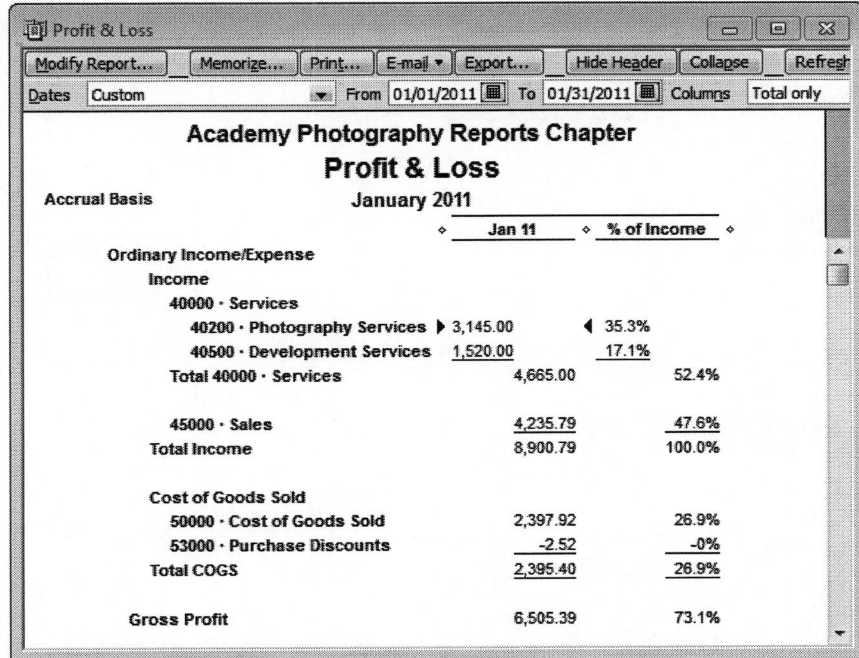

Academy Photography Reports Chapter

Profit & Loss

Accrual Basis — January 2011

	Jan 11	% of Income
Ordinary Income/Expense		
Income		
40000 · Services		
40200 · Photography Services	3,145.00	35.3%
40500 · Development Services	1,520.00	17.1%
Total 40000 · Services	4,665.00	52.4%
45000 · Sales	4,235.79	47.6%
Total Income	8,900.79	100.0%
Cost of Goods Sold		
50000 · Cost of Goods Sold	2,397.92	26.9%
53000 · Purchase Discounts	-2.52	-0%
Total COGS	2,395.40	26.9%
Gross Profit	6,505.39	73.1%

Figure 6-7 Modified Profit & Loss report

Step 4. To find the details behind any of these numbers, you can use **QuickZoom** (explained on page 266). Double-click the *Cost of Goods Sold* line item amount of **2,397.92** in the report (see Figure 6-7).

The report shown in Figure 6-8 shows each transaction coded to the *Cost of Goods Sold* account. Double-click on any of these numbers to see the actual transaction.

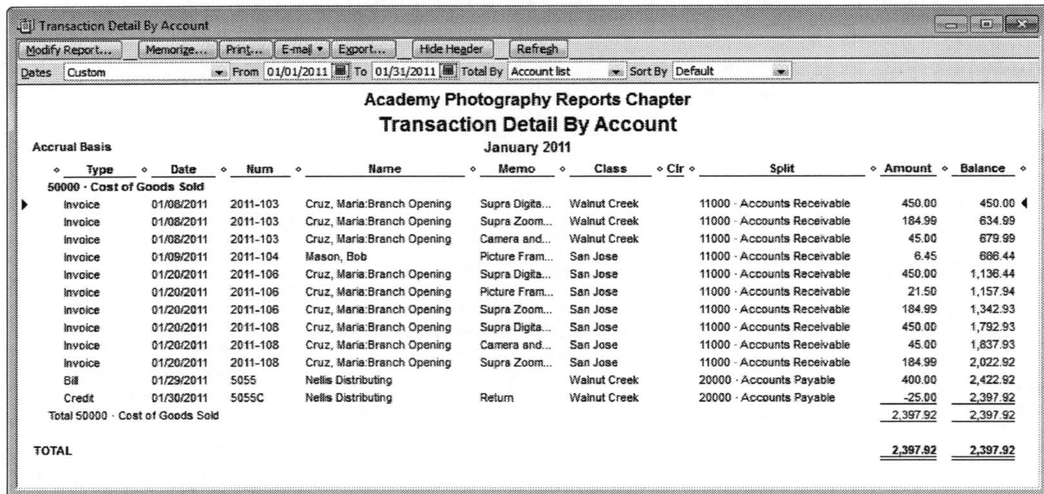

Transaction Detail By Account

Modify Report... | Memorize... | Print... | E-mail | Export... | Hide Header | Refresh

Dates Custom From 01/01/2011 To 01/31/2011 Total By Account list Sort By Default

Academy Photography Reports Chapter

Transaction Detail By Account

January 2011

Accrual Basis

Type	Date	Num	Name	Memo	Class	Clr	Split	Amount	Balance
50000 · Cost of Goods Sold									
Invoice	01/08/2011	2011-103	Cruz, Maria:Branch Opening	Supra Digita...	Walnut Creek		11000 · Accounts Receivable	450.00	450.00
Invoice	01/08/2011	2011-103	Cruz, Maria:Branch Opening	Supra Zoom...	Walnut Creek		11000 · Accounts Receivable	184.99	634.99
Invoice	01/08/2011	2011-103	Cruz, Maria:Branch Opening	Camera and...	Walnut Creek		11000 · Accounts Receivable	45.00	679.99
Invoice	01/09/2011	2011-104	Mason, Bob	Picture Fram...	San Jose		11000 · Accounts Receivable	6.45	686.44
Invoice	01/20/2011	2011-106	Cruz, Maria:Branch Opening	Supra Digita...	San Jose		11000 · Accounts Receivable	450.00	1,136.44
Invoice	01/20/2011	2011-106	Cruz, Maria:Branch Opening	Picture Fram...	San Jose		11000 · Accounts Receivable	21.50	1,157.94
Invoice	01/20/2011	2011-106	Cruz, Maria:Branch Opening	Supra Zoom...	San Jose		11000 · Accounts Receivable	184.99	1,342.93
Invoice	01/20/2011	2011-108	Cruz, Maria:Branch Opening	Supra Digita...	San Jose		11000 · Accounts Receivable	450.00	1,792.93
Invoice	01/20/2011	2011-108	Cruz, Maria:Branch Opening	Camera and...	San Jose		11000 · Accounts Receivable	45.00	1,837.93
Invoice	01/20/2011	2011-108	Cruz, Maria:Branch Opening	Supra Zoom...	San Jose		11000 · Accounts Receivable	184.99	2,022.92
Bill	01/29/2011	5055	Nellis Distributing		Walnut Creek		20000 · Accounts Payable	400.00	2,422.92
Credit	01/30/2011	5055C	Nellis Distributing	Return	Walnut Creek		20000 · Accounts Payable	-25.00	2,397.92
Total 50000 · Cost of Goods Sold								2,397.92	2,397.92
TOTAL								2,397.92	2,397.92

Figure 6-8 Transaction Detail by Account report for the Cost of Goods Sold account

Step 5. Close both open reports.

Profit & Loss by Class Report

To divide your **Profit & Loss** report into departments (or classes), use the **Profit & Loss by Class** report.

COMPUTER PRACTICE

Step 1. From the *Report Center*, click the list view (see Figure 6-9)

Step 2. Select **Company & Financial** from the menu on the left, then double click the **Profit & Loss By Class** report in the *Profit & Loss (income statement)* section.

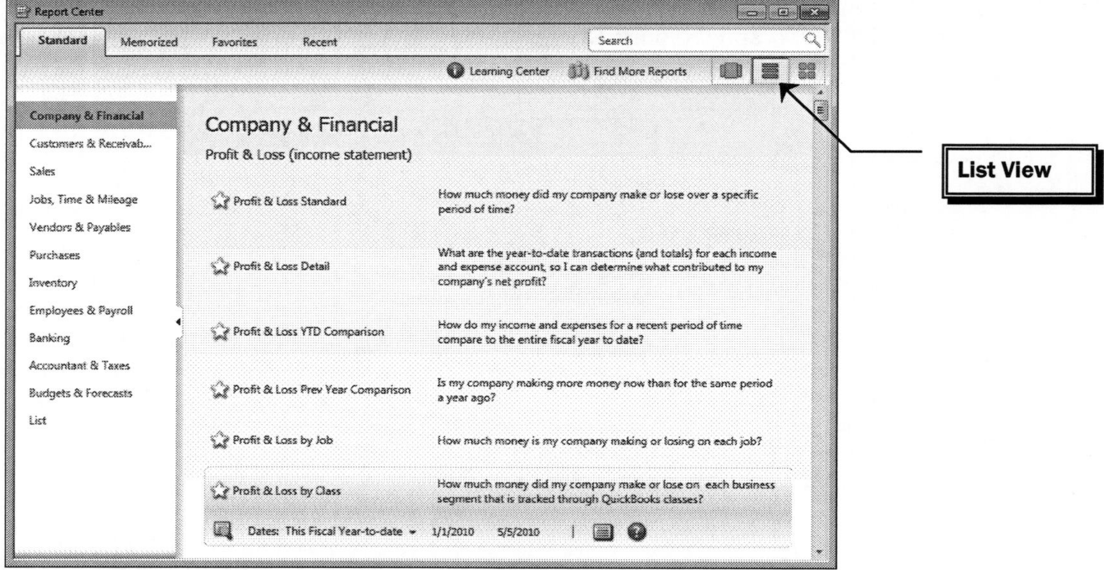

Figure 6-9 List View in the Report Center

Step 3. Enter ***01/01/2011*** in the *From* field and enter ***01/31/2011*** in the *To* field at the top of the report and press **Tab**.

Step 4. Compare your screen to the report shown in Figure 6-10. Notice that totals for each Class are displayed in a separate column.

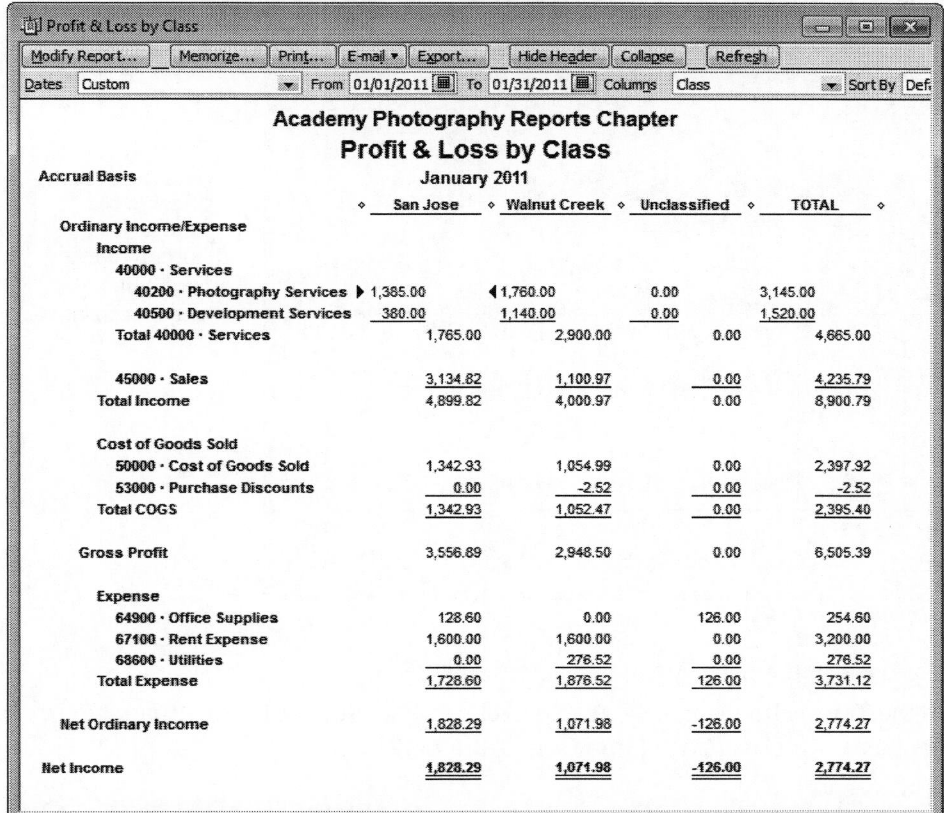

Academy Photography Reports Chapter

Profit & Loss by Class

Accrual Basis — January 2011

	San Jose	Walnut Creek	Unclassified	TOTAL
Ordinary Income/Expense				
Income				
40000 · Services				
40200 · Photography Services	1,385.00	1,760.00	0.00	3,145.00
40500 · Development Services	380.00	1,140.00	0.00	1,520.00
Total 40000 · Services	1,765.00	2,900.00	0.00	4,665.00
45000 · Sales	3,134.82	1,100.97	0.00	4,235.79
Total Income	4,899.82	4,000.97	0.00	8,900.79
Cost of Goods Sold				
50000 · Cost of Goods Sold	1,342.93	1,054.99	0.00	2,397.92
53000 · Purchase Discounts	0.00	-2.52	0.00	-2.52
Total COGS	1,342.93	1,052.47	0.00	2,395.40
Gross Profit	3,556.89	2,948.50	0.00	6,505.39
Expense				
64900 · Office Supplies	128.60	0.00	126.00	254.60
67100 · Rent Expense	1,600.00	1,600.00	0.00	3,200.00
68600 · Utilities	0.00	276.52	0.00	276.52
Total Expense	1,728.60	1,876.52	126.00	3,731.12
Net Ordinary Income	1,828.29	1,071.98	-126.00	2,774.27
Net Income	**1,828.29**	**1,071.98**	**-126.00**	**2,774.27**

Figure 6-10 Profit and Loss by Class report

This report includes an *Unclassified* column, as shown in Figure 6-10, it means that some of the transactions were not assigned a class. To classify the unclassified transactions, follow these steps:

Step 5. Double-click to QuickZoom on the 126.00 amount in the unclassified column under Office Supplies.

This will bring up the Transaction Detail by Account report.

Step 6. Double-click to QuickZoom on the 126.00 amount again. This opens the bill from Ace Supply..

Step 7. Assign the Class Walnut Creek to the bill as shown in Figure 6-11.

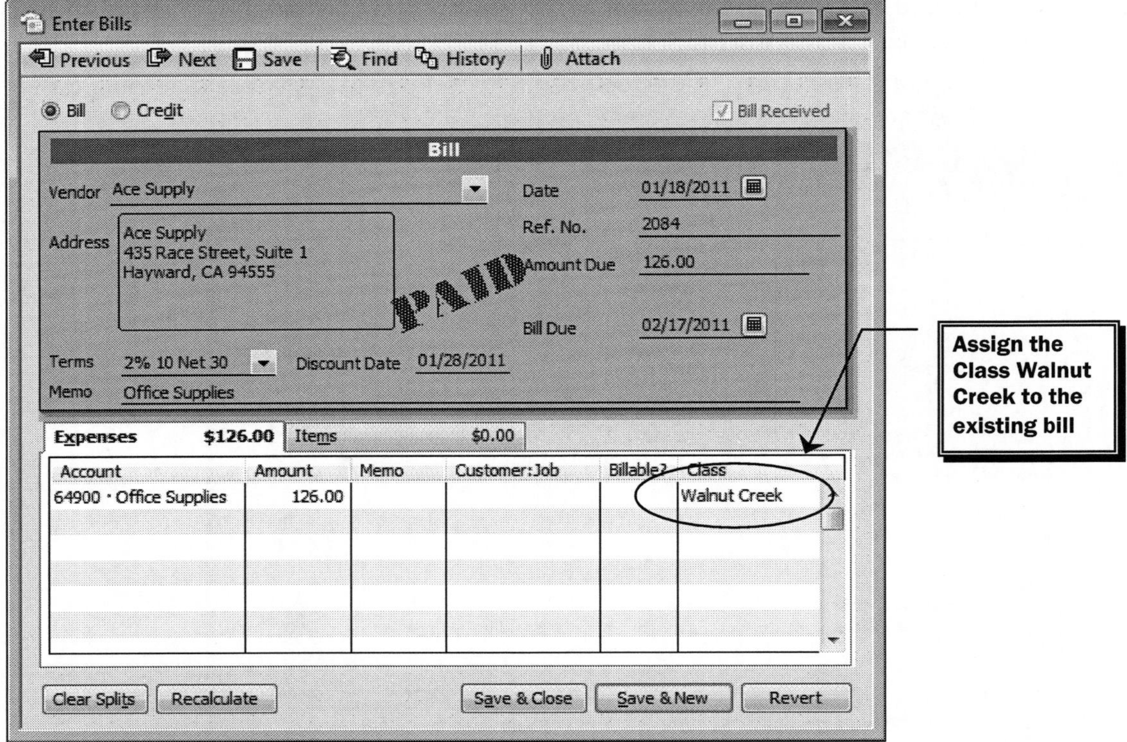

Figure 6-11 Bill from Ace Supply with Class

Step 8. Save and Close the Bill.

Step 9. Close the Transaction Detail By Account report. The Profit & Loss by Class report no longer has an Unclassified column (see Figure 6-12).

Step 10. Close this report.

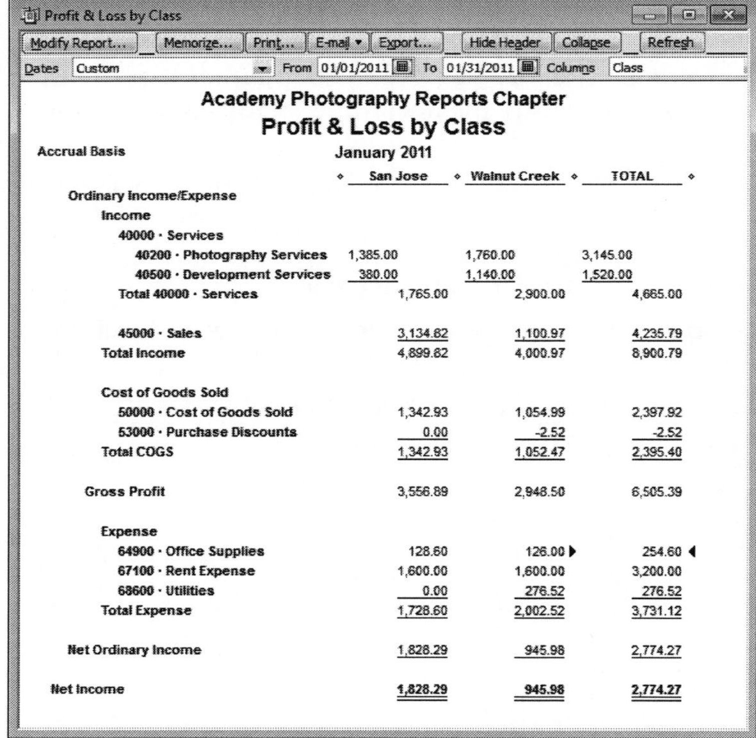

Profit & Loss by Class

Modify Report... Memorize... Print... E-mail Export... Hide Header Collapse Refresh

Dates Custom From 01/01/2011 To 01/31/2011 Columns Class

Academy Photography Reports Chapter

Profit & Loss by Class

Accrual Basis

January 2011

	San Jose	Walnut Creek	TOTAL
Ordinary Income/Expense			
Income			
40000 · Services			
40200 · Photography Services	1,385.00	1,760.00	3,145.00
40500 · Development Services	380.00	1,140.00	1,520.00
Total 40000 · Services	1,765.00	2,900.00	4,665.00
45000 · Sales	3,134.82	1,100.97	4,235.79
Total Income	4,899.82	4,000.97	8,900.79
Cost of Goods Sold			
50000 · Cost of Goods Sold	1,342.93	1,054.99	2,397.92
53000 · Purchase Discounts	0.00	-2.52	-2.52
Total COGS	1,342.93	1,052.47	2,395.40
Gross Profit	3,556.89	2,948.50	6,505.39
Expense			
64900 · Office Supplies	128.60	126.00	254.60
67100 · Rent Expense	1,600.00	1,600.00	3,200.00
68600 · Utilities	0.00	276.52	276.52
Total Expense	1,728.60	2,002.52	3,731.12
Net Ordinary Income	1,828.29	945.98	2,774.27
Net Income	1,828.29	945.98	2,774.27

Figure 6-12 Profit & Loss by Class without Unclassified Column

Note:
When using classes, be sure to always enter the class as you are recording each transaction. This prevents any transaction from being recorded as "unclassified." For transactions that do not fall within the normal operating activities of one of the classes in your company file, use a generic class such as Overhead.

To ensure that transactions are always assigned to classes, set preferences so that QuickBooks will prompt you to assign a class before completing the transaction.

COMPUTER PRACTICE

Follow these steps:

Step 1. Select the **Edit** menu, and then select **Preferences**.

Step 2. Click on the **Accounting** preference.

Step 3. Click the Company Preferences tab.

Step 4. Leave the **Prompt to assign classes** box checked (see Figure 6-13).

You can uncheck this box if you no longer want QuickBooks to prompt you when you forget to assign classes. For now leave it checked.

Step 5. Click **OK** to save your changes and to close the *Preferences* window.

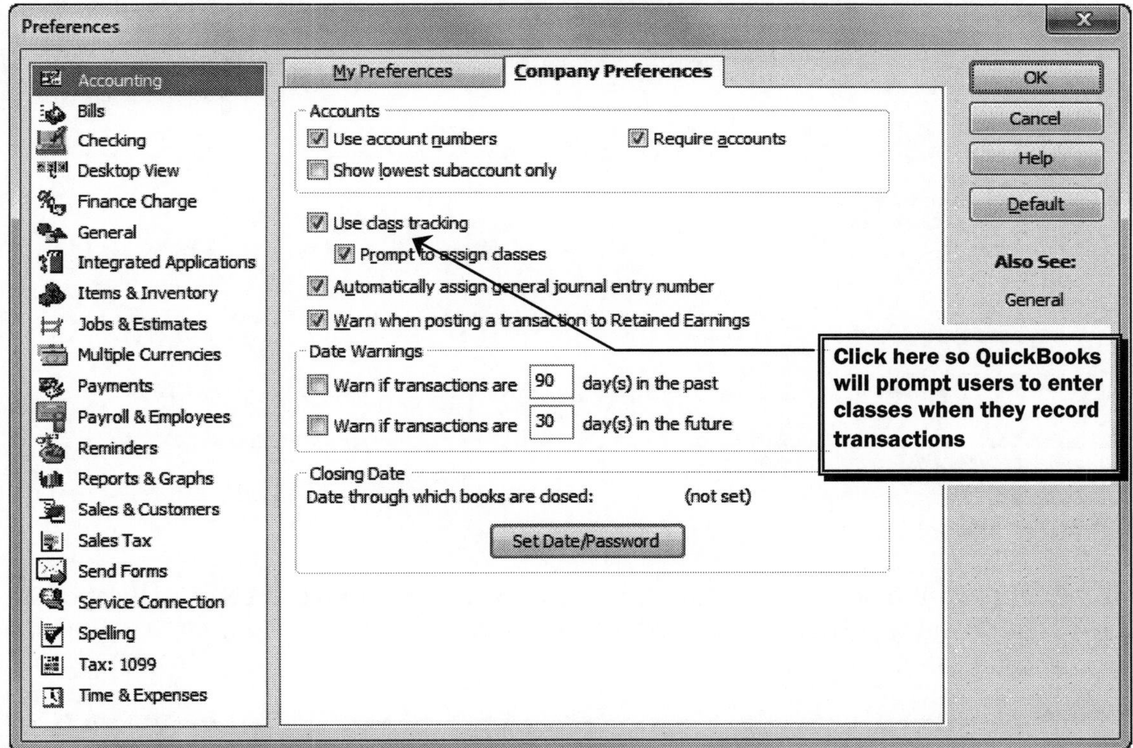

Figure 6-13 Accounting Company Preferences

Profit & Loss by Job Report

To divide your Profit & Loss report into **Customers** or **Jobs**, use the **Profit & Loss by Job** report. This report, sometimes called the Job Cost report, allows you to see your profitability for each customer or job. This information helps you to spot pricing problems, as well as costs that are out of the ordinary. For example, if this report showed that you lost money on all the jobs where you did an outdoor session, you would probably want to adjust your prices for outdoor photo shoots. Similarly, if the cost on one job is significantly higher or lower than other jobs of similar size, you might look closer at that job to see if adjustments are needed to control costs.

COMPUTER PRACTICE

To create a **Profit & Loss by Job** report, follow these steps:

Step 1. From the *Report Center*, select **Company & Financial** and then double click the **Profit & Loss By Job** link in the *Profit & Loss (income statement)* section.

Step 2. Enter ***01/01/2011*** in the *From* field and enter ***01/31/2011*** in the *To* field and press **Tab** (see Figure 6-14).

Step 3. After you view the **Profit & Loss by Job** report, close all open report windows.

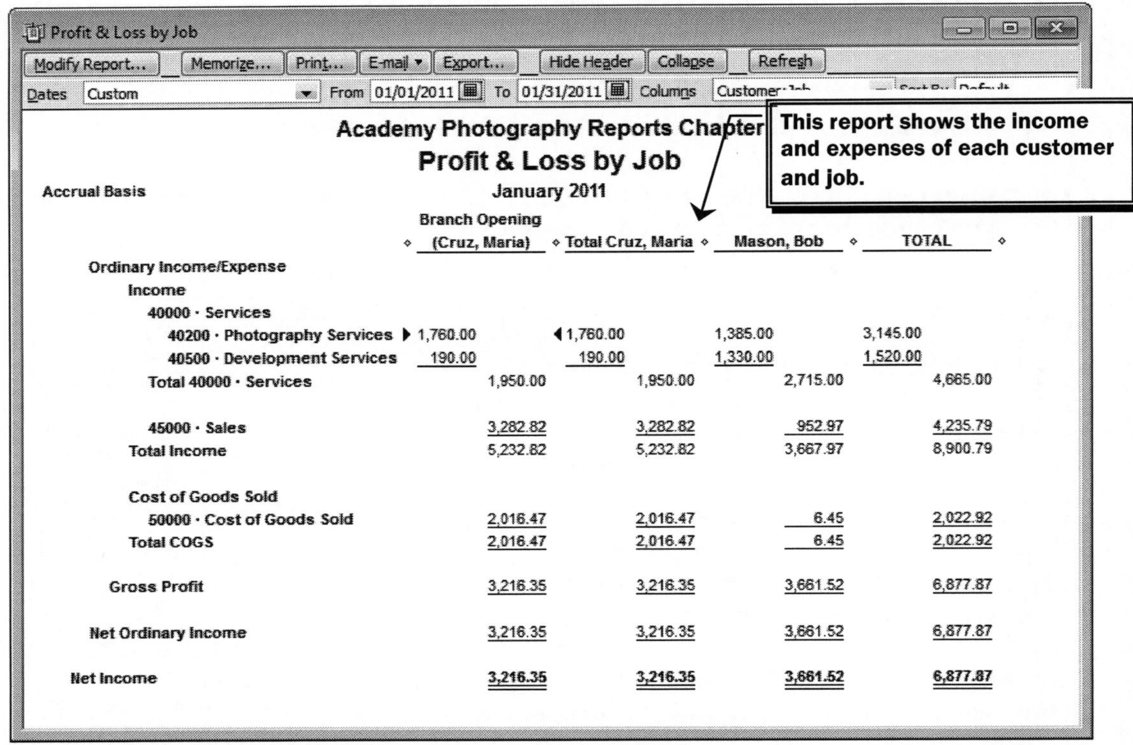

Academy Photography Reports Chapter
Profit & Loss by Job
January 2011
Accrual Basis

	Branch Opening (Cruz, Maria)	Total Cruz, Maria	Mason, Bob	TOTAL
Ordinary Income/Expense				
Income				
40000 · Services				
40200 · Photography Services	1,760.00	1,760.00	1,385.00	3,145.00
40500 · Development Services	190.00	190.00	1,330.00	1,520.00
Total 40000 · Services	1,950.00	1,950.00	2,715.00	4,665.00
45000 · Sales	3,282.82	3,282.82	952.97	4,235.79
Total Income	5,232.82	5,232.82	3,667.97	8,900.79
Cost of Goods Sold				
50000 · Cost of Goods Sold	2,016.47	2,016.47	6.45	2,022.92
Total COGS	2,016.47	2,016.47	6.45	2,022.92
Gross Profit	3,216.35	3,216.35	3,661.52	6,877.87
Net Ordinary Income	3,216.35	3,216.35	3,661.52	6,877.87
Net Income	3,216.35	3,216.35	3,661.52	6,877.87

Figure 6-14 Profit & Loss by Job report

Balance Sheet

Another important report for analyzing your business is the **Balance Sheet**. The Balance Sheet shows your financial position, as defined by the balances in each of your asset, liabilities, and equity accounts on a given date.

COMPUTER PRACTICE

Step 1. From the *Report Center*, select **Company & Financial** and then double click the **Balance Sheet Standard** report in the *Balance Sheet & Net Worth* section. You may need to scroll down.

Step 2. Enter ***01/31/2011*** in the *As of* field and press **Tab**.

In Figure 6-15, you can see a portion of the **Balance Sheet** for Academy Photography on 01/31/2011.

Tip:
Familiarize yourself with how your Balance Sheet changes throughout the year. Banks examine this report very closely before approving loans. Often, the bank will calculate the ratio of your current assets divided by your current liabilities. This ratio, known as the **current ratio**, measures your ability to satisfy your debts.

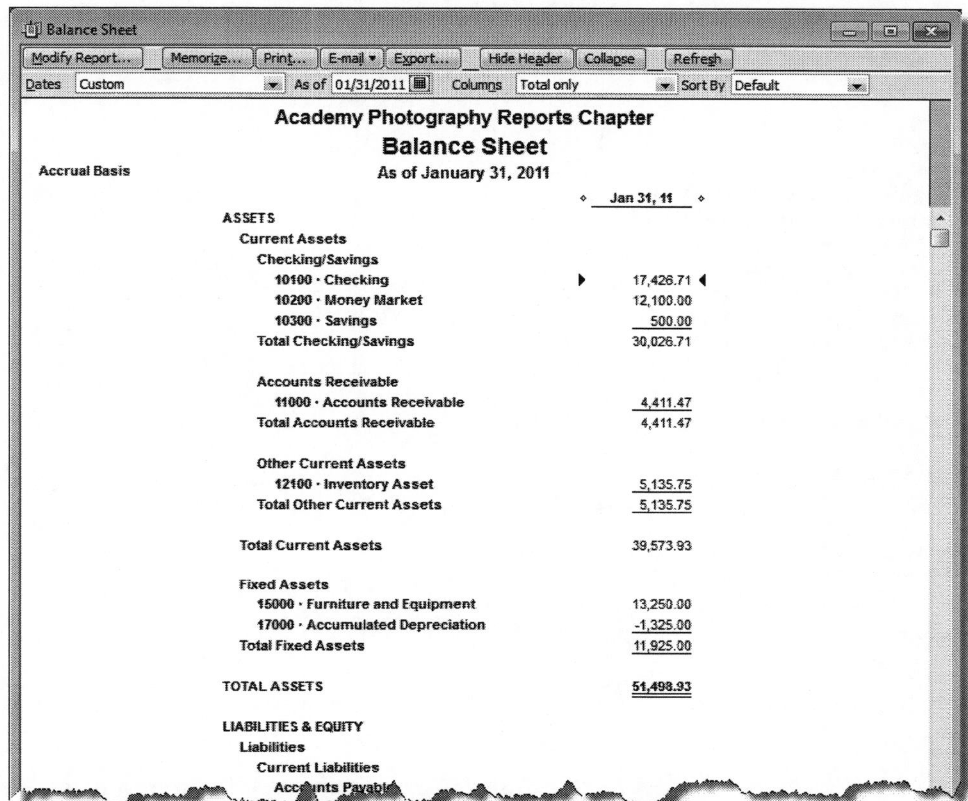

Academy Photography Reports Chapter
Balance Sheet
As of January 31, 2011

Accrual Basis

	Jan 31, 11
ASSETS	
Current Assets	
Checking/Savings	
10100 · Checking	17,426.71
10200 · Money Market	12,100.00
10300 · Savings	500.00
Total Checking/Savings	30,026.71
Accounts Receivable	
11000 · Accounts Receivable	4,411.47
Total Accounts Receivable	4,411.47
Other Current Assets	
12100 · Inventory Asset	5,135.75
Total Other Current Assets	5,135.75
Total Current Assets	39,573.93
Fixed Assets	
15000 · Furniture and Equipment	13,250.00
17000 · Accumulated Depreciation	-1,325.00
Total Fixed Assets	11,925.00
TOTAL ASSETS	51,498.93
LIABILITIES & EQUITY	
Liabilities	
Current Liabilities	
Accounts Payable	

Figure 6-15 Balance Sheet for Academy Photography on 01/31/2011

Statement of Cash Flows

The **Statement of Cash Flows** provides information about the cash receipts and cash payments of your business during a given period. In addition, it provides information about investing and financing activities, such as purchasing equipment or borrowing. The Statement of Cash Flows shows the detail of how you spent the cash shown on the company's Balance Sheet.

COMPUTER PRACTICE

Step 1. From the *Report Center*, select **Company & Financial** and then double click the **Statement of Cash Flows** report in the *Cash Flow* section.

Step 2. Enter ***01/01/2011*** in the *From* field and enter ***01/31/2011*** in the *To* field and press **Tab**.

On the report shown in Figure 6-16, you can see that although there was a net income of $2,774.27, there was a net decrease in cash of $532.89 during the first month of the year. Bankers look closely at this report to determine if your business is able to generate a positive cash flow, or if your business requires additional capital to satisfy its cash needs.

Step 3. After you view the **Statement of Cash Flows** report, close all open report windows.

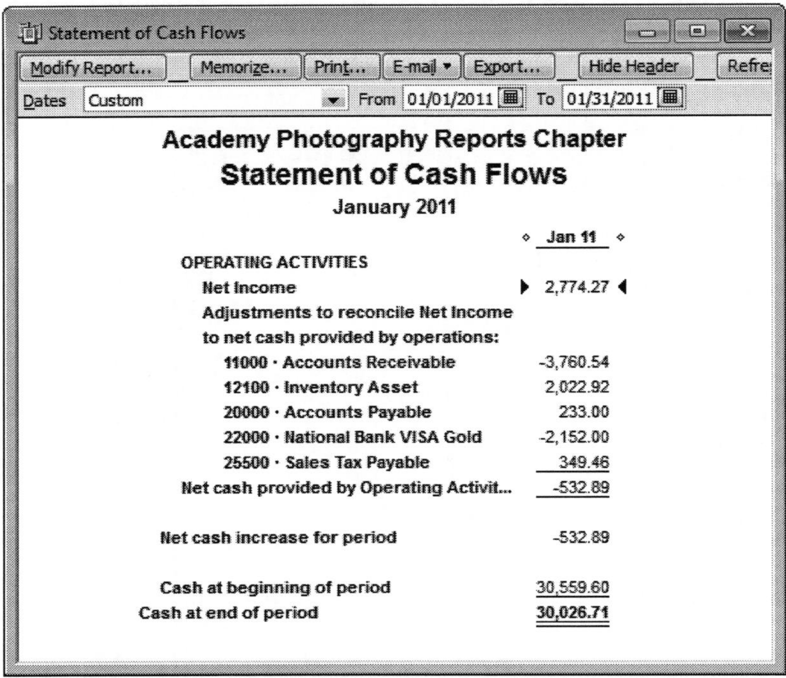

Academy Photography Reports Chapter
Statement of Cash Flows
January 2011

	Jan 11
OPERATING ACTIVITIES	
Net Income	2,774.27
Adjustments to reconcile Net Income to net cash provided by operations:	
11000 · Accounts Receivable	-3,760.54
12100 · Inventory Asset	2,022.92
20000 · Accounts Payable	233.00
22000 · National Bank VISA Gold	-2,152.00
25500 · Sales Tax Payable	349.46
Net cash provided by Operating Activit...	-532.89
Net cash increase for period	-532.89
Cash at beginning of period	30,559.60
Cash at end of period	30,026.71

Figure 6-16 Statement of Cash Flows report

General Ledger

The **General Ledger** shows you all of the activity in all of your accounts for a specific period.

COMPUTER PRACTICE

Step 1. From the *Report Center*, select **Accountant & Taxes** from the list of report categories on the left of the window and then double click the **General Ledger** report in the *Account Activity* section.

Step 2. Enter ***01/01/2011*** in the *From* field and enter ***01/31/2011*** in the *To* field and press **Tab** (see Figure 6-17).

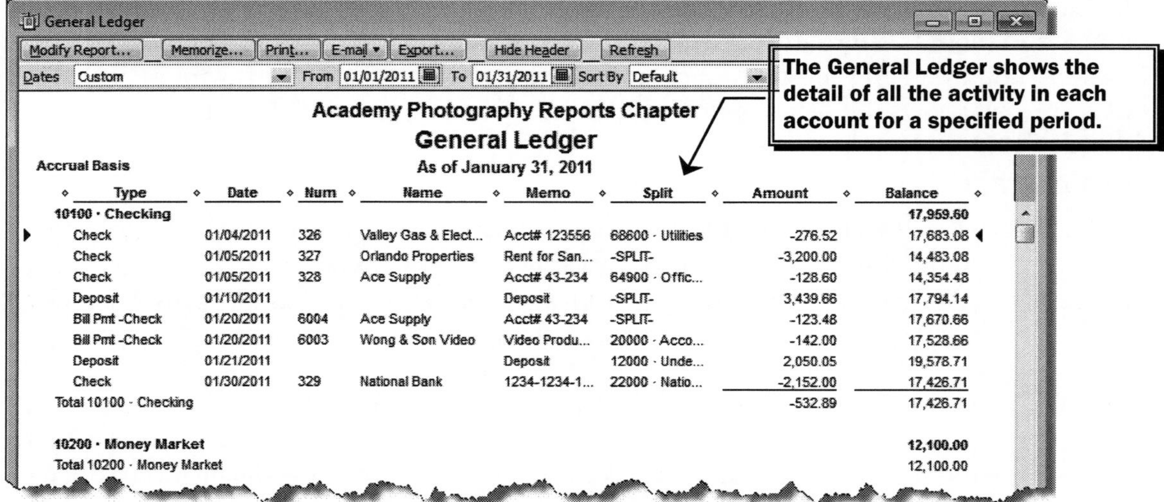

Academy Photography Reports Chapter
General Ledger
As of January 31, 2011
Accrual Basis

Type	Date	Num	Name	Memo	Split	Amount	Balance
10100 · Checking							17,959.60
Check	01/04/2011	326	Valley Gas & Elect...	Acct# 123556	68600 · Utilities	-276.52	17,683.08
Check	01/05/2011	327	Orlando Properties	Rent for San...	-SPLIT-	-3,200.00	14,483.08
Check	01/05/2011	328	Ace Supply	Acct# 43-234	64900 · Offic...	-128.60	14,354.48
Deposit	01/10/2011			Deposit	-SPLIT-	3,439.66	17,794.14
Bill Pmt -Check	01/20/2011	6004	Ace Supply	Acct# 43-234	-SPLIT-	-123.48	17,670.66
Bill Pmt -Check	01/20/2011	6003	Wong & Son Video	Video Produ...	20000 · Acco...	-142.00	17,528.66
Deposit	01/21/2011			Deposit	12000 · Unde...	2,050.05	19,578.71
Check	01/30/2011	329	National Bank	1234-1234-1...	22000 · Natio...	-2,152.00	17,426.71
Total 10100 · Checking						-532.89	17,426.71
10200 · Money Market							12,100.00
Total 10200 · Money Market							12,100.00

Figure 6-17 General Ledger - Activity in all accounts for a specific period

Trial Balance

The **Trial Balance** report shows the balance of each of the accounts as of a certain date. The report shows these balances in a Debit and Credit format. Your accountant will usually prepare this report at the end of each fiscal year.

COMPUTER PRACTICE

Step 1. From the *Report Center*, select **Accountant & Taxes** and then double click the **Trial Balance** report in the *Account Activity* section.

Step 2. Enter ***01/01/2011*** in the *From* field and enter ***01/31/2011*** in the *To* field and press **Tab** (see Figure 6-18).

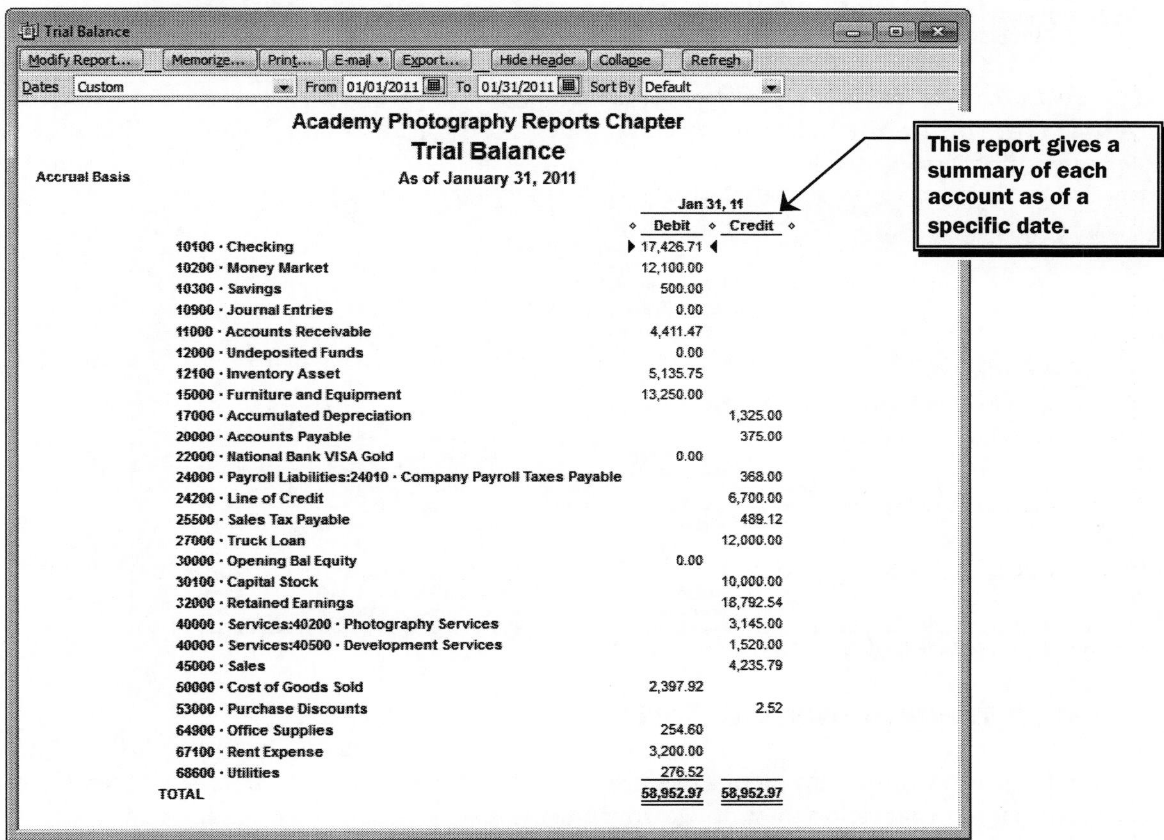

Academy Photography Reports Chapter
Trial Balance
Accrual Basis — As of January 31, 2011

	Jan 31, 11 Debit	Credit
10100 · Checking	17,426.71	
10200 · Money Market	12,100.00	
10300 · Savings	500.00	
10900 · Journal Entries	0.00	
11000 · Accounts Receivable	4,411.47	
12000 · Undeposited Funds	0.00	
12100 · Inventory Asset	5,135.75	
15000 · Furniture and Equipment	13,250.00	
17000 · Accumulated Depreciation		1,325.00
20000 · Accounts Payable		375.00
22000 · National Bank VISA Gold	0.00	
24000 · Payroll Liabilities:24010 · Company Payroll Taxes Payable		368.00
24200 · Line of Credit		6,700.00
25500 · Sales Tax Payable		489.12
27000 · Truck Loan		12,000.00
30000 · Opening Bal Equity	0.00	
30100 · Capital Stock		10,000.00
32000 · Retained Earnings		18,792.54
40000 · Services:40200 · Photography Services		3,145.00
40000 · Services:40500 · Development Services		1,520.00
45000 · Sales		4,235.79
50000 · Cost of Goods Sold	2,397.92	
53000 · Purchase Discounts		2.52
64900 · Office Supplies	254.60	
67100 · Rent Expense	3,200.00	
68600 · Utilities	276.52	
TOTAL	58,952.97	58,952.97

Figure 6-18 Trial Balance - Balance of each account as of a specific date

Step 3. Close all open reports.

Voided/Deleted Transactions Summary Reports

The *Voided/Deleted Transactions Summary* report shows transactions that have been voided or deleted in the data file. This assists Accountants in detecting errors or fraud. This feature is very useful when you have a number of users in a file and transactions seem to "disappear" or change without explanation. The standard version of this report presents the transaction in a summary format (see Figure 6-19).

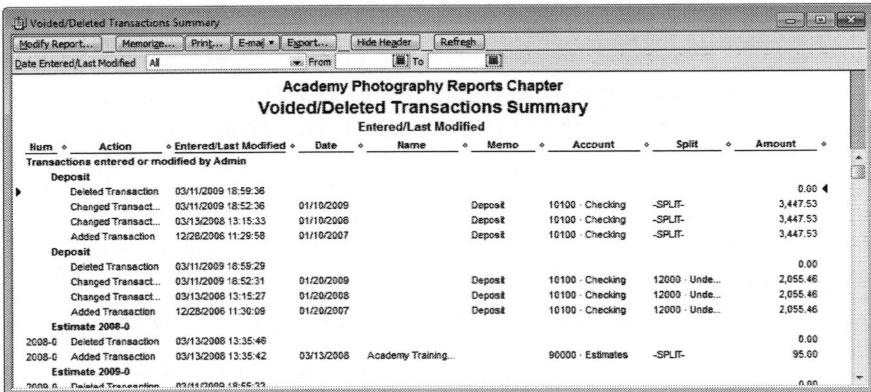

Voided/Deleted Transactions Summary

Academy Photography Reports Chapter
Voided/Deleted Transactions Summary
Entered/Last Modified

Num	Action	Entered/Last Modified	Date	Name	Memo	Account	Split	Amount
Transactions entered or modified by Admin								
Deposit								
	Deleted Transaction	03/11/2009 18:59:36						0.00
	Changed Transact...	03/11/2009 18:52:36	01/10/2009		Deposit	10100 · Checking	-SPLIT-	3,447.53
	Changed Transact...	03/13/2008 13:15:33	01/10/2008		Deposit	10100 · Checking	-SPLIT-	3,447.53
	Added Transaction	12/28/2006 11:29:58	01/10/2007		Deposit	10100 · Checking	-SPLIT-	3,447.53
Deposit								
	Deleted Transaction	03/11/2009 18:59:29						0.00
	Changed Transact...	03/11/2009 18:52:31	01/20/2009		Deposit	10100 · Checking	12000 · Unde...	2,055.46
	Changed Transact...	03/13/2008 13:15:27	01/20/2008		Deposit	10100 · Checking	12000 · Unde...	2,055.46
	Added Transaction	12/28/2006 11:30:09	01/20/2007		Deposit	10100 · Checking	12000 · Unde...	2,055.46
Estimate 2008-0								
2008-0	Deleted Transaction	03/13/2008 13:35:46						0.00
2008-0	Added Transaction	03/13/2008 13:35:42	03/13/2008	Academy Training...		90000 · Estimates	-SPLIT-	95.00
Estimate 2009-0								

Figure 6-19 Voided/Deleted Transactions Report

The *Voided/Deleted Transaction History* report shows all of the line items associated with the transaction. This feature makes the original transaction information available so that it can be recreated if necessary (see Figure 6-20).

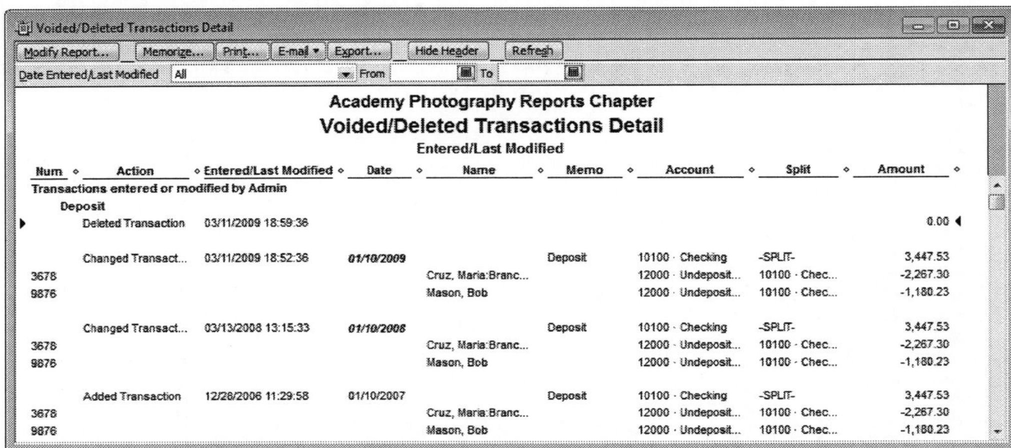

Voided/Deleted Transactions Detail

Academy Photography Reports Chapter
Voided/Deleted Transactions Detail
Entered/Last Modified

Num	Action	Entered/Last Modified	Date	Name	Memo	Account	Split	Amount
Transactions entered or modified by Admin								
Deposit								
	Deleted Transaction	03/11/2009 18:59:36						0.00
	Changed Transact...	03/11/2009 18:52:36	*01/10/2009*		Deposit	10100 · Checking	-SPLIT-	3,447.53
3678				Cruz, Maria:Branc...		12000 · Undeposit...	10100 · Chec...	-2,267.30
9876				Mason, Bob		12000 · Undeposit...	10100 · Chec...	-1,180.23
	Changed Transact...	03/13/2008 13:15:33	*01/10/2008*		Deposit	10100 · Checking	-SPLIT-	3,447.53
3678				Cruz, Maria:Branc...		12000 · Undeposit...	10100 · Chec...	-2,267.30
9876				Mason, Bob		12000 · Undeposit...	10100 · Chec...	-1,180.23
	Added Transaction	12/28/2006 11:29:58	01/10/2007		Deposit	10100 · Checking	-SPLIT-	3,447.53
3678				Cruz, Maria:Branc...		12000 · Undeposit...	10100 · Chec...	-2,267.30
9876				Mason, Bob		12000 · Undeposit...	10100 · Chec...	-1,180.23

Figure 6-20 Voided/Deleted Transactions History Report

Business Management Reports

In the following Computer Practice exercises, you will use QuickBooks to create several different reports that help you manage your business.

Customer Phone List

The **Customer Phone List** shown in Figure 6-21 is a listing of each of your customers and their phone numbers. To create this report, follow these steps:

COMPUTER PRACTICE

Step 1. From the *Report Center*, select **Lists** and then double click the **Customer Phone List** report in the *Customer* section to display the report (see Figure 6-21).

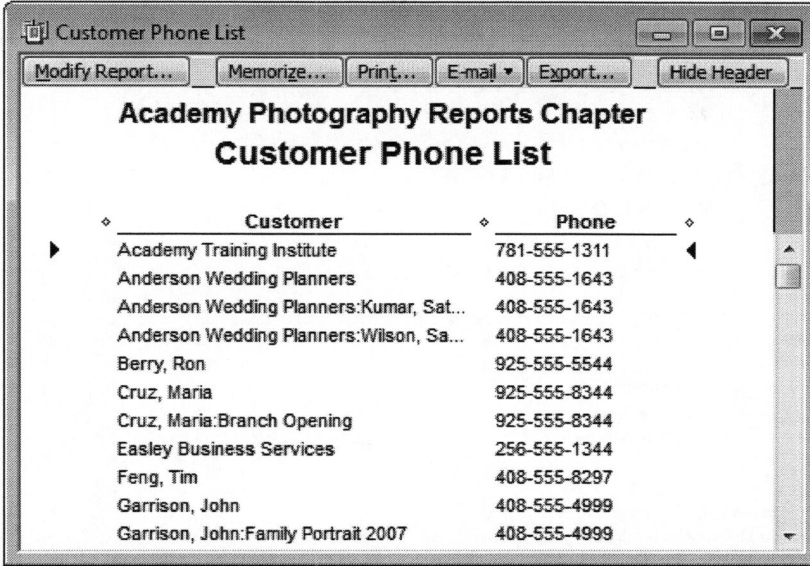

Academy Photography Reports Chapter
Customer Phone List

Customer	Phone
Academy Training Institute	781-555-1311
Anderson Wedding Planners	408-555-1643
Anderson Wedding Planners:Kumar, Sat...	408-555-1643
Anderson Wedding Planners:Wilson, Sa...	408-555-1643
Berry, Ron	925-555-5544
Cruz, Maria	925-555-8344
Cruz, Maria:Branch Opening	925-555-8344
Easley Business Services	256-555-1344
Feng, Tim	408-555-8297
Garrison, John	408-555-4999
Garrison, John:Family Portrait 2007	408-555-4999

Figure 6-21 Customer Phone List report

Vendor Contact List

The **Vendor Contact List** shown in Figure 6-22 is a listing of your vendors along with each vendor's contact information. To create this report, follow these steps:

COMPUTER PRACTICE

Step 1. From the *Report Center,* select **Lists** and then double click the **Vendor Contact List** report in the *Vendor* section to display the report (see Figure 6-22).

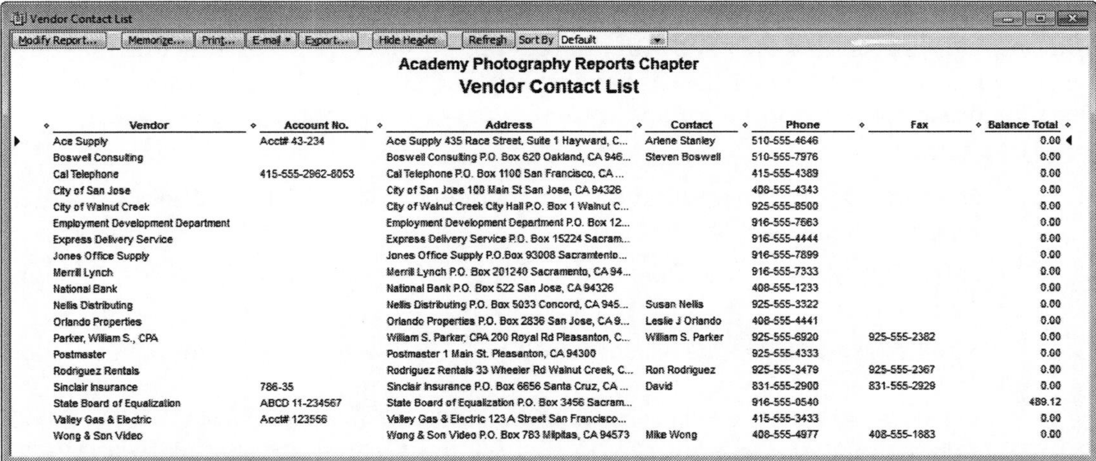

Academy Photography Reports Chapter
Vendor Contact List

Vendor	Account No.	Address	Contact	Phone	Fax	Balance Total
Ace Supply	Acct# 43-234	Ace Supply 435 Race Street, Suite 1 Hayward, C...	Arlene Stanley	510-555-4646		0.00
Boswell Consulting		Boswell Consulting P.O. Box 620 Oakland, CA 946...	Steven Boswell	510-555-7976		0.00
Cal Telephone	415-555-2962-8053	Cal Telephone P.O. Box 1100 San Francisco, CA ...		415-555-4389		0.00
City of San Jose		City of San Jose 100 Main St San Jose, CA 94326		408-555-4343		0.00
City of Walnut Creek		City of Walnut Creek City Hall P.O. Box 1 Walnut C...		925-555-8500		0.00
Employment Development Department		Employment Development Department P.O. Box 12...		916-555-7663		0.00
Express Delivery Service		Express Delivery Service P.O. Box 15224 Sacram...		916-555-4444		0.00
Jones Office Supply		Jones Office Supply P.O.Box 93008 Sacramtento...		916-555-7899		0.00
Merrill Lynch		Merrill Lynch P.O. Box 201240 Sacramento, CA 94...		916-555-7333		0.00
National Bank		National Bank P.O. Box 522 San Jose, CA 94326		408-555-1233		0.00
Nellis Distributing		Nellis Distributing P.O. Box 5033 Concord, CA 945...	Susan Nellis	925-555-3322		0.00
Orlando Properties		Orlando Properties P.O. Box 2836 San Jose, CA 9...	Leslie J Orlando	408-555-4441		0.00
Parker, William S., CPA		William S. Parker, CPA 200 Royal Rd Pleasanton, C...	William S. Parker	925-555-6920	925-555-2382	0.00
Postmaster		Postmaster 1 Main St. Pleasanton, CA 94300		925-555-4333		0.00
Rodriguez Rentals		Rodriguez Rentals 33 Wheeler Rd Walnut Creek, C...	Ron Rodriguez	925-555-3479	925-555-2367	0.00
Sinclair Insurance	786-35	Sinclair Insurance P.O. Box 6656 Santa Cruz, CA ...	David	831-555-2900	831-555-2929	0.00
State Board of Equalization	ABCD 11-234567	State Board of Equalization P.O. Box 3456 Sacram...		916-555-0540		489.12
Valley Gas & Electric	Acct# 123556	Valley Gas & Electric 123 A Street San Francisco...		415-555-3433		0.00
Wong & Son Video		Wong & Son Video P.O. Box 783 Milpitas, CA 94573	Mike Wong	408-555-4977	408-555-1883	0.00

Figure 6-22 Vendor Contact List report

Item Price List

The **Item Price List** shown in Figure 6-23 is a listing of your items. To create this report, follow these steps:

COMPUTER PRACTICE

Step 1. From the *Report Center,* select **Lists** and then double click the **Item Price List** report in the *Listing* section to display the report (see Figure 6-23).

Step 2. After viewing the **Item Price List** report, close all open report windows. Click **No** if QuickBooks prompts you to memorize the reports.

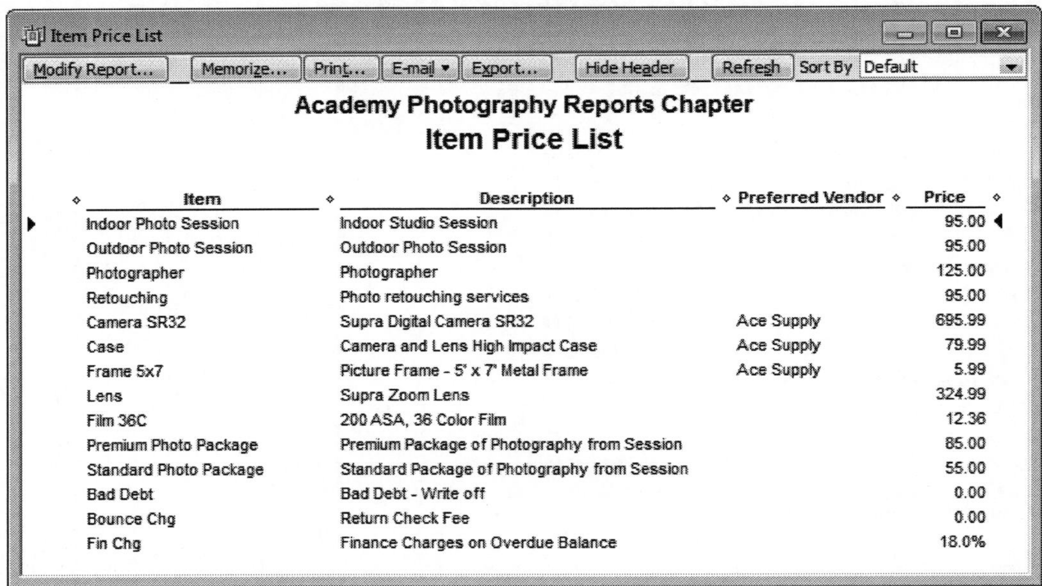

Item Price List

Modify Report... | Memorize... | Print... | E-mail ▾ | Export... | Hide Header | Refresh | Sort By Default

Academy Photography Reports Chapter

Item Price List

Item	Description	Preferred Vendor	Price
Indoor Photo Session	Indoor Studio Session		95.00
Outdoor Photo Session	Outdoor Photo Session		95.00
Photographer	Photographer		125.00
Retouching	Photo retouching services		95.00
Camera SR32	Supra Digital Camera SR32	Ace Supply	695.99
Case	Camera and Lens High Impact Case	Ace Supply	79.99
Frame 5x7	Picture Frame - 5' x 7' Metal Frame	Ace Supply	5.99
Lens	Supra Zoom Lens		324.99
Film 36C	200 ASA, 36 Color Film		12.36
Premium Photo Package	Premium Package of Photography from Session		85.00
Standard Photo Package	Standard Package of Photography from Session		55.00
Bad Debt	Bad Debt - Write off		0.00
Bounce Chg	Return Check Fee		0.00
Fin Chg	Finance Charges on Overdue Balance		18.0%

Figure 6-23 Item Price List report

Check Detail Report

The **Check Detail** report is quite valuable if you use Accounts Payable or Payroll. It is frequently necessary to see what expense account(s) are associated with a Bill Payment. However, the Register report only shows that Bill Payments are associated with Accounts Payable. That's because a Bill Payment only involves the Checking account and Accounts Payable. Similarly, Paychecks only show in the register report as "Split" transactions because several accounts are associated with each paycheck. The Check Detail report shows the detailed expense account information about these types of transactions.

COMPUTER PRACTICE

Step 1. From the *Report Center*, select **Banking** and then double click the **Check Detail** report in the *Banking* section.

Step 2. Enter ***01/01/2011*** in the *From* field and enter ***01/31/2011*** in the *To* field. Then, press **Tab**.

Step 3. Scroll down until you see Bill Payment Check #6004 (near the bottom of the report).

In Figure 6-24, notice Bill Payment number 6004. The report shows that QuickBooks split the total payment of $126.00 between the Accounts Payable account ($2.52) and the Checking account ($123.48).

The amount for $-2.52 is the discount that you took when you paid the Bill. Although this report does not show it, you coded this amount to Purchase Discounts.

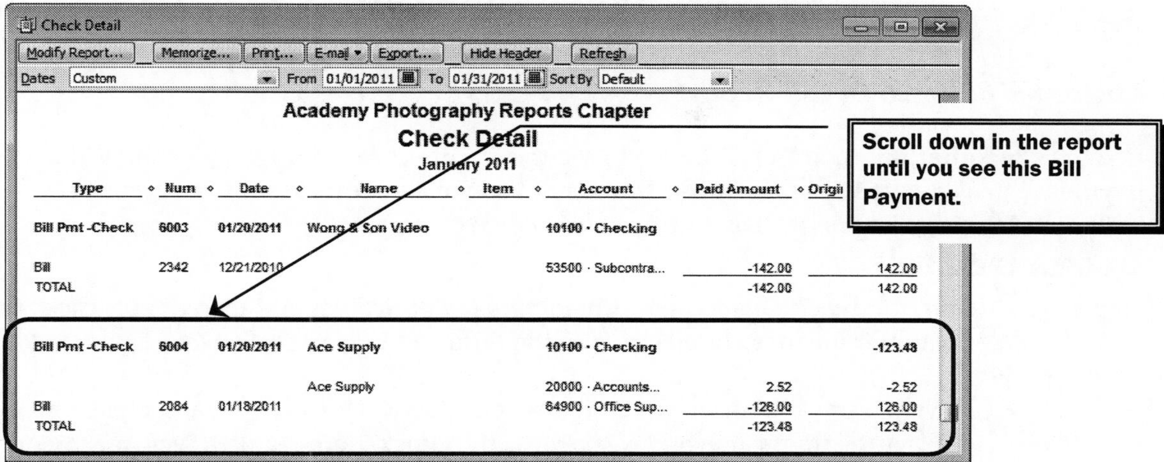

Figure 6-24 Check Detail report

Step 4. Close all open report windows. Click **No** if QuickBooks prompts you to memorize the reports.

> **Tip:**
> In order to make your *Check Detail* reports easier to read and understand, consider recording your purchase discounts differently. Instead of taking the discount on the *Pay Bills* window (as you did in the example on page 144), consider recording your purchase discounts using Bill Credits.

Accounts Receivable and Accounts Payable Reports

There are several reports that you can use to keep track of the money that your customers owe you (Accounts Receivable) and the money that you owe to your vendors (Accounts Payable).

Collections Report

The **Collections Report** is a report that shows each customer's outstanding Invoices along with the customer's telephone number.

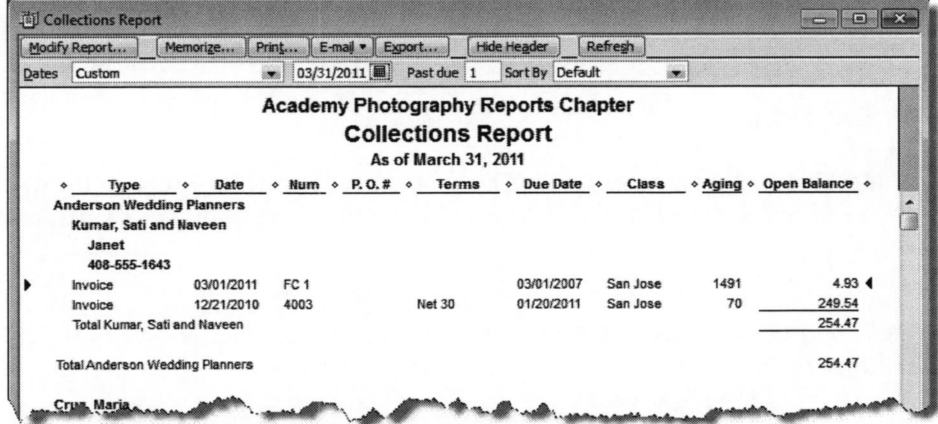

Figure 6-25 Accounts Receivable Collections report

COMPUTER PRACTICE

Step 1. From the *Report Center*, select **Customers & Receivables** and then double click the **Collections Report** in the *A/R Aging* section.

Step 2. Enter ***03/31/2011*** in the *Dates* field and press **Tab** (see Figure 6-25).

Customer Balance Detail Report

Use the **Customer Balance Detail** report to see the details of each customer's transactions and payments. This report shows all transactions that use the Accounts Receivable account, including Invoices, Payments, Discounts, and Finance Charges.

COMPUTER PRACTICE

Step 1. From the *Report Center*, select **Customers & Receivables** and then double click the **Customer Balance Detail** report in the *Customer Balance* section (see Figure 6-26).

To view a transaction shown on this report, double-click on the transaction. This displays the transaction and is known as the **QuickZoom** feature (See page 266 for more about QuickZoom).

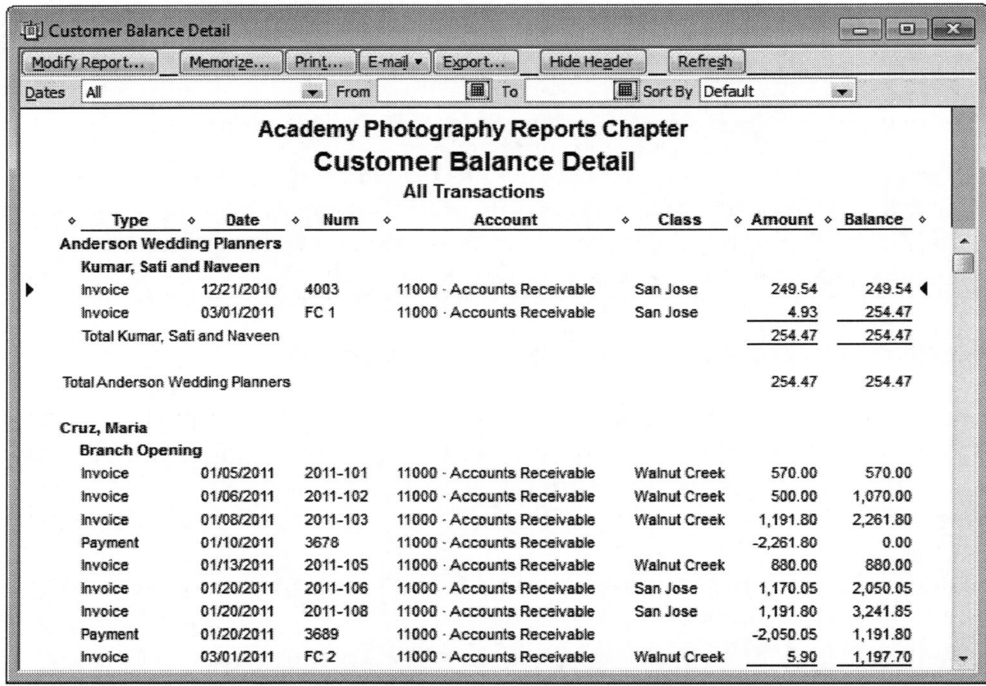

Academy Photography Reports Chapter
Customer Balance Detail
All Transactions

Type	Date	Num	Account	Class	Amount	Balance
Anderson Wedding Planners						
Kumar, Sati and Naveen						
Invoice	12/21/2010	4003	11000 · Accounts Receivable	San Jose	249.54	249.54
Invoice	03/01/2011	FC 1	11000 · Accounts Receivable	San Jose	4.93	254.47
Total Kumar, Sati and Naveen					254.47	254.47
Total Anderson Wedding Planners					254.47	254.47
Cruz, Maria						
Branch Opening						
Invoice	01/05/2011	2011-101	11000 · Accounts Receivable	Walnut Creek	570.00	570.00
Invoice	01/06/2011	2011-102	11000 · Accounts Receivable	Walnut Creek	500.00	1,070.00
Invoice	01/08/2011	2011-103	11000 · Accounts Receivable	Walnut Creek	1,191.80	2,261.80
Payment	01/10/2011	3678	11000 · Accounts Receivable		-2,261.80	0.00
Invoice	01/13/2011	2011-105	11000 · Accounts Receivable	Walnut Creek	880.00	880.00
Invoice	01/20/2011	2011-106	11000 · Accounts Receivable	San Jose	1,170.05	2,050.05
Invoice	01/20/2011	2011-108	11000 · Accounts Receivable	San Jose	1,191.80	3,241.85
Payment	01/20/2011	3689	11000 · Accounts Receivable		-2,050.05	1,191.80
Invoice	03/01/2011	FC 2	11000 · Accounts Receivable	Walnut Creek	5.90	1,197.70

Figure 6-26 Customer Balance Detail report

Vendor Balance Detail Report

The **Vendor Balance Detail** report is similar to the **Customer Balance Detail** report, but it shows transactions that use Accounts Payable, including Bills, Bill Credits, Bill Payments, and Discounts.

COMPUTER PRACTICE

Step 1. From the *Report Center*, select **Vendors & Payables** and then double click the **Vendor Balance Detail** report in the *Vendor Balances* section (see Figure 6-27).

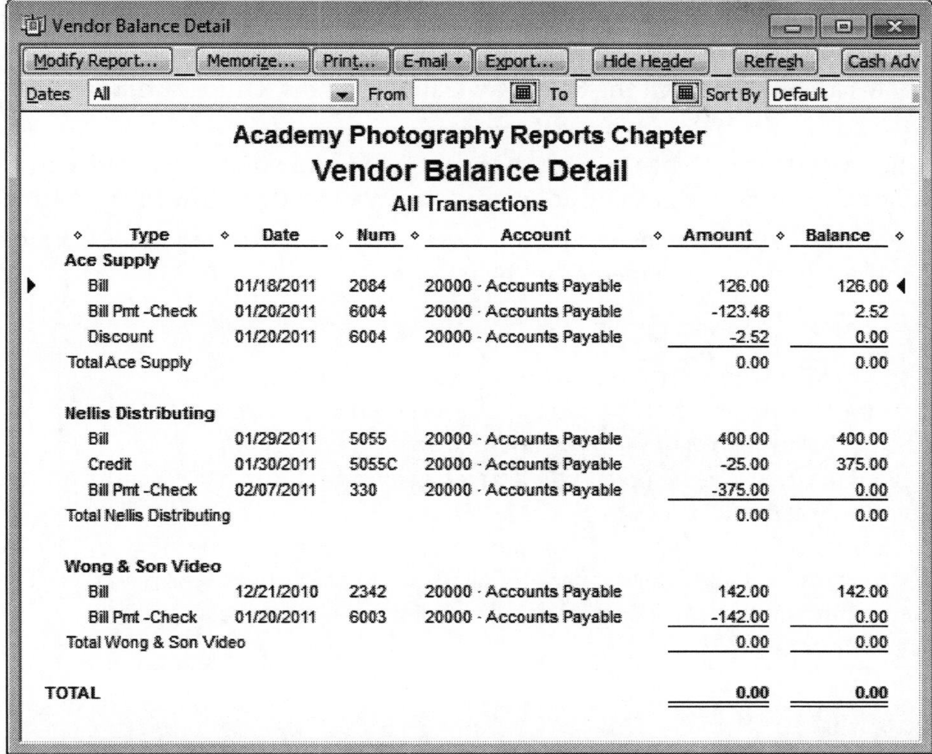

Vendor Balance Detail

Modify Report... | Memorize... | Print... | E-mail | Export... | Hide Header | Refresh | Cash Adv

Dates: All | From | To | Sort By: Default

Academy Photography Reports Chapter

Vendor Balance Detail

All Transactions

Type	Date	Num	Account	Amount	Balance
Ace Supply					
Bill	01/18/2011	2084	20000 · Accounts Payable	126.00	126.00
Bill Pmt -Check	01/20/2011	6004	20000 · Accounts Payable	-123.48	2.52
Discount	01/20/2011	6004	20000 · Accounts Payable	-2.52	0.00
Total Ace Supply				0.00	0.00
Nellis Distributing					
Bill	01/29/2011	5055	20000 · Accounts Payable	400.00	400.00
Credit	01/30/2011	5055C	20000 · Accounts Payable	-25.00	375.00
Bill Pmt -Check	02/07/2011	330	20000 · Accounts Payable	-375.00	0.00
Total Nellis Distributing				0.00	0.00
Wong & Son Video					
Bill	12/21/2010	2342	20000 · Accounts Payable	142.00	142.00
Bill Pmt -Check	01/20/2011	6003	20000 · Accounts Payable	-142.00	0.00
Total Wong & Son Video				0.00	0.00
TOTAL				**0.00**	**0.00**

Figure 6-27 Vendor Balance Detail report

Sales Tax Liability Report

The **Sales Tax Liability** report shows a breakdown of your sales by locality and how much sales tax you have collected for the period you specify.

COMPUTER PRACTICE

Step 1. From the *Report Center*, select **Vendors & Payables** and then double click the **Sales Tax Liability** report in the *Sales Tax* section.

Step 2. Enter ***01/01/2011*** in the *From* field and enter ***03/31/2011*** in the *To* field. Then, press **Tab** (see Figure 6-28).

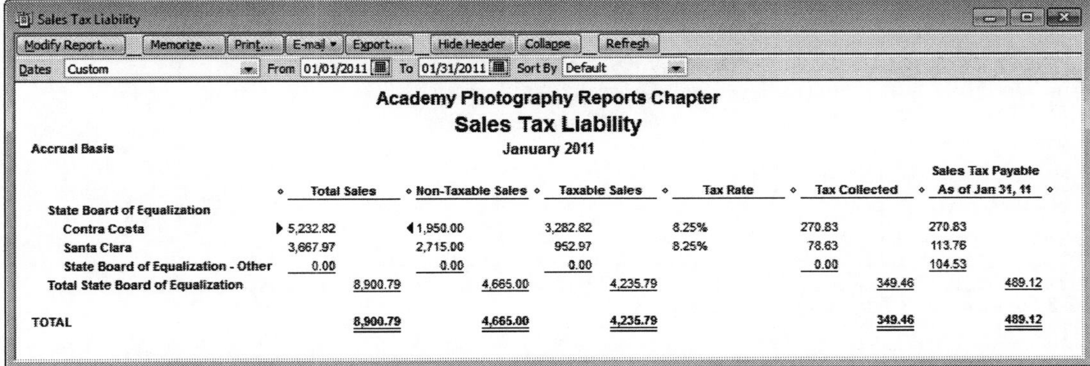

Sales Tax Liability

Modify Report... | Memorize... | Print... | E-mail | Export... | Hide Header | Collapse | Refresh

Dates: Custom | From 01/01/2011 | To 01/31/2011 | Sort By: Default

Academy Photography Reports Chapter

Sales Tax Liability

January 2011

Accrual Basis

	Total Sales	Non-Taxable Sales	Taxable Sales	Tax Rate	Tax Collected	Sales Tax Payable As of Jan 31, 11
State Board of Equalization						
Contra Costa	5,232.82	1,950.00	3,282.82	8.25%	270.83	270.83
Santa Clara	3,667.97	2,715.00	952.97	8.25%	78.63	113.76
State Board of Equalization - Other	0.00	0.00	0.00		0.00	104.53
Total State Board of Equalization	8,900.79	4,665.00	4,235.79		349.46	489.12
TOTAL	**8,900.79**	**4,665.00**	**4,235.79**		**349.46**	**489.12**

Figure 6-28 Sales Tax Liability report

The **Sales Tax Liability** report shows total sales in each county (e.g., Sales Tax Item), and shows the taxable sales separately from the nontaxable sales. In addition, you can see the tax rates and tax collected in each county. You use this information to prepare your sales tax return. The column to the far right shows how much you owe of the tax you've collected. If you have made any sales tax payments, the amount due will reflect those payments. For more information on sales tax, see the Sales Tax Chapter beginning on page 407.

To see the detail of transactions that feed the Sales Tax Liability report, **QuickZoom** on any number in the report.

The **State Board of Equalization – Other** line on the report shows the opening balance in your Sales Tax Payable account, as well as any adjustments you've made to Sales Tax Payable.

Step 3. When you are finished viewing the report, close all open report windows. Click **No** if QuickBooks prompts you to memorize the reports.

> **Note:**
> The Total Sales, Non-Taxable Sales, and Taxable Sales columns will show different information depending on your sales tax preferences. If you select **As of invoice date** in the *When do you owe sales tax?* section of the sales tax preferences (see Figure 6-29), this report will show all sales, including Invoices that your customers have not paid. On the other hand, if you select **Upon receipt of payment** in the *When do you owe sales tax?* section of the sales tax preferences, this report will only show those sales for which you have received payment. Check your state's sales tax regulations and set your sales tax preferences accordingly.

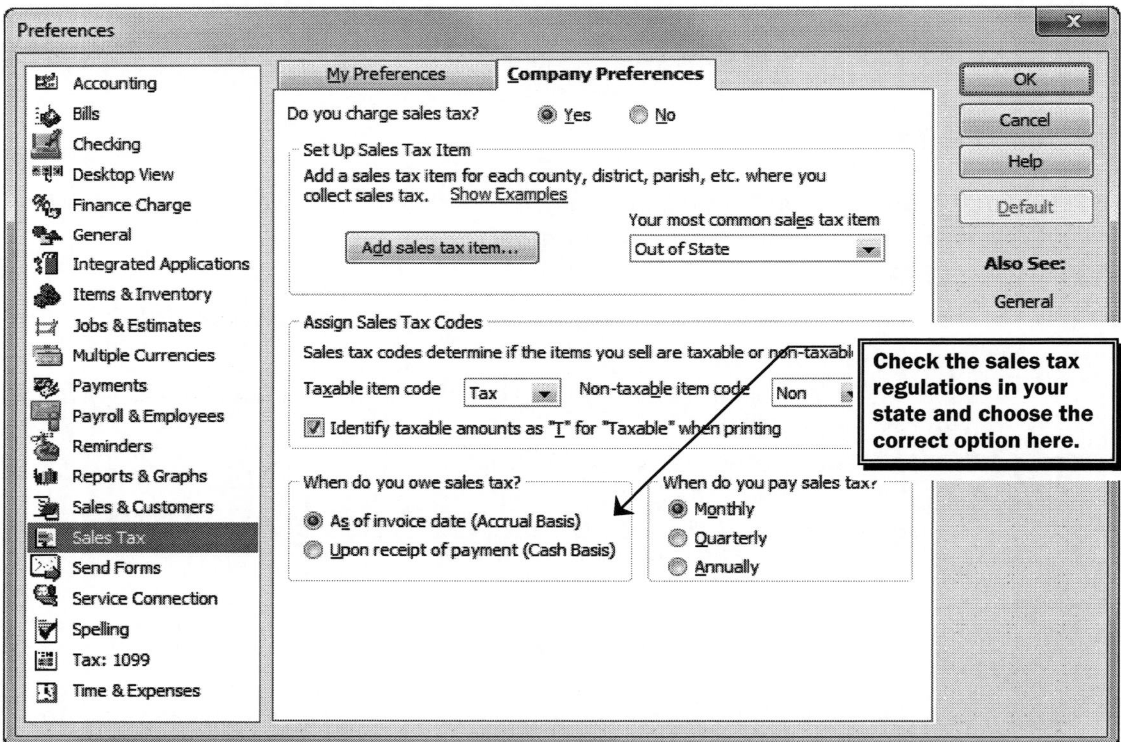

Figure 6-29 Set the Sales Tax Company Preferences

QuickBooks Graphs

One of the best ways to quickly get information from QuickBooks is to create a graph.

The **Income and Expense Graph** shows your income and expenses by month as well as a pie chart showing a summary of your expenses.

COMPUTER PRACTICE

Step 1. From the *Report Center*, select **Company & Financial** and then double click **Income and Expense Graph** in the *Income & Expenses* section.

Step 2. Click **Dates** at the top left of the graph.

QuickBooks will display the *Change Graph Dates* window (see Figure 6-30).

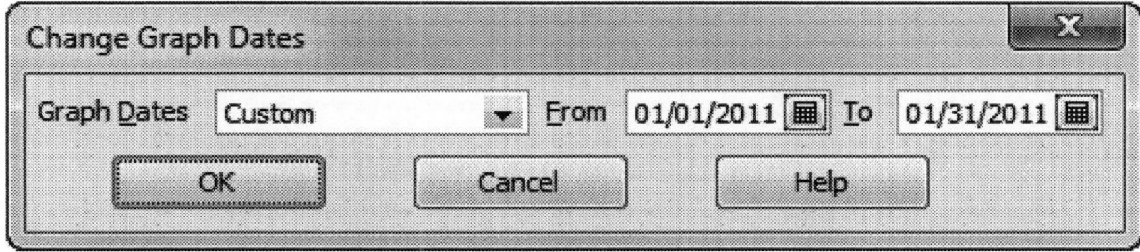

Figure 6-30 Enter the dates for your graph in the window.

Step 3. Enter ***01/01/2011*** in the *From* field and enter ***01/31/2011*** in the *To* field. Then, click **OK**.

Step 4. QuickBooks displays the graph shown in Figure 6-31.

Step 5. After viewing the graph, close the graph window.

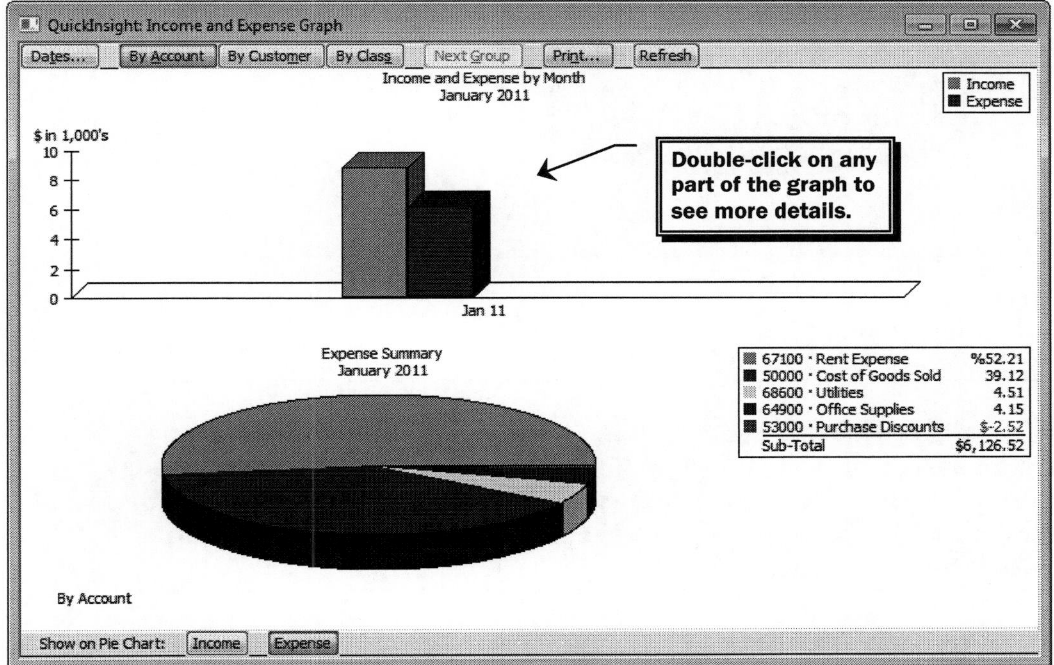

Figure 6-31 Income and Expense by Month graph

QuickBooks graphs highlight interesting facts about your company that are not easy to see from normal reports. For example, you can create a graph that shows your largest customers or your biggest selling items and then you can visually inspect the relative sizes of each section of the graph.

COMPUTER PRACTICE

Step 1. From the *Report Center*, select **Sales** and then double click **Sales Graph** in the *Sales by Customer* section (see Figure 6-32).

Step 2. Click **Dates** at the top left of the graph. QuickBooks will display the *Change Graph Dates* window. Press **Tab**.

Step 3. Enter ***01/01/2011*** in the *From* field and enter ***02/28/2011*** in the *To* field and click **OK**.

Step 4. Click the **By Customer** button on the top of the *QuickInsight: Sales Graph* window. This redraws the graph to show sales by customer.

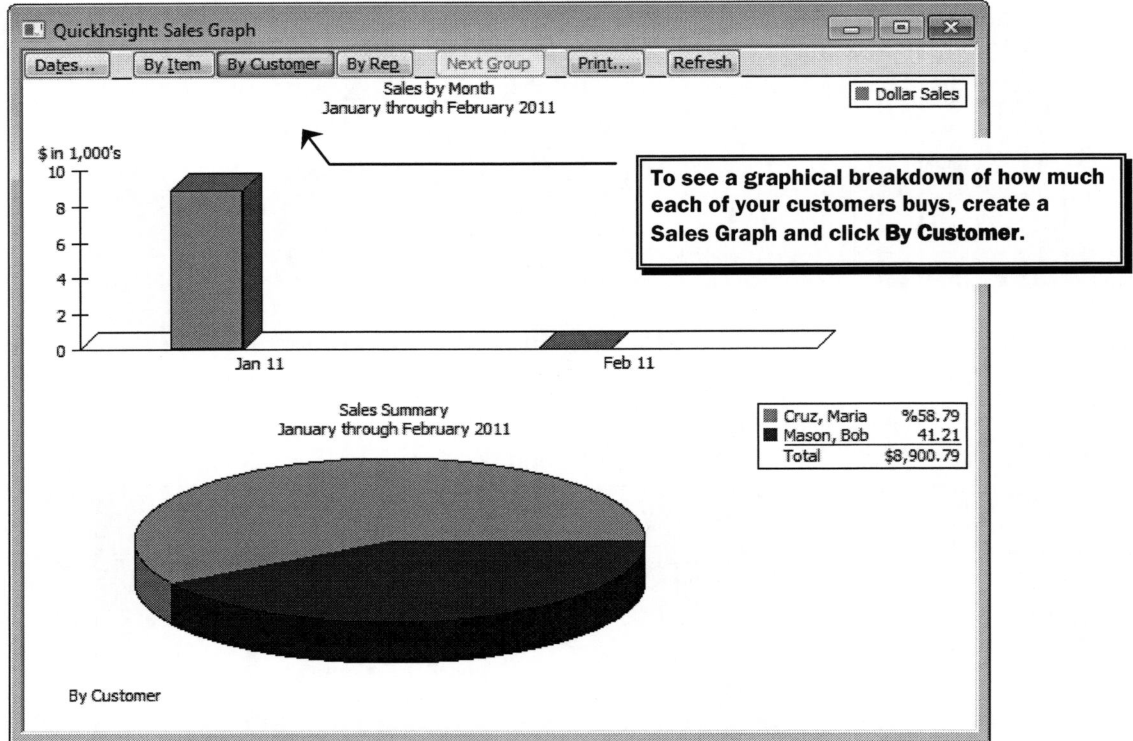

Figure 6-32 Create a Sales Graph by Customer

Step 5. After viewing the graph, close the window.

> **Tip:**
> You can display the number behind the graph section by holding down the right mouse button on that section. In some cases, it is faster to create filtered reports by starting with a graph and zooming in on sections of the graph until QuickBooks creates the report you want. If you are having trouble filtering reports, try viewing a graph first.

Building Custom Reports

To make your reports show only the information you want, you can modify (i.e., *customize*) the report. All reports include at least some modification and filtering options, so familiarize yourself with tabs in the *Modify Report* window as they are described below. In the *Computer Practice* section you will create a sample report and then customize it using the *Modify Report* options available.

The *Modify Report* window displays when you click the **Modify Report** button on any report. Four tabs make up the Modify Report window. In order to effectively learn how to modify reports, familiarize yourself with each tab as they are described below.

Use the **Display** tab to change the date range, select a report basis, add or delete columns, change how columns are displayed, or add subcolumns on a report. The **Display** tab will show different sections depending upon the report being modified. For example, the **Display** tab for a Profit and Loss report does not allow you to select or deselect columns for the report (see Figure 6-33), while the **Display** tab for an Item Price List only allows you to select or deselect columns for the report (see Figure 6-34). The **Display** tab shows those sections particular to the report being modified.

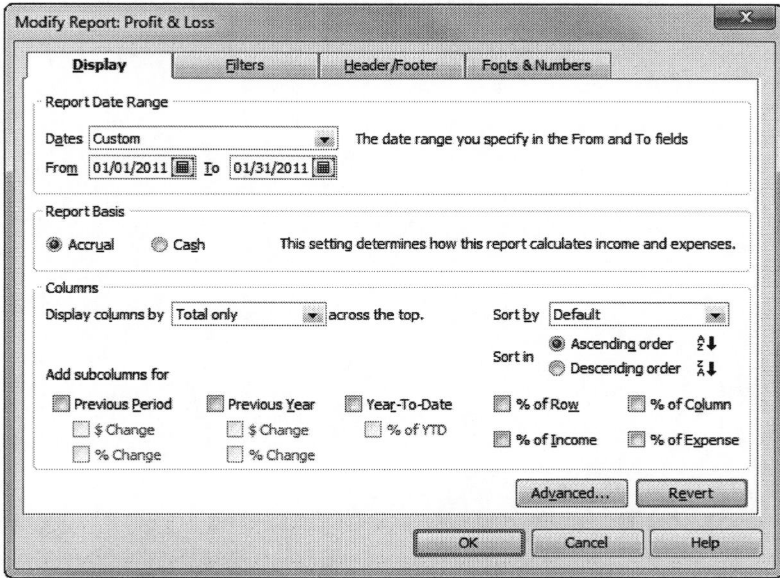

Figure 6-33 Display tab on the Modify Report: Profit & Loss window

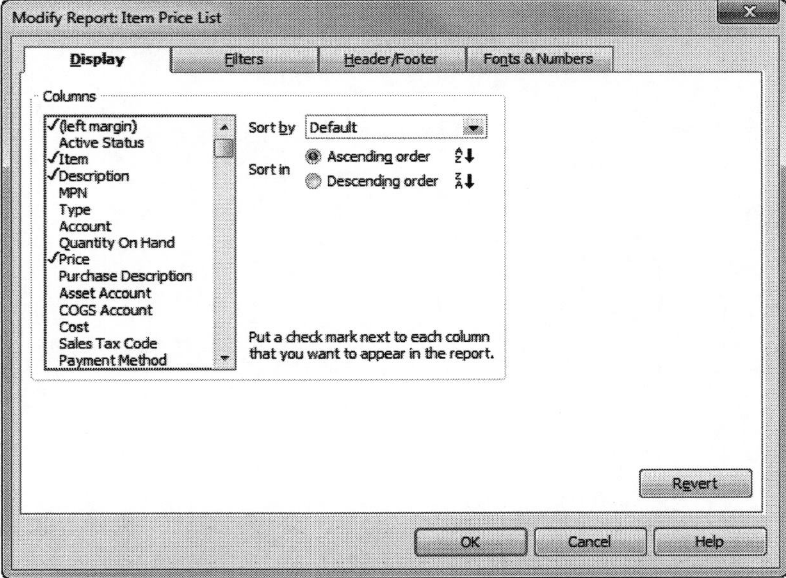

Figure 6-34 Display tab on the Modify Report: Item Price List window

Use the **Filters** tab to narrow the contents of the report so that you can analyze specific areas of your business. On the **Filters** tab, you can filter or choose specific accounts, dates, names, or items to include in the report (see Figure 6-35). Report filtering works similarly to the *Find* Command described on page 259.

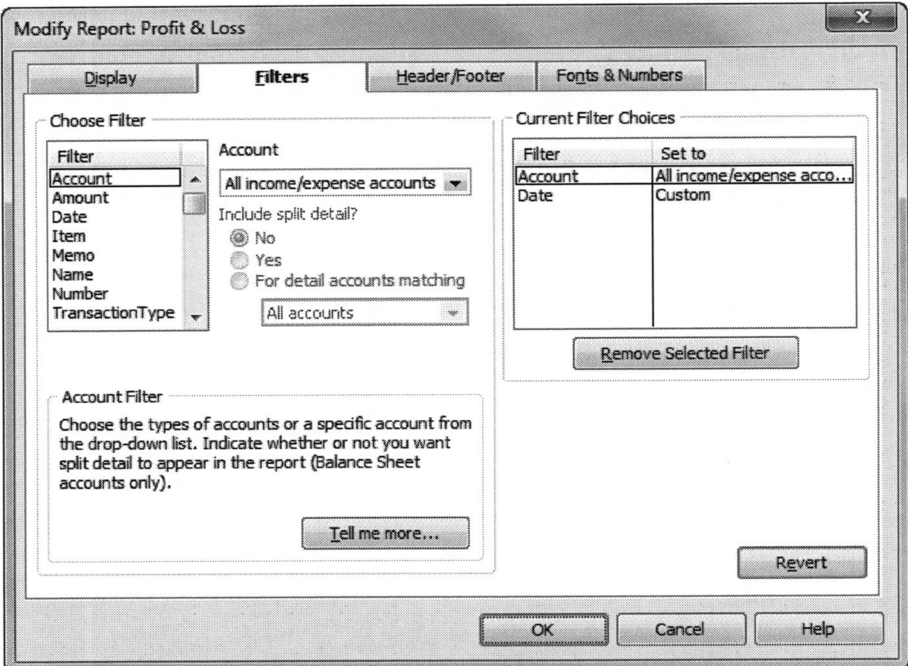

Figure 6-35 Filters tab on The Modify Report: Profit & Loss window

Use the **Header/Footer** tab to select which headers and footers will display on the report. In addition, the **Header/Footer** tab allows you to modify the Company Name, Report Title, Subtitle, Date Prepared, Page Number, and Extra Footer Line (see Figure 6-36).

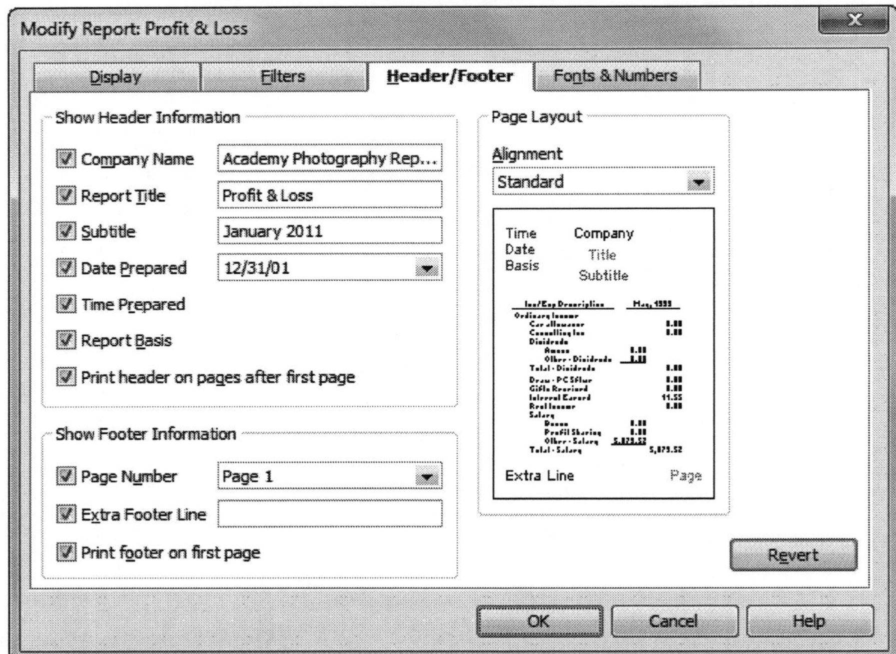

Figure 6-36 Header/Footer tab on The Modify Report: Profit & Loss window

Use the **Fonts & Numbers** tab to change the font and how numbers are displayed on the report. In addition, the **Fonts & Numbers** tab allows you to reduce numbers to multiples of 1000, hide amounts of 0.00, and show dollar amounts without cents (see Figure 6-37).

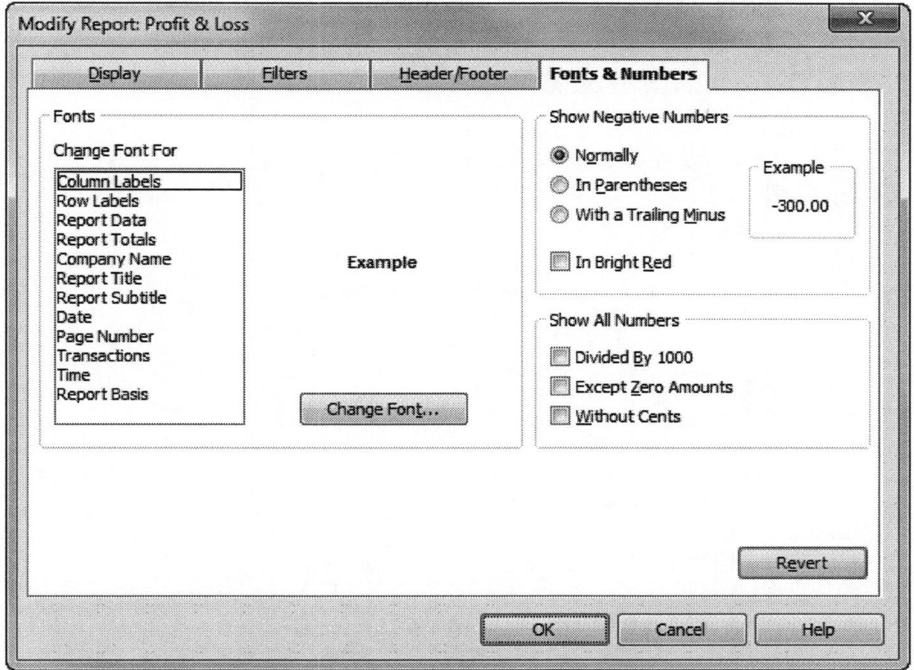

Figure 6-37 Fonts & Numbers tab on The Modify Report: Profit & Loss window

To practice modifying reports, suppose you want to get a report of all transactions that include all Service Items (Photography Service and Development Services) that you sold to customers who live in Walnut Creek during January and February of 2011. In addition, you want QuickBooks to sort and total the report by customer. The report should only display the type of transaction, the date, transaction number, customer name, city, item, account, and amount. Finally, the report should be titled *Sales of Services to Walnut Creek Customers.*

> **Note:**
> Although Academy Photography uses classes to track which store their customers buy from, we want a report about where customers *live*. Specifically, we want the *City* from the customer's address. This information comes from the field called "Name City" that is used as part of the customer's billing address.

COMPUTER PRACTICE

Begin by creating a **Custom Transaction Detail** report and then modify the report so that it provides the information you need. Since we cannot access the Custom Transaction Detail Report from the Report Center, we will begin by using the *Reports* menu.

Step 1. From the *Reports* menu, select **Custom Transaction Detail Report.** The **Modify Report: Custom Transaction Detail Report** window displays.

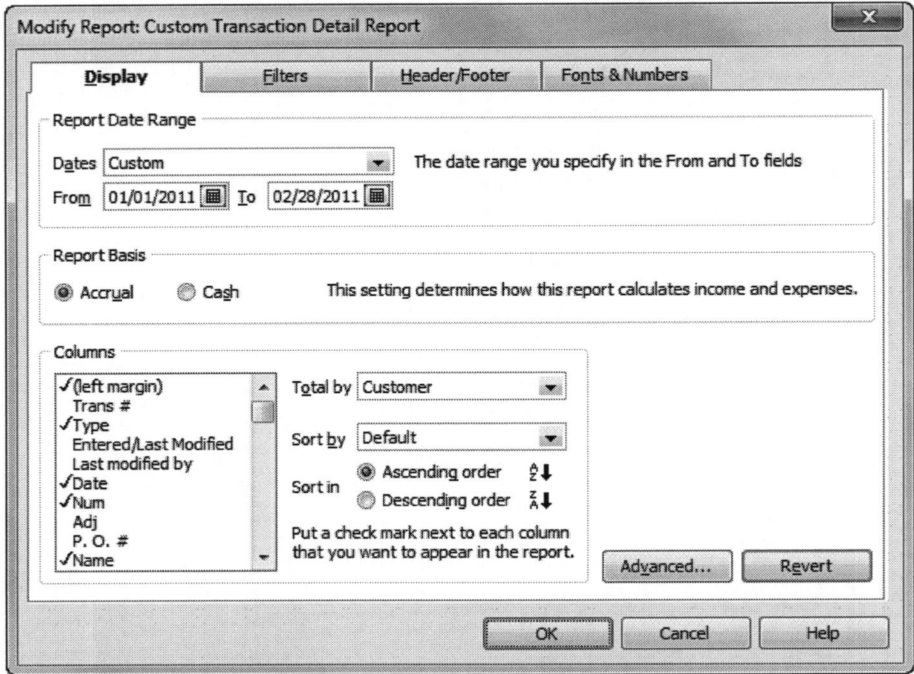

Figure 6-38 Modify Report: Custom Transaction Detail Report window

Step 2. Enter ***01/01/2011*** in the *From* field and enter ***02/28/2011*** in the *To* field.

Step 3. Select **Customer** from the *Total by* drop-down list and click **OK**.

This report will now show all transactions during January and February totaled by customer (see Figure 6-39).

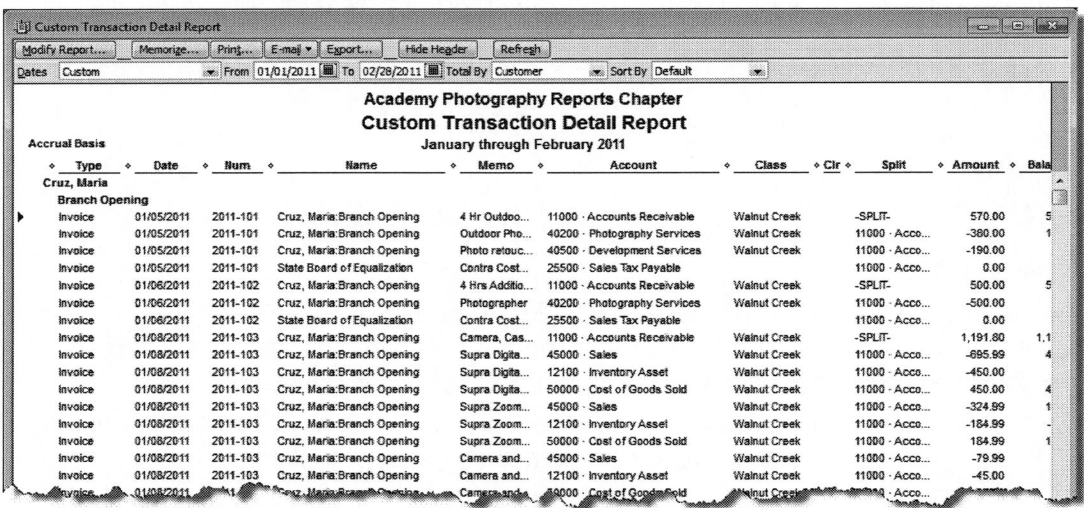

Custom Transaction Detail Report

Academy Photography Reports Chapter
Custom Transaction Detail Report
Accrual Basis
January through February 2011

Type	Date	Num	Name	Memo	Account	Class	Clr	Split	Amount
Cruz, Maria									
Branch Opening									
Invoice	01/05/2011	2011-101	Cruz, Maria:Branch Opening	4 Hr Outdoo...	11000 · Accounts Receivable	Walnut Creek		-SPLIT-	570.00
Invoice	01/05/2011	2011-101	Cruz, Maria:Branch Opening	Outdoor Pho...	40200 · Photography Services	Walnut Creek		11000 · Acco...	-380.00
Invoice	01/05/2011	2011-101	Cruz, Maria:Branch Opening	Photo retouc...	40500 · Development Services	Walnut Creek		11000 · Acco...	-190.00
Invoice	01/05/2011	2011-101	State Board of Equalization	Contra Cost...	25500 · Sales Tax Payable			11000 · Acco...	0.00
Invoice	01/06/2011	2011-102	Cruz, Maria:Branch Opening	4 Hrs Additio...	11000 · Accounts Receivable	Walnut Creek		-SPLIT-	500.00
Invoice	01/06/2011	2011-102	Cruz, Maria:Branch Opening	Photographer	40200 · Photography Services	Walnut Creek		11000 · Acco...	-500.00
Invoice	01/06/2011	2011-102	State Board of Equalization	Contra Cost...	25500 · Sales Tax Payable			11000 · Acco...	0.00
Invoice	01/08/2011	2011-103	Cruz, Maria:Branch Opening	Camera, Cas...	11000 · Accounts Receivable	Walnut Creek		-SPLIT-	1,191.80
Invoice	01/08/2011	2011-103	Cruz, Maria:Branch Opening	Supra Digita...	45000 · Sales	Walnut Creek		11000 · Acco...	-695.99
Invoice	01/08/2011	2011-103	Cruz, Maria:Branch Opening	Supra Digita...	12100 · Inventory Asset	Walnut Creek		11000 · Acco...	-450.00
Invoice	01/08/2011	2011-103	Cruz, Maria:Branch Opening	Supra Digita...	50000 · Cost of Goods Sold	Walnut Creek		11000 · Acco...	450.00
Invoice	01/08/2011	2011-103	Cruz, Maria:Branch Opening	Supra Zoom...	45000 · Sales	Walnut Creek		11000 · Acco...	-324.99
Invoice	01/08/2011	2011-103	Cruz, Maria:Branch Opening	Supra Zoom...	12100 · Inventory Asset	Walnut Creek		11000 · Acco...	-184.99
Invoice	01/08/2011	2011-103	Cruz, Maria:Branch Opening	Supra Zoom...	50000 · Cost of Goods Sold	Walnut Creek		11000 · Acco...	184.99
Invoice	01/08/2011	2011-103	Cruz, Maria:Branch Opening	Camera and...	45000 · Sales	Walnut Creek		11000 · Acco...	-79.99
Invoice	01/08/2011	2011-103	Cruz, Maria:Branch Opening	Camera and...	12100 · Inventory Asset	Walnut Creek		11000 · Acco...	-45.00

Figure 6-39 Transaction Detail by Account report totaled by customer

For our purposes there are four problems with this report:

1. The report shows more columns than we want to display.
2. The report shows all transactions, not just the Service Items sold to customers.
3. The report is not filtered to only show customers who live in Walnut Creek.
4. The report has the wrong title.

We will modify the report to correct the four problems listed above.

Step 4. Click Modify Report.

Step 5. In the **Columns** section of the *Display* tab, notice that several fields have check marks (see Figure 6-40). The checkmarks indicate which columns show on the report. Select **Name City** and **Item** to turn those columns on. Then deselect **Memo, Class, Clr, Split,** and **Balance**. You will need to scroll up and down in the list to find each field.

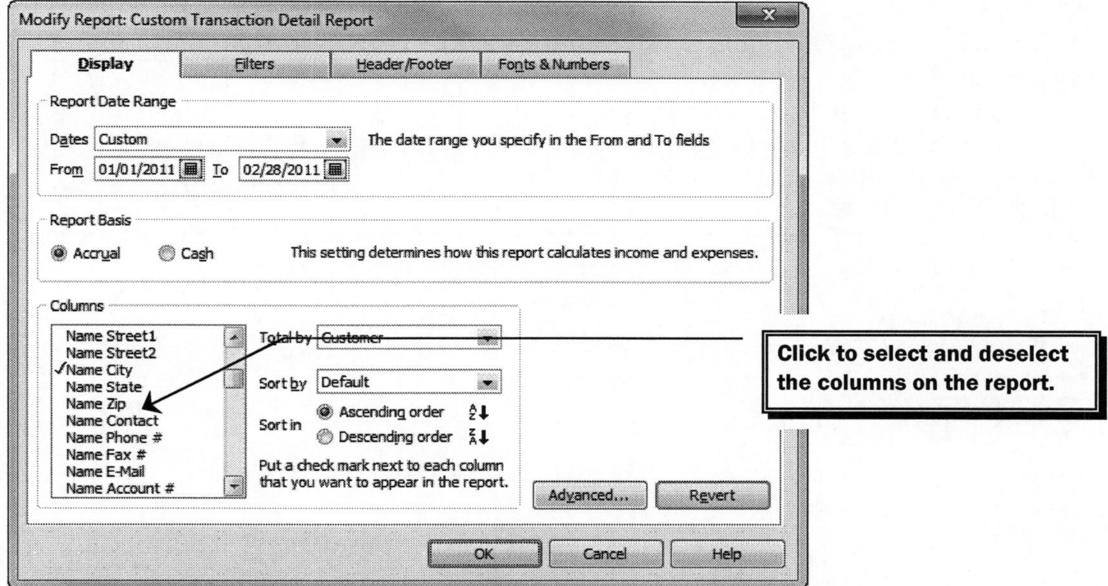

Figure 6-40 Modify columns by checking and unchecking lines in the Columns list

> **Note:**
> There are several other settings on the **Display** tab that you can choose to modify the report further. For example, you could change the basis of the report from Accrual to Cash, or you could set the sorting preferences. Click the **Advanced** button for even more settings. Explore these settings to learn how they affect your reports. For descriptions of each selection, use the QuickBooks **Help** menu.

Step 6. Click the **Filters** tab.

Step 7. To filter the report so that it includes only Service Items, select the **Item** filter in the *Choose Filter* section and select **All services** from the *Item* drop-down list (see Figure 6-41).

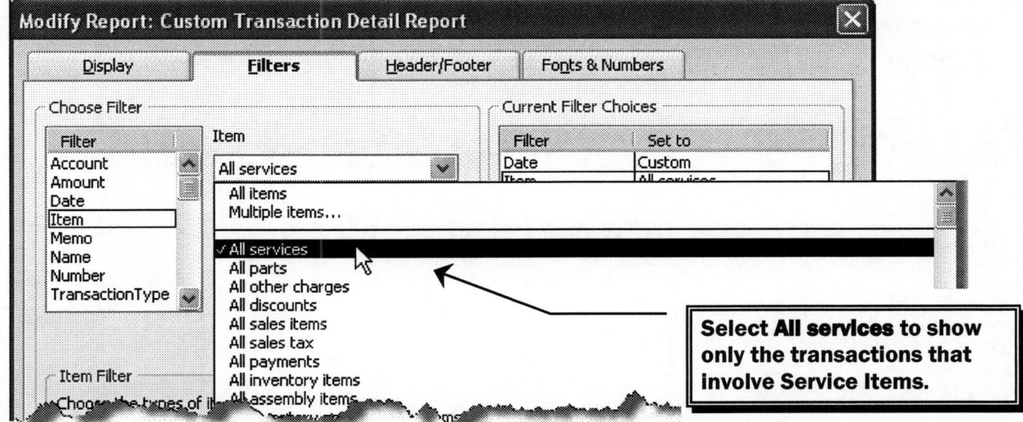

Figure 6-41 Item drop-down list in the Filters window

Step 8. To filter the report so that it includes only those customers who live in Walnut Creek, scroll down the *Choose Filter* section and select the **Name City** filter. This displays a **Name City** field to the right of the *Choose Filter* section. Enter ***Walnut Creek*** in the **Name City** field (see Figure 6-42).

Did You Know?
Many fields on the Filter tab act like wildcards. If you enter a portion of the text in a field for a particular filter, QuickBooks will display all records containing that text. For example, if you only type in ***nut*** or ***eek*** in the *City* field, all customer records in the city of Walnut Creek will still display. Be careful when using a wildcard in a field because it can produce an unintended result if used carelessly.

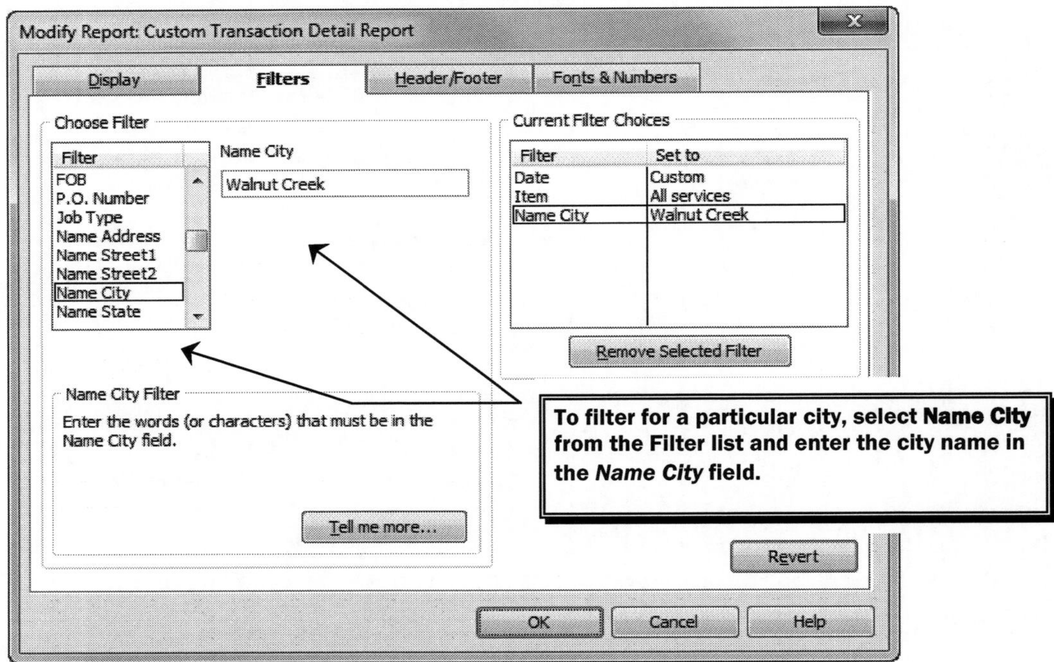

Figure 6-42 Entering a filter for a report

Step 9. Click the **Header/Footer** tab on the *Modify Report* window.

Step 10. To modify the title of the report so that it accurately describes the content of the report, enter ***Sales of Services to Walnut Creek Customers*** in the *Report Title* field as shown in Figure 6-43.

Step 11. Click **OK** on the *Modify Report* window.

DO NOT CLOSE THE REPORT. YOU WILL USE IT IN THE NEXT PRACTICE.

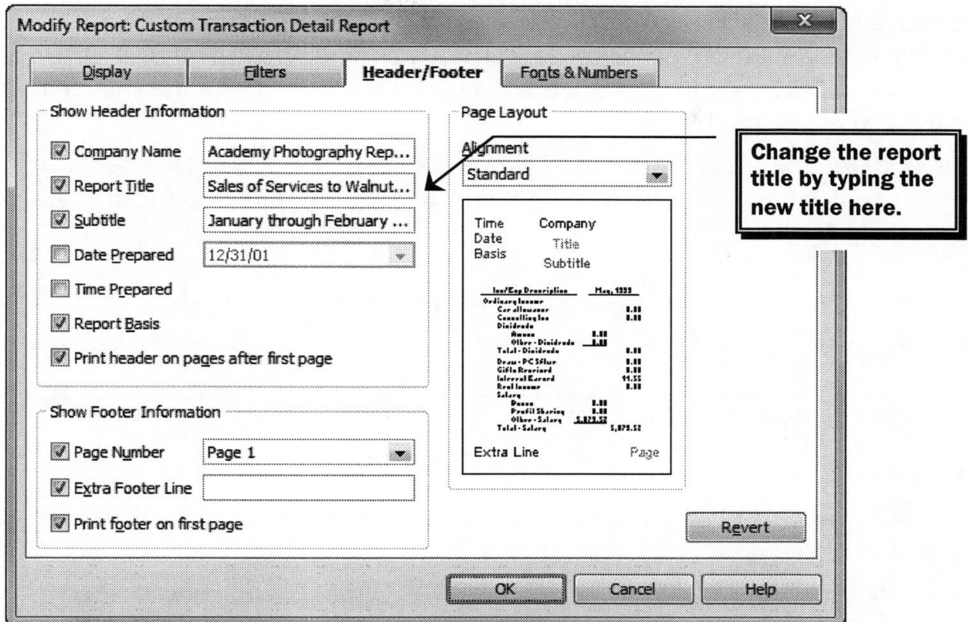

Figure 6-43 Change the report title on the Header/Footer tab

In Figure 6-44 you can see your modified report. Notice that its heading reflects its new content. You can modify the width of columns by dragging the diamond on the top right of the column to reduce or expand the width. Also, if you want to move a column left or right, move your curser over the column header until you see the hand icon. Then, hold your left mouse button down as you drag the column to the left or right.

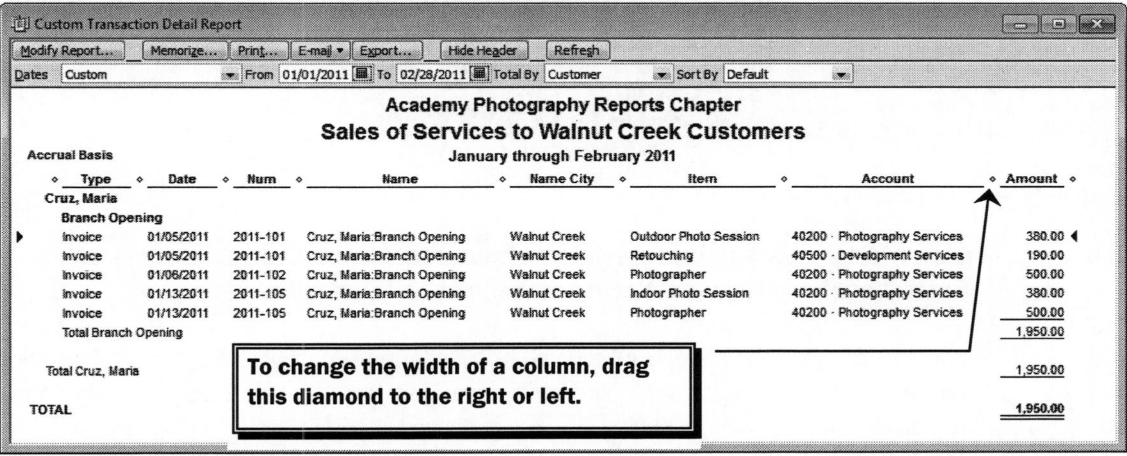

Figure 6-44 The customized report

Memorizing Reports

After you have modified a report, you can *memorize* the format and filtering so that you don't have to perform all of the modification steps the next time you want to view the report.

> **Note:**
> Memorizing a report does not memorize the data on the report, only the format, dates, and filtering.

If you enter specific dates, QuickBooks will use those dates the next time you bring up the report. However, if you select a *relative* date range in the *Dates* field (e.g., Last Fiscal Quarter, Last Year, or This Year to Date) before memorizing a report, QuickBooks will use the relative dates the next time you create the report.

For example, if you memorize a report with the *Dates* field set to **Last Fiscal Quarter**, that report will always use dates for the fiscal quarter prior to the current date (see Figure 6-45).

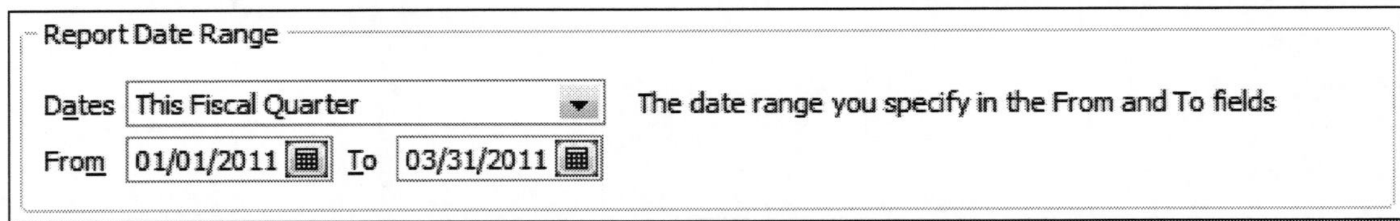

Figure 6-45 The Dates field showing a relative date range

COMPUTER PRACTICE

Step 1. With the *Sales of Services to Walnut Creek Customers* report displayed, click **Memorize** at the top of the report.

Step 2. In the *Memorize Report* window, the name for the report is automatically filled in. QuickBooks uses the report title as the default name for the memorized report (see Figure 6-46). The name can be modified if desired.

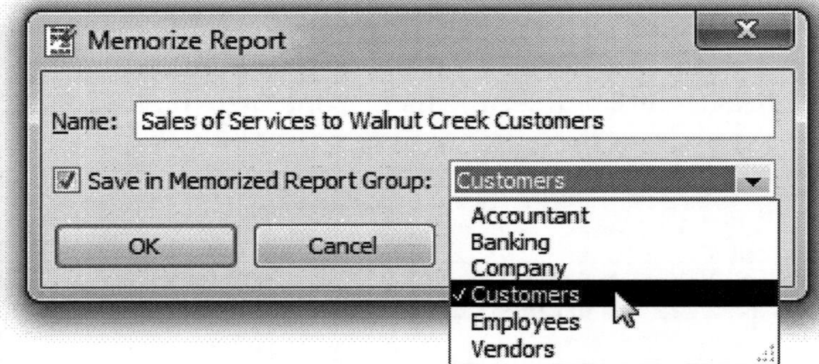

Figure 6-46 Memorize Report window

Step 3. Click the Checkbox next to **Save in Memorized Report Group:** and select **Customers** from the drop-down list as shown in Figure 6-46.

You can group your reports into similar types when you memorize them. This allows you to run several reports in a group by selecting them in the *Process Multiple Reports* window.

Step 4. Click **OK** and close the report.

Viewing Memorized Reports

The next time you want to see this report follow these steps:

Step 1. From the *Report Center*, click on the **Memorized** tab at the top of the window.

Notice that QuickBooks displays the reports in groups according to how you memorized them.

Step 2. Select the report you just memorized by selecting **Customer** on the menu on the left of the window and double click **Sale of Services to Walnut Creek Customers** (see Figure 6-47).

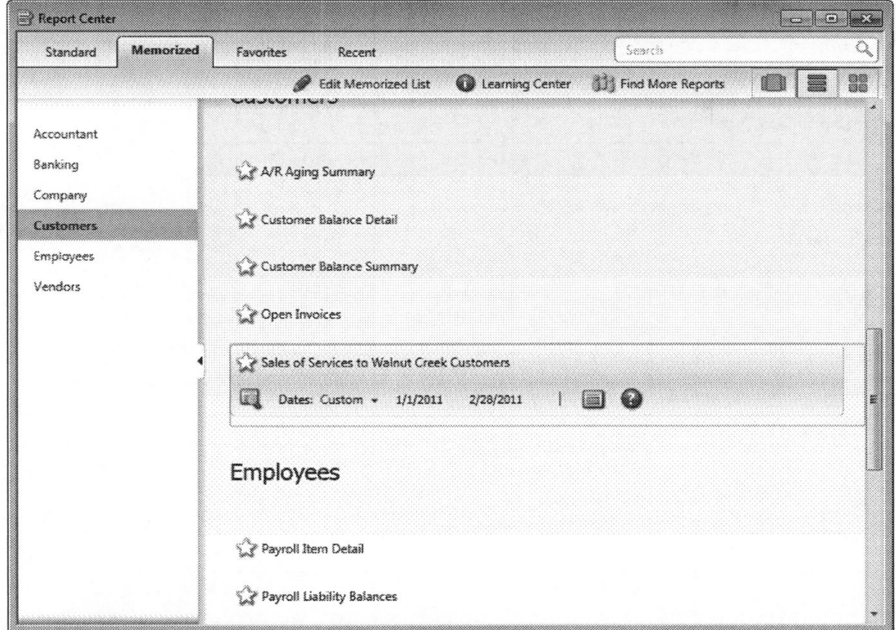

Figure 6-47 Memorized Report in the Report Center

Step 3. Close all open report windows.

Processing Multiple Reports

QuickBooks allows you to combine several reports into a group, so that you can later display and/or print the reports in the group as a batch.

Report Groups

As you can see in the Memorized Report list shown in Figure 6-47, you can have as many reports as you want in a group by memorizing the report and assigning it to the group. If you want to reassign a report to another group, click on the diamond to the left of the report in the Memorized Reports list and drag the mouse up or down until the report appears under the desired group. If you drag it to where it is no longer below a group name, it will not belong to any group.

Processing Multiple Reports

QuickBooks allows you to print reports as a batch. You may want to use this feature to print a series of monthly reports for your files (e.g., monthly Profit and Loss and Balance Sheet reports). Since we cannot process multiple reports from the Report Center, we will begin with the *Reports* menu.

COMPUTER PRACTICE

Step 1. From the **Reports** menu select **Process Multiple Reports** (see Figure 6-48).

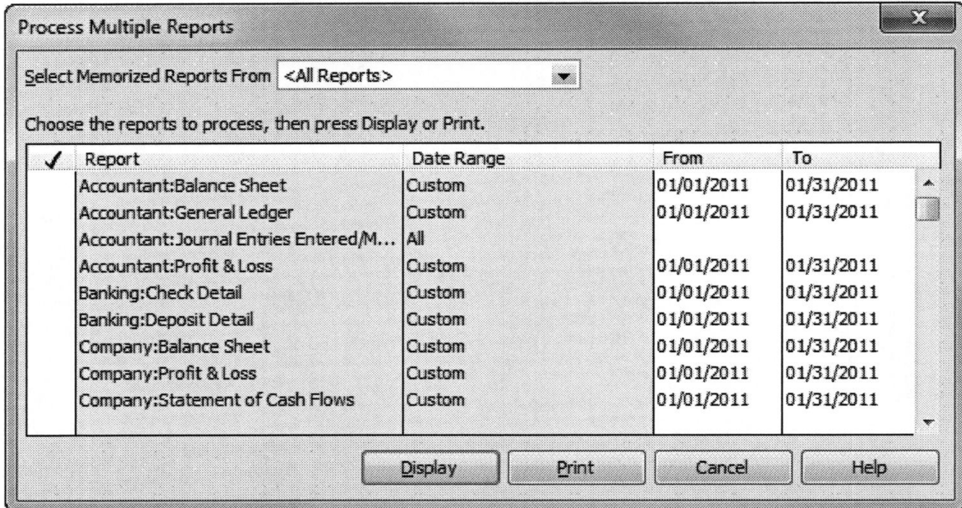

Figure 6-48 Process Multiple Reports window

> **Note:**
> Click in the column to the left of the report you want to include when you print or display your reports. Select the *From* and *To* date ranges of the report you wish to print in the columns on the right. Your date ranges will not match the ones displayed in Figure 6-48 and Figure 6-49. If you print the same group of reports on a regular basis, create a new Report Group in the *Memorize Reports List* window to combine the reports under a single group. Then you can select the group name in the *Select Memorized Reports From* field.

Step 2. Select **Customers** from the *Select Memorized Reports From* drop-down list (see Figure 6-49).

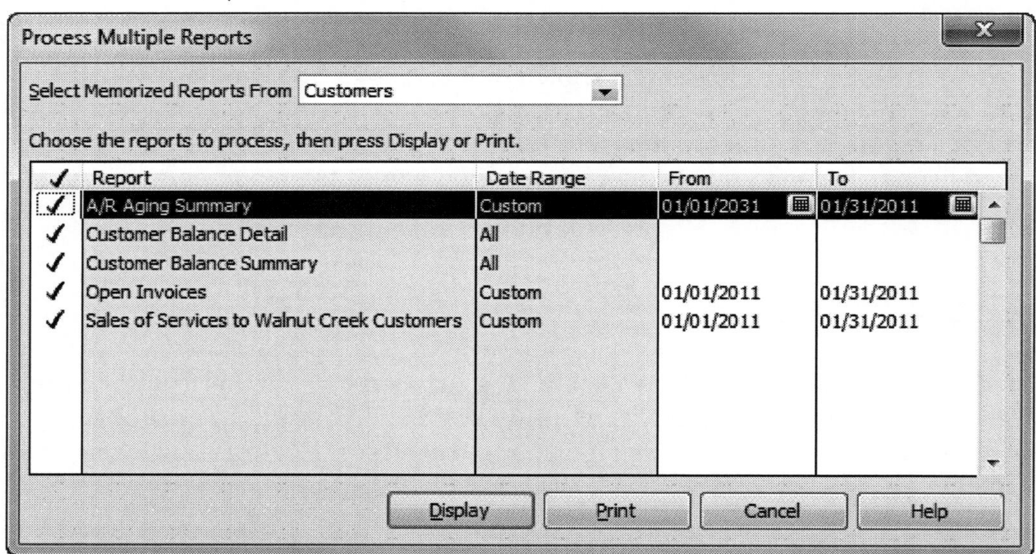

Figure 6-49 Customers Report Group

Step 3. If you do not want to display or print all the reports in the group, uncheck (√) the left column to deselect the reports you want to omit. Click **Display** to show the reports on the window (see Figure 6-50) or click **Print** to print all the reports.

> If your *Home* page is maximized, make sure to **Restore Down** ( ) the window so that your reports will display in the cascade style shown in Figure 6-50.

Step 4. Close all open report windows. Click **No** if QuickBooks prompts you to memorize the reports.

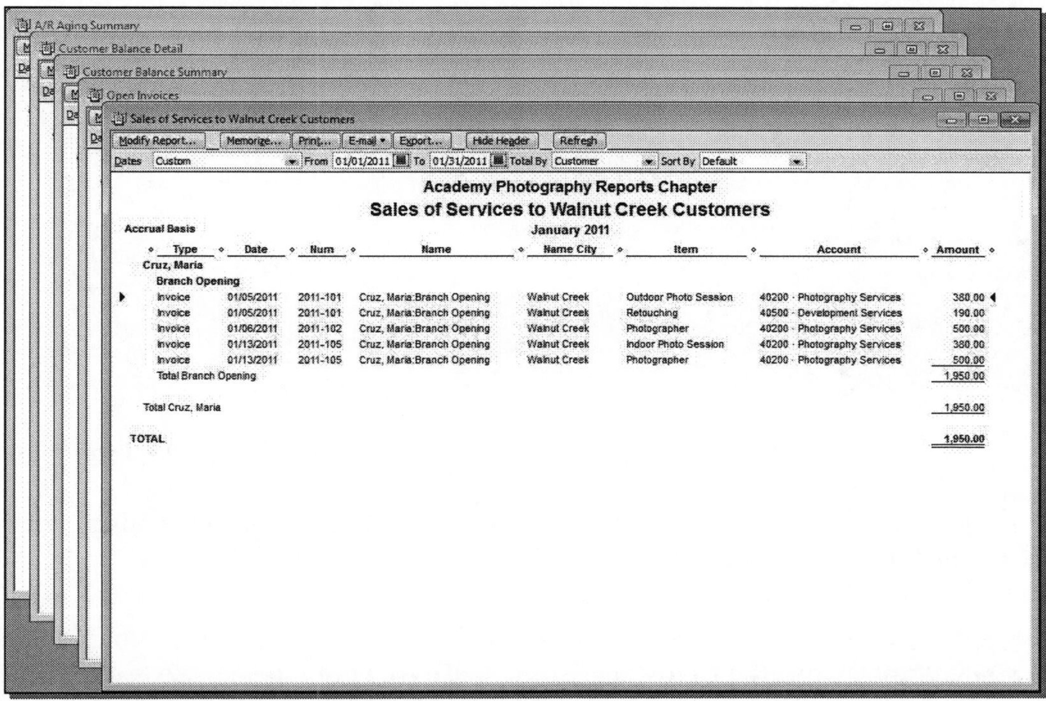

Academy Photography Reports Chapter

Sales of Services to Walnut Creek Customers

Accrual Basis — January 2011

Type	Date	Num	Name	Name City	Item	Account	Amount
Cruz, Maria							
Branch Opening							
Invoice	01/05/2011	2011-101	Cruz, Maria:Branch Opening	Walnut Creek	Outdoor Photo Session	40200 · Photography Services	380.00
Invoice	01/05/2011	2011-101	Cruz, Maria:Branch Opening	Walnut Creek	Retouching	40500 · Development Services	190.00
Invoice	01/06/2011	2011-102	Cruz, Maria:Branch Opening	Walnut Creek	Photographer	40200 · Photography Services	500.00
Invoice	01/13/2011	2011-105	Cruz, Maria:Branch Opening	Walnut Creek	Indoor Photo Session	40200 · Photography Services	380.00
Invoice	01/13/2011	2011-105	Cruz, Maria:Branch Opening	Walnut Creek	Photographer	40200 · Photography Services	500.00
Total Branch Opening							1,950.00
Total Cruz, Maria							1,950.00
TOTAL							1,950.00

Figure 6-50 All of the reports in the Customer report group

Printing Reports

Every report in QuickBooks is printable. When you print reports, QuickBooks allows you to specify the orientation (landscape or portrait) and page-count characteristics for the reports.

COMPUTER PRACTICE

Step 1. Create a **Profit & Loss by Job** report dated ***01/01/2011*** to ***01/31/2011*** (see page 233).

Step 2. To print the report, click **Print** at the top of the window.

> **Another Way:**
> To print a report, press Ctrl+P or select the **File** menu and then select **Print Report.**

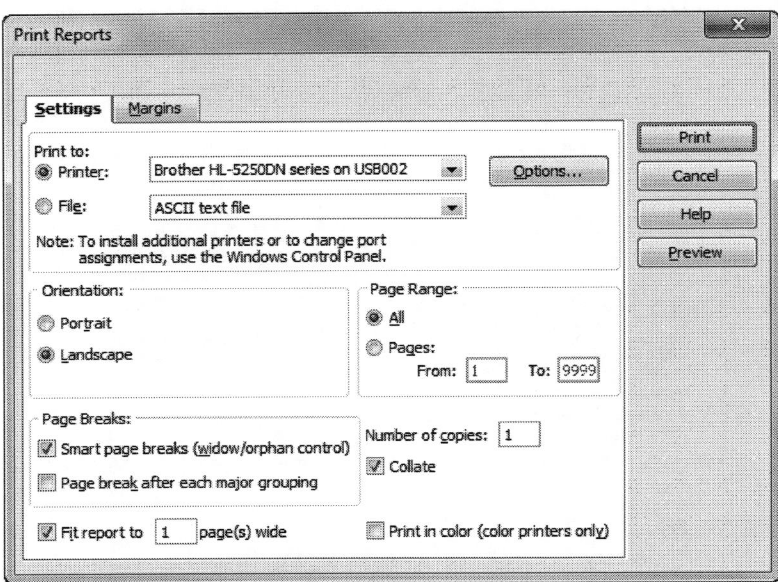

Figure 6-51 Print Report window – your screen may vary

Step 3. The **Print Reports** window displays. Your settings will be different than the settings shown in Figure 6-51.

Step 4. QuickBooks normally selects your default printer, but you can select another printer from the *Printer* drop-down list.

Step 5. Select **Landscape** in the *Orientation* section.

The Portrait setting makes the print appear from left to right across the 8½-inch dimension of the page ("straight up"), while the Landscape setting makes the print appear across the 11-inch dimension of the page ("sideways").

Step 6. Confirm that the **Smart page breaks (widow/orphan control)** setting is selected (see Figure 6-52). This setting keeps related data from splitting across two pages.

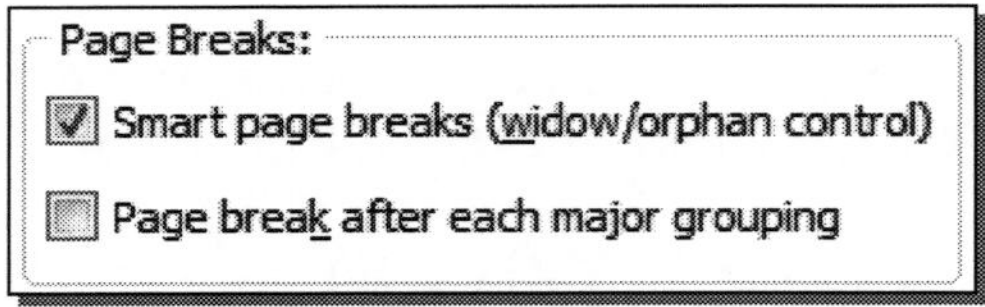

Figure 6-52 Page Breaks setting

Using **Smart page breaks,** you can control (to some extent) where page breaks occur on reports so that your pages don't break in inappropriate places. Using **Page break after each major grouping,** you can have QuickBooks break the pages after each major grouping of accounts. For example, in the Profit & Loss report, all Income and Cost of Goods Sold accounts will be on the first page (or pages), and all the Expense accounts will begin on a new page. In other reports, like the Customer Balance Detail and Vendor Balance Detail reports, this setting will cause each Customer and Vendor to begin on a new page, respectively.

Step 7. Select **Fit report to 1 pages wide** (see Figure 6-53). When **you select this option,** QuickBooks reduces the font size of the report so the width of all columns does not exceed 8½" (in portrait mode) or 11" (in landscape mode).

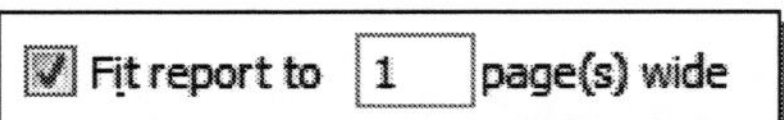

Figure 6-53 Select Fit report to 1 page(s) wide

Before you print any report, it's a good idea to preview the report to make sure it will print the way you want.

Step 8. Click the **Preview** button on the *Print Reports* window.

Step 9. If everything looks right, click **Print** to print the report.

Step 10. Close all open report windows.

> **Note:**
> QuickBooks saves the setting on the *Print Reports* window for memorized reports.

Finding Transactions

There are several ways to find transactions in QuickBooks depending on what you are trying to find. Sometimes you only know the date of a transaction and other times you know only the customer, item, or amount. You can search for a transaction by finding it in the register, using the **Find** command, using **QuickReports**, or using **QuickZoom**.

Using the Find Command

If you are looking for a transaction and you do not know which register to look in, or if you want to find more than just a single transaction, you can use the **Find** command. You can search by several criteria in order to find the transaction(s) you want.

There are two tabs on the Find window: Simple and Advanced. Use the **Simple** tab if you want to search for any of the following information: the transaction type, Customer:Job name used on the transaction, exact or approximate date of the transaction, the transaction number (e.g., Invoice #), or amount. If you need to search based on any other criteria (e.g., account name, item name, memo, etc.), use the **Advanced** tab.

> **Note:**
> *QuickBooks Search* using *Google Desktop* was discontinued with QuickBooks 2010.

Using the Find Command to Find an Invoice

If you need to find a particular Invoice, many QuickBooks users will open the *Create Invoice* window and click **Previous** until they find the Invoice they need. This is often a very time consuming and inefficient way to locate a specific transaction. Instead, to find an Invoice for $2,020.13 that you issued to Bob Mason between January and February 2011, use the **Simple** tab of the *Find* window.

COMPUTER PRACTICE

Step 1. Select **Find** from the *Edit* menu (or press Ctrl+F).

Step 2. Make sure that the **Simple** tab is selected and that **Invoice** displays in the *Transaction Type* field. Press **Tab**.

Step 3. Select **Mason, Bob** from the *Customer:Job* drop-down list and press **Tab**.

Step 4. Since you do not know the exact date of the Invoice, but you know that you created the Invoice during the first quarter of 2011, enter ***01/01/2011*** and ***02/28/2011*** in the *Dates* fields and press **Tab**.

Step 5. Press **Tab** to skip the *Invoice #* field.

If you know the Invoice number, you can enter it in this field. For this practice, we will assume that you do not know the number.

Step 6. Enter ***2,020.13*** in the *Amount* field and press **Tab**.

Step 7. Click **Find** to search for all Invoices for Bob Mason in the amount of $2,020.13 (see Figure 6-54).

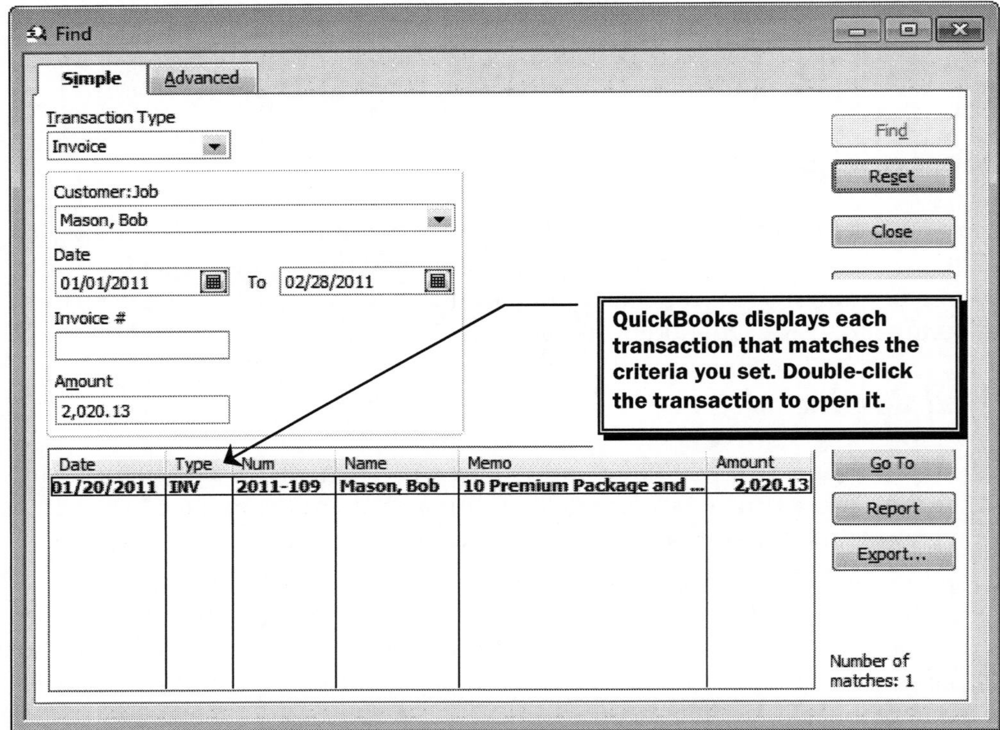

Figure 6-54 Use the Simple tab of the Find window to locate an Invoice for Bob Mason

Step 8. Click **Reset**.

To find all transactions that use the Photographer Item, use the **Advanced** tab in the *Find* window.

COMPUTER PRACTICE

Step 1. Click the **Advanced** tab. QuickBooks adds the *Posting status* criteria by default.

Step 2. In the *Choose Filter* section, select **Item** and the press **Tab**.

Step 3. Enter ***Photographer*** in the *Item* field (see Figure 6-55). Press **Tab**.

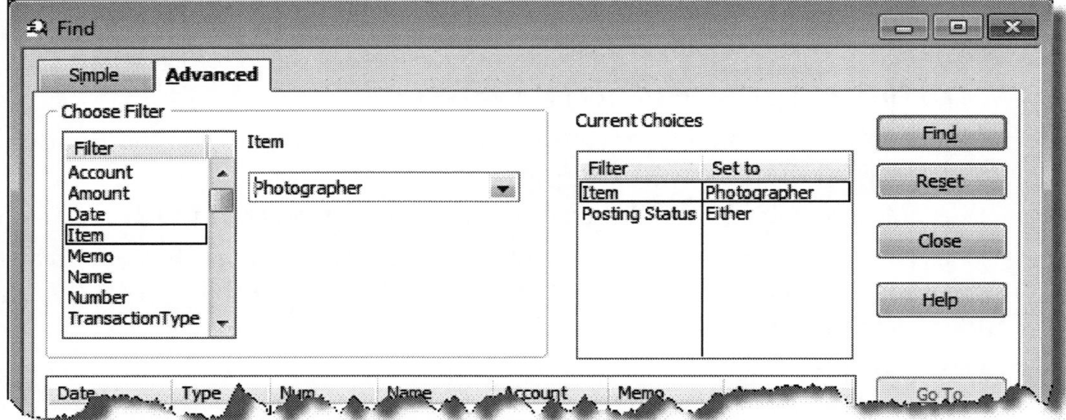

Figure 6-55 Enter Photographer in the Item field

Step 4. Click the **Find** button.

QuickBooks finds all of the transactions that match your criteria and then displays them at the bottom of the *Find* window (see Figure 6-56).

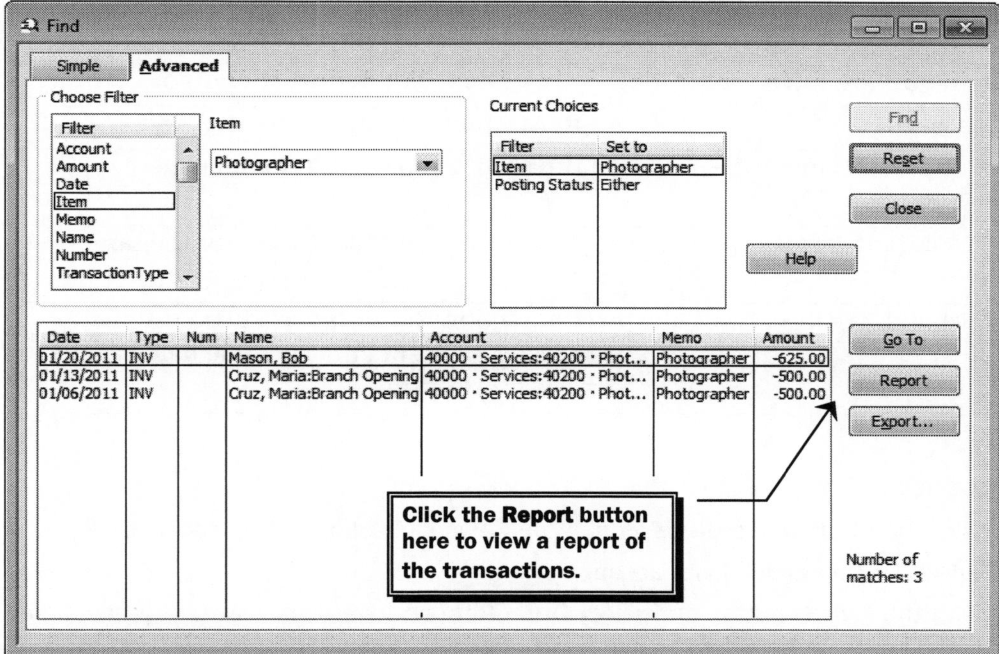

Figure 6-56 Advanced tab of the Find window

Step 5. To view these transactions in a report format, click **Report**.

The report shown in Figure 6-57 includes all transactions that involve the Photographer Item. If you want to look at one of these transactions, double-click it in the report.

Figure 6-57 Find Report for Photographer Items

Step 6. Close the *Find Report* and *Find* windows.

QuickReports

A **QuickReport** can quickly give you detailed transactions about an account, item, customer, vendor, or other payee. You can generate QuickReports from the Chart of Accounts, lists, account registers, or forms. Table 6-2 shows different types of QuickReports.

When you are in...	The QuickReport shows you...
Chart of Accounts	All transactions involving that account.
List (with an Item or Name selected)	All transactions for that Item or Name.
Register (with a transaction selected)	All transactions in that register for the same name.
Form (Invoice, Bill, or Check)	All transactions for that particular customer, vendor, or payee within the same name as the current transaction.

Table 6-2 Types of QuickReports

COMPUTER PRACTICE

Step 1. Click the **Chart of Accounts** icon in the *Company* section of the **Home** page.

Step 2. Select the **Inventory Asset** account.

Step 3. Click the *Reports* button and select **Quick Report: Inventory Asset**. Alternately, press **Ctrl+Q** (see Figure 6-58).

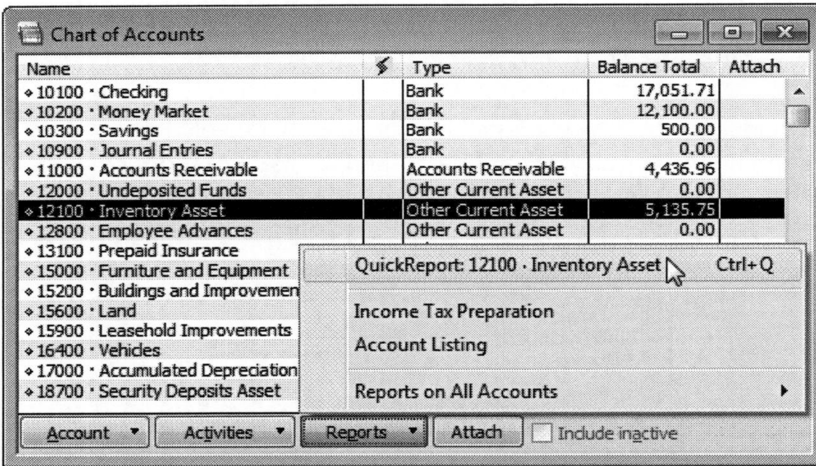

Figure 6-58 QuickReport of the Inventory Asset account

Step 4. QuickBooks displays all transactions involving the **Inventory Asset** account (see Figure 6-59).

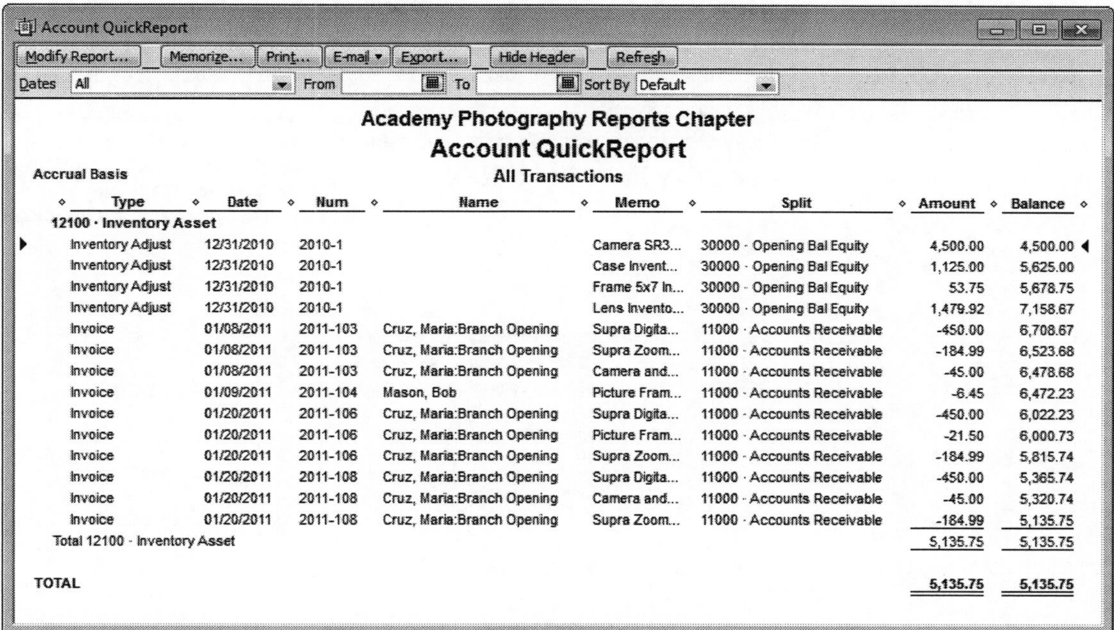

Academy Photography Reports Chapter
Account QuickReport
All Transactions

Accrual Basis

Type	Date	Num	Name	Memo	Split	Amount	Balance
12100 · Inventory Asset							
Inventory Adjust	12/31/2010	2010-1		Camera SR3...	30000 · Opening Bal Equity	4,500.00	4,500.00
Inventory Adjust	12/31/2010	2010-1		Case Invent...	30000 · Opening Bal Equity	1,125.00	5,625.00
Inventory Adjust	12/31/2010	2010-1		Frame 5x7 In...	30000 · Opening Bal Equity	53.75	5,678.75
Inventory Adjust	12/31/2010	2010-1		Lens Invento...	30000 · Opening Bal Equity	1,479.92	7,158.67
Invoice	01/08/2011	2011-103	Cruz, Maria:Branch Opening	Supra Digita...	11000 · Accounts Receivable	-450.00	6,708.67
Invoice	01/08/2011	2011-103	Cruz, Maria:Branch Opening	Supra Zoom...	11000 · Accounts Receivable	-184.99	6,523.68
Invoice	01/08/2011	2011-103	Cruz, Maria:Branch Opening	Camera and...	11000 · Accounts Receivable	-45.00	6,478.68
Invoice	01/09/2011	2011-104	Mason, Bob	Picture Fram...	11000 · Accounts Receivable	-6.45	6,472.23
Invoice	01/20/2011	2011-106	Cruz, Maria:Branch Opening	Supra Digita...	11000 · Accounts Receivable	-450.00	6,022.23
Invoice	01/20/2011	2011-106	Cruz, Maria:Branch Opening	Picture Fram...	11000 · Accounts Receivable	-21.50	6,000.73
Invoice	01/20/2011	2011-106	Cruz, Maria:Branch Opening	Supra Zoom...	11000 · Accounts Receivable	-184.99	5,815.74
Invoice	01/20/2011	2011-108	Cruz, Maria:Branch Opening	Supra Digita...	11000 · Accounts Receivable	-450.00	5,365.74
Invoice	01/20/2011	2011-108	Cruz, Maria:Branch Opening	Camera and...	11000 · Accounts Receivable	-45.00	5,320.74
Invoice	01/20/2011	2011-108	Cruz, Maria:Branch Opening	Supra Zoom...	11000 · Accounts Receivable	-184.99	5,135.75
Total 12100 · Inventory Asset						5,135.75	5,135.75
TOTAL						5,135.75	5,135.75

Figure 6-59 All transaction involving the Inventory Asset account

Step 5. Close the Account QuickReport and Chart of Accounts window.

Step 6. From the *Lists* menu select **Item List.**

Step 7. Select **Camera SR32** from the *Item list.*

Step 8. Click the *Reports* button and select **Quick Report: Camera SR32**. Alternately, press **Ctrl+Q** (see Figure 6-60).

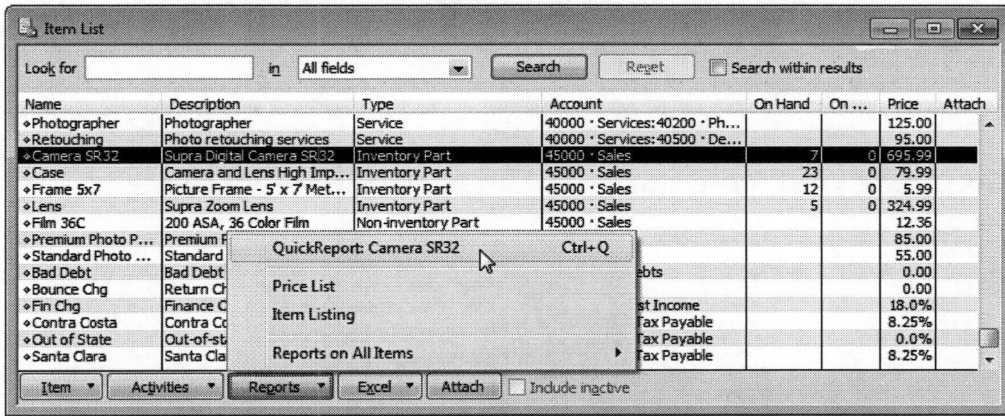

Figure 6-60 QuickReport for Camera SR32 Item

Step 9. Change the *Dates* range to **All.** QuickBooks displays all transactions involving the **Camera SR32** Item (see Figure 6-61).

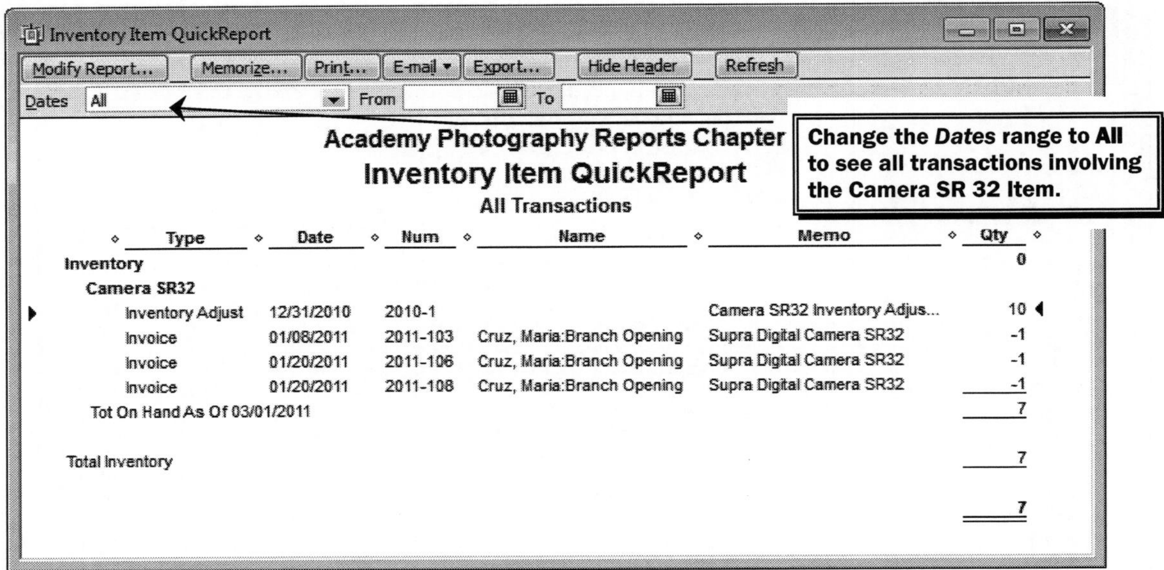

Figure 6-61 All transactions involving the Camera SR32 Item

Step 10. Close the Item QuickReport and Item List window.

Step 11. Click the **Check Register** icon in the *Banking* section of the **Home** page.

Step 12. Confirm that **Checking** displays in the **Select Account** field of the *Use Register* dialog box. Click **OK**.

Step 13. Scroll up and select **BILLPMT #6003**.

Step 14. Click the **QuickReport** icon at the top of the register (see Figure 6-62).

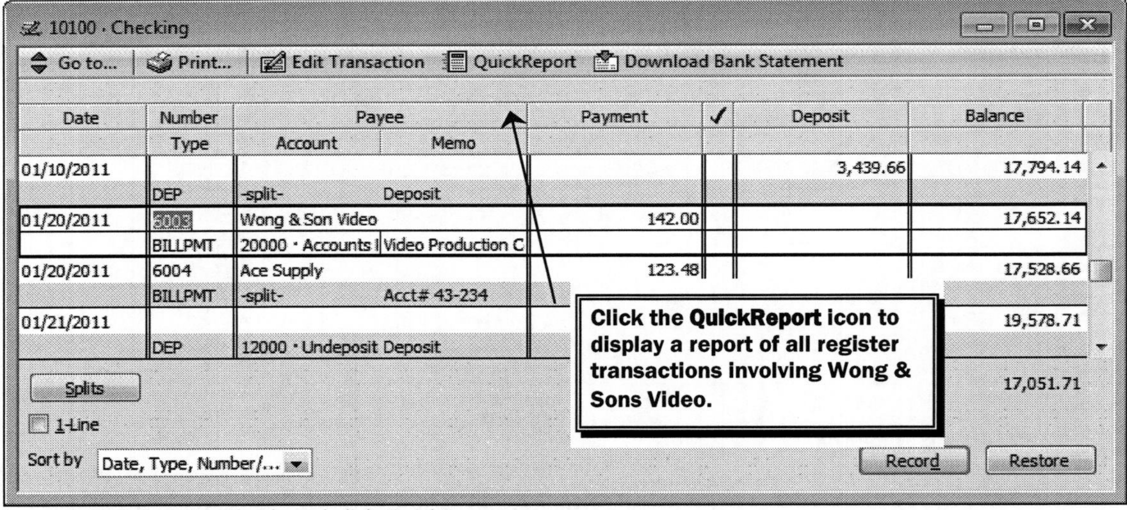

Figure 6-62 Select the Check and click QuickReport icon

Step 15. QuickBooks displays a report of all transactions in the Checking register using the same name as the selected transaction (see Figure 6-63).

Figure 6-63 QuickReport for Vendor Wong & Son Video

Step 16. Close the Register QuickReport and Checking register.

Step 17. Click the **Invoices** icon on the *Home Page.*

Step 18. The **Create Invoices** window displays.

Step 19. Click the **Previous** button once to display invoice **FC 3** for *Bob Mason* Finance Charge (see Figure 6-64).

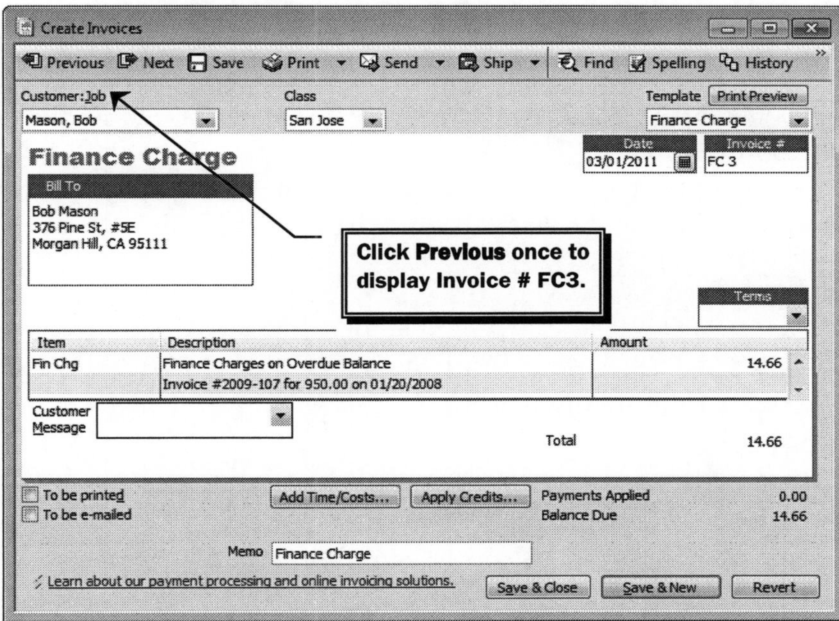

Figure 6-64 Create Invoices window

Step 20. Press **Ctrl+Q** to display the QuickReport window for *Mason, Bob.*

Step 21. Select **All** in the *Dates* field to display all transactions for *Mason, Bob.*

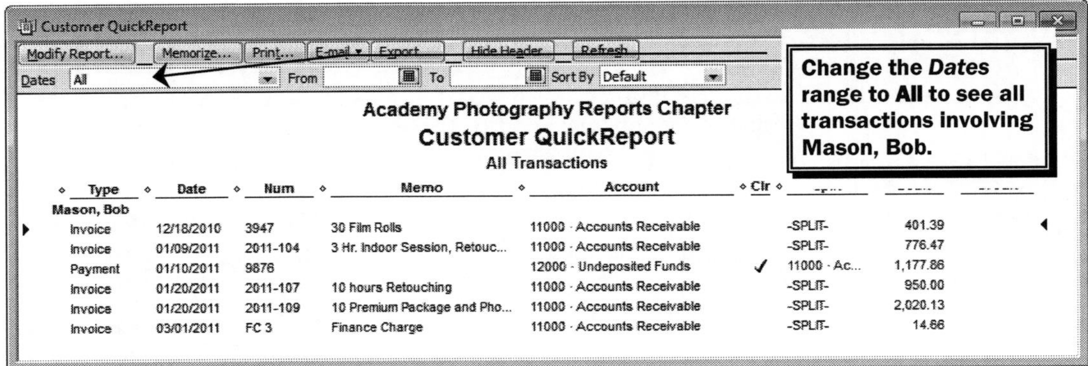

Figure 6-65 QuickReport Mason, Bob

Step 22. Close the QuickReport and Create Invoices windows.

> **Did You Know?**
> You can also generate QuickReports from the Customer Center, Vendor Center, or Employee Center by selecting the customer, vendor, or employee and clicking on the **QuickReport** link in the upper right-hand corner of the window.

Using QuickZoom

QuickBooks provides a convenient feature called **QuickZoom**, which allows you to see the details behind numbers on reports.

For example, the Profit & Loss report in Figure 6-66 shows $3,145.00 of Photography Services income. Double-click on the amount to see the details behind the number.

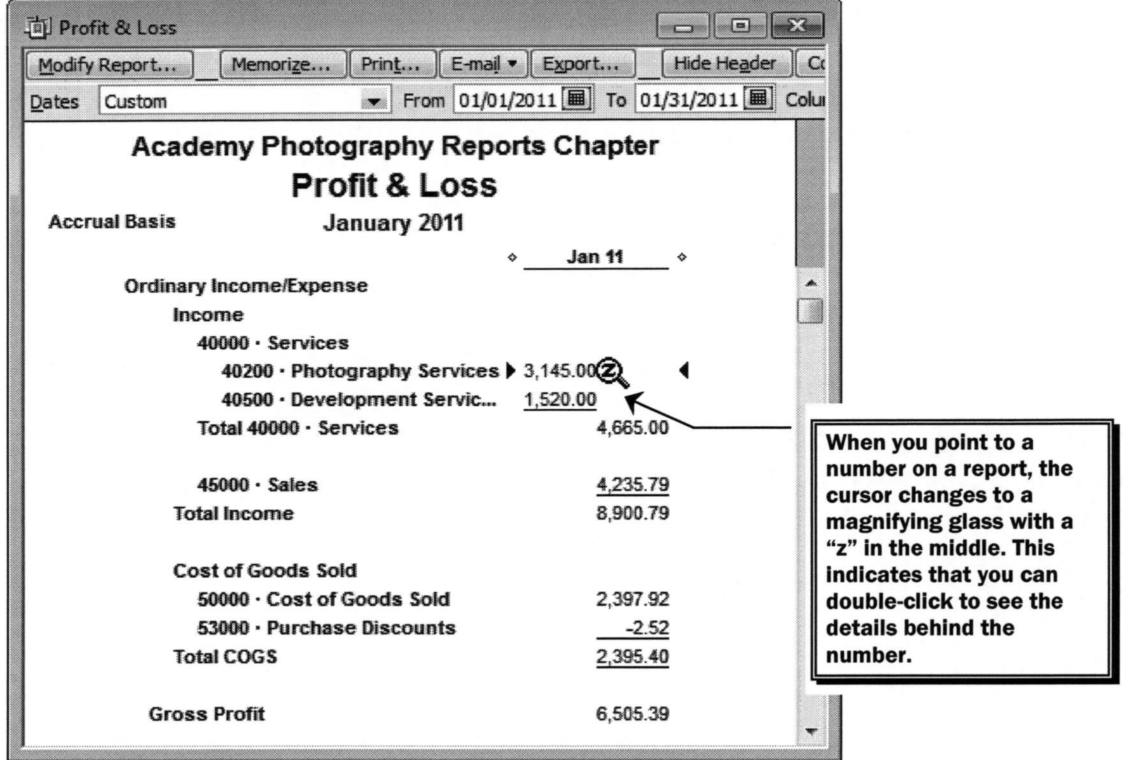

Figure 6-66 QuickZoom allows you to see the details behind a number

As your cursor moves over numbers on the report, it will turn into a magnifying glass with a "z" in the middle. The magnifying icon indicates that you can double-click to see the details behind the number on the report.

After you double-click the number, **QuickZoom** displays a **Transaction Detail By Account** report (see Figure 6-67) that shows the details of each transaction in the account that you zoomed in on.

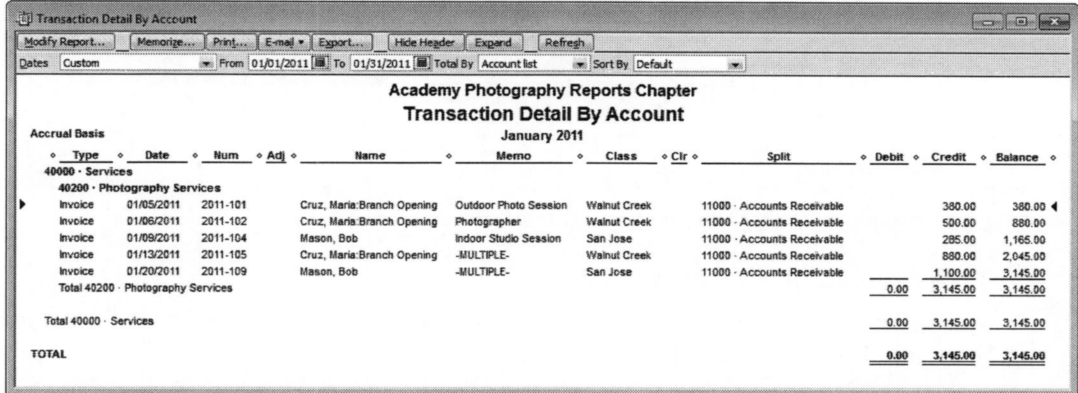

Academy Photography Reports Chapter
Transaction Detail By Account
Accrual Basis
January 2011

Type	Date	Num	Adj	Name	Memo	Class	Clr	Split	Debit	Credit	Balance
40000 · Services											
40200 · Photography Services											
Invoice	01/05/2011	2011-101		Cruz, Maria:Branch Opening	Outdoor Photo Session	Walnut Creek		11000 · Accounts Receivable		380.00	380.00
Invoice	01/06/2011	2011-102		Cruz, Maria:Branch Opening	Photographer	Walnut Creek		11000 · Accounts Receivable		500.00	880.00
Invoice	01/09/2011	2011-104		Mason, Bob	Indoor Studio Session	San Jose		11000 · Accounts Receivable		285.00	1,165.00
Invoice	01/13/2011	2011-105		Cruz, Maria:Branch Opening	-MULTIPLE-	Walnut Creek		11000 · Accounts Receivable		880.00	2,045.00
Invoice	01/20/2011	2011-109		Mason, Bob	-MULTIPLE-	San Jose		11000 · Accounts Receivable		1,100.00	3,145.00
Total 40200 · Photography Services									0.00	3,145.00	3,145.00
Total 40000 · Services									0.00	3,145.00	3,145.00
TOTAL									0.00	3,145.00	3,145.00

Figure 6-67 Transaction Detail by Account report

The columns in this report show the transaction Type, Date, Num (Number), Name, Memo, Class, Clr (Cleared), Split, Amount, and Balance. You can modify the report to add or delete columns as needed. See *Building Custom Reports* page 246 for details on how to modify reports.

The **Clr** column on these reports shows a checkmark (√) when the transaction has a cleared status. If it is a transaction for a bank account, a checkmark means that the transaction has cleared the bank.

Exporting Reports to Spreadsheets

When you need to modify reports in ways that QuickBooks does not allow (e.g., changing the name of a column heading), you will need to export the report to a spreadsheet program.

> Note:
> *Intuit Statement Writer* is a utility for creating reports in Excel using live QuickBooks data. It is available for an additional cost with most editions and in included in the Accountant editions of QuickBooks Premier and QuickBooks Enterprise Solutions.

Exporting a Report to Microsoft Excel

COMPUTER PRACTICE

Step 1. From the *Report Center*, select **Sales** and then double click the **Sales by Customer Detail** report in the *Sales by Customer* section to display the report.

Step 2. Enter ***01/01/2011*** in the *From* field and enter ***01/31/2011*** *in the To* field. Press **Tab** twice (see Figure 6-68).

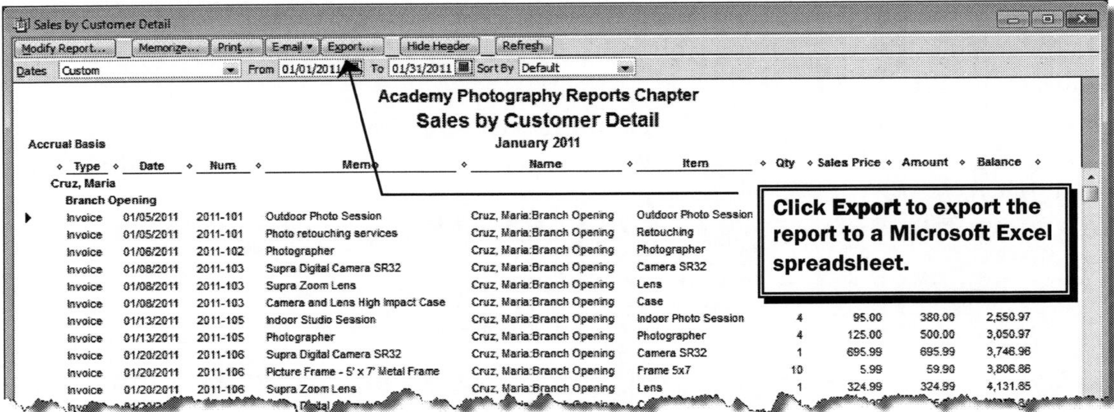

Figure 6-68 Click Export to export the report to a Microsoft Excel spreadsheet

Step 3. Click **Export** at the top of the report.

Step 4. In the Basic tab of the Excel Report window, select ***a new Excel workbook*** to export your report to a new Excel worksheet (see Figure 6-69).

> **Note:**
> The Advanced tab of the Export Report window has many useful features for working with your QuickBooks data in Excel, including Auto Outline, which allows you to collapse and expand detail.

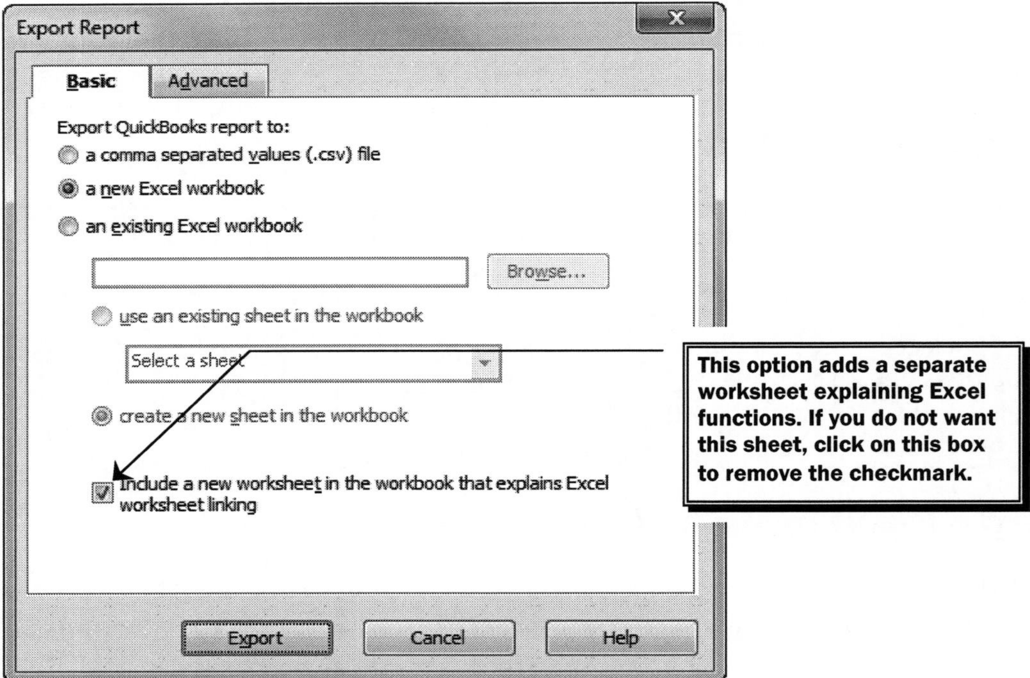

Figure 6-69 Export Report window

Step 5. Click **Export** in the *Export Report* window. QuickBooks will export your report directly to an Excel spreadsheet (see Figure 6-70).

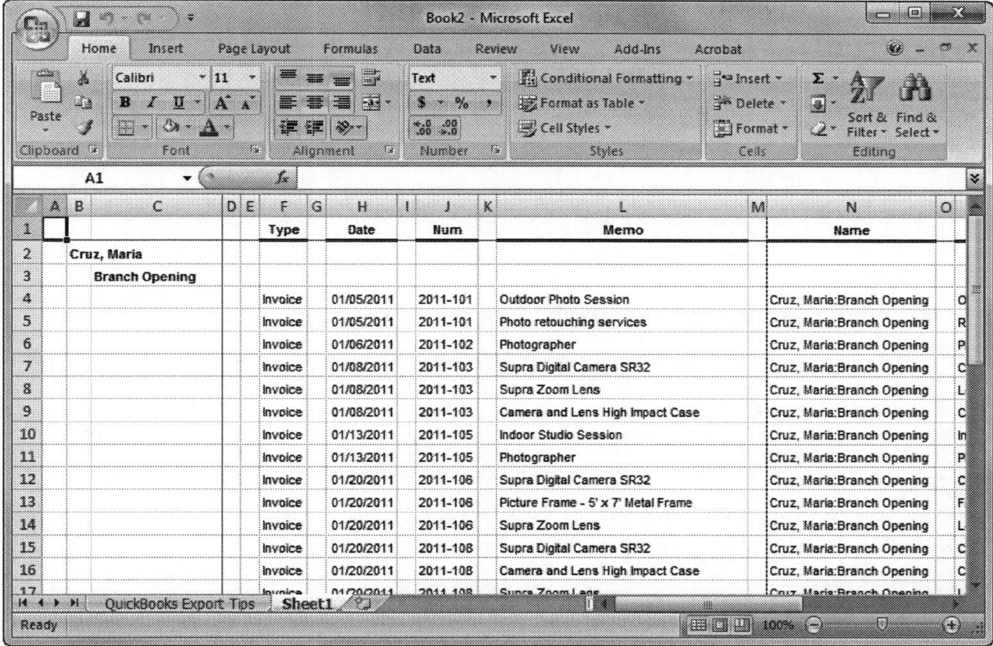

Figure 6-70 The report is now in an Excel spreadsheet.

Chapter Summary and Review

Summary of Key Points

In this chapter, you learned about QuickBooks reports. There are literally thousands of reports that you can generate from QuickBooks by modifying the standard reports. You should now be familiar with how to use QuickBooks to do all of the following:

- Describe several types of QuickBooks reports (page 223).
- Set QuickBooks preferences for cash or accrual basis reports (page 224).
- Create several different accounting reports (page 227).
- Create several different business management reports (page 238).
- Create graphs (page 244).
- Customize the look of reports and filter the data on reports (page 246).
- Memorize and group reports (page 253).
- Process and print multiple reports in batches (page 255).
- Print reports (page 257).
- Use the Find command to find transactions (page 259).
- Use QuickZoom to see the "numbers behind the numbers" on reports (page 266).
- Export reports to spreadsheets for further analysis (page 267).

Comprehension Questions

Answers to these review questions are available with the supplemental material. See page xiii for details.

1. Explain how the *QuickZoom* feature helps you see more detail about a report.
2. Name an example of how the *Check Detail* report is valuable.
3. How can you hide the subaccounts on the *Profit & Loss* report?
4. Explain how using *Filters* helps you get the reports you want.
5. Explain how memorized reports help you save time.

Multiple Choice

Choose the best answer(s) for each of the following:

1. What are the two major types of reports in QuickBooks?
   a) Register and List.
   b) Monthly and Annual.
   c) Accounting and Business Management.
   d) Balance Sheet and Profit & Loss.
2. Use the **Modify Report** button on any report to:
   a) Add or delete columns or to change the accounting basis of the report.
   b) Change the width of columns on the report.
   c) Print the report on blank paper.
   d) Memorize the report for future use.
3. You cannot create a **QuickReport** for:
   a) Customers.
   b) Vendors.
   c) Items.
   d) Incorrectly posted entries.
4. To create a report which lists each of your vendors along with their address and telephone information:
   a) Display the *Vendor Contact List.*
   b) Open the *Find* window and do a search for Vendors and the corresponding Address and Phone Numbers.
   c) Customize the Vendor database.
   d) You must create a *Modified Report* to see this information.
5. In order to analyze the profitability of your company, you should:
   a) Only analyze if the company is profitable.
   b) Create a **Profit & Loss** report.
   c) Review all detailed transaction reports.
   d) Review the financial exceptions report.

6. Which statement is false? You may analyze your income and expenses for a given period:
   a) By class.
   b) By job.
   c) By vendor.
   d) For the whole business.
7. Which report shows monies owed to your company by customer?
   a) The **Balance Sheet** report.
   b) The **Accounts Receivable Collections** report.
   c) The **Accounts Payable Aging** report.
   d) The **Daily Charges** report.
8. In order to modify the header and footer of your report:
   a) Click the **Modify Report** button and then click the **Filters** tab.
   b) Click the **Titles** button and then click the **Customization** tab.
   c) Click the **Header/Footer** button.
   d) Click the **Modify Report** button and then click the **Header/Footer** tab.
9. Report Groups allow you to:
   a) Rearrange the report center.
   b) Organize the memorized report list into groups of related reports.
   c) Create groups of filters for your reports.
   d) Group reports by date.
10. The **Profit & Loss** report shows which of the following:
    a) Assets, Liabilities, and Equity accounts.
    b) Checks written for the period.
    c) Income, Cost of Goods Sold, Expenses, Other Income, and Other Expenses.
    d) A/R increases for the period.
11. If the **Profit & Loss by Class** report has an *Unclassified* column:
    a) There is an error in the filters on the report.
    b) You must refresh the report.
    c) You should eliminate the column using the **Modify Report** window.
    d) Some of the transactions for the period were not assigned to a class.
12. The report that shows total sales in each sales tax district (item) and shows the taxable sales separately from the nontaxable sales is called:
    a) The **Sales Tax Liability** report.
    b) **Tax by County** report.
    c) **Balance Sheet** report.
    d) **Sales by Tax Location** report.
13. Which is <u>not</u> a feature of the **Filters** tab on the *Modify Report* window?
    a) Filters allow you to narrow the contents of reports so that you can analyze specific areas of your business.
    b) Filters allow you to change how reports total and subtotal.
    c) Filters allow you to choose specific accounts, dates, names, or items to include on a report.
    d) Filters allow you to modify the date range on most reports.

14. To modify which columns are displayed on a report, click **Modify Report** and then check the names of columns to be displayed on the:
    a) Header/Footer tab.
    b) Display tab.
    c) Filters tab.
    d) Fonts & Numbers tab.
15. The **Fit report to 1 pages wide** feature does the following:
    a) Fits the report into a single page for each column.
    b) Eliminates columns from the report until it fits on a single page.
    c) Reduces the font size of the report so the width of all columns does not exceed 8½" (in portrait mode) or 11" (in landscape mode).
    d) Increases the margins on reports to make sure everything fits on one page.

Completion Statements

1. The ________ ________ ________ is a listing of your vendors along with each vendor's address and telephone information.
2. To modify the contents of a report, you can ________ it to include certain accounts, names, columns, or transaction types.
3. QuickBooks provides a convenient feature called ________, which allows you to see the detail behind numbers on reports.
4. If you're looking for a transaction and you don't know which register to look in, or if you want to find more than just a single transaction, you can use the _______ command.
5. The ________ ________ is a report that shows your financial position, as defined by the balances in each of your asset, liabilities, and equity accounts on a given date.

Reports-Problem 1

APPLYING YOUR KNOWLEDGE

Restore the Reports-10Problem1.QBM file and store it on your hard disk according to your instructor's directions.

1. Print the reports listed below for Academy Photography.
    a) Customer Phone List.
    b) Check Detail Report for January and February of 2011 with split detail
    c) Customer QuickReport for Maria Cruz's Branch Opening for January and February 2011.
    d) Profit & Loss Report (standard) for January through February 2011.
    e) Profit & Loss Report by Job for January through February 2011.
    f) Trial Balance Report for 01/31/2011.
    g) Balance Sheet Standard Report for January 31, 2011.

2. Create a modified report showing the sales of all services to customers who live in Morgan Hill. Show sales from January through February 2011 only. Modify the report so that it totals by Customer and includes the title and columns displayed in Figure 6-71.

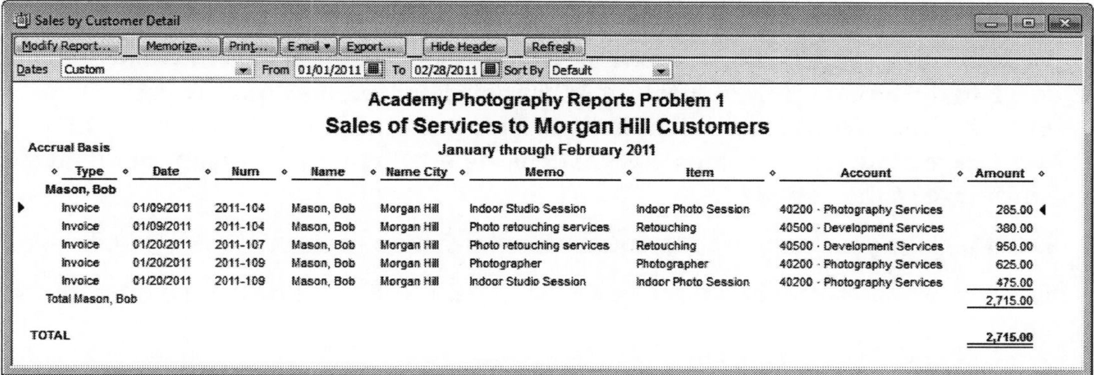
Sales by Customer Detail

Modify Report... Memorize... Print... E-mail Export... Hide Header Refresh

Dates Custom From 01/01/2011 To 02/28/2011 Sort By Default

Academy Photography Reports Problem 1

Sales of Services to Morgan Hill Customers

Accrual Basis

January through February 2011

Type	Date	Num	Name	Name City	Memo	Item	Account	Amount
Mason, Bob								
Invoice	01/09/2011	2011-104	Mason, Bob	Morgan Hill	Indoor Studio Session	Indoor Photo Session	40200 · Photography Services	285.00
Invoice	01/09/2011	2011-104	Mason, Bob	Morgan Hill	Photo retouching services	Retouching	40500 · Development Services	380.00
Invoice	01/20/2011	2011-107	Mason, Bob	Morgan Hill	Photo retouching services	Retouching	40500 · Development Services	950.00
Invoice	01/20/2011	2011-109	Mason, Bob	Morgan Hill	Photographer	Photographer	40200 · Photography Services	625.00
Invoice	01/20/2011	2011-109	Mason, Bob	Morgan Hill	Indoor Studio Session	Indoor Photo Session	40200 · Photography Services	475.00
Total Mason, Bob								2,715.00
TOTAL								2,715.00

Figure 6-71 *Customize your report to look like this.*

Important:
When you complete #2, do not close the report. You will use the modified report in the next step.

3. Print the report you created in Step 2 and then memorize it in the Customers report group. Name the memorized report "Sales of Services to Morgan Hill Customers."

4. Create and print a graph of your Income and Expenses (by Account) for January and February 2011.

Workplace Applications

Discussion Questions

These questions are designed to stimulate discussion about how you can apply QuickBooks to your own organization. They may help you think through some of the issues you'll encounter when using QuickBooks in your company.

1. Reports generally fall into two categories — accounting and business management. You use accounting reports to determine the financial position and profitability of the company. You use business management reports to manage customers, vendors, and employees. You also use business management reports to help set prices, prepare forecasts, and create budgets. What accounting reports would help your company to determine its financial position and profitability? What business management reports would help you better manage your company?

2. Select some accounting reports and identify individuals or entities that are likely to use them.

3. Select some business management reports and identify individuals or entities that are likely to use them. How do you use business management reports in the day-by-day operations of the company? How do you use management reports to manage your relationships with your customers and vendors?

4. How does your company set prices on the products and services it offers? What information would you need to set prices for your products and services? Can you get this information from QuickBooks? If so, what reports would you use?

5. Describe how your organization uses or could use the **A/R Collections** report. What area in your company receives the report? How frequently? What is the average number of days an invoice remains unpaid? What is the benefit if your company reduces that period by one day? One week? What terms are worth offering to make that happen?
6. Describe how your company uses the **A/P Aging** report. What area in your company receives the report? How frequently? What policies affect how quickly your organization pays its bills? What kinds of terms are offered to your company to encourage more rapid payment? What determines whether your organization takes advantage of the terms?
7. Describe how your organization could use information from the **Profit & Loss** report.
8. Describe whether your organization would benefit from the **Profit & Loss by Job** report.
9. How can an accountant use the *Voided/Deleted* Reports to monitor authorized QuickBooks users behavior?

Case Study

Software Support, Incorporated

Software Support, Inc is a company that provides computer consulting services for clients throughout the Chicago metropolitan area. The company provides computer setup, training, and troubleshooting services for small business clients.

They use classes to track their income and expenses separately for each area of the business. The classes are Training, Consulting, and Troubleshooting.

The owners of the company have contracted you to help them analyze their business and to create reports from their QuickBooks file to help them.

1. Which reports would you use to present the financial position of the company at the end of last month?
2. Which report would you use to show all income and expenses separately for each class?
3. Which report would you use to show a list of open invoices, sorted by customer and totaled at the bottom?

Chapter 7 Company File Setup and Maintenance

Objectives

After completing this chapter, you should be able to:

- Perform a Complete Company File Setup Using the 12-step Process (page 275).
- Choose a Start Date (page 275).
- Use the EasyStep Interview to set up your Company File (page 276).
- Setup Accounts in the Chart of Accounts List (page 287).
- Gather Your Information for Setting up Opening Balances (page 298).
- Enter Opening Balances (page 301).
- Enter Year-to-Date Income and Expenses (page 308).
- Adjust the Opening Balance for Sales Tax Payable (page 309).
- Adjust Inventory for Physical Quantities on Hand (page 310).
- Verify your Opening Balances (page 312).
- Close Opening Balance Equity into Retained Earnings (page 313).
- Back up the File and Setting the Closing Date (page 315).
- Set Up Users and Passwords (page 315).

In this chapter, you will learn how to create a new QuickBooks data file, set up the Chart of Accounts, and enter opening balances. You will also learn how to set up user access rights and passwords for each person who will use QuickBooks.

Complete Company File Setup: A 12-Step Process

In this section, you will learn about the 12-Step setup process for completing your QuickBooks file setup.

Choosing a Start Date – Step 1

Before you create your company file, choose a start date for your company file. Your start date is the day before you start using QuickBooks to track your daily transactions. You will need complete information for your opening balances as of this start date.

The 12-Step Setup Checklist

1. Choose a QuickBooks **start date.** See page 275.
2. Create a new QuickBooks **company file** through the EasyStep Interview. See page 276.
3. Edit your **Chart of Accounts** and set up other company lists. See page 287.
4. Enter opening balances for **Balance Sheet** accounts (except Accounts Receivable, Accounts Payable, Inventory, Sales Tax Payable, and Retained Earnings). See page 298.
5. Enter outstanding transactions including **Checks, Deposits**, open **Invoices**, and unpaid **Bills** as of the start date. See page 305.
6. If you are setting up in mid-year, enter your **year-to-date income** and **expenses.** See page 308.
7. Adjust **Sales Tax Payable**. See page 309.
8. Adjust **Inventory** to match your physical counts and set up **Fixed Assets**. See page 311.
9. Set up **payroll lists** and **year-to-date** (YTD) **payroll** information. See page 312.
10. Verify that your **Trial Balance** report matches your accountant's Trial Balance on your **start date**. See page 312.
11. Close the **Opening Bal Equity** account into Retained Earnings. See page 313.
12. Set the **Closing Date** and the **Closing Date Password** to lock the file as of your start date, set up **Users** and **Passwords**, and backup your company file. See page 315.

Table 7-1 The 12-Step Setup Checklist

Assuming you file taxes on a calendar-year basis, the best start date for most companies is December 31st. If you file taxes on a fiscal year, choose the last day of your fiscal year as your start date.

Do not use January 1 (or the first day of your fiscal year) for your start date, because doing so would cause the opening balances to affect your first year's Profit & Loss report. This could affect your taxes and distort the picture of the company's financial history.

Keep in mind that you will need to enter all of the transactions (Checks, Invoices, Deposits, etc.) between your start date and the day you perform the QuickBooks setup. Because of this, your start date has a big impact on how much work you will do during setup. If you do not want to go back to the end of last year, choose a more recent date, such as the end of last quarter or the end of last month.

> **Note:**
> In order for your records to be complete and accurate, you should enter every transaction (Check, Invoice, Deposit, etc.) that your company performed between the start date and the day you perform the QuickBooks setup. For example, if you are setting up the file on January 5 with a start date of December 31, you will need to enter all transactions that the company performed on January 1 through January 5 for your records to be complete and accurate.

If you are starting a new business, your start date is the day you formed the company.

The EasyStep Interview – Step 2

The *EasyStep Interview* walks you through the basic tasks of setting up the file. It helps you create a data file, sets up income and expense accounts from a suggested list based on industry type and assists with configuring preferences to customize QuickBooks for your business. The

EasyStep Interview is designed to make the process of creating a company file as simple as possible.

Launching the EasyStep Interview

COMPUTER PRACTICE

Step 1. Select the **File** menu and then select **New Company**.

Step 2. The *EasyStep Interview* window appears (see Figure 7-1). Click the **Start Interview** button.

> Note:
> The *Getting Started* window also provides the option to skip the EasyStep Interview. Only users who are familiar with QuickBooks Preferences should consider skipping the *EasyStep Interview* (see page 331). If you chose to skip the *EasyStep Interview*, QuickBooks will still display the windows shown in Step 1 through Step 10 of this exercise.

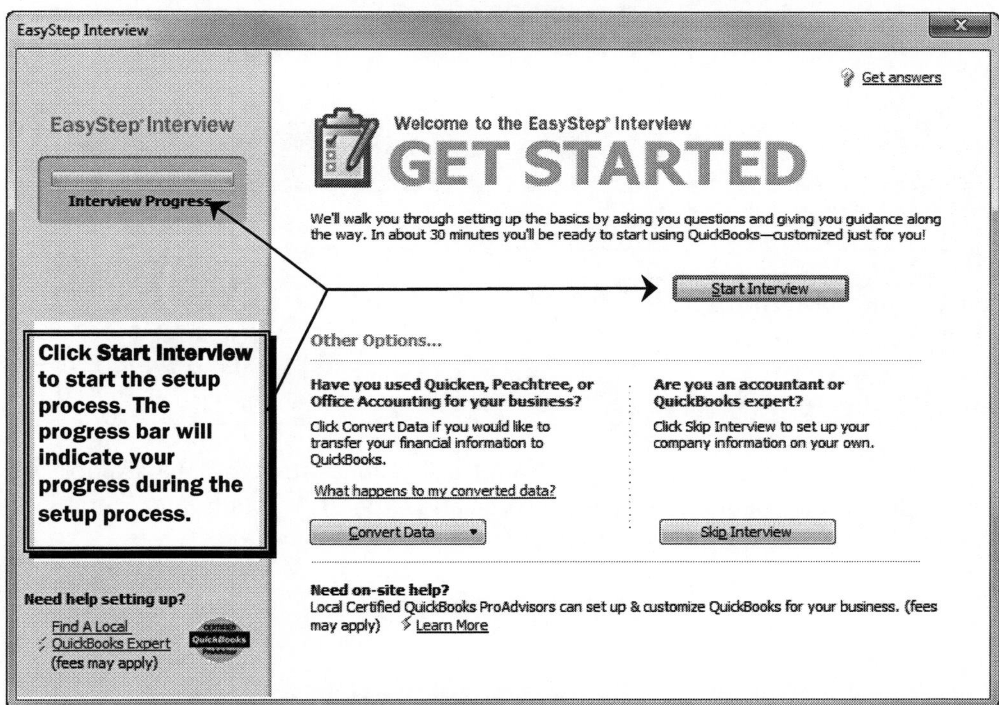

Figure 7-1 The opening window of the EasyStep Interview

> Tip:
> *QuickBooks ProAdvisors* are bookkeepers, accountants, software consultants, and CPAs who offer QuickBooks-related consulting services. In addition, *QuickBooks Certified ProAdvisors* are those *ProAdvisors* who have completed a comprehensive training and testing program. For more information on QuickBooks *ProAdvisors* and *Certified ProAdvisors*, refer to QuickBooks Onscreen Help. The Sleeter Group also certifies professionals who help clients with QuickBooks. To find a consultant near you, go to www.sleeter.com.

Step 3. Enter the information in the Company information screen as shown in Figure 7-2. Click **Next** when done

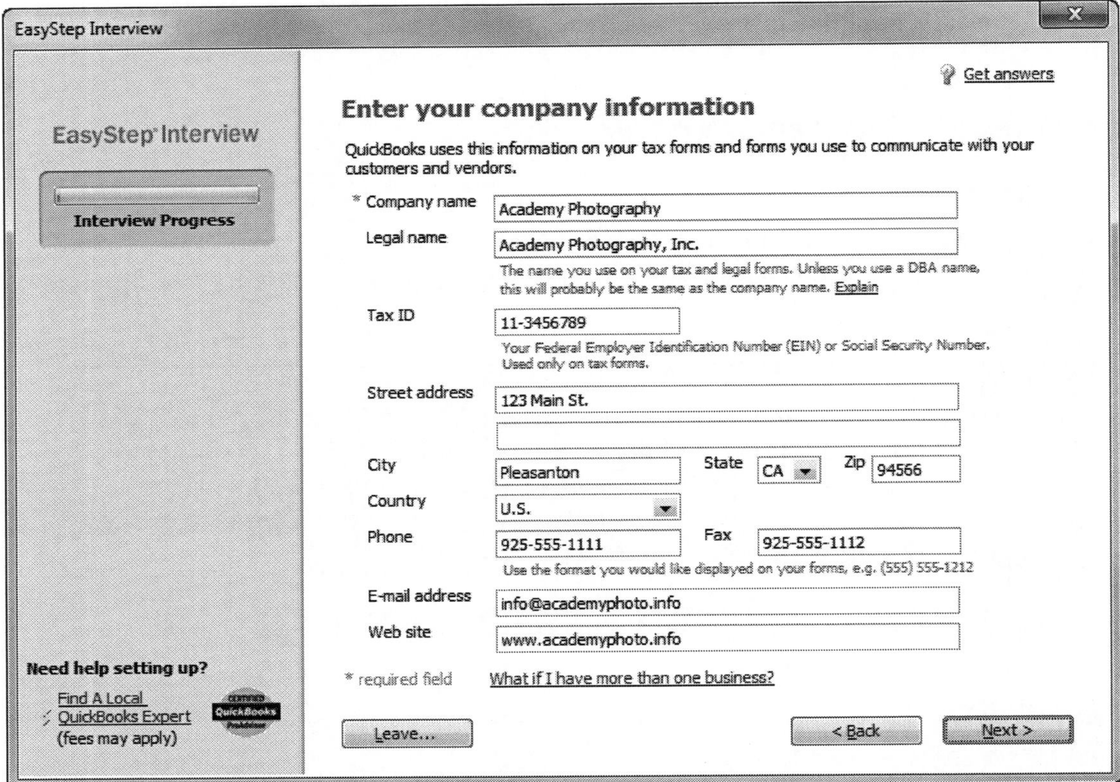

Figure 7-2 Company Information in EasyStep Interview

> **Note:**
> As you answer questions in the *EasyStep Interview*, QuickBooks creates your file, lists, and preferences. To proceed to the next step in the process click **Next**. To go back to a previous window in the interview, click **Back**. To exit the Interview and retain all changes, click **Leave....**

Step 4. Select **Art, Writing or Photography** from the list of industry types. QuickBooks uses the industry information to suggest Income and Expense accounts later in the *EasyStep Interview*. Press **Next** when finished.

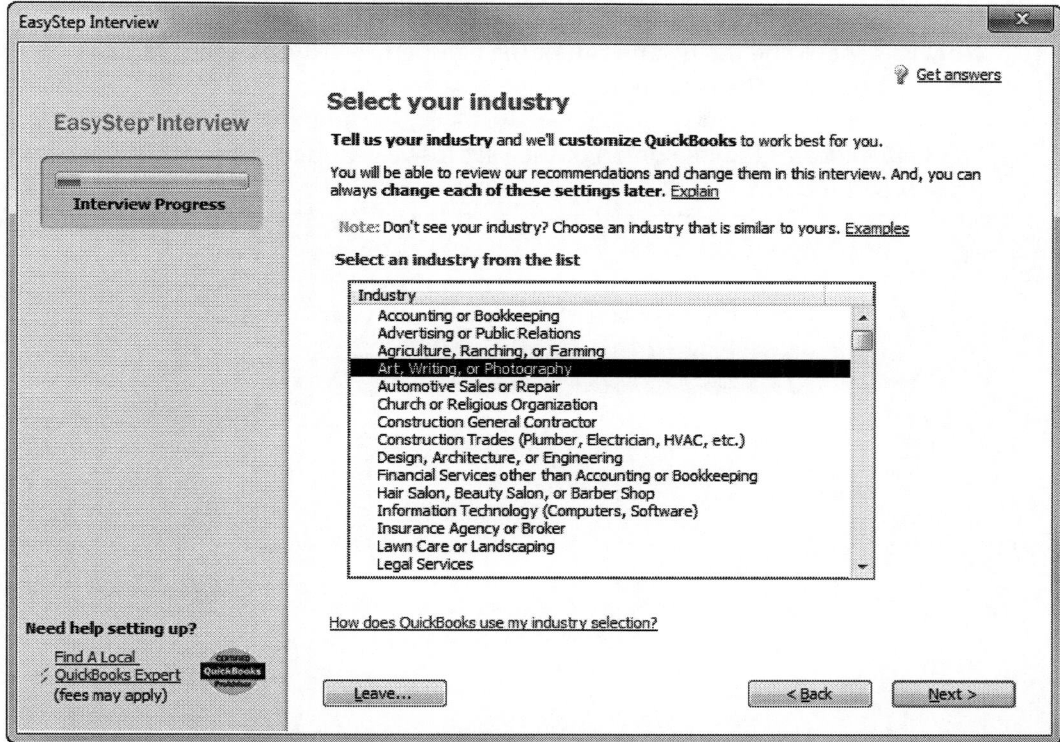

Figure 7-3 Select your industry in EasyStep Interview

Step 5. The *How is your company organized?* screen appears. Select the **S Corporation** radio button and press **Next.**

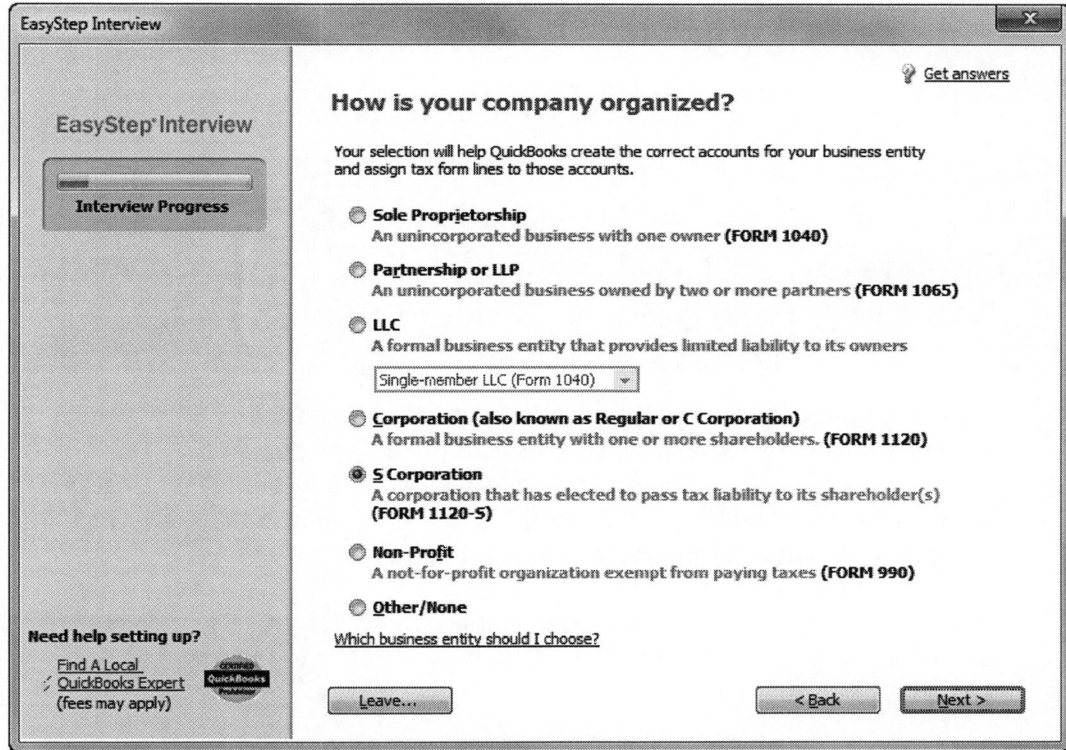

Figure 7-4 How your company is organized window in the EasyStep Interview

Step 6. The next window prompts the user to select the first month of the company's fiscal year. This should be the first month of the company's tax year. Leave **January** selected and press the **Next** button.

This field indicates the beginning of the year for year-to-date reports, such as the *Profit & Loss* report.

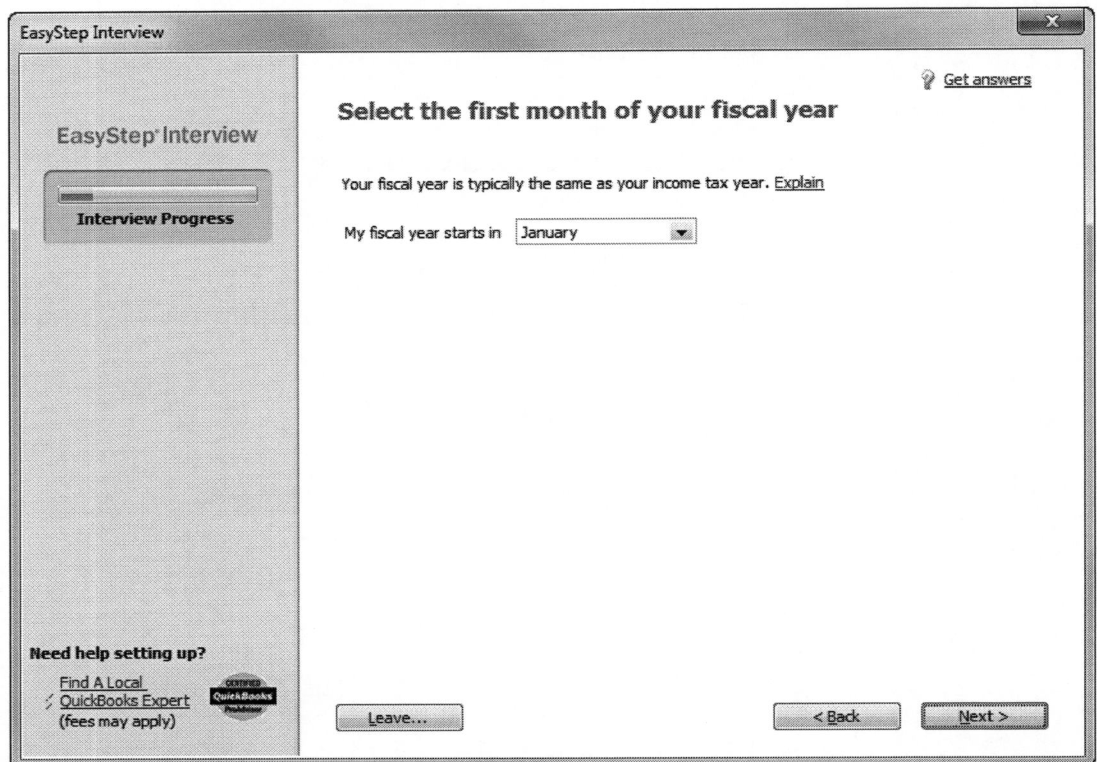

Figure 7-5 Select the first month of your fiscal year window in the EasyStep Interview

> **Note for new businesses:**
> The first month of your fiscal or income tax year is **NOT** necessarily the month you started your business. The first month in your fiscal year specifies the default date range for accounting reports such as the Profit & Loss and Balance Sheet. The first month in your tax year specifies the default date range for **Income Tax Summary** and **Detail** reports.

Step 7. The Administrator password setup screen will appear (see Figure 7-6). Although it's optional, creating an Administrator password is highly recommended. The Administrator is the only person who has access to all functions within a data file. Establishing an Administrator password restricts other users so that they cannot execute tasks that are normally reserved for the Administrator.

However, since you are just creating a sample data file for this lesson, do not create an Administrator password this time. Click **Next** to move to the next step.

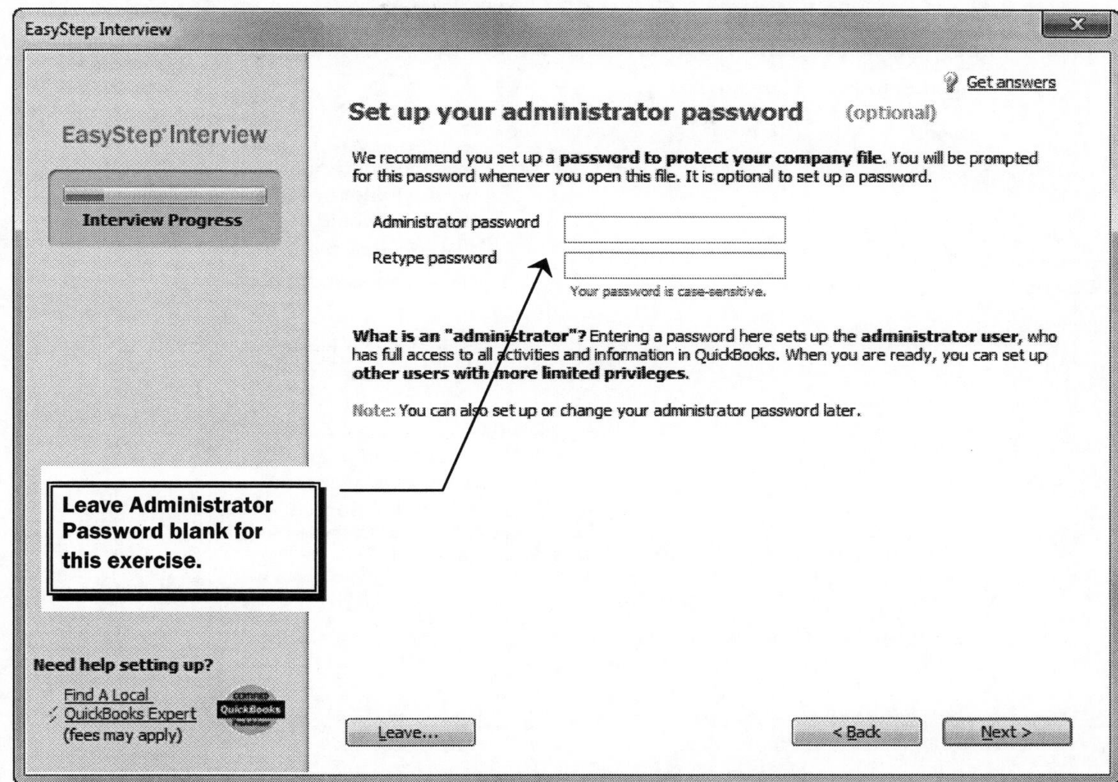

Figure 7-6 The Administrator Password Screen in the EasyStep Interview

> **Tip:**
> If you need help during the interview, click the **Get answers** button at the top of the interview window.

Step 8. The next window in the *EasyStep Interview* window contains a message about creating your company file (see Figure 7-7). Click **Next** to create the file.

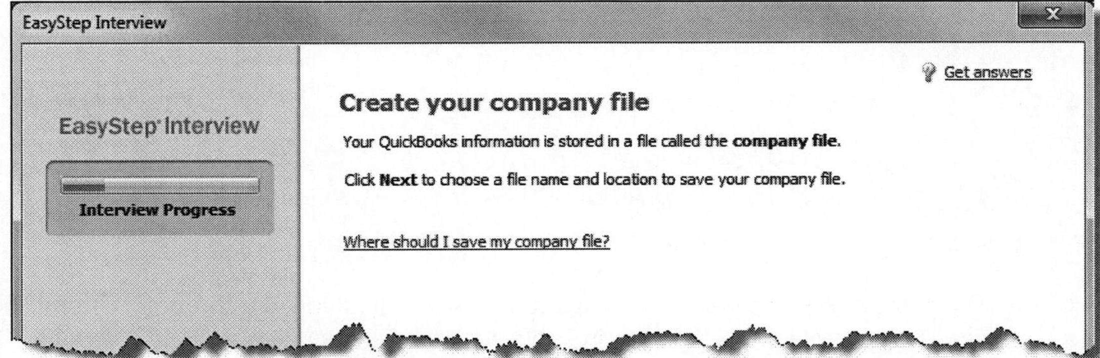

Figure 7-7 Create your company file screen

Step 9. The *Filename for New Company* window (see Figure 7-8) is where you specify the filename and location for your company file. QuickBooks enters your company name and adds .QBW to the end of your filename.

In the *Save in* field, select your student data folder. Use the default file name, Academy Photography.QBW.

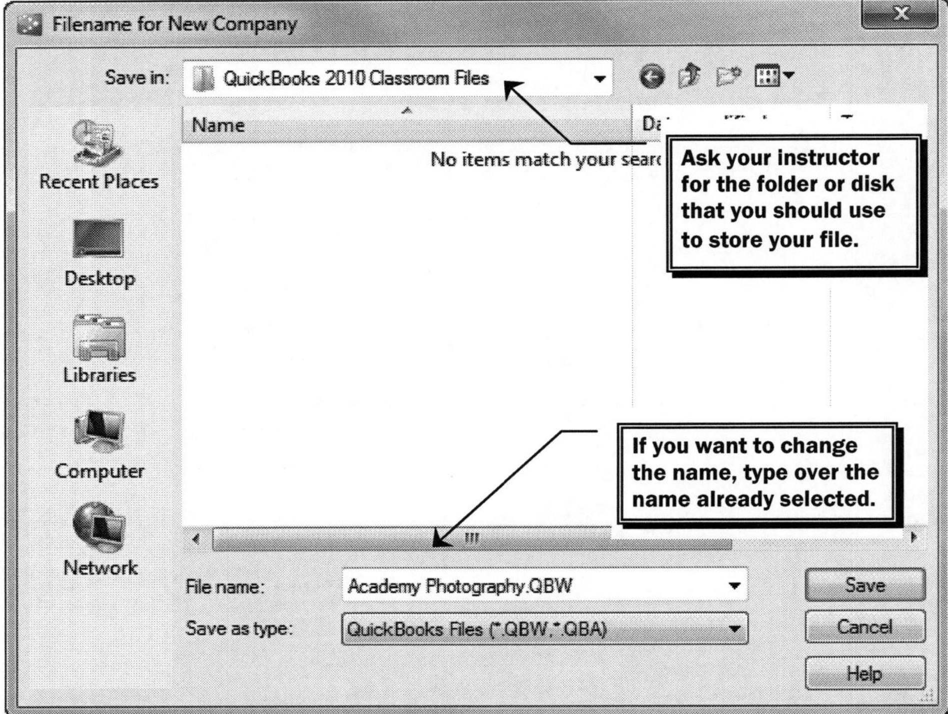

Figure 7-8 Filename for New Company window

Step 10. Click **Save** to create your company file.

Step 11. QuickBooks displays the *Customizing QuickBooks for your business* step. Click **Next** to begin the customizing process.

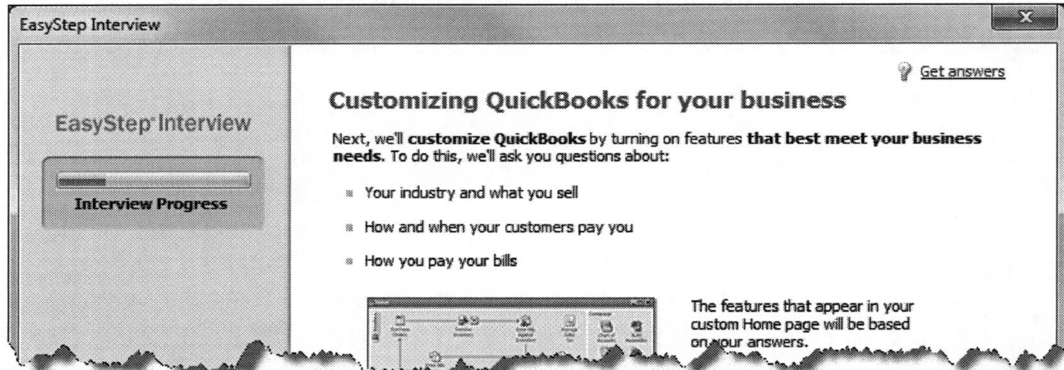

Figure 7-9 Customizing QuickBooks for your business screen

Step 12. The next several screens of the *EasyStep Interview* will guide you through customizing your company file. Use the data in Table 7-2 to answer initial questions about your business.

EasyStep Interview Data	
Question From EasyStep Interview	Response
What do you sell?	Both Services and Products
Do you sell products online?	I don't sell online, and I am not interested in doing so.

Table 7-2 Your Company's industry type

Step 13. The next set of questions relate to how QuickBooks sets up *Preferences* in your company file. Use Table 7-3 to complete these questions.

Company Preferences	
Do you charge sales tax?	Yes
Do you want to create estimates in QuickBooks?	Yes
Do you want to track sales orders before you invoice your customers?	Yes (Note: This option is not available in QuickBooks Pro.)
Do you want to use sales receipts in QuickBooks?	Yes
Do you want to use billing statements in QuickBooks?	Yes
Do you want to use progress invoicing?	Yes
Do you want to keep track of bills you owe?	Yes
Do you print checks?	I print checks.
Do you want to track inventory in QuickBooks?	Yes
Do you accept credit cards?	I accept credit cards and debit cards.
Do you want to track time in QuickBooks?	Yes
Do you have employees?	Yes (check the boxes for both W-2 employees and 1099 contractors)
Do you want to track multiple currencies in QuickBooks	No

Table 7-3 Data for the Preferences

Step 14. In the next section of the interview, QuickBooks creates your Chart of Accounts. Click **Next** on the *Using accounts in QuickBooks* screen (see Figure 7-10).

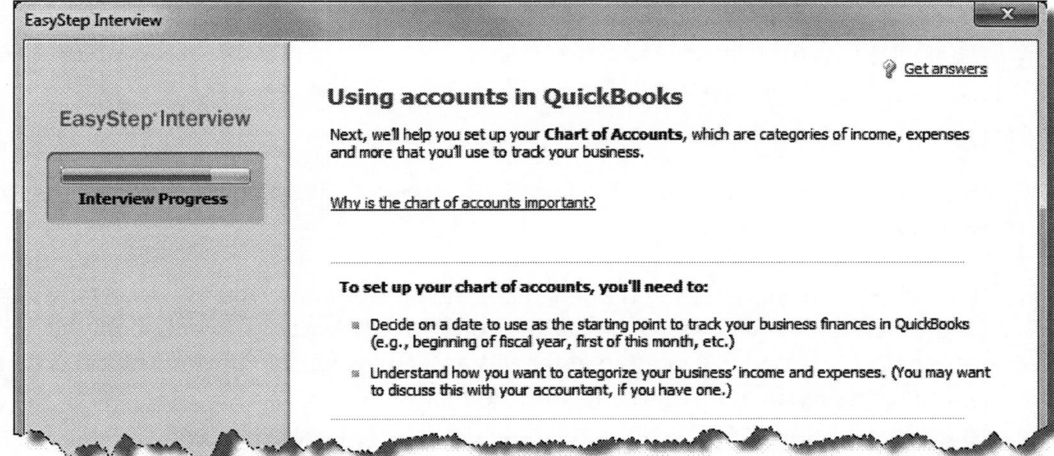

Figure 7-10 Using accounts in QuickBooks section

Step 15. In the *Select a date to start tracking your finances* screen, select **Use today's date or the first day of the quarter or month.** Then enter 12/31/10 in the date field. Click Next.

If you are setting up your file to begin at the start of the fiscal year, it is best to choose the last day of the previous fiscal year as the start date. (see *Choosing a Start Date – Step 1* on page 275).

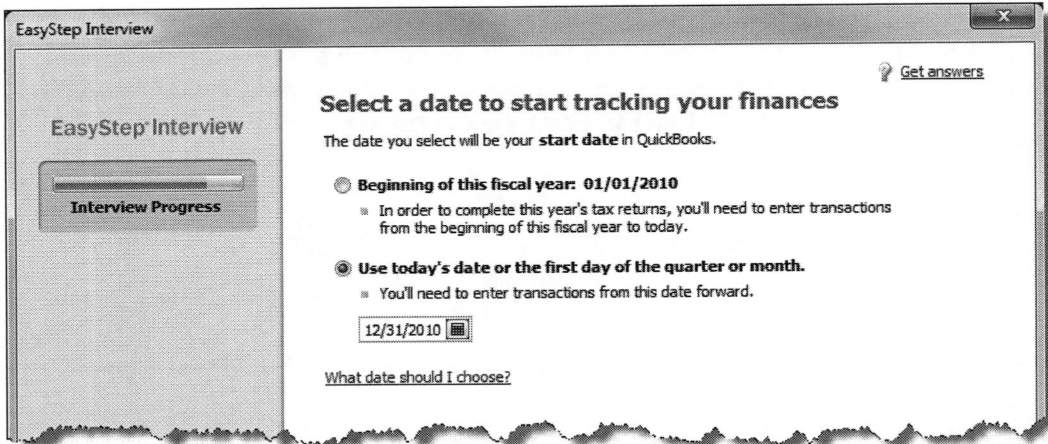

Figure 7-11 Select a date to start tracking your finances window in EasyStep Interview

Step 16. The *Add your bank account* screen prompts you to enter existing bank accounts. If you choose not to add bank accounts during the *EasyStep Interview,* you will be able to create them after the Interview is complete. Select the *Yes.* and press **Next**.

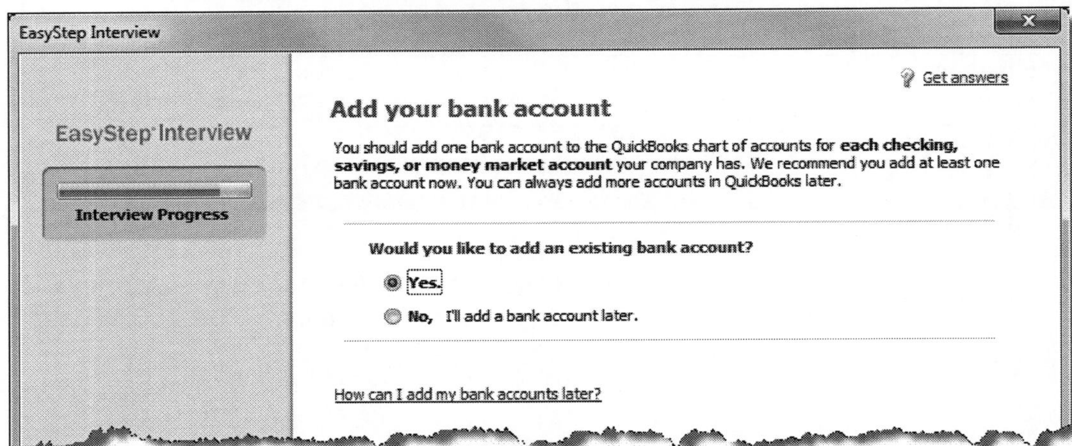

Figure 7-12 Add your bank account window in EasyStep Interview

Step 17. Enter the information in Figure 7-13 in the *Enter your bank account information* window and Press **Next**.

Even when a bank account was opened before the start date, you may want to select *On or After 12/31/10* in the *When did you open this bank account?* field. If you select Before 12/31/10 you will need to enter all transactions for the previous reconciliation period for the first reconciliation to work correctly.

Step 18. The *About the account balance* window is displayed. Press **Next**.

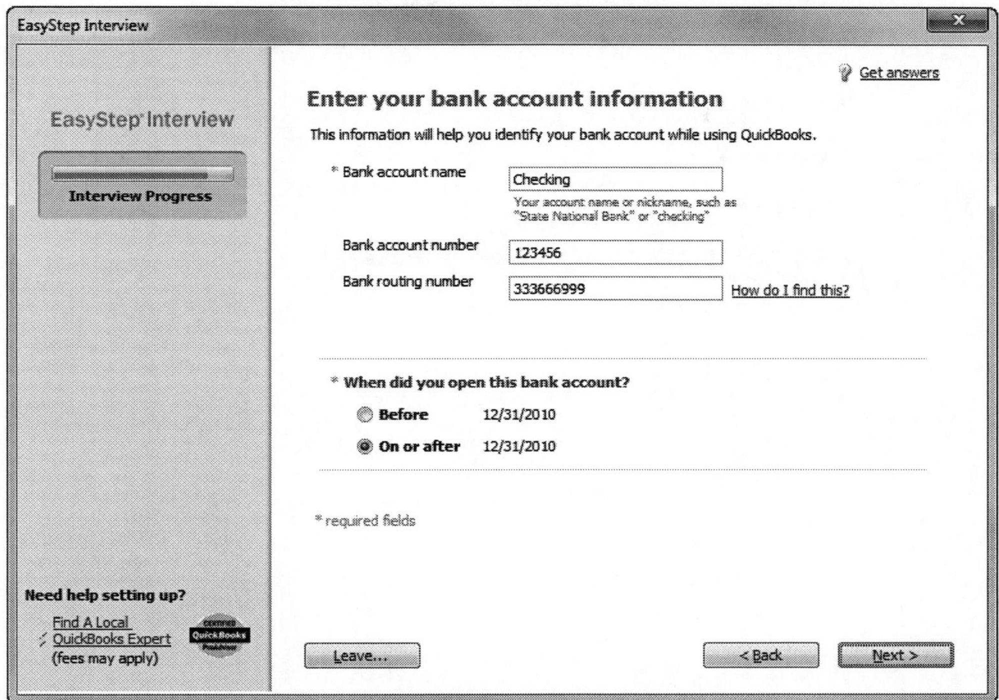

Figure 7-13 Enter your bank account information window in the EasyStep Interview

Step 19. The next screen displays a list of entered bank accounts. Click **No, I'm done or will add more later.** in the *Do you want to add another bank account?* field and Press **Next**.

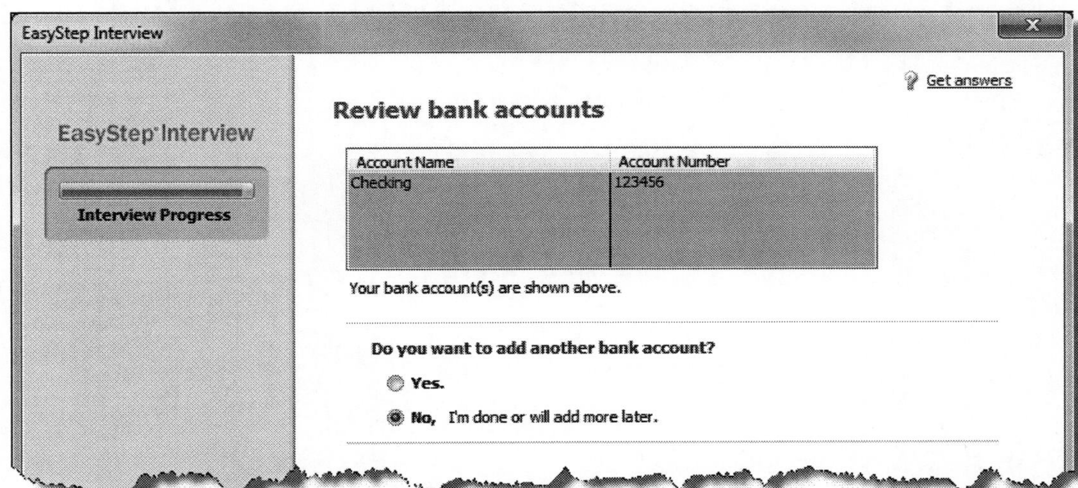

Figure 7-14 Review bank accounts window in the EasyStep Interview

Step 20. The following screen contains a list of suggested income and expense accounts based on the industry selected earlier in the *EasyStep Interview*. These accounts can be edited after completing the *EasyStep Interview*.

Leave the default accounts checked and click **Next**.

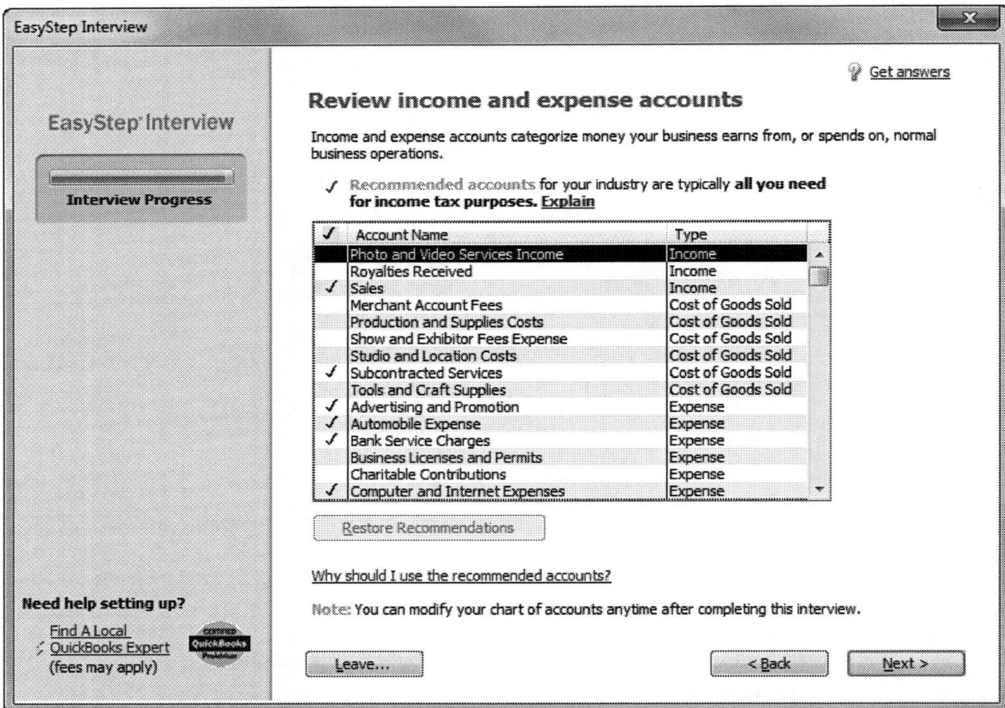

Figure 7-15 Review income and expense accounts window in the EasyStep Interview

Step 21. Click **Finish** to complete the interview.

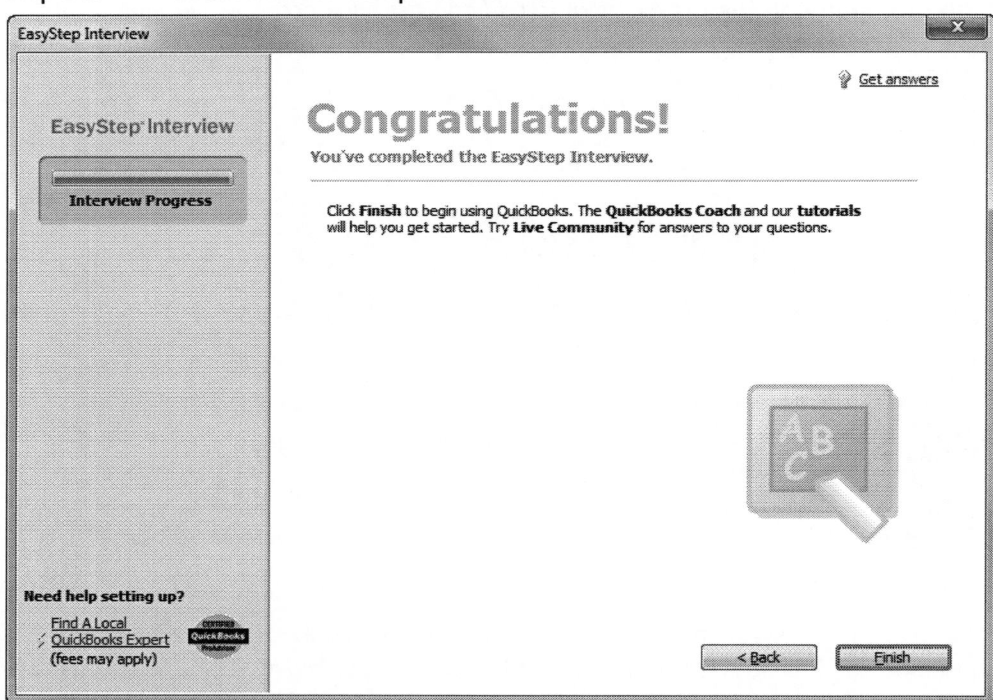

Figure 7-16 Final screen in EasyStep interview

Step 22. When you leave the *EasyStep Interview*, you will see the QuickBooks Coach window shown in Figure 7-17. For more information on the QuickBooks Coach, see page 30. For this exercise, close the QuickBooks Coach window. Once closed, the QuickBooks coach embeds into the Home Page.

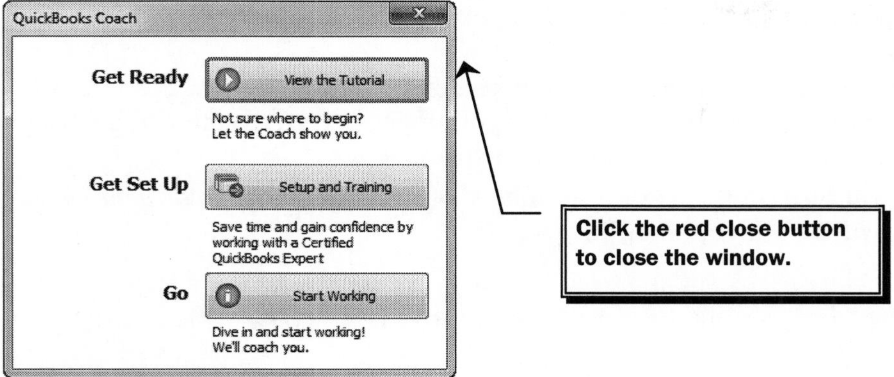

Figure 7-17 QuickBooks Coach window

Step 23. Depending on your system date, you may see a number of *Alert* dialog boxes displayed and the *Alert* message on your screen may be different than the one shown in Figure 7-18. Click **Mark as Done** on any *Alert* dialog box, if necessary.

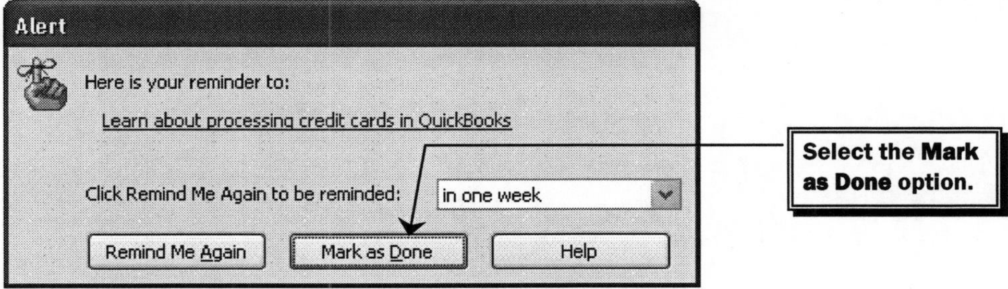

Figure 7-18 Alert Window

Step 24. QuickBooks has now created your company file with a default chart of accounts and has configured your company preferences.

Setting Up the Chart of Accounts and Other Lists – Step 3

Restore the **Setup-10.QBW** file and store it in your student data folder according to your instructor's directions.

Setting Up the Chart of Accounts

The Chart of Accounts is one of the most important lists in QuickBooks. It is a list of all the accounts in the General Ledger. If you are not sure how to design your Chart of Accounts, ask your accountant or QuickBooks ProAdvisor for help.

Account Types

There are five basic account **types** in accounting: assets, liabilities, equity, income, and expenses.

QuickBooks breaks these basic account types into subtypes. For example, QuickBooks uses five types of asset accounts: **Bank**, **Accounts Receivable**, **Other Current Asset**, **Fixed Asset**, and **Other Asset**. QuickBooks offers four types of liability accounts: **Accounts Payable**, **Credit Card**, **Loan**, **Other Current Liability**, and **Long Term Liability**. Income accounts can be divided into **Income** or **Other Income** types. Expenses can be classified as **Expense**, **Other Expense**, or **Cost of Goods Sold. Equity** doesn't have subtypes.

Activating Account Numbers

QuickBooks does not require account numbers. If you prefer, you can use just the account *name* to differentiate between accounts. However, if you prefer to have account numbers, you can activate them in the Accounting Company Preferences.

For this section, you will turn on the account numbers, but at the end of *Setting up the Chart of Accounts* section, you will turn them off again.

COMPUTER PRACTICE

Step 1. Select the **Edit** menu and then select **Preferences** (see Figure 7-19).

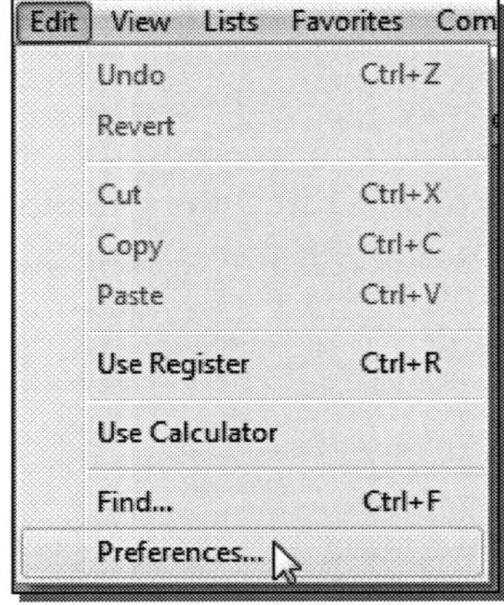

Figure 7-19 Choose Preferences from the Edit menu

Step 2. On the *Preferences* window, click on the **Accounting** option and select the **Company Preferences** tab.

Step 3. Check the **Use account numbers** box and click **OK**.

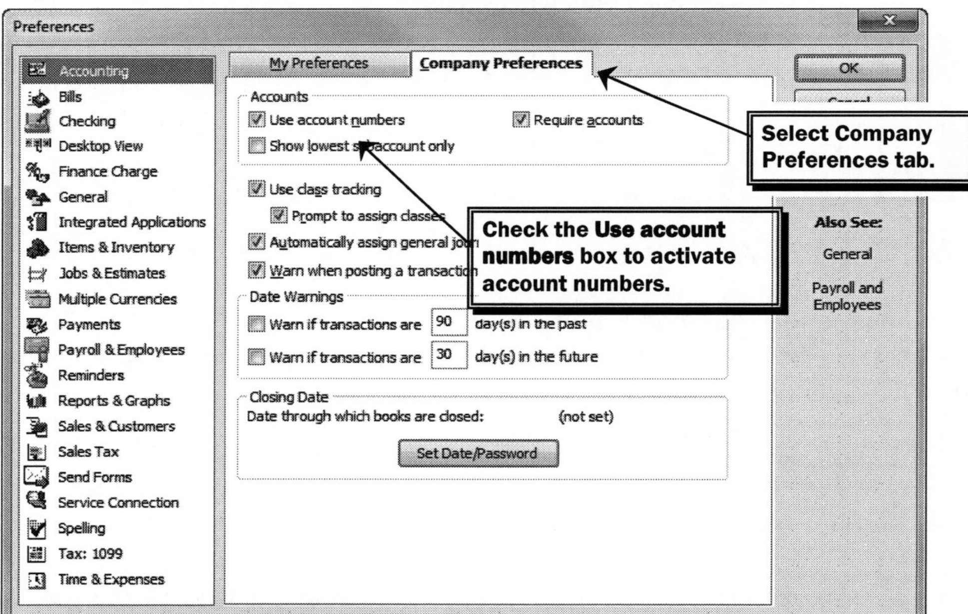

Figure 7-20 The Accounting—Company Preferences window

> **Did You Know?**
> All of the preferences in Figure 7-20 are used to configure the way QuickBooks operates. For more information on these and other preferences, see page 331.

Adding Accounts

COMPUTER PRACTICE

Step 1. Select the **Chart of Accounts** icon on the Company section of the *Home page.*

The *Chart of Accounts* list from your sample file is displayed which shows account numbers as well as account names (see Figure 7-21).

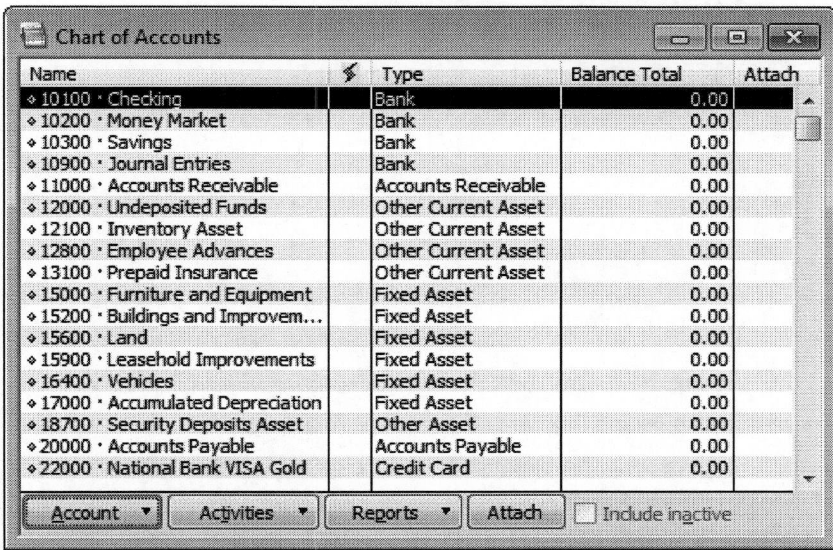

Figure 7-21 Chart of Accounts with account numbers

> **Another way:**
> To open the Chart of Accounts, select **Chart of Accounts** from the *List* menu or press **Ctrl+A.**

Step 2. Select the **Account** drop-list button at the bottom of the *Chart of Accounts* window and select **New** (see Figure 7-22). Another way to add a new account is to press **Ctrl+N**.

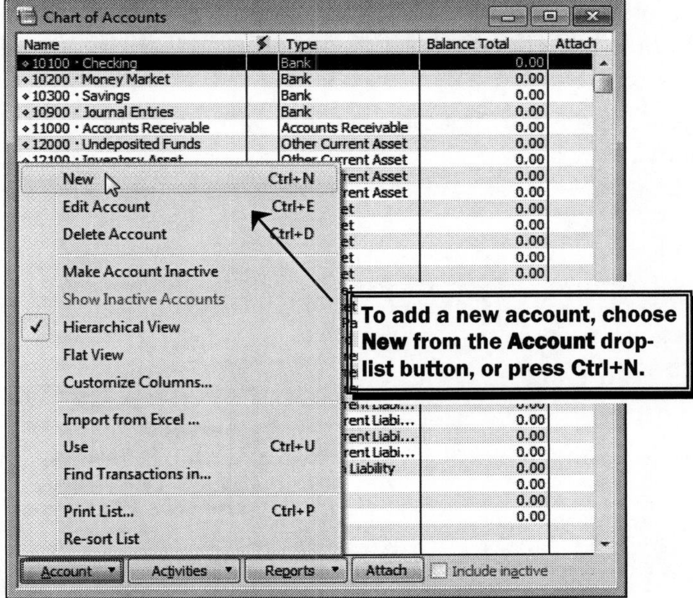

Figure 7-22 Adding an account

Step 3. Select **Expense** from the choice of account types in the *Add New Account: Choose Account Type* window (see Figure 7-23). Click Continue.

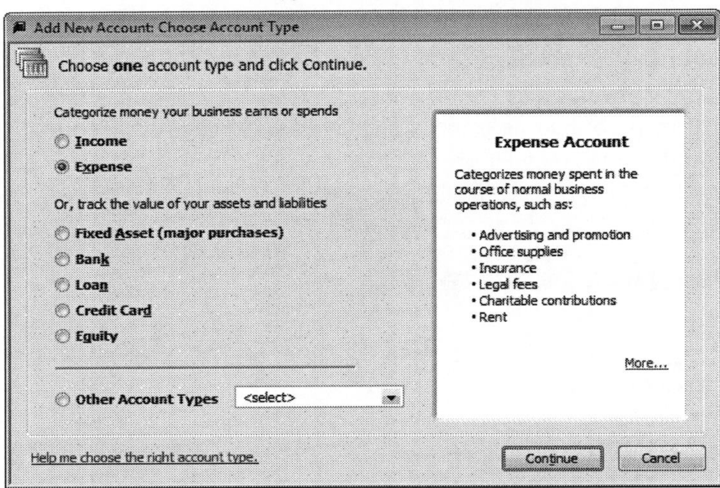

Figure 7-23 Add New Account: Choose Account Type Window

Step 4. Enter ***62600*** in the *Number* field and then press **Tab**.

Step 5. Enter ***Entertainment*** in the *Name* field and then press **Tab** twice.

Step 6. Enter ***Entertainment Expenses*** in the *Description* field and then press **Tab** twice.

The *Description* field is optional. In previous versions, the Description field had a limited length requiring short descriptions. Starting with the QuickBooks 2007, you can enter descriptions with up to 200 characters.

Step 7. Select **Deductions: Other miscellaneous taxes** from the *Tax-Line Mapping* drop-down list.

If you or your accountant uses TurboTax, ProSeries, Lacerte, or other QuickBooks-compatible tax software to prepare your tax return, specify the line on your tax return that this account will feed. This allows the tax software to fill out your tax return automatically, based on the data in QuickBooks. If you do not use one of the supported tax programs to prepare your taxes, or if you do not wish to take advantage of any of the income tax reports in QuickBooks, you can leave this field blank.

Step 8. Your screen should look like Figure 7-24. Click **Save & Close** at the bottom of the window to save the account.

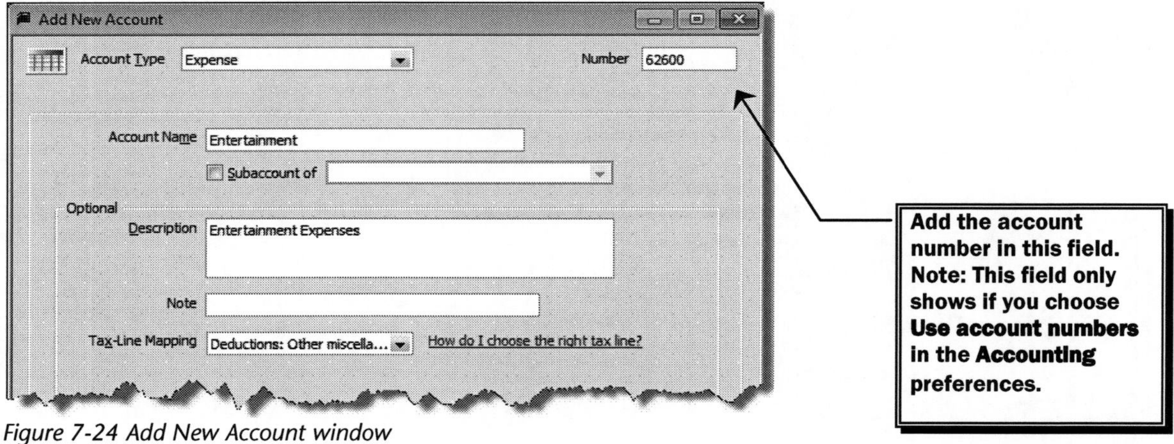

Figure 7-24 Add New Account window

Adding Subaccounts

If you want more detail in your *Chart of Accounts*, you can add *Subaccounts.* Account types for the main account and its subaccounts *must* be same. You can add up to 5 levels of subaccounts.

> **Did You Know?**
> Clicking the **Collapse** button on reports that include Subaccounts (e.g., Balance Sheet and Profit & Loss reports) removes the Subaccount detail from the report. The balance of each primary account on the collapsed report is the total of its Subaccount balances.

COMPUTER PRACTICE

Step 1. Display the *Chart of Accounts* using any method shown previously.

Step 2. Select the **Account** drop-list button at the bottom of the *Chart of Accounts* window and select **New**.

Step 3. Select the **Expense** option from *the Add New Account: Choose Account Type* window. Click Continue.

Step 4. Fill out the *New Account* window as shown in Figure 7-25. Notice that the *Subaccount of* field is checked and the main account is selected in its field.

Step 5. Click **OK** to save the record.

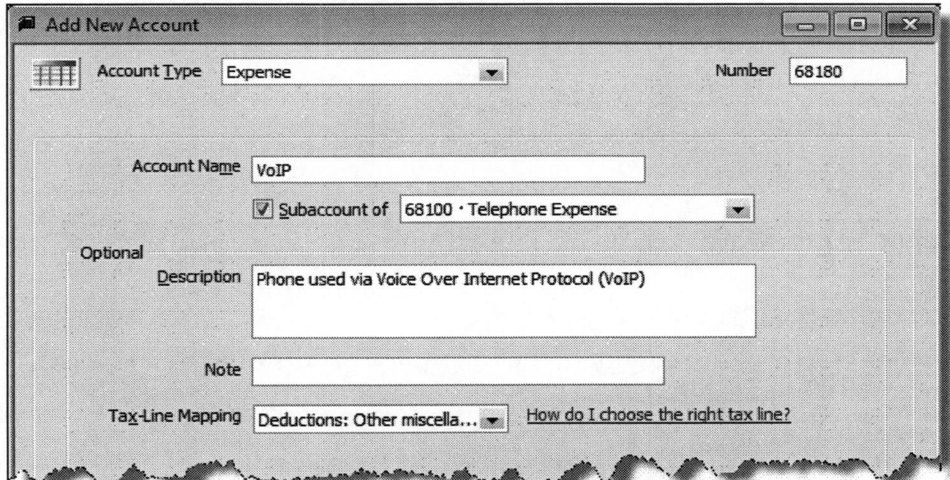

Figure 7-25 Add a Subaccount for more detail in the Chart of Accounts.

Step 6. Now the Chart of Accounts shows your new subaccount slightly indented under its master account (see Figure 7-26).

> **Tip**
> Once subaccounts are set up under a main account, you should only use subaccounts and not the main account in transactions. Using main account defeats the purpose of getting more detail. Also, in reports, whenever you see an account name with the string "-Other", it means that you used main account instead of a subaccount. To see only subaccounts and not the main account in the drop-down list, select the **Show lowest subaccount only** checkbox in **Accounting** *Company preference* (see Figure 7-27).

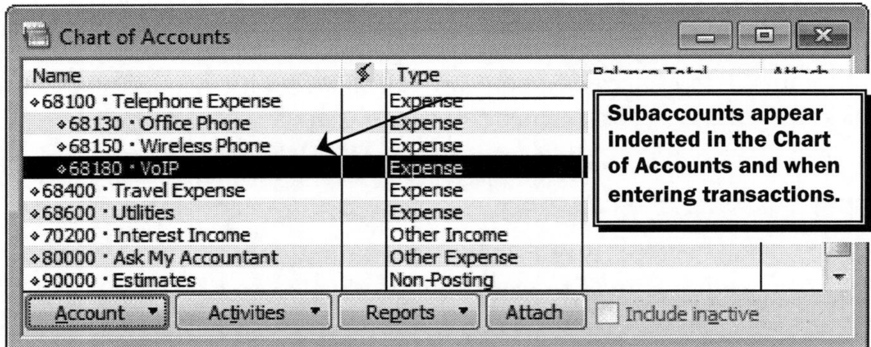

Figure 7-26 Subaccounts appearance in the Chart of Accounts

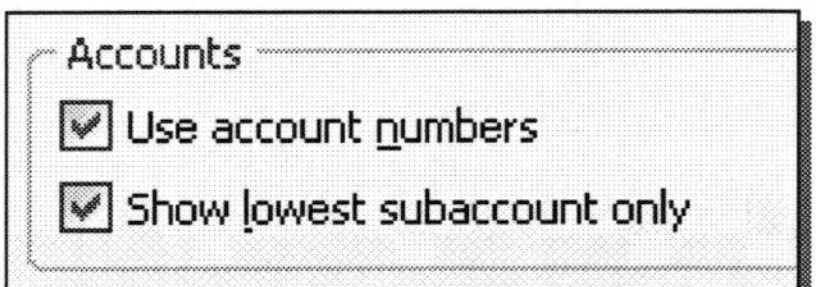

Figure 7-27 Account Numbers Preferences

Removing Accounts from the Chart of Accounts

When you no longer need an account, it is best to remove the account from the Chart of Accounts List. Removing unnecessary accounts helps avoid data entry errors by ensuring that no transactions are accidentally posted to these accounts. There are three ways to remove an account from the Chart of Accounts List: deleting the account, deactivating the account, or merging the account with another account.

Deleting Accounts – Option 1

To delete an account, follow these steps:

DO NOT PERFORM THESE STEPS NOW. THEY ARE FOR REFERENCE ONLY.

1. Select the account in the Chart of Accounts List.
2. Select the **Account** menu at the bottom of the Chart of Accounts window and select **Delete** or press Ctrl+D (see Figure 7-28).

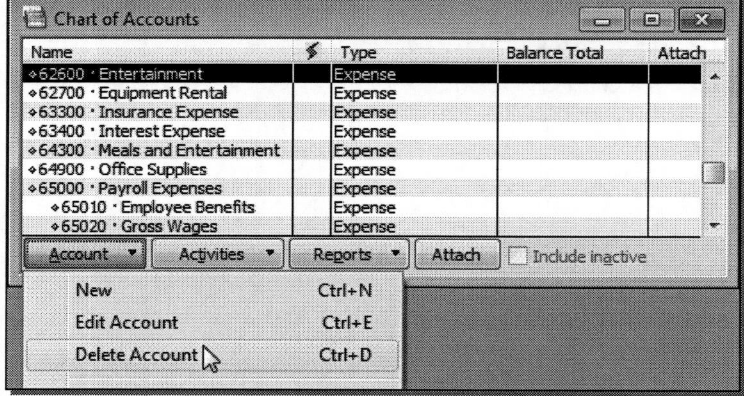

Figure 7-28 Deleting an account from the Chart of Accounts

It is important to note that QuickBooks will not allow you to delete an account if you have used the account in an item record or a transaction. If this is the case and you still want to remove the account, use either Option 2 or Option 3 below.

Deactivating Accounts – Option 2

If you cannot delete an account but you still want to remove it from your list, you can deactivate it. Deactivating an account causes it to be hidden in the Chart of Accounts list. Deactivating an old account reduces the clutter in your lists while preserving your ability to see the account in historical transactions and reports.

> **Note:**
> Even if an account (or item, or name) is inactive, all transactions using that account (or item, or name) will show on reports.

To make an account inactive, follow these steps:

> **DO NOT PERFORM THESE STEPS NOW. THEY ARE FOR REFERENCE ONLY.**

1. Select the account in the Chart of Accounts list.
2. Select the **Account** button and then select **Make Inactive** from the menu (see Figure 7-29).

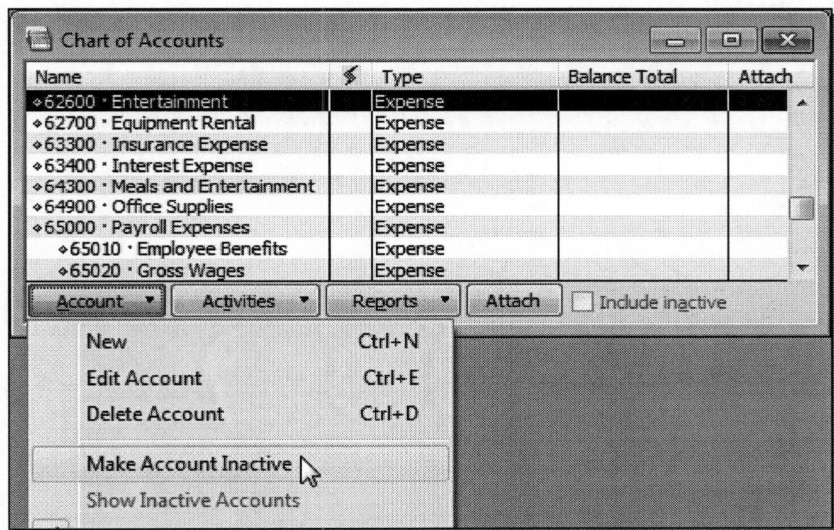

Figure 7-29 Making an account inactive in the Chart of Accounts

To view all accounts in the Chart of Accounts, including the inactive accounts, click **Include inactive** at the bottom of the Chart of Accounts window (see Figure 7-30). The icon in the far left column indicates that an account is inactive. To reactivate the account, click on the ✖ icon.

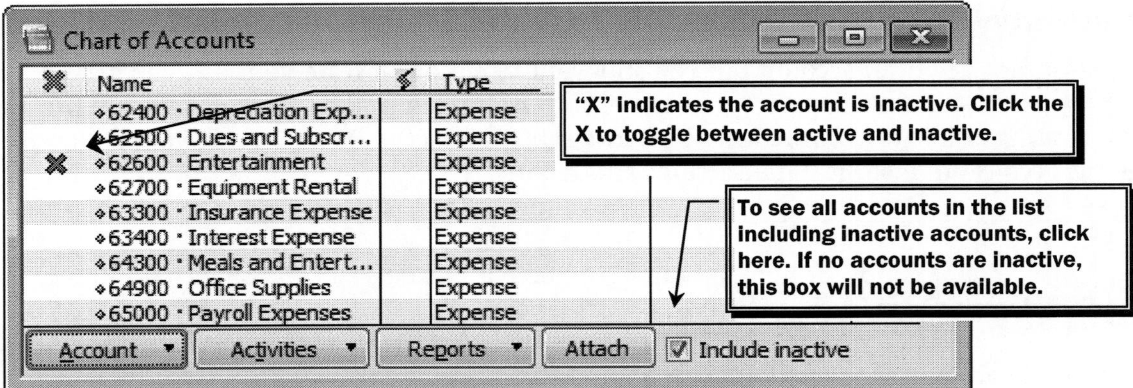

Figure 7-30 When the Show All Field is checked, all accounts appear in the list.

> **Did You Know?**
> You can also deactivate customers, vendors, employees, or items using this same method. Click in the ✖ column to make lines on any list active or inactive.

Merging Accounts – Option 3

When you merge two accounts, QuickBooks edits each transaction from the merging account so that it posts to the merged (combined) account. For example, if you merge the *Entertainment* account into the *Meals and Entertainment* account, QuickBooks will edit each transaction that had been posted to *Entertainment*, making it post to *Meals and Entertainment* instead. Then QuickBooks will remove the *Entertainment* account from the *Chart of Accounts* list.

> **Important:**
> Merging cannot be undone. Once you merge accounts together, there is no way to find out which account the old transactions used (except by reviewing from a backup file). In this example, all transactions that were originally coded to *Entertainment* will post to *Meals and Entertainment.*

COMPUTER PRACTICE

Step 1. Display the Chart of Accounts list.

Step 2. Select the account whose name you do not want to keep. Here you will merge the *Entertainment* account into *Meals and Entertainment*, so select **62600 Entertainment**.

Step 3. Right-click on **62600 Entertainment** and then select **Edit Account**. Alternatively, press **Ctrl+E**.

Step 4. Enter **Meals and Entertainment** in the *Name* field (see Figure 7-31) and then click **Save & Close**. You must enter the account name exactly as it appears in the Chart of Accounts. One way of ensuring this is to copy and paste the account name from the merged account to the merging account.

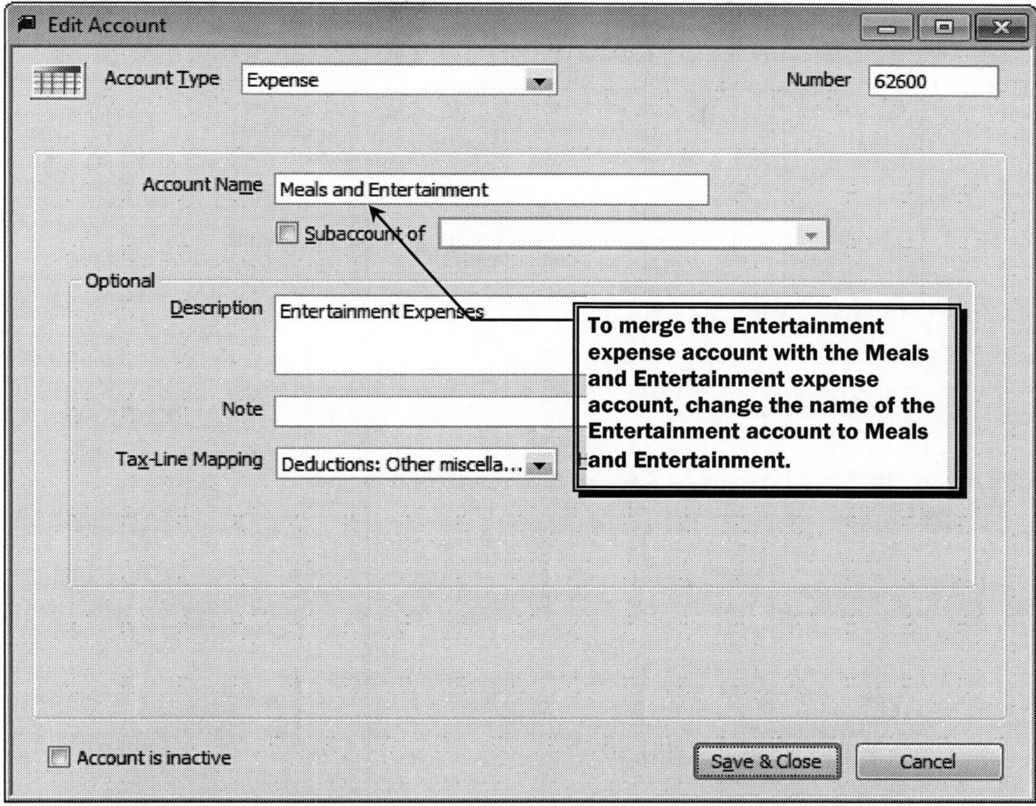

Figure 7-31 Change the name of the account to exactly match the name of another account.

Step 5. Now that this account has the same name as the other account, QuickBooks asks if you want to merge the two accounts (see Figure 7-32). Click **Yes**.

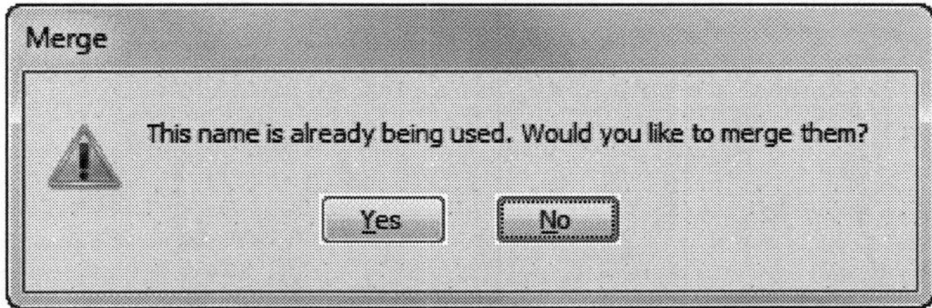

Figure 7-32 Click Yes to merge the accounts.

Did You Know?
If account numbers are in use, another way to merge accounts is to change the account number of one account to match the account number of another. This has the same effect as replacing the account name of the merging account with the account name of the merged account.

Note:
The merge feature is not limited to just the Chart of Accounts List; it can be used on most lists within QuickBooks.

Reordering the Account List

There are several ways to reorder the *Chart of Accounts* list. By default, the Chart of Accounts list sorts first by account type and then alphabetically by account name within the account type (if account numbers are not in use) or numerically by account number within the account type (if account numbers are in use). For example, all of the bank accounts come first, followed by Accounts Receivable, Other Current Assets, and so on. The account types are arranged in the order they appear on financial statements.

You can sort the Chart of Accounts list by the account name or number, by the (online status), or by the balance total column.

DO NOT PERFORM THESE STEPS NOW. THEY ARE FOR REFERENCE ONLY.

1. Display the *Chart of Accounts* (see Figure 7-33).
2. Click the **Name** column heading to sort the list.

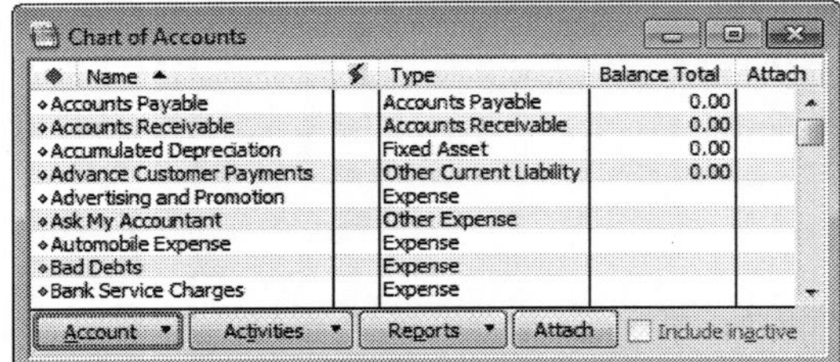

Figure 7-33 Chart of Accounts sorted by name

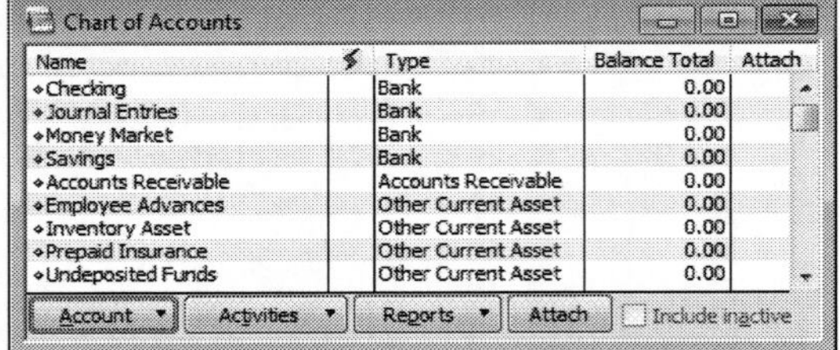

Figure 7-34 Chart of Accounts sorted by number

Note:
When account numbers are inactive and you click the *Name* header, QuickBooks sorts the account list alphabetically by account name.

However, when account numbers are active and you click the *Name* header, QuickBooks sorts the list by account number. Click the other headers to sort by *(Online status)*, *Type*, or *Balance*.

Tip:
When you assign account numbers, set numbering breaks that correspond to the account types. For example, number all of your asset accounts 10000-19999 and all of your liability accounts 20000-29999, and so forth. When you click the Name header to sort the Chart of Accounts, QuickBooks does not also sort the list by account type. Therefore, if you assign an account number of 70000 to a Bank account, QuickBooks will place that account near the bottom of the Chart of Accounts, regardless of its type. If you do not use account numbers, it is best not to use the *Name* header to sort the Chart of Accounts. Instead, select the **Account** menu and choose **Re-sort List**. This will sort the list by Account name (or number) while respecting the account types.

You can also use the mouse to drag the accounts up or down within the same account type. Within each account type, the order of the accounts in the Chart of Accounts determines the order of the accounts in financial statements and other reports.

Tip:
Once you have manually reordered the Chart of Accounts, all new accounts will automatically be added to the top of the list within its type rather than in alphabetical order.

To reorder the Chart of Accounts List using the mouse, follow these steps:

DO NOT PERFORM THESE STEPS NOW. THEY ARE FOR REFERENCE ONLY.

1. If you have sorted the list by *Name, Online Status, Type,* or *Balance* by clicking on the column headers, click on the diamond to the left of the **Name** column header. This will remove the sorting (see Figure 7-35).

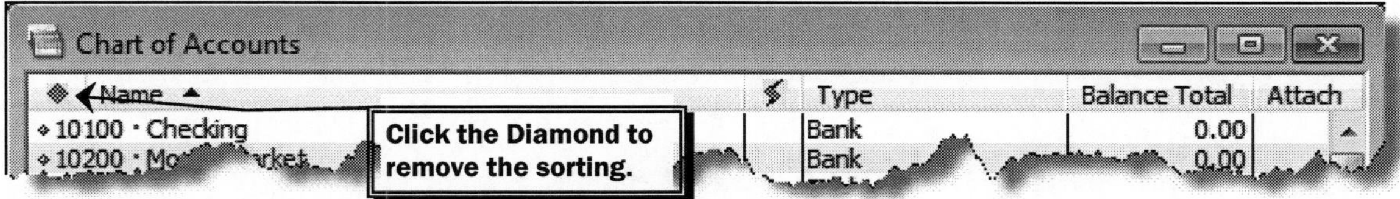

Figure 7-35 Chart of Accounts, sorted by account number

2. While holding down the mouse button, drag the account up or down (see Figure 7-36).

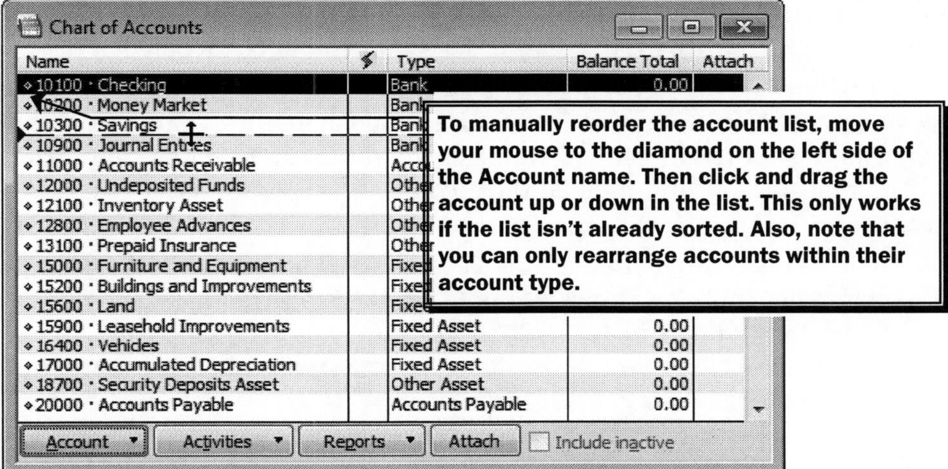

Figure 7-36 Reorder the list by moving an account with the mouse.

> **Tip:**
> To preserve proper financial statement presentation, you can only rearrange accounts within their account type. In addition, QuickBooks treats accounts with Subaccounts as a group, so if you want to move your account above or beneath an account with Subaccounts, you'll need to drag it above or below the group.
>
> **Tip:**
> If you use account numbers, it may be best to edit the numbers to move accounts up or down in the list. For example, if you want account #10400 to be above account #10300, you can edit its account number so that it is #10200. Then, you may need to select the **Account** menu and then select **Re-sort List**.

Turning Off Account Numbers

For the rest of this chapter, we'll turn off the display of account numbers in the Chart of Accounts.

COMPUTER PRACTICE

Step 1. Select the **Edit** menu and then select **Preferences.**

Step 2. In the *Preferences* window, click on the **Accounting** icon and then select the **Company Preferences** tab.

Step 3. Deselect the *Use account numbers* box and then click **OK**.

Setting Up Other Lists

At this point in the 12 Step process, you would enter additional information in lists, such as customers and vendors. For this exercise, the Setup-10.QBM file you restored earlier already has this data entered. Refer to page 43 and 124 for more information on adding Customers and Vendors.

Setting Up Opening Balances – Step 4

Gathering Your Information

After you've set up your Chart of Accounts, you're ready to enter your opening balances. To set up your opening balances, you will need to gather several documents, prepared as of your start date. The following is a list of items needed to complete your setup:

Trial Balance: Ask your accountant to provide you with a Trial Balance for your start date. If your start date is the end of your fiscal year, ask your accountant for an "after-closing" Trial Balance. The term "after-closing" means "after all the income and expenses have been closed into Retained Earnings."

If a Trial Balance is not available, use an after closing Balance Sheet and a year-to-date income statement as of your start date. Table 7-4 shows a sample after-closing Trial Balance for Academy Photography on the start date of 12/31/2010.

Academy Photography		
Trial Balance December 31, 2010		
	Debit	**Credit**
Checking	$17,959.60	
Money Market	$12,100.00	
Savings	$ 500.00	
Accounts Receivable	$ 1,253.41	
Inventory	$ 7,158.67	
Furniture and Equipment	$13,250.00	
Fixed Assets: Accumulated Depreciation		$ 1,325.00
Accounts Payable		$ 142.00
National Bank VISA Gold		$ 2,152.00
Payroll Liabilities:Company PR Taxes		$ 368.00
Sales Tax Payable		$ 141.79
Line of Credit		$ 6,700.00
Truck Loan		$12,000.00
Common Stock		$10,000.00
Retained Earnings		$19,392.89
TOTAL	**$52,221.68**	**$52,221.68**

Table 7-4 Trial Balance on Academy Photography's start date

Bank Statement (for all bank accounts): You will need the most recent bank statement prior to your start date. For example, if your start date is 12/31/2010 you will need the 12/31/2010 bank statements for all of your accounts.

Business Checking Account

Statement Date: **December 31, 2010** *Page 1 of 1*

Summary:

Previous Balance as of 11/30/10:	$	12,155.10
Total Deposits and Credits: 2	+ $	10,157.28
Total Checks and Debits: 9	- $	7,027.40
Total Interest Earned	+ $	8.62
Total Service Charge:1	- $	10.00
Statement Balance as of 12/31/10:	**= $**	**15,283.60**

Deposits and Other Credits:

DEPOSITS

Date	Description		Amount
8-Dec	Customer Deposit	$	6,150.00
20-Dec	Customer Deposit	$	4,007.28
	2 Deposits:	**$**	**10,157.28**

INTEREST

Date	Description		Amount
31-Dec	Interest Earned	$	8.62
	Interest:	**$**	**8.62**

Checks and Other Withdrawals:

CHECKS PAID:

Check No.	Date Paid		Amount
316	2-Dec	$	324.00
317	3-Dec	$	128.60
318	5-Dec	$	83.00
319	8-Dec	$	285.00
320	10-Dec	$	1,528.00
321	12-Dec	$	3,000.00
322	13-Dec	$	276.52
323	15-Dec	$	142.00
324	28-Dec	$	1,260.28
	6 Checks Paid:	**$**	**7,027.40**

SERVICE CHARGES

Date	Description		Amount
31-Dec	Service Charge	$	10.00
	1 Service Charge:	**$**	**10.00**

Figure 7-37 Bank Statement for Academy Photography on 12/31/2010

> **Tip:**
> If your bank statements are not dated on the end of each month, ask your bank to change your statement date to the end of the month.

Unpaid Bills: List each vendor bill by date of the bill, amount due, and what items or expenses you purchased on the bill (see Table 7-5).

Bill Number	Bill Date	Vendor	Amt. Due	Account/Item	Job	Class
2342	12/21/10	Wong & Son Video	$142.00	Subcontractors Expense	Mason, Bob	San Jose

Table 7-5 Unpaid bills on Academy Photography's start date

Outstanding Checks and Deposits: You'll need a list of all your checks and deposits that have not cleared the bank as of the bank statement dated on or prior to your start date.

OUTSTANDING DEPOSTIS AT 12/31/10				
Date	Descriptions			Amount
12/30/10		Customer Deposit	$	3,000.00
		1 Deposit:	**$**	**3,000.00**
OUTSTANDING CHECKS AT 12/31/10				
Check No.	Date Paid	Payee		Amount
325	12/26/10	National Bank	$	324.00
	1 Check:		**$**	**324.00**

Table 7-6 Outstanding deposits and checks on Academy Photography's start date

Open Invoices: List each customer invoice including the date of the invoice, amount due, and the Items sold on the invoice (see Table 7-7).

Inv #	Invoice Date	Customer:Job	Class	Terms	Item	Qty	Amt Due
3947	12/18/10	Mason, Bob	San Jose	Net 30	Camera	1	$695.99
					Santa Clara Tax		8.25%
					Total		$753.41
4003	12/21/10	Cruz, Maria: Branch Opening	San Jose	2% 10 Net 30	Photographer 4 Hrs.	125/hr	$500.00
					Total		$500.00

Table 7-7 Open Invoices on Academy Photography's start date

Employee List and W-4 information for each employee Gather complete name, address, social security number, and withholding information for each employee.

> Note:
> The next three payroll-related lists are necessary only if your start date is in the middle of a calendar year and you want to track payroll details with QuickBooks. If your start date is 12/31, skip these lists and enter the opening balances for payroll liabilities in the liability accounts as shown later in this section.
>
> If your start date is 12/31, you need to enter the detail from these lists only if you want to use QuickBooks to create payroll reports, Form 940, Form 941, or W-2s for the previous year.
>
> All payroll setup instructions are covered in the Payroll Setup chapter beginning on page 481.

Payroll Liabilities by Item: List the amount due for each of your payroll liabilities as of your start date. For example, list the amounts due for federal withholding tax, Social Security (employer), Social Security (employee), and any other payroll liabilities.

Year-to-Date Payroll Detail by Employee: If your start date is not 12/31 and you want QuickBooks to track your payroll, you will need gross earnings, withholdings, employer taxes, and any other deductions for each employee so far this year. For the most detail, this list should include each employee's earnings *for each month* this year.

Year-to-Date Payroll Tax Deposits: If your start date is not 12/31, list each payroll tax deposit during the year by Payroll Item.

Physical Inventory by Inventory Part: List the quantity and cost for each product in inventory (see Table 7-8).

> **Tip:**
> If you don't have actual counts and costs for your inventory, you'll need to estimate. However, the accuracy of your reports will be compromised if you don't have accurate setup numbers. If possible, we strongly recommend conducting a physical inventory as of your QuickBooks start date.

Physical Inventory at 12/31/10		
Item	Quantity on Hand	Value
Camera	10	$4500.00
Case	25	$1125.00
Frame	25	$ 53.75
Lenses	8	$1475.92

Table 7-8 Physical inventory on Academy Photography's start date

Opening Balances for Accounts

To enter opening balances, you can either edit the account in the *New Account* or *Edit Account* window or create a *General Journal Entry*. Entering the *Opening Balance* in the *New Account* or *Edit Account* window is a good method for setting up a single account. General Journal Entries allow you to set up the Opening Balances for several accounts at once.

When entering opening balances for bank accounts and credit cards, it is very important to use the ending balance from the bank statement dated on (or just prior to) your start date.

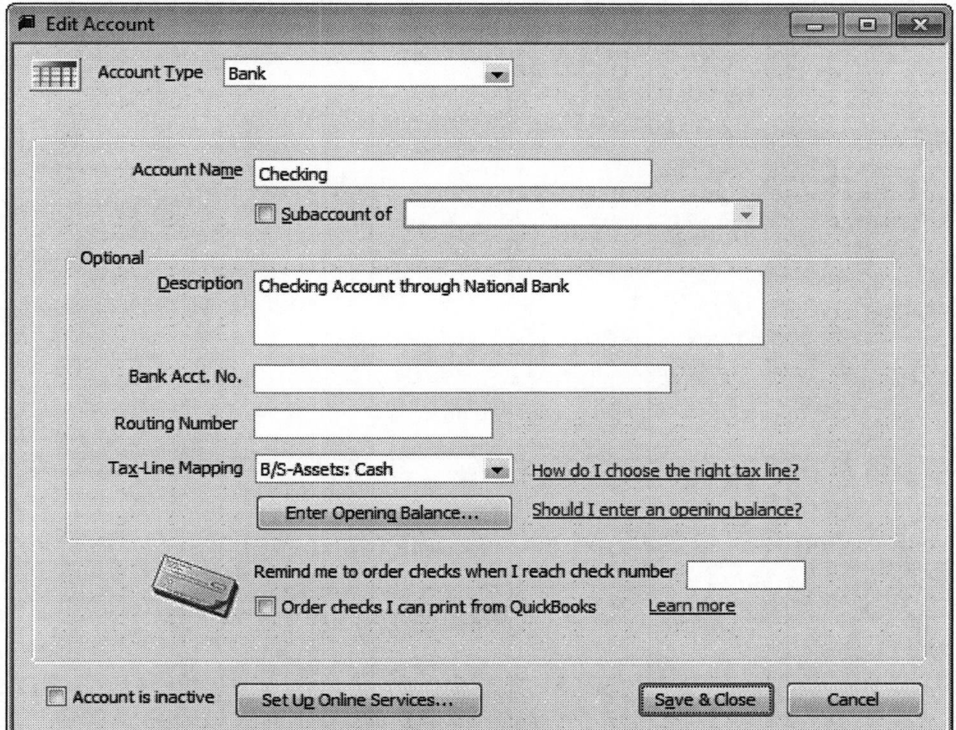

Figure 7-38 Enter an opening balance in the Edit Account window.

Directly Editing the Account

To enter the opening balances, repeat the following steps for each of your Balance Sheet accounts:

COMPUTER PRACTICE

Step 1. Display the Chart of Accounts.

Step 2. Select the **Checking** Bank account by clicking on it.

Step 3. Select the **Account** menu at the bottom of the list and then select **Edit Account**.

Step 4. Click on the **Enter Opening Balance** Button (see Figure 7-38).

Step 5. In the *Enter Opening Balance: Bank Account* window (see Figure 7-39), enter ***15,283.60*** in the *Statement Ending Balance field.*

Step 6. Enter **12/31/10** in the *Statement Ending Date* field.

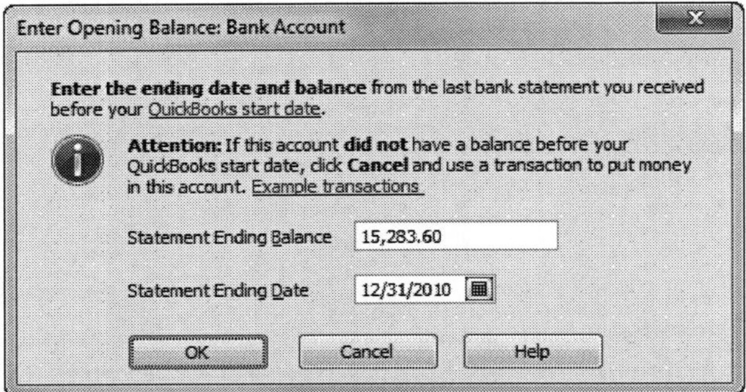

Figure 7-39 Enter Opening Balance for a Bank Account window

Step 7. Click **OK** to finalize the *Enter Opening Balance: Bank Account* window. Then, click **Save & Close** on the *Edit Account Window.* Repeat Steps 2 through 7 for the *Money Market* account. Enter an opening balance of ***$12,100.00*** as of ***12/31/2010*** (see Figure 7-40).

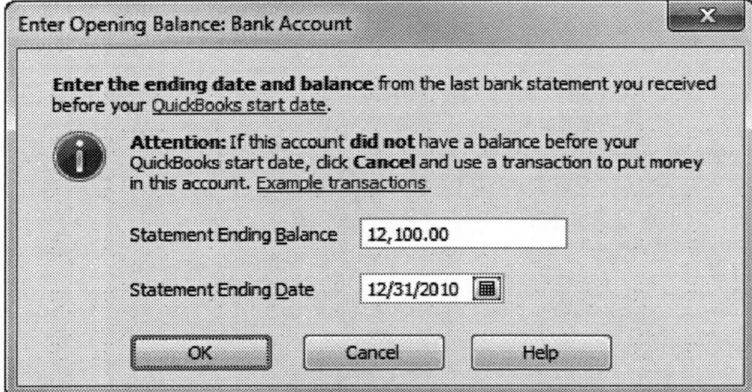

Figure 7-40 Edit the Money Market account to enter an opening balance

> **Accounting Behind the Scenes:**
> When you enter an opening balance in an account, a transaction posts to the account and to *Opening Balance Equity*. Also, the opening balance in the account becomes the *Beginning Balance* for the first bank reconciliation.
>
> **Note:**
> QuickBooks does not allow you to directly enter the opening balance for *Accounts Receivable*, *Undeposited Funds*, *Accounts Payable*, *Sales Tax Payable*, or *Opening Balance Equity*. To enter opening balances for these accounts, see later in this chapter.

Recording Opening Balances in a General Journal Entry

General Journal Entries allow you to record debits and credits to specific accounts. Other forms in QuickBooks, such as Invoices or Bills, take care of the credits and debits for you, behind the scenes (See page 2). Journal Entries record transactions that couldn't otherwise be recorded using QuickBooks forms.

Because total debits always equal total credits, the total of the debit column and the total of the credit column must be equal or you will not be able to save the *Journal Entry*. QuickBooks automatically calculates the amount required to make these entries balance as you create each new line in the General Journal Entry. On the last line of the General Journal Entry, code the amount QuickBooks calculates to the Opening Bal Equity account. This amount may be a debit or a credit, depending on the other figures in the entry.

Although the Trial Balance doesn't show any balance in *Opening Bal Equity*, you use this account during setup to keep everything in balance. At the end of the setup process, you'll transfer the balance from this account into Retained Earnings, as shown later in the setup steps.

You can use a *General Journal Entry* to record some, but not all, of your opening balances. Do not include the following accounts in the *General Journal Entry*: *Accounts Receivable, Accounts Payable, Inventory, Sales Tax Payable*, and *Retained Earnings*. You will enter the opening balance for these accounts later in the 12-Step setup.

COMPUTER PRACTICE

Use the information from the Trial Balance on page 298 to complete the following steps:

Step 1. Select the **Company** menu and then select **Make General Journal Entries.** If necessary, click **OK** in the *Assign Numbers to Journal Entries* dialog box.

Step 2. Fill in the *Make General Journal Entries* window as shown in Figure 7-41.

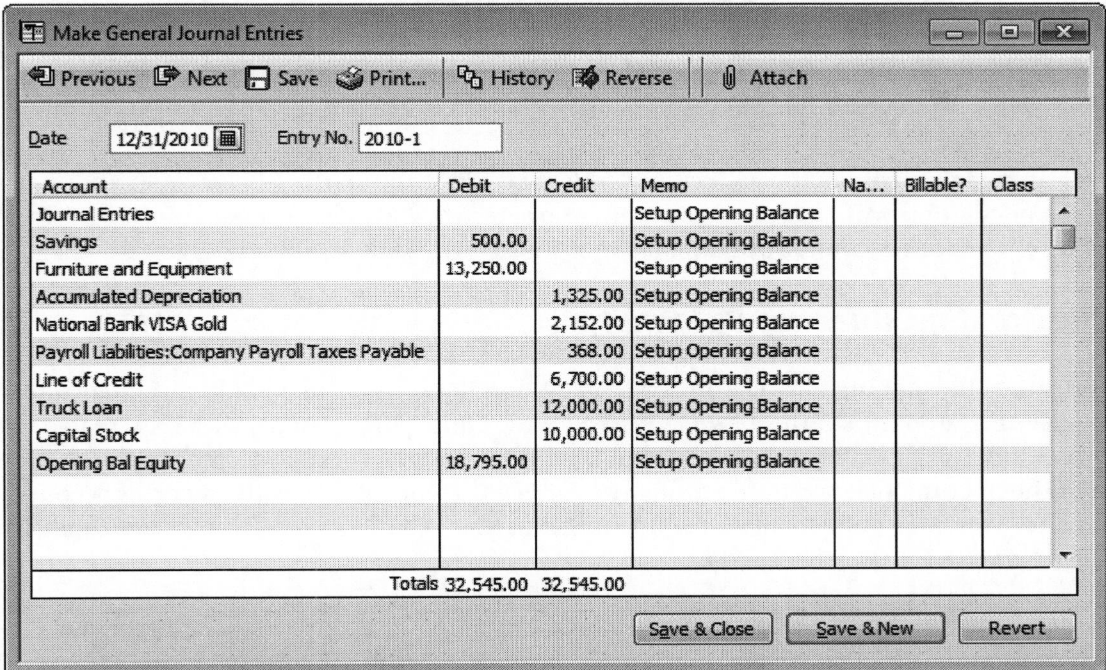

Account	Debit	Credit	Memo	Na...	Billable?	Class
Journal Entries			Setup Opening Balance			
Savings	500.00		Setup Opening Balance			
Furniture and Equipment	13,250.00		Setup Opening Balance			
Accumulated Depreciation		1,325.00	Setup Opening Balance			
National Bank VISA Gold		2,152.00	Setup Opening Balance			
Payroll Liabilities:Company Payroll Taxes Payable		368.00	Setup Opening Balance			
Line of Credit		6,700.00	Setup Opening Balance			
Truck Loan		12,000.00	Setup Opening Balance			
Capital Stock		10,000.00	Setup Opening Balance			
Opening Bal Equity	18,795.00		Setup Opening Balance			
Totals	32,545.00	32,545.00				

Figure 7-41 Enter opening balances using a General Journal Entry.

> **Note:**
> On the top line of each General Journal Entry, use an account called *Journal Entries*, as shown in Figure 7-41. Use the *Bank* account type when setting up this account in your Chart of Accounts. The *Journal Entries* account will never have a balance, so it will never show on financial statements, but it will have a register where you'll be able to look at all of your General Journal Entries.

Step 3. Click **Save & Close** to save the entry.

Step 4. QuickBooks will warn you that you can set up Fixed Asset Items from the *Fixed Asset Item* List. Click **OK**. If you see the *Items not assigned classes* dialog box, click the **Save Anyway** button.

> **Important Note:**
> In this example, you're setting up the opening balances for payroll liabilities directly in the accounts instead of first setting up the payroll function. This way, you can finalize your opening balances before worrying about the payroll setup, and you can separate the tasks of company setup and payroll setup.
>
> Remember though, because we've set up the liabilities outside of the payroll system, your first payroll liability payment (for last year's liability), must be entered using the *Write Checks* window instead of the *Pay Liabilities* window. Alternatively, you could set up the payroll liability balances using the *Adjust Liabilities* window with the *Do not Affect Accounts* setting. Then, you would use the *Pay Liabilities* window to pay your opening payroll liability balances.

The General Journal Entry in Figure 7-41 will set up the opening balances in *most* of the asset, liability, and equity accounts. You will not include some of the assets and liabilities in this General Journal Entry because you will enter their balances later in the 12 Step setup. For example, you'll exclude Accounts Receivable and Accounts Payable because you will create Invoices and Bills to enter these accounts, respectively. See Entering Open Bills (Accounts Payable) on page 305.

If you enter bank accounts through a *General Journal Entry*, the starting balance on your first Bank Reconciliation will be zero. If you want your Starting Balance to equal your Opening Balance, enter bank account's opening balance in the *Edit Account* window.

Understanding Opening Bal Equity

As you enter the opening balances for your assets and liabilities, QuickBooks automatically adds offsetting amounts in the *Opening Bal Equity* account. This account, which is created automatically by QuickBooks, is very useful if used properly. As you'll see later in this section, each of the opening balance transactions you enter into QuickBooks will affect this account. Then, after you have entered all of the opening balances, you'll "close" *Opening Bal Equity* into *Retained Earnings* (or *Owner's Equity*).

> **Tip:**
> By using the *Opening Bal Equity* account during setup, you will quickly be able to access the detail of your setup transactions by looking at the *Opening Bal Equity* register.

Entering Open Items – Step 5

Entering Outstanding Checks and Deposits

To help with the first reconciliation, you want all of the outstanding checks and deposits to show in QuickBooks so that you can match them with your first bank statement after the start date. If you don't enter the individual transactions, you won't see them in the QuickBooks reconciliation window. In addition, if a transaction never clears the bank, you won't know which transaction it was without going back to your old records.

COMPUTER PRACTICE

For each of your bank accounts and credit cards, enter all outstanding checks (or charges) and deposits (or payments) as additional transactions in the account register. Enter each outstanding check and deposit with the date the check was written or the deposit was made, and post each transaction to *Opening Bal Equity*.

Step 1. With the *Chart of Accounts* open, double-click on the **Checking** account to display its register.

Step 2. Enter new transactions directly in the register for each outstanding check and deposit (see Figure 7-42). See the list of outstanding checks and deposits in Table 7-6 on page 300.

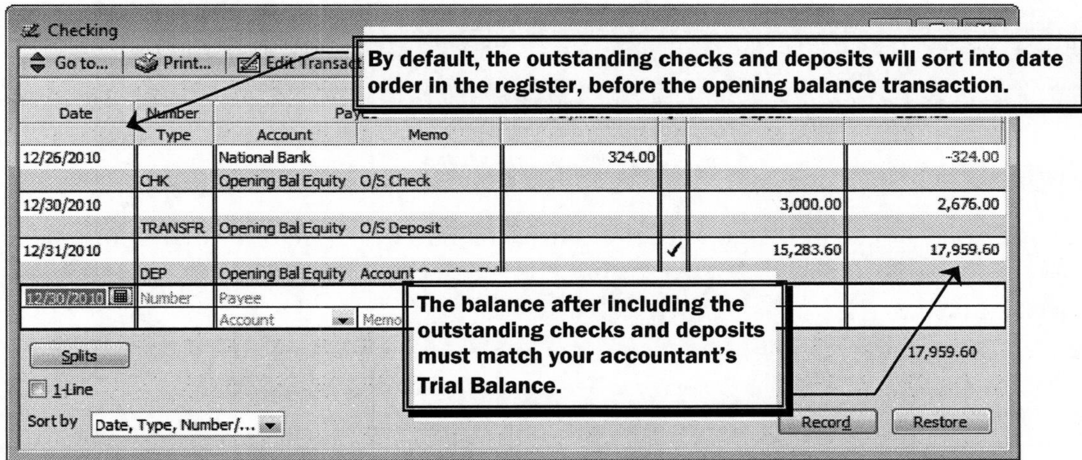

Figure 7-42 Checking account register with outstanding checks and deposits

Entering Open Bills (Accounts Payable)

COMPUTER PRACTICE

Enter your **Unpaid Bills** and **Vendor Credits** as of the start date. Use the original date of the bill (or credit) along with all of the details (terms, vendor, etc.) of the bill. By entering the individual bills, you can preserve detailed job costing and class tracking data if needed.

Step 1. Click **Enter Bill** on the *Home page*, or select the **Vendors** menu and then select **Enter Bills**.

Step 2. Enter the bill as shown in Figure 7-43.

Step 3. Click **Save & Close** to save the transaction.

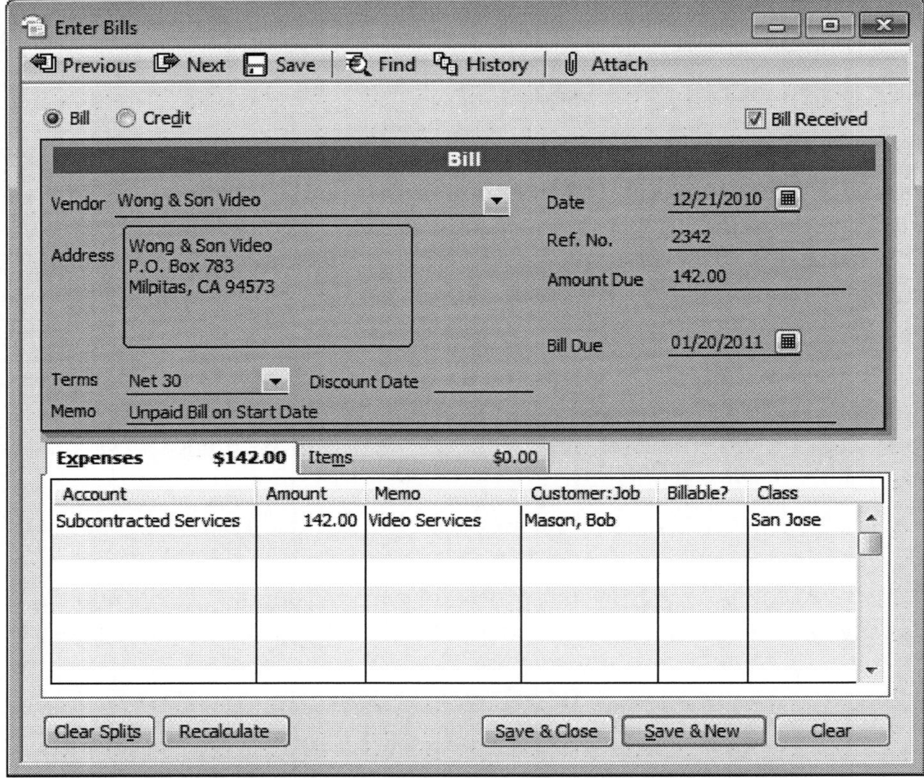

Figure 7-43 Enter the open Bill with the actual Bill date and the Bill due date.

Entering Open Invoices (Accounts Receivable)

Enter each Invoice or Credit Memo as of the Start Date. Enter each Invoice with its original date along with all of the details (terms, customer, etc.) of the original Invoice.

COMPUTER PRACTICE

Step 1. From the *Home page* click **Invoices** or select **Create Invoices** from the *Customer menu.* If you see the *Professional Services Form* dialog box, click **OK.**

Step 2. Enter the Invoice as shown in Figure 7-44. When you see the warning about insufficient quantities, click OK. If you receive a warning about tracking backorders, click OK.

Step 3. Make sure you use the date of the original invoice on this invoice along with all of the detail from that invoice, exactly as shown in Figure 7-44. Make sure the **Academy Photo Service Template** is selected in the *Template* field.

Step 4. Click **Save & New** to save the transaction and display a new Invoice.

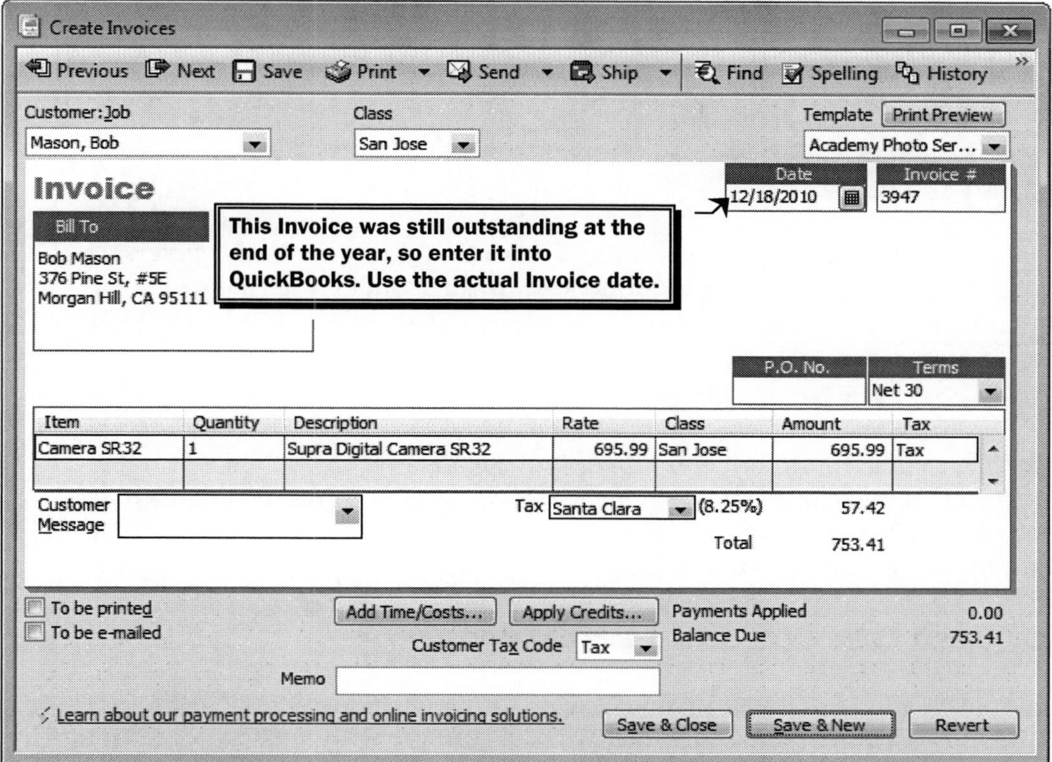

Figure 7-44 Enter the open Invoice with the original Invoice date.

Step 5. Enter another Invoice as shown in Figure 7-45. Click **Save & Close** to save the Invoice.

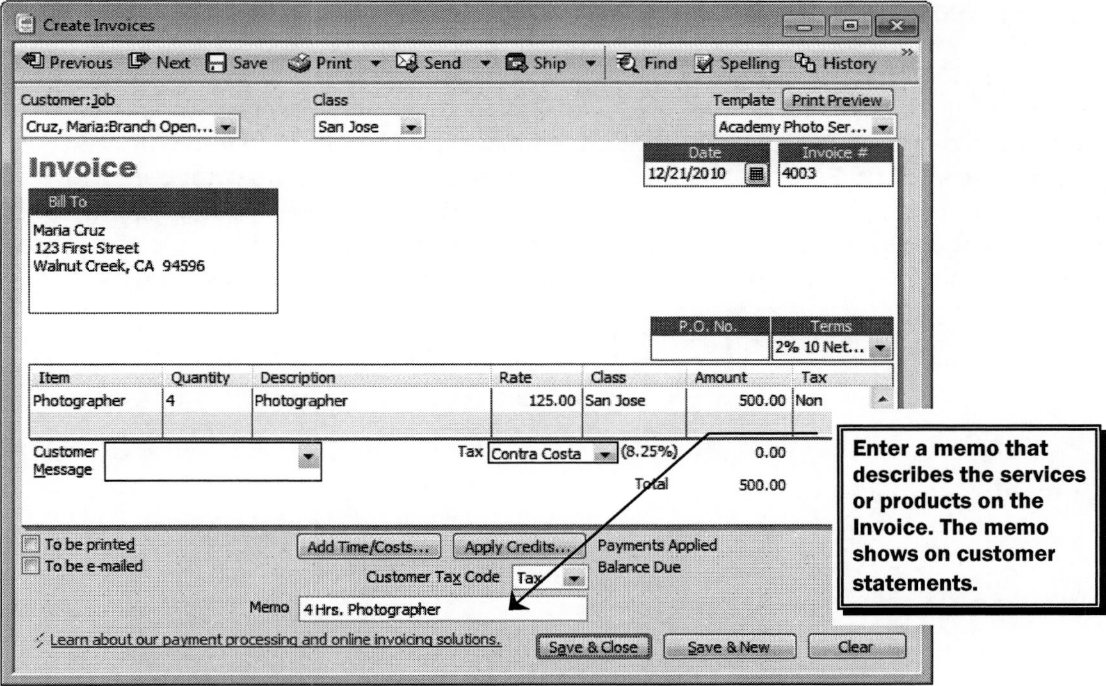

Figure 7-45 Enter this open Invoice.

> **Note:**
> When you set up your company file, it is important that you enter all Invoices, Credit Memos, Bills, and Bill Credits separately. QuickBooks needs the details of the transactions, such as the date, the terms, and the customer or vendor, to prepare accurate aging reports (e.g., Unpaid Bills Detail and A/R Aging Summary).
>
> In addition, when you receive money against one of your prior-year Invoices or pay a prior-year Bill, you will need individual Invoices and Bills against which to match the receipts and payments.

Entering Open Purchase Orders

If you have open Purchase Orders, enter them individually, just as you did with Bills, Bill Credits, Invoices, and Credit Memos. Enter each Purchase Order with its original date and all of its details. If you have partially received items on the Purchase Order, enter only the quantities yet to be received from the vendor.

Entering Open Estimates and Sales Orders

If you have open Estimates (for all versions except for Basic) and/or Sales Orders (for Premier and Enterprise only), enter them individually, just as you did with Bills, Bill Credits, Invoices, and Credit Memos. Enter each Estimate and/or Sales Order with its original date and all of its details. If you have already progress-billed a portion of the Estimate or delivered part of the Sales Order, enter only the remaining amount to be Invoiced.

Entering Year-to-Date Income and Expenses – Step 6

Earlier you learned that Income and Expense accounts are totaled at the end of the fiscal year as the Net Profit (or Loss) and is combined with Retained Earnings (see page 2). In this chapter's exercise the start date is the end of the fiscal year. Later in the 12 step process you will see the Income and Expense accounts zeroed out and their balances combined with Retained Earnings on the first day of the year (1/1/11). However, when your company file has a start date that is *not* the end of the fiscal year, the year-to-date amounts for the Income and Expense accounts will need to be entered as a Journal Entry (see Figure 7-46).

THE JOURNAL ENTRY SHOWN IN FIGURE 7-46 IS FOR REFERENCE ONLY. IT SHOWS A MID-YEAR SETUP ENTRY. DO NOT ENTER IT NOW.

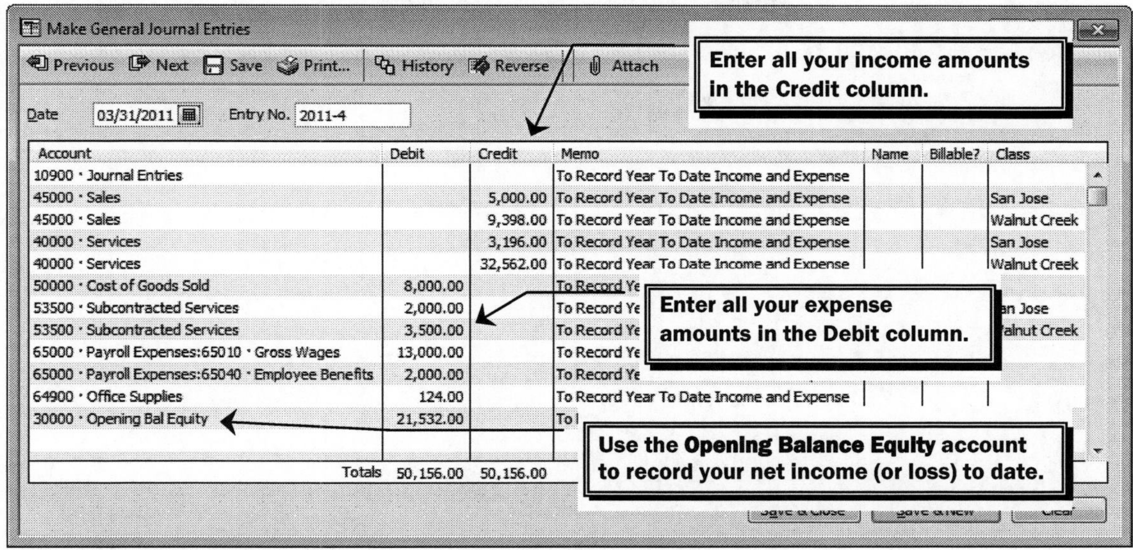

Figure 7-46 The General Journal Entry for a start date after the beginning of the year

Adjusting Opening Balance for Sales Tax Payable – Step 7

To enter the opening balance for *Sales Tax Payable*, begin by opening the *Sales Tax Payable* register to view the activity in the account. Notice that there are entries for each of the Invoices you just entered. This is your *uncollected* tax. Since the total Sales Tax Liability is a combination of the *collected* tax and the *uncollected* tax, you will need to subtract the current balance in the account (the *uncollected* tax) from the amount shown on Trial Balance from your accountant (or your 12/31/2010 sales tax return) to arrive at the unpaid *collected* tax.

$$TotalTaxDue = CollectedTax + UncollectedTax$$
$$CollectedTax = AmountsAlreadyCollectedButNotPaid$$
$$UncollectedTax = TaxOnOpenInvoices$$
$$...therefore$$
$$AdjustmentAmount = Collectedtax = TotalTaxDue - UncollectedTax$$

Equation 7-1 Calculating the amount of your sales tax adjustment

For example, you know from the Trial Balance that Academy Photography's Total Tax Due is $141.79. The Uncollected Tax has already been entered with Invoice 3947. The sales tax on this invoice was $57.42. By subtracting the Uncollected Sales Tax ($57.42) from the Total Tax Due ($141.79) you can calculate the Collected Tax, $84.37.

Then create a *Sales Tax Adjustment* for this collected tax amount.

COMPUTER PRACTICE

Step 1. Select the **Vendors** menu, then select **Sales Tax**, and then select **Adjust Sales Tax Due**.

Step 2. Complete the *Sales Tax Adjustment* window as shown in Figure 7-47 and then click **OK**. If you see the *Items not assigned classes* dialog box, click the **Save Anyway** button.

If you pay sales tax to more than one vendor (sales tax agency), you will need to enter a separate adjustment for each vendor.

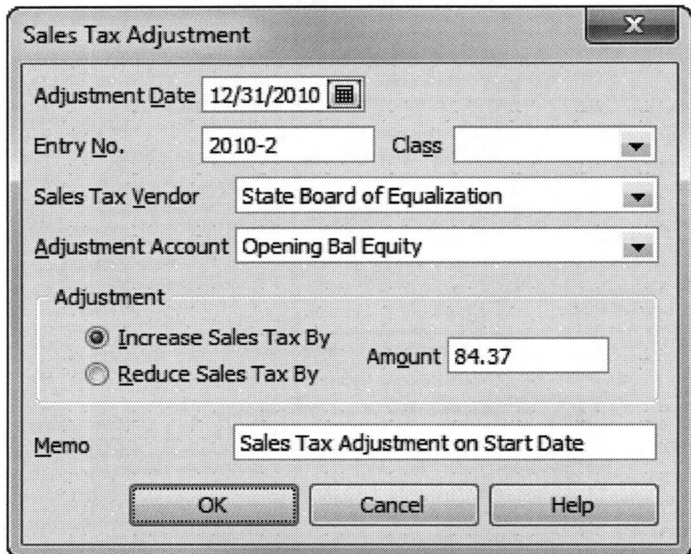

Figure 7-47 The Sales Tax Adjustment window

> **Did You Know?**
> The *Sales Tax Adjustment* window creates a *General Journal Entry* transaction in QuickBooks. Therefore, the Entry No. field will display the next Journal Entry number in sequence. If you prefer, you could enter this adjustment using a *General Journal Entry.*

Adjusting Inventory and Setting up Fixed Assets – Step 8

If you have inventory, you will need to create an inventory adjustment to enter the actual quantity and value on hand as of your start date. This is done *after* you enter your outstanding Bills and Invoices, so that the actual inventory counts and costs will be accurate even if some of the Bills and/or Invoices include Inventory Items.

As with the adjustment to Sales Tax Payable, begin by opening the *Inventory* register to view the activity and the current balance. Also, open the Item List to view the current stock status of each Inventory Item. Then adjust the quantity on hand and value of each item so that inventory will agree with the physical inventory counts and the company's Trial Balance as of your start date.

Adjusting Inventory for Actual Counts

COMPUTER PRACTICE

Step 1. Select the *Vendors* menu, then select **Inventory Activities**, and then select **Adjust Quantity/Value on Hand.**

Step 2. Enter ***12/31/2010*** in the *Adjustment Date* field. Press **Tab**.

Step 3. Enter ***2010-3*** in the *Ref. No.* field. Press **Tab**.

Step 4. Select **Opening Bal Equity** in the *Adjustment Account* field (see Figure 7-48).

Step 5. Click **OK** on the *Income or Expense expected* warning window.

Step 6. Enter in **10** in the *New Qty* column for the *Camera*. Press **Tab** twice.

Step 7. Enter in **25** in the *New Qty* column for the *Case*. Press **Tab** twice.

Step 8. Enter in **25** in the *New Qty* column for the *Frame*. Press **Tab** twice.

Step 9. Enter in **8** in the *New Qty* column for the *Lenses*. Press **Tab**.

Step 10. Check **Value Adjustment** in the lower left hand corner of the window to see the new value column.

Step 11. Click **Save & Close** to record the transaction. If you see the *Items not assigned classes* dialog box, click the **Save Anyway** button.

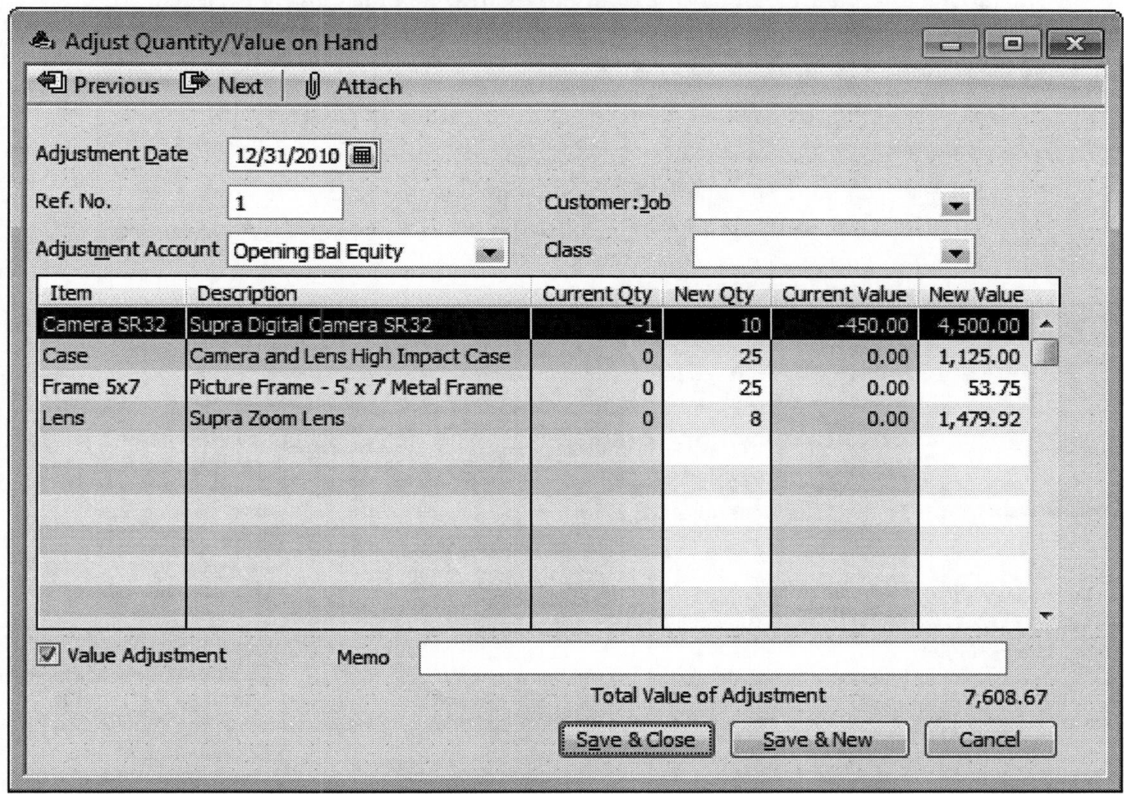

Figure 7-48 Adjust inventory as of the start date

Setting up Fixed Assets

If you have QuickBooks Pro or Premier, you can track detailed information about your company's Fixed Assets. You can set up detailed information about each asset using the Fixed Asset Item list. Then, if your accountant uses QuickBooks Premier: Accountant Edition, he or she can use the Fixed Asset Manager to individually calculate and track depreciation on each asset.

Setting up Loans

If you have QuickBooks Pro or Premier, you can track detailed information about your loans. You can individually track and amortize each of your loans so that QuickBooks will automatically allocate the principal and interest on each payment. For instructions on setting up your loans in the **Loan Manager**, see page 171.

Setup Payroll and YTD Payroll Information – Step 9

Setting up payroll in QuickBooks is a lengthy and involved process. Refer to the Payroll Setup chapter beginning on page 481 for more information about setting up the payroll feature.

Verifying your Trial Balance – Step 10

Before you transfer the balance of *Opening Bal Equity* into *Retained Earnings*, make sure the account balances in QuickBooks match your accountant's Trial Balance.

COMPUTER PRACTICE

Step 1. Select the **Reports** menu, then select **Accountant & Taxes**, and then select **Trial Balance**.

Step 2. Set the *From* and *To* date field to your start date as shown in Figure 7-49.

Step 3. After reviewing the *Trial Balance*, write down the balance of the *Opening Bal Equity* account, and close the window.

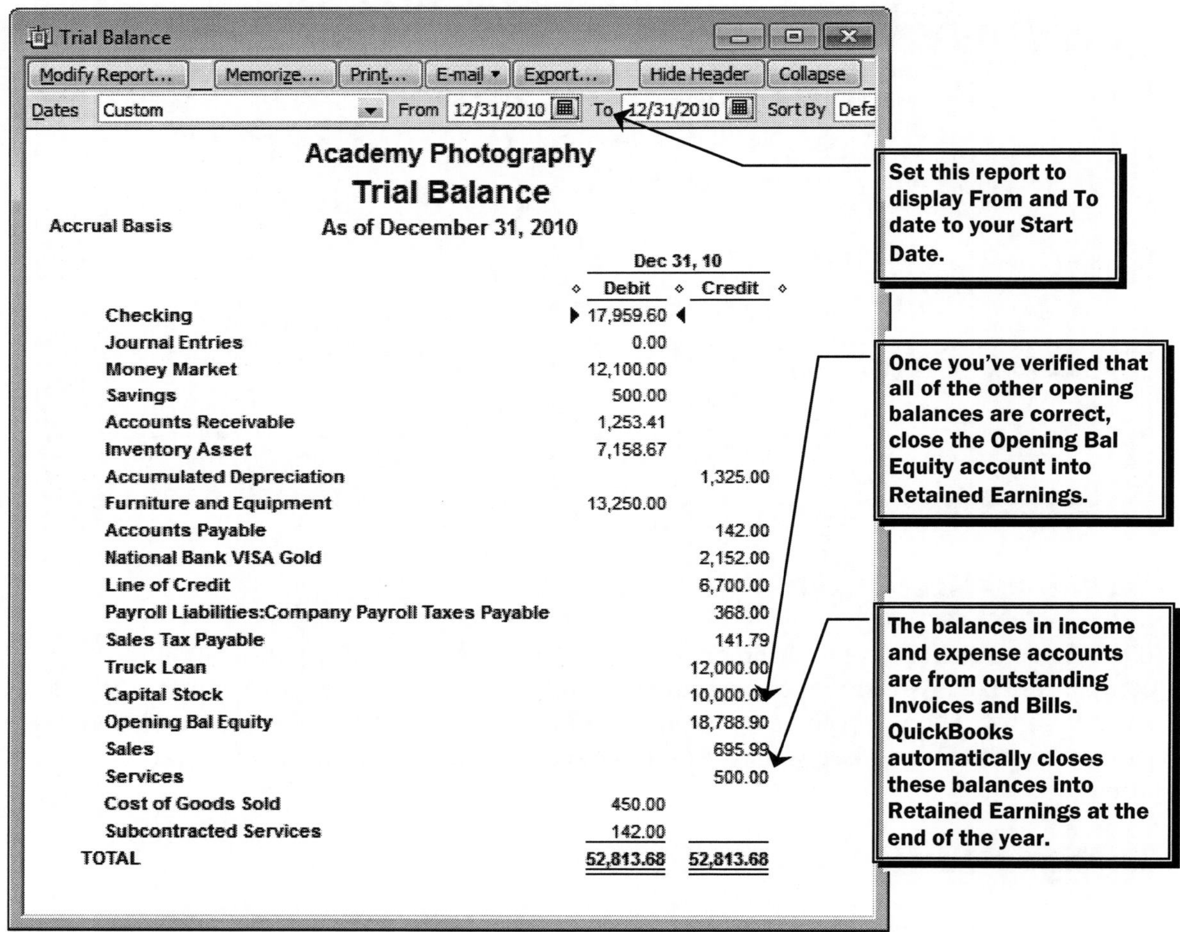

Academy Photography
Trial Balance
Accrual Basis — As of December 31, 2010

	Dec 31, 10 Debit	Credit
Checking	17,959.60	
Journal Entries	0.00	
Money Market	12,100.00	
Savings	500.00	
Accounts Receivable	1,253.41	
Inventory Asset	7,158.67	
Accumulated Depreciation		1,325.00
Furniture and Equipment	13,250.00	
Accounts Payable		142.00
National Bank VISA Gold		2,152.00
Line of Credit		6,700.00
Payroll Liabilities:Company Payroll Taxes Payable		368.00
Sales Tax Payable		141.79
Truck Loan		12,000.00
Capital Stock		10,000.00
Opening Bal Equity		18,788.90
Sales		695.99
Services		500.00
Cost of Goods Sold	450.00	
Subcontracted Services	142.00	
TOTAL	52,813.68	52,813.68

Figure 7-49 Trial Balance for Academy Photography as of the start date

Notice that the *Trial Balance* in Figure 7-49 looks slightly different from your accountant's report (in Table 7-4). For example, there are balances in several income and expense accounts, as well as in *Opening Bal Equity*. Do not worry about this difference at this point; you are not finished with the setup yet. Your *Trial Balance* could also differ from your accountant's report if the reporting basis on the two reports is not the same. For example, if you create an accrual basis *Trial Balance* and your accountant's *Trial Balance* is cash basis, the balances in the income and expense accounts may be different. Regardless of which method of accounting you use, QuickBooks will automatically close the balances in the income and expense accounts at the end of each year. Therefore, at this point in your setup, you should create an accrual basis *Trial Balance*, regardless of which basis you will ultimately use on reports. Just verify that all of the *Balance Sheet* account balances are accurate.

The income and expense accounts have balances because you just entered Invoices and Bills for the open Invoices and unpaid Bills. Those Invoices and Bills were dated during the prior year, so those transactions add to income and expenses for that year.

> Note:
> To learn more about the cash or accrual basis of accounting see the section beginning on page 224.

Closing Opening Bal Equity – Step 11

Once you have compared your Trial Balance report to your accountant's report, use a *General Journal Entry* to transfer (close) the balance in *Opening Bal Equity* into *Retained Earnings.*

> Note:
> If your company is a sole proprietorship, use this same process, but instead of *Retained Earnings*, the account should be called *Owner's Equity*. If your company is a partnership, split the balance of *Opening Bal Equity* between each of the partners' profit accounts.

COMPUTER PRACTICE

Step 1. Select the **Company** menu and then select **Make General Journal Entry**. If necessary, click **OK** in the *Assign Numbers to Journal Entries* dialog box.

Step 2. Set the *Date* field to your start date.

Step 3. Enter the *General Journal Entry* as shown in Figure 7-50 and then click **Save & Close**.

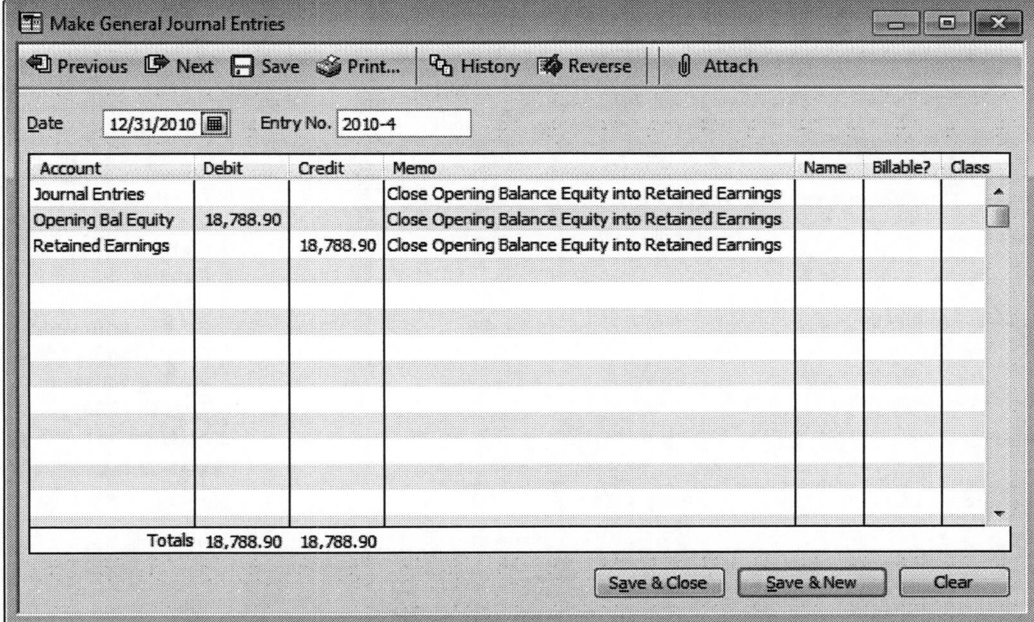

Figure 7-50 General Journal Entry to close Opening Bal Equity into Retained Earnings

Step 4. The *Retained Earnings* window as shown in Figure 7-51 will appear. Click **OK**. If you see the *Items not assigned classes* dialog box, click the **Save Anyway** button.

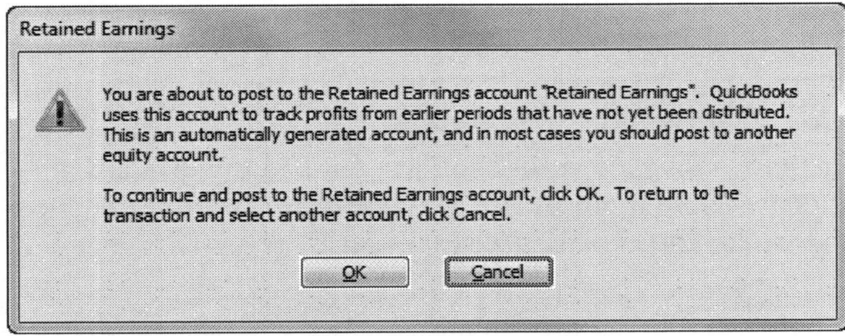

Figure 7-51 Posting to Retained Earnings

When you are finished entering all of the opening balances and you have closed the *Opening Bal Equity* account into *Retained Earnings*, verify your Balance Sheet. Create a Balance Sheet for **the day after** your start date and verify that the numbers match your accountant's Trial Balance.

COMPUTER PRACTICE

Step 1. Select the **Reports** menu, then select **Company & Financial**, and then select **Balance Sheet Standard**.

Step 2. Set the *As of* field to ***01/01/2011***, the day after your start date (see Figure 7-52).

Step 3. Print the report and then close the window.

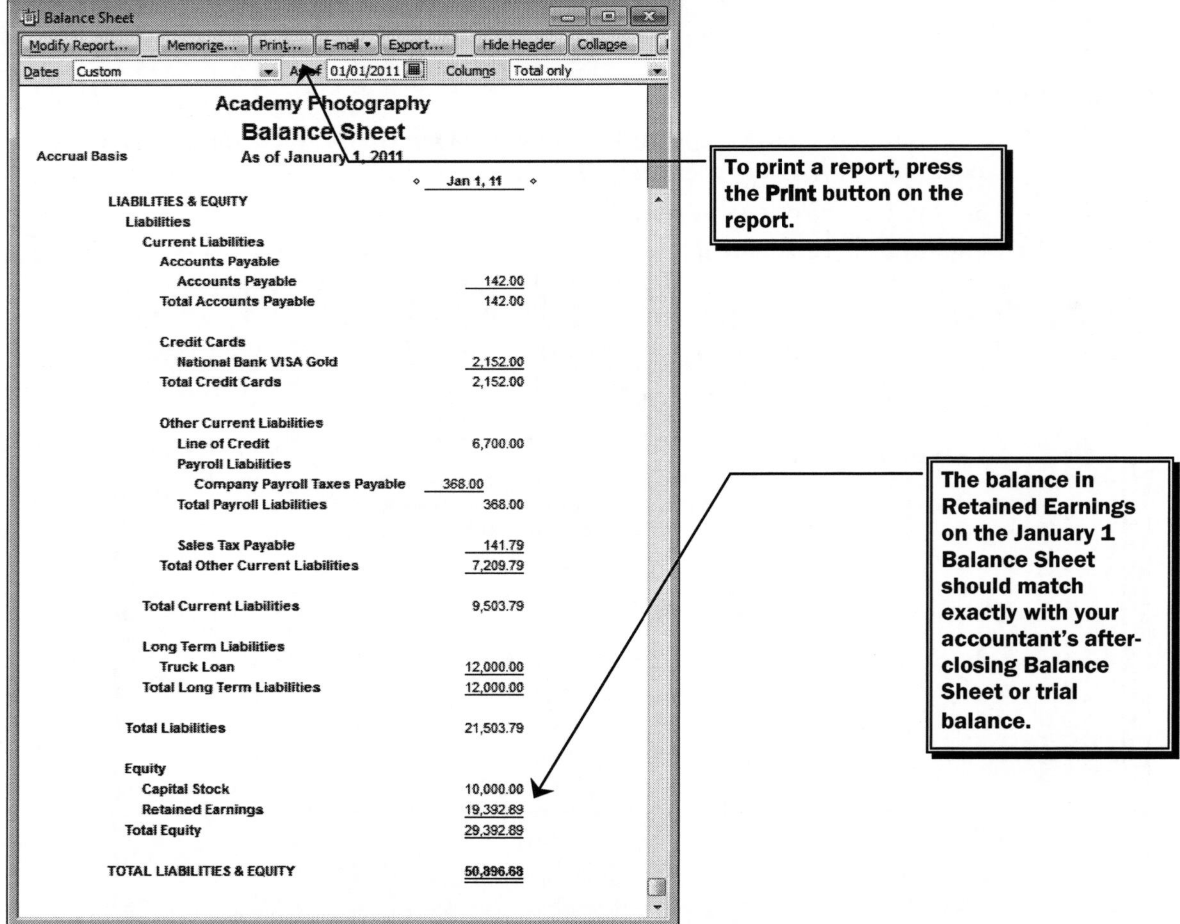

Academy Photography
Balance Sheet
Accrual Basis — As of January 1, 2011

		Jan 1, 11
LIABILITIES & EQUITY		
Liabilities		
Current Liabilities		
Accounts Payable		
Accounts Payable		142.00
Total Accounts Payable		142.00
Credit Cards		
National Bank VISA Gold		2,152.00
Total Credit Cards		2,152.00
Other Current Liabilities		
Line of Credit		6,700.00
Payroll Liabilities		
Company Payroll Taxes Payable	368.00	
Total Payroll Liabilities		368.00
Sales Tax Payable		141.79
Total Other Current Liabilities		7,209.79
Total Current Liabilities		9,503.79
Long Term Liabilities		
Truck Loan		12,000.00
Total Long Term Liabilities		12,000.00
Total Liabilities		21,503.79
Equity		
Capital Stock		10,000.00
Retained Earnings		19,392.89
Total Equity		29,392.89
TOTAL LIABILITIES & EQUITY		50,896.68

Figure 7-52 Academy Photography Balance Sheet

Setting the Closing Date - Backing up the File – Step 12

Now that you have entered all of your opening balances in the file, create a backup of the file. After you begin entering transactions you should back up your file on a regular basis, but keep the backup you perform in Step 12 of the setup on a separate disk or in a separate folder on your computer's hard drive, so that you always have a clean record of your setup transactions.

Setting the Closing Date to Protect your Setup Balances

For details on setting the *Closing Date* and the *Closing Date password*, see the Adjustments Chapter, available with this book's supplemental material (see page xiii for more information).

Congratulations! You have finished the setup of your company file. You are now ready to set up users of the file, modify your sales forms, and begin entering transactions. The process for setting up users and passwords is in the next section, but the setup of your sales forms is covered on page 355.

Users and Passwords

QuickBooks provides a feature for defining "users" of the file. This feature allows the "administrator" (the owner of the file) to set privileges for each user of the file. This provides security and user tracking when several people have access to the same data file.

Setting Up Users in the Company File

Each user should have a separate user name and password. Once users have been setup, when a company file is opened, QuickBooks will require a user name and password. The privileges granted to that user by the administrator determine what functions of QuickBooks they can access. For example, a user might have access to Accounts Receivable, Accounts Payable, and Banking functions, but not payroll or "sensitive activities" like online banking. For a complete description of each privilege, click the **Help** button on the *User Setup* windows.

COMPUTER PRACTICE

Step 1. First you will setup the Administrator's password. Select the **Company** menu, select **Set Up Users and Passwords**, and then select **Change Your Password.** The Change Password window will appear (Figure 7-53).

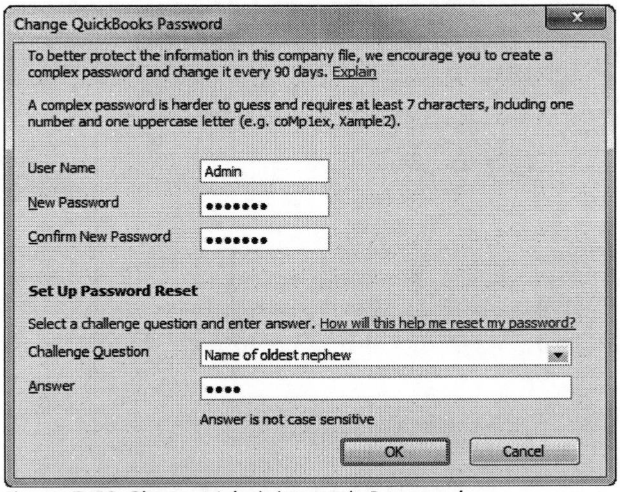

Figure 7-53 Change Administrator's Password

Step 2. Leave **Admin** in the *Administrator's Name* field and then press **Tab** (see Figure 7-53).

You could, of course, change the Administrator's name, but even if you do, you'll always be able to log in (or open the file) as the administrator if you enter ***Admin*** in the user name field and if you enter the administrator's correct password.

Step 3. Enter ***Abc1234*** in the *Administrator's Password* and *Confirm Password* fields. Once you enter this password, you will need to remember this password to open this exercise file in the future.

Several privileges are reserved for the Administrator of the file. For example, the Administrator is the only one who can view or change the company information (name, address, etc) for the file. Also, the Administrator is the only one who can make any changes to the *Company Preferences* tabs in the preference section. For more information about the file administrator, see QuickBooks online Help.

> **Note:**
> To protect and secure your QuickBooks data file, always use a complex password. Complex passwords use seven characters, including letters, numbers and special characters. At least one of the characters should be a number, and another an uppercase letter. Some examples of secure passwords include good2Go, 4mmLens and 3Four56,

Step 4. In the *Challenge Question* field, select **Name of oldest nephew**.

Step 5. Enter **Bill** in the Answer field. Click OK.

Step 6. Now you will setup the user's privileges. Select **Set Up Users** from the *Set Up Users and Passwords* submenu of the *Company* menu. The QuickBooks Login window displays (see Figure 7-54).

Step 7. Type ***Abc1234*** in the *Password* field and click **OK**.

Figure 7-54 QuickBooks Login window

Step 8. The window in Figure 7-55 shows the *User list* for this company file. To create an additional user, click **Add User**.

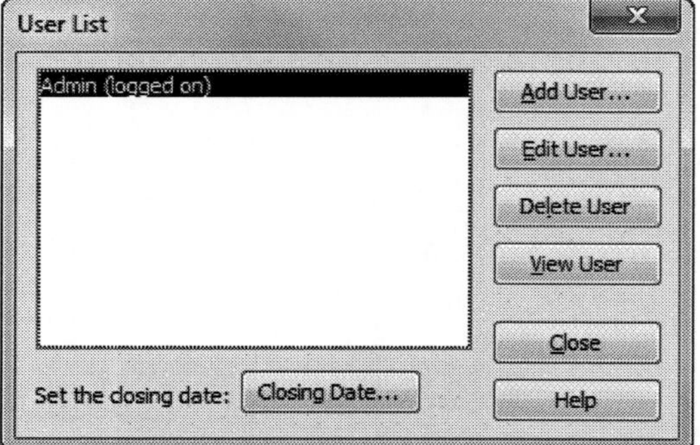

Figure 7-55 The User list for a company file

Step 9. When you click **Add User**, QuickBooks walks you through a series of windows (a Wizard) where you set privileges for each user (see Figure 7-56). Make your selections as appropriate.

Step 10. On the *User Name and Password* window, enter ***Kathy*** in the *User Name* field, and enter ***Abc4321*** in the *Password* and *Confirm Password* fields. Click **Next**.

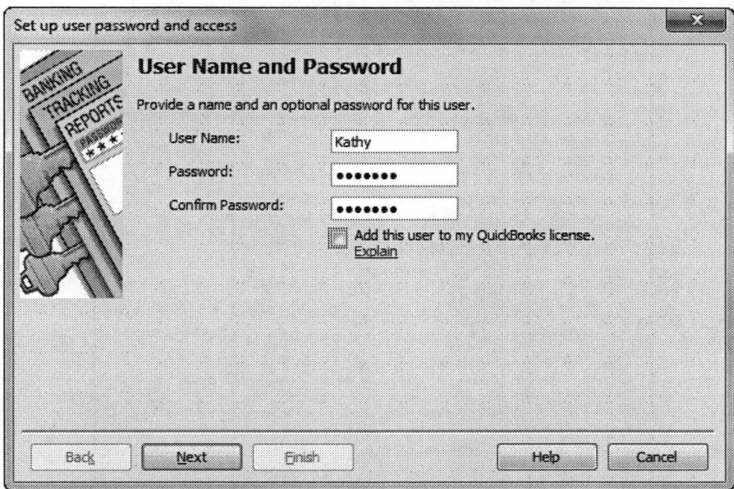

Figure 7-56 The User Name and Password window

Step 11. On the *Access for user: Kathy* window, select **Selected areas of QuickBooks** (see Figure 7-57). Click **Next**.

As the Administrator, you can give users access to all areas of QuickBooks or you can restrict access to selected areas of the program.

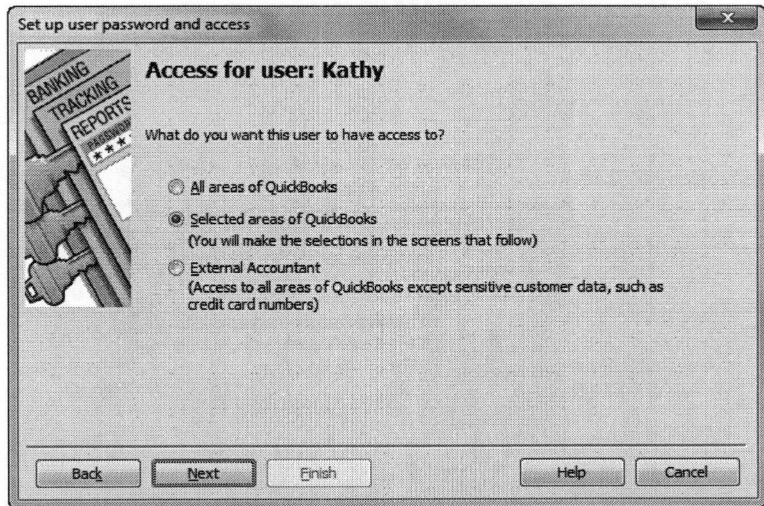

Figure 7-57 You can restrict a user's access

Did you know?
By selecting *Access to All areas of QuickBooks,* you give a user permission to change transactions in closed periods. Choosing *Selected areas* for all users allows you to protect your prior period accounting data without limiting the users' access to any other transactions or reporting (see Figure 7-59).

Step 12. On the *Sales and Accounts Receivable* window, select **Full Access** and click **Next** (see Figure 7-58).

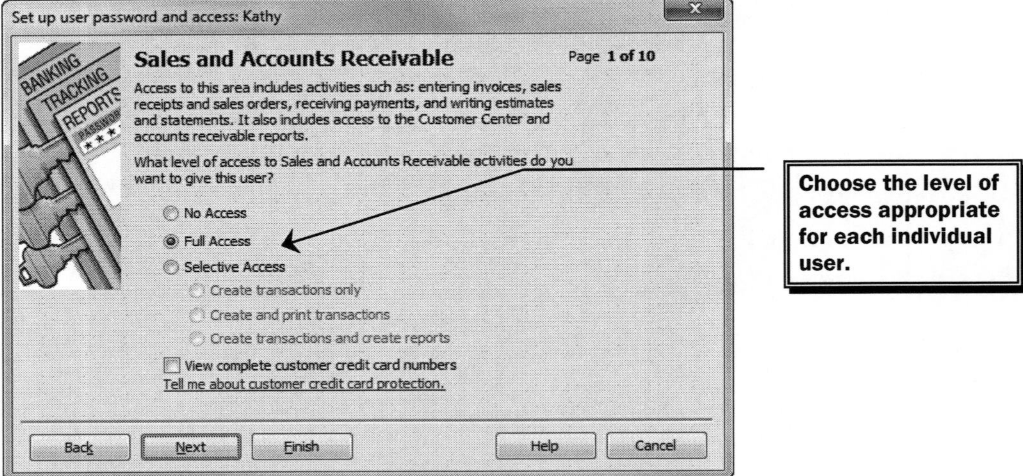

Figure 7-58 The Sales and Accounts Receivable window

Step 13. Click **Next** on each of the following windows to view the default settings.

When setting up your own file, set access rights for each new user as appropriate. If you are not sure what to select, click **Help**. Online Help will fully explain each privilege.

Each user should be restricted from *changing or deleting transactions before the closing date* (see Figure 7-59). This setting creates additional protection for your accounting data once you have closed the books for a period.

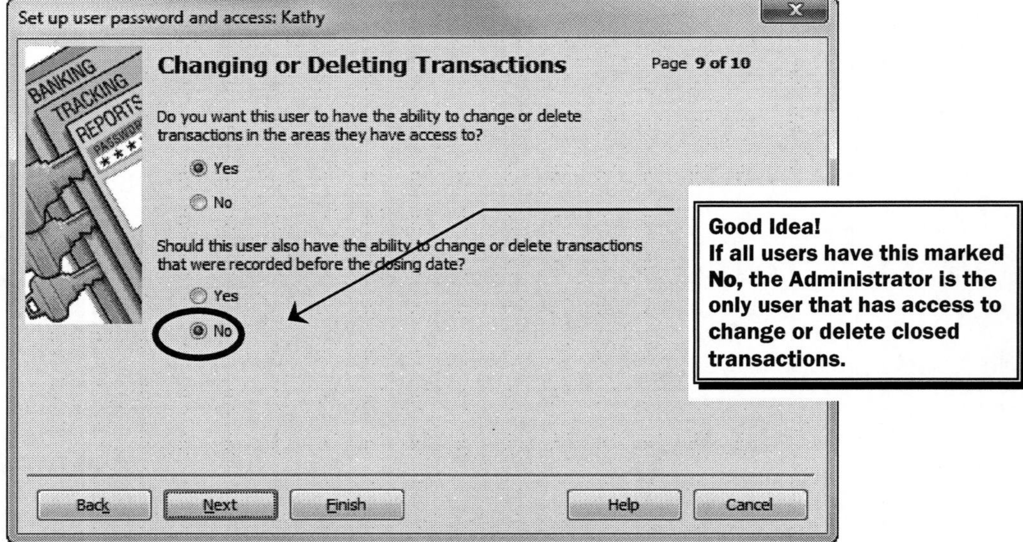

Figure 7-59 Changing or Deleting Transactions window

Step 14. On the final window, review the privileges that you have set for this user (see Figure 7-60). If you want to make any changes, click **Prev** until you see the window you want to change. To save your new user settings, click **Finish**.

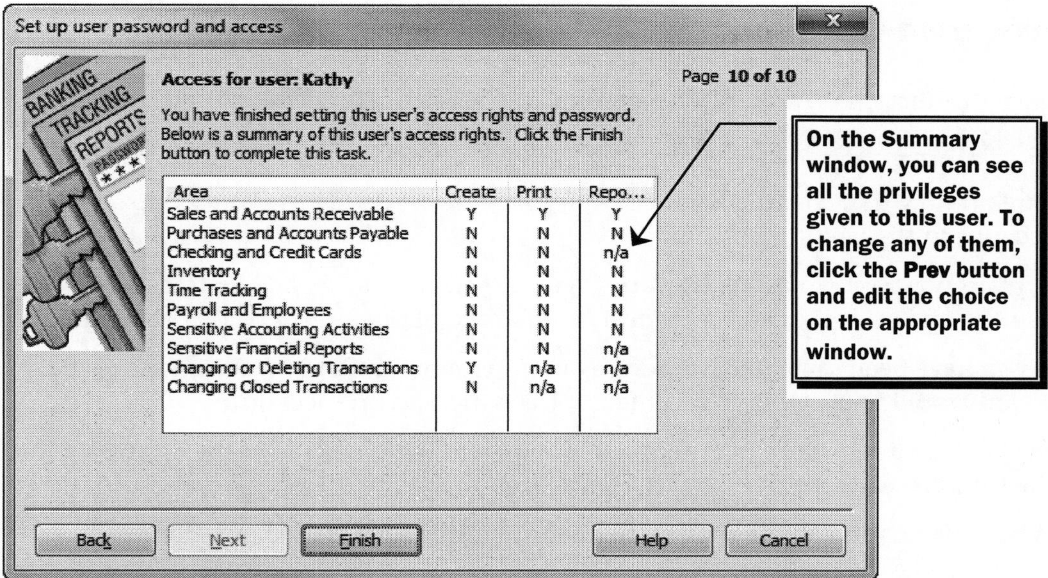

Figure 7-60 The Summary window

Step 15. Click **Close** on the *User List* window.

> Tip:
> Some tasks, such as changing the Customer Preferences, can only be done in Single-User mode. To turn off Multi-User mode, choose *Switch to Single-user Mode* from the *File* menu.

Chapter Summary and Review

Summary of Key Points

In this chapter, you learned how to set up a company file in QuickBooks. Setting up the file is the most important part of making QuickBooks work well for you. Don't forget to verify that all your balances are correct before using your data file.

Topics covered in this chapter include:

- Perform a Complete Company File Setup Using the 12-step Process (page 275).
- Choose a Start Date (page 275).
- Use the EasyStep Interview to set up your Company File (page 276).
- Setup Accounts in the Chart of Accounts List (page 287).
- Gather Your Information for Setting up Opening Balances (page 298).
- Enter Opening Balances (page 301).
- Enter Year-to-Date Income and Expenses (page 308).
- Adjust the Opening Balance for Sales Tax Payable (page 309).
- Adjust Inventory for Physical Quantities on Hand (page 310).
- Verify your Opening Balances (page 312).
- Close Opening Balance Equity into Retained Earnings (page 313).
- Back up the File and Setting the Closing Date (page 315).
- Set Up Users and Passwords (page 315).

Comprehension Questions

> Answers to these review questions are available with the supplemental material. See page xiii for details.

1. Explain how the Opening Balance Equity account is used when you set up a new bank account in the Chart of Accounts.
2. Explain how you would set up your Chart of Accounts to separately track state, county, and city taxes and provide a summary total of all taxes paid at the same time.
3. If you have been separately tracking your entertainment and meal expenses, what action would you take if you wanted to track them as one account?
4. Explain the importance of entering your outstanding checks as of the Start Date into the *Checking* account.
5. What information should you gather before setting up a QuickBooks file?

Multiple Choice

Select the best answer(s) for each of the following:

1. If you're setting up QuickBooks and plan to begin using it at the beginning of the next calendar year, the best start date for your company file setup is:
   a) The first day of the year (01/01/xx).
   b) The day you are starting to use QuickBooks, regardless of the fiscal year.
   c) The last day of the previous year (12/31/xx).
   d) The first day of the quarter chosen for conversion.
2. This chapter suggests that the best way to set up A/R and A/P balances in QuickBooks is to:
   a) Enter the total amount of A/R and A/P on a journal entry dated on your start date.
   b) Enter the balance of each account by editing the accounts in the Chart of Accounts.
   c) Use a special account called A/R Setup (or A/P Setup) to record the opening balances.
   d) Enter a separate Invoice for each open invoice and enter a separate Bill for each unpaid bill.
3. Setting up a company file does not include:
   a) Obtaining a business license.
   b) Selecting the appropriate chart of accounts for your type of business.
   c) Adding accounts to the chart of accounts.
   d) Entering Invoices.
4. A good example of a liability account is:
   a) Inventory.
   b) Accounts Receivable.
   c) Advertising.
   d) Accounts Payable.

5. To ensure the accuracy of the information entered during setup, it is important to:
   a) Know your Retained Earnings.
   b) Verify that your Trial Balance matches the one provided by your accountant.
   c) Start at the beginning of the fiscal period.
   d) Know everything there is to know about accounting.

6. Close Opening Bal Equity into Retained Earnings by:
   a) Starting to enter new daily transactions.
   b) Creating a General Journal Entry.
   c) Setting the Closing Date. QuickBooks will then make the entry for you.
   d) Selecting **Close Opening Balance** on the **Activities** menu.

7. If you no longer need an account in the Chart of Accounts, you can delete it. However, if it has transactions posted to it, you cannot delete it. Instead:
   a) You should ignore it.
   b) You should rename it.
   c) You can merge it with another account, or you can deactivate it.
   d) You can move it to the bottom of the chart of accounts, which will cause it to no longer appear on reports.

8. Which of the following is NOT a way to deactivate an account?
   a) Right-click on the account and select **Make Inactive.**
   b) Select **Make Account Inactive** from the **Account** menu at the bottom of the Chart of Accounts.
   c) Edit the account and click **Account is Inactive.**
   d) Select the account and check the **Include Inactive** checkbox at the bottom of the Chart of Accounts.

9. When account numbers are inactive and you click the *Name* header:
   a) QuickBooks sorts the account list alphabetically by account name.
   b) You can rename the selected account.
   c) You will see all account names.
   d) You can rename the Chart of Accounts list.

10. As the administrator, you can set up new users of the file and restrict access to several areas in the program. Which is something you CANNOT restrict?
    a) Access to all bank accounts.
    b) Access to A/P transactions.
    c) Access to Payroll.
    d) Access to one bank account, but no access to another bank account.

11. When verifying your setup, create a Balance Sheet and verify that Retained Earnings matches the Trial Balance from the accountant. If your start date is 12/31, what date should you use on this Balance Sheet?
    a) Always use the Start Date.
    b) December 31.
    c) January 1.
    d) December 30.

12. To set up the opening balance in your *Sales Tax Payable* account, wait until after you've entered your open invoices. Then adjust the *Sales Tax Payable* account for the additional sales tax due. Why is this adjustment necessary?
    a) Because Opening Bal Equity is not involved.
    b) Because the total amount in Sales Tax Payable is the sum of the *uncollected* sales tax (from the open invoices) plus the *collected* sales tax. Since you already entered the open invoices, the Sales Tax Payable account only has the *uncollected*

sales tax and you have to add in the *collected* sales tax by adjusting the account balance.
c) Because there is no other way to set up the opening balance in Sales Tax Payable.
d) All of the above.

13. Where does QuickBooks place new accounts in the Chart of Accounts after it has been manually reordered?
    a) Alphabetically within its account type.
    b) Alphabetically in the list, regardless of account type.
    c) At the top of the list, within its account type.
    d) At the bottom of the Chart of Accounts.

14. If you have an open Invoice for an inventory item on your start date, to properly set up your Inventory balances (Quantity and Value):
    a) Use a Journal Entry to debit Inventory for the total value of the inventory and then select **Setup Inventory Quantities** from the **Inventory** menu.
    b) Use an Inventory Adjustment transaction *after* you enter in your opening Invoices and Bills.
    c) Use an Inventory Adjustment transaction *before* you enter in your opening Invoices and Bills.
    d) Use the *Opening Balance* field in the *Edit Account* window.

15. Which of the following do you set up using the *EasyStep Interview*?
    a) Default Accounts.
    b) Outstanding Checks and Deposits.
    c) Inventory.
    d) Sales Tax.

Completion Statements

1. There are five basic account types in accounting: __________, __________, __________, __________, and ____________.
2. It is impossible to _________ a QuickBooks account if you have used it in transactions.
3. At the end of your setup, close the ___________ _____________ ___________ account into Retained Earnings.
4. You can use a _______ _________ ________ to record multiple accounts' opening balances at one time.
5. The account balances on your __________ ____________ from your previous books and your QuickBooks file should match at the end of your file setup.

Setup-Problem 1

APPLYING YOUR KNOWLEDGE

Create a **new** QuickBooks company file for Academy Photography. Use the information from the following tables and figures to completely set up the file using 12/31/2010 as your start date. Use the 12-step setup process discussed in this chapter.

Company Info	
Company Name	Academy Photography
Legal Name	Academy Photography, Inc.
Federal ID	11-1111111
Address	123 Main Street Pleasanton, CA 94588
Country	US
Phone	925-555-1111
Fax	925-555-1112
Email	info@academyphoto.biz
Web site	http://www.academyphoto.biz
First Month of Fiscal Year	January
Income Tax Form	S Corporation
Industry	Art, Writing or Photography
Administrative Password	*Leave Blank*

Table 7-9 Company Information

EasyStep Interview Settings	
Products and Services	Academy Photography sells both products and services, although they do not sell products online.
Sales	Academy Photography charges sales tax and creates estimates. They want to track sales orders (if using Premier) and use both sales receipts and progress invoicing.
Purchases & Vendors	Academy Photography will need to create billing statements and track bills. They will also want to print checks. They will be tracking inventory. They do not plan to accept credit or debit cards.
Employees	Academy Photography has both W-2 employees and 1099 contractors. They will want to track time.
Currency	Academy Photography does not need to track multiple currencies.

Table 7-10 EasyStep Interview settings

Additional Accounts for the Chart of Accounts		
Acct #	**Account Name**	**Account Type**
10100	Checking	Bank
10200	Money Market	Bank
10900	Journal Entries	Bank
22000	National Bank VISA Gold	Credit Card
24010	Payroll Liabilities:Company Payroll Taxes Payable	Other Current Liability
24020	Payroll Liabilities:Employee Payroll Taxes Payable	Other Current Liability
24030	Payroll Liabilities:Other Payroll Liabilities	Other Current Liability
27000	Truck Loan	Long Term Liability
40000	Services	Income
45000	Sales (*note: change number of existing account*)	Income

Table 7-11 Additional Accounts for the Chart of Accounts

Accounts – In addition to the default Chart of Accounts, add the accounts listed in Table 7-1. Since QuickBooks automatically created a Sales Income Account, you will only need to change the Account Number for this account. It is not necessary to enter descriptions, bank account numbers, or assign tax line items to any of these accounts for this problem. You will also create subaccounts, whose names are separated from the main account by a colon (:). For example, Company Payroll Taxes Payable is a subaccount of Payroll Liabilities. For a full recommended Chart of Accounts, see Setup Problem 2.

Items – Table 7-12 is the Item list that will be used to track products and services sold by Academy Photography.

Type	Item	Description	Tax Code	Account	Cost	Price
Service	Indoor Photo Session	Indoor Studio Session	Non	Services		$ 95.00
Service	Retouching	Photo retouching services	Non	Services		$ 95.00
Inventory Part	Camera SR32	Supra Digital Camera SR32	Tax	Sales	$ 450.00	$ 695.99
Inventory Part	Case	Camera and Lens High Impact Case	Tax	Sales	$ 45.00	$ 79.99
Non-Inventory Part	Standard Photo Package	Standard Package of Photography from Session	Tax	Sales		$ 55.00
Sales Tax Item	Contra Costa	Contra Costa Sales Tax Vendor: State Board of Equalization (QuickAdd)	Non	Sales Tax Payable		8.25%
Sales Tax Item	Out of State (Automatically Created)	Out of State Sales Tax exempt from sales tax	Non	Sales Tax Payable		0%
Sales Tax Item	Santa Clara	Santa Clara Sales Tax Vendor: State Board of Equalization (QuickAdd)	Non	Sales Tax Payable		8.25%

Table 7-12 Item List

Classes – Academy Photography uses classes to separately track revenues and expenses from each of their locations. You will need to turn on class tracking in the Accounting Company Preferences.

Class Names	San Jose	Walnut Creek	Overhead

Table 7-13 Class Tracking

Terms – Verify the following terms in the Terms list.

Net 30	Net 15	2% 10, Net 30	Due on Receipt

Table 7-14 Terms List

Bank Statements – Figure 7-61 shows the Checking account bank statement for Academy Photography on their Start Date of 12/31/2010. There is no bank statement available for the money market account, but you've been told that there are no outstanding deposits or checks in that account. Enter the Bank Ending Balance as the opening balance for Checking account.

Business Checking Account

Statement Date:	December 31, 2010	Page 1 of 1

Summary:

Previous Balance as of 11/30/10:	$	32,624.52
Total Deposits and Credits: 2	+ $	10,157.28
Total Checks and Debits: 9	- $	7,027.40
Total Interest Earned: 1	+ $	8.62
Total Service Charge: 1	- $	10.00
Statement Balance as of 12/31/10:	**= $**	**35,753.02**

Deposits and Other Credits:

DEPOSITS

Date	Description		Amount
8-Dec	Customer Deposit	$	6,150.00
20-Dec	Customer Deposit	$	4,007.28
	2 Deposits:	**$**	**10,157.28**

INTEREST

Date	Description		Amount
31-Dec	Interest Earned	$	8.62
	Interest:	**$**	**8.62**

Checks and Other Withdrawals:

CHECKS PAID:

Check No.	Date Paid		Amount
3466	2-Dec	$	324.00
3467	3-Dec	$	128.60
3468	5-Dec	$	83.00
3469	8-Dec	$	285.00
3470	10-Dec	$	1,528.00
3471	12-Dec	$	3,000.00
3472	13-Dec	$	276.52
3473	15-Dec	$	142.00
3474	28-Dec	$	1,260.28
	9 Checks Paid:	**$**	**7,027.40**

SERVICE CHARGES

Date	Description		Amount
31-Dec	Service Charge	$	10.00
	1 Service Charge:	**$**	**10.00**

Figure 7-61 Bank statement for checking account on 12/31/2010

Outstanding Checks and Deposits – Table 7-15 shows a list of outstanding checks and deposits in the Checking account on 12/31/2010. Enter outstanding check and deposit in the checking account register using the original date and Opening Balance Equity as the offsetting account. Don't worry if payee information is not available.

Outstanding Deposits at 12/31/10			Outstanding Checks at 12/31/10		
Date	**Amount**		**Date**	**Check #**	**Amount**
12/30/2010	$2000.00		12/26/2010	3475	3462.85

Table 7-15 Outstanding checks and deposits.

Open Invoices - Table 7-16 shows a list of all open Invoices for Academy Photography on 12/31/2010. Enter open invoices using the original information and Intuit Product Invoice template. "QuickAdd" each of the customer names when prompted. Save the tax information to be used again.

Inv #	Invoice Date	Customer:Job	Class	Terms	Item/Qty/Amt Due
2010-955	12/18/2010	Doughboy Donuts	San Jose	Net 30	Indoor Photo Session 3 Hours $ 285.00 Retouching 1 Hour $ 95.00 Total: $ 380.00
2010-942	12/21/2010	Scotts Shoes	San Jose	Net 30	Camera $695.99 Santa Clara Sales Tax Total : $ 753.41

Table 7-16 Open Invoices

Unpaid Bills - Academy Photography had one unpaid Bill at 12/31/2010. Enter the bill with original information. "QuickAdd" each of the vendor names when prompted. Save the terms information to be used again.

Bill #	Bill Date	Terms	Vendor	Amt Due	Account/Item	Job	Class
52773	12/21/10	Net 15	Boswell Consulting	438.00	Subcontracted Services	Scotts Shoes	San Jose

Table 7-17 Unpaid bills

Physical Inventory by Inventory Part – Below is the physical Inventory counts and values at 12/31/2010. Enter the Ref. No. as 2010-1 and Opening Balance Equity as Adjusting account. Select **Save Anyway** option when a dialog box appears asking for class information.

Physical Inventory at 12/31/2010		
Item	**Quantity on Hand**	**Value**
Camera	20	$ 9000.00
Case	20	$ 900.00

Table 7-18 Physical Inventory by Inventory Part

Trial Balance – Table 7-19 shows the ending Trial Balance for Academy Photography on 12/31/2010. Enter opening balances for Asset, Liabilities and Equity accounts to match the Trial Balance amounts.

Adjust Sales Tax Payable to match Trial Balance amount, using Vendor: State Board of Equalization and Account: Opening Balance Equity.

Close the Opening Balance Equity account to Retained Earnings.

You will notice that the Trial Balance does not exactly match the one in Table 7-19. The income and expenses from the open Invoices and unpaid Bills shows in the income and expense accounts. This is CORRECT! When QuickBooks "closes" the year, those numbers will be posted into Retained Earnings. To see it work, change the date on the Trial Balance to 01/01/2011.

Academy Photography		
Trial Balance		
December 31, 2010		
	Debit	Credit
Checking	$34,290.17	
Money Market	$68,100.00	
Accounts Receivable	$1,133.41	
Inventory	$9,900.00	
Furniture and Equipment	$85,365.00	
Accumulated Depreciation		$43,550.00
Accounts Payable		$438.00
National Bank VISA Gold		$2,152.00
Payroll Liabilities: Company Payroll Taxes Payable		$83.00
Payroll Liabilities: Employee Payroll Taxes Payable		$285.00
Sales Tax Payable		$327.03
Truck Loan		$28,625.00
Capital Stock		$10,000.00
Retained Earnings		$113,328.55
TOTAL	$198,788.58	$198,788.58

Table 7-19 Trial balance on 12/31/2010

After completing the setup, print the following reports:

1. Account Listing
2. Item Listing
3. Open Invoices Report at 12/31/2010
4. Unpaid Bills Detail Report at 12/31/2010
5. Inventory Valuation Summary Report at 12/31/2010
6. Trial Balance as of 12/31/2010
7. Trial Balance as of 01/01/11
8. Balance Sheet Standard on 01/01/2011

Notice that Retained Earnings on the 01/01/2011 Balance Sheet has been adjusted for the income and expenses from last year. This shows how QuickBooks automatically calculates Retained Earnings. If you change the date on the Balance Sheet to 12/31/2010, you'll see Net Income on the Balance Sheet and the Retained Earnings number will change back to the "before closing" amounts. Try it.

Optional Setup-Problem 2

In Setup-Problem 1 you used the default Chart of Accounts with a few additions. We recommend further customization to the Chart of Accounts when you setup a company file. For this problem, create a Chart of Accounts using the file you created in Problem 1.

The Chart of Accounts is listed in Table 7-11. It is not necessary to enter descriptions, bank account numbers, or assign tax line items to any of these accounts for this problem. When you create the new data file, QuickBooks will create some accounts on the chart of accounts for you. Your goal in this exercise is to add, delete, or modify the existing chart of accounts as necessary so that it agrees to the list below. As in Problem 1, you will also create subaccounts, whose names are separated from the main account by a colon (:).

After completing the setup, print an Account Listing.

Chart of Accounts		
Acct #	**Account Name**	**Account Type**
10100	Checking	Bank
10200	Money Market	Bank
10300	Savings	Bank
10900	Journal Entries	Bank
11000	Accounts Receivable	Accounts Receivable
12100	Inventory Asset	Other Current Asset
12800	Employee Advances	Other Current Asset
13100	Prepaid Insurance	Other Current Asset
15000	Furniture and Equipment	Fixed Asset
15200	Buildings and Improvements	Fixed Asset
15600	Land	Fixed Asset
15900	Leasehold Improvements	Fixed Asset
16400	Vehicles	Fixed Asset
17000	Accumulated Depreciation	Fixed Asset
18700	Security Deposits Asset	Other Asset
20000	Accounts Payable	Accounts Payable
22000	National Bank VISA Gold	Credit Card
24000	Payroll Liabilities	Other Current Liability
24010	Payroll Liabilities:Company Payroll Taxes Payable	Other Current Liability
24020	Payroll Liabilities:Employee Payroll Taxes Payable	Other Current Liability
24030	Payroll Liabilities:Other Payroll Liabilities	Other Current Liability
24200	Line of Credit	Other Current Liability
24500	Advance Customer Payments	Other Current Liability
25500	Sales Tax Payable	Other Current Liability
27000	Truck Loan	Long Term Liability
30000	Opening Bal Equity	Equity
30100	Capital Stock	Equity
31400	Shareholder Distributions	Equity
32000	Retained Earnings	Equity
40000	Services	Income
45000	Sales	Income
50000	Cost of Goods Sold	Cost of Goods Sold
53000	Purchase Discounts	Cost of Goods Sold
53500	Subcontracted Services	Cost of Goods Sold
54000	Inventory Variance	Cost of Goods Sold
60000	Advertising and Promotion	Expense
60200	Automobile Expense	Expense
60300	Bad Debts	Expense
60400	Bank Service Charges	Expense
61700	Computer and Internet Expenses	Expense
62400	Depreciation Expense	Expense
62500	Dues and Subscriptions	Expense
62600	Equipment Rental	Expense

63300	Insurance Expense	Expense
63400	Interest Expense	Expense
64300	Meals and Entertainment	Expense
64900	Office Supplies	Expense
66000	Payroll Expenses	Expense
66010	Payroll Expenses:Employee Benefits	Expense
66020	Payroll Expenses:Gross Wages	Expense
66040	Payroll Expenses:Officer's Compensation	Expense
66060	Payroll Expenses:Payroll Tax Expense	Expense
66500	Postage and Delivery	Expense
66700	Professional Fees	Expense
67100	Rent Expense	Expense
67200	Repairs and Maintenance	Expense
68100	Telephone Expense	Expense
68130	Telephone Expense:Office Phone	Expense
68150	Telephone Expense:Cell Phone	Expense
68400	Travel Expense	Expense
68600	Utilities	Expense
70200	Interest Income	Other Income
80000	Ask My Accountant	Other Expense
90000	Estimates	Non-Posting

Table 7-20 The Chart of Accounts

Workplace Applications

Discussion Questions

These questions are designed to stimulate discussion about how you can apply QuickBooks to your own organization. They may help you think through some of the issues you'll encounter when using QuickBooks in your company.

1. What would be the best start date for using QuickBooks in your organization? Why?
2. How many accounts are in your organization's Chart of Accounts? How many subaccounts are there? What is the advantage of subaccounts to your organization? Or, if you do not use subaccounts, could there be a benefit to using them and what would it be?
3. Consider the accounts that have outlived their usefulness to your company. Is the best approach to merge them, delete them, or deactivate them? Explain your answer.
4. As your company sets up QuickBooks, what do you think the approach should be for enter opening balances for customers and vendors? Why?

ACTIVITY

Evaluate your company's Chart of Accounts and how well it fits your company's needs. Identify accounts that could be setup as subaccounts or merged into others to better track company income or expenses. Design a Chart of Accounts based on your findings that would best fit your company's needs.

Case Study

Music Central

Music Central sells and services musical instruments and offers music lessons. They track several of each type of instrument in inventory but they do not track replacement parts in inventory. All of the piano and guitar lessons are subcontracted to Thomas Teaches Tunes; and all piano maintenance is subcontracted to Key Tuning Company. However, all wind instruments are taught by Music Central employees. The company is located in downtown Boston and is required to charge state, county, and local sales tax. They have just hired you to convert their manual accounting system to QuickBooks.

The company inventories the following types of instruments, and they stock several different brands of each:

Trumpets (2 brands)	Saxophones (3 brands)
Flutes (1 brand)	Clarinets (3 brands)
Guitars (6 brands)	Pianos (3 brands)

Table 7-21 Inventory of instruments

The company stocks (but does not track in inventory), the following replacement parts:

Key Pads – Various Sizes
Strings – Various sizes
Valves - Various types and sizes
Reeds – Various types and sizes

Table 7-22 Replacement parts

The company performs the following services:

Trumpet Lesson
Flute Lesson
Saxophone Lesson
Clarinet Lesson
Guitar Lesson (subcontracted)
Piano Tuning/Maint (subcontracted)
Piano Lesson (subcontracted)

Table 7-23 Company Services Performed

1. Describe how you would approach the setup of the Item list for this company. Discuss the trade-offs of tracking each brand of instrument as a separate inventory part, and the impact it will have on the amount of data entry for the bookkeeper. Make recommendations on how you would set up the Item list for the company.
2. How would you set up the system to separately track the income and expenses for the subcontracted services?
3. What information would you need from the owner of the company to set up the opening balances for the company, assuming they are a calendar year company and you chose to set them up on 12/31/2010?
4. The owner wants only two people in the company to be able to use Payroll in QuickBooks. How would you set up their access differently from others who are not allowed to use Payroll?

Chapter 8 Customizing QuickBooks

After completing this chapter, you should be able to:

- Modify QuickBooks Preferences (page 332).
- Customize QuickBooks Menus and Windows (page 333).
- Customize the Icon Bar and Display settings (page 336).
- Use the Item List and Other Lists (page 342).
- Use Custom Fields to Track Extra Data on Transactions (page 353).
- Create and Customize Sales Forms (page 355).

> **Restore this File:**
> This chapter uses the Customizing-10.QBW. To open this file, restore the Customizing-10.QBM file to your hard disk. See page 10 for instructions on restoring files.

QuickBooks has many customizable options that allow you to configure the program to meet your own needs and preferences. This chapter introduces you to many of the ways you can make these configurations in QuickBooks using Preferences, customizing the toolbars, and creating templates for forms. This chapter also introduces some new lists, including the *Item* list, the *Terms* list, and the *Template* list.

QuickBooks Preferences

There are two types of preferences in QuickBooks:

1. **User Preferences.** In QuickBooks, user preferences are specific to the user that is currently logged onto the file. You can identify User Preferences on the *My Preferences* tab in the Preferences window. A user can make changes to his or her user preferences as desired. The changes will not affect other users of the data file. Examples of user preferences include changing displays setting (e.g., colors), report settings, and spell check settings.

2. **Company Preferences.** Use Company Preferences to make global changes to the features and functionality of an individual company's data file. For example, the preference that turns Sales Tax Tracking on or off is a Company Preference. Only the *Administrator* of the data file can make changes to Company Preferences. Note that each company's preferences are independent of the preferences established for other QuickBooks companies on your computer.

In this section, you will learn about a few of these preferences and how they affect QuickBooks. Clicking the *Help* button in the *Preferences* window will launch QuickBooks Help with specific topics relevant to the preference in the open window.

> **Note:**
> Many of the preferences are discussed in detail in other chapters, so they are not repeated here. For example, the payroll preferences are discussed in the Payroll Setup chapter, beginning on page 481.

Setting User Preferences

COMPUTER PRACTICE

To access QuickBooks Preferences, follow these steps:

Step 1. Select the *Edit* menu, and then select **Preferences**.

User Preferences – Desktop View

Step 2. Click the **Desktop View** icon. See Figure 8-1.

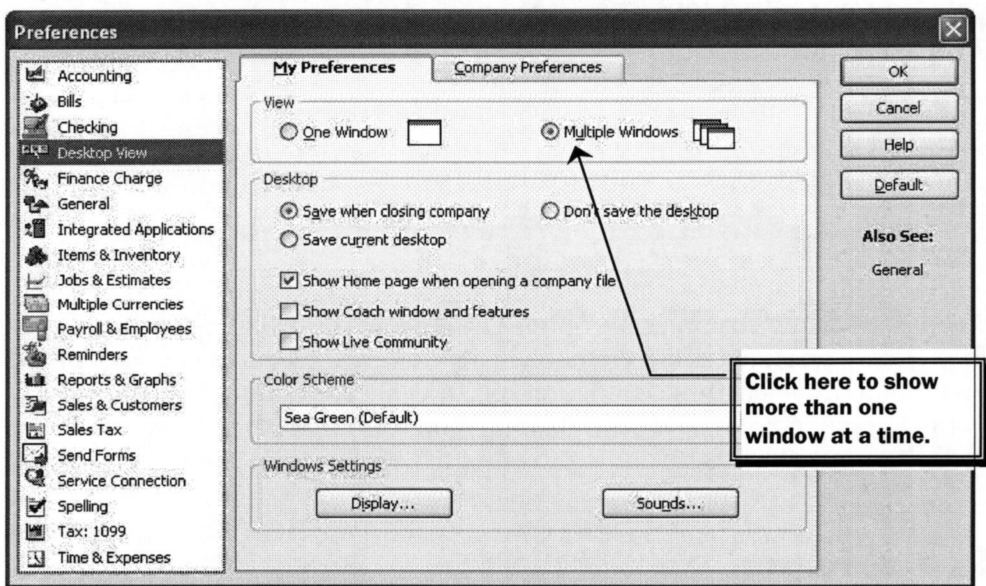

Figure 8-1 User Preferences - Desktop View

The user preferences for **Desktop View** allow you to customize the default windows that show when you open QuickBooks. We recommend selecting **Multiple Windows** as shown on Figure 8-1. When you first create a data file, QuickBooks selects **One Window** as the default preference. Unless you change the preference to **Multiple Windows**, you will not be able to display more than one QuickBooks window at a time, and you will not be able to change the size of QuickBooks windows. You will probably find the program much easier to navigate if you select **Multiple Windows**. You can also change the color and graphics of QuickBooks toolbars and windows by selecting a different default from the *Color Scheme* drop down menu.

There is also the **Show Home page when opening a company file** option. Activating this preference causes the new *Home* page window to be displayed whenever the company file is opened.

> **Tip:**
> If you use QuickBooks in a multi-user environment, it may be best to check the *Don't save the desktop* box on the window shown in Figure 8-1. If you save the desktop, each time you open QuickBooks it will re-open all of the windows and reports you were viewing when you last used the program. If you save the desktop, this may negatively impact performance for other users when they open the data file.

You can also turn on and off the *Show Coach window and features* as well as the *Live Community* option in the Desktop View preferences window. For more on the QuickBooks Coach features see page 30.

Company Preferences – Accounting

Step 3. Click the **Accounting** preference and then click the **Company Preferences** tab (see Figure 8-2).

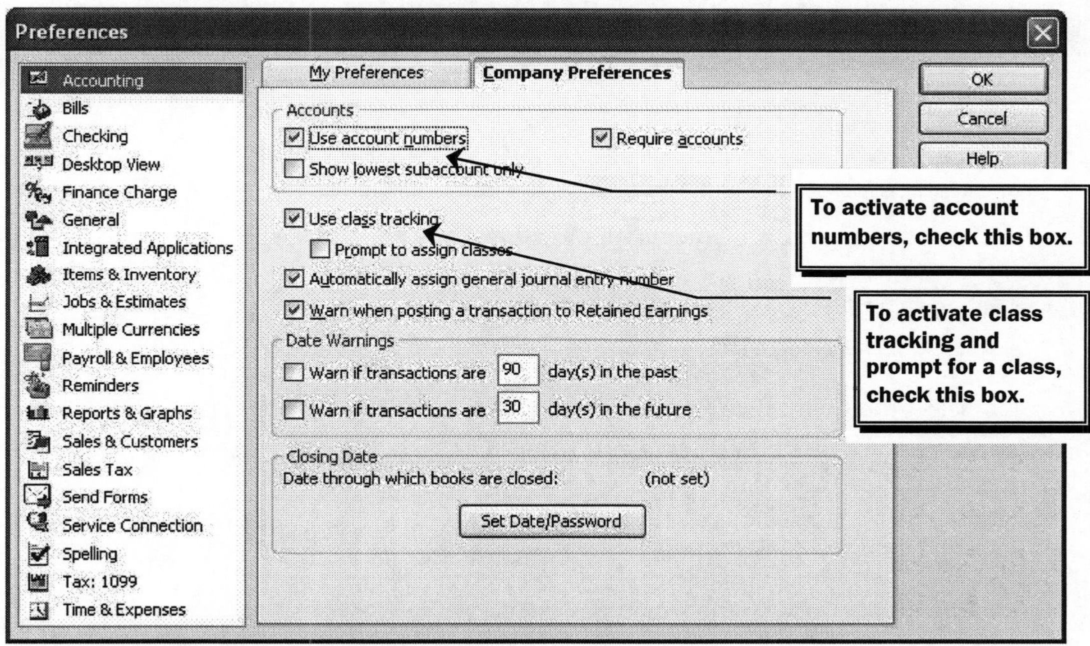

Figure 8-2 The Accounting—Company Preferences window

Use the *Accounting* Company Preferences to control many fundamental features of QuickBooks, such as turning on class tracking and using account numbers.

To see a complete list of each preference and each of the features, see the Appendix included with the supplemental material available online.

Step 4. Click **OK** to close the *Preferences* window.

Customizing QuickBooks Menus and Windows

QuickBooks gives you the ability set up some special customized features. You can create a *Favorites Menu* for your regular activities. You can access the *Open Window List*, which allows you to quickly access various open windows which is particularly important when your windows are maximized. You can also customize the *Icon Bar*, which gives you easy access various commands.

Favorites Menu

The *Favorites* menu is a customizable menu where you can place your common QuickBooks commands.

COMPUTER PRACTICE

Step 1. Locate the *Favorites* Menu between the *Lists* and *Company* menu. (Those using the QuickBooks Premier Accountant Edition will see it between the *Lists* and *Accountant* menu).

If you do not see the *Favorites* menu, you can turn it on by selecting **Favorites Menu** from the *View* menu (see Figure 8-3).

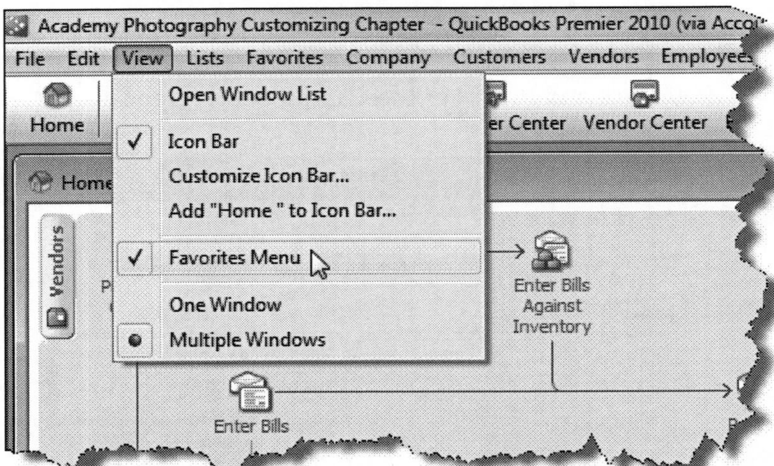

Figure 8-3 Favorites Menu option in the View menu

Step 2. Select the **Customize Favorites** option from the *Favorites* menu (see Figure 8-4).

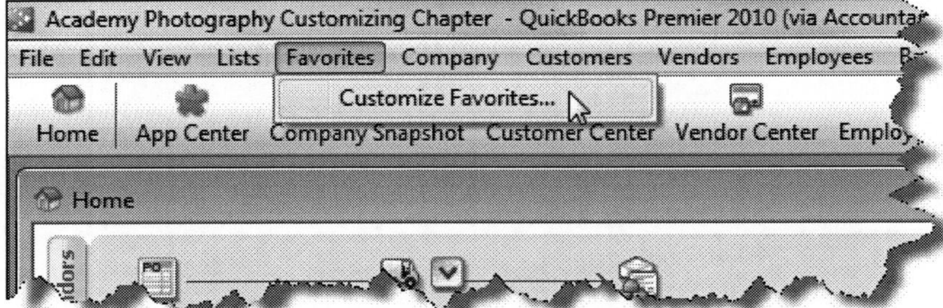

Figure 8-4 Customize Favorites option in the Favorites menu

Step 3. The *Customize Your Menus* window includes all available menu items. You can select an item to be easily accessed through the *Favorites* Menu. Click the **Sales Rep List** and Click **Add** (see Figure 8-5).

You can use the *Sales Rep List* to identify employees who receive commission as a percentage of sales. This list is usually only available through the *Customer Vendor Profile Lists* submenu under the *Lists* menu. By adding it the *Favorites* menu, the can be accessed outside a submenu.

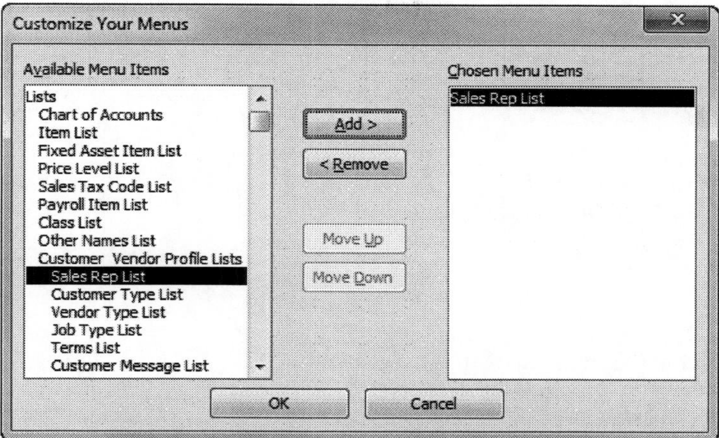

Figure 8-5 Sales Rep List added to Favorites menu in the Customize Your Menus window

Step 4. Click **OK** to close the *Customize Your Menus* window.

Step 5. Select the *Favorites* menu and chose **Sales Rep List** (see Figure 8-6).

Figure 8-6 Sales Rep List in the Favorites menu

Step 6. Close the Sales Rep List.

Open Window List

The QuickBooks **Open Window List** displays all open windows on the far left of the screen. To display the window, select **Open Window List** from the *View* menu (see Figure 8-7).

Figure 8-7 Open Window List menu option

QuickBooks displays the **Open Window List** at the far left of the screen (see Figure 8-8). The Open Window List includes window titles that are currently open, allowing you to quickly toggle between reports, forms, lists, or registers. This window is very helpful if you set your **Desktop** User Preferences to view *One Window* at a time. You cannot customize the Open Windows List.

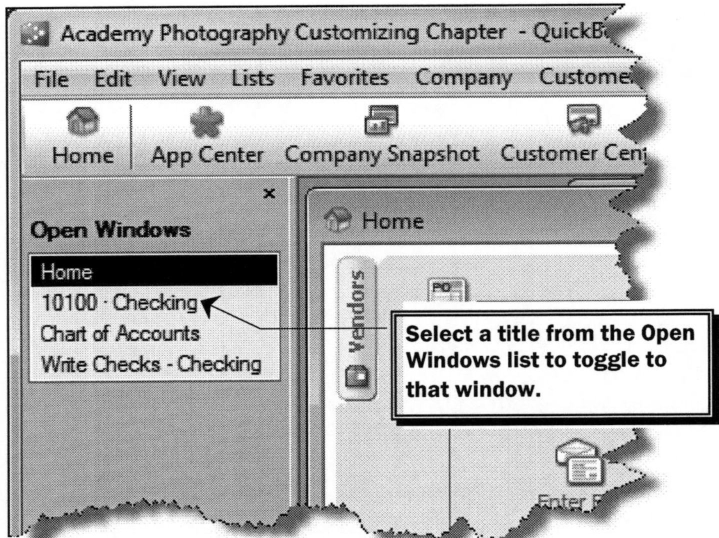

Figure 8-8 Open Window List

QuickBooks Icon Bar

The *Icon Bar* appears at the top of the screen below the menu (see Figure 8-9). The icons on the *Icon Bar* are shortcuts to QuickBooks windows. The *Icon Bar* allows you to create an icon shortcut to almost any window in QuickBooks. The *Icon Bar* can be selected or deselected from the *View* menu and can be customized.

Figure 8-9 Icon Bar

Customizing the Icon Bar

There are two ways to customize the Icon Bar: using the *Customize Icon Bar* window or using the *Add* "window-name" *to Icon Bar* option.

Using the Customize Icon Bar Window

Use the *Customize Icon Bar* window to add icons to the Icon Bar or to edit or delete existing icons. You can also use this window to add separators between icons and to reposition icons.

COMPUTER PRACTICE

Step 1. Select **Customize Icon Bar** from the *View* menu. QuickBooks displays the *Customize Icon Bar* window shown in Figure 8-10.

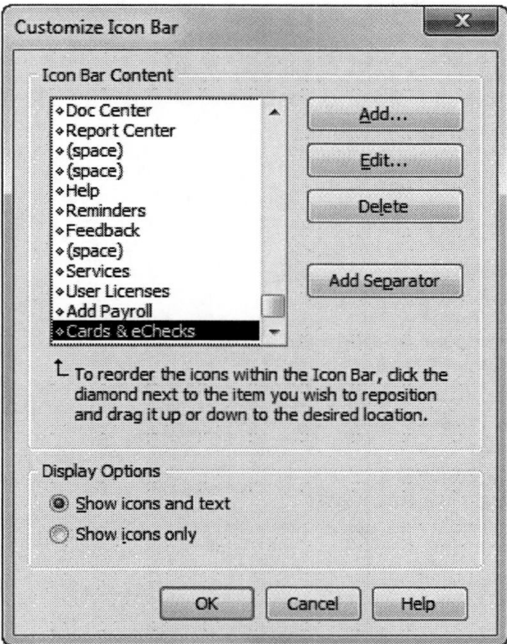

Figure 8-10 Customize Icon Bar window

Step 2. To add an Icon to the Icon Bar click **Add**. QuickBooks opens the window shown in Figure 8-11.

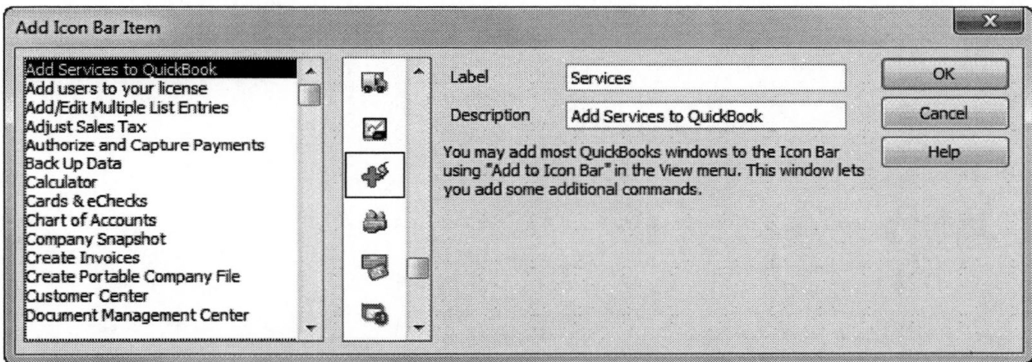

Figure 8-11 Add Icon Bar Item window

Step 3. Select **Calculator** from the list of icons as shown in Figure 8-12. Notice that QuickBooks automatically selects the preferred icon for calculator and recommends the label name and description.

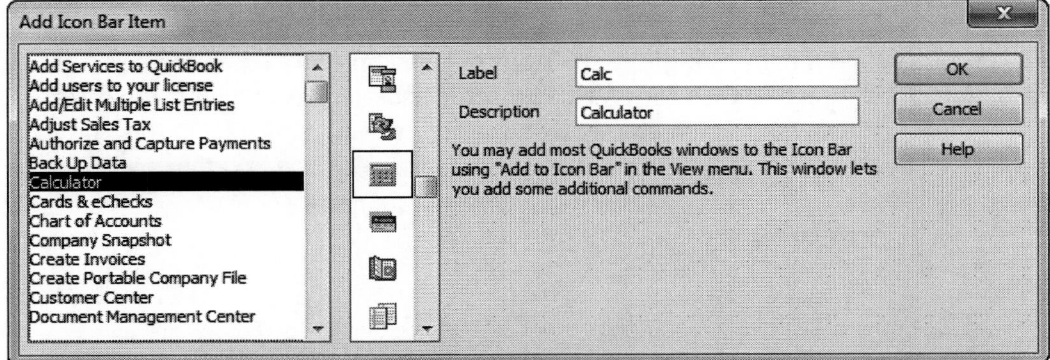

Figure 8-12 Add Icon Bar Item window with Calculator selected

Step 4. Click **OK** to create the Calculator icon.

Step 5. The order of the icons on this list dictates the order of the icons on the icon bar. To move the Calc icon, click the diamond next to **Calc** and then drag and drop Calc to move it above the **User Licenses** icon as shown in Figure 8-13.

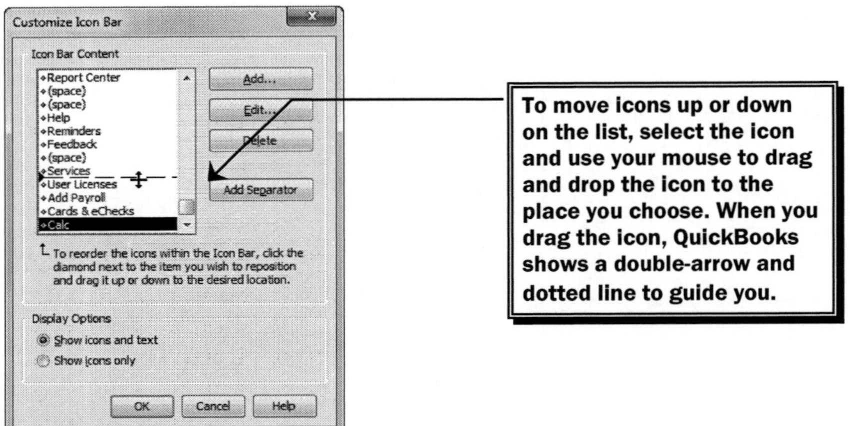

Figure 8-13 Use your mouse to move icons up or down in the list.

Step 6. You can edit the label, description, or icon for any item on the Icon Bar. Highlight the **Calc** item and then click **Edit**. QuickBooks opens the *Edit Icon Bar Item* window shown in Figure 8-14.

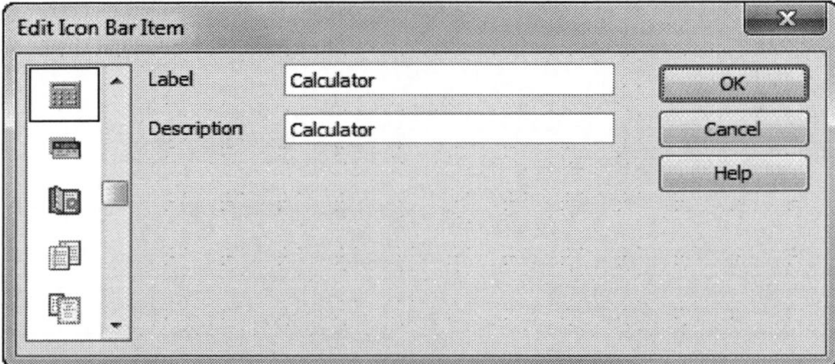

Figure 8-14 Edit Icon Bar Item window

Step 7. Enter ***Calculator*** in the *Label* field and click **OK**. QuickBooks updates the *Icon Bar Content* section of the **Customize Icon Bar** window with the edited label.

Step 8. To remove an icon from the Icon Bar, select the icon in the list and click **Delete**. Highlight the **Feedback** item and then click **Delete**.

Step 9. You may find it helpful to group the icons by type. To add a separator, select the **Calculator** icon and then click **Add Separator**. QuickBooks will insert the word "(space)" below the **Calculator** icon on the list (see Figure 8-15). On the Icon Bar, QuickBooks adds a vertical line between the **Calculator** icon and the **Payroll** icon.

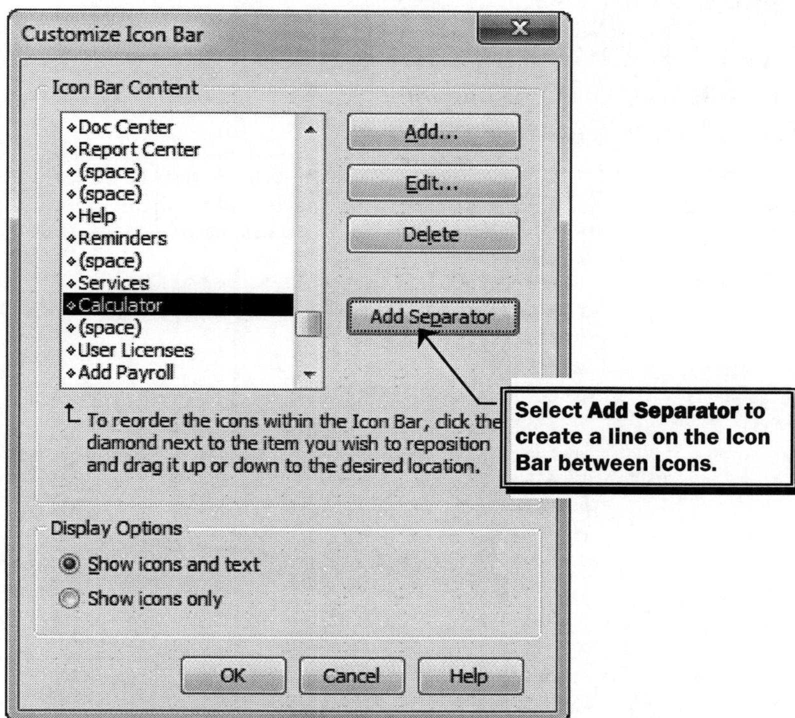

Figure 8-15 Icon List with Separator

Step 10. To accommodate additional icons, or to reduce the height of your Icon Bar, you can select **Show icons only** in the *Display Options* section shown in Figure 8-15. Leave the **Show icons and text** option selected.

Step 11. Click **OK** to save your changes. Figure 8-16 displays the customized Icon Bar.

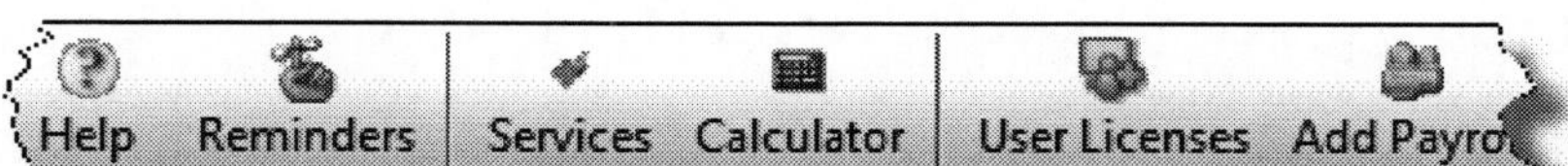

Figure 8-16 Customized Icon Bar

Customizing the Icon Bar – Using Add "window-name" to Icon Bar

You can add Icons to the Icon Bar using the **Add "window-name" to Icon Bar** option from the *View* menu. For example, Academy Photography wants an icon for the **Customer Phone List** report, customized to include the customers' phone and total balance. Follow these steps to add this report to your Icon bar:

COMPUTER PRACTICE

Step 1. From the *Reports* menu select **List**, and then select **Customer Phone List**. See Figure 8-17.

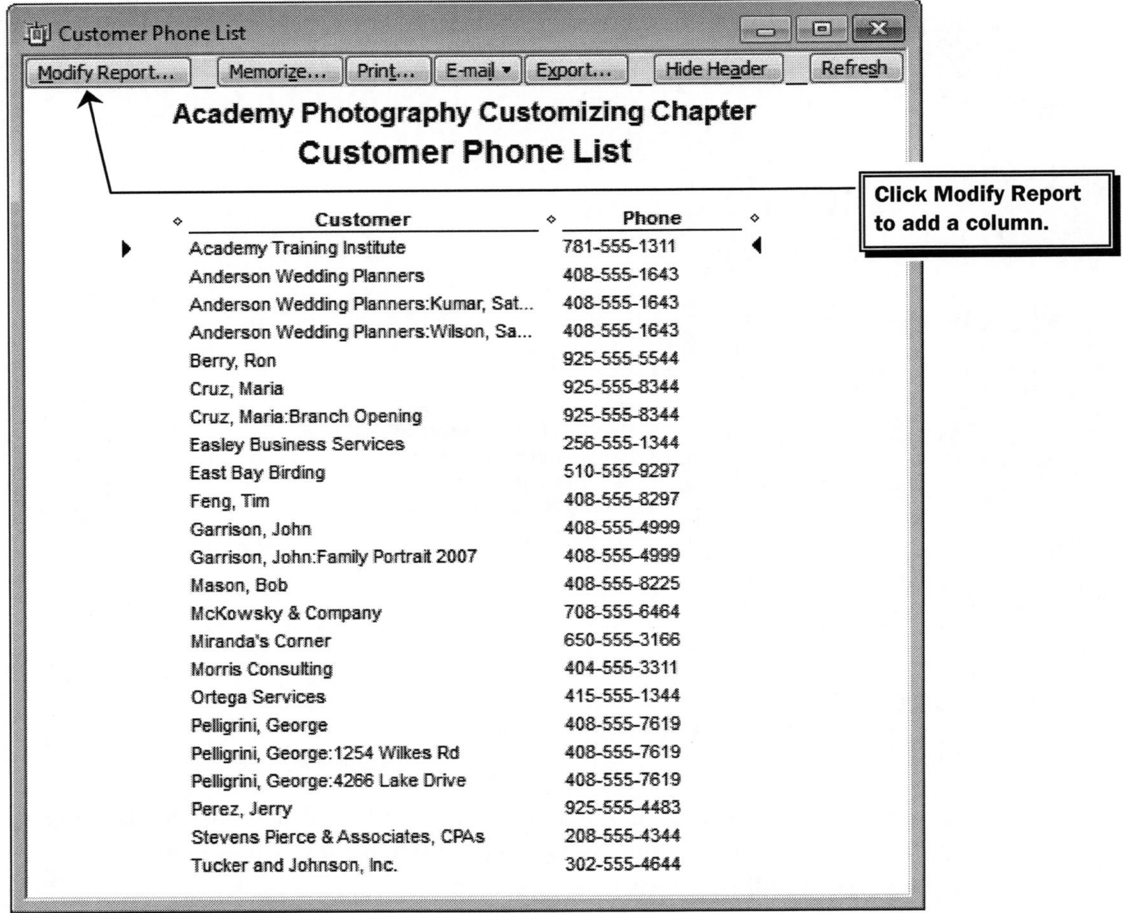

Figure 8-17 Customer Phone List Report

Step 2. Click **Modify Report** and select the **Balance Total** field in the *Columns* list (see Figure 8-18). Click **OK** to save your changes.

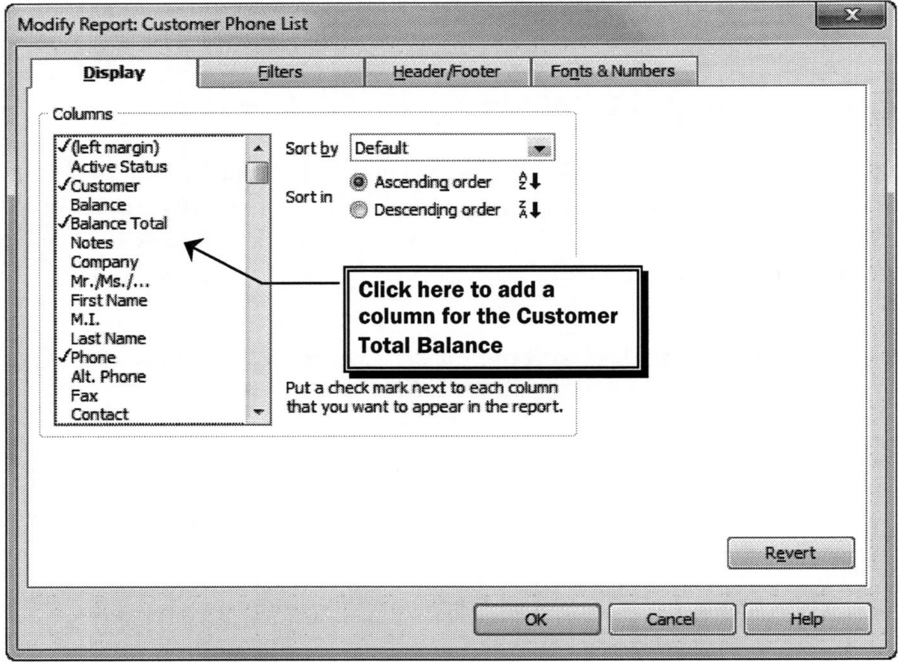

Figure 8-18 Select Balance Total on the Columns List

Step 3. With the modified report displayed, select the *View* menu and then select **Add "Customer Phone List" to Icon Bar**. QuickBooks displays the *Add Window to Icon Bar* window shown in Figure 8-19.

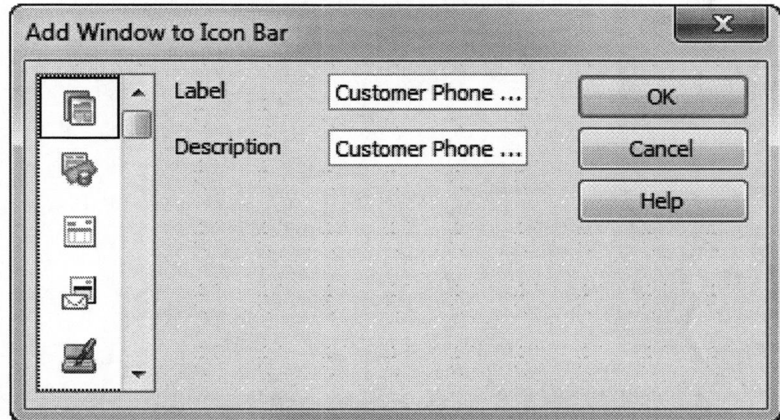

Figure 8-19 Add Window to Icon Bar window

Step 4. Enter Cust Ph List in the Label field as shown in Figure 8-20. Click OK to save your changes.
QuickBooks enters the title of your report in the Label and Description fields. It is usually best to condense the Label so the icon does not use as much space on the Icon Bar.

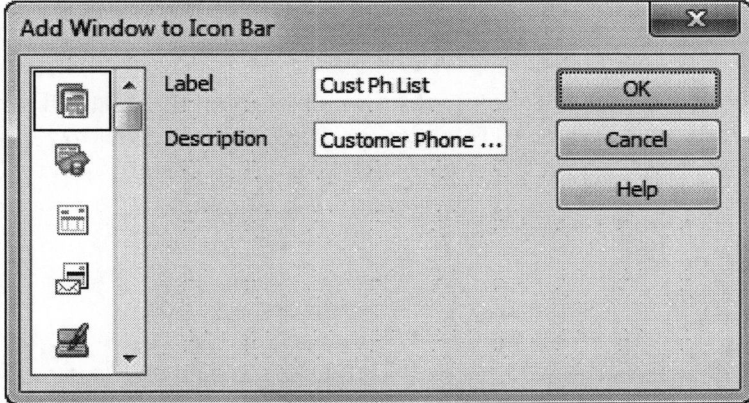

Figure 8-20 Select an icon from the list and edit the Label field.

Step 5. You may need to click on the display-arrows (>>) on the upper right-hand-side of the Icon Bar to see the **Cust Ph List** icon. Figure 8-21 displays the Icon Bar (expanded to the far right) showing the Cust Ph List icon.

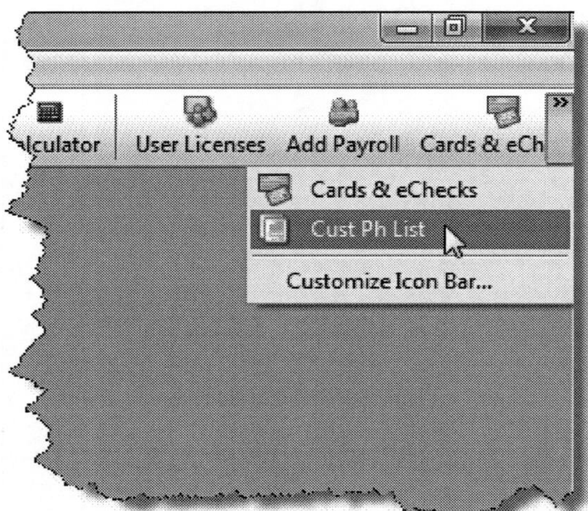

Figure 8-21 Expanded Icon Bar with Cust Ph List icon added

> **Note:**
> QuickBooks adds new icons to the right side of the Icon Bar. If you want to reposition them, select the *View* menu and then select **Customize Icon Bar**. See page 338 for more information.

Step 6. Close the Customer Phone List.

QuickBooks Items and Other Lists

To help you track more details about your sales, QuickBooks provides several lists that allow you to add more information to each transaction. In this section, you will learn how to create items in the *Item list*, *Terms list*, *Price Level list*, and *Templates list*. You will also learn how **Custom fields** can be used to add more detail to several of your lists and reports in QuickBooks.

QuickBooks Items

The **Item List** is used to identify the products and services your business purchases and/or sells. Items in the Item List are also used as part of the Sales Tax tracking process as a means of generating subtotals and as a method of calculating discounts. In this section, you will learn more about QuickBooks items and how they affect the "accounting behind the scenes" as you create transactions.

The Item list shows all items you have already created (see Figure 8-22).

Name	Description	Type	Account	On Hand	On Sales Order	Price	Attach
Indoor Photo Session	Indoor Studio Session	Service	40000 · Services			95.00	
Outdoor Photo Session	Outdoor Photo Session	Service	40000 · Services			95.00	
Photographer	Photographer	Service	40000 · Services			125.00	
Retouching	Photo retouching services	Service	40000 · Services			95.00	
Camera SR32	Supra Digital Camera SR32	Inventory Part	45000 · Sales	9	0	695.99	
Case	Camera and Lens High Impact Case	Inventory Part	45000 · Sales	24	0	79.99	
Frame 5x7	Picture Frame - 5' x 7' Metal Frame	Inventory Part	45000 · Sales	22	0	5.99	
Lens	Supra Zoom Lens	Inventory Part	45000 · Sales	7	0	324.99	
Film 36C	200 ASA, 36 Color Film	Non-inventory Part	45000 · Sales			12.36	
Premium Photo Package	Premium Package of Photography from Session	Non-inventory Part	45000 · Sales			85.00	
Standard Photo Package	Standard Package of Photography from Session	Non-inventory Part	45000 · Sales			55.00	
Bad Debt	Bad Debt - Write off	Other Charge	60300 · Bad Debts			0.00	
Bounce Chg	Return Check Fee	Other Charge	45000 · Sales			0.00	
Fin Chg	Finance Charges on Overdue Balance	Other Charge	70200 · Interest Income			18.0%	
Contra Costa	Contra Costa County Sales Tax	Sales Tax Item	25500 · Sales Tax Payable			8.25%	
Out of State	Out-of-state sale, exempt from sales tax	Sales Tax Item	25500 · Sales Tax Payable			0.0%	
Santa Clara	Santa Clara County Sales Tax	Sales Tax Item	25500 · Sales Tax Payable			8.25%	

Figure 8-22 The Item list

Item Types

There are several different types of items in QuickBooks (see Figure 8-23). When you create an Item, you indicate the Item type along with the name of the Item and the account with which the Item is associated.

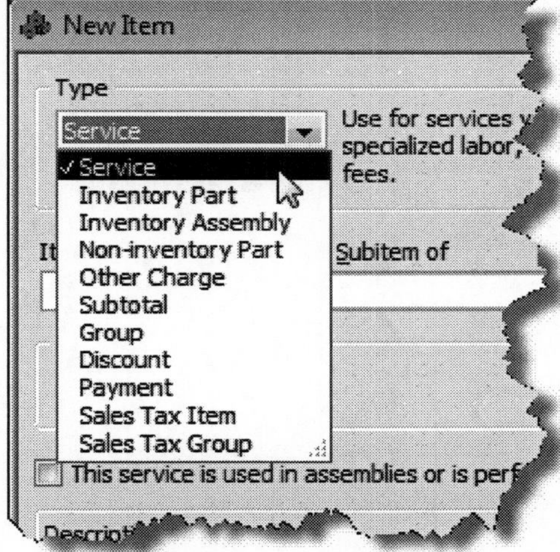

Figure 8-23 The Type menu in the New Item window

Service Items: Used to track services you buy and/or sell.

Inventory Part Items: Used to track your purchases and sales of inventory.

Inventory Assembly Items: Used to track items that contain assemblies of other items. You must have QuickBooks Premier or QuickBooks Enterprise Solutions to use Inventory Assemblies.

Non-inventory Part Items: Used to track products you buy and/or sell but don't keep in inventory.

Other Charge Items: Used to track miscellaneous charges such as shipping and finance charges.

Subtotal Items: Used to calculate and display subtotals on sales forms.

Group Items: Allows you to use one item to "bundle" several items together. Group items are similar to Inventory Assembly items, but Group items do not track quantity on hand (or sold) of the Group. Each item within the Group is tracked separately.

Discount Items: Used to calculate and display discounts on sales forms.

Payment Items: Used to show payments collected on the face of Invoices and refunds given on the face of Credit Memos.

Sales Tax Item: Used to track sales taxes in each location where you sell taxable goods and services.

Sales Tax Group Items: Used when you pay sales tax to more than one tax agency. The Sales Tax Group allows you to group several Sales Tax items together into one total. The total tax from each Sales Tax Item in the group is the amount of tax charged when you use the group on sales forms, but QuickBooks tracks each Sales Tax item in the group separately. In most states, you don't need to use Sales Tax Groups. Use these Group items only if you pay sales tax to more than one agency.

Service Items

Academy Photography sells photo sessions by the hour. To track the sales of a *Service* Item, create an Item called **Photo Session**, and associate the item with the Services income account.

COMPUTER PRACTICE

Step 1. Select the *Lists* menu and then select **Item List**.

Step 2. Select the *Item* menu and then select **New**.

Step 3. Select **Service** from the *Type* drop-down list shown in Figure 8-23, and fill in the detail of the Item as shown in Figure 8-24.

Step 4. Click **OK** to save the Item.

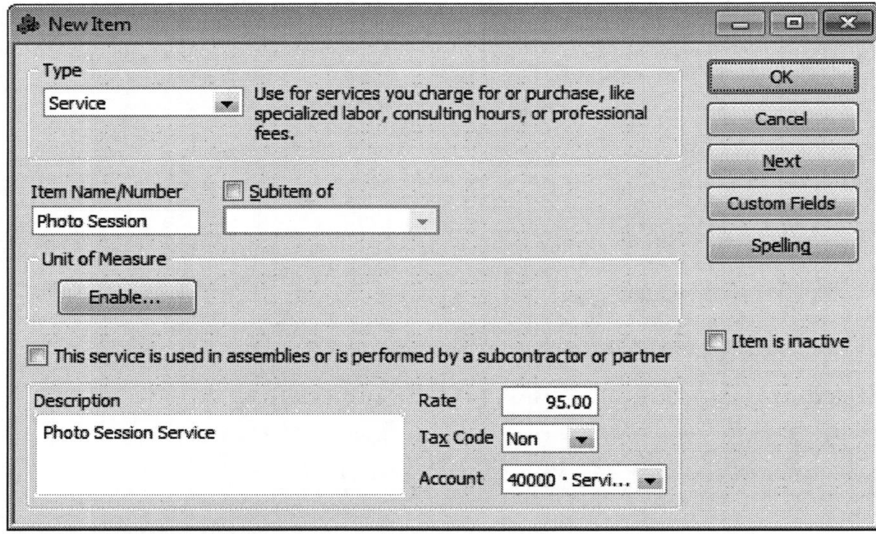

Figure 8-24 Selecting items

If the price for this service fluctuates, you can override this amount when you use it on a sales form. Therefore, when you set up the Item, enter the rate you normally charge.

Subcontracted Services

To track your subcontracted services, you can set up a special "two-sided" service Item to track both the income and the expense of the subcontractor. By using a single Item to track both the income and expense for the subcontracted service, you can automatically track the profitability of your subcontractors. You might want to have a separate Item for each subcontractor.

COMPUTER PRACTICE

Step 1. With the Item List displayed, press **Ctrl+N**.

Step 2. Select **Service** from the *Type* drop-down list and press **Tab**.

Step 3. Enter **Video Photographer** in the Item Name/Number field and check the Subitem of box.

Step 4. Select **Photographer** from the *Subitem of* drop-down list.

Step 5. Check the box next to *This service is used in assemblies or is performed by a subcontractor or partner.*
This box allows you to use the same Item on purchase transactions and sales transactions, but have the Item affect different accounts depending on the transaction.

Step 6. Enter the *Description on Purchase Transactions*, *Cost* (purchase price), *Expense Account*, and *Preferred Vendor* for this Item as shown in Figure 8-25.

Step 7. Select **Non** in the *Tax Code* field.

Step 8. Enter the *Description on Sales Transactions*, *Sales Price*, and *Income Account* for this Item as shown in Figure 8-25.

Step 9. Click **OK** to save the Item.

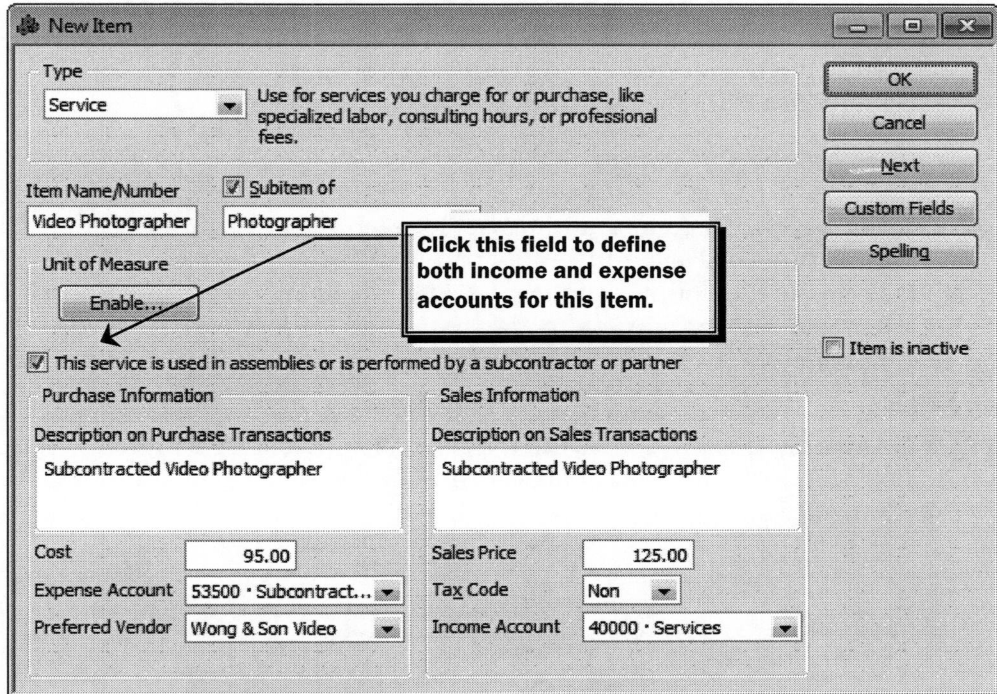

Figure 8-25 Subcontracted Service Item

Non-Inventory Parts

To track products that you sell but don't keep in inventory, set up **Non-Inventory Part** Items.

Academy Photography doesn't track custom photo packages in inventory, so they use one generic Item called Custom Photo Package.

COMPUTER PRACTICE

Step 1. With the **Item List** displayed, press **Ctrl+N**. Select **Non-Inventory Part** from the *Type* drop-down list.

Step 2. Enter **Custom Photo Package** in the Item Name/Number field.

Step 3. Fill in the detail of the Item as shown in Figure 8-26.

Step 4. Click **OK** to save the item.

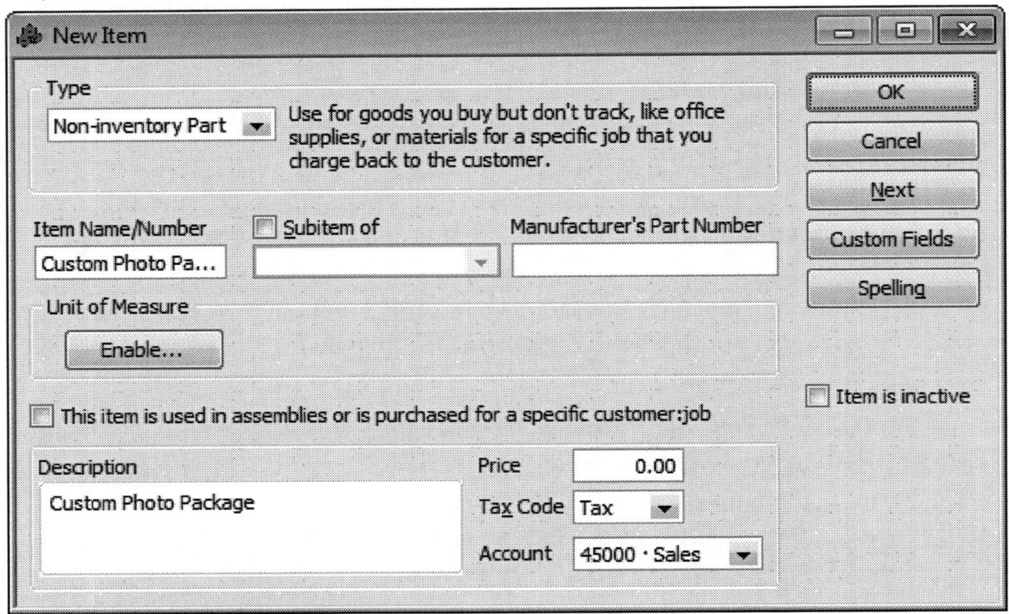

Figure 8-26 Non-inventory Part Item

Non-Inventory Parts - Passed Through

You can also specifically track the income and expenses for each **Non-Inventory Part**. In this case, you should create a "two-sided" Non-Inventory part item to track the purchase costs in a Cost of Goods Sold (or Expense) account, and the sales amounts in an income account. This is particularly useful when you pass the costs on to your customers for special-ordered parts. For example, Academy Photography tracks Camcorder orders with one Non-Inventory Part Item.

COMPUTER PRACTICE

Step 1. With the Item List displayed, press **Ctrl+N**. Select **Non-Inventory Part** from the *Type* drop-down list. Fill in the detail of the Item as shown in Figure 8-27.

Step 2. Click **OK** to save the item.

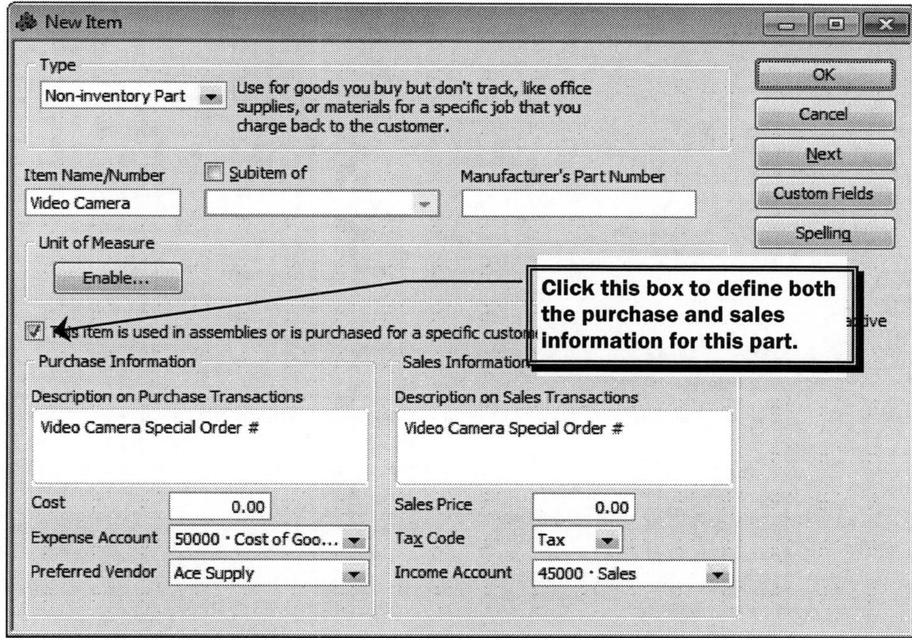

Figure 8-27 Non-inventory Part Item - passed through

Other Charge Items

To track charges like freight, finance charges, or expense reimbursements on your Invoices, use **Other Charge Items.**

COMPUTER PRACTICE

Step 1. With the Item List displayed, press **Ctrl+N**. Select **Other Charge** from the Type drop-down list and fill in the detail of the Item as shown in Figure 8-28.

Step 2. Click **OK** to save the Item.

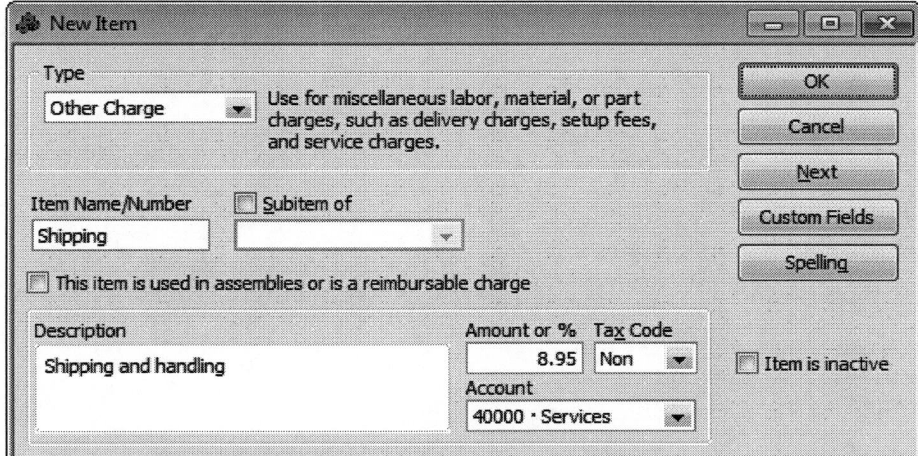

Figure 8-28 Track shipping charges with an Other Charge Item

Sales Tax Items

The **Sales Tax** Items in this section have already been set up in the practice template file, but when you create your own company file, follow the steps below to create the appropriate items for your company:

COMPUTER PRACTICE

Step 1. With the Item List displayed, press **Ctrl+N**. Select **Sales Tax Item** from the *Type* drop-down list and fill in the detail of the Item as shown in Figure 8-29.

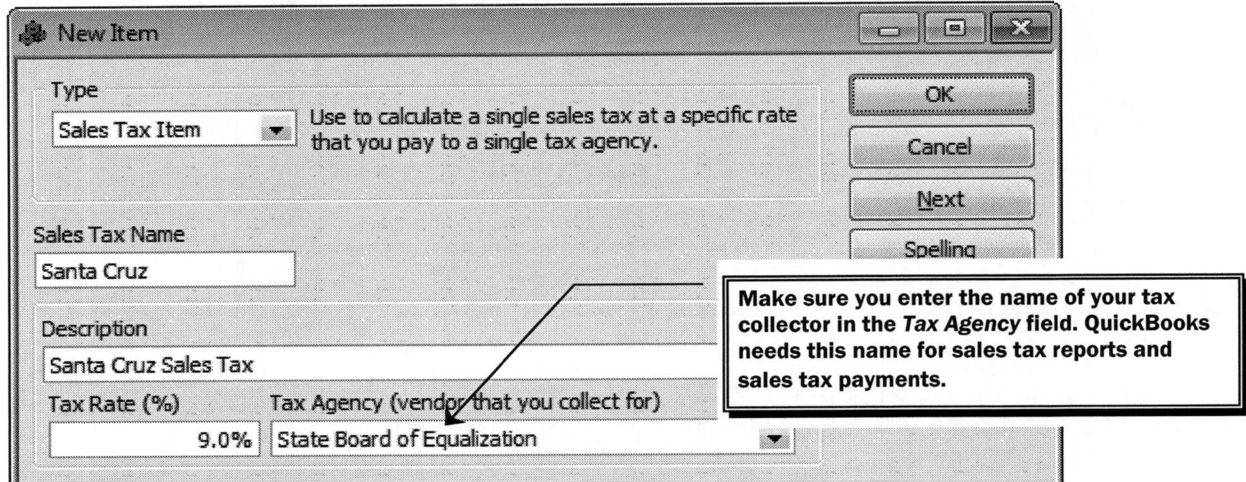

Figure 8-29 Track sales tax with the Sales Tax Item.

Step 2. Click **OK**.

You should create a separate **Sales Tax** Item for each tax imposed by each taxing jurisdiction. For example, if you have both state and county sales taxes, then create Sales Tax Items for the state taxes and each of the county taxes. If multiple Sales Tax Items are to be billed on a particular sales transaction, then create a Sales Tax Group item to join the individual Sales Tax Items together for billing purposes. This allows QuickBooks to correctly track sales taxes by taxing jurisdiction.

> Note:
> If you need to import a large number of Items (or other list entries) you can paste in a spreadsheet using the *Add/Edit Multiple List Entries* option, located in the *Lists* menu.

Printing the Item List

COMPUTER PRACTICE

Step 1. To print the Item List, follow these steps:

Step 2. Select the *Reports* menu, select **List**, and then select **Item Listing** (see Figure 8-30).

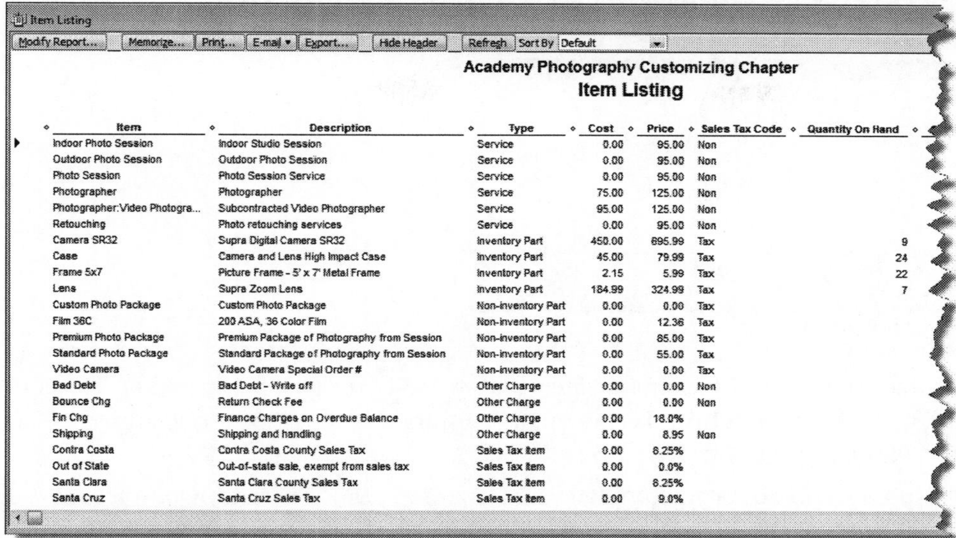

Academy Photography Customizing Chapter
Item Listing

Item	Description	Type	Cost	Price	Sales Tax Code	Quantity On Hand
Indoor Photo Session	Indoor Studio Session	Service	0.00	95.00	Non	
Outdoor Photo Session	Outdoor Photo Session	Service	0.00	95.00	Non	
Photo Session	Photo Session Service	Service	0.00	95.00	Non	
Photographer	Photographer	Service	75.00	125.00	Non	
Photographer:Video Photogra...	Subcontracted Video Photographer	Service	95.00	125.00	Non	
Retouching	Photo retouching services	Service	0.00	95.00	Non	
Camera SR32	Supra Digital Camera SR32	Inventory Part	450.00	695.99	Tax	9
Case	Camera and Lens High Impact Case	Inventory Part	45.00	79.99	Tax	24
Frame 5x7	Picture Frame - 5' x 7' Metal Frame	Inventory Part	2.15	5.99	Tax	22
Lens	Supra Zoom Lens	Inventory Part	184.99	324.99	Tax	7
Custom Photo Package	Custom Photo Package	Non-inventory Part	0.00	0.00	Tax	
Film 36C	200 ASA, 36 Color Film	Non-inventory Part	0.00	12.36	Tax	
Premium Photo Package	Premium Package of Photography from Session	Non-inventory Part	0.00	85.00	Tax	
Standard Photo Package	Standard Package of Photography from Session	Non-inventory Part	0.00	55.00	Tax	
Video Camera	Video Camera Special Order #	Non-inventory Part	0.00	0.00	Tax	
Bad Debt	Bad Debt - Write off	Other Charge	0.00	0.00	Non	
Bounce Chg	Return Check Fee	Other Charge	0.00	0.00	Non	
Fin Chg	Finance Charges on Overdue Balance	Other Charge	0.00	18.0%		
Shipping	Shipping and handling	Other Charge	0.00	8.95	Non	
Contra Costa	Contra Costa County Sales Tax	Sales Tax Item	0.00	8.25%		
Out of State	Out-of-state sale, exempt from sales tax	Sales Tax Item	0.00	0.0%		
Santa Clara	Santa Clara County Sales Tax	Sales Tax Item	0.00	8.25%		
Santa Cruz	Santa Cruz Sales Tax	Sales Tax Item	0.00	9.0%		

Figure 8-30 The Item Listing report

Step 3. Click **Print** at the top of the report (or select **Print Report** from the *File* menu).

Other Lists

In addition to the Item List, there are several additional lists in QuickBooks that you will use when setting up customers and recording sales transactions. An understanding of how to set up and use these lists is essential to operating QuickBooks for your company.

The Terms List

The **Terms List** is where you define the payment terms for Invoices and Bills. QuickBooks uses terms to calculate when an Invoice or Bill is due. If the terms specified on the transaction include a discount for early payment, QuickBooks also calculates the date on which the discount expires.

QuickBooks allows you to define two types of terms:

Standard terms calculate based on how many days from the Invoice or Bill date the payment is due or a discount is earned.

Date-Driven terms calculate based on the day of the month that an Invoice or Bill is due or a discount is earned.

You can override the default terms on each sale as necessary. When you create reports for Accounts Receivable or Accounts Payable, QuickBooks takes into account the terms on each Invoice or Bill.

COMPUTER PRACTICE

Step 1. Select the *Lists* menu, select **Customers & Vendor Profile Lists,** and then select **Terms List** (see Figure 8-31).

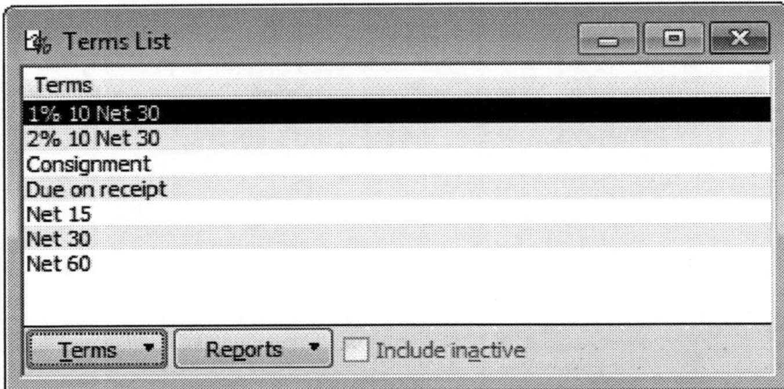

Figure 8-31 The Terms List window

Step 2. The practice template file already includes several terms (see Figure 8-31). To set up additional terms, select the **Terms** menu from the *Terms List* window, and then select **New**, or press **Ctrl+N**.

Step 3. To setup a standard term, complete the *New Terms* window as shown in Figure 8-32, and click **OK**.

The window in Figure 8-32 shows how the 2% 7 Net 30 item is defined. It is a standard terms item that indicates full payment is due in 30 days. If the customers pay within 7 days of the Invoice date, they are eligible for a 2% discount.

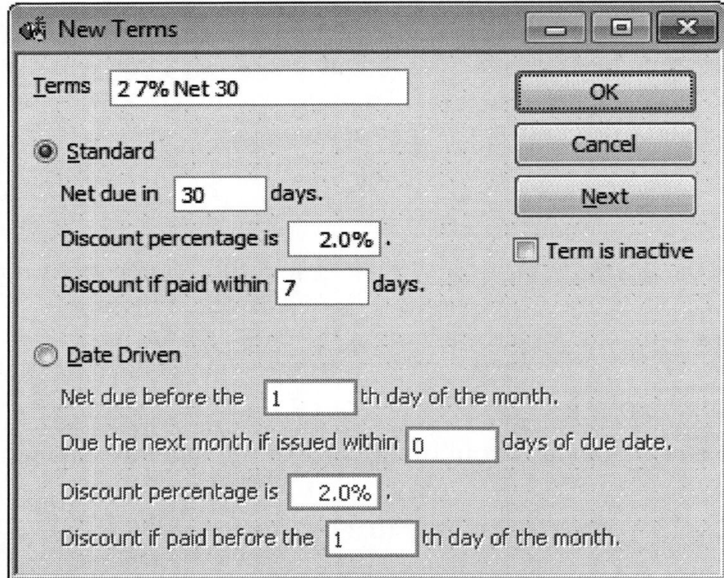

Figure 8-32 The New Terms window with standard terms

Step 4. To set up a date-driven term, press **Ctrl+N**.

Step 5. Select the **Date Driven** radio button.

Step 6. Fill in the fields as shown in Figure 8-33. Then click **OK**.

The terms in Figure 8-33 are an example of date-driven terms, where payment is due on the 10th of the month (e.g. February 10th). If the Invoice is dated less than 10 days before the due date, the Invoice (or Bill) is due on the 10th of the following month.

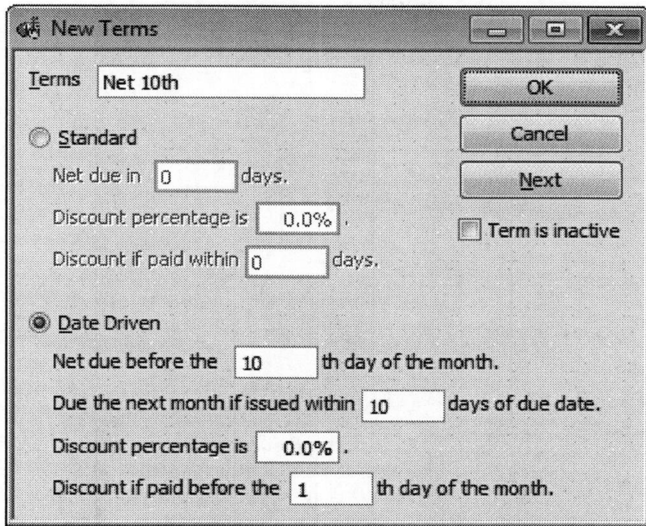

Figure 8-33 The New Terms window with date-driven terms

Step 7. Close the *Term List* window.

Price Levels

> **Note:**
> Per Item Price Levels are only available in QuickBooks Premier and above.

Price Levels allow you to define custom pricing for different customers. Use Price Levels on Invoices or Sales Receipts to adjust the sales amount of particular items. There are several ways to use Price Levels on sales forms:

1. You can adjust each item individually by selecting the applicable Price Level in the *Rate* column drop-down list (see Figure 8-34).

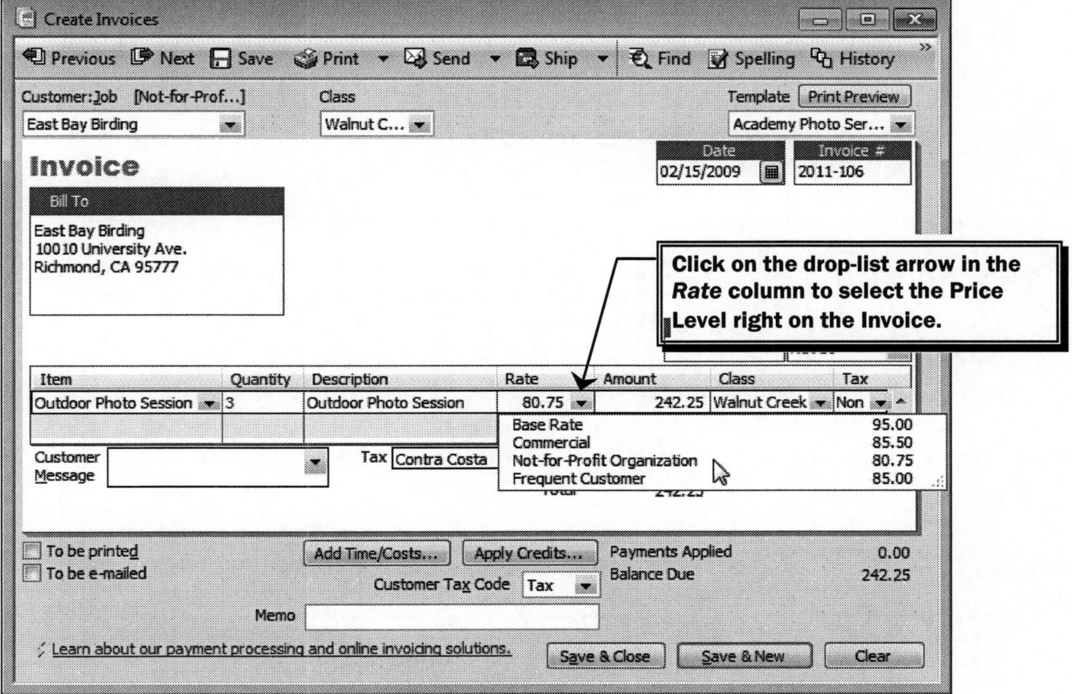

Figure 8-34 Selecting a Price Level on an Invoice

2. You can assign a Price Level to a Customer's record so that when you use the customer's name in a sales form, QuickBooks will change the default sales price for each sales item on the form (see Figure 8-35).

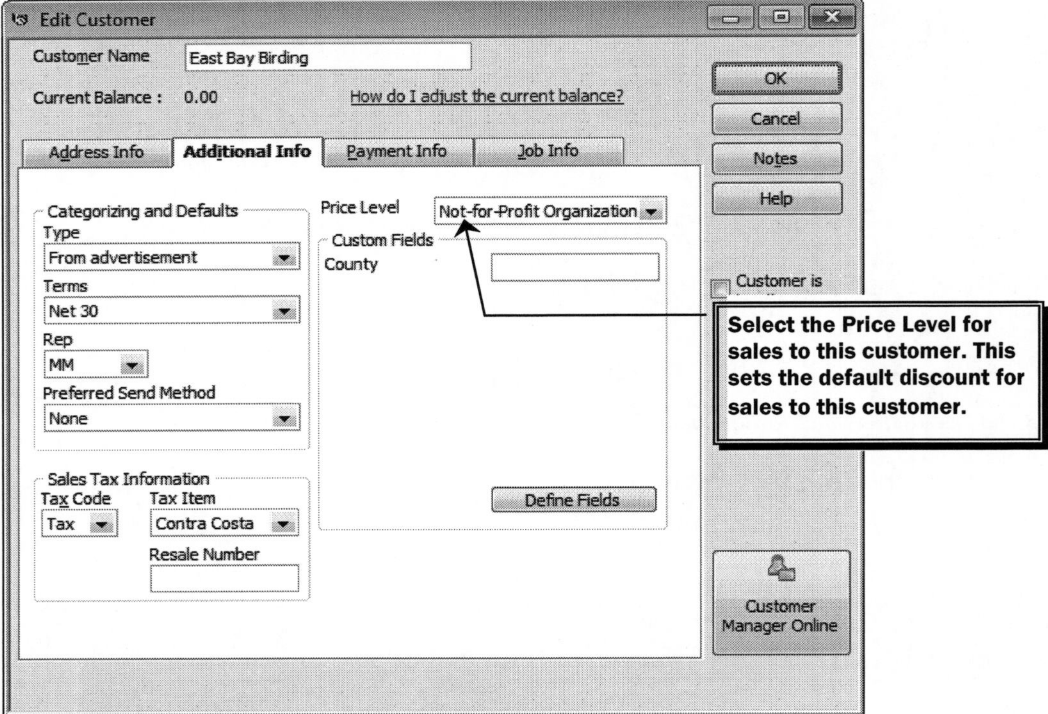

Figure 8-35 Setting a Price Level on a Customer's Record

You can create new Price Levels by opening the Price Levels List and selecting New from the Price Levels Menu or press **Ctrl+N** with the Price Levels List active. Depending on the type of Price Level you select, QuickBooks will:

- Increase or decrease the default sales price by a fixed percentage (see Figure 8-36). Fixed percentage price levels allow you to increase or decrease prices of items for a customer or job by a fixed percentage. For customers that you always give a discount to, use this option so that the discount will be generated automatically.

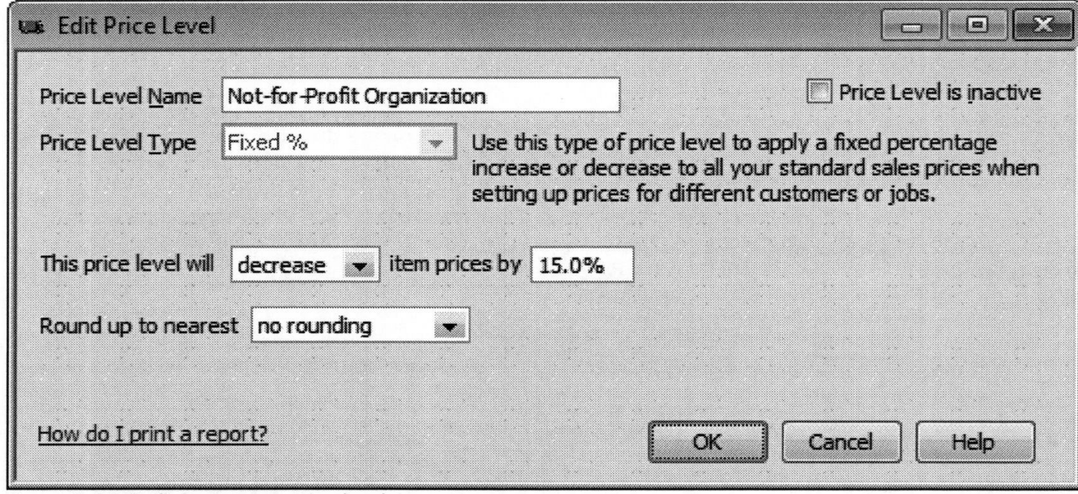

Figure 8-36 Defining a new price level

- Adjust the sales price to an amount you define when setting up the Price Level. Per Item Price Levels let you set different prices for items that are associated with different customers or jobs.

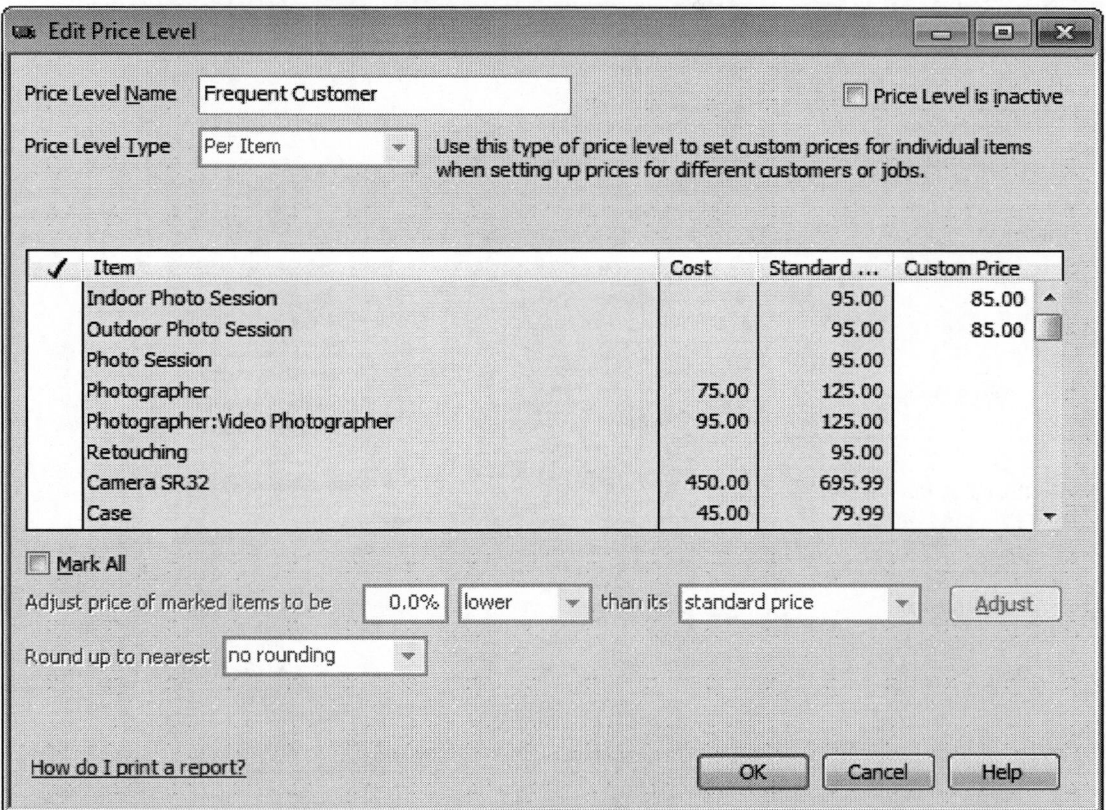

Figure 8-37 New Price Level window - Per Item Price Level Type

Custom Fields

When you set up a new Customer record, you can define **custom fields** for tracking additional information specific to your customers, vendors, and employees.

Academy Photography tracks each customer and vendor by county in order to create reports of total purchases and sales in a city or county. This information allows them to determine the best area to expand business operations.

You can access the **Define Fields** button on the *Additional Info* tab of a Customer or Vendor record (see Figure 8-38).

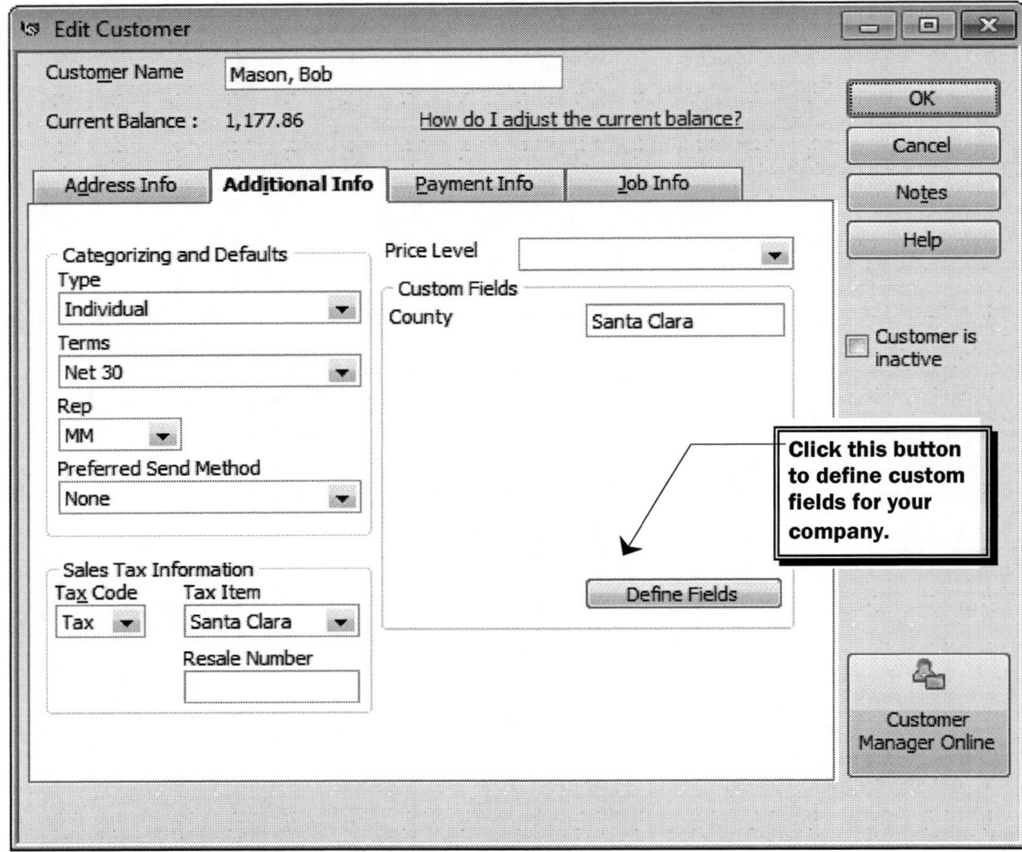

Figure 8-38 Click Define Fields in the Additional Info Tab.

In the window shown in Figure 8-39, you can define up to fifteen custom fields in the QuickBooks data file, and any one field, i.e. customer, vendor, or employee, can have up to seven custom fields.

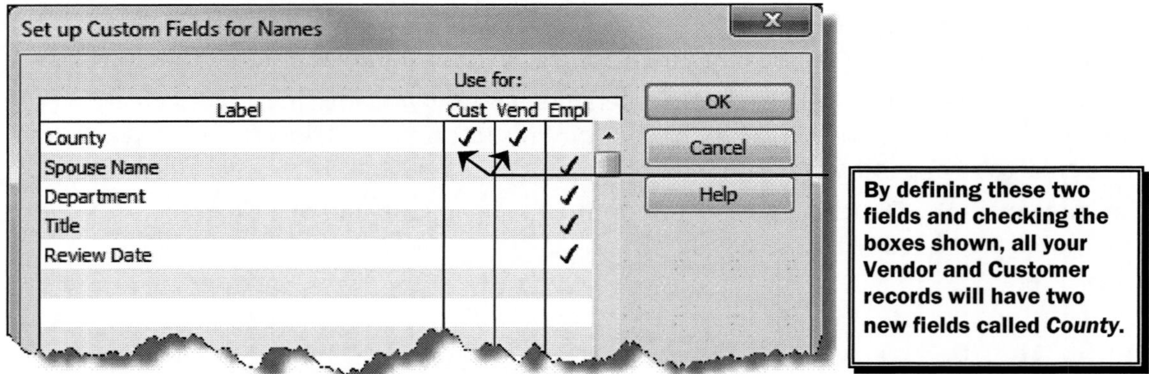

Figure 8-39 The Define Fields window

Adding Custom Field Data to Customer Records

After you have defined a custom field and checked the box in the *Customer:Job* column, the field appears on the Customer record (see Figure 8-40). Fill in the data just as you did for the other fields.

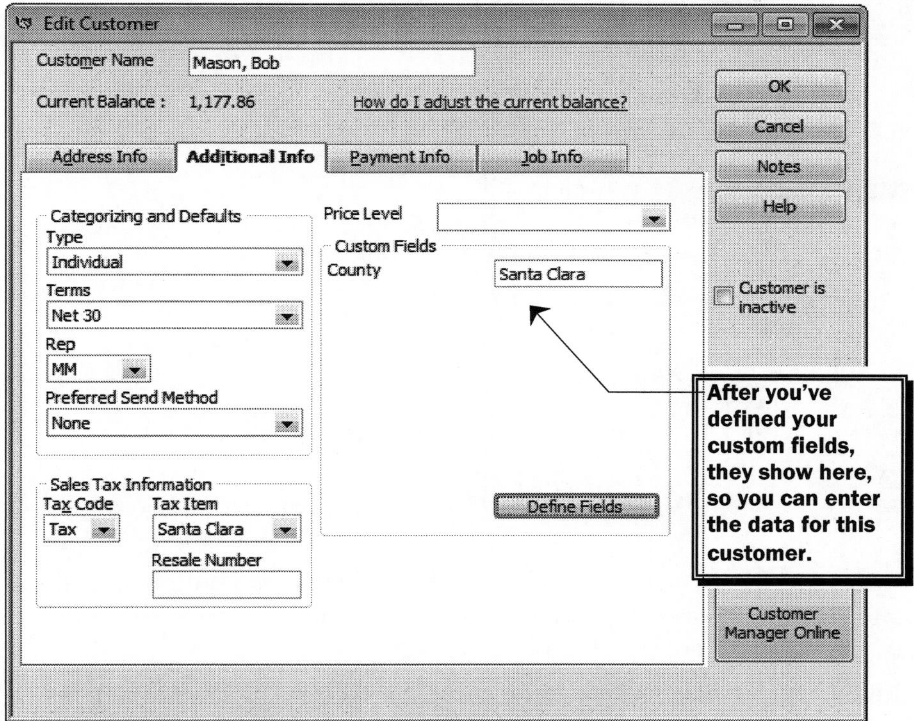

Figure 8-40 Fill in the Custom Fields for each customer.

Modifying Sales Form Templates

QuickBooks provides templates so that you can customize your sales forms. You can select from the standard forms that QuickBooks provides or you can customize the way your forms appear on both the screen and the printed page. The first step in modifying your forms is to create a template for the form you want. The templates for all forms are in the Templates list.

COMPUTER PRACTICE

Step 1. Select the *Lists* menu, and then select **Templates** (see Figure 8-41).

This list shows the standard templates that come with QuickBooks, as well as any form templates the user may have created.

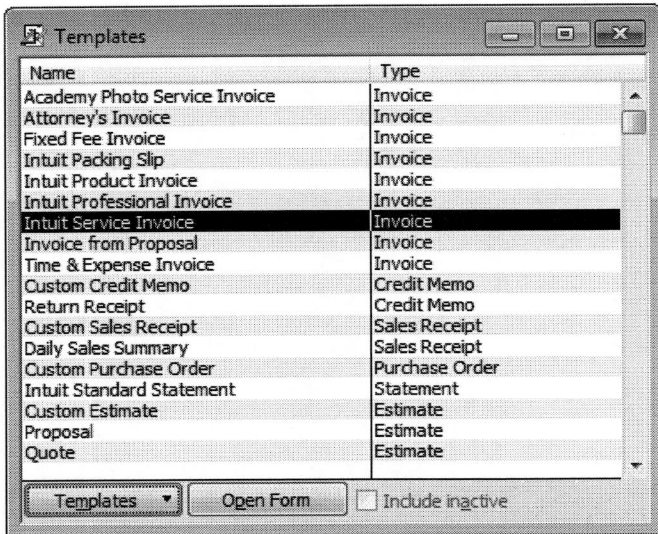

Figure 8-41 The Templates list

Step 2. Select **Intuit Service Invoice.** Then select the **Templates** menu button and select **Duplicate.** The Intuit Service Invoice is the template you are using as the basis for your custom template.

Step 3. Select **Invoice** on the *Select Template Type* window and click **OK** (see Figure 8-42).

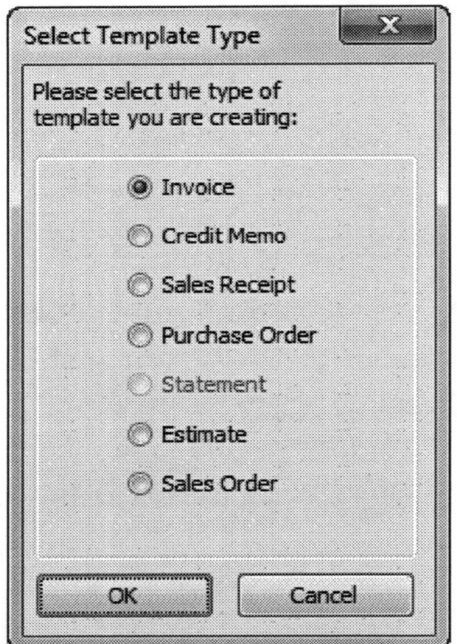

Figure 8-42 Select Template Type window

Step 4. **Copy of: Intuit Service Invoice** should already be selected. Select the *Templates* menu and select **Edit Template.**

Step 5. Click the **Manage Template** button in the *Basic Customization Window* (see Figure 8-43).

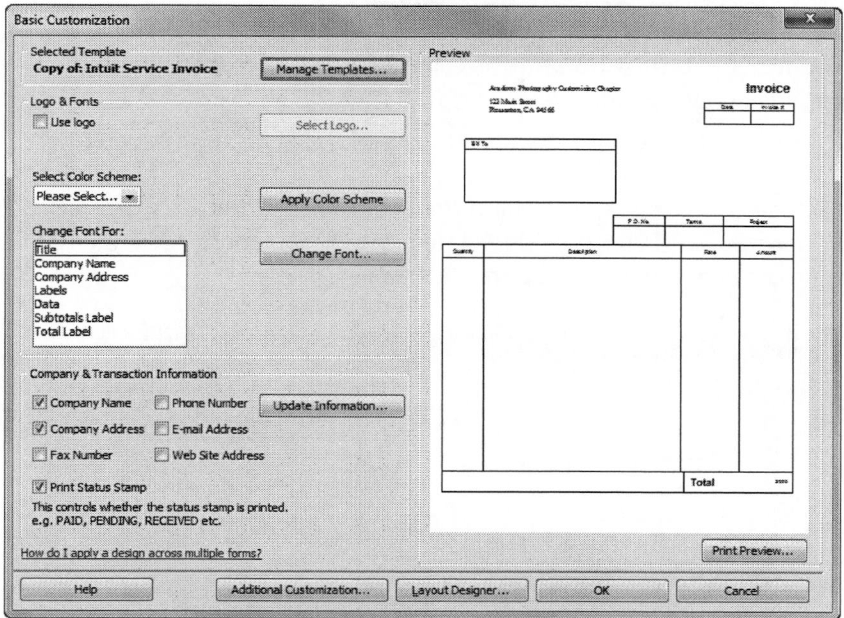

Figure 8-43 Basic Customization Window

Step 6. In the **Manage Templates** window, enter ***My Invoice Template*** in the *Template Name* field (see Figure 8-44).

You must enter a unique template name. You must give your template a descriptive name so that you will easily recognize it when selecting it from a form list.

> Note:
> You can download templates from the Intuit website. You can browse through the selection of pre-designed templates by clicking the **Download Templates** button on the *Manage Templates* window.

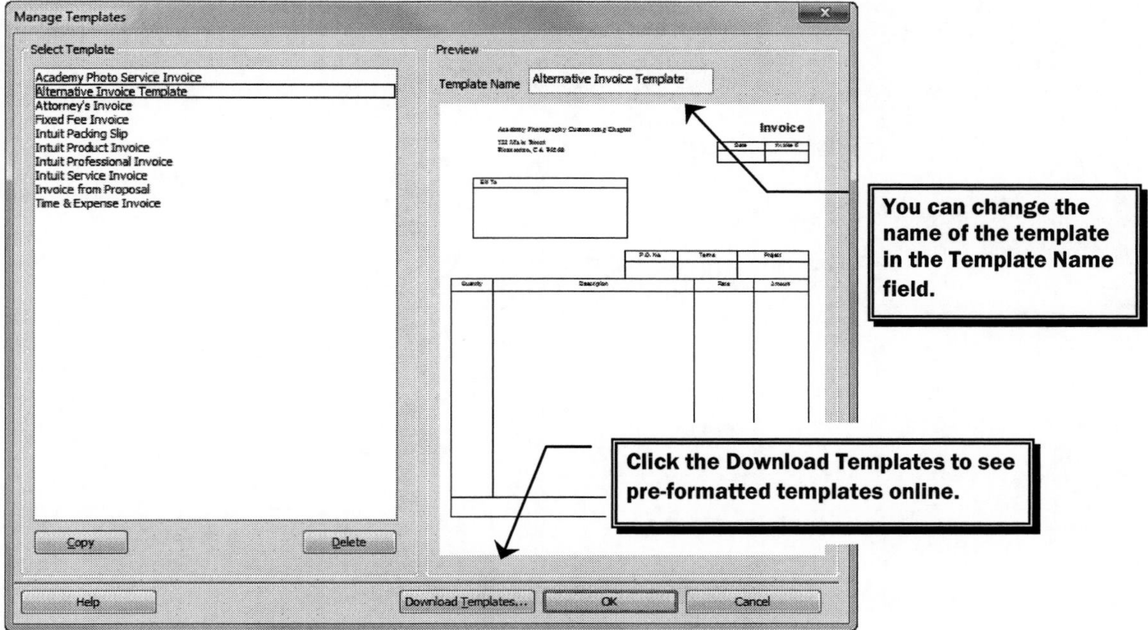

Figure 8-44 Manage Templates window

Step 7. Click **OK** to accept the name change and close the *Manage Templates* window.

Step 8. Click the **Additional Customization** button. The *Basic Customization* window changes to the *Additional Customization* window.

Step 9. Review the fields in the *Header* tab. Do not edit any of the fields on this window.

You would click the boxes in the *Screen* and *Print* columns to indicate which fields will show on the screen and which fields will be printed. You could also modify the titles for each field by changing the text in the *Title* fields.

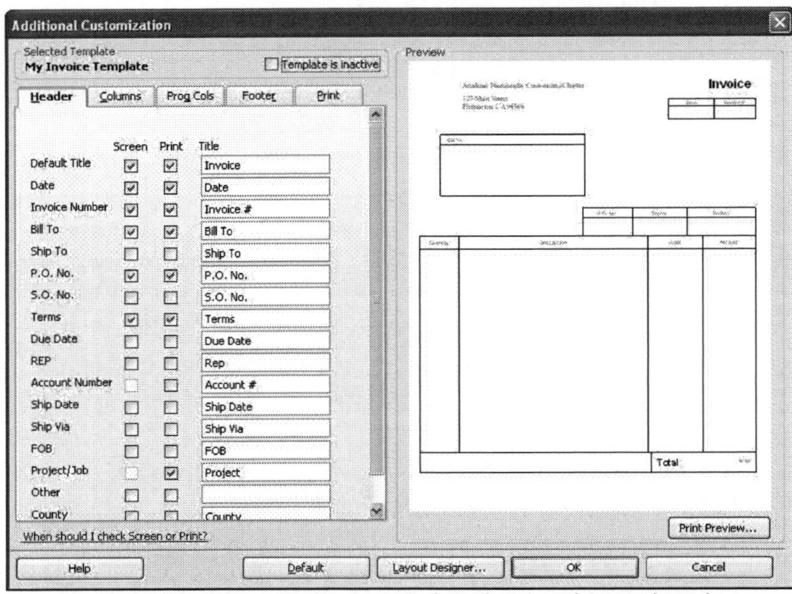

Figure 8-45 Additional Customization window showing the Header tab

Step 10. Click the **Columns** tab to modify how the columns display on the Invoice. Change the order of the columns by entering the numbers in the *Order* column as shown in Figure 8-46. If you see the Layout Designer warning box, click OK.

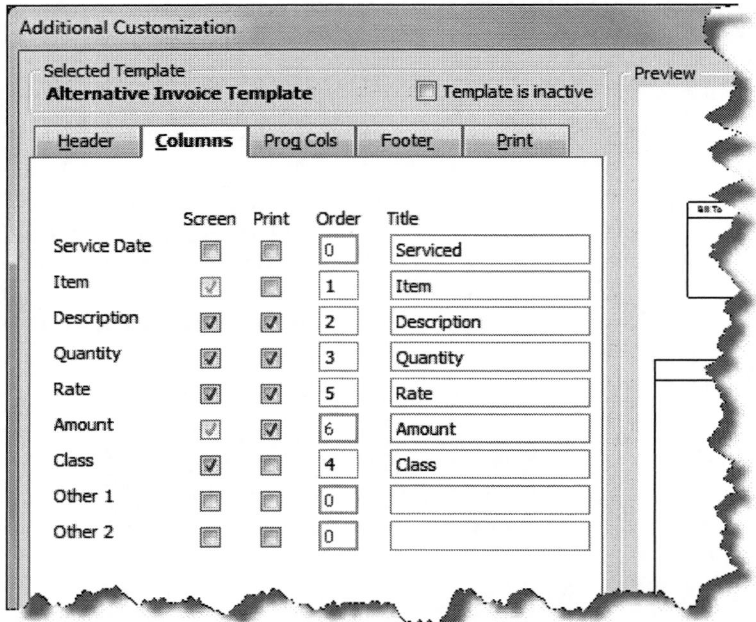

Figure 8-46 Additional Customization window showing the Columns tab

Step 11. Click the **OK** button to return to the Basic Customization window.

Step 12. Next, add a logo to the template by checking the **Use Logo** checkbox (see Figure 8-47).

Adding a business logo to an invoice helps customers familiarize themselves with your company. It can also help them identify your invoice.

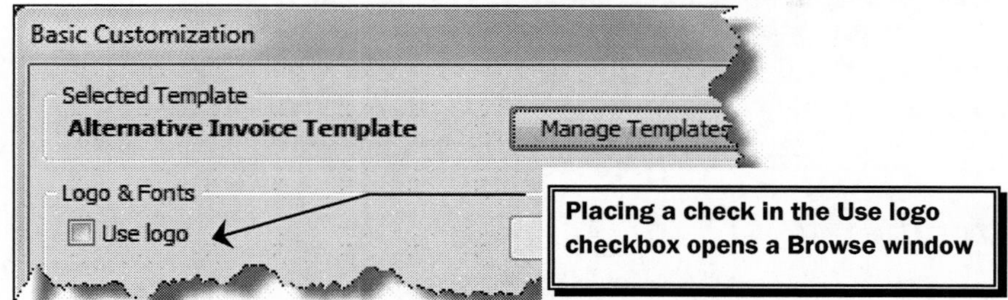

Figure 8-47 The Use logo option in the Basic Customization window

Step 13. In the *Select Image* dialog box, navigate to your student files. Select **logo.gif** and click **Open**.

Step 14. A dialog box warns that the logo graphic file will be copied to a subfolder of the location of your working file. Click **OK** to accept. You should see the logo in the upper left side of the preview pane of the *Managing Templates* window.

Step 15. Click the **Select Color Scheme** drop down menu. You can choose six preset colors. Choose **Maroon** and then click the **Apply Color Scheme** button. The text and border lines on the invoice change to the selected color.

Step 16. Next, change the color of the invoice title to black. Verify that **Title** is selected in the *Change Font for:* box and click the **Change Font** button.

Step 17. The *Example* window opens (Figure 8-48). You can use this window to change font, size, style, and color of the title of the invoice. In the **Color** field, choose **Black**. When finished, click **OK**.

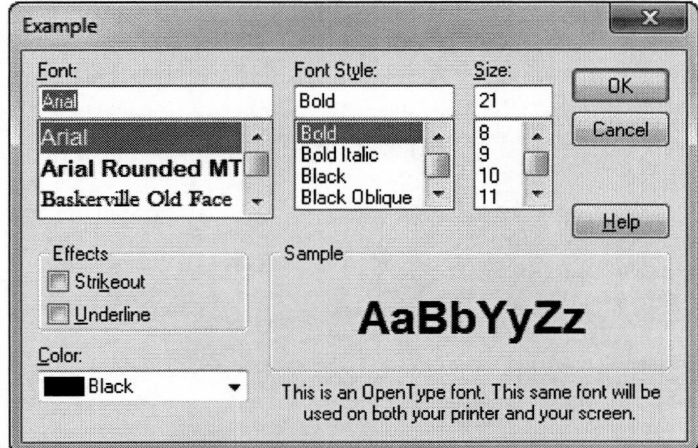

Figure 8-48 Example dialog box for changing font of labels on a template

Step 18. Click **OK** to close the *Basic Customization* window.

Step 19. From the *Home Page*, click the Create **Invoices** icon.

Step 20. To use the new template, choose **My Invoice Template** from the *Template* drop down list.

Step 21. To view how the invoice will print, click the down arrow next to **Print** button at the top of the *Create Invoices* window and select **Preview**.

Step 22. Click **Close** to close the *Print Preview* window.

Step 23. Close the *Invoice* window.

> **Note:**
> You can make further changes to the position of elements in the form by opening the *Layout Designer*. Click the **Layout Designer** button on the bottom of the *Basic Customization* window. From the *Layout Designer*, you can change the position of design elements, such as the textboxes and the logo.

Online Forms Customization

The *Online Forms Customization* allows you to create and customize sales forms using preformatted templates you can access online from within QuickBooks.

COMPUTER PRACTICE

Step 1. Create an *Invoice*.

Step 2. Click the **Customize** button at the top of the window (see Figure 8-49).

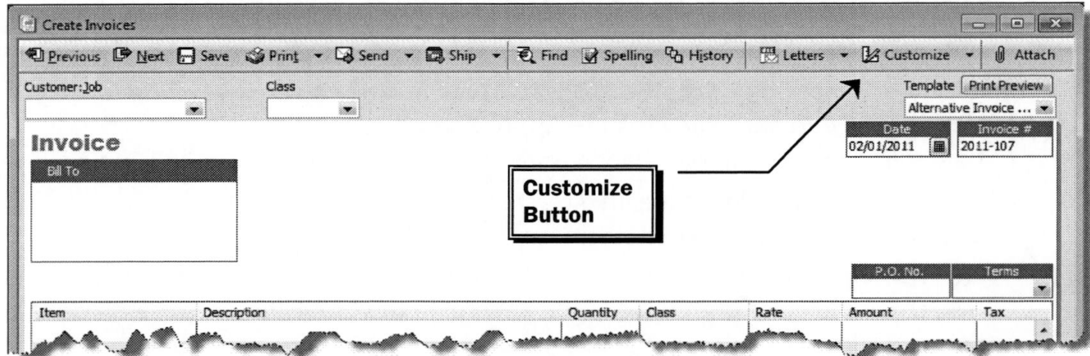

Figure 8-49 Customize Button in the Create Invoice window

Step 3. The *Customize Your QuickBooks Forms* window appears. Click **Create New Design** (see Figure 8-50).

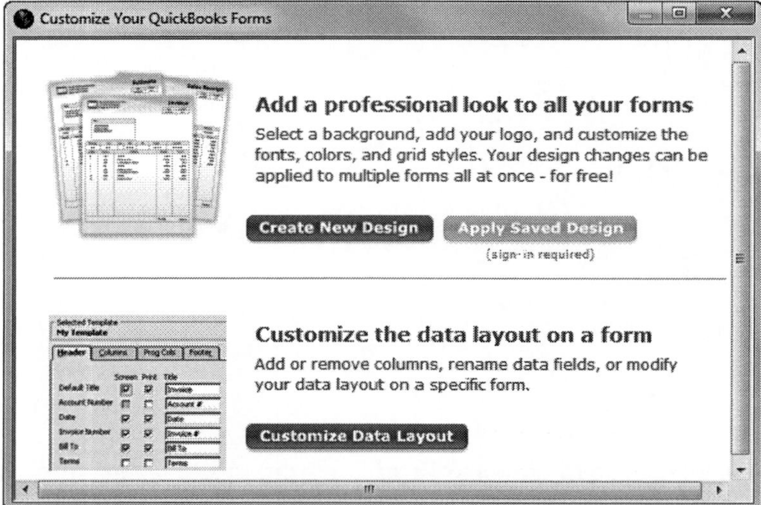

Figure 8-50 Customize Your QuickBooks Forms window

Step 4. The *Intuit Forms – Customize My Forms 1* window appears. In this window you can select a pre-designed form. Select a form of your choosing. In the screenshots below, we have chosen the *BlueCircles* design (see Figure 8-51).

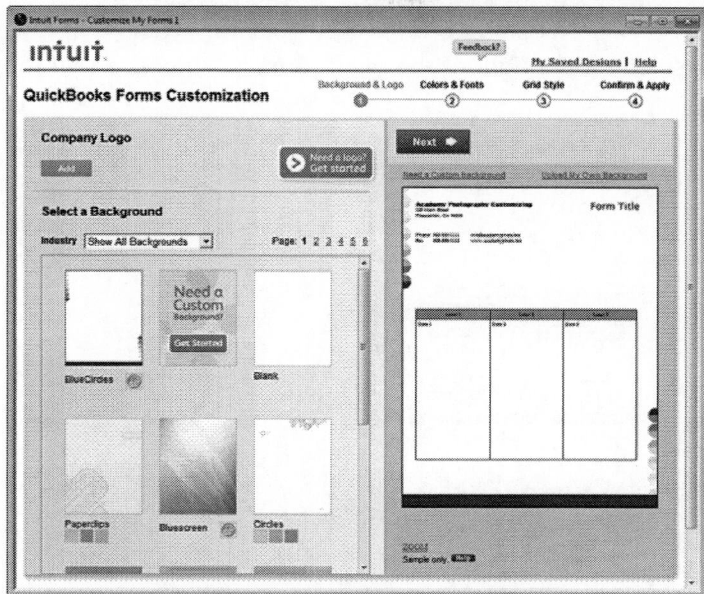

Figure 8-51 Intuit Forms - Customize My Forms 1

Step 5. After choosing a form design, click **Next**.

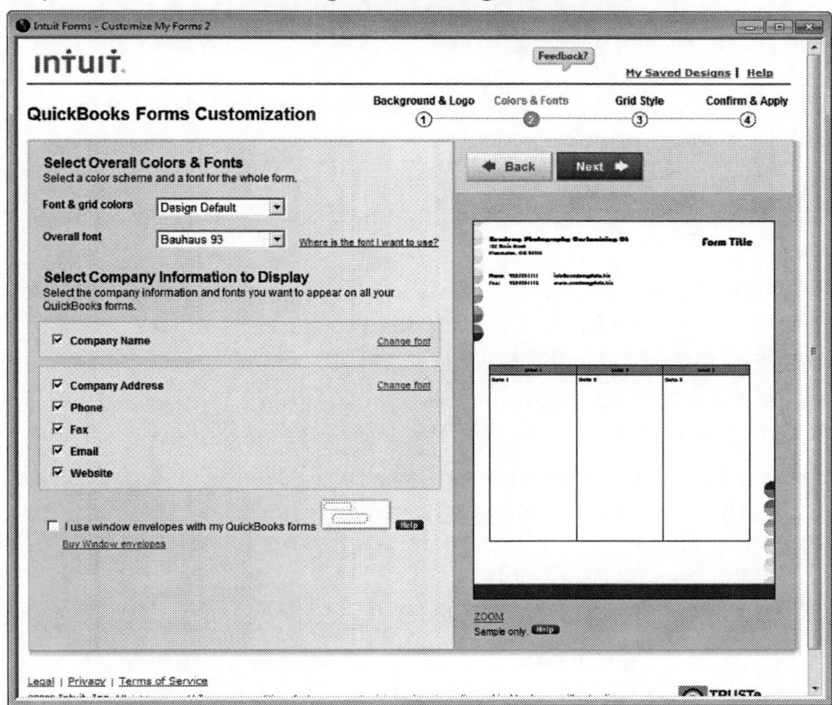

Figure 8-52 Intuit Forms - Customize My Forms 2

Step 6. You can customize the colors and fonts used on this form. You can also set up the form to place the company's and recipient's name and address in the correct position to print in an envelope window.

Select **Bauhuas 93** (or another font of your choosing) from the *Overall font* drop down list. When finished select **Next**.

Step 7. The *Select a grid style* option on the *Intuit Forms – Customized My Forms 3* window displays. We will use the default grid style. Click **Next**.

Step 8. The finalized form is previewed on the right of the *Intuit Forms – Customize My Forms 4* window. Click **Next**.

Step 9. You can apply the new design to various sales forms. Leave all the forms selected in the *Apply Design* window (see Figure 8-53). Click **Apply**.

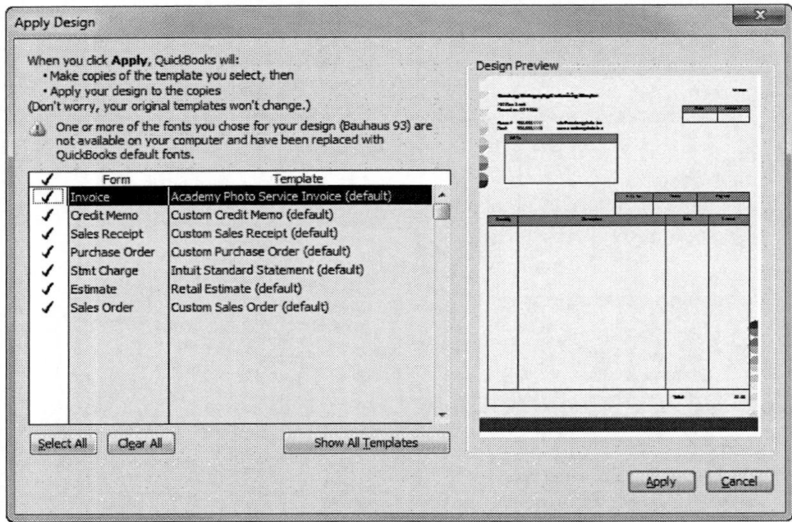

Figure 8-53 The Apply Design window

Step 10. The *Design Applied* window displays telling you that you have completed creating a customized design for your forms. Click **OK**.

Step 11. The *Intuit Forms – Rename Page* offers you the option to save the template online. You will need to have a registered account with Intuit to save your design online. Close the window.

Step 12. If a web browser launches offering sales of items to match your form design, close the window and return to QuickBooks. You will need to close the *Intuit Forms – Rename Page* window, rather than clicking *No Thanks.*

Step 13. The new design has been applied a new default template that begins with "MyDesign...". Click **Yes** in the *New Default Template Detected* window.

Step 14. The new template design is now applied to the invoice. To see the changes, click the **Print** button at the top of the *Invoice* window (see Figure 8-54).

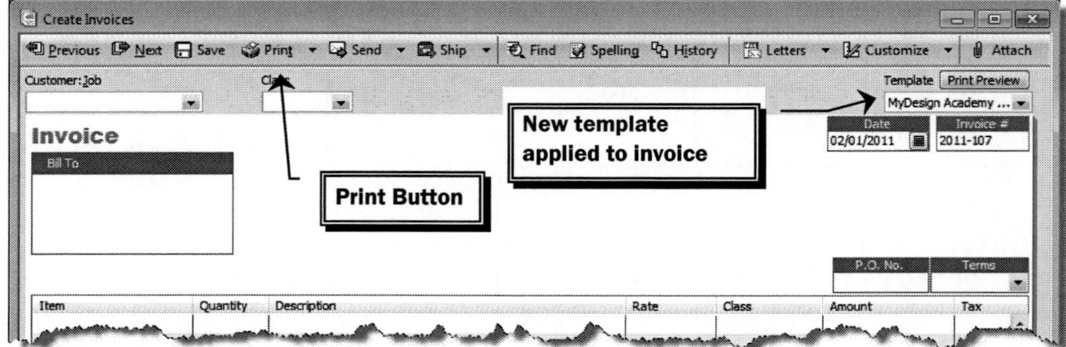

Figure 8-54 New template applied to Invoice

Step 15. Click the **Preview** button to the right of the *Print One Invoice* window.

Step 16. The *Print Preview* displays the new design template on the invoice. Click **Close** to close the *Print Preview* window.

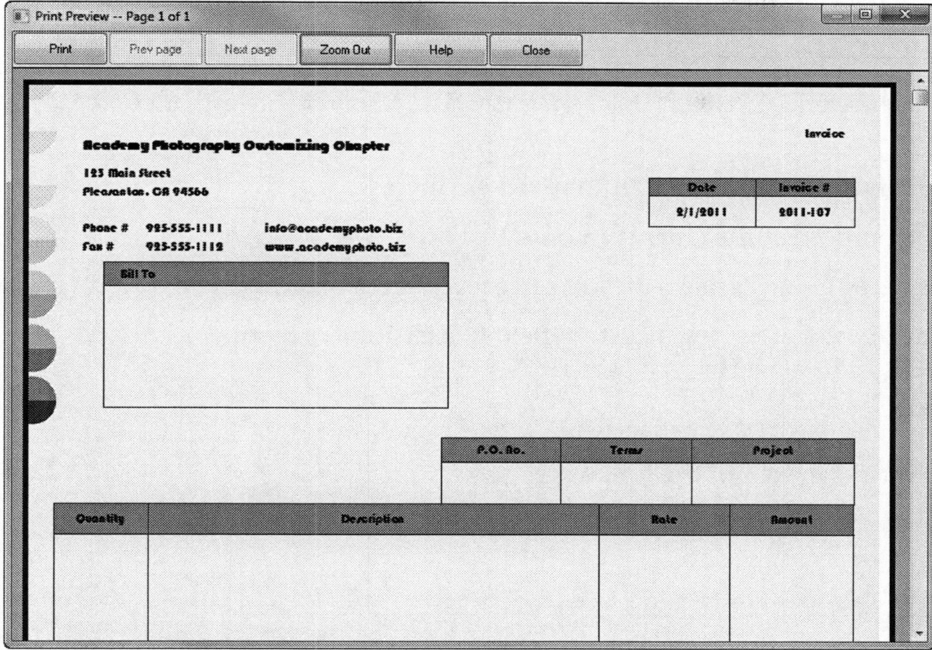

Figure 8-55 Print Preview including new customized design

Step 17. Click **Cancel** to close the *Print One Invoice* window.

Step 18. Close the Invoice.

Chapter Summary and Review

Summary of Key Points

In this chapter, you learned how to customize the QuickBooks interface and how to customize the lists to make QuickBooks work for different types of businesses.

Topics covered in this chapter include:

- Modify QuickBooks Preferences (page 332).
- Customize QuickBooks Menus and Windows (page 333).
- Customize the Icon Bar and Display settings (page 336).
- Use the Item List and Other Lists (page 342).
- Use Custom Fields to Track Extra Data on Transactions (page 353).
- Create and Customize Sales Forms (page 355).

Comprehension Questions

> Answers to these review questions are available with the supplemental material. See page xiii for details.

1. Describe the difference between *User Preferences* (i.e., My Preferences) and *Company Preferences.*
2. What commands should you put in the *Favorites* menu?
3. Describe the purpose of the **Open Window List**.
4. How would setting a customer's default price level affect their future invoices?
5. Describe the process of adding a custom field to a customer record.

Multiple Choice

Select the best answer(s) for each of the following:

1. You can create custom fields for:
   a) Customers.
   b) Templates.
   c) Vendors.
   d) Both a and c.
2. The two types of preferences are:
   a) User and Company Preferences.
   b) User and Accountant Preferences.
   c) Favorite and General Preferences.
   d) Income and Expense Preferences.
3. If you don't see the Favorites menu in your menu bar, you can turn it on in the
   a) Customize Templates window.
   b) Customize Icon Bar window.
   c) List menu.
   d) Windows menu.
4. Which of the following is typically displayed vertically on the far left side of the screen:
   a) The Navigation Bar.
   b) The Icon Bar.
   c) The Open Window List.
   d) None of the above.
5. You cannot customize which of the following:
   a) The layout of Statements.
   b) The Icon Bar.
   c) The layout of the Estimate forms.
   d) The Open Window List.
6. To add an Icon to the Icon Bar, you can use:
   a) The *Add* "window-name" *to Icon Bar* option.
   b) The *Customize Icon Bar* Window.
   c) The User Preferences for Desktop View.
   d) Either a or b.

7. Which of the following menu bars gives you the option of showing icons only:
   a) The Favorites Menu.
   b) The Open Window List.
   c) The Icon Bar.
   d) The Accounting Toolbar.

8. Which of the following is not an available Template Type in QuickBooks:
   a) Credit Memo.
   b) Statement.
   c) Check.
   d) Sales Receipt.

9. If you pay sales tax to more than once agency you should use which of the following item types:
   a) Sales Tax Group.
   b) Group.
   c) Inventory Assembly.
   d) Subtotal.

10. Use which of the following to manually design the layout of an Invoice:
    a) The *Company* tab of the *Customize Invoice* window.
    b) The *Format* tab of the *Customize Invoice* window.
    c) QuickBooks *Company Preferences*.
    d) *The Layout Designer*.

11. The two types of Price Levels are:
    a) Fixed percentage and per item.
    b) Fixed percentage and per customer.
    c) Per item and per customer.
    d) Per customer and per vendor.

12. The *Online Forms Customization* gives you the option to:
    a) Add a professional look to existing QuickBooks templates.
    b) Get started advertising online through a simple four step process.
    c) Process your transactions through the internet using a customizable automated process.
    d) All of the above.

13. The simplest way to offer a regular discount to a customer is to:
    a) Set the price level on the customer's invoices.
    b) Add a Discount Item to each of the customer's invoices.
    c) Enter the discount in the *Customer Discount* field in the *Edit Customer* window.
    d) Set the default price level for that customer

14. To include shipping charges on an Invoice, it is best to use which type of item:
    a) Inventory Part.
    b) Other Charge.
    c) Service.
    d) Non-inventory Part.

15. You can rearrange the order of columns in a template using the:
    a) *Managing Templates* window.
    b) *Template List*.
    c) *Basic Customization* window
    d) *Advanced Customization* window.

Completion Statements

1. Use a(n) __________ Item (item type) to track subcontracted labor.
2. Use the ________ ___________ *User Preferences* to set default windows that show when you open QuickBooks and to change the color and graphics of QuickBooks toolbars and windows.
3. The _________ _________ displays common commands along with a symbolized representing that command along the top of the QuickBooks window.
4. __________-____________ terms calculate based on the day of the month that an Invoice or Bill is due or a discount is earned.
5. Use a _________ Item on Invoices or Sales Receipts to calculate the subtotal of the Items above that line.

Customizing-Problem 1

APPLYING YOUR KNOWLEDGE

Restore the Customizing-10Problem1.QBM file and store it on your hard disk according to your instructor's directions.

1. Set up the following terms:
   a) 2% 7 Net 20
   b) 2% 2nd Net 20th (Due next month if issued within 10 days of the due date)
   c) Net 45
   d) 1% 15th Net 30th (Due next month if issued within 10 days *of the d*ue date)
2. Create a **Terms Listing** report (Select *the Reports menu, **Lists**,* and then ***Terms Listing***). Add the *Discount on Day of Month* and *Min Days to Pay* columns. Expand the columns so you can see the entire column headers. Print the report.
3. Add a custom **field to your** customers called **Web Site**. Add the Web sites to the *following cus*tomer records:

Customer:Job Name	**Web Site**
Anderson Wedding Planners: Kumar, Sati and Naveen	*www.andweddingbliss.net*
Anderson Wedding Planners: Wilson, Sarah and Michael	*www.andweddingbliss.net*
Anderson Wedding Planners	*www.andweddingbliss.net*
Pelligrini, George	*www.pelligrini_build.net*
Pelligrini, George:2354 Wilkes Rd	*www.pelligrini_build.net*
Pelligrini, George: 4266 Lake Drive	*www.pelligrini_build.net*

Table 8-1 Web site data for custom fields

4. Create a Customer Contact list, modified to display the Customer Name and Web Site only.

5. Create a Sales Tax Item for Santa Cruz. The sales tax rate is 9%.

6. Create a duplicate of the Intuit Service Invoice Template. Then, make the following changes:

    a) Change the name of the template to ***Academy Photo Studio Invoice***.
    b) Add the **Web site** custom field to the screen and printed invoice using the *Additional Customization Header* tab.
    c) When prompted, click **Default Layout.**

7. Create a new non-inventory part called ***Specialized Package***. Set up the new item using the following information:

Field Name	Data
Item Name/Number	*Specialized Package*
Description	*Customized Package of Photography from Session*
Price	*0 (leave 0 because it's a custom package)*
Tax Code	*Tax*
Account	*Sales*

Table 8-2 Item setup data

8. Create an Invoice for Pelligrini, George, for the 1254 Wilkes Rd job, using the Academy Photography Studio Invoice template. Enter the following information on header of the invoice:

Field Name	Data
Class	*San Jose*
Date	*02/28/2011*
Invoice #	*2011-106*
Terms	*2% 7 Net 20*
Tax	*Santa Cruz*

Table 8-3 Use this data for the invoice header.

9. Enter the following information into the body of the invoice.

Item	Qty	Description	Rate	Amount	Tax
Indoor Photo Session	*1*		*95.00*	*95.00*	*Non*
Specialized Package	*2*	*Customized Package of Photography from Session*	*700.00*	*1400.00*	*Tax*

Table 8-4 Item descriptions

10. Accept the default for all other fields on the invoice and print the invoice.
11. Save the new terms and tax items when prompted.

Workplace Applications

Discussion Questions

These questions are designed to stimulate discussion about how you can apply QuickBooks to your own organization. They may help you think through some of the issues you'll encounter when using QuickBooks in your company.

1. Discuss how you might use the Price Levels feature in QuickBooks.

Chapter 9 Inventory

Objectives

After completing this chapter, you should be able to:

- Activate the Inventory function (page 372).
- Set up Inventory Items in the Item list (page 373).
- Use QuickBooks to calculate the average cost of inventory (page 378).
- Record sales of Inventory using sales forms (page 378).
- View the accounting entries behind the scenes of inventory sales using the Transaction Journal report (page 379).
- Use purchase orders to order inventory (page 382).
- Receive inventory against purchase orders (page 384).
- Enter bills for received inventory (page 389).
- Adjust your inventory (page 394).
- Set up Group Items to bundle products and/or services (page 396).
- Create reports about inventory (page 398).
- Units of Measure and Inventory Assemblies (Supplemental Material)

Restore this File

This chapter uses Inventory-10.QBW. To open this file, restore the Inventory-10.QBM file to your hard disk. See page 10 for instructions on restoring files.

In this chapter, you will learn how to set up and manage your inventory in QuickBooks.

QuickBooks Tools for Tracking Inventory

The *Vendors* section, located on the *Home* page, shows a graphical representation of the steps involved in managing inventory. The Purchasing Workflow is highlighted Figure 9-1, is visible with the QuickBooks Couch (for more on the QuickBooks Coach see page 30).

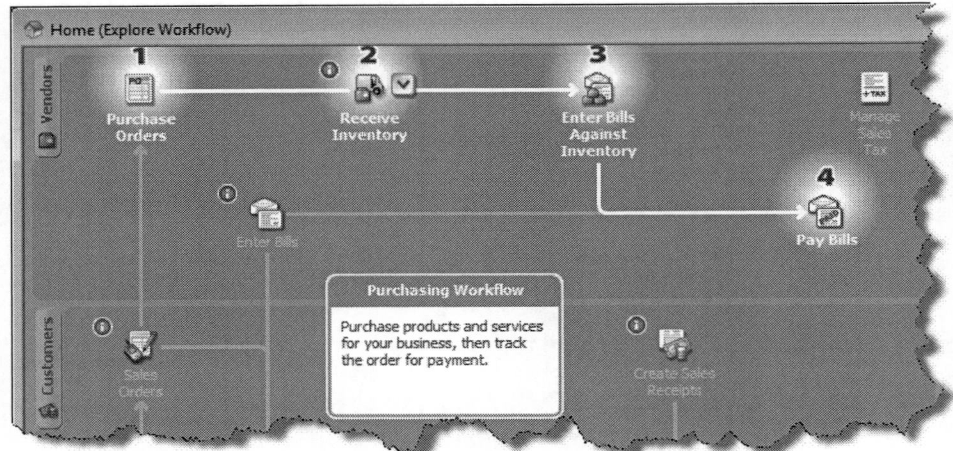

Figure 9-1 Vendors section of the Home page

Table 9-1 shows an overview of the **accounting behind the scenes** for different business transactions that involve inventory. Familiarize yourself with this table, and refer to it when you encounter business transactions involving inventory.

Business Transaction	QuickBooks Transaction	Accounting Entry	Comments
Purchasing Inventory with Purchase Orders	Purchase Orders	Non-posting entry used to record Purchase Orders.	You do not have to use purchase orders. If you do, QuickBooks tracks the status of your orders and matches them with the bill from your vendor.
Receiving Inventory (without Bill from Vendor)	Receive Inventory **Select Receive Inventory without Bill**	Increase (debit) **Inventory**, increase (credit) **Accounts Payable**. Increase inventory counts for each item received.	Use this transaction when you receive inventory items that are not accompanied by a bill. This transaction enters an *item receipt* in the Accounts Payable account. Although it increases A/P, no bill shows in the Pay Bills window.
Receiving Inventory (with Bill from Vendor)	Receive Inventory **Select Receive Inventory with Bill**	Increase (debit) **Inventory**, increase (credit) **Accounts Payable**. Increase inventory counts for each item received.	Use this transaction when you receive inventory accompanied by a Bill from the vendor.
Entering a Bill for Previously Received Inventory Items	Enter Bills Against Inventory	No change in debits and credits. This transaction only changes an **Item Receipt** transaction into a **bill**.	When an item receipt is turned into a bill, QuickBooks shows the bill in the Pay Bills window.
Build Inventory assemblies from individual parts **(Premier Only)**	Build Assemblies	Reduce inventory on hand for each component item, and increase inventory on hand for the assembly item. No net effect on total inventory dollar balance.	Use this transaction to record the assembly of component parts into a finished assembly.

Table 9-1 Summary of inventory transactions

Tracking Inventory with QuickBooks

It is critical to think through your company's information needs before tackling inventory. New users sometimes try to use inventory parts to track products they don't really need to track in detail. You must separately enter every purchase and sale for each inventory part. That might not seem like too much work at first, but if you have hundreds of small products with even a moderate turnover, you might overwhelm your bookkeeping system with detailed transactions.

When you use **Inventory Part** Items to track inventory, QuickBooks handles all the accounting for you automatically, depending upon how you set up Inventory Part Items in the Item list. Inventory is defined as goods that are purchased from a vendor that will be sold at a future date. For example, a retailer has inventory until they sell the merchandise to customers. When the inventory is sold, it is removed from the *Inventory Asset* account and expensed through *Cost of Goods Sold*. This enables the sale to be properly matched to the expense in the right accounting period.

QuickBooks keeps a **perpetual** inventory, meaning that every purchase and every sale of inventory immediately updates all your account balances and reports.

When QuickBooks calculates the cost of inventory, it uses the *average cost* method, explained on page 378. QuickBooks does not support the first-in, first-out (FIFO) or last-in, first-out (LIFO) methods.

> **Key Term:** *Perpetual Inventory* in QuickBooks keeps a continuous record of increases, decreases, and balance on hand of inventory items.
> **Key Term:** *Average Cost* method divides the cost of inventory by the number of units in stock. It is most appropriate when prices paid for inventory do not vary significantly over time, and when inventory turnover is high (i.e., products sell through quickly). QuickBooks calculates the cost of inventory using this method.

In order to keep your inventory system working smoothly, it is critical that you use Inventory Parts Items on all transactions involving inventory. This means you must use the Items tab on every purchase transaction that involves *Inventory Part* type Items. Figure 9-2 illustrates entering a Bill using Inventory Part Items.

DO NOT ENTER THIS BILL NOW. IT IS FOR REFERENCE ONLY.

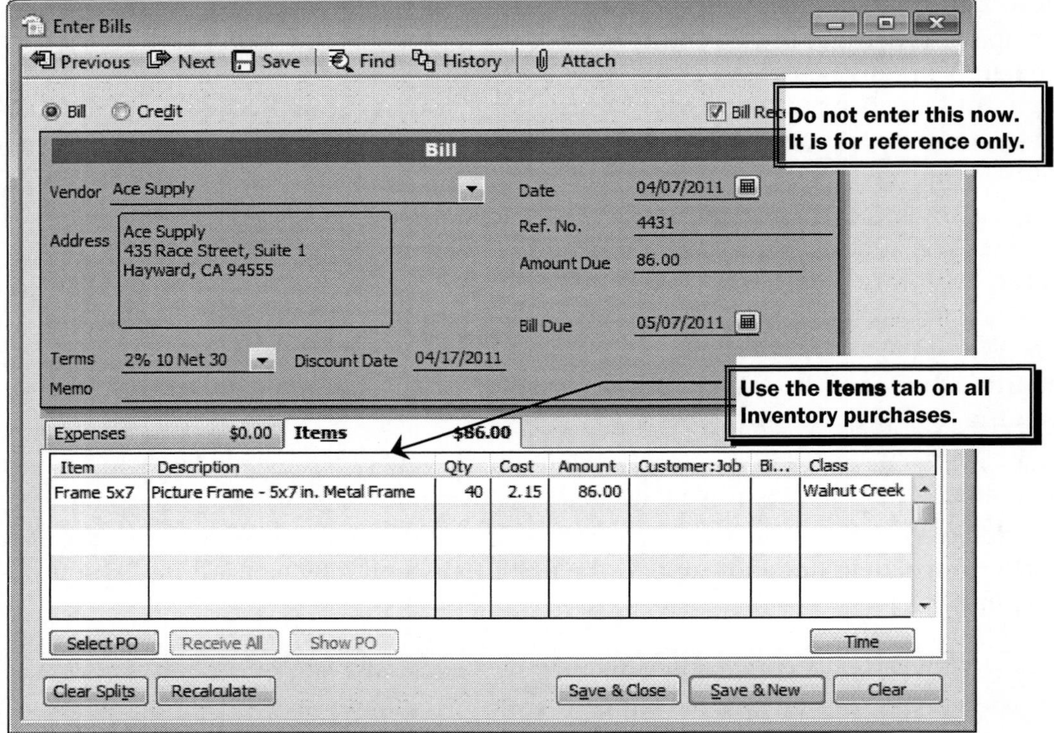

Figure 9-2 The Items tab is used for inventory transactions

Activating the Inventory Function

The first step in using QuickBooks for inventory is to activate **Inventory** in your company **Preferences.**

COMPUTER PRACTICE

Step 1. Select **Preferences** from the *Edit* menu.

Step 2. Select the **Items & Inventory** Preference and then select the **Company Preferences** tab.

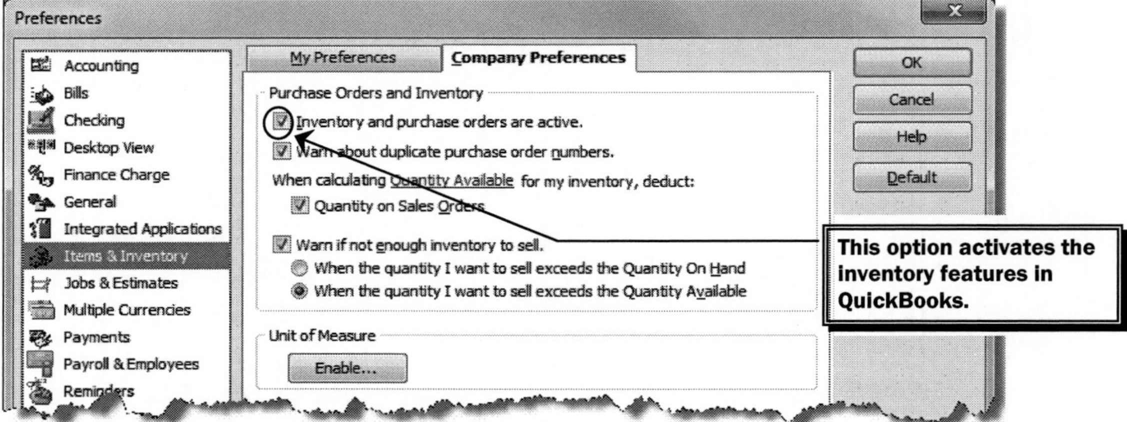

Figure 9-3 Company Preferences for Items & Inventory

Step 3. Verify that *Inventory and purchase orders are active* is checked (see Figure 9-3).

> **Note:**
> When inventory is activated, Purchase Orders are also activated. However, you are not required to use Purchase Orders when tracking inventory.

Step 4. Click the **OK** in the *Preferences* window.

After you activate the Inventory function, the Item List shows a new Item type called **Inventory Part**.

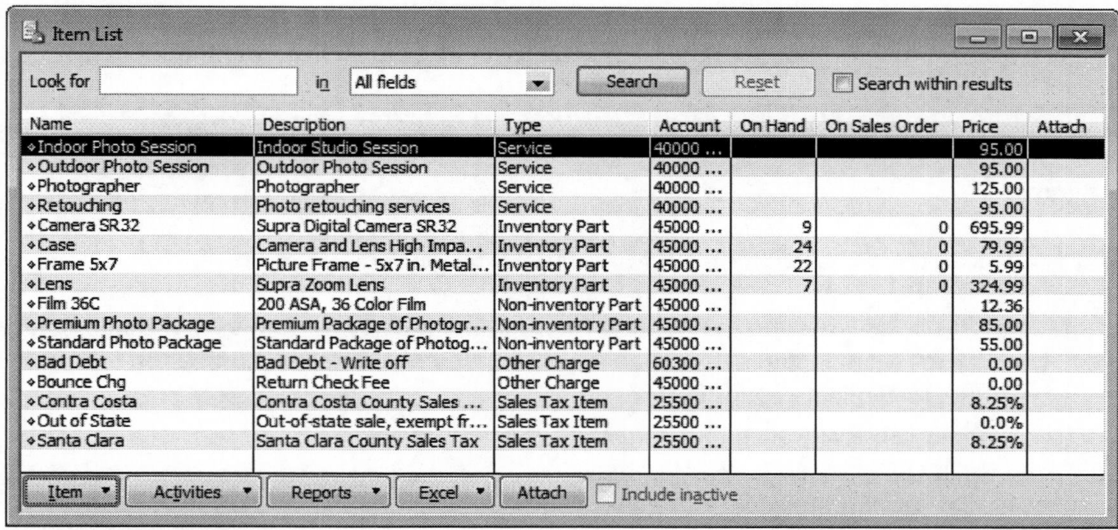

Figure 9-4 Item List window

The first time you create an Inventory Part Item in the Item list, QuickBooks automatically creates two accounts in your **Chart of Accounts**: An *Other Current Asset* account called **Inventory Asset** and a *Cost of Goods Sold* account called **Cost of Goods Sold**. QuickBooks uses these two important accounts to track inventory (see Table 9-2). The Inventory Asset account holds the value of your inventory until you sell it. The Cost of Goods Sold account records the cost of the inventory *when* you sell it.

Accounts for Tracking Inventory	
Inventory Asset	A special *Other Current Asset* account that tracks the cost of each inventory Item purchased. This account increases (by the actual purchase cost) when inventory is purchased, and decreases (by the weighted average cost) when inventory Items are sold.
Cost of Goods Sold	**Cost of Goods Sold** is subtracted from total Income on the **Profit & Loss** report to show **Gross Profit**. QuickBooks automatically increases **Cost of Goods Sold** each time you sell an inventory Item.

Table 9-2 Two accounts that track inventory

Setting up Inventory Parts Items

To set up an inventory part in the Item list, follow these steps:

COMPUTER PRACTICE

Step 1. Select the *Lists* menu and then select **Item List**. Alternatively, click **Items & Services** on the *Company* section of the *Home* page.

Step 2. Select the *Item* menu at the bottom of the list and then select **New**. Alternatively, press **Ctrl+N**.

Step 3. Select **Inventory Part** from the *Type* drop-down list and press **Tab**).

Step 4. Enter ***Frame 8x10*** in the *Item Name/Number* field and press **Tab**.

You might want to give each item in your inventory a part number, and then use the part numbers in the *Item Name/Number* field.

Step 5. Skip the *Subitem of* field by pressing **Tab**.

This field allows you to create subitems of items. If you use subitems, the **Sales by Item** reports and graphs will show totals for all sales and costs of the subitems.

> **Key Term:** *Subitems* help to organize the Item list. Use subitems to group and subtotal information about similar products or services in sales reports and graphs.

Step 6. Skip the *Manufacturer's Part Number* field by pressing **Tab** again.

This field allows you to enter the Part Number that the vendor uses or that is listed by the Manufacturer. This enables you to reference the same number on POs and Bills to eliminate confusion.

Step 7. Press **Tab** to advance to the *Purchase Information* field.

Step 8. Enter ***Picture Frame - 8x10 in. Metal Frame*** in the *Description on Purchase Transactions* field and press **Tab**.

The description you enter here appears as the default description when you use this item on purchase orders and bills.

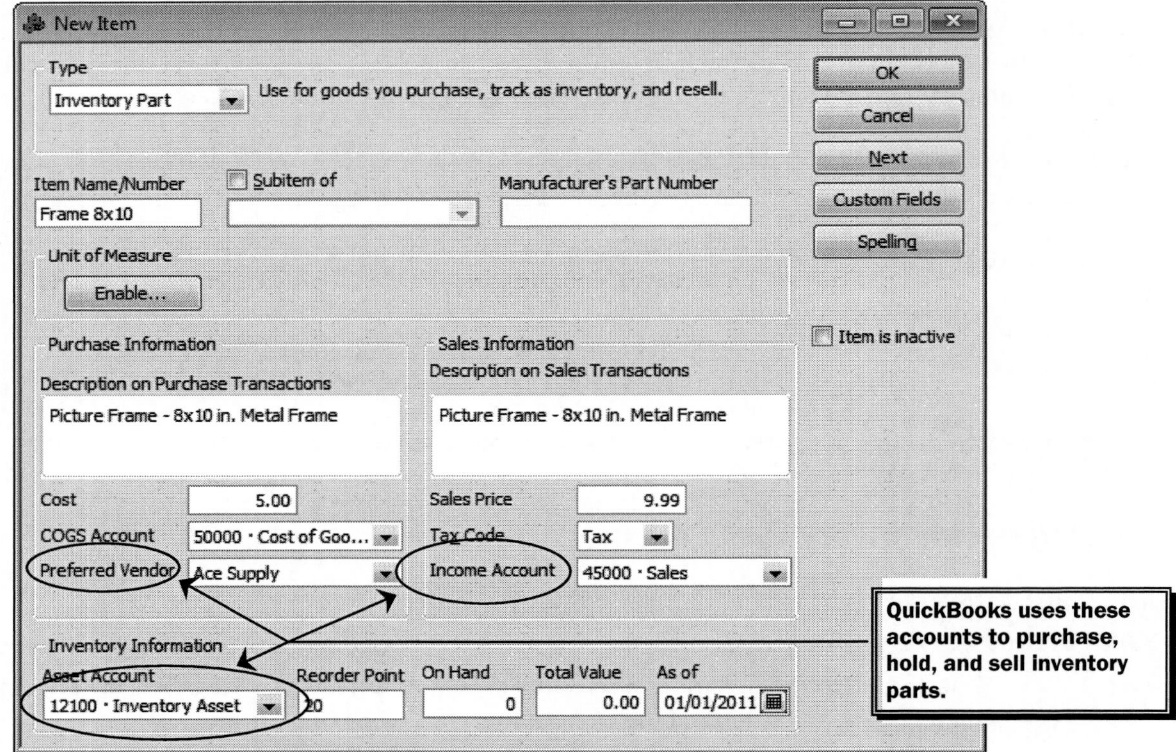

Figure 9-5 The completed New Item window

> **Note:**
> Notice that there are three account fields on the New Item window (**COGS** Account, **Asset** Account, and **Income** Account). In each of these fields, enter the accounts that QuickBooks should use when you purchase, hold, and sell this item. You are specifying how QuickBooks should account for the item when it is used in an inventory transaction. Each field is covered separately in this chapter.

Step 9. Enter ***5.00*** in the *Cost* field and press **Tab**.

Use this field to track the price you pay to your vendor for the item. QuickBooks takes this amount as the default price when you enter this item on purchase orders and bills. If the price changes, you can override the amount on the purchase order and bill or you can edit the amount here.

Step 10. In the *COGS Account* field **Cost of Goods Sold** is already selected. Press **Tab**.

QuickBooks uses the **Cost of Goods Sold** account to record the average cost of this item when you sell it. For more information on average cost, see page 378.

Step 11. Select **Ace Supply** from the *Preferred Vendor* drop-down list and press **Tab**.

The *Preferred Vendor* field is used to associate the item with the vendor from whom you normally purchase this part. It is an optional field and you can leave it blank without compromising the integrity of the system.

Step 12. Press **Tab** to leave the *Description on Sales Transactions* field unchanged. The text in this field defaults to whatever you entered in the *Description on Purchase Transactions* field.

QuickBooks allows you to have two descriptions for this item: one for purchase forms and one for sales forms. You can use your vendor's description when purchasing the item and a more customer-oriented description on your sales forms.

Step 13. Enter ***9.99*** in the *Sales Price* field. Press **Tab**.

In order for the Sales Price field to automatically calculate a price based on the cost of the item, modify the *Default Markup Percentage* field in the **Company Preferences** tab for the Time & Expenses preference (See Figure 9-6).

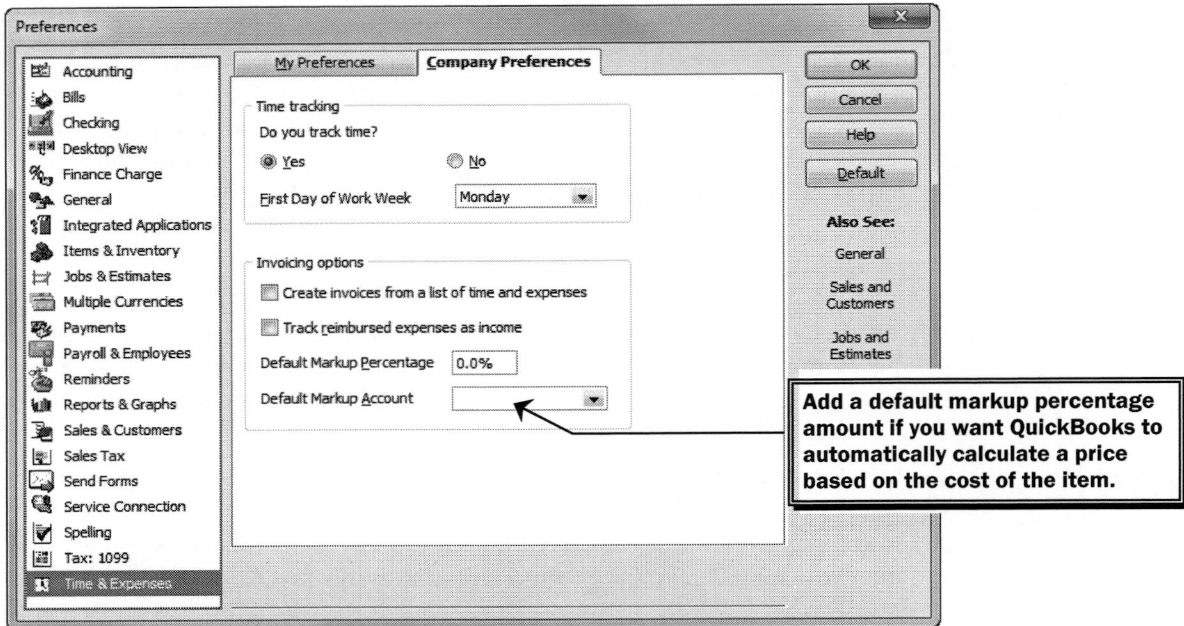

Figure 9-6 Modifying the default markup percentage in the Preferences window

Step 14. The *Sales Price* is how much you normally charge your customers for the item. You can enter a default here and later override it on sales forms.

Step 15. The **Tax** Code is already selected. Press **Tab**.

Tax Codes determine the default taxable status of the item. Since the Tax Code called **Tax** is taxable, QuickBooks calculates sales tax on this item when it appears on sales forms. You can override the default Tax Code on each sales form. For more information on Sales Tax Codes see page 413.

Step 16. Select **Sales** from the Income Account drop-down list. Press **Tab**.

Choose the income account to which you want to post sales of this Item.

Step 17. In the *Asset Account* field, **Inventory Asset** is already selected. Press **Tab**.

The Inventory Asset account is the account that tracks the cost of your inventoried products between the time you purchase them and the time you sell them.

The accounting behind the scenes:
When you purchase inventory, QuickBooks increases (debits) the **Inventory Asset** account by the amount of the purchase price. When you sell inventory, QuickBooks decreases (credits) the **Inventory Asset** account and increases (debits) the Cost of Goods Sold account for the average cost of that item at the time it is sold. For details on how QuickBooks calculates average cost, see page 378.

Step 18. Enter ***20*** in the *Reorder Point* field and press **Tab** (see Figure 9-7).

The QuickBooks Reminders list reminds you when it's time to reorder inventory items based on the *Reorder Point*.

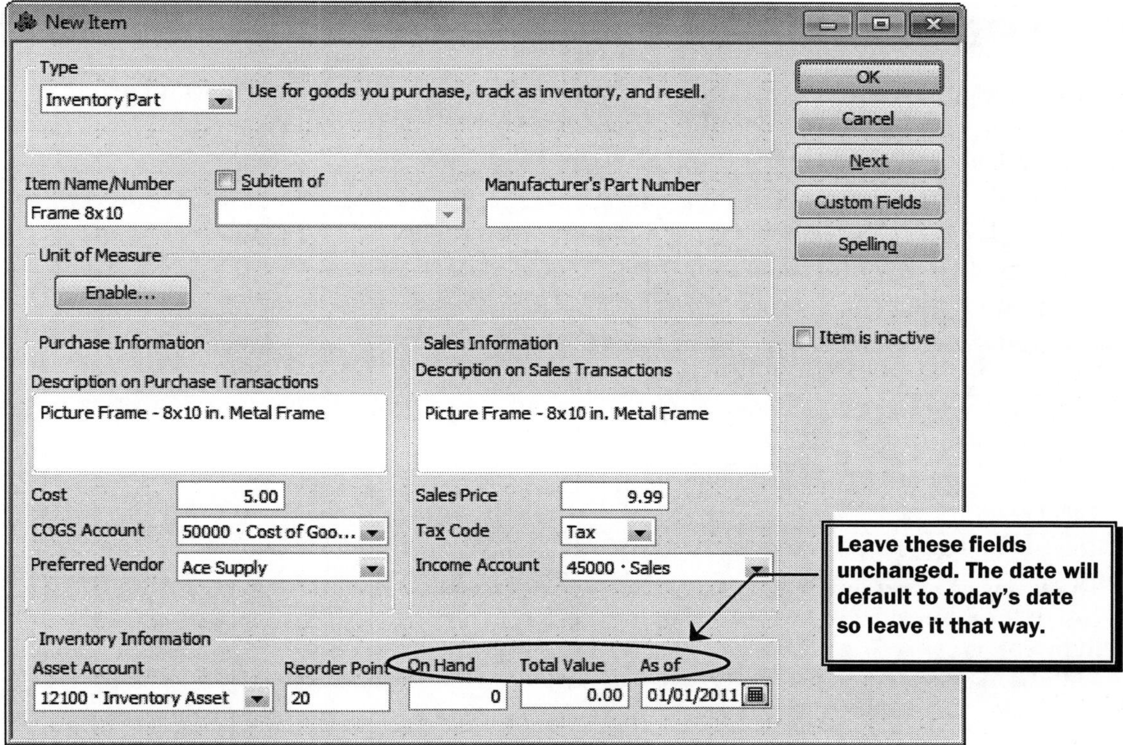

Figure 9-7 When inventory drops below the reorder point, QuickBooks reminds you to reorder

Step 19. Leave the *On Hand, Total Value,* and *As of* fields unchanged.

Note:
Do not enter the *On Hand*, *Total Value*, and *As of* fields. These fields are intended for use during the initial setup of the data file.

The accounting behind the scenes:
If you enter a quantity and value in this window, QuickBooks increases (debits) Inventory for the total value, and increases (credits) Opening Bal Equity.

However, even if you are setting up the data file it is better to leave the *On Hand* and *Total Value* fields set to zero when you set up the item. Then, as you will see later, use a single inventory adjustment transaction to set up the quantity and value on hand for **all** the inventory items.

Step 20. Click **OK** to save the new Item.

Tip:
Before setting up inventory, think about what products you will track as Inventory Parts. It may not be necessary to separately track *every* product you sell as an Inventory Part. If you do not need detailed reports and inventory status information about certain products you sell, consider using Non-inventory Part items to track those products. In general, use Inventory Part items only when you really need to track the stock status of a product.

Calculating Average Cost of Inventory

When you use an inventory item on a purchase form (e.g., a Bill), QuickBooks increases (Debits) the Inventory Asset account for the *actual* cost of the inventory purchase. At the same time, it recalculates the **average cost** of all items in inventory.

When you use an inventory item on a sales form (e.g., an Invoice), in addition to recording income and accounts receivable, QuickBooks increases (debits) Cost of Goods Sold and decreases (credits) Inventory Asset for the average cost of the items.

Table 9-3 shows how QuickBooks calculates the average cost of inventory Items.

Situation/Transaction	Calculation
You have ten 8x10 picture frames in stock. Each originally costs $5.00.	10 units X $5.00 per unit = $50.00 total cost
You buy ten new 8x10 picture frames at $6.00 each.	10 units X $6.00 per unit = $60.00 total cost
The combined cost in inventory.	$50.00 + $60.00 = $110.00
The average cost per unit is equal to the total cost of inventory divided by the total units in inventory.	total cost/total units = average cost/unit $110.00 / 20 = $5.50 avg. cost/unit

Table 9-3 QuickBooks calculates the average cost of inventory items.

Each time you sell inventory items, the average cost per unit is multiplied by the number of units sold. Then this amount is deducted from the **Inventory Asset** account and added to the **Cost of Goods Sold** account.

Invoicing for Inventory Items

Selling Inventory Items Using an Invoice Form

When you sell inventory, always use an Invoice or a Sales Receipt to record the sale. This ensures that QuickBooks updates your inventory records and your financial reports at the same time.

COMPUTER PRACTICE

Step 1. Enter the Invoice as shown in Figure 9-8, recording a sale of two 5x7 frames.

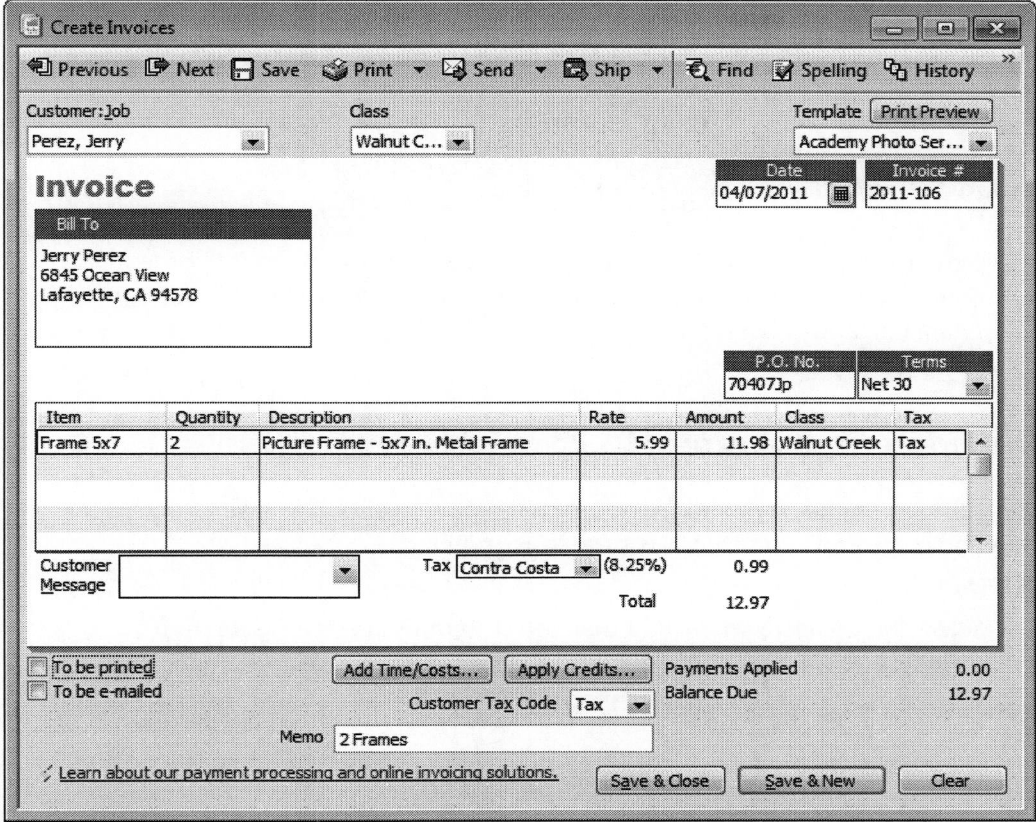

Figure 9-8 Enter this data in your Invoice.

Step 2. Click **Save & New** to save the Invoice.

Creating a Transaction Journal Report

To see how this Invoice affects the **General Ledger**, use a **Transaction Journal** report.

COMPUTER PRACTICE

Step 1. Display the Invoice 2011-106 (shown previously in Figure 9-8).

Step 2. Select the *Reports* menu and then select **Transaction Journal** (or press Ctrl+Y).

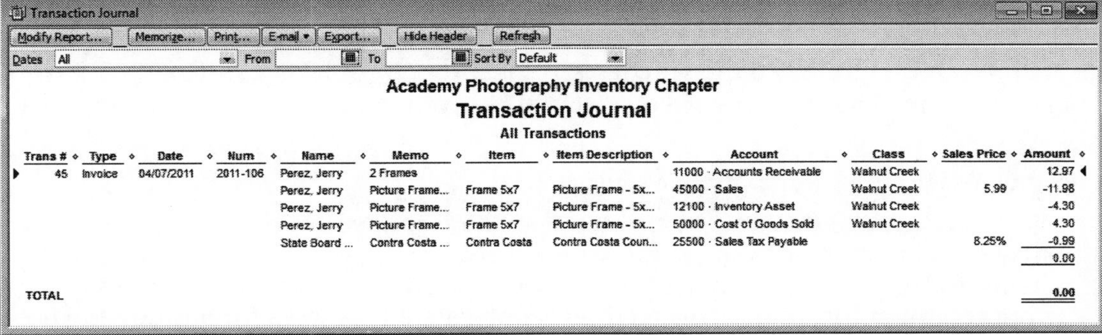

Academy Photography Inventory Chapter

Transaction Journal

All Transactions

Trans #	Type	Date	Num	Name	Memo	Item	Item Description	Account	Class	Sales Price	Amount
45	Invoice	04/07/2011	2011-106	Perez, Jerry	2 Frames			11000 · Accounts Receivable	Walnut Creek		12.97
				Perez, Jerry	Picture Frame...	Frame 5x7	Picture Frame - 5x...	45000 · Sales	Walnut Creek	5.99	-11.98
				Perez, Jerry	Picture Frame...	Frame 5x7	Picture Frame - 5x...	12100 · Inventory Asset	Walnut Creek		-4.30
				Perez, Jerry	Picture Frame...	Frame 5x7	Picture Frame - 5x...	50000 · Cost of Goods Sold	Walnut Creek		4.30
				State Board ...	Contra Costa ...	Contra Costa	Contra Costa Coun...	25500 · Sales Tax Payable		8.25%	-0.99
											0.00
TOTAL											0.00

Figure 9-9 Transaction Journal report

The accounting behind the scenes:
When you sell an Inventory Part, QuickBooks increases (credits) the income account defined for the item sold on the **Invoice** or **Sales Receipt** form. The **Transaction Journal** report (Figure 9-9) shows the accounting behind the scenes of the invoice. You can use the **Transaction Journal** report to see the accounting behind ***any*** QuickBooks transaction.

Step 3. Close the report by clicking the close box (☒) in the upper right corner. If the *Memorize Report* dialog box appears, check the *Do not display this message in the future* box and click **No**.

Step 4. Close the Invoice.

Using Reminders for Inventory

Because you sold two Frame 5x7s and inventory fell below twenty-five units (its reorder point), QuickBooks reminds you that it is time to reorder.

COMPUTER PRACTICE

Step 1. Select the *Company* menu and then select **Reminders** (see Figure 9-10).

Step 2. Double-click on the *Inventory to Reorder* line.

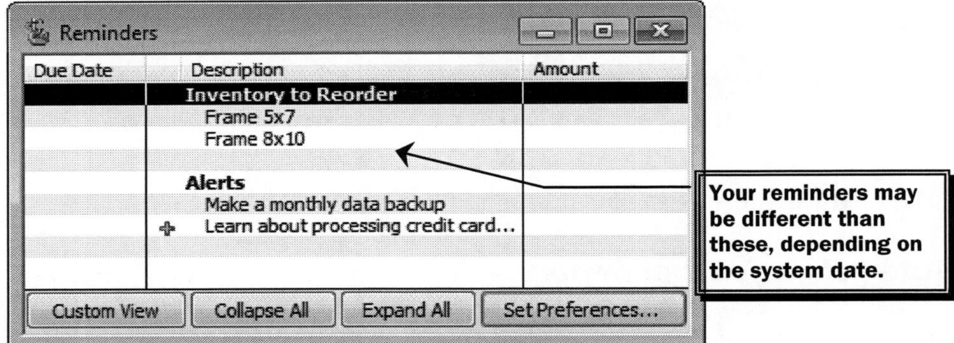

Figure 9-10 Reminders list

Step 3. Close the window by clicking the close box (☒) in the upper right corner.

Purchasing Inventory

There are several ways to record the purchases of inventory in QuickBooks. How you record receiving inventory depends on *when* you receive the inventory and *how* you intend to pay for it.

You have two options for purchasing inventory:

1. You could pay for items at the time you purchase and receive them. For example, you may be at your vendor's store and write a check or charge your credit card for the items. In this case, you will use **Write Checks** or **Enter Credit Card Charges** to record your receipt of inventory. This method is not generally advised for businesses who want a complete system for tracking purchases, receipts, and payments for inventory purchases.
2. Alternatively, you could use the inventory ordering and receiving process displayed in the *Vendors* section of the *Home* page shown in Figure 9-11. If you choose this method for processing inventory, you will issue a purchase order (PO) for each purchase and later receive part or all of the order by recording an Item Receipt or a Bill.

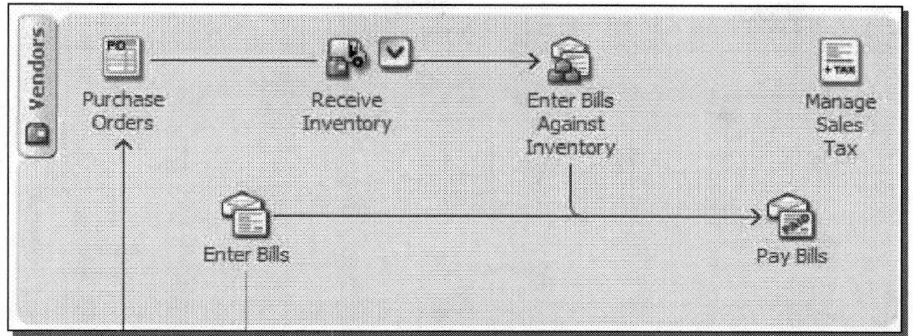

Figure 9-11 The Vendors Section Includes a Flowchart for Ordering and Receiving Inventory

3. If the bill does not accompany the shipment, use the **Receive Inventory without Bill** option from the *Receive Inventory* icon drop-down list (see Figure 9-12). This creates an **Item Receipt** in QuickBooks. When the bill comes, use the **Enter Bill for Received Items** option from the *Vendor* menu. This converts the **Item Receipt** into a Bill.
4. If you receive the bill when you receive the order, use the **Receive Inventory with Bill** option from the *Receive Inventory* drop-down list (see Figure 9-12). This creates a Bill in QuickBooks.

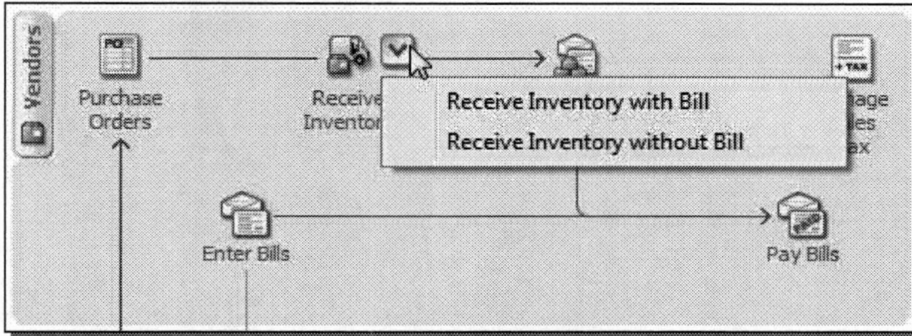

Figure 9-12 Receive Inventory drop-down list option

The **Receive Inventory** options from the *Receive Inventory* drop-down list and the **Receive Items** functions from the *Vendor* menu all record transactions that are *connected* to **Purchase Orders**. This connection is used by QuickBooks to track whether a purchase order is open or not.

Purchasing Inventory at a Retail Store with Check or Credit Card

If you buy inventory at a retail store, use the **Write Checks** or **Enter Credit Card Charges** functions to record the purchase. Record the purchased items using the *Items* tab at the bottom of the check or credit card charge window (see Figure 9-13).

DO NOT ENTER THIS CHECK NOW. IT IS FOR REFERENCE ONLY.

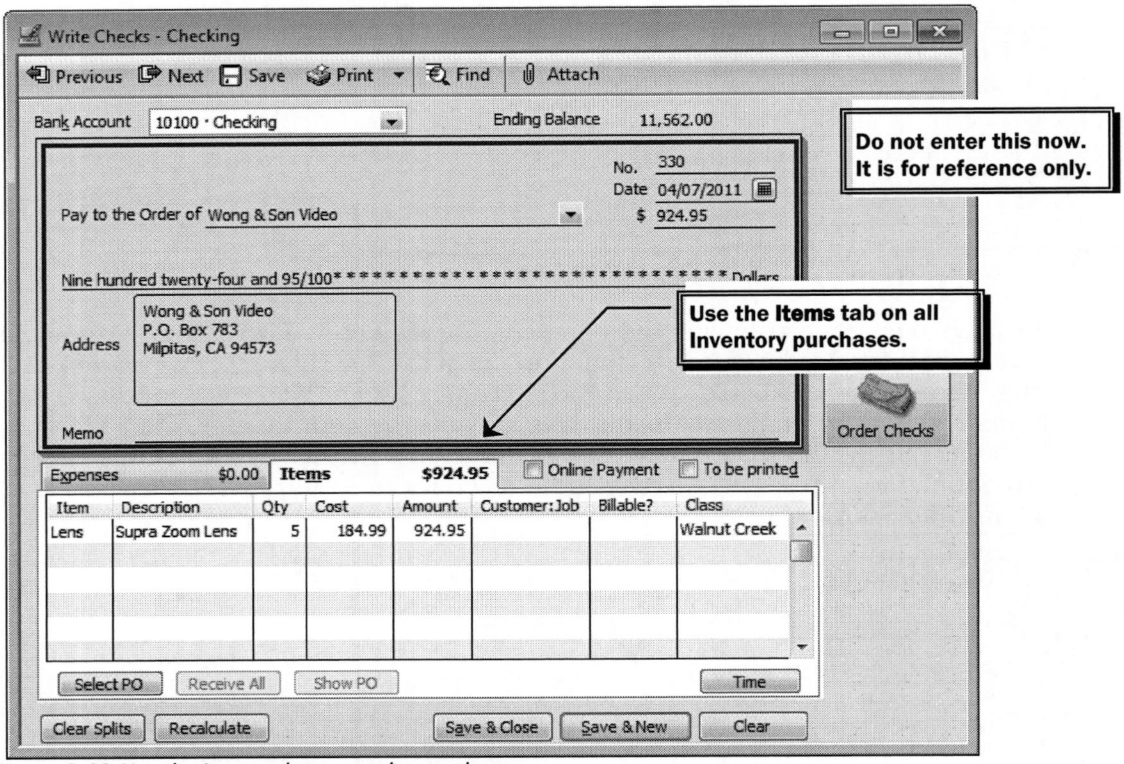

Figure 9-13 Use the Items tab to record a purchase.

Purchase Orders

Use Purchase Orders to track inventory purchases and to easily determine which items you have on order.

If you use Purchase Orders, you will be able to create reports that show what is on order and when it is due to arrive from your supplier. In addition, you can create a list of open purchase orders.

Purchase Orders do not post to the **Chart of Accounts.** However, QuickBooks tracks Purchase Orders in a non-posting account called **Purchase Orders**. You can see this account at the bottom of your **Chart of Accounts**.

Creating a Purchase Order

Create a Purchase Order to reorder inventory, filling out each item and quantity.

> Note:
> Since **Purchase Orders** are non-posting, QuickBooks does not include them on the Pay Bills windows.

COMPUTER PRACTICE

Step 1. Select **Create Purchase Orders** from the *Vendors* menu. Alternately, click the **Purchase Orders** icon on the *Home* page. This displays the *Create Purchase Orders* window (see Figure 9-14).

Step 2. Select **Ace Supply** from the *Vendor* drop-down list or type the name into the *Vendor* field. Press **Tab**.

Step 3. Enter ***Walnut Creek*** in the *Class* field. Press **Tab**.

Step 4. Press **Tab** three times to leave the *Ship To* field blank and to accept **Custom Purchase Order** as the default form template.

If you want the order shipped directly to one of your customers, select your customer from the drop-down list of the *Ship To* field next to the Class field. By default, QuickBooks enters your company's address from the **Company Information** window. To change your *Ship To* address, override it on this form here or select **Company Information** from the *Company* menu. Click the **Ship to Address** button to add your changes.

Step 5. Enter ***04/07/2011*** in the *Date* field (if not displayed already) and press **Tab**.

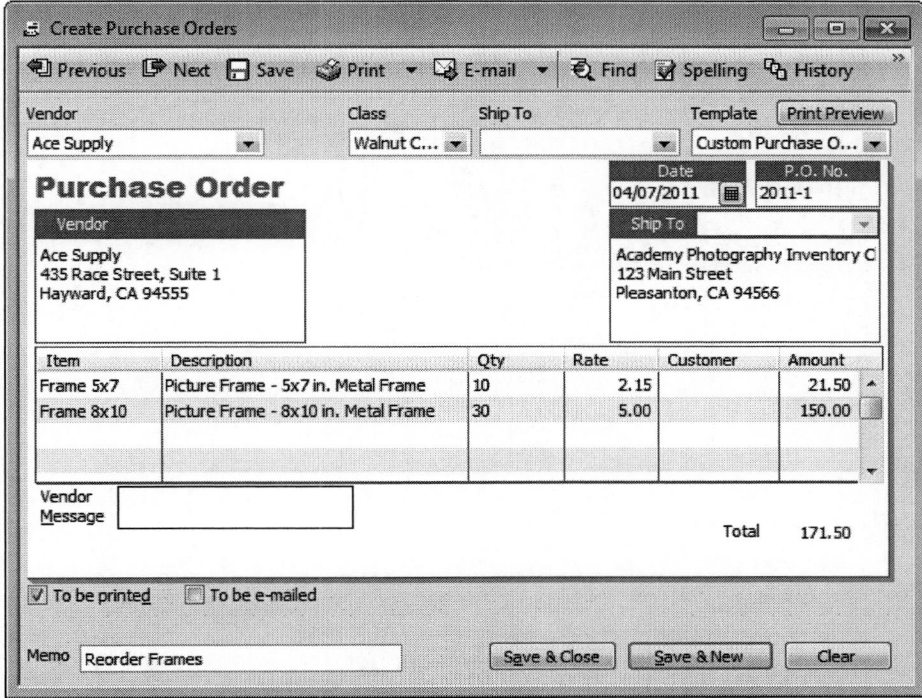

Figure 9-14 Create Purchase Orders window

Step 6. Enter **2011-1** in the *P.O. NO.* field and press **Tab**.
QuickBooks automatically numbers your **Purchase Orders** in the same way it numbers Invoices. It increases the number by one for each new **Purchase Order**. However, you can override this number if necessary.

Step 7. Press **Tab** twice to accept the default vendor address and ship-to address.

Step 8. Enter the **Frame 5x7 (Qty 10)** and **Frame 8x10 (Qty 30)** items in the body of the **Purchase Order** as shown in Figure 9-14.

The Customer column allows you to associate your purchases with the customer or job to which you want to assign the expense for this purchase. Since you are purchasing inventory, you do not know the customer information, so do not use this column.

Step 9. Enter ***Reorder Frames*** in the *Memo* field.

Step 10. Click **Save & Close.**

Receiving Shipments against Purchase Orders

If you use **Purchase Orders** and you receive a shipment that is not accompanied by a Bill, follow these steps:

COMPUTER PRACTICE

Step 1. Select the *Vendors* menu and then select **Receive Items**. Alternatively, click **Receive Inventory** and then select **Receive Inventory without Bill** from the drop-down menu on the *Vendor* section of the *Home* page.

Step 2. The *Create Item Receipts* window opens (see Figure 9-15). Enter ***Ace Supply*** in the *Vendor* field and press **Tab.**

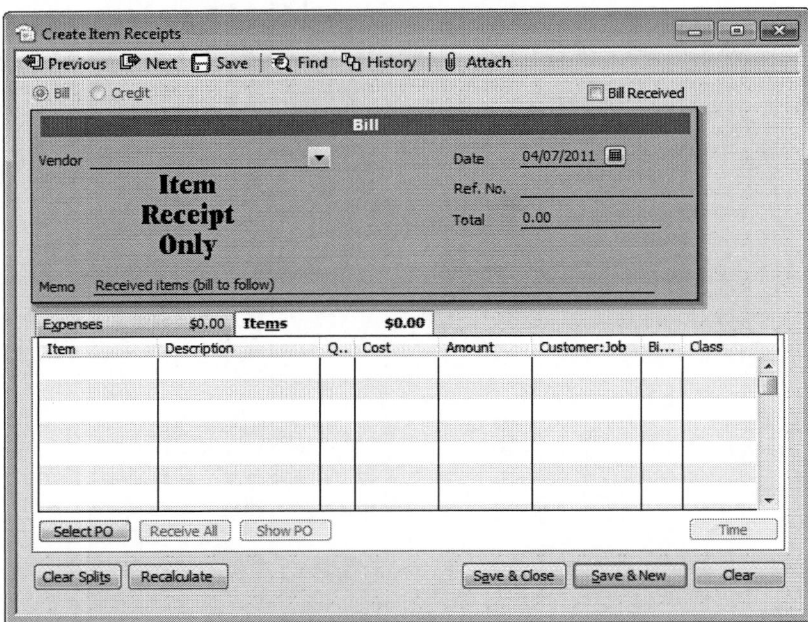

Figure 9-15 The Create Item Receipts window

Step 3. Since there is an open **Purchase Order** for this vendor, QuickBooks displays the message in Figure 9-16. Click **Yes.**

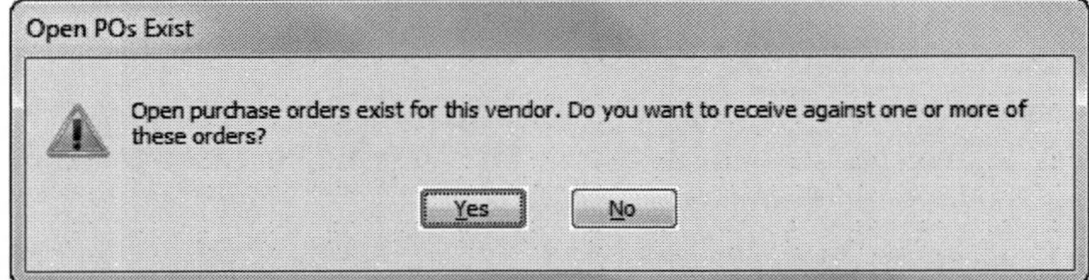

Figure 9-16 QuickBooks displays an Open POs Exist message, if applicable

Step 4. Select the **Purchase Order** you are receiving against from the list in Figure 9-17 by clicking in the √ column. Then click **OK.**

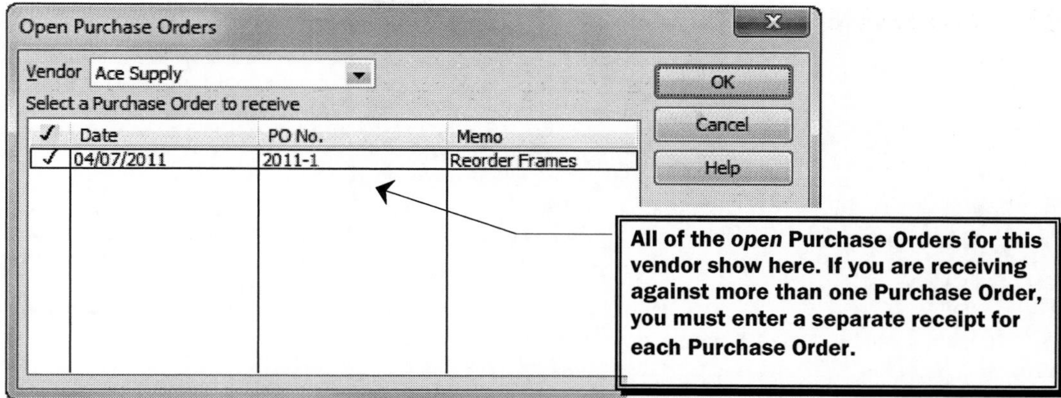

Figure 9-17 Open Purchase Orders window

Step 5. QuickBooks fills in the **Item Receipt** with the information from the **Purchase Order** as shown in Figure 9-18.

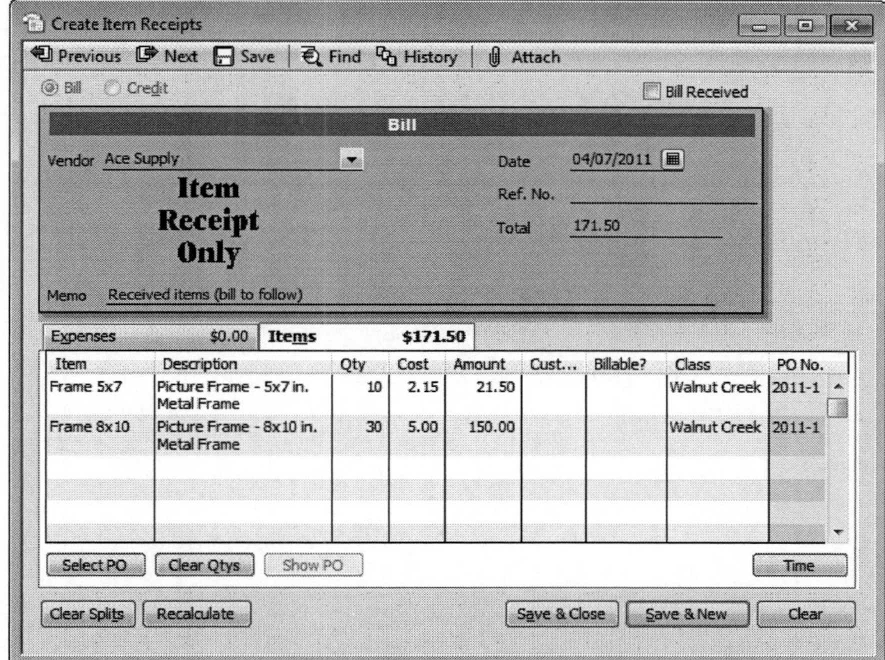

Figure 9-18 QuickBooks automatically completes the Bill using the information from the purchase order

Step 6. Leave ***04/07/2011*** in the *Date* field. Press **Tab**.

Step 7. Enter ***4431*** in the *Ref. No.* field (see Figure 9-19).

In the *Ref. No.* field you enter the shipper number on the packing slip that accompanies the shipment. This helps you match the receipt with the vendor's bill when you receive it.

Step 8. **Tab** to the *Qty* column. Change the quantity to ***5*** for the Frame 5x7, and to ***15*** for the Frame 8x10 (see Figure 9-19).

Do not worry about the Cost column. You have not received the bill yet, so QuickBooks uses the amounts you entered on the **Purchase Order**. When you get the actual bill for this shipment, you will correct or adjust the *Cost* column if necessary.

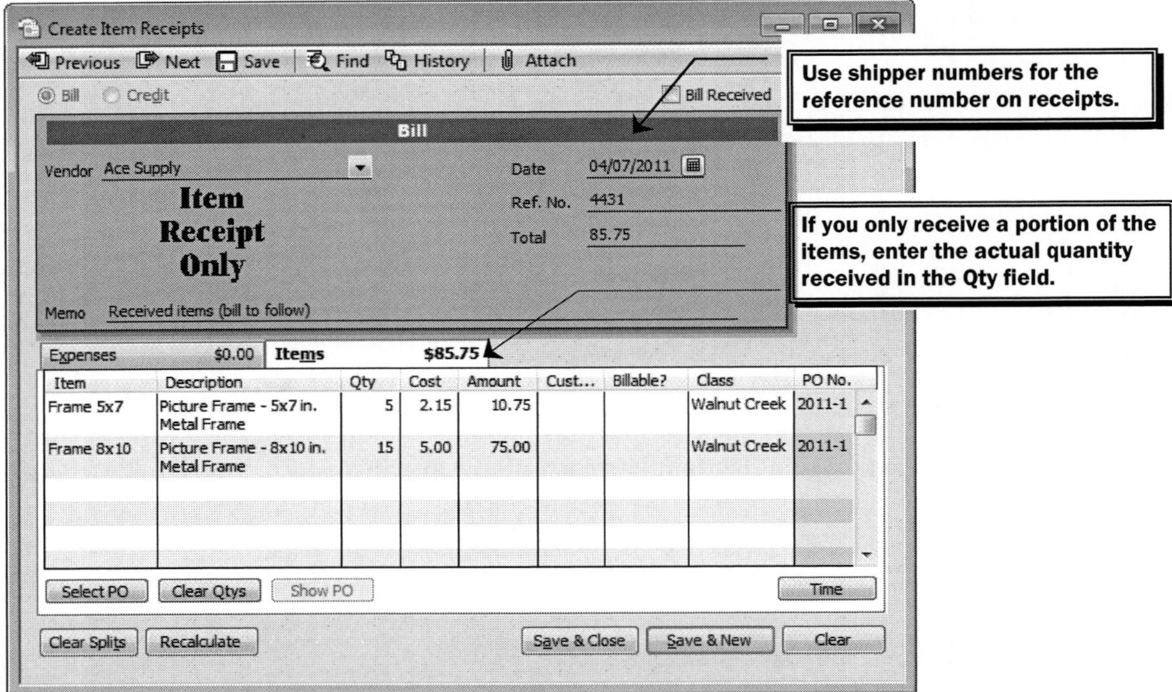

Figure 9-19 Use the shipper number in the Ref. No. field.

Step 9. To save the Item Receipt, click **Save & Close**.

The accounting behind the scenes:
When you record an **Item Receipt**, QuickBooks increases (credits) **Accounts Payable** for the total amount of the **Item Receipt**. It also increases (debits) **Inventory** for the same amount.

However, since you have not received the **Bill**, your *Pay Bills* window will not yet show the **Bill**, even though the balance in Accounts Payable was increased by the **Item Receipt**. This may seem strange at first because you normally expect the total in **Pay Bills** to match the balance in **Accounts Payable**. However, Item Receipts never show in the *Pay Bills* window. This properly accrues the liability in the right period.

It turns out that **Item Receipts** and **Bills** are exactly the *same transaction*. The only difference is that the *Bill Received* box is not checked on **Item Receipts**, and it is checked on **Bills**.

Note:
You will see that **Item Receipt** does show up on the *Unpaid Bills Detail* and *A/P Aging* Reports. This lets you know that you have a payable to a vendor that you have not received a **Bill** for. For Cash Forecasting purposes, it is important that these reports detail out everything you owe, even if a **Bill** has not yet been received.

Creating Open Purchase Orders Reports

COMPUTER PRACTICE

Step 1. Select the *Reports* menu, select **Purchases**, and then select **Open Purchase Orders**.

This report (see Figure 9-20) shows the total dollar amount for *all* open purchase orders, not just the open balance of each **Purchase Order**. To see the open balance on a **Purchase Order**, double-click on it from this report.

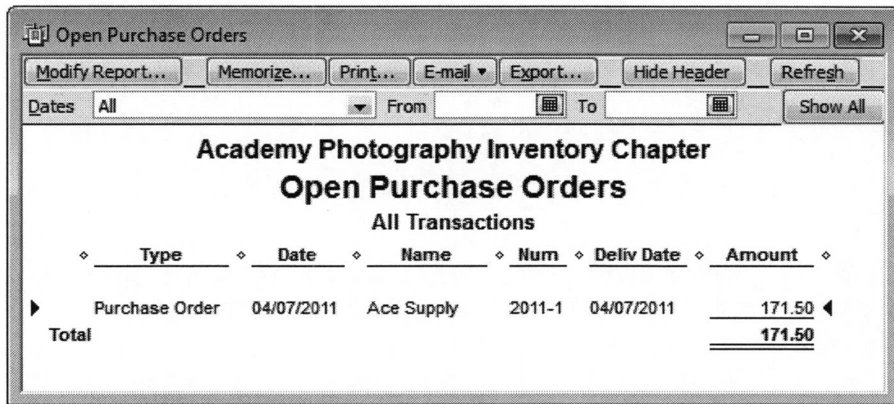

Figure 9-20 The Open Purchase Orders report

Checking Purchase Order Status

To check the status of a **Purchase Order**, to change it, or to cancel it, edit the **Purchase Order** directly.

COMPUTER PRACTICE

Step 1. Display the **Purchase Order** by double-clicking on it from the **Open Purchase Orders** report shown in Figure 9-20.

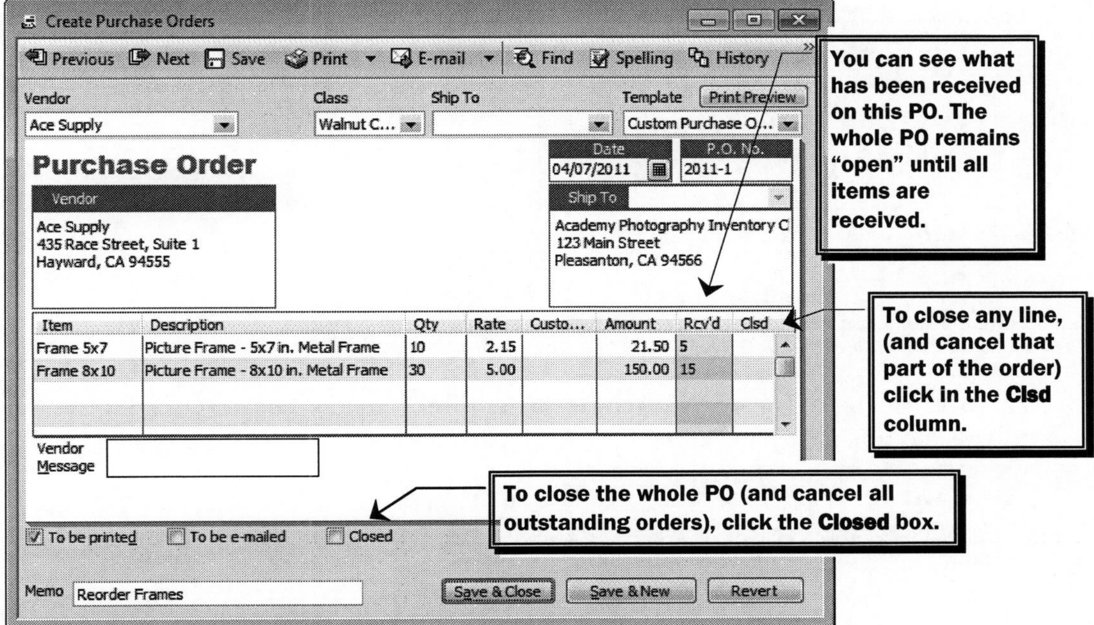

Figure 9-21 Edit the purchase order as necessary.

Step 2. Review the quantity of each Item in the *Rcv'd* column.

On the **Purchase Order** in Figure 9-21, you can see that Academy Photography has received 5 Frame 5x7s and 15 Frame 8x10s.

If you know you will not receive the backorder items on a **Purchase Order**, you can close specific line items or close the whole order. To close any line of the order, click in the **Clsd** column. To close the whole order and cancel the rest of the order, click the **Closed** box at the bottom of the form. If you cancel an order, do not forget to notify the vendor.

Step 3. Close the window without making any changes to the purchase order. Close the *Open Purchase Orders* report.

Entering the Final Shipment

When the final shipment arrives, enter another **Item Receipt**.

COMPUTER PRACTICE

Step 1. Select the *Vendors* menu and then select **Receive Items**. Alternatively, click **Receive Inventory without Bill** on the *Vendor* section of the *Home* page.

Step 2. The *Create Item Receipts* window opens (see Figure 9-22).

Step 3. Enter ***Ace Supply*** in the *Vendor* field and then press **Tab**.

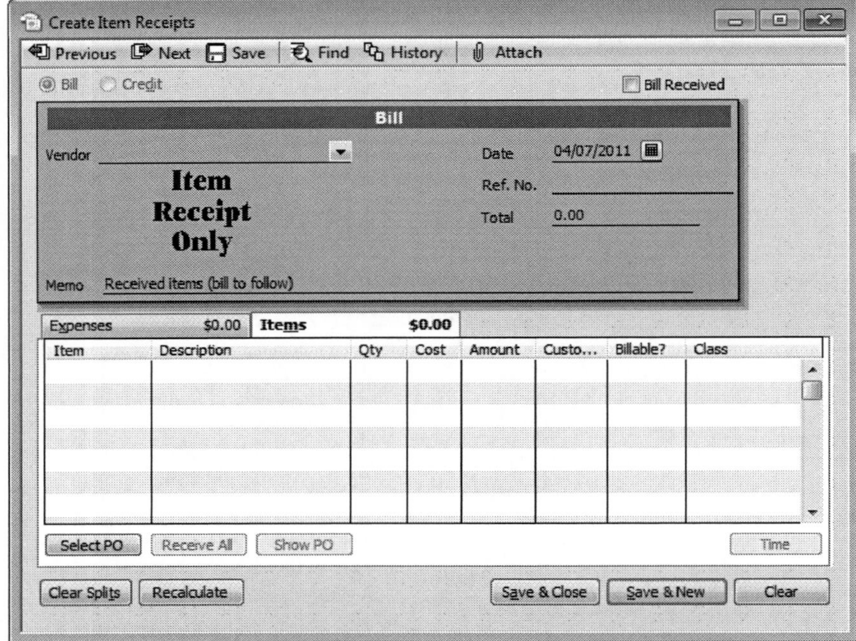

Figure 9-22 Enter the Vendor name in the Create Item Receipts window

Step 4. Because there is an open **Purchase Order** for this vendor, QuickBooks displays the dialog box shown in Figure 9-23. Click **Yes**.

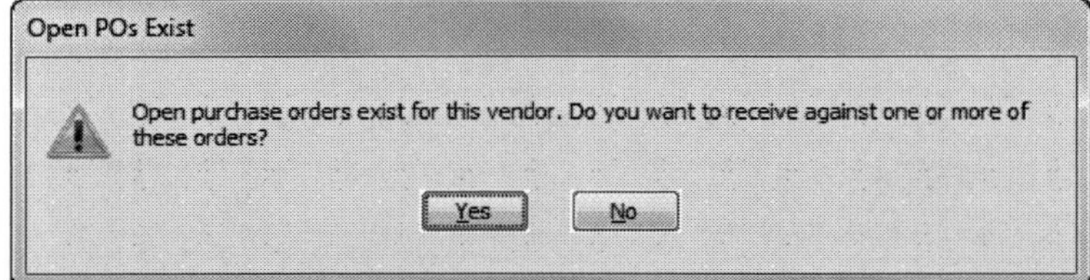

Figure 9-23 The Open PO's Exist window appears

Step 5. Select the **Purchase Order** you are receiving against from the list (see Figure 9-24) and click **OK**.

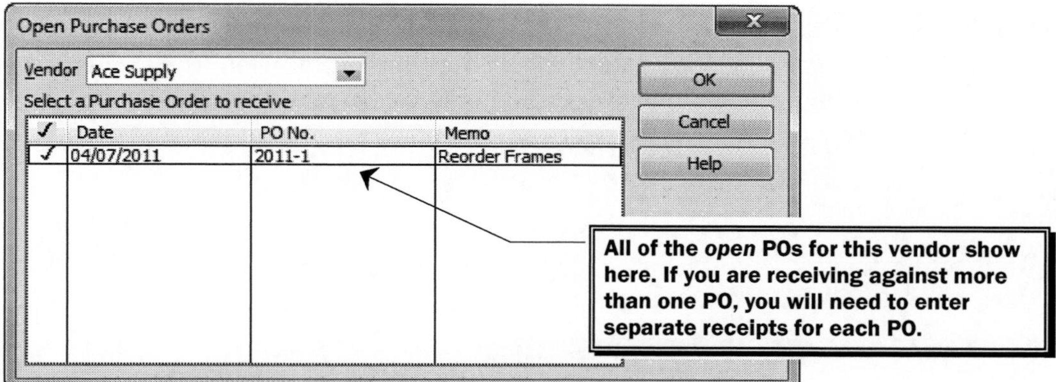

Figure 9-24 Open Purchase Orders window

Step 6. QuickBooks automatically fills in the item receipt with the information from the **Purchase Order**.

Step 7. Leave ***04/14/2011*** in the *Date* field.

Step 8. Enter ***4441*** in the *Ref. No.* field (see Figure 9-25).

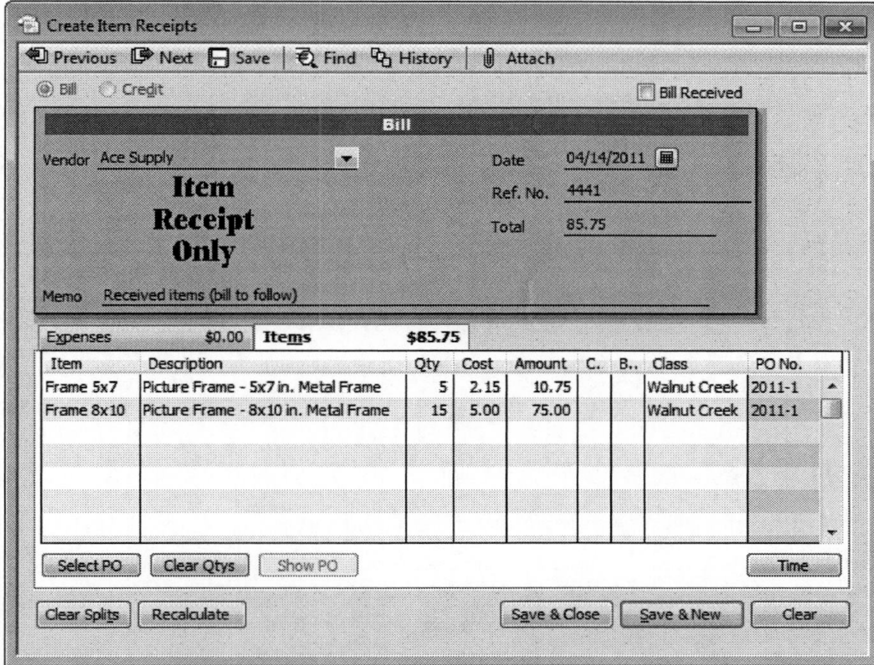

Figure 9-25 Item Receipt #4441

Step 9. Click **Save & Close** to record the receipt.

Entering Bills for Received Inventory

Now that you have recorded **Item Receipts** for your inventory shipments, the next step in the process is to record the bills when they arrive from the vendor.

Converting an Item Receipt into a Bill

COMPUTER PRACTICE

Step 1. Select the *Vendors* menu and then select **Enter Bill for Received Items**. Alternatively, click **Enter Bills Against Inventory** icon in the *Vendor* section of the *Home* page.

Step 2. Enter ***Ace Supply*** in the *Vendor* field and then press **Tab**.

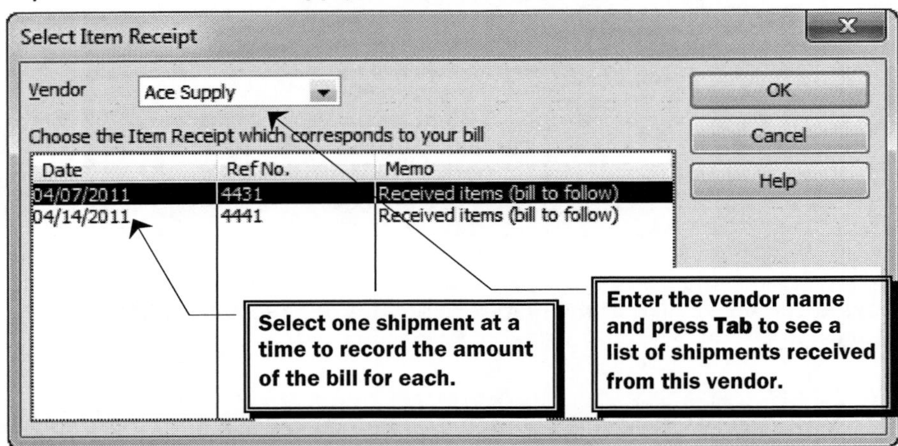

Figure 9-26 Select one shipment at a time

Step 3. Select the first line on the window shown in Figure 9-26. Click **OK**.

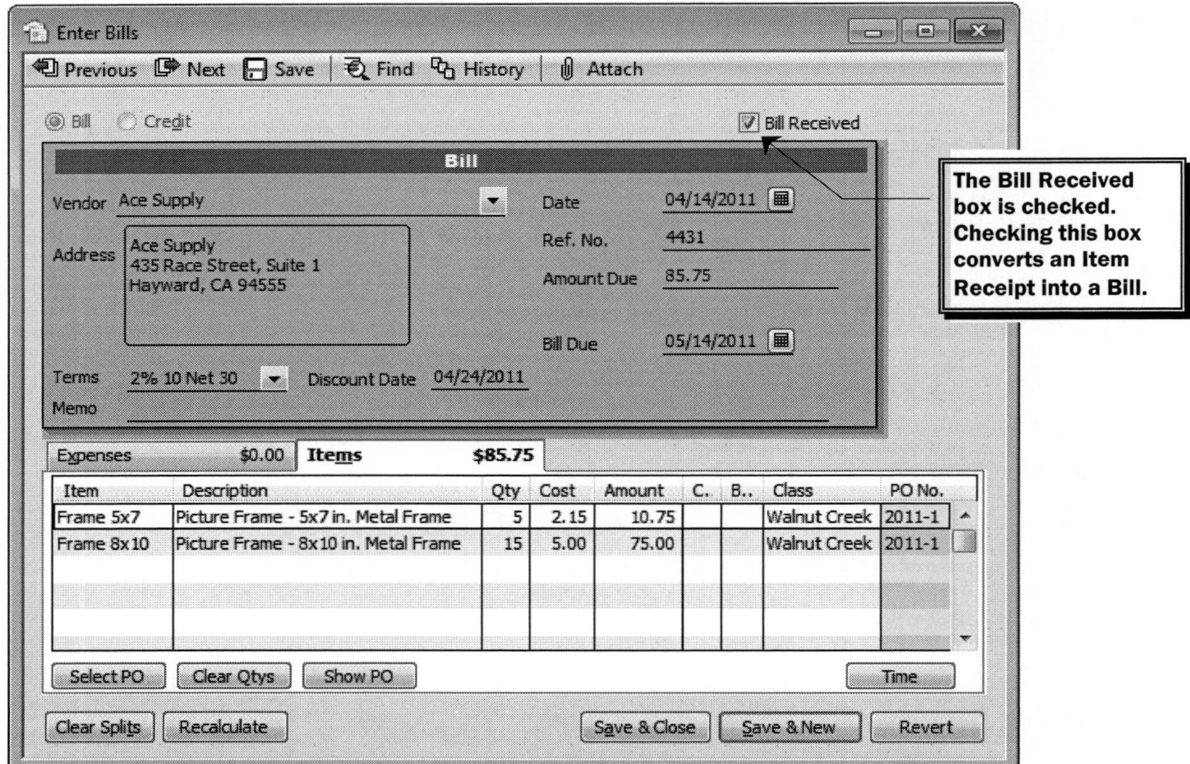

Figure 9-27 Enter Bills window

Step 4. QuickBooks displays the **Item Receipt** and automatically checks the *Bill Received* box (see Figure 9-27). Checking the *Bill Received* box converts the **Item Receipt** into a **Bill.** Verify that the Bill matches your records and make changes to price, terms, due date, or any other field that does not match the vendor's bill.

> **Note:**
> QuickBooks does not add a new transaction when you use the **Enter Bill for Received Items** function. That is because you have already recorded an **Item Receipt**, which increases Inventory and Accounts Payable. This function simply converts your Item Receipt into a Bill.

Step 5. Click **Save & Close** to record the **Bill**.

Step 6. Click **Yes** if the *Recording Transaction* message displays.

Step 7. Repeat Step 1 through Step 6 for Item Receipt #4441 and accept the defaults for all quantities and amounts.

> **Note:**
> QuickBooks does not allow you to "group" multiple **Item Receipts** into one **Bill** if only one vendor bill is received for the entire **PO**. If you receive one vendor bill and have multiple **Item Receipts**, in the reference number of the **Bill** make sure to enter the same number. This will enable you to easily identify all the **Bills** that add up to the vendor bill received when creating the vendor's **Bill Payment** check.

Handling Overshipments

If your vendor ships more than you ordered on a **Purchase Order**, you have three choices.

1. You could refuse the extra shipment and send it back to the vendor without recording anything in QuickBooks.
2. You could receive the extra shipment into inventory and keep it (and pay for it).
3. You could receive the extra shipment into inventory, and then send it back and record a **Bill Credit** in QuickBooks.

If you keep the overshipment (and pay for it):

> DO NOT PERFORM THESE STEPS NOW. THEY ARE FOR REFERENCE ONLY.

1. Override the number in the *Qty* column on the **Item Receipt** so that it exceeds the quantity on your **Purchase Order**. This increases the **Inventory Asset** and **Accounts Payable** accounts for the total amount of the shipment, including the overshipment.
2. When the bill arrives from the vendor, match it with the **Item Receipt** and pay the amount actually due. Unless you edit the **Purchase Order**, it will not match the **Item Receipt** or **Bill**. This may be important later when you look at **Purchase Orders** and actual purchase costs, so consider updating your **Purchase Order** to match the actual costs.

If you send the overshipment back after receiving it into inventory:

> DO NOT PERFORM THESE STEPS NOW. THEY ARE FOR REFERENCE ONLY.

1. Override the number in the *Qty* column on the **Item Receipt** so that it exceeds the quantity on your **Purchase Order**. This increases the **Inventory Asset** and **Accounts Payable** accounts for the total amount of the shipment, including the overshipment. However, you do not plan to actually pay the vendor for this "overshipment." Instead, you will return the extra items, and ask the vendor to credit your account.

2. When you return the excess items, create a **Bill Credit** for the vendor. On the **Bill Credit**, enter the quantity returned and the cost for each item. We use a **Bill Credit** here because we want to reflect the proper financial transactions between us and our vendor.
3. At this point, the vendor may apply your credit towards a future invoice on items they send to you, or they may send you a refund if you have paid for the shipment.
4. If you receive a refund from the vendor, record the refund directly onto your next deposit transaction. You can manually add a line to the deposit using the vendor's name in the **Received from** column, and Accounts Payable in the *From Account* column. Then, after recording the deposit, use the Pay Bills screen to apply the deposit line to the **Bill Credit**.
5. To apply the **Bill Credit** to an unpaid bill for that vendor, use the **Pay Bills** window.

Handling Vendor Overcharges

If you have a discrepancy between your purchase order and the vendor's bill, there are several ways to handle it.

If the vendor overcharged you, the vendor might agree to revise the bill and send you a new one. In this case, wait for the new bill before recording anything in QuickBooks.

On the other hand, you might decide to pay the incorrect bill and have the vendor adjust the next bill. In that case, use the *Expenses* tab on the *Bill* to track the error.

In this example, assume you were overcharged by $10.00.

COMPUTER PRACTICE

Step 1. Select the *Vendors* menu and then select **Enter Bills**. Alternatively, click **Enter Bills** on the *Vendor* section of the *Home* page.

Step 2. Click **Previous** on the *Enter Bills* window to display Bill #4441.

Step 3. Select the **Expenses** tab to record a $10.00 overcharge from the vendor. Use the **Cost of Goods Sold** account and the **Overhead** class to track the overcharge. Alternately, you could record the overcharge to a *Current Asset* account call **Due from Vendors** so that the error does not affect the Profit & Loss statement.

Step 4. Click **Recalculate** to update the *Amount Due* field (see Figure 9-28).

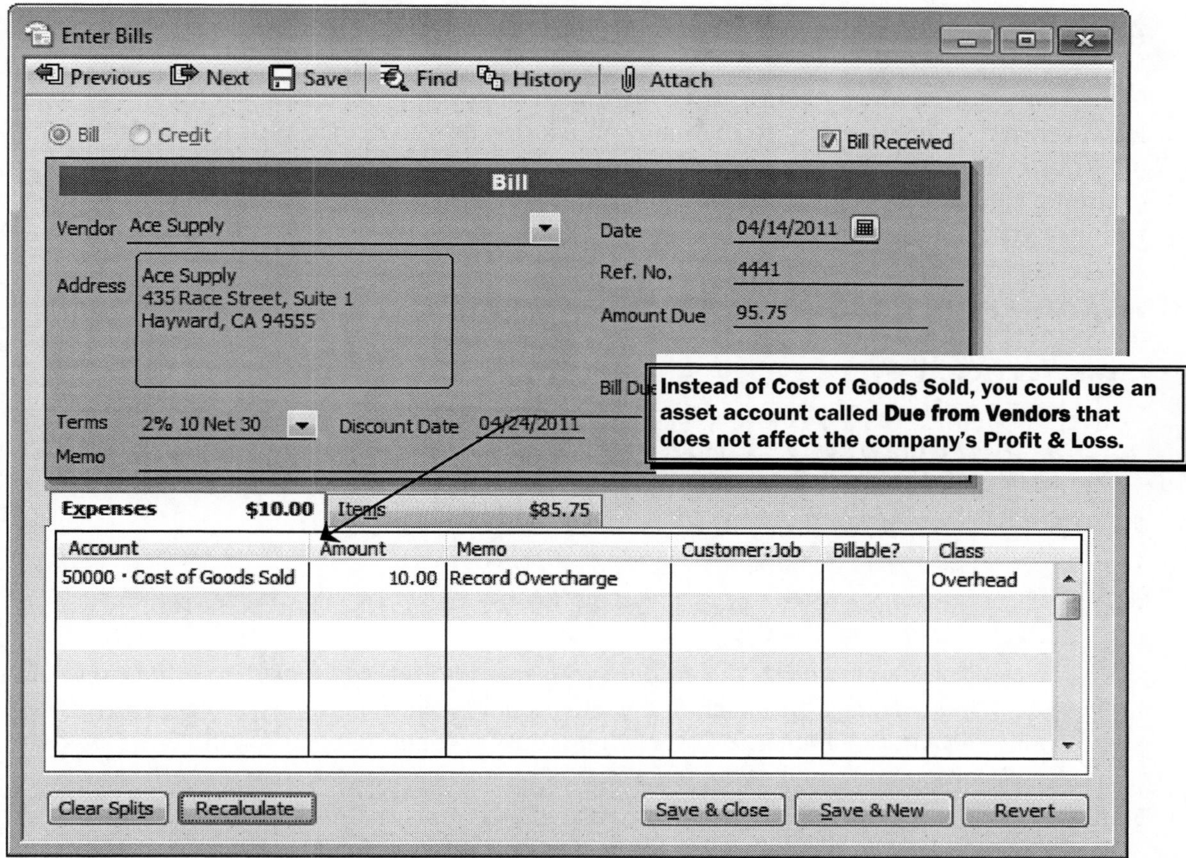

Figure 9-28 Record a vendor overcharge in the Expenses tab

Step 5. Click **Save & Close**. Click **Yes** on the *Recording Transaction* message window.

Since the **Bill** in Figure 9-28 is $10.00 too much, contact the vendor to discuss the overage on the **Bill**. The vendor will either issue you a Credit, or if you have already paid the **Bill**, send you a refund check. The vendor may also apply the overpayment to your account to be applied to a future bill.

Depending upon the vendor's action, do one of the following:

- If the vendor refunds your money, add the refund directly onto your next deposit. Code the deposit to the **Cost of Goods Sold** account and the **Overhead** class (the account and class you used when you recorded the overage on the bill).
- If the vendor sends you a credit memo, enter a **Bill Credit**. Code the **Bill Credit** to the **Cost of Goods Sold** account and **Overhead** class (the account and class you used when you recorded the overage on the **Bill**).

> **Note:**
> Always use the same account when you record the overcharge and the refund or credit. In the example above, the **Expenses** tab of the **Bill** for Ace Supply increases **Cost of Goods Sold** by $10.00 and the deposit or credit from the vendor reduces **Cost of Goods Sold** by the same amount. Alternatively, you could use an **Other Current Asset** account called **Due from Vendors** discussed above.

Adjusting Inventory

QuickBooks automatically adjusts inventory each time you purchase or sell Inventory Items. However, it may be necessary to manually adjust inventory after a physical count of your inventory, or in case of an increase or decrease in the value of your inventory on hand. For example, you might decrease the value of your inventory if it has lost value due to new technology trends.

Adjusting the Quantity of Inventory on Hand

COMPUTER PRACTICE

Step 1. Select the *Vendors* menu, select **Inventory Activities**, and then select **Adjust Quantity/Value on Hand**. Alternatively, click the **Adjust Quantity on Hand** icon on the *Home* page. QuickBooks displays the window shown in Figure 9-30.

Step 2. Enter ***04/30/2011*** in the *Adjustment Date* field and press **Tab**.

Step 3. Enter ***2011–1*** in the *Ref. No.* field and press **Tab**.

Step 4. Enter ***Inventory Variance*** in the *Adjustment Account* field and press **Tab**.

QuickBooks adjusts the account you enter into the *Adjustment Account* field to offset the change in the Inventory Asset account balance. In this example, we are using ***Inventory Variance,*** a Cost of Goods Sold account, but you can use whichever account is best for your records.

Step 5. The *Income or Expense expected* dialog box displays. Check the box next to *Do not display this message* in the future and click **OK** (see Figure 9-29).

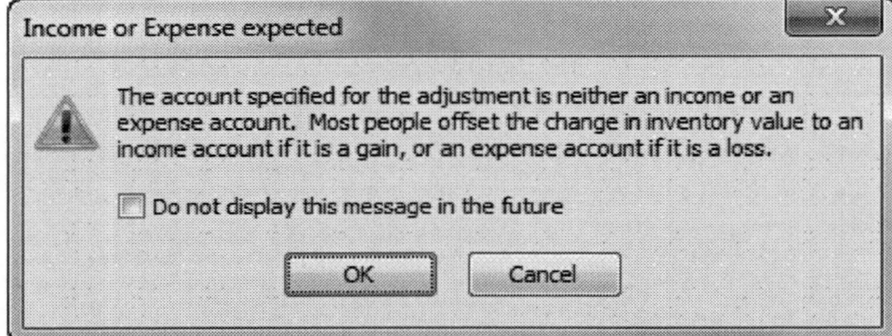

Figure 9-29 Income of Expense expected dialog box

> **Note:**
> The dialog box displays because QuickBooks is looking for an expense account to record the offsetting decrease in the inventory asset. Although the entry can be made to an expense account (decrease in inventory) or an income account (increase in inventory), many people find that offsetting inventory variances to the Cost of Goods Sold account (for either inventory increases or decreases) more accurately reflects the recording of variances.

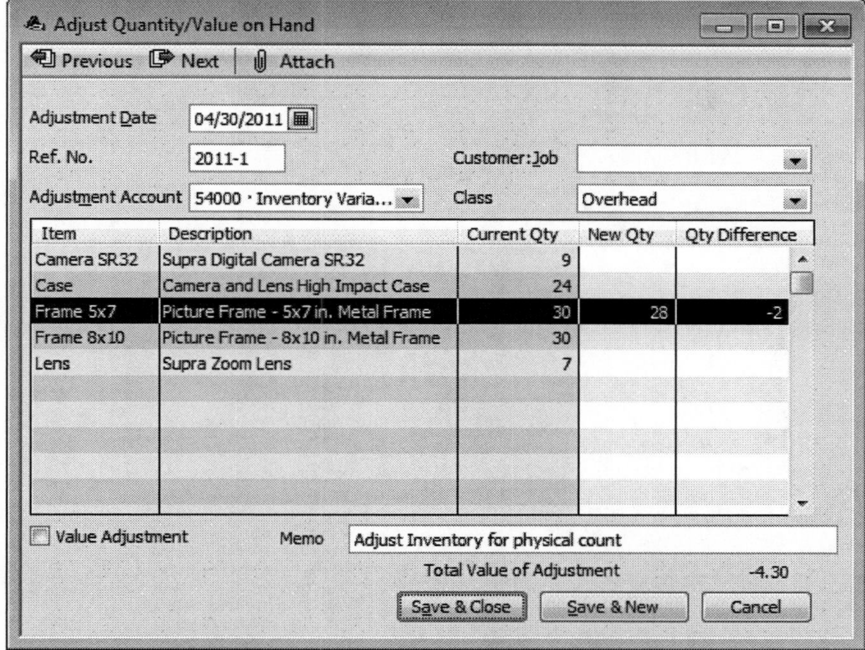

Figure 9-30 Adjust Quantity/Value on Hand window

Step 6. Enter ***Overhead*** in the *Class* field.

Step 7. Skip to the *New Qty* column. Enter ***28*** on the *Frame 5x7* line and press **Tab**.

Notice that QuickBooks calculates the quantity difference (-2) in the *Qty Difference* column. Also, notice that QuickBooks automatically calculates the *Total Value of Adjustment* in the bottom right corner. QuickBooks uses the *average cost method* to calculate this value. Look at the **Inventory Valuation Detail** report later in this chapter to see how the average cost changes each time you adjust inventory in this way.

Step 8. Enter ***Adjust Inventory for physical counts*** in the *Memo* field.

Step 9. To save the adjustment, click **Save & New**.

Adjusting the Value of Inventory

COMPUTER PRACTICE

With the Adjust Quantity/Value on Hand window displayed, follow these steps to record a *value* adjustment to your inventory.

Step 1. At the bottom left of the *Adjust Quantity/Value on Hand* window, click the *Value Adjustment* box (see Figure 9-31).

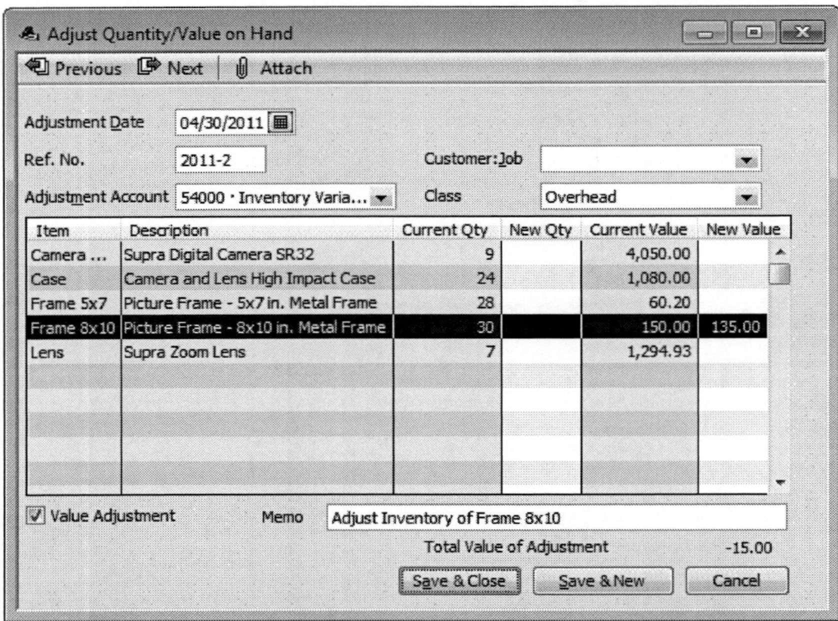

Figure 9-31 Click on the Value Adjustment box to change inventory value

Step 2. Confirm that **04/30/2011** is already selected in the *Adjustment Date* field. Press **Tab**.

Step 3. Leave ***2011-2*** *in the Ref. No.* field. Press **Tab**.

Step 4. Confirm that **Inventory Variance** is already selected in the *Adjustment Account* field.

Step 5. Enter ***Overhead*** in the *Class* field.

Step 6. Enter ***135.00*** in the New Value column on the Frame 8x10 line and press **Tab**.

Notice that QuickBooks calculates the Total Value of Adjustment.

Step 7. Enter ***Adjust Inventory Value of Frame 8x10*** in the *Memo* field.

Step 8. Click **Save & Close** to save the adjustment.

QuickBooks will post the amount of this adjustment ($15.00) to the **General Ledger**. Since this adjustment lowers the value of the Frame 8x10, it reduces the average cost of each unit on hand. Therefore, the next time you sell a Frame 8x10, QuickBooks will transfer the new (lower) average cost out of **Inventory** and into **Cost of Goods Sold**.

> **The accounting behind the scenes:**
> Inventory value adjustments always affect your **Inventory Asset** account. If the *Total Value of Adjustment* is a positive number, the **Inventory** account increases (debit) by that amount and the **Adjustment Account** decreases (credit). If the *Total Value of Adjustment* is a negative number, the debits and the credits are reversed.

Setting up Group Items

Sometimes, you sell items in bundles. For example, every time Academy Photography sells three hours of services for retouching of a 5x7 size photo, it also includes a 5x7 metal frame. Therefore, they sell the 5x7 frame along with 3 hours of retouching service. Academy Photography uses *Group Items* to bundle products and/or services on sales forms. Alternatively, you may also purchase items in a bundle from a vendor, so setting up a group item may make the purchasing process easier as well.

COMPUTER PRACTICE

Step 1. The *Item List* window should still be open on your screen. If not, Select the *Lists* menu and then select **Item List,** or click **Items & Services** on the *Company* section of the *Home* page.

Step 2. Select the **Item** button at the bottom of the *Item List* window and select **New.** Alternatively, press Ctrl+N.

Step 3. Select **Group** from the *Type* drop-down list and press **Tab.**

Step 4. Enter ***5x7 Retouching*** in the *Group Name/Number* field and press **Tab** to advance to the *Description* field.

Step 5. Enter ***Retouching photograph and placing it in a 5x7 metal frame*** in the *Description* field and press **Tab.**

Step 6. Click the *Print items in group* box (see Figure 9-32). Press **Tab.**

Step 7. On the first line at the bottom of the window, select **Frame 5x7** from the *Item* drop-down list. Press **Tab.**

Step 8. Enter ***1*** in the *Qty* column and press **Tab.**

The *Qty* column indicates how many of each item is included in the group.

Step 9. On the second line at the bottom of the window, select **Retouching** from the *Item* drop-down list. Press **Tab.**

Step 10. Enter ***3*** in the *Qty* column. Press **Tab.**

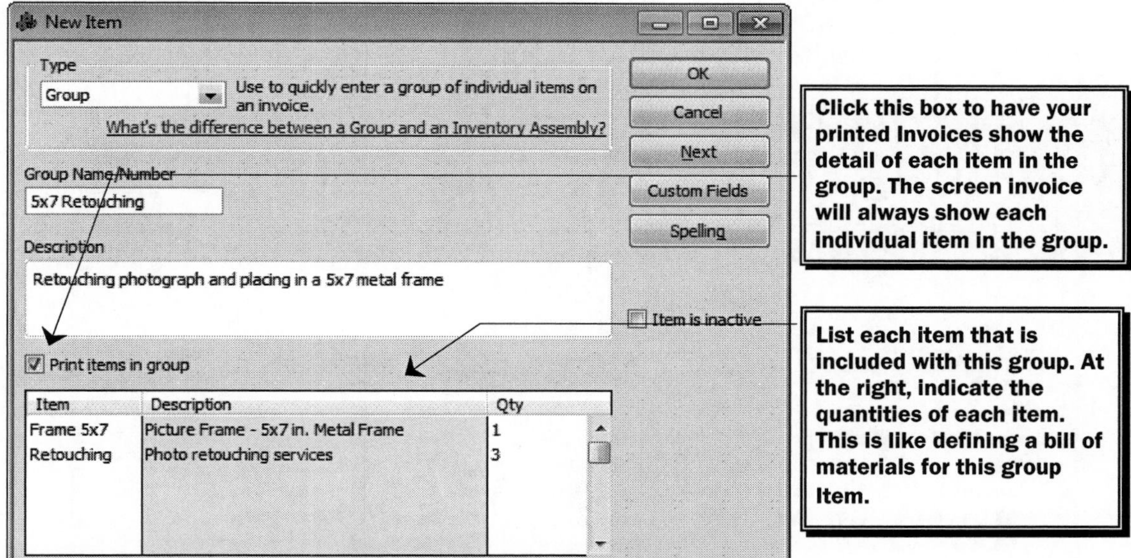

Figure 9-32 Specify Items in the group and whether to print Items on the sales form

> **Note:**
> The *New Item* window in Figure 9-32 does not include a *Sales Price* field. When you enter a Group item on sales forms, QuickBooks uses the sales prices of the Items within the group to calculate a total price for the group. You can override the price of each item within the group directly on the sales form.

> In addition, the printed sales form will only show the group item detail only if the *Print items in group* box is checked. However, you will always see the items in this group on the screen version of the sales form.

Step 11. Click **OK** to save the Group Item and then close the *Item List* window.

> Note:
> QuickBooks Premier includes an "Assemblies" feature which is quite useful if you want to track individual items and then group them into an assembly. The feature is similar to Groups shown above, but it allows you to group several inventory items into a single inventory "assembly" item. See the supplemental material to this chapter available at www.sleeter.com.

Inventory Reports

QuickBooks provides several reports for inventory analysis, all of which are customizable in ways similar to other reports.

For daily management of inventory, use the **Stock Status by Item** report, the **Stock Status by Vendor** report, or the **Inventory Valuation Summary** report. These reports give a quick overview of inventory counts, inventory values, and pending orders.

For detailed research about transactions involving Inventory, use the **Inventory Item QuickReport** or the **Inventory Valuation Detail** report.

Inventory Item QuickReport

The Inventory Item QuickReport is useful for seeing all transactions involving an Inventory Item.

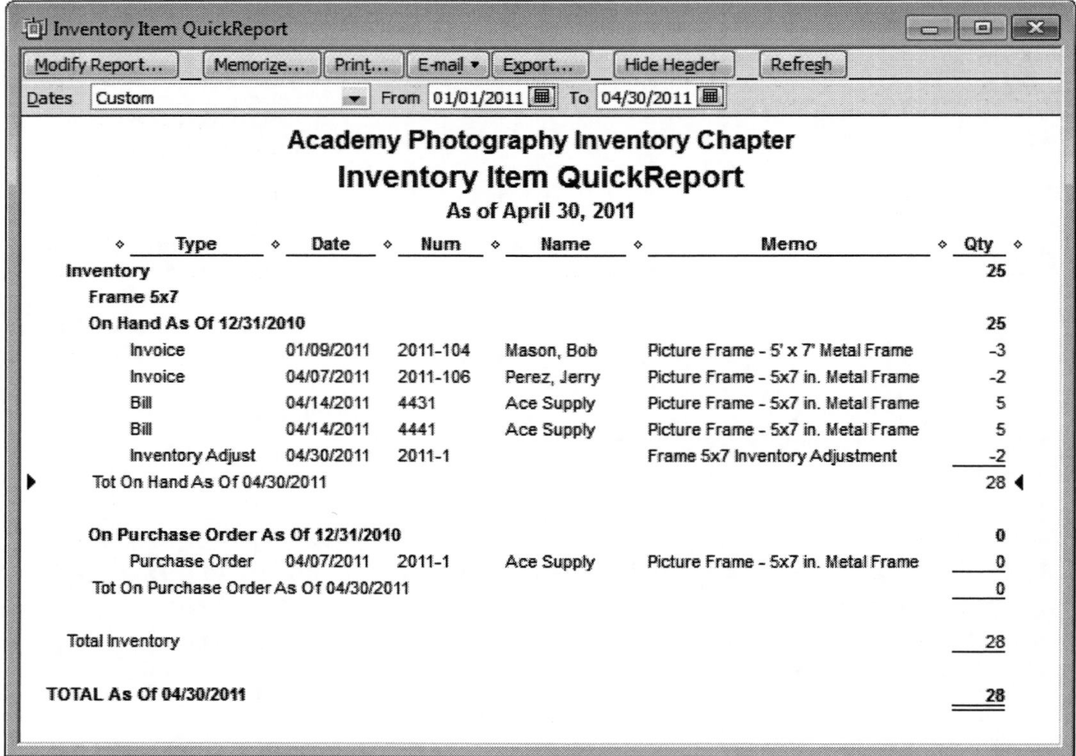

Inventory Item QuickReport

Modify Report... | Memorize... | Print... | E-mail | Export... | Hide Header | Refresh

Dates: Custom | From 01/01/2011 | To 04/30/2011

Academy Photography Inventory Chapter

Inventory Item QuickReport

As of April 30, 2011

Type	Date	Num	Name	Memo	Qty
Inventory					25
Frame 5x7					
On Hand As Of 12/31/2010					25
Invoice	01/09/2011	2011-104	Mason, Bob	Picture Frame - 5' x 7' Metal Frame	-3
Invoice	04/07/2011	2011-106	Perez, Jerry	Picture Frame - 5x7 in. Metal Frame	-2
Bill	04/14/2011	4431	Ace Supply	Picture Frame - 5x7 in. Metal Frame	5
Bill	04/14/2011	4441	Ace Supply	Picture Frame - 5x7 in. Metal Frame	5
Inventory Adjust	04/30/2011	2011-1		Frame 5x7 Inventory Adjustment	-2
Tot On Hand As Of 04/30/2011					28
On Purchase Order As Of 12/31/2010					0
Purchase Order	04/07/2011	2011-1	Ace Supply	Picture Frame - 5x7 in. Metal Frame	0
Tot On Purchase Order As Of 04/30/2011					0
Total Inventory					28
TOTAL As Of 04/30/2011					28

Figure 9-33 Inventory Item QuickReport

COMPUTER PRACTICE

Step 1. Select the *Lists* menu and then select **Item List.**

Step 2. Click on the **Frame 5x7** Item to select it.

Step 3. Select the *Reports* menu at the bottom of the Item list and then select **QuickReport: Frame 5x7**. Alternatively, press Ctrl+Q.

Step 4. Set the *From* date to ***01/01/2011*** and the *To* date to ***04/30/2011*** and press **Tab**. The QuickReport for the Frame 5x7 displays (see Figure 9-33).

Step 5. Close the report by clicking the close box (X) in the upper right corner of the window.

> **Another Way:**
> You can also close reports (and most other windows) in QuickBooks by pressing the ESC key.

Inventory Stock Status by Item Report

The **Stock Status by Item** report is useful for getting a quick snapshot of each inventory part, and the number of units on hand and on order. In addition, this report gives you information about your inventory turnover, showing a column for sales per week.

COMPUTER PRACTICE

Step 1. Select the *Reports* menu, select **Inventory**, and then select **Inventory Stock Status by Item**.

Step 2. Set the *From* date to ***01/01/2011*** and the *To* date to ***04/30/2011*** and press **Tab**. The Inventory Stock Status by Item report displays (see Figure 9-34).

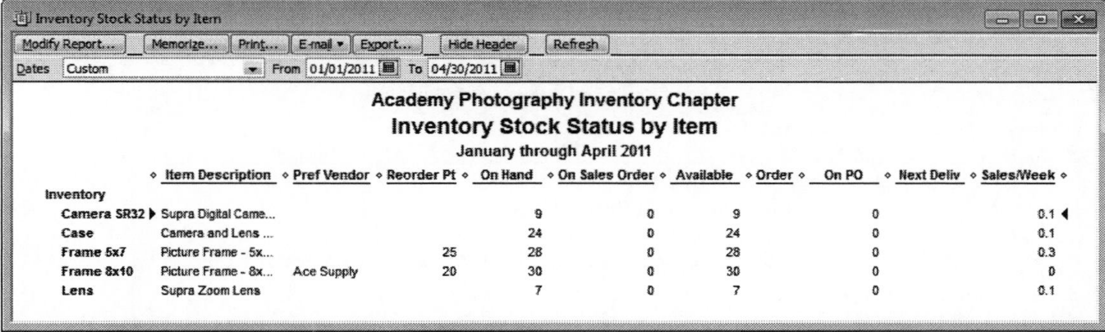

Academy Photography Inventory Chapter
Inventory Stock Status by Item
January through April 2011

	Item Description	Pref Vendor	Reorder Pt	On Hand	On Sales Order	Available	Order	On PO	Next Deliv	Sales/Week
Inventory										
Camera SR32	Supra Digital Came...			9	0	9		0		0.1
Case	Camera and Lens ...			24	0	24		0		0.1
Frame 5x7	Picture Frame - 5x...		25	28	0	28		0		0.3
Frame 8x10	Picture Frame - 8x...	Ace Supply	20	30	0	30		0		0
Lens	Supra Zoom Lens			7	0	7		0		0.1

Figure 9-34 Inventory Stock Status by Item report

Step 3. To close the report, click the close box (X) at the top right corner of the window.

Inventory Stock Status by Vendor Report

The **Stock Status by Vendor** report gives you information about your inventory parts, including how many are on hand, and how many are on order. This report is sorted by the *Preferred Vendor* field in the item.

COMPUTER PRACTICE

Step 1. Select the *Reports* menu, select **Inventory**, and then select **Inventory Stock Status by Vendor**.

Step 2. Set the *From* date to ***01/01/2011*** and the *To* date to ***04/30/2011*** and press **Tab**. The Inventory Stock Status by Vendor report displays (see Figure 9-35).

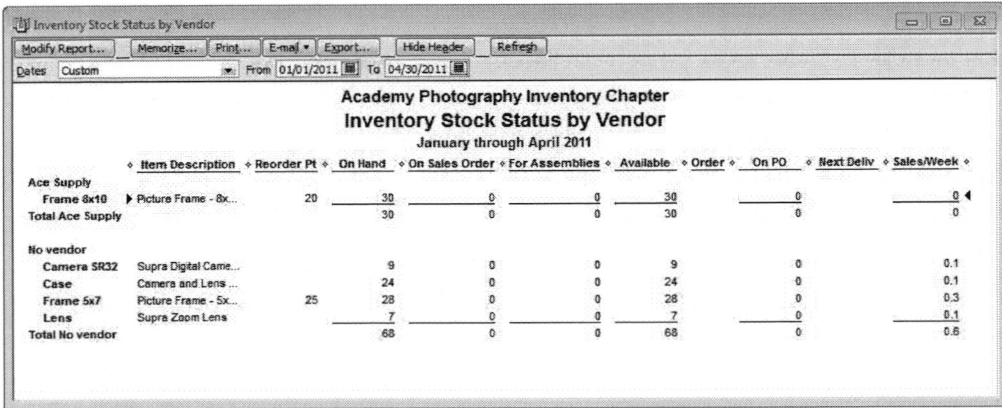

Academy Photography Inventory Chapter
Inventory Stock Status by Vendor
January through April 2011

	Item Description	Reorder Pt	On Hand	On Sales Order	For Assemblies	Available	Order	On PO	Next Deliv	Sales/Week
Ace Supply										
Frame 8x10	Picture Frame - 8x...	20	30	0	0	30		0		0
Total Ace Supply			30	0	0	30		0		0
No vendor										
Camera SR32	Supra Digital Came...		9	0	0	9		0		0.1
Case	Camera and Lens ...		24	0	0	24		0		0.1
Frame 5x7	Picture Frame - 5x...	25	28	0	0	28		0		0.3
Lens	Supra Zoom Lens		7	0	0	7		0		0.1
Total No vendor			68	0	0	68		0		0.6

Figure 9-35 Inventory Stock Status by Vendor report

Step 3. To close the report, click the close box (☒) at the top right corner of the window. Click **No** if you are prompted to memorize the report.

Inventory Valuation Reports

The Inventory Valuation Summary report gives you information about the value of your inventory Items on a certain date. This report shows each item in inventory, the quantity on-hand, the average cost, and the retail value of each item. See the supplemental material (explained on page xiii) for this chapter for an example of an *Inventory Valuation Detail Report.* The following steps generate an *Inventory Valuation Summary Report.*

COMPUTER PRACTICE

Step 1. Select the *Reports* menu, select **Inventory**, and then select **Inventory Valuation Summary**.

Step 2. Set the *Date* field to ***04/30/2011*** and press **Tab** (see Figure 9-36).

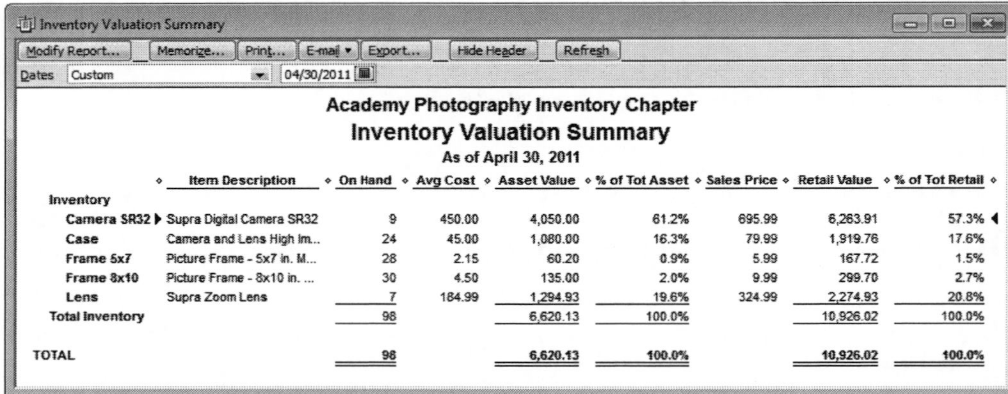

Academy Photography Inventory Chapter
Inventory Valuation Summary
As of April 30, 2011

	Item Description	On Hand	Avg Cost	Asset Value	% of Tot Asset	Sales Price	Retail Value	% of Tot Retail
Inventory								
Camera SR32	Supra Digital Camera SR32	9	450.00	4,050.00	61.2%	695.99	6,263.91	57.3%
Case	Camera and Lens High Im...	24	45.00	1,080.00	16.3%	79.99	1,919.76	17.6%
Frame 5x7	Picture Frame - 5x7 in. M...	28	2.15	60.20	0.9%	5.99	167.72	1.5%
Frame 8x10	Picture Frame - 8x10 in. ...	30	4.50	135.00	2.0%	9.99	299.70	2.7%
Lens	Supra Zoom Lens	7	184.99	1,294.93	19.6%	324.99	2,274.93	20.8%
Total Inventory		98		6,620.13	100.0%		10,926.02	100.0%
TOTAL		98		6,620.13	100.0%		10,926.02	100.0%

Figure 9-36 Inventory Valuation Summary report

Step 3. To close the report, click the close box (☒) at the top right corner of the window.

Inventory Assemblies and Units of Measure

Many businesses purchase items using one unit of measure and sell the same item using a different unit of measure. For example, a retail store may purchase items by the case, but sell the items individually (or by *each*). QuickBooks Premier and Enterprise includes the *Unit of Measure* feature to help in these situations.

Inventory Assembly Items help to track assembled inventory, or inventory that is created from items from raw materials. An Inventory Assembly is defined by specifying which components (must be Inventory Part, Inventory Assembly, Non-inventory Part, Service, or Other Charge type items) are needed to produce it. Essentially, you define the *Bill of Materials* for each **Inventory Assembly** Item when you set up the item.

Both of these topics are covered in the supplemental material for this chapter. Details for accessing this material are available on page xiii.

> **Note:**
> Both *Units of Measure* and *Inventory Assemblies* are available only in QuickBooks **Premier** and **Enterprise** Editions. Download the supplemental material for this chapter to complete several exercises using these features (Premier version required). If you are using the QuickBooks Pro Edition, you can read through this supplement, but you will not be able to complete the exercises.

Chapter Summary and Review

In this chapter, you learned about how to set up and manage your inventory in QuickBooks. You should now be familiar with how to use QuickBooks to do all of the following:

- Activate the Inventory function (page 372).
- Set up Inventory Items in the Item list (page 373).
- Use QuickBooks to calculate the average cost of inventory (page 378).
- Record sales of Inventory using sales forms (page 378).
- View the accounting entries behind the scenes of inventory sales using the Transaction Journal report (page 379).
- Use purchase orders to order inventory (page 382).
- Receive inventory against purchase orders (page 384).
- Enter bills for received inventory (page 389).
- Adjust your inventory (page 394).
- Set up Group Items to bundle products and/or services (page 396).
- Create reports about inventory (page 398).
- Units of Measure and Inventory Assemblies (Supplemental Material)

Comprehension Questions

> Answers to these review questions are available with the supplemental material. See page xiii for details.

1. Why does an item receipt add to the balance in Accounts Payable but not show up in the *Pay Bills* window?
2. What accounts will QuickBooks automatically create when you first create an Inventory Part Item in the Item list?
3. Describe the purpose of the Inventory Asset and Cost of Goods Sold account in QuickBooks.

4. Describe the purpose of using Purchase Orders in QuickBooks.

Multiple Choice

Select the best answer(s) for each of the following:

1. If your vendor ships more than you ordered on a Purchase Order (an overshipment), which of the following actions would not be appropriate?
   a) You could refuse the extra shipment and send it back to the vendor without recording anything in QuickBooks.
   b) You could receive the extra shipment using an Inventory Adjustment transaction.
   c) You could receive the extra shipment into inventory and keep it (and pay for it).
   d) You could receive the extra shipment into inventory, and then send it back and record a Bill Credit in QuickBooks.
2. When setting up a group item, where do you enter the sales price?
   a) Enter the price in the *Sales Price* field.
   b) Enter the price in the *Item Pricing* list.
   c) The Group Item does not include a *Sales Price* field.
   d) Enter the price in the *Set Price* window.
3. To activate QuickBooks inventory:
   a) Select the **File** menu and then select **Preferences.**
   b) Select **Purchases - Vendors.**
   c) Consult your accountant to determine the proper inventory valuation method.
   d) Select the **Edit** menu, then select **Preferences**, then click on **Items & Inventory** Preference and then click the **Company** Preferences tab. Then click on the option that activates inventory.
4. The inventory asset account:
   a) Tracks open purchase orders of inventory items.
   b) Decreases when inventory is purchased.
   c) Increases when inventory is sold.
   d) Increases when inventory is purchased.
5. QuickBooks inventory can do all of the following except:
   a) Provide reports on the status of each item in inventory including how many are on hand and how many are on order.
   b) Use the LIFO or FIFO method of determining inventory cost.
   c) Calculate gross profit on inventory sold.
   d) Track the open purchase orders for every inventory item.
6. A convenient way to track the status of orders for your inventory items is to:
   a) List the items ordered on a sheet and review it each morning.
   b) Analyze your transaction journal report monthly.
   c) Use purchase orders for all inventory purchases.
   d) Hire an outside consultant to monitor your inventory levels.
7. Which of the following statements is false regarding Purchase Orders (POs)?
   a) POs are held in a special non-posting account until you receive the item(s) ordered.
   b) POs that include inventory items are posted to the inventory account at the end of each month.
   c) You can list your open purchase orders at any time.
   d) You may close a purchase order in part or in full at any time.

8. To display the window used to record inventory adjustments in QuickBooks:
   a) Select the **Company** menu and then select **Adjust Inventory for actual counts.**
   b) No adjustments should be made. QuickBooks automatically adjusts inventory each time you purchase or sell inventory items.
   c) Select the **Vendors** menu, select **Inventory Activities**, and then select **Adjust Quantity/Value on Hand.**
   d) Perform a physical inventory count.

9. QuickBooks maintains the value of inventory under which method?
   a) First in First Out, FIFO.
   b) Last in First Out, LIFO.
   c) Cost/retail method of inventory.
   d) Average Cost.

10. Which of the following is NOT a report available through QuickBooks?
   a) Goods-In-Process Inventory by Item.
   b) Inventory Stock Status by Item.
   c) Inventory Valuation Summary.
   d) Item QuickReport.

11. Which of the following statements is true regarding the recording of receipts of inventory items?
   a) How you record inventory received does not depend on how you pay for the items.
   b) Directly writing checks for inventory purchases is generally advised as a best practice.
   c) You can record a receipt against a purchase order even before you receive *all* the items ordered.
   d) You cannot enter the receipt of inventory items before entering the bill from the vendor.

12. When entering a bill for the purchase of inventory part items, what tab of the Enter Bills window should you use?
   a) Items
   b) Expenses
   c) Accounts
   d) Any of the above

13. Before setting up your inventory, it is a good idea to think about what products you will track as Inventory Parts because:
   a) It is necessary to separately track *every* product you sell as an Inventory Part.
   b) You could use **Non-inventory Part** items if you do not need detailed reports and inventory status information about certain products you sell.
   c) It is better to use Inventory Part items rather than Non-inventory Part items when you really need to track the cost of a product.
   d) Your accountant needs the detail information on Inventory Part numbers to be able to close your books for the year.

14. You can adjust the inventory in by
   a) Adjusting the Accounts.
   b) Adjusting the Item Quantity.
   c) Adjusting the Inventory Valuation.
   d) Both (b) and (c).

15. When processing a Vendor overcharge, what do you NOT want to do?
    a) Wait for a new bill from the vendor before recording the bill in QuickBooks, if the vendor agrees to revise the bill and send you a new one.
    b) Use the *Expenses* tab on the **Bill** to track the error, if you decide to pay the overcharge and have the vendor adjust the next bill.
    c) Use two separate accounts when recording the overcharge and the refund or credit to keep the transactions from becoming confusing.
    d) Contact the vendor to discuss the overage on the bill.

Completion Statements

1. The _____ _____ ___ _______report is useful for getting a quick snapshot of each inventory part and the number of units on hand and on order. Also, this report gives you information about your inventory turnover, showing a *sales per week* column.
2. In order to track inventory purchases by item and to easily determine which items you have on order, use _______ ________ when you purchase inventory.
3. QuickBooks keeps a _________ inventory, meaning that every purchase and every sale of inventory immediately updates all of your reports.
4. For detailed research about transactions involving inventory, use the _________ _________ or the ______ _________ ______ report.
5. The _____ ________ _______report gives you information about the value of your inventory items on a certain date. This report shows all values and average cost of items as of the date of the report.

Inventory Problem 1

APPLYING YOUR KNOWLEDGE

Restore the Inventory-10Problem1.QBM file and store it on your hard disk according to your instructor's directions.

1. Create new **Inventory Items** in the *Item* list with the following data.

Item Type	Inventory Part
Item Name	Frame 4x6 Black
Purchase Description	Picture Frame - 4x6 Black
Cost	$3.95
COGS Account	Cost of Goods Sold
Preferred Vendor	Leave blank
Sales Description	Picture Frame - 4x6 Black
Price	$8.49
Tax Code	Tax
Income Account	Sales
Asset Account	Inventory Asset
Reorder Point	25
Qty on Hand	Leave zero
Total Value	Leave zero
As of	Leave current date

Item Type	Inventory Part
Item Name	Frame 4x6 Red
Purchase Description	Picture Frame - 4x6 Red
Cost	$4.99
COGS Account	Cost of Goods Sold
Preferred Vendor	Leave blank
Sales Description	Picture Frame - 4x6 Red
Price	$9.99
Tax Code	Tax
Income Account	Sales
Asset Account	Inventory Asset
Reorder Point	25
Qty on Hand	Leave zero
Total Value	Leave zero
As of	Leave current date

2. Create Purchase Order #2011-1 dated 04/06/2011 to Ace Supply using the Walnut Creek class for 10-Frame 5x7, 40-Frame 4x6 Black, and 40-Frame 4x6 Red. Leave the *Ship To* drop-down field at the top blank. The total PO amount is $379.10. Print the purchase order on blank paper.

3. Record the transactions below. On these transactions, unless you're told differently, keep all defaults on transactions for prices, and sales tax item.

April 10, 2011	Create an item receipt for 10-Frame 5x7, 15-Frame 4x6 Black, and 20-Frame 4x6 Red from Ace Supply against PO #2011-1. The product came without a bill, but the packing slip number was #3883. The total Item Receipt amount is $180.55.
April 13, 2011	Create an item receipt for the remaining items from Ace Supply against PO #2011-1. The product came without a bill, but the packing slip number was #7622. The total Item Receipt amount is $198.55.
April 17, 2011	Create Invoice #2011-106 to Jerry Perez for 5-Frame 5x7 (use list price). Use the **Walnut Creek** class. The total Invoice amount is $32.42.
April 20, 2011	Received bill for Item Receipt #3883 from Ace Supply. Additional $8.50 delivery charges were added to the bill. Use the expenses tab on the bill to record delivery charges (coded to Postage and Delivery expense) and allocate the cost to the **Walnut Creek** class. The total Bill amount is $189.05. (**Hint**: Use the **Recalculate** button if necessary to adjust the Amount Due.)
April 20, 2011	Received bill for Item Receipt #7622 from Ace Supply. The total Bill amount is $198.55.
April 30, 2011	Enter an Inventory Adjustment for a Frame 5x7 item. Use the **Inventory Variance** account and the **Walnut Creek** class to record the adjustment. Inventory Adjustment Reference # 2011-101. Quantity on hand is 26. The total Value of Adjustment is -$2.15.

4. Create and print the following reports:
   a) **Frame 5x7 Item QuickReport** for 01/01/2011 through 04/30/2011
   b) **Inventory Stock Status by Item** for 01/01/2011 through 04/30/2011

c) **Inventory Valuation Detail** for 01/01/2011 through 04/30/2011
d) **Inventory Valuation Summary** as of 04/30/2011

Workplace Applications

Discussion Questions

These questions are designed to stimulate discussion about how you can apply QuickBooks to your own organization. They may help you think through some of the issues you'll encounter when using QuickBooks in your company.

1. How many different items does your organization have in inventory? What is the total number of pieces in your organization's inventory? What is the highest priced item? What is the lowest? What is the total value of your inventory?

2. How do you currently determine when it is time to re-supply each of these items? Does going below a certain amount on-hand trigger an order? Or do you order items after you make a sale that requires them?

Case Study

Fans 4 Fans, Inc.

Fans 4 Fans, Inc. is a small company in Oakland, California, that specializes in selling and installing home ceiling fans with professional sports team logos on them. The company purchases the parts to build the fan from two different vendors. The logo parts, including team helmets that appear to sit on top of the fan, are purchased from the official respective sports associations, and the rest of the fan assembly is purchased from a hardware supply company.

The assembly parts are stocked under two separate SKUs (Stock-Keeping Units) called **Helmet** and **Fan**.

The company keeps the assembly parts in stock and assembles the fans shortly before they are installed at the customer location. Because of the need to ensure the fan is properly assembled and safe, they do not let customers install their own fans. All labor is included in the purchase price of the fan.

1. What items should the company use to track the Helmet and Fan inventory?

2. A company has been so impressed with the Fans 4 Fans Company that it has offered to purchase the company. Fans 4 Fans, Inc. is required to find the value of the inventory on hand before further discussion of selling the business. What reports should they use?

3. If each fan requires the bundling of 4 hours of labor with the item, discuss how Fans 4 Fans, Inc. should set up a Group Item to track the sales of the fans.

Chapter 10 Sales Tax

Objectives

After completing this chapter, you should be able to:

- Activate Sales Tax and set Sales Tax Preferences (page 407).
- Use Sales Tax Items on Sales Forms (page 411).
- Set up Sales Tax Items (page 411).
- Use Sales Tax Codes on Sales Forms (page413).
- Set up Sales Tax Codes (page 414).
- Assign Sales Tax Codes to Items (page 414).
- Assign Sales Tax Codes to Customers (page 416).
- Use QuickBooks reports to assist in preparing your sales tax return (page 419).
- Adjust Sales Tax Payable (page 420).
- Pay Sales Tax (page 422).
- Set up and use Sales Tax Groups (page 424).
- Categorize Revenue by Sales Tax Code (page 425).

Restore this File

This chapter uses Sales Tax-10.QBW. To open this file, restore the Sales Tax-10.QBM file to your hard disk. See page 10 for instructions on restoring files.

If you sell products and certain types of services, chances are you will need to collect and remit sales tax. In many states, aside from the state tax, each county or city may impose an additional tax that businesses are required to track and report.

If you sell non-taxable goods and services, or if you sell to customers that are exempt from paying sales tax, your state will probably require a breakdown of non-taxable sales and the reason sales tax was not imposed.

These differing conditions may not apply in all jurisdictions, but QuickBooks allows you to track sales tax for all of these different situations.

If you are not familiar with the sales tax rates or reporting requirements in your area, consult your state agency, your local QuickBooks advisor, or accountant for guidance.

Setting up Sales Tax

Activating Sales Tax and Setting Preferences

You must set up your **Sales Tax Preferences** before using the Sales Tax feature in QuickBooks.

COMPUTER PRACTICE

Step 1. Click the **Manage Sales Tax** button on the *Home Page*. Or you can choose **Manage Sales Tax** from the *Sales Tax* option on the *Vendors* menu.

Step 2. The *Manage Sales Tax* dialog box will appear (see Figure 10-1).

Step 3. Click the **Sales Tax Preferences...**button in the *Get Started* section.

Alternatively, you could select Preferences from the Edit menu, then select the Sales Tax Company preferences.

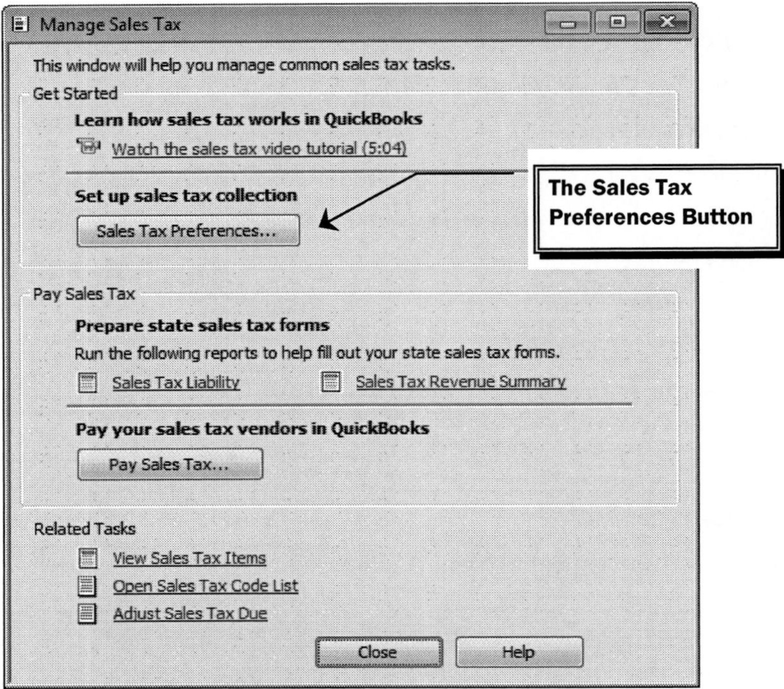

Figure 10-1 The Manage Sales Tax Dialog Box

Step 4. The Sales Tax Company Preferences dialog box appears.

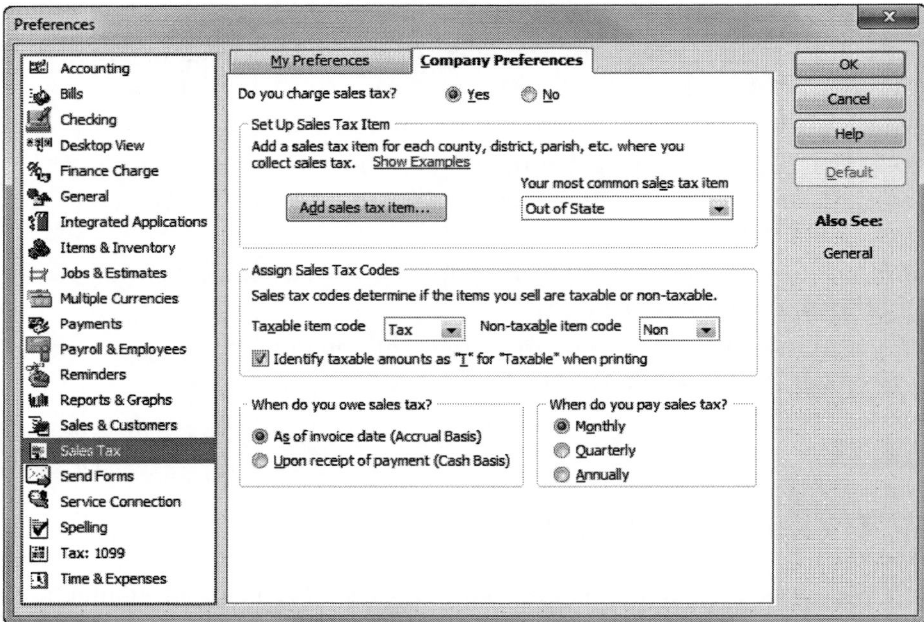

Figure 10-2 Sales Tax Company Preferences

Step 5. Leave **Yes** selected in the *Do You Charge Sales Tax* section.

> **Note:**
> In your practice file, Sales Tax is already activated. However, if you setup your own data file you will need to activate it by clicking **Yes** either in the Sales Tax Preferences or when prompted in the EasyStep Interview.

Step 6. In the *Set Up Sales Tax Items* section, notice *Out of State* is selected in the *Most common sales tax* field. Change this field to **Contra Costa** (see Figure 10-3).

> **Note:**
> The sales tax item listed in the *Most common sales tax* field becomes the default sales tax item on new customer records, and on Sales receipts and Invoices.

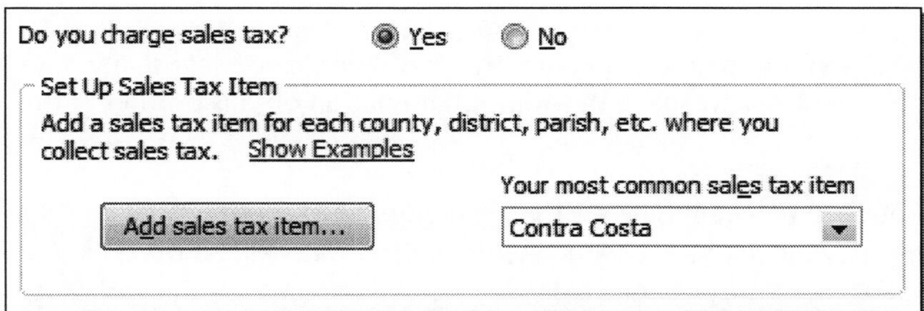

Figure 10-3 Select the most common Sales Tax Item you use on sales forms

Step 7. In the *Assign Sales Tax Codes* section, **Tax** is the default code in the *Taxable item code* field and **Non** is the default for the *Non-Taxable item code* field (see Figure 10-4).

The codes you enter here will become the default codes when you set up new Customers and Items. You can supply the appropriate *Sales Tax Code* on exempt customer records and non-taxable Items. For more information about *Sales Tax Codes,* see page 413.

Step 8. The *Mark taxable amounts with "T" when printing* box is checked (see Figure 10-4).

When you use taxable items on sales forms (e.g., Inventory Parts marked taxable in the Item setup), QuickBooks will print a **T** on that line of the invoice, sales receipt, or credit memo. It is usually best to leave this box checked to clearly distinguish which items are subject to sales tax on printed forms.

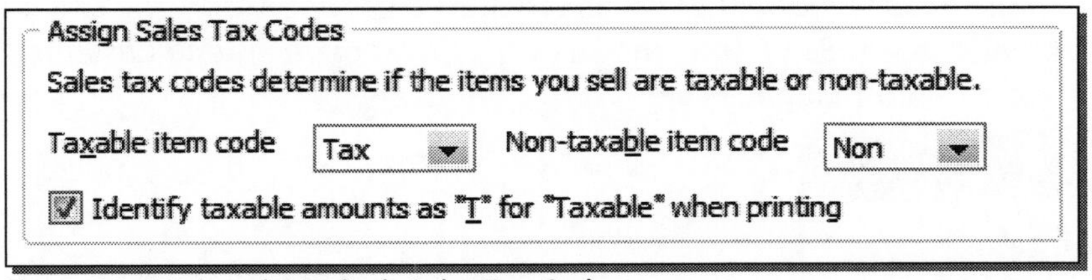

Assign Sales Tax Codes
Sales tax codes determine if the items you sell are taxable or non-taxable.
Taxable item code: Tax — Non-taxable item code: Non
☑ Identify taxable amounts as "T" for "Taxable" when printing

Figure 10-4 Select the Default Sales Tax Codes

Step 9. In the *When do you owe sales tax* section, leave **As of invoice date (Accrual Basis)** selected as shown in Figure 10-5.

With *As of Invoice date* selected in this section, sales tax reports will show that you owe sales tax for all taxable sales, including unpaid amounts from your open

Invoices.

If you select **Upon receipt of payment (Cash Basis)**, the reports will reflect sales tax only from sales on which payments have been received. Check your state sales tax rules and set this *Sales Tax Preference* accordingly.

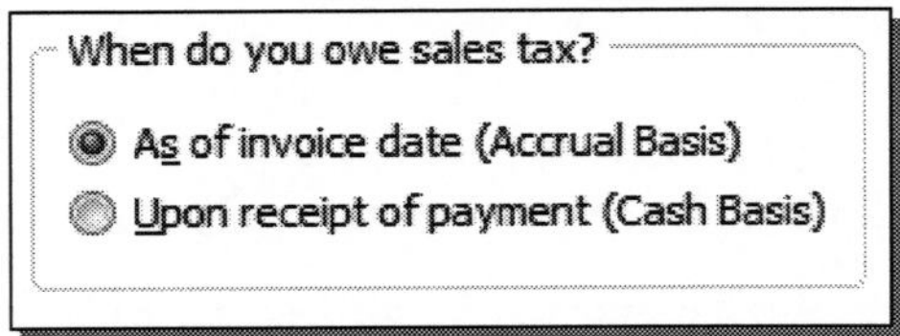

Figure 10-5 Owe Sales Tax on Accrual or Cash Basis

Step 10. In the ***When do you pay sales tax?*** section, **Monthly** is already selected (see Figure 10-6).

Many states require you to pay sales tax monthly. However, if your company pays its sales tax quarterly or annually, select the appropriate option on this portion of the window.

This setting controls the default date for the *Show sales tax due through* field of the *Pay Sales Tax* window. If you select **Monthly**, the default date will be the end of last month. If you select **Quarterly** or **Annually**, the default date will be the end of last calendar quarter or year respectively.

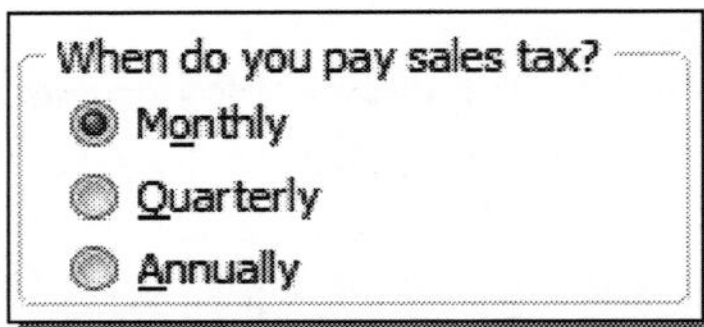

Figure 10-6 Pay Sales Tax section

Step 11. Click **OK** to save your changes.

Step 12. If you made changes on the preference screen before clicking **OK**, QuickBooks may display the *Updating Sales Tax* window (see Figure 10-7).

When you turn on *Sales Tax Tracking*, QuickBooks provides the option to automatically enter the **Tax** *Sales Tax Code* in existing customer records and Inventory and Non-inventory Part Items. If the majority of your customers and items are taxable, it is best to leave both of these boxes checked. If necessary, you can edit customer records and Items. See *Editing the Sales Tax Codes on Items and Customers* on page 414 for more information.

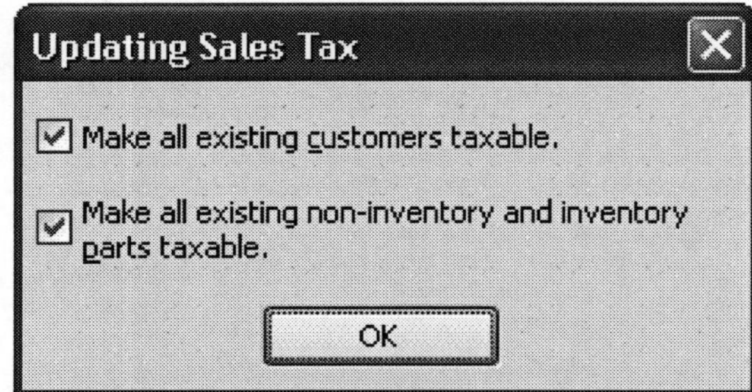

Figure 10-7 Updating Sales Tax window

Step 13. Click **OK** on the *Updating Sales Tax* window.

Sales Tax Items

Sales Tax Items are used on sales forms to calculate the amount of sales tax due on each sale.

Using Sales Tax Items on Sales Forms

On sales forms, Sales Tax is calculated at the bottom of the form, separately from the rest of the Items on the form. To see this, display Invoice 2011-106 (*Customer* menu→*Create Invoice*→ **Previous** button). See Figure 10-8. Close the window after reviewing the form.

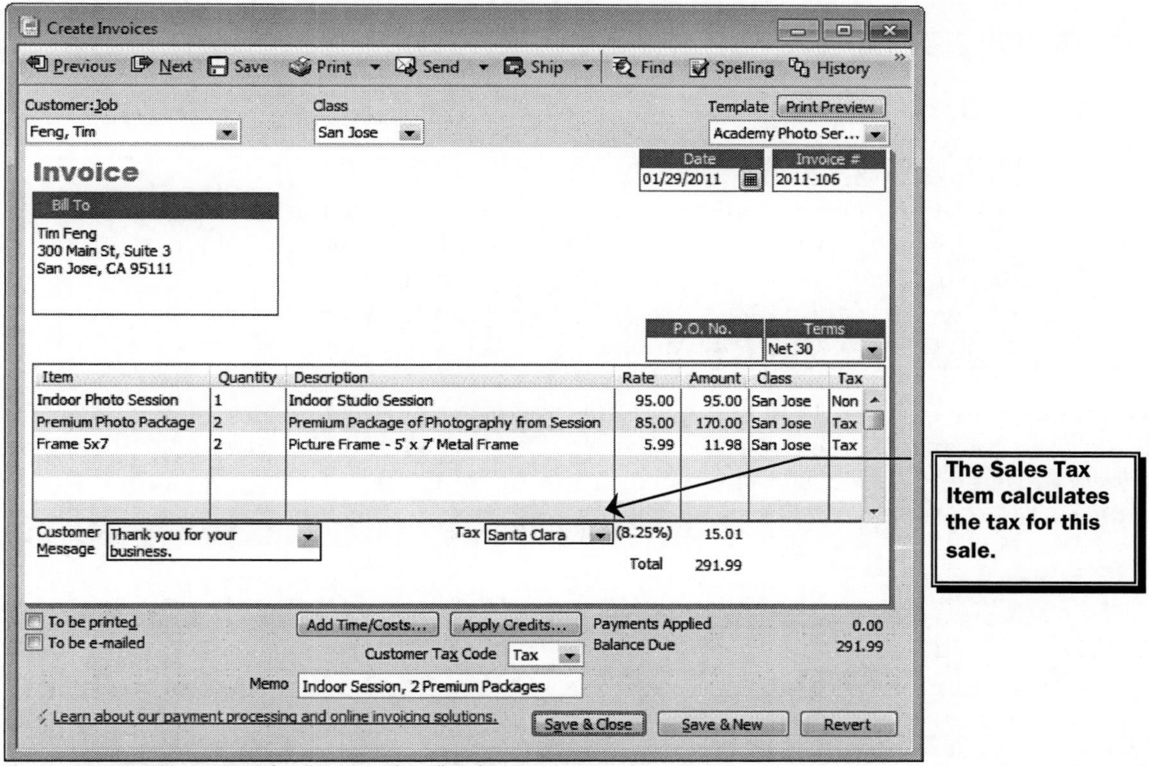

Figure 10-8 Invoice using the "Santa Clara" Sales Tax Item

Setting Up Sales Tax Items

To set up your Sales Tax Items, follow these steps:

COMPUTER PRACTICE

Step 1. Select the *Lists* menu and then select **Item List**. Alternatively, click the **Items & Services** icon on the *Home* page.

Step 2. To add a new Item, select the **Item** button at the bottom of the *Item list* and then select **New**.

Step 3. Select **Sales Tax Item** in the *Type* drop-down list and press **Tab**.

Step 4. Enter the *Tax Name, Description, Tax Rate,* and *Tax Agency*, as shown in Figure 10-9. This item will track all sales activity (taxable and nontaxable) for Alameda County and will charge each customer 8.75% in sales tax. The sales taxes collected using the *Alameda Sales Tax Item* will increase the amount due to the *State Board of Equalization.*

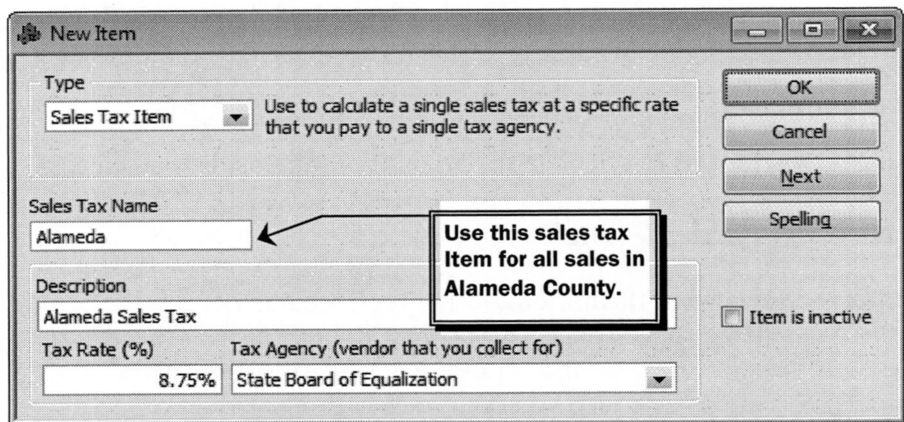

Figure 10-9 Setting up a Sales Tax item

Step 5. Click **OK** to save the Item.

> **The accounting behind the scenes:**
> **Sales Tax Items** automatically calculate the sales tax on each sales form by applying the sales tax rate to all taxable items on that sale. QuickBooks increases (credits) Sales Tax Payable for the amount of sales tax on the sale. Also, QuickBooks tracks the amount due by *Tax Agency* in the **Sales Tax Liability** report and in the *Pay Sales Tax* window.

Your sample file includes three additional *Sales Tax Items* for tracking sales in *Contra Costa* and *Santa Clara* counties as well as *Out of State* sales. After you add the *Alameda Sales Tax Item*, as shown in Figure 10-9, your Item list will look like Figure 10-10.

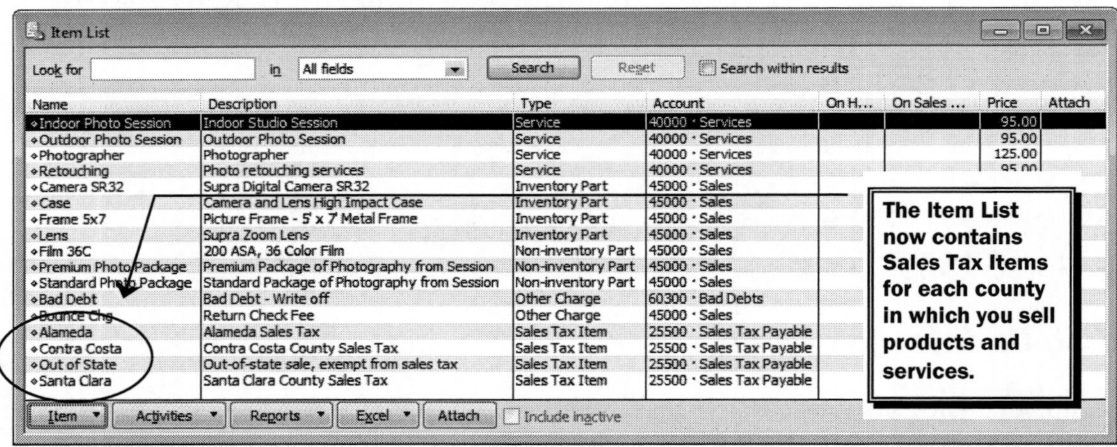

Name	Description	Type	Account	On H...	On Sales ...	Price	Attach
Indoor Photo Session	Indoor Studio Session	Service	40000 · Services			95.00	
Outdoor Photo Session	Outdoor Photo Session	Service	40000 · Services			95.00	
Photographer	Photographer	Service	40000 · Services			125.00	
Retouching	Photo retouching services	Service	40000 · Services			95.00	
Camera SR32	Supra Digital Camera SR32	Inventory Part	45000 · Sales				
Case	Camera and Lens High Impact Case	Inventory Part	45000 · Sales				
Frame 5x7	Picture Frame - 5' x 7' Metal Frame	Inventory Part	45000 · Sales				
Lens	Supra Zoom Lens	Inventory Part	45000 · Sales				
Film 36C	200 ASA, 36 Color Film	Non-inventory Part	45000 · Sales				
Premium Photo Package	Premium Package of Photography from Session	Non-inventory Part	45000 · Sales				
Standard Photo Package	Standard Package of Photography from Session	Non-inventory Part	45000 · Sales				
Bad Debt	Bad Debt - Write off	Other Charge	60300 · Bad Debts				
Bounce Chg	Return Check Fee	Other Charge	45000 · Sales				
Alameda	Alameda Sales Tax	Sales Tax Item	25500 · Sales Tax Payable				
Contra Costa	Contra Costa County Sales Tax	Sales Tax Item	25500 · Sales Tax Payable				
Out of State	Out-of-state sale, exempt from sales tax	Sales Tax Item	25500 · Sales Tax Payable				
Santa Clara	Santa Clara County Sales Tax	Sales Tax Item	25500 · Sales Tax Payable				

Figure 10-10 Item list

> **Note:**
> If you remit sales tax to **only one agency** (e.g., California's State Board of Equalization) but you collect sales tax in several different counties or cities, create a separate *Sales Tax Item* for each taxable location in which you sell products. This allows you to track different sales tax rates for each locale.
>
> **Note:**
> If you pay sales tax to **more than one agency**, you should use *Sales Tax Groups* to combine several different Sales Tax Items into a group tax rate. See page 424 for more information.

Sales Tax Codes

Sales Tax Codes are an additional classification for calculating and reporting sales tax. A Sales Tax Code is assigned to each product or service item, as well as to each customer.

Sales Tax Codes serve two purposes. First, Sales Tax Codes indicate whether a specific product or service is taxable or non-taxable. Secondly, Sales Tax Codes categorize revenue based on the reason you charged or did not charge sales tax.

If your sales tax agency requires reporting for different types of exempt sales, you may wish to create several non-taxable Sales Tax Codes for each type of non-taxable sale (e.g., **RSR** for non-taxable resellers).

Using Sales Tax Codes on Sales Forms

If you use a taxable *Sales Tax Code* in the *Customer Tax Code* field on sales forms, QuickBooks will charge sales tax (see Figure 10-11). If you use a non-taxable *Sales Tax Code*, QuickBooks will not charge sales tax unless you override the sales tax code (to a taxable code) on one of the lines in the body of the form.

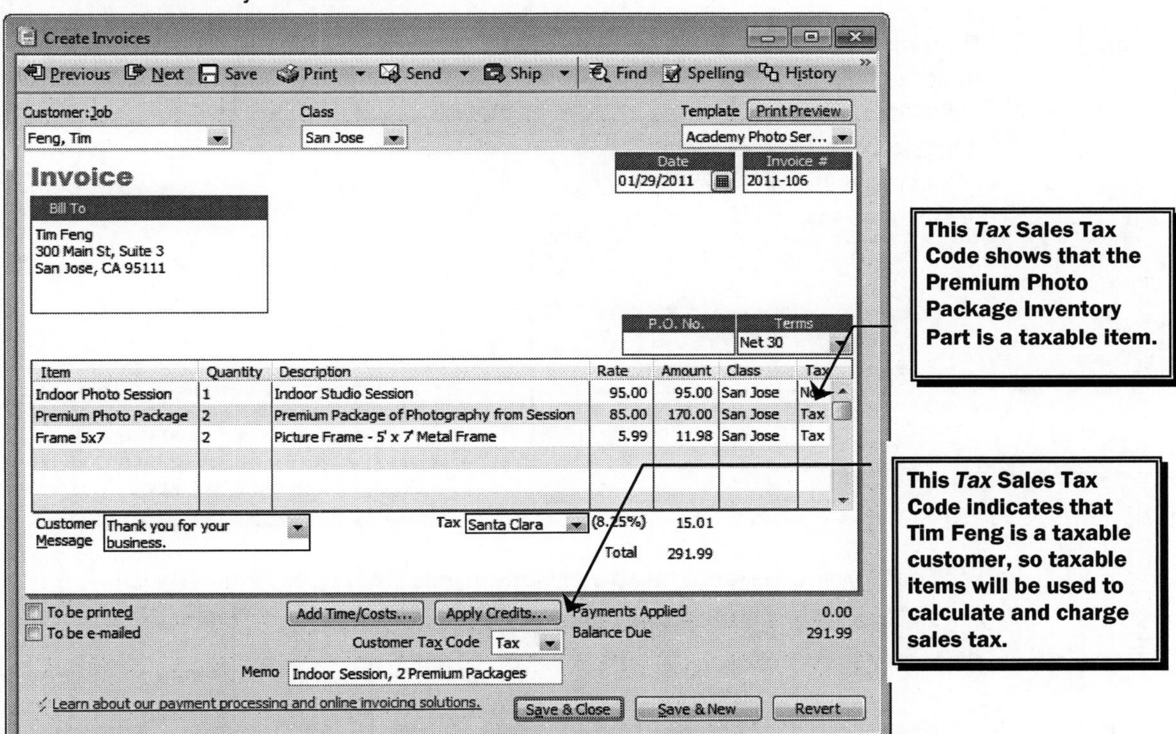

Figure 10-11 Invoice with taxable items

When you set up a customer record, the *Sales Tax Code* you enter in the customer record becomes the default in the *Customer Tax Code* field on sales forms (see Figure 10-11).

Similarly, when you set up Items, the *Sales Tax Code* you enter in the Item record becomes the default Tax Code in the body of sales forms (Figure 10-16).

You can override the *Sales Tax Code* at the bottom of sales forms (by using the *Customer Tax Code* drop-down list), or on each line in the body of the Invoice.

For more information on using Sales Tax Codes to categorize revenue, see page 425.

Setting up Sales Tax Codes

COMPUTER PRACTICE

To set up a Sales Tax Code, follow these steps:

Step 1. From the *Lists* menu select **Sales Tax Code List**. QuickBooks displays the Sales Tax Code List window (see Figure 10-12).

Figure 10-12 Sales Tax Code List

Step 2. The sample file already has two Sales Tax Codes (Tax and Non), so you do not need to add a new one now. However, to add a new one, you would select **New** from the *Sales Tax Code* button at the bottom of the list. To edit a Sale Tax Code, double-click it in the list.

Step 3. Double-click the first Tax Code (**Tax**) in the list.

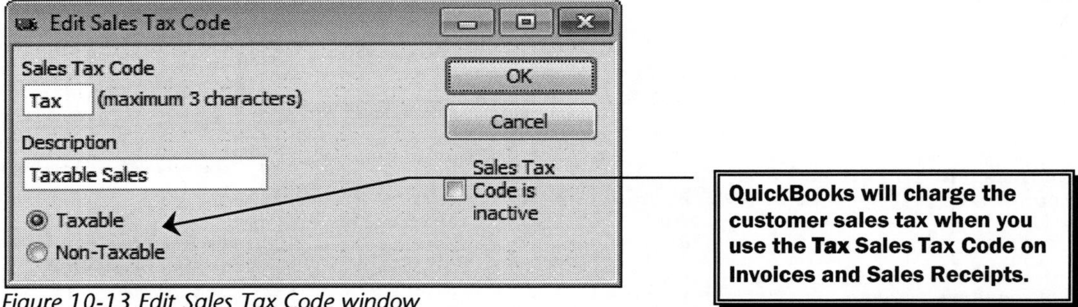

Figure 10-13 Edit Sales Tax Code window

Step 4. Each *Sales Tax Code* has a taxable or non-taxable status (see Figure 10-13).

Step 5. Click **Cancel**. For this example, you will not create a new Tax Code.

Step 6. Close the *Sales Tax Code List* window.

Editing the Sales Tax Codes on Items and Customers

Assigning Sales Tax Codes to Items

To assign a default Sales Tax Code to an Item, follow these steps:

COMPUTER PRACTICE

Step 1. From the *Reports* menu, select **List** and then select **Item Listing**.

Step 2. To make the report more useful for viewing the Sales Tax Code on each Item, click **Modify Report** and remove all columns except **Item**, **Description**, **Type**, and **Sales Tax Code** as shown in Figure 10-14. You will need to scroll down to deselect additional items.

Step 3. Select **Type** from the *Sort by* drop-down list.

Step 4. Click **OK** when finished.

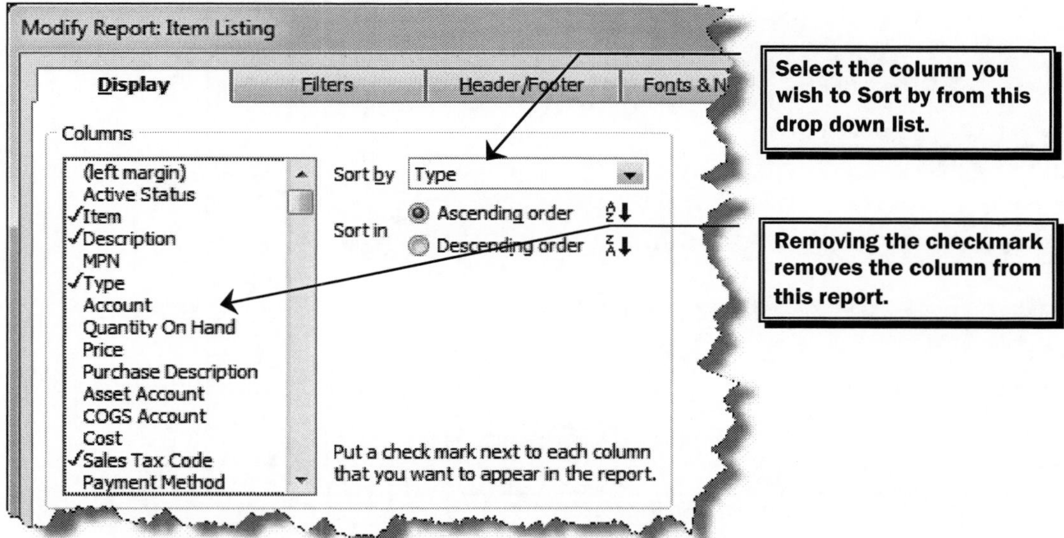

Figure 10-14 Changing Display settings for the Item Listing

Step 5. Move your cursor over the *Sales Tax Code* column header. Your cursor will appear as a "hand." Click and drag the column so that it appears immediately to the right of the **Item** column (see Figure 10-15).

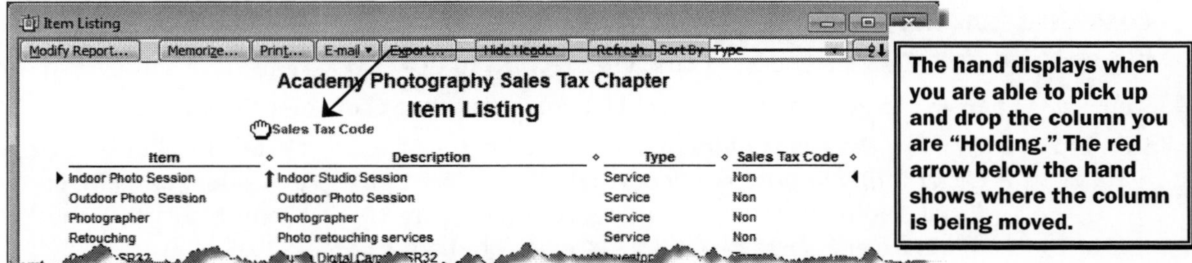

Figure 10-15 Item Listing showing Sales Tax Codes for each Item

To edit the *Sales Tax Code* for an Item in the list, double-click the Item name.

Step 6. Double-click on the **Indoor Photo Session** Item.

Step 7. Leave the *Tax Code* field set to Non as shown in Figure 10-16.

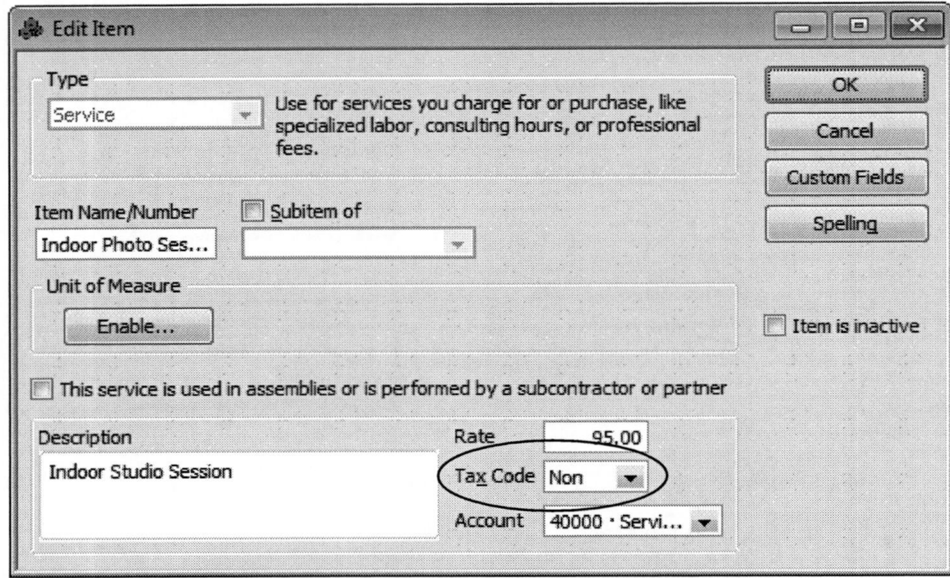

Figure 10-16 Edit the Sales Tax Code on each Item as necessary

Step 8. Click **OK** to close the *Edit Item* window.

Step 9. Close the *Item Listing* report.

Assigning Sales Tax Codes to Customers

COMPUTER PRACTICE

To view and edit Sales Tax Codes on customer records, follow these steps:

Step 1. From the *Reports* menu, select **List** and then select **Customer Contact List**.

Step 2. To make the report more useful for viewing the Sales Tax Code for each Customer, click **Modify Report.** Scroll down the list to select **Sales Tax Code, Tax item,** and **Resale Num** from the *Columns* section (see Figure 10-17). Remove all other check marks except **Customer**. Click **OK** when finished.

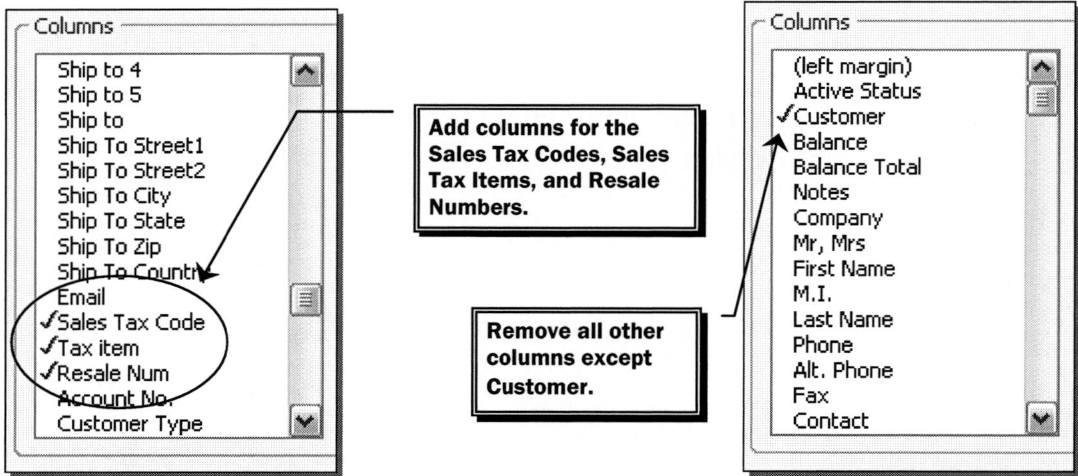

Figure 10-17 Modify Report window for the Customer Contact list

Step 3. To the right of the *Sales Tax Code* column header, click and drag the diamond to widen the column to view the data. Your cursor will be replaced with a cross symbol and a dotted line will indicate the column edge. Repeat this step for the *Tax Item* column and the *Resale Num* column if needed (see Figure 10-18).

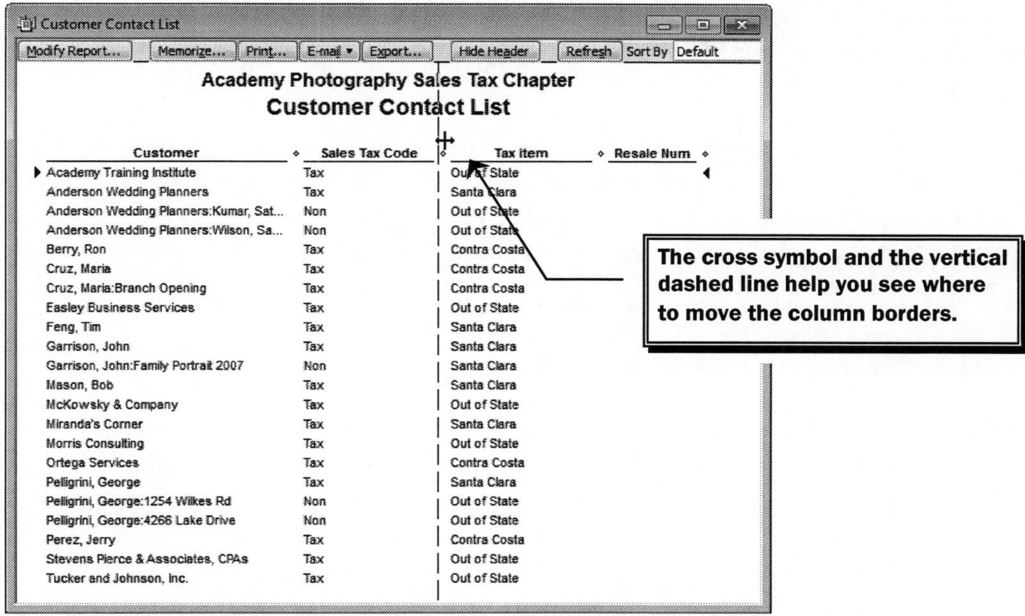

Figure 10-18 Customer Contact List with Sales Tax Code and Tax item columns

To edit the sales tax information for a customer, double-click the customer name in the report.

Step 4. Double-click on **Berry, Ron** in the Customer Contact report.

Step 5. Click the **Additional Information** tab to edit the *Tax Code, Tax Item,* and *Resale Number* as necessary (see Figure 10-19). You don't need to change them in the sample file.

Step 6. Click **OK** when finished. Then close the *Customer Contact List* report and the *Item Listing* report by clicking the (☒) in the upper right corner of the report. If the Memorize Reports window appears, check *Do not display this message in the future* and click **OK**.

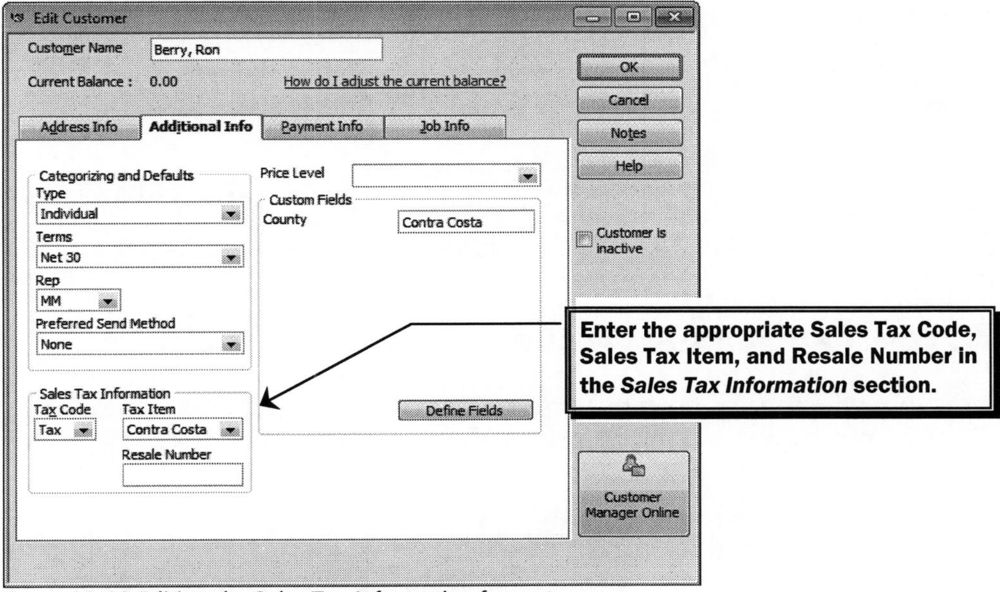

Figure 10-19 Editing the Sales Tax Information for customers

Did you know?
Jobs follow the sales tax status of their parent Customer, so no sales tax information is shown on the Additional Info tab of a Job record. Jobs show on reports with a colon (:) after the customer name.

Tip:
If the customer is not subject to sales tax, select **Non** and enter the customer's resale or other exemption number in the *Resale Number* field. While this is helpful for you when you review your records, your state may require you to retain written proof of this status. Consult your sales tax agency or accountant for more detailed information.

Calculating Sales Tax on Sales Forms

When you properly set up your QuickBooks items, Customers, Sales Tax Codes, and Preferences, QuickBooks automatically calculates and tracks sales tax on each sale.

As illustrated in Figure 10-20 and detailed in the steps above, each line on a sale shows a separate Item that is taxed according to the combination of how the Item, Tax Code, and Customer is set up. When you set up Items, you indicate which Sales Tax Code normally applies to that item. In addition, when you set up a customer record, you indicate the Sales Tax Item and Sales Tax Code to be used for that customer.

Then, when you create a sale (Invoice or Sales Receipt), the Customer Tax Code and the Sales Tax Item are taken from the customer's record and filled into the Customer Tax Code and Tax fields on the form. The Customer Tax Code overrides the Tax Code on each line item. If necessary, you can override the Tax Code on each line of the sales form or at the bottom of the form. The Tax Item, which can also be overridden, determines the rate to charge on the sum of all taxable line items on the sale.

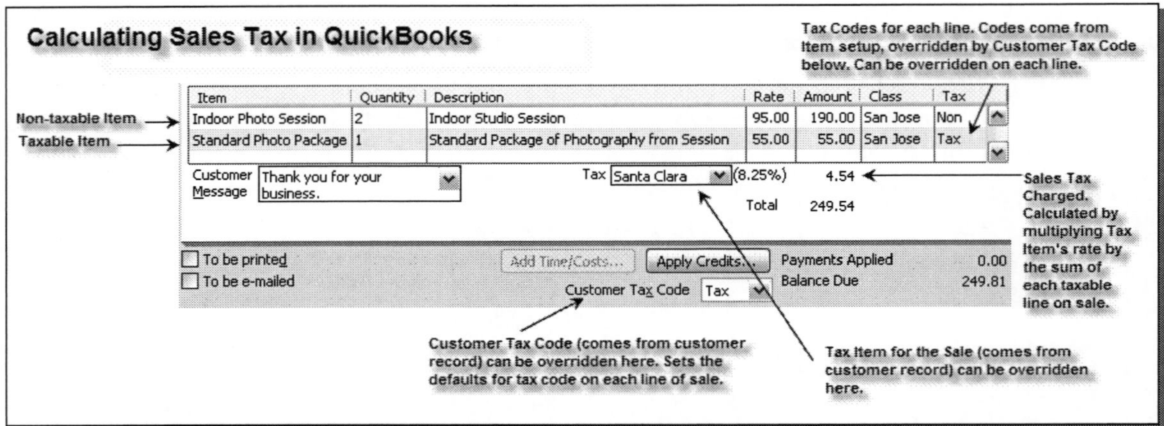

Figure 10-20 Calculating Sales Tax in QuickBooks

QuickBooks and Your Sales Tax Return

Academy Photography files its sales tax return to a single vendor called the State Board of Equalization. In this example, we will run reports for the first quarter of 2011.

The Sales Tax Liability Report

The *Sales Tax Liability* report provides you with the information you need to prepare your sales tax return, including a breakdown of sales and sales tax collected by county and sales tax agency.

COMPUTER PRACTICE

Step 1. If necessary, open the Manage Sales Tax dialog box.

Step 2. Click the **Sales Tax Liability** link under the *Pay Sales Tax* section (see Figure 10-21).

You can also open the *Sales Tax Liability* report by selecting *Vendors & Payables* from the *Reports* menu and then selecting *Sales Tax Liability*.

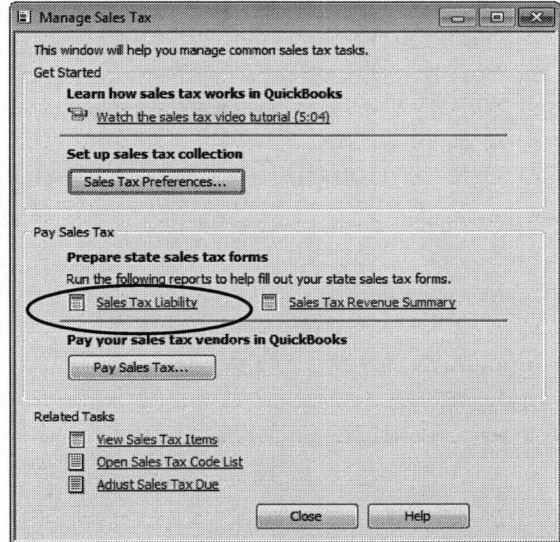

Figure 10-21 The Sales Tax Liability link in the Manage Sales Tax dialog box

Step 3. Set date fields to ***01/01/2011*** through ***03/31/2011*** and then press **Tab** (see Figure 10-22).

> **Tip:**
> If you file sales taxes quarterly, be sure to choose the *Quarterly* option in *Pay Sales Tax* section of the *Sales Tax* Preferences. Your reports will default to the last calendar quarter automatically. Similarly, for *Month* or *Annual* choices they will default to those period dates as well.

Step 4. You should print this report for your records. Keep the report open for now.

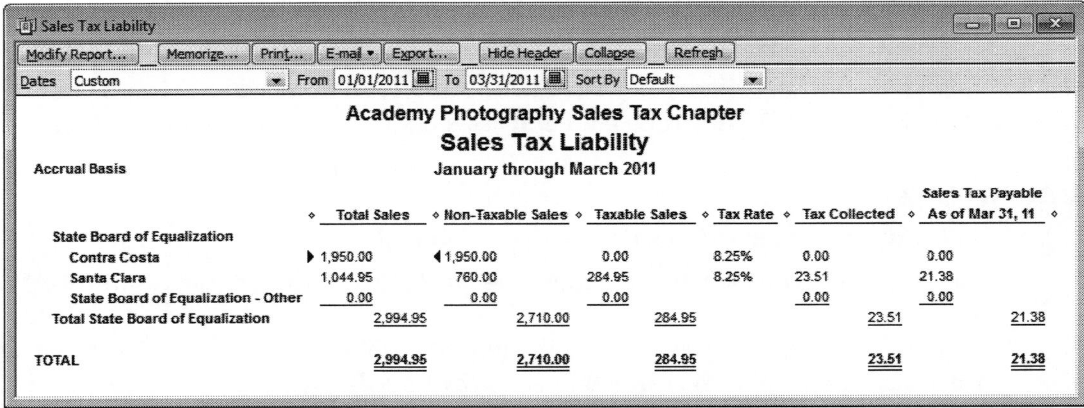

Academy Photography Sales Tax Chapter
Sales Tax Liability
Accrual Basis January through March 2011

	Total Sales	Non-Taxable Sales	Taxable Sales	Tax Rate	Tax Collected	Sales Tax Payable As of Mar 31, 11
State Board of Equalization						
Contra Costa	1,950.00	1,950.00	0.00	8.25%	0.00	0.00
Santa Clara	1,044.95	760.00	284.95	8.25%	23.51	21.38
State Board of Equalization - Other	0.00	0.00	0.00		0.00	0.00
Total State Board of Equalization	2,994.95	2,710.00	284.95		23.51	21.38
TOTAL	2,994.95	2,710.00	284.95		23.51	21.38

Figure 10-22 Sales Tax Liability report

The *Sales Tax Liability* report shows total sales in each county (e.g., Sales Tax Items Contra Costa & Santa Clara), and shows the taxable sales separately from the nontaxable sales. In addition, you can see the tax rates and tax collected in each county.

The *Tax Collected* column shows how much tax you have collected on sales for the period. If you have made any sales tax payments for this period or owe tax from prior periods, the *Sales Tax Payable* column will reflect these activities.

To see the detail of transactions that comprise the *Sales Tax Liability* report, double-click on any dollar amount in the report.

The **State Board of Equalization – Other** line on the report shows any adjustments to the Sales Tax Payable account that you make using a *General Journal Entry* or the *Sales Tax Adjustment* window (see Figure 10-23). This line is zero because there are no sales tax adjustments recorded for this period.

Recording Discounts, Penalties, Interest and Rounding

The amount of sales tax you owe on the sales tax return will often not match the amount accrued in QuickBooks. This could be caused by several factors:

- Some sales tax agencies require you to round sales tax to the nearest dollar when preparing the return.
- Many sales tax agencies offer discounts for timely filing.
- Many sales tax agencies charge interest and penalties for filing late. Though interest and penalties are often paid separately, many agencies provide an option for including them with the return.

While you are preparing your sales tax return, you may need to create a *Sales Tax Adjustment.* If so, create the adjustment *before* you record the sales tax payment so that QuickBooks will show the correct amount to pay. For example, Academy Photography's sales tax payment for the first quarter of 2011 will be rounded to the nearest dollar. Since the amount due is $21.38, you will need to make an adjustment of $0.38, changing the amount owed from $21.38 (see Figure 10-22) to $21.00.

COMPUTER PRACTICE

Step 1. From the *Vendors* menu, select **Sales Tax** and then select **Adjust Sales Tax Due.**

You could also click the **Adjust Sales Tax** link in the *Manage Sales Tax* dialog box.

Step 2. This opens the *Sales Tax Adjustment* window shown in Figure 10-23.

Step 3. Enter ***03/31/2011*** in the *Adjustment Date* field and press **Tab**.

In the *Adjustment Date* field, enter the last day of the month for which you are filing your sales tax returns and making sales tax payments.

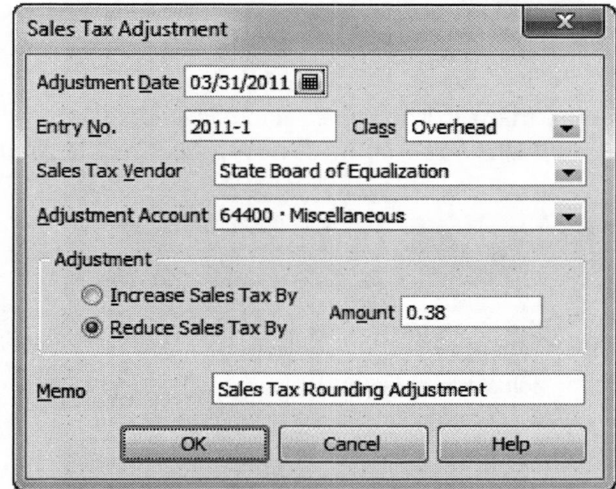

Figure 10-23 Sales Tax Adjustment window

Step 4. Select **Overhead** in the *Class* field and press **Tab**.

Make sure you assign a class to your adjustments. Otherwise, the adjustment will show in the *Unclassified* column on the Profit & Loss by Class report. If the adjustment is related to a specific class (e.g., tax paid on the purchase of a resale item for a specific location), you can enter the appropriate class in this field. If your adjustment to sales tax affects more than one class, you should enter separate adjustments for each class that is affected. As an alternative, you can make this adjustment using a *General Journal Entry*, which will allow you to designate multiple classes on a single adjustment.

Step 5. Leave **2011-1** in the *Entry No.* field and press **Tab**.

When you record an adjustment to sales tax on the *Sales Tax Adjustment* window, QuickBooks creates a General Journal Entry transaction. Therefore, QuickBooks enters this number sequentially using the same numbering sequence as the General Journal Entry window.

Step 6. Select **State Board of Equalization** from the *Sales Tax Vendor* drop-down list and press **Tab**.

This is the agency to which you pay sales tax. If you file sales tax returns to more than one agency, you should enter a separate Sales Tax Adjustment for each sales tax return you file.

Step 7. Select the **Miscellaneous** account from the *Adjustment Account* drop-down list.

If you are adjusting your sale tax to record a timely filing discount, select an appropriate account such as *Other Income* or *Sales Tax Discount*. If you are recording Interest, choose *Interest Expense* or *Fines & Penalties* for late filing fees.

Step 8. Select **Reduce Sales Tax By** in the *Adjustment* section.

Since you are rounding up to the nearest dollar, you need to reduce the amount of sales tax you owe. If you are recording interest or penalties, select **Increase Sales Tax By** in this section. If you are recording timely filing discounts, select **Reduce Sales Tax By**.

Step 9. Enter ***0.38*** in the *Amount* field and then press **Tab**.

Step 10. Enter ***Sales Tax Rounding Adjustment*** in the *Memo* field.

Step 11. Click **OK** to record the adjustment.

The Sales Tax Liability report now shows the adjustment in the *State Board of Equalization – Other* row (see Figure 10-24). The total in the *Sales Tax Payable* column now agrees to the total sales tax due on the return.

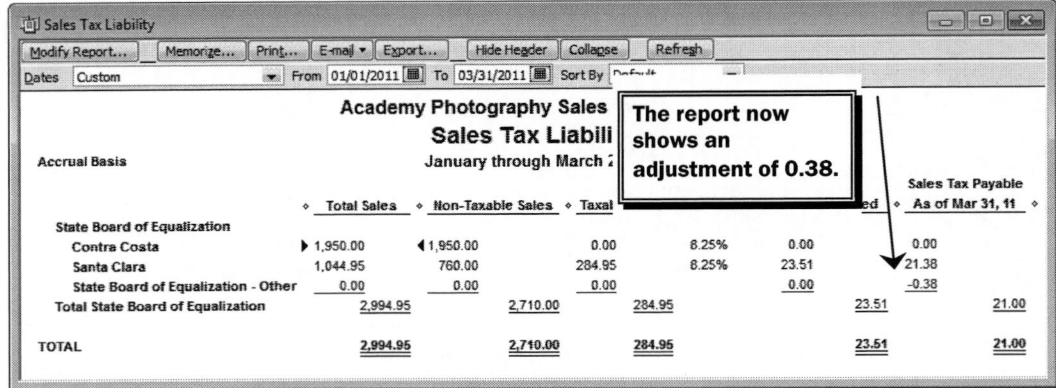

Figure 10-24 The Sales Tax Liability Report now shows the timely filing discount.

Step 12. Close the report by clicking the (☒) in the upper right corner of the report.

> **The accounting behind the scenes:**
> If the adjustment reduces (debits) Sales Tax Payable, QuickBooks will credit the account you enter in the *Adjustment Account* field. If the adjustment increases (credits) Sales Tax Payable, QuickBooks will debit the account you enter in the *Adjustment Account* field.

Paying Sales Tax

After you prepare your sales tax return and make necessary adjustments for discounts, interest, penalties, or rounding, create a sales tax payment for the amount you owe.

When you pay your sales tax, do not use the *Write Checks* window because the payment will not affect the *Sales Tax Items*. It also will not show properly on the Sales Tax Liability reports. To correctly pay your sales tax liability, use the **Pay Sales Tax** window.

COMPUTER PRACTICE

Step 1. From the *Home* page, select the **Manage Sales Tax** icon, if necessary.

Step 2. Click the **Pay Sales Tax...** button in the center of the *Manage Sales Tax* dialog box.

Alternatively, from the *Vendors* menu, select **Sales Tax** and then select **Pay Sales Tax.**

Step 3. The ***Pay Sales Tax*** window displays. In the *Pay From Account* field, **Checking** already displays so press **Tab**.

This field allows you to select the account from which you wish to pay your sales tax.

Step 4. Enter ***04/15/2011*** in the *Check Date* field and press **Tab**.

This field is the date of *when* you are paying the sales tax.

Step 5. Enter ***03/31/2011*** in the *Show sales tax due through* field and press **Tab**.

Enter the last day of the sales tax reporting period in this field. For example, if you are filing your sales tax return for the first quarter, enter the last day of March in this field.

Step 6. Leave **6008** in the *Starting Check No* field and press **Tab**.

QuickBooks automatically enters the next check number sequentially. Since the last check written on the Checking account was #6007, QuickBooks entered **6008** in this field.

Step 7. Click in the **Pay** column (see Figure 10-25) on all the lines that have a balance.

The last line shows the rounding adjustment you recorded using the Sales Tax Adjustment window.

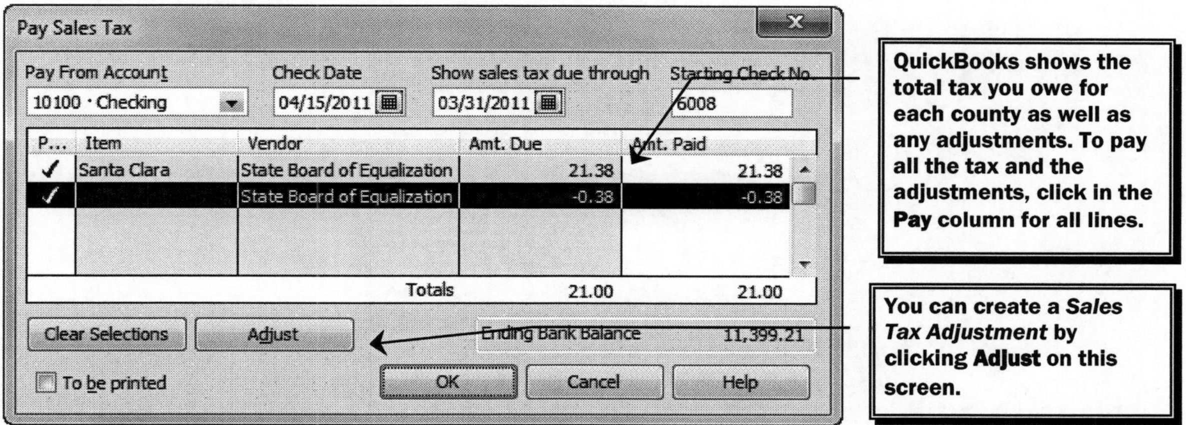

Figure 10-25 Pay Sales Tax window

Step 8. QuickBooks now shows a total of $21.00 for this Sales Tax Payment. Click **OK** to record the Sales Tax Payment.

After you record the sales tax payment, QuickBooks will create a special type of check called a Sales Tax Payment (TAXPMT) in your checking account for the total tax due to each sales tax agency (Vendor).

Important:
QuickBooks allows you to adjust the amounts in the *Amt. Paid* column. However, if you do you will retain an incorrect (overstated) balance in Sales Tax Payable for the period. If you need to change the amount of sales tax due, use a Sales Tax Adjustment, as shown in Figure 10-23. To quickly access the Sales Tax Adjustment window, click **Adjust** on the Pay Sales Tax window (see Figure 10-25).

Advanced Sales Tax Topics

Sales Tax Groups

In many states, multiple sales taxes must be collected and paid to separate agencies. In this case, you should use Sales Tax Groups to combine individual Sales Tax Items into a total tax.

Sales Tax Group Items allow you to combine multiple Sales Tax Items together so that each city, district, county, and state tax is tracked separately, while only the combined rate of all the Sales Tax Items shows on sales forms.

For example, if the county charges sales tax at a rate of 4% and the state charges sales tax at a rate of 4.25%, the combined rate collected from the customer would be 8.25%.

Setting up Sales Tax Group Items

DO NOT PERFORM THESE STEPS NOW. THEY ARE FOR REFERENCE ONLY.

1. Create separate Sales Tax Items for the county and the state, as shown in Figure 10-26 and Figure 10-27.

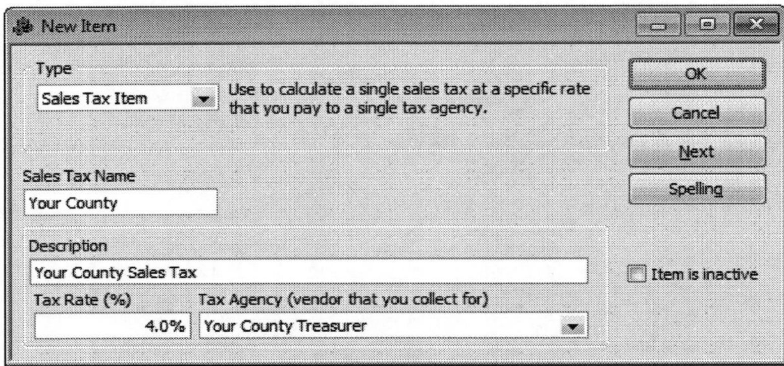

Figure 10-26 Sales Tax Item for Your County

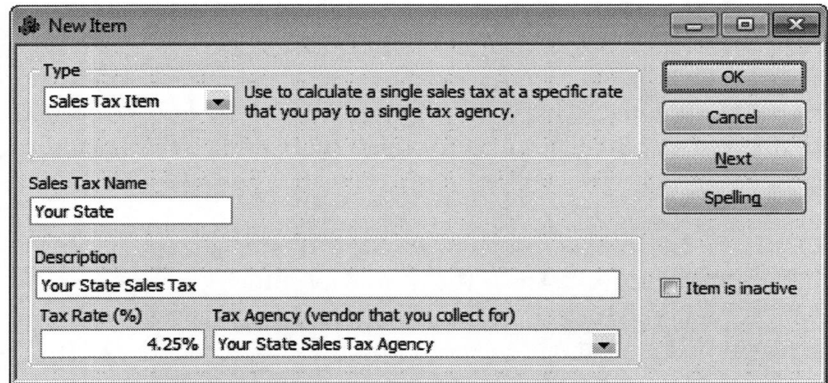

Figure 10-27 Sales Tax Item for Your State

2. With the Item list displayed, select the **Item** menu and select **New**.
3. Select **Sales Tax Group** from the *Type* drop-down list.
4. Using Figure 10-28 for reference, enter the *Group Name/Number* and *Description* and then select the county and state Sales Tax Items in the *Tax Item* field at the bottom of the window.

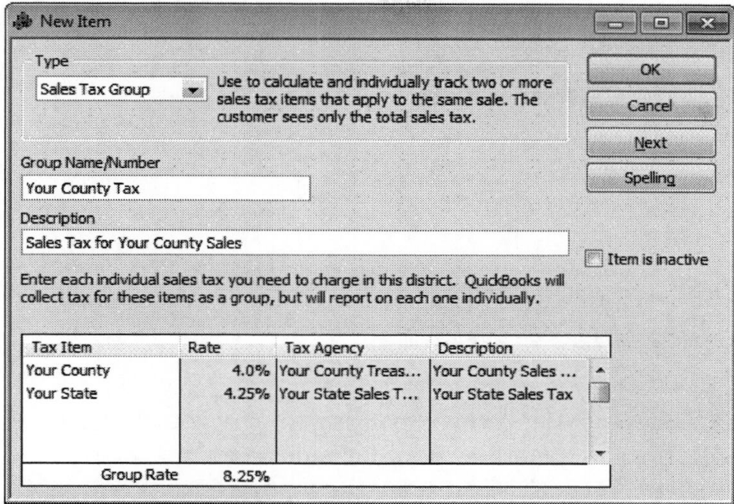

Figure 10-28 Sales Tax Group Item

5. Click **OK** to save the *Sales Tax Group* Item.

Notice in Figure 10-28 that the combined rate of these two Sales Tax Items is 8.25%. This rate will appear on Invoices and Sales Receipts when you use this *Sales Tax Group* Item. On each sale, QuickBooks will allocate 4.0% to the county item and 4.25% to the state item. When you pay sales tax, QuickBooks will create separate checks to the county agency and the state agency for the appropriate amounts.

Categorizing Revenue Based on Sales Tax Codes

QuickBooks provides a breakdown of revenue by Sales Tax Code on the **Sales Tax Revenue Summary** report (see Figure 10-29). To display the report, select **Vendors & Payables** from the *Reports* menu and then select **Sales Tax Revenue Summary**.

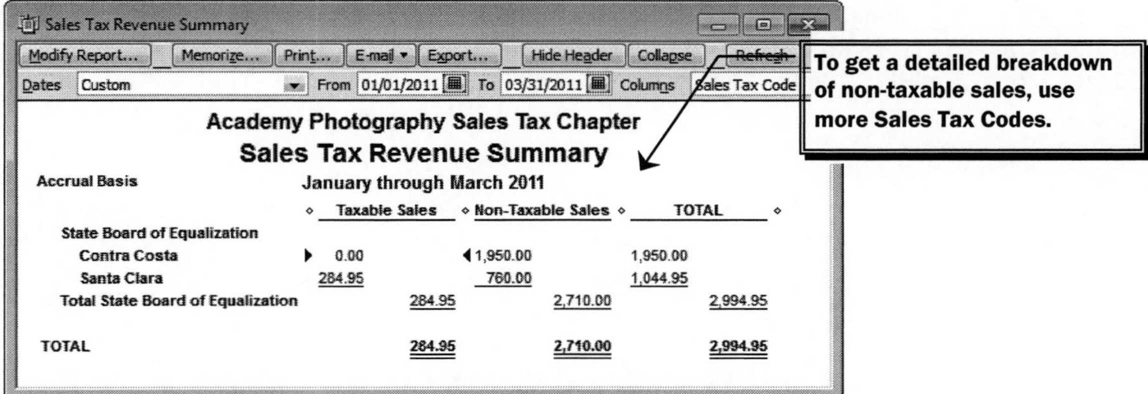

Figure 10-29 Sales Tax Revenue Summary with QuickBooks default Sales Tax Codes

If your sales tax agency requires a detailed breakdown of tax exempt sales, use Sales Tax Codes to produce the information you need. Use Sales Tax Codes to categorize your sales by the reason you charged, or did not charge, sales tax.

If you create separate Sales Tax Code for each type of non-taxable customer, like government agencies, not-for-profit organizations, or resellers, your Sales Tax Code list will look similar to the one in Figure 10-30. To display the list, select **Sales Tax Code List** from the *List* menu.

Figure 10-30 Sales Tax Code List

Then, when you use these Sales Tax Codes on sales forms according to why you charge or do not charge sales tax, QuickBooks will show a separate column for each Sales Tax Code in the *Sales Tax Revenue Summary* report (see Figure 10-31). To display the report, select **Vendors & Payables** from the *Reports* menu and then select **Sales Tax Revenue Summary**.

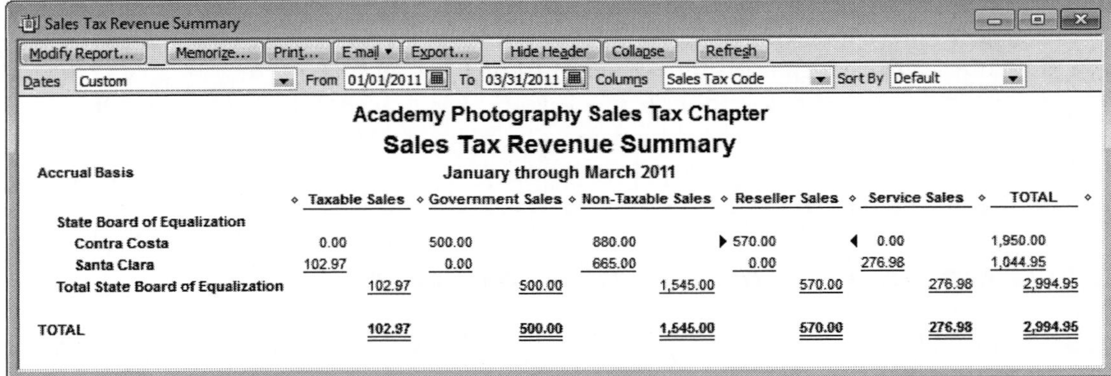

Academy Photography Sales Tax Chapter
Sales Tax Revenue Summary
Accrual Basis
January through March 2011

	Taxable Sales	Government Sales	Non-Taxable Sales	Reseller Sales	Service Sales	TOTAL
State Board of Equalization						
Contra Costa	0.00	500.00	880.00	570.00	0.00	1,950.00
Santa Clara	102.97	0.00	665.00	0.00	276.98	1,044.95
Total State Board of Equalization	102.97	500.00	1,545.00	570.00	276.98	2,994.95
TOTAL	102.97	500.00	1,545.00	570.00	276.98	2,994.95

Figure 10-31 Sales Tax Revenue Summary with additional Sales Tax Codes

To view each individual sale, double-click on any amount in the **Sales Tax Revenue Summary** report. This will display a **Transaction Detail** report showing each transaction affecting that Sales Tax Code.

Chapter Summary and Review

Sales tax tracking is automatic and runs smoothly if you set up and operate QuickBooks correctly.

If your QuickBooks file was not set up correctly, or if the Sales Tax feature has not been properly used in the past, you will probably have to diagnose and repair the problems before sales tax will operate correctly for the future. It is very important that your setup and data entry procedures are accurate in order to keep the sales tax feature working smoothly.

In this chapter, you learned that QuickBooks allows you to track sales tax that you collect from your customers. You should now be familiar with how to use QuickBooks to do all of the following:

- Activate Sales Tax and Set Sales Tax Preferences (page 407).
- Use Sales Tax Items on Sales Forms (page 411).
- Set up Sales Tax Items (page 411).
- Use Sales Tax Codes on Sales Forms (page 413).
- Set up Sales Tax Codes (page 414).
- Assign Sales Tax Codes to Items (page 414).
- Assign Sales Tax Codes to Customers (page 416).
- Use QuickBooks reports to assist in preparing your sales tax return (page 419).
- Adjust Sales Tax Payable (page 420).
- Pay Sales Tax (page 422).
- Set up and use Sales Tax Groups (page 424).
- Categorize Revenue by Sales Tax Code (page 425).

Comprehension Questions

Answers to these review questions are available with the supplemental material. See page xiii for details.

1. Explain how QuickBooks Sales Tax Codes help classify your non-taxable revenue.
2. Explain why you must use the *Pay Sales Tax* function instead of the *Write Checks* function to pay your sales tax.
3. Under what circumstances should you use *Sales Tax Groups*?

Multiple Choice

Select the best answer(s) for each of the following:

1. If you select **Upon receipt of payment (Cash Basis)** in the *When do you owe sales tax* section of the *Sales Tax Preferences*:
   a) The sales tax reports will show sales tax for *Sales Receipts* and paid *Invoices*.
   b) The sales tax reports will show that you owe sales tax for all taxable sales, including amounts from your open Invoices.
   c) The Sales Tax Payable account will not ever show a balance.
   d) QuickBooks will only calculate sales tax on Sales Receipts.

2. What is the purpose of the *Your most common sales tax item* field in the *Set Up Sales Tax Items* section of the *Sales Tax Preferences window*?
   a) It sets the default sales tax code on *Invoices*.
   b) It sets the default sales tax item on new *Sales Receipt* transactions.
   c) It sets the default sales tax item on new customer records.
   d) Both b and c.

3. You can select any of the following in the *When do you pay sales tax?* section of the Sales Tax Preferences, except:
   a) Monthly.
   b) Quarterly.
   c) Semi-annually.
   d) Annually.

4. Sales Tax Items credit which account?
   a) Sales Tax Income.
   b) Sales Tax Payable.
   c) Sales Tax Equity.
   d) Sales Tax Expense.

5. Sales Tax Items track the amount of sales tax due:
   a) By Tax Agency.
   b) By Customer.
   c) By Job.
   d) By Employee.

6. You should use Sales Tax Groups:
   a) Always.
   b) When Sales Tax exceeds $1000 in any month.
   c) When you pay sales tax to more than one agency.
   d) Never.

7. Sales Tax Codes serve which of the following purposes?
   a) They indicate whether a product or service is taxable or non-taxable.
   b) They categorize revenue based on the reason you charged or didn't charge sales tax.
   c) They define the percentage of tax to charge.
   d) Both a and b.

8. If you sell to resellers and do not charge them sales tax, you should:
   a) Set up a taxable sales tax code and assign that code to the resellers' customer records.
   b) Set up a non-taxable sales tax code and assign that code to the resellers' customer records.
   c) Set up a non-taxable sales tax group and assign that group to the resellers' customer records.
   d) Set up a taxable sales tax group and assign that group to the resellers' customer records.

9. You can override Sales Tax Codes:
   a) On Invoices.
   b) On Sales Receipts.
   c) In the *Pay Sales Tax* window.
   d) Both a and b.

10. To charge sales tax, you must do all of the following, except:
   a) Add your **Sales Tax Agency** to your Customer list.

b) Activate the *Sales Tax* function.
c) Set up one or more **Sales Tax Items.**
d) Set up one or more taxable **Sales Tax Codes.**

11. If you record a sale on which tax is charged, which of the following is false:
    a) The balance in Sales Tax Payable will increase.
    b) Sales Tax Payable will be credited for the amount of sales tax.
    c) Sales Tax Payable will be debited for the amount of sales tax.
    d) The amount due for the Tax Agency(ies) for the sales tax item(s) on the sale will increase in the *Pay Sales Tax* window.

12. To correctly pay your sales tax:
    a) Enter a Bill to the Sales Tax agency.
    b) Use the *Write Checks* window to write and print a check.
    c) Use the *Pay Sales Tax* function.
    d) Use the Sales Tax Adjustment function.

13. Which report shows a breakdown of revenues by Sales Tax Code?
    a) **Sales Tax Liability** report.
    b) **Sales Tax by Code** report.
    c) **Sales Tax Revenue Summary** report.
    d) All of the above.

14. To see a detailed listing of taxable sales transactions, do the following:
    a) Create a **Sales Tax Transaction Detail** report.
    b) Open the **Sales Tax Payable** register.
    c) Create a **Sales Tax Revenue Summary** report. Then double-click on the taxable sales total.
    d) None of the above.

15. To record a discount for Sales Tax:
    a) Select **Manage Sales Tax** in the *Vendor* section of the *Home* page.
    b) Select the **Vendors** menu, then select **Sales Tax**, and then select **Adjust Sales Tax Due.**
    c) From the **Sales Tax** menu, select **Adjust Sales Tax.**
    d) Either a or b.

Completion Statements

1. By selecting ___ ___ ______ ______ in the *When do you owe sales tax?* section of the Sales Tax Preferences, sales tax reports will show that you owe sales tax for all taxable sales, including unpaid amounts from your open Invoices.

2. In the *When do you pay sales tax?* section of the *Sales Tax Preferences* window, if you select ________, the default date in the *Show sales tax due through* field of the *Pay Sales Tax* window will be the end of last month.

3. When you record a taxable sale, QuickBooks increases (________) Sales Tax Payable for the amount of sales tax on the sale.

4. When you set up a customer record, the *Sales Tax Code* you enter in the customer record becomes the default in the *Customer* ____ ______ field on sales forms.

5. On the **Sales Tax Liability** report, the ____ __________ column shows how much tax you've collected on sales for the period.

Sales Tax Problem 1

APPLYING YOUR KNOWLEDGE

Restore the SalesTax-10Problem1.QBM file and store it on your hard disk according to your instructor's directions.

1. Create a new Sales Tax Item for San Francisco County.

Item Type	Sales Tax Item
Item Name	San Francisco
Description	San Francisco County Sales Tax
Tax Rate	9.5%
Tax Agency	State Board of Equalization

Table 10-1 Details of the San Francisco Sales Tax Item

2. Create an **Item Listing** report and modify it to display only the following columns: Item, Description, Type, Sales Tax Code, and Tax Agency. Print the **Item Listing** report.
3. Create a new Sales Tax Code for non-taxable resellers.

Sales Tax Code Name	RSR
Description	Reseller Sales
Taxable or Non-Taxable	Non-Taxable

Table 10-2 Details of the RSR Sales Tax Code

4. Print the **Sales Tax Code** list. To print the list, display the **Sales Tax Code List** and then select **Print List** from the *File* menu.
5. Edit the Berry, Ron customer record and set the default **Sales Tax Item** to San Francisco.
6. Edit the Perez, Jerry customer record and set the default **Sales Tax Code** to ***RSR***, the resale number to **abcd1234**, and the default **Sales Tax Item** to San Francisco.

7. Create a Sales Receipt for Ron Berry using the data in Table 10-3. Print the Sales Receipt.

Field	Data
Customer:Job	*Berry, Ron*
Class	*Walnut Creek*
Date	*04/05/2011*
Sale #	*2011-101*
Check No	*322*
Payment Method	*Check*
Item	*Camera SR32, Qty 2, $695.99*
Item	*Case, Qty 2, $79.99*
Sales Tax	San Francisco *(9.5%) – Auto Calculates*
Total Sale	*$1,699.40*
Customer Tax Code	*Tax*

Table 10-3 Details for the Ron Berry sale

8. Create a Sales Receipt for Jerry Perez using the data in Table 10-4. Print the Sales Receipt.

Field	Data
Customer:Job	*Perez, Jerry*
Class	*Walnut Creek*
Date	*04/05/2011*
Sale #	*2011-102*
Check No	*105*
Payment Method	*Check*
Item	*Camera SR32, Qty 2, $695.99*
Item	*Case, Qty 2, $79.99*
Sales Tax	San Francisco *(9.5%) – Auto Calculates*
Total Sale	*$1551.96*
Customer Tax Code	*RSR*

Table 10-4 Details for the Jerry Perez sale

9. Print the **Sales Tax Revenue Summary** report for April 2011.
10. Print the **Sales Tax Liability** report for April 2011.

Workplace Applications

Discussion Questions

These questions are designed to stimulate discussion about how you can apply QuickBooks to your own organization. They may help you think through some of the issues you'll encounter when using QuickBooks in your company.

1. Discuss how to set up Sales Tax in a company file so that the Sales Tax Revenue Summary report will show separate columns for Taxable Sales, Reseller Sales, Government (non-taxable) Sales, and Non-Profit (non-taxable) Sales.
2. Discuss how Sales Tax Items are different from Sales Tax Codes.
3. Discuss how many Sales Tax Codes you'll use in your company.

Chapter 11 Time and Billing

Objectives

After completing this chapter, you should know:

- What makes an expense Billable, Not Billable, or Billed (page 433).
- How to add reimbursable Expenses, Items, Mileage, and Time to Invoices (page 435).
- How to use two-sided Items to track reimbursable expenses (page 441).
- How to use two-sided Items to track subcontracted services (page 448).
- Activate Time Tracking (page 451).
- Pass billable time onto an Invoice (page 454).
- Create reports to analyze timesheet data (page 458).
- How to use the Vehicle Mileage Tracker in QuickBooks (page 461).
- How to handle Multiple Pass-Throughs on a single Invoice (page 468).

Restore this File

This chapter uses TimeBilling-10.QBW. To open this file, restore the TimeBilling-10.QBM file to your hard disk. See page 10 for instructions on restoring files.

The following features, discussed in this chapter are available to users of QuickBooks Pro or higher editions only:

- Time Tracking
- Two-sided Items for advanced Item tracking and Pass-Throughs
- Mileage Tracking
- Reports about Time Tracking, Item Profitability, or Mileage

Reimbursable (Billable) Expenses

QuickBooks allows you to pass expenses through to customers for reimbursement.

To track a reimbursable cost, you'll first need to record the expense. Enter a transaction such as a *Bill*, *Check*, or *Credit Card Charge* to record the original expense, and then assign the customer or job to which the expense applies.

On expense transactions, the *Billable?* option indicates that the expense will be passed through to the customer or job (see Figure 11-1). In other words, this option indicates the expense is can be billed to the customer when a sales form is created. This option only appears after you enter a name into the Customer:Job field in the expense (or item) tab area of the expense transaction. Also, the *Billable?* option only appears if you code the transaction to one of the following account types:

- Other Current Asset

- Expense
- Other Expense

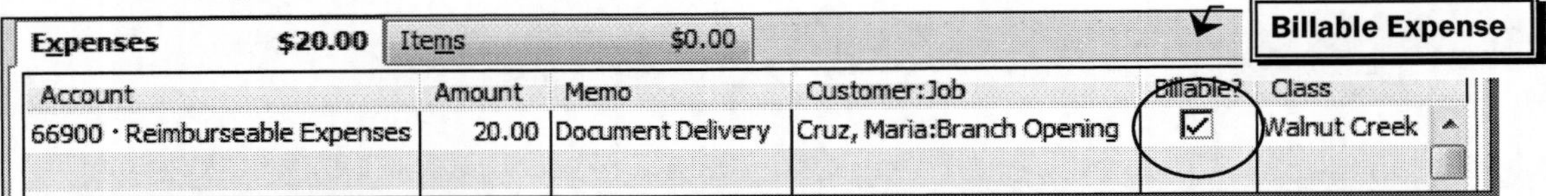

Figure 11-1 Billable Expense item

> **Note:**
> The *Billable?* option will NOT appear if you code the expense transaction to an Income or Cost of Goods Sold type account.
> **Tip:**
> If you need to use the pass-through process for Cost of Goods sold transactions, you can create an item that points to a Cost of Goods Sold account and then use that item on the original transaction by clicking on the **Items** tab. This will allow you to pass the expense through to invoices. See *Using Two-Sided Items* on page 441 for an example of using items to track pass-throughs.

Sometimes you want to assign expenses to jobs so you can track all of the related costs to the job, but you do not intend to pass them through for reimbursement. In this case, you can uncheck the *Billable?* option so that the line item is "Non Billable."

COMPUTER PRACTICE

For simplicity, in this example, we'll use an expense account called *Reimbursable Expenses* to hold the expenses until they are reimbursed. However, you may want to use an *Other Current Asset* type account to hold all of your reimbursable expenses. If you're unsure about which account type to use for your reimbursable expenses, consult with your accountant.

Step 1. Select the **Write Checks** icon on the *Banking* section of the *Home* page.

Step 2. From the *Write Checks* window, enter the *Check* shown in Figure 11-2.

When you select the Branch Opening Job for Maria Cruz in the *Customer:Job* column of the *Expenses* tab, the Billable? Option appears with the checkmark already selected.

Step 3. Click **Save & Close** to record.

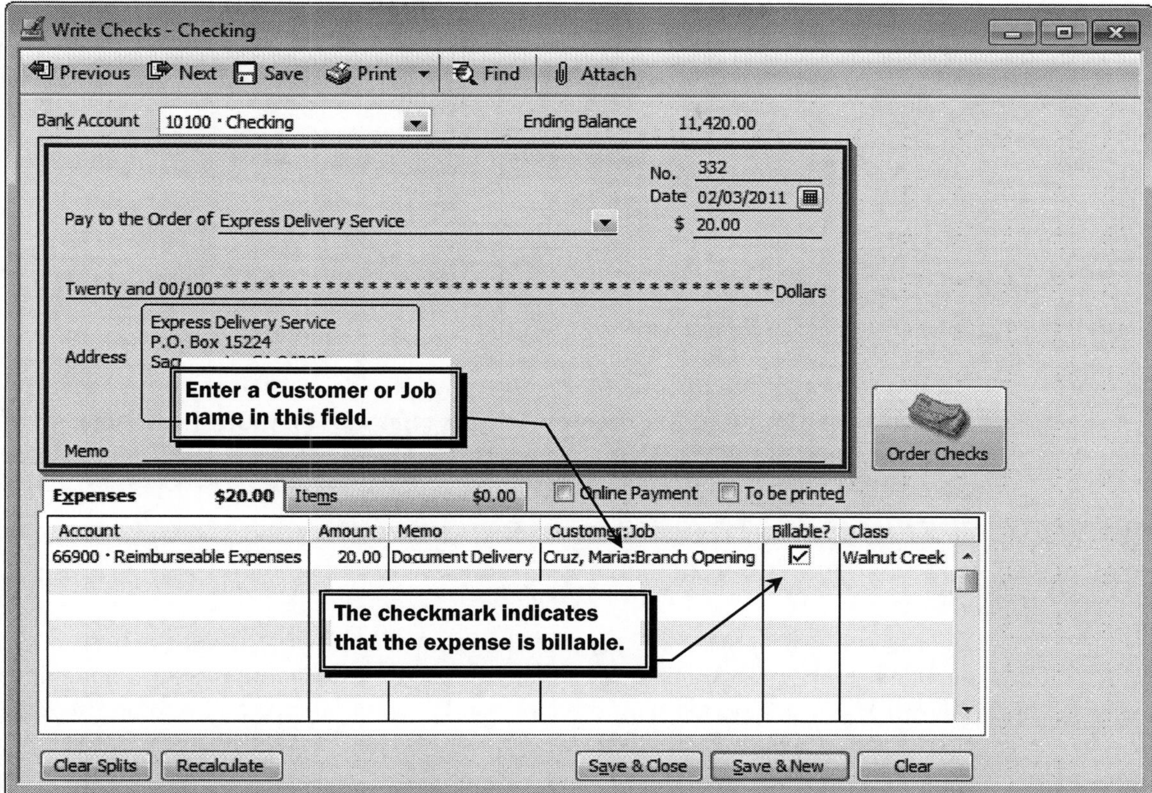

Figure 11-2 Record a reimbursable expense

The next time you create an invoice for the customer, you can pass the cost through to the invoice by following the next steps.

Step 4. Select the **Invoices** icon on the *Customer* section of the ***Home* page**.

Step 5. Enter **Cruz, Maria: Branch Opening** for the *Customer:Job* field.

Once the name is entered, the message in Figure 11-3 appears to prompt you to select the expenses that you designated as billable.

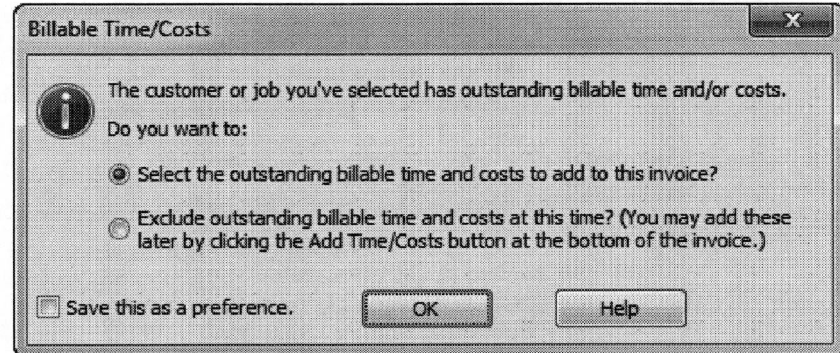

Figure 11-3 Billable Time/Costs option window

Step 6. Click **OK**.

Step 7. The *Choose Billable Time and Costs* window opens for Maria Cruz's Branch Opening Job (see Figure 11-4).

Figure 11-4 Top section of the Choose Billable Time and Costs screen

Step 8. The top section of the *Choose Billable Time and Costs* screen shows four tabs where you can view pass-through expenses. The *Expenses* tab will show the billable expenses (such as the check you just wrote) that were recorded using the *Expenses* tab on checks, bills, and credit card charges.

Step 9. Click the **Expenses** tab (see Figure 11-5).

Step 10. Verify that ***20%*** is entered in the *Markup Amount or %* field.

The Markup will increase the amount due by the customer to cover the costs of processing this expense. You can either enter a static dollar amount or a percentage that will change depending on the amount. Default Markup can be set in the Time & Expense Company Preference.

Step 11. Enter ***Expense Markup*** in the *Markup Account* field.

Step 12. In the middle section of the *Expenses* tab (see Figure 11-5), click a checkmark in the far left column on the line for **Express Delivery Service** to pass the expense, with the 20% markup, to Maria Cruz's invoice.

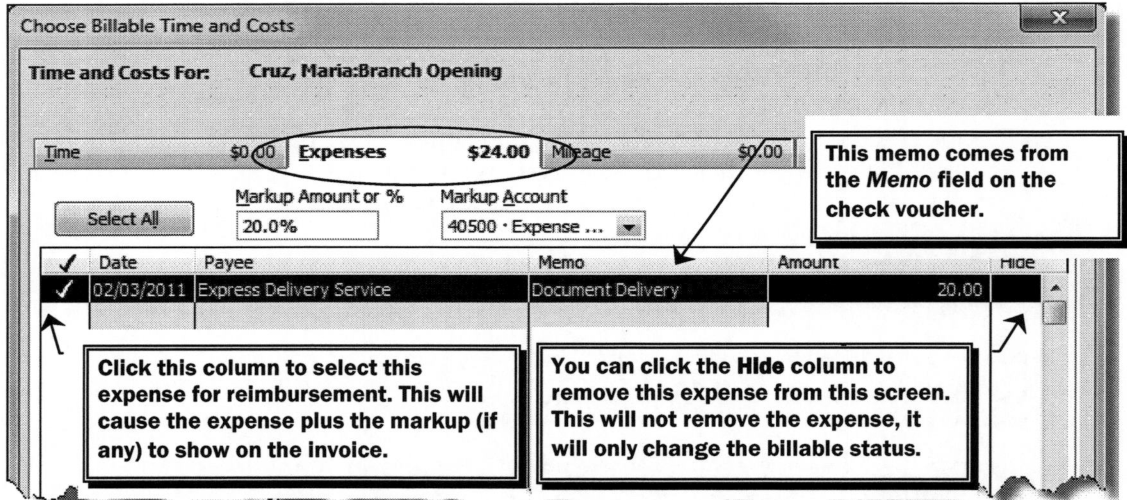

Figure 11-5 Middle section of the Choose Billable Time and Costs screen

Step 13. Select the **Print selected time and costs as one invoice item** option (see Figure 11-6). Then click **OK**.

When you select this option, QuickBooks prints all reimbursable expenses on a single line in the body of the invoice rather than listing each expense separately. You'll always see the details of the reimbursable expenses, including the markup, on the screen even if you chose **Print selected costs as one invoice item**.

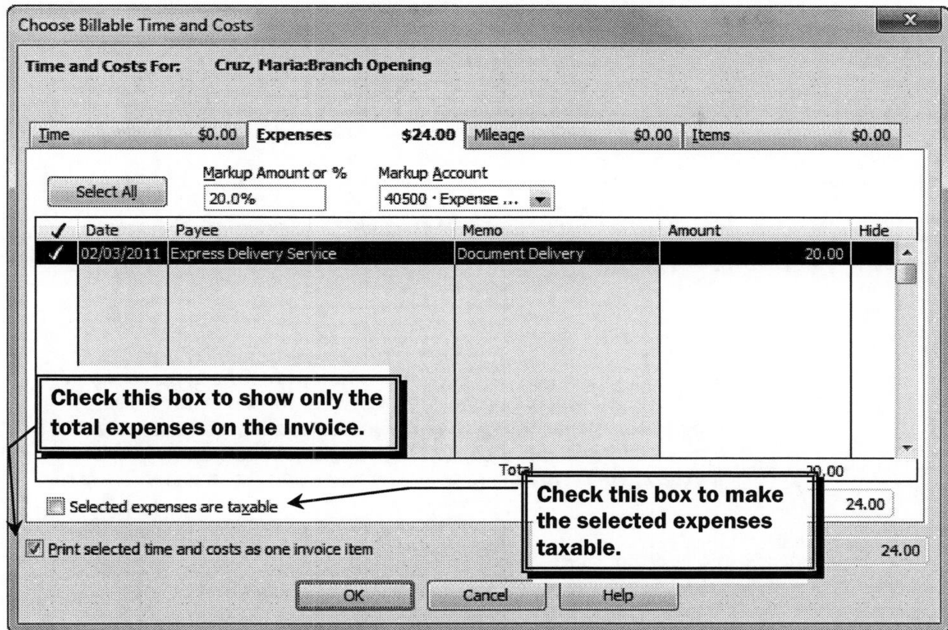

Figure 11-6 The Expenses tab of the Choose Billable Time and Costs screen

Step 14. Once you are returned to the invoice, enter the **Template**, **Class**, **Date**, and **Invoice #** as shown in Figure 11-7. The *Invoice* now includes the reimbursable expense.

Step 15. To see what the *Invoice* will look like when you print it, click **Print,** and then click **Preview** (see Figure 11-8).

Step 16. When you are finished reviewing, click **Close** in the *Print Preview* window, and click **Save & Close** to record the *Invoice.*

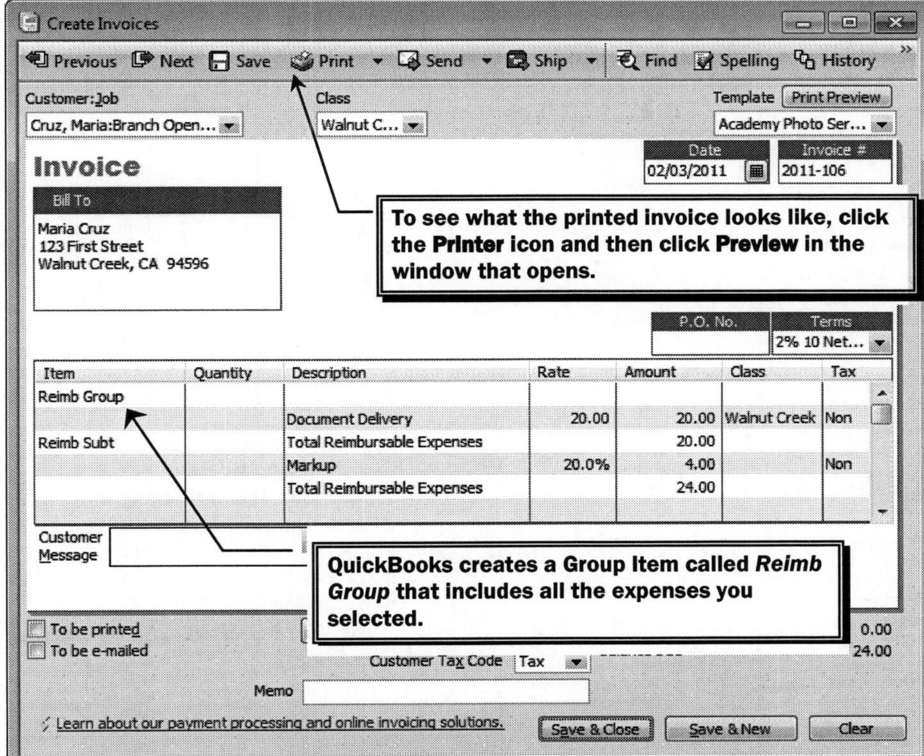

Figure 11-7 Reimbursable expenses shown on an Invoice

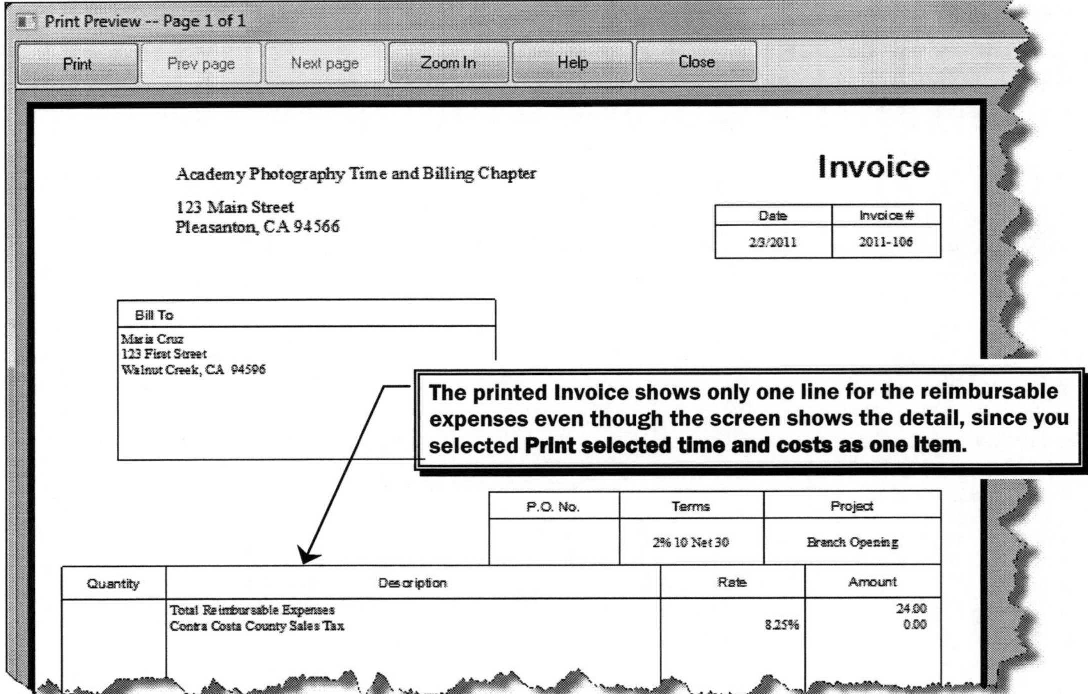

Figure 11-8 Print Preview of invoiced billable expenses

The completed example of pass-through expenses shows on your Profit & Loss statement with the date range set for February 3rd, 2011 to February 3rd, 2011 so as to only include the transaction entered earlier in this chapter and as shown in Figure 11-9.

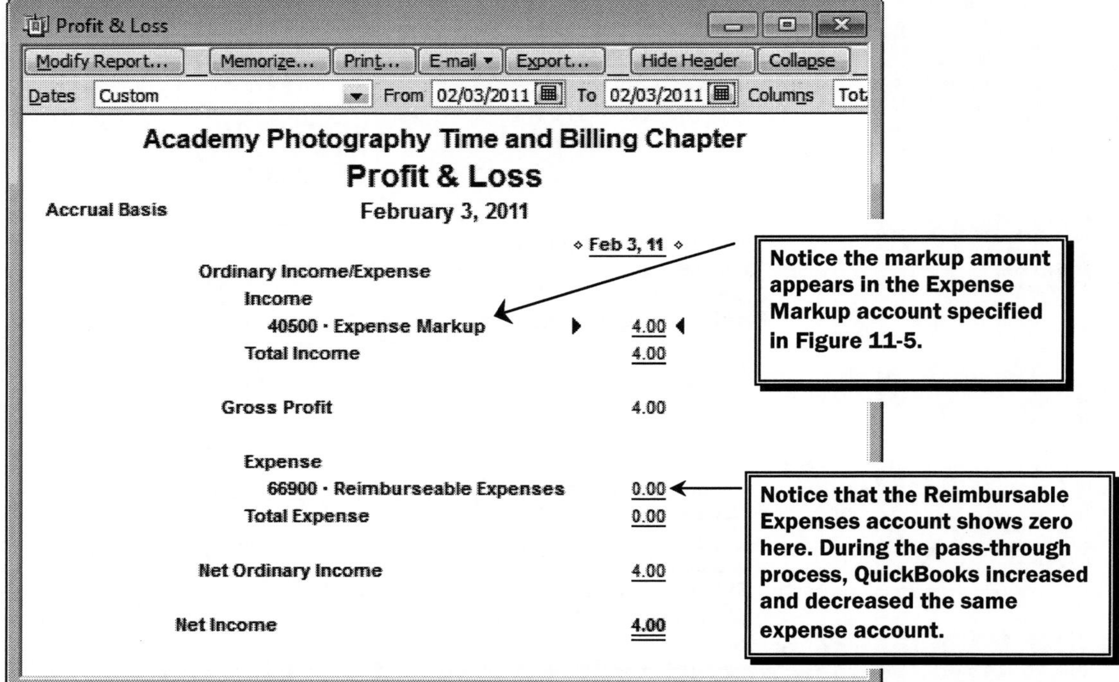

Figure 11-9 Reimbursable Expenses on the Profit & Loss report

> **The Accounting Behind the Scenes:**
> The *Reimbursable Expenses* account has a zero balance because QuickBooks increased (debited) the balance when you recorded the *Check* shown in Figure 11-2 and then decreased (credited) the account when you recorded the *Invoice* shown in Figure 11-7.

Sometimes it is more appropriate to track reimbursable expenses in one account and the reimbursements in another account. For example, you could record all reimbursable expenses in the expense account called "Reimbursable Expenses," and you could track the reimbursements in an income account called "Expenses Reimbursed." For QuickBooks to handle reimbursements in this way, you will need to make changes to your *Time & Expense Company Preferences*.

> **Note:**
> Ask your accountant if you should treat reimbursements as income before making these changes to your company's QuickBooks file.

COMPUTER PRACTICE

Step 1. Select the ***Edit*** menu and choose **Preferences.**

Step 2. Select **Time & Expense** on the left icon bar.

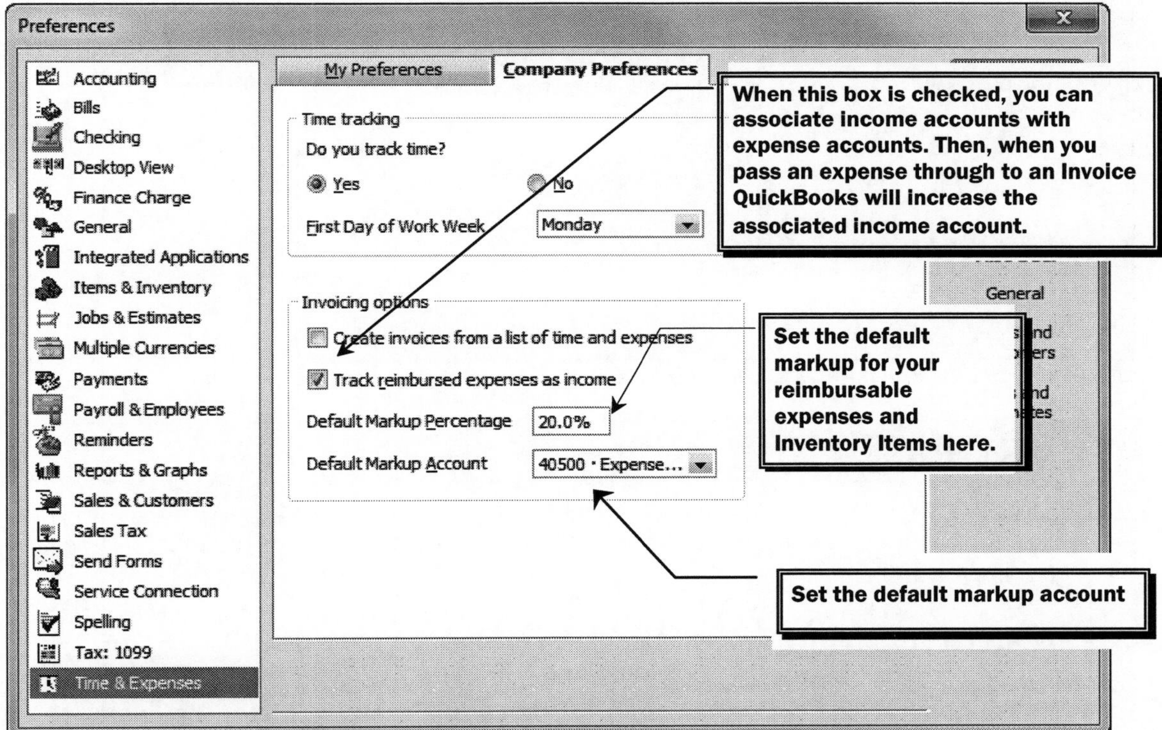

Figure 11-10 Time & Expense Company Preferences

Step 3. Select the **Company Preferences** tab.

Step 4. Notice that the box next to **Track reimbursed expenses as income** is checked.

Step 5. Notice the **20%** in the *Default Markup Percentage* field is preselected.

This field sets the default markup percentage for pass-through expenses.

Step 6. Notice that Expense Markup is selected as the Default Markup Account

Step 7. Click **OK** to close the window.

Now you need to associate each reimbursable expense account with an appropriate income account. You should note that for each reimbursable expense account you create, you will need to create a separate income account. You cannot have mutliple reimbursable expense accounts that tie to only one income account.

Step 1. Display the *Chart of Accounts* list and select the **Reimbursable Expenses** account (See Figure 11-11).

Step 2. Select the *Edit* menu and then select **Edit Account**.

Step 3. Click **Track reimbursed expenses in Income Acct.** and then select the **Expenses Reimbursed** income account from the *Income Account* field drop-down menu.

Step 4. Click **Save & Close** to save your changes.Close the Chart of Accounts.

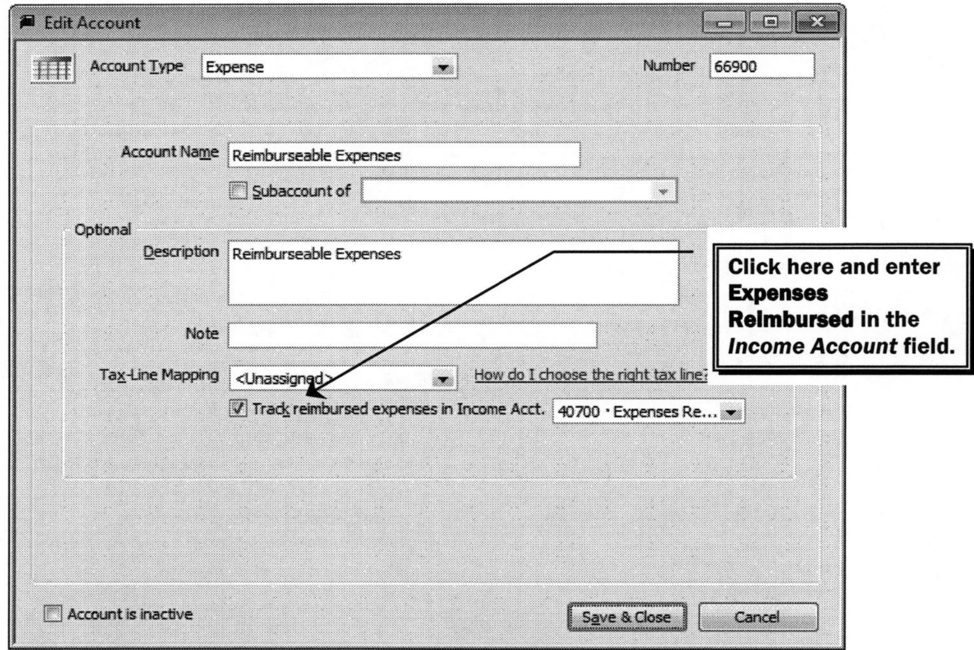

Figure 11-11 Edit the Reimbursable Expense account.

The Accounting Behind the Scenes:
Now when you post an expense to *Reimbursable Expenses* and pass the expense through on an invoice, QuickBooks will increase the *Expenses Reimbursed* income account. From our previous example, the results would be as seen in Figure 11-12.

Important accounting consideration:
If you used an existing expense account in a closed accounting period (a period for which you have filed tax returns or prepared financial statements) do not select the **Track Reimbursed Expenses in Income Acct.** option on that account. Doing so will cause discrepancies between your QuickBooks reports and the company's tax returns and/or financial statements. Instead, create a new account for tracking reimbursable expenses and make the change to that account.

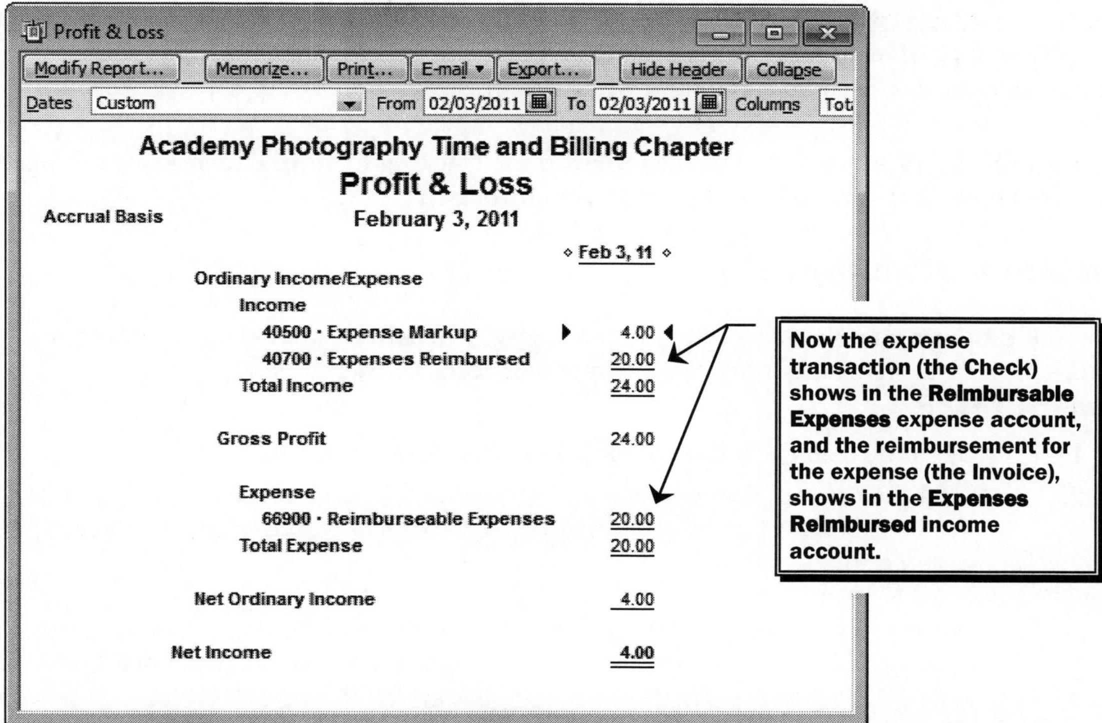

Figure 11-12 Profit & Loss report with separate income and expenses for reimbursable expenses

Using Two-Sided Items

QuickBooks Pro and above allows you to use the same item on expense forms (e.g. checks and bills) and sales forms (e.g. invoices and sales receipts). When you use items to track both expenses and revenue, you can generate reports showing the profitability of each item.

> **Key Term: Two Sided Item** – An item used on both types of forms (expenses and sales) is commonly called a "Two-Sided Item" because the *Item setup* screen includes purchase information on the left side (Expense Account field) and sales information on the right (Income Account field).

Possible uses of two-sided items include:

Reimbursable Expenses: If you have numerous reimbursable expenses and you need detailed reports about those expenses (such as a report showing which expenses have or have not been reimbursed), or if you want the ability to summarize billable costs on invoices by category. To summarize by category, you can create two-sided Other Charge Items to designate categories of expenses (e.g. transportation, clerical, or material expenses). Use these items on both expense transactions and sales forms as on described in the *Reimbursable (Billable) Expenses* section beginning on page 433.

Custom Ordered Parts: If you sell custom-ordered parts, you might want to create two-sided Non-Inventory Part Items to track both the purchase and the sale of each part. Doing so will show you which of the sales were profitable, and by how much.

Subcontracted Labor: If you hire subcontractors, you probably want to use two-sided Service Items to track both the expense and the revenue for the work they perform. Then, you can find out which subcontracted services are profitable, and by how much.

Cost of Goods Sold postings: As discussed earlier, if you use the Expenses tab on expense transactions (bills, checks, credit card charges), you can only record a pass-through expense when you code the transaction to an *Other Current Asset, Expense,* or *Other Expense* account type. If *Cost of Goods Sold* (or another account type) is the appropriate choice for your reimbursements, create a two-sided item with Cost of Goods Sold in the Expense Account field.

Our first example of the use of two-sided items is for Tracking Custom Orders. This example also shows how Cost of Goods Sold postings can be passed-through.

Tracking Custom Orders

If you sell products that you don't hold in inventory, you can use QuickBooks Pro's "two-sided items" to automatically track the revenue and costs for each item.

COMPUTER PRACTICE

Step 1. Open the *Item List* and select **New Item** from the *Item* menu.

Step 2. Enter the **Custom Camera** item as displayed in Figure 11-13. Make sure you select the checkbox next to *This item is used in assemblies or is purchased for a specific customer:job.*

When you select this option, QuickBooks provides the following additional fields: *Description on Purchase Transactions, Cost, Expense Account,* and *Preferred Vendor.*

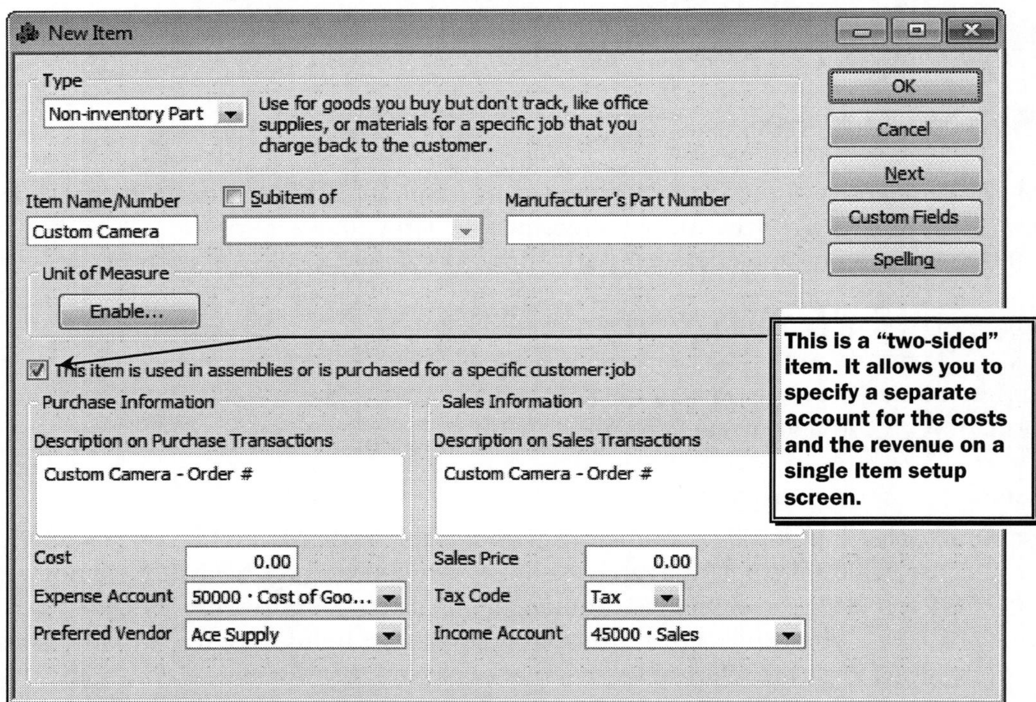

Figure 11-13 A "two-sided" Non-inventory Part Item

> **The Accounting Behind the Scenes:**
> When you use a two-sided item on expense forms, QuickBooks increases (debits) the Expense account you enter in the *Expense Account* field. When you use a two-sided item on sales forms QuickBooks increases (credits) the Income account you enter in the *Income Account* field.

Step 3. Notice that the *Cost* and *Sales Price* for this item are both **0.00**.

Customer Ordered parts will have a different cost and sales price every time you sell them. If you enter cost and sales price amounts in the original item, you'll need to override the numbers for each individual purchase or sale. For this reason, it's best to just leave them zero.

Step 4. Click **OK** to close this window.

> **Tip:**
> Once you set up the Custom Camera Item, you can use the item for all special orders of cameras, regardless of the make or model. You can override the description of the item each time you use it on a transaction.

After creating the two-sided *Non-Inventory Part*, you are now ready to use the item on expense forms.

Step 1. Select the **Purchase Orders** icon on the *Vendors* section of the *Home* page.

Step 2. Prepare a Purchase Order as shown in Figure 11-14.

Notice that QuickBooks uses the default description you entered when setting up the item. Add the number in the *P.O. NO.* field to the end of this description. Choose **No** when asked whether you want to update the *Custom Camera* item with a new cost.

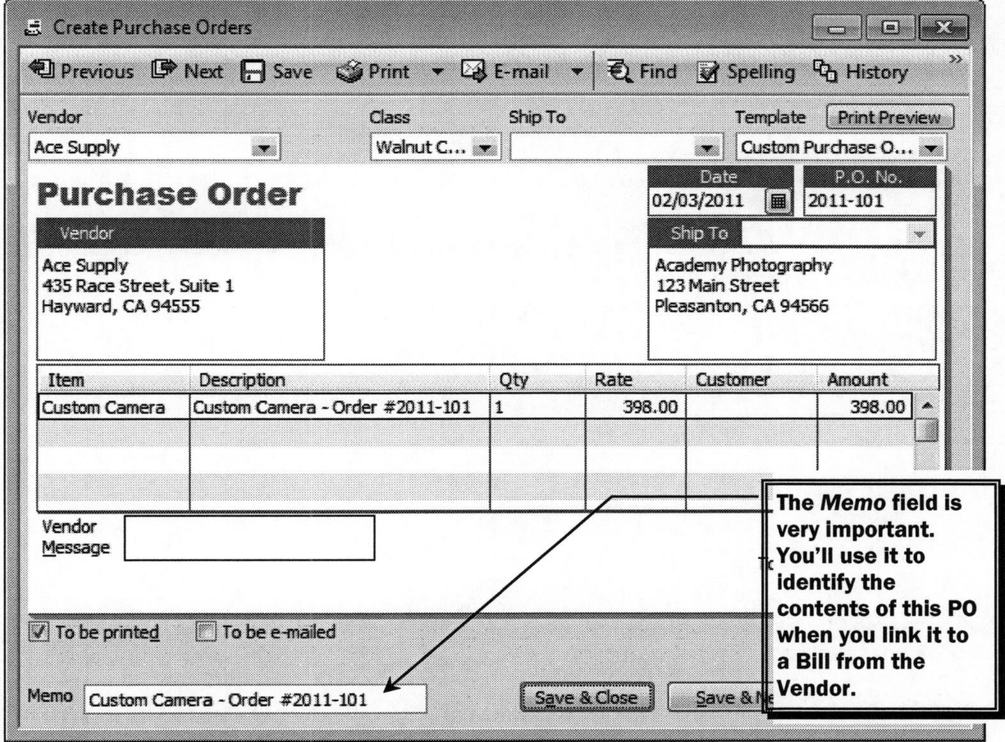

Figure 11-14 A purchase order for a two-sided Non-inventory Part

Tip:
Make sure you enter the description in the *Memo* field so that you'll be able to identify the Purchase Order in the list of *Open Purchase Orders* when you receive the Bill.

Tip:
Use the Windows copy and paste commands to duplicate the description to the Memo field at the bottom of the *Purchase Order* and other forms. Highlight the completed description on the PO form and press Ctrl+C. Then click in the *Memo* field and press Ctrl+V.

Step 3. Click **Save & Close** to record the *Purchase Order.*

When you receive a bill from the vendor, record it as follows:

Step 1. Chose the **Enter Bills** icon on the **Vendor** section of the *Home* page.

Step 2. On the Bill, enter **Ace Supply** in the *Vendor* field. Then press **Tab.**

Step 3. Because there are open **Purchase Orders** for Ace Supply, QuickBooks displays the message shown in Figure 11-15. Click **Yes.**

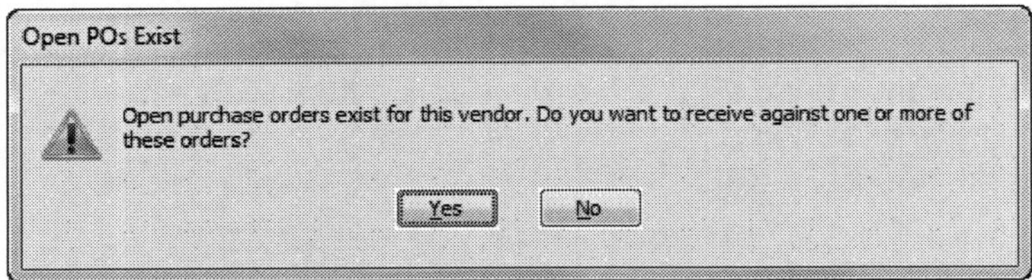

Figure 11-15 Open POs exist message

Step 4. Select PO #2011-101 by placing a checkmark in the column to the left of the date and click **OK.**
If you had several open Purchase Orders for this Vendor, each would appear in the list shown in Figure 11-16.

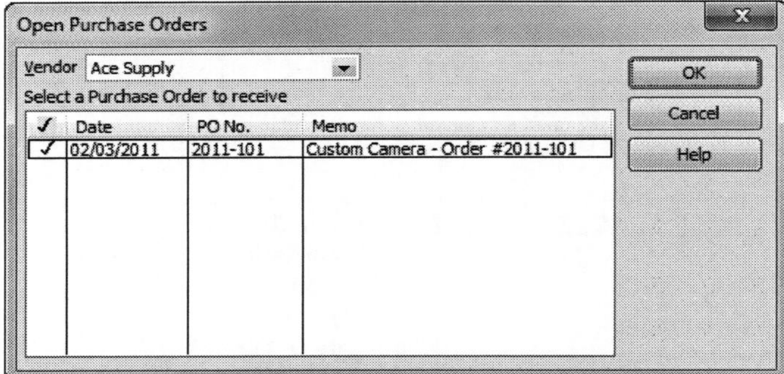

Figure 11-16 Select on open Purchase Order from the list

Step 5. QuickBooks automatically fills out the bill with the data from your PO as shown in Figure 11-17.
Continue filling out the rest of the fields on the Bill.

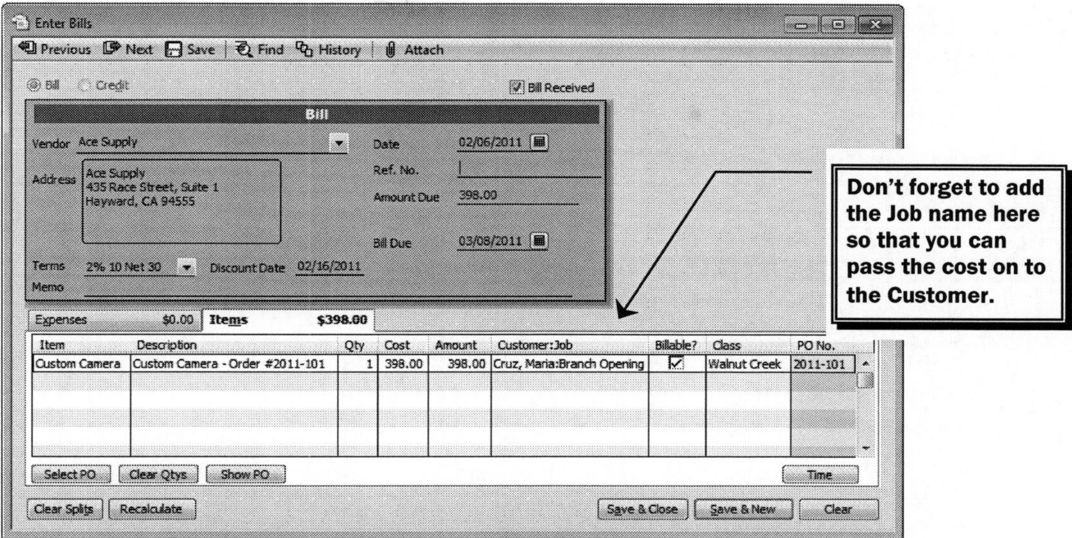

Figure 11-17 QuickBooks automatically fills in the details of the Bill.

Step 6. Verify that ***Cruz, Maria:Branch Opening Job*** is in the *Customer:Job* column of the *Items* tab.

Step 7. Click **Save & Close** to record the *Bill.*

> **The Accounting Behind the Scenes**
> This bill increases (credits) Accounts Payable and increases (debits) Cost of Goods Sold. Cost of Goods Sold is the account in the *Expense Account* field of the Custom Camera Item.

When you create an invoice for this job, you can pass the cost of the Custom Camera Item through to the customer's invoice and mark it up.

Step 1. Select the **Invoices** icon on the *Customer* section of the *Home* page.

Step 2. Enter **Cruz, Maria:Branch Opening** for the *Customer:Job* field.

Step 3. Click **OK** on the *Billable Time/Costs* reminder message.

Step 4. The *Choose Billable Time and Costs* screen opens for Maria Cruz's Branch Opening Job. Choose the **Item** tab (see Figure 11-18).

Step 5. Click the far left column on the first line to select the **Custom Camera** Item (see Figure 11-18). Then click **OK**.

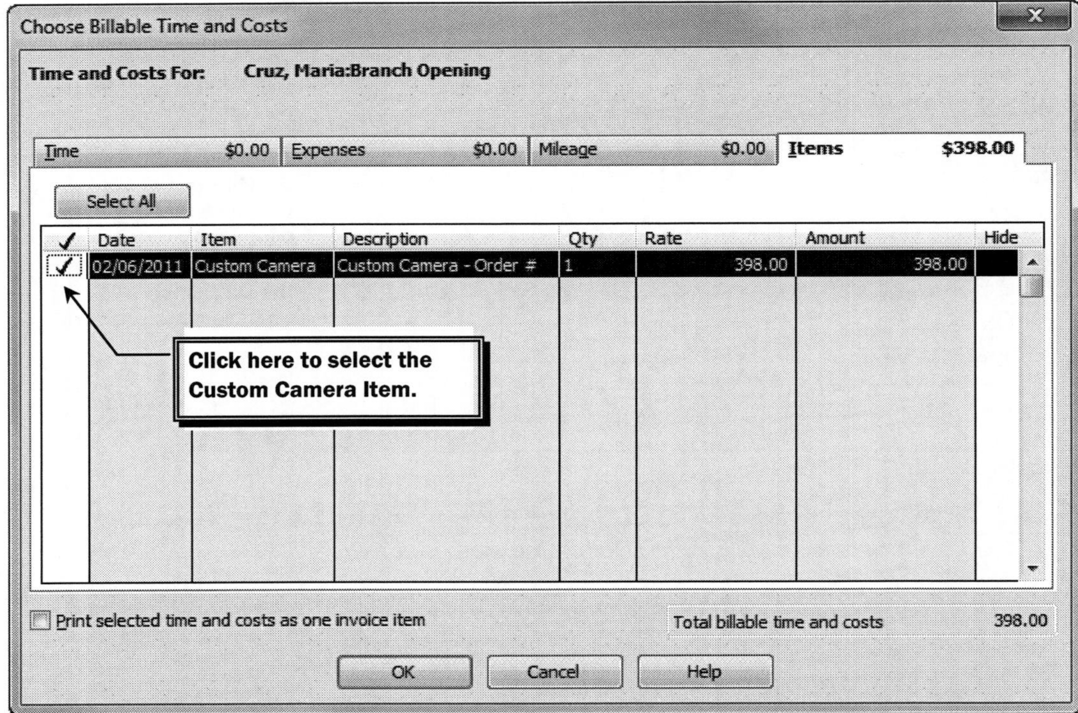

Figure 11-18 Select the Custom Camera Item.

Step 6. When you click **OK**, QuickBooks adds the Custom Camera Item to the customer's invoice. Enter the invoice information as seen in Figure 11-19.

Step 7. Complete the description so it reads **Custom Camera Order #** ***2011-101*** and copy this information to the *Memo* field.

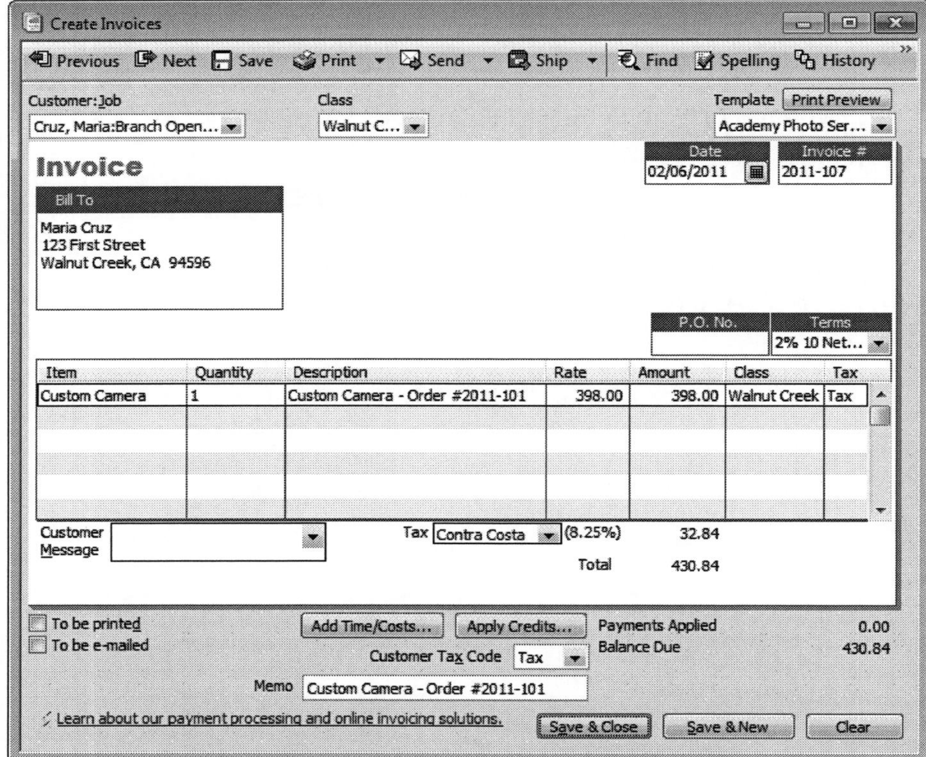

Figure 11-19 The Custom Camera Item now shows in the Customer's Invoice.

Since the Custom Camera Item shown in Figure 11-13 doesn't include an amount in the *Sales Price* field, the item passes through at the cost amount recorded on the bill shown in Figure 11-17, in this case $398.00.

To record the markup you'll need to manually adjust the price that shows on the invoice. You can use the *QuickMath* function that allows you to do calculations without using your calculator. In this example, the Custom Camera cost was $398. Using *QuickMath*, we'll mark this item up by 20%.

Step 8. Place the cursor in the *Rate* column on the *Invoice* (anywhere in this field).

Step 9. Press the * (asterisk) key on the keyboard to access the *QuickMath* function. Since your cursor was in the rate field when you pressed the asterisk, QuickBooks copies the first number ($398) onto the adding machine tape (see Figure 11-20).

Step 10. Enter ***1.2*** (multiply by 120%) and press **Tab** to insert the adjusted (calculated) amount into the *Rate* column.

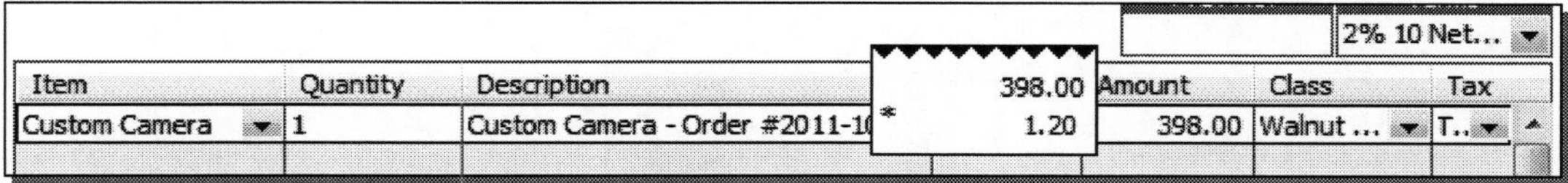

Figure 11-20 The QuickMath adding machine tape

> **Note:**
> The asterisk (*) opens the QuickMath feature because QuickBooks recognizes the asterisk as a multiplication key. You can also access QuickMath by typing a plus (+), minus (-), or back slash (/) to add, subtract or divide by any number, respectively.

Step 11. The invoice now includes the adjusted amount of **$477.60** (see Figure 11-21).

Step 12. Click **Save & Close** to save the invoice.

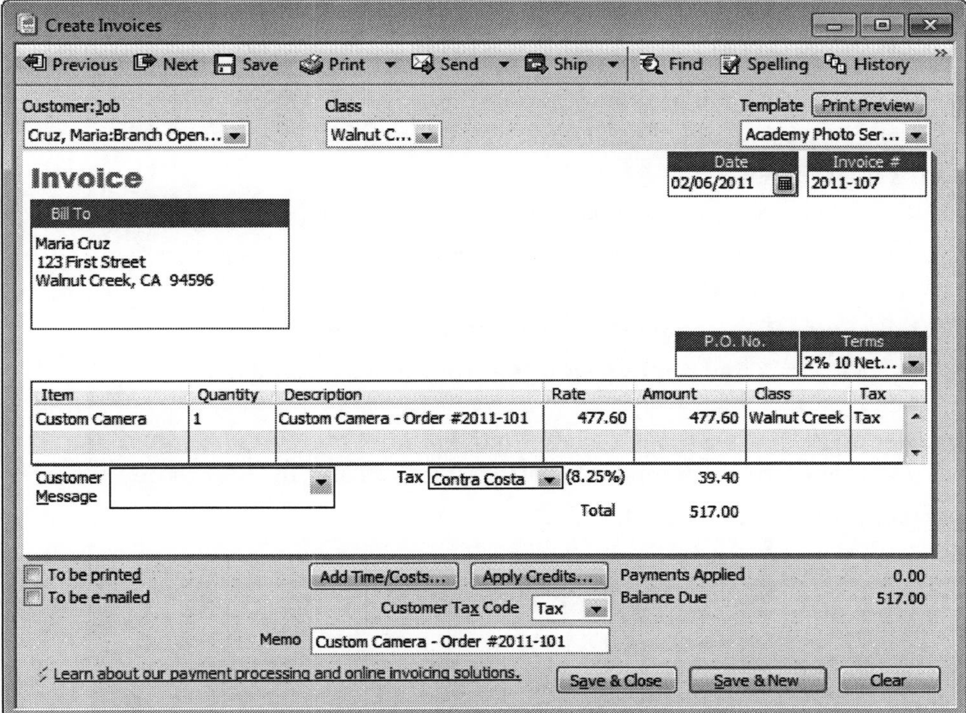

Figure 11-21 Final Invoice including the markup on the Custom Camera Item

Using Service Items to Track Subcontracted Labor

If you hire subcontractors, you may want to create a two-sided *Service Item* for each subcontracted service. This will allow you to pass subcontractor costs through to invoices and it will allow you to create reports showing the profitability of your subcontracted services.

COMPUTER PRACTICE

In this example, we'll use a two-sided service item for Photographer services that are subcontracted to East Bay Photographers. The item is already set up.

Step 1. Open the *Item List* and double-click the **Photographer** Item. This will open the *Edit Item* screen for this item (see Figure 11-22).

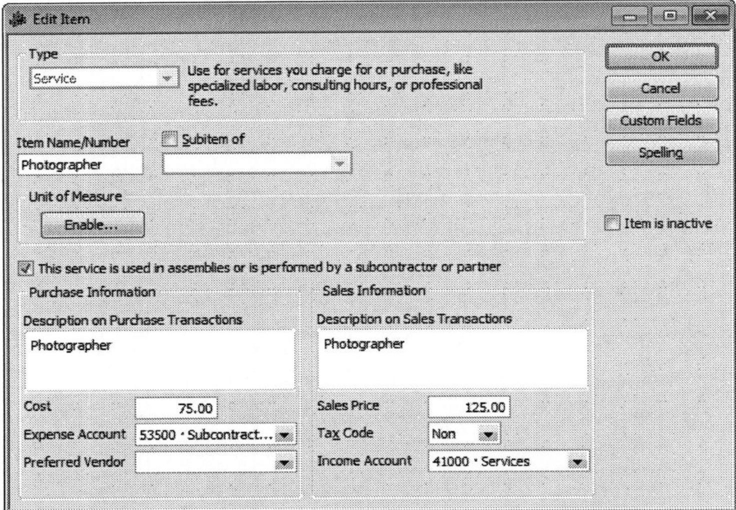

Figure 11-22 A "two-sided" Service Item for tracking subcontracted labor

Step 2. Notice that the box entitled **This service is used in assemblies or is performed by a subcontractor or partner** is selected.

Just as in the last example, when you click this box, QuickBooks opens the other side of the item revealing additional fields for entering the *purchase description, cost, expense account,* and *preferred vendor.*

Step 3. Click **OK** to close the *Photographer* item.

When you receive a bill from, write a check or enter credit charges for a subcontractor, use the Photographer item to record the expense.

Step 4. Select the **Enter Bills** icon on the *Vendors* section of the *Home* page.

Step 5. Enter a Bill for **East Bay Photographers** as shown in Figure 11-23.

The checkmark in the *Billable?* column to the right of the *Customer:Job* column indicates that each line of the bill is billable (i.e., available for pass-through).

Step 6. Click **Save & Close** to record the Bill.

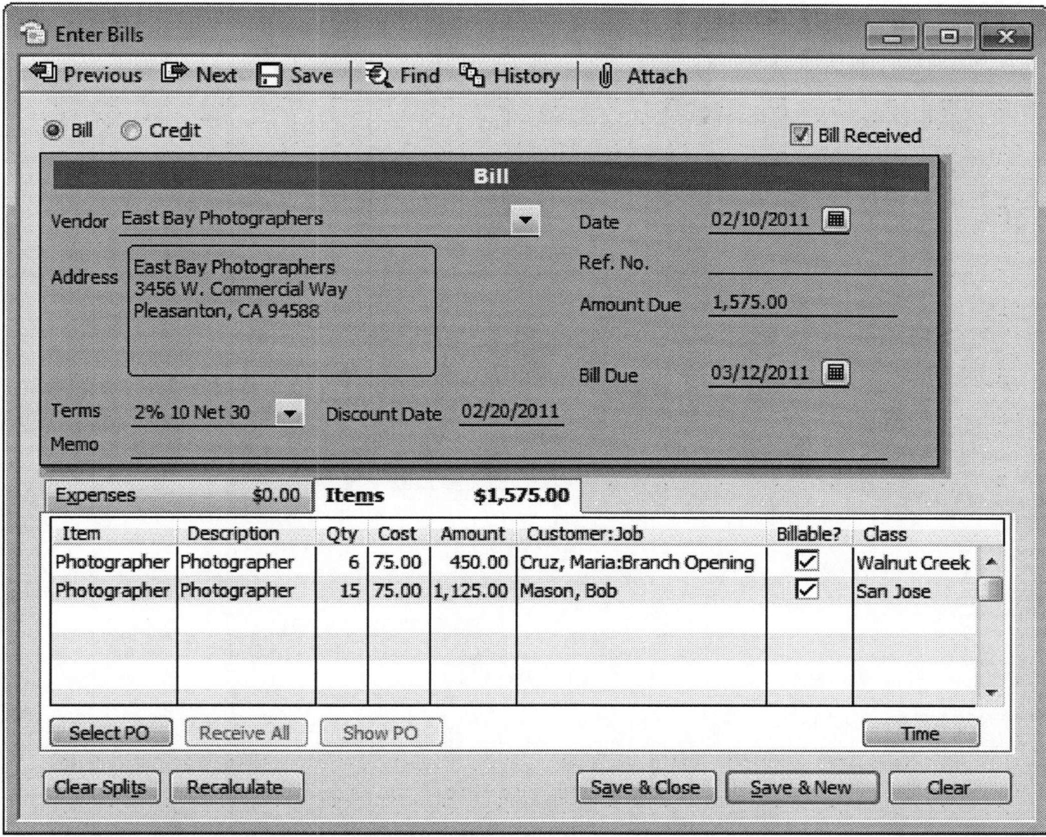

Figure 11-23 Enter a Bill for subcontracted services.

The next time you create an invoice for Bob Mason or Maria Cruz's Branch Opening Job, the Photographer Service Item will show on the *Choose Billable Time and Costs* screen.

Step 1. Select the **Invoices** icon on the *Customer* section of the *Home* page.

Step 2. Enter **Cruz, Maria:Branch Opening** for the *Customer:Job* field.

Step 3. Click **OK** on the *Billable Time/Costs* reminder message. The *Choose Billable Time and Costs* screen opens.

Step 4. Click the *Items* tab. Figure 11-24 shows the *Photographer Service Item* you recorded on the bill shown in Figure 11-23. Notice that the *Rate* column shows $125.00/hour, not the purchase price of $75.00/hour. The $125.00 amount comes from the *Sales Price* field on the Item setup screen (see Figure 11-22).

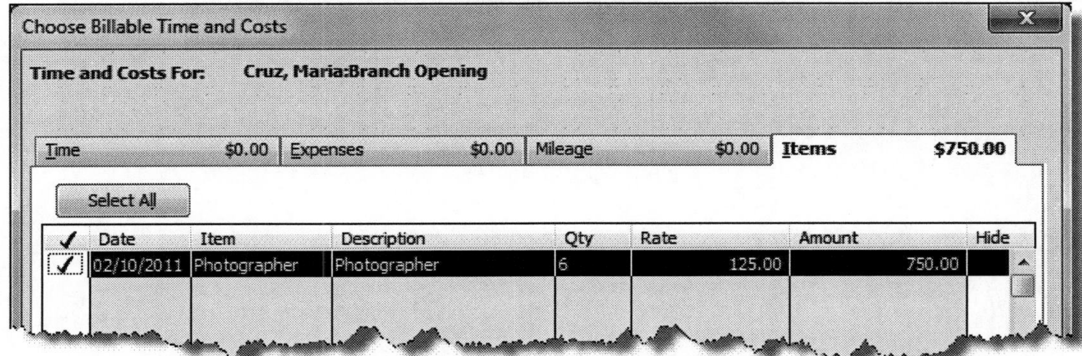

Figure 11-24 The Billable Time and Costs screen shows the two-sided Service Item.

Step 5. Click the far left column on the first line to select the *Photographer* Item (see Figure 11-24). Then click **OK**.

QuickBooks adds the Photographer Item in the body of the *Invoice* as shown in Figure 11-25.

Step 6. Once you are returned to the invoice, enter the **Template**, **Class**, **Date**, and **Invoice #** as shown in Figure 11-25.

Step 7. Click **Save & Close** to record the invoice.

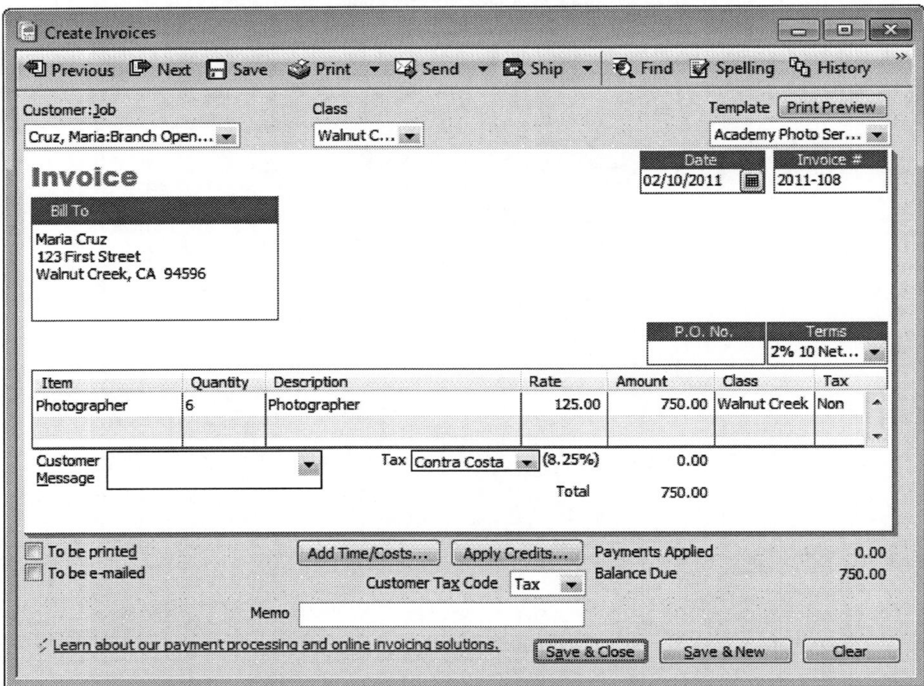

Figure 11-25 The Invoice with the subcontracted service passed-through.

> **Another Way:**
> If you want to track subcontractors time, you can record timesheets for each subcontractor (being sure to mark the transactions as billable) just as you do with your employees. You can then pass the time information through to the invoice instead of passing the expense from the bill. In this case, when you later enter the vendor name in the **Bill** or **Check** window, QuickBooks will prompt you to use the time you entered in the timesheet. If you choose to do so, the payment item will populate with the item you entered from the timesheets. This time will come through with a non-billable status which is correct. If you choose not to pass the time through to the payment, you should still enter the job name on the bill, but you should mark the expense Not Billable by unchecking the Billable? Option.

Unbilled Costs by Job Report

Create an *Unbilled Cost by Job* report to view all of the billable expenses and items that you haven't passed through to invoices.

COMPUTER PRACTICE

Step 1. Select the **Reports** menu, choose **Jobs, Time & Mileage,** and then choose **Unbilled Costs by Job**.

Step 2. Close the report.

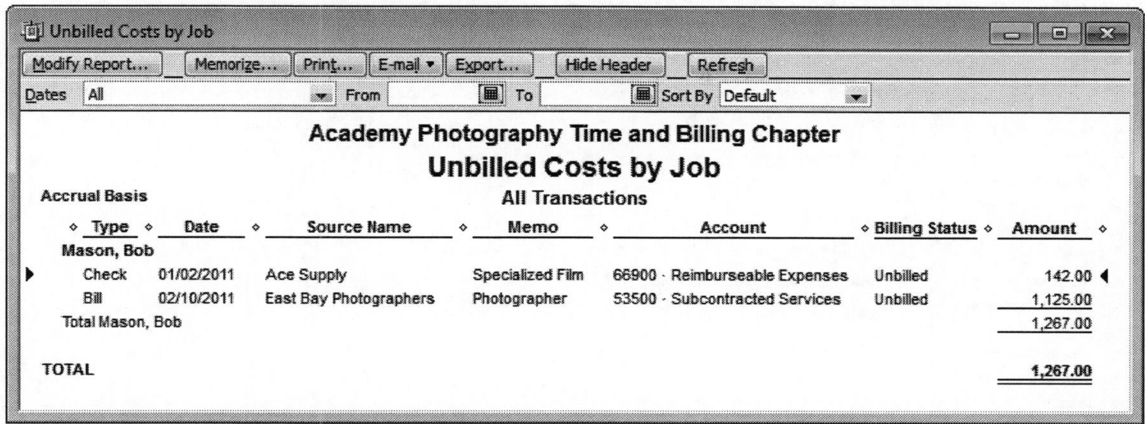

Academy Photography Time and Billing Chapter
Unbilled Costs by Job
Accrual Basis
All Transactions

Type	Date	Source Name	Memo	Account	Billing Status	Amount
Mason, Bob						
Check	01/02/2011	Ace Supply	Specialized Film	66900 · Reimburseable Expenses	Unbilled	142.00
Bill	02/10/2011	East Bay Photographers	Photographer	53500 · Subcontracted Services	Unbilled	1,125.00
Total Mason, Bob						1,267.00
TOTAL						1,267.00

Figure 11-26 The Unbilled Costs by Job report

Billable Time

If you enter timesheet information into QuickBooks that includes a customer or job name, you can pass the time through to the customer's invoice. This example shows how to pass billable hours on timesheets through to invoices.

The time tracking feature in QuickBooks is quite simple on the surface, but very powerful for streamlining businesses that pay hourly employees through QuickBooks payroll, or for businesses that provide time-based services to customers. The time tracking feature requires QuickBooks Pro or above.

The time tracking feature allows you to track how much time each employee, owner, partner, or subcontractor spends working on each job. In addition, you can track which service the person performs and which job and/or class the time should apply to. Then, once you record timesheet information, you can use it to calculate paychecks and to create invoices for the billable time.

When you use timesheets as the basis for paychecks and/or for invoicing, QuickBooks tracks everything required to create detailed job cost reports based on the timesheets.

Although the time tracking features in QuickBooks are quite powerful, there are also several "add-ons" (extra costs apply) to QuickBooks that provide even more features for time tracking, and their data can be synchronized with QuickBooks. For example, there are add-ons that provide time-clock integration, web-based time data entry, and even more flexible tracking features than you can find in QuickBooks (e.g. www.billquick.com). For a complete list of add-ons, go to http://marketplace.intuit.com, and search for time tracking.

Activating Time Tracking in QuickBooks

Before you can use the Time Tracking feature, you must activate Time Tracking in the *Company* tab of the *Time & Expense Preferences* window.

COMPUTER PRACTICE

To activate the Time Tracking feature, follow these steps:

Step 1. Select the **Edit** menu and then select **Preferences.** Select the **Time & Expense** item on the left and click the *Company Preferences* tab (see Figure 11-27).

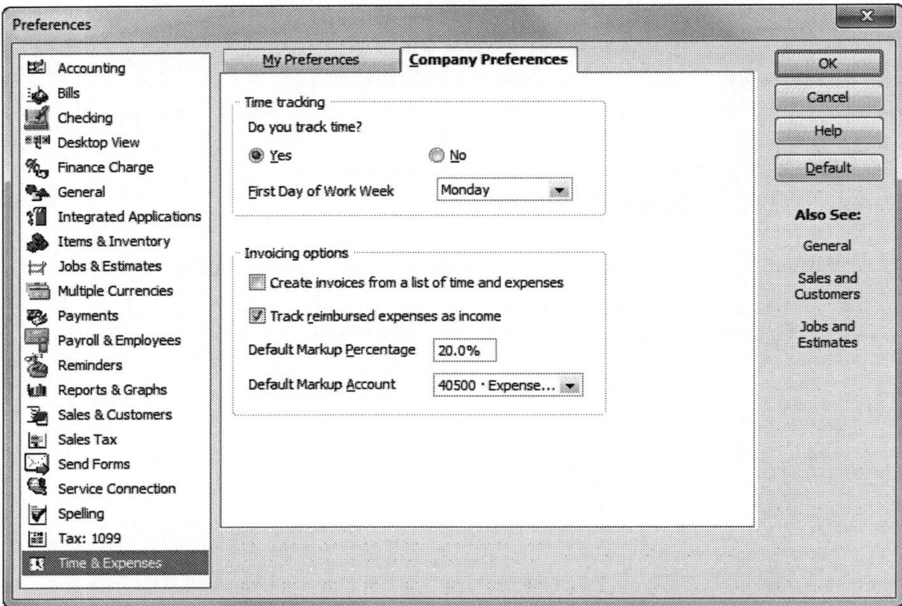

Figure 11-27 Time & Expense preferences

Step 2. Confirm that **Yes** in the *Do you Track Time?* section is already selected.

When working with your company's data file you will need to turn on Time Tracking by clicking **Yes** either on the window shown in Figure 11-27 or in the EasyStep Interview.

Step 3. Confirm that **Monday** is selected in the *First Day of Work Week* field. Monday is the first day that QuickBooks will display on the weekly timesheet

Step 4. Click **OK** to close Preferences.

Entering Time on Timesheets

To track your employees' time, you'll enter *activities* on timesheets.

An *activity* is the time spent by a single person performing a single service on a single date. For example, an attorney might enter an activity on the timesheet to record a phone conversation that she will bill to one of her clients. When an hourly employee performs a service for a customer you should include the customer or job name in the time activity. Each activity is recorded on a separate line of the timesheet and you can mark each time activity as billable if you wish to pass that activity through to a customer's invoice.

A weekly timesheet is a record of several activities performed during a one-week period by a single employee, owner, or subcontractor. Enter weekly timesheet information using the Weekly Timesheet window.

COMPUTER PRACTICE

To enter time *activities*, follow these steps:

Step 1. Select the **Employees** menu, select **Enter Time**, and then select **Use Weekly Timesheet.**

Alternatively, you can click the **Enter Time** button in the *Employee Center.*

Step 2. Enter ***Mike Mazuki*** in the *Name* field

Step 3. Click the **Calendar icon** and choose ***January 10, 2011***.

Step 4. Enter each activity on a separate line in the timesheet as shown in Figure 11-28. Be sure to select the ***Kumar*** job for *Anderson Wedding Planners* and the ***Branch Opening*** job for Maria Cruz in the Customer:Job column.

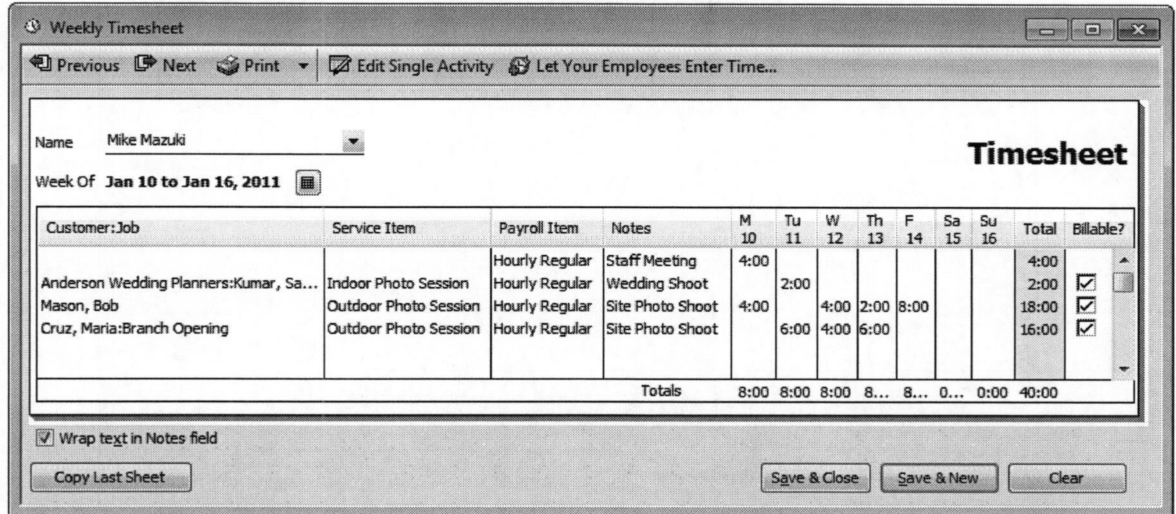

Figure 11-28 Weekly timesheet for Jim Moen

Step 5. Click **Save & Close** to record the timesheet activity.

> **Note:**
> If you plan to use timesheets to create Paychecks, you should record all of the time for each employee, including non-billable time (e.g., sick, vacation, and administrative time).

Printing Timesheets

In some companies, you may need to print several copies of your employee's timesheets for review by owners or managers.

COMPUTER PRACTICE

To print timesheets, follow these steps:

Step 1. From the *File* menu, select **Print Forms** and then select **Timesheets.**

Step 2. Set the dates to ***01/10/2011*** through ***01/16/2011*** (see Figure 11-29).

Step 3. Select **Print full activity notes** at the bottom of the window and then click **OK** (see Figure 11-29).

Step 4. Click **Print** on the *Print Timesheets* window (see Figure 11-30).

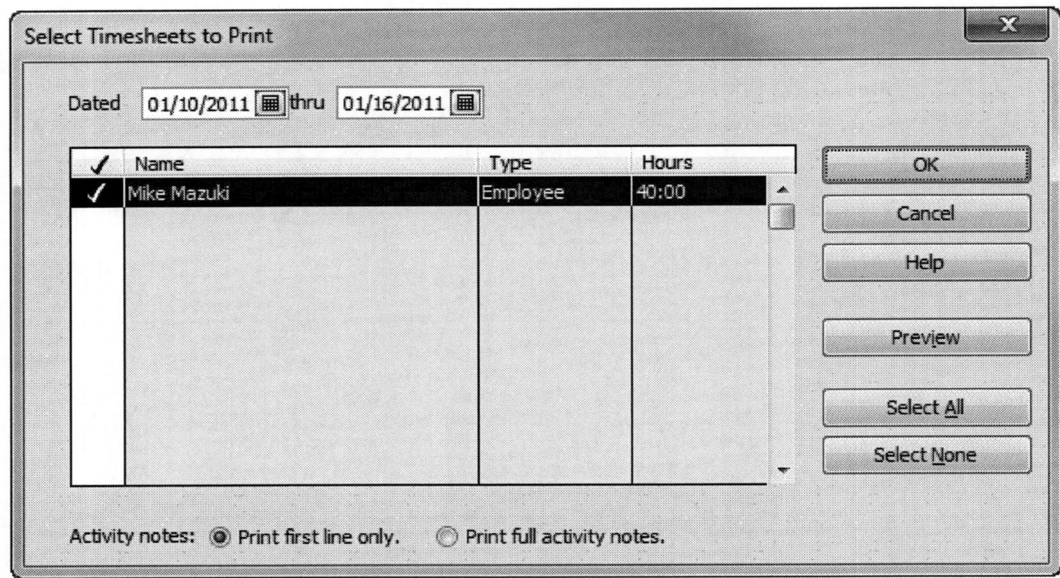

Figure 11-29 Select Timesheets to Print window

Timesheet

Name: Mike Mazuki

Jan 10 to Jan 16, 2011

Customer:Job	Service Item	Payroll Item	Notes	M	Tu	W	Th	F	Sa	Su	Total	Bill*
		Hourly Regular	Staff Meeting	4:00							4:00	N
Anderson Wedding Planners:Kumar, Sati and Naveen	Indoor Photo Session	Hourly Regular	Wedding Shoot		2:00						2:00	B
Cruz, Maria:Branch Opening	Outdoor Photo Session	Hourly Regular	Site Photo Shoot		6:00	4:00	6:00				16:00	B
Mason, Bob	Outdoor Photo Session	Hourly Regular	Site Photo Shoot	4:00		4:00	2:00	8:00			18:00	B
			Totals	8:00	8:00	8:00	8:00	8:00	0:00	0:00	40:00	

Signature ____________________

Figure 11-30 Printed timesheet for Mike Mazuki

Invoicing Customers for Time

You can also pass timesheet information through to invoices. When you mark time activities as "billable," QuickBooks allows you to transfer the time information onto the next invoice for that Customer.

COMPUTER PRACTICE

To create an invoice to a customer, and pass the timesheet data onto the invoice, follow these steps:

Step 1. From the *Customer* menu, select **Create Invoices** or click **Invoices** on the *Home* page.

Step 2. In the **Customer:Job** section select **Cruz, Maria:Branch Opening**.

Step 3. QuickBooks displays the *Billable Time/Costs* window (see Figure 11-31). Click **OK** to continue.

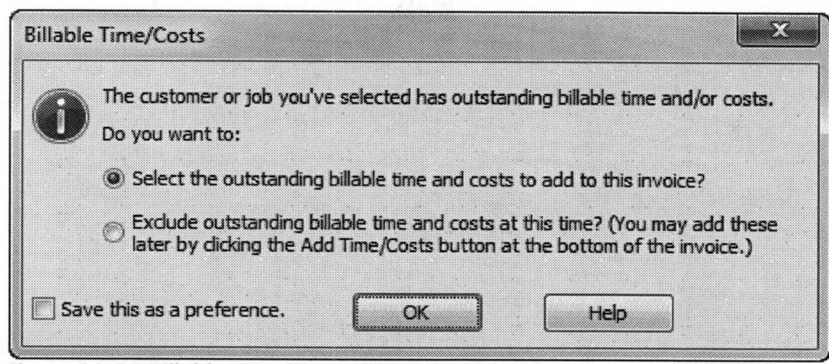

Figure 11-31 Billable Time/Cost window

Step 4. Click the **Time** tab in the *Choose Billable Time and Costs* window (Figure 11-32).

Step 5. Click **Select All** to use all of the time activity for this Customer.

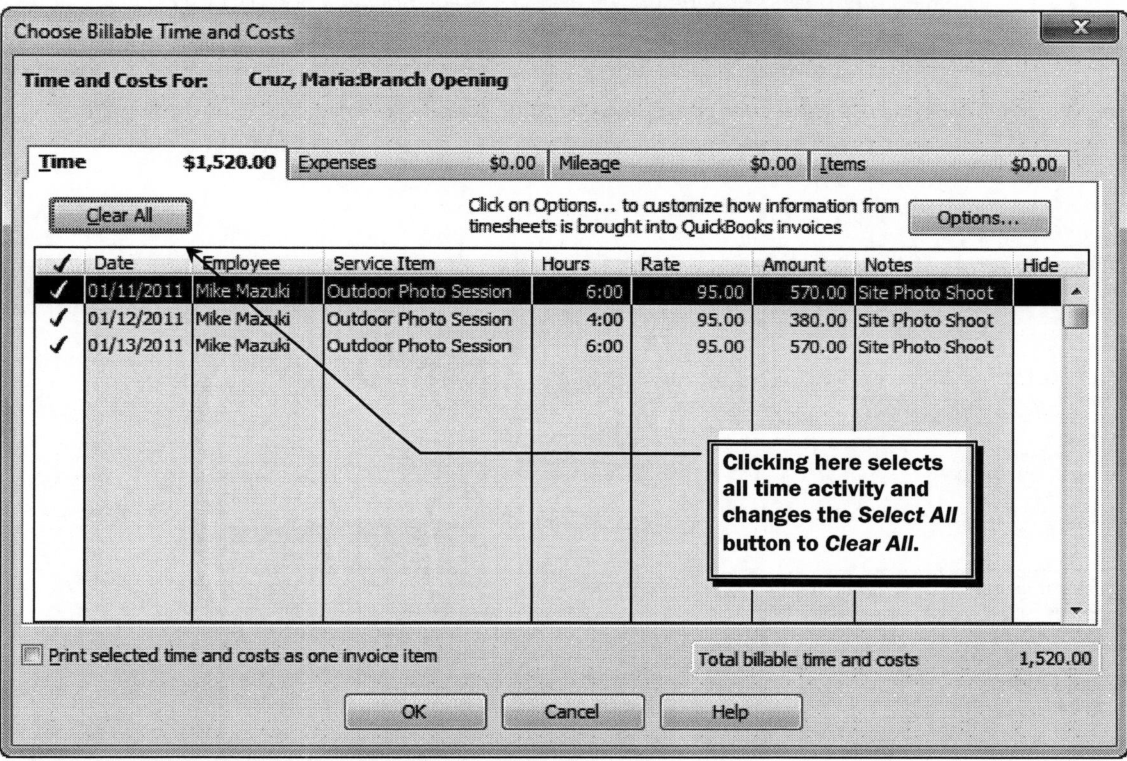

Figure 11-32 Billable time for Maria Cruz's Branch Opening job

Step 6. Click **Options** to modify the way time activities are passed through to invoices.

This window allows you to change the way time is transferred onto invoices. The default setting is shown below, and you'll probably want to leave the setting alone. However, you can modify it to use either the information from the *Notes* field on the employee's timesheet or the information from the *Description* field of the service items. This information will show in the *Description* column of the completed invoice. If you check ***Combine activities with the same service items***, your invoices will not show any notes from individual time records.

Figure 11-33 Options for transferring billable time screen

Step 7. Leave *Enter a separate line on the invoice for each activity* and *Transfer activity notes* selected. Click **OK** to close the *Options for Transferring Billable Time* window. Click **OK** to close the *Choose Billable Time and Costs* window to transfer the time to the invoice.

Step 8. The invoice now shows the time activity from Mike Mazuki's timesheets. Enter ***Walnut Creek*** in the *Class* field and 2/10/11 for the date so your invoice matches Figure 11-34.

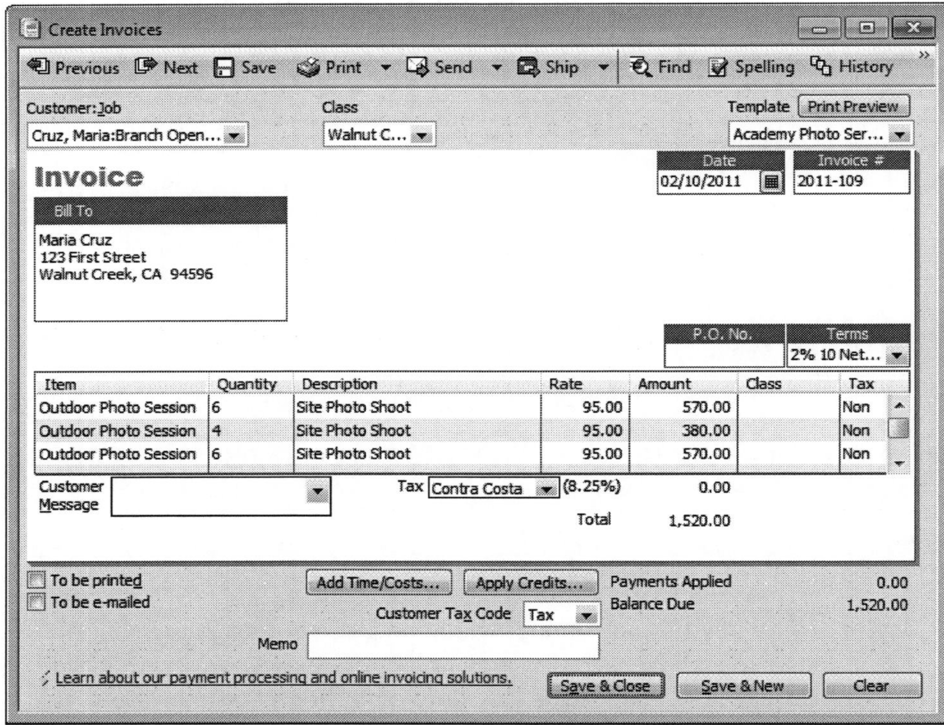

Figure 11-34 Invoice with billable time passed through

> **Note:**
> After you post timesheet information to paychecks and invoices, the timesheet will affect income (because of the invoice), expenses (because of the paycheck), and Job Cost reports (because of the job information on both the paycheck and the invoice).

Step 9. Click **Save & Close** to record the invoice.

Making Activities Billable Again

After you pass time (or items) through to an invoice, QuickBooks removes the check in the *Billable* column in the *Choose Billable Time and Costs* window and replaces it with a small gray icon. If you void or delete an invoice that contains billable time or items, you'll need to go back to the original time activity and click the gray icon to make the time activity billable again.

> **Note:**
> When you transfer time activities onto an invoice, QuickBooks changes the billable status of the time activities to "billed." However, if you void or delete the invoice, QuickBooks **does not automatically** change the status backed to "unbilled".
>
> **Tip:**
> If you have billable time, cost or item activity that you wish to clear from your unbilled reports (e.g., Unbilled Costs by Job), you can pass the time through to an invoice, save the invoice, and then delete the invoice. This method is much faster than editing each billable item, cost or time activity individually.

COMPUTER PRACTICE

To make time activities billable again edit each time activity as described in the following steps:

Step 1. Select the **Employees** menu, select **Enter Time**, and then select **Use Weekly Timesheet**.

Step 2. Enter ***Mike Mazuki*** in the *Name* field.

Step 3. Click the **calendar icon** and choose ***01/10/2011***

Step 4.
Because you passed the time through to an invoice, QuickBooks grayed the Invoice icon on the timesheet activity for Maria Cruz's Branch Opening job (see Figure 11-35).

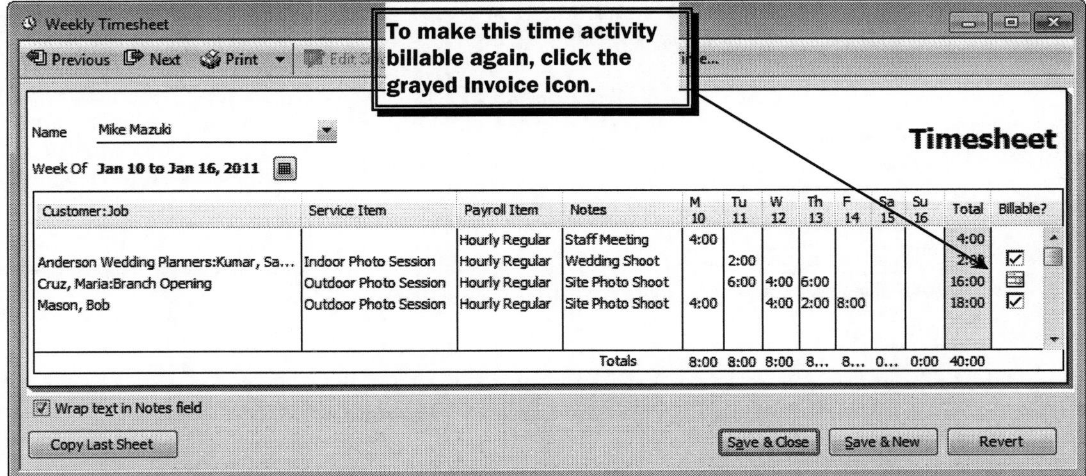

Figure 11-35 Timesheet for Mike Mazuki showing that the time for Maria Cruz's Job has been billed

Step 5. Click the gray icon in the *Billable* column to make the time activity for the Branch Opening job billable again.

Step 6. Click **Yes** on Billing Status window shown in Figure 11-36.

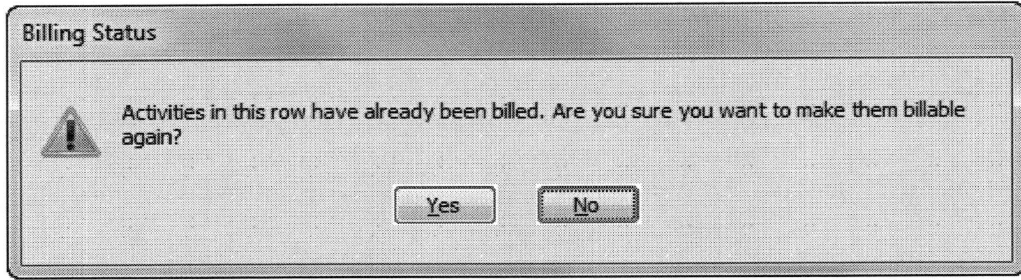

Figure 11-36 Billing Status window

Step 7. Click **Save & Close** on the *Weekly Timesheet* window to save your changes.

Time Reports

There are several reports that help you summarize and track time activities.

Time by Name Report

The Time by Name report shows how many hours each employee, owner, or partner worked for each Customer or Job.

COMPUTER PRACTICE

To create the Time by Name report, follow these steps:

Step 1. From the *Reports* menu, select **Jobs, Time & Mileage**, and then select **Time by Name.**

Step 2. Set the date range for the report to ***01/01/2011*** through ***01/31/2011***.

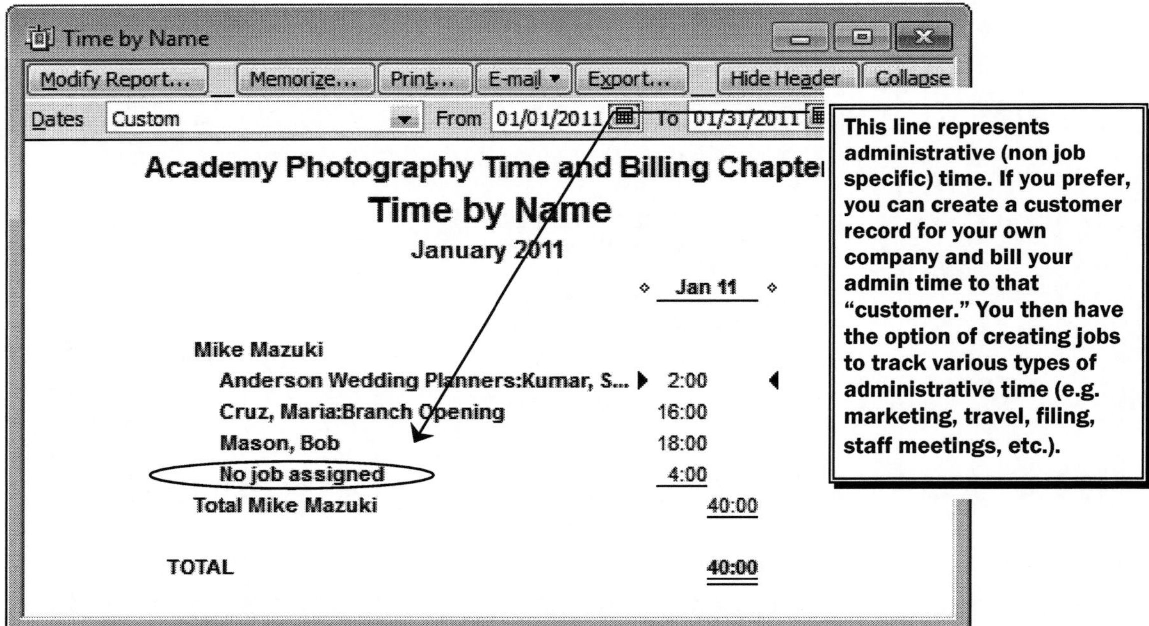

Figure 11-37 Time by Name report

Step 3. Click the **Modify Reports** button in the upper left corner of the *Time by Name* report window.

Step 4. Click the checkbox next to the **Billed** and **Unbilled** options in the *Modify Report* window (see Figure 11-38). Click **OK**.

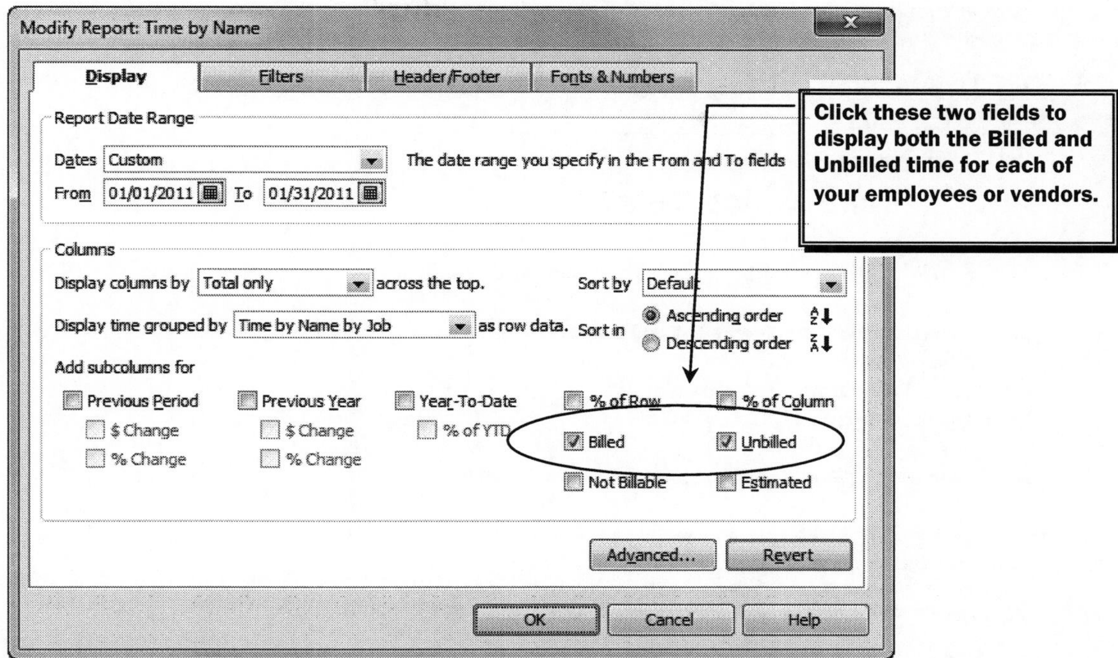

Figure 11-38 Modify the Time by Name report to include Billed and Unbilled columns.

Step 5. The *Time by Name* report now differentiates between the **Billed** and **Unbilled** time.

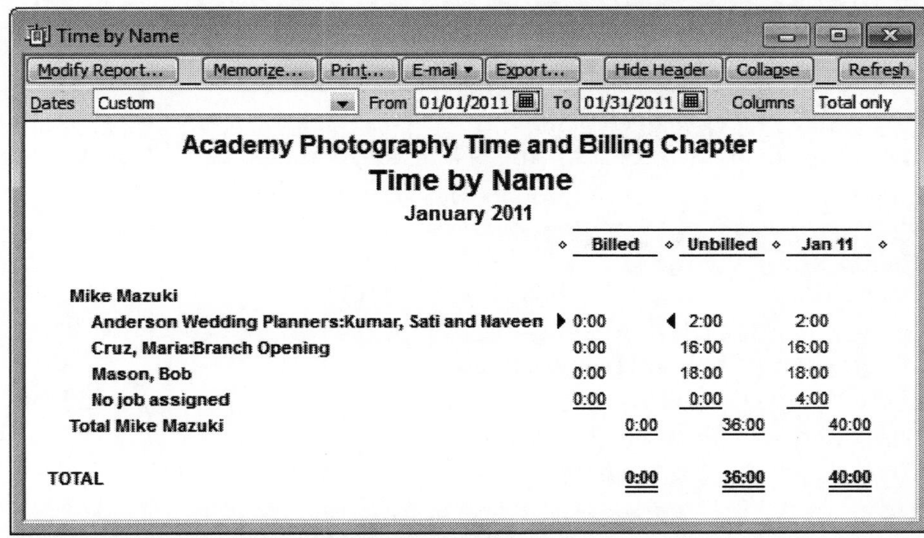

Academy Photography Time and Billing Chapter
Time by Name
January 2011

	Billed	Unbilled	Jan 11
Mike Mazuki			
Anderson Wedding Planners:Kumar, Sati and Naveen	0:00	2:00	2:00
Cruz, Maria:Branch Opening	0:00	16:00	16:00
Mason, Bob	0:00	18:00	18:00
No job assigned	0:00	0:00	4:00
Total Mike Mazuki	0:00	36:00	40:00
TOTAL	0:00	36:00	40:00

Figure 11-39 The customized Time by Name report

Step 6. Close the report.

Time by Job Detail Report

The Time by Job Detail report shows the detail of each Service Item, totaled by Customer or Job.

COMPUTER PRACTICE

Step 1. From the *Reports* menu, select **Jobs, Time & Mileage**, and then select **Time by Job Detail**.

Step 2. Set the date range to ***01/01/2011*** through ***01/31/2011***.

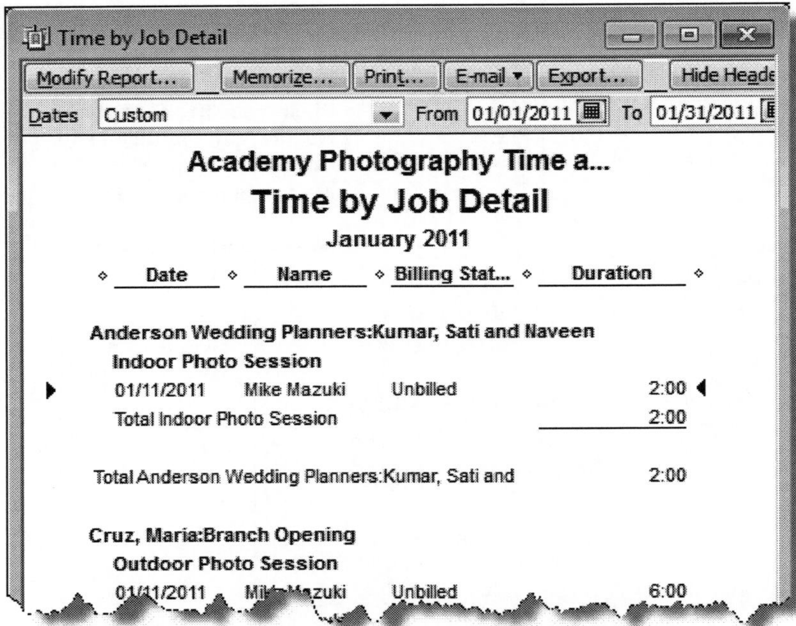

Figure 11-40 Time by Job Detail report

Time by Item Report

The **Time by Item** report shows the detail of each Customer, totaled by Service Item.

COMPUTER PRACTICE

To create a Time by Item report, follow these steps:

Step 1. From the *Reports* menu, select **Jobs, Time & Mileage,** and then select **Time by Item**.

Step 2. Set the date range to ***01/01/2011*** through ***01/31/2011***.

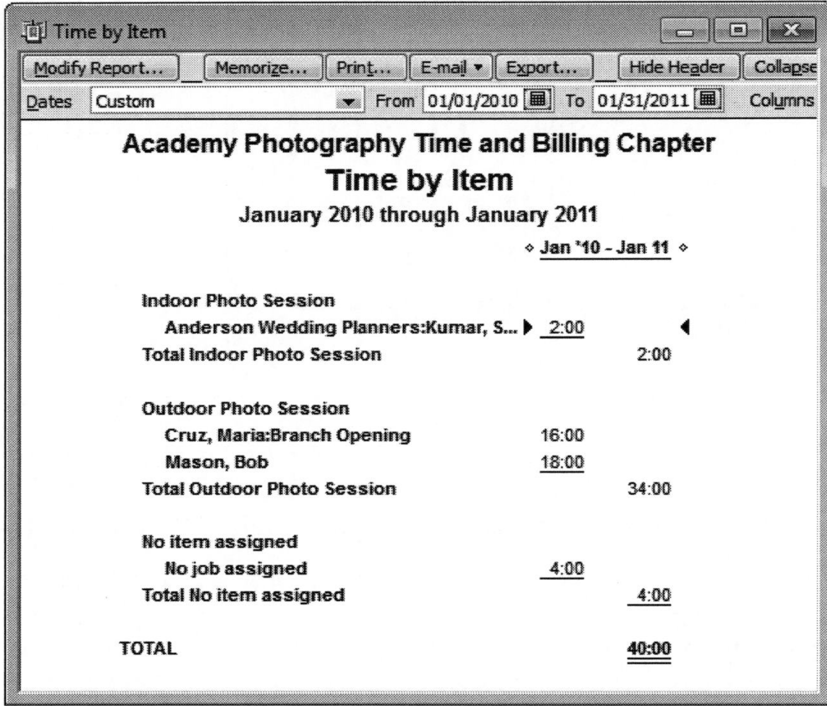

Figure 11-41 Time by Item report

Tracking an Owner's or Partner's Time

In some businesses, owners and partners do not receive paychecks, but they still need to track their time activity, record the labor costs to specific jobs, and then pass the time through to their customers' invoices.

COMPUTER PRACTICE

To track an owner or partner's time for billing purposes, follow these steps:

Step 1. Display the *Other Names* list by selecting the **Lists** menu and then selecting **Other Names List**.

Step 2. Select **New** from the **Other Names** menu at the bottom of the *Other Names List* window.

Step 3. Create an *Other Name* record for Vern Black, the owner of Academy Photography as shown in Figure 11-42.

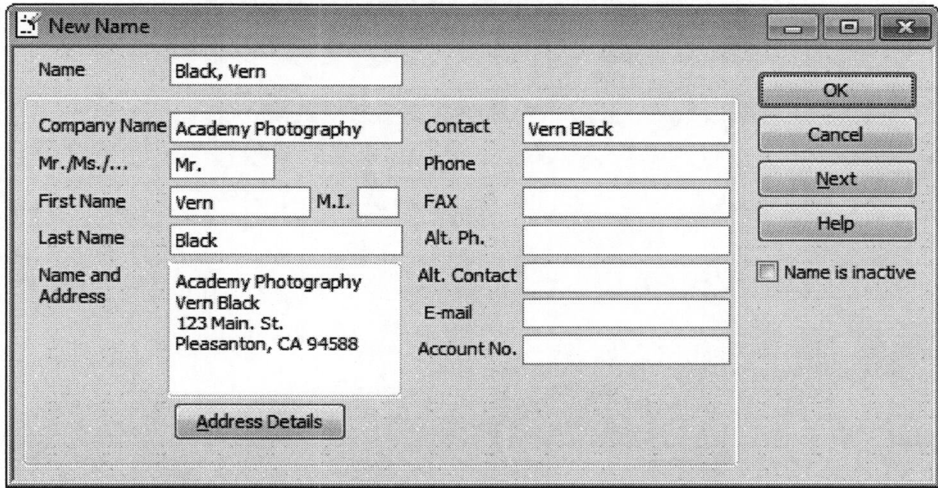

Figure 11-42 Other Name record for owner Vern Black

Step 4. Click **OK** to save Vern Black's record, and then close the *Other Names* list.

Step 5. Open the *Weekly Timesheet* window and enter the timesheet activity for Vern Black as shown in Figure 11-43.

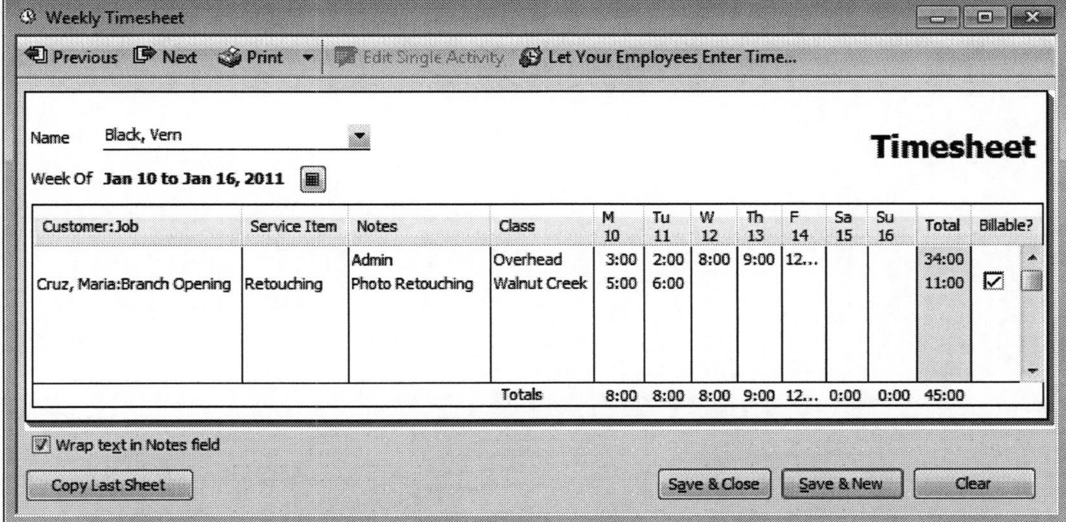

Figure 11-43 Time activity for Vern Black

Step 6. Click **Save & Close** to record the timesheet activity.

Step 7. To pass this time through to an invoice for the customer, open the *Create Invoices* window and enter the Maria Cruz's Branch Opening Job in the Customer:Job field. Click OK in the *Billable Time/Costs* window.

Step 8. Click the **Time** tab in the Choose Billable Time and Costs window (see Figure 11-44). Notice that QuickBooks shows the time for Vern Black as well as the timesheet activity for Mike Mazuki that you made billable again on the Weekly Timesheet window shown in Figure 11-35.

Step 9. Click **Select All** and then click **OK** to transfer the timesheet information through to the customer's invoice (see Figure 11-44).

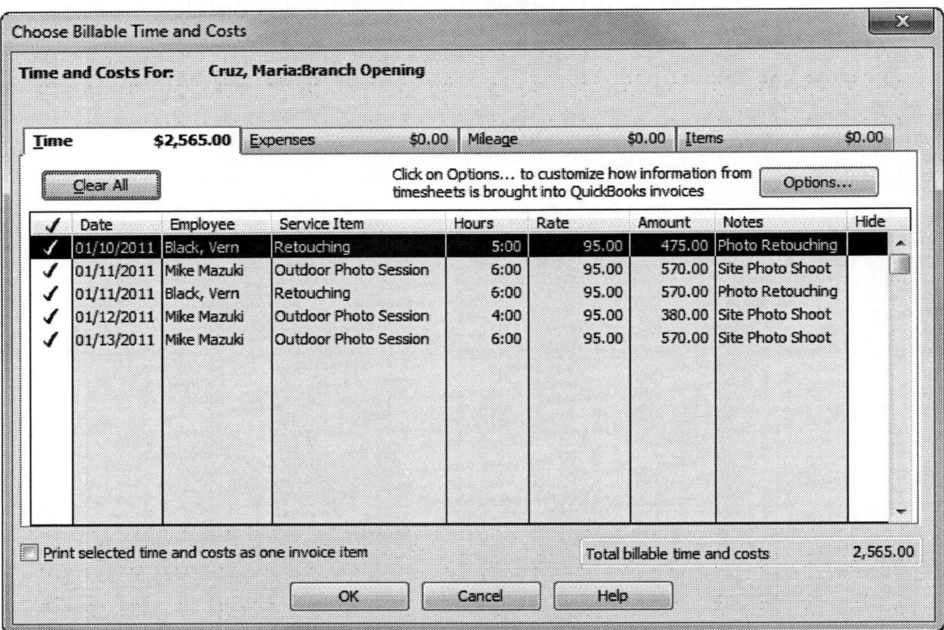

Figure 11-44 Billable Time and Costs window including owner's time

Step 10. Enter the class and date information so that your invoice matches Figure 11-45.

Step 11. Click **Save & Close** to record the invoice.

Step 12. The *Recording Transaction* window displays that Maria Cruz is over his credit limit. Click **Yes**.

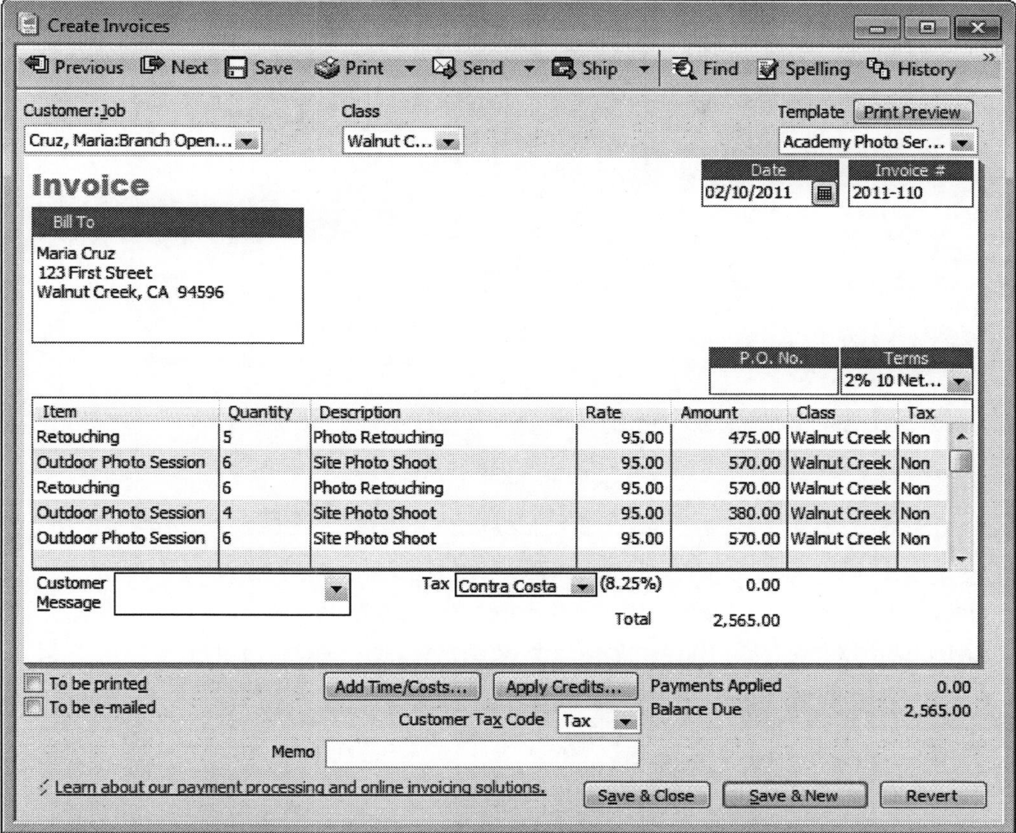

Figure 11-45 The Invoice now shows the time activity for Mike Mazuki and Vern Black.

> **Note:**
> You will not usually "pay" the owner for their time because owners generally take a "draw" (a check coded to Owner's Drawing) instead of getting paid through payroll. Therefore, the timesheet information for Vern Black will not get recorded as labor costs on Maria Cruz's Branch Opening Job.

Vehicle Mileage Tracking

QuickBooks has a Vehicle Mileage tracker that allows you to track vehicle mileage, post mileage to invoices, and run reports to assist with tax preparation.

To set up mileage tracking, you'll need to create one or more items and at least one Vehicle in the Vehicle list.

> **Note:** You cannot use vehicle mileage tracking to reimburse your employees for mileage on their paycheck, a bill or check.

COMPUTER PRACTICE

Step 1. Create an *Other Charge* item called **Mileage** with the information shown in Figure 11-46. Set the *Expense Account* to ***Automobile Expense*** and the *Income Account* to ***Expenses Reimbursed***.

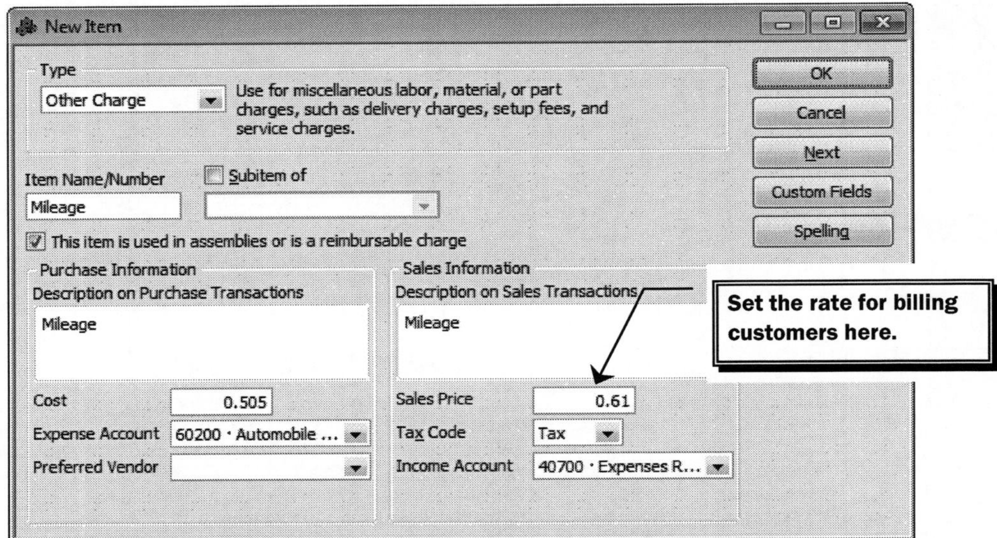

Figure 11-46 Create an Other Charge item for passing mileage costs through to customers

Step 2. Select the *Company* menu and select **Enter Vehicle Mileage**.

Step 3. Select **Add New** from the *Vehicle* drop-down list (see Figure 11-47).

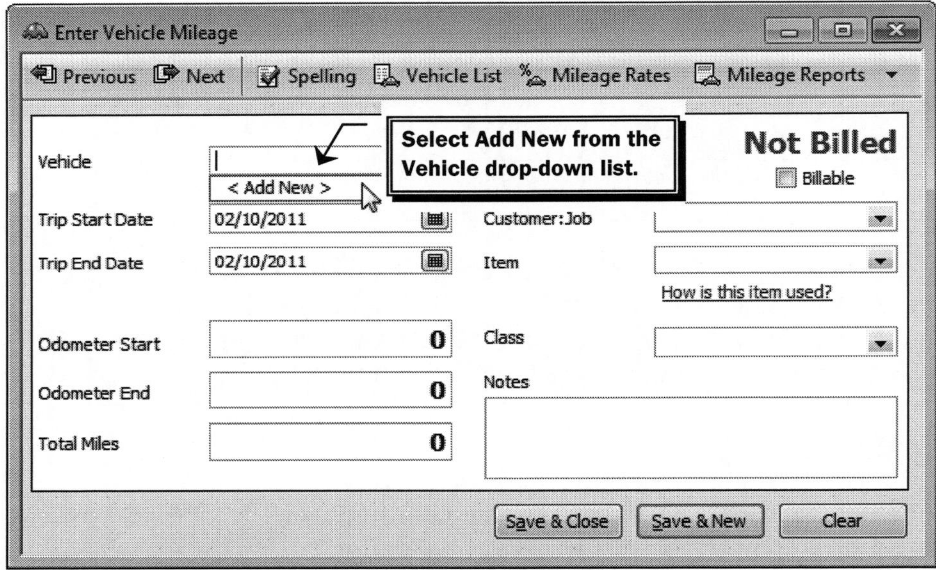

Figure 11-47 Add New Vehicle to Vehicle List

Step 4. Enter ***2008 Toyota Prius*** in the *Vehicle* field and ***2008 Toyota Prius*** in the *Description* field of the **New Vehicle** window (see Figure 11-48). Then click **OK** to save the entry.

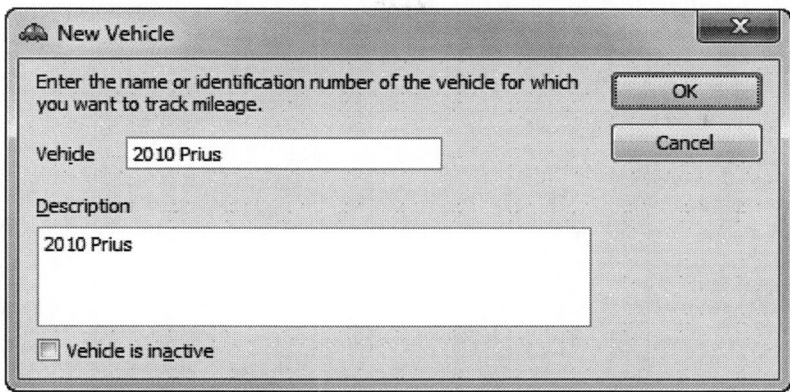

Figure 11-48 New Vehicle window

This creates a new item on the *Vehicle* list. See Figure 11-49.

You can access the *Vehicle* list by selecting the **Lists** menu, then select **Customer & Vendor Profile Lists**, and then select **Vehicle list**. Alternatively, you can click the Vehicle List button on the top of the *Enter Vehicle Mileage* window.

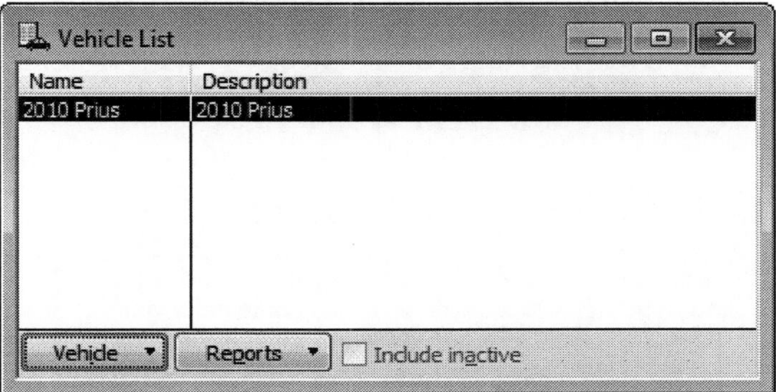

Figure 11-49 Vehicle List accessed through Enter Vehicle Mileage window

Step 5. To set up your mileage rates, click the **Mileage Rates** button on the top of the *Enter Vehicle Mileage* window (see Figure 11-50).

Figure 11-50 Mileage Rates button in Enter Vehicle Mileage window

Step 6. Enter the mileage rate designated by the IRS for the appropriate tax year on the first blank line of the *Mileage Rates* window as shown in Figure 11-51).

Step 7. Click **Close** to close the Mileage Rate window.

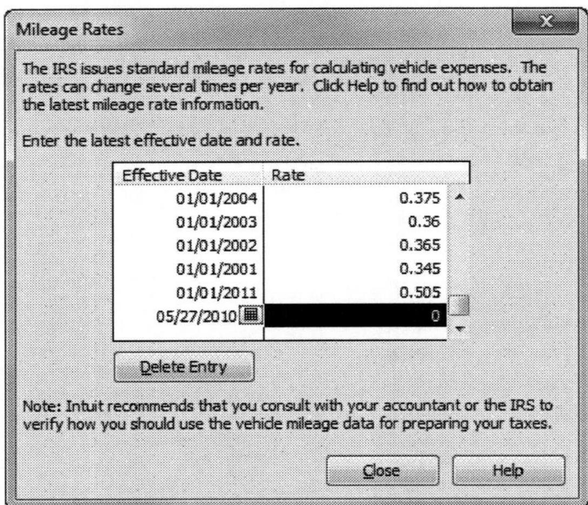

Figure 11-51 Enter Mileage rates to calculate vehicle expenses

> **Note:**
> The rates you enter on the *Mileage Rates* window (Figure 11-51) are for reporting purposes only. These rates help you with preparing your company's income tax return. When you record mileage, you'll use the Other Charge item you set up earlier (see Figure 11-46) and QuickBooks will use the rate you entered in the *Sales Price* field of the Item setup (Step 5 above).

Step 8. Complete the *Enter Vehicle Mileage* window as shown in Figure 11-52.

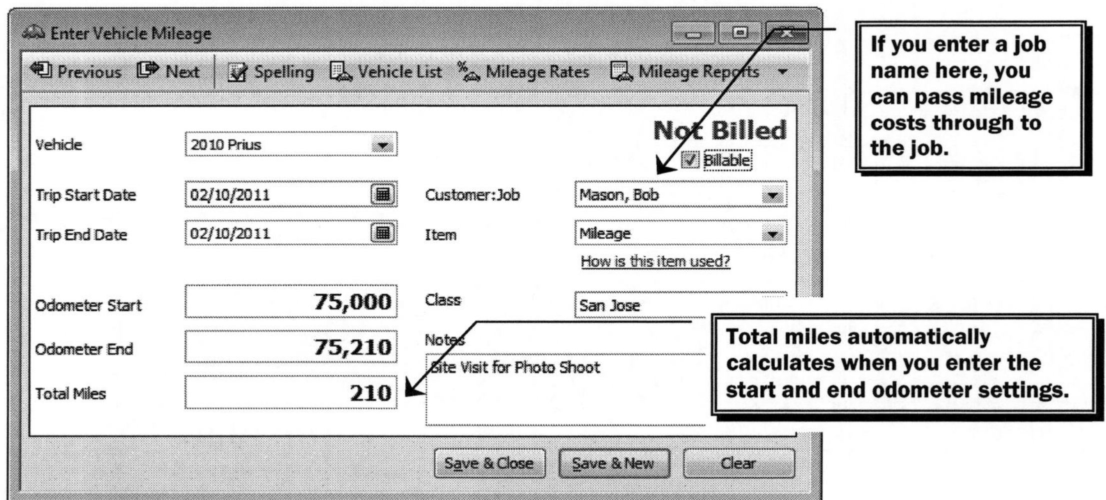

Figure 11-52 Enter Vehicle Mileage window

Step 9. Click **Save & Close** to save your mileage entry.

To create reports about your mileage, follow these steps:

COMPUTER PRACTICE

Step 1. Select the **Reports** menu, then select **Jobs, Time & Mileage,** and then select **Mileage by Vehicle Detail** (see Figure 11-53).

Step 2. Set the date range to ***01/01/2011*** through ***02/28/2011***.

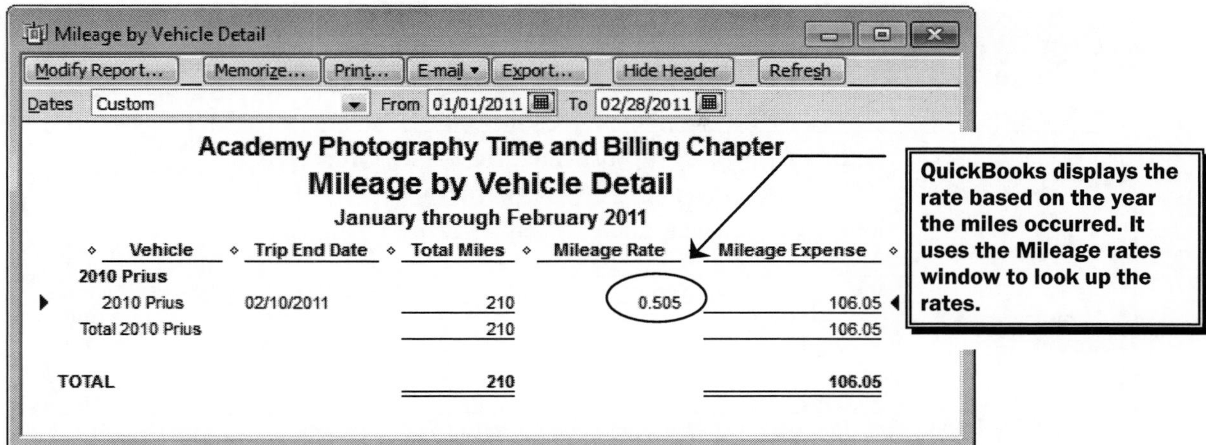

Figure 11-53 Mileage by Vehicle Detail report

Step 3. Close the **Mileage by Vehicle Detail** report.

To see all mileage that has not yet been billed, use a Mileage report such as *Mileage by Job Summary*.

Step 1. Select the **Reports** menu, then select **Jobs, Time & Mileage,** and then select **Mileage by Job Summary**.

Step 2. Set the date fields to ***01/01/2011*** through ***02/28/2011***.

Step 3. Click **Modify Report** to format the report to display the *Billed, Unbilled, and Not Billable* columns as shown in Figure 11-55).

Step 4. Click **OK** to save your changes.

Step 5. Close all report windows.

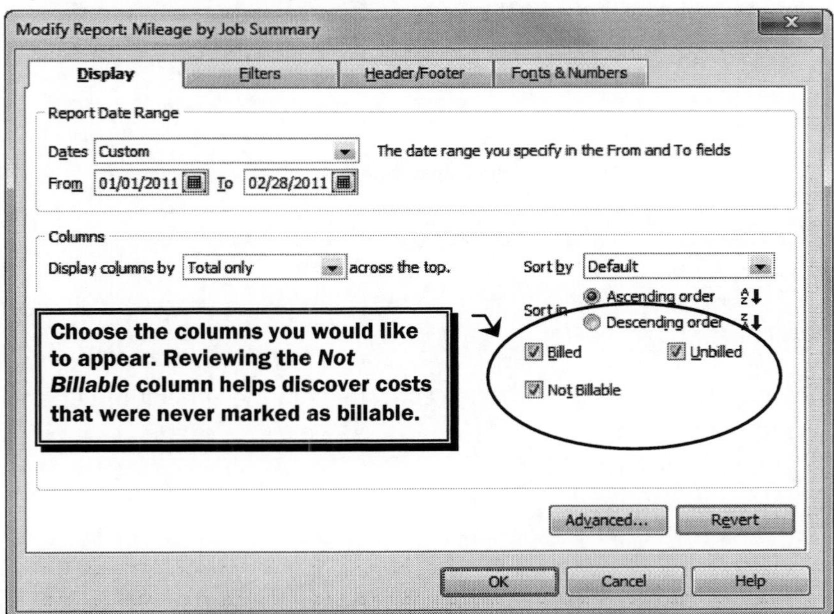

Figure 11-54 Modifying the Mileage by Job Report

By reviewing this report (see Figure 11-55), you can see which mileage items have not been billed. If you find a line with *No name,* double-click on it to see whether the mileage should be assigned to a job or not.

Not Billable Miles can also be investigated to see if some of those entries should be billable.

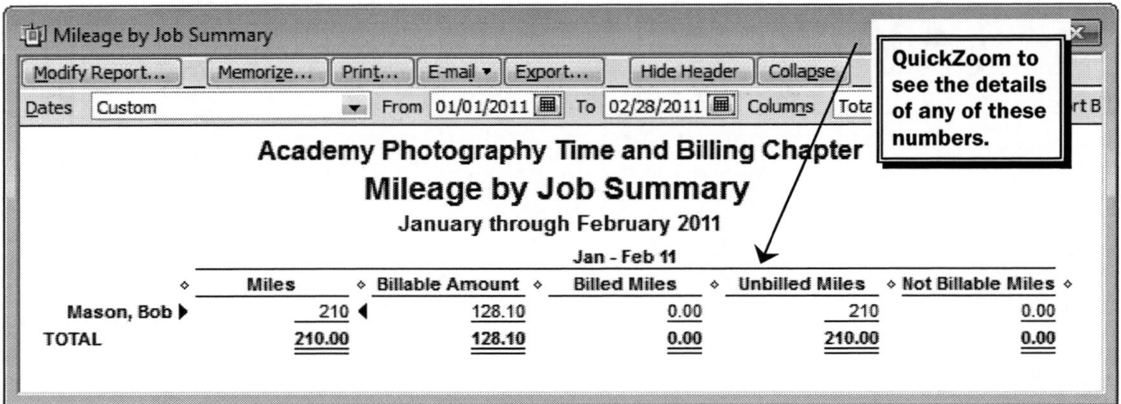

	Miles	Billable Amount	Billed Miles	Unbilled Miles	Not Billable Miles
Mason, Bob	210	128.10	0.00	210	0.00
TOTAL	210.00	128.10	0.00	210.00	0.00

Figure 11-55 Mileage by Job Summary Report showing Bob Mason's billable mileage

Multiple Pass-Throughs on One Invoice

As before, to pass these costs through to the customer, create an invoice and use the *Time/Costs* button to post the entries onto the invoice.

COMPUTER PRACTICE

Step 1. Select the **Invoices** icon on the *Customer* section of the *Home* page.

Step 2. Select **Bob Mason** from the *Customer:Job* list and click **OK** in the *Billable Time/Costs* window to open the *Choose Billable Time and Costs* window.

Step 3. Click the *Mileage* tab (see Figure 11-56).

Step 4. Click to place a checkmark in the left column on the *Mileage* item for 02/10/2011.

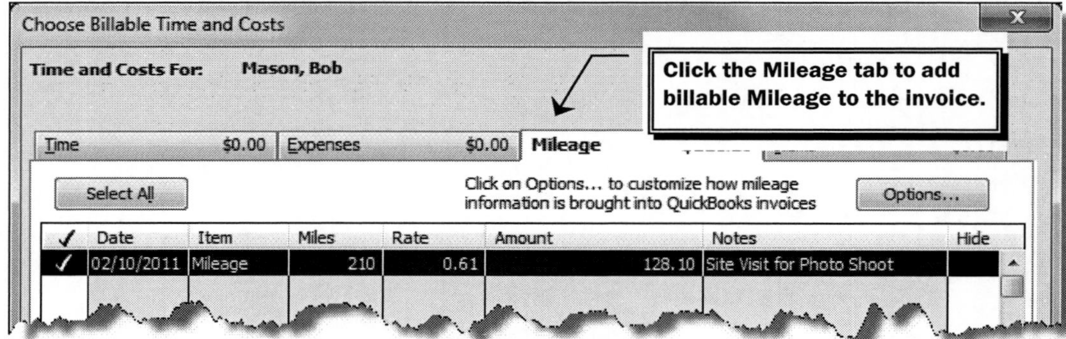

Figure 11-56 Mileage tab of Billable Time and Costs window

Step 5. Next, select the *Items* Tab and click to place a checkmark in the left column on the unbilled items (see Figure 11-57).

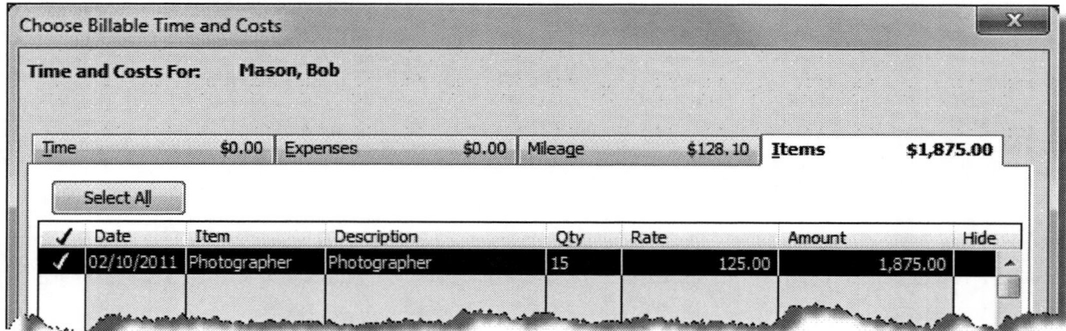

Figure 11-57 Items tab of Billable Time and Costs window

Step 6. Next, select the *Expenses* Tab and click to place a checkmark in the left column on the unbilled Expenses (see Figure 11-58). Leave the *Markup Amount* ***20%*** and the *Markup Account* set to ***Expense Markup***.

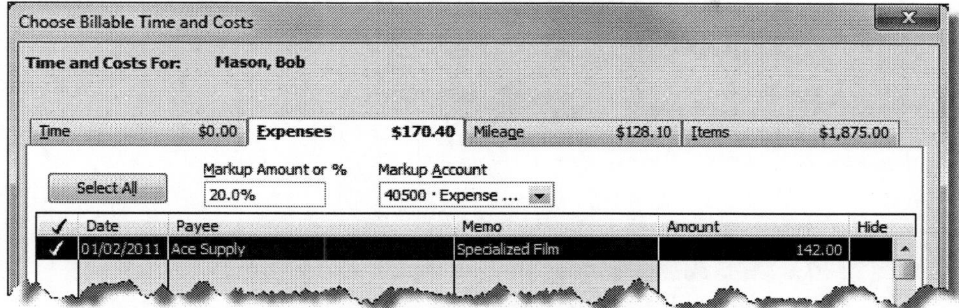

Figure 11-58 Expenses tab of Billable Time and Costs window

Step 7. Click **OK** to post all selected pass-throughs to the invoice. This step is necessary because we want to add one more summary line with all of the time records selected. But first, we have to post each of the selected expenses to the invoice so they will appear on separate lines.

Step 8. Click the **Add Time/Costs** button on the lower part of the invoice to re-display the *Billable Time and Costs* window.

You can always display the *Choose Billable Time and Costs* window by clicking the **Add Time/Costs** button on an invoice.

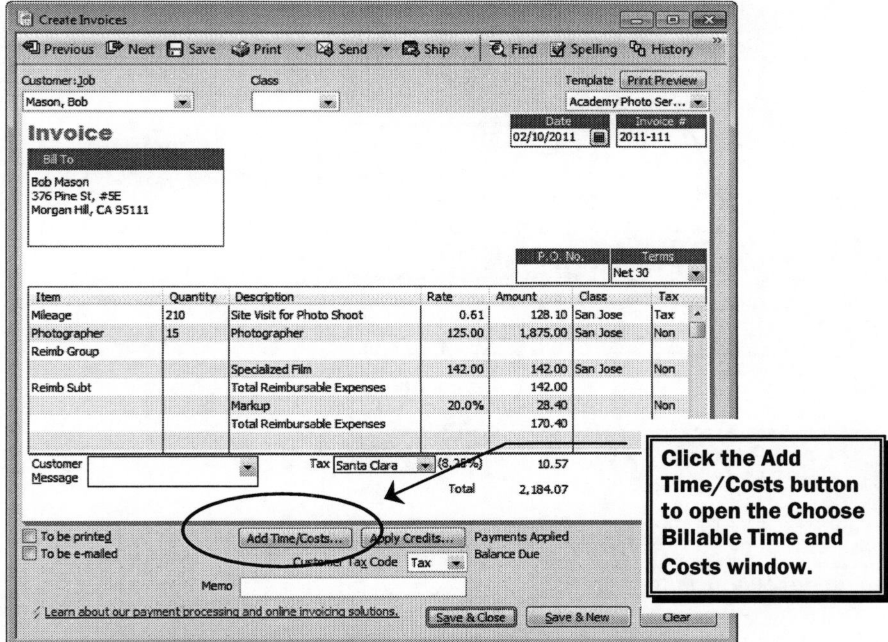

Figure 11-59 Bob Mason's invoice before adding Time

Step 9. Click the *Time* Tab and click **Select All** on the unbilled Expenses (see Figure 11-60).

Step 10. Then click ***Print Selected time and costs as one invoice item***. This ensures that the invoice only has one line for the billable time *when it is printed*. This summarizes billable time into one entry so the printed invoice is shorter, but it doesn't show the customer the detail that you might need. Decide what's best for you when you do your own invoices.

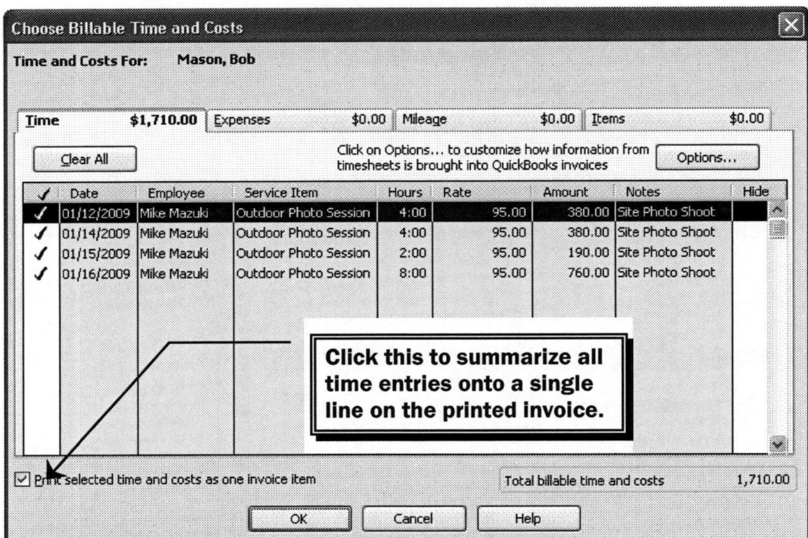

Figure 11-60 Time tab of Billable Time and Costs window

Step 11. Click **OK** to post all of the selected pass-throughs to the invoice.

Step 12. Then scroll down to the bottom of the invoice and change the description from ***Total Reimbursable Expenses*** to ***Total Services.***

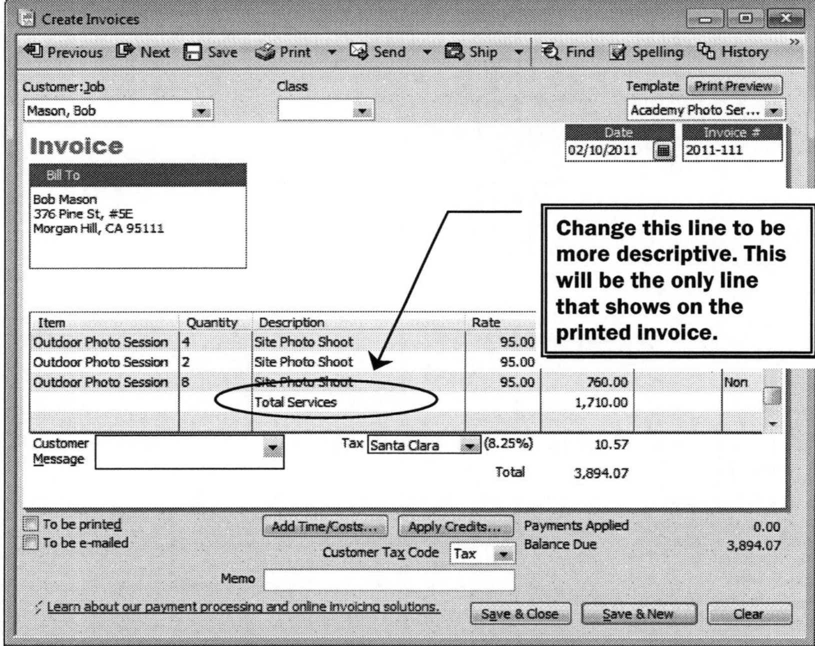

Figure 11-61 Bottom of invoice with Total Services entered.

Step 13. Preview the resulting invoice by choosing **Print** and **Preview** as seen in Figure 11-62.

Step 14. Click **Close** to close the Print Preview window.

Step 15. Click **Save & Close** to close the window.

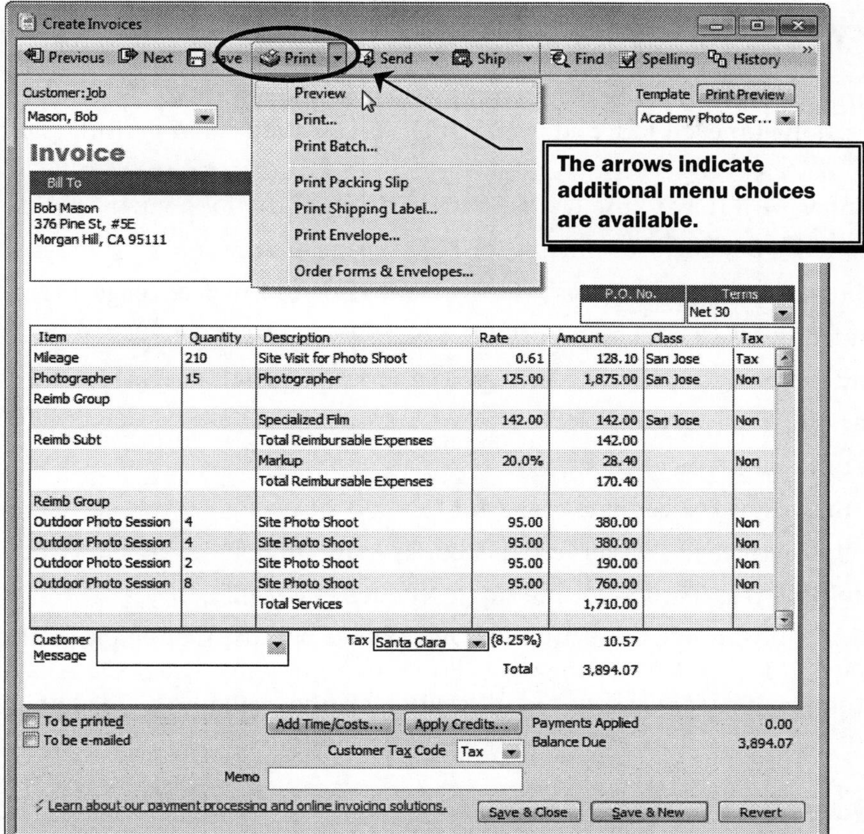

Figure 11-62 Bob Mason's completed Invoice

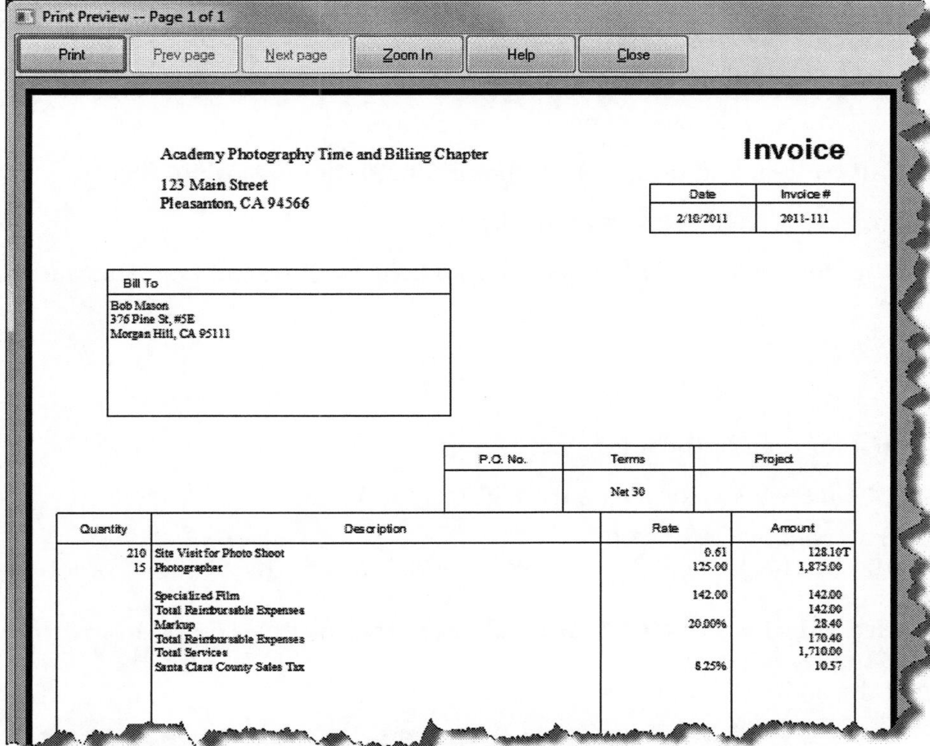

Academy Photography Time and Billing Chapter
123 Main Street
Pleasanton, CA 94566

Invoice

Date	Invoice #
2/18/2011	2011-111

Bill To
Bob Mason
376 Pine St, #5E
Morgan Hill, CA 95111

P.O. No.	Terms	Project
	Net 30	

Quantity	Description	Rate	Amount
210	Site Visit for Photo Shoot	0.61	128.10T
15	Photographer	125.00	1,875.00
	Specialized Film	142.00	142.00
	Total Reimbursable Expenses		142.00
	Markup	20.00%	28.40
	Total Reimbursable Expenses		170.40
	Total Services		1,710.00
	Santa Clara County Sales Tax	8.25%	10.57

Figure 11-63 Print Preview of final Invoice

Chapter Summary and Review

In this chapter, you learned how to track how much time each employee, owner, partner or subcontractor spends working on each Job; and even which service the person performs on that Job.

You should now be familiar with how to use QuickBooks to do all of the following:

- What makes an expense Billable, Not Billable, or Billed (page 433).
- How to add reimbursable Expenses, Items, Mileage, and Time to Invoices (page 435).
- How to use two-sided Items to track reimbursable expenses (page 441).
- How to use two-sided Items to track subcontracted services (page 448).
- Activate Time Tracking (page 451).
- Pass billable time onto an Invoice (page 454).
- Create reports to analyze timesheet data (page 458).
- How to use the Vehicle Mileage Tracker in QuickBooks (page 461).
- How to handle Multiple Pass-Throughs on a single Invoice (page 468).

Time Tracking is one of the most powerful features of QuickBooks because it streamlines the entry of Invoices and Paychecks, while enabling QuickBooks to automatically associate labor costs with specific Customers, Jobs, or Classes. Time tracking is only available in QuickBooks Pro and above.

Comprehension Questions

> Answers to these review questions are available with the supplemental material. See page xiii for details.

1. Explain how to track reimbursable expenses.
2. How do you pass-through billable expenses to customers?
3. What is a *Two-sided* item and under what circumstances should you use them?
4. What is the purpose of Vehicle Mileage Tracker?
5. Explain how the *Use time data to create paychecks* option can be used to streamline your payroll system.

Multiple Choice

Select the best answer(s) for each of the following:

1. In QuickBooks you are allowed to pass-through billable expenses to customers:
   a) Only if you paid by credit card.
   b) If you paid by check or credit card, but you don't assign the customer or job to the expense.
   c) If you used bill, check or credit card and assign the customer or job to which the expense applies.
   d) None of the above.

2. Which account types CANNOT be used in the expense tab of a purchase transaction to make the expense billable:
   a) Cost of Goods Sold.
   b) Expense.
   c) Other Expense.
   d) All the above.
3. If you want to assign expenses to a Customer:Job, but do not want to pass them for reimbursement, do the following in a purchase transaction:
   a) Do not assign the Customer:Job, just enter the information in the Memo field.
   b) Assign the Customer:Job and then click the checkbox in the Billable column, so that you remove the checkmark.
   c) Delete the Invoice icon.
   d) a or b.
4. Which of the following tabs appear in the **Choose Billable Time and Costs** window:
   a) Items.
   b) Expenses.
   c) Time.
   d) All of the above.
5. In an invoice, you can automatically markup the Pass-through expenses, using the Markup Account option. It is available in the **Choose Billable Time and Costs** window on:
   a) Items tab.
   b) Expenses tab.
   c) Time tab.
   d) All of the above.
6. To track reimbursable expenses in one expense account and the reimbursements in another income account:
   a) Select **Track reimbursed expenses as income** option in the *Time & Expense Company Preference*.
   b) Associate each reimbursable expense account with an appropriate income account.
   c) Both a and b.
   d) None of the above.
7. If you select **Print selected time and costs as one invoice item**, which of the following will be true:
   a) All reimbursable expenses will be printed on a single line in the body of the printed invoice.
   b) A group called **Reimb Group** will be created on the invoice displayed.
   c) **Reimb Group** will include the details of all the expenses you selected on the invoice displayed.
   d) All of the above.
8. Two-sided items can be used for:
   a) Reimbursable expenses.
   b) Custom order parts.
   c) Subcontracted labor.
   d) All of the above.

9. For a two-sided non-inventory item set up without a specific cost/sales price, how will you record the markup in the sales price:
   a) Set the markup in the Time & Expense Company Preference.
   b) Set the markup in the Items tab of **Choose Billable Time and Costs** window.
   c) Manually adjust the price on the sales forms for markup.
   d) All of the above.

10. To see a detailed listing all the billable expenses and items that you have not passed through to invoices:
    a) Create **Unbilled expenses** report.
    b) Create **Unbilled Items** report.
    c) Create **Unbilled Costs by Job** report.
    d) None of the above.

11. Vehicle Mileage Tracker (Pro and above) allows you to:
    a) Track vehicle mileage, post mileage to invoices, run reports to assist with tax preparation.
    b) Reimburse your employees for mileage on their paycheck, a bill or a check.
    c) Track scheduled maintenance of a vehicle.
    d) All of the above.

12. Before you can use the Time Tracking feature, you must:
    a) Enter in time activity for each employee into QuickBooks.
    b) Go through the Payroll Setup Wizard to set up each employee.
    c) Turn on Time & Expense in the *Company Preferences* tab of the *Preferences* window.
    d) Update your payroll tax tables using the *Get Payroll Updates* command.

13. If you plan to use timesheets to create paychecks, you should:
    a) Make sure that you know which employees are hourly and which are salaried.
    b) Record all of the time for each employee, including non-billable time (e.g., sick, vacation, and administrative time), on the timesheet.
    c) Create a Customer:Job assignment for each employee so that their time can be allocated correctly.
    d) Purchase a time-clock in order to backup record the employees' time.

14. Timesheets provide the basic information for job costing, but they do not actually record job costs. To use the timesheet information to record job costs you have to pass the timesheet information onto a:
    a) Paycheck, Check, Bill, or Credit Card Charge.
    b) Invoice.
    c) Sales Receipt.
    d) All the above.

15. After you post timesheet information to paychecks and invoices, the timesheet will affect:
    a) Income.
    b) Job Cost Reports.
    c) Expenses.
    d) All the above.

Completion Statements

1. Choose Billable Time and Costs window allows you to setup *Markup Amount or %* and *Markup Account,* in the __________ tab.
2. An item used on both expenses and sales for is commonly called a ______-_______ ______.
3. A(n) _______ is the time spent by a single person performing a single service on a single date.
4. A(n) _______ _______ is a record of several activities performed during a one-week period by a single employee, owner, or subcontractor.
5. The _______ _______ _______ report shows the total number of hours each employee worked for each Customer or Job.

Time and Billing Problem 1

APPLYING YOUR KNOWLEDGE

Open This File
This chapter uses Time_and_Billing-10Problem1.QBW. To open this file, restore the Time_and_Billing-10Problem1.QBM file to your hard disk.

1. Create the following two-sided *Service* item:

Field	Data
Item Type	Service
Item Name	Videographer
Option Selected	This item is used in assemblies or is performed by a subcontractor or partner
Description on Purchase	Subcontracted Videography Service
Description on Sales	Videography Service
Cost	$100
Sale Price	$175
Expense Account	Subcontracted Services
Preferred Vendor	Wong & Son Video
Tax Code	Non
Income Account	Services

Table 11-1 Details of the Installation Service Item

2. Create the following two-sided *Other Charge* item:

Field	Data
Item Type	Other Charge
Item Name	Freight & Delivery
Option Selected	This is used in assemblies or is a reimbursable charge
Description on Purchase	Freight and Delivery Charges
Description on Sales	Freight and Delivery Charges
Cost	$30
Sale Price	$60
Expense Account	Reimbursable Expenses
Tax Code	Non
Income Account	Services

Table 11-2 Details of the Other Charge Item

3. Create the following two-sided *Non-inventory Part* item:

Field	Data
Item Type	Non-inventory Part
Item Name	Custom Lens
Option Selected	This item is used in assemblies or is purchased for a specific Customer:Job
Description on Purchase	Custom Lens Order #
Description on Sales	Custom Lens Order #
Cost	$0
Sale Price	$0
Expense Account	Cost of Goods Sold
Tax Code	Tax
Income Account	Sales

Table 11-3 Details of the Non-inventory Part Item

4. Create a Purchase Order by entering the following, Total: **$900.00**:

Field	Data
Vendor	Ace Supply
Class	Walnut Creek
Date	4/1/11
P.O. No.	2011-101
Item	Custom Lens
Description	Custom Lens Order #2011-101
Qty	3
Rate	$300
Customer	Cruz, Maria: Branch Opening
Memo	Custom Lens Order #2011-101

Table 11-4 Details of the Purchase Order

5. A new partner, Sonya Mercado, has joined Academy Photography. Open the **Other Names List** and add Sonya Mercado to the list.

6. Enter a bill (**Ref # A1234**) on **4/5/2011** from **Ace Supply** after receiving the custom lens order. Use the P.O. **#2011-101**, Customer:job: **Maria Cruz's Branch Opening job**, Class: **Walnut Creek**, Memo: **Custom Lens order #2011-101**. This item expense is billable. Add freight charge of **$30.00** using the **Freight & Delivery** item, Customer:job: **Maria Cruz's Branch Opening** job and Class: **Walnut Creek**. This item expense is also billable. Total: **$930.00**.

7. Print **Unbilled Costs by Job Report** for all transactions.

8. Create an invoice on **4/5/2011** for **Maria Cruz's Branch Opening** job, Class: **Walnut Creek**, Invoice #: **2011-106**, Description and Memo: **Custom Lens order #2011-101**. Select all the open billable items for this job. Use **QuickMath** to markup the Custom Lens item by **20%**. Total **$1,229.10**. Print the **invoice**.

9. Enter **Vehicle Mileage** for **Ford Escape** (use **Quick Add** to add the vehicle), Trip start date: **4/17/2011**, Trip End Date: **4/17/2011**, Odometer Start: **15283**, Odometer End: **15983**, Total Miles: **700**, Customer:Job: **Bob Mason**, Item: **Mileage** (Create new item: *Other Charge* Item, Two-sided, Cost: **.505**, Expense account: **Automobile Expense**, Sale Price: .61, non-taxable, Income account: **Expenses Reimbursed**), Class: **San Jose**, Note: **Site trip for shoot**. Make the mileage **billable. Set the Mileage Rates for 2011 to $.505**.

10. Create an invoice for **Bob Mason** on **4/21/2011** for expenses and mileage charges. Class: **San Jose**, Invoice #: **2011-107**, Memo: **Expenses and Mileage Invoice**. Select the billable charges on the **Mileage** tab. Then select the billable charge on the **Expenses** tab and have QuickBooks mark up the expense by 20%, coded to **Expense Markup** Income. Invoice Total: $597.40. Print the **Invoice**.

11. Use the Weekly Timesheet to record hours from the table below for Sonya Mercado from 04/23/11 through 04/29/11.

Date	Day	Hrs	Customer:Job	Service	Notes	Class	Billable
4/23/11	Mon	8.0	Anderson Wedding Planners: Wilson, Sarah and Michael	Indoor Photo Session	Photo Shoot	Walnut Creek	Yes
4/24/11	Tues	8.0	Anderson Wedding Planners: Wilson, Sarah and Michael	Indoor Photo Session	Photo Shoot	Walnut Creek	Yes
4/25/11	Wed	8.0	Perez, Jerry	Outdoor Photo Session	Photo Shoot	Walnut Creek	Yes
4/26/11	Thurs	8.0			Admin	San Jose	No
4/27/11	Fri	8.0	Miranda's Corner	Indoor Photo Session	Product Photos	San Jose	Yes

Figure 11-64 Sonya Mercado's time log

12. Create a Sales Receipt Anderson Wedding Planners' Wilson job.
    a) Include all of Sonya Mercado's time, and post it to the Sales Receipt.
    b) Class is **Walnut Creek.**
    c) Date is **04/27/2011.**
    d) Sales No. is **2011-101.**
    e) Check No. is **10987.**
    f) Payment Method is **Check.**
    g) Add one (1) **Photographer** Item for **$125.00** to the Sales Receipt.
    h) Sales Receipt total is **$1645.00.**
13. Print **Mileage by Job Detail** Report for **April 2011.**
14. Print **Mileage by Vehicle Detail** Report for **April 2011.**
15. Print the **Profit and Loss by Job** for **April 2011.**

Workplace Applications

Discussion Questions

These questions are designed to stimulate discussion about how you can apply QuickBooks to your own organization. They may help you think through some of the issues you'll encounter when using QuickBooks in your company.

1. Does your organization incur expenses that it later bills to customers? What type of expenses (i.e. items, mileage, time, etc.) does your organization pass along to customers? Under what circumstances might your organization incur expenses but not pass them along to customers?
2. Does your organization use items that it buys and sells to customers? Does your organization use subcontracted labor? Does your organization bill customers for employees' time?
3. Does your organization reimburse for mileage? Does your organization bill customers for mileage?
4. How do employees in your organization fill out timesheets? How does/would your timesheet information get into QuickBooks in your company? Record your last weeks' time activity into a Weekly Timesheet in QuickBooks. Are you able to allocate all your hours to a Customer or Job? If not, how would you use the timesheet to pass all your hours through to your paycheck?
5. How would you show the activity of the boss' time on the *Time by Name* report? On the *Profit and Loss by Job* report? Does the boss have a single billable rate? If not, how would you track time activity for the various rates?
6. How many customers does your company have? List the various types of administrative activities in your company (i.e. accounting, marketing, human resources, etc.). Describe the benefits of tracking the administrative time of each employee. If you decided to begin tracking administrative time, discuss how you would set up each activity.

Case Study

The Law Offices of Kathy Roach

Kathy L. Roach is a premier commercial litigation attorney. Her law office focuses on business torts and contract litigation and she has clients throughout the Chicago metropolitan area. The law office uses QuickBooks Premier to track billable expenses for its clients. All partners and associates pass through all client-related costs to their clients using QuickBooks.

On November 6, 2011, Ms. Roach received a call from Troy Dillon, a client of the firm since 1982, to complain that he has not received a bill for services in over three months. Mr. Dillon is trying to close out his fiscal year and wants an invoice right away to include in his financials. Mr. Dillon also reminds Ms. Roach that they have agreed that he will no longer be billed for internet charges relating to costs associated with email communications.

Ms. Roach asked her associate, Susie Lambert, to produce an invoice for Troy Dillon so that she could review it and send it to him immediately.

1. What report should Susie Lambert produce before creating the invoice for Troy Dillon?

2. What steps would Susie Lambert take so that the internet charges do not appear on the invoice?

Chapter 12 Payroll Setup

Objectives

After completing this chapter, you should be able to:

- Activate the payroll feature and configure payroll preferences (page 483).
- Set up payroll accounts in the Chart of Accounts (page 485).
- Enable the data file for payroll processing (page 486).
- Use the *Payroll Setup Interview* to add payroll items, vendors, employee records, and year-to-date amounts (page 490).
- Understand the accounting behind the scenes of payroll items (page 525).
- Add payroll items from the Payroll Item list (page 528).
- Edit payroll items in the Payroll Item list (page 531).
- Release, deactivate, and reactivate employees (page 539).

> **Restore this File**
> This chapter uses PRSetup-10.QBW. To open this file, restore the PRSetup-10.QBM file to your hard disk. See page 10 for instructions on restoring files.

In this chapter, you will learn how to set up QuickBooks to track your payroll. In order to use QuickBooks to track your payroll, you must properly set up your payroll accounts, payroll items, employees, and opening balances. If you plan to process payroll manually or use an outside payroll service, you will still need to set up QuickBooks to correctly record your payroll transactions.

You have five choices for using QuickBooks to track your payroll:

1. **Manual Payroll.** You can prepare your own payroll manually in QuickBooks without the use of any tax tables. This option is not recommended for most users, but it is provided if you want to manually calculate your Payroll. You may also want to prepare payroll manually if you use an outside payroll service (i.e. ADP or Paychex). With an outside payroll service you would be required to re-enter payroll details into QuickBooks. *This chapter uses Manual Payroll.*
2. **Basic Payroll.** You can prepare your own payroll in-house using QuickBooks Standard Payroll. This option is recommended for users who want a cost-effective way to maintain control and flexibility of their payroll process. Basic Payroll utilizes up-to-date tax tables that automatically calculate employee deductions and fills out the company's federal tax forms.
3. **Enhanced Payroll.** This option is recommended for users who need a comprehensive in-house payroll solution that offers all the features of Standard Payroll plus additional features like state payroll forms, workers' compensation tracking, and one-step net to gross calculations. Like the Basic Payroll option, Enhanced Payroll utilizes up-to-date tax tables that automatically calculate employee deductions and fills out the company's federal tax forms.

4. **Online Payroll.** Intuit Online Payroll offers many of the same features as Enhanced Payroll, including state payroll forms, workers' compensation tracking and tax tables. Because it is available online, this payroll option doesn't require QuickBooks and can be accessed when you are away from your QuickBooks data.
5. **Assisted Payroll.** This option is recommended for users that want all the flexibility of processing their own payroll that is offered using Enhanced Payroll, but would like for QuickBooks to complete all of their tax filings, deposits, and W-2s.

For detailed information on the differences between these options, select the *Employees* menu, select **Payroll**, and then select **Learn About Payroll Options**. Intuit occasionally makes changes to their Payroll options between version releases, and there may be changes since the publication of this book.

Checklist for Setting up Payroll

The setup of your payroll, just like the setup of your company file itself, is the most important factor in getting it to work well for you. Table 12-1 provides you with a checklist for your payroll setup. Make sure that you complete each step in the order given unless it really does not apply.

Payroll Setup Checklist

1. Gather information about each of your employees, including the name, address, social security number, and W-4 information.
2. Activate the Payroll function in *Preferences*.
3. Set up payroll accounts in the Chart of Accounts. Example accounts: Gross Wages, Payroll Tax Expense, Federal PR Tax Liabilities, and State PR Tax Liabilities.
4. Enable your QuickBooks file for payroll processing either manually, or by signing up for one of QuickBooks payroll services.
5. Using the *Payroll Setup Interview*, set up payroll items, payroll vendors, employee defaults, employee records, and year-to-date payroll figures.
6. Add additional payroll items directly from the Payroll Item list.
7. Edit payroll items to modify the vendor information and the way the items affect the Chart of Accounts.
8. If setting up mid-year, enter year-to-date information for additional payroll items on the Payroll list for each employee and enter year-to-date liability payments.
9. Verify payroll item setup, employee setup, and the vendor list.
10. Proof your setup. Use the *Payroll Checkup* wizard and compare reports with your accountant's or payroll service's reports. The *Payroll Checkup* wizard is not covered in this chapter.

Table 12-1 Payroll Setup Checklist

> **Key Term: W-4:** Form W-4 is the IRS form that each of your employees must fill out when you hire them. The IRS requires employees to provide you with their name, address, social security number, and their withholding information on this form. The Internal Revenue service has many payroll forms available online at www.irs.gov. For form W-4, enter ***W4*** in *Search* field.

Activating Payroll

COMPUTER PRACTICE

To activate the Payroll function and configure your Payroll preferences, follow these steps:

Step 1. Select the **Edit** menu, and then select **Preferences.**

Step 2. Select the **Payroll & Employee** preference and then select the **Company Preferences** tab (see Figure 12-1).

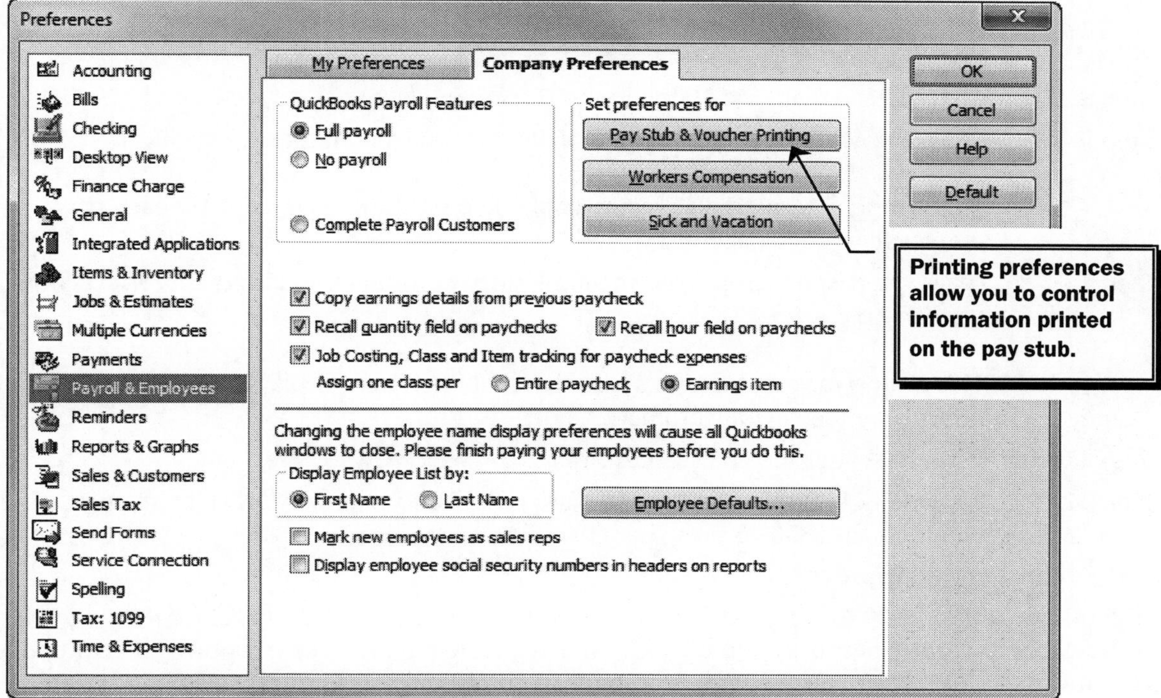

Figure 12-1 Company Preferences tab for Payroll & Employees

Step 3. Leave the **Full payroll** feature selected.

In the practice file, the Payroll function is already activated. In your company file, choose the **Full payroll** feature if you want to calculate paychecks, print paychecks, track liabilities by Payroll Item, and prepare Forms 941, 940, W-2, and W-3.

Step 4. Check the box next to the **Copy last paycheck earnings when creating new one** field.

If you check this box, QuickBooks automatically carries forward earnings items, their rates, and the hours from the previous paycheck. Sick or Vacation payroll items are also carried forward from the previous paycheck. You might want to check this preference if your employees' hours usually do not change or if the split-lines for job costing and class tracking remain the same from paycheck to paycheck.

Step 5. Leave the **Recall quantity field on paychecks** box checked.

If you check this box, QuickBooks remembers the quantities you entered on the last paycheck, and pre-fills those quantities on each new paycheck. Check this preference when you have a fixed quantity that recurs from paycheck to paycheck.

Step 6. Leave the **Job Costing, Class and Item tracking for paycheck expenses** box checked.

If you check this box, QuickBooks will track payroll costs (additions, deductions, and company taxes) by job, class, or service item. The costs will be allocated in the same proportion as the gross wages.

Step 7. Check **Earnings item** next to *Assign one class per.*

If you have employees who work in different departments, and you want to allocate their payroll expenses to separate departments (classes), select **Earnings item**. Classes allow you to track separate departments, profit centers, or store locations in one QuickBooks file.

Step 8. Check to see that **First Name** in the *Display Employee List by:* section.

Step 9. Leave the **Mark new employee as sales reps** box unchecked.

This setting automatically creates a Sales Rep (in the sales rep list) for each new employee.

Step 10. Leave the **Display employee social security numbers in headers on reports** box unchecked.

This setting makes employees' social security numbers display at the top of each column on the Payroll Summary report.

Step 11. Verify that your screen matches Figure 12-1. Click **OK** to save.

Step 12. If QuickBooks displays a *Warning* dialog box stating that it must close all open windows, click **OK** to save your changes.

Federal and State Employer IDs

If you have not already set up your Federal Employer Identification Number (FEIN), you will not be able to complete the signup process for any of the payroll service options. QuickBooks will automatically enter your Federal Employer ID in the payroll signup windows. To enter your taxpayer ID, select the **Company** menu and then select **Company Information** (see Figure 12-2). After verifying your company data, click **OK** to save.

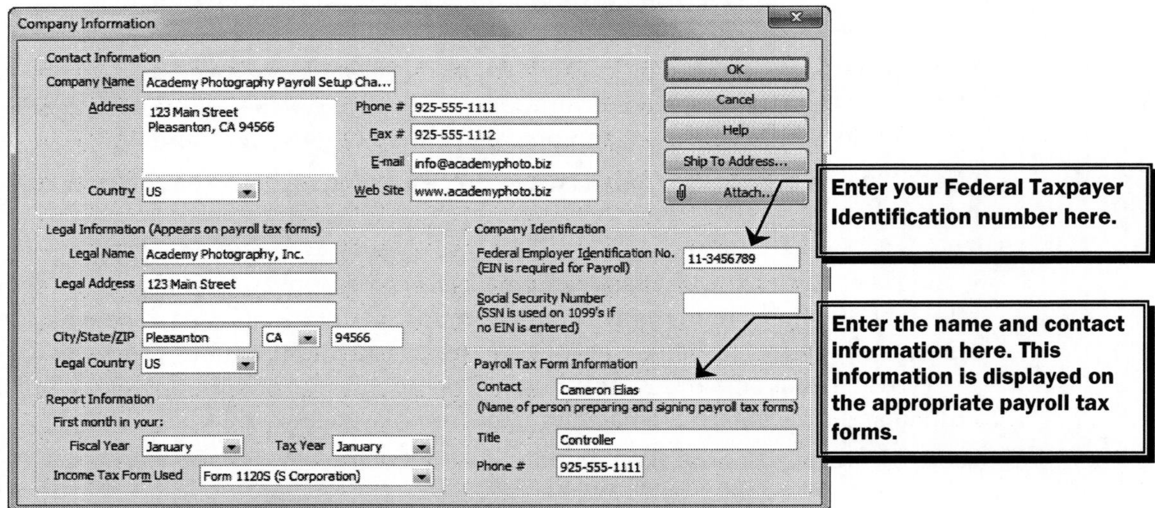

Figure 12-2 Company Information window

Your State taxpayer ID will be entered when you set up your State Payroll Tax Items, and can be modified at any time as discussed on page 535.

Payroll Accounts

In your Chart of Accounts, confirm that you have all of the accounts you want to see on your Balance Sheet and Profit and Loss reports. Academy Photography uses the following accounts for payroll. These accounts are already set up in the practice file.

Example Liability Accounts for Payroll

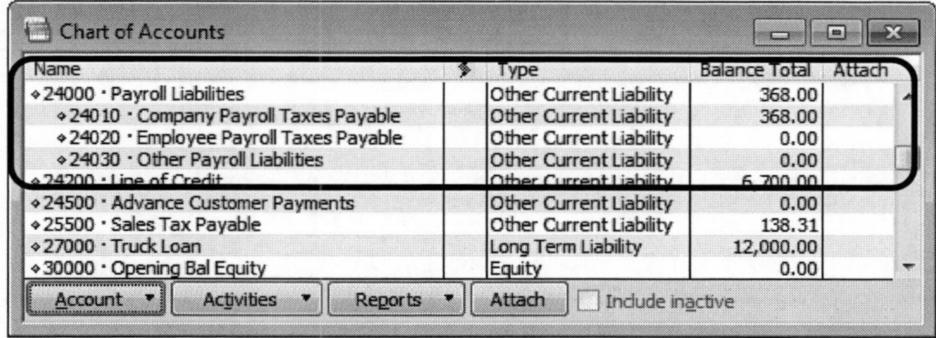

Figure 12-3 Payroll Liability Accounts

Example Expense Accounts for Payroll

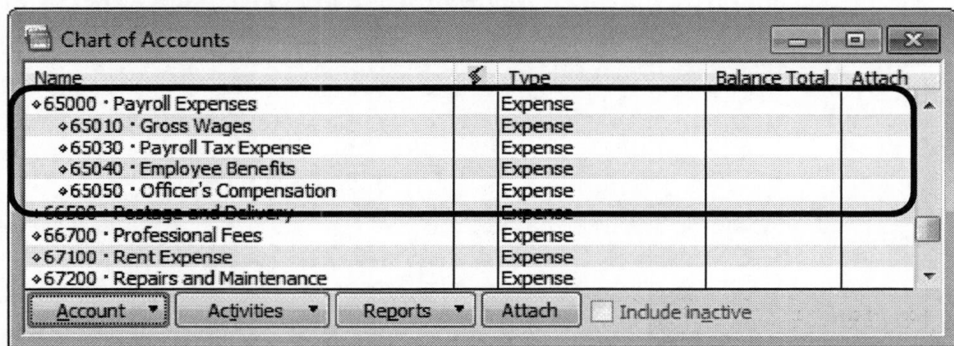

Figure 12-4 Payroll Expense Accounts

If you are not sure which accounts you should include in your **Chart of Accounts**, ask your accountant. However, you should normally have only a few Subaccounts associated with the Payroll Liabilities account, and a few Subaccounts associated with the Payroll Expenses account. Do not add unnecessary accounts and Subaccounts to the **Chart of Accounts**, since the detailed tracking of payroll comes from Payroll Items and not accounts.

If your **Chart of Accounts** already has too many accounts or Subaccounts, you can merge some accounts until you have a manageable number of accounts.

Payroll Items

Payroll items are used to track the compensation, additions, deductions, and other employer-paid expenses listed on the employee's paycheck. These items include wages, commissions, tips, benefits, taxes, dues, retirement plans, and any other additions and deductions to an employee's paycheck. Like other QuickBooks items, payroll Items are connected to the Chart of Accounts so that as paychecks are created, the accounting behind the scenes is handled automatically. In addition, payroll Items are used to accumulate payroll liabilities. Figure 12-5 shows the Payroll Item List after the Payroll Setup Interview--discussed beginning on page 490--has been completed.

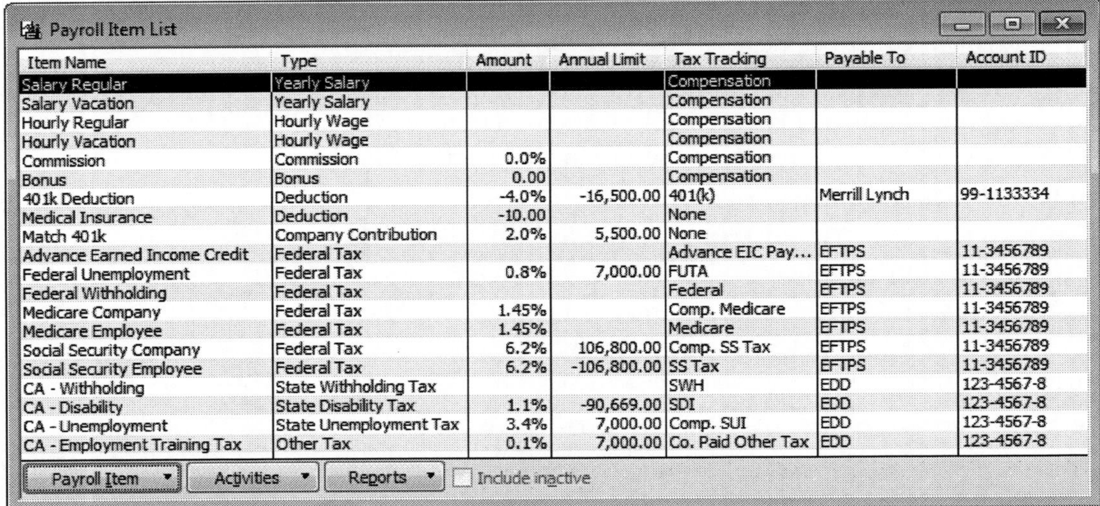

Payroll Item List

Item Name	Type	Amount	Annual Limit	Tax Tracking	Payable To	Account ID
Salary Regular	Yearly Salary			Compensation		
Salary Vacation	Yearly Salary			Compensation		
Hourly Regular	Hourly Wage			Compensation		
Hourly Vacation	Hourly Wage			Compensation		
Commission	Commission	0.0%		Compensation		
Bonus	Bonus	0.00		Compensation		
401k Deduction	Deduction	-4.0%	-16,500.00	401(k)	Merrill Lynch	99-1133334
Medical Insurance	Deduction	-10.00		None		
Match 401k	Company Contribution	2.0%	5,500.00	None		
Advance Earned Income Credit	Federal Tax			Advance EIC Pay...	EFTPS	11-3456789
Federal Unemployment	Federal Tax	0.8%	7,000.00	FUTA	EFTPS	11-3456789
Federal Withholding	Federal Tax			Federal	EFTPS	11-3456789
Medicare Company	Federal Tax	1.45%		Comp. Medicare	EFTPS	11-3456789
Medicare Employee	Federal Tax	1.45%		Medicare	EFTPS	11-3456789
Social Security Company	Federal Tax	6.2%	106,800.00	Comp. SS Tax	EFTPS	11-3456789
Social Security Employee	Federal Tax	6.2%	-106,800.00	SS Tax	EFTPS	11-3456789
CA - Withholding	State Withholding Tax			SWH	EDD	123-4567-8
CA - Disability	State Disability Tax	1.1%	-90,669.00	SDI	EDD	123-4567-8
CA - Unemployment	State Unemployment Tax	3.4%	7,000.00	Comp. SUI	EDD	123-4567-8
CA - Employment Training Tax	Other Tax	0.1%	7,000.00	Co. Paid Other Tax	EDD	123-4567-8

Figure 12-5 Payroll Item List

Enabling the Data File for Payroll Processing

There are two ways to enable your data file for payroll processing in QuickBooks: either using the Internet, or manually without an Internet connection.

> **Activating vs. Enabling**
> *Activating* the data file for payroll processing means that you "turn on" payroll features in the QuickBooks preferences. *Enabling* the data file for payroll processing means that QuickBooks will display the menu options and icons needed for payroll processing.

Enable Intuit Payroll

Most users enable their data file over the Internet by signing up for a QuickBooks payroll service or selecting the option to process their payroll manually. If you have an Internet connection, follow these steps to enable your data file for payroll processing:

> **DO NOT PERFORM THESE STEPS NOW. THEY ARE FOR REFERENCE ONLY.**

1. From the *Home* page click on the **Learn about Payroll Options** icon. Alternatively, select the *Employees* menu, select **Payroll**, and then select **Learn About Payroll Options.**
2. QuickBooks displays the *Launch Web Browser?* dialog box. Click **OK**.
3. QuickBooks displays the *QuickBooks Payroll Services* window shown in Figure 12-6 (your window may have changed since the writing of this book). If you want to sign up for a payroll service, select the *Learn More* link from one of the options below and follow the online steps.

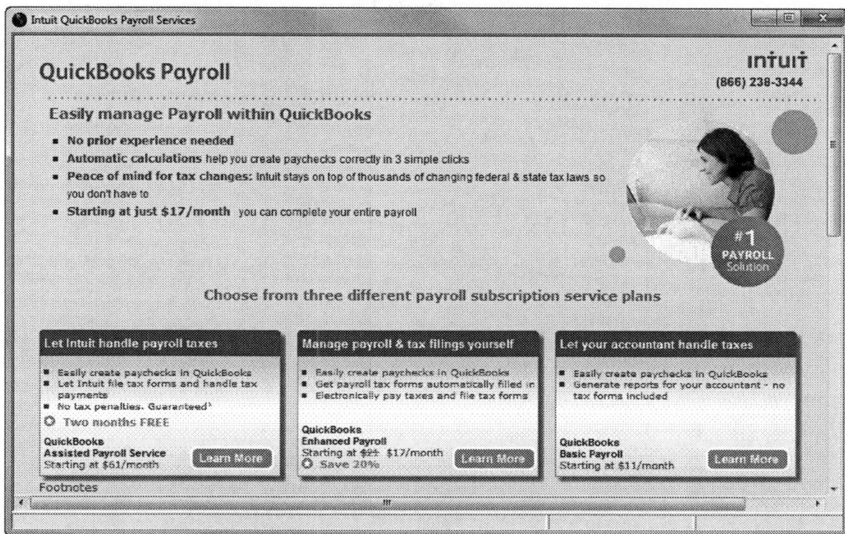

Figure 12-6 QuickBooks Payroll Services window

4. Once you sign up for a QuickBooks payroll service, a Payroll Service Key will be emailed to you. You can then select the **Enter Payroll Service Key** option from the *Employees* menu as illustrated below in Figure 12-7 to add your service key and activate your payroll subscription.

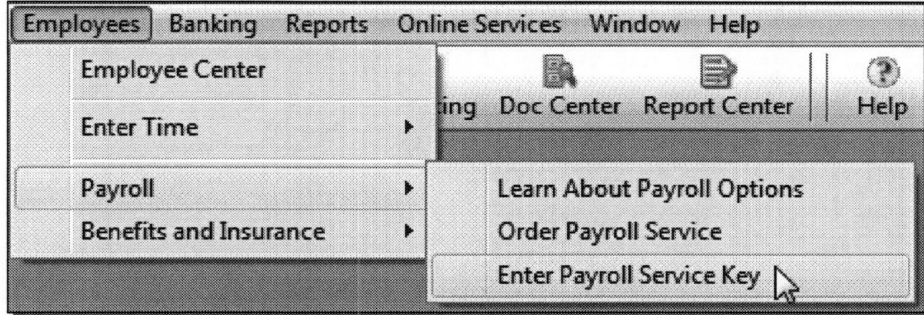

Figure 12-7 Activate Service Key option

> **Note:**
> QuickBooks no longer offers a free one-time download of the current payroll tax tables as it did in times past. In order to receive current payroll tax tables you will have to enroll in one of Intuit's Payroll Service options.

5. After activating the Service Key, the *Home* page should now display the **Payroll Center, Pay Employees, Pay Liabilities**, and **Process Payroll Forms** icons in the *Employees* section (see Figure 12-8). In addition, the *List* and *Employees* menus will now display payroll processing options.

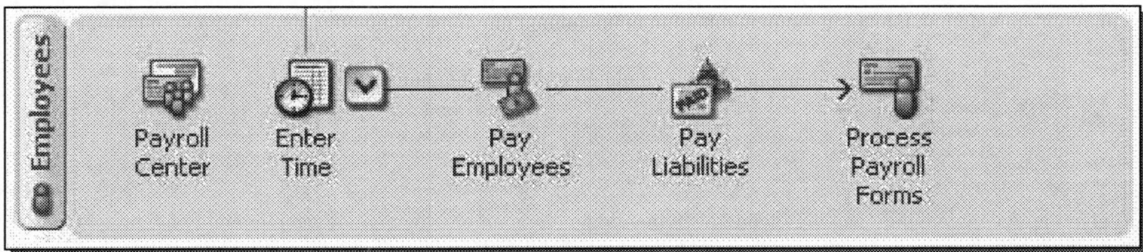

Figure 12-8 Employees section of the Home page after enabling payroll

Enable Manual Payroll

The exercises in this chapter use Manual Payroll. Follow the steps below to enable your QuickBooks data file to process payroll manually:

COMPUTER PRACTICE

Step 1. From the *Help* menu, select **QuickBooks Help**. Alternatively, press **F1**.

Step 2. Click the **Search** tab, type in ***manual payroll*** in the search box, and press the **arrow** button (see Figure 12-9).

Step 3. Select **Process payroll manually (without a subscription to QuickBooks payroll)** from the topics displayed.

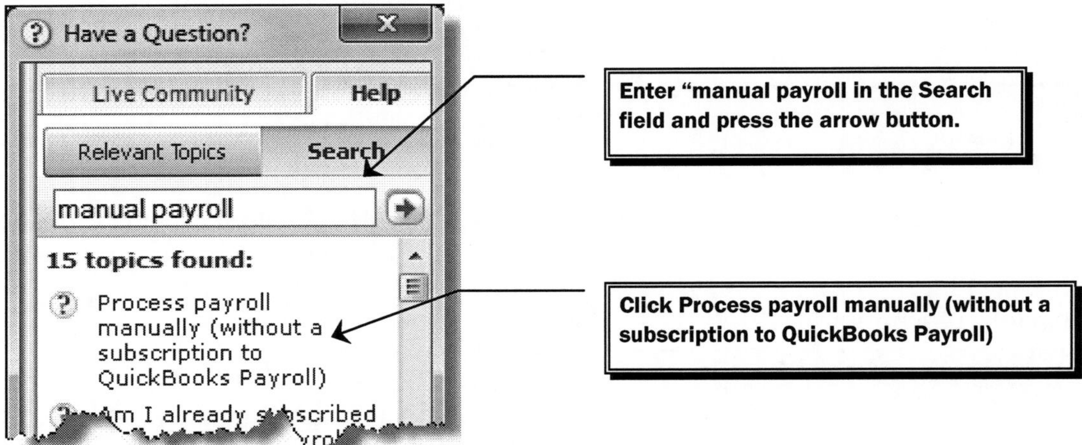

Figure 12-9 QuickBooks Help - Process Payroll Manually

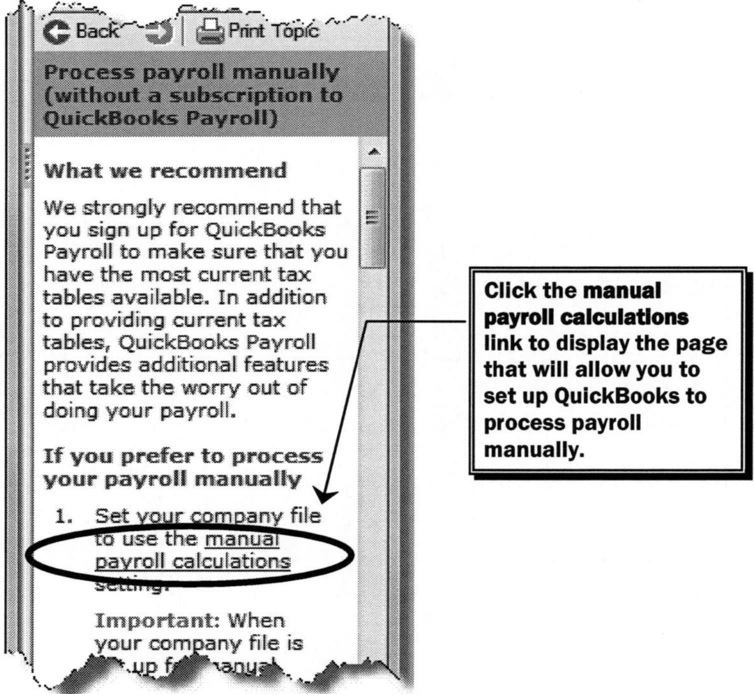

Figure 12-10 Manual payroll search in QuickBooks Help

Step 4. Click on the **manual payroll calculations** link in the *If you prefer to process your payroll manually* section (see Figure 12-10).

Step 5. QuickBooks displays the message: *Are you sure you want to set your company file to use manual calculation?* Click the **Set my company file to use manual calculations** link at the bottom (see Figure 12-11).

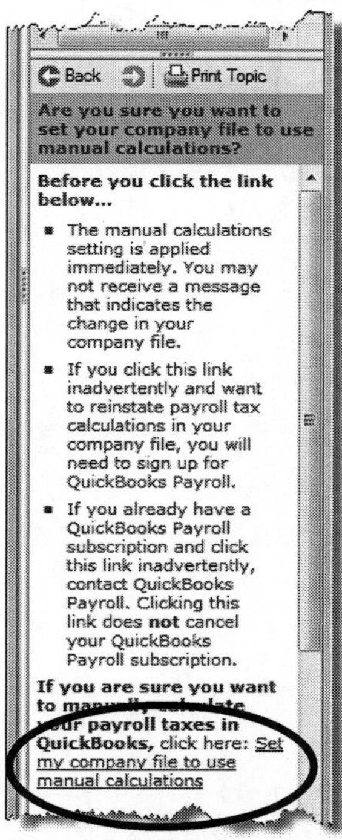

Figure 12-11 Option to set company file for manual payroll processing

Step 6. Your QuickBooks file is now set up to calculate payroll manually. QuickBooks displays the dialog box in Figure 12-12 to inform the user that paychecks will now have to be calculated manually. Click **OK**.

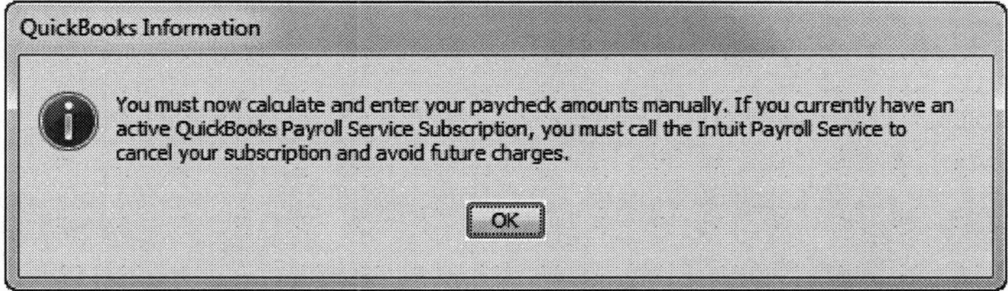

Figure 12-12 Dialog box informing the user that paycheck amount will have to be calculated manually

Step 7. Close the **QuickBooks Help** window.

Step 8. Verify that the *Home* page displays the **Pay Employees** and **Pay Liabilities** icons in the *Employees* section (see Figure 12-13). In addition, the *List* and *Employees* menus will now display additional payroll options. Note that when payroll is processed manually, the Payroll Center icon in the Employee section of the *Home* page does not display as it does in Figure 12-8.

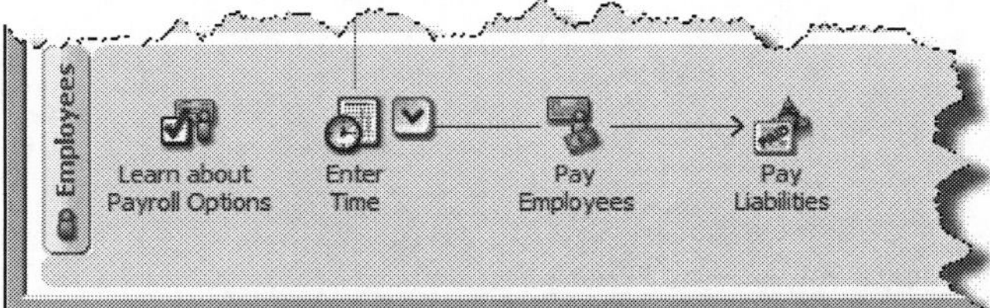

Figure 12-13 Employee section after manual payroll in QuickBooks has been enabled

The Payroll Setup Interview

The *Payroll Setup Interview* is a set of windows similar to the *EasyStep Interview* that walks you through the setup of payroll. This wizard is optional, but if you are starting from scratch (as shown here), you will probably find it helpful. Even if you have existing payroll, the wizard can take the guesswork out of setting up new benefits and wages for your employees.

COMPUTER PRACTICE

Step 1. From the *Employees* menu, select **Payroll Setup** (see Figure 12-14).

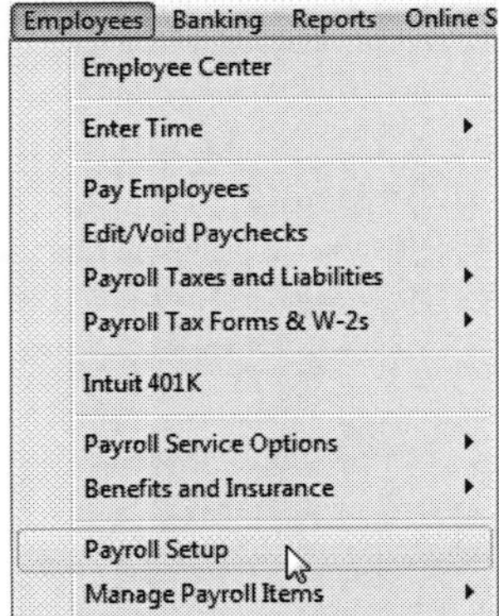

Figure 12-14 Payroll Setup menu option

Step 2. QuickBooks displays the *QuickBooks Payroll Setup* window shown in Figure 12-15. Click the **Close** link on the upper right side of the window to close the *Live Community.*

Live Community is support features Intuit offers to QuickBooks users. It allows you to ask questions of other QuickBooks users. We won't be using *Live Community* during this exercise.

Step 3. Click **Continue.**

The Payroll Setup Interview takes you through a 6-step process to complete the setup of your payroll. If you need to leave the payroll process at any point during setup, click the **Finish Later** button and QuickBooks will display a message to let you know that you can return to the setup process at any time. When you select **Payroll Setup** from the *Employee* menu again, QuickBooks will return you to the last point where you left off in the setup process.

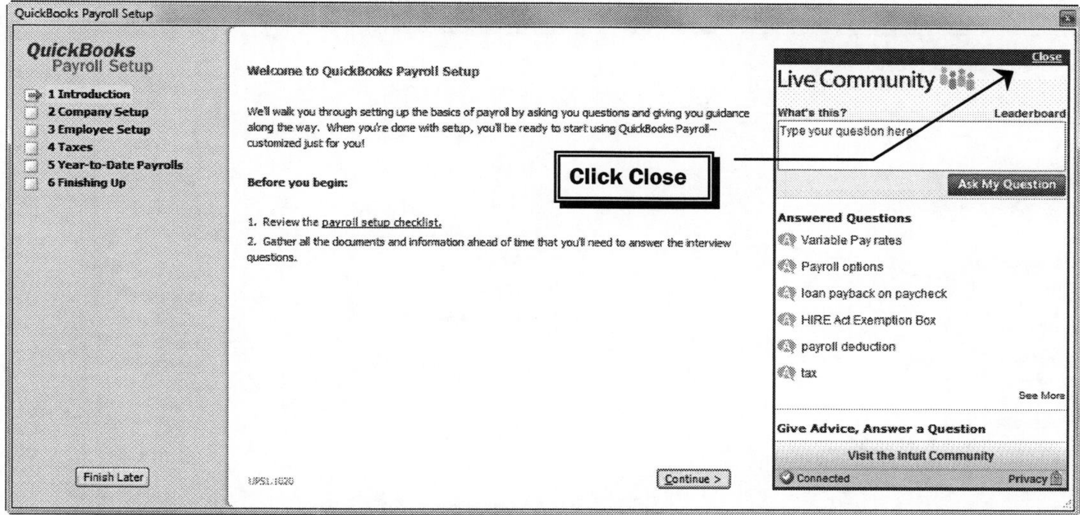

Figure 12-15 Payroll Setup Interview window

Setting up Compensation and Benefits Payroll Items

In this section of the setup wizard, you will set up compensation items (i.e. hourly wages, salary wages, bonuses, commissions, etc).

COMPUTER PRACTICE

Step 1. QuickBooks displays the Compensation and Benefits section in shown in Figure 12-16. Click **Continue.**

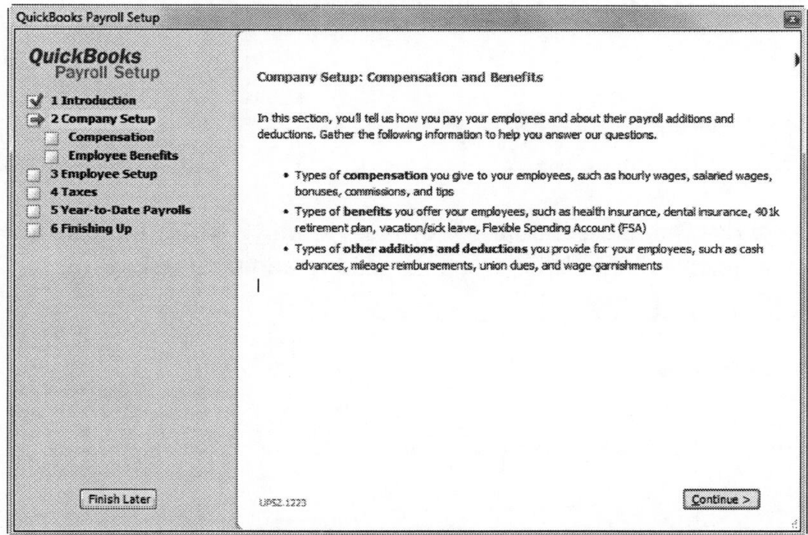

Figure 12-16 Payroll Setup Interview – Step 2 - Compensation and Benefits

Step 2. QuickBooks displays the *Add New* window and pre-selects **Salary, Hourly wage and overtime**, and **Bonus, award, or one-time compensation** (see Figure 12-17). Select the **Commission** compensation item and click **Next.**

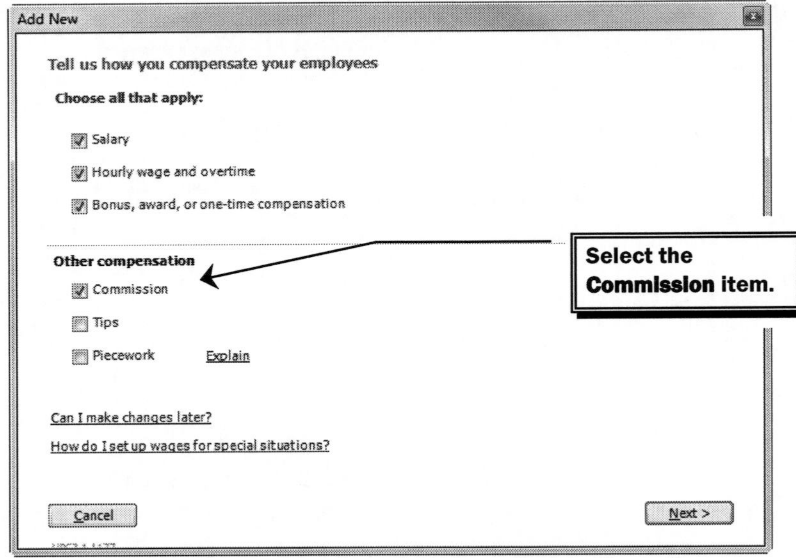

Figure 12-17 Payroll Setup Interview - Add New compensation options

Step 3. In the next screen, QuickBooks wants to know how commissions should be calculated. Select **Percentage of sales (or other amount)** and click **Finish** (see Figure 12-18).

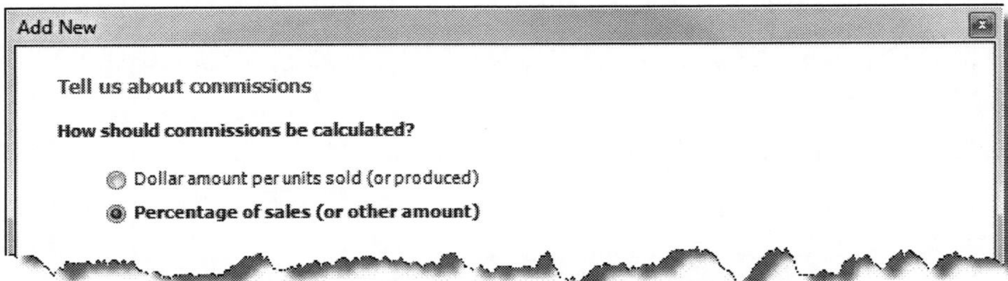

Figure 12-18 Payroll Setup Interview – commissions calculations

Step 4. QuickBooks displays the **Compensation list** shown in Figure 12-19. At this point, we need to modify this list by editing some of the names and adding new ones.

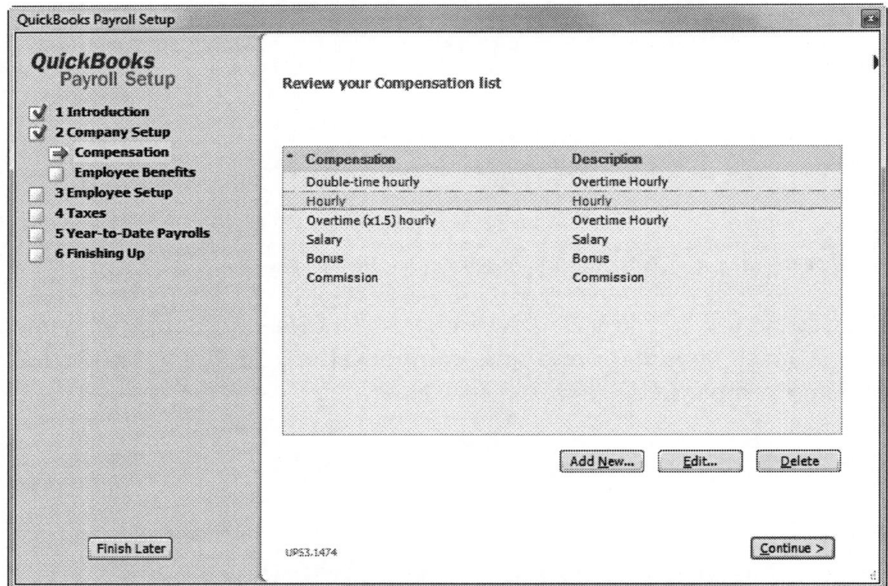

Figure 12-19 Payroll Setup Interview – Review the Compensation list

Step 5. To change the name of the **Hourly** payroll item to **Hourly Regular**, select **Hourly** from the *Compensation list* and click **Edit**.

Step 6. Type ***Hourly Regular*** in the *Show on paychecks as* field (see Figure 12-20) and select **Payroll Expenses:Gross Wages** from the Account name drop-down list. You may need to scroll up once the Account name list is open. Then click **Finish**.

Figure 12-20 Edit Hourly Pay window

Step 7. Edit or delete all of the rest of the default compensation items, renaming and editing the accounts to match the table shown in Table 12-2. Leave all other fields set to their defaults as you edit the items.

Default Item Name	Change to this Name	Change to this Account
Double-time hourly	**Delete this item**	**Delete this item**
Hourly	Hourly Regular	Payroll Expenses:Gross Wages
Overtime (x1.5) hourly	**Delete this item**	**Delete this item**
Salary	Salary Regular	Payroll Expenses:Gross Wages
Bonus	Bonus	Payroll Expenses:Gross Wages
Commission	Commission	Payroll Expenses:Gross Wages

Table 12-2 Compensation Item Names and Accounts

Step 8. When the Commission item is edited, QuickBooks displays the *Edit COMMISSION: Commission* window. Leave the default rate or amount at 0% and click **Finish** to return to the Compensation List (see Figure 12-21).

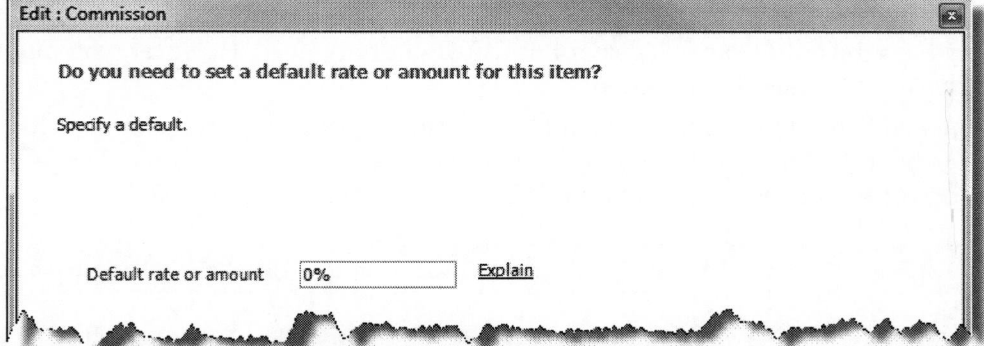

Figure 12-21 Default rate window for commissions

Step 9. When you're finished editing the default payroll items, your list will look like the one in Figure 12-22.

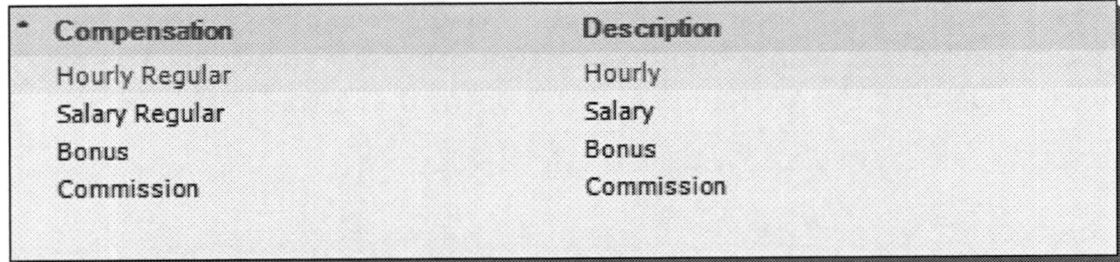

Compensation	Description
Hourly Regular	Hourly
Salary Regular	Salary
Bonus	Bonus
Commission	Commission

Figure 12-22 Compensation items after renaming

Step 10. Click **Continue** to set up employee benefits.

Medical Insurance Deduction

Step 1. QuickBooks displays the Set up employee benefits window. Click Continue.

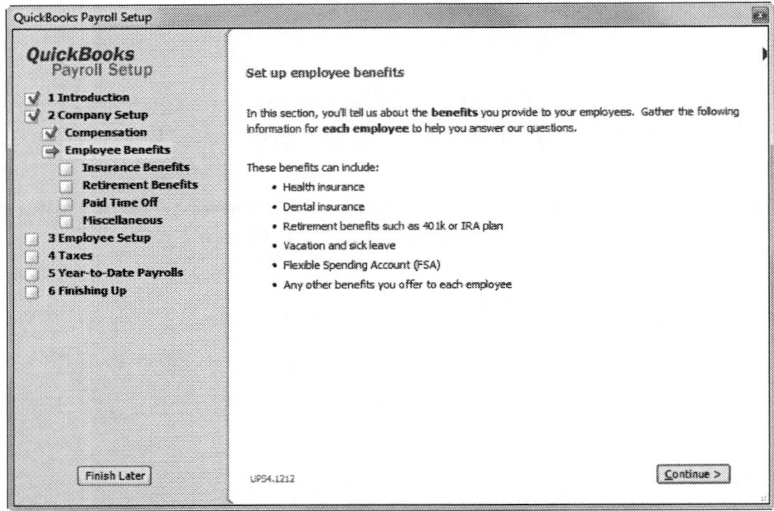

Figure 12-23 Payroll Setup Interview – Set up employee benefits

In this section of the setup wizard, you will set up the benefits you offer (health insurance, dental insurance, retirements plans, etc.), and any other additions or deductions that affect the employees gross income (i.e. expense reimbursements, dues, garnishments, etc.). If your company provides benefits, there are three options for allocating the costs between the company and the employee. First, the company could pay the entire expense; second, the company and employee could share the expense; and third, the employee could pay the entire expense.

If your company pays the entire expense, payroll is usually not involved. However, you might need to adjust the W-2s to include the benefits.

If the costs are shared between the company and the employees, or if the employees pay for the entire cost via payroll deductions, use a *Deduction Item* to track the deductions. The following method is the simplest way to handle this type of deduction in payroll:

DO NOT PERFORM THESE STEPS NOW. THEY ARE FOR REFERENCE ONLY.

1. When you receive the bill from the provider of benefits, enter it in QuickBooks just like any other bill. Code the bill to the appropriate expense account, (in this case, *Health Insurance Expense*). Then just pay this bill normally.

2. Set up a *Payroll Deduction Item* for the benefit, (in this case, Medical Insurance) and use the same expense account for this Payroll Item as you use to code the bill (*Health Insurance Expense*). This deduction reduces the *Health Insurance Expense* account each time you withhold from employees' paychecks (as shown in this section).

> **Tip:**
> Setting up and using the Medical Insurance Deduction item in this way simplifies the tracking of medical insurance costs. By not accruing the deductions to a liability account, this method avoids the necessity of using **Payroll Liability Payments** to pay the medical insurance bills. Instead, you'll use the normal process of entering and paying bills, which directly expenses the whole amount of the insurance expense (both employer and employee portion), and the payroll deductions will reduce the total insurance expense (employee portion) as paychecks are written.
>
> **The accounting behind the scenes:**
> The bill entered in Step 1 increases (debits) the *Health Insurance Expense* account. When you use the *Medical Insurance Deduction Item* on a paycheck, it reduces (credits) the *Health Insurance Expense* account. The net amount left in the expense account represents the company portion for health insurance.

Now, we will resume the exercise.

COMPUTER PRACTICE

Step 1. In the *Set up insurance benefits* page (Figure 12-24), click **Health insurance** and then click **Next**.

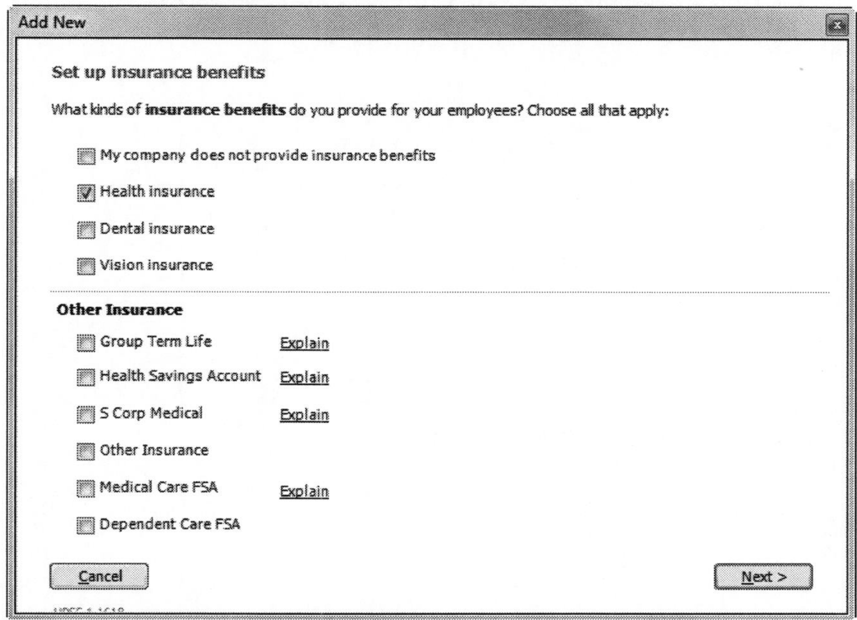

Figure 12-24 Set up insurance benefits page

Step 2. Select the option for **Both the employee and company pay portions** shown in Figure 12-25 and then click **Next**.

Even though Academy Photography pays most of the health insurance costs, this item will be set up to deduct a portion of the expense after taxes from paychecks.

We'll have to modify it later to connect the payroll item to the health insurance expense account. Make sure to leave the **Payment is deducted after taxes** option selected.

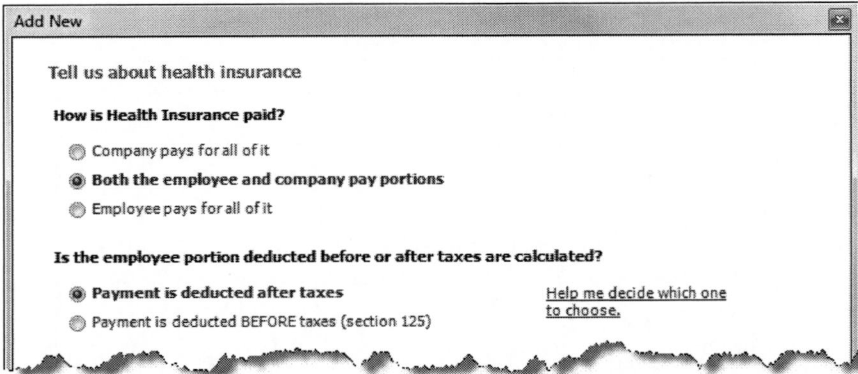

Figure 12-25 The health insurance payroll item setup screen

Step 3. In Figure 12-26 the Payroll Setup Interview asks if you want to setup the Payee, account number, and Payment frequency. Leave **I don't need a regular payment schedule for this item** selected and click **Finish**.

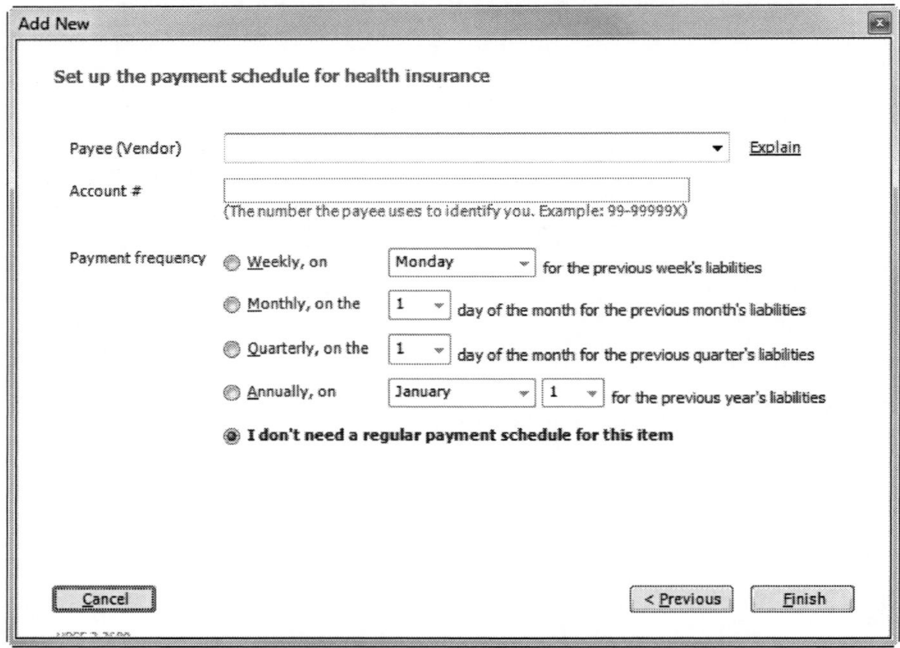

Figure 12-26 Setting up the payment schedule window

Step 4. The *Insurance Item* window displays.

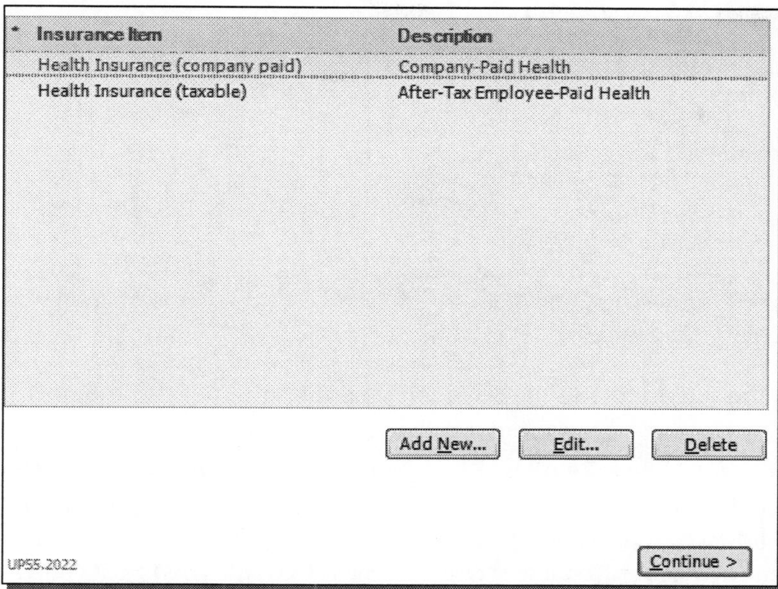

Figure 12-27 Insurance Items list

Notice in Figure 12-27 that QuickBooks has added two Payroll items. One item, *Health Insurance (company paid)*, was added to track the accruals for the employer portion of the health insurance costs, and the other item, *Health Insurance (taxable)*, to track the employee deductions. However, for our example, the employer pays the health insurance bill by directly coding the bill to *Health Insurance* expense. Then, the employer deducts the employee's portion of the health insurance costs from their paychecks. So we'll delete the *Health Insurance (company paid)* item because we won't accrue the employer's portion of the health insurance costs through payroll.

Step 5. Select the *Health Insurance (company paid)* item (see Figure 12-27), and then click **Delete.**

Step 6. Click **Yes** on the *Delete Payroll Item* window shown in Figure 12-28.

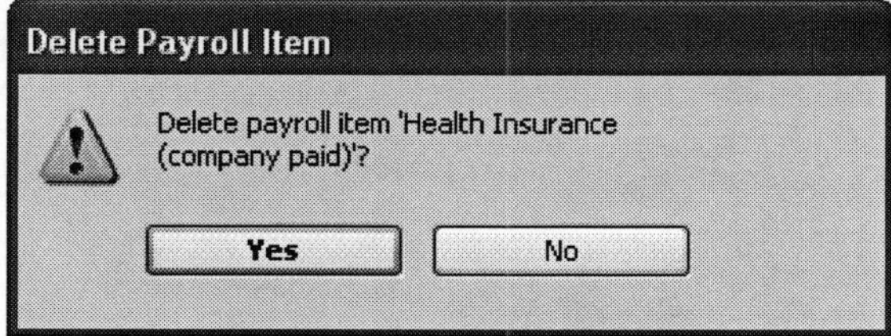

Figure 12-28 Delete Payroll Item dialog box

Step 7. Next, select the *Health Insurance (taxable)* item and click **Edit** (see Figure 12-29). Change the name to ***Medical Insurance*** in the *Show on paychecks as* field and click **Next.**

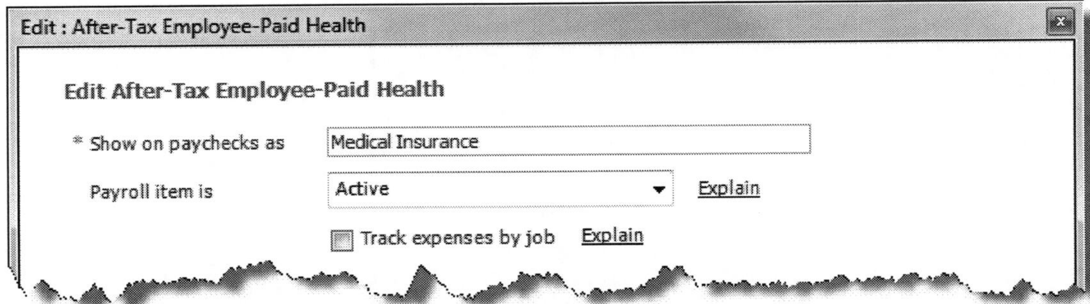

Figure 12-29 Edit: After-Tax Employee-Paid Health window

Step 8. Click **Next** to skip the option to edit the payment schedule and move to the next window.

Step 9. In the **Edit After-Tax Employee-Paid Health** section, change the Account type to **Expense**, and select Insurance Expense:Health Insurance Expense from the Account name drop-down list (see Figure 12-30). Ignore the warning displayed next to the Account name that the Account type must be a liability account. Then click **Next.**

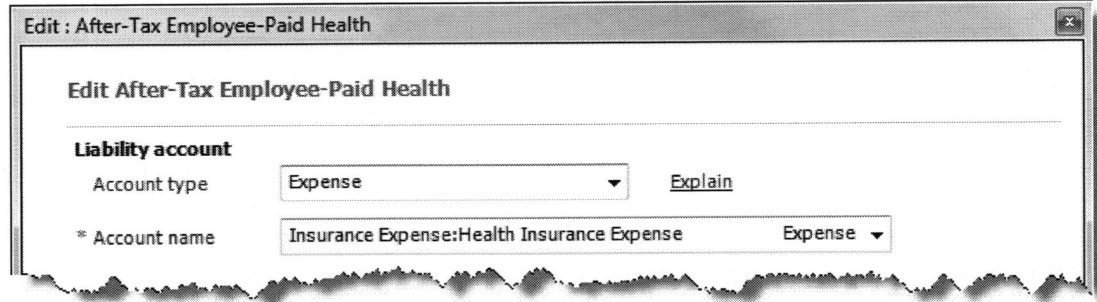

Figure 12-30 Account type and Account name window

Step 10. Leave the defaults in the tax tracking type window and click **Next** (see Figure 12-31).

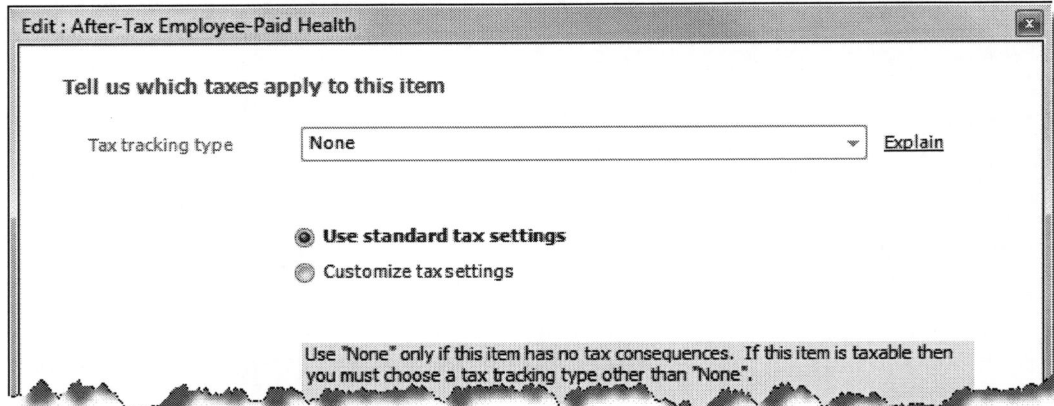

Figure 12-31 Tax tracking type window

Step 11. Change the default rate to 10.00 and click **Finish** (see Figure 12-32).

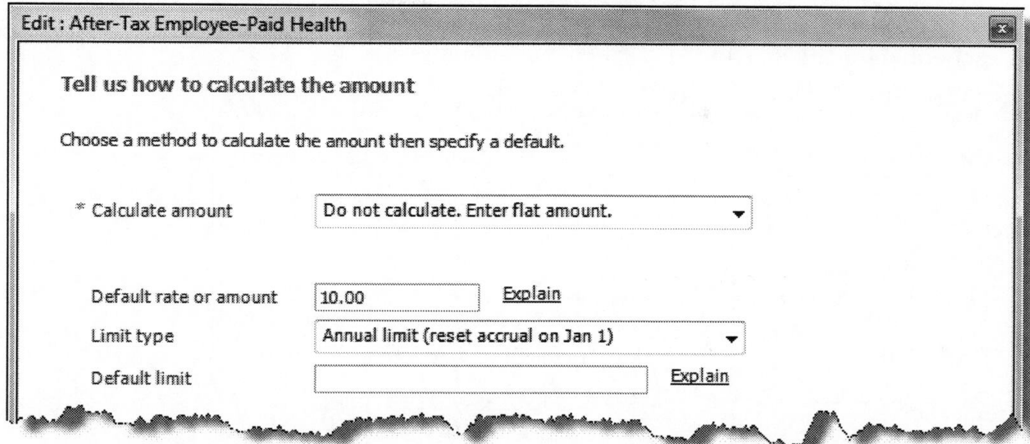

Figure 12-32 Setting the default rate

Step 12. You will return to the *Insurance Benefits list*. Click **Continue**.

401(k) Employee Deduction and Company Match Items

If you have a 401(k) plan, you can set up Payroll Items to track the employer contributions and the employee contributions (salary deferral) to the plan.

COMPUTER PRACTICE

Step 1. On the *Tell us about your retirement benefits* screen (Figure 12-33), click on the **401(k)** Item and click **Next**.

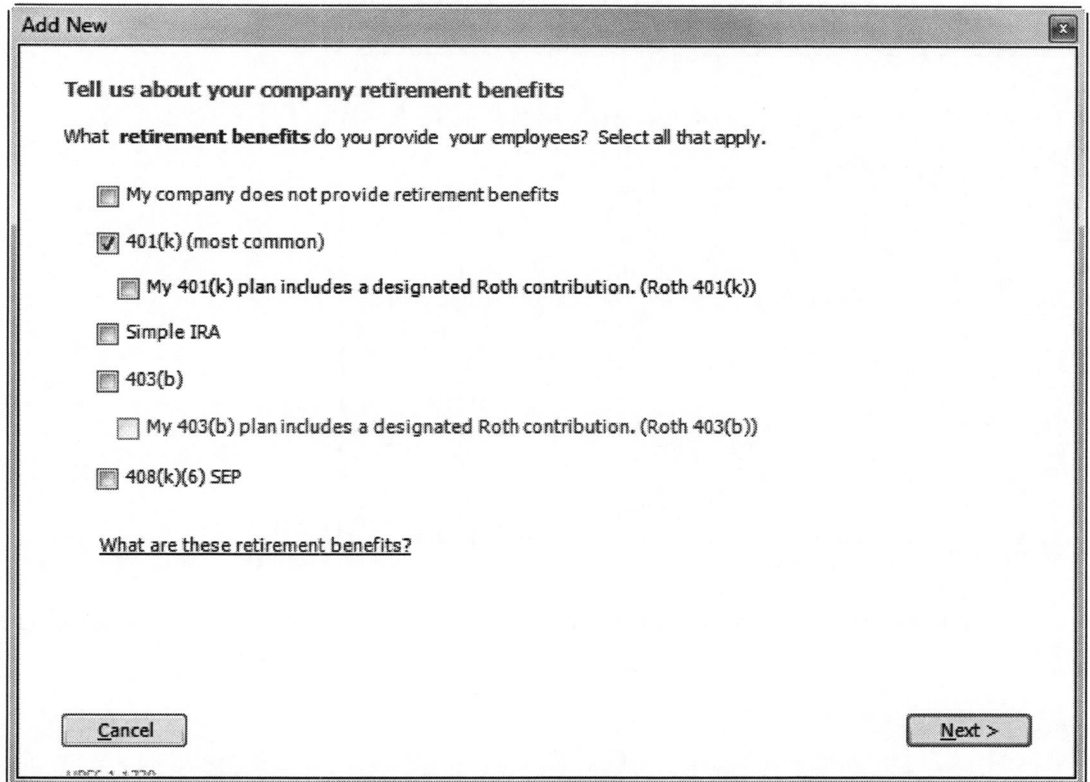

Figure 12-33 Adding the 401(k) Payroll Items

Step 2. Click **Finish** to accept the default selection and not set up a regular payment schedule for the 401(k).

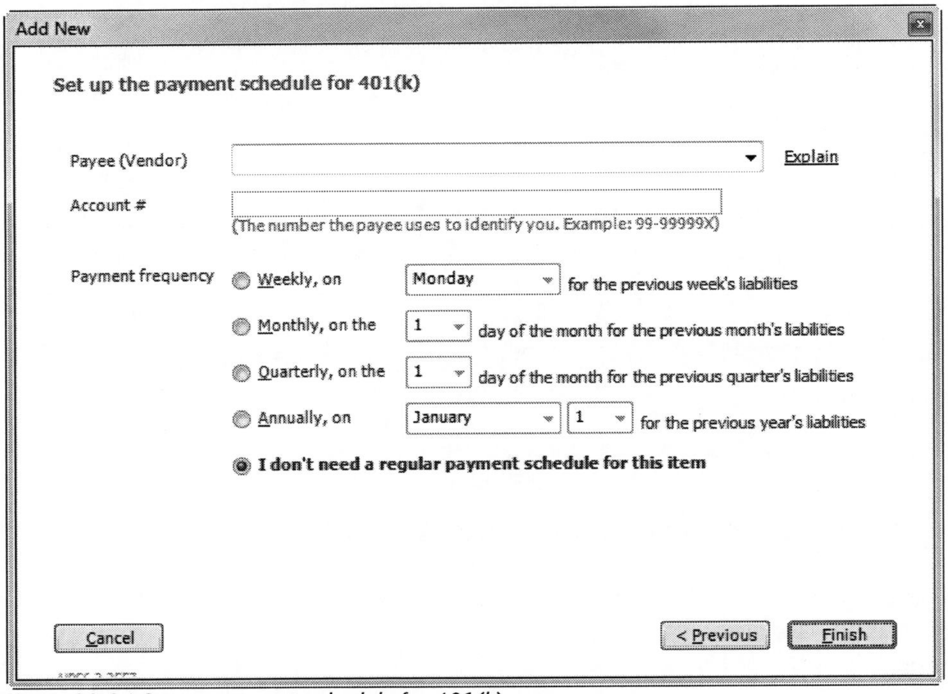

Figure 12-34 Set up payment schedule for 401(k)

Step 3. Next, edit each of the default items shown in Figure 12-35. First, select the *401k Co. Match* item and click **Edit**.

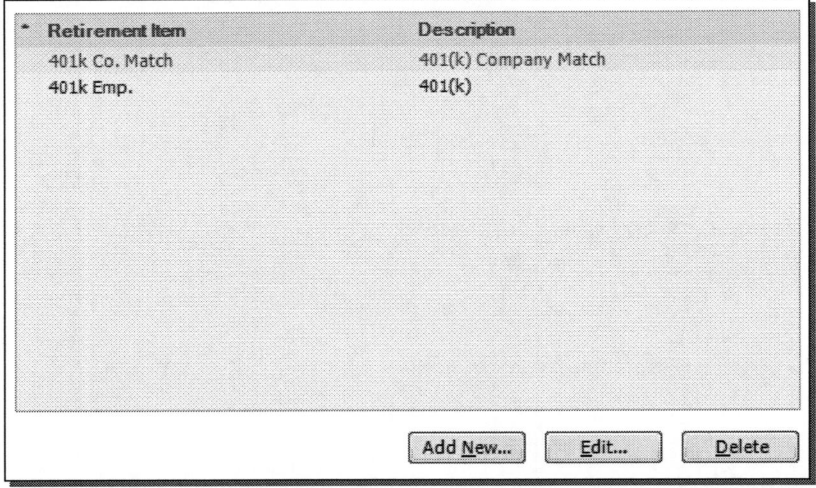

Figure 12-35 The default item names for 401k

Step 4. Type ***Match 401k*** in the *Show on paychecks as* field (see Figure 12-36). Click **Next**.

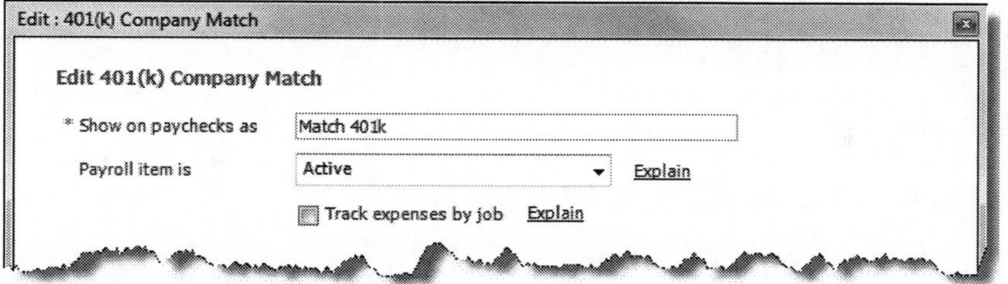

Figure 12-36 Modifying the company match item name for 401k

Step 5. Type ***Merrill Lynch*** in the Payee (Vendor) field and ***99-1133334*** in the Account # field and click **Next** (see Figure 12-37.

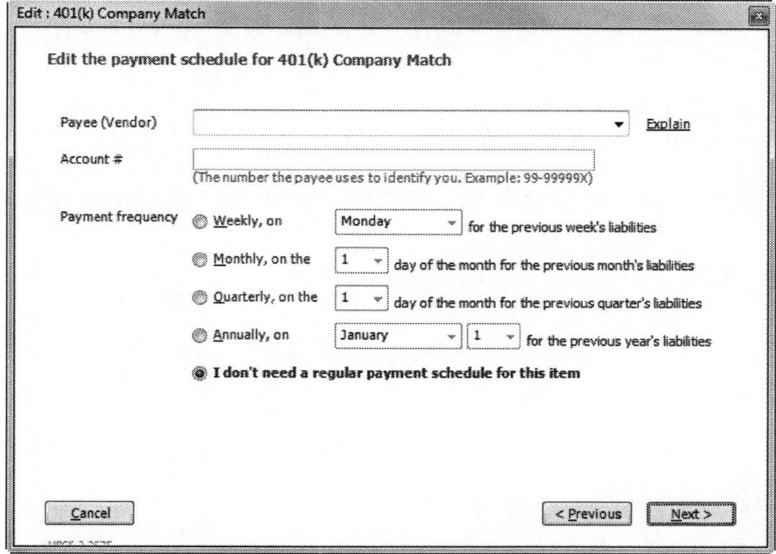

Figure 12-37 Modifying the company match item Payee and Account # for 401k

Step 6. In the *Expense account* section, select **Payroll Expenses: Employee Benefits** from the drop-down list in the Account name field. You may need to scroll up to find this selection. In the *Liability account* section, select **Payroll Liabilities: Other Payroll Liabilities** from the drop-down list in the Account name field. (See Figure 12-38.) Click **Next.**

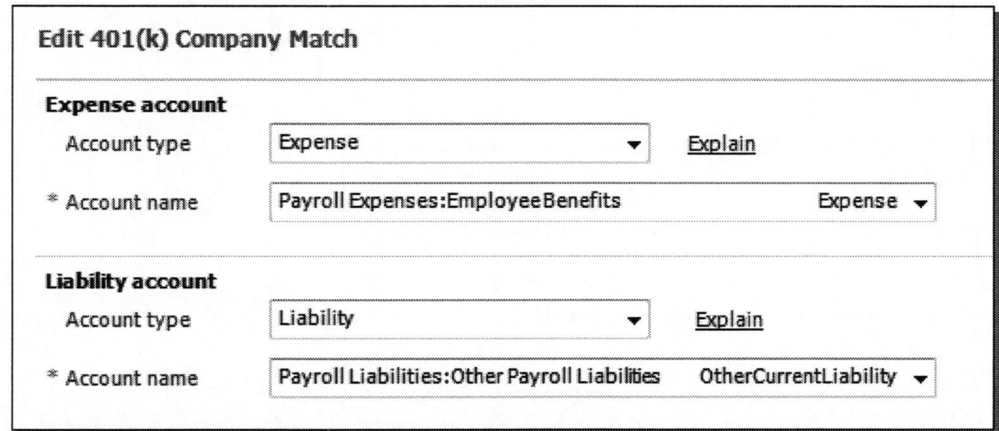

Figure 12-38 Modifying the Expense account and Liability account information

Step 7. On the next window, leave the **Use standard tax settings** checked and click **Next.**

Step 8. On the *Tell us how to calculate the amount* screen, enter the information shown in Figure 12-39 and then click **Finish**.

Tell us how to calculate the amount

Choose a method to calculate the amount then specify a default.

* Calculate amount	as a percentage of pay	
Default rate or amount	2%	Explain
Limit type	Annual limit (reset accrual on Jan 1)	
Default limit	5,500.00	Explain

Figure 12-39 Setting the calculation method, amounts, and limit for 401(k) contribution item

Step 9. You will return to the **Retirement Benefit list** window. Select the *401k Emp.* item and click **Edit**.

Step 10. Enter the data as shown in Figure 12-40 and then click **Next**.

Edit 401(k)

* Show on paychecks as	401k Deduction	
Payroll item is	Active	Explain
	Track expenses by job	Explain

Figure 12-40 401(k) deduction item

Step 11. Enter the data as shown in Figure 12-41 and then click **Next**.

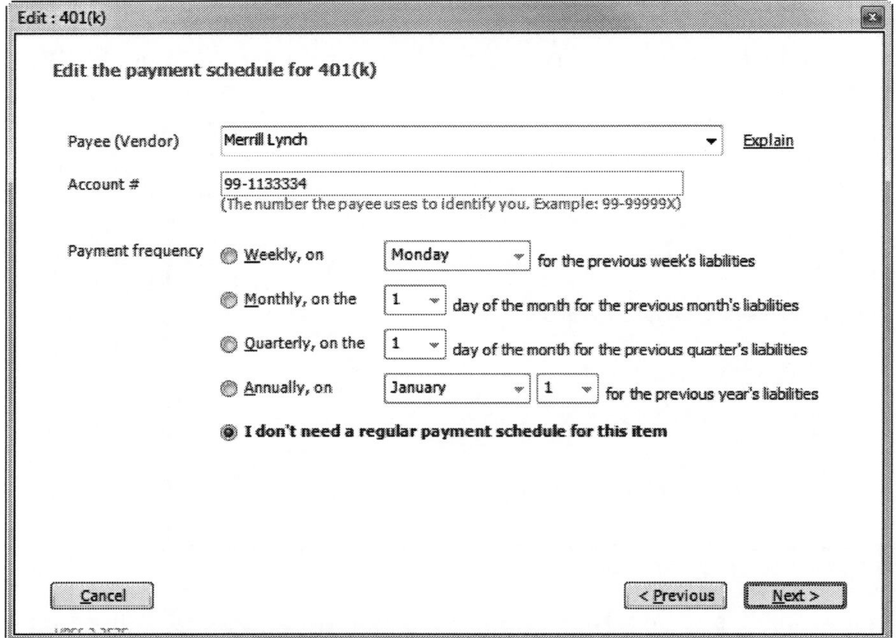

Figure 12-41 401(k) Payee and Account #

Step 12. Enter the data as shown in Figure 12-42 and then click **Next.**

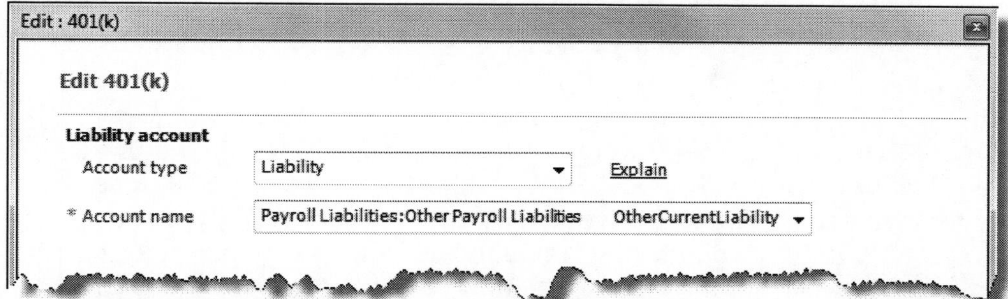

Figure 12-42 Setting the payee and account for the 401(k) Deduction item.

Step 13. Leave the **Use standard tax settings** checked and click **Next.**

Step 14. Enter the data as shown in Figure 12-43 and then click **Finish.**

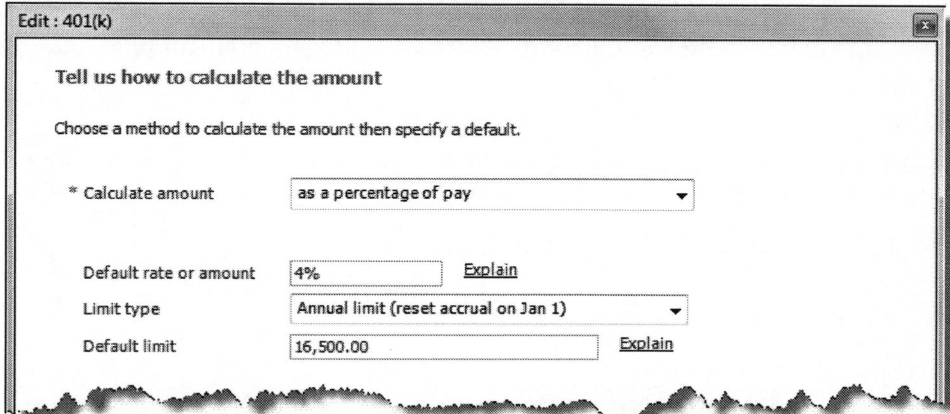

Figure 12-43 Setting the calculation method, amounts, and limit for 401(k) deduction item

You're now finished with setting up the retirement benefits portion of your payroll item list. Your Payroll Setup Interview should now look like Figure 12-44.

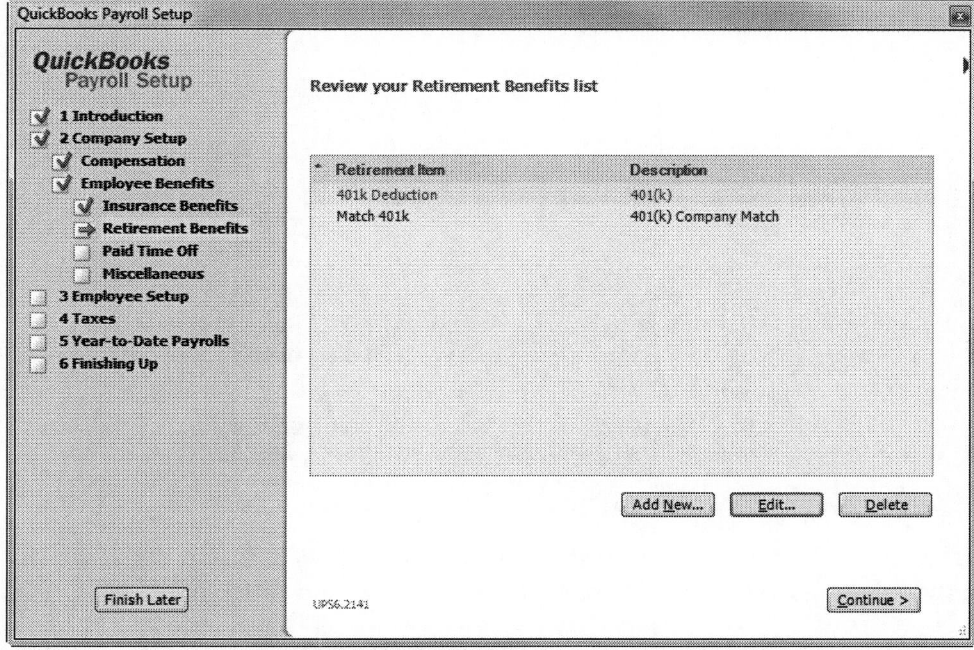

Figure 12-44 Progress in the Payroll Setup Interview.

Step 15. Click **Continue** to proceed to the next section of the setup.

> **Note:**
> If you have 401(k) deductions for several employees, you'll probably want to set up separate Deduction Items for each employee. Enter the employee's account number in the **Enter the number that identifies you to agency** field. That way, when you pay your liabilities, the voucher of the liability check lists deductions separately for each employee. Alternatively, you could use just one Deduction Item and send a printout of your Payroll Summary report with your payment to the 401(k) administrator. Filter that report to show only the *401(k) Deduction* and the *Match 401(k)* items. You'll have to handwrite the account numbers for each employee on the report.

Paid Time Off Payroll Items

If you pay employees for time off, the Payroll Setup Interview will walk you through creating items to track and pay vacation or sick pay.

COMPUTER PRACTICE

Step 1. On the *Set up paid time off* screen (Figure 12-45), click on the **Paid vacation time off** Item and click **Finish.**

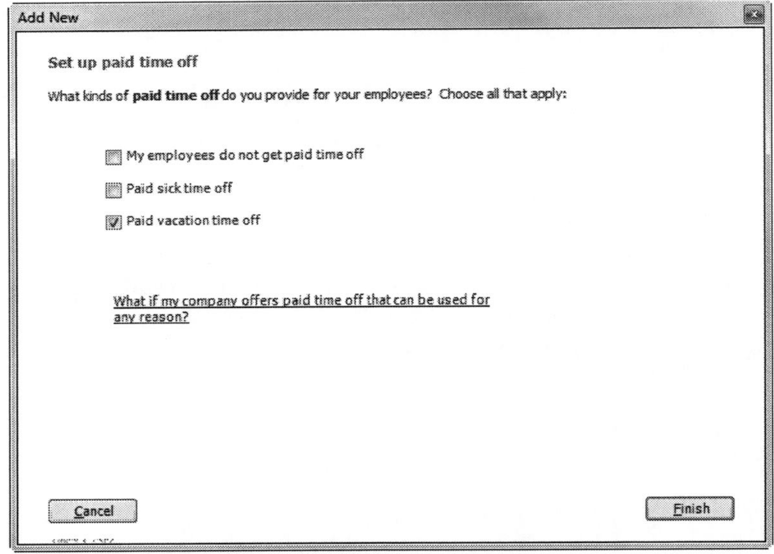

Figure 12-45 Adding Paid vacation Payroll Items

> **Note:**
> If you have a "Paid Time Off (PTO)" policy instead of separate sick and vacation time, you can use either Sick or Vacation time to keep track of how much PTO you offer your employees. Rename it on the payroll preferences so that when it prints on your paychecks and pay stubs, it appears as Paid Time Off. In QuickBooks, however, it continues to appear as either Sick or Vacation, depending on which one you used.

Step 2. Next, edit each of the default items shown in Figure 12-46 to match the data shown in the subsequent screens. First, select *Hourly Vacation* and click **Edit.**

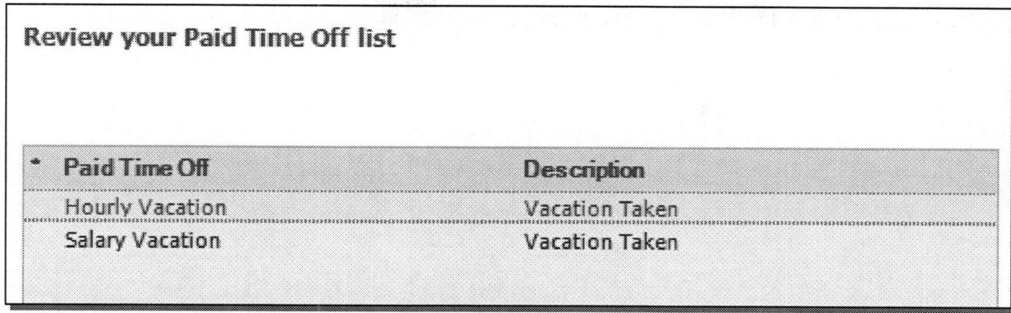

Figure 12-46 The default item names for vacation tracking

Step 3. Set the expense account to **Payroll Expenses:Gross Wages** as shown in Figure 12-47. Then click **Finish**.

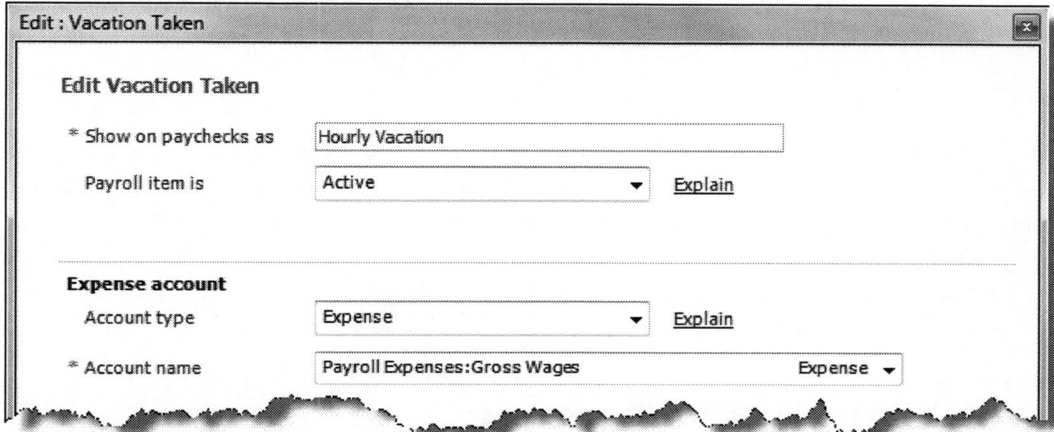

Figure 12-47 Modifying the Hourly Vacation item

Step 4. Next, edit the Salary Vacation item to match the *Account* shown in Figure 12-48. Then click **Finish**.

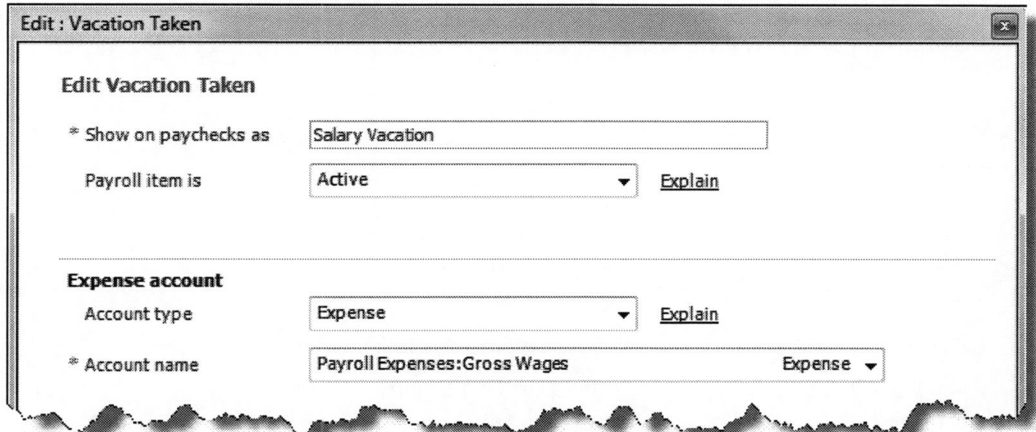

Figure 12-48 Modifying the Salary Vacation item

You're now finished with setting up the Paid Time Off portion of your payroll item list. Your Payroll Setup Interview should now look like Figure 12-49.

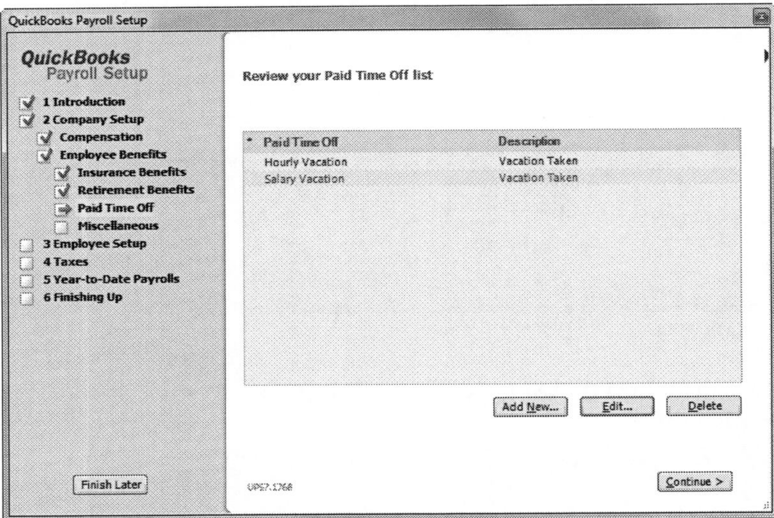

Figure 12-49 Progress in the Payroll Setup Interview.

Step 5. Click **Continue** to proceed to the next section of the setup.

In the next section, you can set up other types of Additions and Deductions that are relevant to your company. The process is similar to the earlier steps and you can follow the onscreen instructions.

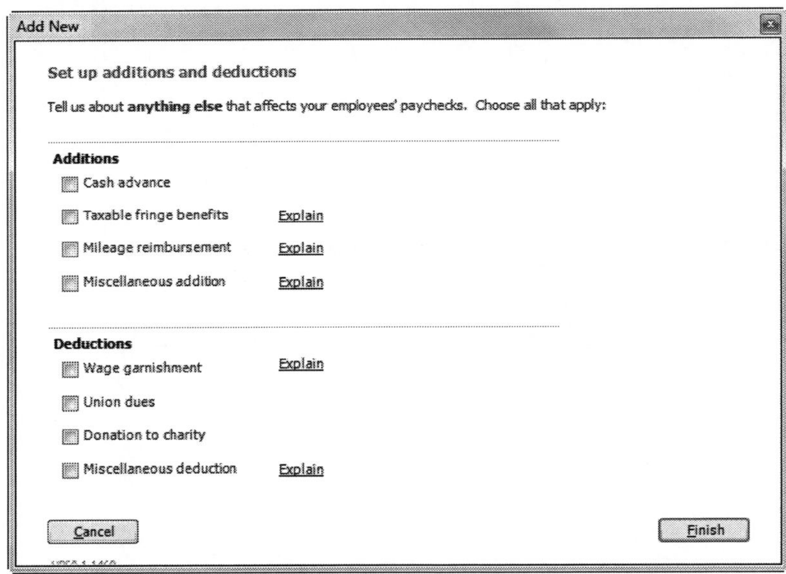

Figure 12-50 Other additions and deductions screen

Step 6. Click **Finish** to skip the screen shown in Figure 12-50.

Step 7. Click **Continue** to advance to setting up Employees.

Setting up Employees

COMPUTER PRACTICE

After you have set up your Payroll Items, the setup wizard takes you through setting up employees.

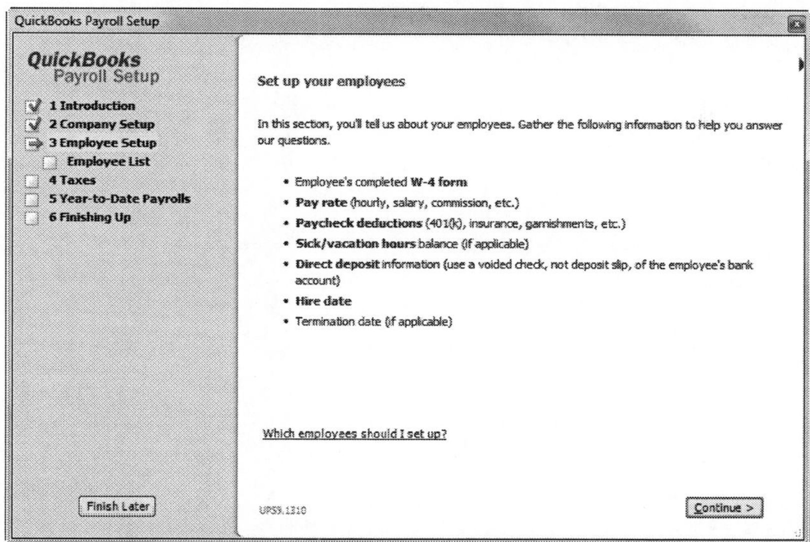

Figure 12-51 Set up Employees starting point in the Payroll Setup Interview.

Step 1. On the *Set up Employees* window (Figure 12-51), click **Continue**.

Step 2. Enter the information shown in Figure 12-52 and then click **Next**.

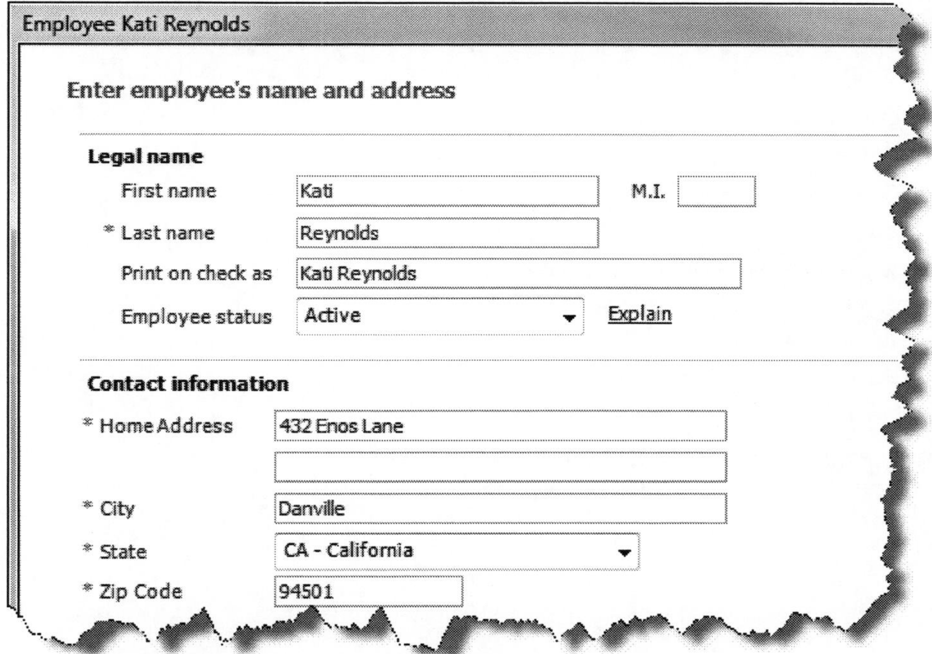

Figure 12-52 Entering Kati Reynolds' address information

> **Note:**
> QuickBooks uses the Employee name fields (first name, middle initial, then last name) to distinguish between employees. Therefore, if two employees have the same name, you must not use their exact names in the Employee list. If necessary, add or omit a middle initial to distinguish between different employees with the same name.

Step 3. In the *hiring information* window, enter the data as shown in Figure 12-53 and then click **Next**.

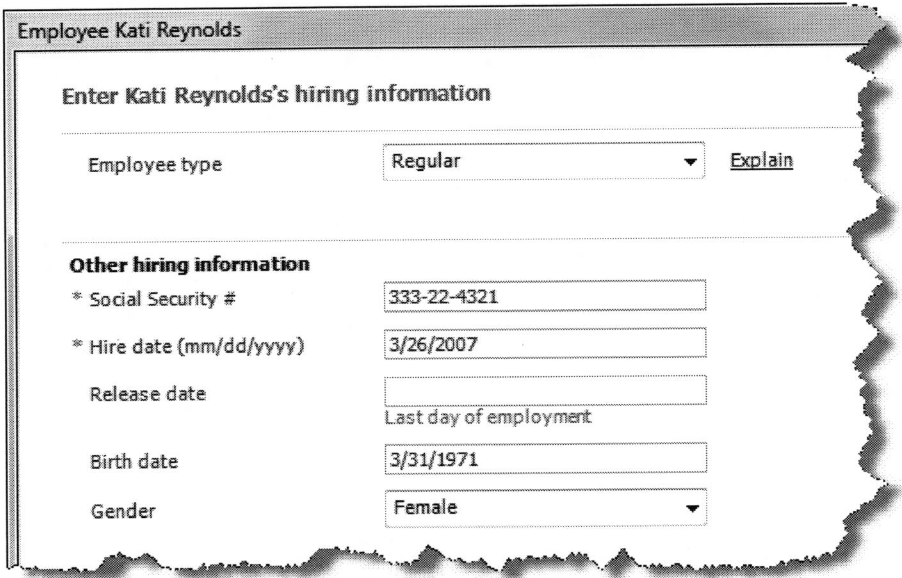

Figure 12-53 Hiring information window for Kati Reynolds

Step 4. In the *wages and compensation for Kati Reynolds* window, enter the information as shown in Figure 12-54. Then click **Next**.

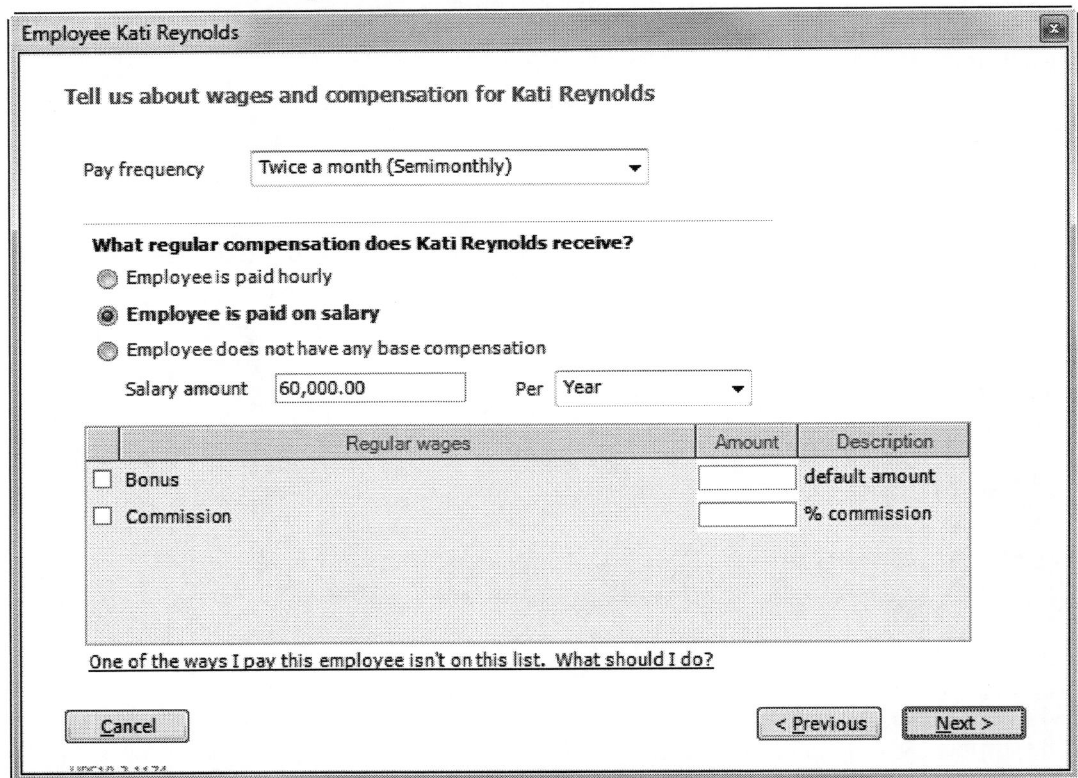

Figure 12-54 Pay frequency and compensation window for Kati Reynolds

Step 5. Select the benefit items as shown in Figure 12-55. Then click **Next**.

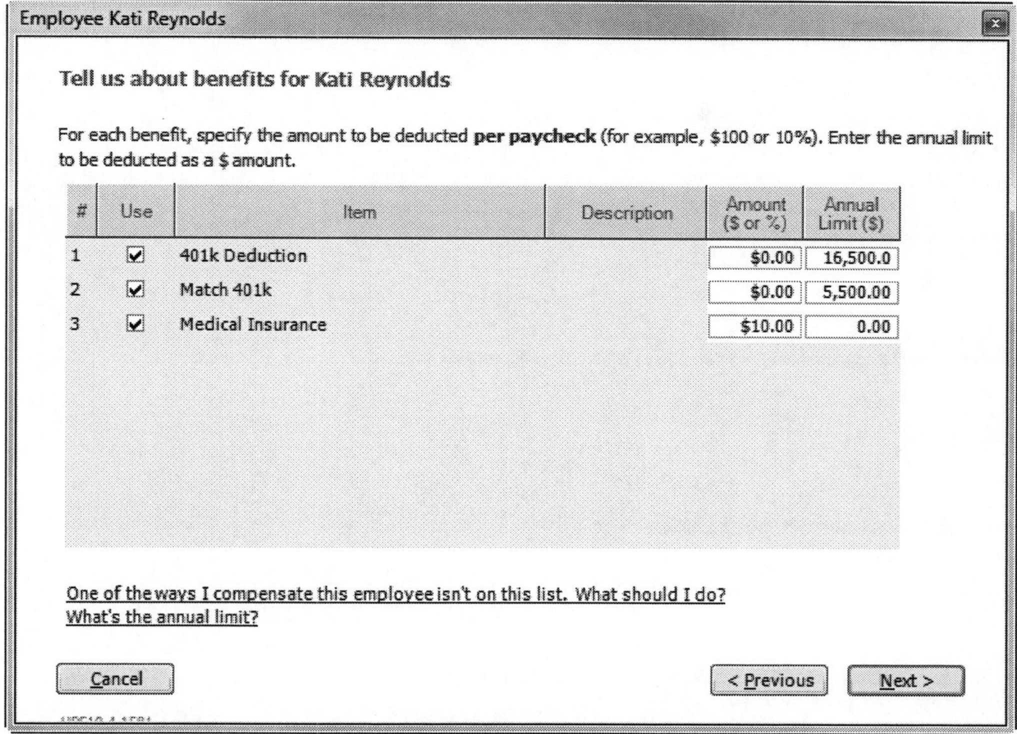

Figure 12-55 Selecting the benefits items to add to Kati Reynolds' paychecks

Step 6. Enter the vacation time calculation method for Kati Reynolds as shown in Figure 12-56. Leave the Current balances blank. Then click **Next**.

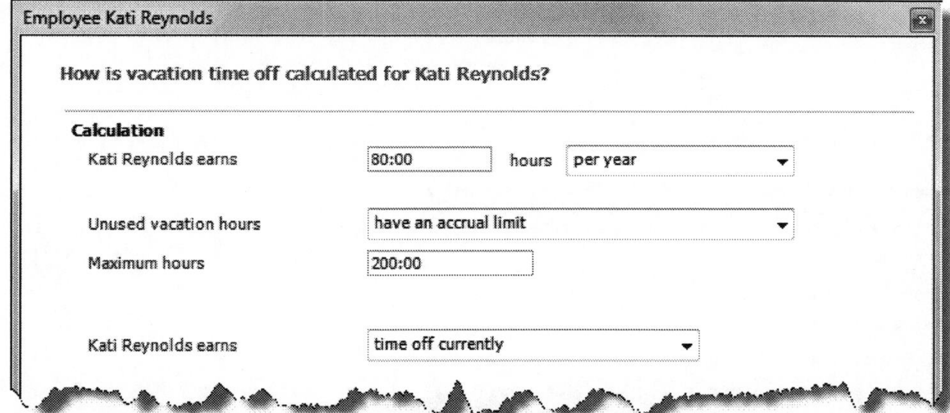

Figure 12-56 Vacation time calculation for Kati Reynolds

Step 7. Click **Next** to skip the *direct deposit information* screen.

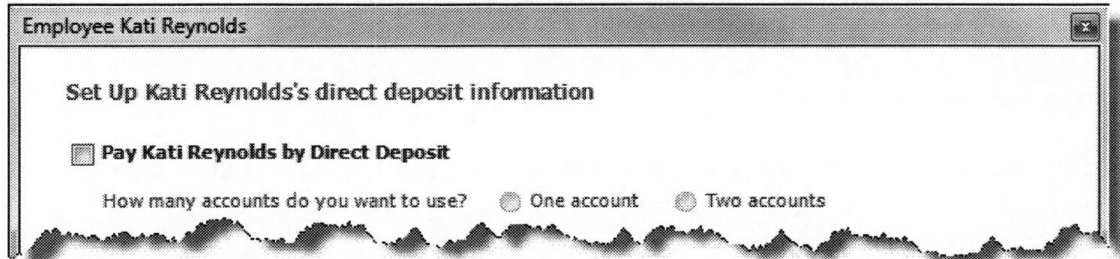

Figure 12-57 Direct Deposit Payroll Setup

Step 8. Enter the information shown in Figure 12-58 and then click **Next**.

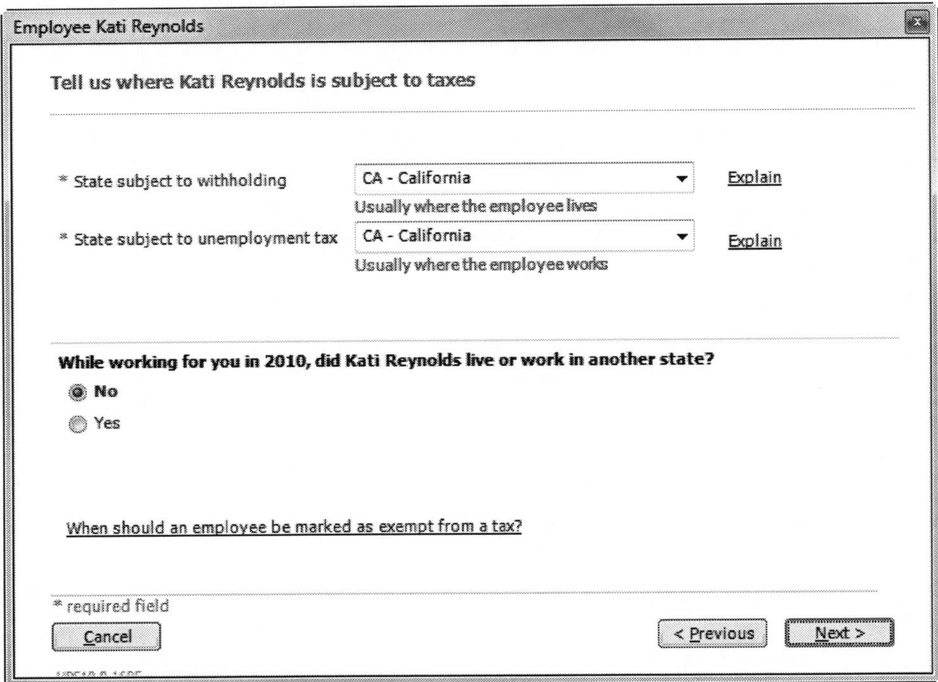

Figure 12-58 State information for Kati Reynolds

Step 9. Enter the federal tax information as shown in Figure 12-59 and then click **Next**.

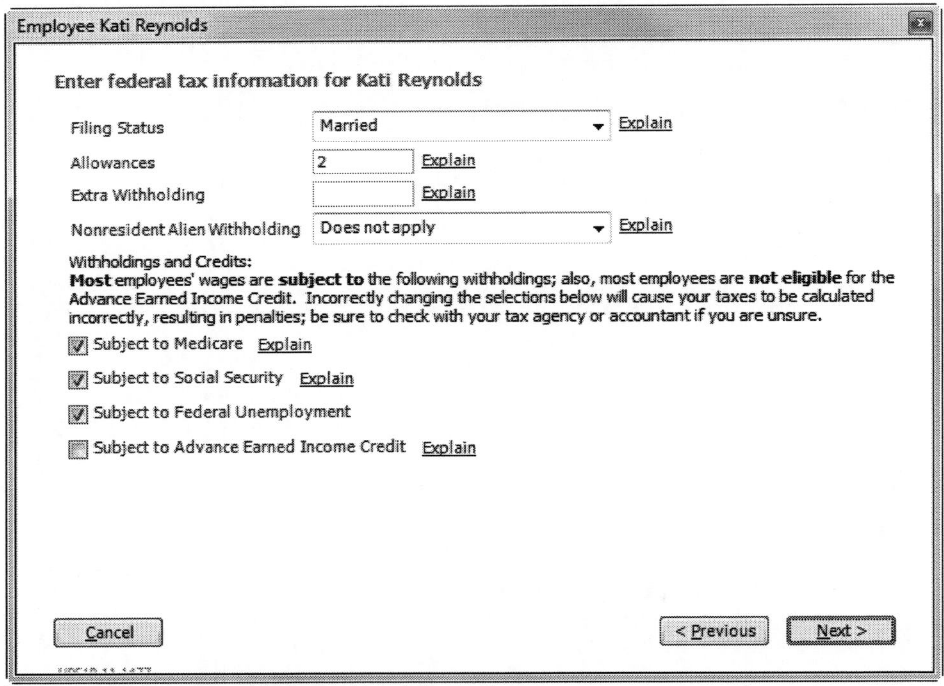

Figure 12-59 Kati Reynolds' federal tax information

Step 10. Enter the state tax information as shown in Figure 12-60 and then click **Next**.

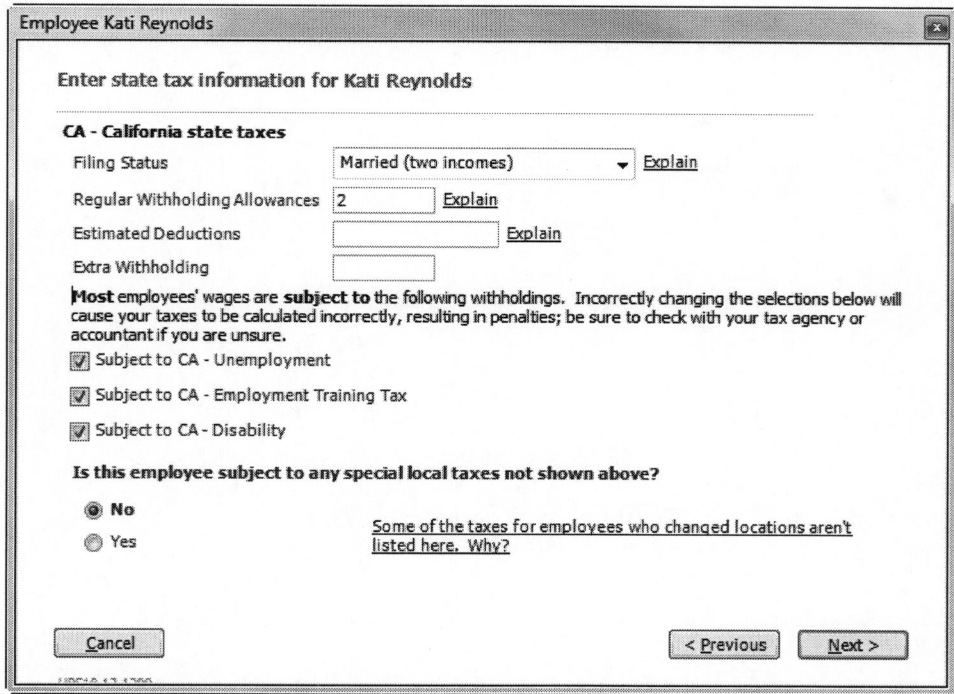

Figure 12-60 Kati Reynolds' state tax information

Step 11. Choose S (State Plan for Both UI and DI) from the *Setup wage plan information for Kati Reynolds* as shown in Figure 12-61.

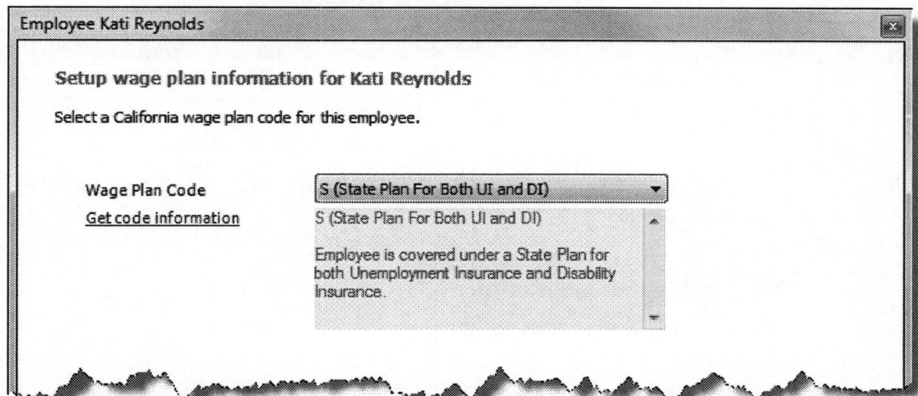

Figure 12-61 Setup wage plan information for Kati Reynolds

Step 12. Click **Finish**.

Step 13. You've finished setting up Kati Reynolds, your screen should look like Figure 12-62.

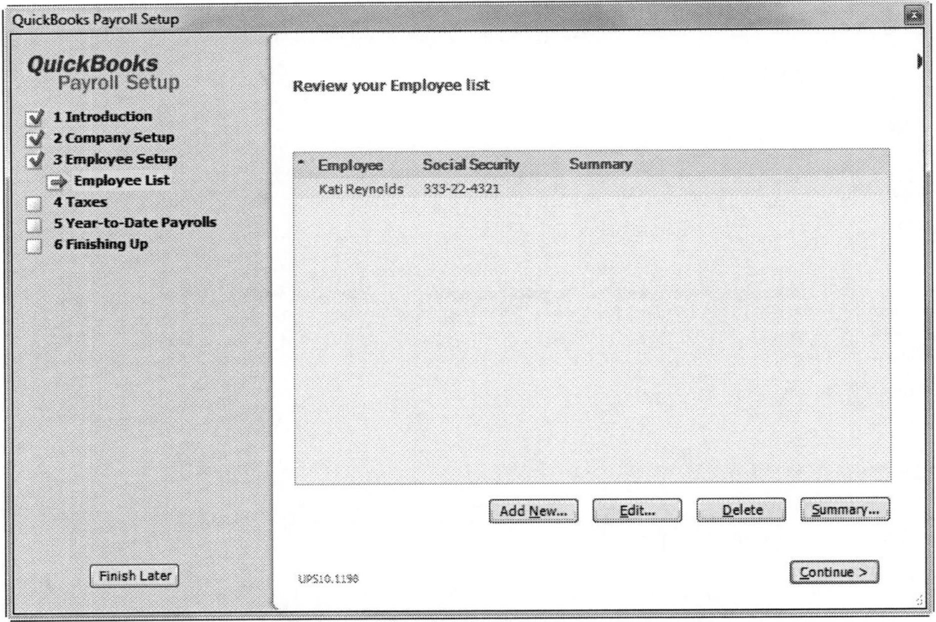

Figure 12-62 Progress in the Payroll Setup Interview.

Adding another Employee

COMPUTER PRACTICE

Step 1. Next, add another employee by clicking **Add New** and enter the information shown in Table 12-3. Click **Finish** when you are done.

Employee Personal Info	Hiring Information	Compensation Info
Mike Mazuki Print As: Mike Mazuki Employee Status: Active 123 Hillsboro Lane Walnut Creek, CA 94569	Employee Type: Regular SS No: 111-22-3333 Hire Date: 4/2/2006 Birth date: 5/5/1965 Gender: Male	Pay frequency: Semi Monthly Employee is paid hourly Hourly wage: 24.00
Benefits info	**Vacation Time Calculation**	
Use: 401(k) Deduction Use: 401(k) Match Use: Medical Insurance	Earns 3:00 hours per paycheck Accrual Limit: 80 hours Earns time off currently	
State Lived and Worked	**Taxes – Federal**	**Taxes – State**
State subject to withholding: CA State subject to unemployment tax: CA Mike did NOT work in another state in 2011.	Filing Status: Married Allowances: 2 Extra Withholding: 0 Nonresident Alien Withholdings: Does not apply Subject to: √ Medicare √ Social Security √ Federal Unemployment Tax	Filing Status: Married (2 incomes) Regular Withholding Allowances: 2 Estimated Deductions: 0 Extra withholding: 0 Subject to: √ CA – Unemployment √ CA – Employment Training Tax √ CA – Disability Employee is not subject to any special local taxes.
Wage Plan		
Wage Plan Code: S		

Table 12-3 New Employee information - Mike Mazuki

Step 2. After adding the second employee, click **Continue** to proceed to the payroll taxes setup.

Payroll Tax Item Setup

COMPUTER PRACTICE

The next section of the Payroll Setup Interview helps you set up the payroll tax items. Continue on with the Payroll Setup Interview, following these steps:

Step 1. The first screen of the payroll taxes setup is shown in Figure 12-63. Click **Continue.**

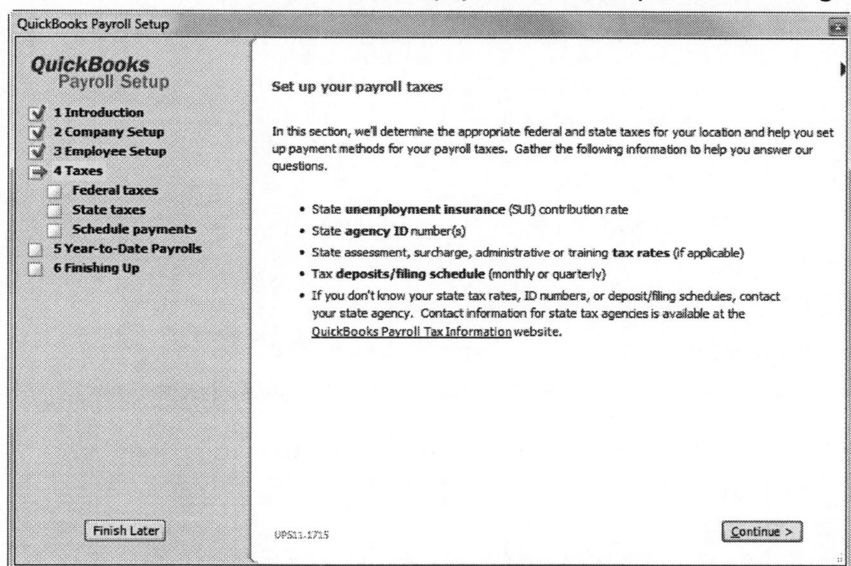

Figure 12-63 Setting up employees completed

Step 2. QuickBooks displays the federal payroll tax items that have been set up for you (see Figure 12-64). Click **Continue.**

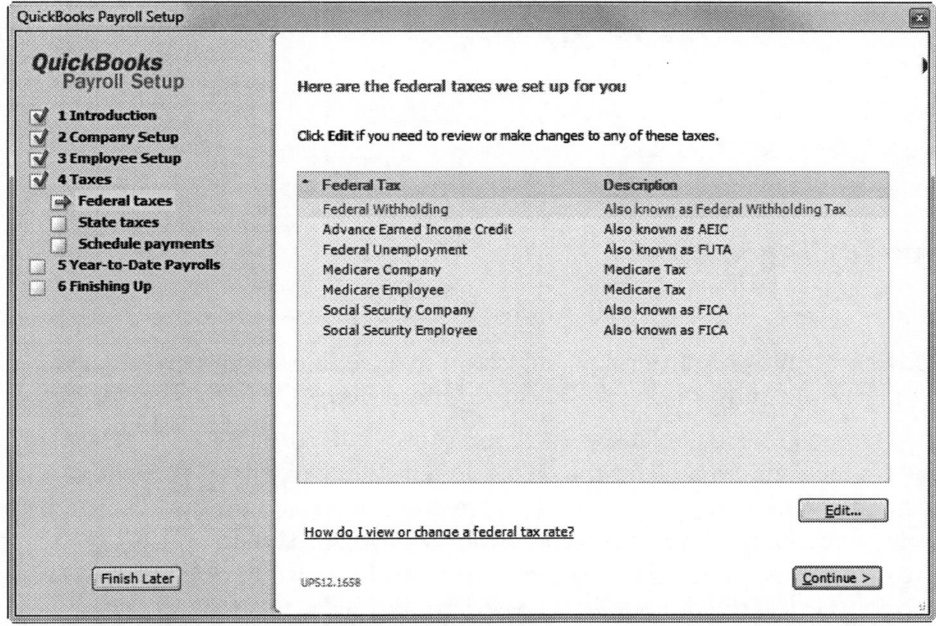

Figure 12-64 Federal payroll tax items

Step 3. In the company file you are using, QuickBooks displays the *Set up state payroll taxes* window because the Unemployment Company Rate must be entered in manually (since we are processing payroll manually). Enter ***3.4%*** in the *CA – Unemployment Company Rate* field (see Figure 12-65). Press **Tab** to accept the entry and **Finish** to move to review your state taxes.

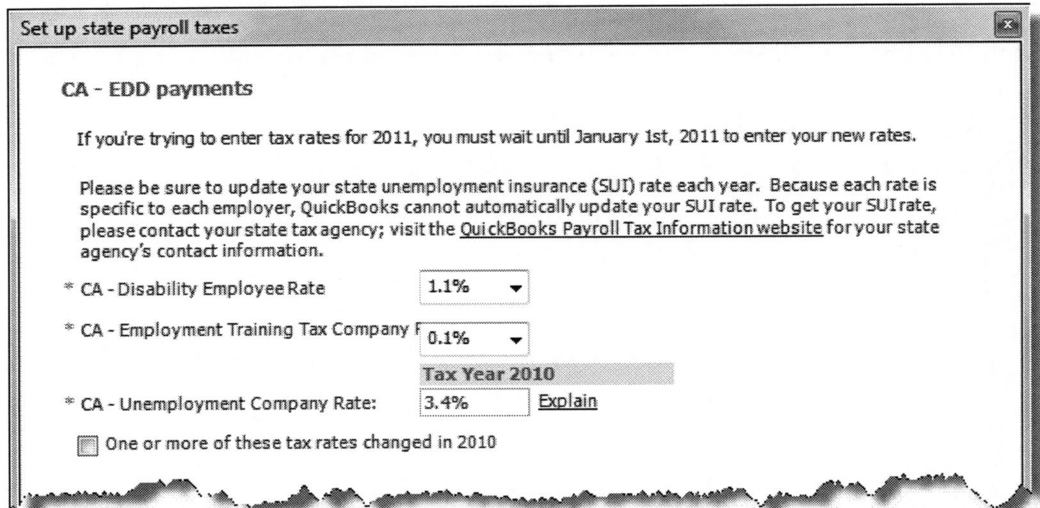

Figure 12-65 Entering in 3.4% in the California Unemployment Company Rate field – your screen may vary

Step 4. Review the state payroll tax items shown in Figure 12-66. Then click **Continue**.

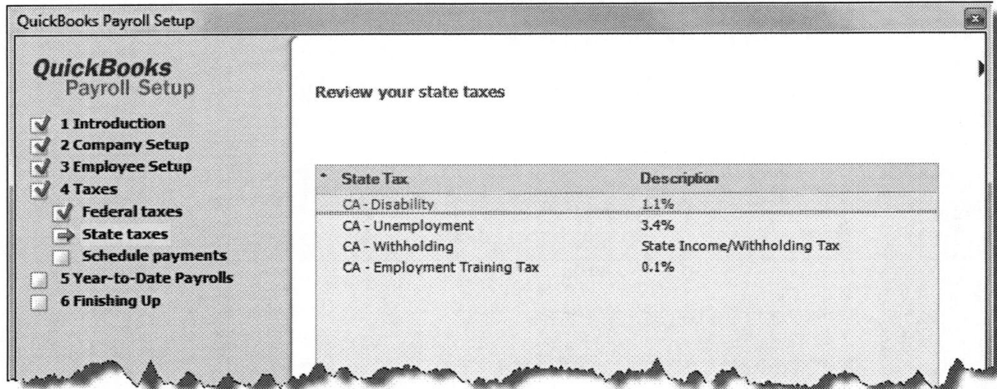

Figure 12-66 State payroll tax items

Scheduling Your Tax Payments

COMPUTER PRACTICE

The next section of the Payroll Setup Interview helps you to schedule your tax payments. Continue on with the Payroll Setup Interview following these steps:

Step 1. The first screen in the payroll taxes section is shown in Figure 12-67. This is where you set up the vendor name for the payee on federal tax payments for Federal 940. The default vendor name is United States Treasury. However, since you'll most likely make payments using the Electronic Federal Tax Payment System (EFTPS), the sample data file has already been set up with a vendor called EFTPS. Select **EFTPS** as the vendor you use to pay your liabilities for Federal taxes. In addition, select **Quarterly** from the drop down list in the *Deposit Frequency* field. Click **Next**.

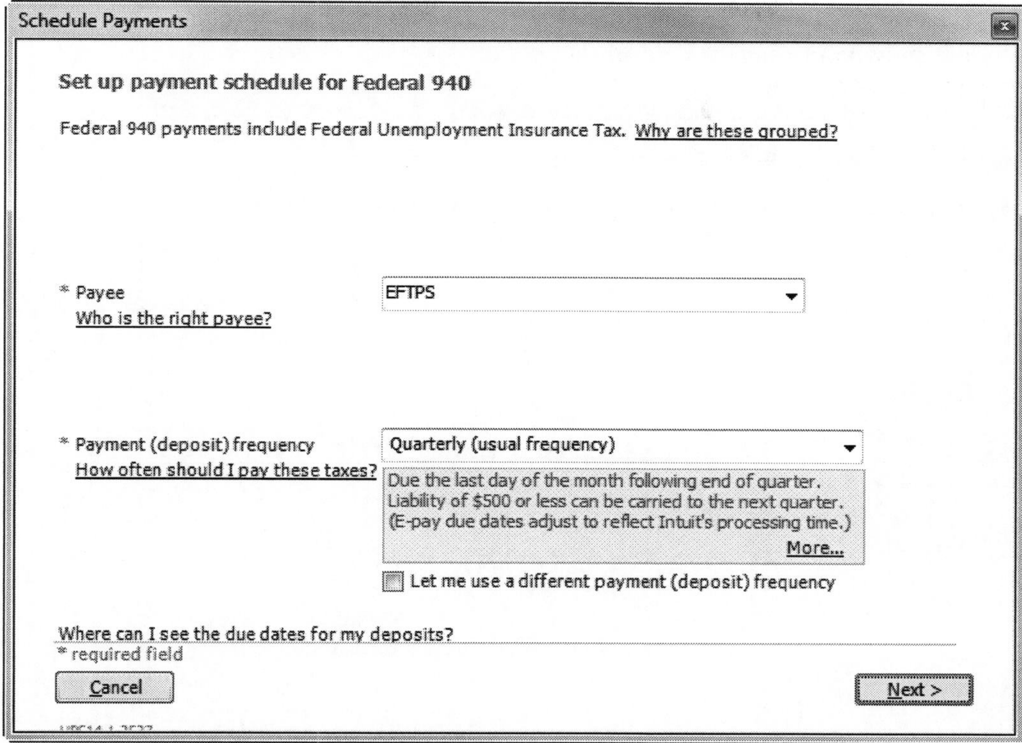

Figure 12-67 Set up payments for Federal 940

Step 2. To set up payments for Federal 941/944, enter in the data shown in Figure 12-68 and click **Next**.

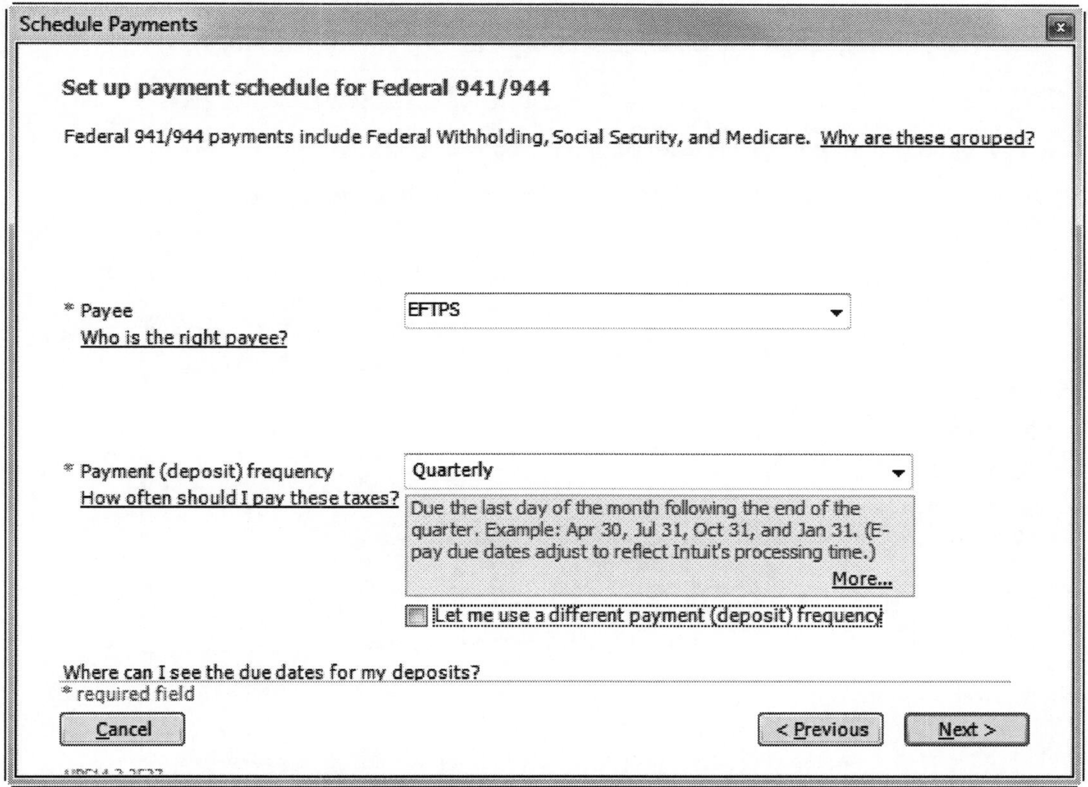

Figure 12-68 Set up payments for Federal 941/944

Step 3. To set up payments for California Withholding and Disability Insurance, enter in the data shown in Figure 12-69 and click **Next**.

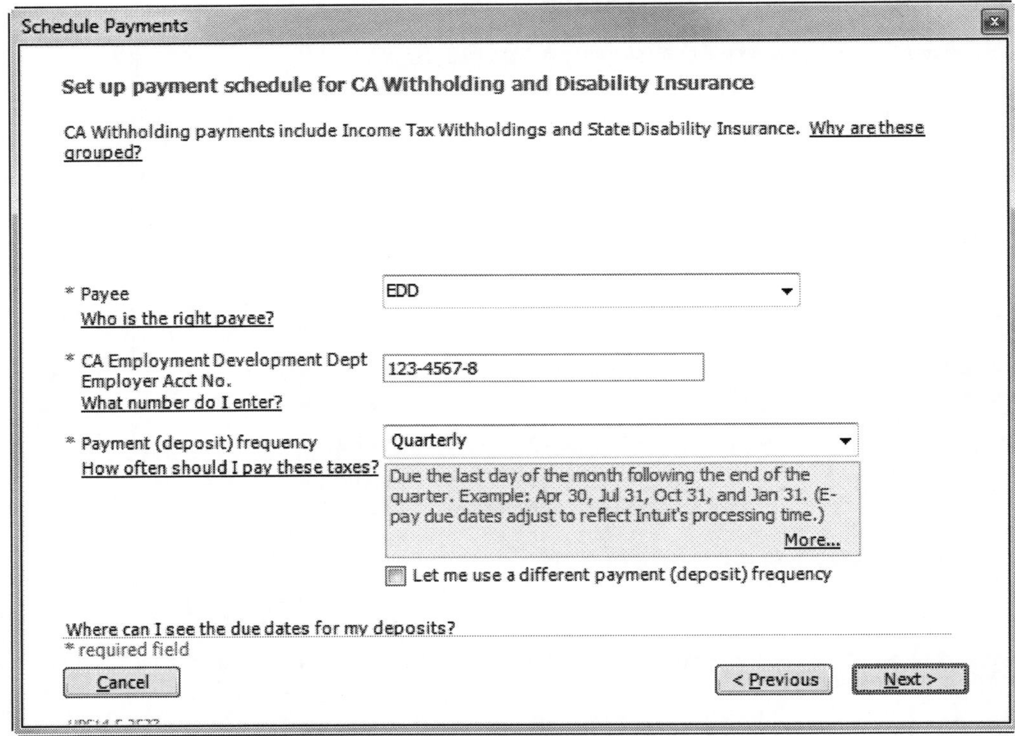

Figure 12-69 Set up payments for CA UI and Employment Training Tax

Step 4. To set up payments for California Unemployment Insurance (UI) and Employment Training Tax, enter the data shown in Figure 12-70 and click **Finish**.

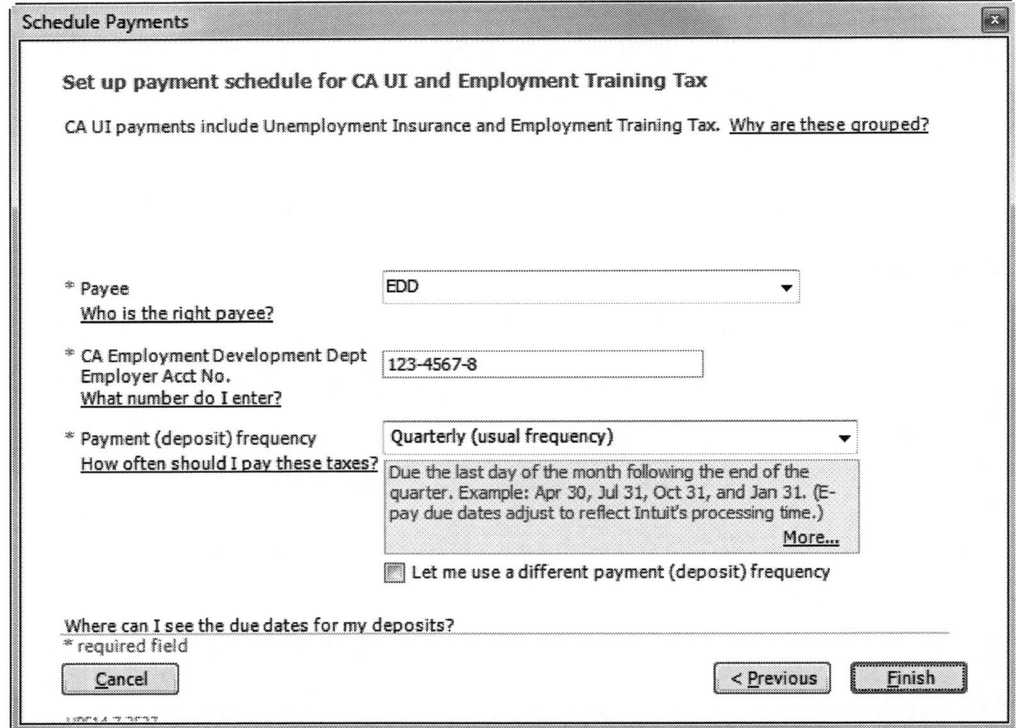

Figure 12-70 Set up payments for CA Withholding and Disability Insurance

Step 5. QuickBooks returns you to window where you can review the list of your scheduled tax payments (see Figure 12-71). Click **Continue** to set up your year-to-date amounts.

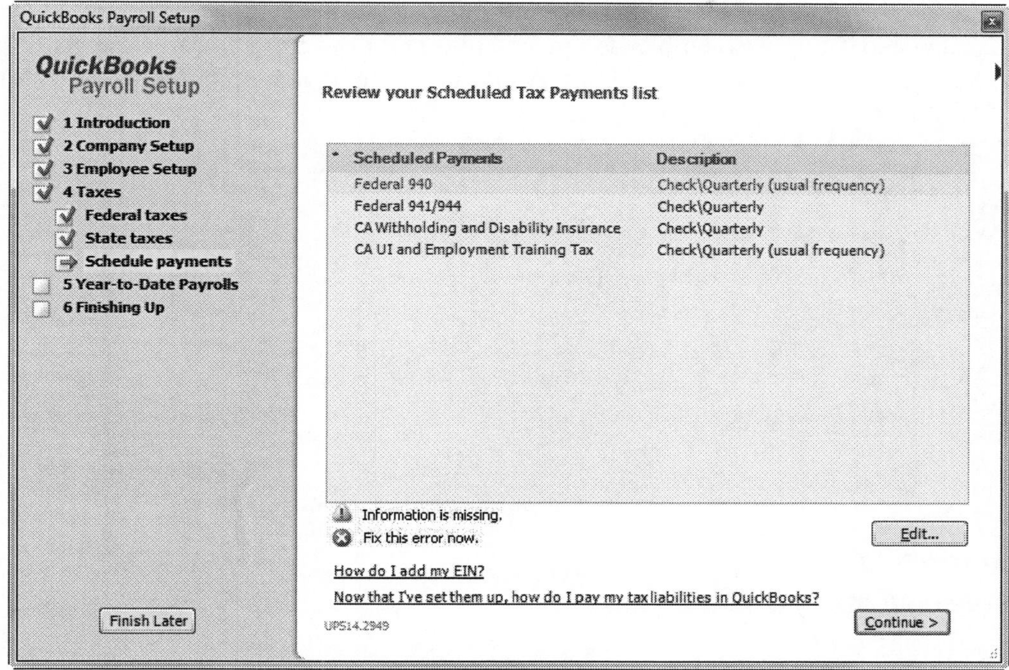

Figure 12-71 Review your Scheduled Tax Payments list

Setting up Year-to-Date Payroll Amounts

COMPUTER PRACTICE

Step 1. Click **Continue** on the *Enter payroll history for the current* year window (Figure 12-72).

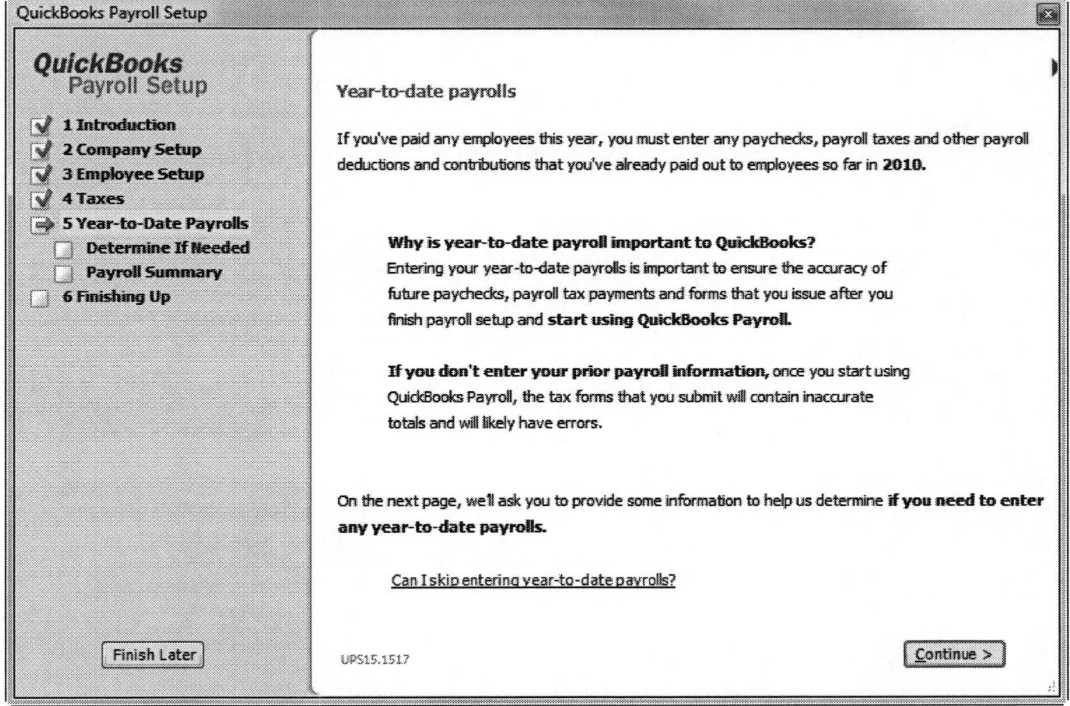

Figure 12-72 Entering YTD Payroll Amounts

Step 2. On the window shown in Figure 12-73, click **No** and then click **Continue**.

If you were setting up your own payroll in the middle of the year, you would click **Yes** on this page and then QuickBooks would lead you down a set of screens where you would set up each employee's payroll history for the current year. However, this example assumes that you're setting up payroll at the beginning of the year, so click **Continue**.

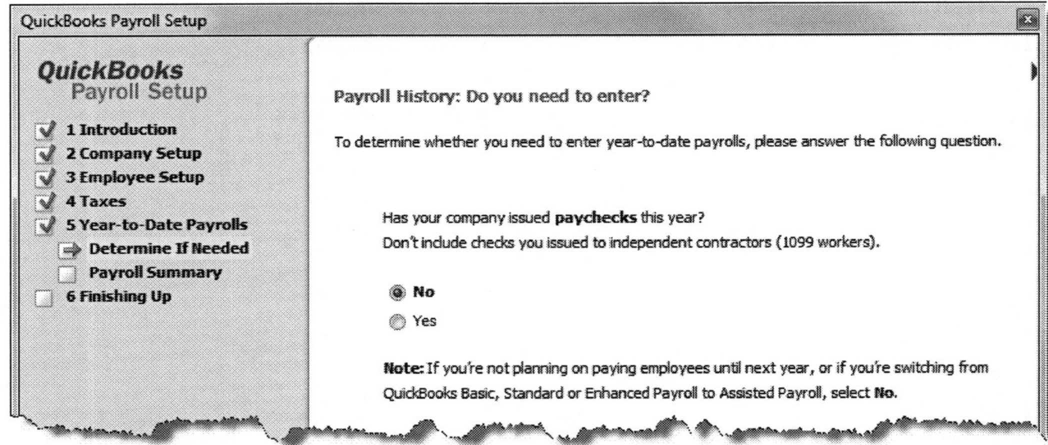

Figure 12-73 Finished with YTD Payroll Amounts completed

Finishing Up The Payroll Setup Interview

COMPUTER PRACTICE

Step 1. Click **Go to Payroll Center** on the Setup is complete window (see Figure 12-74).

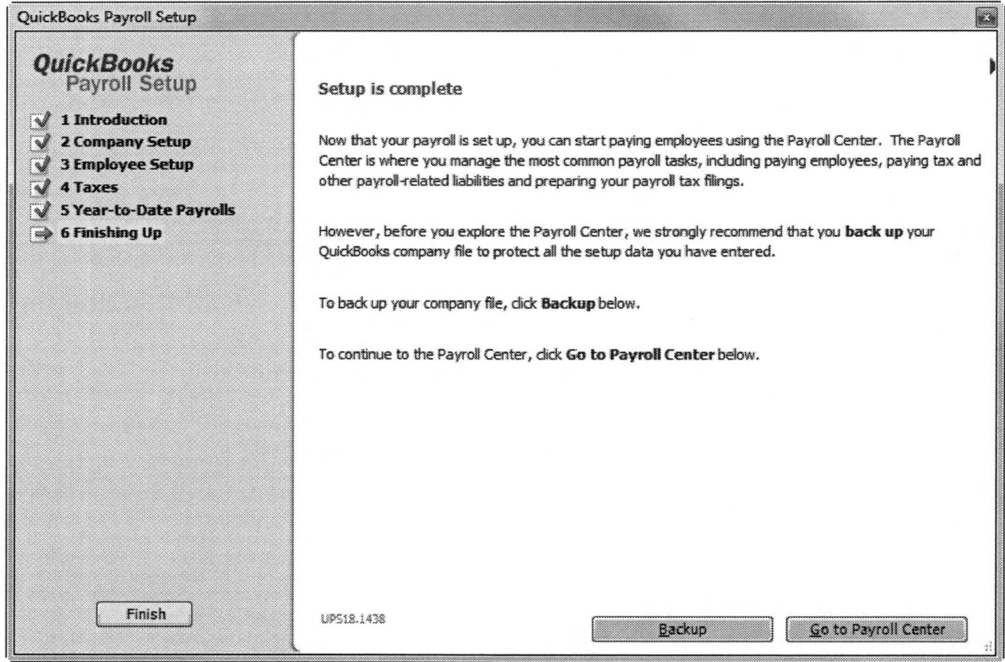

Figure 12-74 The Congratulations window

Step 2. The Employee Center is shown in Figure 12-75.

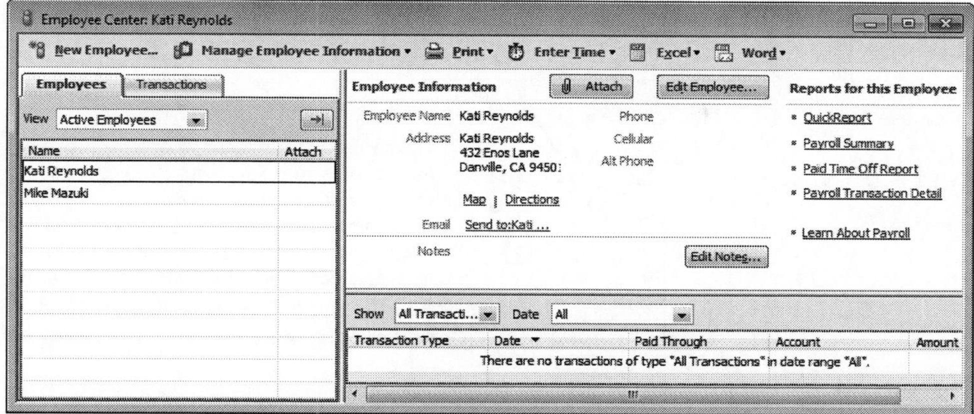

Figure 12-75 Employee Center

> **Note:**
> Because we are processing payroll manually, the Employee Center does not display the Payroll tab. This tab displays only when payroll is activated using a payroll activation key.

Finalizing the Payroll Setup

After finishing the Payroll Setup Interview, you can set up custom fields and employee defaults. Also, you can add, delete, or modify Payroll Items from the Payroll item list. For example, if you want to link the payroll taxes to specific categories in the chart of accounts, you will need to edit each of the payroll tax items.

Custom Fields for Payroll

If you want to track more detailed information about your employees, use custom fields (see Figure 12-77). You can create up to 15 fields to be used for customers, vendors, or employees. In the practice file, several custom fields have already been added.

Step 1. From the **Employees** tab in the *Employee Center*, double-click on Mike Mazuki and then click the *Additional Information* tab. See Figure 12-76.

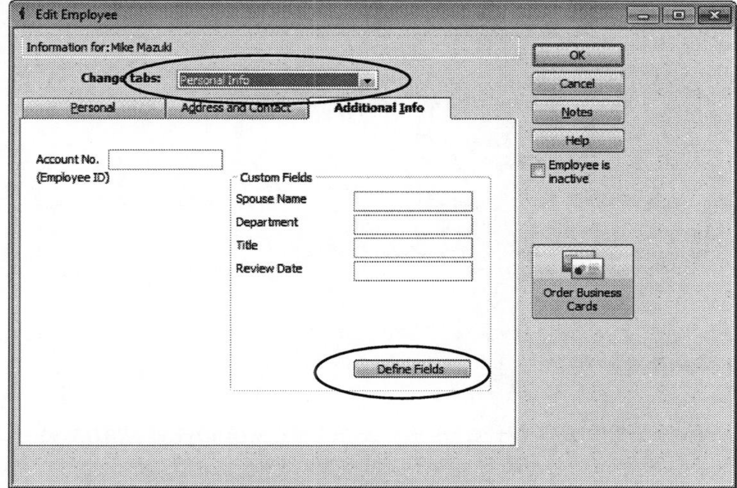

Figure 12-76 Editing an employee record

Step 2. Click **Define Fields** on the *Additional Info* tab of the *New Employee* window.

Step 3. When you're finished reviewing the field names that are already entered in your sample file, click **OK**. Then click **Cancel** to close the *Edit Employee* window.

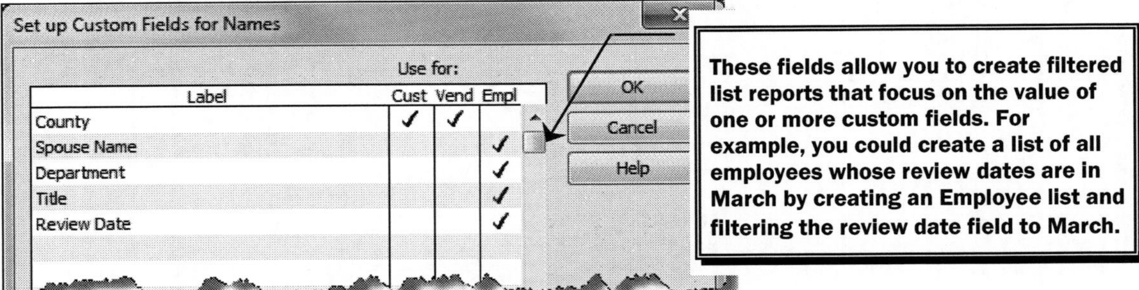

Figure 12-77 Defining custom fields

Setting Up Employee Defaults

The *Employee Defaults* feature allows you to define defaults for your employee records so that each time you add a new employee, you don't have to enter the same information over and over. For example, if you pay all your employees weekly, you can set up the defaults for weekly payroll and that way you won't have to enter the pay period on each new employee record. You don't have to use the *Employee Defaults*, but if you do, it will save you time and reduce the likelihood of errors.

COMPUTER PRACTICE

To set up the employee defaults, follow these steps:

Step 1. From the *Employee Center*, select the *Manage Employee Information* drop-down and select **Change New Employee Default Settings** as shown in Figure 12-78.

> Note:
> Although Mike Mazuki appears to be selected from the list, setting up employee defaults only apply to new employees you will set up after default settings are in place.

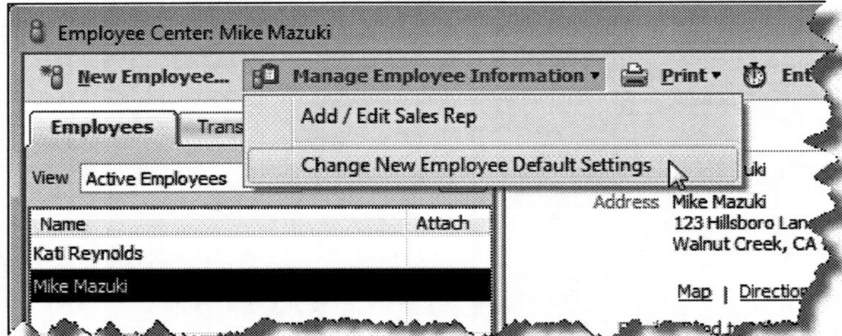

Figure 12-78 Selecting Employee Defaults from the Employee Center

Step 2. In the *Employee Defaults* window, Select **<Add New>** from the Payroll Schedule drop-down list as shown in Figure 12-79.

The Payroll Schedule function allows you to group together employees with the same pay frequency (i.e. weekly, bi-weekly, monthly, etc.) in order to make processing employees with various payroll schedules convenient and easy.

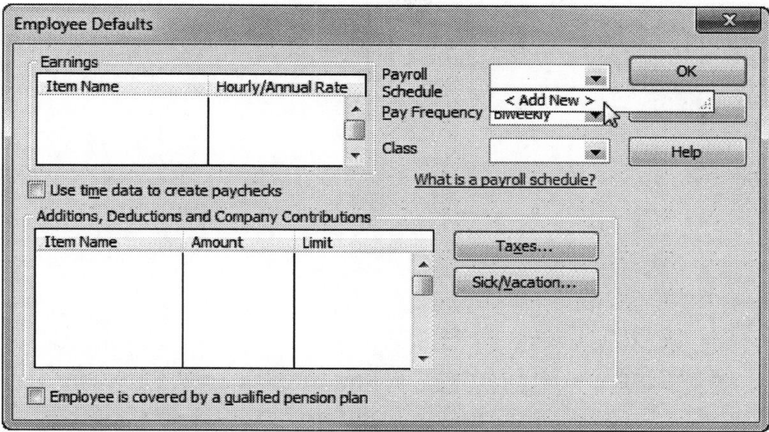

Figure 12-79 Adding a new Payroll Schedule

Step 3. QuickBooks displays the *New Payroll Schedule* window. Complete the schedule based upon entries in Figure 12-80. Click **OK** to continue.

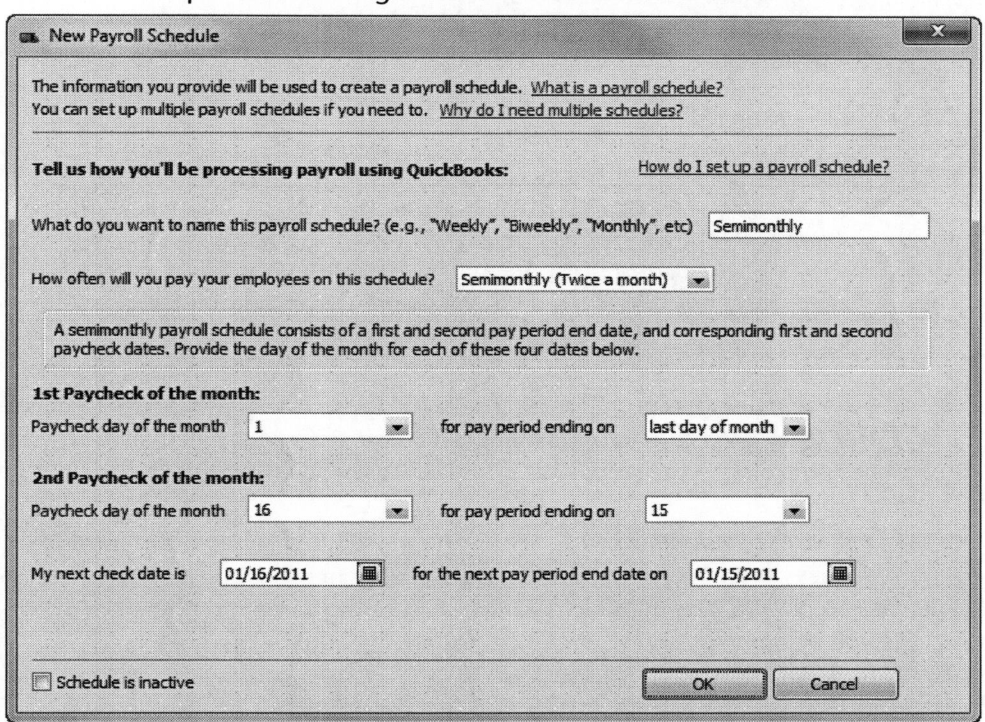

Figure 12-80 New Payroll Schedule

Step 4. If QuickBooks displays the dialog box in Figure 12-81, it is because you have you are doing this exercise before January 16, 2011. This won't affect your exercise. Click **Yes**.

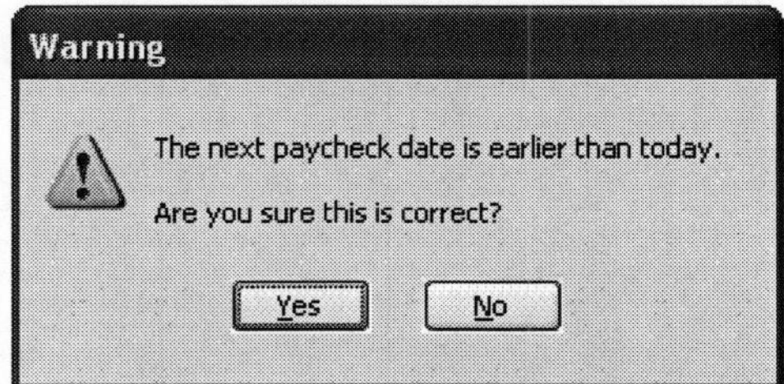

Figure 12-81 Next paycheck date dialog box

Step 5. In Figure 12-82 QuickBooks asks if you would like to assign the new schedule to all employees with the Semimonthly pay frequency. Click **Yes**.

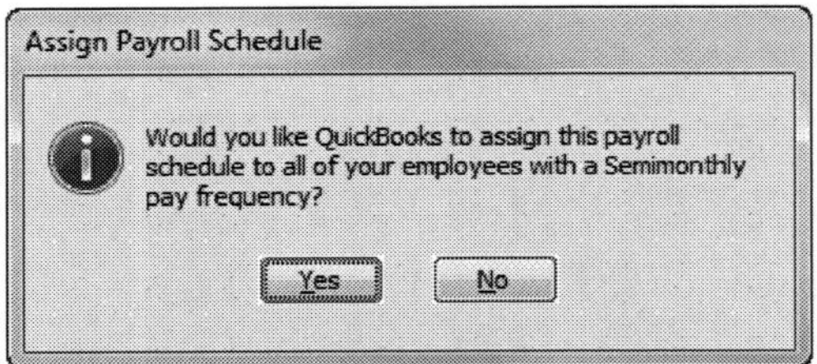

Figure 12-82 Assign Payroll Schedule dialog box

Step 6. Figure 12-83 displays the number of employees assigned to the new schedule. This information is helpful because it can alert you to assignment errors. Unfortunately, there is no way to undo global assignments. Click **OK**.

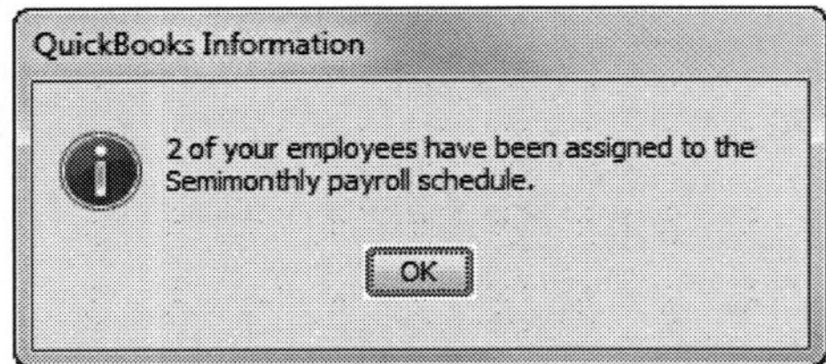

Figure 12-83 Number of employees assigned a schedule dialog box

> **Note:**
> The Payroll Schedules list can be viewed in the *Payroll* tab of the Employee Center, which requires a payroll subscription service from QuickBooks. In addition, Payroll Schedules cannot be deleted or modified without a payroll subscription from QuickBooks.

Step 7. Complete the remaining information as shown in Figure 12-84. Make sure to check the box, **Use time data to create paychecks**, so that timesheet data can automatically transfer to the employee's *Preview Paycheck* window.

Use the *Employee Defaults* window to set up the payroll information that most of your employees have in common. In the pay period, enter how often most employees are paid. These are only defaults, so entering something here does not preclude you from overriding your choices for an individual employee.

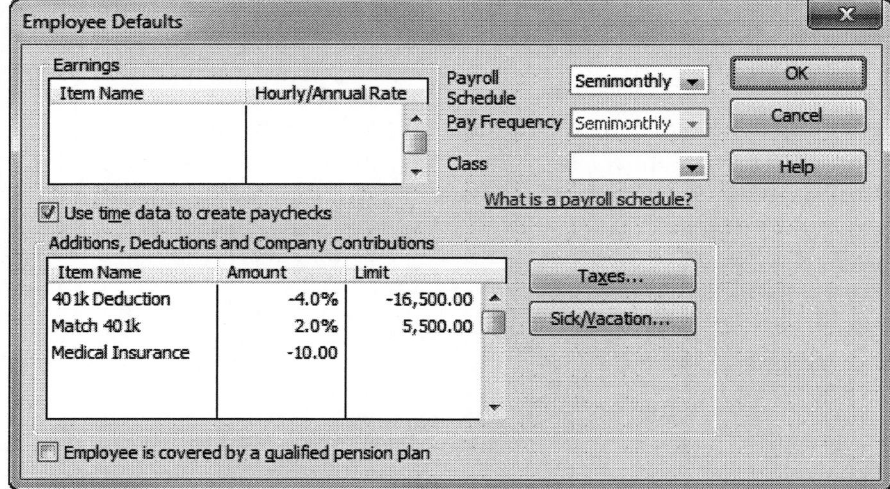

Figure 12-84 Employee Defaults window

Step 8. Verify that your screen matches Figure 12-84, and then click **Taxes.**

Default settings for taxes

COMPUTER PRACTICE

Step 1. In the *Taxes Defaults* window, leave the default *Federal tax settings* as shown in Figure 12-85 and click the **State** tab.

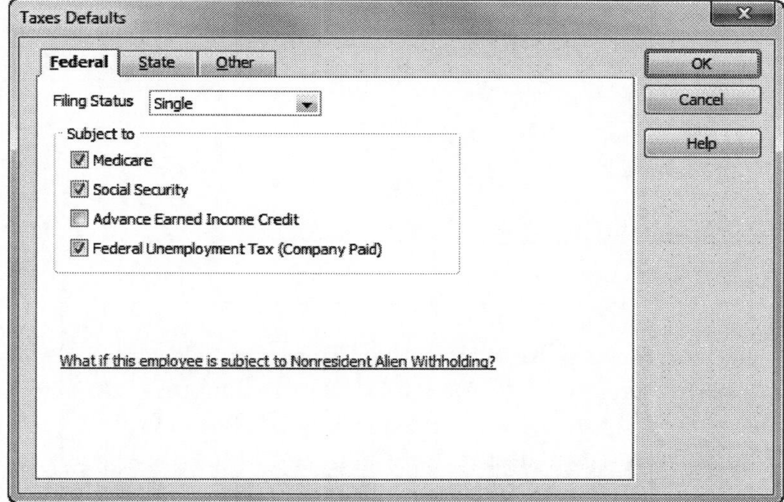

Figure 12-85 Taxes Defaults - Federal

Step 2. On the *State taxes default* window, select **CA** from the State drop-down list in both the **State Worked** and **State Subject to Withholding** sections (see Figure 12-86). This window will vary depending on the states you choose. Then click the **Other** tab.

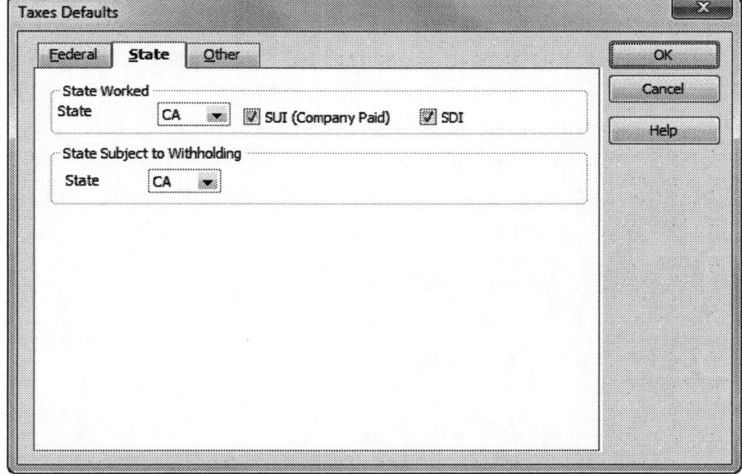

Figure 12-86 Taxes Defaults - State

Step 3. Select **CA – Employment Training Tax** in the *Item Name* section as shown in Figure 12-87. Then click **OK.**

If your State has local taxes, the *Other* tab should include the local taxes you must withhold or accrue.

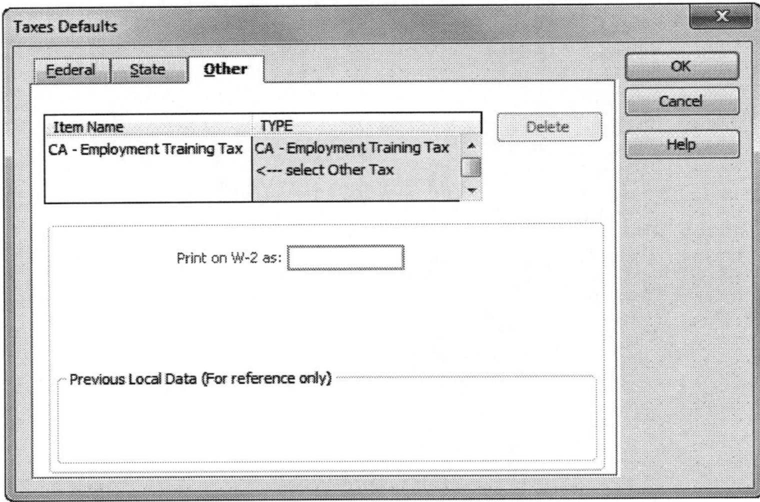

Figure 12-87 Taxes Defaults - Other

> **Note:**
> If your employees are subject to any of the local taxes that are supported by QuickBooks, you can add those taxes here. If your local tax is not supported directly by QuickBooks, you should set up a *User Defined* **Other** tax. See Payroll Taxes (Local) in the QuickBooks onscreen help for more information on these taxes.

Default settings for sick/vacation time

COMPUTER PRACTICE

Step 1. On the *Employee Defaults* window, click **Sick/Vacation** (Figure 12-88).

This is where you choose sick and vacation time settings to match your company policies. You can choose **Beginning of year** if your policy is to give each employee a set number of hours per year. If employees earn sick or vacation time for each pay period, then choose **Every paycheck**. You can also choose to accrue sick and vacation based on the number of hours worked or just once per year. Select the appropriate option from the *Accrual period* drop-down list.

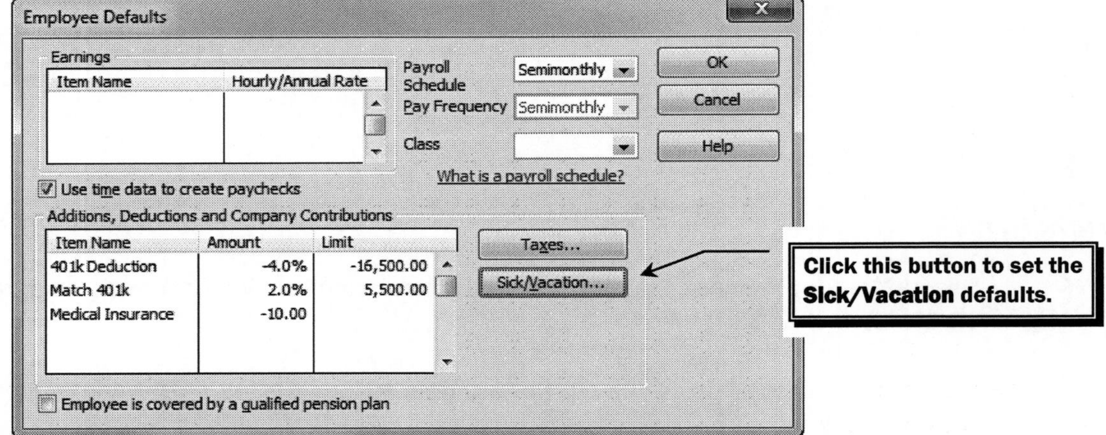

Figure 12-88 Employee Defaults window

Step 2. Since Academy Photography only offers its employees vacation time, we will only set up vacation defaults.

Step 3. In the *Vacation* section, select **Every paycheck** from the *Accrual period* drop-down list to indicate how often you want vacation hours accrued.

Step 4. Enter ***3:00*** in the *Hours accrued per paycheck* field and press **Tab**.

Step 5. Enter ***200:00*** in the *Maximum number of hours* field.

Step 6. Leave *Reset hours each new year?* unchecked.

Step 7. Leave *Sick and vacation hours paid* unchecked.

Step 8. Leave *Overtime hours paid* checked.

Step 9. Verify your results match Figure 12-89. Click **OK** to save your work on this window, then click **OK** on the *Employee Defaults* window to save your changes.

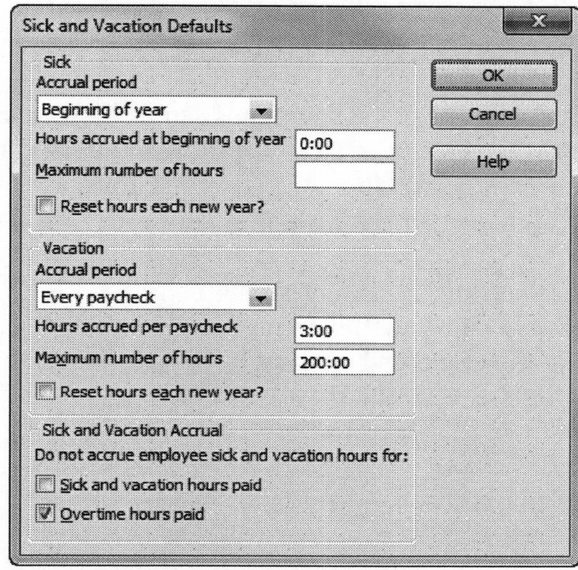

Figure 12-89 Sick and Vacation Defaults

The Accounting Behind the Scenes — Payroll Items

Now that you've finished with the *Payroll Setup Interview*, consider the accounting behind the scenes involving payroll items.

Payroll Items define the relationship between items you put on paychecks and the Chart of Accounts. QuickBooks uses Payroll Items to track each kind of compensation, withholding tax, employer tax, addition, and deduction from paychecks. Using Payroll Items, QuickBooks tracks the detail it needs to calculate paychecks, look up taxes in the tax table, prepare detailed reports, and prepare your payroll tax forms.

Some Payroll Items accumulate payroll liabilities (withholdings and company taxes) into liability accounts according to which tax vendor collects the tax. For example, the Federal Withholding Payroll Item accumulates Federal taxes withheld into the Federal PR Taxes liability account. Since the Federal Withholding Item shows ***EFTPS*** in the *Paid to* field, the withheld taxes are accumulated and tracked as being payable to ***EFTPS***.

Payroll Items are set up so that QuickBooks automatically makes all the accounting entries when you process paychecks and payroll liability payments.

Wage Items: There are two types of **Earnings Items: Salary Wage** Items and **Hourly Wage** Items. Earnings Items track regular, sick, or vacation pay. For example, if you pay an employee for 50 regular hours and 10 hours of vacation, you'll use a regular pay Item and a vacation pay Item, with the corresponding number of hours for each.

Salary Wage Items are used to track payments of gross wages to salaried employees. Since these items represent company expenses, these items increase (debit) an expense account, usually Gross Wages or Officer's Compensation expense.

Hourly Wage Items are used to track payments to hourly employees. Just like the Yearly Salary Items, these items increase (debit) an expense account, usually Gross Wages or Officer's Compensation Expense.

> **Note:**
> QuickBooks automatically accumulates sick and vacation hours, but it does not record a liability for this unpaid expense in the General Ledger. If you want to accrue expenses and liabilities for unpaid sick and vacation time, you'll need to make an adjustment using a General Journal entry.

Commission Items are used to track payments of commissions. These items can be defined as a percentage of the number that you enter when you create paychecks. Commission Items increase (debit) an expense account, usually Gross Wages expense.

Bonus Items are used to track bonuses paid to employees (e.g. performance bonuses or annual bonuses). You calculate the employee's bonus before you process payroll for the period. For example, if you give your employees a bonus based on the sales they generate for the company, you would create a Sales by Rep report and calculate the bonus based on the information in the report. Then, you would enter the calculated amount in the employee's next paycheck. Bonus Items increase (debit) an expense account, usually Gross Wages expense.

Other Payments

Addition Items are used to track amounts added to paychecks beyond gross wages. For example, you might set up an Addition Item to track Tips or employee expense reimbursements. Additions increase (debit) an expense account.

Deduction Items are used to track deductions from paychecks. You can create separate deduction items for each deduction you use on paychecks. For example, if you have a retirement plan with salary deferrals, you can create a 401(k) Deduction Item that calculates a percentage of the total gross wages to be deducted before QuickBooks calculates the Federal and State income tax. Employee contributions such as the 401(k) would be excluded from taxable earning when calculating federal withholding. Since deductions are withheld from paychecks, they increase (credit) a liability account. The Item also accumulates a balance due to the vendor to whom the deductions are paid.

Company Contribution Items are used to track additional money that the company contributes as a result of a paycheck. A company contribution is not paid to the employee, but to a vendor on behalf of an employee. For example, if your company matches employees' 401(k) contributions, use a Company Contribution Item to track it. Since this item represents additional company expense but is not paid directly to the employee, the item increases (debits) an expense account and increases (credits) a liability account. The item also accumulates a balance due to the vendor to whom the contribution is paid.

Federal Tax Items are used to track Federal taxes that are withheld from paychecks or are paid by the employer.

The following Federal Tax Items are employee taxes and are withheld from paychecks: **Federal Withholding**, **Social Security Employee**, and **Medicare Employee**. These Items are associated with a liability account and with the vendor to whom the tax is paid (usually EFTPS or your local bank).

The following Federal Tax Items are company taxes: **Federal Unemployment, Social Security Company**, and **Medicare Company**. These Items are company-paid taxes; they increase (debit) an expense account, usually **Payroll Taxes**, and increase (credit) a liability account, usually **Federal PR Taxes Payable**.

State Tax Items are used to track State taxes that are withheld from paychecks or paid by the employer. Each State has different taxes, so depending on your State, you might have a **State Withholding, State Disability**, and/or **State Unemployment Tax** Item.

State Withholding taxes are employee taxes and are withheld from paychecks. These Items are associated with a liability account and with the vendor to whom the tax is paid — usually the State Department of Revenue or Taxation.

State Disability taxes are usually employee taxes, but this varies by State.

State Unemployment taxes are usually company taxes, but this also varies by State.

Other Tax Items are used to track other State or local taxes that are withheld from paychecks or paid by the employer. Each locality has different taxes, so check in your State for which local taxes apply to payroll. If your local tax is not directly supported by QuickBooks (i.e., if you don't see the tax in the Other Tax List), you'll need to set up a *User-Defined Tax* to track it.

Calculated Items Based on Quantity

Deduction Items, Addition Items, and Company Contribution Items can be used to withhold or contribute a percentage of gross or net pay, or as a fixed amount. However, sometimes you want these Items to calculate a percentage of some other number. For example, a wage garnishment might need to be created to withhold 20% of the net paycheck. To track this, create a new deduction item with the **Based on Quantity** button checked (see Figure 12-90). Then, when the garnishment item is added to a paycheck, you'll manually enter the amount (in this example, enter net pay in the quantity field) on which the calculation should be based.

Calculate based on quantity

Calculate this item based on quantity

Select this item if you want this payroll item to be calculated based on a quantity that you enter manually on paychecks.

Figure 12-90 You can setup some items based on quantity.

Based on Hours

You can also use Deduction Items, Addition Items, and Company Contribution Items to withhold or contribute a fixed amount or a percentage of gross pay – based on the number of hours the employee worked. In this case, setup the payroll item with the Based on Hours radio button checked (see Figure 12-91). QuickBooks gives you the option of including or excluding sick and vacation hours when calculating the employee's deduction, addition, or company contribution.

Figure 12-91 You can setup some items based on hours.

Adding Payroll Items from the Payroll Item List

The *Payroll Setup Interview* set up most of your items, but you'll probably need to set up a few more on your own. The *Custom Payroll Item Setup* feature allows you to add or edit Payroll Items. This feature is accessible from the Payroll Item List and is described in the next section

Adding a Wage (Compensation) Item

If your company is a corporation, the IRS requires you to report compensation of officers separately from the rest of the employees. To track officers' compensation separately from the rest of your employees, you should create an additional *Compensation* Payroll Item called **Officer's Salary.** Follow these steps:

COMPUTER PRACTICE

Step 1. Display the Payroll Items list by selecting the *Lists* menu and then selecting **Payroll Item List.**

Step 2. Because you did not sign up for a payroll service when working with the sample data file for this chapter, QuickBooks may display the window shown in Figure 12-92. If you signed up for a payroll service when using your own data file you will not see this window. Click **No.**

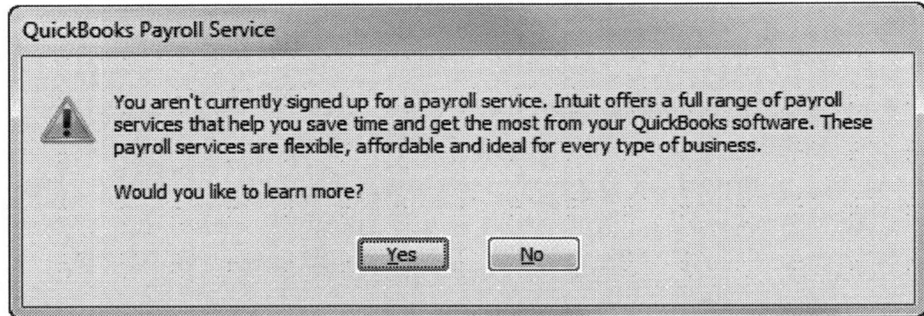

Figure 12-92 QuickBooks Payroll Service window

Step 3. The *Payroll Item List* (Figure 12-93) shows all the items that you have set up using the *Payroll Setup Interview.*

Payroll Item List

Item Name	Type	Amount	Annual Limit	Tax Tracking	Payable To	Account ID
Salary Regular	Yearly Salary			Compensation		
Salary Vacation	Yearly Salary			Compensation		
Hourly Regular	Hourly Wage			Compensation		
Hourly Vacation	Hourly Wage			Compensation		
Commission	Commission	0.0%		Compensation		
Bonus	Bonus	0.00		Compensation		
401k Deduction	Deduction	-4.0%	-16,500.00	401(k)	Merrill Lynch	99-1133334
Medical Insurance	Deduction	-10.00		None		
Match 401k	Company Contribution	4.0%	5,500.00	None	Merrill Lynch	99-1133334
Advance Earned Income ...	Federal Tax			Advance EIC Payment	EFTPS	11-3456789
Federal Unemployment	Federal Tax	0.8%	7,000.00	FUTA	EFTPS	11-3456789
Federal Withholding	Federal Tax			Federal	EFTPS	11-3456789
Medicare Company	Federal Tax	1.45%		Comp. Medicare	EFTPS	11-3456789
Medicare Employee	Federal Tax	1.45%		Medicare	EFTPS	11-3456789
Social Security Company	Federal Tax	6.2%	106,800.00	Comp. SS Tax	EFTPS	11-3456789
Social Security Employee	Federal Tax	6.2%	-106,800.00	SS Tax	EFTPS	11-3456789
CA - Withholding	State Withholding Tax			SWH	EDD	123-4567-8
CA - Disability	State Disability Tax	1.1%	-90,669.00	SDI	EDD	123-4567-8
CA - Unemployment	State Unemployment Tax	3.4%	7,000.00	Comp. SUI	EDD	123-4567-8
CA - Employment Training...	Other Tax	0.1%	7,000.00	Co. Paid Other Tax	EDD	123-4567-8

Payroll Item ▾ | Activities ▾ | Reports ▾ | Include inactive

Figure 12-93 Payroll Item list

Step 4. To add a new item, select **New** from the *Payroll Item* menu at the bottom of the *Payroll Item List*, or press **Ctrl+N** (see Figure 12-94).

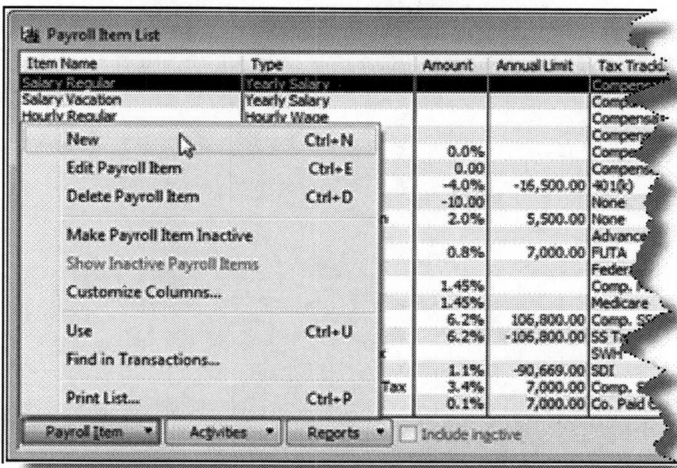

Figure 12-94 Select New from Payroll Item menu

Step 5. Select **Custom Setup** in the *Add new payroll item* window (see Figure 12-95). Then click **Next**.

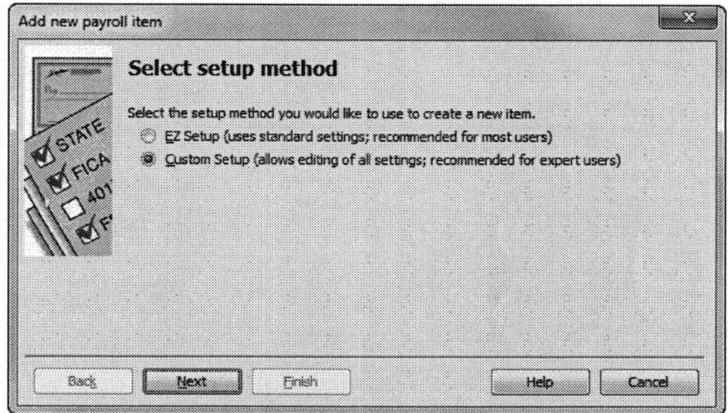

Figure 12-95 Select Custom Payroll Item setup

Step 6. Select **Wage (Hourly Wages, Annual Salary, Commission, Bonus)** on the *Payroll item type* window and click **Next** (see Figure 12-96).

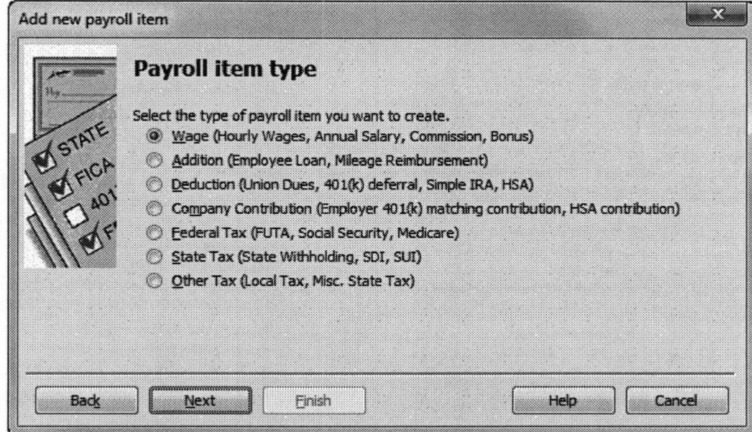

Figure 12-96 Payroll Item types

Step 7. Select **Annual Salary** on the *Wages* window (as shown in Figure 12-97) and click **Next**.

You can set up hourly wage items on this window too. Also, each Wage Item can be for regular pay, overtime pay, sick pay, or vacation pay. When you pay an employee for sick or vacation time, you'll use a Sick or Vacation Pay Item in addition to the regular pay item.

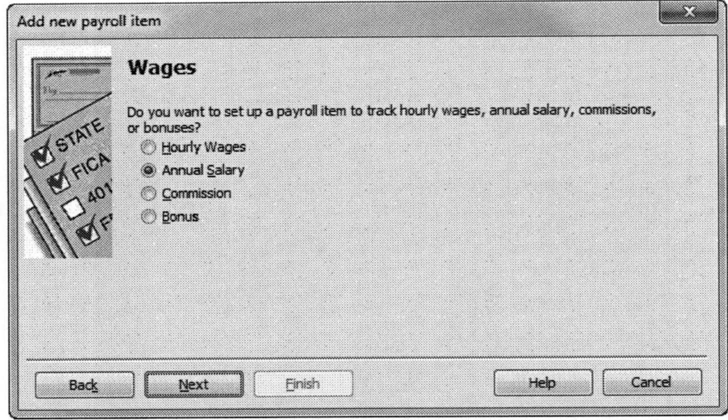

Figure 12-97 Use this window to set up salary and hourly wages.

Step 8. Leave **Regular Pay** selected and click **Next** (see Figure 12-98).

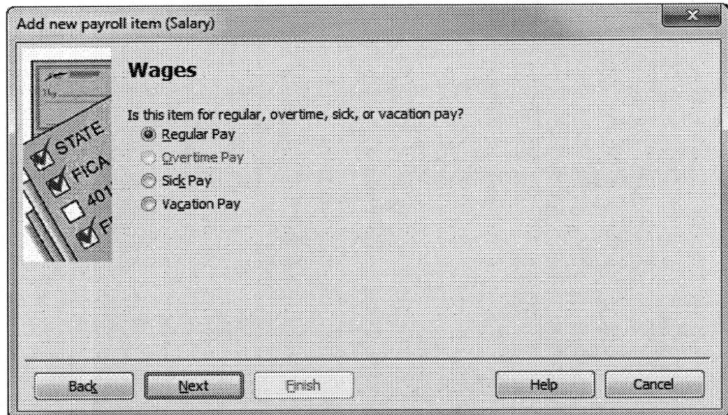

Figure 12-98 Use this window to set up regular, sick, or vacation pay.

Step 9. Enter ***Officer's Salary*** on the *Enter name for salary item* field and click **Next** (see Figure 12-99).

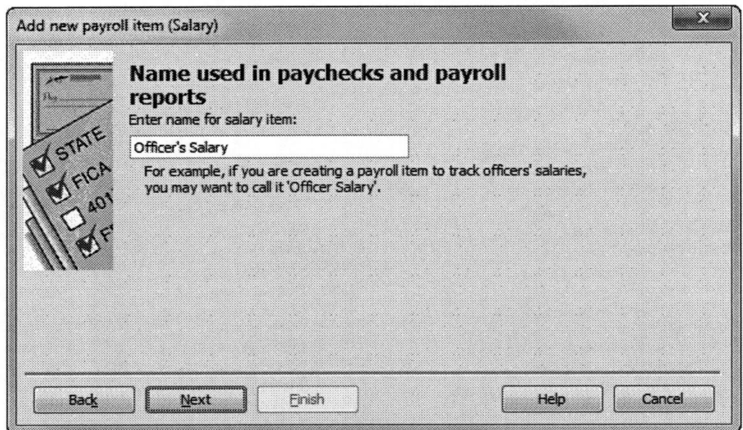

Figure 12-99 Use this window to name the Item.

Step 10. Select **Payroll Expenses:Officer's Compensation** on the *Expense account* window and click **Finish** (see Figure 12-100).

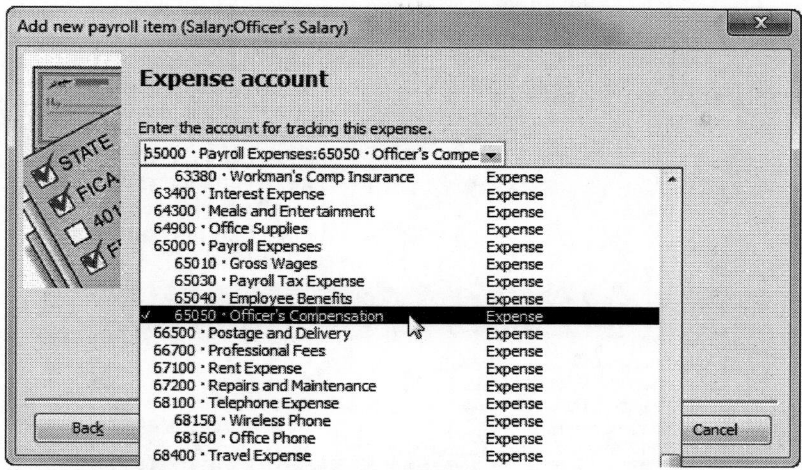

Figure 12-100 Expense account for payroll item

Editing Payroll Items

You will need to edit several of the items created by the *Payroll Setup Interview* so that they will affect the appropriate accounts in the Chart of Accounts. For example, the Federal withholding tax is set up to affect the *Payroll Liabilities* account instead of one of its Subaccounts (Employee Payroll Taxes Payable). You will make these changes by double-clicking each Payroll item in the Payroll Item list and then making the needed changes.

COMPUTER PRACTICE

Editing the Federal Withholding Payroll item

Step 1. Display the *Payroll Items List* by selecting the **Lists** menu, then selecting **Payroll Item List** (see Figure 12-101).

Step 2. QuickBooks may display a payroll service message. Click **No** to move to the next screen.

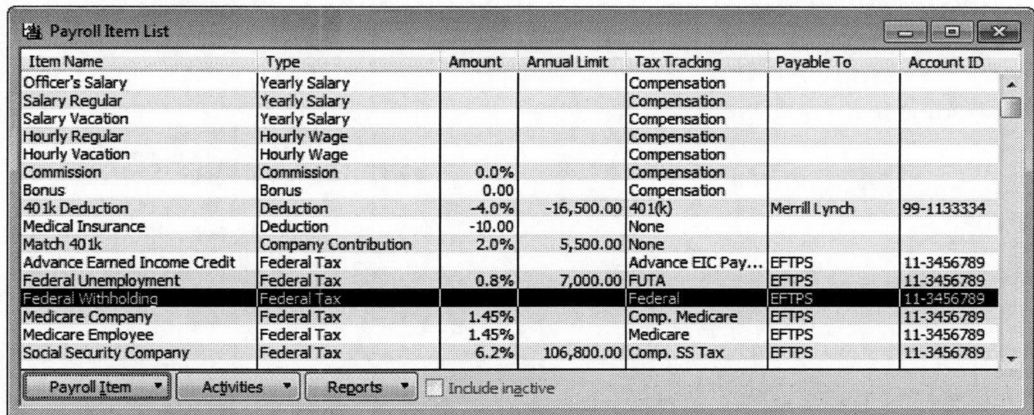

Item Name	Type	Amount	Annual Limit	Tax Tracking	Payable To	Account ID
Officer's Salary	Yearly Salary			Compensation		
Salary Regular	Yearly Salary			Compensation		
Salary Vacation	Yearly Salary			Compensation		
Hourly Regular	Hourly Wage			Compensation		
Hourly Vacation	Hourly Wage			Compensation		
Commission	Commission	0.0%		Compensation		
Bonus	Bonus	0.00		Compensation		
401k Deduction	Deduction	-4.0%	-16,500.00	401(k)	Merrill Lynch	99-1133334
Medical Insurance	Deduction	-10.00		None		
Match 401k	Company Contribution	2.0%	5,500.00	None		
Advance Earned Income Credit	Federal Tax			Advance EIC Pay...	EFTPS	11-3456789
Federal Unemployment	Federal Tax	0.8%	7,000.00	FUTA	EFTPS	11-3456789
Federal Withholding	Federal Tax			Federal	EFTPS	11-3456789
Medicare Company	Federal Tax	1.45%		Comp. Medicare	EFTPS	11-3456789
Medicare Employee	Federal Tax	1.45%		Medicare	EFTPS	11-3456789
Social Security Company	Federal Tax	6.2%	106,800.00	Comp. SS Tax	EFTPS	11-3456789

Figure 12-101 Payroll Item list

Step 3. Double-click on the **Federal Withholding** Payroll Item.

Step 4. Click **Next** on the *Name used in paychecks and payroll* reports window.

Step 5. On the following window (see Figure 12-102), choose which liability account you want this Item to affect. In this example, select **Payroll Liabilities:Employee Payroll Taxes Payable** from the *Liability account* drop-down list.

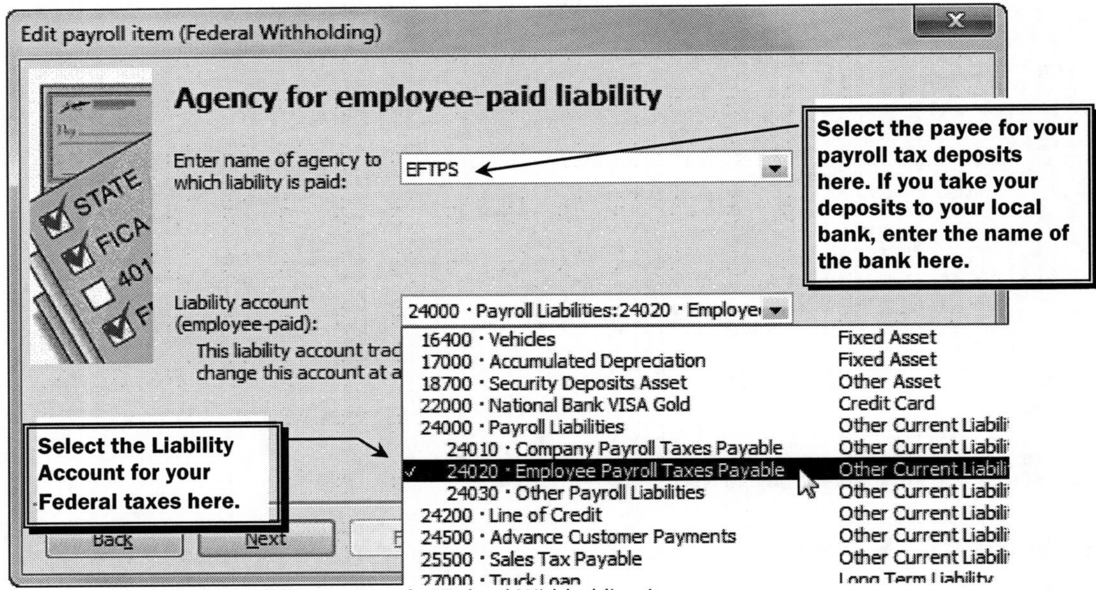

Figure 12-102 Edit the Liability Account for Federal Withholding item.

Step 6. Click **Next** twice and then click **Finish** to save the change.

COMPUTER PRACTICE

Editing the Federal Unemployment item

Step 1. To modify the Federal Unemployment item, double-click on the **Federal Unemployment** item in the *Payroll Item List*.

Step 2. Click **Next**.

Step 3. On the *Agency for company-paid liability* window of the *Edit Payroll Item* wizard, change the account information as shown in Figure 12-103. Choose **Company Payroll Taxes Payable** for the *Liability account* and **Payroll Tax Expense** for the *Expense account*. Then click **Next**.

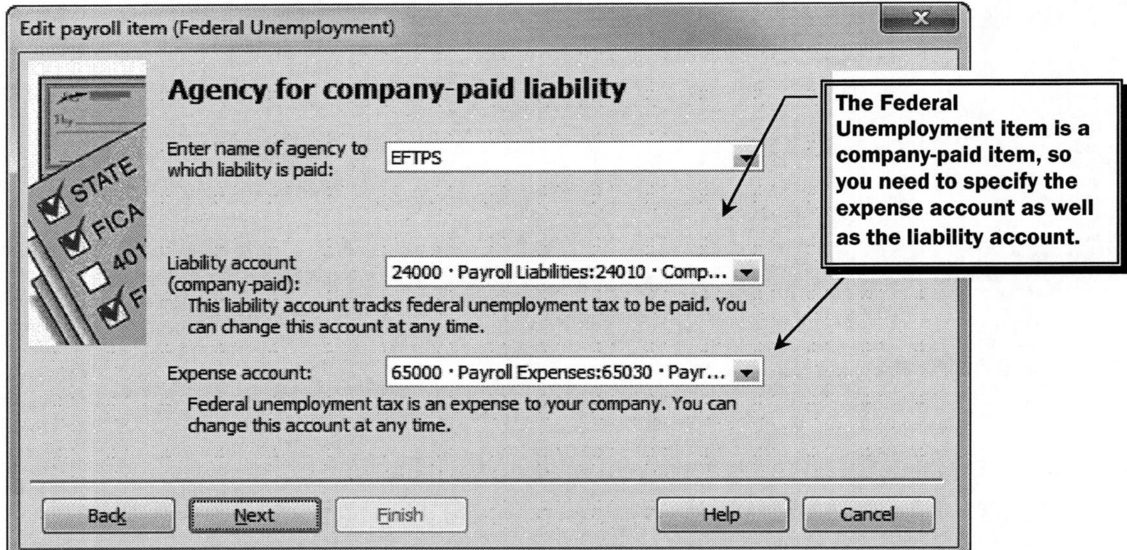

Figure 12-103 Edit the Federal Unemployment Item's accounts.

Since Federal Unemployment is an employer-paid tax, you need to enter two account names, one for the liability account and one for the expense account.

Step 4. The tax rate of **0.8%** is already selected (Figure 12-104). Click **Next** twice and then click **Finish**.

If your State has a *State Unemployment Tax* you may be eligible for a Federal Unemployment or FUTA tax reduction, making your FUTA tax 0.8% instead of 6.2%. Select the appropriate button on this window. If you're not sure if you're eligible for this reduction, ask your accountant.

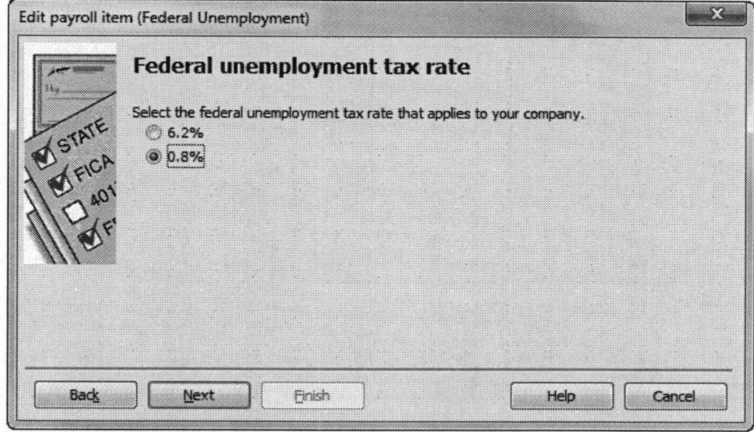

Figure 12-104 Setting the Unemployment tax rate

In the *Payroll Item List,* there are two Medicare and two Social Security Items (Figure 12-105). Although QuickBooks has two Medicare and two Social Security items in the Payroll Items list to track employer and employee taxes separately, the two sets of items are grouped together in QuickBooks and are modified using a single edit window. Therefore, when you change the Medicare Company account, the Medicare Employee account is automatically updated and vice versa. The same applies to the Social Security accounts.

Medicare Company	Federal Tax
Medicare Employee	Federal Tax
Social Security Company	Federal Tax
Social Security Employee	Federal Tax

Figure 12-105 Medicare and Social Security tax items

COMPUTER PRACTICE

Editing the Medicare and **Social Security items**

Step 1. Double-click the **Medicare Company** or **Medicare Employee** payroll item in the *Payroll Item List* window. Since both items will be modified at the same time, either one can be selected.

Step 2. QuickBooks displays the *Edit payroll item (Medicare Taxes)* window (see Figure 12-106). Click **Next**.

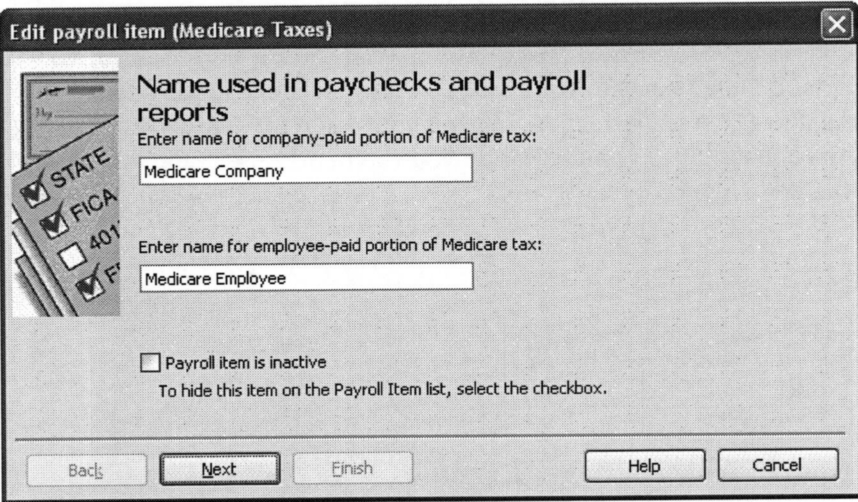

Figure 12-106 Edit Payroll Item (Medicare Taxes)

Step 3. Select **Company Payroll Taxes Payable** from the drop-down box next to the company-paid liability account field, and **Employee Payroll Taxes Payable** from the drop-down box next to the employee-paid liability account field as shown in Figure 12-107. Click **Next**.

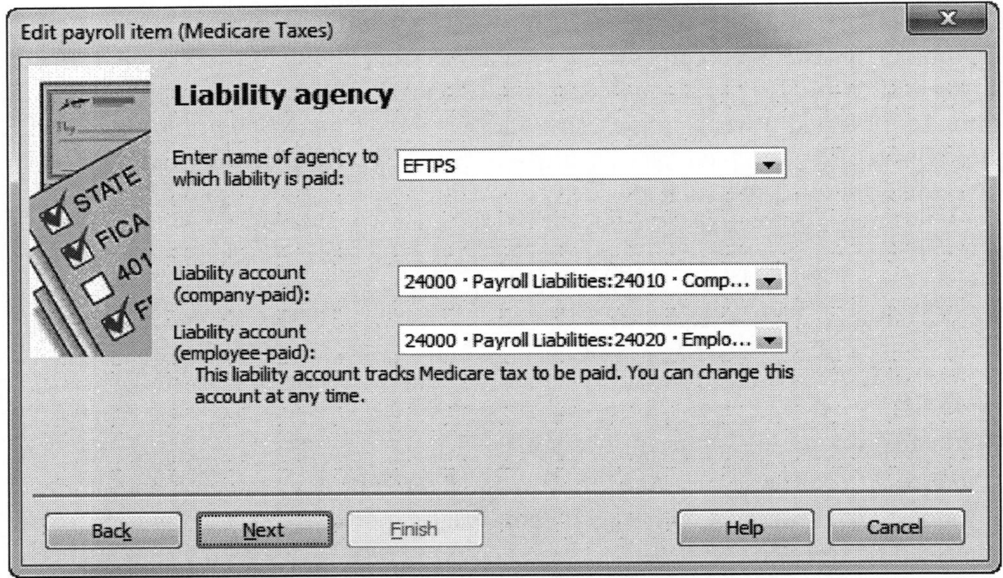

Figure 12-107 Editing Liability accounts for the employer and employee Medicare items

Step 4. Select **Payroll Expenses:Payroll Tax Expense** from the drop-down list in the *Enter the account for tracking this expense* field (see Figure 12-108). Then click **Next** three times through the remaining windows and click **Finish** on the last window.

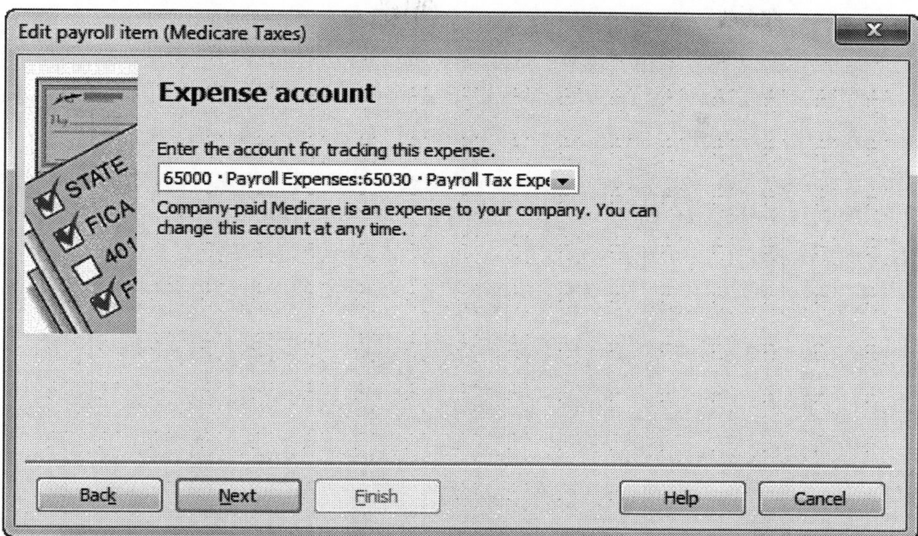

Figure 12-108 Enter the Expense account.

Step 5. Double-click the **Social Security Company** or **Social Security Employee** payroll item in the *Payroll Item List* window. Since both items will be modified at the same time, either one can be selected. Repeat steps 2 through 4 above to modify these two payroll items.

COMPUTER PRACTICE

Editing the State Withholding item

Step 1. To modify the State Withholding Item, double-click on **CA- Withholding** in the *Payroll Item List.*

Step 2. Click **Next.**

Step 3. On the *Agency for employee-paid liability* window, change the *Liability account (employee-paid)* by selecting **Payroll Liabilities:Employee Payroll Taxes Payable** from the drop-down list. Your screen should look like Figure 12-109.

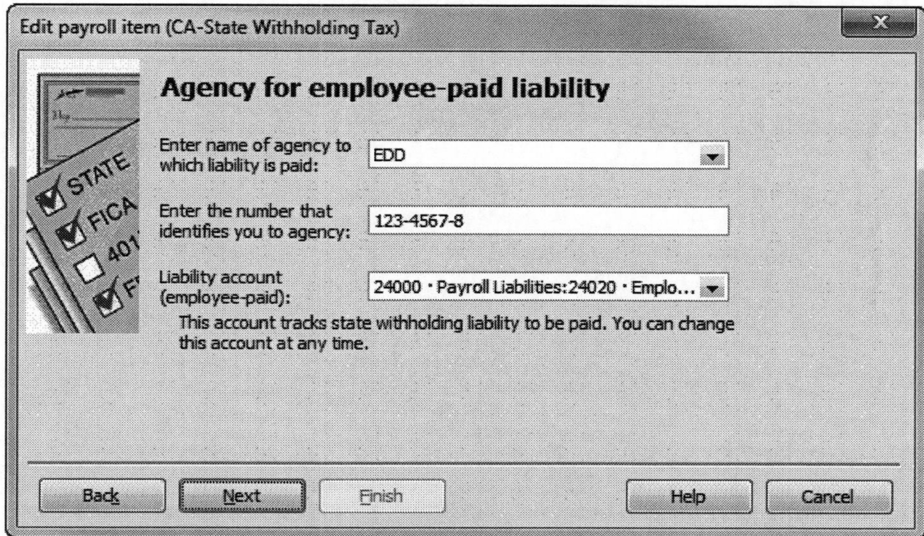

Figure 12-109 Editing the State Withholding item

Step 4. Click **Next** twice and then click **Finish.**

COMPUTER PRACTICE

Editing the State Disability item

QuickBooks creates a State Disability Item only if your State collects disability tax. Since California collects State Disability tax, the *Payroll Setup Interview* created a State Disability Item. You'll now need to edit the item to make it affect the appropriate accounts.

Step 1. Double-click **CA – Disability** in the *Payroll Item List*, and then click **Next.**

Step 2. Verify that ***123-4567-8*** is entered in the *Enter the number that identifies you to agency* box. This is your State Tax ID# that you receive from your tax agency.

Step 3. In the *Liability account (employee-paid)* field, select **Payroll Liabilities: Employee Payroll Taxes Payable** from the drop-down list. Your screen should look like Figure 12-110.

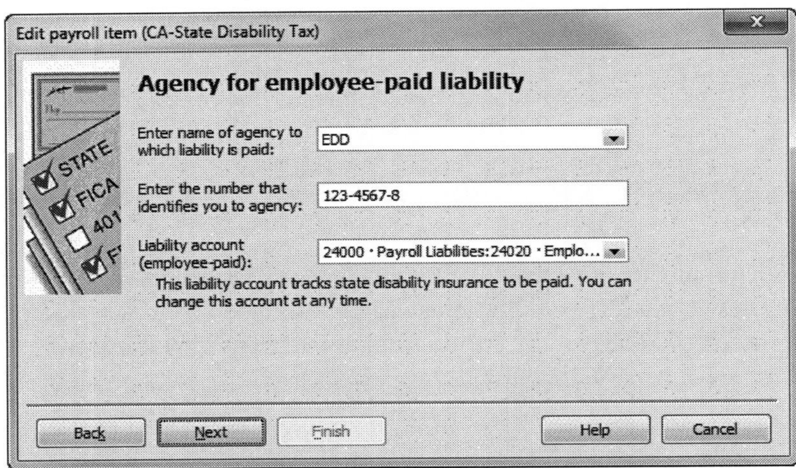

Figure 12-110 Change the liability account for the disability item.

Step 4. Click **Next.**

Step 5. On the *Employee tax rate* window, QuickBooks automatically fills in the rate from the tax table (see Figure 12-111). Leave the default Employee rate and click **Next.**

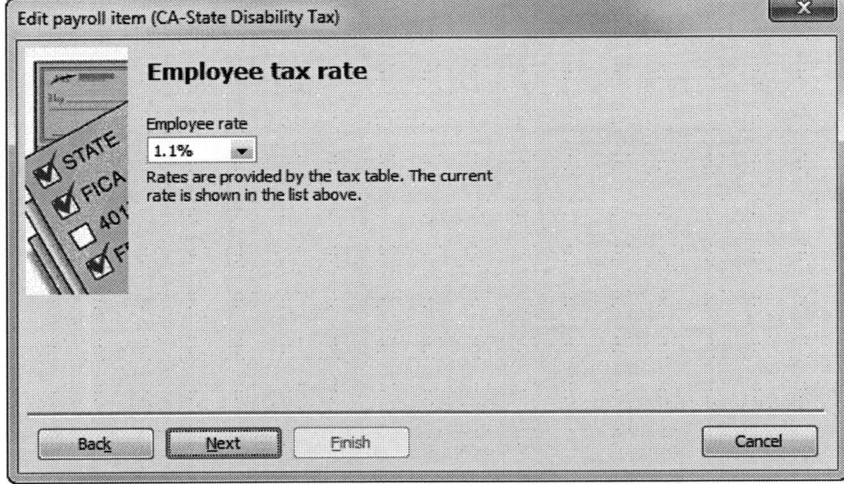

Figure 12-111 QuickBooks supplies the tax rate from tax tables.

Step 6. On the *Taxable compensation* window, QuickBooks automatically checks all of the *Wage items* that are subject to State disability tax. Leave all of these checked. Click **Next** and then click **Finish.**

COMPUTER PRACTICE

Editing the State Unemployment item

For State Unemployment, you'll also need to edit the payroll item to make it affect the proper accounts.

Step 1. Double-click the **CA – Unemployment** item. Then click **Next**.

Step 2. On the *Agency for company-paid liability* window, change the liability account to **Payroll Liabilities:Company Payroll Taxes Payable**. Change the expense account to **Payroll Expenses:Payroll Tax Expense**. Your screen should look like Figure 12-112.

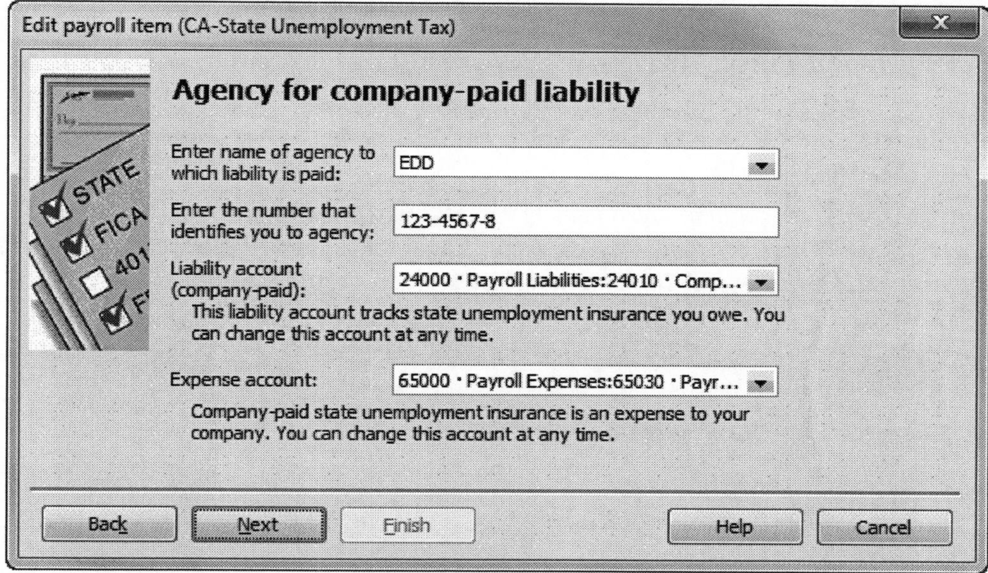

Figure 12-112 Edit payroll item window for the State Unemployment Tax

Step 3. Click **Next**.

Step 4. On the *Company tax rate* window (Figure 12-113), leave the tax rates as you entered them in the *Payroll Setup Interview*, or change them here if necessary. Click **Next**.

If your State unemployment tax rate changes, return to this window to update QuickBooks. The state unemployment tax rate is not supplied by the tax table because each employer has a different rate. Therefore, you must enter it here.

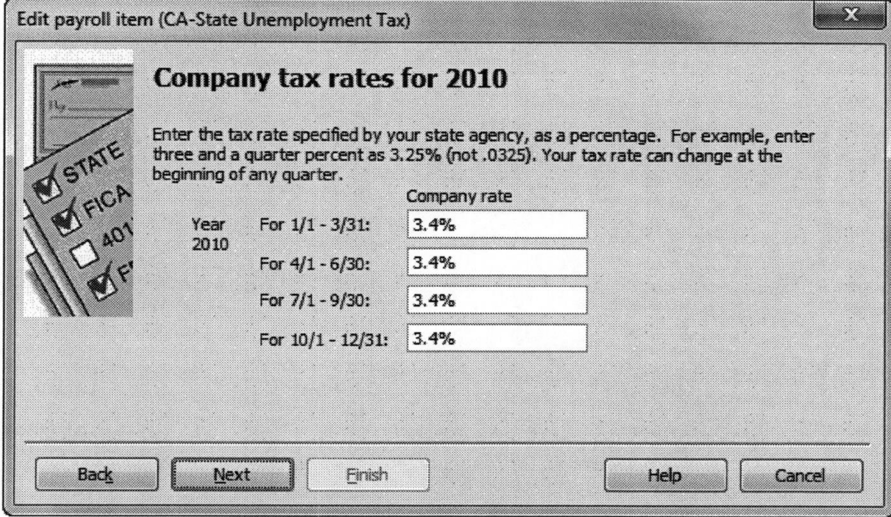

Figure 12-113 Unemployment tax rates

Step 5. On the *Taxable compensation* window, QuickBooks automatically checks all of the *Wage Items* that are subject to state unemployment tax. Leave them all checked. Click **Next** and then click **Finish**.

COMPUTER PRACTICE

Editing Other Tax items

If you have other State-specific taxes or local taxes, set up Other Tax Items. For example, in California set up an Other Tax Item to track California Employment Training Tax (ETT).

You created the *Employment Training Tax item* in the *Payroll Setup Interview*. Now follow these steps to edit it:

Step 1. Double-click on the **CA – Employment Training Tax** item in the *Payroll Item List*. Then click **Next**.

Step 2. On the *Agency for company-paid liability* window, change the liability account to **Payroll Liabilities:Company Payroll Taxes Payable**. Change the expense account to **Payroll Expenses:Payroll Tax Expense**. Your screen should look like Figure 12-114. Click **Next**.

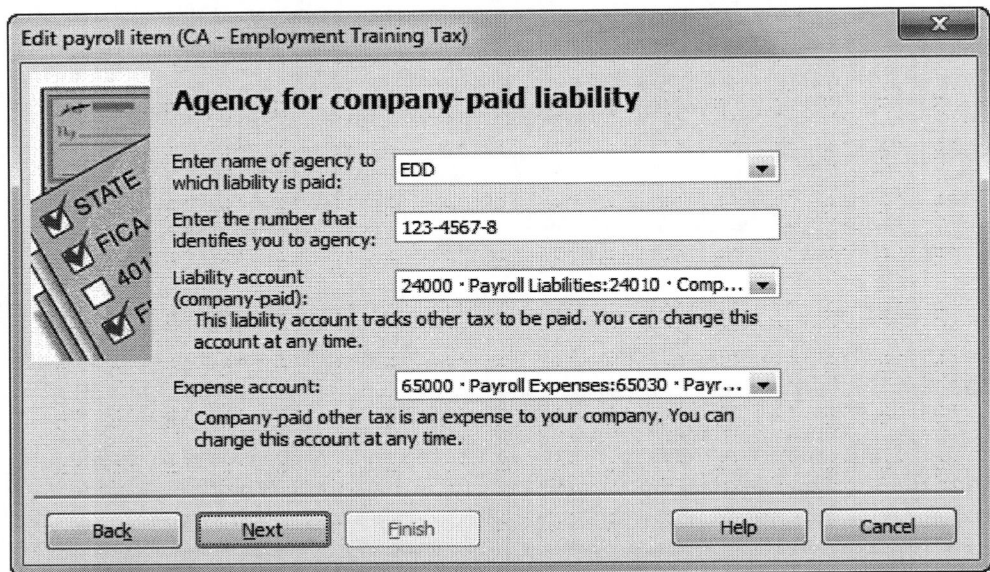

Figure 12-114 Edit the liability and expense account for the ETT tax item.

Step 3. On the *Company tax rate* window accept the default rate of **0.1%** and click **Next**.

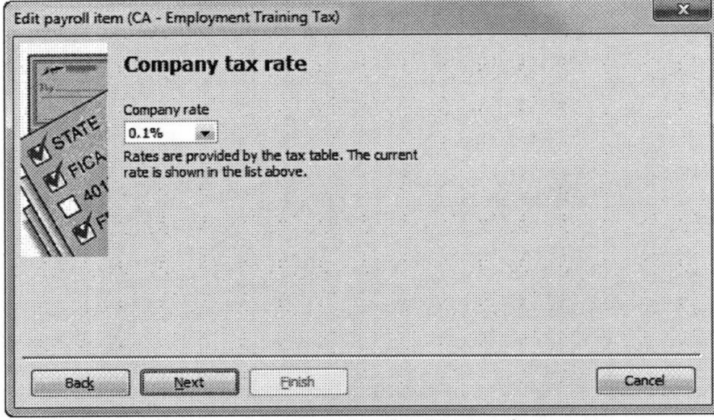

Figure 12-115 Company tax rate for Unemployment

Step 4. On the *Taxable compensation* window, QuickBooks automatically checks all of the Wage Items that are subject to this local tax. Leave all of these checked. Click **Next** and then click **Finish.** Then close the Payroll Item list.

Releasing Employees

When you release an employee, edit the employee record and fill in the **Released** field with the date on which the employee separated from the company (see Figure 12-117). A released employee no longer appears in the *Select Employees to Pay* window when you run your payroll.

COMPUTER PRACTICE

Step 1. Select the **Employee Center** icon on the *Icon Bar.*

Step 2. Double-click on **Mike Mazuki** from the *Name* list.

Step 3. Select **Employment Info** from the *Change tabs* drop-down list (Figure 12-116).

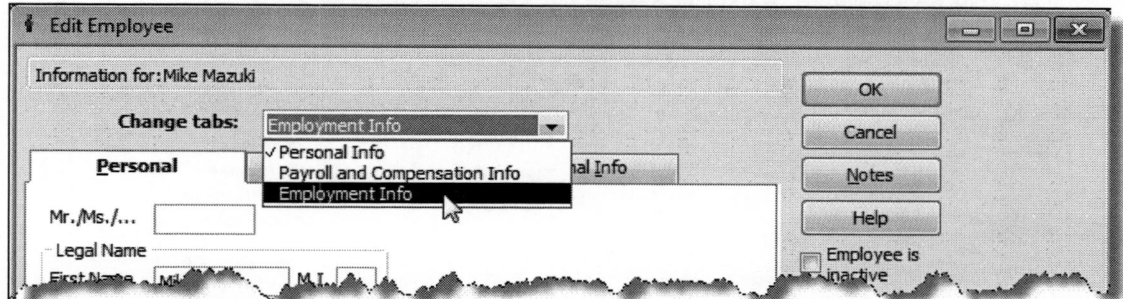

Figure 12-116 Selecting Employment Info from Change tabs

Step 4. Enter ***2/28/11*** in the *Release Date* field (Figure 12-117) and press **Tab.**

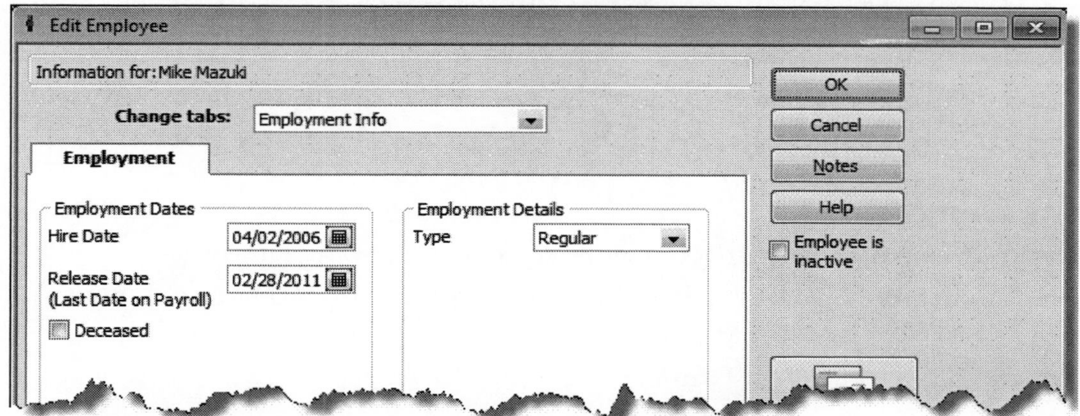

Figure 12-117 Releasing an employee

Step 5. A *Warning* window appears stating that the released employee will not show up on the Select Employees to Pay list after the release date (Figure 12-118).

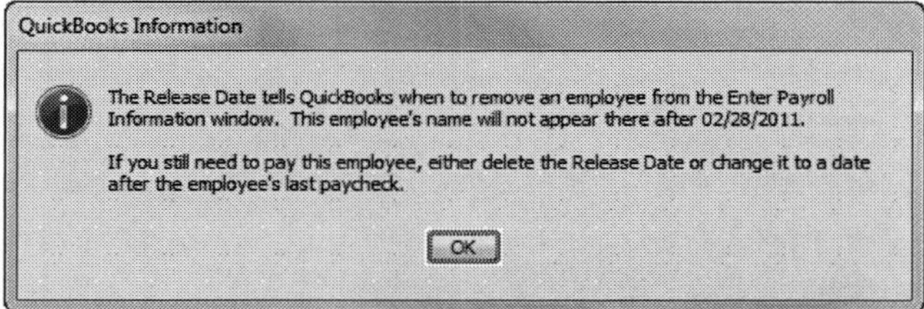

Figure 12-118 Warning Window that employee will not show on Select Employees to Pay list

Step 6. Click **OK** to close the warning window

Step 7. Click **Cancel** to prevent this change from taking effect in your sample file.

Deactivating and Reactivating Employees

After you've released an employee, you may wish to delete that employee from your *Employee list*. However, if an employee's name is used in any transactions (e.g., paychecks) or if the name is used in the *Rep* field on any customer record or sales transaction, QuickBooks won't allow you to delete the employee from the *Employee list*. However, you can "deactivate" the employee so it will no longer appear in your list.

To deactivate an employee, follow these steps:

Step 1. Right-click Mike Mazuki in the Employee Center and select **Make Employee Inactive** (see Figure 12-119). This removes this employee from the list, but it doesn't delete the employee from your company file.

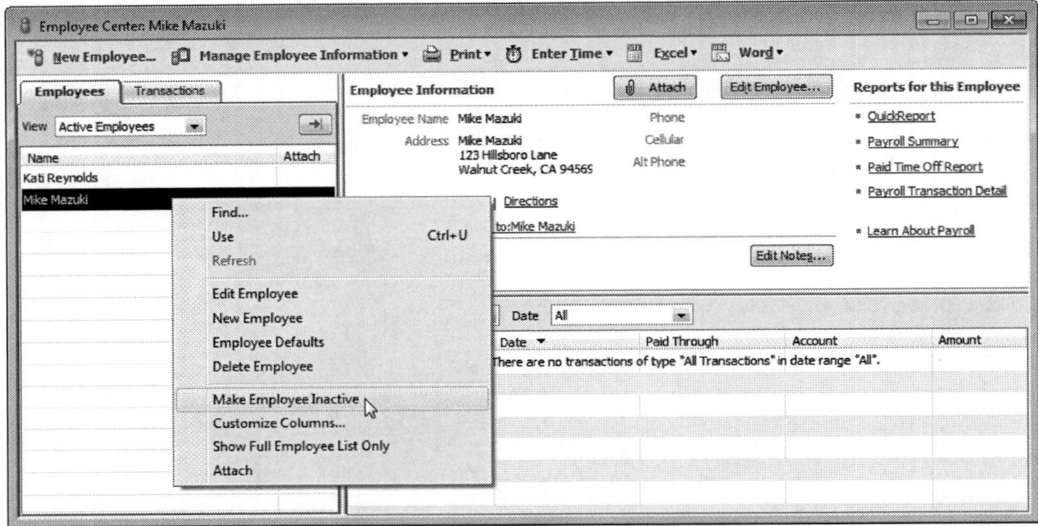

Figure 12-119 Deactivating an employee

COMPUTER PRACTICE

To reactivate an employee, first set your Employee Center to view All Employees.

Step 1. Select **All Employees** from the **View** menu in the *Employee Center* (see Figure 12-120).

Figure 12-120 Viewing ALL employees including inactive ones

Step 2. To reactive Mike Mazuki, right-click on his name and select **Make Employee Active.** Alternatively, click on the ✖ icon in the *Employee List* as shown in Figure 12-121 (or edit the employee record and uncheck the **Employee is inactive** box).

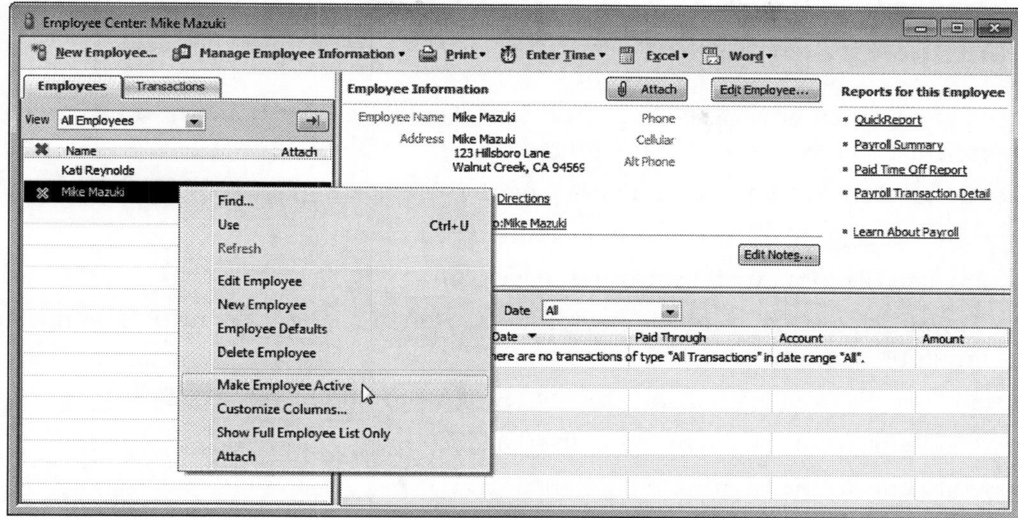

Figure 12-121 Reactivating an inactive employee

The Employee Contact List report

You can print a list of employees by following the steps below.

COMPUTER PRACTICE

Step 1. Select the **Reports** menu, select **List**, and then select **Employee Contact List** (see Figure 12-122).

> **Important:**
> If you made "Mike Mazuki" inactive in the preceding section, you will need to reactivate his record, so that your report matches Figure 12-122. In the *Edit Employee* window, uncheck the **Employee is inactive** box.

Employee Contact List

Academy Photography Payroll Setup Chapter

Employee Contact List

Employee	SS No.	Phone	Address	Gender
Kati Reynolds	333-22-4321		432 Enos Lane Danville, CA 94501	Female
Mike Mazuki	111-22-3333		123 Hillsboro Lane Walnut Creek, CA 94569	Male

Figure 12-122 Employee Contact List

Step 2. Click **Print** at the top of the report and follow the prompts to print the report. Then, close the *Employee Contact List* report.

Chapter Summary and Review

In this chapter, you learned how to set up payroll in QuickBooks. You should now be familiar with how to use QuickBooks to do all of the following:

- Activate the payroll feature and configure payroll preferences (page 483).
- Set up payroll accounts in the Chart of Accounts (page 485).
- Enable the data file for payroll processing (page 486).
- Use the *Payroll Setup Interview* to add payroll items, vendors, employee records, and year-to-date amounts (page 490).
- Understand the **accounting behind the scenes** of payroll items (page 525).
- Add payroll items from the Payroll Item list (page 528).
- Edit payroll items in the Payroll Item list (page 531).
- Release, deactivate, and reactivate employees (page 539).

Comprehension Questions

Answers to these review questions are available with the supplemental material. See page xiii for details.

1. What type of payroll item should you set up to track additional money contributed by the company as a result of a paycheck?
2. Why do you need to edit several of your payroll items (e.g., Payroll Tax Items) after you complete the *Payroll Setup Interview*?
3. Name an example of a payroll item that should be "Based on Quantity"?

Multiple Choice

Select the best answer(s) for each of the following:

1. An easy and convenient way to process payroll in QuickBooks for employees on different payroll schedules would be to:
   a) Move all employees onto a single schedule.
   b) Use the Payroll Schedule function in QuickBooks.
   c) Outsource payroll.
   d) Make all employees independent contractors.

2. You enter the Federal ID for your company:
   a) In **Payroll Preferences** on the *Company Preferences* tab.
   b) On Step 3 of the *Payroll Setup Interview* – "Set up Company Information."
   c) In the *Company Information* window.
   d) In **General Preferences** on the *Company Preferences* tab.
3. Use a **Payroll Deduction** Item to track medical insurance costs when:
   a) The employees pay part of (or all of) the cost.
   b) Costs exceed $100 per month for the employee.
   c) The employer pays the total cost.
   d) You do not track medical insurance costs as a Payroll Deduction Item.

4. Which of the following would QuickBooks exclude from taxable earnings when calculating federal withholding?
   a) Vacation salary
   b) Sick leave salary
   c) Overtime earnings
   d) Employee contributions to a 401(k)

5. Why are there two **Medicare** and two **Social Security** items in the **Payroll Items** list?
   a) Different tax rates apply to employee and employer portions.
   b) You use separate accounts because you must write separate checks for employee and employer portions.
   c) QuickBooks tracks the employee and employer portions separately.
   d) You maintain separate ledger accounts for the two portions of each tax.

6. Which of the following payroll periods is not an option in QuickBooks?
   a) Quarterly
   b) Biweekly
   c) Daily
   d) Semiannually

7. Which of the following is *not* a feature of QuickBooks Standard Payroll Service?
   a) Tracks individual employees for hours worked and gross pay.
   b) Writes and prints paychecks on standard checks.
   c) Calculates and electronically remits federal payroll tax liabilities using EFTPS.
   d) Automatically calculates Federal, State and some local taxes using tax tables supplied through the QuickBooks Standard Payroll Service.

8. QuickBooks uses Payroll Items to:
   a) Accumulate payroll liabilities.
   b) Track each different kind of compensation.
   c) Define the relationship between items you put on paychecks and the chart of accounts.
   d) All of the above.

9. Which payroll item cannot be created in the *Payroll Setup Interview*:
   a) Commissions.
   b) Bonus.
   c) Medical Insurance Deduction.
   d) You can create all items above during the *Payroll Setup Interview*.

10. If you no longer want an employee to show in the *Select Employees to Pay* list:
    a) Stop paying the employee.
    b) Deselect the employee for payments.
    c) Enter a Release Date in the employee's record.
    d) Remove all wage items from the employee's record.

11. Which is *not* an option when setting the accrual period for sick and vacation time?
    a) Beginning of year
    b) Every Month
    c) Every Paycheck
    d) Every hour on paycheck

12. Which of the following payroll options does not require you to sign up for an Intuit Payroll Service?
    a) Manual
    b) Standard
    c) Assisted
    d) Complete
13. The *Payroll Setup Interview* will not allow you to:
    a) Edit the default name for payroll items.
    b) Associate deduction and withholding items with vendors.
    c) Set the pay rate for an employee.
    d) Add two employees with exactly the same name.
14. To set up local taxes for employees that are not supported by QuickBooks:
    a) Choose the *Other* tab under Tax Defaults.
    b) Set up New **Payroll Item** , and select *OtherTax*
    c) You cannot set up taxes not supported by QuickBooks tax tables.
    d) A or B .
15. You need to set up a custom field to track which of the following for your employees?
    a) Social Security number
    b) Spouse's Name
    c) Date of Birth
    d) Email address

Completion Statements

Record in your notebook the best answer(s) for each of the following:

1. The _____ _______ feature allows you to define defaults for your employee records so that you do not have to enter the same information each time you add a new employee.
2. To set up custom fields for adding more detailed information about your employees, click the ________ ___________ button on the *Additional Information* tab of the *New Employee* or *Edit Employee* window.
3. QuickBooks uses _____________ items to track amounts withheld from gross or net pay of employees. Since these payroll items represent amounts withheld, these items usually credit a ________ account.
4. When you release an employee, edit the employee record and fill in the _______ ________ field with the date on which the employee separated from the company. QuickBooks will no longer show the employee in the *Select Employees to Pay* list.
5. When you pay semi-monthly wages, you can assign employees to a ________ *Schedule.* This allows you to group together all employees with semi-monthly wages.

Payroll Setup Problem 1

APPLYING YOUR KNOWLEDGE

> Restore the PRSetup-10Problem1.QBM file and store it on your hard disk according to your instructor's directions.

1. Verify that your Chart of Accounts has the accounts shown in Table 12-4 below. These accounts have already been set up for you in the problem template.

◆24000 · Payroll Liabilities	Other Current Liability
◆24010 · Company Payroll Taxes Payable	Other Current Liability
◆24020 · Employee Payroll Taxes Payable	Other Current Liability
◆24030 · Other Payroll Liabilities	Other Current Liability

◆65000 · Payroll Expenses	Expense
◆65010 · Gross Wages	Expense
◆65030 · Payroll Tax Expense	Expense
◆65040 · Employee Benefits	Expense
◆65050 · Officer's Compensation	Expense

Table 12-4 Chart of Accounts for Payroll Setup

2. Using the *Payroll Setup Interview*, add the payroll items shown in Table 12-5.

Item Name	Setup Notes
(a) Salary Regular	This item should point to Gross Wages, a subaccount of the Payroll Expenses account.
(b) Hourly Regular	This item should point to Gross Wages, a subaccount of the Payroll Expenses account.
(c) Hourly Double-time	This item should point to Gross Wages, a subaccount of the Payroll Expenses account.
(d) Hourly Time-and-a-half	This item should point to Gross Wages, a subaccount of the Payroll Expenses account.
(e) Commission	Add a 4% commission item. This item should point to Gross Wages Expense, a subaccount of the Payroll Expenses account. Commissions are calculated based upon percentage of sales.
(f) Health Insurance	Use Health Insurance (taxable) item to set up this item. Leave the payee and account number fields blank. Use "Payroll Liabilities:Other Payroll Liabilities" to track the withholding. Employee pays for all of it and it is deducted after taxes at a flat rate of $50.00. Select all other defaults.
(g) 401(k) Employee	Payee is Merrill Lynch: Account number with Merrill Lynch is "99-1123456." Liability account is "Payroll Liabilities:Other Payroll Liabilities," Tax Tracking type is "401(k)," and you should use the standard tax settings. The default rate is 4% as a percentage of pay and the default limit is $16,000. This is a traditional 401(k) and not a Roth 401(k).
(h) Match 401(k)	Track this expense by Job. Payee is Merrill Lynch; Account number is "99-1123456." Expense account is "Payroll Expenses: Employee Benefits." Liability account is "Payroll Liabilities:Other Payroll Liabilities." Expense is "Payroll Expenses: Employee Benefits." Tax Tracking type is "None." Use standard tax settings. The default rate is 2% and the default limit is $5,500.00.
(i) Salary Vacation	This item should point to Gross Wages, a subaccount of the Payroll Expenses account.
(j) Hourly Vacation	This item should point to Gross Wages, a subaccount of the Payroll Expenses account.
(k) Salary Sick	This item should point to Gross Wages, a subaccount of the Payroll Expenses account.
(l) Hourly Sick	This item should point to Gross Wages, a subaccount of the Payroll Expenses account.

Table 12-5 Add these payroll items.

3. Set up a new employee with the following information:

Field	Data
First Name	*Malcolm*
M.I.	
Last Name	*Heath*
Print on check as	*Malcolm Heath*
Employee Status	*Active*
Address	*444 Adams Ave.* *Pleasanton, CA 94555*
Employee Tax Type	*Regular*
SS No.	*123-12-3123*
Hire Date	*10/7/1999*
Release Date	
Date of Birth	*04/16/1961*
Gender	*Male*
Pay Period	*Weekly*
Earnings	*Hourly Regular – Rate $28 per hour (leave all other fields blank)*
Additions, Deductions, and Company Contributions	*401(k) Employee (4%), limit $16,000.00* *Match 401(k) (2%), limit $5,500.00* *Health Insurance ($50)*
Sick/Vacation Settings	*3 hours sick time per paycheck, maximum 80 hours* *3 hours vacation time per paycheck, maximum 200 hours*
Employee Works and lives	*Works - CA; Lives - CA; Did not live or work in another state*
Federal Filing Status	*Single, 0 Allowances, Nonresident Alien Withholding: Does not apply, Subject to Social Security, FUTA, Medicare*
State Filing Status	*CA – Filing Status Single 0 regular withholding allowances; subject to SUI, Employment Training tax, and Disability; not subject to any special local taxes*
Wage Plan Code	*S (State Plan For Both UI and DI)*

Table 12-6 New employee setup information

4. Enter the Unemployment Rate for State Payroll Taxes as shown in Table 12-7.

Item Name	Setup Notes
Payee	EDD
California Tax ID	123-4567-8
Deposit Frequency	Quarterly
State Unemployment Rate	3.4%

Table 12-7 Setup for state payroll taxes EDD Payments

5. Select **EFTPS** as the payee (vendor) for United States Treasury Payments. You deposit your taxes quarterly. You use this to pay your liabilities for Federal taxes. Click **Continue** to skip Federal Taxes window.

6. For the State payroll taxes, setup the Payee, Employer Account number, and Deposit Frequency from Table 12-7 above.

7. Do not set up YTD amounts. On the *Determine if you need to enter payroll history* screen, select **No** for the *Has your company issues paychecks in 2011* option. Click **Continue** till you reach *Go to Payroll Center to manage your payroll* button and then click **Go to the Payroll Center** to complete the Interview.

8. Set up your Employee Defaults for the following:

Field Name	Setup Notes
(a) Payroll Schedule	Weekly
(b) Additions, Deductions and Company Contributions	401(k) Employee (-4%), Maximum -16,000.00 Match 401(k) (2%), Maximum $5,500.00 Health Insurance (-$50 per paycheck)
(c) Federal Taxes	Filing Status: Single Subject to: Social Security, FUTA, Medicare
(d) State Taxes	Default State Worked: CA Default State Subject to Withholding: CA
(e) Other Taxes	CA – Employment Training Tax
(f) Sick Hours Accruals	Accrual Period: Beginning of Year Hours Accrued at Beginning of Year: 40 Maximum number of hours: 80 Reset hours each new year
(g) Vacation Hours Accruals	Accrual Period: Beginning of Year Hours Accrued at Beginning of Year: 80 Maximum number of hours: 200 Do not reset hours each new year.

Table 12-8 Employee default settings

9. Create a Payroll Item Listing report. Select the ***Reports*** menu, then choose **List** and then choose **Payroll Item Listing**. Modify the report to include the Payable to column and then print the report. Set the report to print on 1 page wide.

10. Create an Employee Listing report.

Payroll Setup Problem 2

EXTENDING YOUR KNOWLEDGE

Restore the PRSetup-10Problem2.QBM file and store it on your hard disk according to your instructor's directions.

1. Use the Payroll Item list to edit the Federal and State tax items. If you see the *QuickBooks Payroll Service* window, select **No** to continue. Edit the tax items to point to the stated accounts and change the vendors as shown in Table 12-9.

Item Name	Account: Set the items to point to the accounts shown below.
(a) Federal Withholding	Liability Account: Employee Payroll Taxes Payable (Subaccount of Payroll Liabilities) *Vendor: EFTPS*
(b) Social Security Medicare	Liability Account: Company Payroll Taxes Payable (company-paid); Employee Payroll Taxes Payable (employee-paid) (Subaccount of Payroll Liabilities) Expense Account: Payroll Tax Expense (Subaccount of Payroll Expenses) *Vendor: EFTPS*
(c) Federal Unemployment	Liability Account: Company Payroll Taxes Payable (Subaccount of Payroll Liabilities) Expense Account: Payroll Tax Expense (Subaccount of Payroll Expenses) *Vendor: EFTPS* *Federal Unemployment Tax Rate is 0.8%*
(d) CA – Income Tax	Liability Account: Employee Payroll Taxes Payable (Subaccount of Payroll Liabilities)
(e) CA – Disability	Liability Account: Employee Payroll Taxes Payable (Subaccount of Payroll Liabilities) *Employee Tax Rate is 1.1%*
(f) CA – Unemployment	Liability Account: Company Payroll Taxes Payable (Subaccount of Payroll Liabilities) Expense Account: Payroll Tax Expense (Subaccount of Payroll Expenses) *Company Tax Rate is 4.5%*
(g) CA – Employment Training Tax	Liability Account: Company Payroll Taxes Payable (Subaccount of Payroll Liabilities) Expense Account: Payroll Tax Expense (Subaccount of Payroll Expenses) *Company Tax Rate is 0.1%*

Table 12-9 Setup vendor for Federal and State tax items

2. Create three *Annual Salary* payroll items called **Officer's Salary, Officer's Vacation Salary and Officer's Sick Salary** using the Payroll Item List. Edit the items to point to an expense account called Payroll Expenses:Officer's Compensation.

3. Create a Payroll Item Listing report. Select the **Reports** menu, then choose **List** and then choose **Payroll Item Listing.** Modify the report to include the **Payable to** column and then print the report. Set the report to print on 1 page wide.

Workplace Applications

Discussion Questions

These questions are designed to stimulate discussion about how you can apply QuickBooks to your own organization. They may help you think through some of the issues you'll encounter when using QuickBooks in your company.

1. How many employees are there in your organization? Of these, how many does your organization pay wages on an hourly basis, and how many does your organization pay on a salary basis?
2. What benefits does your company offer? Do your employees contribute to any of these benefits? If so, which ones? Do the employees contribute all or part of the cost associated with the benefit?
3. What payroll taxes does your organization have to pay? Are there different taxes or tax rates for different cities, counties, states, or countries in which your company operates? List some of the taxes and the rates that apply.
4. Go to the IRS Web site and find form W-4. Fill out the form by following the directions on the form – using your own payroll information. What is the total number of allowances you claim? Discuss how this form affects employees' net paychecks.

Case Study

Hardware Easycare, Inc.

Hardware Easycare, Inc. is a new hardware service company that travels to your work location and performs routine maintenance on computer hardware. They respond within thirty minutes on all service calls within a 10-mile radius of the company headquarters. There are 3 salaried employees and 8 service technicians (hourly employees) who will come to your home or office. All salaried employees receive a quarterly bonus of 1% of gross profit.

The company has a 401(k) plan in which all employees can participate.

Fran, the bookkeeper for the company wants your advice on setting up her payroll.

1. Advise Fran how to set up QuickBooks payroll if she wants to deduct 2% of gross pay from employees for 401(k) contributions.
2. How should Fran set up QuickBooks to track the bonus for salaried employees?
3. How will Fran use the Bonus item on her employees' paychecks?

Chapter 13 Payroll Processing

Objectives

After completing this chapter, you should be able to:

- Use the Employee Center to view previous payroll activity (page 552).
- Update your Payroll Tax Tables (page 553).
- Create Paychecks and override default calculations (page 556).
- Edit, Void, and Delete Paychecks (page 565).
- Pay Payroll Liabilities (page 570).
- Adjust Payroll Liabilities (page 574).
- Create Payroll Reports (page 575).
- Paying Payroll Taxes (Supplemental Material).

Restore this File

This chapter uses PRProcessing-10.QBW. To open this file, restore the PRProcessing-10.QBM file to your hard disk. See page 10 for instructions on restoring files.

In this chapter, you'll learn to process your payroll smoothly using QuickBooks payroll. This chapter presents the use of *QuickBooks Standard Payroll,* which helps you create your paychecks by automatically calculating the payroll taxes on each paycheck.

The exercise file for this chapter is a Sample File, a special file that will allow you to interact with the automated payroll options without requiring a payroll subscription. All sample files will set the current date to December 15, 2011 while using the sample file (Figure 13-1). You can identify sample files by a warning on the upper right corner of the Home page (Figure 13-2).

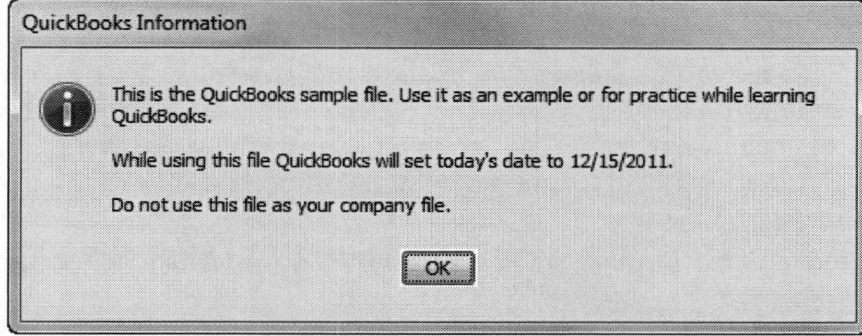

Figure 13-1 Sample File Date Warning

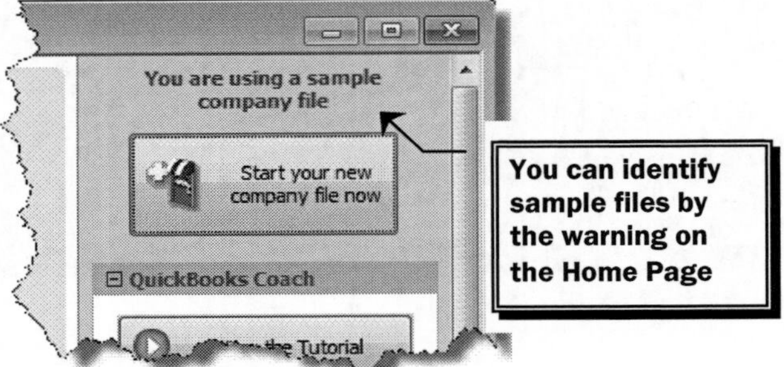

Figure 13-2 Sample File's Home Page

Payroll Processing Checklists

To keep your payroll running smoothly and to minimize errors, you should complete the following steps at the prescribed intervals:

Every Payday

- Review the previous payroll activity in the Employee Center.
- Verify that your tax tables are current and update them if necessary.
- Create, review, and correct (if necessary) paychecks.
- Print paychecks and pay stubs.

Every Tax Deposit Due Date (monthly or semi-weekly)

- Create, review, and correct (if necessary) liability payments.
- Print liability payment checks.

Every Quarter (after the end of the quarter)

- Verify the accuracy of all payroll transactions for the previous quarter.
- Create payroll reports for the previous quarter and year-to-date.
- Create payroll tax returns (Federal Form 941 and State Quarterly Returns).

Every January

- Verify the accuracy of all payroll transactions for the entire previous year.
- Create payroll reports for the previous quarter and year-to-date.
- Create payroll tax returns (Federal Form 941, 940, and State Quarterly and Yearly Returns).

Using the Employee Center

The **Employee Center** displays a list of all employees and related transactions such as paychecks, liability checks, and payroll liability adjustments. Before processing payroll each pay period, it is a good idea to open up the Employee Center and review the latest payroll activity for each employee. Doing so will help reduce payroll processing errors like creating duplicate checks or processing payroll checks with incorrect data.

To open the Employee Center, click the **Employee Center** icon on the *Navigation Bar*, or the **Employees** button on the *Home* page.

Payroll Center

If you have an active QuickBooks payroll service subscription, the Employee Center will contain an additional Payroll tab called the Payroll Center. You can use this window to pay employees, pay taxes and other liabilities, and process payroll forms (see Figure 13-3).

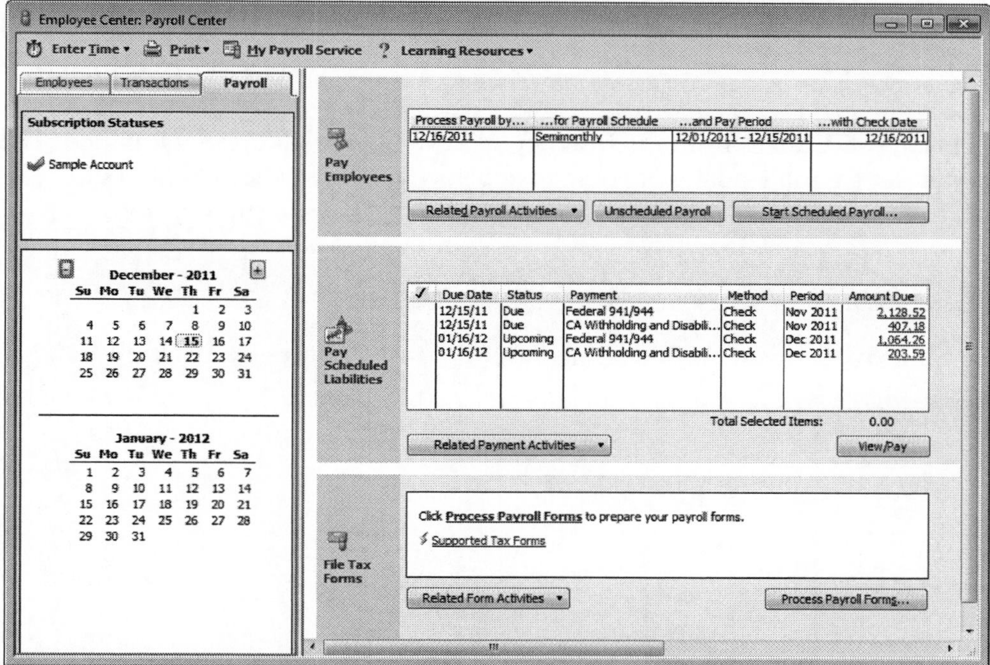

Figure 13-3 Employee Center with active subscription showing Payroll tab

Payroll Tax Tables

Key Term: *Payroll Tax Tables* include the tax rates necessary to calculate an employee's paycheck. This calculation affects the amounts of taxes that are withheld from an employee's check (e.g., Federal and State income tax) as well as the amounts of taxes the company must pay for the employee (e.g., Federal and State Unemployment tax). The Payroll Tax Table also includes data that updates the forms that print directly from QuickBooks (e.g., 940, 941, and W-2).

In order for your paychecks to calculate automatically and your forms to print properly, you must have a current payroll service subscription. Intuit recommends that you connect to their Web site frequently (at least every 45 days) to ensure that you're using the latest tax tables.

Updating your tax tables

If you do not have access to the Internet to download tax tables, you can subscribe to Intuit's QuickBooks Standard Payroll or QuickBooks Enhanced Payroll service with the additional option for disk delivery. Or, if you do have a payroll service subscription but do not have the latest updates, you will be prompted in the Payroll tab of the Employee Center to update your subscription (see Figure 13-4).

Figure 13-4 Check Subscription Status section of Payroll tab

To download the latest tax tables from the Internet, use the *Get Payroll Updates* function. The steps for using the Get Payroll Updates are described below, however, they cannot be completed with the exercise file, since sample files do not have payroll subscriptions.

DO NOT PERFORM THESE STEPS NOW. THEY ARE FOR REFERENCE ONLY.

1. Select the **Employees** menu and then select **Get Payroll Updates** (see Figure 13-5).

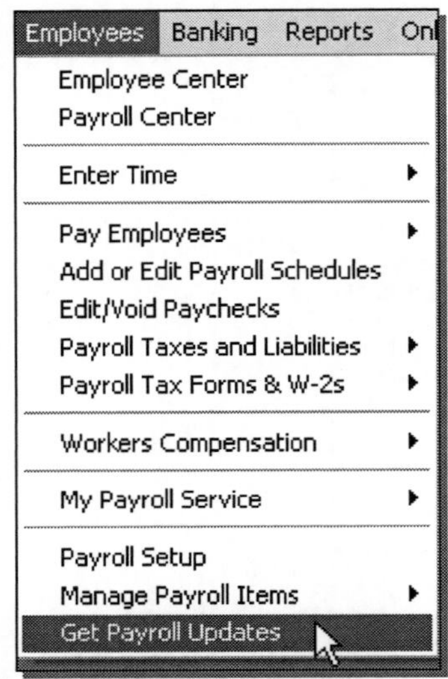

Figure 13-5 Get Payroll Updates command

> **Note:**
> If you do not have a payroll service subscription, the **Get Payroll Updates** option will not be available on the *Employees* menu.

2. In the Get Payroll Updates window, download the tax tables by clicking **Update** in Figure 13-6.

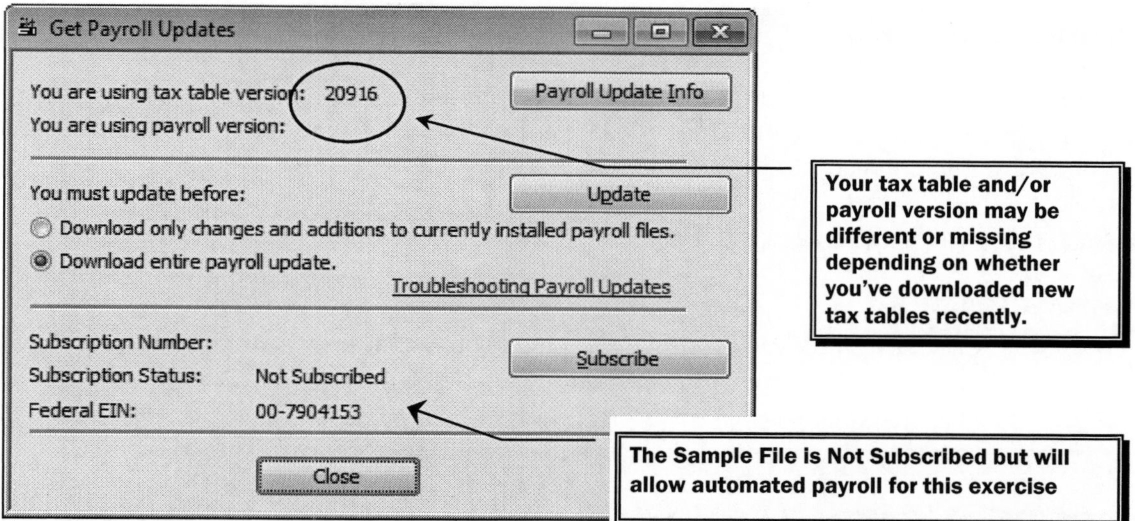

Figure 13-6 Get Payroll Updates window

3. QuickBooks displays the Intuit Payroll Services stating that your payroll subscription will be verified online (see Figure 13-7).

Figure 13-7 Intuit Payroll Services window

4. After the tax tables have been updated QuickBooks displays the window in Figure 13-8.

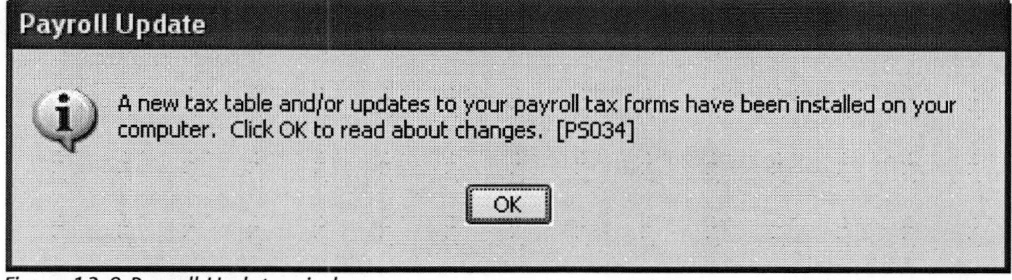

Figure 13-8 Payroll Update window

Important:
QuickBooks relies on the data from the payroll tax tables to accurately calculate, pay, and report tax withholdings and company tax liabilities. This is why it is so important that your payroll items are set up correctly (as discussed in the previous chapter) and that you update your tax tables regularly. As the tax rates change, updating your tax tables keeps your payroll calculations and forms up to date and accurate.

Paying Employees

In the previous chapter, you set up payroll for Academy Photography. Once the payroll setup is complete, and you have downloaded the latest tax tables (not required in the sample file for this chapter), you are ready to process payroll.

Selecting the Employees to Pay

COMPUTER PRACTICE

Step 1. Click **Pay Employees** on the *Home* page. The *Employee Center* opens with the *Payroll* tab selected and the *Pay Employees* section highlighted. (Figure 13-9)

Step 2. Click the *Start Scheduled Payroll* button.

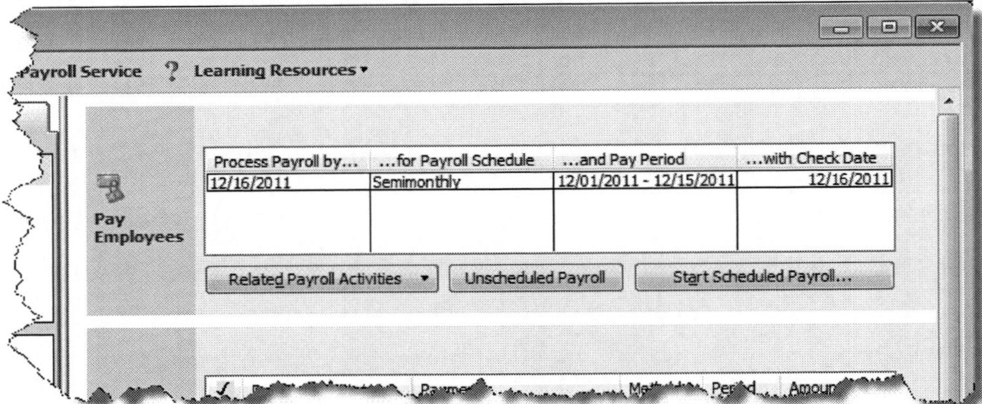

Figure 13-9 Pay Employees Section of Employee Center

Step 3. The Enter Payroll Information window opens (Figure 13-10). Leave the default dates in the *Pay Period Ends* and *Check Date* fields.

The two date fields on this window are very important. The first one indicates the last day of the pay period included on the paychecks, and the second one sets the date of the actual paycheck. Make sure you always check these dates before creating your paychecks.

> **Important:**
> The check date on paychecks determines when the payroll expenses show on all reports. For example, if you pay employees on the 16th of the month for wages earned during the first half of the month, the reports will show the expenses for that payroll on the 16th.

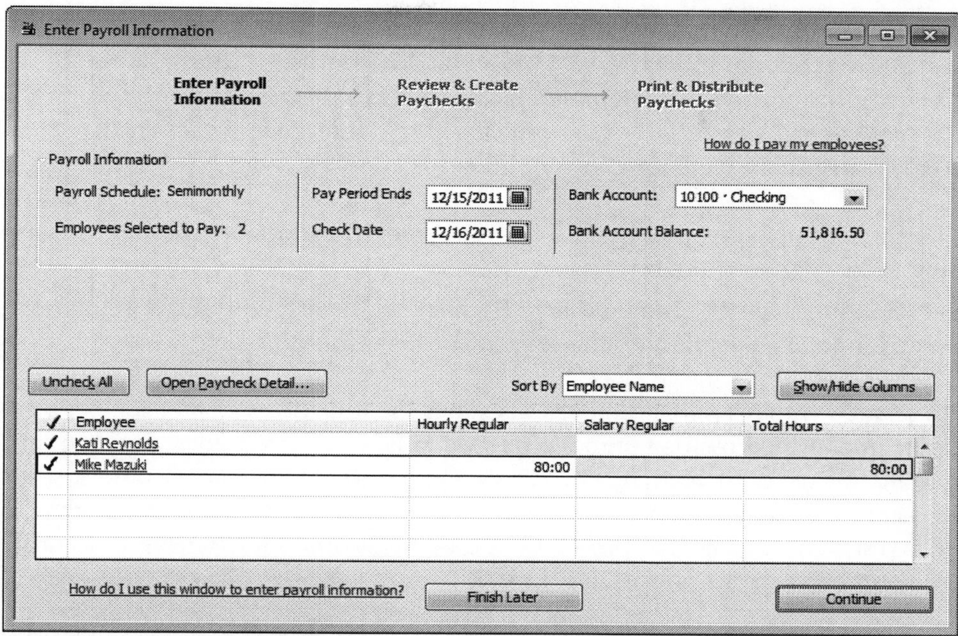

Figure 13-10 Enter Payroll Information window

Step 4. Click the *Kati Reynolds* link in the list of employees to open the *Preview Paycheck* window (Figure 13-11). Alternatively you can select **Kati Reynolds** and click **Open Paycheck Detail** button.

The Preview Paycheck window displays the automatic deductions that QuickBooks has calculated for the payroll liabilities based on the tax tables and settings entered in the previous chapter. Kati Reynolds is a salaried employee and therefore receives *Salary Regular* earnings.

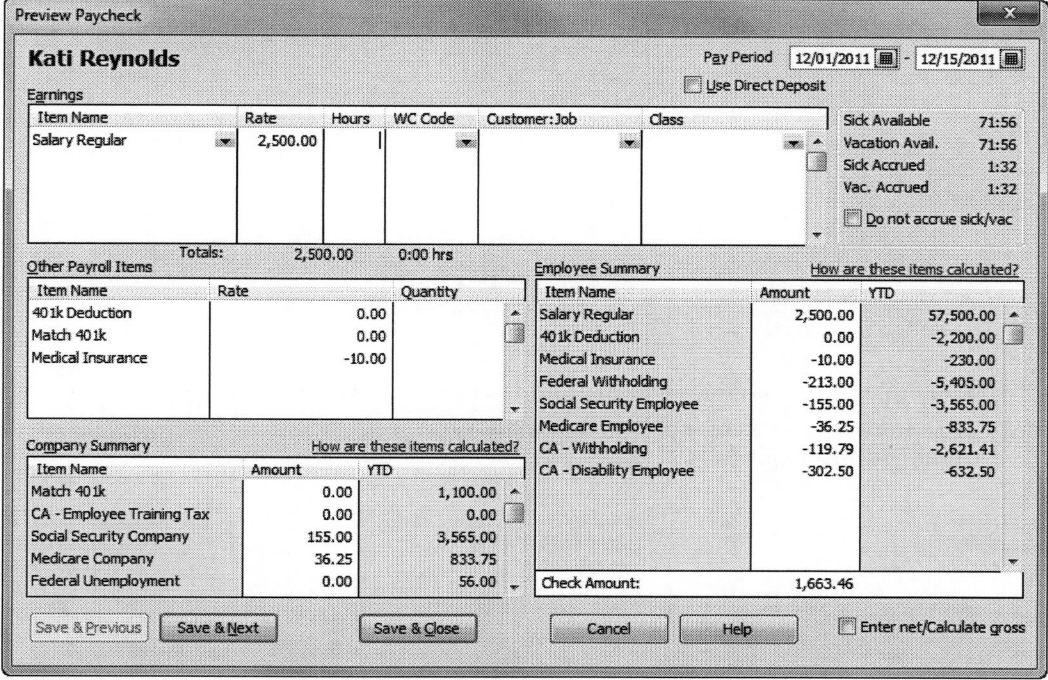

Figure 13-11 Preview Paycheck window for Kati Reynolds

> **Note:**
> The tax withholdings shown in Figure 13-11 may be different than what you see on your screen. Withholdings are calculated using the tax tables loaded on your computer. Some readers with different tax tables will see differences between their exercise file and the screenshots throughout this chapter.

Step 5. In the *Earnings* section, add a second line for **Salary Vacation**. Notice that the salary is split evenly between the two lines.

Step 6. Enter ***85*** in the *Hours* column for **Salary Regular** on the first line, and **3** in the *Hours* column for **Salary Vacation** on the second line (see Figure 13-12).

With salaried employees, QuickBooks calculates the total gross pay for the period (annual rate divided by the number of pay periods) and then divides that amount equally into each of the Earnings Items listed in the *Earnings* Section. To track sick and vacation hours used, enter the number of hours for each on separate lines in the earnings section. QuickBooks prorates the total salary amount to each line according to the number of hours on that line.

Earnings

Item Name	Rate	Hours	WC Code	Customer:Job	Class
Salary Regular	2,414.77	85:00			
Salary Vacation	85.23	3:00			
Totals:	2,500.00	88:00 hrs			

Figure 13-12 Earnings section in Preview Paycheck window

Step 7. Enter **-4%** in the *Rate* column next to *401k Deduction* and **2%** in the *Rate* column next to *Match 401k* in the *Other Payroll Items* section of the *Preview Paychecks* window (Figure 13-13).

Other Payroll Items

Item Name	Rate	Quantity
401k Deduction	-4.0%	
Match 401k	2.0%	
Medical Insurance	-10.00	

Figure 13-13 Other Payroll Items in Preview Paycheck window

Step 8. Verify that your screen matches Figure 13-14 (tax items may vary). Notice that the *401k Deduction* in the Employee Summary section has been automatically calculated. When finished click **Save & Next**.

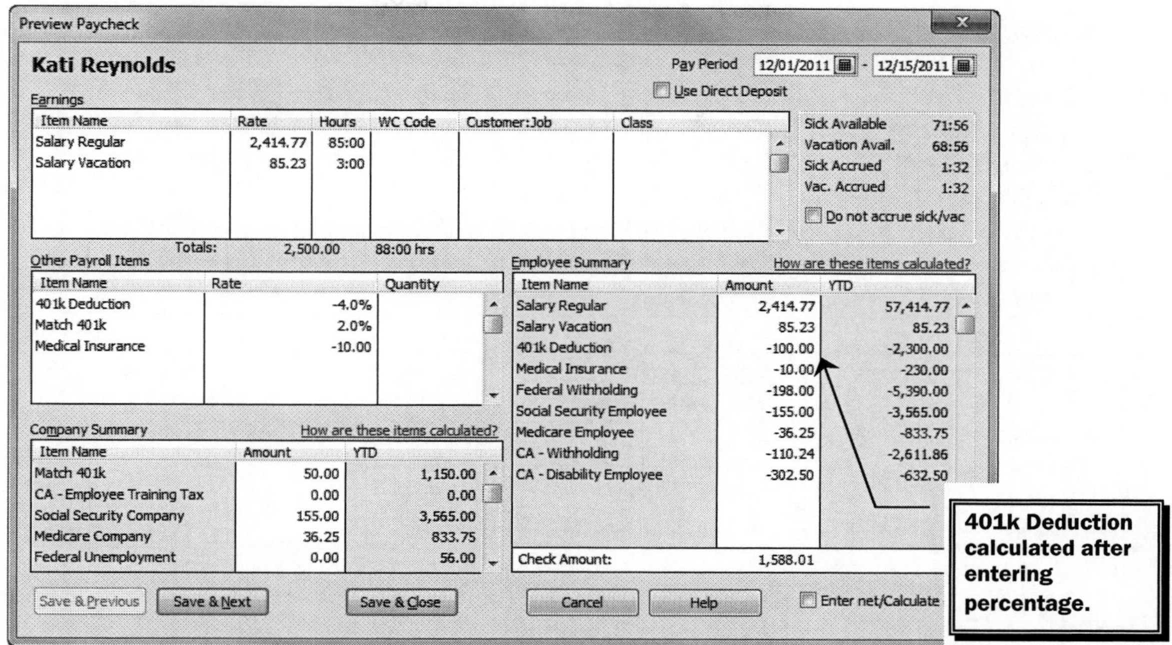

Figure 13-14 Preview Paychecks window after data entry – tax items on your screen may vary

Step 9. The other employee, Mike Mazuki's *Preview Paycheck* window opens (Figure 13-15).

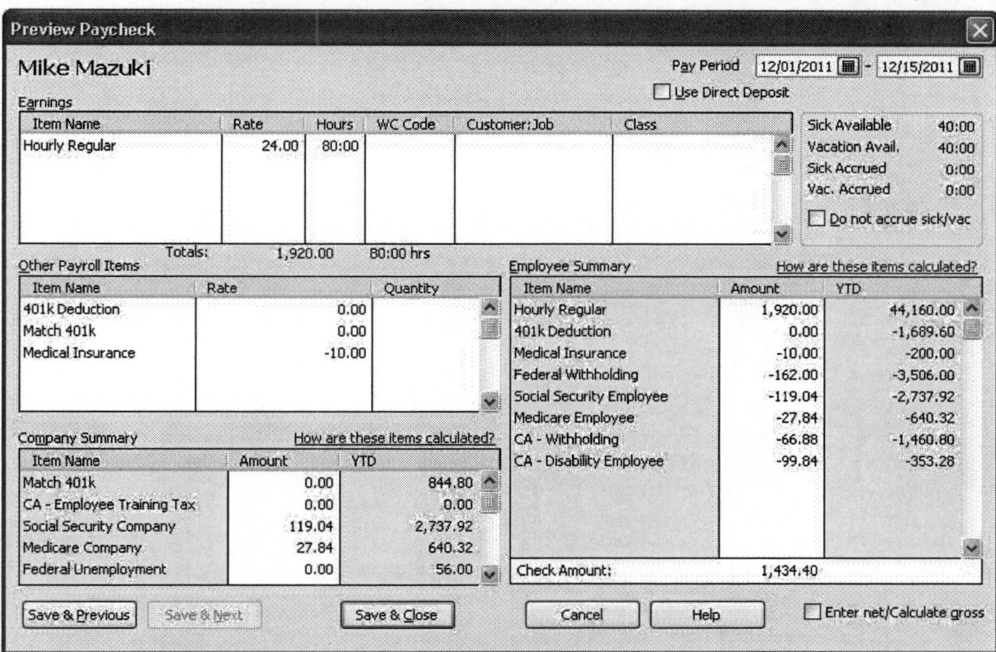

Figure 13-15 Mike Mazuki's Preview Paycheck window

Step 10. Notice that *Earnings* section is set to *Hourly Regular* and *80* hours. The number of hours is automatically set from the previous Paycheck.

Note:
If the default setting was set up to *Use Time Data to Create Paychecks* (see page 522), QuickBooks would fill the earnings section of the paycheck with data entered in the *Weekly Timesheet*. An example is shown in Figure 13-16. You can override any of the information that was automatically copied from the timesheet. However, any changes you make here will not change the original timesheet. If you discover errors at this point, you might want to cancel out of the *Create Paycheck* window, then correct the timesheet, and then recreate the paycheck.

Item Name	Rate	Hours	Customer:Job	Class	Service Item
Hourly Regular	24.00	10:00	Garrison, John:Kitchen	San Jose	Design
Hourly Regular	24.00	8:00		San Jose	
Hourly Regular	24.00	36:00	Young, Bill:Window Re...	Walnut Creek	Labor
Hourly Regular	24.00	18:00	Mason, Bob	San Jose	Design
Hourly Regular	24.00	8:00		Walnut Creek	

Figure 13-16 Example Earnings section of the Review Paycheck window including Timesheet data

Step 11. Enter ***4%*** in the *Rate* column next to *401k Deduction* in the *Other Payroll Items* section of the *Preview Paychecks* window (Figure 13-13). Press **Tab** to leave the Rate field. Notice that QuickBooks automatically adds a negative sign, because most payroll deductions are negative.

Step 12. Enter 2% in the Rate column next to Match 401k. Press **Tab** to leave the Rate field. The Match 401k is left as a positive number, since the Company Match is not deducted from the paycheck.

Step 13. Verify that your window matches (tax items may vary) and press the **Save & Close** button.

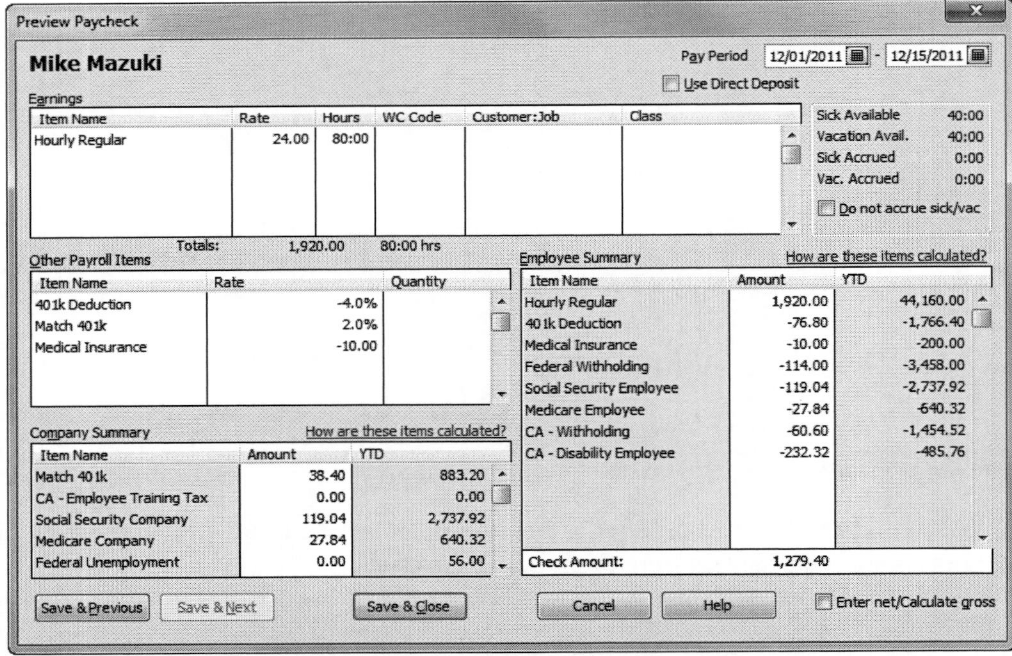

Figure 13-17 Preview Paycheck window after data entry – tax items on your screen may vary

Step 14. Click **Continue** in the *Enter Payroll Information* window. The *Review and Create Paychecks* window appears.

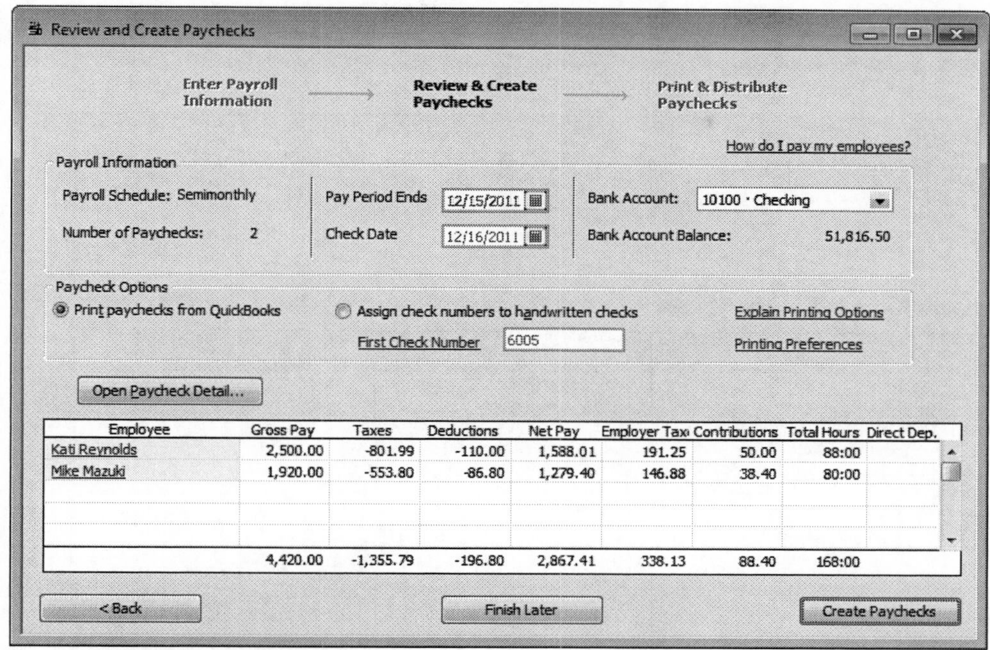

Figure 13-18 Review and Create Paychecks window

Step 15. Verify that your screen matches Figure 13-18 (taxes may vary) and click **Create Paychecks**. The *Confirmation and Next Steps* window appears. Leave this window open for the next exercise.

Printing Paychecks

When you're finished creating all of the paychecks, QuickBooks displays the *Confirmation and Next Steps* window (Figure 13-19). From this window, you can print paychecks or print pay stubs. The next exercise prints paychecks.

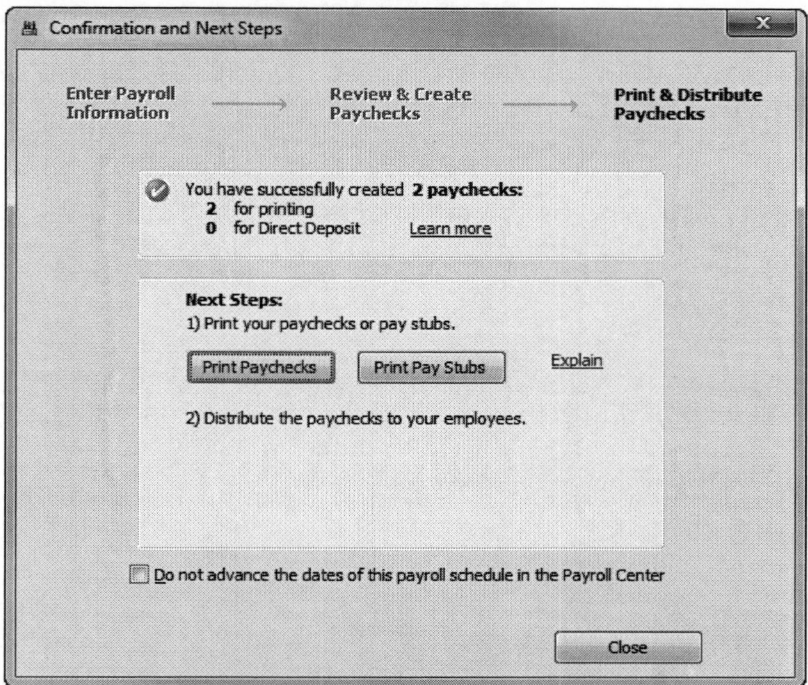

Figure 13-19 Confirmation and Next Steps window

COMPUTER PRACTICE

Step 1. Click the Print Paychecks button on the *Confirmation and Next Steps* window.

> **Another Way:**
> If you want to print the checks after you have left the *Confirmation and Next Steps* window, select the **File** menu, select **Print Forms**, and then select **Paychecks.**

Step 2. Leave **6067** in the *First Check Number* field (see Figure 13-20). Click **OK.**

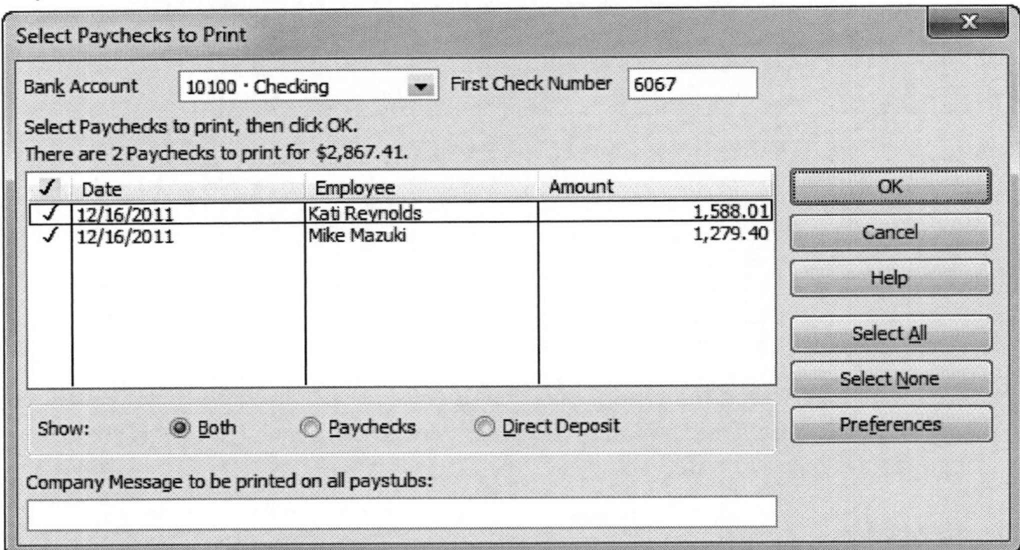

Figure 13-20 Select the paychecks to be printed.

Step 3. In the *Print Checks* window, QuickBooks lets you know that there are two checks to print and gives the total amount of those checks (see Figure 13-21).

You can also select the check style in the *Print Checks* window. Select **Voucher** as your choice of check style. When you use voucher checks, QuickBooks prints the pay stub information on the voucher portion of the checks.

> **Note:**
> For this class you'll print on blank paper instead of real checks. When you're printing on real checks, make sure to load the checks into the printer before you click **Print.**
>
> **Tip:**
> It's best to use voucher checks for payroll. Make sure your checks are oriented correctly in the printer. With some printers, you feed the top of the page in first, and for others you feed the bottom in first. With some printers, you need to insert the check face up, and with others, you insert it face down.

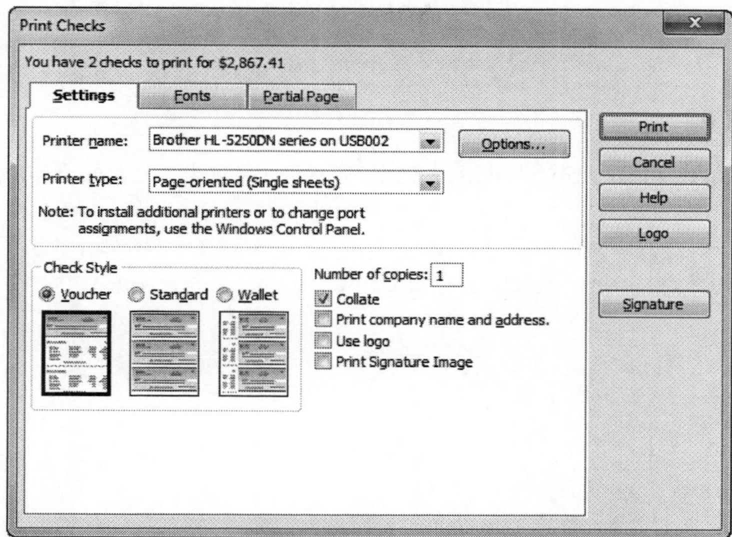

Figure 13-21 Print Checks window

The paycheck and voucher pay stubs for Mike Mazuki are shown as printed on blank paper in Figure 13-22.

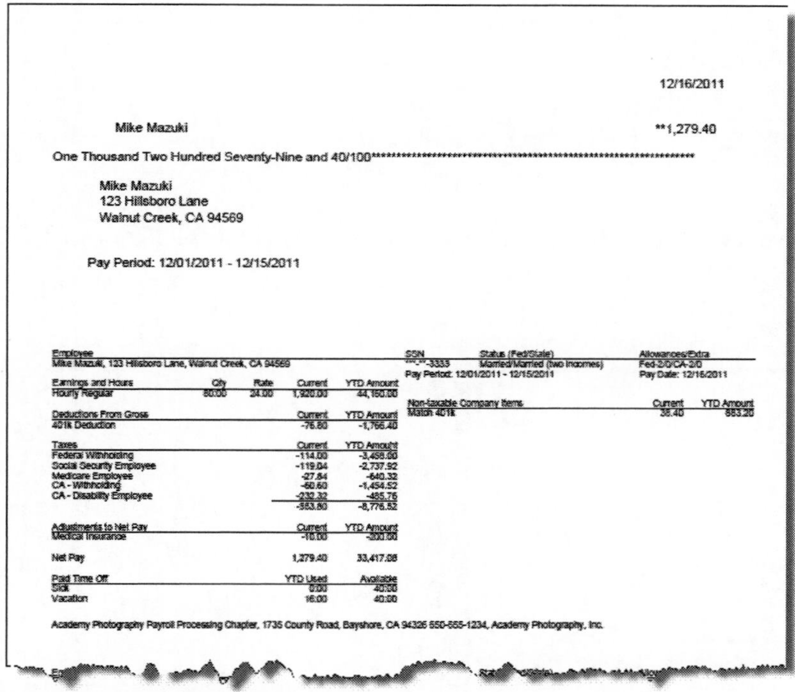

12/16/2011

Mike Mazuki **1,279.40

One Thousand Two Hundred Seventy-Nine and 40/100***

Mike Mazuki
123 Hillsboro Lane
Walnut Creek, CA 94569

Pay Period: 12/01/2011 - 12/15/2011

Employee					SSN	Status (Fed/State)	Allowances/Extra
Mike Mazuki, 123 Hillsboro Lane, Walnut Creek, CA 94569					***-**-3333	Married/Married (two incomes)	Fed-2/0/CA-2/0
					Pay Period: 12/01/2011 - 12/15/2011		Pay Date: 12/16/2011

Earnings and Hours	Qty	Rate	Current	YTD Amount
Hourly Regular	80:00	24.00	1,920.00	44,160.00

Deductions From Gross	Current	YTD Amount
401k Deduction	-76.80	-1,766.40

Taxes	Current	YTD Amount
Federal Withholding	-114.00	-3,458.00
Social Security Employee	-119.04	-2,737.92
Medicare Employee	-27.84	-640.32
CA - Withholding	-60.60	-1,454.52
CA - Disability Employee	-232.32	-465.76
	-553.80	-8,776.52

Adjustments to Net Pay	Current	YTD Amount
Medical Insurance	-10.00	-200.00

Net Pay	1,279.40	33,417.08

Paid Time Off	YTD Used	Available
Sick	0:00	40:00
Vacation	16:00	40:00

Non-taxable Company Items	Current	YTD Amount
Match 401k	38.40	883.20

Academy Photography Payroll Processing Chapter, 1735 County Road, Bayshore, CA 94326 650-555-1234, Academy Photography, Inc.

Figure 13-22 Mike Mazuki's Paycheck

Step 4. Verify the printer settings and then click **OK**. Click **OK** on the *Print Checks - Confirmation* message.

Step 5. Click **Close** on the *Confirmation and Next Steps* window.

Printing Pay Stubs

If you don't print checks from QuickBooks, you can still print pay stubs for your employees on blank paper.

> **Note:**
> You can print pay stubs at any time, even after you have printed the paychecks.

COMPUTER PRACTICE

Step 1. Select the **File** menu, then select **Print Forms**, and then select **Pay Stubs** (see Figure 13-23).

Step 2. Leave the default date of ***12/14/2011*** for the beginning date and ***3/13/12*** for the thru date for the pay stubs to print. Paychecks dated in the date range you specify will show in the list.

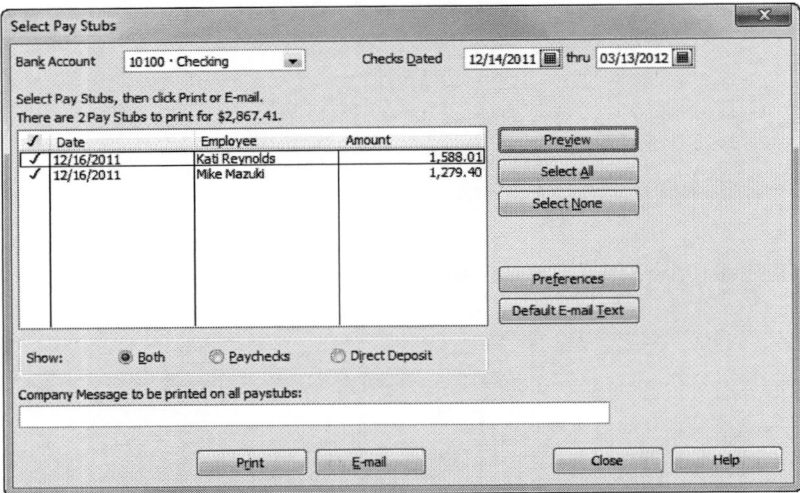

Figure 13-23 Select Pay Stubs window

Step 3. Click **Preview** to see what the pay stubs look like when they print (see Figure 13-24). QuickBooks prints one Pay stub per page.

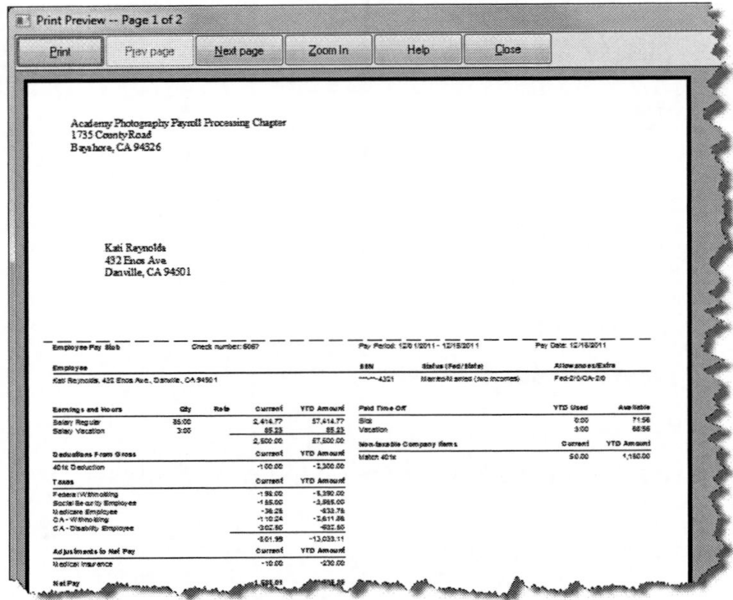

Figure 13-24 Print Preview of a pay stub

Step 4. After previewing the pay stub, click **Print** to print the pay stubs.

Job-Costing Wages

> **Key Term:** *Job Costing*
> Tracking income and expenses separately for each job or project is known as *Job Costing*. Allocating income and expenses to specific jobs allows you to create reports showing detailed or summarized financial information about each job. (e.g., Profit & Loss by Job) If your company needs to track job costs, make sure you enter the *Customer:Job* name for every income and expense transaction that you enter.

To manually allocate this employee's wages to each of the jobs and classes that they worked on, enter a separate line for each combination of Earnings Item, Rate, Hours, Customer:Job, and Class. QuickBooks calculates the amount of gross wages that should be allocated to each job and class based on the total pay for each Payroll Item. In addition, QuickBooks allocates the company paid payroll taxes, company contributions, and other payroll items for this paycheck based on the proportion of wages assigned to each job and class.

> **Did You Know?**
> To add a line between two existing lines, you can use the Insert Line command. Place the cursor on the second line of the *Earnings* section. Then press Ctrl+INSERT. Notice that a blank line is inserted before the existing lines. This works on all forms in QuickBooks.

Editing, Voiding, and Deleting Paychecks

If you find errors on paychecks, you can edit, void, or delete the paychecks. However, be careful when you do any of these actions because changing transactions may adversely affect your records. When in doubt, ask your accountant.

> **Note:**
> If you edit a paycheck that you have already printed, make sure your changes don't affect the net pay amount. Also, if this employee has other paychecks dated after this check, the changes you make may invalidate the tax calculations on the newer checks. It's best to avoid editing, voiding, or deleting any paycheck except the most recent paycheck for each employee. If you're unsure about any adjustments you need to make, check with your accountant.

Editing Paychecks

It's not considered good accounting practice to edit paychecks after they've been printed and sent to the employee. However, it is possible to edit paychecks in QuickBooks, even after they've been printed. Editing paychecks should only be done if you haven't sent the paycheck to the employee.

COMPUTER PRACTICE

Step 1. From the *Payroll Center*, select the **Related Payroll Activities** button. Select **Edit or Void Paychecks** from the drop down menu.

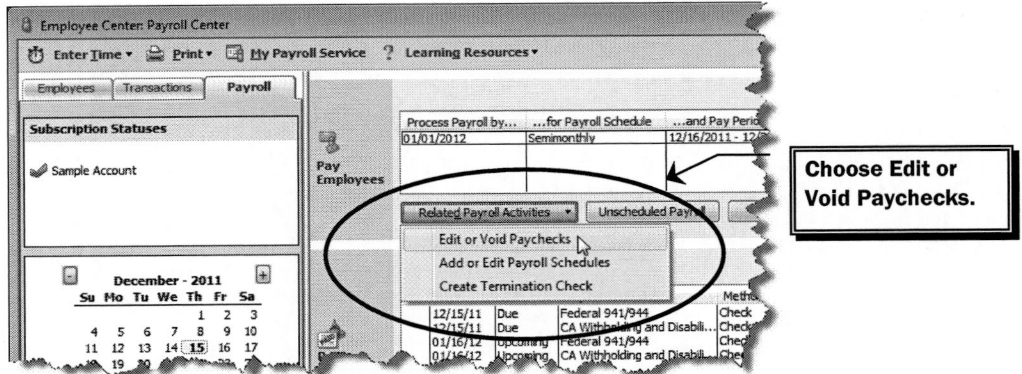

Figure 13-25 Edit Paychecks in the Payroll Center

Step 2. Set the *Edit/Void Paychecks from* date to ***12/01/2011*** and the *through* date to ***12/31/2011***. Then press **Tab** (see Figure 13-26).

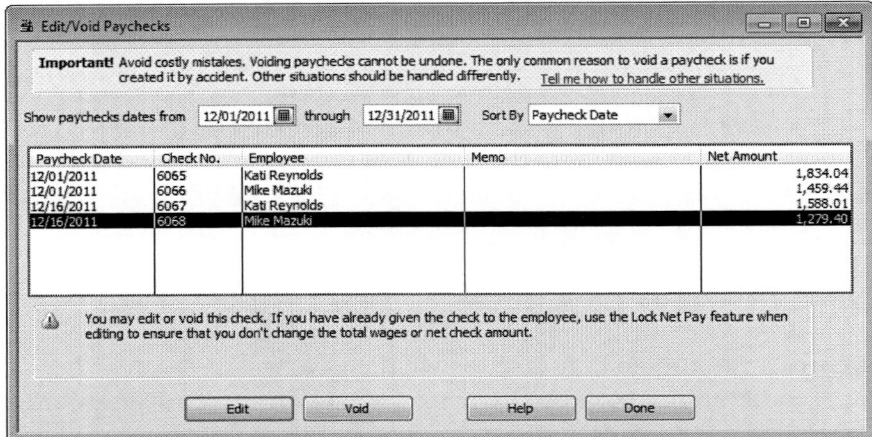

Paycheck Date	Check No.	Employee	Memo	Net Amount
12/01/2011	6065	Kati Reynolds		1,834.04
12/01/2011	6066	Mike Mazuki		1,459.44
12/16/2011	6067	Kati Reynolds		1,588.01
12/16/2011	6068	Mike Mazuki		1,279.40

Figure 13-26 Edit/Void Paychecks window

Step 3. Press **Tab** to leave **Paycheck Date** in the *Sort By* field.

Step 4. Highlight **Mike Mazuki's paycheck** dated ***12/16/2011*** and then click **Edit** (see Figure 13-26).

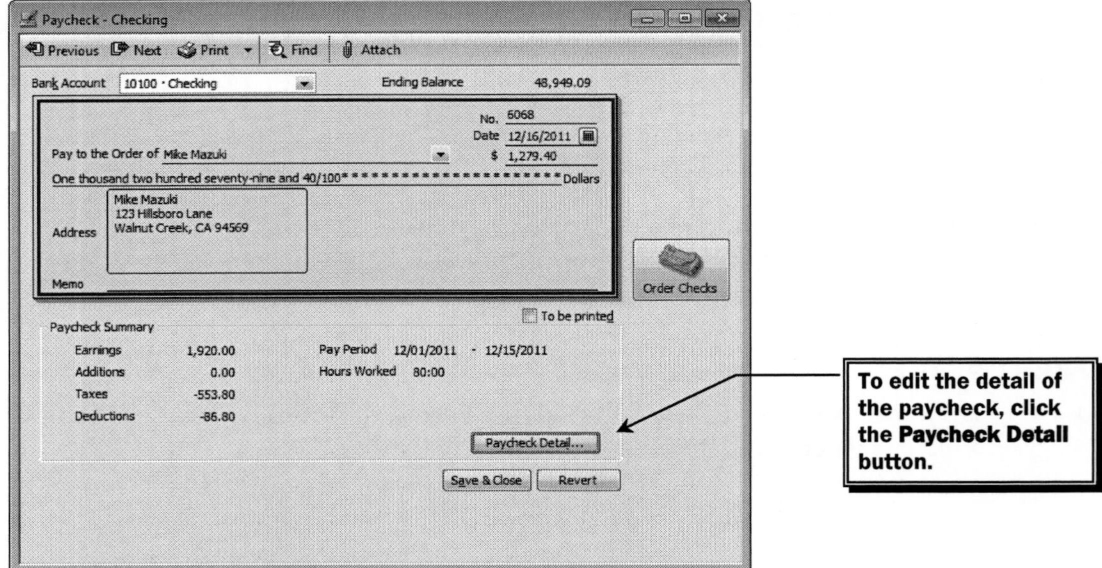

Figure 13-27 Click Paycheck Detail to edit the items on the paycheck

Step 5. To edit the items on the paycheck, click **Paycheck Detail** (see Figure 13-27).

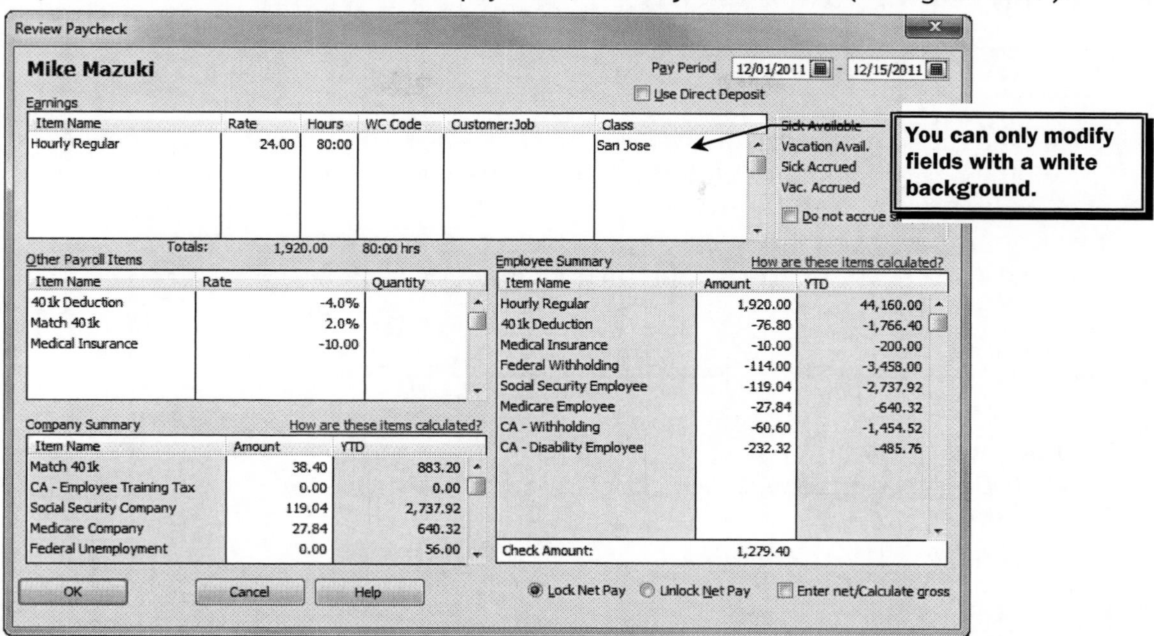

Figure 13-28 Any of the fields with a white background can be edited.

Step 6. Change the class of the *Hourly Regular Earnings* item to the **San Jose** class.

Step 7. The Net Pay Locked window is displayed (Figure 13-29). Changing the class will not affect the Net Pay of this Paycheck. Click **No**.

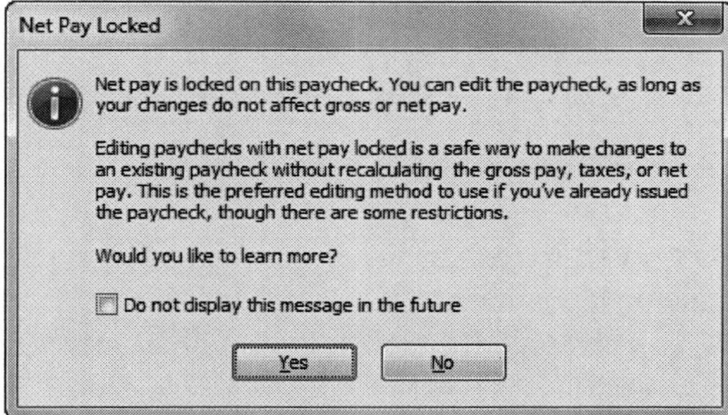

Figure 13-29 Net Pay Locked warning

> **Note:**
> You can edit only the fields with a white background on the *Review Paycheck* window. To edit the year-to-date amounts, use the *Adjust Liabilities* window (see page 574), or override the amounts on a future paycheck for this employee.

Step 8. Click **Cancel** and then click **Save & Close** to leave the check unchanged. Click **Done** to leave the *Edit/Void Paychecks* window.

> **Another Way:**
> You can also edit a paycheck by double-clicking on the paycheck in the checking account register and then continue from Step 5 above.

Replacing Lost or Stolen Checks

DON'T PERFORM THESE STEPS NOW. THEY ARE FOR REFERENCE ONLY.

1. Find the check in the *Employee Center* or the *Checking* account register, then double-click to edit the check, and then click the **To be printed** box in the *Paycheck* window (see Figure 13-30). This clears the check number field, and replaces it with "To Print."

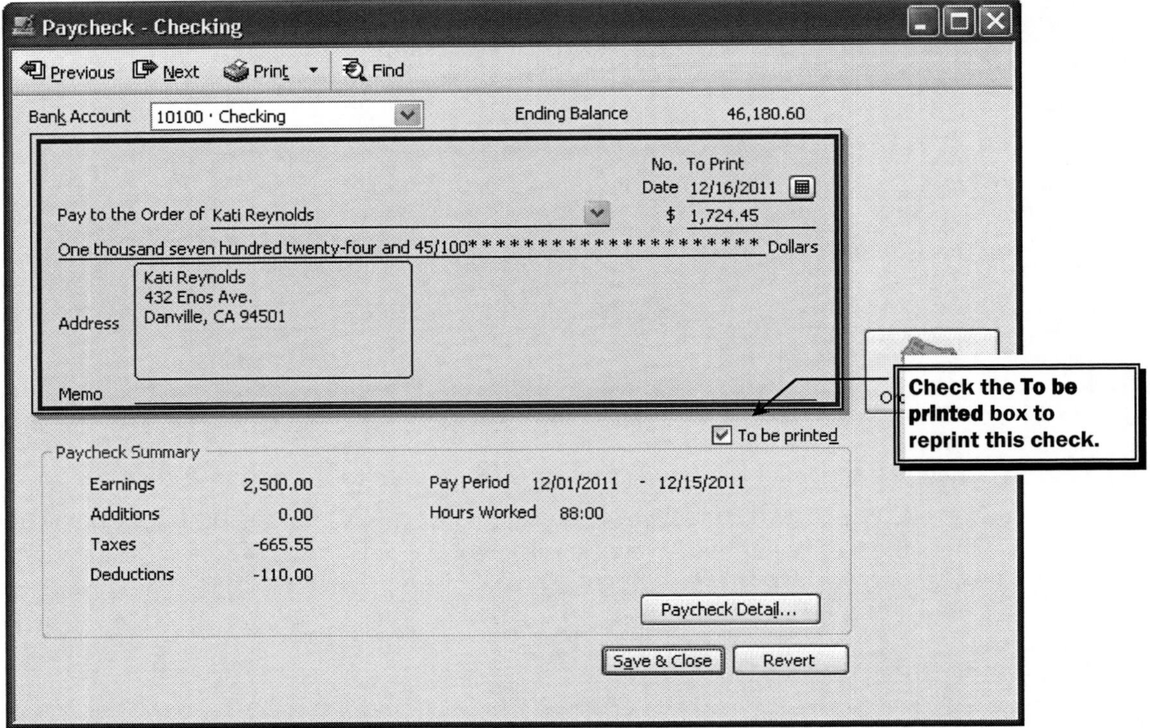

Figure 13-30 Payroll Check to be reprinted

2. Click **Save & Close** and then **Yes** to save your change.
3. Reprint the check and then give it a new check number.
4. Enter a *new* check directly in the *Checking* account register with the same date, payee, amount, and check number as the lost check. Code it to the *Miscellaneous Expense* account.
5. Void the new check you just created. This converts the check into a *voided* check with the same date, payee, amount and check number as the lost or stolen check.

Tip:
The reason you don't void the original transaction and create a new paycheck is a little tricky to understand. In the event that the paycheck to be replaced was not the *most recent paycheck* for that employee, QuickBooks would not be able to recreate the check exactly as the original. That's because the year-to-date information is calculated on each paycheck by taking all paychecks (regardless of their date) and adding their amounts together. The method shown here avoids this problem by simply reprinting the original paycheck using a new check number.

Voiding Paychecks

If you need to void a paycheck, make sure it's the most recent paycheck for this employee. If it's not the most recent paycheck, see the tip above.

Before you edit or void old paychecks, make a backup of your file.

DON'T PERFORM THESE STEPS NOW. THEY ARE FOR REFERENCE ONLY.

1. From the *Payroll Center*, select the **Related Payroll Activities** button and then select **Edit or Void Paychecks**.
2. Verify that the *Show Paychecks from* date is set to your desired date range. Press **Tab**.
3. On the list of paychecks, select the paycheck you want to void.
4. Click **Void**. Don't actually void the check now. These are just the steps you will take when you void paychecks.
5. Click **Done** to close the *Edit/Void Paychecks* window.

This updates the employee's year-to-date payroll information. However, if this employee has paychecks already entered and dated after this paycheck, you won't see any changes to the year-to-date amounts on those paychecks. The next paycheck you create for this employee will show the correct year-to-date amounts, as will the payroll reports and tax forms.

Deleting Paychecks

The only time you should delete a paycheck is when you created it in error and you haven't printed the check. Otherwise, you should void the paycheck so you can keep a record of it.

DON'T PERFORM THESE STEPS NOW. THEY ARE FOR REFERENCE ONLY.

1. From the *Employee*s menu, select **Edit/Void Paychecks**.
2. Set the *Show paychecks from* date to the desired date range. Then press **Tab**.
3. On the list of paychecks, click the paycheck you want to delete and then click **Edit**.
4. At the top of the *QuickBooks Company* window, select the **Edit** menu and then select **Delete Paycheck** (or press Ctrl+D).
5. Click **OK**.

Another Way:
You can also void (or delete) paychecks by selecting the paycheck in the *Checking* account register. Then select **Void (or Delete) Paycheck** from the **Edit** menu.

Important note:
If the paycheck you're voiding or deleting isn't the most recent paycheck, keep in mind that the year-to date information (and possibly other calculations) on all paychecks dated after a voided or deleted paycheck will be incorrect. This is because those checks were calculated using the information from this check, and now that the check is void (or deleted), those paychecks are incorrect.

To avoid this problem, delete all the paychecks for this employee dated after the paycheck. Then, after you void or delete the paycheck, recreate the paychecks that were dated after the voided (or deleted) paycheck. When you recreate those paychecks, QuickBooks recalculates all the year-to-date amounts and taxes.

If you use Assisted Payroll or Direct Deposit:
If you use the Assisted Payroll service, or if you have direct deposit service, any transactions that have been sent to the payroll service cannot be deleted. To resolve these problems, contact payroll technical support.

Paying Payroll Liabilities

Paying your payroll liabilities correctly is a critical part of maintaining accurate payroll information in QuickBooks.

When you pay the liabilities, don't use the *Write Checks* window because doing so won't affect the *Payroll Items*. It also won't show the liability payments on tax forms 940 or 941. To correctly pay your payroll liabilities, use the *Pay Liabilities* section of the *Payroll Center* window.

The accounting behind the scenes:
You must use the *Pay Liabilities* feature to record liability payments. Payroll Liability payments decrease (debit) the payroll liability accounts in addition to reducing the balance due for the payroll items. If you don't use the *Pay Liabilities* feature, QuickBooks won't track your payments in the liabilities reports or tax forms such as the 941.

Note:
The IRS publication *Circular E, Employer's Tax Guide* specifies the rules for when your payroll taxes must be paid. Depending on the size of your payroll, you will be either a "Monthly" depositor or a "Semi-weekly" depositor. Monthly depositors are required to pay all payroll liabilities by the 15th of the month following the payroll date. Semi-weekly depositors are required to pay all payroll liabilities by the Wednesday after the payroll date if the payroll date is Wednesday, Thursday, or Friday. Semi-weekly depositors are required to pay all payroll liabilities by the Friday after the payroll date, if the payroll date is Saturday, Sunday, Monday, or Tuesday.

COMPUTER PRACTICE

Step 1. Click the Pay Liabilities button on the Home page. The *Payroll Center* opens with the Pay Scheduled Liabilities section highlighted.

Step 2. Place checkmarks next to the two Liabilities due on 12/15/11 (Figure 13-31).

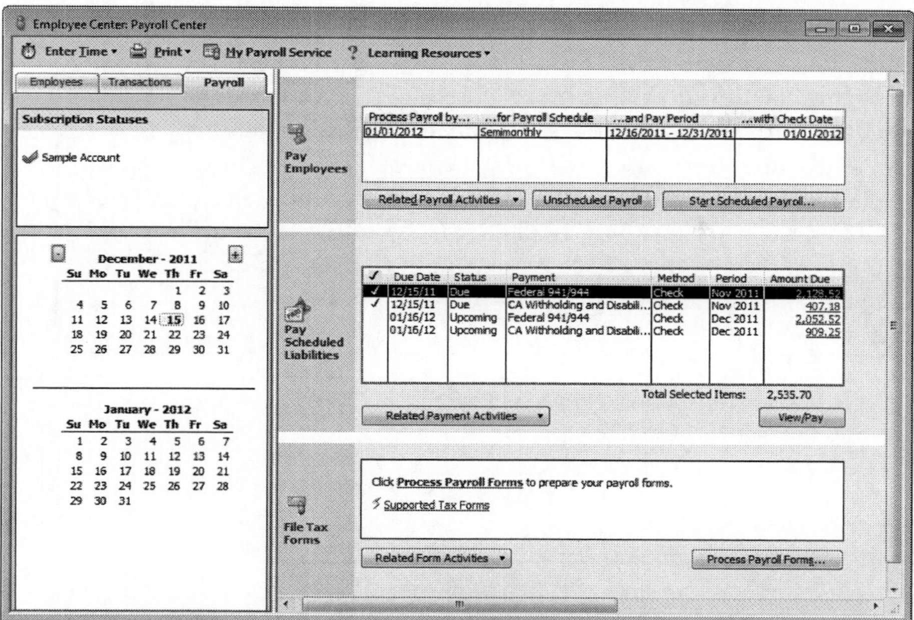

Figure 13-31 Payroll Center

Step 3. Click the View/Pay button.

Step 4. The first of two *Liability Payment – Checking* windows opens with the fields entered to pay the EFTPS for accumulated payroll liabilities (Figure 13-32).

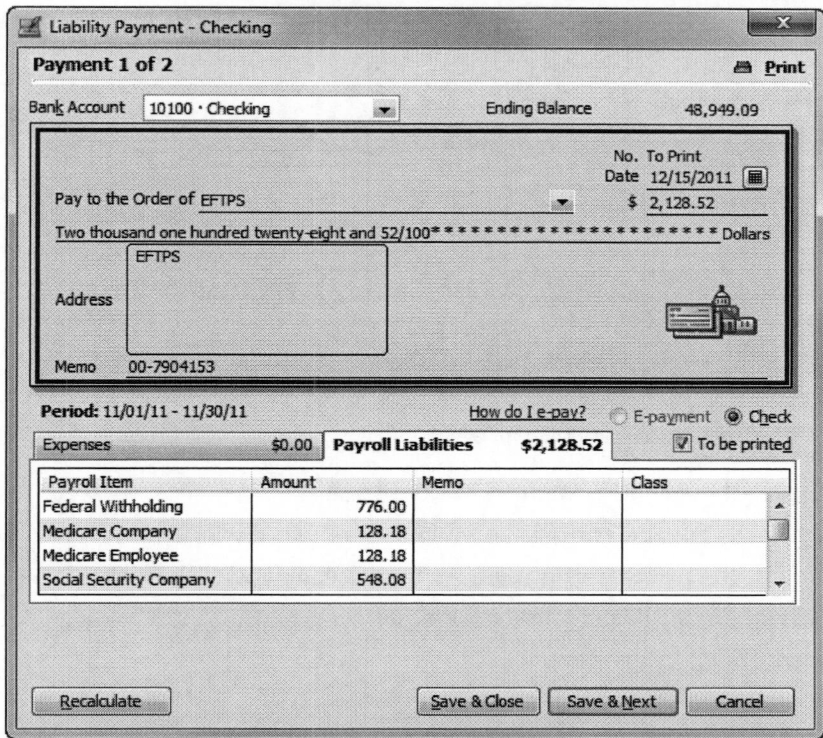

Figure 13-32 Reviewing the liability check before saving

> **Note:**
> QuickBooks allows you to modify the amounts in the *Amount* column of the *Pay Liabilities* window but you should avoid this if possible. Discrepancies here indicate incorrect payroll calculations or misapplication of prior liability payments. These situations should be corrected at the payroll item or transaction level to avoid repetition of the same errors in the future. Instead, if you need to make a small change to the amount you're paying (e.g., adjust for rounding), enter an adjustment on the liability check using the **Expenses** tab. If you consistently have trouble in this area, contact your accountant or QuickBooks Pro Advisor for help.

Step 5. Click **Save & Next**. The second *Liabilities Payment – Checking* window opens.

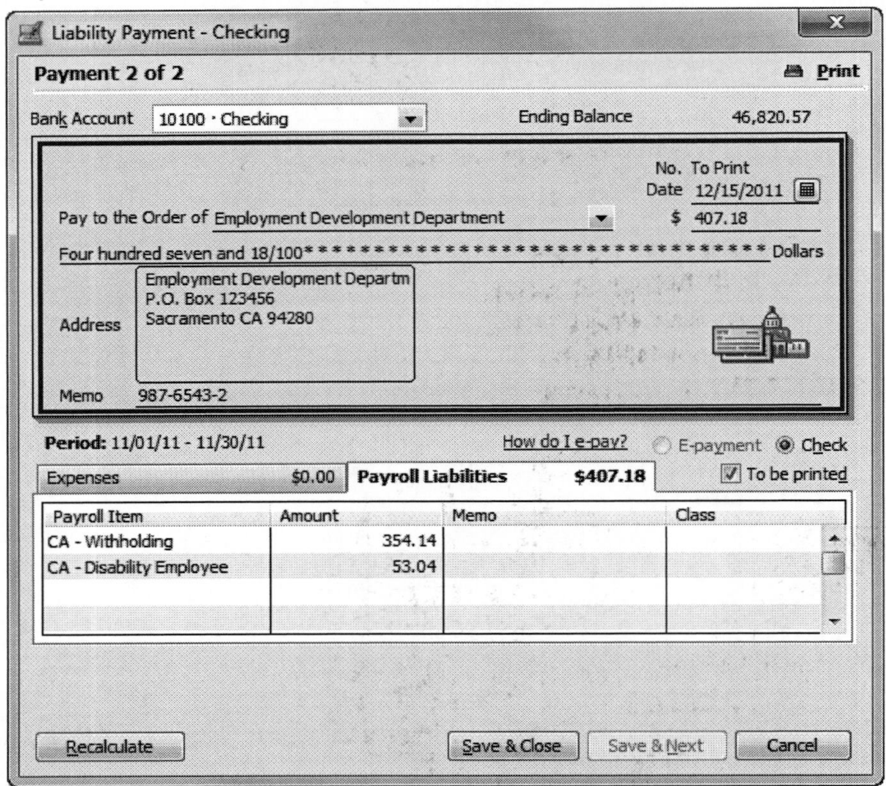

Figure 13-33 Employment Development Department Liability Payment window

Step 6. Click **Save & Close**. The *Payment Summary* window opens.

Step 7. Click the **Print Checks** button. The *Select Checks to Print* window opens.

Step 8. Click **OK**. Verify that the printer settings are set up correctly and click **Print**.

Step 9. Click **OK** in the *Print Checks – Confirmation* window.

Step 10. Close the *Payment Summary* window.

Tip for correcting payroll liabilities:
If you find an error in the amount that QuickBooks suggests you owe, it could be for several reasons. For example, if your state unemployment rate has changed in this period, the amount due may still be calculating at the old rate. In this case, the Payroll Item needs to be corrected and a *Liability Adjustment* could be made to correct the period in question. Another reason *Pay Liabilities* accruals may appear wrong is that prior payments were not made through *Pay Liabilities* or were dated incorrectly in the *Payment for Payroll liabilities through* field. In this case, the payments may need to be created, with the improper payments voided. Finally, you could check each paycheck to see which one created the error. When you find the erroneous paycheck or paychecks, modify the Payroll Items on the paycheck. Of course, if you've already printed the paycheck, you should never make adjustments affecting net pay. Instead, use the *Adjust Liabilities* function discussed later in the chapter, or make an adjustment on the next check for the affected employees.

Step 11. Display the *Checking* account register by double-clicking it in the Chart of Accounts list.

Notice the transaction type is *LIAB CHK*, as shown in Figure 13-34. The *LIAB CHK* transaction is the only type of transaction that properly records payment of payroll liabilities. That's because *LIAB CHK* transactions record the details of which payroll liabilities *and* Payroll Items are paid by that check and the date they are relieved. Any other type of payment can't lower the balance due shown on the Payroll Liabilities report.

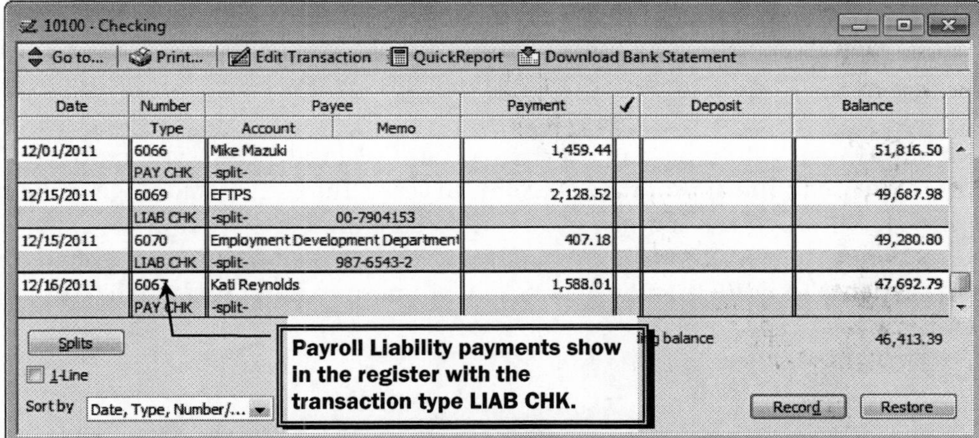

Figure 13-34 A payroll liability payment in the Check Register

Note:
If this is the first time you record a liability payment after setting up your data file, there will probably be balances due for Federal and State payroll taxes on your start date that do not show in the *Pay Liabilities* window.

Editing a Liability Payment

If you need to edit an existing liability payment, you can edit it as shown below. However, make sure you only do this if you haven't yet submitted the payment to the tax agency. If you have submitted the payment to the tax agency, you should use the *Adjust Liabilities* window instead of editing the payment.

DON'T PERFORM THESE STEPS NOW. THEY ARE FOR REFERENCE ONLY.

1. Select the liability payment in the account register and click **Edit Transaction**.
2. The liability payment is displayed as when first created (see Figure 13-33). Edit any of the fields on the Payroll Liability Check and then click **Save & Close**.

Adjusting Payroll Liabilities

If your payroll liabilities need adjusting, you can use the ***Liability Adjustment*** window.

To avoid significant tax penalties, when you adjust payroll liabilities you must fully understand all the accounting and tax implications of the adjustment. Consult with your accountant or QuickBooks Pro Advisor if think your payroll liabilities need adjusting.

DON'T PERFORM THESE STEPS NOW. THEY ARE FOR REFERENCE ONLY.

1. From the *Payroll Center*, click the **Related Payment Activities** button. Select **Adjust Payroll Liabilities** from the button's drop down menu.
2. On the *Liability Adjustment* window (see Figure 13-35), enter ***12/15/2011*** as the *Date* for your adjustment and ***12/15/2011*** as the *Effective Date* of the adjustment.

   The *Date* field is the date you actually enter the transaction. The *Effective Date* field is the date you want this adjustment to affect your liability balances on payroll reports. Use the *Memo* field to explain your adjustment.
3. Enter **San Jose** in the *Class* field.

   Since your adjustment will impact an expense account (Payroll Taxes), you need to allocate the expense to the appropriate class. In this case, the overrstated wages were for services provided through the San Jose location. To determine the appropriate class, you will need to review the paycheck(s) on which the overstatement occurred. If you need to allocate the expense to more than one class, you will need to enter separate liability adjustments for each class.

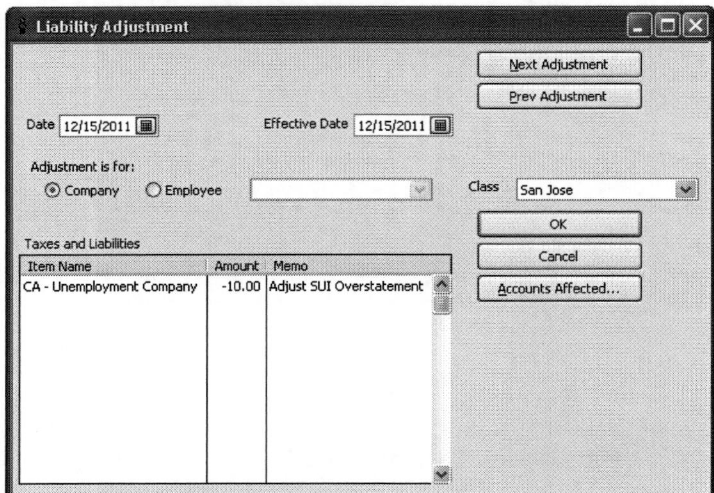

Figure 13-35 Liability Adjustment window

4. Leave **Company** selected in the *Adjustment is for:* field.
5. In the *Taxes and Liabilities* section, select **CA – Unemployment Company** as the *Item Name*, enter ***-10.00*** in the *Amount* column, and enter ***Adjust SUI Overstatement*** in the *Memo* column.

   Use positive numbers to increase the balance of the Payroll Item and negative numbers to reduce the balance of the Payroll Item.
6. Click **Cancel** to prevent this adjustment from being saved. **Do not save the adjustment** shown in Figure 13-35. It is for illustration only.

Creating Payroll Reports

Payroll Summary Report

There are several reports that you can use to analyze your payroll. The *Payroll Summary* report shows the detail of each employee's earnings, taxes, and net pay.

COMPUTER PRACTICE

Step 1. Select the **Reports** menu, then select **Employees & Payroll**, and then select **Payroll Summary**.

Step 2. Leave the date range *From **10/01/2011** to **12/15/2011*** and press **Tab**.

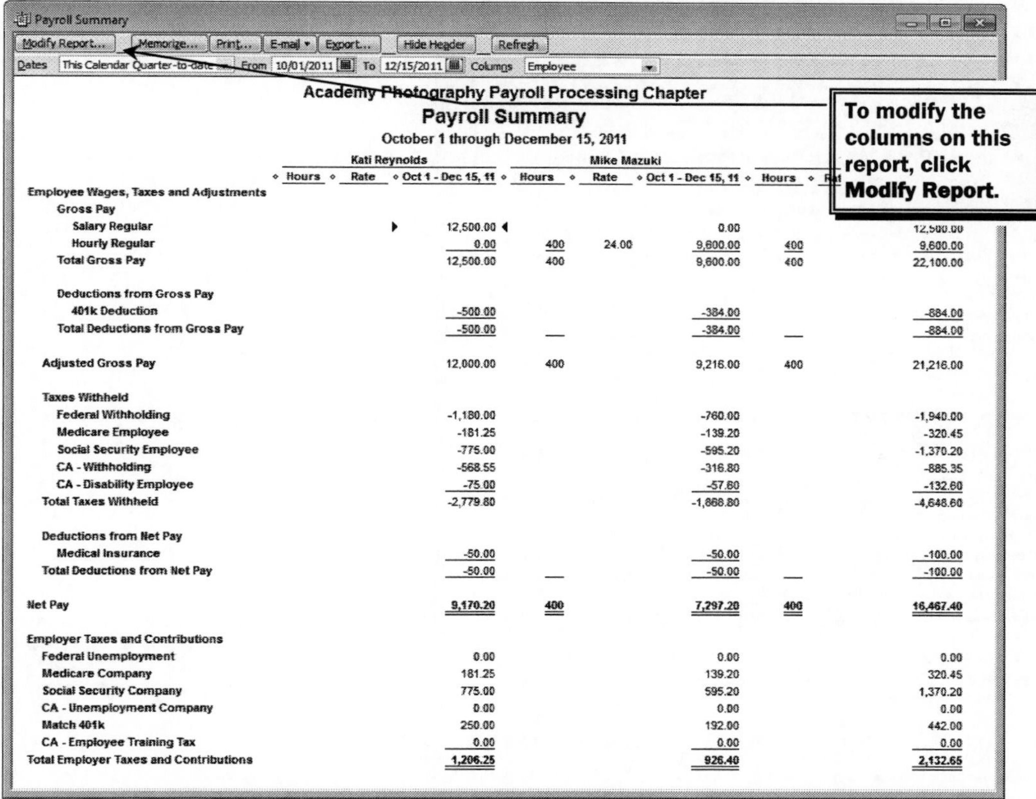

Academy Photography Payroll Processing Chapter
Payroll Summary
October 1 through December 15, 2011

	Kati Reynolds			Mike Mazuki					
	Hours	Rate	Oct 1 - Dec 15, 11	Hours	Rate	Oct 1 - Dec 15, 11	Hours		
Employee Wages, Taxes and Adjustments									
Gross Pay									
Salary Regular			12,500.00			0.00			12,500.00
Hourly Regular			0.00	400	24.00	9,600.00	400		9,600.00
Total Gross Pay			12,500.00	400		9,600.00	400		22,100.00
Deductions from Gross Pay									
401k Deduction			-500.00			-384.00			-884.00
Total Deductions from Gross Pay			-500.00			-384.00			-884.00
Adjusted Gross Pay			12,000.00	400		9,216.00	400		21,216.00
Taxes Withheld									
Federal Withholding			-1,180.00			-760.00			-1,940.00
Medicare Employee			-181.25			-139.20			-320.45
Social Security Employee			-775.00			-595.20			-1,370.20
CA - Withholding			-568.55			-316.80			-885.35
CA - Disability Employee			-75.00			-57.60			-132.60
Total Taxes Withheld			-2,779.80			-1,868.80			-4,648.60
Deductions from Net Pay									
Medical Insurance			-50.00			-50.00			-100.00
Total Deductions from Net Pay			-50.00			-50.00			-100.00
Net Pay			9,170.20	400		7,297.20	400		16,467.40
Employer Taxes and Contributions									
Federal Unemployment			0.00			0.00			0.00
Medicare Company			181.25			139.20			320.45
Social Security Company			775.00			595.20			1,370.20
CA - Unemployment Company			0.00			0.00			0.00
Match 401k			250.00			192.00			442.00
CA - Employee Training Tax			0.00			0.00			0.00
Total Employer Taxes and Contributions			1,206.25			926.40			2,132.65

Figure 13-36 Payroll Summary report

The **Payroll Summary** report (see Figure 13-36) shows columns for each employee, along with their hours and rates of pay. If you want to see more employees on a page, you can customize this report not to show the *Hours* and *Rate* columns.

Step 3. Click **Modify Report** at the top of the *Payroll Summary* report.

Step 4. Clear the **Hours** and **Rate** boxes and then click **OK** (see Figure 13-37).

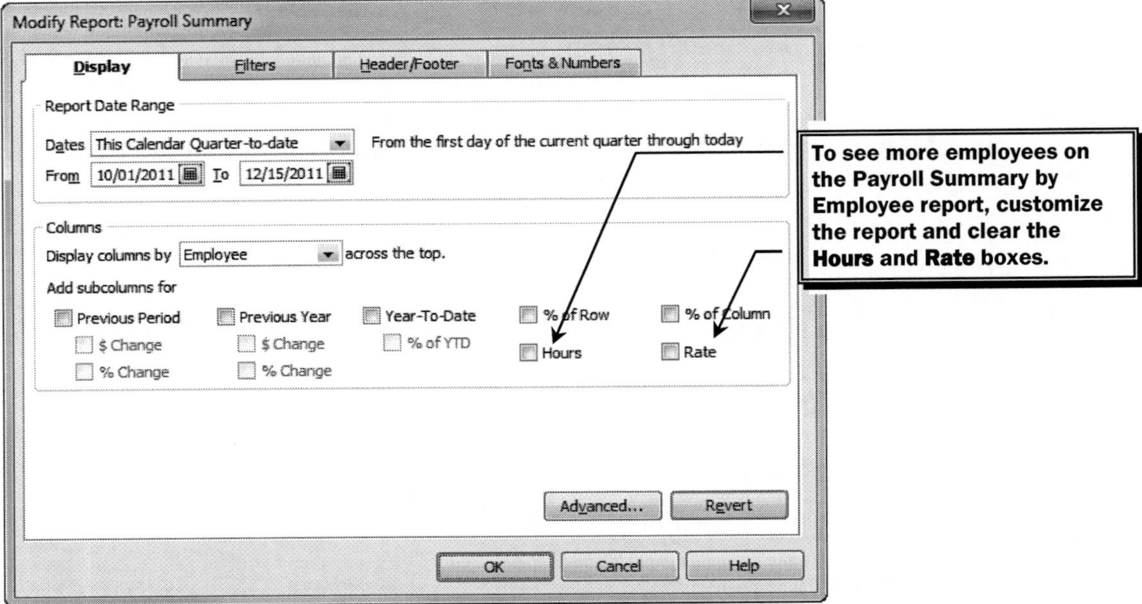

Figure 13-37 The Modify Report window

Step 5. Your report will now look like Figure 13-38. To print the report, click **Print** (or press Ctrl+P).

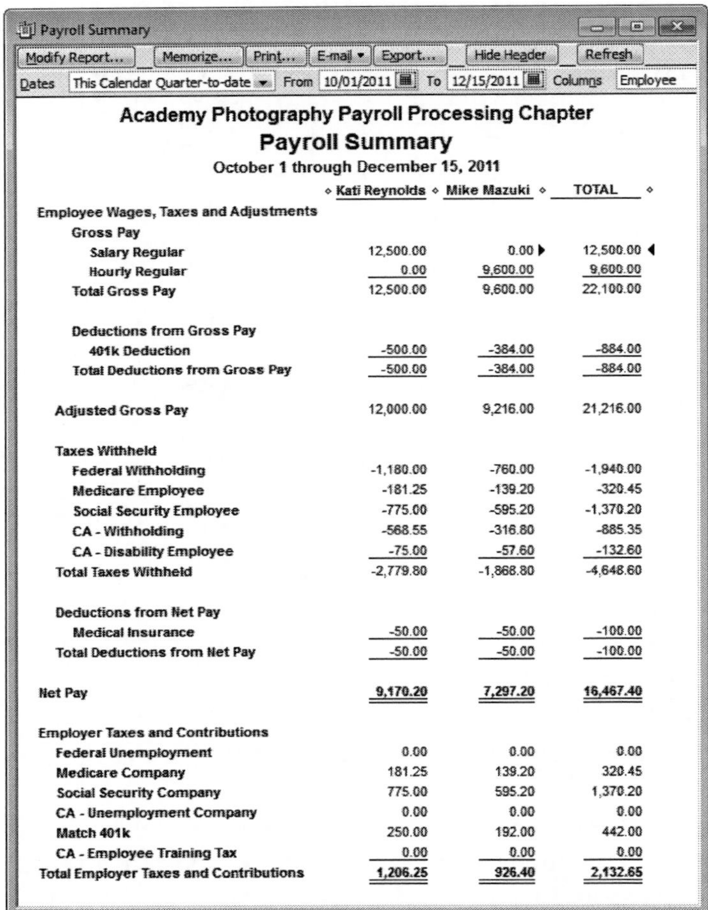

Academy Photography Payroll Processing Chapter
Payroll Summary
October 1 through December 15, 2011

	Kati Reynolds	Mike Mazuki	TOTAL
Employee Wages, Taxes and Adjustments			
Gross Pay			
Salary Regular	12,500.00	0.00	12,500.00
Hourly Regular	0.00	9,600.00	9,600.00
Total Gross Pay	12,500.00	9,600.00	22,100.00
Deductions from Gross Pay			
401k Deduction	-500.00	-384.00	-884.00
Total Deductions from Gross Pay	-500.00	-384.00	-884.00
Adjusted Gross Pay	12,000.00	9,216.00	21,216.00
Taxes Withheld			
Federal Withholding	-1,180.00	-760.00	-1,940.00
Medicare Employee	-181.25	-139.20	-320.45
Social Security Employee	-775.00	-595.20	-1,370.20
CA - Withholding	-568.55	-316.80	-885.35
CA - Disability Employee	-75.00	-57.60	-132.60
Total Taxes Withheld	-2,779.80	-1,868.80	-4,648.60
Deductions from Net Pay			
Medical Insurance	-50.00	-50.00	-100.00
Total Deductions from Net Pay	-50.00	-50.00	-100.00
Net Pay	9,170.20	7,297.20	16,467.40
Employer Taxes and Contributions			
Federal Unemployment	0.00	0.00	0.00
Medicare Company	181.25	139.20	320.45
Social Security Company	775.00	595.20	1,370.20
CA - Unemployment Company	0.00	0.00	0.00
Match 401k	250.00	192.00	442.00
CA - Employee Training Tax	0.00	0.00	0.00
Total Employer Taxes and Contributions	1,206.25	926.40	2,132.65

Figure 13-38 Payroll Summary report without hours and rates

Sales Rep Commissions

If you pay commissions to your employees, you can create a *Sales by Rep Summary* or *Sales by Rep Detail* report to help calculate the commissions due.

COMPUTER PRACTICE

Step 1. Select the **Reports** menu, then select **Sales,** and then select **Sales by Rep Summary** (see Figure 13-39).

Step 2. Leave the date range *From **12/01/2011*** *To **12/15/2011*** and then press TAB.

> **Important:**
> The *Sales by Rep Summary* or *Detail* report requires you to first tag each sale with the employee who gets credit. To set this up, modify your *Invoice* and *Sales Receipts* template to include the *Rep* field. In the *Rep* field on each sales form, make sure you enter the initials of the employee who gets credit for the sale. The *Sales by Rep* report will show the total sales for each sales rep.

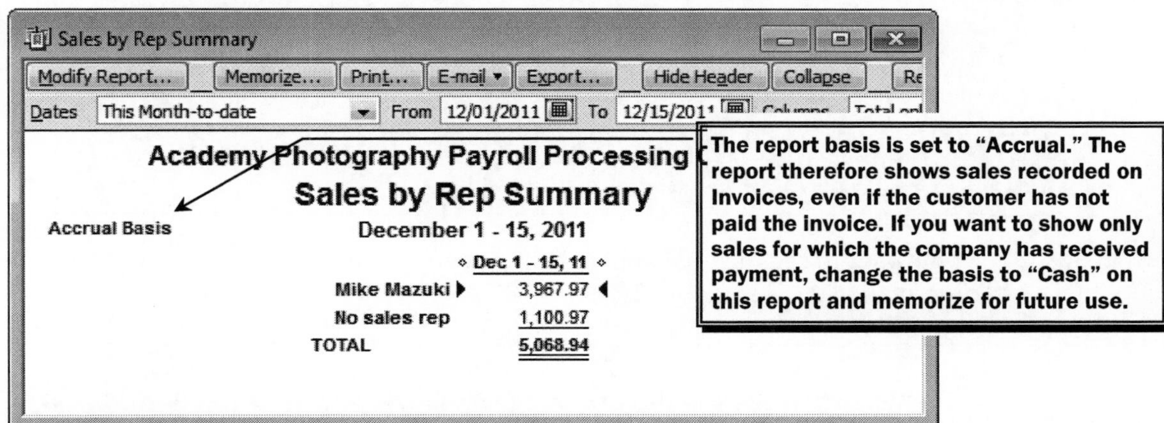

Figure 13-39 Sales by Rep Summary report

Payroll Liabilities Report

The **Payroll Liabilities** report is used to track the status of your payroll liabilities by Payroll Item.

COMPUTER PRACTICE

Step 1. From the **Reports** menu, select **Employees & Payroll,** and then select **Payroll Liability Balances.**

> **Did You Know?**
> QuickBooks Payroll does not offer state forms for its Standard Payroll service. Even with the Enhanced Payroll service, not all state forms are supported. See http://www.quickbooks.com/taxforms for supported state forms.

Step 2. Leave the *From* date to ***01/01/2011*** and the *To* date to ***11/30/2011***. Then press **Tab** (see Figure 13-40).

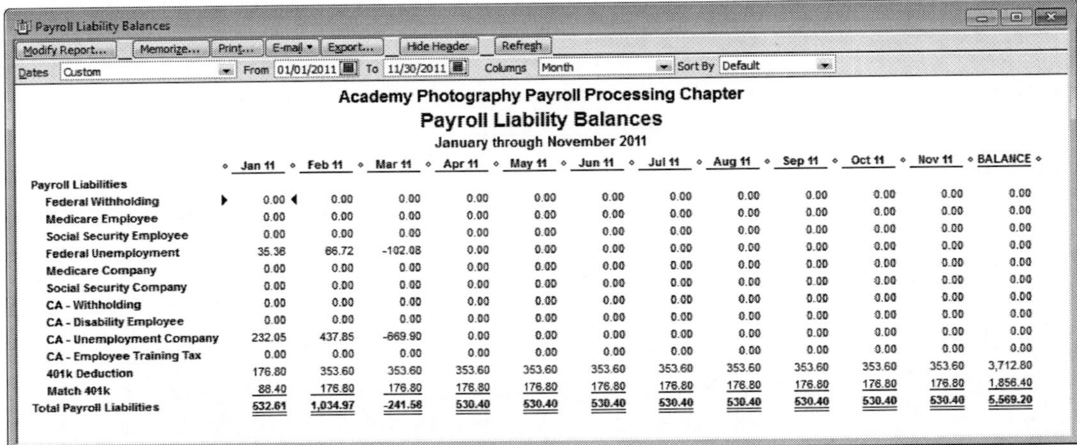

Payroll Liability Balances

Modify Report... | Memorize... | Print... | E-mail ▾ | Export... | Hide Header | Refresh

Dates: Custom | From: 01/01/2011 | To: 11/30/2011 | Columns: Month | Sort By: Default

Academy Photography Payroll Processing Chapter

Payroll Liability Balances

January through November 2011

	Jan 11	Feb 11	Mar 11	Apr 11	May 11	Jun 11	Jul 11	Aug 11	Sep 11	Oct 11	Nov 11	BALANCE
Payroll Liabilities												
Federal Withholding	0.00	0.00	0.00	0.00	0.00	0.00	0.00	0.00	0.00	0.00	0.00	0.00
Medicare Employee	0.00	0.00	0.00	0.00	0.00	0.00	0.00	0.00	0.00	0.00	0.00	0.00
Social Security Employee	0.00	0.00	0.00	0.00	0.00	0.00	0.00	0.00	0.00	0.00	0.00	0.00
Federal Unemployment	35.36	66.72	-102.08	0.00	0.00	0.00	0.00	0.00	0.00	0.00	0.00	0.00
Medicare Company	0.00	0.00	0.00	0.00	0.00	0.00	0.00	0.00	0.00	0.00	0.00	0.00
Social Security Company	0.00	0.00	0.00	0.00	0.00	0.00	0.00	0.00	0.00	0.00	0.00	0.00
CA - Withholding	0.00	0.00	0.00	0.00	0.00	0.00	0.00	0.00	0.00	0.00	0.00	0.00
CA - Disability Employee	0.00	0.00	0.00	0.00	0.00	0.00	0.00	0.00	0.00	0.00	0.00	0.00
CA - Unemployment Company	232.05	437.85	-669.90	0.00	0.00	0.00	0.00	0.00	0.00	0.00	0.00	0.00
CA - Employee Training Tax	0.00	0.00	0.00	0.00	0.00	0.00	0.00	0.00	0.00	0.00	0.00	0.00
401k Deduction	176.80	353.60	353.60	353.60	353.60	353.60	353.60	353.60	353.60	353.60	353.60	3,712.80
Match 401k	88.40	176.80	176.80	176.80	176.80	176.80	176.80	176.80	176.80	176.80	176.80	1,856.40
Total Payroll Liabilities	532.61	1,034.97	-241.58	530.40	530.40	530.40	530.40	530.40	530.40	530.40	530.40	5,569.20

Figure 13-40 Payroll Liabilities report

> **Note:**
> The *To* date field at the top of the Payroll Liabilities report is very important. It tells QuickBooks to report on liabilities for wages paid through that date. Even if liabilities have been paid after the "To" date, the balances in the report reflect the payments. For example, even if you paid February's Federal liabilities in March, the report above would show zero balances for the Federal liabilities in the Feb 11 column. Therefore, this report really shows your unpaid liabilities for paychecks created before the "To" date.

Step 3. If you want to see the total unpaid balances only, select **Total only** from the *Columns* drop-down list. See Figure 13-41.

> **Tip:**
> If you are a semi-weekly depositor, select **Week** from the *Columns* drop-down list. The report will then provide a breakdown of your payroll liabilities by week instead of by month.

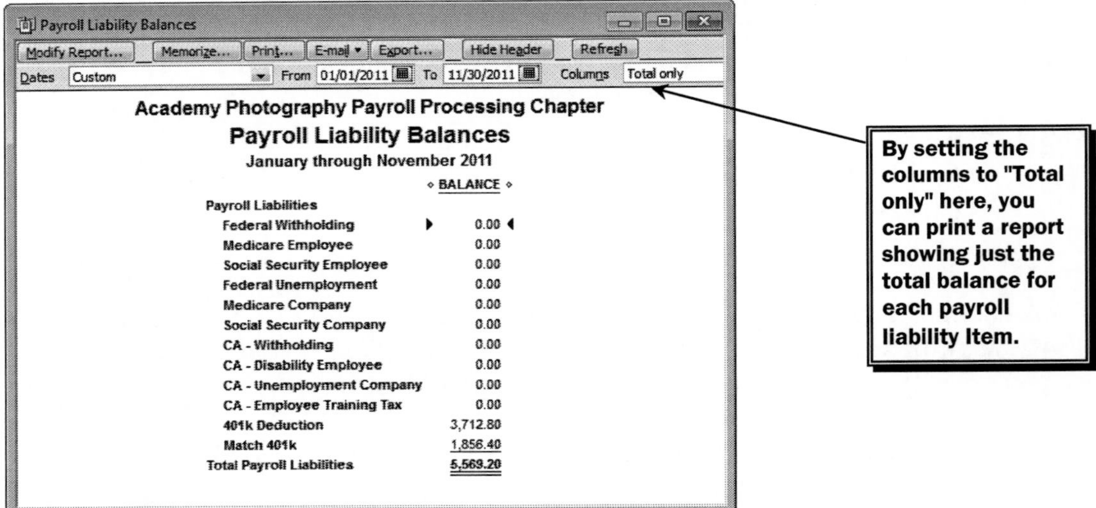

Payroll Liability Balances

Modify Report... | Memorize... | Print... | E-mail ▾ | Export... | Hide Header | Refresh

Dates: Custom | From: 01/01/2011 | To: 11/30/2011 | Columns: Total only

Academy Photography Payroll Processing Chapter

Payroll Liability Balances

January through November 2011

	BALANCE
Payroll Liabilities	
Federal Withholding	0.00
Medicare Employee	0.00
Social Security Employee	0.00
Federal Unemployment	0.00
Medicare Company	0.00
Social Security Company	0.00
CA - Withholding	0.00
CA - Disability Employee	0.00
CA - Unemployment Company	0.00
CA - Employee Training Tax	0.00
401k Deduction	3,712.80
Match 401k	1,856.40
Total Payroll Liabilities	5,569.20

By setting the columns to "Total only" here, you can print a report showing just the total balance for each payroll liability Item.

Figure 13-41 Payroll Liabilities report showing total unpaid accruals only

COMPUTER PRACTICE

You can filter the report to show only certain liabilities. For example, if you only want to see the Federal liabilities, follow these steps:

Step 1. Click **Modify Report** and then click the **Filters** tab (see Figure 13-42).

Step 2. Scroll down the *Filter* list on the left side of the window and then select **Payroll Item**.

Step 3. Select **All Federal** from the *Payroll Item* drop-down list in the center of the window (see Figure 13-42).

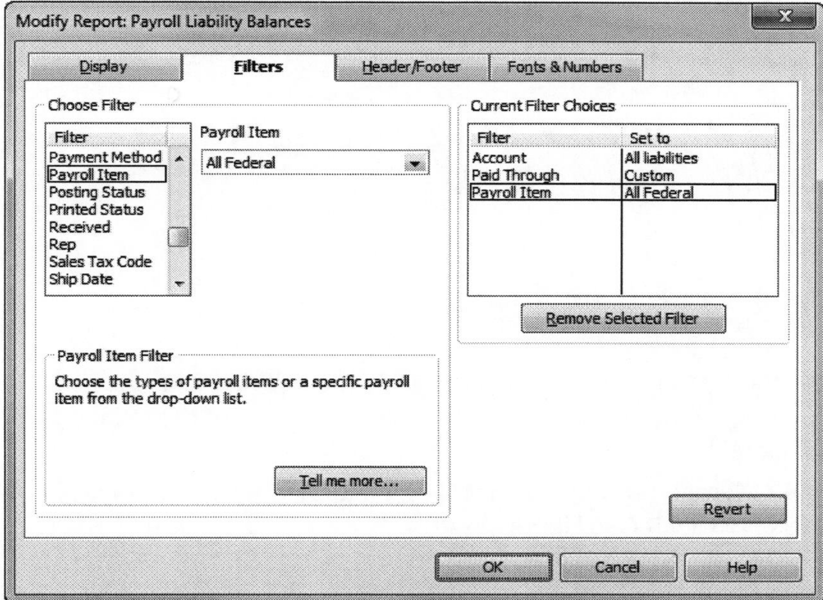

Figure 13-42 Payroll Item filter for all Federal items

To give the report a new title to match the filtered content of the report, follow these steps:

Step 1. Click the **Header/Footer** tab.

Step 2. Enter ***Federal Payroll Liability*** in the *Report Title* field and then click **OK** (see Figure 13-43).

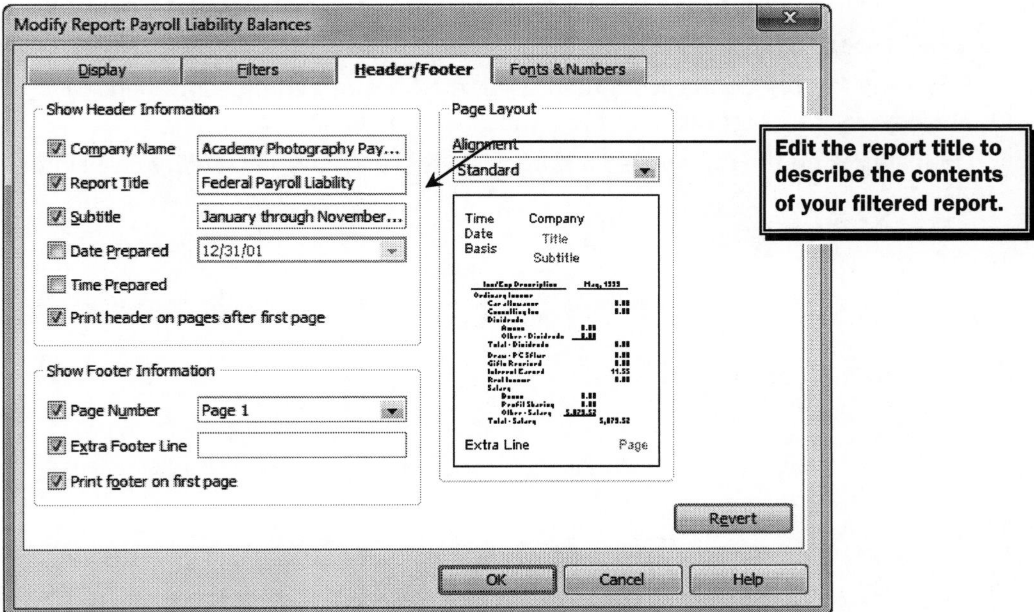

Figure 13-43 The Report Title field allows you to enter a new title

Step 3. Verify that the *Columns* field shows **Total only**.

Now the report title matches the content of the report. To memorize this report so you can save the current settings, follow these steps:

Step 1. Click the **Memorize** button shown in Figure 13-44.

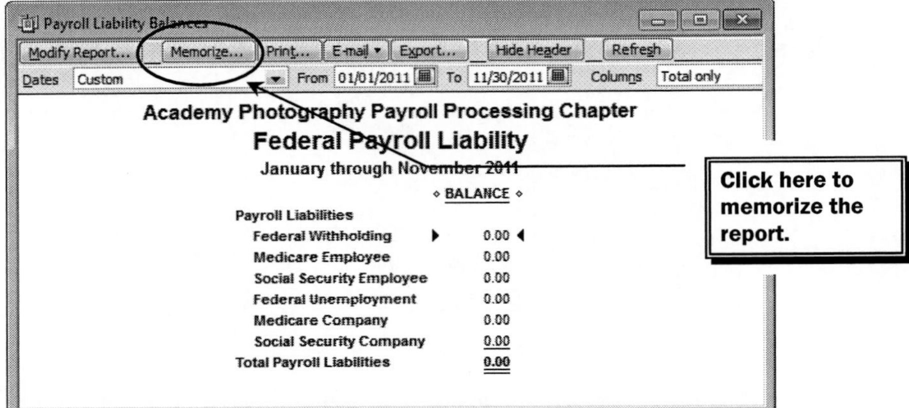

Figure 13-44 Custom Report called "Federal Payroll Liabilities."

Step 2. QuickBooks uses the customized report header as the default name for the Memorized Report, as shown in Figure 13-45. Press **Tab** to accept the default name **Federal Payroll Liability**.

Step 3. Check the **Save in Memorized Report Group** box and then select **Employees** from the drop-down list. Click **OK** (see Figure 13-45).

Figure 13-45 Save the memorized report in the Employees group.

Then, to create this report again:

Step 1. Select the **Report Center** icon, then select the **Memorized** tab, and then select **Employees** from the menu on the right side of the *Center*.

Step 2. Double-click on the memorized report called **Federal Payroll Liability** (see Figure 13-46).

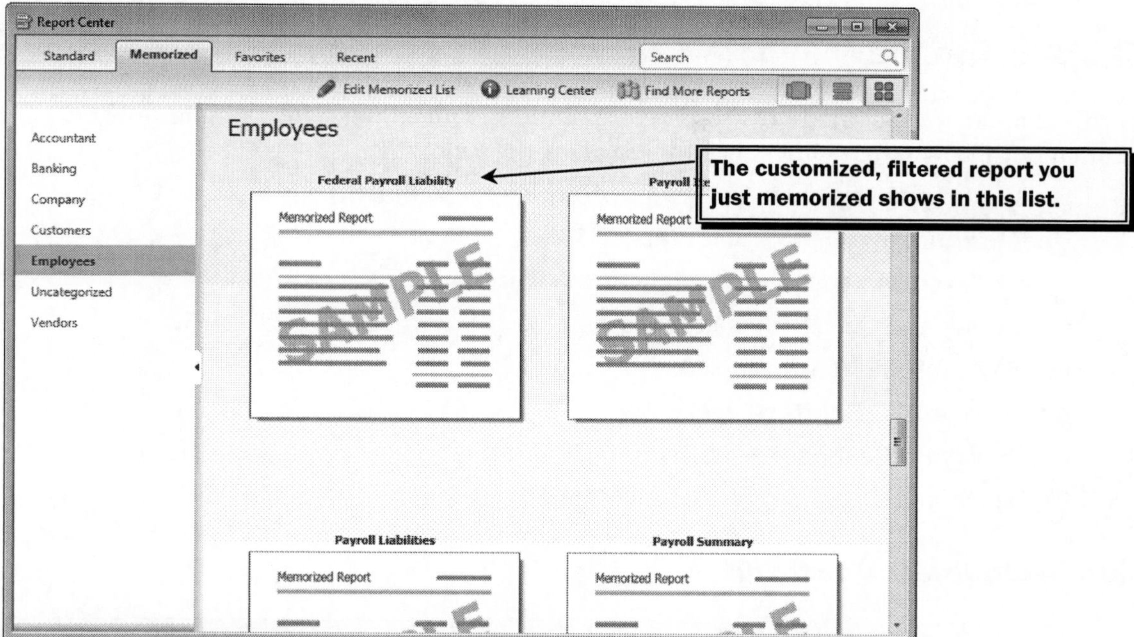

Figure 13-46 Select the report to create

Paying Payroll Taxes

Paying payroll taxes is an important part of payroll processing. This subject is covered in the supplemental material to this chapter. See page xiii for more information about accessing the supplemental material.

Chapter Summary and Review

In this chapter, you learned how to process payroll in QuickBooks. You should now be familiar with how to use QuickBooks to do all of the following:

- Use the Employee Center to view previous payroll activity (page 552).
- Update your Payroll Tax Tables (page 553).
- Create Paychecks and override default calculations (page 556).
- Edit, Void, and Delete Paychecks (page 565).
- Pay Payroll Liabilities (page 570).
- Adjust Payroll Liabilities (page 574).
- Create Payroll Reports (page 575).
- Paying Payroll Taxes (Supplemental Material).

Comprehension Questions

> Answers to these review questions are available with the supplemental material. See page xiii for details.

1. When should you update your payroll tax tables?
2. How can you override the Federal income tax withholding on a paycheck?
3. What type of checks (standard, voucher, or wallet) is the best choice for printing paychecks? Why?
4. Should you ever delete a paycheck that was printed and given to the employee? Why?
5. Explain how to update your tax tables and the impact of failing to update them.

Multiple Choice

Select the best answer(s) for each of the following:

1. To properly affect the payroll items, which function (from the **Employee** section of the *Home* page) should you use to pay the payroll taxes?
   a) Write Checks.
   b) Pay Bills.
   c) Pay Employees.
   d) Pay Liabilities.
2. Voucher style checks, when used for processing payroll may contain:
   a) Earnings and tax withholdings.
   b) Adjustments to earnings.
   c) Federal filing status.
   d) All of the above.
3. The Payroll Liability Balances report identifies:
   a) Liability payments made during the payment period.
   b) Liability amounts by Payroll Item.
   c) Liabilities for employee deductions only.
   d) Liabilities for employer taxes only.

4. The payroll tax return that reports Social Security, Medicare, and Federal Income Tax is submitted quarterly on:
   a) Form 940.
   b) Form 941.
   c) Form W-2.
   d) Payroll Liabilities Report.

5. To begin processing your payroll:
   a) Select **Write Checks** from the Home page.
   b) Select the *Employees* menu and then select **Pay Scheduled Liabilities.**
   c) Select the *Payroll* menu and then select **Process Payroll.**
   d) Choose **Pay Employees** from the *Employees* section of the *Home* page.

6. QuickBooks automatically calculates paychecks using information from all of the following sources except:
   a) Amounts on all previous paychecks.
   b) The employee's current earnings shown in the earnings section of the paycheck.
   c) The employee's tax settings in the employee record.
   d) The employee's expense report.

7. With a Standard QuickBooks payroll subscription, which forms *cannot* be printed directly from QuickBooks?
   a) State Payroll Tax forms from most states.
   b) 940.
   c) W3.
   d) All of the above can be printed if you have a Standard QuickBooks payroll subscription.

8. Which statement is true?
   a) You can print pay stubs at any time.
   b) Pay stubs print two per page.
   c) If you find an error in a past paycheck, you should delete and recreate the paycheck to ensure accuracy.
   d) You cannot void a paycheck.

9. To correctly pay your payroll liabilities, choose one of the following options:
   a) Write a check for the taxes and code it to payroll liabilities.
   b) Use the *Pay Scheduled Liabilities* section of the *Payroll Center.*
   c) Enter the tax authorities as payroll agencies.
   d) Enter a *Bill* for all taxes due. Then use *Pay Bills.*

10. The payroll summary by employee report shows:
    a) The detail of each employee's earnings only.
    b) The YTD employee's earnings by job.
    c) The detail of each employee's biographical information.
    d) The detail of each employee's hours, earnings, taxes, and net pay.

11. If the *Pay Liabilities* window shows incorrect tax amounts due, the problem could be caused by:
    a) Incorrect user entry of payroll item rates.
    b) Using Write checks to pay taxes.
    c) Users overriding calculated taxes.
    d) Any of the above.

12. To have data from the weekly timesheet affect an employee's paychecks:
    a) The timer must be used for all employees.
    b) Select *Use time Data to create Paychecks* on the employee record.
    c) Employees must enter their own time into QuickBooks.
    d) Use job costing.
13. What is shown in the Company Summary section of the *Preview Paycheck* window?
    a) Earnings and deductions.
    b) Insurance withheld from employee checks.
    c) Employer paid taxes and contributions.
    d) All tax and liability payments due.
14. How do you pay a salaried employee for vacation time?
    a) Vacation time is not available for salaried employees.
    b) Use a salary vacation payroll item and enter the vacation hours in the *Hours* column.
    c) Enter vacation time in the employee's record.
    d) Enter vacation hours on the pay stub.
15. Every payday, you should
    a) Create liability payments.
    b) Process employees' W-2 forms.
    c) Create payroll tax returns.
    d) Verify your tax tables are current and update them if necessary.

Completion Statements

Record in your notebook the best answer(s) for each of the following:

1. To manually job-cost or classify wages, enter a separate line in the earnings section of the paycheck for each combination of Earnings Item, Rate, Hours, ____:___, and _______.
2. The Payroll Tab in the Employee Center is also known as the _________ ___________.
3. In order to edit the items on a paycheck, display the paycheck and click the ______ ______ button in the Paycheck window.
4. QuickBooks prints state payroll tax forms only if you subscribe to its Enhanced Payroll service. However, if you do not subscribe to QuickBooks Enhanced payroll service, you can create reports, such as the _________ ________ ________ ________ report that help you prepare your state payroll tax returns.

Payroll Processing Problem 1

APPLYING YOUR KNOWLEDGE

Restore the PRProcessing-10Problem1.QBM file and store it on your hard disk according to your instructor's directions.

1. Process paychecks for both Mike Mazuki and Kati Reynolds with the information shown below. Create printable paychecks, dated 12/31/2011 drawn on the Checking bank account for the payroll period ending on 12/31/2011.

Mike Mazuki's Paycheck

Field	Data
Check Date	*12/31/2011*
Pay Period	*12/16/2011 through 12/31/2011*
Earnings	*20 hours – Hourly Regular – San Jose Class.* *52 hours – Hourly Regular – Walnut Creek Class* *8 hours –Hourly Vacation – Overhead Class*
Other Payroll Items (Deductions)	*401k Employee, -4%* *Match 401k, 2%* *Medical Insurance,-$10*

Table 13-1 Mike Mazuki's Paycheck

Kati Reynolds' Paycheck

Field	Data
Check Date	*12/31/2011*
Pay Period	*12/16/2011 through 21/31/2011*
Earnings	*Salary Regular, 64 hours, San Jose Class* *Salary Vacation, 16 hours, Overhead*
Other Payroll Items (Deductions)	*401k Employee, -4%* *Match 401k, 2%* *Medical Insurance,-$10*

Table 13-2 Kati Reynolds's Paycheck

2. Print both paychecks on blank paper. Use voucher checks for the format of the printed checks. Assign the checks to number 6071 and 6072.
3. On 1/4/2012, pay all liabilities for all State and Federal. Print the payroll liability checks on blank paper, beginning with check number 6073.
4. Print a Payroll Summary report for the last quarter of 2011. In the Print Reports settings window, select the option to fit the report to 1 page wide.
5. Print a Payroll Liability Balances report for 9/1/2011 through 12/31/2011.

Workplace Applications

Discussion Questions

These questions are designed to help you apply what you are learning about QuickBooks to your own organization. Some of your answers may lead to more questions you would like to ask about your organization.

1. What type of checks does your organization use to print paychecks? If it does not use voucher checks, how does your organization print pay stubs? How many paychecks does your company issue every week, every month, and every year?

2. Does your company keep track of payroll costs by job or project? How many different jobs or projects does your company track?
3. How often does your company make tax payroll deposits? Monthly? Semiweekly?

Case Study

Software Answers, Incorporated

Software Answers, Inc is a company that sells and provides online support for over 200 software packages. The company also uses its expertise to write code for software solutions that customize other applications.

The company has 12 customer-support representatives earning hourly wages, and four founding members of the company who are salaried. The company pays a commission to its customer-support representatives for each software package they sell.

1. How would you set up payroll items for employees on commission?
2. How would you ensure the commissions on software sales are correctly paid to the employees?

Chapter 14 Estimates

Objectives

After completing this chapter, you should be able to:

- Prepare Estimates (page 587).
- Prepare Invoices from Estimates (page 589).
- Use the Progress Invoicing Feature (page 591).
- Create Purchase Orders from Estimates (page 595).
- Create Reports about Estimates (page 599).
- Create Sales Orders (Supplemental Material).

> **Restore this File**
>
> This chapter uses Estimates-10.QBW. To open this file, restore the Estimates-10.QBM file to your hard disk. See page 10 for instructions on restoring files.

QuickBooks has two features that help you track "bids" for your sales or projects. Depending on the type of business you have, you might use either the Estimate or the Sales Order feature to prepare written estimates (or bids) for the work you propose to do. Then, when you perform the work, you can transfer the information from the Estimates or Sales Orders onto Invoices.

Some businesses (e.g., contractors) prefer to use Estimates while others (e.g., retailers) prefer to use Sales Orders. These two features allow you to accomplish essentially the same function of tracking proposed versus actual revenues and expenses, as well as active (or open) and inactive (or closed) bids.

QuickBooks also provides a "Progress Invoicing" feature that allows you to prepare several invoices for a job as each stage of the job is completed. To reduce errors and provide fast data entry, QuickBooks automates the process of copying portions of an Estimate or Sales Order onto each progress invoice.

In this chapter, you'll learn how these features help you track the various stages of sales transactions.

Creating Estimates and Progress Invoicing can be done using QuickBooks Pro or higher editions. However, Sales Orders require QuickBooks Premier or higher editions, and cannot be created using QuickBooks Pro. Sales Orders are covered in supplemental material for this chapter available online (see page xiii).

Creating Estimates

Entering an **Estimate** into QuickBooks is similar to entering an Invoice. You fill out all the customer and item information just as when you create an invoice. The big difference is that Estimates do not post to the general ledger, and therefore they do not affect any of your financial reports. They do help you track your future sales and they do help you track how your actual revenues and costs compare with what was estimated, but **Estimates** do not record any financial information themselves. Additionally, you can create and print **Estimates** for your proposals and then use QuickBooks reports to help you follow up with each prospect during the sales process.

COMPUTER PRACTICE

To create an Estimate, follow these steps:

Step 1. Select the **Customers** menu and then select **Create Estimates**. Alternatively, click the **Estimates** icon on the *Home* page.

Step 2. Enter **Garrison, John: Family Portrait** in the *Customer:Job* field and press **TAB**.

Step 3. Enter the remaining information shown in Figure 14-1 on the Estimate form.

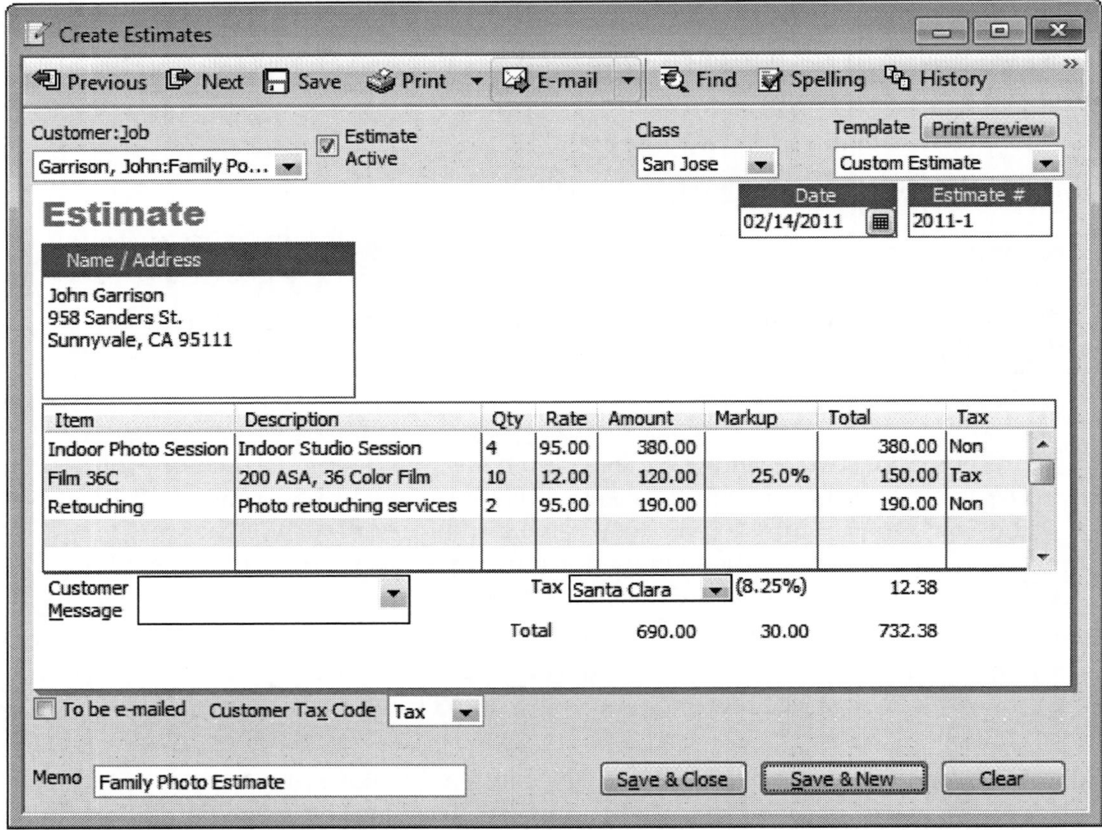

Figure 14-1 Creating an estimate

Step 4. If QuickBooks displays the Price Levels dialog box as displayed in Figure 14-2, check the *Do not display this message in the future box* and click **OK**.

Figure 14-2 Dialog box about Price Levels

Step 5. Click **Save & Close** to record the Estimate.

> **Note:**
> You can customize your Estimates by creating or editing templates in the same way you customize your Invoices as illustrated on page 355.

Creating Invoices from Estimates

When an Estimate is approved or accepted by a customer, you can import the information from the Estimate into an Invoice. Doing so eliminates the need to manually enter the detail on the Invoice.

COMPUTER PRACTICE

To create an Invoice from and Estimate, follow these steps:

Step 1. From the **Customers** menu, select **Create Invoices**.

Step 2. Enter **Garrison, John: Family Portrait** in the *Customer:Job* field and press **TAB**.

QuickBooks displays the *Available Estimates* window (see Figure 14-3).

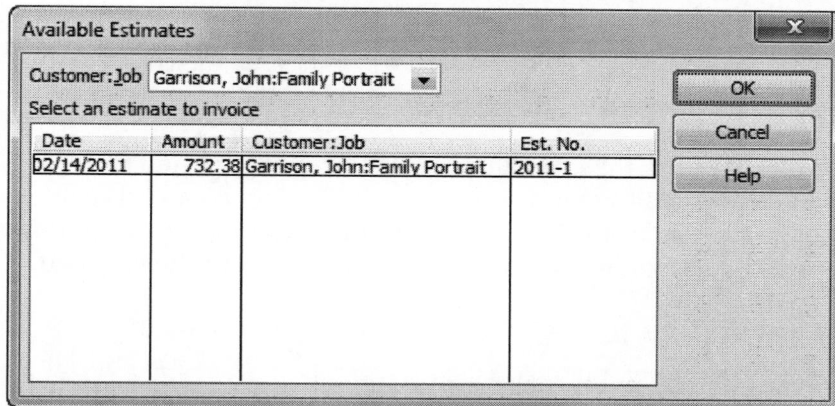

Figure 14-3 The Available Estimates window

> **Note:**
> When you work with a prospect, you may need to create several Estimates (i.e., bids) showing different alternatives for the job. If you do, QuickBooks will show each of the open, active Estimates in the *Available Estimates* window.

Step 3. Select Estimate #2011-1 on the *Available Estimates* window and click **OK**.

QuickBooks transfers the information from the Estimate onto the Invoice. If necessary, you can make changes to the Invoice before saving it.

Step 4. Change the Quantity column for the Retouching Item on the Invoice from 2 to 1 (see Figure 14-4) and then press **TAB**.

The Estimate was for 2 hours of retouching, but Academy Photo actually completed the work in 1 hour, so you're making this change to reflect the actual charge. You will be able to compare the actual revenues with the estimated revenues on your reports later in this chapter.

Step 5. Edit the *Memo* field so that the memo reads ***Family photo***.

Step 6. Click **Save & Close** to record the Invoice.

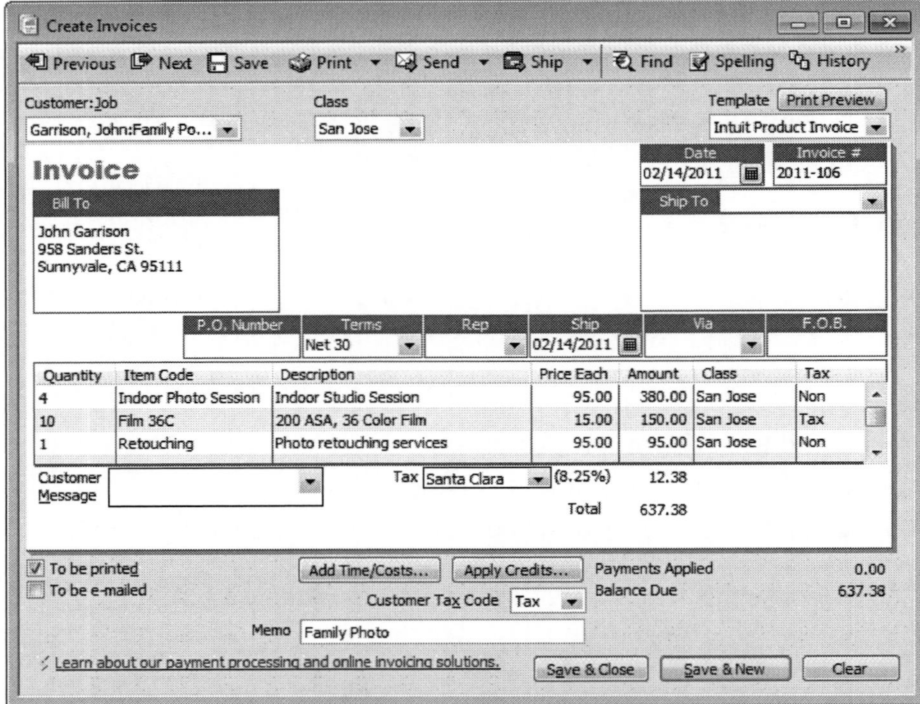

Figure 14-4 Modify the Invoice as Necessary to Reflect the Actual Charges.

Invoices can also be created directly from the Estimates window. You might find this procedure to be streamlined as compared to that described above. To convert an Estimate into an Invoice using this method, click the **Create Invoice** icon in the *Create Estimates* window as shown in Figure 14-5. This will transfer all of the line item information from the Estimate to an Invoice.

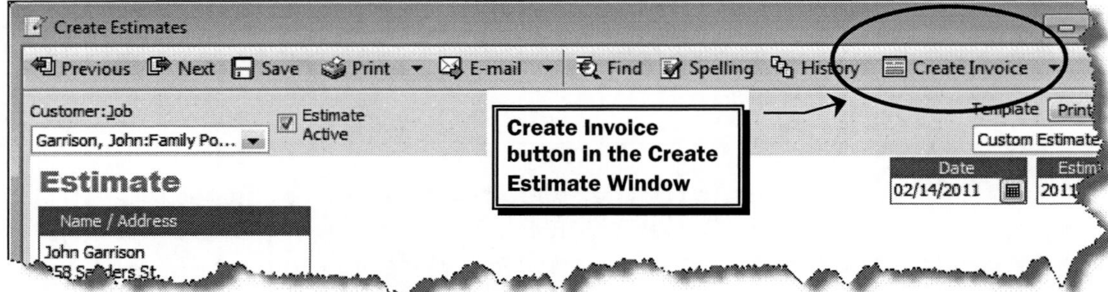

Figure 14-5 Creating an Invoice from the Estimate Window

If you choose to create an Invoice directly from an Estimate, QuickBooks will display the dialog box shown in Figure 14-6, advising that the entire Estimate has been copied to an invoice.

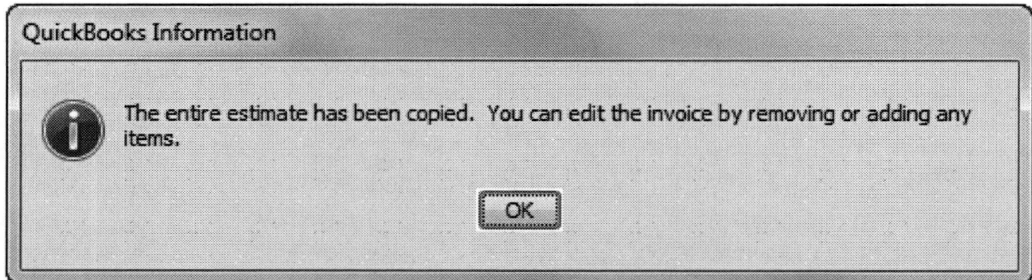

Figure 14-6 Message Received After Converting Estimate Information Into an Invoice

Progress Invoicing

Progress Invoicing allows you to charge your customers a portion of the total Estimate for each stage of a project. QuickBooks tracks how much of the Estimate has been invoiced, and how much remains to be invoiced.

COMPUTER PRACTICE

To create a progress invoice from an estimate, first modify your preferences. Follow these steps:

Step 1. Select the **Edit** menu and then select **Preferences.**

Step 2. Select **Jobs & Estimates** and click the **Company Preferences** tab (see Figure 14-7).

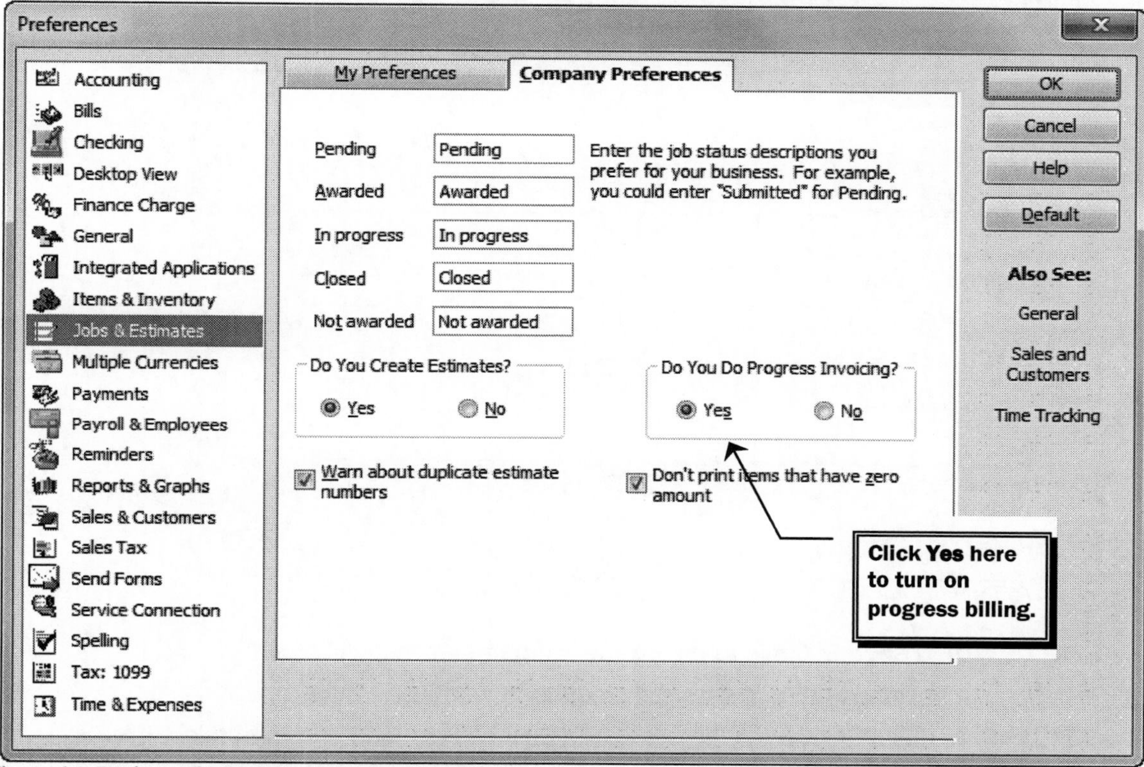

Figure 14-7 Jobs and Estimates Company Preferences

Step 3. Click **Yes** in the *Do You Do Progress Invoicing?* Section as shown in Figure 14-7

Step 4. Click **OK** to save your changes.

Step 5. QuickBooks displays the dialog box in Figure 14-8 warning that all windows will be closed to change the preference. Click **OK.**

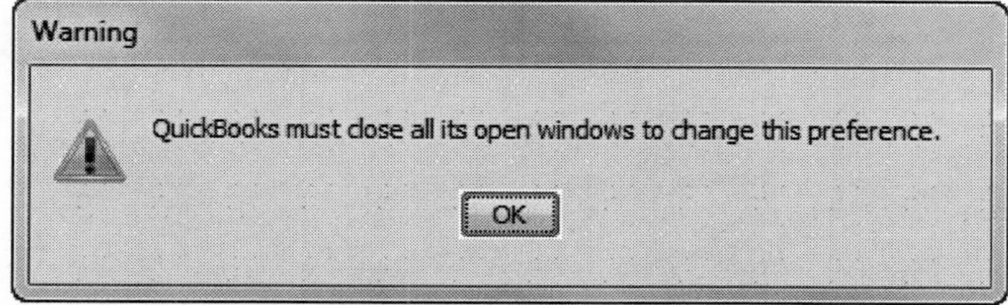

Figure 14-8 Warning window to close all open windows

Step 6. Click the *Home* icon on the Navigation Bar to display the *Home* page (see Figure 14-9).

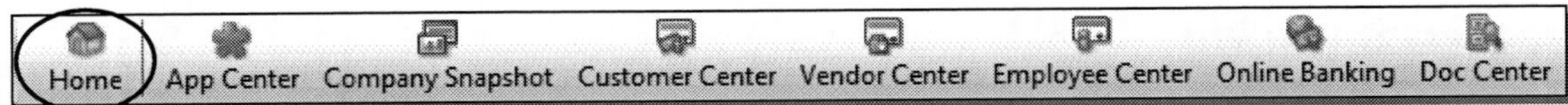

Figure 14-9 Home icon on the Navigation bar

Step 7. Click the **Estimates** icon on the *Home* page.

Step 8. Create an Estimate for **Anderson Wedding Planners: Wilson, Sarah and Michael** job with the data shown in Figure 14-10.

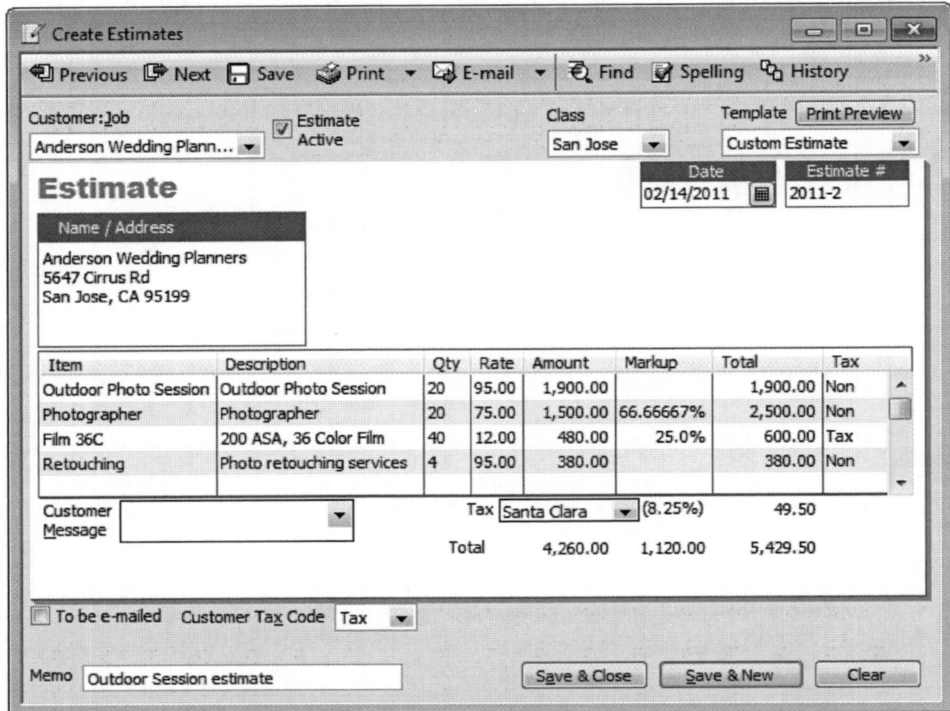

Figure 14-10 Estimate for Wilson, Sarah and Michael Job to be Progress Invoiced

Step 9. Click **Save & Close** to record the Estimate.

Step 10. If necessary, click **Yes** on the credit limit warning.

Step 11. To create a Progress Bill, select the **Customers** menu and then select **Create Invoices.**

Step 12. Select the **Anderson Wedding Planners: Wilson, Sarah and Michael** job from the *Customer:Job* drop-down menu and press **TAB**.

Step 13. QuickBooks displays the *Available Estimates* window. Select Estimate **2011-2** and click **OK** (see Figure 14-11).

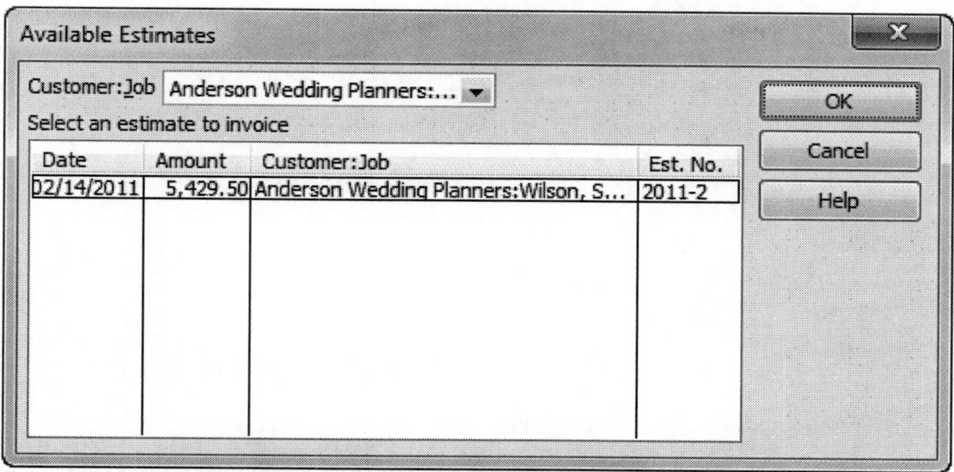

Figure 14-11 Select the Estimate on the Available Estimates Window.

Step 14. QuickBooks displays the *Create Progress Invoice Based on Estimate* window. Select **Create invoice for a percentage of the entire estimate** and enter ***25.0%*** in the *% of estimate* field as shown in Figure 14-12.

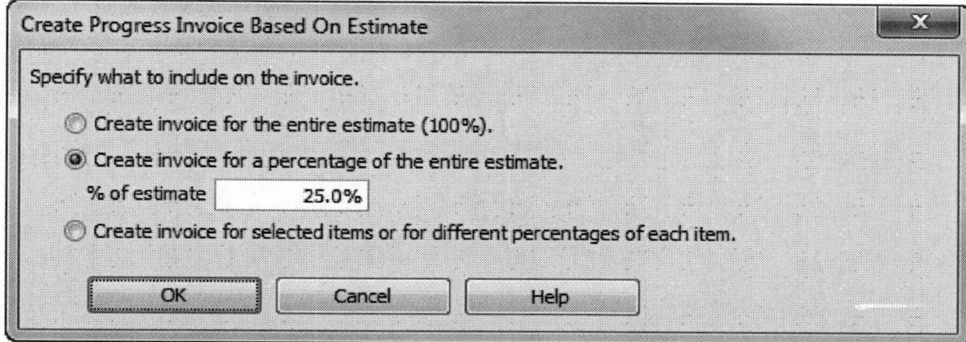

Figure 14-12 Enter the Percentage of the Estimate to be Billed

> **Note**
> As you can see in Figure 14-12, you can also create an Invoice for the entire Estimate (i.e., no Progress Invoicing) or different percentages of each item. Select the option that applies to your situation.

Step 15. QuickBooks displays the *Create Invoice* window (see Figure 14-13) and automatically reduces the quantities for products and services to 25% of the estimated amount.

Step 16. Click **OK**.

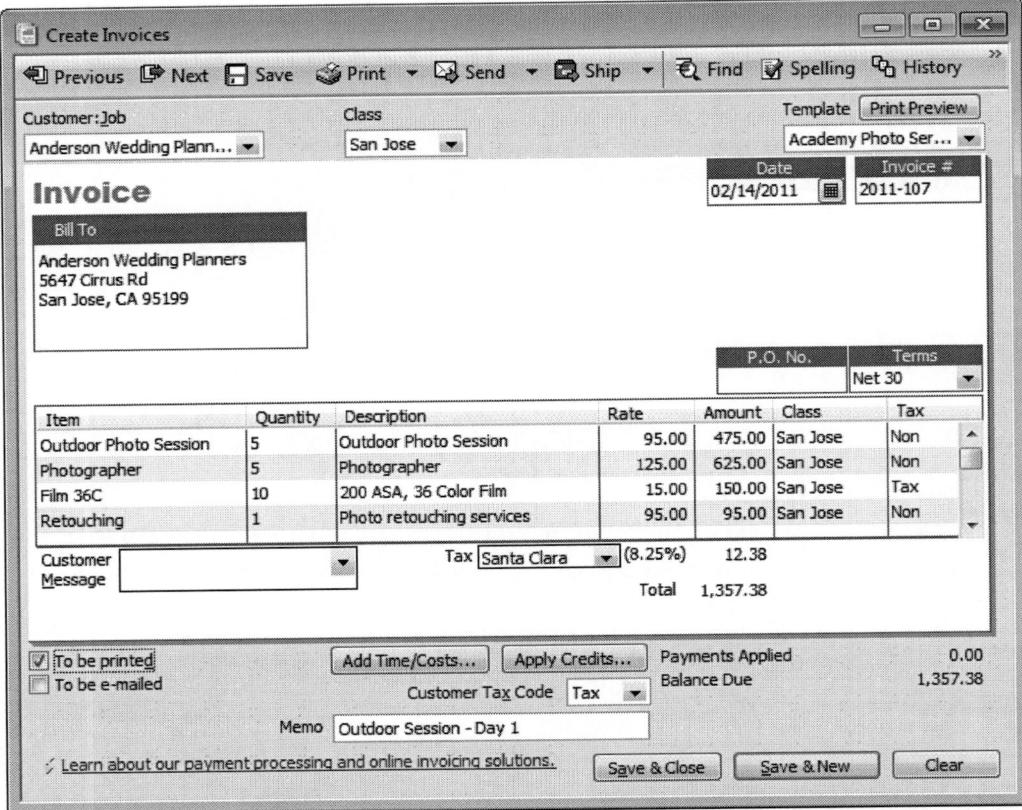

Figure 14-13 Progress Billed Invoice for Anderson Wedding Planners: Wilson, Sarah and Michael Job

Step 17. Edit the *Memo* as shown in Figure 14-13 and then click **Save & Close** to save the progress invoice.

Progress Invoices can be adjusted directly from the Invoice window. Click the **Progress** icon in the *Create Invoices* window as shown in Figure 14-14. This will open the *Specify Invoice Amounts for Items on Estimate* window show in Figure 14-15, where you can make corrections or adjustments to the progress invoice quantity or percentage.

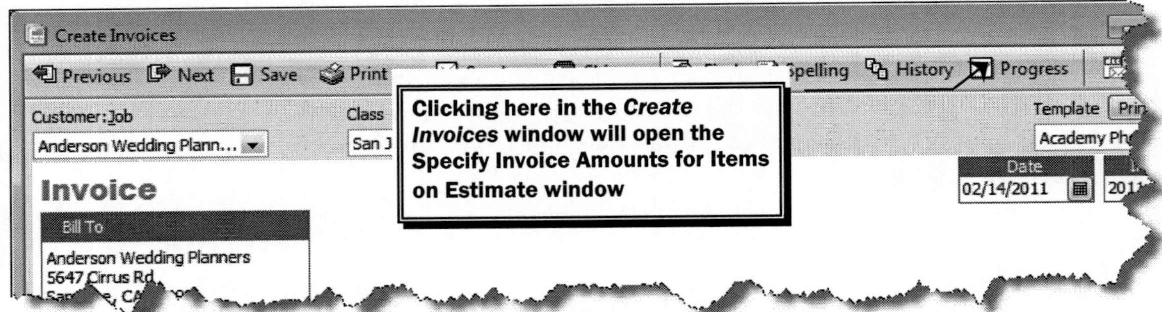

Figure 14-14 Clicking on Progress icon in Create Invoices window

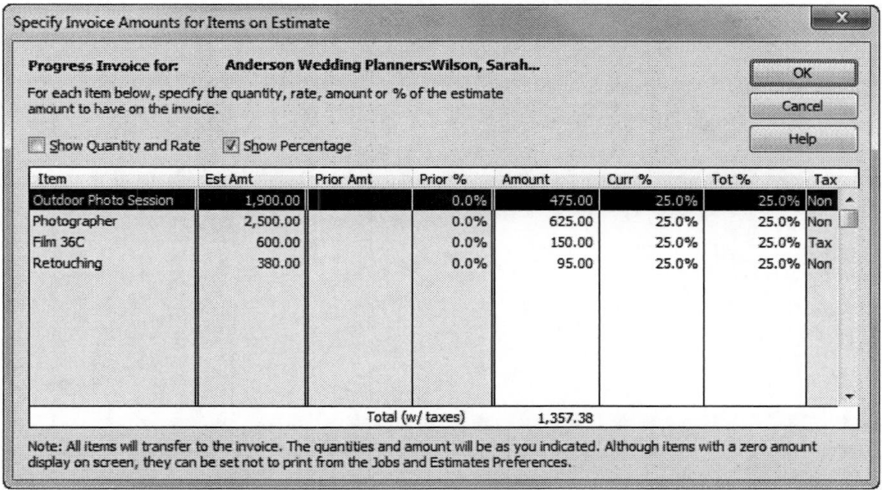

Figure 14-15 Specify Invoice Amounts for Items on Estimate window (showing percentage)

Creating Purchase Orders from Estimates

Occasionally Academy Photo sells custom photo frames to their customers. When they do, they create an Estimate and then when the customer approves the Estimate, they order the frame to complete the job. In cases like this, QuickBooks Premier and QuickBooks Enterprise Solutions allow you to create a Purchase Order using all or part of the information on the Estimate for the job.

> QuickBooks Pro does not have the ability to create Purchase Orders directly from Estimates. The following Computer Practice will only work with QuickBooks Premier and QuickBooks Enterprise. **Readers using QuickBooks Pro should read through but not complete the following exercise.**

COMPUTER PRACTICE

To create a Purchase Order from an Estimate, first create the Estimate and then create a Purchase Order based on the Estimate. Follow these steps:

Step 1. Click the **Estimates** icon on the *Home* page.

Step 2. Enter **Cruz, Maria: Branch Opening** in the *Customer:Job* field and press **TAB.**

Step 3. Enter the remaining information as shown in Figure 14-16.

Step 4. Click **Save & New** to save the Estimate, and then click **Previous** to redisplay the same Estimate.

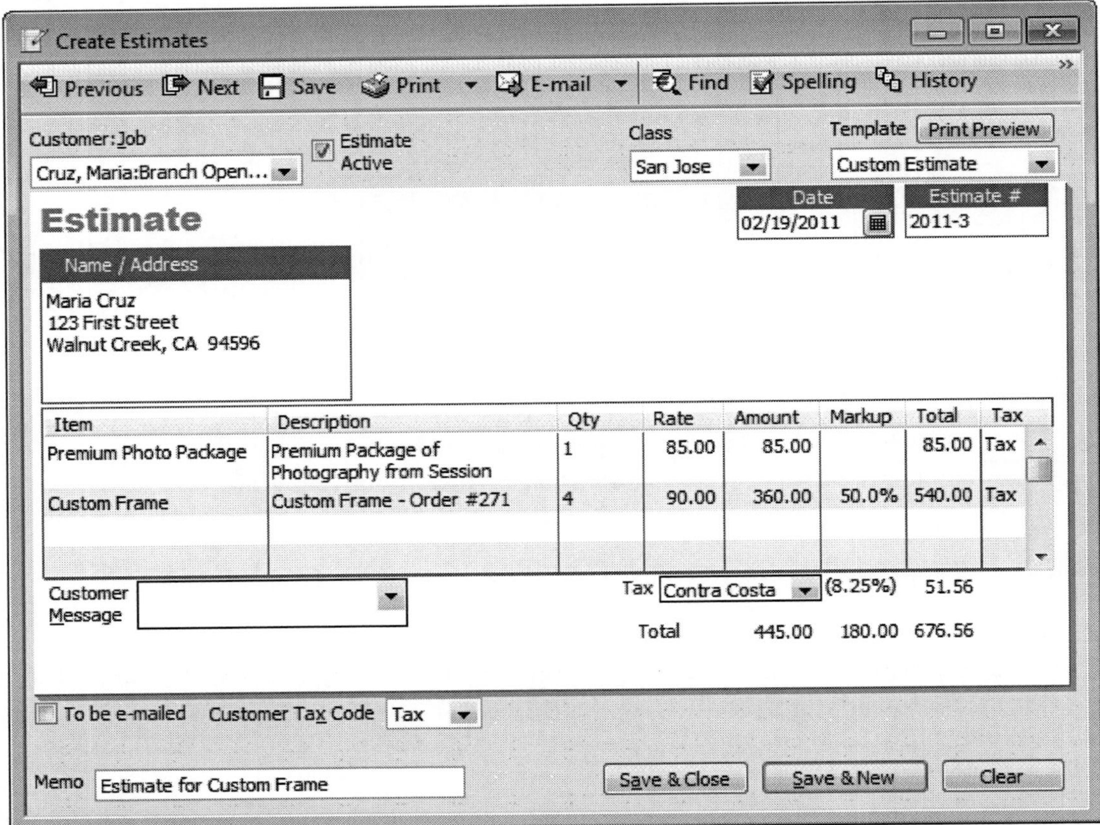

Figure 14-16 Estimate for Custom Frame

Step 5. Select the *Create Invoice* drop-down menu at the top of the Estimate, and then select **Purchase Order** as shown in Figure 14-17.

You have to make sure you click the down-arrow to the right of the Create Invoice button. Otherwise, it will prompt you to create an Invoice instead of a Purchase Order.

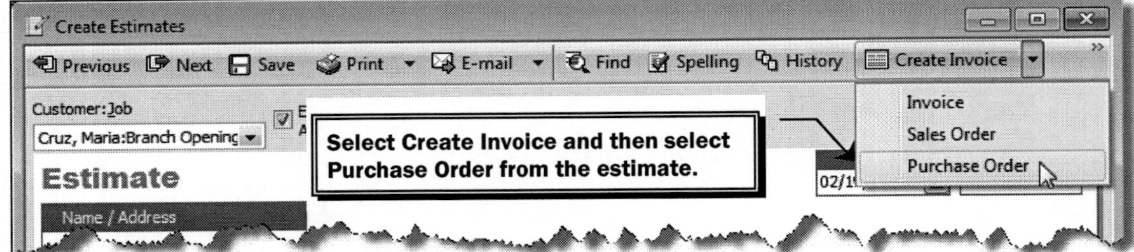

Figure 14-17 Select Purchase Order from the Create Invoice Button Drop-Down Menu

Step 6. QuickBooks displays the *Create Purchase Order Based on the Sales Transaction* window. Select **Create purchase order for selected items** as shown in Figure 14-18. Then, click **OK**.

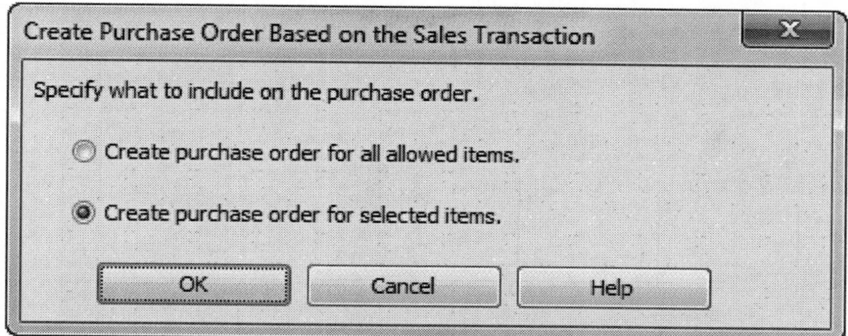

Figure 14-18 Use this Window to Create a Purchase Order from the Estimate Detail.

> **Note**
> You should only select **Create purchase order for all allowed items** if you want QuickBooks to include all Service, Non-inventory Part and Inventory Part items on the Purchase Order *and* if you purchase all of the items from the same vendor. Since that situation will probably be rare, you'll usually select **Create purchase order for selected items** as shown in Figure 14-18. Selecting this option will allow you to control which items post to the Purchase Order and to create multiple Purchase Orders from this Estimate, if necessary.

Step 7. QuickBooks displays the *Specify Purchase Order Quantities for Items on the Sales Transaction* window. Select the ***Custom Frame*** line as shown in Figure 14-19. Then, click **OK**.

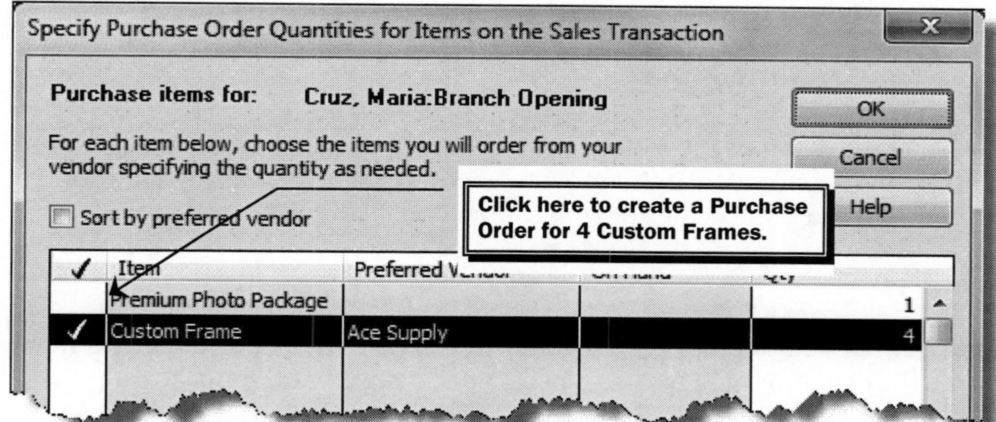

Figure 14-19 Use this Window to Select the Specific Items to Include on the Purchase Order

> **Note:**
> If the items on the Estimate are *Inventory Parts*, QuickBooks will show the stock status for the part in the **On Hand** column. If necessary, you can override the amount in the **Qty** column.

Step 8. QuickBooks creates a Purchase Order for 4 custom frames as shown in Figure 14-20. If necessary, modify the Description to include the Order #.

Step 9. Click **Save & Close** to save the Purchase Order.

Step 10. Click **Save & Close** on the *Create Estimates* window.

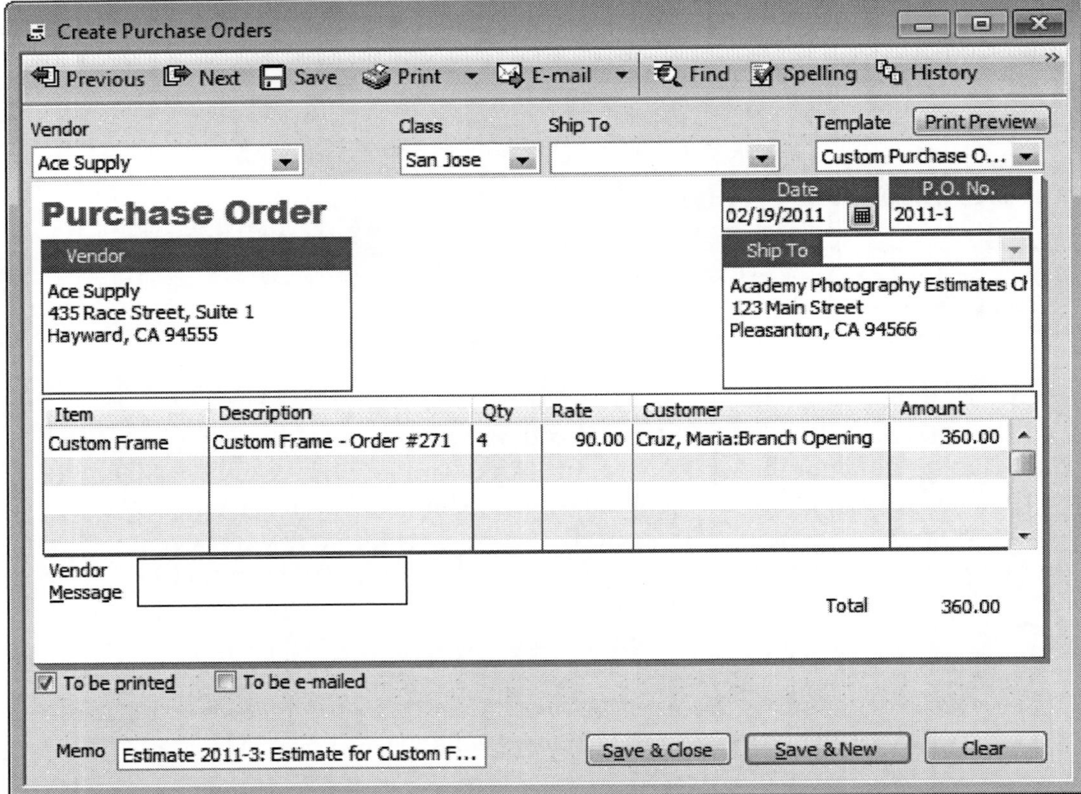

Figure 14-20 QuickBooks Creates the Purchase Order Using the Information Entered on the Estimate

Viewing and Tracking Estimates

QuickBooks provides tools that enable you to quickly view the details of an existing Estimate or to re-print an Estimate. QuickBooks also provides reports that help you manage your proposals and to determine the accuracy of your estimating.

Viewing Estimates

In the ***Customer Center***, you can see each Customer or Job that has an outstanding Estimate. If you need to see the details of the Estimate, you can do so directly from this list.

COMPUTER PRACTICE

To view an Estimate from the Customer Center, follow these steps:

Step 1. Open the *Customer Center*, click on the *Transactions* tab, and click **Estimates** to open the window shown in Figure 14-21.

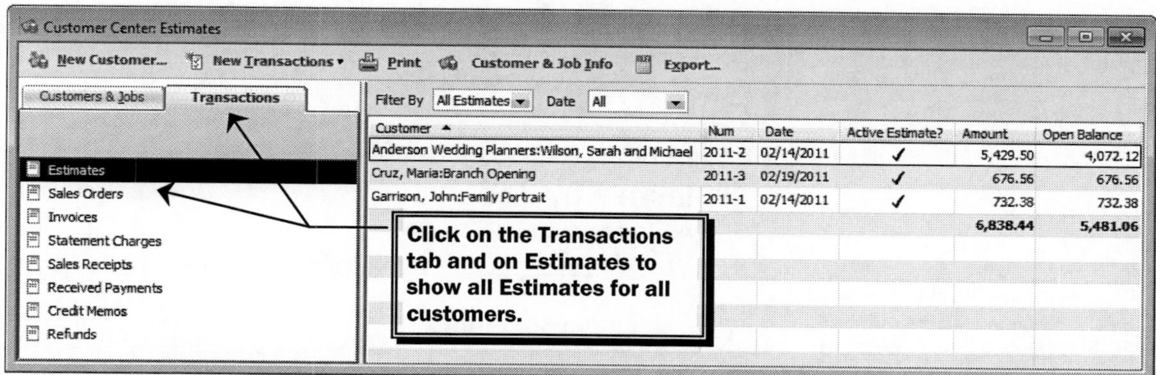

Customer	Num	Date	Active Estimate?	Amount	Open Balance
Anderson Wedding Planners:Wilson, Sarah and Michael	2011-2	02/14/2011	✓	5,429.50	4,072.12
Cruz, Maria:Branch Opening	2011-3	02/19/2011	✓	676.56	676.56
Garrison, John:Family Portrait	2011-1	02/14/2011	✓	732.38	732.38
				6,838.44	5,481.06

Figure 14-21 Viewing all Estimates from the Customer Center – Your screen may vary

Step 2. Double-click on John Garrison's Family Portrait Job and the Estimate form for that job is opened (see Figure 14-22).

Step 3. Close **Customer Center** and **Estimate** windows.

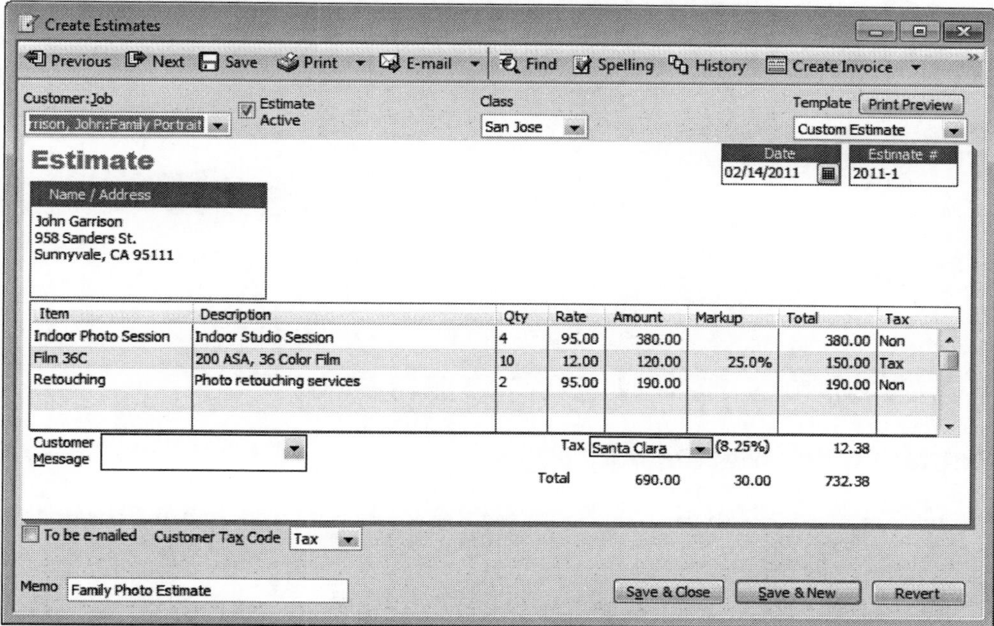

Item	Description	Qty	Rate	Amount	Markup	Total	Tax
Indoor Photo Session	Indoor Studio Session	4	95.00	380.00		380.00	Non
Film 36C	200 ASA, 36 Color Film	10	12.00	120.00	25.0%	150.00	Tax
Retouching	Photo retouching services	2	95.00	190.00		190.00	Non

Figure 14-22 Estimate for John Garrison: Family Portrait Job

Tracking Estimates

There are several reports that help you track Estimates and analyze the accuracy of your estimating.

Estimates by Job Report

If you want to see a list of Estimates for all your Jobs, create the *Estimates by Job Report.*

COMPUTER PRACTICE

To create the Estimates by Job report, follow these steps:

Step 1. Select the **Reports** menu, select **Jobs, Time & Mileage**, and then select **Estimates by Job**.

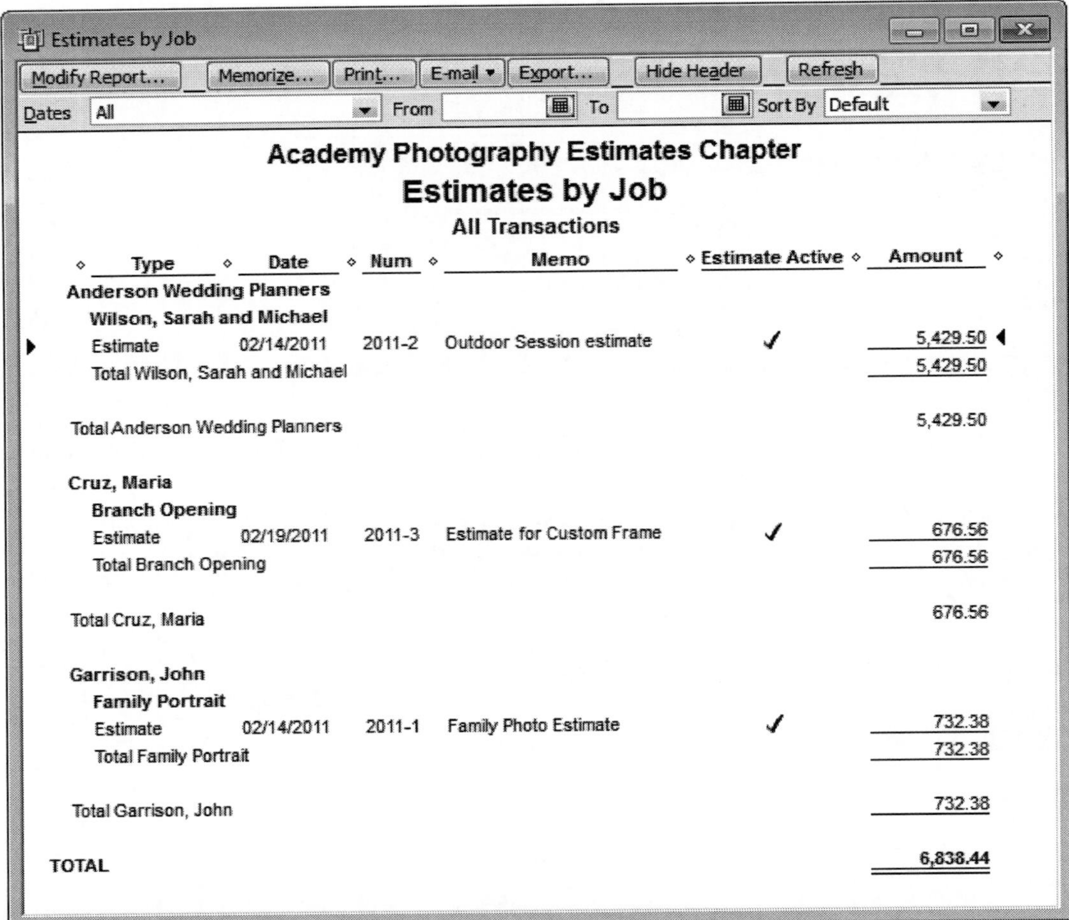

Academy Photography Estimates Chapter

Estimates by Job

All Transactions

Type	Date	Num	Memo	Estimate Active	Amount
Anderson Wedding Planners					
Wilson, Sarah and Michael					
Estimate	02/14/2011	2011-2	Outdoor Session estimate	✓	5,429.50
Total Wilson, Sarah and Michael					5,429.50
Total Anderson Wedding Planners					5,429.50
Cruz, Maria					
Branch Opening					
Estimate	02/19/2011	2011-3	Estimate for Custom Frame	✓	676.56
Total Branch Opening					676.56
Total Cruz, Maria					676.56
Garrison, John					
Family Portrait					
Estimate	02/14/2011	2011-1	Family Photo Estimate	✓	732.38
Total Family Portrait					732.38
Total Garrison, John					732.38
TOTAL					6,838.44

Figure 14-23 Estimates by Job report - All Customers and Jobs - Your screen may vary

The Job Estimates vs. Actuals Summary Report

Use the *Job Estimates vs. Actuals Summary* report to see the total estimated amount compared with the actual charges for Jobs.

COMPUTER PRACTICE

To create the Job Estimates vs. Actuals Summary report, follow these steps:

Step 1. Select the **Reports** menu, select **Jobs, Time & Mileage**, and then select **Job Estimates vs. Actuals Summary.**

Step 2. Click the **Collapse** button to display the report in Figure 14-24.

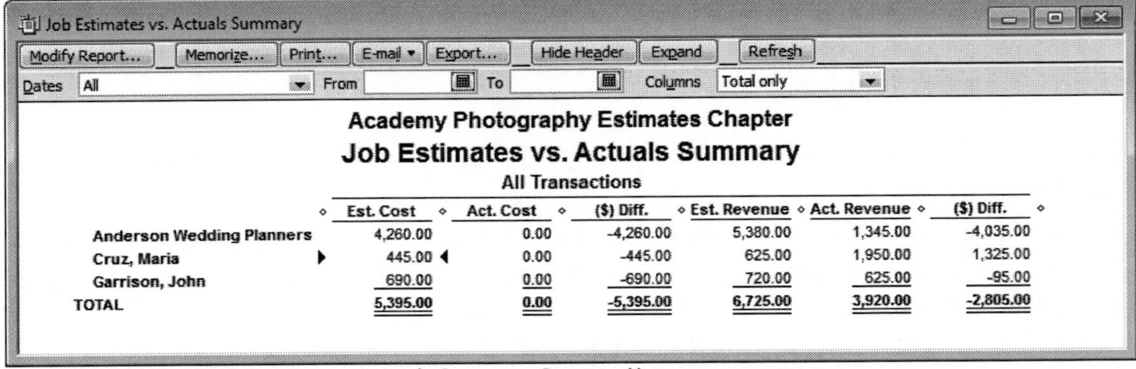

Academy Photography Estimates Chapter

Job Estimates vs. Actuals Summary

All Transactions

	Est. Cost	Act. Cost	($) Diff.	Est. Revenue	Act. Revenue	($) Diff.
Anderson Wedding Planners	4,260.00	0.00	-4,260.00	5,380.00	1,345.00	-4,035.00
Cruz, Maria	445.00	0.00	-445.00	625.00	1,950.00	1,325.00
Garrison, John	690.00	0.00	-690.00	720.00	625.00	-95.00
TOTAL	5,395.00	0.00	-5,395.00	6,725.00	3,920.00	-2,805.00

Figure 14-24 The Job Estimates vs. Actuals Summary Report - Your screen may vary

> **Note:**
> In the report shown in Figure 14-24, notice that the Actual Revenue for Anderson Wedding Planners job is exactly 25% of the Estimated Revenue. In the Progress Invoicing section beginning on page 591, you were instructed to "progress bill" this customer for 25% of the Estimate. The actual revenue will increase and the difference in Estimates vs. Actual will decrease as you create future progress invoices for this customer.

Job Progress Invoices vs. Estimates Report

If you Progress Invoice customers, you can use the *Job Progress Invoices vs. Estimates* report to track your progress billing. The report shows the amount of the original Estimates, the total of the progress Invoices and the percentage of the Estimate you have currently billed the customer.

COMPUTER PRACTICE

To create the Job Progress Invoices vs. Estimates report, follow these steps:

Step 1. Select the **Reports** menu, select **Jobs, Time & Mileage**, and then select **Job Progress Invoices vs. Estimates.**

Step 2. Select **All** in the *Dates* box and press **Tab.**

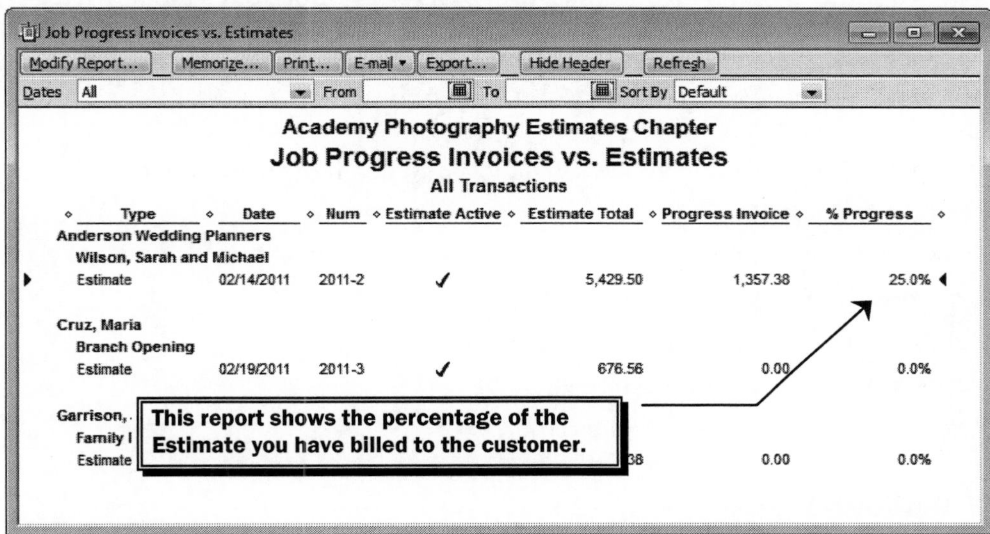

Figure 14-25 Job Progress Invoices vs. Estimates report - Your screen may vary

> **Note:**
> The *Job Progress Invoices vs. Estimates* report only shows active Estimates. After you bill 100% of an Estimate, or if you manually "close" an Estimate, QuickBooks no longer displays the estimate on this report. To track open and closed estimates as they relate to billings use the *Job Estimates vs. Actuals Summary* report shown in Figure 14-24.

Step 3. Close all open reports.

Sales Orders

Sales Orders are very similar to Estimates. You use them to track orders from customers while you are processing the order, or otherwise waiting to fulfill the order. As with Estimates, Sales

Orders do not post to the General Ledger and therefore they do not affect any of your financial reports.

You can print Sales Orders for use as pick lists. Pick lists are often used in warehouses or other distribution type businesses. Warehouse staff uses these lists to "pick" items from the warehouse shelves and package them into a single shipment. Sales Orders can be customized much the same as other sales forms. Once the order is ready to ship, the Sales Orders is used to create an Invoice for the order. You can also use QuickBooks reports to keep track of open sales orders and back ordered items.

> Note:
> Sales Orders are available only in QuickBooks **Premier** and **Enterprise** Editions. Download the supplemental material for this chapter to complete several exercises using Sales Orders (Premier version required). If you are using the QuickBooks Pro Edition, you can read through this supplement, but you will not be able to complete the exercises. To download the supplemental materials, see xiii.

Chapter Summary and Review

QuickBooks has two features that help you track proposals or bids for your sales or projects. Depending on the type of business you have, you might use either the Estimate or the Sales Order feature to prepare written proposals or bids for the work you propose to do. Then, when you perform the work, you can transfer the information from the Estimates or Sales Orders onto Invoices.

You should now be familiar with how to use QuickBooks to do all of the following:

- Prepare Estimates (page 587).
- Prepare Invoices from Estimates (page 589).
- Use the Progress Invoicing Feature (page 591).
- Create Purchase Orders from Estimates (page 595).
- Create Reports about Estimates (page 599).
- Create Sales Orders (Supplemental Material).

Comprehension Questions

> Answers to these review questions are available with the supplemental material. See page xiii for details.

1. Explain the primary difference between an **Estimate** and an **Invoice** and describe what **Estimates** help you do.
2. Explain what **Progress Invoicing** allows you to do in QuickBooks.
3. Explain the similarities between **Sales Orders** and **Estimates** and describe what **Sales Orders** allow you to do.

Multiple Choice

Select the best answer(s) for each of the following:

1. Estimates help you to:
   a) Track your future sales.
   b) Track how your actual revenues and costs compare with what was estimated.
   c) Track and record financial information.
   d) Answers (a) and (b).

2. Creating an Invoice from an Estimate:
   a) Has little or no effect on the financial statements since *Estimates* do not post to the General Ledger.
   b) Eliminates the need to manually enter *Estimate* details on the Invoice.
   c) Can affect the P&L because creating an *Estimate* itself affects the P&L.
   d) Can take up to several hours because it may be difficult to locate the ***Create Invoice*** button on the *Estimate* form.

3. Which statement is false:
   a) Progress invoicing allows you to charge your customers a portion of the total Estimate for each stage of the Job.
   b) QuickBooks can track how much of the *Estimate* has been invoiced, and how much remains to be invoiced.
   c) Progress invoicing can create an *Invoice* for the entire *Estimate* (i.e., no progress invoicing) but only after the *Estimate* is closed.
   d) Progress invoicing allows you to create an Invoice for some Estimate items.

4. *After* the customer approves the Estimate you can create the following form(s) using QuickBooks Premier:
   a) Purchase Order.
   b) Sales Order.
   c) Both (a) and (b).
   d) Neither (a) and (b).

5. You should usually select ***Create** purchase order for selected items* button when creating *Purchase Orders* from *Estimates* because:
   a) Selecting this option bypasses the **Specify Purchase Order Quantities for Items on the Sales Transaction** window.
   b) Selecting this option records your items and directly opens up the Purchase Order form.
   c) Inventory and non-inventory parts will display on the *Purchase Order* number.
   d) It is rare that you will include all service items on the purchase order and acquire the purchase items from the same vendor.

6. You can view estimates:
   a) In the *Customer Center.*
   b) On the Estimates by Job report.
   c) Job Estimates vs. Actuals Summary report.
   d) All of the above.

7. If you want to see a list of Estimates for all your Jobs, create:
   a) The **Estimate** form.
   b) The **Estimates by Job** report.
   c) The **Job Progress Invoices vs. Estimates** reports.
   d) All the above.

8. Which statement is true:
   a) To track open and closed estimates as they relate to billings use the *Job Estimates vs. Actuals Summary* report.
   b) You have to manually "close" an Estimate in order for QuickBooks to display the estimate on the *Job Progress Invoices vs. Estimates* report.

c) The *Job Progress Invoices vs. Estimates* report shows all Estimates.
d) None of the above.

9. For General Ledger activity, Sales Orders closely resemble which other form in QuickBooks:
   a) Bills.
   b) Estimates.
   c) Invoices.
   d) Sales Receipts.

10. If you do not have enough stock on hand to fill orders, you can:
    a) Create a Purchase Order from a Sales Order using QuickBooks Premier.
    b) Send the Customer an Order Delay receipt from QuickBooks.
    c) Replace the order with another item the customer did not ask for.
    d) Both b) and c).

11. If you wish to create multiple Purchase Orders from a single Sales Order:
    a) Select various Vendors from the Purchase Order form.
    b) Make copies of the Purchase Order.
    c) Select **Create purchase order for all allowed items** button in the *Create Purchase Order Based on the Sales Transaction* window.
    d) Select **Create purchase order for selected items** button in the *Create Purchase Order Based on the Sales Transaction* window.

12. If you want to see a list of all open Sales Orders for all your customers, create:
    a) The *Open Customer Orders by Sales* report.
    b) The *Open Sales Orders by Item* report.
    c) The *Open Sales Orders by Customer* report.
    d) The *Open Sales Orders List of all Customers* report.

Completion Statements

1. When you work with a prospective customer you may need to create several Estimates showing different alternatives for the job. If you do, QuickBooks will show each of the open, active Estimates in the ______ ______ window.

2. When creating Purchase Orders from an Estimate, if the items on the Estimate are inventory parts, QuickBooks will show the stock status for the part in the ______ ______ column. If necessary, you can override the amount in the ______ column.

3. Sales Orders are available only in QuickBooks ______ and ______ Editions.

4. You can create ______ ______ from Sales Orders just as you can with Estimates using QuickBooks Premier.

5. If you want to track the details of partially invoiced Sales Orders (i.e., Sales Orders that include back ordered items), create a(n) ______ ______ ______ ______ ______ report.

Estimates-Problem 1

APPLYING YOUR KNOWLEDGE

Restore the Estimates-10Problem1.QBM file and store it on your hard disk according to your instructor's directions.

1. Jerry Perez is looking to buy some photo equipment and service. He wants you to submit an Estimate. Use the information in Table 14-1 to create an Estimate for Jerry Perez. Total for the estimate should be $13,628.62.

Information	Data
Customer	Jerry Perez
Class	Walnut Creek
Date	5/1/2011
Estimate #	2011-1
Camera SR32	15 @ $450.00 each with a 25% markup
Lens	15 @ $184.99 each with a $500 total markup
Retouching services	10 hours @ $95 per hour, No markup

Table 14-1 Jerry Perez's Estimate information

2. Create an *Estimates by Job* report. Set the date range to *All.*
3. To complete Estimate 2011-1, you will need to order additional inventory. Create a Purchase Order to Ace Supply on 05/02/2011 for the 9 Camera and 7 Lenses that Academy Photo does not have in stock. Place order for 15 of each. Customer is Jerry Perez. Use purchase order number 2011-1.
4. Jerry Perez has agreed to pay 30% of the job on the date the project is started, but he wants you to bring an invoice for 30% of the amount. Use the Estimate to create a Progress Invoice of 30% of the total. Date the invoice 05/03/2011 and number it 2011-106. Ignore the warning that you don't have enough inventory to sell to Jerry Perez. If needed, turn on the Progress Invoicing preference.
5. Create a *Job Progress Invoices vs. Estimates* report from **01/01/2011** to **05/31/2011**.

Workplace Applications

Discussion Questions

These questions are designed to stimulate discussion about how you can apply QuickBooks to your own organization. They may help you think through some of the issues you'll encounter when using QuickBooks in your company.

1. How do employees in your organization track sales? Does your organization provide estimates, bids, or proposals? Locate a sales invoice for your organization. Use this to create a fictitious estimate. From this estimate create a Sales Order. Who in your organization would be responsible for creating estimates like the ones being used in this chapter?

2. Does your organization always receive 100% payment as services are provided? If not, how does or organization keep track of payments, customer deposits, estimates, bids, or proposals? How would you write a QuickBooks procedure manual for Estimates and Sales Orders for your company using the techniques you learned in this chapter?

3. How does your organization obtain new customers? Which QuickBooks form (Estimates, Purchase Orders, Sales Orders, or Invoice) does your organization use the most (or would use the most at this point)? Which form would your organization benefit from the most if your company would use it more often?

Case Study

Software Support, Incorporated

Software Support, Inc. is a company that provides computer consulting services for clients throughout the Chicago metropolitan area. The company provides computer setup, training, and troubleshooting services for small business clients.

On April 6, 2011, Stephanie Rosenberg, Software Support's long-time customer, called to complain that she received an invoice for $4,000.00 when it was agreed that Software Support would only bill as the work progressed. According to Ms. Rosenberg the invoice should have only been $1,000.00 because only 25% of the work had been completed. The invoice was created from CEA #50212, Software Support's Client Engagement Agreement that was customized from a QuickBooks Estimate template form. Software Support always provides CEAs to their customers before working on any project.

Investigating the matter, David Samuels, Software Support's Senior Training Technician, discovered that Kovak Williamson did indeed bill Ms. Rosenberg for the full project amount. David asked Kovak to correct the situation and give him a report showing the progress of this and all projects.

1. How does Kovak Williamson correct the invoice to Stephanie Rosenberg?

2. What report does Kovak Williamson give to David Samuels after the invoice is corrected?

Chapter 15 Horizon Financial Planning Business Scenario

Description of Company – Horizon Financial Planning

After many years with his company, Barry Williams was caught by the entrepreneurial spirit. After carefully saving up enough seed capital and convincing a recently unemployed colleague to join him, he developed a well thought-out business plan and started Horizon Financial Planning (HFP).

Barry saw great opportunities. He lives in a large metropolitan city in Texas, close to several regional colleges and large universities, as well as hundreds of medium to large corporations. He plans to offer financial planning, investment, and estate planning seminars, plus related consulting services to individual, corporate, and institutional clients. Furthermore, his business plan includes the purchase and promotion of planning kits, along with several popular books and instructional DVDs related to achieving financial stability and success, which he will sell at corporate and collegiate brown-bag lunch seminars. Several times a year he conducts large seminars on financial planning and building wealth. He also offers companion seminars on estate planning and minimizing taxes.

To control his new start-up, he selected QuickBooks software to help manage the business operations while fulfilling fiduciary responsibilities from an accounting, tax, and record-keeping perspective. To launch the company, he has hired a full time employee, Shelly James and a part-time employee, Atasha Williams. He has leased 1,200 square feet of downtown office space.

Goals

Using QuickBooks and the sample file (Horizon-10.QBW), you will perform the following:

- Record initial start-up costs.
- Record two complete months and a partial third month of business transactions, including purchases, sales, deposits, Accounts Receivable, Accounts Payable, payroll, and taxes.
- Track inventory
- Reconcile bank accounts
- Answer several questions about the finances for Horizon Financial Planning

Revenue and expense transactions will be recorded into one of the three classes that HFP uses to track performance. At the end of each period, you will reconcile the bank statement and then produce financial statements and sales analysis reports, including a report of business performance by class.

Company Set Up

> **Restore this File**
>
> This chapter uses Horizon-10.QBW. To open this file, restore the Horizon-10.QBM file to your hard disk.

The company file for this exercise is mostly set up for you. Begin by familiarizing yourself with the setup of the file so you can correctly record the transactions for October through November and complete the exercises as instructed below.

Classes

In order to separately track profit centers, Horizon Financial Planning uses the following classes:

- Consulting/Seminars
- Product Sales
- Admin/Other

All sales and expenses of books, DVDs, and planning kits are tracked in the Product Sales class.

All sales and expenses of Consulting and Seminars are tracked in the Consulting/Seminars class.

All other revenues and expenses are tracked in the Admin/Other class.

Items

To track products, services, and inventory items, Horizon Financial Planning has the following Items set up in QuickBooks.

HFP – Item List		
Services	**Inventory Parts**	**Non-Inventory Parts**
Consultation Seminar	Books DVDs	Planning Kits
Other Charge	**Sales Tax**	**Fixed Asset Items**
Bounce Chg Misc Office Supplies	Out of State TX Sales Tax	Copier Fax Machine Laptop PC Projector

Table 15-1 Items for Horizon Financial Planning

Many products are sold at seminars. Sales of products are recorded on **Sales Receipts** and sales of Consulting and Seminars are recorded on **Invoices**.

Payroll Setup

Initially, there are three employees set up on the HFP Employee list. Barry Williams is the owner of the company. Atasha Williams is a part-time hourly employee with the following hourly rates:

- Regular wages $12.50
- Overtime Wages $18.75

She is single, has no dependents, and claims zero federal allowances. Payroll costs are allocated to the Admin/Other class.

Shelly James is a salaried employee with an annual salary of $52,000.

She is married and claims zero federal allowances. Payroll costs are allocated to the Consulting/Seminars class.

All employees are paid on a semimonthly basis. All employees live and work in Texas.

Texas State Unemployment Insurance (SUI) is assessed on the first $9,000 in wages for each employee. HFP's tax rate is 0.67%, and it is an employer expense (i.e., not withheld). This tax is paid to the Texas Workforce Commission quarterly.

All regular employees are covered under the company-sponsored medical insurance plan underwritten by Longhorn American Insurance Company. HFP remits its premium monthly to Longhorn American. The company and the employees share the cost of monthly premiums equally. Deductions are made from net pay for the employee portion of the premium. Longhorn American charges HFP monthly premiums.

- No dependants $200.00 per month
- One or more dependants $400.00 per month

> Note:
> Payroll taxes are calculated based on the tax tables. Some amounts in this exercise may vary depending on changes to these tax tables.

Customer List

The QuickBooks Customer list is already set up for you. The following institutions all have customer records:

HFP Customer List	
Central Texas University Computer Manufacturers USA Energy Alternatives and Operations, Inc. Energy Corporation of Texas Houston Community Campus Texas Sky University	These customers receive Invoices and make payments on terms.
John R. Clark M. L. Kountz	These customers are individual seminar participants. Their product purchases are recorded on **Sales Receipts**.
Seminar Sales Summary	This customer record is used to record summary transactions of product sales at each seminar.

Table 15-2 Customer List

Vendor List

The QuickBooks Vendor list is already set up for you. Below is a listing of each vendor and their relationship with HFP.

HFP Vendor List	
Braten Investments	Landlord
Clover Computing	Computer service
Education & Medical Fund	Charitable organization
EFTPS	Payroll liabilities
Hotel Legacy	Seminar host
Image Contacts, Inc.	Printing and mailers
Lone Star Office Supply	Office supplies
Longhorn American Insurance	Insurance underwriter
Office Furniture Rentals	Furniture rental
Office Supply Depot	Office supplies and equipment
Provident Texas Investors	Investment consultant
Rash Productions, Inc.	Marketing consultant
South Texas Bell	Telephone and communications provider
Texas Light & Power	Electrical power provider
Texas Media & Publications	Distributor of books, DVDs, and planning kits
Texas State Comptroller	Texas Sales tax
Texas Workforce Commission	State Unemployment tax

Table 15-3 Vendor List

All bills from vendors are held until the last working day of each month, sorted by due date, and paid in a batch.

All payments received are grouped into the **Undeposited Funds** account to be deposited together.

Instructions

1. Restore the Horizon-10.QBM file to Horizon-10.QBW file.
2. Enter the transactions for October 2011 beginning on page 611.
3. Reconcile the bank statement for October for the statement shown on page 625.
4. Prepare the following reports and graphs:
   a) Standard Balance Sheet as of 10/31/2011
   b) Standard Profit and Loss for October 2011
   c) Profit and Loss by Class for October 2011
   d) Statement of Cash Flows for October 2011
   e) Sales by Item Summary for October 2011
   f) Graph – Sales by Month by Customer for October 2011
5. Back up your data file to Horizon-10AfterOctober.QBM, and then continue entering the remaining transactions for November 2011 beginning on page 617.
6. Reconcile the bank statement for November using as shown on page 626.
7. Prepare the following reports and graphs:
   a) Standard Balance Sheet as of 11/30/2011
   b) Standard Profit and Loss for November 2011
   c) Profit and Loss by Class for November 2011
   d) Statement of Cash Flows for November 2011

e) Sales by Item Summary for November 2011
f) Graph – Sales by Month by Customer for November 2011
g) Inventory Valuation Summary as of 11/30/11

8. Complete the analysis questions on page 624.

9. Backup your file to Horizon-10Final.QBM.

Business Transactions

October 2011

Oct	Business Transaction	Transaction Details
1	Deposit owner investment from Barry Williams to provide cash for operations.	Transaction type: **Deposit** Deposit to: **Checking-Texas National Bank** Date: **10/1/2011** Memo: ***Deposit Owner's Investment*** From Account: **Investments** (Equity Account) Check #401 Class: **Admin/Other** Amount: **$50,000.00**
1	Issued **Purchase Order** to Texas Media and Publications to order Books and DVDs.	Transaction type: **Purchase Order** Vendor: **Texas Media & Publications** Class: **Product Sales** Date: **10/1/2011** PO#: **2011–101** Items: **Books (110 @ $25.00)** **DVDs (110 @ $15.00)** Memo: ***Order Books and DVDs*** Total purchase order is **$4,400.00**
1	Paid rent plus refundable deposit to Braten Investments.	Transaction type: **Check** Pay to the Order of: **Braten Investments** Check#: **1001** Memo: ***October Rent plus $300 Deposit*** Expense: **Rent - $1,500.00** Expense: **Refundable Deposits** (Other Current Asset) - **$300.00** Total Check: **$1,800.00** Class: **Admin/Other**
1	Issued Purchase Order to Office Supply Depot for office equipment.	Transaction type: **Purchase Order** Vendor: **Office Supply Depot** Class: **Admin/Other** Date: **10/1/2011** PO#: **2011–102** Items: **Laptop PC $2,500.00, Copier $1,100.00, Fax Machine $750.00, Projector $2,500.00** Memo: ***Purchase office equipment*** Total purchase order is **$6,850.00** ***Note:*** **The items are already added to the Fixed Asset Item list.**

Oct	Business Transaction	Transaction Details
1	Issued Purchase Order to Lone Star Office Supply for office supplies.	Transaction type: **Purchase Order** Vendor: **Lone Star Office Supply** Class: **Admin/Other** Date: **10/1/2011** PO#: **2011–103** Item: **Office Supplies ($650.00)** Memo: ***Purchase office supplies*** Total purchase order is **$650.00**
4	Received bill from Office Supply Depot.	Transaction type: **Receive Items & Enter Bill** Vendor: **Office Supply Depot** PO #: **2011-102 ⇨ Items and Class auto fill from PO.** Date: **10/4/2011** Bill Due: **11/3/2011** Amount: **$6,850.00** Terms: **Net 30** Ref No: **68-20** Memo: ***Office Equipment***
4	Received bill from Lone Star Office Supply for supply items.	Transaction type: **Receive Items & Enter Bill** Vendor: **Lone Star Office Supply** PO #: **2011-103 ⇨ Items and Class auto fill from PO.** Date: **10/4/2011** Bill Due: **11/3/2011** Amount: **$650.00** Terms: **Net 30** Ref No: **6433** Memo: ***Office Supplies***
4	Issued check to Office Furniture Rentals, Inc. for rental of office furniture for October.	Transaction type: **Check** Pay to the Order of: **Office Furniture Rentals, Inc.** Check#: **1002** Memo: ***Furniture Rental*** Expense: **Equipment Rental ($910.00)** Class: **Admin/Other** Memorize the check, using *Don't Remind me* option.
4	Received bill from Texas Media and Publications.	Transaction type: **Receive Items & Enter Bill** Vendor: **Texas Media & Publications** PO #: **2011-101 ⇨ Items and Class auto fill from PO.** Date: **10/4/2011** Bill Due: **11/3/2011** Amount: **$4,400.00** Terms: **Net 30** Ref No: **8736** Memo: ***Books and DVDs***

Oct	Business Transaction	Transaction Details
6	Enter a Weekly timesheet for Atasha Williams' hours.	Transaction type: **Weekly timesheet** Name: **Atasha Williams** Week of: **Oct 3 to 9** Payroll Item: **Regular Wages** WC Code: **Leave Blank** Class: **Admin/Other** Mon: **8 hours** Tues: **4 hours** Wed: **8 hours** Thurs: **4 hours** Fri, Sat, Sun: **0 hours** Billable?: **Not Billable**
13	Enter a Weekly timesheet for Atasha Williams' hours.	Transaction type: **Weekly timesheet** Name: **Atasha Williams** Week of: **October 10 to 16** Payroll Item: **Regular Wages** Class: **Admin/Other** Mon: **8 hours** Tues: **4 hours** Wed: **8 hours** Thurs: **4 hours** Fri, Sat, Sun: **0 hours** Billable?: **Not Billable**
14	Received bill from Texas Media & Publications. These non- inventory products were ordered by telephone without issuing a PO.	Transaction type: **Bill** Vendor: **Texas Media and Publications** Date: **10/14/2011** Bill Due: **11/13/2011** Amount: **$1,250.00** Terms: **Net 30** Ref No: **8100** Memo: ***Planning Kits*** Item: **Planning Kits – 50 Units @ $25** Class: **Product Sales**
17	Pay employees for payroll period 10/01/2011 – 10/15/2011.	Pay Period Ends: **10/15/11** Paycheck Date: **10/17/2011** Bank Account: **Checking – Texas National Bank** Atasha Williams: **48 hours** Shelly James: **Salary** Starting Check Number: **1003**
19	Received bill from Image Contacts, Inc. for printing and mailing of flyers.	Transaction type: **Bill** Vendor: **Image Contacts, Inc.** Date: **10/19/2011** Bill Due: **11/18/2011** Amount: **$1,200.00** Terms: **Net 30** Ref No: **8869** Memo: ***Printing and Mailing Flyers*** Expense: **Advertising and Promotion** Class: **Consulting/Seminars**

Oct	Business Transaction	Transaction Details
20	Enter a Weekly timesheet for Atasha Williams' hours.	Transaction type: **Weekly timesheet** Name: **Atasha Williams** Week of: **October 17 to 23** Payroll Item: **Regular Wages** Class: **Admin/Other** Mon: **8 hours** Tues: **4 hours** Wed: **8 hours** Thurs: **4 hours** Fri, Sat, Sun: **0 hours** Billable?: **Not Billable**
21	Received bill from Rash Productions for consulting fees for an upcoming seminar to be conducted.	Transaction type: **Bill** Vendor: **Rash Productions** Date: **10/21/2011** Bill Due: **11/20/2011** Amount: **$2,000.00** Terms: **Net 30** Ref No: **8248** Memo: ***Consulting Fees*** Expense: **Professional Fees** Class: **Consulting/Seminars**
24	Conducted an on-site brown-bag lunch seminar at Computer Manufacturers USA.	Transaction type: **Sales Receipt** Customer: **Seminar Sales Summary** Class: **Product Sales** Date: **10/24/2011** Sale No: **2011-101** Check No.: Leave Blank Payment Method: **Check** Items: **Books (44 @ $50.00)** **DVDs (12 @ $40.00)** **Planning Kits (21 @ $100.00)** Texas sales tax applies. Total: **$5,174.35** Memo: **Computer Manufacturers USA Seminar Sales**
24	Prepare Invoice to Computer Manufacturers USA for on-site seminar conducted on this date.	Transaction type: **Invoice** Customer: **Computer Manufacturers USA** Class: **Consulting/Seminars** Template: **Horizon Invoice** Date: **10/24/2011** Invoice #: **2011-101** Terms: **Due on Receipt** Items: **Seminar (1 @ $5,000.00)** Total: **$5,000.00** Memo: ***Computer Manufacturers USA Onsite Seminar***

Oct	Business Transaction	Transaction Details
25	Received check from Computer Manufacturers.	Transaction type: **Payment** Customer: **Computer Manufacturers USA** Date: **10/25/2011** Amount: **$5,000.00** Check No: **1069** Payment Method: **Check** Memo: ***Payment Received – Inv. #2011-101*** Apply to: **Invoice #2011-101**
26	Issued check to Education & Medical Fund for contributions.	Transaction type: **Check** Check#: **1005** Date: **10/26/2011** Pay to the Order of: **Education & Medical Fund** Amount: **$250.00** Memo: ***Charitable Contribution*** Expense: **Charitable Contributions** Class: **Consulting/Seminars**
27	Enter a Weekly timesheet for Atasha Williams' hours.	Transaction type: **Weekly timesheet** Name: **Atasha Williams** Week of: **October 24 to 30** Payroll Item: **Regular Wages** Class: **Admin/Other** Mon: **8 hours** Tues: **4 hours** Wed: **8 hours** Thurs: **4 hours** Fri, Sat, Sun: **0 hours** Billable?: **Not Billable**
28	Enter a Sales Receipt to record the product sales at the seminar given at Energy Corporation of Texas	Transaction type: **Sales Receipt** Customer: **Seminar Sales Summary** Class: **Product Sales** Date: **10/28/2011** Sale No: **2011-102** Check No.: Leave Blank Payment Method: **Check** Items: **Books (26 @ $50.00)** **DVDs (18 @ $40.00)** **Planning Kits (8 @ $100.00)** Texas sales tax applies. Total: **$3,052.65** Memo: ***Energy Corp. of Texas Seminar Sales***
28	Prepare Invoice for Energy Corporation of Texas for on-site seminar conducted on this date.	Transaction type: **Invoice** Customer: **Energy Corporation of Texas** Class: **Consulting/Seminars** Date: **10/28/2011** Invoice #: **2011-102** Terms: **Due on Receipt** Items: **Seminar (1 @ $5,000.00)** Total: **$5,000.00** Memo: ***Energy Corp of Texas Onsite Seminar***

Oct	Business Transaction	Transaction Details
28	Received bill from Texas Light & Power.	Transaction type: **Bill** Vendor: **Texas Light & Power** Date: **10/28/2011** Bill Due: **11/27/2011** Amount: **$815.00** Terms: **Net 30** Ref No: **925586** Memo: ***Utility Bill*** Expense: **Utilities** Class: **Admin/Other**
28	Received bill from South Texas Bell for telephone.	Transaction type: **Bill** Vendor: **South Texas Bell** Date: **10/28/2011** Bill Due: **11/27/2011** Amount: **$282.00** Terms: **Net 30** Ref No: **987543** Memo: ***Telephone Bill*** Expense: **Telephone Expense:Office Phone** Class: **Admin/Other**
31	Enter a Weekly timesheet for Atasha Williams' hours. (Enter timesheet early due to pay cycle)	Transaction type: **Weekly timesheet** Name: **Atasha Williams** Week of: **October 31 to November 6** Payroll Item: **Regular Wages** Class: **Admin/Other** Mon: **8 hours** Tues: **4 hours** Wed: **8 hours** Thurs: **4hours** Fri, Sat, Sun: **0 hours** Billable?: **Not Billable**
31	Received check from Energy Corporation of Texas.	Transaction type: **Payment** Customer: **Energy Corporation of Texas** Date: **10/31/2011** Amount: **$5,000.00** Check No: **2021** Payment Method: **Check** Memo: ***Payment Received – Inv #2011-102*** Apply to: **Invoice #2011-102**
31	Pay employees for time worked during payroll period 10/16/2011 through 10/31/2011.	Pay Period Ends: **10/31/11** Paycheck Date: **10/31/11** Bank Account: **Checking – Texas National Bank** Atasha Williams: **56 hours** Shelly James: **Salary** Starting Check Number: **1006**
31	Deposit funds held in Undeposited Funds account to Texas State Bank.	Transaction type: **Deposit** Deposit to: **Checking-Texas National Bank** Memo: **Deposit** Date: **10/31/2011** Total Deposit Amount: **$18,227.00**

Oct	Business Transaction	Transaction Details
31	Pay all bills in a batch sorted by Vendor. Pay from the Checking-Texas National Bank account, and create "To be Printed" checks.	Select **Pay Bills**, and then pay the following bills: Image Contacts, Inc., for $1,200.00 Lone Star Office Supply for $650.00 Office Supply Depot for $6,850.00 Rash Productions, Inc. for $2,000.00 South Texas Bell 1013 for $282.00 Texas Light & Power for $815.00 Texas Media & Publications for $4,400.00 Texas Media & Publications for $1,250.00 Total payments: $17,447.00 Bill Payment Date: **10/31/2011**
31	Print all checks (Chk#1008-1014).	#1008 – Image Contacts, Inc. #1009 – Lone Star Office Supply #1010 – Office Supply Depot #1011 – Rash Productions, Inc. #1012 – South Texas Bell #1013 – Texas Light & Power #1014 – Texas Media & Publications
31	Issued check to Clover Computing for computer repairs.	Transaction type: **Check** Pay to the Order of: **Clover Computing** Check#: **1015** Date: **10/31/2011** Memo: ***Computer Repairs*** Expense: **Computer & Internet Expenses** Class: **Admin/Other** Total: **$492.00**

November 2011

Nov	Business Transaction	Transaction Details
1	Issue PO for books from Texas Media & Publications.	Transaction type: **Purchase Order** Vendor: **Texas Media & Publications** Class: **Product Sales** Date: **11/1/2011** PO#: **2011–104** Items: **Books (70 @ $25.00)** Memo: ***Reorder Books*** Total purchase order is **$1,750.00**
1	Issued check to Braten Investments for rent.	Transaction type: **Check** Vendor: **Braten Investments** Check#: **1016** Date: **11/1/2011** Memo: ***November Rent*** Expense: **Rent - $1,500.00** Total Check: **$1,500.00** Class: **Admin/Other**
2	Paid October sales tax.	Transaction type: **Sales Tax Payment** Check Date: **11/2/2011** Account: **Checking – Texas National Bank** Show Sales tax due through: **10/31/2011** Vendor: **Texas State Comptroller** Check#: **1017** Total Check: **$627.00**

Nov	Business Transaction	Transaction Details
3	Received bill from Texas Media & Publications.	Transaction type: **Receive Items & Enter Bill** Vendor: **Texas Media & Publications** PO #: **2011-104 ⇨ Items and Class from PO** Date: **11/3/2011** Bill Due: **12/3/2011** Amount: **$1,750.00** Terms: **Net 30** Ref No: **5989** Memo: ***Books***
4	Pay Medical Insurance Payroll Liabilities to Longhorn American Insurance.	Transaction type: **Payroll Liabilities** Account: **Checking – Texas National Bank** Pay to the Order of: **Longhorn American Insurance** Date: **11/4/2011** Memo: ***99-99999X (Account Number)*** Payroll Item: Medical Insurance **$600.00** Expense: Insurance Expense **$600.00 (Use Expense Tab for this)** Total: **$1,200.00** Class: **Admin/Other** Check No.: **1018**
10	Enter a Weekly timesheet for Atasha Williams' hours.	Transaction type: **Weekly timesheet** Name: **Atasha Williams** Week of: **November 7 to 13** Payroll Item: **Regular Wages** Class: **Admin/Other** Mon: **8 hours** Tues: **4 hours** Wed: **8 hours** Thurs: **4 hours** Fri, Sat, Sun: **0 hours** Billable?: **Not Billable**
11	Conducted an on-site seminar at Texas Sky University.	Transaction type: **Sales Receipt** Customer: **Seminar Sales Summary** Class: **Product Sales** Date: **11/11/2011** Sale No: **2011-103** Check No.: Leave Blank Payment Method: **Check** Items: **Books (71 @ $50.00)** **DVDs (44 @ $40.00)** **Planning Kits (31 @ $100.00)** Texas sales tax applies. Total: **$9,103.83** Memo: ***Texas Sky University Seminar Sales***

Nov	Business Transaction	Transaction Details
11	Prepare Invoice to Texas Sky University for on-site seminar conducted on this date.	Transaction type: **Invoice** Customer: **Texas Sky University** Class: **Consulting/Seminars** Date: **11/11/2011** Invoice #: **2011-103** Terms: **Net 30** Items: **Seminar (1 @ $5,000.00)** Total: **$5,000.00** Memo: ***Texas Sky University Onsite Seminar***
14	Enter a Weekly timesheet for Atasha Williams' hours. (enter early due to pay cycle)	Transaction type: **Weekly timesheet** Name: **Atasha Williams** Week of: **November 14 to 20** Payroll Item: **Regular Wages** Class: **Admin/Other** Mon: **8 hours** Tues: **4 hours** Wed: **8 hours** Thurs: **4 hours** Fri, Sat, Sun: **0 hours** Billable?: **Not Billable**
14	Received check from Texas Sky University.	Transaction type: **Payment** Customer: **Texas Sky University** Date: **11/14/2011** Amount: **$5,000.00** Check No: **5091** Payment Method: **Check** Memo: ***Payment Received – Inv. #2011-103*** Apply to: **Invoice #2011-103**
15	Pay employees for time worked during payroll period 11/01/2011 through 11/15/2011.	Pay Period Ends: **11/15/11** Paycheck Date: **11/16/2011** Bank Account: **Checking – Texas National Bank** Atasha Williams: **52 hours** Shelly James: **Salary** Starting Check No.: **1019**
15	Prepare Invoice Energy Alternatives and Operations, Inc. for a consultation	Transaction type: **Invoice** Customer: **Energy Alternatives and Operations, Inc.** Class: **Consulting/Seminars** Date: **11/15/2011** Invoice #: **2011-104** Terms: **Net 30** Items: **Consultation (20 @ $250.00)** Total: **$5,000.00** Memo: ***Energy Alternatives Consulting Hrs.***
15	Pay 941 Payroll Liabilities	Transaction Type: **Payroll Liabilities** Account: **Checking – Texas National Bank** Check No.: **1021** Date: **11/15/11** Pay to the Order of: **EFTPS** Amount: **$1,187.10** (Amount may vary depending on tax tables. See note on page 609)

Nov	Business Transaction	Transaction Details
16	Issued PO for books and DVDs from Texas Media & Publications.	Transaction type: **Purchase Order** Vendor: **Texas Media & Publications** Class: **Product Sales** Date: **11/16/2011** PO#: **2011–105** Items: **Books (100 @ $25.00)** **DVDs (100 @ $15.00)** Memo: ***Reorder Books and DVDs*** Total purchase order is **$4,000.00**
17	Received check from Energy Alternatives and Operations, Inc.	Transaction type: **Payment** Customer: **Energy Alternatives and Operations, Inc.** Date: **11/17/2011** Amount: **$5,000.00** Check No: **1015** Payment Method: **Check** Memo: ***Payment Received – Inv. #2011-104*** Apply to: **Invoice #2011-104**
18	Received bill from Texas Media & Publications	Transaction type: **Receive Items & Enter Bill** Vendor: **Texas Media & Publications** PO #: **2011-105 ⇨ Items and Class auto fill from PO.** Date: **11/18/2011** Bill Due: **12/18/2011** Amount: **$4,000.00** Terms: **Net 30** Ref No: **5990** Memo: ***Books and DVDs***
18	Deposit funds held in Undeposited Funds account to Texas State Bank.	Transaction type: **Deposit** Deposit to: **Checking-Texas National Bank** Memo: **Deposit** Date: **11/18/2011**
21	Conducted an on-site seminar at Central Texas University.	Transaction type: **Sales Receipt** Customer: **Seminar Sales Summary** Class: **Product Sales** Date: **11/21/2011** Sale No: **2011-104** Check No.: Leave Blank Payment Method: **Check** Items: **Books (44 @ $50.00)** **DVDs (36 @ $40.00)** **Planning Kits (5 @ $100.00)** Texas sales tax applies. Total: **$4,481.55** Memo: **Central Texas University Seminar Sales**

Nov	Business Transaction	Transaction Details
21	Prepare Invoice for Central Texas University for on-site seminar conducted on this date.	Transaction type: **Invoice** Customer: **Central Texas University** Class: **Consulting/Seminars** Date: **11/21/2011** Invoice #: **2011-105** Terms: **Net 30** Items: **Seminar (1 @ $5,000.00)** Total: **$5,000.00** Memo: ***Central Texas University Onsite Seminar***
23	Enter a Weekly timesheet for Atasha Williams' hours.	Transaction type: **Weekly timesheet** Name: **Atasha Williams** Week of: **November 21 to 27** Payroll Item: **Regular Wages** Class: **Admin/Other** Mon: **8 hours** Tues: **4 hours** Wed: **8 hours** Thurs: **0 hours** Fri, Sat, Sun: **0 hours** Billable?: **Not Billable**
23	Received check from Central Texas University.	Transaction type: **Payment** Customer: **Central Texas University** Date: **11/23/2011** Amount: **$5,000.00** Check No: **4551** Payment Method: **Check** Memo: ***Payment Received – Inv. #2011-105*** Apply to: **Invoice #2011-105**
28	Entered Bill–Credit from Texas Media & Publications for DVDs returned due to damage in shipment.	Transaction type: **Bill Credit** Vendor: **Texas Media & Publications** Date: **11/28/2011** Credit Amount: **$30.00** Ref No: **5990-C** Memo: ***Credit for Damaged DVDs*** Item: **DVDs (2 @ $15.00)** Class: **Product Sales**
28	Issue Credit Memo to customer John R. Clark, who returned a book purchased at the seminar at Texas Central University on 11/21/2011.	Transaction type: **Credit Memo** Customer: **John R. Clark** Class: **Product Sales** Date: **11/28/2011** Credit No: **2011-106** Items: **Books** (1 @ $50.00 taxable) Total Credit Amount: **$54.13** Memo: ***Returned Book*** ***(Refund check is issued in next step)***
28	Issued refund check to John R. Clark. Applied this refund to the Credit Memo.	Transaction type: **Check (created from Credit Memo using "Give a refund" option button)** Refund Amount: **$54.13** Check Number: **1022** Date: **11/28/2011** Class: **Product Sales** Memo: ***Refund***

Nov	Business Transaction	Transaction Details
28	Received bill from Texas Light & Power.	Transaction type: **Bill** Vendor: **Texas Light & Power** Date: **11/28/2011** Bill Due: **12/28/2011** Amount: **$560.00** Terms: **Net 30** Ref No: **8310** Memo: ***Utility Bill*** Expense: **Utilities** Class: **Admin/Other**
28	Received bill from South Texas Bell for telephone expenses.	Transaction type: **Bill** Vendor: **South Texas Bell** Date: **11/28/2011** Bill Due: **12/28/2011** Amount: **$422.00** Terms: **Net 30** Ref No: **6058** Memo: ***Telephone Bill*** Expense: **Telephone Expense:Office Phone** Class: **Admin/Other**
30	Enter a Weekly timesheet for Atasha Williams' hours.	Transaction type: **Weekly timesheet** Name: **Atasha Williams** Week of: **November 28 to December 4** Payroll Item: **Regular Wages** Class: **Admin/Other** Mon: **8 hours** Tues: **4 hours** Wed: **8 hours** Thurs: **4 hours** Fri, Sat, Sun: **0 hours** Billable?: **Not Billable**
29	A physical count verified books on hand but showed 95 DVDs (a loss of 3 DVDs). Therefore, the Quantity On Hand for DVDs was adjusted down 3 to match the physical count.	Transaction type: **Inventory Adjustment** Date: **11/29/2011** Ref No: **2011-1** Account: **Inventory Variance** Class: **Product Sales** New Quantity for DVDs Item: **95** Quantity Difference: **-3** Memo: ***Adjust for Actual Quantity on Hand***
29	Customer M.L. Kountz purchased a planning kit at the seminar at Texas Central University on 11/21/2011, but the bank returned his check unpaid.	Transaction type: **Check** Check#: **Bounce** Date: **11/29/2011** Pay to the Order of: **M. L. Kountz** Memo: ***Bounced Check #34566 11/21/11*** Expense: **Accounts Receivable** Customer:Job: **M. L. Kountz** Amount: **$107.25** Class: **Product Sales** Total: **$107.25**

Nov	Business Transaction	Transaction Details
29	Record the bank service charges in the checking account.	Transaction type: **Check** Check#: **BounceChg** Date: **11/29/2011** Pay to the Order of: **M. L. Kountz** Memo: ***Bounced Check Charge for M.L. Kountz*** Expense: **Bank Service Charges** Customer:Job: **M. L. Kountz** Amount: **$10.00** Class: **Product Sales**
30	Deposit funds held in Undeposited Funds account to Texas State Bank.	Transaction type: **Deposit** Deposit to: **Checking-Texas National Bank** Date: **11/30/2011** Memo: **Deposit**
30	Pay employees for time worked during payroll period 11/15/2011 through 11/30/2011.	Pay Period Ends: **11/30/2011** Paycheck Date: **11/30/2011** Bank Account: **Checking – Texas National Bank** Atasha Williams: **52 hours** Shelly James: **Salary** Starting Check: **1023**
30	Pay all bills in a batch sorted by Vendor. Pay from the Checking-Texas National Bank account, and create "To be Printed" checks.	Select **Pay Bills** and pay all existing bills. Bill Payment Date: **11/30/2011**
30	Print all checks (Chk#1025-1027).	#1025 – South Texas Bell #1026 – Texas Light & Power #1027 – Texas Media & Publications

Analysis Questions

Use the completed reports and template file to answer the following questions. Write your answer in the space to the left of each question.

1. ________ What is the net income or net loss for October?
2. ________ What is the total Cost of Goods Sold for October?
3. ________ What is the total amount of payroll expenses (gross wages and payroll taxes) for October?
4. ________ What is the gross profit for October?
5. ________ What is the total Product Revenue for November?
6. ________ What is the amount of rent paid for October?
7. ________ What is the total payroll expense for November?
8. ________ What is the Total Income for the Consulting/Seminars class for November?
9. ________ What is the net income or net loss for November?
10. ________ What is the Total Liabilities on October 31?
11. ________ What is the net cash increase for October?
12. ________ What is the cash balance at the end of November?
13. ________ What percentage of November total sales was the Seminar Item?
14. ________ What percentage of October total sales was sold to Energy Corporation of Texas in October?
15. ________ How much does Horizon Financial Planning have in total assets on October 31?
16. ________ How many books does Horizon Financial Planning have on hand as of November 30?

Business Checking Account

Statement Date:	October 31, 2011	*Page 1 of 1*
Summary:		**Horizon Financial Planning**

Previous Balance as of 9/30/11	$	-
Total Deposits and Credits: 2	+ $	68,227.00
Total Checks and Debits: 15	- $	20,407.00
Total Interest Earned	+ $	-
Total Service Charge:1	- $	10.00
Statement Balance as of 10/31/11:	**= $**	**47,810.00**

Deposits and Other Credits:

DEPOSITS

Date	Description		Amount
1-Oct	Customer Deposit	$	50,000.00
31-Oct	Customer Deposit	$	18,227.00
	2 Deposits:	**$**	**68,227.00**

INTEREST

Date	Description		Amount
	Interest:	**$**	**-**

Checks and Other Withdrawals:

CHECKS PAID:

Check No.	Date Paid		Amount
1001	1-Oct	$	1,800.00
1002	5-Oct	$	910.00
1005	28-Oct	$	250.00
1008	31-Oct	$	1,200.00
1009	31-Oct	$	650.00
1010	31-Oct	$	6,850.00
1011	31-Oct	$	2,000.00
1012	31-Oct	$	282.00
1013	31-Oct	$	815.00
1014	31-Oct	$	5,650.00
	15 Checks Paid:	**$**	**20,407.00**

OTHER WITHDRAWALS/PAYMENTS

Date	Description		Amount
	0 Other Withdrawals/Payments:	**$**	**-**

SERVICE CHARGES

Date	Description		Amount
31-Oct	Service Charge	$	10.00
	1 Service Charge:	**$**	**10.00**

Figure 15-1 October Bank Statement

Business Checking Account

Statement Date:	**November 30, 2011**		*Page 1 of 1*
Summary:			**Horizon Financial Planning**

Previous Balance as of 10/31/11:	$	**47,810.00**
Total Deposits and Credits: 2	+ $	28,585.38
Total Checks and Debits: 11	- $	10,722.38
Total Interest Earned	+ $	-
Total Service Charge:1	- $	10.00
Statement Balance as of 11/30/11:	= $	**65,663.00**

Deposits and Other Credits:

DEPOSITS

Date	Description		Amount
19-Nov	Customer Deposit	$	19,103.83
30-Nov	Customer Deposit	$	9,481.55
	2 Deposits:	**$**	**28,585.38**

INTEREST

Date	Description		Amount
	Interest:	**$**	**-**

Checks and Other Withdrawals:

CHECKS PAID:

Check No.	Date Paid		Amount
1015	1-Nov	$	492.00
1016	1-Nov	$	1,500.00
1017	3-Nov	$	627.00
1018	3-Nov	$	1,200.00
1022	26-Nov	$	54.13
1025	30-Nov	$	422.00
1026	30-Nov	$	560.00
1027	30-Nov	$	5,750.00
	8 Checks Paid:	**$**	**10,605.13**

OTHER WITHDRAWALS/PAYMENTS

Date	Description		Amount
29-Nov	Bounce	$	107.25
29-Nov	Service Charge	$	10.00
	2 Other Withdrawals/Payments:	**$**	**117.25**

SERVICE CHARGES

Date	Description		Amount
30-Nov	Service Charge	$	10.00
	1 Service Charge:	**$**	**10.00**

Figure 15-2 November Bank Statement

> **Note:**
> Paychecks are calculated using the tax tables loaded on your computer. In this scenario, we have intentionally not included the paychecks and the payroll liability payments in these bank statements to make the reconciliation consistent for readers using different tax tables.

Budgeting, Forecasting and Business Planning

After completing this chapter, you should be able to:

- Create Budgets.
- Create Budget Reports by Customer/job or by Class.
- Create Forecasts and Forecast Reports.
- Utilize the Cash Flow Projector.
- Develop a Business Plan for your business.

uickBooks provides several budgeting, forecasting, and business planning tools that help you make operational decisions in your business. In this chapter, you will learn how to use these tools to help you manage your business and stay on top of your financial performance.

Note:
This chapter is included with the supplemental material for this book, available online. Directions for downloading this chapter are available on page xiii.

Adjustments and Year-End Procedures

Objectives

After completing this chapter, you should be able to:

- Process 1099 forms for vendors.
- Print 1099 and 1096 forms.
- Edit, void, and delete transactions.
- Enter general journal entries.
- Track fixed assets.
- Memorize and schedule transactions to be automatically entered.
- Close the year and enter special transactions for sole proprietorships and partnerships.
- Set the closing date to lock the company file.

In this chapter, you will learn how to process 1099s, edit and void transactions in current and closed periods, and you'll learn how to use journal entries and zero-dollar checks to adjust balances and close the year. You will also learn how to track your fixed assets, memorize transactions, and use the closing date in QuickBooks.

> **Note:**
> This chapter is included with the supplemental material for this book, available online. Directions for downloading this chapter are available on page xiii.

Appendix

The appendix includes:

- A list of keyboard shortcuts
- A detailed description of QuickBooks Preferences
- Answer Key to the End of Chapter Review Questions
- Glossary of QuickBooks and Accounting terminology

Note:
This appendix is included with the supplemental material for this book, available online. Directions for downloading this chapter are available on page xiii.

Index